A Treasury of the

THEATRE

Volume Two

MODERN EUROPEAN DRAMA
FROM HENRIK IBSEN TO JEAN-PAUL SARTRE

Revised Edition, Edited by

JOHN GASSNER

SIMON AND SCHUSTER, NEW YORK

THIS VOLUME IS REVISED AND EXPANDED FROM THE ORIGINAL

"A TREASURY OF THE THEATRE" EDITED BY BURNS MANTLE AND JOHN GASSNER

PUBLISHED BY SIMON AND SCHUSTER

A DIVISION OF GULF & WESTERN CORPORATION

SIMON & SCHUSTER BUILDING

ROCKEFELLER CENTER

1230 AVENUE OF THE AMERICAS

NEW YORK, NEW YORK 10020

ISBN 0-671-75610-9

MANUFACTURED IN THE UNITED STATES OF AMERICA

14   15   16   17   18   19   20   21   22   23

The editor and publishers of A TREASURY OF THE THEATRE are grateful to the following publishers, playwrights, and translators for permission to reprint many of the plays in this volume:

To Charles Scribner's Sons for their consent to the inclusion of *Ghosts* and *Hedda Gabler* by Henrik Ibsen, as translated by William Archer and Edmund Gosse. Published by Charles Scribner's Sons, New York.

To John W. Luce and Company for their consent to the inclusion of *The Father* by August Strindberg, as translated by Edith and Warner Oland. Copyright 1907 by John W. Luce and Company, Boston, Mass.

To The Viking Press, Inc., for their consent to the inclusion of *The Weavers* by Gerhart Hauptmann, as translated by Mary Morison, and published as Volume I of *The Dramatic Works of Gerhart Hauptmann*. Copyright 1912 and published by The Viking Press, Inc., New York.

To George Rapall Noyes and George Z. Patrick for their consent to the inclusion of their translation of *The Power of Darkness* by Leo Tolstoy. Reprinted by permission of George Rapall Noyes from *Masterpieces of the Russian Drama* by George Rapall Noyes, D. Appleton & Co., 1933. *Caution:* No performance, professional or amateur, no public reading, no radio broadcast, and no television performance may be given without permission from and payment of royalty to Mr. George R. Noyes, 1486 Greenwood Terrace, Berkeley, Calif.

To Morris Gest for his consent to the inclusion of the Jenny Covan translation of *The Lower Depths* by Maxim Gorki, and to Oliver M. Sayler for consent to the inclusion, in part, of his introduction to the same play.

To Random House, Inc., for their consent to the inclusion of *The Intruder* by Maurice Maeterlinck.

To Henry Holt and Company, Inc., for their consent to the inclusion of *Cyrano de Bergerac* by Edmond Rostand, as translated by Brian Hooker. Reprinted by permission of the publishers. Copyright, 1923, by Henry Holt and Company, Inc., New York.

To Charles Scribner's Sons for their consent to the inclusion of *There Are Crimes and Crimes*. Reprinted from *Plays, Second Series* by August Strindberg, translated by Edwin Bjorkman; copyright 1913 by Charles Scribner's Sons, 1942 by Edwin Bjorkman; used by permission of the publishers, Charles Scribner's Sons, New York.

To Liveright Publishing Corporation, for their consent to the inclusion of *Liliom* by Ferenc Molnár. Copyright 1921 by Boni and Liveright, Inc., New York.

To E. P. Dutton and Company, Inc., for their consent to the inclusion of *Six Characters in Search of an Author* by Luigi Pirandello, as translated by Edward Storer. Copyright 1922 by E. P. Dutton and Company, Inc., New York.

To Samuel French for consent to the inclusion of *R. U. R.* by Karel Capek, English version by Paul Selver and Nigel Playfair. Copyright, 1923, by Doubleday, Page & Co. All Rights Reserved. *Caution:* Professionals and amateurs are hereby warned that *R. U. R.*, being fully protected under the copyright laws of the United States of America, the British Empire, including the Dominion of Canada, and all other countries of the Copyright Union, is subject to a royalty. All rights, including professional, amateur, motion pictures, recitation, public reading, radio broadcasting, televising, and the rights of translation into foreign languages are strictly reserved. Amateurs may produce this play upon payment of a royalty of Twenty-Five Dollars for each performance, payable one week before the play is to be given, to Samuel French, at 25 West 45th Street, New York 19, or 7623 Sunset Blvd., Hollywood 46, Calif., or, if in Canada, to Samuel French (Canada) Ltd., 480 University Ave., Toronto.

To New Directions for their consent to the inclusion of *Blood Wedding* by Federico García Lorca. Copyright, 1947, by New Directions, Norfolk, Conn.

To New Directions for their permission to include excerpts of *The Private Life of the Master Race* by Bertolt Brecht, as translated by Eric R. Bentley. Copyright 1944 by E. R. Bentley. Published by New Directions, Norfolk, Conn.

To Alfred A. Knopf, Inc., for their consent to the inclusion of *The Flies* by Jean-Paul Sartre, as translated by Stuart Gilbert. Copyright 1946 by Stuart Gilbert. Also to Hamish Hamilton, Ltd., London, for Canadian distribution permission. Reprinted from *No Exit and The Flies*, by Jean-Paul Sartre, by permission of Alfred A. Knopf, Inc.

TO
THE MEMORY OF MY FATHER

CONTENTS

PREFACE

THE SUBJECT of the present volume is the modern drama written on the European continent. That this gives us anything but a bedside book will soon be apparent.

The reader who is familiar with the older drama or has dipped into the first volume of *A Treasury of the Theatre,* subtitled *From Aeschylus to Turgenev,* will observe some decided differences in matter and treatment. The modern dramatists have been sensible of a sharper separation between the community and the individual than many older writers. T. S. Eliot expressed the problem well in writing that writers "need to assume some moral attitude in common with their audience. Aeschylus and Sophocles, the Elizabethans, and the Restoration dramatists had this. But this must be already given; it is not the job of the dramatist to impose it." Many plays in the present volume reflect the plight of the modern individual in an age of complex and turbulent transition.

Nevertheless, the troubled brood of European playwrights from Ibsen to Sartre can be seen striving to make the same inquiries into human nature and destiny as their predecessors, even if they have not been as successful in finding answers as Sophocles, the Periclean Greek who "saw life steadily and saw it whole." The modern playwrights, too, have tried to connect man with his fellowman, his society, and his universe.

Although making the connection became increasingly difficult as the century began to reel like a drunkard under its burdens, the modern dramatists also have attempted to provide the consolations and conciliations of art. For consolation and conciliation have been functions of art from the beginning. The circumstances under which the playwrights wrote their plays—the wars, revolutions, counter-revolutions, initial liberations and subsequent tyrannies, the uncertainties and the deluding certainties—did not wrench the writers hopelessly loose from their weather-worn humanistic moorings. We may not forget that great drama was written before in periods of catastrophic war and of defeats sustained by the values we call civilization. Many of the plays of Sophocles and Euripides were produced in the midst of dissensions, betrayals, military setbacks, and alternate rule by demagogues and oligarchs. The traitors and the war-makers, the demagogues and the oligarchs vanished long ago; the humanism of Sophocles and Euripides survived them all. "As a matter of fact," Brooks Atkinson wrote in the days when Hitler's triumphs dismayed civilization, "men of letters have rarely had the pleasure of practicing their trade in time of peace, public rest, and well-being." Nor is it too surprising that dramatists, who specialize in "conflict," that special province of dramatic art, should have managed to face the brawling world without being intimidated into incoherence. Their greatest danger as artists has always come from other sources—from perverted values and from the dubious "blisses of the commonplace" and a too ready consent to them.

It can be said, at least, that the reader of this "Ibsen to Sartre" collection will not find much inducement to slothful ease. Moreover, if he weathers this modern European section of *A Treasury of the Theatre,* he will be braced for the next volume—the collection of modern drama in English subtitled *From Oscar Wilde to Arthur Miller.*

J. G.

June 1951

Introduction

THE DRAMA OF MODERN TIMES has been a literature of the valleys and plateaus rather than of the heights. This has been its chief limitation, but it has also been its greatest strength, for humanity will be found mostly in the valleys and on the plateaus. One of America's earliest pioneers in modern drama, Arthur Hopkins, once expressed a conviction that the theatre can "ultimately reach a place where it helps mankind to a better human understanding, to a deeper social pity, and to a wider tolerance of all that is life." That much, although in artistry a good deal more than that, has been attained by the theatre of modern times. Even in its intellectualism and skepticism it has remained a humanistic enterprise.

Until the modern age there were only three truly major periods of dramatic art in some twenty-four centuries of Western theatre: the fifth-century B.C. Athenian, the Elizabethan, and the seventeenth-century French. Ours is the fourth great period. It began during the last quarter of the nineteenth century and has not yet ended. The modern period has already lasted as long as the Greek, longer than the seventeenth-century French, and twice as long as the Elizabethan. And it has already established its main claims to importance.

Among these is the very extensiveness of modern drama. Classic tragedy was the achievement of a few men in one city; great Renaissance drama was mainly the work of Englishmen during the reigns of Elizabeth and James I; memorable neoclassic drama was the product of three French writers of the age of Louis XIV. Significant modern playwriting has come from virtually all Europe and the United States.

After preliminary efforts chiefly in France, the modern drama took shape as a critical and analytical instrument of realism in Scandinavia, largely in the hands of Henrik Ibsen and August Strindberg. It was simultaneously and subsequently employed in France by a number of able practitioners of less stature—Henry Becque, Eugène Brieux, François de Curel, Georges de Porto-Riche, and Paul Hervieu; in Central Europe, by Gerhart Hauptmann, Frank Wedekind, and Arthur Schnitzler; in Russia, by Leo Tolstoy, Anton Chekhov, and Maxim Gorki; in Southern Europe, by Jacinto Benavente and other Spaniards and Italians; and, finally, in England, Ireland, and America. In each instance, moreover, the realistic style underwent some modification or augmentation as it spread across the Western world. It acquired precision in France, humanization in Russia, poetic intensification in Ireland, robustness in America, intellectual nimbleness in England. The possibility of variation was inherent in modern realism and was made apparent by writers so different in temperament and endowment as Becque, Chekhov, George Bernard Shaw, Sean O'Casey, and Eugene O'Neill. This cannot be said of Greek tragedy, which was only vulgarized and sterilized in Rome; of Elizabethan drama, which was not for export and lost vitality very quickly even in England; of seventeenth-century French tragedy, which shriveled when exposed to a different national climate.

A similar capacity for dissemination and variation appeared in the second and, after 1890, parallel movement of dramatic modernism, which diverged from realism. The movement away from realism began in France with the Belgian symbolist Maurice Maeterlinck and the romanticist Edmond Rostand. It spread to Scandinavia, affecting the later work of Ibsen and Strindberg as well as their successors in the North. It drew Central European playwrights such as Hauptmann.

Wedekind, Ferenc Molnár, Bertolt Brecht, and a variety of "expressionists" into its orbit. It moved east toward Russia and south to Italy and Spain, where it found a memorable response from Luigi Pirandello and Federico García Lorca. It advanced to the Irish drama of William Butler Yeats, John Millington Synge, and O'Casey; to the English theatre of James M. Barrie; and to the American stage of O'Neill, Thornton Wilder, Tennessee Williams, and Arthur Miller. No Western nation, in fact, failed to respond to the possibilities of imaginative theatre. Although it remained poorer in poetic texture than the older major dramatic literatures, the modern drama acquired poetic overtones everywhere in its course. Realistic writing, too, became interpenetrated with poetry. And, as a result of imaginative techniques, a poetry of the theatre came into being.

The varied interests of modern playwrights led to a vast exploration of dramatic forms and styles. By comparison with the modern theatre's readiness to experiment, the older theatres had been conservative. Whoever wishes to call the state of the modern stage anarchic may do so, but we may also call it remarkably exploratory. We need point only to a few representative developments—the one-act play as an art form; the discussion piece; the naturalistic but also poetic "slice-of-life" play, free from contrived plotting; the "mass drama," or group drama; the "memory play"; the theatricalist form, which presents the staging of a play, or the "play within the play." To this list we must add the various other styles represented in this anthology, such as symbolism and expressionism. If the modern theatre did not actually invent any or all of these forms of the drama, it employed and developed them with freedom and skill.

With these and other means, the modern drama swept into its orbit an extensive knowledge of man and his world, including the multiple advances of modern times in the fields of sociology and psychology. The creators of modern playwriting were men whose horizons were broad and not confined to the theatre. Many, indeed, received their training in other fields. (Ibsen had studied pharmacy; Hauptmann, science and astronomy; John Galsworthy, law; Chekhov, Schnitzler, and Somerset Maugham, medicine; Pirandello, Karel Capek, and Jean-Paul Sartre, philosophy and psychology. Shaw had cut his eyeteeth on music and economics.) Many were also intensely occupied at one time or another with politics. Playwrights brought into the theatre the intellectual seeds of Schopenhauer, Nietzsche, Kierkegaard, Darwin, Marx, the Webbs, Freud, and other leaders of Western thought. A cartoon intended by Max Beerbohm as a jest at Shaw's expense may stand as a summary of the dramatists' responsiveness to the busy world of modern ideas. Beerbohm shows Shaw presenting a parcel of clothes to the famous nineteenth-century critic Georg Brandes, who is called a *marchand d'idées*. The "merchant of ideas" asks Shaw what he wants for the parcel. The latter sanguinely answers, "Immortality." Brandes protests, "Come, I've handled these goods before! Coat, Mr. Schopenhauer's; waistcoat, Mr. Ibsen's; Mr. Nietzsche's trousers. . . ." Shaw's rejoinder is, "Ah, but look at the patches." In the work of most playwrights, perhaps even the patches had been taken from the thinkers of the age. Yet the combined effect was frequently interesting and exciting.

There also entered into the drama some of the qualities and elements of the novel, the major literary medium of modern times. It was the nineteenth-century writers of fiction who taught the best lessons of naturalness, documentation, psychological probing, and clinical reporting. It was from the novel, and not from the weak eighteenth-century examples of bourgeois drama, that playwrights could discover the true possibilities of commonplace characters and environments.

Flaubert alone supplied a conclusive example with *Madame Bovary*. It was from the novel, too, that playwrights could learn the art of letting the small events of life express human experience without theatrical fireworks or *coups de théâtre*. Some extremely effective theatre was created by these means, from 1890, when Maeterlinck wrote *The Intruder* as evidence that uneventful drama could be tremendously moving, to 1950, when Carson McCullers transferred her warm novel of adolescence, *The Member of the Wedding,* to the stage. Dramatists learned, in short, that untheatrical theatre could make good theatre.

The grand manner of romanticism and later the more efficient theatricality of the "well-made play" were discredited chiefly by the example of the powerful novelists of the nineteenth century. It was to the naturalistic novel that Emile Zola pointed in the eighteen-seventies when he tried to inculcate a new approach to playwriting. Not only were naturalness and verisimilitude furthered by the lessons of the novel but dramatists were enabled to introduce new material that did not suit the grand manner and the contrived dramaturgy of Ibsen's forerunners. There was room now for sociology, for clinical data, for the interchange of ideas, for the evaluation and transvaluation of values. When fiction became experimental in a nonrealistic manner, moreover, with Conrad, Proust, Kafka, and Joyce, dramatists had new lessons to learn.

There is surely some interest in the fact that the modern theatre should have played host to so many dramatizations of novels, not only because it indicates an enrichment of the drama by the most ample and progressive medium of modern literature but because it shows the modern stage capable of assimilating the rich matter of modern fiction. It was apparently unable to do so in the Victorian period, for example, when fiction made much progress while the theatre floundered in a morass of banality. It is remarkable, indeed, how many modern playwrights began as novelists and short-story writers or wrote fiction and drama concurrently. (Among them were Tolstoy, Chekhov, Gorki, Strindberg, Zola, Barrie, Galsworthy, Maugham, Pirandello, Sartre, Molnár, Capck, Wilder, and William Saroyan.) It is also noteworthy how many novelists made forays into the theatre, from Henry James to James Joyce, Thomas Wolfe, Ernest Hemingway, John Steinbeck, Gertrude Stein, and André Gide.

Virtually everything in modern culture found its way, in fact, into the theatre. The poets came into it—directly, as in the case of Yeats, T. S. Eliot, Robinson Jeffers, Lorca, and Brecht, and indirectly. (The influence of poetry on symbolist drama is an obvious example.) Modern music contributed its advances, not merely in serving as accompaniment or in playing an important part in musical comedy and music drama but in enlarging the possibilities of a poetry of the theatre. Nor has this contribution been limited to an enrichment of texts that would otherwise have made banal theatre. A musical element is potent in Shaw's and Chekhov's plays, for example; we may observe the undulation of arguments and themes in Shavian drama and the counterpointing of characters and situations in Chekhovian drama. And an even stronger influence radiated from the emphasis on nuance, atmosphere, and unification of the play and the stage production by mood in Wagner's music-drama cycle *The Ring of the Nibelung*. Nor can it be said that modern developments in the fine arts, from nineteenth-century impressionism to twentieth-century surrealism, failed to make an impression on playwriting and stage art.

Enrichment and provocation, as well as considerable confusion, came, then, into the modern theatre. The fourth major phase of Western drama owes its importance largely to its comprehensiveness. Only a small portion of the culture and social reality of Roman civilization found expression in Roman comedy and tragedy. Hardly anything pertinent to the age of Darwin, Faraday, Huxley, Mill, Dickens, and George Eliot will be found in the work of the Victorian playwrights. In few periods did the drama assimilate the substance that made the age historically and culturally important. Even the medieval drama, so close to the interests and religion of the masses, failed to express medieval culture and life as did Dante's *Divine Comedy.* Only the major dramatic literatures provide a sufficient summation and distillation of their times. This is true of Greek tragedy and comedy and of Elizabethan playwriting. It is also true of the modern drama. From the plays included in *A Treasury of the Theatre* and from the others dealt with in the introductions and the appendix we may derive not only a picture of our age but perspectives on its civilization.

The modern passion for showing things just as they are—that is, for verisimilitude—has indeed had many consequences. It has, for one thing, made our dramatic literature prose, if not necessarily prosaic. Modern playwrights have not written any sublime masterpieces in which the greatest dramatic insights and conflicts find expression in the greatest poetry. Because the drama, unlike the novel, is a concentrated form and a highly selective art, it aspires inherently to the state of poetry. The greatest drama has also been great poetry. Modern poets have written in both prose and verse, but they have not reached the towering heights of an Aeschylus, Sophocles, or Shakespeare. It may also be said that there is less memorable writing in many good modern plays than in many poor ones written in Athens or in Elizabethan England. The use of prose, however, has not only helped to give modern plays verisimilitude and the effect of authenticity but it has discouraged the reliance on rant and rhetoric that vitiated the work of many earlier playwrights. It has also compelled modern writers to dramatize rather than to narrate events. Our theatre has been an imitation of an action in the form of action more completely than much of the playwriting of the past, and dramatists have found it necessary to build plays more logically and convincingly than when they could dazzle audiences with verbal pyrotechnics. Prose, admittedly a deterrent to the highest flights of dramatic art, has served as a discipline and a challenge.

The concern with verisimilitude has had also an effect on dramatic style for which the term "realism" is inadequate. In the past, a realism of content and thought was often achieved without the instrumentality of a realistic technique. Who shall say that there is a less realistic attitude and understanding in the tragedies of Euripides and Shakespeare than in the plays of Ibsen, Strindberg, and Chekhov? Yet the former employed such formal devices as choruses, narrations, soliloquies, and asides to signify experience instead of presenting it as it would appear in a photographic and phonographic record. Modern playwrights have generally tried, however, to create the illusion that we are watching events exactly as they occurred. The older playwrights distilled experience, whereas most recent writers have reproduced it. To use the terms introduced by the critic Alexander Bakshy, modern playwrights have *represented* dramatic experience whereas the older playwrights *presented* it. The older theatre tended to be a rite; the modern theatre has been, as a rule, a picture.

Even poetic plays, such as those of Maeterlinck and Rostand, have been essentially *representational,* and their action is meant to be staged as a picture unveiled for the spectator. The effort to project or signify rather than actually to reproduce experience has been the unconventional procedure in our theatre. Although some of the results, as in *Our Town,* have been singularly effective, the *presentational* style has been the secondary one in our drama. It has also been more or less at odds with our picture-frame stage, which, lacking a forestage, creates a physical gulf between the actor and the spectator, who is invited to look on and overhear rather than to participate in the dramatic action. The history of the modern drama, as well as of the stage, has been, to a degree, a battle between realism and antirealism and, more especially, between the representational and presentational styles.

In our unstable age we observe, finally, as we might well have expected, much erosion of boundaries between the types of drama created in the past; that is, many plays are not sharply distinguishable as comedy or tragedy. Tragicomedy may be as old as some of the plays of Euripides (to the well-known Elizabethan vogue of tragicomedy even Shakespeare succumbed), and sentimental comedy (*comédie larmoyante,* or "tearful comedy") was a middle-class creation of the eighteenth century. But the mixed drama of modern times has a different quality. It often consists of an analysis or challenge carried to a consistent conclusion. It offers no happy endings as a salve for suffering characters or as an evasion of an issue; nor does it substitute sentimentality for stern confrontations of reality. Yet, whether it concludes in victory or disaster for the protagonist, this type of drama falls between the provinces of comedy and tragedy.

Even high seriousness on the part of the modern playwright is not apt to be exalting or has been exalting only to those who are roused by its message. No one is likely to be uplifted by *The Little Foxes*—or, for that matter, by *Ghosts,* although it was possible enough in the eighteen-eighties to become excited over the issue it presented. Characters in a play may command the full range of our sympathy, as they do in *The Cherry Orchard* and *The Lower Depths,* without exhilarating us. For this intermediate kind of play no entirely adequate term has yet been discovered. "Tragicomedy" can apply accurately only to plays that develop tragically but conclude happily. "Drama," the term generally favored, is perhaps broad enough to be serviceable.

Since most people are neither comic nor tragic, neither heroes nor villains, they fall into intermediate classifications. There is much truth in the modern playwrights' observation of such personalities, but it is the kind of truth that produces drama of intermediate effect. So does the veracious playwriting that shows us small men falling from small heights or characters vitiated by their environment (as is the young prize fighter in *Golden Boy*), destroyed by a pathological condition, or doomed to stalemate and disintegration. Intermediate, too, is the play in which the author is more interested in discussing a subject or in demonstrating a situation than in providing a unitary experience of joy or grief.

Truthful observation, verisimilitude, and common reality have led playwrights away from the glory that was Greek, Elizabethan, and seventeenth-century French tragedy. Even greatly tried characters—such as Ibsen's Mrs. Alving in *Ghosts,* the starved workers of *The Weavers,* the derelicts of *The Lower Depths,* or the bewildered stoker of *The Hairy Ape*—suffer with vastly more genuineness than magnificence of mind and spirit. Modern drama is not heroic drama in the high tragic sense of the other great ages of the theatre. The language of prose, although it can be poetically colored, suits the characters of modern drama best, just as the language of poetry suits Antigone and Hamlet.

If poetry has not been altogether absent from the modern theatre, it is partly because some playwrights have cast backward glances at a romantic past and rejected the workaday world, as did Rostand, or because they have found sources of poetic feeling and language in a people not yet completely drawn into the modern world, as did Synge in Ireland and Lorca in Spain. For the most part, however, the poetry of the moderns has been wrung from the plain life they have observed with tender or passionate awareness. They have found little grandeur in modern reality; but in feeling the common pulse, they have found that it somehow throbbed with the splendor of all life that seeks and suffers, and that feels lost in the world and nonetheless tries to find meaning and purpose in it. As they have listened to men and women, they have heard no thunderous symphonies of the universe, but they have heard the still, small voice of humanity. Sometimes that voice has become a song. And the song has risen at times to a higher pitch and become impassioned. If it has celebrated no glories of a traditional heroic nature, who shall say that it has not been heroic in the unassuming manner in which a great deal of common life is, and is compelled to be, heroic?

Realism and Naturalism

Realism and Naturalism

The first important advances in modern drama and theatre were made in the direction variously known as realism and naturalism. "Realism" was the general tendency; "naturalism," the specialized, extreme style developed by militant champions of realism who created a program and a movement. Neither realism nor naturalism was a new style in literature when dramatists and stage directors promoted it during the last quarter of the nineteenth century. But the stage had lagged considerably behind the other literary culture of Europe. Consequently, principles were trumpeted in the theatre as though they had never been heard before, and vanguards marched out to do battle with the entrenched proprietors of the old-fashioned stage. When the clash of arms ended and the smoke receded, the first battalion of "modernists" could claim complete victory.

Almost immediately, many Europeans began to wonder whether the victory had been worth winning. Realism and naturalism were decried as commonplace or arid, and a second battalion of "modernists," dedicated to recovering poetry and imagination for dramatic art, swept over the stage. Nevertheless, the pioneering realists had not labored in vain, and their victories were never actually dissipated by later experimentation, so that today the dominant theatre of the Western world is still realistic. Before 1895, realism brought forth masterpieces that have rarely been equaled by the nonrealistic plays of the twentieth century. And in spite of successive waves of theatrical stylization since 1895, most of the durable dramas since then have been essentially realistic or have owed much of their power to elements introduced into the theatre during the eighteen-seventies and 'eighties.

The world since then has belonged to the middle classes and the working classes, for whom the facts of daily life are immediate and momentous. In no previous period have both ordinary citizens and artists been so greatly occupied with science and sociology, and with political and economic realities. No other age has been so materialistic in its thinking, even though science lost a good deal of its nineteenth-century mechanistic philosophy and sociology was invaded by conflicting ideologies heatedly maintained by their socialist, communist, and fascist proponents.

Concreteness became the modern passion. And the theatre, in which things must always be shown and shouted or they simply do not exist, in which a hint is illuminated with thousand-watt power and a whisper reaches every ear—the theatre lent itself to the presentation of the concrete more than any of the other arts before the photographic medium of motion pictures reached maturity. Whether or not we approve of a dramatic art devoted to the prose of life, that is what we receive from the realists and from the naturalists.

THE ARRIVAL OF DRAMATIC REALISM

Until the advent of realistic styles and techniques, the nineteenth-century stage was a flimsy anachronism, made tolerable by some brilliant virtuoso acting. Up to the eighteen-seventies, most of the plays clung to the conventions of a decadent romanticism, even when they dealt with contemporary characters and problems. Alert and earnest men of the theatre could not fail to realize that a wide rift had occurred between these conventions and the realities of the nineteenth century. It was time to end the cleavage, as John Mason Brown has said, "between the grotesque and the commonplace, the picturesque and the factual, the Gothic revival and the scientific spirit, the cloak and swords of yesteryear and the slums of today." The novelists were already facing the modern world, as anyone could see in the work of such masters as Balzac, Flaubert, and Tolstoy. The dramatists could not trail behind them any longer.

Adapting the drama to reality was more difficult than attuning the novel to modern times, because a playwright is dependent upon the stage for which he is writing. And the stage held on to antiquated styles of production. Its stock scenery represented the vested interests of playhouse proprietors, and the acting profession would not willingly, and could not easily, unlearn lifetime habits of theatrical declamation and ostentatious performance. Dramaturgy, moreover, presents more intricate problems than narrative art. No matter how strongly the playwright tries to make his play conform to life, he has to provide effective exits and entrances, convincing time-covering scenes, and act endings that will bring the audience back into the theatre after the intermissions. He must also telescope events that the novelist would present in separate chapters, and intermingle characters whom a novelist would keep separate. Kitty and Anna, for example, can live apart for long periods in Tolstoy's *Anna Karenina* and still belong to the same book, whereas a stage version in which their lives merely ran parallel to each other would disintegrate and fail to sustain interest. In truth, the dramatist had, and still has, a hard time of it whenever he tries to realize standards of absolute realism. Nevertheless, playwrights began to infuse their work with the breath of life and to give their art a greater degree of verisimilitude than earlier dramatists had usually attained or had considered necessary.

From their effort to approximate reality, moreover, the drama acquired more or less special attributes, and these are of signal importance in differentiating the modern realistic play from the dramatic work of previous ages. Not even the casual reader or playgoer can overlook the emphatic contrasts between plays written for the realistic stage and those written for the romantic theatre of Schiller and Goethe, for the renaissance theatre of Shakespeare and Lope de Vega, or for the classic theatre of Sophocles and Euripides.

Poetry, the dominant vehicle for high drama in earlier periods, gave way to prose dialogue. Prose had entered the theatre long before the middle of the last century, but now it became the medium for exalted feeling as well as for commonplace experience, for tragedy as well as for comedy. Authentic dialect also came into frequent use, and was employed not merely for comic effect, as it was in Shakespearean drama. Whether the theatre suffered a setback from the triumph of prose has been a subject for debate for many decades and will probably remain so for a long time to come.

Playwrights began to introduce detailed stage directions into their work in order to authenticate the background and behavior of their characters, as well as to voice opinions they could no longer relegate to declamation by the actor as in the more artificially written earlier drama. The audience would not, of course, hear directions and undramatized comments of the author. Yet their effect could be felt in the stage productions, insofar as the stage director and the scene designer carried out the intentions thus indicated by the playwright. The reader —and plays began to be read on a larger scale than hitherto, except for national classics or the Greek and Latin drama taught in school—could re-create the dramatist's world more faithfully when he followed descriptions of the setting, costuming, and appearance of the characters; and he could acquaint himself more closely with the playwright's mind. He now received a printed text that bore a closer resemblance to a novel than to a dramatic poem. (What intelligent reader would forego the pleasure of Shaw's directions and comments?) More important, however, was the fundamental approach of the playwright, for he was now dominated by the consuming desire to study life more scientifically and more specifically than hitherto. He began to document his work, to present his material objectively, and to pay close attention to the role of instinct and milieu in human behavior. The study of so-called instinct gave rise to modern psychological drama, the study of background to modern social drama.

No one familiar with the drama since Sophocles would maintain that "psychological drama" was invented by realists and naturalists. Not even in the clinical sense of the term was psychology unknown in the theatre until the advent of modern playwrights such as Strindberg and O'Neill. The intuitions of Sophocles, Euripides, and Shakespeare were just as valid and penetrating as O'Neill's schematizations, if not indeed more so. (As Freud himself pointed out, the world's artists had discovered the "unconscious" long before clinicians, including himself, found a place for it in their case reports.) But the realistic dramatists were the first to represent psychological deviations or complexities directly rather than suggestively or symbolically and to locate them in familiar, contemporary backgrounds rather than to imply them in the context of myth or history.

If authors, in addition, often tended to view their subjects with a disconcerting indifference to moral judgments, this, too, reflected an essentially new attitude. Once playwrights conceived the notion of bringing a scientific view into the theatre, they could no more hesitate to fill the stage with unappetizing exhibitions than an anatomist would to perform a dissection in the operating room of a hospital or a medical school. The modernists who called themselves naturalists were dedicated to the cause of evolving a "natural science" of human behavior and considered themselves "determinists." Men, the writers tended to imply, behave as they must; that is, their hereditary traits and their instincts shape and determine their character and frequently overpower their reason or moral scruples. If this is so, man is not responsible for his actions, and moral indignation is out of order. For a dramatist to register disapproval of a person who succumbs to his sexual or criminal drives would be as absurd as for a physician to upbraid a patient for developing a cancer. This was the extreme view, and its illogicality became transparent to all writers but those who refused to make a distinction between inorganic matter or animal life and human beings. But the scientific attitude made itself generally felt in the playwright's concern with psychology, heredity, and instinct, in his matter-of-fact treatment of these matters, and in his air of playing the role of a detached observer.

As important as the growth of psychological and clinical studies, finally, was the advent of modern social drama, and here too the scientific attitude of the age of Darwin and Marx played a part. Enthusiasts of naturalistic doctrine proposed to study man as a creature inexorably determined by his social situation, or milieu. The earlier romantic playwrights had introduced "local color" into the drama. The realists went one great step further and introduced environment.

Writers now tended to treat the environment not merely as the background for a dramatic complication but as the foreground itself. They regarded society as a reality interesting and important in its own right. If the idea that character is to a great degree a product of social factors already existed in European thought, it was still new in the theatre. And if romantic dramatists had already pitted characters against social convention as long ago as the third quarter of the eighteenth century, it was nonetheless an innovation for the new playwrights to treat the subject with attention to contemporary life and with sociological interest. The problem play that maintains a thesis directly and the drama of social agitation that openly promotes a cause won more and more adherents in the modern theatre.

In an increasing number of instances, moreover, social drama no longer presented an individual as the central character. From such early plays as Hauptmann's *The Weavers* and Gorki's *The Lower Depths* to such comparatively recent examples as Rice's *Street Scene* and Odets' *Waiting for Lefty,* one can trace a trend toward representing a collective character or "mass hero"—a group of weavers, sailors, taxicab drivers, and the like. In such instances, we may well wonder how much has been lost or gained by the change of focus. If "the proper study of mankind is man," is he better understood or more meaningfully presented as a singular individual or as a collective entity? Debate over these questions can range far and wide. But the "collective character" has remained important in the theatre since *The Weavers* appeared in 1892.

As an inevitable consequence of the new social outlook, it was the common man who came to hold "stage center"—not merely in comedies of intrigue and sentimental pieces, but in tragedy and in serious plays concerned with his problems. The "little man," who had been usually presented in the older drama as the roguish servant, the lumpish peasant, or the upstart and absurd bourgeois, acquired dignity and importance in the new democratic theatre. He was not entirely new to his honors, it is true. He had been invested with them to some degree in Elizabethan plays such as *Arden of Feversham* and *The Yorkshire Tragedy,* and in such peasant dramas as Lope de Vega's *The Sheep-Well* and Calderon's *The Mayor of Zalamea.* The French encyclopedist of the eighteenth century, Diderot, had promulgated the need for "middle-class tragedy," and had written ineffectual samples himself. Other writers of "bourgeois" or of "liberal" persuasion—such as Lillo in England and Lessing and Schiller in Germany—had followed his example. But their plays had been exceptions to the unwritten, and also written, rule that only the highborn were worthy of heroic treatment. It was the realists who made the commoner completely at home in the theatre and gave him the tragic stature hitherto reserved for the aristocracy, insofar as it was within the province of realism to endow anyone with such stature. In time, too, the lowly hero was apt to be found more and more in working-class circles and among the peasantry rather than in middle-class circumstances.

FROM REALISM TO NATURALISM

The stages by which dramatic realism moved to supremacy would have to be traversed through many centuries. The conscientious chronicler would carry us as far back as the farces and religious dramas of the Middle Ages. (We have already noted the appearance of peasant drama in Spain's Golden Age and of middle-class drama in Shakespeare's day and in the eighteenth century.) Then he would deposit us on the threshold of modern drama in France. Here, shortly after Victor Hugo won a signal victory for romanticism with his *Hernani* in 1830, the increasingly bourgeois world of Louis Philippe and Louis Napoleon found a remarkably proficient entertainer in Eugène Scribe (1791–1861). His characters belonged to this workaday world, even if they only went through the motions of life as their author dangled them from the strings of artificial plots. Scribe, however, managed to create the illusion of reality on the stage with surface effects, and he taught a generation how to hold audiences with any kind of material. He did so by spinning out intrigues, by tangling up and then unwinding situations, and by producing discoveries and unexpected twists of circumstance. He turned playwriting into a virtuoso performance like tightrope-walking and sword-swallowing. The artificial pattern he evolved has been aptly named "the well-made play," for it was made rather than lived, and it was made well in the sense that it "worked" on the playgoer by keeping him on emotional tenterhooks. Scribe's clever craftsmanship was adopted by such younger playwrights as Emile Augier (1820–1889) and Alexandre Dumas *fils* (1824–1895), the illegitimate son of the great romancer of *The Three Musketeers.* They were followed by the most proficient of all the contrivers, Victorien Sardou (1831–1908). It must be remembered that all these manufacturers of plot found adapters and imitators throughout the Western world. The young Ibsen himself served an apprenticeship in Scribe's workshop when he stage-managed twenty-one plays by Scribe at the theatre in Bergen where he got his first practical experience. The Scribian technique of surprise discoveries and turns of intrigue appeared in Ibsen's work as late as 1877, when he composed his social drama *The Pillars of Society.*

Within the artificial circle of the well-made play, Augier (alone and in collaboration) painted objective pictures of his times such as *The Son-in-Law of Monsieur Poirier* (1854) and *The Marriage of Olympia* (1855), and Dumas *fils* delivered sermons on social reform after having first created a sensation with his famous tragedy—or pseudo tragedy—of a courtesan, *The Lady of the Camellias* (1852). Augier and the younger Dumas were, in fact, full-fledged realists, according to their own view, and what we call their artificial technique struck them as simply good craftsmanship. They dealt with facets of the life of their times that they considered important, employed prose dialogue, and made their plots revolve around ordinary people instead of knights of old or creatures of fancy. They regarded themselves as modernists and held what they believed to be advanced ideas, although these may strike us today as singularly old-fashioned, quaint, and narrow. Augier appointed himself the arch-defender of middle-class values that we now call mid-Victorian. He thought he was treating a momentous issue when he showed courtesans snaring youths of good family in marriage and thus infiltrating respectable society. Dumas' zeal for moral edification and for "useful theatre," as he called it, led him to lecture the public on a variety of then current problems ranging from illegitimacy to corrupt journalism.

Whether the well-made play was always an evil is arguable. Insofar as construction was concerned, the plays were assuredly not an abomination but a boon to the theatre. No one who is aware of the chaotic character of much Elizabethan and romantic drama can think otherwise. The multiple plots, static narrations, and long declamations in these nonrealistic plays could cause only confusion and boredom except in the hands of very able craftsmen. Indeed, with the advent of realism, dramatists tended to favor classic clarity and order. The well-made play assured effectiveness. Any number of admirable modern plays—*The Father, Hedda Gabler, The Power of Darkness, Loyalties, Desire Under the Elms,* and *The Little Foxes,* for example—are "well made." The adjective acquired a pejorative meaning as a result of the practice of superficial playwrights who strove only for theatrical effect and of didactic dramatists who were more intent upon delivering a message than upon presenting life on the stage.

In a bumbling fashion, another current of realism also began when Balzac produced his unflattering study of finance and usury, *Mercadet,* in 1851. The De Goncourt brothers left the security of the novel to write a play about a daughter who falls in love with her mother's lover, *Henriette Maréchal* (1865). The poet Villiers de L'Isle Adam anticipated *A Doll's House* with *The Revolt* in 1870, and the great Flaubert floundered with a drama, *Le Candidat,* in 1874. None of the authors belonged to the theatre by profession. Nor did Emile Zola (1840–1902), who, having already started his study of heredity and environment in the celebrated "Rougon-Macquart" series of family novels, wrote a sordid case history of adultery, *Thérèse Raquin,* in 1867, dramatized it in 1873, and defended it with a proclamation of principles for a new dramatic art. None of these plays won any immediate success, but they indicated a trend toward naturalism. They were not as contrived as the plays of Dumas and Augier, if only because their authors were less skillful in the theatre. The material was for the most part unsavory and was presented without the spice of moralization. The treatment of social reality or human nature was regarded as naturalistic because the objective reporting could be said to parallel the methods of the natural sciences.

In the meantime, there were stirrings in the theatre elsewhere: all the way from Russia, where Gogol's stinging satire on bureaucracy, *The Inspector General,* was produced as early as 1836, to England, where Thomas William Robertson (1829–1871) presented the tepid social dramas *Society* in 1865 and *Caste* in 1867. In Germany, the short-lived genius George Büchner (1813–1837) left a fragment that is a curious naturalistic masterpiece, *Wozzeck,* in 1836. (It remained unknown for many decades and was first produced in 1913.) In Germany, too, Friedrich Hebbel (1813–1863) developed his theory that tragedy is the product of the individual's clash with his society and wrote the powerful middle-class prose tragedy *Maria Magdalena* (1845). With *The League of Youth* published in 1869 and *The Pillars of Society* in 1877, Ibsen was on the way to turning his individual genius into the channels of genuinely modern realism, as was that other individualist, Henry Becque, when he wrote *The Vultures* in the same year, 1877, in Paris. Neither of these men needed any prodding from proclamations by Zola. They did need a new style of theatre for their plays, but would have to wait some ten years before it came into being.

A program was nonetheless needed to bring the formative drama into focus, and Zola, who had a gift for polemics among his varied talents, provided it first in the preface he wrote for the published version of *Thérèse Raquin* in 1873, then in prefaces to other unsuccessful plays the next year, and in his collected essays, *Le Naturalisme au théâtre,* printed in 1881. Zola was particularly impressed with the researches of Claude Bernard, who was investigating the relationship between the nervous system and nutrition in experiments on living animals and had published his *Introduction to the Study of Experimental Medicine* in 1865. Making extravagant claims for a truly modern drama, Zola took his stand on the side of what he called "nature" and found a suitable name for his conception of "scientific" realism in the term "naturalism," already familiar in other fields.

In order to "bring the theatre into closer relation with the great movement toward truth and experimental science," Zola maintained that the drama would have to apply the "new methods of science" to the study of human nature and behavior. Natural laws were in operation throughout the universe and applied to man as well as to the rest of creation. "A like determinism," wrote Zola, "will govern the stones of a highway and the brain of man." The moral life was no exception to this rule, and the French critic Taine had already expressed this view in declaring that "vice and virtue are products like sugar and vitriol."

Zola's notions of determinism were no sounder than his understanding of scientific method, and his attempt to apply animal reflexes to human behavior was a flagrant oversimplification. He had merely picked up scraps of materialistic philosophy and mechanistic science as a means for justifying an un-varnished picture of raw passion in *Thérèse Raquin*. He stated that "given a strong man and unsatisfied woman," he had tried "to see in them the beast [or animal], to see nothing but the beast, to throw them into a violent drama and note scrupulously the sensations and acts of these creatures." He concluded with a flourish, "I have simply done on two living bodies the work which surgeons do on corpses." This was, however, only his way of justifying a clinical approach that was soon to become frequent in dramatic realism; and in spite of making excessive claims for his procedure in the play, he did strike a blow in behalf of the modern dramatist's right to uncover sordid realities in the interest of truth.

It may be noted, too, that Zola extended the range of observation beyond the narrow limits of the clinic, just as he himself went beyond them in *Thérèse Raquin* when he allowed his murdering couple to be overcome with devastating remorse; the "beast" he proposed to study turned into a human creature after all. Zola expressed his crusade for naturalism most satisfactorily when he stated it most flexibly, as when he proposed to submit "man and his work to a system of precise analysis, taking into account all circumstances, environment, and 'organic causes.'" If the phrase "system of precise analysis" is dropped from these lines as a procedure impossible to art, Zola's sentence leaves room for considerable variation in the drama. It was the variation or deviation from rigid naturalism that was generally interesting or successful in the theatre. The variations grew in number and the deviations multiplied, leaving pure Zolaism in the lurch. Truly creative playwrights did not feel tethered to the program of Zola, and even those who thought they followed it merely approximated it. If Hauptmann, for example, thought he had written a completely dispassionate play when he composed *The Weavers,* that was not the effect it had on its audiences, who were roused to pity and revolutionary ardor by his account of the miseries of the Silesian weavers.

Zola's polemics helped to put an end to the rule of the degenerate romantic drama and discredited the "well-made plays" of sheer artifice. He incited, instead, and gave honorable status to, the uncontrived document of reality that he called a *lambeau d'existence,* or fragment of life, which a younger minor dramatist, Jean Jullien, popularized under the term *tranche de vie,* or slice of life. Dramatists, not excluding Zola himself, in spite of his fulminations against *any* kind of "arrangement," continued to "arrange" life more or less. To be an art, how could the drama fail to be an arrangement? The same question would arise when enthusiasts of stage naturalism thought that they were creating a completely natural art of theatre, free of all conventions. How could the theatre fail to abide by some degree and some kind of convention? A realistic, even naturalistic, stage production only created its own conven-

tion. It based its acting style on the hypothesis that the large open space framed by the proscenium arch was a "fourth wall" that shut the actor off completely from the audience. If the front of the set had been an *actual* fourth wall, how could an actor have been seen or heard from the auditorium? Nevertheless, the natural, "unarranged" (that is, inconspicuously arranged) dramatic style was to give us after Zola's trumpetings such persuasive and affecting works as the best plays of Chekhov and O'Casey. And the "unconventional" (that is, inconspicuously conventional) theatre was to yield the memorable productions of the Moscow Art Theatre and the early Abbey Theatre in Dublin.

No program is more valuable than the uses to which it is put. Zola's propaganda challenged the old romantic and contrived styles of the drama and justified a more natural art of playwriting, as well as greater fidelity to life, than had been considered desirable in dramatic writing before 1870. The playwrights and stage producers who put his proposals into successful practice in their own way were the genuine artists of the theatre. Their creativity at its best was always individual, sometimes intensely personal.

Always, indeed, it was the personal talent of an Ibsen, Strindberg, or Chekhov that made realism and naturalism important on the stage and between the covers of a book. Realism was undoubtedly promoted by a change in the theatre audiences of the nineteenth century, which became increasingly middle class after 1830. Understandably, they favored plays that dealt with the world they knew and that presented a real environment on the stage. Naturalism was unquestionably aided in Europe by advances in science (Zola wanted the French intellect to keep in step with scientific advances being made throughout Europe, especially in Germany). The decline of idealism as a consequence of political corruption during the reign of Louis Philippe and the failure of the revolutionary movements of 1848 no doubt inclined men toward the deterministic and unemotional view of reality held by the naturalists. But it was the creativity of playwrights and stage directors in response to these and other developments that gave us a theatre vital enough to deserve our interest and respect.

THE NEW THEATRE

A new drama requires a new theatre, and a new theatre was born by the last decade of the nineteenth century. Its history, like that of the drama, consists of at first half-understood, gradual advances within the province of the older theatre itself, of some skirmishing at the borders by a hardy forerunner of new stagecraft (the Duke of Saxe-Meiningen), and, finally, of decisive victories by leaders who were articulate and wholly aware of their mission.

As for the initial trends, they may be summarized best as responses to the failure of romantic theatre in the nineteenth century. Ever since the Renaissance in Italy, the European theatre had tried to simulate backgrounds by combining architecture and painting on the stage. "Side wings" of painted canvas stretched on wooden frames were placed in grooves at the sides of the stage. They were arranged in accordance with the laws of perspective so as to form a stage picture, which was completed by the addition of a painted backdrop. The feats of Renaissance and seventeenth-century scene designers were often extraordinarily beautiful, especially when viewed from the front rows center in the auditorium. These "wing-and-backdrop" settings were in effect architectural forms in the contemporary Baroque style and created illusion conventionally. Most of the acting took place in front of the setting, so that there was no great discrepancy between the real actors and the simulated street scene or interior on the stage. In the nineteenth century, the platform in front of the setting began to disappear and the actors played more and more within the set. But they continued to indulge in soliloquies and asides, to act in a declamatory style, and to address themselves to the audience, as though they were not sitting and moving within the scenic environment. This alone would have made the performance flagrantly artificial, and the formal style of acting actually became absurd when the subject was middle-class life and the characters were ordinary persons.

The artificiality of the theatre was made transparent by the nature of the settings themselves. These continued to be built of canvas, yet the flats were now used to create the impression of real rooms instead of being arranged by means of a backdrop and side wings to create an essentially formal effect. The flats were put together to form the walls of a room. Since these walls were made of canvas, however, they were flimsy and the actors had to be warned not to lean against them lest they destroy the illusion by shaking the set. Canvas doors with the cloth shivering on them when they were opened or closed could reduce an entrance or an exit to an absurdity. Worse still, some doors and part of the furniture were painted on the walls, and sometimes entire scenes were painted on backdrops. If the actor backed up far enough he might tower over the objects diminished in perspective, and there would also be a discrepancy between the shadows the living person cast under the lights and the painted shadows. Here, then, was a theatre that tried to create illusion with illusion-destroying means. It was doomed by its own ineptitude.

Meanwhile the trend toward making stage production more realistic was already under way. It started with an antiquarian movement that introduced authentic costuming into the theatre and tried to make the painted setting an accurate re-production of a classic background or a medieval scene. Producers were indeed so proud of such achievements that they publicized them, citing authorities to prove that their costumes, stage properties, scenery, spectacles, and dances were authentic. In time, too, the old painted flats vanished and were supplanted by solid scenery, and when ceilings were placed across the walls of the setting, the theatre acquired the "box set" still in use when interiors are represented. Once the old "apron," or forestage, was eliminated, all the acting was cut off from the audience. A distinct environment became possible for the performance on the stage, and the presentation of environment assumed increasing importance to realists and naturalists. Stock scenery was discarded, and special scenery which was solid and practical was constructed for each play.

Once the box set came into use, it was plain, too, that a new convention had arisen. Since the setting was now enclosed on three sides by walls, a "fourth wall" had to be assumed. Inevitably, given the stage, the empty space framed by the proscenium arch had to be assumed to represent the fourth wall of a room, and, in time, the actor was expected to treat it as such. He had to perform as though he were living not in the theatre but in privacy behind the "wall." Much as it distressed the old-time actor, he could no longer ogle the audience and declaim to it. He could not even take "stage center" on every occasion without violating the naturalness expected of actions behind the "wall." A modern director would actually expect him to turn his back to the public from time to time, as if oblivious that he was being observed by an audience "out front," and the scene designer might place a piece of furniture against the imaginary partition. The playwright was also importantly affected by the new convention. He became conscious of the absurdity of writing the time-honored soliloquies and asides of the older styles of drama once the actor was no longer on terms of intimacy with the public and could not take it into his confidence concerning his state of mind or secret intentions. Acting and stage production consequently became increasingly "natural." These changes, accelerated by the introduction of gas and electric illumination, were tantamount to a revolution in the theatre.

The important changes were effectuated by far-seeing leaders who created their own acting companies while the established theatre held on to outworn practices as long as possible. Among the pioneers, four or five were particularly influential, and the history of realism on the stage is largely the history of their efforts. In chronological order, they are the Duke of Saxe-Meiningen, André Antoine, Otto Brahm, Constantin Stanislavsky, and his associate, Vladimir Nemirovitch-Dantchenko.

In the eighteen-seventies the Duke of Saxe-Meiningen created an acting company for the court theatre of his little duchy, and for seventeen seasons between 1874 and 1890 the troupe made notable advances in authentic costuming, carefully designed scenery, and effective ensemble acting. In staging a battle scene, for example, the Duke went so far in his passion for realism as to place a stuffed horse on the stage. He employed the famous realistic painters Israels and Liebermann as scenic artists. For exterior scenes the Duke broke up the stage floor into different levels, creating a realistic effect of uneven ground. But his crowning achievement was his meticulous treatment of crowds on the stage. He was so intent upon individualizing these that he would even place important members of his company in the mob whenever they were not playing major roles. When a prominent actress refused to do "mob duty" she was summarily dismissed. By emphasizing ensemble performances, the Duke actually abolished the time-honored "star" system, and he gave full sway to the stage director as the autocrat of the stage, responsible for a unified production. There was nothing regimental about the Meiningen crowds; symmetrical arrangements were abolished; the actors were ordered to look at one another or at the events transpiring in their presence instead of facing the audience. Antoine, who saw a performance of the Meiningen company in Brussels in the summer of 1888, was particularly impressed with the crowd scenes and tableaux. Although the Duke also produced some of Ibsen's dramas (*Pillars of Society* and *A Doll's House*), his repertory consisted mostly of plays by Shakespeare and later romantic works by Schiller, Kleist, and others. But his stagecraft marked the first major advance toward realistic theatre. Among those who were stimulated by the Meiningen company's achievements were Antoine and Stanislavsky, who saw its performances in Moscow in 1885. Since the Duke made every effort to display his troupe outside his own little territory (his capital city had no more than eight thousand inhabitants), he was a remarkably effective missionary for early realism. He brought the company to Berlin on May 1, 1874, and to Vienna and Budapest in 1875. Between 1874 and 1890 the Meiningen group played 385 times in Berlin and 2,206 times on tours through Germany, Switzerland, Poland, Russia, Denmark, Sweden, Holland, Belgium, and England.

Antoine's contributions to realistic theatrical art occurred in Paris, the capital of European culture. An employee of the Paris Gas Company, he had trained himself for an acting career and joined a small amateur group, the Cercle Gaulois. At first he had only vague aspirations and no program, but when he tried to produce a realistic one-act play based on a story by Zola he found it necessary to break with the Cercle Gaulois. He formed his own group, named it Le Théâtre Libre (The Free Theatre) and presented a first bill of one-acters on May 30, 1887. As Zola and his followers gave the project their support, the Théâtre Libre became the outpost of French naturalism. Soon Antoine produced the work of Ibsen, Strindberg, Tolstoy, and Hauptmann, among others; his little subscription theatre became the seat of European naturalism. Subsequently he founded another, larger theatre for the general public, the Théâtre Antoine, and ran it for nine years (1897–1906). He also took charge of the state theatre, the Odéon, for some eight years, until 1914. He won fame as an actor and became an effective drama critic.

Antoine's influence continued long after he resigned from the Théâtre Libre in 1894, but it was there that he inaugurated realistic stagecraft. In the course of his work as manager, actor, and stage director he banished the false theatricality of the conventional French theatre. He abolished the declamatory style, introduced realistic settings, going so far as to hang real meat on hooks in a butcher-shop scene, and he even had his actors now and then turn their backs on the audience. He was willing to grant that the stage setting was a matter of secondary importance for the performance of a classic drama, but he considered it of major significance in the staging of "works written in the vein of realism and naturalism, where the theory of environment and the influence of exterior things have become so important." "Should it not assume on the stage," he added, "the same importance as a description in a novel?" Antoine's work at the Théâtre Libre, as well as its extension into the larger theatres of France and its dissemination in other little theatres, was the second round of the battle for a realistic stage.

The third round was fought under the leadership of a critic turned director, Otto Brahm, who opened a little theatre in Berlin on September 29, 1889, in imitation of Antoine's project. The Freie Bühne (literally the Free Stage) began by producing Ibsen's *Ghosts*. Then followed a native naturalistic play, Hauptmann's *Before Sunrise*, the De Goncourt brothers' *Henriette Maréchal*, Tolstoy's *The Power of Darkness*, and three other native dramas. In its second season, the Freie Bühne gave seven plays, including Zola's *Thérèse Raquin*, Becque's *The Vultures*, Strindberg's *The Father*, and Hauptmann's *Lonely Lives*. When this last play was accepted in 1892 by the citadel of conventional art, the Deutsches Theater of Berlin, victory was in sight. In 1894, Otto Brahm was made the director of the Deutsches Theater, the new realistic style triumphed, and Brahm completed the renovation of theatrical art in Germany. The Freie Bühne ceased operations, having accomplished its pioneering task.

Brahm introduced into Central Europe practically the same realistic innovations that Antoine had developed in France. He achieved many triumphs with his famous "Brahm style" of plain and natural stagecraft, which made the actors underplay their roles and speak as casually as the scene permitted. A declared enemy of theatricalism and artifice, he strove for authenticity rather than theatrical effect, forbidding his cast to indulge in any emphases not absolutely required by a situation. Brahm got rewarding results whenever he staged a realistic play. He failed only when he mistakenly applied the principles of realism to Shakespearean drama.

The widening arc of the free-theatre movement in Europe reached its farthest points when it touched Moscow and London. The Independent Theatre, founded in London in 1891 by Jacob T. Grein, a native of Holland, is less important for its founder's innovations of theatrical art than for its hospitality to the new drama. Grein's theatre never had more than 175 supporters, but among these were such important men as George Meredith, Thomas Hardy, George Moore, Frank Harris, William Archer, Bernard Shaw, Arthur Wing Pinero, and Henry Arthur Jones. The Independent Theatre lasted from 1891 to 1897 and produced twenty-six plays. Like Brahm, Grein selected *Ghosts* for his opening salvo. His second production was Zola's *Thérèse Raquin*, and to Grein goes the credit for having introduced Shaw as a playwright with *Widowers' Houses* (1893). In Moscow, six years after the establishment of a free theatre in London, there was born an enterprise of greater and more lasting importance, the Moscow Art Theatre, which developed the art of inner realism in addition to adopting external realism in the stage picture.

Stanislavsky and Dantchenko's theatre became notable on many counts. Founded in 1897, it has lasted up to the present time. It reached large audiences in Russia and it also toured Europe and the United States extensively. It fathered other enterprises, including a second studio devoted to musical productions. It also made Anton Chekhov a dramatist of international renown after successfully reviving his failure *The Sea Gull,* and it introduced Maxim Gorki to the world with *The Lower Depths.* Its most important achievement, however, was its development of the art of acting. Largely owing to the genius of Stanislavsky as a director and teacher

of acting, the Moscow company carried realistic performance beyond mimicry and verisimilitude.

Actors were trained to achieve an "inner justification" for their roles, to make a complete identification with the characters they played. Step by step, an actor was expected to lose his own personality as something that stands apart from the role. But this was to be done not by destroying the individuality of the performer but by exploring it for elements of experience and emotion that would enable him to re-create himself as a character in the play. And for this purpose, the Moscow Art Theatre actors followed processes in preparing their parts that have come to be known as the "Stanislavsky system," although the word "system" must be employed with the widest possible latitude. The preparation of a role included exercises before and during rehearsals: "sense memory," by means of which the actor gained mastery of the physical actions he was expected to perform; "affective memory," through which he made his feeling genuine by drawing upon memories of his own experience, emotions, or states of mind which paralleled the feelings he was expected to express on the stage; and "improvisations," with which he imagined or performed actions that he would not exhibit on the stage after the rehearsals but that he would have performed if he had been the same character outside the text of the play. By means of such intensive preparation over a period of many months, the actors were fully justified in calling their art "a theatre of inner feeling." In becoming the world's foremost theatre, in maintaining that position for half a century, inspiring other groups with its example, and revolutionizing the training of actors, the Moscow Art Theatre brought the advances of the earlier pioneers of the stage to their ultimate realization.

A revolution was needed in theatrical art before the revolution in playwriting could be made complete and effectual. The free-theatre movement effected this revolution between 1887 and 1900, concluding the first major phase of the modernization of the stage and drama.

Henrik Ibsen

(1828–1906)

To the unwary, Ibsen can be one of the most deceptive of dramatists. He was an advocate of causes who was apt to reverse himself disconcertingly. A flouter of middle-class convention in his writings, he was nevertheless very much of the middle class himself. He dressed meticulously, liked to display the orders of merit that governments and royalty bestowed on him, and invested his royalties in railroad securities and other sound businesses with the care of a conservative banker. For a cosmopolitan artist who spent much of his adult life in foreign lands, he was singularly provincial in many respects. As a political thinker, he gave comfort at different times to both the liberals and conservatives of his native Norway, and both were mistaken in claiming his undivided allegiance. A poet of distinction, he wrote some of the most outwardly prosaic masterpieces of the drama, and he continued to write lyric poetry during the decisive period when he made the prose play the norm for modern playwriting. He injected realism into his early, romantic dramas, and introduced symbolism into his late, realistic work. Ibsen was uniquely a writer who could sing like a thrush and croak like a raven—sometimes simultaneously. Only a full-length study can chart the contradictions of the man and the artist.

If Ibsen was nonetheless portrayed by many of his champions as a modern realist with a reformer's zeal and simple sociological outlook, the reason is that there was a need to create this concept of a fighting realist in the late nineteenth century. The simplified Ibsen was an invention, or "construct," of history as a result of the interest in science and sociology, the emancipation of women, and the liberalization of religion and government that started well before 1875 but became particularly marked after that date. Since Ibsen responded intensely to his times, he collaborated with history in the style and content of about a dozen of his plays, even if the collaboration was on his own terms as man and artist. Especially after 1875, he wrote a series of plays that were explicit enough, at least on the surface, to be praised or denounced as realistic vehicles of modern problems and ideas.

For convenience his plays may be divided into three categories: romantic drama, from his first play, *Catiline,* in 1850, to *Emperor and Galilean* in 1873; realistic drama, from *The Pillars of Society* in 1877 to *Hedda Gabler* in 1890; and symbolist drama, from *The Lady from the Sea* in 1888 to his last work, *When We Dead Awaken,* in 1899. He was as much an artist in one phase as he was in another, but it was the Ibsen of the middle period who was, and still is, singled out as the dramatist important, for better or worse, to society and the theatre. Of the plays in this segment of his career, moreover, there were several—*Pillars of Society, A Doll's House, Ghosts,* and *An Enemy of the People*—that presented social problems of importance to their times and did so in an unorthodox manner that could not be ignored. Ibsen became a hero to progressives and Antichrist to the conservatives. He kept his own counsel more often than either side realized, but this did not matter to his supporters and enemies. He became the central figure of the modern drama because he incorporated modern tensions. *Peer Gynt,* a play that belongs essentially to the romantic theatre, is his greatest work. But it is *Ghosts* that made Ibsen the most influential dramatist of the modern theatre.

Born and reared in the town of Skien in southeastern Norway, Ibsen was to experience the narrowness of provincial society from the moment his wealthy merchant family lost its fortune when he was eight years old. Poverty brought social ostracism in its wake, and the lad, who had to be sent to a poor people's school where he received an inferior education, became ingrown and embittered. Nor did he find much sympathy in his family—in later life he maintained virtually no connection with its members except for one sister, Hedwig. His father was always absorbed in his own troubles, and his mother's religious dogmatism created a gulf which her son was disinclined to bridge.

Ibsen began to reveal a talent for painting, dreamed of going to Dresden or Rome to study art, and took some instruction from a local landscape painter. Since art was no career for a poor boy, he fixed his eyes on medicine, but lacking both the means and the educational prerequisites, he became apprenticed in 1844 to a pharmacist in Grimstad, a small town in the south, a day's travel by steamer from Skien. He was fifteen, thin and undersized, when he left his parents, and he returned to Skien for a visit only once in his life, six years later.

A community lacking cultural activities, with only one teacher for over a hundred children, Grimstad was no improvement upon Skien. For three years Ibsen lived alone with his dreams, growing into the taciturn and dour individual he remained even in the days when he was feted by royalty and pursued by admirers of both sexes. But Grimstad was on the sea and on its shores Ibsen fed poetry into his soul.

besides, the town had a little lending library which enabled him to immerse himself in the Danish comedies of Holberg and the romantic literature of Goethe, Schiller, and Heine. He grew a huge black seaman's beard and began to write verse. In his fourth year in Grimstad he found a congenial friend in a young customs inspector, Christopher Due, who in turn introduced him to a law student, Schulerud. They soon formed a little circle of radicals and called for a Scandinavian union against Prussian expansionism, then threatening to wrest the province of Schleswig-Holstein from Denmark. Ibsen's contribution to the cause consisted of impassioned tirades and the poem "Awake, Ye Scandinavians" (1849). Less innocent were his pranks on Grimstad citizens, his drinking and card parties, and his consorting with a servant girl whose illegitimate child he had to support for fourteen years. It was in Grimstad, moreover, that he began to think of a literary career; he was encouraged by Due, who had his nature poem "In Autumn" published in the *Christiania Post.*

Revolution was in the air in 1848 and the failure of the uprisings that broke out at the time in Germany and Hungary strengthened his conviction that he was called upon to express the momentous struggles of the day. "Deeper I must thrust and lower, Till I hear the ring of ore," he wrote in a poem entitled "The Miner." And taking his cue from his reading in Cicero and Sallust, he wrote his first verse drama, *Catiline,* under the pen name of Brynjolf Bjarme. It was a historical play in the romantic vein that glorified the Roman traitor as an enemy of convention and a man who "burns in freedom's holy zeal." His law-student friend Schulerud took it to Christiania, but was unable to place it with either a theatre or a publisher; he finally printed it at his own expense as a token of his faith in Ibsen, who was then in despair over an unsuccessful love affair. Confident of his friend's future, Schulerud also encouraged him to leave Grimstad and enroll at the University of Christiania.

To prepare for the entrance examinations he entered a "student factory," where he met other young men with literary ambitions, among them Björnstjerne Björnson, who became Norway's leading man of letters while Ibsen still lived in obscurity. Unable to matriculate at the University, however, he gave up his ambition to study medicine, and enrolled only for special lectures given by a prominent poet. He joined a short-lived liberal weekly, to which he contributed sarcastic articles and caricatures. He signed political protests and joined a secret revolutionary society, whose leaders were arrested within the year and sentenced to long prison terms. Ibsen was shocked by this turn of events and, never possessing much physical courage, thereafter refrained scrupulously from political activities. He finished a romantic medieval play, *The Warrior's Barrow,* and saw it performed three times in Christiania in September and October 1850. Attracting attention with a patriotic verse prologue written for the opening of a national theatre in Bergen, the young playwright suddenly found himself launched upon a career that was to make him world famous.

Invited to serve as theatre poet and stage manager at the Bergen theatre by its founder and director, the famous Norwegian violinist and national hero Ole Bull, Ibsen left Christiania in the fall of 1851. He spent six years at Bergen, learning more about the theatre from his experience there than he could teach the more or less inexperienced actors whom he timidly directed. Fortunately, too, the trustees of the theatre subsidized him to study the stage in Copenhagen and Dresden the next year, on the condition that he would obligate himself to stage-manage in Bergen for a period of five years. He returned from his travels a well-informed young man and brought with him the first of the plays he wrote for the National Theatre, a fairy play, *St. John's Night,* inspired by a continental production of *A Midsummer Night's Dream.* Henceforth, his work as stage manager was notable for efficiency, as he prepared each scene for the stage in "production books" with illustrations of the background and notations for the stage movement. As he put into production 145 plays by Holberg, Scribe, Shakespeare, and others, assigning the roles to the actors and supervising their rehearsals, he acquired a practical knowledge possessed by few important playwrights since Molière. As his contract also required him to write one play a year for performance on the anniversary of the theatre, he had, in addition, an unusual incentive for playwriting. The national idealism of his historical play *Lady Inger of Ostrat* won favor in 1855, and the piece he wrote for the season of 1856, *The Feast at Solhoug,* a lyrical drama based on medieval Norwegian balladry, proved successful not only in Bergen but subsequently in Christiania. In that same happy year he met and proposed to Susannah Thoresen, daughter of the dean of a church in Bergen, who was to prove a staunch companion during the rest of his life. The young woman became the model for the *femme fatale* of his next drama, *The Vikings of Helgeland,* produced in Christiania in 1857 and considered the outstanding Norwegian play of its time.

During that summer, Ibsen became director of the Norwegian Theatre in Christiania, and in this capacity he spent his next five years until the theatre went bankrupt in 1862. In Christiania, Ibsen married his fiancée (1858), and became the father of a son, Sigurd. Throwing himself wholeheartedly into the world of the large city, he founded with Björnson a Norwegian society for the promotion of national culture, joined an iconoclastic literary circle that called itself "The Hollanders," and participated in its alcoholic and intellectual revelries, neglecting his stage duties and his writing. He did not publish another play till 1862, when *Love's Comedy* appeared. Regarded as scandalous, it proved a fiasco, although this verse satire on conventional love and marriage later came to be considered the first important step in Ibsen's development as a realist and social critic. On top of this fiasco came the bankruptcy of the Norwegian Theatre, and Ibsen found himself in desperate straits. He became shabby and moody, took to drink, and was often found lying in the gutter late at night.

Fortunately his spirits rallied and, fired by his dream of a Scandinavian union against Prussia, he composed a historical drama, *The Pretenders*, in two months of excited writing during 1863. The production at the Christiania Theatre was successful, and this profound drama won him a government stipend of four hundred dollars for travel. He began to envision himself once more as his nation's bard and conscience, publishing a fiery poem in favor of aid to Denmark; but the failure of Norway to rise to his heroic demands, and the defeat of the Danes by Prussia depressed him when he left the country in the spring of 1864. He remained a voluntary exile from Norway for twenty-seven years.

Brooding in Rome on the cautious Philistinism of his countrymen, and stirred by the liberation movement in Italy under Garibaldi, Ibsen wrote his ringing verse drama *Brand,* whose clerical hero rejects all compromise and tries to lead his flock to the heights regardless of consequences. The entire Scandinavian world, which could hardly have missed the implications of this dramatic epic, was excited when *Brand* was published in 1866. Its author was voted a lifelong pension by the Norwegian parliament, and the demand for the book was so great that it had to be republished numerous times. Relieved of financial pressure, Ibsen wrote a reverse treatment of the theme of heroism in *Peer Gynt,* whose hero never commits himself to anything and is deficient in integrity. In *Peer Gynt,* published in 1867 with tremendous success, Ibsen produced an amalgam of humor and pathos, folklore and fantasy. The careless hero of the play became the incarnation of the spinelessness and opportunism that Ibsen deplored in his country, and, by extension, the play became the classic indictment of the antiheroic modern man. For a romantic drama it was an unusually devastating social exposé, and it remains a modern masterpiece. For a satire, however, it was a singularly imaginative and poetic drama, and it towers above the topical plays of the modern theatre engendered largely by Ibsen's own later social dramas. With this work, moreover, he brought the long first period of his career to its peak. After 1867, he wrote only two more verse plays, the uneven philosophical double-drama *Emperor and Galilean* (1873), which called for a fusion of Christian and pagan ideals, and *When We Dead Awaken* (1899), a feeble last effort before illness incapacitated him for the rest of his life.

After *Peer Gynt,* Ibsen was to establish a second claim to fame, this time as a realist rather than as a dramatic poet whose ideas were modern but whose artistic ties were with the older theatre of romanticism. In 1869 came his prose satire on political opportunism or pseudo liberalism, *The League of Youth,* and its reception indicated that Ibsen had started on a difficult new road. The riots that greeted the play in Norway were dress rehearsals for the fury that was to be unleashed by Ibsen's later social problem plays. *The Pillars of Society* (1877), an attack on the unscrupulous practices of shipbuilders and on the shaky foundations of respectability in general, was the exception. Five theatres played it simultaneously in Berlin early in 1878, and it was with this play that Ibsen became the most popular modern dramatist in Germany. The years 1876 to 1878 were, indeed, roseate for Ibsen; in 1876 *Peer Gynt,* with incidental music by the young Edvard Grieg, enjoyed an unprecedented run in Christiania, and in 1877 the University of Upsala awarded Ibsen an honorary doctor's degree, so that he proudly could list himself henceforth as "Doctor" Henrik Ibsen. And it is just as well that he collected his harvest of reputation and royalties at that time. Two years later, in 1879, his name was anathema to conservatives as the author of *A Doll's House;* and four years later, when he published *Ghosts,* he was pilloried as the perpetrator of the greatest scandal of modern times.

A Doll's House was the fruit of reflection on woman's dependent status in society and a response to the growing clamor for "women's rights," a subject to which Ibsen had been introduced ten years earlier by Georg Brandes' translation of John Stuart Mill's treatise *The Subjection of Women.* The production of *A Doll's House* in Christiania drew a storm of protest against his heroine Nora's leaving her husband, and other managements refused to produce the play at all until Ibsen obliged them by composing an alternate ending in which Nora stayed home for the sake of her children. (Ibsen, incidentally, left an unfinished play, hitherto unpublished, which traces Nora's career after she left her "doll's house.") To the opposition, it seemed as if Ibsen had taken an ax not merely to the "doll's house" Nora abandoned in search of self-realization but to the foundations of the church and state. Nevertheless, Ibsen won a victory for himself and for realism in the theatre. The Christiania playhouse gave twenty-five performances of the work in the winter of 1879–1880 and it was triumphantly staged, without the alternate ending, at Munich in March 1880.

Ghosts (1881) was a logical sequel to *A Doll's House.* In the earlier play a wife had left her home after discovering that she was the useless property of her husband and had been reared in ignorance of the world outside her household. And for this Nora had been roundly denounced, especially by clergymen, as having behaved "unnaturally." In

Ghosts, Ibsen reversed the situation. In heeding the clergyman, Pastor Manders, and not leaving her husband, Mrs. Alving had been guilty of an act far more "unnatural" than anything that could have been charged against Nora. Irony could go no further than Mrs. Alving's reward for obeying conventional precepts. The wages of "virtue" here are paresis for the son and desperation for the mother. It is not difficult to understand why the play should have outraged the circumspect, for whom the mere mention of Oswald's "social disease" on the stage would have been sufficient provocation.

In the perspective of time, *Ghosts* is important for reasons other than the scandal it caused. Ibsen was under the influence of Zola when he wrote the play. By incorporating environment and heredity as decisive factors in his drama, and by admitting the scientific knowledge of his day into the theatre, Ibsen gave naturalism its most controversial work. No other stage piece disseminated the naturalists' program so widely or so arrestingly. Ibsen proved himself a greater craftsman than any of the confirmed modernists. "Natural" dramaturgy was as much a part of the naturalist program as the candid presentation of life, no matter how sordid the details. But no one else except Henry Becque (whose exemplary drama *The Vultures* was still unproduced in 1881) was as yet capable of dispensing entirely with artificial dialogue, suspensive intrigue, and theatrical trickery.

Ibsen went so far toward abolishing "plot" that he eliminated all events antecedent to the critical situation. He dramatized only the harvest of Mrs. Alving's conformity to the conventional code. The past is shown dramatically in those parts of the play in which Mrs. Alving reacts to drastic developments and exposes her situation to the pastor who sent her back to a dissipated husband. Ibsen's procedure was, in fact, radical even for the naturalists who congregated in Antoine's theatre nine years later. When, at Zola's suggestion, Antoine produced the play at the Théâtre Libre on May 30, 1890, the playwright Henry Céard complained that it was too obscure "for our Latin brains." He suggested using a prologue in which Oswald's father would be surprised by the young Mrs. Alving in the act of making love to Regina's mother. After this, "a French public would enter into the significance of the play perfectly."

That was not, of course, the "significance" that Ibsen strove for in *Ghosts,* any more than he was particularly concerned with venereal disease or with the question of mercy killing. (When asked whether Mrs. Alving administered the lethal pills to her imbecile son after the final curtain, Ibsen invariably replied that he did not know.) As a work of art, indeed, Ibsen's drama still eludes the superficial reader and stage director. *Ghosts* became famous as a model naturalistic document and social-problem play, but it is both less and more than that. As a

"problem play" about heredity and disease, it has been outdated for many decades and, for all its realism, it is not a mere slice-of-life exercise, since Ibsen contrived the action to enforce his argument. His skill is so great that everything seems entirely natural in the play, and yet it consists of coincidences like the fire in the orphan asylum, the revelation that Regina is Oswald's illegitimate half sister, and the discovery of Oswald's ailment. Blow after blow is struck by the hammer of dramaturgy in order to destroy the rotten edifice that convention had reared. Behind the mask of Ibsen's prosaic dialogue and pretence of ordinariness hides the face of an ironist and poet.

The ironist, who mocks Pastor Manders on every occasion, becomes as mordant as Jonathan Swift in piling up the sequence of events. Mrs. Alving does not want to touch the money left by her husband, therefore she erects an orphan asylum in his name—a curious monument to a man who was a profligate all his life and whose illegitimate child is a servant girl in Mrs. Alving's household. The dedication ceremony is to be performed by the same Pastor Manders who has congratulated himself for many years on having saved Mrs. Alving's marriage! The institution must not be insured against fire, according to Manders, because it is under the protection of God. And it burns down! The late Alving's legacy goes up in smoke. But he has left another legacy—in the diseased bloodstream of his son. Mrs. Alving erected a last façade of respectability for her unhappy marriage, and it vanishes in a few minutes, whereas her "reward" for submission to convention is a grief that will endure to the end of her days. The traditionalists who were outraged by *Ghosts* had more reason than we are apt to concede today. If they complained that the play was cynical, they were actually more penetrative than latter-day innocents for whom it is a very simple tract.

The poet in Ibsen transmutes the simple idea of heredity into the Nemesis or Fate of Greek tragedy, and a bleak background and sultry weather brood over the proceedings; the atmosphere is that of the "haunted house" theme of romanticism. Ibsen here recalls the Aeschylus of the Oresteian trilogy and the Sophocles of *Oedipus Rex,* as well as the Poe of *The Fall of the House of Usher.* And the poetry has a dry, modern quality, for the haunted house is a bourgeois home in provincial Norway and the classic Fury or "domestic Ate" is now a streptococcus in the circulatory system. This is "bourgeois tragedy," antiheroic drama. The poet, moreover, transcends the simple social reformer with his grisly symbolism of the orphan asylum as the vain façade of respectability and of Oswald's ailment as the hidden reality. The very title of the play is symbolic and its story carries us beyond the manifest drama of hereditary disease. Mrs. Alving is haunted by the "ghosts" of the past—not only by Regina, the child of Alving's indiscretions, and by the unfortunate

Oswald, but by all the conformities she finally recognizes as unfortunate and evil. One of these ghosts of convention even goes as far back as her girlhood, for it was her early training that made her an inadequate wife and started Alving on his extramarital adventures. Even if Mrs. Alving had left her husband permanently after the first year of marriage there would have been ghosts of miseducation and false values to haunt her. The dark tones of the play, in sum, are overtones never present in humdrum topical plays that offer us a simple demonstration of a problem and one specific remedy.

Curiously enough, the first production of *Ghosts* was given in America, where not a single earlier play of Ibsen's had yet been produced. It was performed in 1882 by a company playing in Danish and Norwegian in Chicago, Minneapolis, and other cities of the Midwest. (The first American production of an Ibsen play in English was a bowdlerized version of *A Doll's House* under the title of *Thora*.) The European *première* of *Ghosts* was in Helsingborg, Sweden, in 1883. That year, too, a provincial company gave performances in Denmark, and another production materialized in the Dramatic Theatre in Stockholm.

The violent attacks on *Ghosts* from all quarters in Norway, its rejection by Norwegian theatres, and the refusal of booksellers to stock copies of the published play drew eloquent rejoinders from Björnson and the great Danish critic Georg Brandes. In April 1886, an enthusiastic Viennese playwright, Felix Philippi, gave the first German production of the play in the Bavarian city of Augsburg, northwest of Munich. It was a private performance, since *Ghosts* was then still banned in Germany as a revolutionary play "with destructive tendencies." Next, the Duke of Saxe-Meiningen, the pioneer of stage realism in Europe, gave the play in his ducal theatre at Meiningen in December 1886 and signalized the occasion by knighting the author. Elsewhere the play became a rallying point for such vigorous modernists as the young Bernard Shaw and Emile Zola, and the critic turned director, Otto Brahm, defiantly started the first season of his Berlin progressive theatre, the Freie Bühne, with *Ghosts* on the afternoon of September 29, 1889. Antoine himself played the part of Oswald seven months later in his Théâtre Libre production. Public productions of *Ghosts* were forbidden in England as late as 1891, but J. T. Grein gave one private performance for the subscribers of his Independent Theatre in London on March 13, 1891.

BIBLIOGRAPHY: William Archer, Introductions to *The Collected Works of Henrik Ibsen*, 1906–1912; Eric Bentley, *The Playwright as Thinker* (pp. 92–94, 102–135, 140–144), 1946; Anita Block, *The Changing World in Plays and Theatre* (pp. 22–33), 1939; Barrett H. Clark and George Freedley, *A History of Modern Drama* (pp. 1–20), 1947; John Gassner, *Masters of the Drama* (pp. 354–386), 1945; Edmund Gosse, *Henrik Ibsen* (with essays by Edward Dowden and James Huneker), 1917; James Huneker, *Iconoclasts* (pp. 1–138), 1905; Halvdan Koht, *The Life of Ibsen*, 1931; A. E. Zucker, *Ibsen the Master-Builder*, 1929.

For additional commentary, see pages 40–41.

GHOSTS

By Henrik Ibsen

TRANSLATED FROM THE NORWEGIAN BY WILLIAM ARCHER [1]

CHARACTERS

MRS. HELEN ALVING, *widow of Captain Alving, late Chamberlain to the King*
OSWALD ALVING, *her son, a painter*
PASTOR MANDERS

JACOB ENGSTRAND, *a carpenter*
REGINA ENGSTRAND, *Mrs. Alving's maid*
The action takes place at Mrs. Alving's country house, beside one of the large fjords in Western Norway.

ACT I

A spacious garden-room, with one door to the left, and two doors to the right. In the middle of the room a round table, with chairs about it. On the table lie books, periodicals, and newspapers. In the foreground to the left a window, and by it a small sofa, with a work-table in front of it. In the background, the room is continued into a somewhat narrower conservatory, the walls of which are formed by large panes of glass. In the right-hand wall of the conservatory is a door leading down into the garden. Through the glass wall a gloomy fjord-landscape is faintly visible, veiled by steady rain. Engstrand, the carpenter, who has a club foot, stands by the garden door. His left leg is somewhat bent; he has a clump of wood under the sole of his boot. Regina, with an empty garden syringe in her hand, hinders him from advancing.

REGINA: [*In a low voice*] What do you want? Stop where you are. You're positively dripping.

ENGSTRAND: It's the Lord's own rain, my girl.

REGINA: It's the devil's rain, *I* say.

ENGSTRAND: Lord, how you talk, Regina. [*Limps a step or two forward into the room*] It's just this as I wanted to say—

REGINA: Don't clatter so with that foot of yours, I tell you! The young master's asleep upstairs.

ENGSTRAND: Asleep? In the middle of the day?

REGINA: It's no business of yours.

ENGSTRAND: I was out on the loose last night—

REGINA: I can quite believe that.

ENGSTRAND: Yes, we're weak vessels, we poor mortals, my girl—

REGINA: So it seems.

ENGSTRAND: —and temptations are manifold in this world, you see. But all the same, I was hard at work, God knows, at half-past five this morning.

REGINA: Very well; only be off now. I won't stop here and have *rendezvous* with you.

ENGSTRAND: What do you say you won't have?

REGINA: I won't have any one find you here; so just you go about your business.

ENGSTRAND: [*Advances a step or two*] Blest if I go before I've had a talk with you. This afternoon I shall have finished my work at the school-house, and then I shall take to-night's boat and be off home to the town.

REGINA: [*Mutters*] Pleasant journey to you!

ENGSTRAND: Thank you, my child. To-morrow the Orphanage is to be opened, and then there'll be fine doings, no doubt, and plenty of intoxicating drink going, you know. And nobody shall say of Jacob Engstrand that he can't keep out of temptation's way.

REGINA: Oh!

ENGSTRAND: You see, there's to be heaps of grand folks here to-morrow. Pastor Manders is expected from town, too.

REGINA: He's coming to-day.

ENGSTRAND: There, you see! And I should be cursedly sorry if he found out anything against me, don't you understand?

REGINA: Oho! is that your game?

ENGSTRAND: Is what my game?

REGINA: [*Looking hard at him*] What are you going to fool Pastor Manders into doing, this time?

ENGSTRAND: Sh! sh! Are you crazy? Do *I* want to fool Pastor Manders? Oh no! Pastor Manders has been far too good a friend to me for that. But I just wanted to say, you know—that I mean to be off home again to-night.

REGINA: The sooner the better, say I.

ENGSTRAND: Yes, but I want you with me, Regina.

REGINA: [*Open-mouthed*] You want me—? What are you talking about?

ENGSTRAND: I want you to come home with me, I say.

REGINA: [*Scornfully*] Never in this world shall you get me home with you.

ENGSTRAND: Oh, we'll see about that.

REGINA: Yes, you may be sure we'll see about it!

[1] Entirely revised by William Archer.

15

Me, that have been brought up by a lady like Mrs. Alving! Me, that am treated almost as a daughter here! Is it me you want to go home with you?—to a house like yours? For shame!

ENGSTRAND: What the devil do you mean? Do you set yourself up against your father, you hussy?

REGINA: [*Mutters without looking at him*] You've said often enough I was no concern of yours.

ENGSTRAND: Pooh! Why should you bother about that—

REGINA: Haven't you many a time sworn at me and called me a—? *Fi donc!*

ENGSTRAND: Curse me, now, if ever I used such an ugly word.

REGINA: Oh, I remember very well what word you used.

ENGSTRAND: Well, but that was only when I was a bit on with drink. Temptations are manifold in this world, Regina.

REGINA: Ugh!

ENGSTRAND: And besides, it was when your mother was that aggravating—I had to find something to twit her with, my child. She was always setting up for a fine lady. [*Mimics*] "Let me go, Engstrand; let me be. Remember I was three years in Chamberlain Alving's family at Rosenvold." [*Laughs*] Mercy on us! She could never forget that the Captain was made a Chamberlain while she was in service here.

REGINA: Poor mother! you very soon tormented her into her grave.

ENGSTRAND: [*With a twist of his shoulders*] Oh, of course! I'm to have the blame for everything.

REGINA: [*Turns away; half aloud*] Ugh—! And that leg too!

ENGSTRAND: What do you say, my child?

REGINA: *Pied de mouton.*

ENGSTRAND: Is that English, eh?

REGINA: Yes.

ENGSTRAND: Ay, ay; you've picked up some learning out here; and that may come in useful now, Regina.

REGINA: [*After a short silence*] What do you want with me in town?

ENGSTRAND: Can you ask what a father wants with his only child? A'n't I a lonely, forlorn widower?

REGINA: Oh, don't try on any nonsense like that with me! Why do you want me?

ENGSTRAND: Well, let me tell you, I've been thinking of setting up in a new line of business.

REGINA: [*Contemptuously*] You've tried that often enough, and much good you've done with it.

ENGSTRAND: Yes, but this time you shall see, Regina! Devil take me—

REGINA: [*Stamps*] Stop your swearing!

ENGSTRAND: Hush, hush; you're right enough there, my girl. What I wanted to say was just this—I've laid by a very tidy pile from this Orphanage job.

REGINA: Have you? That's a good thing for you.

ENGSTRAND: What can a man spend his ha'pence on here in this country hole?

REGINA: Well, what then?

ENGSTRAND: Why, you see, I thought of putting the money into some paying speculation. I thought of a sort of a sailor's tavern—

REGINA: Pah!

ENGSTRAND: A regular high-class affair, of course; not any sort of pig-sty for common sailors. No! damn it! it would be for captains and mates, and—and—regular swells, you know.

REGINA: And I was to—?

ENGSTRAND: You were to help, to be sure. Only for the look of the thing, you understand. Devil a bit of hard work shall you have, my girl. You shall do exactly what you like.

REGINA: Oh, indeed!

ENGSTRAND: But there must be a petticoat in the house; that's as clear as daylight. For I want to have it a bit lively-like in the evenings, with singing and dancing, and so on. You must remember they're weary wanderers on the ocean of life. [*Nearer*] Now don't be a fool and stand in your own light, Regina. What's to become of you out here? Your mistress has given you a lot of learning; but what good is that to you? You're to look after the children at the new Orphanage, I hear. Is that the sort of thing for you, eh? Are you so dead set on wearing your life out for a pack of dirty brats?

REGINA: No; if things go as I want them to— Well there's no saying—there's no saying.

ENGSTRAND: What do you mean by "there's no saying"?

REGINA: Never you mind.—How much money have you saved?

ENGSTRAND: What with one thing and another, a matter of seven or eight hundred crowns.

REGINA: That's not so bad.

ENGSTRAND: It's enough to make a start with, my girl.

REGINA: Aren't you thinking of giving me any?

ENGSTRAND: No, I'm blest if I am!

REGINA: Not even of sending me a scrap of stuff for a new dress?

ENGSTRAND: Come to town with me, my lass, and you'll soon get dresses enough.

REGINA: Pooh! I can do that on my own account, if I want to.

ENGSTRAND: No, a father's guiding hand is what you want, Regina. Now, I've got my eye on a capital house in Little Harbour Street. They don't want much ready-money; and it could be a sort of a Sailors' Home, you know.

REGINA: But I will not live with you! I have nothing whatever to do with you. Be off!

ENGSTRAND: You wouldn't stop long with me, my girl. No such luck! If you knew how to play your cards, such a fine figure of a girl as you've grown in the last year or two—

REGINA: Well?

ENGSTRAND: You'd soon get hold of some mate—or maybe even a captain—

REGINA: I won't marry any one of that sort. Sailors have no *savoir vivre*.

ENGSTRAND: What's that they haven't got?

REGINA: I know what sailors are, I tell you. They're not the sort of people to marry.

ENGSTRAND: Then never mind about marrying them. You can make it pay all the same. [*More confidential*] He—the Englishman—the man with the yacht—he came down with three hundred dollars, he did; and she wasn't a bit handsomer than you.

REGINA: [*Making for him*] Out you go!

ENGSTRAND: [*Falling back*] Come, come! You're not going to hit me, I hope.

REGINA: Yes, if you begin talking about mother I shall hit you. Get away with you, I say! [*Drives him back towards the garden door*] And don't slam the doors. Young Mr. Alving—

ENGSTRAND: He's asleep; I know. You're mightily taken up about young Mr. Alving— [*More softly*] Oho! you don't mean to say it's him as—?

REGINA: Be off this minute! You're crazy, I tell you! No, not that way. There comes Pastor Manders. Down the kitchen stairs with you.

ENGSTRAND: [*Towards the right*] Yes, yes, I'm going. But just you talk to him as is coming there. He's the man to tell you what a child owes its father. For I am your father all the same, you know. I can prove it from the church register.

[*He goes out through the second door to the right, which* Regina *has opened, and closes again after him.* Regina *glances hastily at herself in the mirror, dusts herself with her pocket handkerchief, and settles her necktie; then she busies herself with the flowers.* Pastor Manders, *wearing an overcoat, carrying an umbrella, and with a small travelling-bag on a strap over his shoulder, comes through the garden door into the conservatory*]

MANDERS: Good-morning, Miss Engstrand.

REGINA: [*Turning round, surprised and pleased*] No, really! Good-morning, Pastor Manders. Is the steamer in already?

MANDERS: It is just in. [*Enters the sitting-room*] Terrible weather we have been having lately.

REGINA: [*Follows him*] It's such blessed weather for the country, sir.

MANDERS: No doubt; you are quite right. We townspeople give too little thought to that. [*He begins to take off his overcoat*]

REGINA: Oh, mayn't I help you?—There! Why, how wet it is! I'll just hang it up in the hall. And your umbrella, too—I'll open it and let it dry.

[*She goes out with the things through the second door on the right.* Pastor Manders *takes off his travelling-bag and lays it and his hat on a chair. Meanwhile* Regina *comes in again*]

MANDERS: Ah, it's a comfort to get under cover. I hope everything is going on well here?

REGINA: Yes, thank you, sir.

MANDERS: You have your hands full, I suppose, in preparation for to-morrow?

REGINA: Yes, there's plenty to do, of course.

MANDERS: And Mrs. Alving is at home, I trust?

REGINA: Oh dear, yes. She's just upstairs, looking after the young master's chocolate.

MANDERS: Yes, by-the-bye—I heard down at the pier that Oswald had arrived.

REGINA: Yes, he came the day before yesterday. We didn't expect him before to-day.

MANDERS: Quite strong and well, I hope?

REGINA: Yes, thank you, quite; but dreadfully tired with the journey. He has made one rush right through from Paris—the whole way on one train, I believe. He's sleeping a little now, I think; so perhaps we'd better talk a little quietly.

MANDERS: Sh!—as quietly as you please.

REGINA: [*Arranging an arm-chair beside the table*] Now, do sit down, Pastor Manders, and make yourself comfortable. [*He sits down; she places a footstool under his feet*] There! Are you comfortable now, sir?

MANDERS: Thanks, thanks, extremely so. [*Looks at her*] Do you know, Miss Engstrand, I positively believe you have grown since I last saw you.

REGINA: Do you think so, sir? Mrs. Alving says I've filled out too.

MANDERS: Filled out? Well, perhaps a little; just enough. [*Short pause*]

REGINA: Shall I tell Mrs. Alving you are here?

MANDERS: Thanks, thanks, there is no hurry, my dear child.—By-the-bye, Regina, my good girl, tell me: how is your father getting on out here?

REGINA: Oh, thank you, sir, he's getting on well enough.

MANDERS: He called upon me last time he was in town.

REGINA: Did he, indeed? He's always so glad of a chance of talking to you, sir.

MANDERS: And you often look in upon him at his work, I daresay?

REGINA: I? Oh, of course, when I have time, I—

MANDERS: Your father is not a man of strong character, Miss Engstrand. He stands terribly in need of a guiding hand.

REGINA: Oh, yes; I daresay he does.

MANDERS: He requires some one near him whom he cares for, and whose judgment he respects. He frankly admitted as much when he last came to see me.

REGINA: Yes, he mentioned something of the sort to me. But I don't know whether Mrs. Alving can spare me; especially now that we've got the new Orphanage to attend to. And then I should be so sorry to leave Mrs. Alving; she has always been so kind to me.

MANDERS: But a daughter's duty, my good girl— Of course, we should first have to get your mistress's consent.

REGINA: But I don't know whether it would be

quite proper for me, at my age, to keep house for a single man.

MANDERS: What! My dear Miss Engstrand! When the man is your own father!

REGINA: Yes, that may be; but all the same— Now, if it were in a thoroughly nice house, and with a real gentleman—

MANDERS: Why, my dear Regina—

REGINA: —one I could love and respect, and be a daughter to—

MANDERS: Yes, but my dear, good child—

REGINA: Then I should be glad to go to town. It's very lonely out here; you know yourself, sir, what it is to be alone in the world. And I can assure you I'm both quick and willing. Don't you know of any such place for me, sir?

MANDERS: I? No, certainly not.

REGINA: But, dear, dear sir, do remember me if—

MANDERS: [*Rising*] Yes, yes, certainly, Miss Engstrand.

REGINA: For if I—

MANDERS: Will you be so good as to tell your mistress I am here?

REGINA: I will, at once, sir. [*She goes out to the left*]

MANDERS: [*Paces the room two or three times, stands a moment in the background with his hands behind his back, and looks out over the garden. Then he returns to the table, takes up a book, and looks at the title-page; starts, and looks at several books*] Ha—indeed!

[Mrs. Alving *enters by the door on the left; she is followed by* Regina, *who immediately goes out by the first door on the right*]

MRS. ALVING: [*Holds out her hand*] Welcome, my dear Pastor.

MANDERS: How do you do, Mrs. Alving? Here I am as I promised.

MRS. ALVING: Always punctual to the minute.

MANDERS: You may believe it was not so easy for me to get away. With all the Boards and Committees I belong to—

MRS. ALVING: That makes it all the kinder of you to come so early. Now we can get through our business before dinner. But where is your portmanteau?

MANDERS: [*Quickly*] I left it down at the inn. I shall sleep there to-night.

MRS. ALVING: [*Suppressing a smile*] Are you really not to be persuaded, even now, to pass the night under my roof?

MANDERS: No, no, Mrs. Alving; many thanks. I shall stay at the inn, as usual. It is so conveniently near the landing-stage.

MRS. ALVING: Well, you must have your own way. But I really should have thought we two old people—

MANDERS: Now you are making fun of me. Ah, you're naturally in great spirits to-day—what with to-morrow's festival and Oswald's return.

MRS. ALVING: Yes; you can think what a delight it is to me! It's more than two years since he was home last. And now he has promised to stay with me all the winter.

MANDERS: Has he really? That is very nice and dutiful of him. For I can well believe that life in Rome and Paris has very different attractions from any we can offer here.

MRS. ALVING: Ah, but here he has his mother, you see. My own darling boy—he hasn't forgotten his old mother!

MANDERS: It would be grievous indeed, if absence and absorption in art and that sort of thing were to blunt his natural feelings.

MRS. ALVING: Yes, you may well say so. But there's nothing of that sort to fear with him. I'm quite curious to see whether you know him again. He'll be down presently; he's upstairs just now, resting a little on the sofa. But do sit down, my dear Pastor.

MANDERS: Thank you. Are you quite at liberty—?

MRS. ALVING: Certainly. [*She sits by the table*]

MANDERS: Very well. Then let me show you— [*He goes to the chair where his travelling-bag lies, takes out a packet of papers, sits down on the opposite side of the table, and tries to find a clear space for the papers*] Now, to begin with, here is— [*Breaking off*] Tell me, Mrs. Alving, how do these books come to be here?

MRS. ALVING: These books? They are books I am reading.

MANDERS: Do you read this sort of literature?

MRS. ALVING: Certainly I do.

MANDERS: Do you feel better or happier for such reading?

MRS. ALVING: I feel, so to speak, more secure.

MANDERS: That is strange. How do you mean?

MRS. ALVING: Well, I seem to find explanation and confirmation of all sorts of things I myself have been thinking. For that is the wonderful part of it, Pastor Manders—there is really nothing new in these books, nothing but what most people think and believe. Only most people either don't formulate it to themselves, or else keep quiet about it.

MANDERS: Great heavens! Do you really believe that most people—?

MRS. ALVING: I do, indeed.

MANDERS: But surely not in this country? Not here among us?

MRS. ALVING: Yes, certainly; here as elsewhere.

MANDERS: Well, I really must say—!

MRS. ALVING: For the rest, what do you object to it these books?

MANDERS: Object to in them? You surely do not suppose that I have nothing better to do than to study such publications as these?

MRS. ALVING: That is to say, you know nothing of what you are condemning?

MANDERS: I have read enough about these writings to disapprove of them.

MRS. ALVING: Yes; but your own judgment—

MANDERS: My dear Mrs. Alving, there are many occasions in life when one must rely upon others.

Things are so ordered in this world; and it is well that they are. Otherwise, what would become of society?

MRS. ALVING: Well, well, I daresay you're right there.

MANDERS: Besides, I of course do not deny that there may be much that is attractive in such books. Nor can I blame you for wishing to keep up with the intellectual movements that are said to be going on in the great world—where you have let your son pass so much of his life. But—

MRS. ALVING: But?

MANDERS: [Lowering his voice] But one should not talk about it, Mrs. Alving. One is certainly not bound to account to everybody for what one reads and thinks within one's own four walls.

MRS. ALVING: Of course not; I quite agree with you.

MANDERS: Only think, now, how you are bound to consider the interests of this Orphanage, which you decided on founding at a time when—if I understand you rightly—you thought very differently on spiritual matters.

MRS. ALVING: Oh, yes; I quite admit that. But it was about the Orphanage—

MANDERS: It was about the Orphanage we were to speak; yes. All I say is: prudence, my dear lady! And now let us get to business. [Opens the packet, and takes out a number of papers] Do you see these?

MRS. ALVING: The documents?

MANDERS: All—and in perfect order. I can tell you it was hard work to get them in time. I had to put on strong pressure. The authorities are almost morbidly scrupulous when there is any decisive step to be taken. But here they are at last. [Looks through the bundle] See! here is the formal deed of gift of the parcel of ground known as Solvik in the Manor of Rosenvold, with all the newly constructed buildings, schoolrooms, master's house, and chapel. And here is the legal fiat for the endowment and for the By-laws of the Institution. Will you look at them? [Reads] "By-laws for the Children's Home to be known as 'Captain Alving's Foundation.'"

MRS. ALVING: [Looks long at the paper] So there it is.

MANDERS: I have chosen the designation "Captain" rather than "Chamberlain." "Captain" looks less pretentious.

MRS. ALVING: Oh, yes; just as you think best.

MANDERS: And here you have the Bank Account of the capital lying at interest to cover the current expenses of the Orphanage.

MRS. ALVING: Thank you; but please keep it—it will be more convenient.

MANDERS: With pleasure. I think we will leave the money in the Bank for the present. The interest is certainly not what we could wish—four per cent. and six months' notice of withdrawal. If a good mortgage could be found later on—of course it must be a first mortgage and an unimpeachable security—then we could consider the matter.

MRS. ALVING: Certainly, my dear Pastor Manders. You are the best judge in these things.

MANDERS: I will keep my eyes open at any rate.— But now there is one thing more which I have several times been intending to ask you.

MRS. ALVING: And what is that?

MANDERS: Shall the Orphanage buildings be insured or not?

MRS. ALVING: Of course they must be insured.

MANDERS: Well, wait a moment, Mrs. Alving. Let us look into the matter a little more closely.

MRS. ALVING: I have everything insured; buildings and movables and stock and crops.

MANDERS: Of course you have—on your own estate. And so have I—of course. But here, you see, it is quite another matter. The Orphanage is to be consecrated, as it were, to a higher purpose.

MRS. ALVING: Yes, but that's no reason—

MANDERS: For my own part, I should certainly not see the smallest impropriety in guarding against all contingencies—

MRS. ALVING: No, I should think not.

MANDERS: But what is the general feeling in the neighbourhood? You, of course, know better than I.

MRS. ALVING: Well—the general feeling—

MANDERS: Is there any considerable number of people—really responsible people—who might be scandalised?

MRS. ALVING: What do you mean by "really responsible people"?

MANDERS: Well, I mean people in such independent and influential positions that one cannot help attaching some weight to their opinions.

MRS. ALVING: There are several people of that sort here, who would very likely be shocked if—

MANDERS: There, you see! In town we have many such people. Think of all my colleagues' adherents! People would be only too ready to interpret our action as a sign that neither you nor I had the right faith in a Higher Providence.

MRS. ALVING: But for your own part, my dear Pastor, you can at least tell yourself that—

MANDERS: Yes, I know—I know; my conscience would be quite easy, that is true enough. But nevertheless we should not escape grave misinterpretation; and that might very likely react unfavourably upon the Orphanage.

MRS. ALVING: Well, in that case—

MANDERS: Nor can I entirely lose sight of the difficult—I may even say painful—position in which I might perhaps be placed. In the leading circles of the town, people take a lively interest in this Orphanage. It is, of course, founded partly for the benefit of the town, as well; and it is to be hoped it will, to a considerable extent, result in lightening our Poor Rates. Now, as I have been your adviser, and have had the business arrangements in my hands,

I cannot but fear that I may have to bear the brunt of fanaticism—

MRS. ALVING: Oh, you mustn't run the risk of that.

MANDERS: To say nothing of the attacks that would assuredly be made upon me in certain papers and periodicals, which—

MRS. ALVING: Enough, my dear Pastor Manders. That consideration is quite decisive.

MANDERS: Then you do not wish the Orphanage to be insured?

MRS. ALVING: No. We will let it alone.

MANDERS: [*Leaning back in his chair*] But if, now, a disaster were to happen? One can never tell— Should you be able to make good the damage?

MRS. ALVING: No; I tell you plainly I should do nothing of the kind.

MANDERS: Then I must tell you, Mrs. Alving—we are taking no small responsibility upon ourselves.

MRS. ALVING: Do you think we can do otherwise?

MANDERS: No, that is just the point; we really cannot do otherwise. We ought not to expose ourselves to misinterpretation; and we have no right whatever to give offence to the weaker brethren.

MRS. ALVING: You, as a clergyman, certainly should not.

MANDERS: I really think, too, we may trust that such an institution has fortune on its side; in fact, that it stands under a special providence.

MRS. ALVING: Let us hope so, Pastor Manders.

MANDERS: Then we will let it take its chance?

MRS. ALVING: Yes, certainly.

MANDERS: Very well. So be it. [*Makes a note*] Then—no insurance.

MRS. ALVING: It's odd that you should just happen to mention the matter to-day—

MANDERS: I have often thought of asking you about it—

MRS. ALVING: —for we very nearly had a fire down there yesterday.

MANDERS: You don't say so!

MRS. ALVING: Oh, it was a trifling matter. A heap of shavings had caught fire in the carpenter's workshop.

MANDERS: Where Engstrand works?

MRS. ALVING: Yes. They say he's often very careless with matches.

MANDERS: He has so much on his mind, that man —so many things to fight against. Thank God, he is now striving to lead a decent life, I hear.

MRS. ALVING: Indeed! Who says so?

MANDERS: He himself assures me of it. And he is certainly a capital workman.

MRS. ALVING: Oh, yes so long as he's sober—

MANDERS: Ah, that melancholy weakness! But he is often driven to it by his injured leg, he says. Last time he was in town I was really touched by him. He came and thanked me so warmly for having got him work here, so that he might be near Regina.

MRS. ALVING: He doesn't see much of her.

MANDERS: Oh, yes; he has a talk with her every day. He told me so himself.

MRS. ALVING: Well, it may be so.

MANDERS: He feels so acutely that he needs some one to keep a firm hold on him when temptation comes. That is what I cannot help liking about Jacob Engstrand: he comes to you so helplessly, accusing himself and confessing his own weakness. The last time he was talking to me— Believe me, Mrs. Alving, supposing it were a real necessity for him to have Regina home again—

MRS. ALVING: [*Rising hastily*] Regina!

MANDERS: —you must not set yourself against it.

MRS. ALVING: Indeed I shall set myself against it. And besides—Regina is to have a position in the Orphanage.

MANDERS: But, after all, remember he is her father—

MRS. ALVING: Oh, I know very well what sort of a father he has been to her. No! She shall never go to him with my goodwill.

MANDERS: [*Rising*] My dear lady, don't take the matter so warmly. You sadly misjudge poor Engstrand. You seem to be quite terrified—

MRS. ALVING: [*More quietly*] It makes no difference. I have taken Regina into my house, and there she shall stay. [*Listens*] Hush, my dear Mr. Manders; say no more about it. [*Her face lights up with gladness*] Listen! there is Oswald coming downstairs. Now we'll think of no one but him.

[Oswald Alving, *in a light overcoat, hat in hand, and smoking a large meerschaum, enters by the door on the left; he stops in the doorway*]

OSWALD: Oh, I beg your pardon; I thought you were in the study. [*Comes forward*] Good-morning, Pastor Manders.

MANDERS: [*Staring*] Ah—! How strange—!

MRS. ALVING: Well now, what do you think of him, Mr. Manders?

MANDERS: I—I—can it really be—?

OSWALD: Yes, it's really the Prodigal Son, sir.

MANDERS: [*Protesting*] My dear young friend—

OSWALD: Well, then, the Lost Sheep Found.

MRS. ALVING: Oswald is thinking of the time when you were so much opposed to his becoming a painter.

MANDERS: To our human eyes many a step seems dubious, which afterwards proves— [*Wrings his hand*] But first of all, welcome, welcome home! Do not think, my dear Oswald—I suppose I may call you by your Christian name?

OSWALD: What else should you call me?

MANDERS: Very good. What I wanted to say was this, my dear Oswald—you must not think that I utterly condemn the artist's calling. I have no doubt there are many who can keep their inner self unharmed in that profession, as in any other.

OSWALD: Let us hope so.

MRS. ALVING: [*Beaming with delight*] I know one who has kept both his inner and his outer self unharmed. Just look at him, Mr. Manders.

OSWALD: [*Moves restlessly about the room*] Yes, es, my dear mother; let's say no more about it.

MANDERS: Why, certainly—that is undeniable. And you have begun to make a name for yourself already. The newspapers have often spoken of you, most favourably. Just lately, by-the-bye, I fancy I haven't seen your name quite so often.

OSWALD: [*Up in the conservatory*] I haven't been able to paint so much lately.

MRS. ALVING: Even a painter needs a little rest now and then.

MANDERS: No doubt, no doubt. And meanwhile he can be preparing himself and mustering his forces for some great work.

OSWALD: Yes.—Mother, will dinner soon be ready?

MRS. ALVING: In less than half an hour. He has a capital appetite, thank God.

MANDERS: And a taste for tobacco, too.

OSWALD: I found my father's pipe in my room—

MANDERS: Aha—then that accounts for it!

MRS. ALVING: For what?

MANDERS: When Oswald appeared there, in the doorway, with the pipe in his mouth, I could have sworn I saw his father, large as life.

OSWALD: No, really?

MRS. ALVING: Oh, how can you say so? Oswald takes after me.

MANDERS: Yes, but there is an expression about the corners of the mouth—something about the lips —that reminds one exactly of Alving: at any rate, now that he is smoking.

MRS. ALVING: Not in the least. Oswald has rather a clerical curve about his mouth, I think.

MANDERS: Yes, yes; some of my colleagues have much the same expression.

MRS. ALVING: But put your pipe away, my dear boy; I won't have smoking in here.

OSWALD: [*Does so*] By all means. I only wanted to try it; for I once smoked it when I was a child.

MRS. ALVING: You?

OSWALD: Yes. I was quite small at the time. I recollect I came up to father's room one evening when he was in great spirits.

MRS. ALVING: Oh, you can't recollect anything of those times.

OSWALD: Yes, I recollect it distinctly. He took me on his knee, and gave me the pipe. "Smoke, boy," he said; "smoke away, boy!" And I smoked as hard as I could, until I felt I was growing quite pale, and the perspiration stood in great drops on my forehead. Then he burst out laughing heartily—

MANDERS: That was most extraordinary.

MRS. ALVING: My dear friend, it's only something Oswald has dreamt.

OSWALD: No, mother, I assure you I didn't dream it. For—don't you remember this?—you came and carried me out into the nursery. Then I was sick, and I saw that you were crying.—Did father often play such practical jokes?

MANDERS: In his youth he overflowed with the joy of life—

OSWALD: And yet he managed to do so much in the world; so much that was good and useful; although he died so early.

MANDERS: Yes, you have inherited the name of an energetic and admirable man, my dear Oswald Alving. No doubt it will be an incentive to you—

OSWALD: It ought to, indeed.

MANDERS: It was good of you to come home for the ceremony in his honour.

OSWALD: I could do no less for my father.

MRS. ALVING: And I am to keep him so long! That is the best of all.

MANDERS: You are going to pass the winter at home, I hear.

OSWALD: My stay is indefinite, sir.—But, ah! it is good to be at home!

MRS. ALVING: [*Beaming*] Yes, isn't it, dear?

MANDERS: [*Looking sympathetically at him*] You went out into the world early, my dear Oswald.

OSWALD: I did. I sometimes wonder whether it wasn't too early.

MRS. ALVING: Oh, not at all. A healthy lad is all the better for it; especially when he's an only child. He oughtn't to hang on at home with his mother and father, and get spoilt.

MANDERS: That is a very disputable point, Mrs. Alving. A child's proper place is, and must be, the home of his fathers.

OSWALD: There I quite agree with you, Pastor Manders.

MANDERS: Only look at your own son—there is no reason why we should not say it in his presence— what has the consequence been for him? He is six or seven and twenty, and has never had the opportunity of learning what a well-ordered home really is.

OSWALD: I beg your pardon, Pastor; there you're quite mistaken.

MANDERS: Indeed? I thought you had lived almost exclusively in artistic circles.

OSWALD: So I have.

MANDERS: And chiefly among the younger artists?

OSWALD: Yes, certainly.

MANDERS: But I thought few of those young fellows could afford to set up house and support a family.

OSWALD: There are many who cannot afford to marry, sir.

MANDERS: Yes, that is just what I say.

OSWALD: But they may have a home for all that. And several of them have, as a matter of fact; and very pleasant, well-ordered homes they are, too.

[Mrs. Alving *follows with breathless interest; nods, but says nothing*]

MANDERS: But I'm not talking of bachelors' quarters. By a "home" I understand the home of a family, where a man lives with his wife and children.

OSWALD: Yes; or with his children and his children's mother.

MANDERS: [*Starts; clasps his hands*] But, good heavens—

OSWALD: Well?

MANDERS: Lives with—his children's mother!

OSWALD: Yes. Would you have him turn his children's mother out of doors?

MANDERS: Then it is illicit relations you are talking of! Irregular marriages, as people call them!

OSWALD: I have never noticed anything particularly irregular about the life these people lead.

MANDERS: But how is it possible that a—a young man or young woman with any decency of feeling can endure to live in that way?—in the eyes of all the world!

OSWALD: What are they to do? A poor young artist—a poor girl—marriage costs a great deal. What are they to do?

MANDERS: What are they to do? Let me tell you, Mr. Alving, what they ought to do. They ought to exercise self-restraint from the first; that is what they ought to do.

OSWALD: That doctrine will scarcely go down with warm-blooded young people who love each other.

MRS. ALVING: No, scarcely!

MANDERS: [*Continuing*] How can the authorities tolerate such things! Allow them to go on in the light of day! [*Confronting* Mrs. Alving] Had I not cause to be deeply concerned about your son? In circles where open immorality prevails, and has even a sort of recognised position—!

OSWALD: Let me tell you, sir, that I have been in the habit of spending nearly all my Sundays in one or two such irregular homes—

MANDERS: Sunday of all days!

OSWALD: Isn't that the day to enjoy one's self? Well, never have I heard an offensive word, and still less have I witnessed anything that could be called immoral. No; do you know when and where I have come across immorality in artistic circles?

MANDERS: No, thank heaven, I don't!

OSWALD: Well, then, allow me to inform you. I have met with it when one or other of our pattern husbands and fathers has come to Paris to have a look round on his own account, and has done the artists the honour of visiting their humble haunts. They knew what was what. These gentlemen could tell us all about places and things we had never dreamt of.

MANDERS: What! Do you mean to say that respectable men from home here would—?

OSWALD: Have you never heard these respectable men, when they got home again, talking about the way in which immorality runs rampant abroad?

MANDERS: Yes, no doubt—

MRS. ALVING: I have too.

OSWALD: Well, you may take their word for it. They know what they are talking about! [*Presses his hands to his head*] Oh! that that great, free, glorious life out there should be defiled in such a way!

MRS. ALVING: You mustn't get excited, Oswald. It's not good for you.

OSWALD: Yes; you're quite right, mother. It's bad for me, I know. You see, I'm wretchedly worn out. I shall go for a little turn before dinner. Excuse me, Pastor: I know you can't take my point of view; but I couldn't help speaking out. [*He goes out by the second door to the right*]

MRS. ALVING: My poor boy!

MANDERS: You may well say so. Then this is what he has come to! [Mrs. Alving *looks at him silently*]

MANDERS: [*Walking up and down*] He called himself the Prodigal Son. Alas! alas!

[Mrs. Alving *continues looking at him*]

MANDERS: And what do you say to all this?

MRS. ALVING: I say that Oswald was right in every word.

MANDERS: [*Stands still*] Right? Right! In such principles?

MRS. ALVING: Here, in my loneliness, I have come to the same way of thinking, Pastor Manders. But I have never dared to say anything. Well! now my boy shall speak for me.

MANDERS: You are greatly to be pitied, Mrs. Alving. But now I must speak seriously to you. And now it is no longer your business manager and adviser, your own and your husband's early friend, who stands before you. It is the priest—the priest who stood before you in the moment of your life when you had gone farthest astray.

MRS. ALVING: And what has the priest to say to me?

MANDERS: I will first stir up your memory a little. The moment is well chosen. To-morrow will be the tenth anniversary of your husband's death. To-morrow the memorial in his honour will be unveiled. To-morrow I shall have to speak to the whole assembled multitude. But to-day I will speak to you alone.

MRS. ALVING: Very well, Pastor Manders. Speak.

MANDERS: Do you remember that after less than a year of married life you stood on the verge of an abyss? That you forsook your house and home? That you fled from your husband? Yes, Mrs. Alving—fled, fled, and refused to return to him, however much he begged and prayed you?

MRS. ALVING: Have you forgotten how infinitely miserable I was in that first year?

MANDERS: It is the very mark of the spirit of rebellion to crave for happiness in this life. What right have we human beings to happiness? We have simply to do our duty, Mrs. Alving! And your duty was to hold firmly to the man you had once chosen, and to whom you were bound by the holiest ties.

MRS. ALVING: You know very well what sort of life Alving was leading—what excesses he was guilty of.

MANDERS: I know very well what rumours there were about him; and I am the last to approve the life he led in his young days, if report did not wrong him. But a wife is not appointed to be her husband's judge. It was your duty to bear with humility the cross which a Higher Power had, in its wisdom, laid upon you. But instead of that you rebelliously throw away the cross, desert the back-slider whom you should have supported, go and risk your good name and reputation, and—nearly succeed in ruining other people's reputation into the bargain.

MRS. ALVING: Other people's? One other person's, you mean.

MANDERS: It was incredibly reckless of you to seek refuge with me.

MRS. ALVING: With our clergyman? With our intimate friend?

MANDERS: Just on that account. Yes, you may thank God that I possessed the necessary firmness; that I succeeded in dissuading you from your wild designs; and that it was vouchsafed me to lead you back to the path of duty, and home to your lawful husband.

MRS. ALVING: Yes, Pastor Manders, that was certainly your work.

MANDERS: I was but a poor instrument in a Higher Hand. And what a blessing has it not proved to you, all the days of your life, that I induced you to resume the yoke of duty and obedience! Did not everything happen as I foretold? Did not Alving turn his back on his errors, as a man should? Did he not live with you from that time, lovingly and blamelessly, all his days? Did he not become a benefactor to the whole district? And did he not help you to rise to his own level, so that you, little by little became his assistant in all his undertakings? And a capital assistant, too—oh, I know, Mrs. Alving, that praise is due to you.—But now I come to the next great error in your life.

MRS. ALVING: What do you mean?

MANDERS: Just as you once disowned a wife's duty, so you have since disowned a mother's.

MRS. ALVING: Ah—!

MANDERS: You have been all your life under the dominion of a pestilent spirit of self-will. The whole bias of your mind has been towards insubordination and lawlessness. You have never known how to endure any bond. Everything that has weighed upon you in life you have cast away without care or conscience, like a burden you were free to throw off at will. It did not please you to be a wife any longer, and you left your husband. You found it troublesome to be a mother, and you sent your child forth among strangers.

MRS. ALVING: Yes, that is true. I did so.

MANDERS: And thus you have become a stranger to him.

MRS. ALVING: No! no! I am not.

MANDERS: Yes, you are; you must be. And in what state of mind has he returned to you? Bethink yourself well, Mrs. Alving. You sinned greatly against your husband;—that you recognise by raising yonder memorial to him. Recognise now, also, how you have sinned against your son—there may yet

be time to lead him back from the paths of error. Turn back yourself, and save what may yet be saved in him. For [*With uplifted forefinger*] verily, Mrs. Alving, you are a guilt-laden mother!—This I have thought it my duty to say to you. [*Silence*]

MRS. ALVING: [*Slowly and with self-control*] You have now spoken out, Pastor Manders; and to-morrow you are to speak publicly in memory of my husband. I shall not speak to-morrow. But now I will speak frankly to you, as you have spoken to me.

MANDERS: To be sure; you will plead excuses for your conduct—

MRS. ALVING: No. I will only tell you a story.

MANDERS: Well—?

MRS. ALVING: All that you have just said about my husband and me, and our life after you had brought me back to the path of duty—as you called it—about all that you know nothing from personal observation. From that moment you, who had been our intimate friend, never set foot in our house again.

MANDERS: You and your husband left the town immediately after.

MRS. ALVING: Yes; and in my husband's lifetime you never came to see us. It was business that forced you to visit me when you undertook the affairs of the Orphanage.

MANDERS: [*Softly and hesitatingly*] Helen—if that is meant as a reproach, I would beg you to bear in mind—

MRS. ALVING: —the regard you owed to your position, yes; and that I was a runaway wife. One can never be too cautious with such unprincipled creatures.

MANDERS: My dear—Mrs. Alving, you know that is an absurd exaggeration—

MRS. ALVING: Well well, suppose it is. My point is that your judgment as to my married life is founded upon nothing but common knowledge and report.

MANDERS: I admit that. What then?

MRS. ALVING: Well, then, Pastor Manders—I will tell you the truth. I have sworn to myself that one day you should know it—you alone!

MANDERS: What is the truth, then?

MRS. ALVING: The truth is that my husband died just as dissolute as he had lived all his days.

MANDERS: [*Feeling after a chair*] What do you say?

MRS. ALVING: After nineteen years of marriage, as dissolute—in his desires at any rate—as he was before you married us.

MANDERS: And those—those wild oats—those irregularities—those excesses, if you like—you call "a dissolute life"?

MRS. ALVING: Our doctor used the expression.

MANDERS: I do not understand you.

MRS. ALVING: You need not.

MANDERS: It almost makes me dizzy. Your whole married life, the seeming union of all these years, was nothing more than a hidden abyss!

MRS. ALVING: Neither more nor less. Now you know it.

MANDERS: This is—this is inconceivable to me. I cannot grasp it! I cannot realize it! But how was it possible to—? How could such a state of things be kept secret?

MRS. ALVING: That has been my ceaseless struggle, day after day. After Oswald's birth, I thought Alving seemed to be a little better. But it did not last long. And then I had to struggle twice as hard, fighting as though for life or death, so that nobody should know what sort of man my child's father was. And you know what power Alving had of winning people's hearts. Nobody seemed able to believe anything but good of him. He was one of those people whose life does not bite upon their reputation. But at last, Mr. Manders—for you must know the whole story—the most repulsive thing of all happened.

MANDERS: More repulsive than what you have told me!

MRS. ALVING: I had gone on bearing with him, although I knew very well the secrets of his life out of doors. But when he brought the scandal within our own walls—

MANDERS: Impossible! Here!

MRS. ALVING: Yes; here in our own home. It was there [Pointing towards the first door on the right], in the dining-room, that I first came to know of it. I was busy with something in there, and the door was standing ajar. I heard our housemaid come up from the garden, with water for those flowers.

MANDERS: Well—?

MRS. ALVING: Soon after, I heard Alving come in too. I heard him say something softly to her. And then I heard—[With a short laugh]—oh! it still sounds in my ears, so hateful and yet so ludicrous—I heard my own servant-maid whisper, "Let me go, Mr. Alving! Let me be!"

MANDERS: What unseemly levity on his part! But it cannot have been more than levity, Mrs. Alving; believe me, it cannot.

MRS. ALVING: I soon knew what to believe. Mr. Alving had his way with the girl; and that connection had consequences, Mr. Manders.

MANDERS: [As though petrified] Such things in this house! in this house!

MRS. ALVING: I had borne a great deal in this house. To keep him at home in the evenings, and at night, I had to make myself his boon companion in his secret orgies up in his room. There I have had to sit alone with him, to clink glasses and drink with him, and to listen to his ribald, silly talk. I have had to fight with him to get him dragged to bed—

MANDERS: [Moved] And you were able to bear all this!

MRS. ALVING: I had to bear it for my little boy's sake. But when the last insult was added; when my own servant-maid—; then I swore to myself: This shall come to an end! And so I took the reins into my own hand—the whole control—over him and everything else. For now I had a weapon against him, you see; he dared not oppose me. It was then I sent Oswald away from home. He was nearly seven years old, and was beginning to observe and ask questions, as children do. That I could not bear. It seemed to me the child must be poisoned by merely breathing the air of this polluted home. That was why I sent him away. And now you can see, too, why he was never allowed to set foot inside his home so long as his father lived. No one knows what that cost me.

MANDERS: You have indeed had a life of trial.

MRS. ALVING: I could never have borne it if I had not had my work. For I may truly say that I have worked! All the additions to the estate—all the improvements—all the labour-saving appliances, that Alving was so much praised for having introduced—do you suppose he had energy for anything of the sort?—he, who lay all day on the sofa, reading an old Court Guide! No; but I may tell you this too: when he had his better intervals, it was I who urged him on; it was I who had to drag the whole load when he relapsed into his evil ways, or sank into querulous wretchedness.

MANDERS: And it is to this man that you raise a memorial?

MRS. ALVING: There you see the power of an evil conscience.

MANDERS: Evil—? What do you mean?

MRS. ALVING: It always seemed to me impossible but that the truth must come out and be believed. So the Orphanage was to deaden all rumours and set every doubt at rest.

MANDERS: In that you have certainly not missed your aim, Mrs. Alving.

MRS. ALVING: And besides, I had one other reason. I was determined that Oswald, my own boy, should inherit nothing whatever from his father.

MANDERS: Then it is Alving's fortune that—?

MRS. ALVING: Yes. The sums I have spent upon the Orphanage, year by year, make up the amount—I have reckoned it up precisely—the amount which made Lieutenant Alving "a good match" in his day.

MANDERS: I don't understand—

MRS. ALVING: It was my purchase-money. I do not choose that that money should pass into Oswald's hands. My son shall have everything from me—everything.

[Oswald Alving enters through the second door to the right; he has taken off his hat and overcoat in the hall]

MRS. ALVING: [Going towards him] Are you back again already? My dear, dear boy!

OSWALD: What can a fellow do out of doors in this eternal rain? But I hear dinner is ready. That's capital!

REGINA: [With a parcel, from the dining-room] A parcel has come for you, Mrs. Alving. [Hands it to her]

MRS. ALVING: [*With a glance at* Mr. Manders] No doubt copies of the ode for to-morrow's ceremony.

MANDERS: H'm—

REGINA: And dinner is ready.

MRS. ALVING: Very well. We will come directly. I will just—[*Begins to open the parcel*]

REGINA: [*To* Oswald] Would Mr. Alving like red or white wine?

OSWALD: Both, if you please.

REGINA: *Bien.* Very well, sir. [*She goes into the dining-room*]

OSWALD: I may as well help to uncork it. [*He also goes into the dining room, the door of which swings half open behind him*]

MRS. ALVING: [*Who has opened the parcel*] Yes, I thought so. Here is the Ceremonial Ode, Pastor Manders.

MANDERS: [*With folded hands*] With what countenance I am to deliver my discourse to-morrow—!

MRS. ALVING: Oh, you will get through it somehow.

MANDERS: [*Softly, so as not to be heard in the dining-room*] Yes; it would not do to provoke scandal.

MRS. ALVING: [*Under her breath, but firmly*] No. But then this long, hateful comedy will be ended. From the day after to-morrow, I shall act in every way as though he who is dead had never lived in this house. There shall be no one here but my boy and his mother.

[*From the dining-room comes the noise of a chair overturned, and at the same moment is heard*]

REGINA: [*Sharply, but in a whisper*] Oswald! take care! are you mad? Let me go!

MRS. ALVING: [*Starts in terror*] Ah——!

[*She stares wildly towards the half-open door. Oswald is heard laughing and humming. A bottle is uncorked*]

MANDERS: [*Agitated*] What can be the matter? What is it, Mrs. Alving?

MRS. ALVING: [*Hoarsely*] Ghosts! The couple from the conservatory—risen again!

MANDERS: Is it possible! Regina—? Is she—?

MRS. ALVING: Yes. Come. Not a word—!

[*She seizes* Pastor Manders *by the arm, and walks unsteadily towards the dining-room*]

CURTAIN

ACT II.

The same room. The mist still lies heavy over the landscape. Manders *and* Mrs. Alving *enter from the dining-room.*

MRS. ALVING: [*Still in the doorway*] *Velbekomme,*[1] Mr. Manders. [*Turns back towards the dining-room*] Aren't you coming too, Oswald?

[1] A phrase equivalent to the German *Prosit die Mahlzeit*—"May good digestion wait on appetite."

OSWALD: [*From within*] No, thank you. I think I shall go out a little.

MRS. ALVING: Yes, do. The weather seems a little brighter now. [*She shuts the dining-room door, goes to the hall door, and calls:*] Regina!

REGINA: [*Outside*] Yes, Mrs. Alving?

MRS. ALVING: Go down to the laundry, and help with the garlands.

REGINA: Yes, Mrs. Alving.

[Mrs. Alving *assures herself that* Regina *goes; then shuts the door*]

MANDERS: I suppose he cannot overhear us in there?

MRS. ALVING: Not when the door is shut. Besides, he's just going out.

MANDERS: I am still quite upset. I don't know how I could swallow a morsel of dinner.

MRS. ALVING: [*Controlling her nervousness, walks up and down*] Nor I. But what is to be done now?

MANDERS: Yes; what is to be done? I am really quite at a loss. I am so utterly without experience in matters of this sort.

MRS. ALVING: I feel sure that, so far, no mischief has been done.

MANDERS: No; heaven forbid! But it is an unseemly state of things, nevertheless.

MRS. ALVING: It is only an idle fancy on Oswald's part; you may be sure of that.

MANDERS: Well, as I say, I am not accustomed to affairs of the kind. But I should certainly think—

MRS. ALVING: Out of the house she must go, and that immediately. That is as clear as daylight—

MANDERS: Yes, of course she must.

MRS. ALVING: But where to? It would not be right to—

MANDERS: Where to? Home to her father, of course.

MRS. ALVING: To whom did you say?

MANDERS: To her— But then, Engstrand is not—? Good God, Mrs. Alving, it's impossible! You must be mistaken after all.

MRS. ALVING: Unfortunately there is no possibility of mistake. Johanna confessed everything to me; and Alving could not deny it. So there was nothing to be done but to get the matter hushed up.

MANDERS: No, you could do nothing else.

MRS. ALVING: The girl left our service at once and got a good sum of money to hold her tongue for the time. The rest she managed for herself when she got to town. She renewed her old acquaintance with Engstrand, no doubt let him see that she had money in her purse and told him some tale about a foreigner who put in here with a yacht that summer. So she and Engstrand got married in hot haste. Why, you married them yourself.

MANDERS: But then how to account for—? I recollect distinctly Engstrand coming to give notice of the marriage. He was quite overwhelmed with contrition and bitterly reproached himself for the misbehaviour he and his sweetheart had been guilty of.

MRS. ALVING: Yes; of course he had to take the blame upon himself.

MANDERS: But such a piece of duplicity on his part! And towards me too! I never could have believed it of Jacob Engstrand. I shall not fail to take him seriously to task; he may be sure of that.—And then the immorality of such a connection! For money—! How much did the girl receive?

MRS. ALVING: Three hundred dollars.

MANDERS: Just think of it—for a miserable three hundred dollars to go and marry a fallen woman!

MRS. ALVING: Then what have you to say of me? I went and married a fallen man.

MANDERS: Why—good heavens!—what are you talking about! A fallen man!

MRS. ALVING: Do you think Alving was any purer when I went with him to the altar than Johanna was when Engstrand married her?

MANDERS: Well, but there is a world of difference between the two cases—

MRS. ALVING: Not so much difference after all—except in the price:—a miserable three hundred dollars and a whole fortune.

MANDERS: How can you compare such absolutely dissimilar cases? You had taken counsel with your own heart and with your natural advisers.

MRS. ALVING: [Without looking at him] I thought you understood where what you call my heart had strayed to at the time.

MANDERS: [Distantly] Had I understood anything of the kind I should not have been a daily guest in your husband's house.

MRS. ALVING: At any rate, the fact remains that with myself I took no counsel whatever.

MANDERS: Well then, with your nearest relatives —as your duty bade you—with your mother and your two aunts.

MRS. ALVING: Yes, that is true. Those three cast up the account for me. Oh, it's marvellous how clearly they made out that it would be downright madness to refuse such an offer. If mother could only see me now, and know what all that grandeur has come to!

MANDERS: Nobody can be held responsible for the result. This, at least, remains clear: your marriage was in full accordance with law and order.

MRS. ALVING: [At the window] Oh, that perpetual law and order! I often think that is what does all the mischief in this world of ours.

MANDERS: Mrs. Alving, that is a sinful way of talking.

MRS. ALVING: Well, I can't help it; I must have done with all this constraint and insincerity. I can endure it no longer. I must work my way out to freedom.

MANDERS: What do you mean by that?

MRS. ALVING: [Drumming on the window-frame] I ought never to have concealed the facts of Alving's life. But at that time I dared not do anything else—

I was afraid, partly on my own account. I was such a coward.

MANDERS: A coward?

MRS. ALVING: If people had come to know anything, they would have said—"Poor man! with a runaway wife, no wonder he kicks over the traces."

MANDERS: Such remarks might have been made with a certain show of right.

MRS. ALVING: [Looking steadily at him] If I were what I ought to be, I should go to Oswald and say, "Listen, my boy: your father led a vicious life—"

MANDERS: Merciful heavens—!

MRS. ALVING: —and then I should tell him all I have told you—every word of it.

MANDERS: You shock me unspeakably, Mrs. Alving.

MRS. ALVING: Yes; I know that. I know that very well. I myself am shocked at the idea. [Goes away from the window] I am such a coward.

MANDERS: You call it "cowardice" to do your plain duty? Have you forgotten that a son ought to love and honour his father and mother?

MRS. ALVING: Do not let us talk in such general terms. Let us ask: Ought Oswald to love and honour Chamberlain Alving?

MANDERS: Is there no voice in your mother's heart that forbids you to destroy your son's ideals?

MRS. ALVING: But what about the truth?

MANDERS: But what about the ideals?

MRS. ALVING: Oh—ideals, ideals! If only I were not such a coward!

MANDERS: Do not despise ideals, Mrs. Alving: they will avenge themselves cruelly. Take Oswald's case: he, unfortunately, seems to have few enough ideals as it is; but I can see that his father stands before him as an ideal.

MRS. ALVING: Yes, that is true.

MANDERS: And this habit of mind you have yourself implanted and fostered by your letters.

MRS. ALVING: Yes; in my superstitious awe for duty and the properties, I lied to my boy, year after year. Oh, what a coward—what a coward I have been!

MANDERS: You have established a happy illusion in your son's heart, Mrs. Alving; and assuredly you ought not to undervalue it.

MRS. ALVING: H'm; who knows whether it is so happy after all—? But, at any rate, I will not have any tampering with Regina. He shall not go and wreck the poor girl's life.

MANDERS: No; good God—that would be terrible!

MRS. ALVING: If I knew he was in earnest, and that it would be for his happiness—

MANDERS: What? What then?

MRS. ALVING: But it couldn't be; for unfortunately Regina is not the right sort of woman.

MANDERS: Well, what then? What do you mean?

MRS. ALVING: If I weren't such a pitiful coward, I should say to him, "Marry her, or make what arrangement you please, only let us have nothing underhand about it."

MANDERS: Merciful heavens, would you let them marry! Anything so dreadful—! so unheard of—

MRS. ALVING: Do you really mean "unheard of"? Frankly, Pastor Manders, do you suppose that throughout the country there are not plenty of married couples as closely akin as they?

MANDERS: I don't in the least understand you.

MRS. ALVING: O yes, indeed you do.

MANDERS: Ah, you are thinking of the possibility that— Alas! yes, family life is certainly not always so pure as it ought to be. But in such a case as you point to, one can never know—at least with any certainty. Here, on the other hand—that you, a mother, can think of letting your son—

MRS. ALVING: But I cannot—I wouldn't for anything in the world; that is precisely what I am saying.

MANDERS: No, because you are a "coward," as you put it. But if you were not a "coward," then—? Good God! a connection so shocking!

MRS. ALVING: So far as that goes, they say we are all sprung from connections of that sort. And who is it that arranged the world so, Pastor Manders?

MANDERS: Questions of that kind I must decline to discuss with you, Mrs. Alving; you are far from being in the right frame of mind for them. But that you dare to call your scruples "cowardly"—!

MRS. ALVING: Let me tell you what I mean. I am timid and faint-hearted because of the ghosts that hang about me, and that I can never quite shake off.

MANDERS: What do you say hangs about you?

MRS. ALVING: Ghosts! When I heard Regina and Oswald in there, it was as though ghosts rose up before me. But I almost think we are all of us ghosts, Pastor Manders. It is not only what we have inherited from our father and mother that "walks" in us. It is all sorts of dead ideas, and lifeless old beliefs, and so forth. They have no vitality, but they cling to us all the same, and we cannot shake them off. Whenever I take up a newspaper, I seem to see ghosts gliding between the lines. There must be ghosts all the country over, as thick as the sands of the sea. And then we are, one and all, so pitifully afraid of the light.

MANDERS: Aha—here we have the fruits of your reading. And pretty fruits they are, upon my word! Oh, those horrible, revolutionary, freethinking books!

MRS. ALVING: You are mistaken, my dear Pastor. It was you yourself who set me thinking; and I thank you for it with all my heart.

MANDERS: I!

MRS. ALVING: Yes—when you forced me under the yoke of what you called duty and obligation; when you lauded as right and proper what my whole soul rebelled against as something loathsome. It was then that I began to look into the seams of your doctrines. I wanted only to pick at a single knot; but when I had got that undone, the whole thing ravelled out. And then I understood that it was all machine-sewn.

MANDERS: [*Softly, with emotion*] And was that the upshot of my life's hardest battle?

MRS. ALVING: Call it rather your most pitiful defeat.

MANDERS: It was my greatest victory, Helen—the victory over myself.

MRS. ALVING: It was a crime against us both.

MANDERS: When you went astray, and came to me crying, "Here I am; take me!" I commanded you, saying, "Woman, go home to your lawful husband." Was that a crime?

MRS. ALVING: Yes, I think so.

MANDERS: We two do not understand each other.

MRS. ALVING: Not now, at any rate.

MANDERS: Never—never in my most secret thoughts have I regarded you otherwise than as another's wife.

MRS. ALVING: Oh—indeed?

MANDERS: Helen—!

MRS. ALVING: People so easily forget their past selves.

MANDERS: I do not. I am what I always was.

MRS. ALVING: [*Changing the subject*] Well well well; don't let us talk of old times any longer. You are now over head and ears in Boards and Committees, and I am fighting my battle with ghosts, both within me and without.

MANDERS: Those without I shall help you to lay. After all the terrible things I have heard from you today, I cannot in conscience permit an unprotected girl to remain in your house.

MRS. ALVING: Don't you think the best plan would be to get her provided for?—I mean, by a good marriage.

MANDERS: No doubt. I think it would be desirable for her in every respect. Regina is now at the age when— Of course I don't know much about these things, but—

MRS. ALVING: Regina matured very early.

MANDERS: Yes, I thought so. I have an impression that she was remarkably well developed, physically, when I prepared her for confirmation. But in the meantime, she ought to be at home, under her father's eye— Ah! but Engstrand is not— That he—that he—could so hide the truth from me!

[*A knock at the door into the hall*]

MRS. ALVING: Who can this be? Come in!

ENGSTRAND: [*In his Sunday clothes, in the doorway*] I humbly beg your pardon, but—

MANDERS: Aha! H'm—

MRS. ALVING: Is that you, Engstrand?

ENGSTRAND: —there was none of the servants about, so I took the great liberty of just knocking.

MRS. ALVING: Oh, very well. Come in. Do you want to speak to me?

ENGSTRAND: [*Comes in*] No, I'm obliged to you,

ma'am; it was with his Reverence I wanted to have a word or two.

MANDERS: [*Walking up and down the room*] Ah—indeed! You want to speak to me, do you?

ENGSTRAND: Yes, I'd like so terrible much to—

MANDERS: [*Stops in front of him*] Well; may I ask what you want?

ENGSTRAND: Well, it was just this, your Reverence: we've been paid off down yonder—my grateful thanks to you, ma'am,—and now everything's finished, I've been thinking it would be but right and proper if we, that have been working so honestly together all this time—well, I was thinking we ought to end up with a little prayer-meeting to-night.

MANDERS: A prayer-meeting? Down at the Orphanage?

ENGSTRAND: Oh, if your Reverence doesn't think it proper—

MANDERS: Oh yes, I do; but—h'm—

ENGSTRAND: I've been in the habit of offering up a little prayer in the evenings, myself—

MRS. ALVING: Have you?

ENGSTRAND: Yes, every now and then—just a little edification, in a manner of speaking. But I'm a poor, common man, and have little enough gift, God help me!—and so I thought, as the Reverend Mr. Manders happened to be here, I'd—

MANDERS: Well, you see, Engstrand, I have a question to put to you first. Are you in the right frame of mind for such a meeting? Do you feel your conscience clear and at ease?

ENGSTRAND: Oh, God help us, your Reverence! we'd better not talk about conscience.

MANDERS: Yes, that is just what we must talk about. What have you to answer?

ENGSTRAND: Why—a man's conscience—it can be bad enough now and then.

MANDERS: Ah, you admit that. Then perhaps you will make a clean breast of it, and tell me—the real truth about Regina?

MRS. ALVING: [*Quickly*] Mr. Manders!

MANDERS: [*Reassuringly*] Please allow me—

ENGSTRAND: About Regina! Lord, what a turn you gave me! [*Looks at* Mrs. Alving] There's nothing wrong about Regina, is there?

MANDERS: We will hope not. But I mean, what is the truth about you and Regina? You pass for her father, eh!

ENGSTRAND: [*Uncertain*] Well—h'm—your Reverence knows all about me and poor Johanna.

MANDERS: Come now, no more prevarication! Your wife told Mrs. Alving the whole story before quitting her service.

ENGSTRAND: Well, then, may—! Now, did she really?

MANDERS: You see we know you now, Engstrand.

ENGSTRAND: And she swore and took her Bible oath—

MANDERS: Did she take her Bible oath?

ENGSTRAND: No; she only swore; but she did it that solemn-like.

MANDERS: And you have hidden the truth from me all these years? Hidden it from me, who have trusted you without reserve, in everything.

ENGSTRAND: Well, I can't deny it.

MANDERS: Have I deserved this of you, Engstrand? Have I not always been ready to help you in word and deed, so far as it lay in my power? Answer me. Have I not?

ENGSTRAND: It would have been a poor look-out for me many a time but for the Reverend Mr. Manders.

MANDERS: And this is how you reward me! You cause me to enter falsehoods in the Church Register, and you withhold from me, year after year, the explanations you owed alike to me and to the truth. Your conduct has been wholly inexcusable, Engstrand; and from this time forward I have done with you!

ENGSTRAND: [*With a sigh*] Yes! I suppose there's no help for it.

MANDERS: How can you possibly justify yourself?

ENGSTRAND: Who could ever have thought she'd have gone and made bad worse by talking about it? Will your Reverence just fancy yourself in the same trouble as poor Johanna—

MANDERS: I!

ENGSTRAND: Lord bless you, I don't mean just exactly the same. But I mean, if your Reverence had anything to be ashamed of in the eyes of the world, as the saying goes. We menfolk oughtn't to judge a poor woman too hardly, your Reverence.

MANDERS: I am not doing so. It is you I am reproaching.

ENGSTRAND: Might I make so bold as to ask your Reverence a bit of a question?

MANDERS: Yes, if you want to.

ENGSTRAND: Isn't it right and proper for a man to raise up the fallen?

MANDERS: Most certainly it is.

ENGSTRAND: And isn't a man bound to keep his sacred word?

MANDERS: Why, of course he is; but—

ENGSTRAND: When Johanna had got into trouble through that Englishman—or it might have been an American or a Russian, as they call them—well, you see, she came down into the town. Poor thing, she'd sent me about my business once or twice before: for she couldn't bear the sight of anything as wasn't handsome; and I'd got this damaged leg of mine. Your Reverence recollects how I ventured up into a dancing saloon, where seafaring men was carrying on with drink and devilry, as the saying goes. And then, when I was for giving them a bit of an admonition to lead a new life—

MRS. ALVING: [*At the window*] H'm—

MANDERS: I know all about that, Engstrand; the ruffians threw you downstairs. You have told me of the affair already. Your infirmity is an honour to you.

ENGSTRAND: I'm not puffed up about it, your Reverence. But what I wanted to say was, that when she came and confessed all to me, with weeping and gnashing of teeth, I can tell your Reverence I was sore at heart to hear it.

MANDERS: Were you indeed, Engstrand? Well, go on.

ENGSTRAND: So I says to her, "The American, he's sailing about on the boundless sea. And as for you, Johanna," says I, "you've committed a grievous sin, and you're a fallen creature. But Jacob Engstrand," says I, "he's got two good legs to stand upon, he has—" You see, your Reverence, I was speaking figurative-like.

MANDERS: I understand quite well. Go on.

ENGSTRAND: Well, that was how I raised her up and made an honest woman of her, so as folks shouldn't get to know how as she'd gone astray with foreigners.

MANDERS: In all that you acted very well. Only I cannot approve of your stooping to take money—

ENGSTRAND: Money? I? Not a farthing!

MANDERS: [Inquiringly to Mrs. Alving] But—

ENGSTRAND: Oh, wait a minute!—now I recollect. Johanna did have a trifle of money. But I would have nothing to do with that. "No," says I, "that's mammon; that's the wages of sin. This dirty gold—or notes, or whatever it was—we'll just fling that back in the American's face," says I. But he was off and away, over the stormy sea, your Reverence.

MANDERS: Was he really, my good fellow?

ENGSTRAND: He was indeed, sir. So Johanna and I, we agreed that the money should go to the child's education; and so it did, and I can account for every blessed farthing of it.

MANDERS: Why, this alters the case considerably.

ENGSTRAND: That's just how it stands, your Reverence. And I make so bold as to say as I've been an honest father to Regina, so far as my poor strength went; for I'm but a weak vessel, worse luck!

MANDERS: Well, well, my good fellow—

ENGSTRAND: All the same, I bear myself witness as I've brought up the child, and lived kindly with poor Johanna, and ruled over my own house, as the Scripture has it. But it couldn't never enter my head to go to your Reverence and puff myself up and boast because even the likes of me had done some good in the world. No, sir; when anything of that sort happens to Jacob Engstrand, he holds his tongue about it. It don't happen so terrible often, I daresay. And when I do come to see your Reverence, I find a mortal deal that's wicked and weak to talk about. For I said it before, and I say it again—a man's conscience isn't always as clean as it might be.

MANDERS: Give me your hand, Jacob Engstrand.

ENGSTRAND: Oh, Lord! your Reverence—

MANDERS: Come, no nonsense. [Wrings his hand] There we are!

ENGSTRAND: And if I might humbly beg your Reverence's pardon—

MANDERS: You? On the contrary, it is I who ought to beg your pardon—

ENGSTRAND: Lord, no, sir!

MANDERS: Yes, assuredly. And I do it with all my heart. Forgive me for misunderstanding you. I only wish I could give you some proof of my hearty regret, and of my good-will towards you—

ENGSTRAND: Would your Reverence do it?

MANDERS: With the greatest pleasure.

ENGSTRAND: Well then, here's the very chance. With the bit of money I've saved here, I was thinking I might set up a Sailors' Home down in the town.

MRS. ALVING: You?

ENGSTRAND: Yes; it might be a sort of Orphanage, too, in a manner of speaking. There's such a many temptations for seafaring folk ashore. But in this Home of mine, a man might feel like as he was under a father's eye, I was thinking.

MANDERS: What do you say to this, Mrs. Alving?

ENGSTRAND: It isn't much as I've got to start with, Lord help me! But if I could only find a helping hand, why—

MANDERS: Yes, yes; we will look into the matter more closely. I entirely approve of your plan. But now, go before me and make everything ready, and get the candles lighted, so as to give the place an air of festivity. And then we will pass an edifying hour together, my good fellow; for now I quite believe you are in the right frame of mind.

ENGSTRAND: Yes, I trust I am. And so I'll say good-bye, ma'am, and thank you kindly; and take good care of Regina for me—[Wipes a tear from his eye]—poor Johanna's child. Well, it's a queer thing, now; but it's just like as if she'd growd into the very apple of my eye. It is, indeed. [He bows and goes out through the hall]

MANDERS: Well, what do you say of that man now, Mrs. Alving? That was a very different account of matters, was it not?

MRS. ALVING: Yes, it certainly was.

MANDERS: It only shows how excessively careful one ought to be in judging one's fellow creatures. But what a heartfelt joy it is to ascertain that one has been mistaken! Don't you think so?

MRS. ALVING: I think you are, and will always be, a great baby, Manders.

MANDERS: I?

MRS. ALVING: [Laying her two hands upon his shoulders] And I say that I have half a mind to put my arms round your neck, and kiss you.

MANDERS: [Stepping hastily back] No, no! God bless me! What an idea!

MRS. ALVING: [With a smile] Oh, you needn't be afraid of me.

MANDERS: [By the table] You have sometimes such an exaggerated way of expressing yourself. Now, let me just collect all the documents, and put them in my bag. [*He does so*] There, that's all right. And now, good-bye for the present. Keep your eyes open when Oswald comes back. I shall look in again later. [*He takes his hat and goes out through the hall door*]

MRS. ALVING: [*Sighs, looks for a moment out of the window, sets the room in order a little, and is about to go into the dining-room, but stops at the door with a half-suppressed cry*] Oswald, are you still at table?

OSWALD: [*In the dining room*] I'm only finishing my cigar.

MRS. ALVING: I thought you had gone for a little walk.

OSWALD: In such weather as this?

[*A glass clinks. Mrs. Alving leaves the door open, and sits down with her knitting on the sofa by the window*]

OSWALD: Wasn't that Pastor Manders that went out just now?

MRS. ALVING: Yes; he went down to the Orphanage.

OSWALD: H'm. [*The glass and decanter clink again*]

MRS. ALVING: [*With a troubled glance*] Dear Oswald, you should take care of that liqueur. It is strong.

OSWALD: It keeps out the damp.

MRS. ALVING: Wouldn't you rather come in here, to me?

OSWALD: I mayn't smoke in there.

MRS. ALVING: You know quite well you may smoke cigars.

OSWALD: Oh, all right then; I'll come in. Just a tiny drop more first.—There! [*He comes into the room with his cigar, and shuts the door after him. A short silence*] Where has the pastor gone to?

MRS. ALVING: I have just told you; he went down to the Orphanage.

OSWALD: Oh, yes; so you did.

MRS. ALVING: You shouldn't sit so long at table, Oswald.

OSWALD: [*Holding his cigar behind him*] But I find it so pleasant, mother. [*Strokes and caresses her*] Just think what it is for me to come home and sit at mother's own table, in mother's room, and eat mother's delicious dishes.

MRS. ALVING: My dear, dear boy!

OSWALD: [*Somewhat impatiently, walks about and smokes*] And what else can I do with myself here? I can't set to work at anything.

MRS. ALVING: Why can't you?

OSWALD: In such weather as this? Without a single ray of sunshine the whole day? [*Walks up the room*] Oh, not to be able to work—!

MRS. ALVING: Perhaps it was not quite wise of you to come home?

OSWALD: Oh, yes, mother; I had to.

MRS. ALVING: You know I would ten times rather forego the joy of having you here, than let you—

OSWALD: [*Stops beside the table*] Now just tell me, mother: does it really make you so very happy to have me home again?

MRS. ALVING: Does it make me happy!

OSWALD: [*Crumpling up a newspaper*] I should have thought it must be pretty much the same to you whether I was in existence or not.

MRS. ALVING: Have you the heart to say that to your mother, Oswald?

OSWALD: But you've got on very well without me all this time.

MRS. ALVING: Yes; I have got on without you. That is true.

[*A silence. Twilight slowly begins to fall. Oswald paces to and fro across the room. He has laid his cigar down*]

OSWALD: [*Stops beside Mrs. Alving*] Mother, may I sit on the sofa beside you?

MRS. ALVING: [*Makes room for him*] Yes, do, my dear boy.

OSWALD: [*Sits down*] There is something I must tell you, mother.

MRS. ALVING: [*Anxiously*] Well?

OSWALD: [*Looks fixedly before him*] For I can't go on hiding it any longer.

MRS. ALVING: Hiding what? What is it?

OSWALD: [*As before*] I could never bring myself to write to you about it; and since I've come home—

MRS. ALVING: [*Seizes him by the arm*] Oswald, what is the matter?

OSWALD: Both yesterday and to-day I have tried to put the thoughts away from me—to cast them off; but it's no use.

MRS. ALVING: [*Rising*] Now you must tell me everything, Oswald!

OSWALD: [*Draws her down to the sofa again*] Sit still; and then I will try to tell you.—I complained of fatigue after my journey—

MRS. ALVING: Well? What then?

OSWALD: But it isn't that that is the matter with me; not any ordinary fatigue—

MRS. ALVING: [*Tries to jump up*] You are not ill, Oswald?

OSWALD: [*Draws her down again*] Sit still, mother. Do take it quietly. I'm not downright ill, either; not what is commonly called "ill." [*Clasps his hands above his head*] Mother, my mind is broken down—ruined—I shall never be able to work again! [*With his hands before his face, he buries his head in her lap, and breaks into bitter sobbing*]

MRS. ALVING: [*White and trembling*] Oswald! Look at me! No, no; it's not true.

OSWALD: [*Looks up with despair in his eyes*] Never to be able to work again! Never!—never! A living death! Mother, can you imagine anything so horrible!

MRS. ALVING: My poor boy! How has this horrible thing come upon you?

OSWALD: [*Sitting upright again*] That's just what I cannot possibly grasp or understand. I have never led a dissipated lif —never, in any respect. You mustn't believe that of me, mother! I've never done that.

MRS. ALVING: I am sure you haven't, Oswald.

OSWALD: And yet this has come upon me just the same—this awful misfortune!

MRS. ALVING: Oh, but it will pass over, my dear, blessed boy. It's nothing but over-work. Trust me, I am right.

OSWALD: [Sadly] I thought so too, at first; but it isn't so.

MRS. ALVING: Tell me everything, from beginning to end.

OSWALD: Yes, I will.

MRS. ALVING: When did you first notice it?

OSWALD: It was directly after I had been home last time, and had got back to Paris again. I began to feel the most violent pains in my head—chiefly in the back of my head, they seemed to come. It was as though a tight iron ring was being screwed round my neck and upwards.

MRS. ALVING: Well, and then?

OSWALD: At first I thought it was nothing but the ordinary headache I had been so plagued with while I was growing up—

MRS. ALVING: Yes, yes—

OSWALD: But it wasn't that. I soon found that out. I couldn't work any more. I wanted to begin upon a big new picture, but my powers seemed to fail me; all my strength was crippled; I could form no definite images; everything swam before me— whirling round and round. Oh, it was an awful state! At last I sent for a doctor—and from him I learned the truth.

MRS. ALVING: How do you mean?

OSWALD: He was one of the first doctors in Paris. I told him my symptoms; and then he set to work asking me a string of questions which I thought had nothing to do with the matter. I couldn't imagine what the man was after—

MRS. ALVING: Well?

OSWALD: At last he said: "There has been something worm-eaten in you from your birth." He used that very word—vermoulu.

MRS. ALVING: [Breathlessly] What did he mean by that?

OSWALD: I didn't understand either, and begged him to explain himself more clearly. And then the old cynic said—[Clenching his fist] Oh—!

MRS. ALVING: What did he say?

OSWALD: He said, "The sins of the fathers are visited upon the children."

MRS. ALVING: [Rising slowly] The sins of the fathers—!

OSWALD: I very nearly struck him in the face—

MRS. ALVING: [Walks away across the room] The sins of the fathers—

OSWALD: [Smiles sadly] Yes; what do you think of that? Of course I assured him that such a thing was out of the question. But do you think he gave in? No, he stuck to it; and it was only when I produced your letters and translated the passages relating to father—

MRS. ALVING: But then—?

OSWALD: Then of course he had to admit that he was on the wrong track; and so I learned the truth— the incomprehensible truth! I ought not to have taken part with my comrades in that light-hearted, glorious life of theirs. It had been too much for my strength. So I had brought it upon myself!

MRS. ALVING: Oswald! No, no; do not believe it!

OSWALD: No other explanation was possible, he said. That's the awful part of it. Incurably ruined for life—by my own heedlessness! All that I meant to have done in the world—I never dare think of it again—I'm not able to think of it. Oh! if I could only live over again, and undo all I have done! [He buries his face in the sofa. Mrs. Alving wrings her hands and walks, in silent struggle, backwards and forwards]

OSWALD: [After a while, looks up and remains resting upon his elbow] If it had only been something inherited—something one wasn't responsible for! But this! To have thrown away so shamefully, thoughtlessly, recklessly, one's own happiness, one's own health, everything in the world—one's future, one's very life—!

MRS. ALVING: No, no, my dear, darling boy; this is impossible! [Bends over him] Things are not so desperate as you think.

OSWALD: Oh, you don't know—[Springs up] And then, mother, to cause you all this sorrow! Many a time I have almost wished and hoped that at bottom you didn't care so very much about me.

MRS. ALVING: I, Oswald? My only boy! You are all I have in the world! The only thing I care about!

OSWALD: [Seizes both her hands and kisses them] Yes, yes, I see it. When I'm at home, I see it, of course; and that's almost the hardest part for me.— But now you know the whole story; and now we won't talk any more about it to-day. I daren't think of it for long together. [Goes up the room] Get me something to drink, mother.

MRS. ALVING: To drink? What do you want to drink now?

OSWALD: Oh, anything you like. You have some cold punch in the house.

MRS. ALVING: Yes, but my dear Oswald—

OSWALD: Don't refuse me, mother. Do be kind, now! I must have something to wash down all these gnawing thoughts. [Goes into the conservatory] And then—it's so dark here! [Mrs. Alving pulls a bell-rope on the right] And this ceaseless rain! It may go on week after week, for months together. Never to get a glimpse of the sun! I can't recollect ever having seen the sun shine all the times I've been at home.

MRS. ALVING: Oswald—you are thinking of going away from me.

OSWALD: H'm—[Drawing a heavy breath] I'm not

thinking of anything. I cannot think of anything! [*In a low voice*] I let thinking alone.

REGINA: [*From the dining-room*] Did you ring, ma'am?

MRS. ALVING: Yes; let us have the lamp in.

REGINA: Yes, ma'am. It's ready lighted. [*Goes out*]

MRS. ALVING: [*Goes across to* Oswald] Oswald, be frank with me.

OSWALD: Well, so I am, mother. [*Goes to the table*] I think I have told you enough.

[Regina *brings the lamp and sets it upon the table*]

MRS. ALVING: Regina, you may bring us a small bottle of champagne.

REGINA: Very well, ma'am. [*Goes out*]

OSWALD: [*Puts his arm round* Mrs. Alving's *neck*] That's just what I wanted. I knew mother wouldn't let her boy go thirsty.

MRS. ALVING: My own, poor, darling Oswald; how could I deny you anything now?

OSWALD: [*Eagerly*] Is that true, mother? Do you mean it?

MRS. ALVING: How? What?

OSWALD: That you couldn't deny me anything.

MRS. ALVING: My dear Oswald—

OSWALD: Hush!

REGINA: [*Brings a tray with a half-bottle of champagne and two glasses, which she sets on the table*] Shall I open it?

OSWALD: No, thanks. I will do it myself.

[Regina *goes out again*]

MRS. ALVING: [*Sits down by the table*] What was it you meant—that I mustn't deny you?

OSWALD: [*Busy opening the bottle*] First let us have a glass—or two. [*The cork pops; he pours wine into one glass, and is about to pour it into the other*]

MRS. ALVING: [*Holding her hand over it*] Thanks; not for me.

OSWALD: Oh! won't you? Then I will! [*He empties the glass, fills, and empties it again; then he sits down by the table*]

MRS. ALVING: [*In expectancy*] Well?

OSWALD: [*Without looking at her*] Tell me—I thought you and Pastor Manders seemed so odd— so quiet—at dinner to-day.

MRS. ALVING: Did you notice it?

OSWALD: Yes. H'm— [*After a short silence*] Tell me: what do you think of Regina?

MRS. ALVING: What do I think?

OSWALD: Yes; isn't she splendid?

MRS. ALVING: My dear Oswald, you don't know her as I do—

OSWALD: Well?

MRS. ALVING: Regina, unfortunately, was allowed to stay at home too long. I ought to have taken her earlier into my house.

OSWALD: Yes, but isn't she splendid to look at, mother? [*He fills his glass*]

MRS. ALVING: Regina has many serious faults—

OSWALD: Oh, what does that matter? [*He drinks again*]

MRS. ALVING: But I am fond of her, nevertheless, and I am responsible for her. I wouldn't for all the world have any harm happen to her.

OSWALD: [*Springs up*] Mother, Regina is my only salvation!

MRS. ALVING: [*Rising*] What do you mean by that?

OSWALD: I cannot go on bearing all this anguish of soul alone.

MRS. ALVING: Have you not your mother to share it with you?

OSWALD: Yes; that's what I thought; and so I came home to you. But that will not do. I see it won't do. I cannot endure my life here.

MRS. ALVING: Oswald!

OSWALD: I must live differently, mother. That is why I must leave you. I will not have you looking on at it.

MRS. ALVING: My unhappy boy! But, Oswald while you are so ill as this—

OSWALD: If it were only the illness, I should stay with you, mother, you may be sure; for you are the best friend I have in the world.

MRS. ALVING: Yes, indeed I am, Oswald; am I not?

OSWALD: [*Wanders restlessly about*] But it's all the torment, the gnawing remorse—and then, the great, killing dread. Oh—that awful dread!

MRS. ALVING: [*Walking after him*] Dread? What dread? What do you mean?

OSWALD: Oh, you mustn't ask me any more. I don't know. I can't describe it.

[Mrs. Alving *goes over to the right and pulls the bell*]

OSWALD: What is it you want?

MRS. ALVING: I want my boy to be happy—that is what I want. He sha'n't go on brooding over things. [*To* Regina, *who appears at the door:*] More champagne—a large bottle.

[Regina *goes*]

OSWALD: Mother!

MRS. ALVING: Do you think we don't know how to live here at home?

OSWALD: Isn't she splendid to look at? How beautifully she's built! And so thoroughly healthy!

MRS. ALVING: [*Sits by the table*] Sit down, Oswald; let us talk quietly together.

OSWALD: [*Sits*] I daresay you don't know, mother, that I owe Regina some reparation.

MRS. ALVING: You!

OSWALD: For a bit of thoughtlessness, or whatever you like to call it—very innocent, at any rate. When I was home last time—

MRS. ALVING: Well?

OSWALD: She used often to ask me about Paris, and I used to tell her one thing and another. Then I recollect I happened to say to her one day, "Shouldn't you like to go there yourself?"

MRS. ALVING: Well?

OSWALD: I saw her face flush, and then she said, "Yes, I should like it of all things." "Ah, well," I replied, "it might perhaps be managed"—or something like that.

MRS. ALVING: And then?

OSWALD: Of course I had forgotten all about it; but the day before yesterday I happened to ask her whether she was glad I was to stay at home so long—

MRS. ALVING: Yes?

OSWALD: And then she gave me such a strange look, and asked, "But what's to become of my trip to Paris?"

MRS. ALVING: Her trip!

OSWALD: And so it came out that she had taken the thing seriously; that she had been thinking of me the whole time, and had set to work to learn French—

MRS. ALVING: So that was why—!

OSWALD: Mother—when I saw that fresh, lovely, splendid girl standing there before me—till then I had hardly noticed her—but when she stood there as though with open arms ready to receive me—

MRS. ALVING: Oswald!

OSWALD: —then it flashed upon me that in her lay my salvation; for I saw that she was full of the joy of life.

MRS. ALVING: [Starts] The joy of life—? Can there be salvation in that?

REGINA: [From the dining-room, with a bottle of champagne] I'm sorry to have been so long, but I had to go to the cellar. [Places the bottle on the table]

OSWALD: And now bring another glass.

REGINA: [Looks at him in surprise] There is Mrs. Alving's glass, Mr. Alving.

OSWALD: Yes, but bring one for yourself, Regina. [Regina starts and gives a lightning-like side glance at Mrs. Alving] Why do you wait?

REGINA: [Softly and hesitatingly] Is it Mrs. Alving's wish?

MRS. ALVING: Bring the glass, Regina.

[Regina goes out into the dining-room]

OSWALD: [Follows her with his eyes] Have you noticed how she walks?—so firmly and lightly!

MRS. ALVING: This can never be, Oswald!

OSWALD: It's a settled thing. Can't you see that? It's no use saying anything against it.

[Regina enters with an empty glass, which she keeps in her hand]

OSWALD: Sit down, Regina.

[Regina looks inquiringly at Mrs. Alving]

MRS. ALVING: Sit down. [Regina sits on a chair by the dining-room door, still holding the empty glass in her hand] Oswald—what were you saying about the joy of life?

OSWALD: Ah, the joy of life, mother—that's a thing you don't know much about in these parts. I have never felt it here.

MRS. ALVING: Not when you are with me?

OSWALD: Not when I'm at home. But you don't understand that.

MRS. ALVING: Yes; yes; I think I almost understand it—now.

OSWALD: And then, too, the joy of work! At bottom, it's the same thing. But that, too, you know nothing about.

MRS. ALVING: Perhaps you are right. Tell me more about it, Oswald.

OSWALD: I only mean that here people are brought up to believe that work is a curse and a punishment for sin, and that life is something miserable, something it would be best to have done with, the sooner the better.

MRS. ALVING: "A vale of tears," yes; and we certainly do our best to make it one.

OSWALD: But in the great world people won't hear of such things. There, nobody really believes such doctrines any longer. There, you feel it a positive bliss and ecstasy merely to draw the breath of life. Mother, have you noticed that everything I have painted has turned upon the joy of life?—always, always upon the joy of life?—light and sunshine and glorious air—and faces radiant with happiness. That is why I'm afraid of remaining at home with you.

MRS. ALVING: Afraid? What are you afraid of here, with me?

OSWALD: I'm afraid lest all my instincts should be warped into ugliness.

MRS. ALVING: [Looks steadily at him] Do you think that is what would happen?

OSWALD: I know it. You may live the same life here as there, and yet it won't be the same life.

MRS. ALVING: [Who has been listening eagerly, rises, her eyes big with thought, and says:] Now I see the sequence of things.

OSWALD: What is it you see?

MRS. ALVING: I see it now for the first time. And now I can speak.

OSWALD: [Rising] Mother, I don't understand you.

REGINA: [Who has also risen] Perhaps I ought to go?

MRS. ALVING: No. Stay here. Now I can speak. Now, my boy, you shall know the whole truth. And then you can choose. Oswald! Regina!

OSWALD: Hush! The Pastor—

MANDERS: [Enters by the hall door] There! We have had a most edifying time down there.

OSWALD: So have we.

MANDERS: We must stand by Engstrand and his Sailors' Home. Regina must go to him and help him—

REGINA: No thank you, sir.

MANDERS: [Noticing her for the first time] What—? You here? And with a glass in your hand!

REGINA: [Hastily putting the glass down] Pardon!

OSWALD: Regina is going with me, Mr. Manders.

MANDERS: Going! With you!

OSWALD: Yes; as my wife—if she wishes it.

MANDERS: But, merciful God—!

REGINA: I can't help it, sir.

OSWALD: Or she'll stay here, if I stay.

REGINA: [Involuntarily] Here!

MANDERS: I am thunderstruck at your conduct, Mrs. Alving.

MRS. ALVING: They will do neither one thing nor the other; for now I can speak out plainly.

MANDERS: You surely will not do that! No, no, no!

MRS. ALVING: Yes, I can speak and I will. And no ideals shall suffer after all.

OSWALD: Mother—what is it you are hiding from me?

REGINA: [Listening] Oh, ma'am, listen! Don't you hear shouts outside. [She goes into the conservatory and looks out]

OSWALD: [At the window on the left] What's going on? Where does that light come from?

REGINA: [Cries out] The Orphanage is on fire!

MRS. ALVING: [Rushing to the window] On fire!

MANDERS: On fire! Impossible! I've just come from there.

OSWALD: Where's my hat? Oh, never mind it— Father's Orphanage—! [He rushes out through the garden door]

MRS. ALVING: My shawl, Regina! The whole place is in a blaze!

MANDERS: Mrs. Alving, it is a judgment upon this abode of lawlessness.

MRS. ALVING: Yes, of course. Come, Regina. [She and Regina hasten out through the hall]

MANDERS: [Clasps his hands together] And we left it uninsured! [He goes out the same way]

ACT III.

The room as before. All the doors stand open. The lamp is still burning on the table. It is dark out of doors; there is only a faint glow from the conflagration in the background to the left. Mrs. Alving, with a shawl over her head, stands in the conservatory, looking out. Regina, also with a shawl on, stands a little behind her.

MRS. ALVING: The whole thing burnt!—burnt to the ground!

REGINA: The basement is still burning.

MRS. ALVING: How is it Oswald doesn't come home? There's nothing to be saved.

REGINA: Should you like me to take down his hat to him?

MRS. ALVING: Has he not even got his hat on?

REGINA: [Pointing to the hall] No; there it hangs.

MRS. ALVING: Let it be. He must come up now. I shall go and look for him myself. [She goes out through the garden door]

MANDERS: [Comes in from the hall] Is not Mrs. Alving here?

REGINA: She has just gone down the garden.

MANDERS: This is the most terrible night I ever went through.

REGINA: Yes; isn't it a dreadful misfortune, sir?

MANDERS: Oh, don't talk about it! I can hardly bear to think of it.

REGINA: How can it have happened—?

MANDERS: Don't ask me, Miss Engstrand! How should I know? Do you, too—? Is it not enough that your father—?

REGINA: What about him?

MANDERS: Oh, he has driven me distracted—

ENGSTRAND: [Enters through the hall] Your Reverence—

MANDERS: [Turns round in terror] Are you after me here, too?

ENGSTRAND: Yes, strike me dead, but I must—! Oh, Lord! what am I saying? But this is a terrible ugly business, your Reverence.

MANDERS: [Walks to and fro] Alas! alas!

REGINA: What's the matter?

ENGSTRAND: Why, it all came of this here prayer-meeting, you see. [Softly] The bird's limed, my girl. [Aloud] And to think it should be my doing that such a thing should be his Reverence's doing!

MANDERS: But I assure you, Engstrand—

ENGSTRAND: There wasn't another soul except your Reverence as ever laid a finger on the candles down there.

MANDERS: [Stops] So you declare. But I certainly cannot recollect that I ever had a candle in my hand.

ENGSTRAND: And I saw as clear as daylight how your Reverence took the candle and snuffed it with your fingers, and threw away the snuff among the shavings.

MANDERS: And you stood and looked on?

ENGSTRAND: Yes; I saw it as plain as a pike-staff, I did.

MANDERS: It's quite beyond my comprehension. Besides, it has never been my habit to snuff candles with my fingers.

ENGSTRAND: And terrible risky it looked, too, that it did! But is there such a deal of harm done after all, your Reverence?

MANDERS: [Walks restlessly to and fro] Oh, don't ask me!

ENGSTRAND: [Walks with him] And your Reverence hadn't insured it, neither?

MANDERS: [Continuing to walk up and down] No, no, no; I have told you so.

ENGSTRAND: [Following him] Not insured! And then to go straight away down and set light to the whole thing! Lord, Lord, what a misfortune!

MANDERS: [Wipes the sweat from his forehead] Ay, you may well say that, Engstrand.

ENGSTRAND: And to think that such a thing should happen to a benevolent Institution, that was to have been a blessing both to town and country, as the saying goes! The newspapers won't be for handling your Reverence very gently, I expect.

MANDERS: No; that is just what I am thinking of. That is almost the worst of the whole matter. All the malignant attacks and imputations—! Oh, it makes me shudder to think of it!

MRS. ALVING: [*Comes in from the garden*] He is not to be persuaded to leave the fire.

MANDERS: Ah, there you are, Mrs. Alving.

MRS. ALVING: So you have escaped your Inaugural Address, Pastor Manders.

MANDERS: Oh, I should so gladly—

MRS. ALVING: [*In an undertone*] It is all for the best. That Orphanage would have done no one any good.

MANDERS: Do you think not?

MRS. ALVING: Do you think it would?

MANDERS: It is a terrible misfortune, all the same.

MRS. ALVING: Let us speak of it plainly, as a matter of business.—Are you waiting for Mr. Manders, Engstrand?

ENGSTRAND: [*At the hall door*] That's just what I'm a-doing of, ma'am.

MRS. ALVING: Then sit down meanwhile.

ENGSTRAND: Thank you, ma'am; I'd as soon stand.

MRS. ALVING: [*To* Manders] I suppose you are going by the steamer?

MANDERS: Yes; it starts in an hour.

MRS. ALVING: Then be so good as to take all the papers with you. I won't hear another word about this affair. I have other things to think of—

MANDERS: Mrs. Alving—

MRS. ALVING: Later on I shall send you a power of attorney to settle everything as you please.

MANDERS: That I will very readily undertake. The original destination of the endowment must now be completely changed, alas!

MRS. ALVING: Of course it must.

MANDERS: I think, first of all, I shall arrange that the Solvik property shall pass to the parish. The land is by no means without value. It can always be turned to account for some purpose or other. And the interest of the money in the Bank I could, perhaps, best apply for the benefit of some undertaking of acknowledged value to the town.

MRS. ALVING: Do just as you please. The whole matter is now completely indifferent to me.

ENGSTRAND: Give a thought to my Sailors' Home, your Reverence.

MANDERS: Upon my word, that is not a bad suggestion. That must be considered.

ENGSTRAND: Oh, devil take considering—Lord forgive me!

MANDERS: [*With a sigh*] And unfortunately I cannot tell how long I shall be able to retain control of these things—whether public opinion may not compel me to retire. It entirely depends upon the result of the official inquiry into the fire—

MRS. ALVING: What are you talking about?

MANDERS: And the result can by no means be foretold.

ENGSTRAND: [*Comes close to him*] Ay, but it can though. For here stands old Jacob Engstrand.

MANDERS: Well well, but—?

ENGSTRAND: [*More softly*] And Jacob Engstrand isn't the man to desert a noble benefactor in the hour of need, as the saying goes.

MANDERS: Yes, but my good fellow—how—?

ENGSTRAND: Jacob Engstrand may be likened to a sort of guardian angel, he may, your Reverence.

MANDERS: No, no; I really cannot accept that.

ENGSTRAND: Oh, that'll be the way of it, all the same. I know a man as has taken others' sins upon himself before now, I do.

MANDERS: Jacob! [*Wrings his hand*] Yours is a rare nature. Well, you shall be helped with your Sailors' Home. That you may rely upon.

[Engstrand *tries to thank him, but cannot for emotion*]

MANDERS: [*Hangs his travelling-bag over his shoulder*] And now let us set out. We two will go together.

ENGSTRAND: [*At the dining-room door, softly to* Regina] You come along too, my lass. You shall live as snug as the yolk in an egg.

REGINA: [*Tosses her head*] Merci! [*She goes out into the hall and fetches* Manders' *overcoat*]

MANDERS: Good-bye, Mrs. Alving! and may the spirit of Law and Order descend upon this house, and that quickly.

MRS. ALVING: Good-bye, Pastor Manders. [*She goes up toward the conservatory, as she sees* Oswald *coming in through the garden door*]

ENGSTRAND: [*While he and* Regina *help* Manders *to get his coat on*] Good-bye, my child. And if any trouble should come to you, you know where Jacob Engstrand is to be found. [*Softly*] Little Harbour Street, h'm—! [*To* Mrs. Alving *and* Oswald] And the refuge for wandering mariners shall be called "Chamberlain Alving's Home," that it shall! And if so be as I'm spared to carry on that house in my own way, I make so bold as to promise that it shall be worthy of the Chamberlain's memory.

MANDERS: [*In the doorway*] H'm—h'm!—Come along, my dear Engstrand. Good-bye! Good-bye! [*He and* Engstrand *go out through the hall*]

OSWALD: [*Goes towards the table*] What house was he talking about?

MRS. ALVING: Oh, a kind of Home that he and Pastor Manders want to set up.

OSWALD: It will burn down like the other.

MRS. ALVING: What makes you think so?

OSWALD: Everything will burn. All that recalls father's memory is doomed. Here am I, too, burning down. [Regina *starts and looks at him*]

MRS. ALVING: Oswald! You oughtn't to have remained so long down there, my poor boy.

OSWALD: [*Sits down by the table*] I almost think you are right.

MRS. ALVING: Let me dry your face, Oswald; you

are quite wet. [*She dries his face with her pocket-handkerchief*]

OSWALD: [*Stares indifferently in front of him*] Thanks, mother.

MRS. ALVING: Are you not tired, Oswald? Should you like to sleep?

OSWALD: [*Nervously*] No, no—not to sleep! I never sleep. I only pretend to. [*Sadly*] That will come soon enough.

MRS. ALVING: [*Looking sorrowfully at him*] Yes, you really are ill, my blessed boy.

REGINA: [*Eagerly*] Is Mr. Alving ill?

OSWALD: [*Impatiently*] Oh, do shut all the doors! This killing dread—

MRS. ALVING: Close the doors, Regina.

[Regina *shuts them and remains standing by the hall door.* Mrs. Alving *takes her shawl off.* Regina *does the same.* Mrs. Alving *draws a chair across to* Oswald's *and sits by him*]

MRS. ALVING: There now! I am going to sit beside you—

OSWALD: Yes, do. And Regina shall stay here too. Regina shall be with me always. You will come to the rescue, Regina, won't you?

REGINA: I don't understand—

MRS. ALVING: To the rescue?

OSWALD: Yes—when the need comes.

MRS. ALVING: Oswald, have you not your mother to come to the rescue?

OSWALD: You? [*Smiles*] No, mother; that rescue you will never bring me. [*Laughs sadly*] You! ha ha! [*Looks earnestly at her*] Though, after all, who ought to do it if not you? [*Impetuously*] Why can't you say "thou" to me, Regina? Why don't you call me "Oswald"?

REGINA: [*Softly*] I don't think Mrs. Alving would like it.

MRS. ALVING: You shall have leave to, presently. And meanwhile sit over here beside us.

[Regina *seats herself demurely and hesitatingly at the other side of the table*]

MRS. ALVING: And now, my poor suffering boy, I am going to take the burden off your mind—

OSWALD: You, mother?

MRS. ALVING: —all the gnawing remorse and self-reproach you speak of.

OSWALD: And you think you can do that?

MRS. ALVING: Yes, now I can, Oswald. A little while ago you spoke of the joy of life; and at that word a new light burst for me over my life and everything connected with it.

OSWALD: [*Shakes his head*] I don't understand you.

MRS. ALVING: You ought to have known your father when he was a young lieutenant. He was brimming over with the joy of life!

OSWALD: Yes, I know he was.

MRS. ALVING: It was like a breezy day only to look at him. And what exuberant strength and vitality there was in him!

OSWALD: Well—?

MRS. ALVING: Well then, child of joy as he was—for he was like a child in those days—he had to live at home here in a half-grown town, which had no joys to offer him—only dissipations. He had no object in life—only an official position. He had no work into which he could throw himself heart and soul; he had only business. He had not a single comrade that could realise what the joy of life meant—only loungers and boon-companions—

OSWALD: Mother—!

MRS. ALVING: So the inevitable happened.

OSWALD: The inevitable?

MRS. ALVING: You told me yourself, this evening, what would become of you if you stayed at home.

OSWALD: Do you mean to say that father—?

MRS. ALVING: Your poor father found no outlet for the overpowering joy of life that was in him. And I brought no brightness into his home.

OSWALD: Not even you?

MRS. ALVING: They had taught me a great deal about duties and so forth, which I went on obstinately believing in. Everything was marked out into duties—into my duties, and his duties, and—I am afraid I made his home intolerable for your poor father, Oswald.

OSWALD: Why have you never spoken of this in writing to me?

MRS. ALVING: I have never before seen it in such a light that I could speak of it to you, his son.

OSWALD: In what light did you see it, then?

MRS. ALVING: [*Slowly*] I saw only this one thing: that your father was a broken-down man before you were born.

OSWALD: [*Softly*] Ah—! [*He rises and walks away to the window*]

MRS. ALVING: And then, day after day, I dwelt on the one thought that by rights Regina should be at home in this house—just like my own boy.

OSWALD: [*Turning round quickly*] Regina—!

REGINA: [*Springs up and asks, with bated breath*] I—?

MRS. ALVING: Yes, now you know it, both of you.

OSWALD: Regina!

REGINA: [*To herself*] So mother was that kind of woman.

MRS. ALVING: Your mother had many good qualities, Regina.

REGINA: Yes, but she was one of that sort, all the same. Oh, I've often suspected it; but— And now, if you please, ma'am, may I be allowed to go away at once?

MRS. ALVING: Do you really wish it, Regina?

REGINA: Yes, indeed I do.

MRS. ALVING: Of course you can do as you like; but—

OSWALD: [*Goes towards* Regina] Go away now? Your place is here.

REGINA: *Merci*, Mr. Alving!—or now, I suppose, I may say Oswald. But I can tell you this wasn't at all what I expected.

MRS. ALVING: Regina, I have not been frank with you—

REGINA: No, that you haven't indeed. If I'd known that Oswald was an invalid, why— And now, too, that it can never come to anything serious between us— I really can't stop out here in the country and wear myself out nursing sick people.

OSWALD: Not even one who is so near to you?

REGINA: No, that I can't. A poor girl must make the best of her young days, or she'll be left out in the cold before she knows where she is. And I, too, have the joy of life in me, Mrs. Alving!

MRS. ALVING: Unfortunately, you have. But don't throw yourself away, Regina.

REGINA: Oh, what must be, must be. If Oswald takes after his father, I take after my mother, I daresay.—May I ask, ma'am, if Pastor Manders knows all this about me?

MRS. ALVING: Pastor Manders knows all about it.

REGINA: [Busied in putting on her shawl] Well then, I'd better make haste and get away by this steamer. The Pastor is such a nice man to deal with; and I certainly think I've as much right to a little of that money as he has—that brute of a carpenter.

MRS. ALVING: You are heartily welcome to it, Regina.

REGINA: [Looks hard at her] I think you might have brought me up as a gentleman's daughter, ma'am; it would have suited me better. [Tosses her head] But pooh—what does it matter! [With a bitter side glance at the corked bottle] I may come to drink champagne with gentlefolks yet.

MRS. ALVING: And if you ever need a home, Regina, come to me.

REGINA: No, thank you, ma'am. Pastor Manders will look after me, I know. And if the worst comes to the worst, I know of one house where I've every right to a place.

MRS. ALVING: Where is that?

REGINA: "Chamberlain Alving's Home."

MRS. ALVING: Regina—now I see it—you are going to your ruin.

REGINA: Oh, stuff! Good-bye. [She nods and goes out through the hall]

OSWALD: [Stands at the window and looks out] Is she gone?

MRS. ALVING: Yes.

OSWALD: [Murmuring aside to himself] I think it was a mistake, this.

MRS. ALVING: [Goes up behind him and lays her hands on his shoulders] Oswald, my dear boy—has it shaken you very much?

OSWALD: [Turns his face towards her] All that about father, do you mean?

MRS. ALVING: Yes, about your unhappy father. I am so afraid it may have been too much for you.

OSWALD: Why should you fancy that? Of course it came upon me as a great surprise; but it can make no real difference to me.

MRS. ALVING: [Draws ner hands away] No difference! That your father was infinitely unhappy!

OSWALD: Of course I can pity him, as I would anybody else; but—

MRS. ALVING: Nothing more! Your own father!

OSWALD: [Impatiently] Oh, "father,"—"father"! I never knew anything of father. I remember nothing about him, except that he once made me sick.

MRS. ALVING: This is terrible to think of! Ought not a son to love his father, whatever happens?

OSWALD: When a son has nothing to thank his father for? has never known him? Do you really cling to that old superstition?—you who are so enlightened in other ways?

MRS. ALVING: Can it be only a superstition—?

OSWALD: Yes; surely you can see that, mother. It's one of those notions that are current in the world, and so—

MRS. ALVING: [Deeply moved] Ghosts!

OSWALD: [Crossing the room] Yes; you may call them ghosts.

MRS. ALVING: [Wildly] Oswald—then you don't love me, either!

OSWALD: You I know, at any rate—

MRS. ALVING: Yes, you know me; but is that all!

OSWALD: And, of course, I know how fond you are of me, and I can't but be grateful to you. And then you can be so useful to me, now that I am ill.

MRS. ALVING: Yes, cannot I, Oswald? Oh, I could almost bless the illness that has driven you home to me. For I see very plainly that you are not mine: I have to win you.

OSWALD: [Impatiently] Yes, yes, yes; all these are just so many phrases. You must remember that I am a sick man, mother. I can't be much taken up with other people; I have enough to do thinking about myself.

MRS. ALVING: [In a low voice] I shall be patient and easily satisfied.

OSWALD: And cheerful too, mother!

MRS. ALVING: Yes, my dear boy, you are quite right. [Goes towards him] Have I relieved you of all remorse and self-reproach now?

OSWALD: Yes, you have. But now who will relieve me of the dread?

MRS. ALVING: The dread?

OSWALD: [Walks across the room] Regina could have been got to do it.

MRS. ALVING: I don't understand you. What is this about dread—and Regina?

OSWALD: Is it very late, mother?

MRS. ALVING: It is early morning. [She looks out through the conservatory] The day is dawning over the mountains. And the weather is clearing, Oswald. In a little while you shall see the sun.

OSWALD: I'm glad of that. Oh, I may still have much to rejoice in and live for—

MRS. ALVING: I should think so, indeed!

OSWALD: Even if I can't work—

MRS. ALVING: Oh, you'll soon be able to work

again, my dear boy—now that you haven't got all those gnawing and depressing thoughts to brood over any longer.

OSWALD: Yes, I'm glad you were able to rid me of all those fancies. And when I've got over this one thing more— [*Sits on the sofa*] Now we will have a little talk, mother—

MRS. ALVING: Yes, let us. [*She pushes an armchair towards the sofa, and sits down close to him*]

OSWALD: And meantime the sun will be rising. And then you will know all. And then I shall not feel this dread any longer.

MRS. ALVING: What is it that I am to know?

OSWALD: [*Not listening to her*] Mother, did you not say a little while ago, that there was nothing in the world you would not do for me, if I asked you?

MRS. ALVING: Yes, indeed I said so!

OSWALD: And you'll stick to it, mother?

MRS. ALVING: You may rely on that, my dear and only boy! I have nothing in the world to live for but you alone.

OSWALD: Very well, then; now you shall hear— Mother, you have a strong, steadfast mind, I know. Now you're to sit quite still when you hear it.

MRS. ALVING: What dreadful thing can it be—?

OSWALD: You're not to scream out. Do you hear? Do you promise me that? We will sit and talk about it quietly. Do you promise me, mother?

MRS. ALVING: Yes, yes; I promise. Only speak!

OSWALD: Well, you must know that all this fatigue —and my inability to think of work—all that is not the illness itself—

MRS. ALVING: Then what is the illness itself?

OSWALD: The disease I have as my birthright— [*He points to his forehead and adds very softly*]— is seated here.

MRS. ALVING: [*Almost voiceless*] Oswald! No—no!

OSWALD: Don't scream. I can't bear it. Yes, mother, it is seated here—waiting. And it may break out any day—at any moment.

MRS. ALVING: Oh, what horror—!

OSWALD: Now, quiet, quiet. That is how it stands with me—

MRS. ALVING: [*Springs up*] It's not true, Oswald! It's impossible! It cannot be so!

OSWALD: I have had one attack down there already. It was soon over. But when I came to know the state I had been in, then the dread descended upon me, raging and ravening; and so I set off home to you as fast as I could.

MRS. ALVING: Then this is the dread—!

OSWALD: Yes—it's so indescribably loathsome, you know. Oh, if it had only been as ordinary mortal disease—! For I'm not so afraid of death—though I should like to live as long as I can.

MRS. ALVING: Yes, yes, Oswald, you must!

OSWALD: But this is so unutterably loathsome. To become a little baby again! To have to be fed! To have to— Oh, it's not to be spoken of!

MRS. ALVING: The child has his mother to nurse him.

OSWALD: [*Springs up*] No, never that! That is just what I will not have. I can't endure to think that perhaps I should lie in that state for many years— and get old and grey. And in the meantime you might die and leave me. [*Sits in* Mrs. Alving's *chair*] For the doctor said it wouldn't necessarily prove fatal at once. He called it a sort of softening of the brain—or something like that. [*Smiles sadly*] I think that expression sounds so nice. It always sets me thinking of cherry-colored velvet—something soft and delicate to stroke.

MRS. ALVING: [*Shrieks*] Oswald!

OSWALD: [*Springs up and paces the room*] And now you have taken Regina from me. If I could only have had her! She would have come to the rescue, I know.

MRS. ALVING: [*Goes to him*] What do you mean by that, my darling boy? Is there any help in the world that I would not give you?

OSWALD: When I got over my attack in Paris, the doctor told me that when it comes again—and it will come—there will be no more hope.

MRS. ALVING: He was heartless enough to—

OSWALD: I demanded it of him. I told him I had preparations to make— [*He smiles cunningly*] And so I had. [*He takes a little box from his inner breast pocket and opens it*] Mother, do you see this?

MRS. ALVING: What is it?

OSWALD: Morphia.

MRS. ALVING: [*Looks at him horror-struck*] Oswald—my boy—

OSWALD: I've scraped together twelve pilules—

MRS. ALVING: [*Snatches at it*] Give me the box, Oswald.

OSWALD: Not yet, mother. [*He hides the box again in his pocket*]

MRS. ALVING: I shall never survive this!

OSWALD: It must be survived. Now if I'd had Regina here, I should have told her how things stood with me—and begged her to come to the rescue at the last. She would have done it. I know she would.

MRS. ALVING: Never!

OSWALD: When the horror had come upon me, and she saw me lying there helpless, like a little newborn baby, impotent, lost, hopeless—past all saving—

MRS. ALVING: Never in all the world would Regina have done this!

OSWALD: Regina would have done it. Regina was so splendidly light-hearted. And she would soon have wearied of nursing an invalid like me.

MRS. ALVING: Then heaven be praised that Regina is not here—

OSWALD: Well then, it is you that must come to the rescue, mother.

MRS. ALVING: [*Shrieks aloud*] I!

OSWALD: Who should do it if not you?

MRS. ALVING: I! your mother!

OSWALD: For that very reason.

MRS. ALVING: I, who gave you life!

OSWALD: I never asked you for life. And what sort of a life have you given me? I will not have it! You shall take it back again!

MRS. ALVING: Help! Help! [*She runs out into the hall*]

OSWALD: [*Going after her*] Do not leave me! Where are you going?

MRS. ALVING: [*In the hall*] To fetch the doctor, Oswald! Let me pass!

OSWALD: [*Also outside*] You shall not go out. And no one shall come in.

[*The locking of a door is heard*]

MRS. ALVING: [*Comes in again*] Oswald! Oswald—my child!

OSWALD: [*Follows her*] Have you a mother's heart for me—and yet can see me suffer from this unutterable dread?

MRS. ALVING: [*After a moment's silence, commands herself, and says:*] Here is my hand upon it.

OSWALD: Will you—

MRS. ALVING: If it should ever be necessary. But it will never be necessary. No, no; it is impossible.

OSWALD: Well, let us hope so. And let us live together as long as we can. Thank you, mother.

[*He seats himself in the arm-chair which* Mrs. Alving *has moved to the sofa. Day is breaking. The lamp is still burning on the table*]

MRS. ALVING: [*Drawing near cautiously*] Do you feel calm now?

OSWALD: Yes.

MRS. ALVING: [*Bending over him*] It has been a dreadful fancy of yours, Oswald—nothing but a fancy. All this excitement has been too much for you. But now you shall have a long rest; at home with your mother, my own blessed boy. Everything you point to you shall have, just as when you were a little child.—There now. The crisis is over. You see how easily it passed! Oh, I was sure it would. —And do you see, Oswald, what a lovely day we are going to have? Brilliant sunshine! Now you can really see your home.

[*She goes to the table and puts out the lamp. Sunrise. The glacier and the snow-peaks in the background glow in the morning light*]

OSWALD: [*Sits in the arm-chair with his back towards the landscape, without moving. Suddenly he says:*] Mother, give me the sun.

MRS. ALVING: [*By the table, starts and looks at him*] What do you say?

OSWALD: [*Repeats, in a dull, toneless voice*] The sun. The sun.

MRS. ALVING: [*Goes to him*] Oswald, what is the matter with you?

[Oswald *seems to shrink together in the chair; all his muscles relax; his face is expressionless, his eyes have a glassy stare*]

MRS. ALVING: [*Quivering with terror*] What is this? [*Shrieks*] Oswald! what is the matter with you? [*Falls on her knees beside him and shakes him*] Oswald! Oswald! look at me! Don't you know me?

OSWALD: [*Tonelessly as before*] The sun.—The sun.

MRS. ALVING: [*Springs up in despair, entwines her hands in her hair and shrieks*] I cannot bear it! [*Whispers, as though petrified*] I cannot bear it! Never! [*Suddenly*] Where has he got them? [*Fumbles hastily in his breast*] Here! [*Shrinks back a few steps and screams:*] No; no; no!—Yes!—No; no!

[*She stands a few steps away from him with her hands twisted in her hair, and stares at him in speechless horror*]

OSWALD: [*Sits motionless as before and says*] The sun.—The sun.

THE END

Henrik Ibsen

(1828–1906)

After the publication of *Ghosts,* Ibsen replied to the critics who had denounced him as an offender against society with a vehement polemic, *An Enemy of the People* (1883). He pitted his idealist Dr. Stockmann against the "compact majority" of the selfish, the timid, and the opportunistic. Ibsen was, indeed, so outspoken at the time that he impressed acquaintances as a thoroughgoing anarchist. But having discharged his spleen with this satire on vested interests, he proceeded to write one of the most sympathetic and beautiful of his plays, *The Wild Duck.* On the surface, it would even appear that he recanted his views in this drama, since he reduced the passion for reform to an absurdity in the case of a provincial Hamlet who destroys people's happiness with "the call of the ideal." Actually, Ibsen's procedure in the play was ironical, since it proposed that morality was relative rather than absolute and that illusions were a necessary part of happiness. Nevertheless, *The Wild Duck* represents an important change in direction for Ibsen. Thereafter he was to concentrate upon the drama of character rather than of social ideas. Social issues and problems still appeared in several of his plays, but they were qualified by the wisdom of one who treats such matters as a student of human nature. Beginning with *The Wild Duck* in 1884, Ibsen, who had introduced the social-problem play into the theatre of realism through his earlier prose works, created modern character drama in play after play— in *Rosmersholm, The Lady from the Sea, Hedda Gabler, The Master Builder, Little Eyolf,* and *John Gabriel Borkman.*

All these works locate the conflict within the characters. This quality does not by itself, of course, indicate any particular modernity to readers familiar with such classics as *Hamlet* and *Phaedra.* But Ibsen presented his character dramas in modern dress by means of prose dialogue, contemporary rather than historical backgrounds, and ordinary persons engaged in prosaic, nonheroic activities. And to these elements he added his concern with the general problem of self-realization and with specific social questions. The "woman question," that is, the problems raised by the so-called liberation of women, is implied in all but two of his last works. *Rosmersholm,* in addition, presents the problem of religious reform, and *John Gabriel Borkman* delineates a Napoleon of modern finance. Ibsen expressed his aims clearly when he wrote that his intention in *Hedda Gabler* had been to present characters, emotions, and human destinies "upon a groundwork of certain of the social conditions and principles [ideas] of the present day."

In most of the late plays, Ibsen relied a good deal on symbolism, and not always successfully. To see character drama in the clearest light we must turn to *Hedda Gabler* (1890), written without benefit of symbolism. Those who insist upon reading symbolism into the play are straining a point. The recurrent references to Hedda's pistols and "vine leaves in one's hair" are essentially punctuation marks in the characterization.

As was his habit, Ibsen based his work on observation of real people; in this case, of young women who considered themselves emancipated without finding proper outlets for their desires or notions of themselves. They thought of themselves as "new women," "Ibsen women," but achieved nothing themselves; posed as superior and mysterious personalities, but had no depths; spoke of freedom in love but were too egotistical to make either freedom or love fruitful. Often, too, they became "harpy women," Ibsen's phrase for those who tried to gratify themselves parasitically by making extreme demands upon men without giving anything substantial in return. Ibsen was not a little disturbed by them, for they were the products of a changing society, and he himself had advocated the change. Were the spiritual daughters of his Nora to be fundamentally unwomanly, sterile, and destructive? Ibsen found himself particularly involved with one of these "modern" girls, the eighteen-year-old Austrian, Emilie Bardach, who once confessed to him that she had no desire to marry but intended to take married men away from their wives. It is not too much to say that the sixty-year-old author was himself captivated for a time. But he was also able to resist her and to study her objectively, and he drew upon his observations to delineate Hedda. His younger contemporary, Strindberg, had warned the world against the "new woman" in *The Father, Comrades,* and *Miss Julie* in 1887 and 1888, and had attacked Ibsen for promoting a vicious "gynolatry." *Hedda Gabler* was in a sense a major qualification of Ibsen's previous championship of the "new woman." He did not, however, turn the qualification into an issue or debate, but made it implicit in the story of Hedda. The result was one of the most rounded characterizations of the modern drama, which has attracted most of the great and, unfortunately, many of the less than great actresses of the theatre.

Because her sisters are to be found everywhere

in the Western world, Hedda deserves more study than is usually given her. Restlessness without direction, self-regard combined with uselessness, desire for a rich life without willingness to enrich her own and others' lives, bold ideas of "living dangerously" nullified by a cold heart—these are some of the elements that went into the making of Ibsen's highly individualized yet decidedly representative portrait. For a complete understanding of the play, moreover, Hedda must be viewed within the constellation of the supplementary characters that Ibsen supplied with more calculation than may be suspected. Judge Brack is her male counterpart, and may serve to remind us that Hedda draws her frailties not merely from woman but from the human race. Tesman, who belongs to a species of pedant less familiar here than in Europe, is significant in several ways. That Hedda married a Tesman instead of joining her fate to the Dionysian Lövborg is surely indicative of fundamental Philistinism. Like so many of her sisters, she plays safe. She is an aristocrat by birth who lacks aristocracy of the spirit, a second-rate Brunhild in furbelows, a very pale shadow of the heroic women of Norse legend whom Ibsen had celebrated in his romantic dramas, even if she rides horses and shoots off pistols. She might have had a different life if she had married someone who was not a Tesman, but would she have been able to marry a man of different mettle? That she repulsed Lövborg and did marry Tesman, is carrying a child by the latter, and must live with him on a social level wounding to her vanity—these are essential factors in her drama.

Hedda's situation stems from her character, a fact Ibsen enforces upon us by drawing her opposite in Mrs. Elvsted. The once mousy girl who claims neither social nor individual superiority is Hedda's superior as a human being. The sophisticated Hedda is cowardly, whereas the "unemancipated," feminine Mrs. Elvsted behaves like a brave "new woman." She leaves husband and children in order to protect the man she saved from drink and despair and inspired to write an important book. It is the "bourgeois" Mrs. Elvsted, who, moved by love, is the free person. Because she has inner resources, moreover, she can continue to live after Lövborg's suicide, and finds self-realization in reconstructing his masterpiece. Hedda can only die.

Ibsen may be charged with returning to old-fashioned dramaturgy in making Hedda commit suicide. He may be defended, it is true, on the ground that Hedda is at the end of her resources, and that she has not been in full command of herself since her pregnancy. Also, she finds herself entirely superfluous when Tesman and Mrs. Elvsted start restoring the manuscript she threw into the fire, and her particular self-esteem makes her incapable of accepting Brack as a lover and buying his silence. Nevertheless, women like Hedda fail more usually, as well as more crushingly, by hanging on to life and avenging their frustration on others. The tragedy of a Hedda in real life, Bernard Shaw remarked, "is not that she commits suicide but that she continues to live."

For additional commentary and bibliography, see pages 10–14.

HEDDA GABLER

By Henrik Ibsen

TRANSLATED FROM THE NORWEGIAN BY EDMUND GOSSE AND WILLIAM ARCHER

CHARACTERS

GEORGE TESMAN
HEDDA TESMAN, *his wife*
MISS JULIANA TESMAN, *his aunt*

MRS. ELVSTED
JUDGE BRACK

EILERT LÖVBORG
BERTA, *servant at the Tesmans*

The scene of the action is Tesman's villa, in the west end of Christiania.

ACT I.

A spacious, handsome, and tastefully furnished drawing-room, decorated in dark colors. In the back, a wide doorway with curtains drawn back, leading into a smaller room decorated in the same style as the drawing-room. In the right-hand wall of the front room, a folding door leading out to the hall. In the opposite wall, on the left, a glass door, also with curtains drawn back. Through the panes can be seen part of a veranda outside, and trees covered with autumn foliage. An oval table, with a cover on it, and surrounded by chairs, stands well forward. In front, by the wall on the right, a wide stove of dark porcelain, a high-backed arm-chair, a cushioned foot-rest, and two footstools. A settee, with a small round table in front of it, fills the upper right-hand corner. In front, on the left, a little way from the wall, a sofa. Further back than the glass door, a piano. On either side of the doorway at the back a whatnot with terra-cotta and majolica ornaments.— Against the back wall of the inner room a sofa, with a table, and one or two chairs. Over the sofa hangs the portrait of a handsome elderly man in a General's uniform. Over the table a hanging lamp, with an opal glass shade.—A number of bouquets are arranged about the drawing-room, in vases and glasses. Others lie upon the tables. The floors in both rooms are covered with thick carpets.—Morning light. The sun shines in through the glass door.

Miss Juliana Tesman, *with her bonnet on and carrying a parasol, comes in from the hall, followed by* Berta, *who carries a bouquet wrapped in paper.* Miss Tesman *is a comely and pleasant-looking lady of about sixty-five. She is nicely but simply dressed in a gray walking-costume.* Berta *is a middle-aged woman of plain and rather countrified appearance.*

MISS TESMAN: [*Stops close to the door, listens, and says softly*] Upon my word, I don't believe they are stirring yet!

BERTA: [*Also softly*] I told you so, Miss. Remem-ber how late the steamboat got in last night. And then, when they got home!—good Lord, what a lot the young mistress had to unpack before she could get to bed.

MISS TESMAN: Well, well—let them have their sleep out. But let us see that they get a good breath of the fresh morning air when they do appear.

[*She goes to the glass door and throws it open*]

BERTA: [*Beside the table, at a loss what to do with the bouquet in her hand*] I declare there isn't a bit of room left. I think I'll put it down here, Miss.

[*She places it on the piano*]

MISS TESMAN: So you've got a new mistress now, my dear Berta. Heaven knows it was a wrench to me to part with you.

BERTA: [*On the point of weeping*] And do you think it wasn't hard for me, too, Miss? After all the blessed years I've been with you and Miss Rina.

MISS TESMAN: We must make the best of it, Berta. There was nothing else to be done. George can't do without you, you see—he absolutely can't. He has had you to look after him ever since he was a little boy.

BERTA: Ah, but, Miss Julia, I can't help thinking of Miss Rina lying helpless at home there, poor thing. And with only that new girl, too! She'll never learn to take proper care of an invalid.

MISS TESMAN: Oh, I shall manage to train her. And, of course, you know I shall take most of it upon myself. You needn't be uneasy about my poor sister, my dear Berta.

BERTA: Well, but there's another thing, Miss. I'm so mortally afraid I shan't be able to suit the young mistress.

MISS TESMAN: Oh, well—just at first there may be one or two things——

BERTA: Most like she'll be terrible grand in her ways.

MISS TESMAN: Well, you can't wonder at that— General Gabler's daughter! Think of the sort of life she was accustomed to in her father's time. Don't you remember how we used to see her riding down

42

the road along with the General? In that long black habit—and with feathers in her hat?

BERTA: Yes, indeed—I remember well enough!— But, good Lord, I should never have dreamt in those days that she and Master George would make a match of it.

MISS TESMAN: Nor I.—But by-the-bye, Berta— while I think of it: in future you mustn't say Master George. You must say Dr. Tesman.

BERTA: Yes, the young mistress spoke of that, too —last night—the moment they set foot in the house. Is it true then, Miss?

MISS TESMAN: Yes, indeed it is. Only think, Berta —some foreign university has made him a doctor— while he has been abroad, you understand. I hadn't heard a word about it, until he told me himself upon the pier.

BERTA: Well, well, he's clever enough for anything, he is. But I didn't think he'd have gone in for doctoring people, too.

MISS TESMAN: No, no, it's not that sort of doctor he is. [Nods significantly] But let me tell you, we may have to call him something still grander before long.

BERTA: You don't say so! What can that be, Miss?

MISS TESMAN: [Smiling] H'm—wouldn't you like to know! [With emotion] Ah, dear, dear—if my poor brother could only look up from his grave now, and see what his little boy has grown into! [Looks around] But bless me, Berta—why have you done this? Taken the chintz covers off all the furniture?

BERTA: The mistress told me to. She can't abide covers on the chairs, she says.

MISS TESMAN: Are they going to make this their everyday sitting-room then?

BERTA: Yes, that's what I understood—from the mistress. Master George—the doctor—he said nothing.

[George Tesman comes from the right into the inner room, humming to himself, and carrying an unstrapped empty portmanteau. He is a middle-sized, young-looking man of thirty-three, rather stout, with a round, open, cheerful face, fair hair and beard. He wears spectacles, and is somewhat carelessly dressed in comfortable indoor clothes]

MISS TESMAN: Good morning, good morning, George.

TESMAN: [In the doorway between the rooms] Aunt Julia! Dear Aunt Julia! [Goes up to her and shakes hands warmly] Come all this way—so early! Eh?

MISS TESMAN: Why, of course I had to come and see how you were getting on.

TESMAN: In spite of your having had no proper night's rest?

MISS TESMAN: Oh, that makes no difference to me.

TESMAN: Well, I suppose you got home all right from the pier? Eh?

MISS TESMAN: Yes, quite safely, thank goodness. Judge Brack was good enough to see me right to my door.

TESMAN: We were so sorry we couldn't give you a seat in the carriage. But you saw what a pile of boxes Hedda had to bring with her.

MISS TESMAN: Yes, she had certainly plenty of boxes.

BERTA: [To Tesman] Shall I go in and see if there's anything I can do for the mistress?

TESMAN: No thank you, Berta—you needn't. She said she would ring if she wanted anything.

BERTA: [Going towards the right] Very well.

TESMAN: But look here—take this portmanteau with you.

BERTA: [Taking it] I'll put it in the attic. [She goes out by the hall door]

TESMAN: Fancy, Auntie—I had the whole of that portmanteau chock full of copies of documents. You wouldn't believe how much I have picked up from all the archives I have been examining—curious old details that no one has had any idea of——

MISS TESMAN: Yes, you don't seem to have wasted your time on your wedding trip, George.

TESMAN: No, that I haven't. But do take off your bonnet, Auntie. Look here! Let me untie the strings —eh?

MISS TESMAN: [While he does so] Well well— this is just as if you were still at home with us.

TESMAN: [With the bonnet in his hand, looks at it from all sides] Why, what a gorgeous bonnet you've been investing in!

MISS TESMAN: I bought it on Hedda's account.

TESMAN: On Hedda's account? Eh?

MISS TESMAN: Yes, so that Hedda needn't be ashamed of me if we happened to go out together.

TESMAN: [Patting her cheek] You always think of everything, Aunt Julia. [Lays the bonnet on a chair beside the table] And now, look here—suppose we sit comfortably on the sofa and have a little chat, till Hedda comes.

[They seat themselves. She places her parasol in the corner of the sofa]

MISS TESMAN: [Takes both his hands and looks at him] What a delight it is to have you again, as large as life, before my very eyes, George! My George—my poor brother's own boy!

TESMAN: And it's a delight for me, too, to see you again, Aunt Julia! You, who have been father and mother in one to me.

MISS TESMAN: Oh yes, I know you will always keep a place in your heart for your old aunts.

TESMAN: And what about Aunt Rina? No improvement—eh?

MISS TESMAN: Oh no—we can scarcely look for any improvement in her case, poor thing. There she lies, helpless, as she has lain for all these years. But heaven grant I may not lose her yet awhile. For if

I did, I don't know what I should make of my life,
George—especially now that I haven't you to look
after any more.

TESMAN: [*Patting her back*] There there
there——!

MISS TESMAN: [*Suddenly changing her tone*] And
to think that here are you a married man, George!
—And that you should be the one to carry off Hedda
Gabler—the beautiful Hedda Gabler! Only think of
it—she, that was so beset with admirers!

TESMAN: [*Hums a little and smiles complacently*]
Yes, I fancy I have several good friends about town
who would like to stand in my shoes—eh?

MISS TESMAN: And then this fine long wedding-
tour you have had! More than five—nearly six
months——

TESMAN: Well, for me it has been a sort of tour
of research as well. I have had to do so much grubbing among old records—and to read no end of
books too, Auntie.

MISS TESMAN: Oh yes, I suppose so. [*More confidentially, and lowering her voice a little*] But listen
now, George,—have you nothing—nothing special
to tell me?

TESMAN: As to our journey?

MISS TESMAN: Yes.

TESMAN: No, I don't know of anything except
what I have told you in my letters. I had a doctor's
degree conferred on me—but that I told you yesterday.

MISS TESMAN: Yes, yes, you did. But what I mean
is—haven't you any—any—expectations——?

TESMAN: Expectations?

MISS TESMAN: Why you know, George—I'm your
old auntie!

TESMAN: Why, of course I have expectations.

MISS TESMAN: Ah!

TESMAN: I have every expectation of being a professor one of these days.

MISS TESMAN: Oh yes, a professor——

TESMAN: Indeed, I may say I am certain of it. But
my dear Auntie—you know all about that already!

MISS TESMAN: [*Laughing to herself*] Yes, of course
I do. You are quite right there. [*Changing the subject*] But we were talking about your journey. It
must have cost a great deal of money, George?

TESMAN: Well, you see—my handsome traveling-
scholarship went a good way.

MISS TESMAN: But I can't understand how you
can have made it go far enough for two.

TESMAN: No, that's not so easy to understand—
eh?

MISS TESMAN: And especially travelling with a
lady—they tell me that makes it ever so much more
expensive.

TESMAN: Yes, of course—it makes it a little more
expensive. But Hedda had to have this trip, Auntie!
She really had to. Nothing else would have done.

MISS TESMAN: No no, I suppose not. A wedding-
tour seems to be quite indispensable nowadays.—

But tell me now—have you gone thoroughly over
the house yet?

TESMAN: Yes, you may be sure I have. I have
been afoot ever since daylight.

MISS TESMAN: And what do you think of it all?

TESMAN: I'm delighted! Quite delighted! Only I
can't think what we are to do with the two empty
rooms between this inner parlor and Hedda's bedroom.

MISS TESMAN: [*Laughing*] Oh my dear George, I
daresay you may find some use for them—in the
course of time.

TESMAN: Why of course you are quite right, Aunt
Julia! You mean as my library increases—eh?

MISS TESMAN: Yes, quite so, my dear boy. It was
your library I was thinking of.

TESMAN: I am specially pleased on Hedda's account. Often and often, before we were engaged, she
said that she would never care to live anywhere but
in Secretary Falk's villa.

MISS TESMAN: Yes, it was lucky that this very
house should come into the market, just after you
had started.

TESMAN: Yes, Aunt Julia, the luck was on our
side, wasn't it—eh?

MISS TESMAN: But the expense, my dear George!
You will find it very expensive, all this.

TESMAN: [*Looks at her, a little cast down*] Yes, I
suppose I shall, Aunt!

MISS TESMAN: Oh, frightfully!

TESMAN: How much do you think? In round numbers?—Eh?

MISS TESMAN: Oh, I can't even guess until all the
accounts come in.

TESMAN: Well, fortunately, Judge Brack has se-
cured the most favorable terms for me,—so he said
in a letter to Hedda.

MISS TESMAN: Yes, don't be uneasy, my dear boy.
—Besides, I have given security for the furniture
and all the carpets.

TESMAN: Security? You? My dear Aunt Julia—
what sort of security could you give?

MISS TESMAN: I have given a mortgage on our
annuity.

TESMAN: [*Jumps up*] What! On your—and Aunt
Rina's annuity!

MISS TESMAN: Yes, I knew of no other plan, you
see.

TESMAN: [*Placing himself before her*] Have you
gone out of your senses, Auntie! Your annuity—it's
all that you and Aunt Rina have to live upon.

MISS TESMAN: Well well—don't get so excited
about it. It's only a matter of form you know—
Judge Brack assured me of that. It was he that was
kind enough to arrange the whole affair for me. A
mere matter of form, he said.

TESMAN: Yes, that may be all very well. But
nevertheless——

MISS TESMAN: You will have your own salary to
depend upon now. And, good heavens, even if we

did have to pay up a little——! To eke things out a bit at the start——! Why, it would be nothing but a pleasure to us.

TESMAN: Oh Auntie—will you never be tired of making sacrifices for me!

MISS TESMAN: [*Rises and lays her hand on his shoulders*] Have I any other happiness in this world except to smooth your way for you, my dear boy? You, who have had neither father nor mother to depend on. And now we have reached the goal, George! Things have looked black enough for us, sometimes; but, thank heaven, now you have nothing to fear.

TESMAN: Yes, it is really marvelous how everything has turned out for the best.

MISS TESMAN: And the people who opposed you— who wanted to bar the way for you—now you have them at your feet. They have fallen, George. Your most dangerous rival—his fall was the worst.—And now he has to lie on the bed he has made for himself—poor misguided creature.

TESMAN: Have you heard anything of Eilert? Since I went away, I mean.

MISS TESMAN: Only that he is said to have published a new book.

TESMAN: What! Eilert Lövborg! Recently—eh?

MISS TESMAN: Yes, so they say. Heaven knows whether it can be worth anything! Ah, when your new book appears—that will be another story, George! What is it to be about?

TESMAN: It will deal with the domestic industries of Brabant during the Middle Ages.

MISS TESMAN: Fancy—to be able to write on such a subject as that!

TESMAN: However, it may be some time before the book is ready. I have all these collections to arrange first, you see.

MISS TESMAN: Yes, collecting and arranging—no one can beat you at that. There you are my poor brother's own son.

TESMAN: I am looking forward eagerly to setting to work at it; especially now that I have my own delightful home to work in.

MISS TESMAN: And, most of all, now that you have got the wife of your heart, my dear George.

TESMAN: [*Embracing her*] Oh yes, yes, Aunt Julia. Hedda—she is the best part of it all! [*Looks towards the doorway*] I believe I hear her coming—eh?

[Hedda *enters from the left through the inner room. She is a woman of nine-and-twenty. Her face and figure show refinement and distinction. Her complexion is pale and opaque. Her steel-gray eyes express a cold, unruffled repose. Her hair is of an agreeable medium brown, but not particularly abundant. She is dressed in a tasteful, somewhat loose-fitting morning gown*]

MISS TESMAN: [*Going to meet Hedda*] Good morning, my dear Hedda! Good morning. and a hearty welcome!

HEDDA: [*Holds out her hand*] Good morning, dear Miss Tesman! So early a call! That is kind of you.

MISS TESMAN: [*With some embarrassment*] Well —has the bride slept well in her new home?

HEDDA: Oh yes, thanks. Passably.

TESMAN: [*Laughing*] Passably! Come, that's good, Hedda! You were sleeping like a stone when I got up.

HEDDA: Fortunately. Of course one has always to accustom one's self to new surroundings, Miss Tesman—little by little. [*Looking towards the left*] Oh —there the servant has gone and opened the veranda door, and let in a whole flood of sunshine.

MISS TESMAN: [*Going towards the door*] Well, then we will shut it.

HEDDA: No no, not that! Tesman, please draw the curtains. That will give a softer light.

TESMAN: [*At the door*] All right—all right.— There now, Hedda, now you have both shade and fresh air.

HEDDA: Yes, fresh air we certainly must have, with all these stacks of flowers——. But—won't you sit down, Miss Tesman?

MISS TESMAN: No, thank you. Now that I have seen that everything is all right here—thank heaven! —I must be getting home again. My sister is lying longing for me, poor thing.

TESMAN: Give her my very best love, Auntie; and say I shall look in and see her later in the day.

MISS TESMAN: Yes, yes, I'll be sure to tell her. But by the by, George—[*Feeling in her dress pocket*] —I had almost forgotten—I have something for you here.

TESMAN: What is it, Auntie? Eh?

MISS TESMAN: [*Produces a flat parcel wrapped in newspaper and hands it to him*] Look here, my dear boy.

TESMAN: [*Opening the parcel*] Well, I declare!— Have you really saved them for me, Aunt Julia! Hedda! isn't this touching—eh?

HEDDA: [*Beside the whatnot on the right*] Well, what is it?

TESMAN: My old morning-shoes! My slippers.

HEDDA: Indeed. I remember you often spoke of them while we were abroad.

TESMAN: Yes, I missed them terribly. [*Goes up to her*] Now you shall see them, Hedda!

HEDDA: [*Going towards the stove*] Thanks, I really don't care about it.

TESMAN: [*Following her*] Only think—ill as she was, Aunt Rina embroidered these for me. Oh you can't think how many associations cling to them.

HEDDA: [*At the table*] Scarcely for me.

MISS TESMAN: Of course not for Hedda, George.

TESMAN: Well, but now that she belongs to the family, I thought——

HEDDA: [*Interrupting*] We shall never get on with this servant, Tesman.

MISS TESMAN: Not get on with Berta?

TESMAN: Why, dear, what puts that in your head? Eh?

HEDDA: [*Pointing*] Look there! She has left her old bonnet lying about on a chair.

TESMAN: [*In consternation, drops the slippers on the floor*] Why, Hedda——

HEDDA: Just fancy, if any one should come in and see it!

TESMAN: But Hedda—that's Aunt Julia's bonnet.

HEDDA: Is it!

MISS TESMAN: [*Taking up the bonnet*] Yes, indeed it's mine. And, what's more, it's not old, Madam Hedda.

HEDDA: I really did not look closely at it, Miss Tesman.

MISS TESMAN: [*Trying on the bonnet*] Let me tell you it's the first time I have worn it—the very first time.

TESMAN: And a very nice bonnet it is too—quite a beauty!

MISS TESMAN: Oh, it's no such great thing, George. [*Looks around her*] My parasol——? Ah, here. [*Takes it*] For this is mine too—[*mutters*]—not Berta's.

TESMAN: A new bonnet and a new parasol! Only think, Hedda!

HEDDA: Very handsome indeed.

TESMAN: Yes, isn't it? Eh? But Auntie, take a good look at Hedda before you go! See how handsome she is!

MISS TESMAN: Oh, my dear boy, there's nothing new in that. Hedda was always lovely.

[*She nods and goes towards the right*]

TESMAN: [*Following*] Yes, but have you noticed what splendid condition she is in? How she has filled out on the journey?

HEDDA: [*Crossing the room*] Oh, do be quiet——!

MISS TESMAN: [*Who has stopped and turned*] Filled out?

TESMAN: Of course you don't notice it so much now that she has that dress on. But I, who can see——

HEDDA: [*At the glass door, impatiently*] Oh, you can't see anything.

TESMAN: It must be the mountain air in the Tyrol——

HEDDA: [*Curtly, interrupting*] I am exactly as I was when I started.

TESMAN: So you insist; but I'm quite certain you are not. Don't you agree with me, Auntie?

MISS TESMAN: [*Who has been gazing at her with folded hands*] Hedda is lovely—lovely—lovely. [*Goes up to her, takes her head between both hands, draws it downwards, and kisses her hair*] God bless and preserve Hedda Tesman—for George's sake.

HEDDA: [*Gently freeing herself*] Oh—! Let me go.

MISS TESMAN: [*In quiet emotion*] I shall not let a day pass without coming to see you.

TESMAN: No you won't, will you, Auntie? Eh?

MISS TESMAN: Good-bye—good-bye!

[*She goes out by the hall door.* Tesman *accompanies her. The door remains half open.* Tesman *can be heard repeating his message to* Aunt Rina *and his thanks for the slippers*]

[*In the meantime,* Hedda *walks about the room, raising her arms and clenching her hands as if in desperation. Then she flings back the curtains from the glass door, and stands there looking out*]

[*Presently* Tesman *returns and closes the door behind him*]

TESMAN: [*Picks up the slippers from the floor*] What are you looking at, Hedda?

HEDDA: [*Once more calm and mistress of herself*] I am only looking at the leaves. They are so yellow—so withered.

TESMAN: [*Wraps up the slippers and lays them on the table*] Well you see, we are well into September now.

HEDDA: [*Again restless*] Yes, to think of it!—Already in—in September.

TESMAN: Don't you think Aunt Julia's manner was strange, dear? Almost solemn? Can you imagine what was the matter with her? Eh?

HEDDA: I scarcely know her, you see. Is she not often like that?

TESMAN: No, not as she was to-day.

HEDDA: [*Leaving the glass door*] Do you think she was annoyed about the bonnet?

TESMAN: Oh, scarcely at all. Perhaps a little, just at the moment——

HEDDA: But what an idea, to pitch her bonnet about in the drawing-room! No one does that sort of thing.

TESMAN: Well you may be sure Aunt Julia won't do it again.

HEDDA: In any case, I shall manage to make my peace with her.

TESMAN: Yes, my dear, good Hedda, if you only would.

HEDDA: When you call this afternoon, you might invite her to spend the evening here.

TESMAN: Yes, that I will. And there's one thing more you could do that would delight her heart.

HEDDA: What is it?

TESMAN: If you could only prevail on yourself to say *du* to her. For my sake, Hedda? Eh?

HEDDA: No no, Tesman—you really mustn't ask that of me. I have told you so already. I shall try to call her "Aunt"; and you must be satisfied with that.

TESMAN: Well well. Only I think now that you belong to the family, you——

HEDDA: H'm—I can't in the least see why——

[*She goes up towards the middle doorway*]

TESMAN: [*After a pause*] Is there anything the matter with you, Hedda? Eh?

HEDDA: I'm only looking at my old piano. It doesn't go at all well with all the other things.

TESMAN: The first time I draw my salary, we'll see about exchanging it.

HEDDA: No, no—no exchanging. I don't want to part with it. Suppose we put it there in the inner room, and then get another here in its place. When it's convenient, I mean.

TESMAN: [*A little taken aback*] Yes—of course we could do that.

HEDDA: [*Takes up the bouquet from the piano*] These flowers were not here last night when we arrived.

TESMAN: Aunt Julia must have brought them for you.

HEDDA: [*Examining the bouquet*] A visiting-card. [*Takes it out and reads*] "Shall return later in the day." Can you guess whose card it is?

TESMAN: No. Whose? Eh?

HEDDA: The name is "Mrs. Elvsted."

TESMAN: Is it really? Sheriff Elvsted's wife? Miss Rysing that was.

HEDDA: Exactly. The girl with the irritating hair, that she was always showing off. An old flame of yours I've been told.

TESMAN: [*Laughing*] Oh, that didn't last long; and it was before I knew you, Hedda. But fancy her being in town!

HEDDA: It's odd that she should call upon us. I have scarcely seen her since we left school.

TESMAN: I haven't seen her either for—heaven knows how long. I wonder how she can endure to live in such an out-of-the-way hole—eh?

HEDDA: [*After a moment's thought, says suddenly*] Tell me, Tesman—isn't it somewhere near there that he—that—Eilert Lövborg is living?

TESMAN: Yes, he is somewhere in that part of the country.

[Berta *enters by the hall door*]

BERTA: That lady, ma'am, that brought some flowers a little while ago, is here again. [*Pointing*] The flowers you have in your hand, ma'am.

HEDDA: Ah, is she? Well, please show her in.

[Berta *opens the door for* Mrs. Elvsted, *and goes out herself.—Mrs. Elvsted* is a woman of fragile figure, with pretty, soft features. Her eyes are light blue, large, round, and somewhat prominent, with a startled, inquiring expression. Her hair is remarkably light, almost flaxen, and unusually abundant and wavy. She is a couple of years younger than Hedda. She wears a dark visiting dress, tasteful, but not quite in the latest fashion]

HEDDA: [*Receives her warmly*] How do you do, my dear Mrs. Elvsted? It's delightful to see you again.

MRS. ELVSTED: [*Nervously, struggling for self-control*] Yes, it's a very long time since we met.

TESMAN: [*Gives her his hand*] And we too—eh?

HEDDA: Thanks for your lovely flowers——

MRS. ELVSTED: Oh, not at all—— I would have

come straight here yesterday afternoon; but I heard that you were away——

TESMAN: Have you just come to town? Eh?

MRS. ELVSTED: I arrived yesterday, about midday. Oh, I was quite in despair when I heard that you were not at home.

HEDDA: In despair! How so?

TESMAN: Why, my dear Mrs. Rysing—I mean Mrs. Elvsted——

HEDDA: I hope that you are not in any trouble?

MRS. ELVSTED: Yes, I am. And I don't know another living creature here that I can turn to.

HEDDA: [*Laying the bouquet on the table*] Come—let us sit here on the sofa——

MRS. ELVSTED: Oh, I am too restless to sit down.

HEDDA: Oh no, you're not. Come here.

[*She draws* Mrs. Elvsted *down upon the sofa and sits at her side*]

TESMAN: Well? What is it, Mrs. Elvsted——?

HEDDA: Has anything particular happened to you at home?

MRS. ELVSTED: Yes—and no. Oh—I am so anxious you should not misunderstand me——

HEDDA: Then your best plan is to tell us the whole story, Mrs. Elvsted.

TESMAN: I suppose that's what you have come for —eh?

MRS. ELVSTED: Yes, yes—of course it is. Well then, I must tell you—if you don't already know—that Eilert Lövborg is in town, too.

HEDDA: Lövborg——!

TESMAN: What! Has Eilert Lövborg come back? Fancy that, Hedda!

HEDDA: Well well—I hear it.

MRS. ELVSTED: He has been here a week already. Just fancy—a whole week! In this terrible town, alone! With so many temptations on all sides.

HEDDA: But, my dear Mrs. Elvsted—how does he concern you so much?

MRS. ELVSTED: [*Looks at her with a startled air, and says rapidly*] He was the children's tutor.

HEDDA: Your children's?

MRS. ELVSTED: My husband's. I have none.

HEDDA: Your step-children's, then?

MRS. ELVSTED: Yes.

TESMAN: [*Somewhat hesitatingly*] Then was he— I don't know how to express it—was he—regular enough in his habits to be fit for the post? Eh?

MRS. ELVSTED: For the last two years his conduct has been irreproachable.

TESMAN: Has it indeed? Fancy that, Hedda!

HEDDA: I hear it.

MRS. ELVSTED: Perfectly irreproachable, I assure you! In every respect. But all the same—now that I know he is here—in this great town—and with a large sum of money in his hands—I can't help being in mortal fear for him.

TESMAN: Why did he not remain where he was? With you and your husband? Eh?

MRS. ELVSTED: After his book was published he was too restless and unsettled to remain with us.

TESMAN: Yes, by the by, Aunt Julia told me he had published a new book.

MRS. ELVSTED: Yes, a big book, dealing with the march of civilization—in broad outline, as it were. It came out about a fortnight ago. And since it has sold so well, and been so much read—and made such a sensation——

TESMAN: Has it indeed? It must be something he has had lying by since his better days.

MRS. ELVSTED: Long ago, you mean?

TESMAN: Yes.

MRS. ELVSTED: No, he has written it all since he has been with us—within the last year.

TESMAN: Isn't that good news, Hedda? Think of that.

MRS. ELVSTED: Ah yes, if only it would last!

HEDDA: Have you seen him here in town?

MRS. ELVSTED: No, not yet. I have had the greatest difficulty in finding out his address. But this morning I discovered it at last.

HEDDA: [Looks searchingly at her] Do you know, it seems to me a little odd of your husband—h'm——

MRS. ELVSTED: [Starting nervously] Of my husband! What?

HEDDA: That he should send you to town on such an errand—that he does not come himself and look after his friend.

MRS. ELVSTED: Oh no, no—my husband has no time. And besides, I—I had some shopping to do.

HEDDA: [With a slight smile] Ah, that is a different matter.

MRS. ELVSTED: [Rising quickly and uneasily] And now I beg and implore you, Mr. Tesman—receive Eilert Lövborg kindly if he comes to you! And that he is sure to do. You see you were such great friends in the old days. And then you are interested in the same studies—the same branch of science—so far as I can understand.

TESMAN: We used to be, at any rate.

MRS. ELVSTED: That is why I beg so earnestly that you—you too—will keep a sharp eye upon him. Oh, you will promise me that, Mr. Tesman—won't you?

TESMAN: With the greatest of pleasure, Mrs. Rysing——

HEDDA: Elvsted.

TESMAN: I assure you I shall do all I possibly can for Eilert. You may rely upon me.

MRS. ELVSTED: Oh, how very, very kind of you! [Presses his hands] Thanks, thanks, thanks! [Frightened] You see, my husband is so very fond of him!

HEDDA: [Rising] You ought to write to him, Tesman. Perhaps he may not care to come to you of his own accord.

TESMAN: Well, perhaps it would be the right thing to do, Hedda? Eh?

HEDDA: And the sooner the better. Why not at once?

MRS. ELVSTED: [Imploringly] Oh, if you only would!

TESMAN: I'll write this moment. Have you his address, Mrs.—Mrs. Elvsted?

MRS. ELVSTED: Yes. [Takes a slip of paper from her pocket, and hands it to him] Here it is.

TESMAN: Good, good. Then I'll go in—— [Looks about him] By the by—my slippers? Oh, here.

[Takes the packet, and is about to go]

HEDDA: Be sure you write him a cordial, friendly letter. And a good long one too.

TESMAN: Yes, I will.

MRS. ELVSTED: But please, please don't say a word to show that I have suggested it.

TESMAN: No, how could you think I would? Eh? [He goes out to the right, through the inner room]

HEDDA: [Goes up to Mrs. Elvsted, smiles, and says in a low voice] There! We have killed two birds with one stone.

MRS. ELVSTED: What do you mean?

HEDDA: Could you not see that I wanted him to go?

MRS. ELVSTED: Yes, to write the letter——

HEDDA: And that I might speak to you alone.

MRS. ELVSTED: [Confused] About the same thing?

HEDDA: Precisely.

MRS. ELVSTED: [Apprehensively] But there is nothing more, Mrs. Tesman! Absolutely nothing!

HEDDA: Oh yes, but there is. There is a great deal more—I can see that. Sit here—and we'll have a cosy, confidential chat.

[She forces Mrs. Elvsted to sit in the easy-chair beside the stove, and seats herself on one of the footstools]

MRS. ELVSTED: [Anxiously, looking at her watch] But, my dear Mrs. Tesman—I was really on the point of going.

HEDDA: Oh, you can't be in such a hurry.—Well? Now tell me something about your life at home.

MRS. ELVSTED: Oh, that is just what I care least to speak about.

HEDDA: But to me, dear——? Why, weren't we schoolfellows?

MRS. ELVSTED: Yes, but you were in the class above me. Oh, how dreadfully afraid of you I was then!

HEDDA: Afraid of me?

MRS. ELVSTED: Yes, dreadfully. For when we met on the stairs you used always to pull my hair.

HEDDA: Did I, really?

MRS. ELVSTED: Yes, and once you said you would burn it off my head.

HEDDA: Oh, that was all nonsense, of course.

MRS. ELVSTED: Yes, but I was so silly in those days.—And since then, too—we have drifted so far —far apart from each other. Our circles have been so entirely different.

HEDDA: Well then, we must try to drift together again. Now listen! At school we said *du* to each other; and we called each other by our Christian names——

MRS. ELVSTED: No, I am sure you must be mistaken.

HEDDA: No, not at all! I can remember quite distinctly. So now we are going to renew our old friendship. [*Draws the footstool closer to* Mrs. Elvsted] There now! [*Kisses her cheek*] You must say *du* to me and call me Hedda.

MRS. ELVSTED: [*Presses and pats her hands*] Oh, how good and kind you are! I am not used to such kindness.

HEDDA: There, there, there! And I shall say *du* to you, as in the old days, and call you my dear Thora.

MRS. ELVSTED: My name is Thea.

HEDDA: Why, of course! I meant Thea. [*Looks at her compassionately*] So you are not accustomed to goodness and kindness, Thea? Not in your own home?

MRS. ELVSTED: Oh, if I only had a home! But I haven't any; I have never had a home.

HEDDA: [*Looks at her for a moment*] I almost suspected as much.

MRS. ELVSTED: [*Gazing helplessly before her*] Yes —yes—yes.

HEDDA: I don't quite remember—was it not as housekeeper that you first went to Mr. Elvsted's?

MRS. ELVSTED: I really went as governess. But his wife—his late wife—was an invalid,—and rarely left her room. So I had to look after the housekeeping as well.

HEDDA: And then—at last—you became mistress of the house.

MRS. ELVSTED: [*Sadly*] Yes, I did.

HEDDA: Let me see—about how long ago was that?

MRS. ELVSTED: My marriage?

HEDDA: Yes.

MRS. ELVSTED: Five years ago.

HEDDA: To be sure; it must be that.

MRS. ELVSTED: Oh those five years——! Or at all events the last two or three of them! Oh, if you [1] could only imagine——

HEDDA: [*Giving her a little slap on the hand*] De? Fie, Thea!

MRS. ELVSTED: Yes, yes, I will try—— Well, if you could only imagine and understand——

HEDDA: [*Lightly*] Eilert Lövborg has been in your neighborhood about three years, hasn't he?

MRS. ELVSTED: [*Looks at her doubtfully*] Eilert Lövborg? Yes—he has.

HEDDA: Had you known him before, in town here?

MRS. ELVSTED: Scarcely at all. I mean—I knew him by name of course.

1 Mrs. Elvsted here uses the formal pronoun *De*, whereupon Hedda rebukes her. In her next speech Mrs. Elvsted says *du*.

HEDDA: But you saw a good deal of him in the country?

MRS. ELVSTED: Yes, he came to us every day. You see, he gave the children lessons; for in the long run I couldn't manage it all myself.

HEDDA: No, that's clear.—And your husband——? I suppose he is often away from home?

MRS. ELVSTED: Yes. Being sheriff, you know, he has to travel about a good deal in his district.

HEDDA: [*Leaning against the arm of the chair*] Thea—my poor, sweet Thea—now you must tell me everything—exactly as it stands.

MRS. ELVSTED: Well then, you must question me.

HEDDA: What sort of a man is your husband, Thea? I mean—you know—in everyday life. Is he kind to you?

MRS. ELVSTED: [*Evasively*] I am sure he means well in everything.

HEDDA: I should think he must be altogether too old for you. There is at least twenty years' difference between you, is there not?

MRS. ELVSTED: [*Irritably*] Yes, that is true, too. Everything about him is repellent to me! We have not a thought in common. We have no single point of sympathy—he and I.

HEDDA: But is he not fond of you all the same? In his own way?

MRS. ELVSTED: Oh I really don't know. I think he regards me simply as a useful property. And then it doesn't cost much to keep me. I am not expensive.

HEDDA: That is stupid of you.

MRS. ELVSTED: [*Shakes her head*] It cannot be otherwise—not with him. I don't think he really cares for any one but himself—and perhaps a little for the children.

HEDDA: And for Eilert Lövborg, Thea.

MRS. ELVSTED: [*Looking at her*] For Eilert Lövborg? What puts that into your head?

HEDDA: Well, my dear—I should say, when he sends you after him all the way to town—— [*Smiling almost imperceptibly*] And besides, you said so yourself, to Tesman.

MRS. ELVSTED: [*With a little nervous twitch*] Did I? Yes, I suppose I did. [*Vehemently, but not loudly*] No—I may just as well make a clean breast of it at once! For it must all come out in any case.

HEDDA: Why, my dear Thea——?

MRS. ELVSTED: Well, to make a long story short: My husband did not know that I was coming.

HEDDA: What! Your husband didn't know it!

MRS. ELVSTED: No, of course not. For that matter, he was away from home himself—he was traveling. Oh, I could bear it no longer, Hedda! I couldn't indeed—so utterly alone as I should have been in future.

HEDDA: Well? And then?

MRS. ELVSTED: So I put together some of my things—what I needed most—as quietly as possible. And then I left the house.

HEDDA: Without a word?

MRS. ELVSTED: Yes—and took the train straight to town.

HEDDA: Why, my dear, good Thea—to think of you daring to do it!

MRS. ELVSTED: [*Rises and moves about the room*] What else could I possibly do?

HEDDA: But what do you think your husband will say when you go home again?

MRS. ELVSTED: [*At the table, looks at her*] Back to him?

HEDDA: Of course.

MRS. ELVSTED: I shall never go back to him again.

HEDDA: [*Rising and going towards her*] Then you have left your home—for good and all?

MRS. ELVSTED: Yes. There was nothing else to be done.

HEDDA: But then—to take flight so openly.

MRS. ELVSTED: Oh, it's impossible to keep things of that sort secret.

HEDDA: But what do you think people will say of you, Thea?

MRS. ELVSTED: They may say what they like, for aught *I* care. [*Seats herself wearily and sadly on the sofa*] I have done nothing but what I had to do.

HEDDA: [*After a short silence*] And what are your plans now? What do you think of doing?

MRS. ELVSTED: I don't know yet. I only know this, that I must live here, where Eilert Lövborg is —if I am to live at all.

HEDDA: [*Takes a chair from the table, seats herself beside her, and strokes her hands*] My dear Thea—how did this—this friendship—between you and Eilert Lövborg come about?

MRS. ELVSTED: Oh it grew up gradually. I gained a sort of influence over him.

HEDDA: Indeed?

MRS. ELVSTED: He gave up his old habits. Not because I asked him to, for I never dared do that. But of course he saw how repulsive they were to me; and so he dropped them.

HEDDA: [*Concealing an involuntary smile of scorn*] Then you have reclaimed him—as the saying goes— my little Thea.

MRS. ELVSTED: So he says himself, at any rate. And he, on his side, has made a real human being of me—taught me to think, and to understand so many things.

HEDDA: Did he give you lessons too, then?

MRS. ELVSTED: No, not exactly lessons. But he talked to me—talked about such an infinity of things. And then came the lovely, happy time when I began to share in his work—when he allowed me to help him!

HEDDA: Oh he did, did he?

MRS. ELVSTED: Yes, he never wrote anything without my assistance.

HEDDA: You were two good comrades, in fact?

MRS. ELVSTED: [*Eagerly*] Comrades! Yes, fancy, Hedda—that is the very word he used!—Oh, I ought

to feel perfectly happy; and yet I cannot; for I don't know how long it will last.

HEDDA: Are you no surer of him than that?

MRS. ELVSTED: [*Gloomily*] A woman's shadow stands between Eilert Lövborg and me.

HEDDA: [*Looks at her anxiously*] Who can that be?

MRS. ELVSTED: I don't know. Some one he knew in his—in his past. Some one he has never been able wholly to forget.

HEDDA: What has he told you about—about this?

MRS. ELVSTED: He has only once—quite vaguely —alluded to it.

HEDDA: Well! And what did he say?

MRS. ELVSTED: He said that when they parted, she threatened to shoot him with a pistol.

HEDDA: [*With cold composure*] Oh, nonsense! No one does that sort of thing here.

MRS. ELVSTED: No. And that is why I think it must have been that red-haired singing-woman whom he once——

HEDDA: Yes, very likely.

MRS. ELVSTED: For I remember they used to say of her that she carried loaded firearms.

HEDDA: Oh—then of course it must have been she.

MRS. ELVSTED: [*Wringing her hands*] And now just fancy, Hedda—I hear that this singing-woman— that she is in town again! Oh, I don't know what to do——

HEDDA: [*Glancing towards the inner room*] Hush! Here comes Tesman. [*Rises and whispers*] Thea— all this must remain between you and me.

MRS. ELVSTED: [*Springing up*] Oh yes—yes! For heaven's sake——!

[George Tesman, *with a letter in his hand, comes from the right through the inner room*]

TESMAN: There now—the epistle is finished.

HEDDA: That's right. And now Mrs. Elvsted is just going. Wait a moment—I'll go with you to the garden gate.

TESMAN: Do you think Berta could post the letter, Hedda dear?

HEDDA: [*Takes it*] I will tell her to.

[Berta *enters from the hall*]

BERTA: Judge Brack wishes to know if Mrs. Tesman will receive him.

HEDDA: Yes, ask Judge Brack to come in. And look here—put this letter in the post.

BERTA: [*Taking the letter*] Yes, ma'am.

[*She opens the door for* Judge Brack *and goes out herself.* Brack *is a man of forty-five; thickset, but well-built and elastic in his movements. His face is roundish with an aristocratic profile. His hair is short, still almost black, and carefully dressed. His eyes are lively and sparkling. His eyebrows thick. His moustaches are also thick, with short-cut ends. He wears a well-cut walking-suit, a little too youthful for his age. He uses an eye-glass, which he now and then lets drop*]

JUDGE BRACK: [*With his hat in his hand, bowing*] May one venture to call so early in the day?

HEDDA: Of course one may.

TESMAN: [*Presses his hand*] You are welcome at any time. [*Introducing him*] Judge Brack—Miss Rysing——

HEDDA: Oh——!

BRACK: [*Bowing*] Ah—delighted——

HEDDA: [*Looks at him and laughs*] It's nice to have a look at you by daylight, Judge!

BRACK: Do you find me—altered?

HEDDA: A little younger, I think.

BRACK: Thank you so much.

TESMAN: But what do you think of Hedda—eh? Doesn't she look flourishing? She has actually——

HEDDA: Oh, do leave me alone. You haven't thanked Judge Brack for all the trouble he has taken——

BRACK: Oh, nonsense—it was a pleasure to me——

HEDDA: Yes, you are a friend indeed. But here stands Thea all impatience to be off—so *au revoir* Judge. I shall be back again presently.

 [*Mutual salutations.* Mrs. Elvsted *and* Hedda *go out by the hall door*]

BRACK: Well,—is your wife tolerably satisfied——

TESMAN: Yes, we can't thank you sufficiently. Of course she talks of a little rearrangement here and there; and one or two things are still wanting. We shall have to buy some additional trifles.

BRACK: Indeed!

TESMAN: But we won't trouble you about these things. Hedda says she herself will look after what is wanting.—Shan't we sit down? Eh?

BRACK: Thanks, for a moment. [*Seats himself beside the table*] There is something I wanted to speak to you about, my dear Tesman.

TESMAN: Indeed? Ah, I understand! [*Seating himself*] I suppose it's the serious part of the frolic that is coming now. Eh?

BRACK: Oh, the money question is not so very pressing; though, for that matter, I wish we had gone a little more economically to work.

TESMAN: But that would never have done, you know! Think of Hedda, my dear fellow! You, who know her so well——. I couldn't possibly ask her to put up with a shabby style of living!

BRACK: No, no—that is just the difficulty.

TESMAN: And then—fortunately—it can't be long before I receive my appointment.

BRACK: Well, you see—such things are often apt to hang fire for a time.

TESMAN: Have you heard anything definite? Eh?

BRACK: Nothing exactly definite—— [*Interrupting himself*] But by the by—I have one piece of news for you.

TESMAN: Well?

BRACK: Your old friend, Eilert Lövborg, has returned to town.

TESMAN: I know that already.

BRACK: Indeed! How did you learn it?

TESMAN: From that lady who went out with Hedda.

BRACK: Really? What was her name? I didn't quite catch it.

TESMAN: Mrs. Elvsted.

BRACK: Aha—Sheriff Elvsted's wife? Of course—he has been living up in their regions.

TESMAN: And fancy—I'm delighted to hear that he is quite a reformed character!

BRACK: So they say.

TESMAN: And then he has published a new book —eh?

BRACK: Yes, indeed he has.

TESMAN: And I hear it has made some sensation!

BRACK: Quite an unusual sensation.

TESMAN: Fancy—isn't that good news! A man of such extraordinary talents——. I felt so grieved to think that he had gone irretrievably to ruin.

BRACK: That was what everybody thought.

TESMAN: But I cannot imagine what he will take to now! How in the world will he be able to make his living? Eh?

 [*During the last words,* Hedda *has entered by the hall door*]

HEDDA: [*To* Brack, *laughing with a touch of scorn*] Tesman is for ever worrying about how people are to make their living.

TESMAN: Well you see, dear—we were talking about poor Eilert Lövborg.

HEDDA: [*Glancing at him rapidly*] Oh, indeed? [*Seats herself in the arm-chair beside the stove and asks indifferently*] What is the matter with him?

TESMAN: Well—no doubt he has run through all his property long ago; and he can scarcely write a new book every year—eh? So I really can't see what is to become of him.

BRACK: Perhaps I can give you some information on that point.

TESMAN: Indeed!

BRACK: You must remember that his relations have a good deal of influence.

TESMAN: Oh, his relations, unfortunately, have entirely washed their hands of him.

BRACK: At one time they called him the hope of the family

TESMAN: At one time, yes! But he has put an end to all that.

HEDDA: Who knows? [*With a slight smile*] I hear they have reclaimed him up at Sheriff Elvsted's——

BRACK: And then this book that he has published——

TESMAN: Well well, I hope to goodness they may find something for him to do. I have just written to him. I asked him to come and see us this evening, Hedda dear.

BRACK: But my dear fellow, you are booked for my bachelors' party this evening. You promised on the pier last night.

HEDDA: Had you forgotten, Tesman?

TESMAN: Yes, I had utterly forgotten.

BRACK: But it doesn't matter, for you may be sure he won't come.

TESMAN: What makes you think that? Eh?

BRACK: [With a little hesitation, rising and resting his hands on the back of his chair] My dear Tesman—and you too, Mrs. Tesman—I think I ought not to keep you in the dark about something that—that——

TESMAN: That concerns Eilert——?

BRACK: Both you and him.

TESMAN: Well, my dear Judge, out with it.

BRACK: You must be prepared to find your appointment deferred longer than you desired or expected.

TESMAN: [Jumping up uneasily] Is there some hitch about it? Eh?

BRACK: The nomination may perhaps be made conditional on the result of a competition——

TESMAN: Competition! Think of that, Hedda!

HEDDA: [Leans further back in the chair] Aha—aha!

TESMAN: But who can my competitor be? Surely not——?

BRACK: Yes, precisely—Eilert Lövborg.

TESMAN: [Clasping his hands] No, no—it's quite inconceivable! Quite impossible! Eh?

BRACK: H'm—that is what it may come to, all the same.

TESMAN: Well but, Judge Brack—it would show the most incredible lack of consideration for me. [Gesticulates with his arms] For—just think—I'm a married man! We have married on the strength of these prospects, Hedda and I; and run deep into debt; and borrowed money from Aunt Julia too. Good heavens, they had as good as promised me the appointment. Eh?

BRACK: Well, well, well—no doubt you will get it in the end; only after a contest.

HEDDA: [Immovable in her arm-chair] Fancy, Tesman, there will be a sort of sporting interest in that.

TESMAN: Why, my dearest Hedda, how can you be so indifferent about it?

HEDDA: [As before] I am not at all indifferent. I am most eager to see who wins.

BRACK: In any case, Mrs. Tesman, it is best that you should know how matters stand. I mean—before you set about the little purchases I hear you are threatening.

HEDDA: This can make no difference.

BRACK: Indeed! Then I have no more to say. Good-bye! [To Tesman] I shall look in on my way back from my afternoon walk, and take you home with me.

TESMAN: Oh yes, yes—your news has quite upset me.

HEDDA: [Reclining, holds out her hand] Good-bye, Judge; and be sure you call in the afternoon.

BRACK: Many thanks. Good-bye, good-bye!

TESMAN: [Accompanying him to the door] Good-bye, my dear Judge! You must really excuse me——

[Judge Brack goes out by the hall door]

TESMAN: [Crosses the room] Oh Hedda—one should never rush into adventures. Eh?

HEDDA: [Looks at him, smiling] Do you do that?

TESMAN: Yes, dear—there is no denying—it was adventurous to go and marry and set up house upon mere expectations.

HEDDA: Perhaps you are right there.

TESMAN: Well—at all events, we have our delightful home, Hedda! Fancy, the home we both dreamed of—the home we were in love with, I may almost say. Eh?

HEDDA: [Rising slowly and wearily] It was part of our compact that we were to go into society—to keep open house.

TESMAN: Yes, if you only knew how I had been looking forward to it! Fancy—to see you as hostess—in a select circle! Eh? Well, well, well—for the present we shall have to get on without society, Hedda—only to invite Aunt Julia now and then.—Oh, I intended you to lead such an utterly different life, dear——!

HEDDA: Of course I cannot have my man in livery just yet.

TESMAN: Oh no, unfortunately. It would be out of the question for us to keep a footman, you know.

HEDDA: And the saddle-horse I was to have had——

TESMAN: [Aghast] The saddle-horse!

HEDDA: ——I suppose I must not think of that now.

TESMAN: Good heavens, no!—that's as clear as daylight.

HEDDA: [Goes up the room] Well, I shall have one thing at least to kill time with in the meanwhile.

TESMAN: [Beaming] Oh thank heaven for that! What is it, Hedda? Eh?

HEDDA: [In the middle doorway, looks at him with covert scorn] My pistols, George.

TESMAN: [In alarm] Your pistols!

HEDDA: [With cold eyes] General Gabler's pistols. [She goes out through the inner room, to the left]

TESMAN: [Rushes up to the middle doorway and calls after her] No, for heaven's sake, Hedda darling—don't touch those dangerous things! For my sake, Hedda! Eh?

ACT II.

The room at the Tesmans as in the first act, except that the piano has been removed, and an elegant little writing-table with book-shelves put in its place. A smaller table stands near the sofa on the left. Most of the bouquets have been taken away. Mrs. Elvsted's bouquet is upon the large table in front.—It is afternoon.

Hedda, *dressed to receive callers, is alone in the room. She stands by the open glass door, loading a revolver. The fellow to it lies in an open pistol-case on the writing-table.*

HEDDA: [*Looks down the garden, and calls*] So you are here again, Judge!

BRACK: [*Is heard calling from a distance*] As you see, Mrs. Tesman!

HEDDA: [*Raises the pistol and points*] Now I'll shoot you, Judge Brack!

BRACK: [*Calling unseen*] No, no, no! Don't stand aiming at me!

HEDDA: This is what comes of sneaking in by the back way.[1] [*She fires*]

BRACK: [*Nearer*] Are you out of your senses!——

HEDDA: Dear me—did I happen to hit you?

BRACK: [*Still outside*] I wish you would let these pranks alone!

HEDDA: Come in then, Judge.

[Judge Brack, *dressed as though for a men's party, enters by the glass door. He carries a light overcoat over his arm*]

BRACK: What the deuce—haven't you tired of that sport, yet? What are you shooting at?

HEDDA: Oh, I am only firing in the air.

BRACK: [*Gently takes the pistol out of her hand*] Allow me, Madam! [*Looks at it*] Ah—I know this pistol well! [*Looks around*] Where is the case? Ah, here it is. [*Lays the pistol in it, and shuts it*] Now we won't play at that game any more to-day.

HEDDA: Then what in heaven's name would you have me do with myself?

BRACK: Have you had no visitors?

HEDDA: [*Closing the glass door*] Not one. I suppose all our set are still out of town.

BRACK: And is Tesman not at home either?

HEDDA: [*At the writing-table, putting the pistol-case in a drawer which she shuts*] No. He rushed off to his aunt's directly after lunch; he didn't expect you so early.

BRACK: H'm—how stupid of me not to have thought of that!

HEDDA: [*Turning her head to look at him*] Why stupid?

BRACK: Because if I had thought of it I should have come a little—earlier.

HEDDA: [*Crossing the room*] Then you would have found no one to receive you; for I have been in my room changing my dress ever since lunch.

BRACK: And is there no sort of little chink that we could hold a parley through?

HEDDA: You have forgotten to arrange one.

BRACK: That was another piece of stupidity.

HEDDA: Well, we must just settle down here—and wait. Tesman is not likely to be back for some time yet.

1 *Bagveje* means both "back ways" and "underhand courses."

BRACK: Never mind; I shall not be impatient.

[Hedda *seats herself in the corner of the sofa. Brack lays his overcoat over the back of the nearest chair, and sits down, but keeps his hat in his hand. A short silence. They look at each other*]

HEDDA: Well?

BRACK: [*In the same tone*] Well?

HEDDA: I spoke first.

BRACK: [*Bending a little forward*] Come, let us have a cosy little chat, Mrs. Hedda.

HEDDA: [*Leaning further back in the sofa*] Does it not seem like a whole eternity since our last talk? Of course I don't count those few words yesterday evening and this morning.

BRACK: You mean since our last confidential talk? Our last *tête-à-tête*?

HEDDA: Well, yes—since you put it so.

BRACK: Not a day has passed but I have wished that you were home again.

HEDDA: And I have done nothing but wish the same thing.

BRACK: You? Really, Mrs. Hedda? And I thought you had been enjoying your tour so much!

HEDDA: Oh, yes, you may be sure of that!

BRACK: But Tesman's letters spoke of nothing but happiness.

HEDDA: Oh, Tesman! You see, he thinks nothing so delightful as grubbing in libraries and making copies of old parchments, or whatever you call them.

BRACK: [*With a spice of malice*] Well, that is his vocation in life—or part of it at any rate.

HEDDA: Yes, of course; and no doubt when it's your vocation——. But I! Oh, my dear Mr. Brack, how mortally bored I have been.

BRACK: [*Sympathetically*] Do you really say so? In downright earnest?

HEDDA: Yes, you can surely understand it——! To go for six whole months without meeting a soul that knew anything of our circle, or could talk about the things we are interested in.

BRACK: Yes, yes—I, too, should feel that a deprivation.

HEDDA: And then, what I found most intolerable of all——

BRACK: Well?

HEDDA: ——was being everlastingly in the company of—one and the same person——

BRACK: [*With a nod of assent*] Morning, noon, and night, yes—at all possible times and seasons.

HEDDA: I said "everlastingly."

BRACK: Just so. But I should have thought, with our excellent Tesman, one could——

HEDDA: Tesman is—a specialist, my dear Judge.

BRACK: Undeniably.

HEDDA: And specialists are not at all amusing to travel with. Not in the long run at any rate.

BRACK: Not even—the specialist one happens to love?

HEDDA: Faugh—don't use that sickening word!

BRACK: [*Taken aback*] What do you say, Mrs. Hedda?

HEDDA: [*Half laughing, half irritated*] You should just try it! To hear of nothing but the history of civilization morning, noon and night——

BRACK: Everlastingly.

HEDDA: Yes, yes, yes! And then all this about the domestic industry of the middle ages——! That's the most disgusting part of it!

BRACK: [*Looks searchingly at her*] But tell me—in that case, how am I to understand your——? H'm——

HEDDA: My accepting George Tesman, you mean?

BRACK: Well, let us put it so.

HEDDA: Good heavens, do you see anything so wonderful in that?

BRACK: Yes and no—Mrs. Hedda.

HEDDA: I had positively danced myself tired, my dear Judge. My day was done—— [*With a slight shudder*] Oh, no—I won't say that; nor think it, either!

BRACK: You have assuredly no reason to.

HEDDA: Oh, reasons—— [*Watching him closely*] And George Tesman—after all, you must admit that he is correctness itself.

BRACK: His correctness and respectability are beyond all question.

HEDDA: And I don't see anything absolutely ridiculous about him.—Do you?

BRACK: Ridiculous? N—no—I shouldn't exactly say so——

HEDDA: Well—and his powers of research, at all events, are untiring.—I see no reason why he should not one day come to the front, after all.

BRACK: [*Looks at her hesitatingly*] I thought that you, like every one else, expected him to attain the highest distinction.

HEDDA: [*With an expression of fatigue*] Yes, so I did.—And then, since he was bent, at all hazards, on being allowed to provide for me—I really don't know why I should not have accepted his offer?

BRACK: No—if you look at it in that light——

HEDDA: It was more than my other adorers were prepared to do for me, my dear Judge.

BRACK: [*Laughing*] Well, I can't answer for all the rest; but as for myself, you know quite well that I have always entertained a—a certain respect for the marriage tie—for marriage as an institution, Mrs. Hedda.

HEDDA: [*Jestingly*] Oh, I assure you I have never cherished any hopes with respect to you.

BRACK: All I require is a pleasant and intimate interior, where I can make myself useful in every way, and am free to come and go as—as a trusted friend——

HEDDA: Of the master of the house, do you mean?

BRACK: [*Bowing*] Frankly—of the mistress first of all; but, of course, of the master, too, in the second place. Such a triangular friendship—if I may call it so—is really a great convenience for all parties, let me tell you.

HEDDA: Yes, I have many a time longed for some one to make a third on our travels. Oh—those railway-carriage *tête-à-têtes*——!

BRACK: Fortunately your wedding journey is over now.

HEDDA: [*Shaking her head*] Not by a long—long way. I have only arrived at a station on the line.

BRACK: Well, then the passengers jump out and move about a little, Mrs. Hedda.

HEDDA: I never jump out.

BRACK: Really?

HEDDA: No—because there is always some one standing by to——

BRACK: [*Laughing*] To look at your ankles, do you mean?

HEDDA: Precisely.

BRACK: Well, but, dear me——

HEDDA: [*With a gesture of repulsion*] I won't have it. I would rather keep my seat where I happen to be—and continue the *tête-à-tête*.

BRACK: But suppose a third person were to jump in and join the couple.

HEDDA: Ah—that is quite another matter!

BRACK: A trusted, sympathetic friend——

HEDDA: ——with a fund of conversation on all sorts of lively topics——

BRACK: ——and not the least bit of a specialist!

HEDDA: [*With an audible sigh*] Yes, that would be a relief, indeed.

BRACK: [*Hears the front door open, and glances in that direction*] The triangle is completed.

HEDDA: [*Half aloud*] And on goes the train.

[*George Tesman in a gray walking-suit, with a soft felt hat, enters from the hall. He has a number of unbound books under his arm and in his pockets*]

TESMAN: [*Goes up to the table beside the corner settee*] Ouf—what a load for a warm day—all these books. [*Lays them on the table*] I'm positively perspiring, Hedda. Hallo—are you there already, my dear Judge? Eh? Berta didn't tell me.

BRACK: [*Rising*] I came in through the garden.

HEDDA: What books have you got there?

TESMAN: [*Stands looking them through*] Some new books on my special subjects—quite indispensable to me.

HEDDA: Your special subjects?

BRACK: Yes, books on his special subjects, Mrs. Tesman.

[*Brack and Hedda exchange a confidential smile*]

HEDDA: Do you need still more books on your special subjects?

TESMAN: Yes, my dear Hedda, one can never have too many of them. Of course, one must keep up with all that is written and published.

HEDDA: Yes, I suppose one must.

TESMAN: [*Searching among his books*] And look

here—I have got hold of Eilert Lövborg's new book, too. [*Offering it to her*] Perhaps you would like to glance through it, Hedda? Eh?

HEDDA: No, thank you. Or rather—afterwards perhaps.

TESMAN: I looked into it a little on the way home.

BRACK: Well, what do you think of it—as a specialist?

TESMAN: I think it shows quite remarkable soundness of judgment. He never wrote like that before. [*Putting the books together*] Now I shall take all these into my study. I'm longing to cut the leaves——! And then I must change my clothes. [*To Brack*] I suppose we needn't start just yet? Eh?

BRACK: Oh, dear, no—there is not the slightest hurry.

TESMAN: Well, then, I will take my time. [*Is going with his books, but stops in the doorway and turns*] By the by, Hedda—Aunt Julia is not coming this evening.

HEDDA: Not coming? Is it that affair of the bonnet that keeps her away?

TESMAN: Oh, not at all. How could you think such a thing of Aunt Julia? Just fancy——! The fact is, Aunt Rina is very ill.

HEDDA: She always is.

TESMAN: Yes, but to-day she is much worse than usual, poor dear.

HEDDA: Oh, then it's only natural that her sister should remain with her. I must bear my disappointment.

TESMAN: And you can't imagine, dear, how delighted Aunt Julia seemed to be—because you had come home looking so flourishing!

HEDDA: [*Half aloud, rising*] Oh, those everlasting Aunts!

TESMAN: What?

HEDDA: [*Going to the glass door*] Nothing.

TESMAN: Oh, all right.

[*He goes through the inner room, out to the right*]

BRACK: What bonnet were you talking about?

HEDDA: Oh, it was a little episode with Miss Tesman this morning. She had laid down her bonnet on the chair there—[*looks at him and smiles*]—and I pretended to think it was the servant's.

BRACK: [*Shaking his head*] Now, my dear Mrs. Hedda, how could you do such a thing? To that excellent old lady, too!

HEDDA: [*Nervously crossing the room*] Well, you see—these impulses come over me all of a sudden; and I cannot resist them. [*Throws herself down in the easy-chair by the stove*] Oh, I don't know how to explain it.

BRACK: [*Behind the easy-chair*] You are not really happy—that is at the bottom of it.

HEDDA: [*Looking straight before her*] I know of no reason why I should be—happy. Perhaps you can give me one?

BRACK: Well—amongst other things, because you

have got exactly the home you had set your heart on.

HEDDA: [*Looks up at him and laughs*] Do you, too, believe in that legend?

BRACK: Is there nothing in it, then?

HEDDA: Oh, yes, there is something in it.

BRACK: Well?

HEDDA: There is this in it, that I made use of Tesman to see me home from evening parties last summer——

BRACK: I, unfortunately, had to go quite a different way.

HEDDA: That's true. I know you were going a different way last summer.

BRACK: [*Laughing*] Oh fie, Mrs. Hedda! Well, then—you and Tesman——?

HEDDA: Well, we happened to pass here one evening; Tesman, poor fellow, was writhing in the agony of having to find conversation; so I took pity on the learned man——

BRACK: [*Smiles doubtfully*] You took pity? H'm——

HEDDA: Yes, I really did. And so—to help him out of his torment—I happened to say, in pure thoughtlessness, that I should like to live in this villa.

BRACK: No more than that?

HEDDA: Not that evening.

BRACK: But afterwards?

HEDDA: Yes, my thoughtlessness had consequences, my dear Judge.

BRACK: Unfortunately that too often happens, Mrs. Hedda.

HEDDA: Thanks! So you see it was this enthusiasm for Secretary Falk's villa that first constituted a bond of sympathy between George Tesman and me. From that came our engagement and our marriage, and our wedding journey, and all the rest of it. Well, well, my dear Judge—as you make your bed so you must lie, I could almost say.

BRACK: This is exquisite! And you really cared not a rap about it all the time?

HEDDA: No, heaven knows I didn't.

BRACK: But now? Now that we have made it so homelike for you?

HEDDA: Uh—the rooms all seem to smell of lavender and dried rose-leaves.—But perhaps it's Aunt Julia that has brought that scent with her.

BRACK: [*Laughing*] No, I think it must be a legacy from the late Mrs. Secretary Falk.

HEDDA: Yes, there is an odor of mortality about it. It reminds me of a bouquet—the day after the ball. [*Clasps her hands behind her head, leans back in her chair and looks at him*] Oh, my dear Judge—you cannot imagine how horribly I shall bore myself here.

BRACK: Why should not you, too, find some sort of vocation in life, Mrs. Hedda?

HEDDA: A vocation—that should attract me?

BRACK: If possible, of course.

HEDDA: Heaven knows what sort of a vocation

that could be. I often wonder whether—— [*Breaking off*] But that would never do, either.

BRACK: Who can tell? Let me hear what it is.

HEDDA: Whether I might not get Tesman to go into politics, I mean.

BRACK: [*Laughing*] Tesman? No, really now, political life is not the thing for him—not at all in his line.

HEDDA: No, I daresay not.—But if I could get him into it all the same?

BRACK: Why—what satisfaction could you find in that? If he is not fitted for that sort of thing, why should you want to drive him into it?

HEDDA: Because I am bored, I tell you! [*After a pause*] So you think it quite out of the question that Tesman should ever get into the ministry?

BRACK: H'm—you see, my dear Mrs. Hedda—to get into the ministry, he would have to be a tolerably rich man.

HEDDA: [*Rising impatiently*] Yes, there we have it! It is this genteel poverty I have managed to drop into——! [*Crosses the room*] That is what makes life so pitiable! So utterly ludicrous!—For that's what it is.

BRACK: Now *I* should say the fault lay elsewhere.

HEDDA: Where, then?

BRACK: You have never gone through any really stimulating experience.

HEDDA: Anything serious, you mean?

BRACK: Yes, you may call it so. But now you may perhaps have one in store.

HEDDA: [*Tossing her head*] Oh, you're thinking of the annoyances about this wretched professorship! But that must be Tesman's own affair. I assure you I shall not waste a thought upon it.

BRACK: No, no, I daresay not. But suppose now that what people call—in elegant language—a solemn responsibility were to come upon you? [*Smiling*] A new responsibility, Mrs. Hedda?

HEDDA: [*Angrily*] Be quiet! Nothing of that sort will ever happen!

BRACK: [*Warily*] We will speak of this again a year hence—at the very outside.

HEDDA: [*Curtly*] I have no turn for anything of the sort, Judge Brack. No responsibilities for me!

BRACK: Are you so unlike the generality of women as to have no turn for duties which——?

HEDDA: [*Beside the glass door*] Oh, be quiet, I tell you!—I often think there is only one thing in the world I have any turn for.

BRACK: [*Drawing near to her*] And what is that, if I may ask?

HEDDA: [*Stands looking out*] Boring myself to death. Now you know it. [*Turns, looks towards the inner room, and laughs*] Yes, as I thought! Here comes the Professor.

BRACK: [*Softly, in a tone of warning*] Come, come, come, Mrs. Hedda!

[George Tesman, *dressed for the party, with his gloves and hat in his hand, enters from the right through the inner room*]

TESMAN: Hedda, has no message come from Eilert Lövborg? Eh?

HEDDA: No.

TESMAN: Then you'll see he'll be here presently.

BRACK: Do you really think he will come?

TESMAN: Yes, I am almost sure of it. For what you were telling us this morning must have been a mere floating rumor.

BRACK: You think so?

TESMAN: At any rate, Aunt Julia said she did not believe for a moment that he would ever stand in my way again. Fancy that!

BRACK: Well, then, that's all right.

TESMAN: [*Placing his hat and gloves on a chair on the right*] Yes, but you must really let me wait for him as long as possible.

BRACK: We have plenty of time yet. None of my guests will arrive before seven or half-past.

TESMAN: Then meanwhile we can keep Hedda company, and see what happens. Eh?

HEDDA: [*Placing Brack's hat and overcoat upon the corner settee*] And at the worst Mr. Lövborg can remain here with me.

BRACK: [*Offering to take his things*] Oh, allow me, Mrs. Tesman!—What do you mean by "at the worst"?

HEDDA: If he won't go with you and Tesman.

TESMAN: [*Looks dubiously at her*] But, Hedda, dear—do you think it would quite do for him to remain with you? Eh? Remember, Aunt Julia can't come.

HEDDA: No, but Mrs. Elvsted is coming. We three can have a cup of tea together.

TESMAN: Oh, yes, that will be all right.

BRACK: [*Smiling*] And that would perhaps be the safest plan for him.

HEDDA: Why so?

BRACK: Well, you know, Mrs. Tesman, how you used to gird at my little bachelor parties. You declared they were adapted only for men of the strictest principles.

HEDDA: But no doubt Mr. Lövborg's principles are strict enough now. A converted sinner——

[Berta *appears at the hall door*]

BERTA: There's a gentleman asking if you are at home, ma'am——

HEDDA: Well, show him in.

TESMAN: [*Softly*] I'm sure it is he! Fancy that!

[Eilert Lövborg *enters from the hall. He is slim and lean; of the same age as* Tesman, *but looks older and somewhat worn-out. His hair and beard are of a blackish brown, his face long and pale, but with patches of color on the cheek-bones. He is dressed in a well-cut black visiting suit, quite new. He has dark gloves and a silk hat. He stops near the door, and makes a rapid bow, seeming somewhat embarrassed*]

TESMAN: [*Goes up to him and shakes him warmly by the hand*] Well, my dear Eilert—so at last we meet again!

EILERT LÖVBORG: [*Speaks in a subdued voice*] Thanks for your letter, Tesman. [*Approaching Hedda*] Will you, too, shake hands with me, Mrs. Tesman?

HEDDA: [*Taking his hand*] I am glad to see you, Mr. Lövborg. [*With a motion of her hand*] I don't know whether you two gentlemen——?

LÖVBORG: [*Bowing slightly*] Judge Brack, I think.

BRACK: [*Doing likewise*] Oh, yes,—in the old days——

TESMAN: [*To Lövborg, with his hands on his shoulders*] And now you must make yourself entirely at home, Eilert! Mustn't he, Hedda?—For I hear you are going to settle in town again? Eh?

LÖVBORG: Yes, I am.

TESMAN: Quite right, quite right. Let me tell you, I have got hold of your new book; but I haven't had time to read it yet.

LÖVBORG: You may spare yourself the trouble.

TESMAN: Why so?

LÖVBORG: Because there is very little in it.

TESMAN: Just fancy—how can you say so?

BRACK: But it has been very much praised, I hear.

LÖVBORG: That was what I wanted; so I put nothing into the book but what every one would agree with.

BRACK: Very wise of you.

TESMAN: Well, but, my dear Eilert——!

LÖVBORG: For now I mean to win myself a position again—to make a fresh start.

TESMAN: [*A little embarrassed*] Ah, that is what you wish to do? Eh?

LÖVBORG: [*Smiling, lays down his hat, and draws a packet, wrapped in paper, from his coat pocket*] But when this one appears, George Tesman, you will have to read it. For this is the real book—the book I have put my true self into.

TESMAN: Indeed? And what is it?

LÖVBORG: It is the continuation.

TESMAN: The continuation? Of what?

LÖVBORG: Of the book.

TESMAN: Of the new book?

LÖVBORG: Of course.

TESMAN: Why, my dear Eilert—does it not come down to our own days?

LÖVBORG: Yes, it does; and this one deals with the future.

TESMAN: With the future! But, good heavens, we know nothing of the future!

LÖVBORG: No; but there is a thing or two to be said about it all the same. [*Opens the packet*] Look here——

TESMAN: Why, that's not your handwriting.

LÖVBORG: I dictated it. [*Turning over the pages*] It falls into two sections. The first deals with the civilizing forces of the future. And here is the second—[*running through the pages towards the end*]—forecasting the probable line of development.

TESMAN: How odd now! I should never have thought of writing anything of that sort.

HEDDA: [*At the glass door, drumming on the pane*] H'm—— I daresay not.

LÖVBORG: [*Replacing the manuscript in its paper and laying the packet on the table*] I brought it, thinking I might read you a little of it this evening.

TESMAN: That was very good of you, Eilert. But this evening——? [*Looking at Brack*] I don't quite see how we can manage it——

LÖVBORG: Well, then, some other time. There is no hurry.

BRACK: I must tell you, Mr. Lövborg—there is a little gathering at my house this evening—mainly in honor of Tesman, you know——

LÖVBORG: [*Looking for his hat*] Oh—then I won't detain you——

BRACK: No, but listen—will you not do me the favor of joining us?

LÖVBORG: [*Curtly and decidedly*] No, I can't—thank you very much.

BRACK: Oh, nonsense—do! We shall be quite a select little circle. And I assure you we shall have a "lively time," as Mrs. Hed—as Mrs. Tesman says.

LÖVBORG: I have no doubt of it. But nevertheless——

BRACK: And then you might bring your manuscript with you, and read it to Tesman at my house. I could give you a room to yourselves.

TESMAN: Yes, think of that, Eilert,—why shouldn't you? Eh?

HEDDA: [*Interposing*] But, Tesman, if Mr. Lövborg would really rather not! I am sure Mr. Lövborg is much more inclined to remain here and have supper with me.

LÖVBORG: [*Looking at her*] With you, Mrs. Tesman?

HEDDA: And with Mrs. Elvsted.

LÖVBORG: Ah—— [*Lightly*] I saw her for a moment this morning.

HEDDA: Did you? Well, she is coming this evening. So you see you are almost bound to remain, Mr. Lövborg, or she will have no one to see her home.

LÖVBORG: That's true. Many thanks, Mrs. Tesman—in that case I will remain.

HEDDA: Then I have one or two orders to give the servant——

[*She goes to the hall door and rings. Berta enters. Hedda talks to her in a whisper, and points towards the inner room. Berta nods and goes out again*]

TESMAN: [*At the same time, to Lövborg*] Tell me, Eilert—is it this new subject—the future—that you are going to lecture about?

LÖVBORG: Yes.

TESMAN: They told me at the bookseller's that

you are going to deliver a course of lectures this autumn.

LÖVBORG: That is my intention. I hope you won't take it ill, Tesman.

TESMAN: Oh no, not in the least! But——?

LÖVBORG: I can quite understand that it must be disagreeable to you.

TESMAN: [Cast down] Oh, I can't expect you, out of consideration for me, to——

LÖVBORG: But I shall wait till you have received your appointment.

TESMAN: Will you wait? Yes, but—yes, but—are you not going to compete with me? Eh?

LÖVBORG: No; it is only the moral victory I care for.

TESMAN: Why, bless me—then Aunt Julia was right after all! Oh, yes—I knew it! Hedda! Just fancy—Eilert Lövborg is not going to stand in our way!

HEDDA: [Curtly] Our way? Pray leave me out of the question.

[She goes up towards the inner room, where Berta is placing a tray with decanters and glasses on the table. Hedda nods approval, and comes forward again. Berta goes out.]

TESMAN: [At the same time] And you, Judge Brack—what do you say to this? Eh?

BRACK: Well, I say that a moral victory—h'm—may be all very fine——

TESMAN: Yes, certainly. But all the same——

HEDDA: [Looking at Tesman with a cold smile] You stand there looking as if you were thunder-struck——

TESMAN: Yes—so I am—I almost think——

BRACK: Don't you see, Mrs. Tesman, a thunder-storm has just passed over?

HEDDA: [Pointing towards the inner room] Will you not take a glass of cold punch, gentlemen?

BRACK: [Looking at his watch] A stirrup-cup? Yes, it wouldn't come amiss.

TESMAN: A capital idea, Hedda! Just the thing! Now that the weight has been taken off my mind——

HEDDA: Will you not join them, Mr. Lövborg?

LÖVBORG: [With a gesture of refusal] No, thank you. Nothing for me.

BRACK: Why bless me—cold punch is surely not poison.

LÖVBORG: Perhaps not for every one.

HEDDA: I will keep Mr. Lövborg company in the meantime.

TESMAN: Yes, yes, Hedda dear, do.

[He and Brack go into the inner room, seat themselves, drink punch, smoke cigarettes, and carry on a lively conversation during what follows. Eilert Lövborg remains standing beside the stove. Hedda goes to the writing-table]

HEDDA: [Raising her voice a little] Do you care to look at some photographs, Mr. Lövborg? You know Tesman and I made a tour in the Tyrol on our way home?

[She takes up an album, and places it on the table beside the sofa, in the further corner of which she seats herself. Eilert Lövborg approaches, stops, and looks at her. Then he takes a chair and seats himself to her left, with his back towards the inner room]

HEDDA: [Opening the album] Do you see this range of mountains, Mr. Lövborg? It's the Ortler group. Tesman has written the name underneath. Here it is: "The Ortler group near Meran."

LÖVBORG: [Who has never taken his eyes off her, says softly and slowly:] Hedda—Gabler!

HEDDA: [Glancing hastily at him] Ah! Hush!

LÖVBORG: [Repeats softly] Hedda Gabler!

HEDDA: [Looking at the album] That was my name in the old days—when we two knew each other.

LÖVBORG: And I must teach myself never to say Hedda Gabler again—never, as long as I live.

HEDDA: [Still turning over the pages] Yes, you must. And I think you ought to practise in time. The sooner the better, I should say.

LÖVBORG: [In a tone of indignation] Hedda Gabler married? And married to—George Tesman!

HEDDA: Yes—so the world goes.

LÖVBORG: Oh, Hedda, Hedda—how could you [1] throw yourself away!

HEDDA: [Looks sharply at him] What? I can't allow this!

LÖVBORG: What do you mean?

[Tesman comes into the room and goes towards the sofa]

HEDDA: [Hears him coming and says in an indifferent tone] And this is a view from the Val d'Ampezzo, Mr. Lövborg. Just look at these peaks! [Looks affectionately up at Tesman] What's the name of these curious peaks, dear?

TESMAN: Let me see. Oh, those are the Dolomites.

HEDDA: Yes, that's it!—Those are the Dolomites, Mr. Lövborg.

TESMAN: Hedda, dear,—I only wanted to ask whether I shouldn't bring you a little punch after all? For yourself, at any rate—eh?

HEDDA: Yes, do, please; and perhaps a few biscuits.

TESMAN: No cigarettes?

HEDDA: No.

TESMAN: Very well.

[He goes into the inner room and out to the right. Brack sits in the inner room, and keeps an eye from time to time on Hedda and Lövborg]

LÖVBORG: [Softly, as before] Answer me, Hedda—how could you go and do this?

HEDDA: [Apparently absorbed in the album] If you continue to say du to me I won't talk to you.

LÖVBORG: May I not say du even when we are alone?

[1] He uses the familiar du.

HEDDA: No. You may think it; but you mustn't say it.

LÖVBORG: Ah, I understand. It is an offence against George Tesman, whom you [1]—love.

HEDDA: [Glances at him and smiles] Love? What an idea!

LÖVBORG: You don't love him then!

HEDDA: But I won't hear of any sort of unfaithfulness! Remember that.

LÖVBORG: Hedda—answer me one thing——

HEDDA: Hush!

[Tesman enters with a small tray from the inner room]

TESMAN: Here you are! Isn't this tempting?

[He puts the tray on the table]

HEDDA: Why do you bring it yourself?

TESMAN: [Filling the glasses] Because I think it's such fun to wait upon you, Hedda.

HEDDA: But you have poured out two glasses. Mr. Lövborg said he wouldn't have any——

TESMAN: No, but Mrs. Elvsted will soon be here, won't she?

HEDDA: Yes, by the by—Mrs. Elvsted——

TESMAN: Had you forgotten her? Eh?

HEDDA: We were so absorbed in these photographs. [Shows him a picture] Do you remember this little village?

TESMAN: Oh, it's that one just below the Brenner Pass. It was there we passed the night——

HEDDA: ——and met that lively party of tourists.

TESMAN: Yes, that was the place. Fancy—if we could only have had you with us, Eilert! Eh?

[He returns to the inner room and sits beside Brack]

LÖVBORG: Answer me this one thing, Hedda——

HEDDA: Well?

LÖVBORG: Was there no love in your friendship for me, either? Not a spark—not a tinge of love in it?

HEDDA: I wonder if there was? To me it seems as though we were two good comrades—two thoroughly intimate friends. [Smilingly] You especially were frankness itself.

LÖVBORG: It was you that made me so.

HEDDA: As I look back upon it all, I think there was really something beautiful, something fascinating—something daring—in—in that secret intimacy—that comradeship which no living creature so much as dreamed of.

LÖVBORG: Yes, yes, Hedda! Was there not?— When I used to come to your father's in the afternoon—and the General sat over at the window reading his papers—with his back towards us——

HEDDA: And we two on the corner sofa——

LÖVBORG: Always with the same illustrated paper before us——

HEDDA: For want of an album, yes.

LÖVBORG: Yes, Hedda, and when I made my confessions to you—told you about myself, things that

at that time no one else knew! There I would sit and tell you of my escapades—my days and nights of devilment. Oh, Hedda—what was the power in you that forced me to confess these things?

HEDDA: Do you think it was any power in me?

LÖVBORG: How else can I explain it? And all those—those roundabout questions you used to put to me——

HEDDA: Which you understood so particularly well——

LÖVBORG: How could you sit and question me like that? Question me quite frankly——

HEDDA: In roundabout terms, please observe.

LÖVBORG: Yes, but frankly nevertheless. Cross-question me about—all that sort of thing?

HEDDA: And how could you answer, Mr. Lövborg?

LÖVBORG: Yes, that is just what I can't understand—in looking back upon it. But tell me now, Hedda—was there not love at the bottom of our friendship? On your side, did you not feel as though you might purge my stains away—if I made you my confessor? Was it not so?

HEDDA: No, not quite.

LÖVBORG: What was your motive, then?

HEDDA: Do you think it quite incomprehensible that a young girl—when it can be done—without any one knowing——

LÖVBORG: Well?

HEDDA: ——should be glad to have a peep, now and then, into a world which——

LÖVBORG: Which——?

HEDDA: ——which she is forbidden to know anything about?

LÖVBORG: So that was it?

HEDDA: Partly. Partly—I almost think.

LÖVBORG: Comradeship in the thirst for life. But why should not that, at any rate, have continued?

HEDDA: The fault was yours.

LÖVBORG: It was you that broke with me.

HEDDA: Yes, when our friendship threatened to develop into something more serious. Shame upon you, Eilert Lövborg! How could you think of wronging your—your frank comrade?

LÖVBORG: [Clenching his hands] Oh, why did you not carry out your threat? Why did you not shoot me down?

HEDDA: Because I have such a dread of scandal.

LÖVBORG: Yes, Hedda, you are a coward at heart.

HEDDA: A terrible coward. [Changing her tone] But it was a lucky thing for you. And now you have found ample consolation at the Elvsteds'.

LÖVBORG: I know what Thea has confided to you.

HEDDA: And perhaps you have confided to her something about us?

LÖVBORG: Not a word. She is too stupid to understand anything of that sort.

HEDDA: Stupid?

LÖVBORG: She is stupid about matters of that sort.

HEDDA: And I am cowardly. [Bends over towards

him, without looking him in the face, and says more softly:] But now I will confide something to you.

LÖVBORG: [*Eagerly*] Well?

HEDDA: The fact that I dared not shoot you down——

LÖVBORG: Yes!

HEDDA: ——that was not my most arrant cowardice—that evening.

LÖVBORG: [*Looks at her a moment, understands, and whispers passionately*] Oh, Hedda! Hedda Gabler! Now I begin to see a hidden reason beneath our comradeship! You and I——! After all, then, it was your craving for life——

HEDDA: [*Softly, with a sharp glance*] Take care! Believe nothing of the sort!

[*Twilight has begun to fall. The hall door is opened from without by* Berta]

HEDDA: [*Closes the album with a bang and calls smilingly:*] Ah, at last! My darling Thea,—come along!

[Mrs. Elvsted *enters from the hall. She is in evening dress. The door is closed behind her*]

HEDDA: [*On the sofa, stretches out her arms towards her*] My sweet Thea—you can't think how I have been longing for you!

[Mrs. Elvsted, *in passing, exchanges slight salutations with the gentlemen in the inner room, then goes up to the table and gives* Hedda *her hand. Eilert Lövborg has risen. He and* Mrs. Elvsted *greet each other with a silent nod*]

MRS. ELVSTED: Ought I to go in and talk to your husband for a moment?

HEDDA: Oh, not at all. Leave those two alone. They will soon be going.

MRS. ELVSTED: Are they going out?

HEDDA: Yes, to a supper-party.

MRS. ELVSTED: [*Quickly, to* Lövborg] Not you?

LÖVBORG: No.

HEDDA: Mr. Lövborg remains with us.

MRS. ELVSTED: [*Takes a chair and is about to seat herself at his side*] Oh, how nice it is here!

HEDDA: No, thank you, my little Thea! Not there! You'll be good enough to come over here to me. I will sit between you.

MRS. ELVSTED: Yes, just as you please.

[*She goes round the table and seats herself on the sofa on* Hedda's *right.* Lövborg *re-seats himself on his chair*]

LÖVBORG: [*After a short pause, to* Hedda] Is not she lovely to look at?

HEDDA: [*Lightly stroking her hair*] Only to look at?

LÖVBORG: Yes. For we two—she and I—we are two real comrades. We have absolute faith in each other; so we can sit and talk with perfect frankness——

HEDDA: Not round about, Mr. Lövborg?

LÖVBORG: Well——

MRS. ELVSTED: [*Softly clinging close to* Hedda]

Oh, how happy I am, Hedda! For, only think, he says I have inspired him, too.

HEDDA: [*Looks at her with a smile*] Ah! Does he say that, dear?

LÖVBORG: And then she is so brave, Mrs. Tesman!

MRS. ELVSTED: Good heavens—am I brave?

LÖVBORG: Exceedingly—where your comrade is concerned.

HEDDA: Ah, yes—courage! If one only had that!

LÖVBORG: What then? What do you mean?

HEDDA: Then life would perhaps be livable, after all. [*With a sudden change of tone*] But now, my dearest Thea, you really must have a glass of cold punch.

MRS. ELVSTED: No, thanks—I never take anything of that kind.

HEDDA: Well, then, you, Mr. Lövborg.

LÖVBORG: Nor I, thank you.

MRS. ELVSTED: No, he doesn't, either.

HEDDA: [*Looks fixedly at him*] But if I say you shall?

LÖVBORG: It would be no use.

HEDDA: [*Laughing*] Then I, poor creature, have no sort of power over you?

LÖVBORG: Not in that respect.

HEDDA: But seriously, I think you ought to—for your own sake.

MRS. ELVSTED: Why, Hedda——!

LÖVBORG: How so?

HEDDA: Or rather on account of other people.

LÖVBORG: Indeed?

HEDDA: Otherwise people might be apt to suspect that—in your heart of hearts—you did not feel quite secure—quite confident in yourself.

MRS. ELVSTED: [*Softly*] Oh, please, Hedda——!

LÖVBORG: People may suspect what they like—for the present.

MRS. ELVSTED: [*Joyfully*] Yes, let them!

HEDDA: I saw it plainly in Judge Brack's face a moment ago.

LÖVBORG: What did you see?

HEDDA: His contemptuous smile, when you dared not go with them into the inner room.

LÖVBORG: Dared not? Of course I preferred to stop here and talk to you.

MRS. ELVSTED: What could be more natural, Hedda?

HEDDA: But the Judge could not guess that. And I saw, too, the way he smiled and glanced at Tesman when you dared not accept his invitation to this wretched little supper-party of his.

LÖVBORG: Dared not! Do you say I dared not?

HEDDA: I don't say so. But that was how Judge Brack understood it.

LÖVBORG: Well, let him.

HEDDA: Then you are not going with them?

LÖVBORG: I will stay here with you and Thea.

MRS. ELVSTED: Yes, Hedda—how can you doubt that?

HEDDA: [*Smiles and nods approvingly to* Lövborg]

Firm as a rock! Faithful to your principles, now and forever! Ah, that is how a man should be! [*Turns to* Mrs. Elvsted *and caresses her*] Well, now, what did I tell you, when you came to us this morning in such a state of distraction——

LÖVBORG: [*Surprised*] Distraction!

MRS. ELVSTED: [*Terrified*] Hedda—oh, Hedda——!

HEDDA: You can see for yourself! You haven't the slightest reason to be in such mortal terror—— [*Interrupting herself*] There! Now we can all three enjoy ourselves!

LÖVBORG: [*Who has given a start*] Ah—what is all this, Mrs. Tesman?

MRS. ELVSTED: Oh, my God, Hedda! What are you saying? What are you doing?

HEDDA: Don't get excited! That horrid Judge Brack is sitting watching you.

LÖVBORG: So she was in mortal terror! On my account!

MRS. ELVSTED: [*Softly and piteously*] Oh, Hedda —now you have ruined everything!

LÖVBORG: [*Looks fixedly at her for a moment. His face is distorted*] So that was my comrade's frank confidence in me?

MRS. ELVSTED: [*Imploringly*] Oh, my dearest friend—only let me tell you——

LÖVBORG: [*Takes one of the glasses of punch, raises it to his lips, and says in a low, husky voice*] Your health, Thea!

[*He empties the glass, puts it down, and takes the second*]

MRS. ELVSTED: [*Softly*] Oh, Hedda, Hedda—how could you do this?

HEDDA: *I* do it? *I*? Are you crazy?

LÖVBORG: Here's to your health, too, Mrs. Tesman. Thanks for the truth. Hurrah for the truth!

[*He empties the glass and is about to re-fill it.*]

HEDDA: [*Lays her hand on his arm*] Come, come —no more for the present. Remember you are going out to supper.

MRS. ELVSTED: No, no, no!

HEDDA: Hush! They are sitting watching you.

LÖVBORG: [*Putting down the glass*] Now, Thea— tell me the truth——

MRS. ELVSTED: Yes.

LÖVBORG: Did your husband know that you had come after me?

MRS. ELVSTED: [*Wringing her hands*] Oh, Hedda— do you hear what he is asking?

LÖVBORG: Was it arranged between you and him that you were to come to town and look after me? Perhaps it was the Sheriff himself that urged you to come? Aha, my dear—no doubt he wanted my help in his office! Or was it at the cardtable that he missed me?

MRS. ELVSTED: [*Softly, in agony*] Oh, Lövborg, Lövborg——!

LÖVBORG: [*Seizes a glass and is on the point of filling it*] Here's a glass for the old Sheriff, too!

HEDDA: [*Preventing him*] No more just now. Remember, you have to read your manuscript to Tesman.

LÖVBORG: [*Calmly, putting down the glass*] It was stupid of me all this, Thea—to take it in this way, I mean. Don't be angry with me, my dear, dear comrade. You shall see—both you and the others—that if I was fallen once—now I have risen again! Thanks to you, Thea.

MRS. ELVSTED: [*Radiant with joy*] Oh, heaven be praised——!

[Brack *has in the meantime looked at his watch. He and* Tesman *rise and come into the drawing room*]

BRACK: [*Takes his hat and overcoat*] Well, Mrs. Tesman, our time has come.

HEDDA: I suppose it has.

LÖVBORG: [*Rising*] Mine too, Judge Brack.

MRS. ELVSTED: [*Softly and imploringly*] Oh, Lövborg, don't do it!

HEDDA: [*Pinching her arm*] They can hear you!

MRS. ELVSTED: [*With a suppressed shriek*] Ow!

LÖVBORG: [*To* Brack] You were good enough to invite me.

BRACK: Well, are you coming after all?

LÖVBORG: Yes, many thanks.

BRACK: I'm delighted——

LÖVBORG: [*To* Tesman, *putting the parcel of MS. in his pocket*] I should like to show you one or two things before I send it to the printers.

TESMAN: Fancy—that will be delightful. But, Hedda dear, how is Mrs. Elvsted to get home? Eh?

HEDDA: Oh, that can be managed somehow.

LÖVBORG: [*Looking towards the ladies*] Mrs. Elvsted? Of course, I'll come again and fetch her. [*Approaching*] At ten or thereabouts, Mrs. Tesman? Will that do?

HEDDA: Certainly. That will do capitally.

TESMAN: Well, then, that's all right. But you must not expect me so early, Hedda.

HEDDA: Oh, you may stop as long—as long as ever you please.

MRS. ELVSTED: [*Trying to conceal her anxiety*] Well, then, Mr. Lövborg—I shall remain here until you come.

LÖVBORG: [*With his hat in his hand*] Pray do, Mrs. Elvsted.

BRACK: And now off goes the excursion train, gentlemen! I hope we shall have a lively time, as a certain fair lady puts it.

HEDDA: Ah, if only the fair lady could be present unseen——!

BRACK: Why unseen?

HEDDA: In order to hear a little of your liveliness at first hand, Judge Brack.

BRACK: [*Laughing*] I should not advise the fair lady to try it.

TESMAN: [*Also laughing*] Come, you're a nice one, Hedda! Fancy that!

BRACK: Well, good-bye, good-bye, ladies.

LÖVBORG: [*Bowing*] About ten o'clock, then.

[*Brack, Lövborg, and Tesman go out by the hall door. At the same time, Berta enters from the inner room with a lighted lamp, which she places on the drawing-room table; she goes out by the way she came*]

MRS. ELVSTED: [*Who has risen and is wandering restlessly about the room*] Hedda—Hedda—what will come of all this?

HEDDA: At ten o'clock—he will be here. I can see him already—with vine-leaves in his hair—flushed and fearless——

MRS. ELVSTED: Oh, I hope he may.

HEDDA: And then, you see—then he will have regained control over himself. Then he will be a free man for all his days.

MRS. ELVSTED: Oh, God!—if he would only come as you see him now!

HEDDA: He will come as I see him—so, and not otherwise! [*Rises and approaches Thea*] You may doubt him as long as you please; *I* believe in him. And now we will try——

MRS. ELVSTED: You have some hidden motive in this, Hedda!

HEDDA: Yes, I have. I want for once in my life to have power to mould a human destiny.

MRS. ELVSTED: Have you not the power?

HEDDA: I have not—and have never had it.

MRS. ELVSTED: Not your husband's?

HEDDA: Do you think that is worth the trouble? Oh, if you could only understand how poor I am. And fate has made you so rich! [*Clasps her passionately in her arms*] I think I must burn your hair off, after all.

MRS. ELVSTED: Let me go! Let me go! I am afraid of you, Hedda!

BERTA: [*In the middle doorway*] Tea is laid in the dining-room, ma'am.

HEDDA: Very well. We are coming.

MRS. ELVSTED: No, no, no! I would rather go home alone! At once!

HEDDA: Nonsense! First you shall have a cup of tea, you little stupid. And then—at ten o'clock— Eilert Lövborg will be here—with vine-leaves in his hair.

[*She drags Mrs. Elvsted almost by force towards the middle doorway*]

ACT III.

The room at the Tesmans'. *The curtains are drawn over the middle doorway, and also over the glass door. The lamp, half turned down, and with a shade over it, is burning on the table. In the stove, the door of which stands open, there has been a fire, which is now nearly burnt out.*

Mrs. Elvsted, *wrapped in a large shawl, and with her feet upon a foot-rest, sits close to the stove, sunk back in the armchair.* Hedda, *fully dressed, lies sleeping upon the sofa, with a sofa-blanket over her.*

MRS. ELVSTED: [*After a pause, suddenly sits up in her chair, and listens eagerly. Then she sinks back again wearily, moaning to herself*] Not yet!— Oh, God—oh, God—not yet!

[*Berta slips cautiously in by the hall door. She has a letter in her hand*]

MRS. ELVSTED: [*Turns and whispers eagerly*] Well —has any one come?

BERTA: [*Softly*] Yes, a girl has just brought this letter.

MRS. ELVSTED: [*Quickly, holding out her hand*] A letter! Give it to me!

BERTA: No, it's for Dr. Tesman, ma'am.

MRS. ELVSTED: Oh, indeed.

BERTA: It was Miss Tesman's servant that brought it. I'll lay it here on the table.

MRS. ELVSTED: Yes, do.

BERTA: [*Laying down the letter*] I think I had better put out the lamp. It's smoking.

MRS. ELVSTED: Yes, put it out. It must soon be daylight now.

BERTA: [*Putting out the lamp*] It is daylight already, ma'am.

MRS. ELVSTED: Yes, broad day! And no one come back yet——!

BERTA: Lord bless you, ma'am—I guessed how it would be.

MRS. ELVSTED: You guessed?

BERTA: Yes, when I saw that a certain person had come back to town—and that he went off with them. For we've heard enough about that gentleman before now.

MRS. ELVSTED: Don't speak so loud. You will waken Mrs. Tesman.

BERTA: [*Looks towards the sofa and sighs*] No, no —let her sleep, poor thing. Shan't I put some wood on the fire?

MRS. ELVSTED: Thanks, not for me.

BERTA: Oh, very well.

[*She goes softly out by the hall door*]

HEDDA: [*Is awakened by the shutting of the door and looks up*] What's that——?

MRS. ELVSTED: It was only the servant——

HEDDA: [*Looking about her*] Oh, we're here—! Yes, now I remember. [*Sits erect upon the sofa, stretches herself, and rubs her eyes*] What o'clock is it, Thea?

MRS. ELVSTED: [*Looks at her watch*] It's past seven.

HEDDA: When did Tesman come home?

MRS. ELVSTED: He has not come.

HEDDA: Not come home yet?

MRS. ELVSTED: [*Rising*] No one has come.

HEDDA: Think of our watching and waiting here till four in the morning——

MRS. ELVSTED: [*Wringing her hands*] And how I watched and waited for him!

HEDDA: [*Yawns, and says with her hand before her mouth*] Well, well—we might have spared ourselves the trouble.

MRS. ELVSTED: Did you get a little sleep?

HEDDA: Oh, yes; I believe I have slept pretty well. Have you not?

MRS. ELVSTED: Not for a moment. I couldn't, Hedda!—not to save my life.

HEDDA: [*Rises and goes towards her*] There, there, there! There's nothing to be so alarmed about. I understand quite well what has happened.

MRS. ELVSTED: Well, what do you think? Won't you tell me?

HEDDA: Why, of course, it has been a very late affair at Judge Brack's——

MRS. ELVSTED: Yes, yes—that is clear enough. But all the same——

HEDDA: And then, you see, Tesman hasn't cared to come home and ring us up in the middle of the night. [*Laughing*] Perhaps he wasn't inclined to show himself either—immediately after a joIlification.

MRS. ELVSTED: But in that case—where can he have gone?

HEDDA: Of course, he has gone to his aunts' and slept there. They have his old room ready for him.

MRS. ELVSTED: No, he can't be with them; for a letter has just come for him from Miss Tesman. There it lies.

HEDDA: Indeed? [*Looks at the address*] Why, yes, it's addressed in Aunt Julia's own hand. Well, then, he has remained at Judge Brack's. And as for Eilert Lövborg—he is sitting, with vine-leaves in his hair, reading his manuscript.

MRS. ELVSTED: Oh, Hedda, you are just saying things you don't believe a bit.

HEDDA: You really are a little blockhead, Thea.

MRS. ELVSTED: Oh, yes, I suppose I am.

HEDDA: And how mortally tired you look.

MRS. ELVSTED: Yes, I am mortally tired.

HEDDA: Well, then, you must do as I tell you. You must go into my room and lie down for a little while.

MRS. ELVSTED: Oh, no, no—I shouldn't be able to sleep.

HEDDA: I am sure you would.

MRS. ELVSTED: Well, but your husband is certain to come soon now; and then I want to know at once——

HEDDA: I shall take care to let you know when he comes.

MRS. ELVSTED: Do you promise me, Hedda?

HEDDA: Yes, rely upon me. Just you go in and have a sleep in the meantime.

MRS. ELVSTED: Thanks; then I'll try to.

[*She goes off through the inner door*]

[Hedda *goes up to the glass door and draws back the curtains. The broad daylight streams into the room. Then she takes a little hand-glass from the writing-table, looks at herself in it, and arranges her hair. Next she goes to the hall door and presses the bell-button*]

[Berta *presently appears at the hall door*]

BERTA: Did you want anything, ma'am?

HEDDA: Yes; you must put some more wood in the stove. I am shivering.

BERTA: Bless me—I'll make up the fire at once. [*She rakes the embers together and lays a piece of wood upon them; then stops and listens*] That was a ring at the front door, ma'am.

HEDDA: Then go to the door. I will look after the fire.

BERTA: It'll soon burn up.

[*She goes out by the hall door*]

[Hedda *kneels on the foot-rest and lays some more pieces of wood in the stove*]

[*After a short pause,* George Tesman *enters from the hall. He looks tired and rather serious. He steals on tiptoe towards the middle doorway and is about to slip through the curtains*]

HEDDA: [*At the stove, without looking up*] Good morning.

TESMAN: [*Turns*] Hedda! [*Approaching her*] Good heavens—are you up so early? Eh?

HEDDA: Yes, I am up very early this morning.

TESMAN: And I never doubted you were still sound asleep! Fancy that, Hedda!

HEDDA: Don't speak so loud. Mrs. Elvsted is resting in my room.

TESMAN: Has Mrs. Elvsted been here all night?

HEDDA: Yes, since no one came to fetch her.

TESMAN: Ah, to be sure.

HEDDA: [*Closes the door of the stove and rises*] Well, did you enjoy yourselves at Judge Brack's?

TESMAN: Have you been anxious about me? Eh?

HEDDA: No, I should never think of being anxious. But I asked if you had enjoyed yourself.

TESMAN: Oh, yes,—for once in a way. Especially the beginning of the evening; for then Eilert read me part of his book. We arrived more than an hour too early—fancy that! And Brack had all sorts of arrangements to make—so Eilert read to me.

HEDDA: [*Seating herself by the table on the right*] Well? Tell me, then——

TESMAN: [*Sitting on a footstool near the stove*] Oh, Hedda, you can't conceive what a book that is going to be! I believe it is one of the most remarkable things that have ever been written. Fancy that!

HEDDA: Yes, yes; I don't care about that—

TESMAN: I must make a confession to you, Hedda. When he had finished reading—a horrid feeling came over me.

HEDDA: A horrid feeling?

TESMAN: I felt jealous of Eilert for having had it in him to write such a book. Only think, **Hedda!**

HEDDA: Yes, yes, I am thinking!

TESMAN: And then how pitiful to think that he—with all his gifts—should be irreclaimable, after all.

HEDDA: I suppose you mean that he has more courage than the rest?

TESMAN: No, not at all—I mean that he is incapable of taking his pleasures in moderation.

HEDDA: And what came of it all—in the end?

TESMAN: Well, to tell the truth, I think it might best be described as an orgy, Hedda.

HEDDA: Had he vine-leaves in his hair?

TESMAN: Vine-leaves? No, I saw nothing of the sort. But he made a long, rambling speech in honor of the woman who had inspired him in his work—that was the phrase he used.

HEDDA: Did he name her?

TESMAN: No, he didn't; but I can't help thinking he meant Mrs. Elvsted. You may be sure he did.

HEDDA: Well—where did you part from him?

TESMAN: On the way to town. We broke up—the last of us at any rate—all together; and Brack came with us to get a breath of fresh air. And then, you see, we agreed to take Eilert home; for he had had far more than was good for him.

HEDDA: I daresay.

TESMAN: But now comes the strange part of it, Hedda; or, I should rather say, the melancholy part of it. I declare I am almost ashamed—on Eilert's account—to tell you——

HEDDA: Oh, go on——!

TESMAN: Well, as we were getting near town, you see, I happened to drop a little behind the others. Only for a minute or two—fancy that!

HEDDA: Yes, yes, yes, but——?

TESMAN: And then, as I hurried after them—what do you think I found by the wayside? Eh?

HEDDA: Oh, how should I know!

TESMAN: You mustn't speak of it to a soul, Hedda! Do you hear! Promise me, for Eilert's sake. [Draws a parcel, wrapped in paper, from his coat pocket] Fancy, dear—I found this.

HEDDA: Is not that the parcel he had with him yesterday?

TESMAN: Yes, it is the whole of his precious, irreplaceable manuscript! And he had gone and lost it, and knew nothing about it. Only fancy, Hedda! So deplorably——

HEDDA: But why did you not give him back the parcel at once?

TESMAN: I didn't dare to—in the state he was then in——

HEDDA: Did you not tell any of the others that you found it?

TESMAN: Oh, far from it! You can surely understand that, for Eilert's sake, I wouldn't do that.

HEDDA: So no one knows that Eilert Lövborg's manuscript is in your possession?

TESMAN: No. And no one must know it.

HEDDA: Then what did you say to him afterwards?

TESMAN: I didn't talk to him again at all; for when we got in among the streets, he and two or three of the others gave us the slip and disappeared. Fancy that!

HEDDA: Indeed! They must have taken him home then.

TESMAN: Yes, so it would appear. And Brack, too, left us.

HEDDA: And what have you been doing with yourself since?

TESMAN: Well, I and some of the others went home with one of the party, a jolly fellow, and took our morning coffee with him; or perhaps I should rather call it our night coffee—eh? But now, when I have rested a little, and given Eilert, poor fellow, time to have his sleep out, I must take this back to him.

HEDDA: [Holds out her hand for the packet] No—don't give it to him! Not in such a hurry, I mean. Let me read it first.

TESMAN: No, my dearest Hedda, I mustn't, I really mustn't.

HEDDA: You must not?

TESMAN: No—for you can imagine what a state of despair he will be in when he wakens and misses the manuscript. He has no copy of it, you must know! He told me so.

HEDDA: [Looking searchingly at him] Can such a thing not be reproduced? Written over again?

TESMAN: No, I don't think that would be possible. For the inspiration, you see——

HEDDA: Yes, yes—I suppose it depends on that—— [Lightly] But, by the by—here is a letter for you.

TESMAN: Fancy——!

HEDDA: [Handing it to him] It came early this morning.

TESMAN: It's from Aunt Julia! What can it be? [He lays the packet on the other footstool, opens the letter, runs his eye through it, and jumps up] Oh, Hedda—she says that poor Aunt Rina is dying!

HEDDA: Well, we were prepared for that.

TESMAN: And that if I want to see her again, I must make haste. I'll run in to them at once.

HEDDA: [Suppressing a smile] Will you run?

TESMAN: Oh, my dearest Hedda—if you could only make up your mind to come with me! Just think!

HEDDA: [Rises and says wearily, repelling the idea] No, no, don't ask me. I will not look upon sickness and death. I loathe all sorts of ugliness.

TESMAN: Well, well, then——! [Bustling around] My hat——? My overcoat——? Oh, in the hall——. I do hope I mayn't come too late, Hedda! Eh?

HEDDA: Oh, if you run——

[Berta appears at the hall door]

BERTA: Judge Brack is at the door, and wishes to know if he may come in.

TESMAN: At this time! No, I can't possibly see him.

HEDDA: But I can. [To Berta] Ask Judge Brack to come in.

[Berta *goes out*]

HEDDA: [*Quickly, whispering*] The parcel, Tesman! [*She snatches it up from the stool*]

TESMAN: Yes, give it to me!

HEDDA: No, no, I will keep it till you come back. [*She goes to the writing-table and places it in the bookcase. Tesman stands in a flurry of haste, and cannot get his gloves on*] [*Judge Brack enters from the hall*]

HEDDA: [*Nodding to him*] You are an early bird, I must say.

BRACK: Yes, don't you think so? [*To Tesman*] Are you on the move, too?

TESMAN: Yes, I must rush off to my aunts'. Fancy—the invalid one is lying at death's door, poor creature.

BRACK: Dear me, is she indeed? Then on no account let me detain you. At such a critical moment——

TESMAN: Yes, I must really rush—— Good-bye! Good-bye!

[*He hastens out by the hall door*]

HEDDA: [*Approaching*] You seem to have made a particularly lively night of it at your rooms, Judge Brack.

BRACK: I assure you I have not had my clothes off, Mrs. Hedda.

HEDDA: Not you, either?

BRACK: No, as you may see. But what has Tesman been telling you of the night's adventures?

HEDDA: Oh, some tiresome story. Only that they went and had coffee somewhere or other.

BRACK: I have heard about that coffee-party already. Eilert Lövborg was not with them, I fancy?

HEDDA: No, they had taken him home before that.

BRACK: Tesman too?

HEDDA: No, but some of the others, he said.

BRACK: [*Smiling*] George Tesman is really an ingenuous creature, Mrs. Hedda.

HEDDA: Yes, heaven knows he is. Then is there something behind all this?

BRACK: Yes, perhaps there may be.

HEDDA: Well then, sit down, my dear Judge, and tell your story in comfort.

[*She seats herself to the left of the table. Brack sits near her, at the long side of the table*]

HEDDA: Now then?

BRACK: I had special reasons for keeping track of my guests—or rather of some of my guests—last night.

HEDDA: Of Eilert Lövborg among the rest, perhaps?

BRACK: Frankly—yes.

HEDDA: Now you make me really curious——

BRACK: Do you know where he and one or two of the others finished the night, Mrs. Hedda?

HEDDA: If it is not quite unmentionable, tell me.

BRACK: Oh no, it's not at all unmentionable. Well, they put in an appearance at a particularly animated *soirée*.

HEDDA: Of the lively kind?

BRACK: Of the very liveliest——

HEDDA: Tell me more of this, Judge Brack——

BRACK: Lövborg, as well as the others, had been invited in advance. I knew all about it. But he declined the invitation; for now, as you know, he has become a new man.

HEDDA: Up at the Elvsteds', yes. But he went after all, then?

BRACK: Well, you see, Mrs. Hedda—unhappily the spirit moved him at my rooms last evening——

HEDDA: Yes, I hear he found inspiration.

BRACK: Pretty violent inspiration. Well, I fancy that altered his purpose; for we menfolk are unfortunately not always so firm in our principles as we ought to be.

HEDDA: Oh, I am sure you are an exception, Judge Brack. But as to Lövborg——?

BRACK: To make a long story short—he landed at last in Mademoiselle Diana's rooms.

HEDDA: Mademoiselle Diana's?

BRACK: It was Mademoiselle Diana that was giving the soirée, to a select circle of her admirers and her lady friends.

HEDDA: Is she a red-haired woman?

BRACK: Precisely.

HEDDA: A sort of a—singer?

BRACK: Oh yes—in her leisure moments. And moreover a mighty huntress—of men—Mrs. Hedda. You have no doubt heard of her. Eilert Lövborg was one of her most enthusiastic protectors—in the days of his glory.

HEDDA: And how did all this end?

BRACK: Far from amicably, it appears. After a most tender meeting, they seem to have come to blows——

HEDDA: Lövborg and she?

BRACK: Yes. He accused her or her friends of having robbed him. He declared that his pocket-book had disappeared—and other things as well. In short, he seems to have made a furious disturbance.

HEDDA: And what came of it all?

BRACK: It came to a general scrimmage, in which the ladies as well as the gentlemen took part. Fortunately the police at last appeared on the scene.

HEDDA: The police too?

BRACK: Yes. I fancy it will prove a costly frolic for Eilert Lövborg, crazy being that he is.

HEDDA: How so?

BRACK: He seems to have made a violent resistance—to have hit one of the constables on the head and torn the coat off his back. So they had to march him off to the police-station with the rest.

HEDDA: How have you learnt all this?

BRACK: From the police themselves.

HEDDA: [*Gazing straight before her*] So that is what happened. Then he had no vine-leaves in his hair.

BRACK: Vine-leaves, Mrs. Hedda?

HEDDA: [*Changing her tone*] But tell me now

Judge—what is your real reason for tracking out Eilert Lövborg's movements so carefully?

BRACK: In the first place, it could not be entirely indifferent to me if it should appear in the police-court that he came straight from my house.

HEDDA: Will the matter come into court then?

BRACK: Of course. However, I should scarcely have troubled so much about that. But I thought that, as a friend of the family, it was my duty to supply you and Tesman with a full account of his nocturnal exploits.

HEDDA: Why so, Judge Brack?

BRACK: Why, because I have a shrewd suspicion that he intends to use you as a sort of blind.

HEDDA: Oh, how can you think such a thing!

BRACK: Good heavens, Mrs. Hedda—we have eyes in our head. Mark my words! This Mrs. Elvsted will be in no hurry to leave town again.

HEDDA: Well, even if there should be anything between them, I suppose there are plenty of other places where they could meet.

BRACK: Not a single home. Henceforth, as before, every respectable house will be closed against Eilert Lövborg.

HEDDA: And so ought mine to be, you mean?

BRACK: Yes. I confess it would be more than painful to me if this personage were to be made free of your house. How superfluous, how intrusive, he would be, if he were to force his way into——

HEDDA: ——into the triangle?

BRACK: Precisely. It would simply mean that I should find myself homeless.

HEDDA: [Looks at him with a smile] So you want to be the one cock in the basket[1]—that is your aim.

BRACK: [Nods slowly and lowers his voice] Yes, that is my aim. And for that I will fight—with every weapon I can command.

HEDDA: [Her smile vanishing] I see you are a dangerous person—when it comes to the point.

BRACK: Do you think so?

HEDDA: I am beginning to think so. And I am exceedingly glad to think—that you have no sort of hold over me.

BRACK: [Laughing equivocally] Well well, Mrs. Hedda—perhaps you are right there. If I had, who knows what I might be capable of?

HEDDA: Come, come now, Judge Brack! That sounds almost like a threat.

BRACK: [Rising] Oh, not at all! The triangle, you know, ought, if possible, to be spontaneously constructed.

HEDDA: There I agree with you.

BRACK: Well, now I have said all I had to say; and I had better be getting back to town. Good-bye, Mrs. Hedda. [He goes towards the glass door]

HEDDA: [Rising] Are you going through the garden?

BRACK: Yes, it's a short cut for me.

1 Eneste hane i kurven—a proverbial saying.

HEDDA: And then it is a back way, too.

BRACK: Quite so. I have no objection to back ways. They may be piquant enough at times.

HEDDA: When there is ball practice going on, you mean?

BRACK: [In the doorway, laughing to her] Oh, people don't shoot their tame poultry, I fancy.

HEDDA: [Also laughing] Oh, no, when there is only one cock in the basket——

[They exchange laughing nods of farewell. He goes. She closes the door behind him]

[Hedda, who has become quite serious, stands for a moment looking out. Presently she goes and peeps through the curtain over the middle doorway. Then she goes to the writing-table, takes Lövborg's packet out of the bookcase, and is on the point of looking through its contents. Berta is heard speaking loudly in the hall. Hedda turns and listens. Then she hastily locks up the packet in the drawer, and lays the key on the inkstand]

[Eilert Lövborg, with his greatcoat on and his hat in his hand, tears open the hall door. He looks somewhat confused and irritated]

LÖVBORG: [Looking towards the hall] And I tell you I must and will come in! There!

[He closes the door, turns, sees Hedda, at once regains his self-control, and bows]

HEDDA: [At the writing-table] Well, Mr. Lövborg, this is rather a late hour to call for Thea.

LÖVBORG: You mean rather an early hour to call on you. Pray pardon me.

HEDDA: How do you know that she is still here?

LÖVBORG: They told me at her lodgings that she had been out all night.

HEDDA: [Going to the oval table] Did you notice anything about the people of the house when they said that?

LÖVBORG: [Looks inquiringly at her] Notice anything about them?

HEDDA: I mean, did they seem to think it odd?

LÖVBORG: [Suddenly understanding] Oh yes, of course! I am dragging her down with me! However, I didn't notice anything.—I suppose Tesman is not up yet?

HEDDA: No—I think not——

LÖVBORG: When did he come home?

HEDDA: Very late.

LÖVBORG: Did he tell you anything?

HEDDA: Yes, I gathered that you had had an exceedingly jolly evening at Judge Brack's.

LÖVBORG: Nothing more?

HEDDA: I don't think so. However, I was so dreadfully sleepy——

[Mrs. Elvsted enters through the curtains of the middle doorway]

MRS. ELVSTED: [Going towards him] Ah, Lövborg! At last——!

LÖVBORG: Yes, at last. And too late!

MRS. ELVSTED: [*Looks anxiously at him*] What is too late?

LÖVBORG: Everything is too late now. It is all over with me.

MRS. ELVSTED: Oh no, no—don't say that!

LÖVBORG: You will say the same when you hear——

MRS. ELVSTED: I won't hear anything!

HEDDA: Perhaps you would prefer to talk to her alone? If so, I will leave you.

LÖVBORG: No, stay—you too. I beg you to stay.

MRS. ELVSTED: Yes, but I won't hear anything, I tell you.

LÖVBORG: It is not last night's adventures that I want to talk about.

MRS. ELVSTED: What is it then——?

LÖVBORG: I want to say that now our ways must part.

MRS. ELVSTED: Part!

HEDDA: [*Involuntarily*] I knew it!

LÖVBORG: You can be of no more service to me, Thea.

MRS. ELVSTED: How can you stand there and say that! No more service to you! Am I not to help you now, as before? Are we not to go on working together?

LÖVBORG: Henceforward I shall do no work.

MRS. ELVSTED: [*Despairingly*] Then what am I to do with my life?

LÖVBORG: You must try to live your life as if you had never known me.

MRS. ELVSTED: But you know I cannot do that!

LÖVBORG: Try if you cannot, Thea. You must go home again——

MRS. ELVSTED: [*In vehement protest*] Never in this world! Where you are, there will I be also! I will not let myself be driven away like this! I will remain here! I will be with you when the book appears.

HEDDA: [*Half aloud, in suspense*] Ah yes—the book!

LÖVBORG: [*Looks at her*] My book and Thea's; for that is what it is.

MRS. ELVSTED: Yes, I feel that it is. And that is why I have a right to be with you when it appears! I will see with my own eyes how respect and honor pour in upon you afresh. And the happiness—the happiness—oh, I must share it with you!

LÖVBORG: Thea—our book will never appear.

HEDDA: Ah!

MRS. ELVSTED: Never appear!

LÖVBORG: Can never appear.

MRS. ELVSTED: [*In agonized foreboding*] Lövborg —what have you done with the manuscript?

HEDDA: [*Looks anxiously at him*] Yes, the manuscript——?

MRS. ELVSTED: Where is it?

LÖVBORG: Oh Thea—don't ask me about it!

MRS. ELVSTED: Yes, yes, I will know. I demand to be told at once.

LÖVBORG: The manuscript——. Well then—I have torn the manuscript into a thousand pieces.

MRS. ELVSTED: [*Shrieks*] Oh no, no——!

HEDDA: [*Involuntarily*] But that's not——

LÖVBORG: [*Looks at her*] Not true, you think?

HEDDA: [*Collecting herself*] Oh well, of course— since you say so. But it sounded so improbable——

LÖVBORG: It is true, all the same.

MRS. ELVSTED: [*Wringing her hands*] Oh God— oh God, Hedda—torn his own work to pieces!

LÖVBORG: I have torn my own life to pieces. So why should I not tear my life-work too——?

MRS. ELVSTED: And you did this last night?

LÖVBORG: Yes, I tell you! Tore it into a thousand pieces—and scattered them on the fjord—far out. There there is cool sea-water at any rate—let them drift upon it—drift with the current and the wind. And then presently they will sink—deeper and deeper—as I shall, Thea.

MRS. ELVSTED: Do you know, Lövborg, that what you have done with the book—I shall think of it to my dying day as though you had killed a little child.

LÖVBORG: Yes, you are right. It is a sort of child-murder.

MRS. ELVSTED: How could you, then——! Did not the child belong to me too?

HEDDA: [*Almost inaudibly*] Ah, the child——

MRS. ELVSTED: [*Breathing heavily*] It is all over then. Well well, now I will go, Hedda.

HEDDA: But you are not going away from town?

MRS. ELVSTED: Oh, I don't know what I shall do. I see nothing but darkness before me. [*She goes out by the hall door*]

HEDDA: [*Stands waiting for a moment*] So you are not going to see her home, Mr. Lövborg?

LÖVBORG: I? Through the streets? Would you have people see her walking with me?

HEDDA: Of course I don't know what else may have happened last night. But is it so utterly irretrievable?

LÖVBORG: It will not end with last night—I know that perfectly well. And the thing is that now I have no taste for that sort of life either. I won't begin it anew. She has broken my courage and my power of braving life out.

HEDDA: [*Looking straight before her*] So that pretty little fool has had her fingers in a man's destiny. [*Looks at him*] But all the same, how could you treat her so heartlessly?

LÖVBORG: Oh, don't say that it was heartless!

HEDDA: To go and destroy what has filled her whole soul for months and years! You do not call that heartless!

LÖVBORG: To you I can tell the truth, Hedda.

HEDDA: The truth?

LÖVBORG: First promise me—give me your word —that what I now confide to you Thea shall never know.

HEDDA: I give you my word.

LÖVBORG: Good. Then let me tell you that what I said just now was untrue.

HEDDA: About the manuscript?

LÖVBORG: Yes. I have not torn it to pieces—nor thrown it into the fjord.

HEDDA: No, no——. But—where it is then?

LÖVBORG: I have destroyed it none the less—utterly destroyed it, Hedda!

HEDDA: I don't understand.

LÖVBORG: Thea said that what I had done seemed to her like a child-murder.

HEDDA: Yes, so she said.

LÖVBORG: But to kill his child—that is not the worst thing a father can do to it.

HEDDA: Not the worst?

LÖVBORG: No. I wanted to spare Thea from hearing the worst.

HEDDA: Then what is the worst?

LÖVBORG: Suppose now, Hedda, that a man—in the small hours of the morning—came home to his child's mother after a night of riot and debauchery, and said: "Listen—I have been here and there—in this place and in that. And I have taken our child with me—to this place and to that. And I have lost the child—utterly lost it. The devil knows into what hands it may have fallen—who may have had their clutches on it."

HEDDA: Well—but when all is said and done, you know—this was only a book——

LÖVBORG: Thea's pure soul was in that book.

HEDDA: Yes, so I understand.

LÖVBORG: And you can understand, too, that for her and me together no future is possible.

HEDDA: What path do you mean to take then?

LÖVBORG: None. I will only try to make an end of it all—the sooner the better.

HEDDA: [A step nearer him] Eilert Lövborg—listen to me.—Will you not try to—to do it beautifully?

LÖVBORG: Beautifully? [Smiling] With vine-leaves in my hair, as you used to dream in the old days——?

HEDDA: No, no. I have lost my faith in the vine-leaves. But beautifully nevertheless! For once in a way!—Good-bye! You must go now—and do not come here any more.

LÖVBORG: Good-bye, Mrs. Tesman. And give George Tesman my love. [He is on the point of going]

HEDDA: No, wait! I must give you a memento to take with you.

[She goes to the writing-table and opens the drawer and the pistol-case; then returns to Lövborg with one of the pistols]

LÖVBORG: [Looks at her] This? Is this the memento?

HEDDA: [Nodding slowly] Do you recognize it? It was aimed at you once.

LÖVBORG: You should have used it then.

HEDDA: Take it—and do you use it now.

LÖVBORG: [Puts the pistol in his breast pocket] Thanks!

HEDDA: And beautifully, Eilert Lövborg. Promise me that!

LÖVBORG: Good-bye, Hedda Gabler.

[He goes out by the hall door]

[Hedda listens for a moment at the door. Then she goes up to the writing-table, takes out the packet of manuscript, peeps under the cover, draws a few of the sheets half out, and looks at them. Next she goes over and seats herself in the arm-chair beside the stove, with the packet in her lap. Presently she opens the stove door, and then the packet]

HEDDA: [Throws one of the quires into the fire and whispers to herself] Now I am burning your child, Thea!—Burning it, curly-locks! [Throwing one or two more quires into the stove] Your child and Eilert Lövborg's. [Throws the rest in] I am burning —I am burning your child.

ACT IV.

The same rooms at the Tesmans'. It is evening. The drawing-room is in darkness. The back room is lighted by the hanging lamp over the table. The curtains over the glass door are drawn close.

Hedda, dressed in black, walks to and fro in the dark room. Then she goes into the back room and disappears for a moment to the left. She is heard to strike a few chords on the piano. Presently she comes in sight again, and returns to the drawing-room.

Berta enters from the right, through the inner room, with a lighted lamp, which she places on the table in front of the corner settee in the drawing-room. Her eyes are red with weeping, and she has black ribbons in her cap. She goes quietly and circumspectly out to the right. Hedda goes up to the glass door, lifts the curtain a little aside, and looks out into the darkness.

Shortly afterwards, Miss Tesman, in mourning, with a bonnet and veil on, comes in from the hall. Hedda goes towards her and holds out her hand.

MISS TESMAN: Yes, Hedda, here I am, in mourning and forlorn; for now my poor sister has at last found peace.

HEDDA: I have heard the news already, as you see. Tesman sent me a card.

MISS TESMAN: Yes, he promised me he would. But nevertheless I thought that to Hedda—here in the house of life—I ought myself to bring the tidings of death.

HEDDA: That was very kind of you.

MISS TESMAN: Ah, Rina ought not to have left us just now. This is not the time for Hedda's house to be a house of mourning.

HEDDA: [*Changing the subject*] She died quite peacefully, did she not, Miss Tesman?

MISS TESMAN: Oh, her end was so calm, so beautiful. And then she had the unspeakable happiness of seeing George once more—and bidding him good-bye.—Has he not come home yet?

HEDDA: No. He wrote that he might be detained. But won't you sit down?

MISS TESMAN: No thank you, my dear, dear Hedda. I should like to, but I have so much to do. I must prepare my dear one for her rest as well as I can. She shall go to her grave looking her best.

HEDDA: Can I not help you in any way?

MISS TESMAN: Oh, you must not think of it! Hedda Tesman must have no hand in such mournful work. Nor let her thoughts dwell on it either—not at this time.

HEDDA: One is not always mistress of one's thoughts——

MISS TESMAN: [*Continuing*] Ah yes, it is the way of the world. At home we shall be sewing a shroud; and here there will soon be sewing too, I suppose—but of another sort, thank God!

[George Tesman *enters by the hall door*]

HEDDA: Ah, you have come at last!

TESMAN: You here, Aunt Julia? With Hedda? Fancy that!

MISS TESMAN: I was just going, my dear boy. Well, have you done all you promised?

TESMAN: No; I'm really afraid I have forgotten half of it. I must come to you again to-morrow. To-day my brain is all in a whirl. I can't keep my thoughts together.

MISS TESMAN: Why, my dear George, you mustn't take it in this way.

TESMAN: Mustn't——? How do you mean?

MISS TESMAN: Even in your sorrow you must rejoice, as I do—rejoice that she is at rest.

TESMAN: Oh yes, yes—you are thinking of Aunt Rina.

HEDDA: You will feel lonely now, Miss Tesman.

MISS TESMAN: Just at first, yes. But that will not last very long, I hope. I daresay I shall soon find an occupant for poor Rina's little room.

TESMAN: Indeed? Who do you think will take it? Eh?

MISS TESMAN: Oh, there's always some poor invalid or other in want of nursing, unfortunately.

HEDDA: Would you really take such a burden upon you again?

MISS TESMAN: A burden! Heaven forgive you, child—it has been no burden to me.

HEDDA: But suppose you had a total stranger on your hands——

MISS TESMAN: Oh, one soon makes friends with sick folk; and it's such an absolute necessity for me to have some one to live for. Well, heaven be praised, there may soon be something in *this* house, too, to keep an old aunt busy.

HEDDA: Oh, don't trouble about anything here.

TESMAN: Yes, just fancy what a nice time we three might have together, if——?

HEDDA: If——?

TESMAN: [*Uneasily*] Oh, nothing. It will all come right. Let us hope so—eh?

MISS TESMAN: Well well, I daresay you two want to talk to each other. [*Smiling*] And perhaps Hedda may have something to tell you too, George. Good-bye! I must go home to Rina. [*Turning at the door*] How strange it is to think that now Rina is with me and with my poor brother as well!

TESMAN: Yes, fancy that, Aunt Julia! Eh? [Miss Tesman *goes out by the hall door*]

HEDDA: [*Follows* Tesman *coldly and searchingly with her eyes*] I almost believe your Aunt Rina's death affects you more than it does your Aunt Julia.

TESMAN: Oh, it's not that alone. It's Eilert I am so terribly uneasy about.

HEDDA: [*Quickly*] Is there anything new about him?

TESMAN: I looked in at his rooms this afternoon, intending to tell him the manuscript was in safe keeping.

HEDDA: Well, did you not find him?

TESMAN: No. He wasn't at home. But afterwards I met Mrs. Elvsted, and she told me that he had been here early this morning.

HEDDA: Yes, directly after you had gone.

TESMAN: And he said that he had torn his manuscript to pieces—eh?

HEDDA: Yes, so he declared.

TESMAN: Why, good heavens, he must have been completely out of his mind! And I suppose you thought it best not to give it back to him, Hedda?

HEDDA: No, he did not get it.

TESMAN: But of course you told him that we had it?

HEDDA: No. [*Quickly*] Did you tell Mrs. Elvsted?

TESMAN: No; I thought I had better not. But you ought to have told him. Fancy, if, in desperation, he should go and do himself some injury! Let me have the manuscript, Hedda! I will take it to him at once. Where is it?

HEDDA: [*Cold and immovable, leaning on the arm-chair*] I have not got it.

TESMAN: Have not got it? What in the world do you mean?

HEDDA: I have burnt it—every line of it.

TESMAN: [*With a violent movement of terror*] Burnt! Burnt Eilert's manuscript!

HEDDA: Don't scream so. The servant might hear you.

TESMAN: Burnt! Why, good God——! No, no, no! It's impossible!

HEDDA: It is so, nevertheless.

TESMAN: Do you know what you have done, Hedda? It's unlawful appropriation of lost property. Fancy that! Just ask Judge Brack, and he'll tell **you** what it is.

HEDDA: I advise you not to speak of it—either to Judge Brack, or to any one else.

TESMAN: But how could you do anything so unheard-of? What put it into your head? What possessed you? Answer me that—eh?

HEDDA: [*Suppressing an almost imperceptible smile*] I did it for your sake, George.

TESMAN: For my sake!

HEDDA: This morning, when you told me about what he had read to you——

TESMAN: Yes yes—what then?

HEDDA: You acknowledged that you envied him his work.

TESMAN: Oh, of course I didn't mean that literally.

HEDDA: No matter—I could not bear the idea that any one should throw you into the shade.

TESMAN: [*In an outburst of mingled doubt and joy*] Hedda! Oh, is this true? But—but—I never knew you show your love like that before. Fancy that!

HEDDA: Well, I may as well tell you that—just at this time—— [*Impatiently, breaking off*] No, no; you can ask Aunt Julia. She will tell you, fast enough.

TESMAN: Oh, I almost think I understand you, Hedda! [*Clasps his hands together*] Great heavens! do you really mean it! Eh?

HEDDA: Don't shout so. The servant might hear.

TESMAN: [*Laughing in irrepressible glee*] The servant! Why, how absurd you are, Hedda. It's only my old Berta! Why, I'll tell Berta myself.

HEDDA: [*Clenching her hands together in desperation*] Oh, it is killing me,—it is killing me, all this!

TESMAN: What is, Hedda? Eh?

HEDDA: [*Coldly, controlling herself*] All this—absurdity—George.

TESMAN: Absurdity! Do you see anything absurd in my being overjoyed at the news! But after all—perhaps I had better not say anything to Berta.

HEDDA: Oh——why not that too?

TESMAN: No, no, not yet! But I must certainly tell Aunt Julia. And then that you have begun to call me George too! Fancy that! Oh, Aunt Julia will be so happy—so happy!

HEDDA: When she hears that I have burnt Eilert Lövborg's manuscript—for your sake?

TESMAN: No, by the by—that affair of the manuscript—of course nobody must know about that. But that you love me so much, Hedda—Aunt Julia must really share my joy in that! I wonder, now, whether this sort of thing is usual in young wives? Eh?

HEDDA: I think you had better ask Aunt Julia that question too.

TESMAN: I will indeed, some time or other. [*Looks uneasy and downcast again*] And yet the manuscript—the manuscript! Good God! it is terrible to think what will become of poor Eilert now.

[Mrs. Elvsted, *dressed as in the first act, with hat and cloak, enters by the hall door*]

MRS. ELVSTED: [*Greets them hurriedly, and says in evident agitation*] Oh, dear Hedda, forgive my coming again.

HEDDA: What is the matter with you, Thea?

TESMAN: Something about Eilert Lövborg again—eh?

MRS. ELVSTED: Yes! I am dreadfully afraid some misfortune has happened to him.

HEDDA: [*Seizes her arm*] Ah,—do you think so?

TESMAN: Why, good Lord—what makes you think that, Mrs. Elvsted?

MRS. ELVSTED: I heard them talking of him at my boarding-house—just as I came in. Oh, the most incredible rumors are afloat about him to-day.

TESMAN: Yes, fancy, so I heard too! And I can bear witness that he went straight home to bed last night. Fancy that!

HEDDA: Well, what did they say at the boarding-house?

MRS. ELVSTED: Oh, I couldn't make out anything clearly. Either they knew nothing definite, or else——. They stopped talking when they saw me; and I did not dare to ask.

TESMAN: [*Moving about uneasily*] We must hope—we must hope that you misunderstood them, Mrs. Elvsted.

MRS. ELVSTED: No, no; I am sure it was of him they were talking. And I heard something about the hospital or——

TESMAN: The hospital?

HEDDA: No—surely that cannot be!

MRS. ELVSTED: Oh, I was in such mortal terror! I went to his lodgings and asked for him there.

HEDDA: You could make up your mind to that, Thea!

MRS. ELVSTED: What else could I do? I really could bear the suspense no longer.

TESMAN: But you didn't find him either—eh?

MRS. ELVSTED: No. And the people knew nothing about him. He hadn't been home since yesterday afternoon, they said.

TESMAN: Yesterday! Fancy, how could they say that?

MRS. ELVSTED: Oh, I am sure something terrible must have happened to him.

TESMAN: Hedda dear—how would it be if I were to go and make inquiries——?

HEDDA: No, no—don't you mix yourself up in this affair.

[Judge Brack, *with his hat in his hand, enters by the hall door, which* Berta *opens, and closes behind him. He looks grave and bows in silence*]

TESMAN: Oh, is that you, my dear judge? Eh?

BRACK: Yes. It was imperative I should see you this evening.

TESMAN: I can see you have heard the news about Aunt Rina?

BRACK: Yes, that among other things.

TESMAN: Isn't it sad—eh?

BRACK: Well, my dear Tesman, that depends on how you look at it.

TESMAN: [*Looks doubtfully at him*] Has anything else happened?

BRACK: Yes.

HEDDA: [*In suspense*] Anything sad, Judge Brack?

BRACK: That, too, depends on how you look at it, Mrs. Tesman.

MRS. ELVSTED: [*Unable to restrain her anxiety*] Oh! it is something about Eilert Lövborg!

BRACK: [*With a glance at her*] What makes you think that, Madam? Perhaps you have already heard something——?

MRS. ELVSTED: [*In confusion*] No, nothing at all, but——

TESMAN: Oh, for heaven's sake, tell us!

BRACK: [*Shrugging his shoulders*] Well, I regret to say Eilert Lövborg has been taken to the hospital. He is lying at the point of death.

MRS. ELVSTED: [*Shrieks*] Oh God! oh God——!

TESMAN: To the hospital! And at the point of death!

HEDDA: [*Involuntarily*] So soon then——

MRS. ELVSTED: [*Wailing*] And we parted in anger, Hedda!

HEDDA: [*Whispers*] Thea—Thea—be careful!

MRS. ELVSTED: [*Not heeding her*] I must go to him! I must see him alive!

BRACK: It is useless, Madam. No one will be admitted.

MRS. ELVSTED: Oh, at least tell me what has happened to him? What is it?

TESMAN: You don't mean to say that he has himself—— Eh?

HEDDA: Yes, I am sure he has.

TESMAN: Hedda, how can you——?

BRACK: [*Keeping his eyes fixed upon her*] Unfortunately you have guessed quite correctly, Mrs. Tesman.

MRS. ELVSTED: Oh, how horrible!

TESMAN: Himself, then! Fancy that!

HEDDA: Shot himself!

BRACK: Rightly guessed again, Mrs. Tesman.

MRS. ELVSTED: [*With an effort at self-control*] When did it happen, Mr. Brack?

BRACK: This afternoon—between three and four.

TESMAN: But, good Lord, where did he do it? Eh?

BRACK: [*With some hesitation*] Where? Well—I suppose at his lodgings.

MRS. ELVSTED: No, that cannot be; for I was there between six and seven.

BRACK: Well then, somewhere else. I don't know exactly. I only know that he was found——. He had shot himself—in the breast.

MRS. ELVSTED: Oh, how terrible! That he should die like that!

HEDDA: [*To* Brack] Was it in the breast?

BRACK: Yes—as I told you.

HEDDA: Not in the temple?

BRACK: In the breast, Mrs. Tesman.

HEDDA: Well, well—the breast is a good place, too.

BRACK: How do you mean, Mrs. Tesman?

HEDDA: [*Evasively*] Oh, nothing—nothing.

TESMAN: And the wound is dangerous, you say—eh?

BRACK: Absolutely mortal. The end has probably come by this time.

MRS. ELVSTED: Yes, yes, I feel it. The end! The end! Oh, Hedda——!

TESMAN: But tell me, how have you learnt all this?

BRACK: [*Curtly*] Through one of the police. A man I had some business with.

HEDDA: [*In a clear voice*] At last a deed worth doing!

TESMAN: [*Terrified*] Good heavens, Hedda! what are you saying?

HEDDA: I say there is beauty in this.

BRACK: H'm, Mrs. Tesman——

TESMAN: Beauty! Fancy that!

MRS. ELVSTED: Oh, Hedda, how can you talk of beauty in such an act!

HEDDA: Eilert Lövborg has himself made up his account with life. He has had the courage to do—the one right thing.

MRS. ELVSTED: No, you must never think that was how it happened! It must have been in delirium that he did it.

TESMAN: In despair!

HEDDA: That he did not. I am certain of that.

MRS. ELVSTED: Yes, yes! In delirium! Just as when he tore up our manuscript.

BRACK: [*Starting*] The manuscript? Has he torn that up?

MRS. ELVSTED: Yes, last night.

TESMAN: [*Whispers softly*] Oh, Hedda, we shall never get over this.

BRACK: H'm, very extraordinary.

TESMAN: [*Moving about the room*] To think of Eilert going out of the world in this way! And not leaving behind him the book that would have immortalized his name.

MRS. ELVSTED: Oh, if only it could be put together again!

TESMAN: Yes, if it only could! I don't know what I would not give——

MRS. ELVSTED: Perhaps it can, Mr. Tesman.

TESMAN: What do you mean?

MRS. ELVSTED: [*Searches in the pocket of her dress*] Look here. I have kept all the loose notes he used to dictate from.

HEDDA: [*A step forward*] Ah——!

TESMAN: You have kept them, Mrs. Elvsted! Eh?

MRS. ELVSTED: Yes, I have them here. I put them in my pocket when I left home. Here they still are——

TESMAN: Oh, do let me see them!

MRS. ELVSTED: [*Hands him a bundle of papers*] But they are in such disorder—all mixed up.

TESMAN: Fancy, if we could make something out of them, after all! Perhaps if we two put our heads together——

MRS. ELVSTED: Oh yes, at least let us try——

TESMAN: We will manage it! We must! I will dedicate my life to this task.

HEDDA: You, George? Your life?

TESMAN: Yes, or rather all the time I can spare. My own collections must wait in the meantime. Hedda—you understand, eh? I owe this to Eilert's memory.

HEDDA: Perhaps.

TESMAN: And so, my dear Mrs. Elvsted, we will give our whole minds to it. There is no use in brooding over what can't be undone—eh? We must try to control our grief as much as possible, and——

MRS. ELVSTED: Yes, yes, Mr. Tesman. I will do the best I can.

TESMAN: Well then, come here. I can't rest until we have looked through the notes. Where shall we sit? Here? No, in there, in the back room. Excuse me, my dear Judge. Come with me, Mrs. Elvsted.

MRS. ELVSTED: Oh, if only it were possible!

[Tesman *and* Mrs. Elvsted *go into the back room. She takes off her hat and cloak. They both sit at the table under the hanging lamp, and are soon deep in an eager examination of the papers.* Hedda *crosses to the stove and sits in the arm-chair. Presently* Brack *goes up to her*]

HEDDA: [*In a low voice*] Oh, what a sense of freedom it gives one, this act of Eilert Lövborg's.

BRACK: Freedom, Mrs. Hedda? Well, of course, it is a release for him——

HEDDA: I mean for me! It gives me a sense of freedom to know that a deed of deliberate courage is still possible in this world,—a deed of spontaneous beauty.

BRACK: [*Smiling*] H'm—my dear Mrs. Hedda——

HEDDA: Oh, I know what you are going to say. For you are a kind of specialist, too, like—you know!

BRACK: [*Looking hard at her*] Eilert Lövborg was more to you than perhaps you are willing to admit to yourself. Am I wrong?

HEDDA: I don't answer such questions. I only know that Eilert Lövborg has had the courage to live his life after his own fashion. And then—the last great act, with its beauty! Ah! that he should have the will and the strength to turn away from the banquet of life—so early.

BRACK: I am sorry, Mrs. Hedda,—but I fear I must dispel an amiable illusion.

HEDDA: Illusion?

BRACK: Which could not have lasted long in any case.

HEDDA: What do you mean?

BRACK: Eilert Lövborg did not shoot himself—voluntarily.

HEDDA: Not voluntarily?

BRACK: No. The thing did not happen exactly as I told it.

HEDDA: [*In suspense*] Have you concealed something? What is it?

BRACK: For poor Mrs. Elvsted's sake I idealized the facts a little.

HEDDA: What are the facts?

BRACK: First, that he is already dead.

HEDDA: At the hospital?

BRACK: Yes—without regaining consciousness.

HEDDA: What more have you concealed?

BRACK: This—the event did not happen at his lodgings.

HEDDA: Oh, that can make no difference.

BRACK: Perhaps it may. For I must tell you—Eilert Lövborg was found shot in—in Mademoiselle Diana's boudoir.

HEDDA: [*Makes a motion as if to rise, but sinks back again*] That is impossible, Judge Brack! He cannot have been there again to-day.

BRACK: He was there this afternoon. He went there, he said, to demand the return of something which they had taken from him. Talked wildly about a lost child——

HEDDA: Ah—so that was why——

BRACK: I thought probably he meant his manuscript; but now I hear he destroyed that himself. So I suppose it must have been his pocket-book.

HEDDA: Yes, no doubt. And there—there he was found?

BRACK: Yes, there. With a pistol in his breast-pocket, discharged. The ball had lodged in a vital part.

HEDDA: In the breast—yes.

BRACK: No—in the bowels.

HEDDA: [*Looks up at him with an expression of loathing*] That, too! Oh, what curse is it that makes everything I touch turn ludicrous and mean?

BRACK: There is one point more, Mrs. Hedda—another disagreeable feature in the affair.

HEDDA: And what is that?

BRACK: The pistol he carried——

HEDDA: [*Breathless*] Well? What of it?

BRACK: He must have stolen it.

HEDDA: [*Leaps up*] Stolen it! That is not true! He did not steal it!

BRACK: No other explanation is possible. He must have stolen it—— Hush!

[Tesman *and* Mrs. Elvsted *have risen from the table in the back room, and come into the drawing-room*]

TESMAN: [*With the papers in both his hands*] Hedda, dear, it is almost impossible to see under that lamp. Think of that!

HEDDA: Yes, I am thinking.

TESMAN: Would you mind our sitting at your writing-table—eh?

HEDDA: If you like [*Quickly*] No, wait! Let me clear it first!

TESMAN: Oh, you needn't trouble, Hedda. There is plenty of room.

HEDDA: No, no, let me clear it, I say! I will take these things in and put them on the piano. There!

[*She has drawn out an object, covered with sheet music, from under the bookcase, places several other pieces of music upon it, and carries the whole into the inner room, to the left.* Tesman *lays the scraps of paper on the writing-table, and moves the lamp there from the corner table. He and* Mrs. Elvsted *sit down and proceed with their work.* Hedda *returns*]

HEDDA: [*Behind* Mrs. Elvsted's *chair, gently ruffling her hair*] Well, my sweet Thea,—how goes it with Eilert Lövborg's monument?

MRS. ELVSTED: [*Looks dispiritedly up at her*] Oh, it will be terribly hard to put in order.

TESMAN: We must manage it. I am determined. And arranging other people's papers is just the work for me.

[Hedda *goes over to the stove, and seats herself on one of the footstools.* Brack *stands over her, leaning on the arm-chair*]

HEDDA: [*Whispers*] What did you say about the pistol?

BRACK: [*Softly*] That he must have stolen it.

HEDDA: Why stolen it?

BRACK: Because every other explanation ought to be impossible, Mrs. Hedda.

HEDDA: Indeed?

BRACK: [*Glances at her*] Of course, Eilert Lövborg was here this morning. Was he not?

HEDDA: Yes.

BRACK: Were you alone with him?

HEDDA: Part of the time.

BRACK: Did you not leave the room whilst he was here?

HEDDA: No.

BRACK: Try to recollect. Were you not out of the room a moment?

HEDDA: Yes, perhaps just a moment—out in the hall.

BRACK: And where was your pistol-case during that time?

HEDDA: I had it locked up in——

BRACK: Well, Mrs. Hedda?

HEDDA: The case stood there on the writing-table.

BRACK: Have you looked since, to see whether both the pistols are there?

HEDDA: No.

BRACK: Well, you need not. I saw the pistol found in Lövborg's pocket, and I knew it at once as the one I had seen yesterday—and before, too.

HEDDA: Have you it with you?

BRACH: No; the police have it.

HEDDA: What will the police do with it?

BRACK: Search till they find the owner.

HEDDA: Do you think they will succeed.

BRACK: [*Bends over her and whispers*] No, Hedda Gabler—not so long as I say nothing.

HEDDA: [*Looks frightened at him*] And if you do not say nothing,—what then?

BRACK: [*Shrugs his shoulders*] There is always the possibility that the pistol was stolen.

HEDDA: [*Firmly*] Death rather than that.

BRACK: [*Smiling*] People say such things—but they don't do them.

HEDDA: [*Without replying*] And supposing the pistol was not stolen, and the owner is discovered? What then?

BRACK: Well, Hedda—then comes the scandal.

HEDDA: The scandal!

BRACK: Yes, the scandal—of which you are so mortally afraid. You will, of course, be brought before the court—both you and Mademoiselle Diana. She will have to explain how the thing happened—whether it was an accidental shot or murder. Did the pistol go off as he was trying to take it out of his pocket, to threaten her with? Or did she tear the pistol out of his hand, shoot him, and push it back into his pocket? That would be quite like her; for she is an able-bodied young person, this same Mademoiselle Diana.

HEDDA: But *I* have nothing to do with all this repulsive business.

BRACK: No. But you will have to answer the question: Why did you give Eilert Lövborg the pistol? And what conclusions will people draw from the fact that you did give it to him?

HEDDA: [*Lets her head sink*] That is true. I did not think of that.

BRACK: Well, fortunately, there is no danger, so long as I say nothing.

HEDDA: [*Looks up at him*] So I am in your power, Judge Brack. You have me at your beck and call, from this time forward.

BRACK: [*Whispers softly*] Dearest Hedda—believe me—I shall not abuse my advantage.

HEDDA: I am in your power none the less. Subject to your will and your demands. A slave, a slave then! [*Rises impetuously*] No, I cannot endure the thought of that! Never!

BRACK: [*Looks half-mockingly at her*] People generally get used to the inevitable.

HEDDA: [*Returns his look*] Yes, perhaps. [*She crosses to the writing-table. Suppressing an involuntary smile, she imitates* Tesman's *intonations*] Well? Are you getting on, George? Eh?

TESMAN: Heaven knows, dear. In any case it will be the work of months.

HEDDA: [*As before*] Fancy that! [*Passes her hands softly through* Mrs. Elvsted's *hair*] Doesn't it seem strange to you, Thea? Here are you sitting with Tesman—just as you used to sit with Eilert Lövborg?

MRS. ELVSTED: Ah, if I could only inspire your husband in the same way!

HEDDA: Oh, that will come, too—in time.

TESMAN: Yes, do you know, Hedda—I really

think I begin to feel something of the sort. But won't you go and sit with Brack again?

HEDDA: Is there nothing I can do to help you two?

TESMAN: No, nothing in the world. [*Turning his head*] I trust to you to keep Hedda company, my dear Brack.

BRACK: [*With a glance at* Hedda] With the very greatest of pleasure.

HEDDA: Thanks. But I am tired this evening. I will go in and lie down a little on the sofa.

TESMAN: Yes, do dear—eh?

[Hedda *goes into the back room and draws the curtains. A short pause. Suddenly she is heard playing a wild dance on the piano*]

MRS. ELVSTED: [*Starts from her chair*] Oh—what is that?

TESMAN: [*Runs to the doorway*] Why, my dearest Hedda—don't play dance-music to-night! Just think of Aunt Rina! And of Eilert, too!

HEDDA: [*Puts her head out between the curtains*] And of Aunt Julia. And of all the rest of them.—After this, I will be quiet. [*Closes the curtains again*]

TESMAN: [*At the writing-table*] It's not good for her to see us at this distressing work. I'll tell you what, Mrs. Elvsted,—you shall take the empty room at Aunt Julia's, and then I will come over in the evenings, and we can sit and work there—eh?

HEDDA: [*In the inner room*] I hear what you are saying, Tesman. But how am *I* to get through the evenings out here?

TESMAN: [*Turning over the papers*] Oh, I daresay Judge Brack will be so kind as to look in now and then, even though I am out.

BRACK: [*In the arm-chair, calls out gaily*] Every blessed evening, with all the pleasure in life, Mrs. Tesman! We shall get on capitally together, we two!

HEDDA: [*Speaking loud and clear*] Yes, don't you flatter yourself we will, Judge Brack? Now that you are the one cock in the basket——

[*A shot is heard within.* Tesman, Mrs. Elvsted, *and* Brack *leap to their feet*]

TESMAN: Oh, now she is playing with those pistols again.

[*He throws back the curtains and runs in, followed by* Mrs. Elvsted. Hedda *lies stretched on the sofa, lifeless. Confusion and cries.* Berta *enters in alarm from the right*]

TESMAN: [*Shrieks to* Brack] Shot herself! Shot herself in the temple! Fancy that!

BRACK: [*Half-fainting in the arm-chair*] Good God!—people don't do such things.

August Strindberg

(1849–1912)

When the British actor-manager Robert Lorraine read *The Father* to his wife, she was on her knees before him at the end of the second act, assuring him that all their children were his own and that he was not to believe a single word of Strindberg's play. This appears to have convinced him that one could give a successful production of this formidable drama even in England, which he proceeded to do in 1927. Strindberg's furious onslaught on the emotions, however, had enabled him to overcome the diffidence of audiences elsewhere as early as the eighteen-eighties and 'nineties—in Germany and France, as well as in his own country, Sweden, which came to acknowledge him as its greatest writer. Ever since the Théâtre Libre produced his drama *Miss Julie* (1892), the European theatre has been fully aware of its debt to this author of some seventy long and short plays. It has even tended to approve the prediction of Ibsen, who, though often berated by his junior colleague, once declared, "He will be greater than I."

Strindberg's fame spread as far east as Japan, where he found imitators, and as far west as America, where O'Neill, his debtor, claimed him in 1924 as "the most modern of moderns, the greatest interpreter of the characteristic spiritual conflicts that constitute the drama." It was during the period of O'Neill's close association with the Provincetown Playhouse that Strindberg was introduced to its small but faithful audiences with one of his most experimental plays, *The Spook Sonata*. Although his virulent dramas were never received with open arms in the English-speaking world, the impression they made upon leaders of the American and English theatre makes Strindberg important to us. His example can be traced in many an O'Neill success and failure. His importance was dinned into the ears of American writers by important critics like James Huneker and H. L. Mencken. Huneker, who predicted in 1905 that the antifeminist Strindberg would find no popularity in America, "a land peopled with gynolatrists," thought of him as a "culture hero" who had "brought us the history of experiences not to be forgotten." Later, when Shaw received the Nobel Prize, which had been withheld from Strindberg himself by the enmity of a committee member, he converted it into a trust fund for English translations of Strindberg's writings—fifty-five volumes of plays, stories, novels, autobiographies, and miscellaneous writings—from the standard Swedish edition.

Johan August Strindberg was born in Stockholm, the fourth of eleven children. His mother had been a barmaid in the city, and his father, a small businessman whose family deplored the *mésalliance,* had married her only a few months before August's birth. Cradled in poverty and reared in an overcrowded three-room household harassed by many births and deaths, August became an oversensitive and rebellious lad. He became even more irritable and suspicious when, in his thirteenth year, his mother died and his father promptly remarried. Fixated on his mother by love and hatred, made insecure for life, and filled with aggressive drives compounded of desire and fear, Strindberg was primed from the start for a life of furious conflict with the world and with himself. He froze and starved at the University of Upsala for a semester in 1867, tried the University of Stockholm for a time, left it to teach at the same grammar school where he had suffered childhood humiliations, served for a while as a physician's assistant, and made a vain attempt to become an actor. Returning in 1870 to the University of Stockholm, he studied literature and science avidly; but winning a stipend from King Charles V of Sweden for a short romantic play, he abandoned his studies in 1872 to pursue a literary career.

Fortunately, although his first full-length drama, *Master Olof,* was rejected by both publishers and theatres, Strindberg received an appointment as assistant in the Royal Library in Stockholm, and here, from 1874 to 1882, he brooded and browsed, studied philosophy, tried to master the Chinese language, produced a scholarly study, and wrote the first naturalistic social novel in Swedish, *The Red Room* (1879), under the influence of Flaubert. During this period he also fell fatefully in love with the wife of a baron, Siri von Essen, whom he married and with whom he had three children before becoming embroiled in as violent a domestic conflict as any ever aired in literature. Leaving his librarian's post, he traveled about Europe with his family between 1883 and 1889, publishing a collection of realistic short stories on marriage, *Married* (1884). The volume was confiscated and its publisher arraigned for blasphemy, but Strindberg won popularity with the Swedish public by hastening home to assume full responsibility for the book. He gained an acquittal from the court and the following year published a second and even more trenchant collection of stories, also entitled *Married*. It contained all the familiar elements of Strindberg's later ultra-realistic plays, including their misogyny and their

75

attack on the cult of feminism which had been promoted by *A Doll's House*. Here first appeared his strange attraction-repulsion pattern in his relations with women, which had been no doubt implanted in him by childhood experiences with a mother of lowly origins who could give him scant attention and died when he was still a boy.

Thereafter "the battle of the sexes" was to consume much of his energy and to find notable expression in *The Father* (1887), *Comrades* (1888), *Miss Julie* (1888), *The Link* (1893), and *The Dance of Death* (1901), as well as in searing, if embarrassing, autobiographical novels. He was finally divorced in 1891 after overpublicized bickerings, but since he married for a second time (1893) and for a third time (1901), there was never any lack of fuel for his analytical and recriminatory studies of marriage. In the war of the sexes, Strindberg contended, "the less honest and more perverse would come out conqueror"; that is, the woman would win, the man being handicapped "by an inbred respect for women." Of Ibsen and the "Ibsenites," or feminists, he declared, "My superior intelligence revolts against the gynolatry which is the latest superstition of the freethinkers," and he expressed a fear that society was going back to a state of matriarchy. His antifeminism often verged on hysteria; nor was it consistent with his own practice as the husband of three wives, each of whom was an "emancipated" woman. Although he made penetrative observations, he hardly qualified as a sociologist. His findings were obviously too colored by personal animus to be accepted as considered judgments. It is for his talent as a dramatist and not as an ineffectual eccentric that Strindberg is remembered.

A number of his plays devoted directly to the sex duel are masterworks of analysis. Although he did not follow naturalism slavishly, he went far toward making it enduringly memorable, and the psychological conflicts in which he specialized led modern playwrights into one of the rewarding channels of their craft. Strindberg advanced dramatic art by writing more probingly and more tautly than Ibsen generally did. He went further than Ibsen in turning out a species of drama in which hardly anything remains of exposition and nearly everything is simply the dramatized climax. To this end, he abolished intermissions and act divisions, virtually giving rise to the modern one-act drama, which is to be distinguished as an art form from the "vaudevilles" or inconsequential curtain-raisers of the popular theatre. (He was anticipated by the authors of short plays for Antoine's Théâtre Libre, it is true, but these precursors had neither his breadth nor his depth.) The masterpiece of this kind of concentrated dramaturgy is the hour-and-a-half-long uninterrupted drama *Miss Julie*, in which the sexual instinct thrusts a fastidious and neurotic noblewoman into a disastrous affair with her father's footman.

In another long one-acter, *The Creditor*, in which he exposed a woman's parasitism, he transferred all the conflict to the psychological plane and conveyed it entirely through analytical conversation before moving on to a shattering conclusion. The extreme example of simplification was *The Stronger*, which is no more than a betrayed but ultimately victorious woman's monologue in the presence of her rival.

Without exemplifying any breadth of vision or sweetness of spirit in his realistic pieces, Strindberg concerned himself with the subject of human relations, especially with the intensified competitiveness of men and women in modern society and their loss of emotional security. Since he placed in the arena of the sex duel "exceptional people in conflict with exceptional circumstance," as the novelist Storm Jameson has noted, the sparks that fly from the collisions illuminate the scene and excite the onlooker. And if Strindberg was often so extreme in utterance as to seem to exceed the bounds of rationality, there is no evidence of a clouded mind in his observations and logic. The difference between him and more relaxed writers is that his lucidity happened to be charged with lightning. His works were more than mere displays of "the sorrows of a hen-pecked Blue Beard," as the British critic Desmond MacCarthy called them; and plays like *The Father* and *Miss Julie* are something else and something more than his pronouncements on women and marriage. His best work distributes justice between its antagonists, takes account of human contradictions, and crackles with sardonic humor. Like other good artists, Strindberg wrote more richly and better than he perhaps knew or intended. In *The Link* and *The Dance of Death* he presented a husband whose behavior was just as deplorable as the wife's, and in *Miss Julie* he made the drama revolve around a girl who was the victim of sexuality welling up from suppression. Miss Julie's compulsively offensive behavior toward a suitor of her own class and her attraction to a valet is fundamentally pitiable in the light of clinical understanding, whereas real ruthlessness emerges in the valet's exploitation of her weakness. Mrs. X, heroine of *The Stronger*, is a wife who managed to retrieve her husband from the clutches of a sterile seductress and proved herself "the stronger woman" by doing what the "emancipated" woman could not do—that is, holding her man. No doubt Strindberg approved of her "unemancipated" conduct, but he was sufficiently objective to refrain from making her lovable. His animosities, in short, did not often lessen his power to create character, whereas many playwrights far more agreeable than he have not hesitated to turn characters into puppets of their argument. Even so relentless a treatment of domestic war as *The Father* reveals at the helm of Strindberg's dramaturgy a steady hand not always noticed by this dramatist's detractors.

In *The Father* Strindberg championed the husband in his struggle against the wife, and, indeed, the husband is more sinned against than sinning. Yet the Captain is hardly a reasonable man either in his dealings with his wife Laura or in his frantic obsession with the possibility that their daughter may not be his own. The old nurse who puts him in a straitjacket is a compassionate woman, and even the ruthless Laura is not an unmitigated serpent of subtlety and evil. For all her diabolical scheming, she is ignorant and obtuse, as well as conventionally religious; she can be, besides, as considerate to others as she is inconsiderate toward her husband when balked by him. Even in the all-consuming struggle of *The Father,* we find the contradictions and divagations that distinguish life from the closed syllogism of argument. Next to the power of a ruling passion, we find here, as in other Strindberg plays, creative flexibility and multifaceted reality.

Although *The Father* follows the dramatic line of an intrigue and has act divisions, so that it is less originally constructed than either *Miss Julie* or *The Creditor,* it exhibits most of the qualities we associate with its author's genius. It is a remarkably compact play, and everything that occurs in it forms a climax in the relations of husband and wife. The quarrel over the education of the daughter is only the spark that explodes the powder keg. We can hardly fail to realize that the domestic struggle has been going on for some time and that the hatred of the couple has been mounting in countless details of daily experience. The man's irritability has been compounding itself and now it pays a heavy interest on its capital; otherwise, he would be nothing but a fool, and he is no fool. The woman has

been smouldering before she becomes demoniacal in the play; otherwise her attitude toward the husband would be inexplicable. An unwritten novel, but one fully traced in Strindberg's distressingly candid autobiographies, underlies *The Father.*

Above all, Strindberg approaches a new concept of tragedy or, more precisely, approximates comparatively new variations on it. More than in the work of any earlier dramatist, man is destroyed in *The Father* (as in other Strindberg dramas, especially in *The Creditor* and in the second-rate one-acter *Simoon*) by his neuroses, and it is by inciting or encouraging a neurotic condition that Laura works her will. Strindberg's destroyed character, moreover, is no longer a hero in the classic or Elizabethan sense of the term, and he falls ignominiously. Miss Julie cuts her throat, the husband in *The Dance of Death* gets an apoplectic stroke, and the Father collapses in a straitjacket, after having waged a struggle over more or less picayune or unheroic matters that became momentous only in his disturbed mind. Nevertheless, because of the substantial amount of passion and will invested by the characters, the effect of the action in Strindberg's work is not inconsequential or devoid of a certain degree of tragic exaltation. For, unlike the followers of Zolaist naturalism, from which Strindberg learned a good deal while living in the Paris of the eighteen-eighties and 'nineties, Strindberg made no virtue of scientific detachment. Strindberg was the dramatist of division in the modern soul, and it splits apart explosively in his characters as it often did in his own person.

For additional commentary and bibliography, see pages 328–329.

THE FATHER

By August Strindberg

TRANSLATED FROM THE SWEDISH BY EDITH AND WARNER OLAND

CHARACTERS

A CAPTAIN OF CAVALRY	DOCTOR ÖSTERMARK	NÖJD
LAURA, *his wife*	THE PASTOR	AN ORDERLY
BERTHA, *their daughter*	THE NURSE	

ACT I.

The sitting-room at the Captain's. *There is a door a little to the right at the back. In the middle of the room, a large, round table strewn with newspapers and magazines. To right a leather-covered sofa and table. In the right-hand corner a private door. At left there is a door leading to the inner room and a desk with a clock on it. Gamebags, guns and other arms hang on the walls. Army coats hang near door at back. On the large table stands a lighted lamp.*

CAPTAIN: [*Rings, an orderly comes in*]

ORDERLY: Yes, Captain.

CAPTAIN: Is Nöjd out there?

ORDERLY: He is waiting for orders in the kitchen.

CAPTAIN: In the kitchen again, is he? Send him in at once.

ORDERLY: Yes, Captain.

[*Goes*]

PASTOR: What's the matter now?

CAPTAIN: Oh, the rascal has been cutting up with the servant-girl again; he's certainly a bad lot.

PASTOR: Why, Nöjd got into the same trouble year before last, didn't he?

CAPTAIN: Yes, you remember? Won't you be good enough to give him a friendly talking to and perhaps you can make some impression on him. I've sworn at him and flogged him, too, but it hasn't had the least effect.

PASTOR: And so you want me to preach to him? What effect do you suppose the word of God will have on a rough trooper?

CAPTAIN: Well, it certainly has no effect on me.

PASTOR: I know that well enough.

CAPTAIN: Try it on *him,* anyway.

[*Nöjd comes in*]

CAPTAIN: What have you been up to now, Nöjd?

NÖJD: God save you, Captain, but I couldn't talk about it with the Pastor here.

PASTOR: Don't be afraid of me, my boy.

CAPTAIN: You had better confess or you know what will happen.

NÖJD: Well, you see it was like this; we were at a dance at Gabriel's, and then—then Ludwig said—

CAPTAIN: What has Ludwig got to do with it? Stick to the truth.

NÖJD: Yes, and Emma said "Let's go into the barn——"

CAPTAIN: ——Oh, so it was Emma who led you astray, was it?

NÖJD: Well, not far from it. You know that unless the girl is willing nothing ever happens.

CAPTAIN: Never mind all that: Are you the father of the child or not?

NÖJD: Who knows?

CAPTAIN: What's that? Don't you know?

NÖJD: Why no—that is, you can never be sure.

CAPTAIN: Weren't you the only one?

NÖJD: Yes, that time, but you can't be sure for all that.

CAPTAIN: Are you trying to put the blame on Ludwig? Is that what you are up to?

NÖJD: Well, you see it isn't easy to know who is to blame.

CAPTAIN: Yes, but you told Emma you would marry her.

NÖJD: Oh, a fellow's always got to say that—

CAPTAIN: [*To* Pastor] This is terrible, isn't it?

PASTOR: It's the old story over again. See here, Nöjd, you surely ought to know whether you are the father or not?

NÖJD: Well, of course, I was mixed up with the girl—but you know yourself, Pastor, that it needn't amount to anything for all that.

PASTOR: Look here, my lad, we are talking about you now. Surely you won't leave the girl alone with the child. I suppose we can't compel you to marry her, but you should provide for the child—that you shall do!

NÖJD: Well, then, so must Ludwig, too.

CAPTAIN: Then the case must go to the courts. I cannot ferret out the truth of all this, nor is it to my liking. So now be off.

PASTOR: One moment, Nöjd. H'm—don't you think it dishonorable to leave a girl destitute like that with her child? Don't you think so? Don't you see that such conduct——h'm—h'm——

NÖJD: Yes, if I only knew for sure that I was father of the child, but you can't be sure of that, Pastor, and I don't see much fun slaving all your life for another man's child. Surely you, Pastor, and the Captain can understand for yourselves.

CAPTAIN: Be off.

NÖJD: God save you, Captain.

[Goes]

CAPTAIN: But keep out of the kitchen, you rascal! [To Pastor] Now, why didn't you get after him?

PASTOR: What do you mean?

CAPTAIN: Why, you only sat and mumbled something or other.

PASTOR: To tell the truth I really don't know what to say. It is a pity about the girl, yes, and a pity about the lad, too. For think if he were not the father. The girl can nurse the child for four months at the orphanage, and then it will be permanently provided for, but it will be different for him. The girl can get a good place afterwards in some respectable family, but the lad's future may be ruined if he is dismissed from the regiment.

CAPTAIN: Upon my soul I should like to be in the magistrate's shoes and judge this case. The lad is probably not innocent, one can't be sure, but we do know that the girl is guilty, if there is any guilt in the matter.

PASTOR: Well, well, I judge no one. But what were we talking about when this stupid business interrupted us? It was about Bertha and her confirmation, wasn't it?

CAPTAIN: Yes, but it was certainly not in particular about her confirmation but about her whole welfare. This house is full of women who all want to have their say about my child. My mother-in-law wants to make a Spiritualist of her. Laura wants her to be an artist; the governess wants her to be a Methodist, old Margret a Baptist, and the servant-girls want her to join the Salvation Army! It won't do to try to make a soul in patches like that. I, who have the chief right to try to form her character, am constantly opposed in my efforts. And that's why I have decided to send her away from home.

PASTOR: You have too many women trying to run this house.

CAPTAIN: You're right! It's like going into a cage full of tigers, and if I didn't hold a red-hot iron under their noses they would tear me to pieces any moment. And you laugh, you rascal! Wasn't it enough that I married your sister, without your palming off your old stepmother on me?

PASTOR: But, good heavens, one can't have stepmothers in one's own house!

CAPTAIN: No, you think it is better to have mothers-in-law in some one else's house!

PASTOR: Oh well, we all have some burden in life.

CAPTAIN: But mine is certainly too heavy. I have my old nurse into the bargain, who treats me as if I ought still to wear a bib. She is a good old soul, to be sure, and she must not be dragged into such talk.

PASTOR: You must keep a tight rein on the women folk. You let them run things too much.

CAPTAIN: Now will you please inform me how I'm to keep order among the women folk?

PASTOR: Laura was brought up with a firm hand, but although she is my own sister, I must admit she was pretty troublesome.

CAPTAIN: Laura certainly has her faults, but with her it isn't so serious.

PASTOR: Oh, speak out—I know her.

CAPTAIN: She was brought up with romantic ideas, and it has been hard for her to find herself, but she is my wife——

PASTOR: And because she is your wife she is the best of wives? No, my dear fellow, it is she who really wears on you most.

CAPTAIN: Well, anyway, the whole house is topsyturvy. Laura won't let Bertha leave her, and I can't allow her to remain in this bedlam.

PASTOR: Oh, so Laura won't? Well, then, I'm afraid you are in for trouble. When she was a child if she set her mind on anything she used to play dead dog till she got it, and then likely as not she would give it back, explaining that it wasn't the thing she wanted, but having her own way.

CAPTAIN: So she was like that even then? H'm— she really gets into such a passion sometimes that I am anxious about her and afraid she is ill.

PASTOR: But what do you want to do with Bertha that is so unpardonable? Can't you compromise?

CAPTAIN: You mustn't think I want to make a prodigy of her or an image of myself. I don't want to be a procurer for my daughter and educate her exclusively for matrimony, for then if she were left unmarried she might have bitter days. On the other hand, I don't want to influence her toward a career that requires a long course of training which would be entirely thrown away if she should marry.

PASTOR: What do you want, then?

CAPTAIN: I want her to be a teacher. If she remains unmarried she will be able to support herself, and at any rate she wouldn't be any worse off than the poor schoolmasters who have to share their salaries with a family. If she marries she can use her knowledge in the education of her children. Am I right?

PASTOR: Quite right. But, on the other hand, hasn't she shown such talent for painting that it would be a great pity to crush it?

CAPTAIN: No! I have shown her sketches to an eminent painter, and he says they are only the kind of thing that can be learned at schools. But then a young fop came here in the summer who, of course, understands the matter much better, and he declared that she had colossal genius, and so that settled it to Laura's satisfaction.

PASTOR: Was he quite taken with Bertha?

CAPTAIN: That goes without saying.

PASTOR: Then God help you, old man, for in that case I see no hope. This is pretty bad—and, of course, Laura has her supporters—in there?

CAPTAIN: Yes, you may be sure of that; the whole house is already up in arms, and, between ourselves, it is not exactly a noble conflict that is being waged from that quarter.

PASTOR: Don't you think I know that?

CAPTAIN: You do?

PASTOR: I do.

CAPTAIN: But the worst of it is, it strikes me that Bertha's future is being decided from spiteful motives. They hint that men better be careful, because women can do this or that now-a-days. All day long, incessantly, it is a conflict between man and woman. Are you going? No, stay for supper. I have no special inducements to offer, but do stay. You know I am expecting the new doctor. Have you seen him?

PASTOR: I caught a glimpse of him as I came along. He looked pleasant and reliable.

CAPTAIN: That's good. Do you think it possible he may become my ally?

PASTOR: Who can tell? It depends on how much he has been among women.

CAPTAIN: But won't you really stay?

PASTOR: No thanks, my dear fellow; I promised to be home for supper, and the wife gets uneasy if I am late.

CAPTAIN: Uneasy? Angry, you mean. Well, as you will. Let me help you with your coat.

PASTOR: It's certainly pretty cold tonight. Thanks. You must take care of your health, Adolf, you seem rather nervous.

CAPTAIN: Nervous?

PASTOR: Yes, you are not really very well.

CAPTAIN: Has Laura put that into your head? She has treated me for the last twenty years as if I were at the point of death.

PASTOR: Laura? No, but you make me uneasy about you. Take care of yourself—that's my advice! Good-bye, old man; but didn't you want to talk about the confirmation?

CAPTAIN: Not at all! I assure you that matter will have to take its course in the ordinary way at the cost of the clerical conscience for I am neither a believer nor a martyr.

PASTOR: Good-bye. Love to Laura.

[Goes]

[The Captain opens his desk and seats himself at it. Takes up account books]

CAPTAIN: [Figuring] Thirty-four—nine, forty-three—seven, eight, fifty-six—

LAURA: [Coming in from inner room] Will you be kind enough?——

CAPTAIN: Just a moment! Sixty-six—seventy-one, eighty-four, eighty-nine, ninety-two, a hundred. What is it?

LAURA: Am I disturbing you?

CAPTAIN: Not at all. Housekeeping money, I suppose?

LAURA: Yes, housekeeping money.

CAPTAIN: Put the accounts down there and I will go over them.

LAURA: The accounts?

CAPTAIN: Yes.

LAURA: Am I to keep accounts now?

CAPTAIN: Of course you are to keep accounts. Our affairs are in a precarious condition, and in case of a liquidation, accounts are necessary, or one is liable to punishment for being careless.

LAURA: It's not my fault that our affairs are in a precarious condition.

CAPTAIN: That is exactly what the accounts will decide.

LAURA: It's not my fault that our tenant doesn't pay.

CAPTAIN: Who recommended this tenant so warmly? You! Why did you recommend a—good-for-nothing, we'll call him?

LAURA: But why did you rent to this good-for-nothing?

CAPTAIN: Because I was not allowed to eat in peace, nor sleep in peace, nor work in peace, till you women got that man here. You wanted him so that your brother might be rid of him, your mother wanted him because I didn't want him, the governess wanted him because he reads his Bible, and old Margret because she had known his grandmother from childhood. That's why he was taken, and if he hadn't been taken, I'd be in a madhouse by now or lying in my grave. However, here is the housekeeping money and your pin money. You may give me the accounts later.

LAURA: [Curtsies] Thanks so much. Do you too keep an account of what you spend besides the housekeeping money?

CAPTAIN: That doesn't concern you.

LAURA: No, that's true—just as little as my child's education concerns me. Have the gentlemen come to a decision after this evening's conference?

CAPTAIN: I had already come to a decision, and therefore it only remained for me to talk it over with the one friend I and the family have in common. Bertha is to go to boarding school in town, and starts in a fortnight.

LAURA: To which boarding school, if I may venture to ask?

CAPTAIN: Professor Säfberg's.

LAURA: That free thinker!

CAPTAIN: According to the law, children are to be brought up in their father's faith.

LAURA: And the mother has no voice in the matter?

CAPTAIN: None whatever. She has sold her birthright by a legal transaction, and forfeited her rights in return for the man's responsibility of caring for her and her children.

LAURA: That is to say she has no rights concerning her child.

CAPTAIN: No, none at all. When once one has sold

one's goods, one cannot have them back and still keep the money.

LAURA: But if both father and mother should agree?

CAPTAIN: Do you think that could ever happen? I want her to live in town, you want her to stay at home. The arithmetical result would be that she remain at the railway station midway between town and home. This is a knot that cannot be untied, you see.

LAURA: Then it must be broken. What did Nöjd want here?

CAPTAIN: That is an official secret.

LAURA: Which the whole kitchen knows!

CAPTAIN: Good, then you must know it.

LAURA: I do know it.

CAPTAIN: And have your judgment ready-made?

LAURA: My judgment is the judgment of the law.

CAPTAIN: But it is not written in the law who the child's father is.

LAURA: No, but one usually knows that.

CAPTAIN: Wise minds claim that one can never know.

LAURA: That's strange. Can't one ever know who the father of a child is?

CAPTAIN: No; so they claim.

LAURA: How extraordinary! How can the father have such control over the children then?

CAPTAIN: He has control only when he has assumed the responsibilities of the child, or has had them forced upon him. But in wedlock, of course, there is no doubt about the fatherhood.

LAURA: There are no doubts then?

CAPTAIN: Well, I should hope not.

LAURA: But if the wife has been unfaithful?

CAPTAIN: That's another matter. Was there anything else you wanted to say?

LAURA: Nothing.

CAPTAIN: Then I shall go up to my room, and perhaps you will be kind enough to let me know when the doctor arrives. [Closes desk and rises]

LAURA: Certainly.

[Captain goes through the private door right]

CAPTAIN: As soon as he comes. For I don't want to seem rude to him, you understand.

[Goes]

LAURA: I understand. [Looks at the money she holds in her hands]

MOTHER-IN-LAW'S VOICE: [Within] Laura!

LAURA: Yes.

MOTHER-IN-LAW'S VOICE: Is my tea ready?

LAURA: [In doorway to inner room] In just a moment.

[Laura goes toward hall door at back as the orderly opens it]

ORDERLY: Doctor Ostermark.

DOCTOR: Madam!

LAURA: [Advances and offers her hand] Welcome, Doctor—you are heartily welcome. The Captain is out, but he will be back soon.

DOCTOR: I hope you will excuse my coming so late, but I have already been called upon to pay some professional visits.

LAURA: Sit down, won't you?

DOCTOR: Thank you.

LAURA: Yes, there is a great deal of illness in the neighborhood just now, but I hope it will agree with you here. For us country people living in such isolation it is of great value to find a doctor who is interested in his patients, and I hear so many nice things of you, Doctor, that I hope the pleasantest relations will exist between us.

DOCTOR: You are indeed kind, and I hope for your sake my visits to you will not often be caused by necessity. Your family is, I believe, as a rule in good health——

LAURA: Fortunately we have been spared acute illnesses, but still things are not altogether as they should be.

DOCTOR: Indeed?

LAURA: Heaven knows, things are not as might be wished.

DOCTOR: Really, you alarm me.

LAURA: There are some circumstances in a family which through honor and conscience one is forced to conceal from the whole world——

DOCTOR: Excepting the doctor.

LAURA: Exactly. It is, therefore, my painful duty to tell you the whole truth immediately.

DOCTOR: Shouldn't we postpone this conference until I have had the honor of being introduced to the Captain?

LAURA: No! You must hear me before seeing him.

DOCTOR: It relates to him then?

LAURA: Yes, to him, my poor, dear husband.

DOCTOR: You alarm me, indeed, and believe me, I sympathize with your misfortune.

LAURA: [Taking out handkerchief] My husband's mind is affected. Now you know all, and may judge for yourself when you see him.

DOCTOR: What do you say? I have read the Captain's excellent treatises on mineralogy with admiration, and have found that they display a clear and powerful intellect.

LAURA: Really? How happy I should be if we should all prove to be mistaken.

DOCTOR: But of course it is possible that his mind might be affected in other directions.

LAURA: That is just what we fear, too. You see he has sometimes the most extraordinary ideas which, of course, one might expect in a learned man, if they did not have a disastrous effect on the welfare of his whole family. For instance, one of his whims is buying all kinds of things.

DOCTOR: That is serious; but what does he buy?

LAURA: Whole boxes of books that he never reads.

DOCTOR: There is nothing strange about a scholar's buying books.

LAURA: You don't believe what I am saying?

DOCTOR: Well, Madam, I am convinced that you believe what you are saying.

LAURA: Tell me, is it reasonable to think that one can see what is happening on another planet by looking through a microscope?

DOCTOR: Does he say he can do that?

LAURA: Yes, that's what he says.

DOCTOR: Through a microscope?

LAURA: Through a microscope, yes.

DOCTOR: This is serious, if it is so.

LAURA: If it is so! Then you have no faith in me, Doctor, and here I sit confiding the family secret to——

DOCTOR: Indeed, Madam, I am honored by your confidence, but as a physician I must investigate and observe before giving an opinion. Has the Captain ever shown any symptoms of indecision or instability of will?

LAURA: Has he! We have been married twenty years, and he has never yet made a decision without changing his mind afterward.

DOCTOR: Is he obstinate?

LAURA: He always insists on having his own way, but once he has got it he drops the whole matter and asks me to decide.

DOCTOR: This is serious, and demands close observation. The will, you see, is the mainspring of the mind, and if it is affected the whole mind goes to pieces.

LAURA: God knows how I have taught myself to humor his wishes through all these long years of trial. Oh, if you knew what a life I have endured with him—if you only knew.

DOCTOR: Your misfortune touches me deeply, and I promise you to see what can be done. I pity you with all my heart, and I beg you to trust me completely. But after what I have heard I must ask you to avoid suggesting any ideas that might make a deep impression on the patient, for in a weak brain they develop rapidly and quickly turn to monomania or fixed ideas.

LAURA: You mean to avoid arousing suspicions?

DOCTOR: Exactly. One can make the insane believe anything, just because they are receptive to everything.

LAURA: Indeed? Then I understand. Yes—yes. [*A bell rings within*] Excuse me, my mother wishes to speak to me. One moment—— ——Ah, here is Adolf.

[Captain *comes in through private door*]

CAPTAIN: Oh, here already, Doctor? You are very welcome.

DOCTOR: Captain! It is a very great pleasure to me to make the acquaintance of so celebrated a man of science.

CAPTAIN: Oh, I beg of you. The duties of service do not allow me to make any very profound investigations, but I believe I am now really on the track of a discovery.

DOCTOR: Indeed?

CAPTAIN: You see, I have submitted meteoric stones to spectrum analysis, with the result that I have found carbon, that is to say, a clear trace of organic life. What do you say to that?

DOCTOR: Can you see that with a microscope?

CAPTAIN: Lord, no—with the spectroscope.

DOCTOR: The spectroscope! Pardon. Then you will soon be able to tell us what is happening on Jupiter.

CAPTAIN: Not what is happening, but what has happened. If only the confounded book-sellers in Paris would send me the books; but I believe all the book-sellers in the universe have conspired against me. Think of it, for the last two months not a single one has ever answered my communications, neither letters nor abusive telegrams. I shall go mad over it, and I can't imagine what's the matter.

DOCTOR: Oh, I suppose it's the usual carelessness; you mustn't let it vex you so.

CAPTAIN: But the devil of it is I shall not get my treatise done in time, and I know they are working along the same lines in Berlin. But we shouldn't be talking about this—but about you. If you care to live here we have rooms for you in the wing, or perhaps you would rather live in the old quarters?

DOCTOR: Just as you like.

CAPTAIN: No, as you like. Which is it to be?

DOCTOR: You must decide that, Captain.

CAPTAIN: No, it's not for me to decide. You must say which you prefer. I have no preference in the matter, none at all.

DOCTOR: Oh, but I really cannot decide.

CAPTAIN: For heaven's sake, Doctor, say which you prefer. I have no choice in the matter, no opinion, no wishes. Haven't you got character enough to know what you want? Answer me, or I shall be provoked.

DOCTOR: Well, if it rests with me, I prefer to live here.

CAPTAIN: Thank you—forgive me, Doctor, but nothing annoys me so much as to see people undecided about anything. [*Nurse comes in*] Oh, there you are, Margret. Do you happen to know whether the rooms in the wing are in order for the Doctor?

NURSE: Yes, sir, they are.

CAPTAIN: Very well. Then I won't detain you, Doctor; you must be tired. Good-bye, and welcome once more. I shall see you tomorrow, I hope.

DOCTOR: Good evening, Captain.

CAPTAIN: I daresay that my wife explained conditions here to you a little, so that you have some idea how the land lies?

DOCTOR: Yes, your excellent wife has given me a few hints about this and that, such as were necessary to a stranger. Good evening, Captain.

CAPTAIN: [*To* Nurse] What do you want, you old dear? What is it?

NURSE: Now, little Master Adolf, just listen——

CAPTAIN: Yes, Margret, you are the only one I can listen to without having spasms.

NURSE: Now, listen, Mr. Adolf. Don't you think you should go half-way and come to an agreement with Mistress in this fuss over the child? Just think of a mother——

CAPTAIN: Think of a father, Margret.

NURSE: There, there, there. A father has something besides his child, but a mother has nothing but her child.

CAPTAIN: Just so, you old dear. She has only one burden, but I have three, and I have her burden, too. Don't you think that I should hold a better position in the world than that of a poor soldier if I had not had her and her child?

NURSE: Well, that isn't what I wanted to talk about.

CAPTAIN: I can well believe that, for you wanted to make it appear that I am in the wrong.

NURSE: Don't you believe, Mr. Adolf, that I wish you well?

CAPTAIN: Yes, dear friend, I do believe it; but you don't know what is for my good. You see it isn't enough for me to have given the child life, I want to give her my soul, too.

NURSE: Such things I don't understand. But I do think you ought to be able to agree.

CAPTAIN: You are not my friend, Margret.

NURSE: I? Oh, Lord, what are you saying, Mr. Adolf? Do you think I can forget that you were my child when you were little?

CAPTAIN: Well, you dear, have I forgotten it? You have been like a mother to me, and always have stood by me when I had everybody against me, but now, when I really need you, you desert me and go over to the enemy.

NURSE: The enemy!

CAPTAIN: Yes, the enemy! You know well enough how things are in this house! You have seen everything from the beginning.

NURSE: Indeed I have seen! But, God knows, why two people should torment the life out of each other; two people who are otherwise so good and wish all others well. Mistress is never like that to me or to others——

CAPTAIN: Only to me, I know it. But let me tell you, Margret, if you desert me now, you will do wrong. For now they have begun to weave a plot against me, and that doctor is not my friend.

NURSE: Oh, Mr. Adolf, you believe evil about everybody. But you see it's because you haven't the true faith; that's just what it is.

CAPTAIN: Yes, you and the Baptists have found the only true faith. You are indeed lucky!

NURSE: Anyway, I'm not unhappy like you, Mr. Adolf. Humble your heart and you will see that God will make you happy in your love for your neighbor.

CAPTAIN: It's a strange thing that you no sooner speak of God and love than your voice becomes hard and your eyes fill with hate. No, Margret, surely you have not the true faith.

NURSE: Yes, go on being proud and hard in your learning, but it won't amount to much when it comes to the test.

CAPTAIN: How mightily you talk, humble heart. I know very well that knowledge is of no use to you women.

NURSE: You ought to be ashamed of yourself. But in spite of everything old Margret cares most for her great big boy, and he will come back to the fold when it's stormy weather.

CAPTAIN: Margret! Forgive me, but believe me when I say that there is no one here who wishes me well but you. Help me, for I feel that something is going to happen here. What it is, I don't know, but something evil is on the way. [Scream from within] What's that? Who's that screaming?

[Bertha enters from inner room]

BERTHA: Father! Father! Help me; save me.

CAPTAIN: My dear child, what is it? Speak!

BERTHA: Help me. She wants to hurt me.

CAPTAIN: Who wants to hurt you? Tell me! Speak!

BERTHA: Grandmother! But it's my fault for I deceived her.

CAPTAIN: Tell me more.

BERTHA: Yes, but you mustn't say anything about it. Promise me you won't.

CAPTAIN: Tell me what it is then.

[Nurse goes]

BERTHA: In the evening she generally turns down the lamp and then she makes me sit at a table holding a pen over a piece of paper. And then she says that the spirits are to write.

CAPTAIN: What's all this—and you have never told me about it?

BERTHA: Forgive me, but I dared not, for Grandmother says the spirits take revenge if one talks about them. And then the pen writes, but I don't know whether I'm doing it or not. Sometimes it goes well, but sometimes it won't go at all, and when I am tired nothing comes, but she wants it to come just the same. And tonight I thought I was writing beautifully, but then Grandmother said it was all from Stagnelius, and that I had deceived her, and then she got terribly angry.

CAPTAIN: Do you believe that there are spirits?

BERTHA: I don't know.

CAPTAIN: But I know that there are none.

BERTHA: But Grandmother says that you don't understand, Father, and that you do much worse things —you who can see to other planets.

CAPTAIN: Does she say that! Does she say that? What else does she say?

BERTHA: She says that you can't work witchery

CAPTAIN: I never said that I could. You know what meteoric stones are—stones that fall from other heavenly bodies. I can examine them and learn whether they contain the same elements as our world. That is all I can tell.

BERTHA: But Grandmother says that there are things that she can see which you cannot see.

CAPTAIN: Then she lies.

BERTHA: Grandmother doesn't tell lies.

CAPTAIN: Why doesn't she?

BERTHA: Then Mother tells lies, too.

CAPTAIN: H'm!

BERTHA: And if you say that Mother lies, I can never believe in you again.

CAPTAIN: I have not said so, and so you must believe in me when I tell you that it is for your future good that you should leave home. Will you? Will you go to town and learn something useful?

BERTHA: Oh, yes, I should love to go to town, away from here, anywhere. If I can only see you sometimes—often. Oh, it is so gloomy and awful in there all the time, like a winter night, but when you come home, Father, it is like a morning in spring when they take off the double windows.

CAPTAIN: My beloved child! My dear child!

BERTHA: But, Father, you'll be good to Mother, won't you? She cries so often.

CAPTAIN: H'm—then you want to go to town?

BERTHA: Yes, yes.

CAPTAIN: But if Mother doesn't want you to go?

BERTHA: But she must let me.

CAPTAIN: But if she won't?

BERTHA: Well, then, I don't know what will happen. But she must! She must!

CAPTAIN: Will you ask her?

BERTHA: You must ask her very nicely; she wouldn't pay any attention to my asking.

CAPTAIN: H'm! Now if you wish it, and I wish it, and she doesn't wish it, what shall we do then?

BERTHA: Oh, then it will all be in a tangle again! Why can't you both——

[Laura comes in]

LAURA: Oh, so Bertha is here. Then perhaps we may have her own opinion as the question of her future has to be decided.

CAPTAIN: The child can hardly have any well-grounded opinion about what a young girl's life is likely to be, while we, on the contrary, can more easily estimate what it may be, as we have seen so many young girls grow up.

LAURA: But as we are of different opinions Bertha must be the one to decide.

CAPTAIN: No, I let no one usurp my rights, neither women nor children. Bertha, leave us.

[Bertha goes out]

LAURA: You were afraid of hearing her opinion, because you thought it would be to my advantage.

CAPTAIN: I know that she wishes to go away from home, but I know also that you possess the power of changing her mind to suit your pleasure.

LAURA: Oh, am I really so powerful?

CAPTAIN: Yes, you have a fiendish power of getting your own way; but so has anyone who does not scruple about the way it is accomplished. How did you get Doctor Norling away, for instance, and how did you get this new doctor here?

LAURA: Yes, how did I manage that?

CAPTAIN: You insulted the other one so much that he left, and made your brother recommend this fellow.

LAURA: Well, that was quite simple and legitimate. Is Bertha to leave home now?

CAPTAIN: Yes, she is to start in a fortnight.

LAURA: That is your decision?

CAPTAIN: Yes.

LAURA: Then I must try to prevent it.

CAPTAIN: You cannot.

LAURA: Can't I? Do you really think I would trust my daughter to wicked people to have her taught that everything her mother has implanted in her child is mere foolishness? Why, afterwards, she would despise me all the rest of her life!

CAPTAIN: Do you think that a father should allow ignorant and conceited women to teach his daughter that he is a charlatan?

LAURA: It means less to the father.

CAPTAIN: Why so?

LAURA: Because the mother is closer to the child, as it has been discovered that no one can tell for a certainty who the father of a child is.

CAPTAIN: How does that apply to this case?

LAURA: You do not know whether you are Bertha's father or not.

CAPTAIN: I do not know?

LAURA: No; what no one knows, you surely cannot know.

CAPTAIN: Are you joking?

LAURA: No; I am only making use of your own teaching. For that matter, how do you know that I have not been unfaithful to you?

CAPTAIN: I believe you capable of almost anything, but not that, nor that you would talk about it if it were true.

LAURA: Suppose that I was prepared to bear anything, even to being despised and driven out, everything for the sake of being able to keep and control my child, and that I am truthful now when I declare Bertha is my child, but not yours. Suppose——

CAPTAIN: Stop now!

LAURA: Just suppose this. In that case your power would be at an end.

CAPTAIN: When you had proved that I was not the father.

LAURA: That would not be difficult! Would you like me to do so?

CAPTAIN: Stop!

LAURA: Of course I should only need to declare the name of the real father, give all details of place and time. For instance—when was Bertha born? In the third year of our marriage.

CAPTAIN: Stop now, or else——

LAURA: Or else, what? Shall we stop now? Think carefully about all you do and decide, and whatever you do, don't make yourself ridiculous.

CAPTAIN: I consider all this most lamentable.

LAURA: Which makes you all the more ridiculous.

CAPTAIN: And you?

LAURA: Oh, we women are really too clever.

CAPTAIN: That's why one cannot contend with you.

LAURA: Then why provoke contests with a superior enemy?

CAPTAIN: Superior?

LAURA: Yes, it's queer, but I have never looked at a man without knowing myself to be his superior.

CAPTAIN: Then you shall be made to see your superior for once, so that you shall never forget it.

LAURA: That will be interesting.

NURSE: [*Comes in*] Supper is served. Will you come in?

LAURA: Very well.

[Captain *lingers; sits down with a magazine in an arm chair near table*]

LAURA: Aren't you coming in to supper?

CAPTAIN: No, thanks. I don't want anything.

LAURA: What, are you annoyed?

CAPTAIN: No, but I am not hungry.

LAURA: Come, or they will ask unnecessary questions—be good now. You won't? Stay there then. [*Goes*] Mr. Adolf! What is this all about?

NURSE: Mr. Adolf! What is this all about?

CAPTAIN: I don't know what it is. Can you explain to me why you women treat an old man as if he were a child?

NURSE: I don't understand it, but it must be because all you men, great and small, are women's children, every man of you.

CAPTAIN: But no women are born of men. Yes, but I am Bertha's father. Tell me, Margret, don't you believe it? Don't you?

NURSE: Lord, how silly you are. Of course you are your own child's father. Come and eat now, and don't sit there and sulk. There, there, come now.

CAPTAIN: Get out, woman. To hell with the hags. [*Goes to private door*] Svärd, Svärd!

[Orderly *comes in*]

ORDERLY: Yes, Captain.

CAPTAIN: Hitch into the covered sleigh at once.

NURSE: Captain, listen to me.

CAPTAIN: Out, woman! At once!

[Orderly *goes*]

NURSE: Good Lord, what's going to happen now? [Captain *puts on his cap and coat and prepares to go out*]

CAPTAIN: Don't expect me home before midnight. [*Goes*]

NURSE: Lord preserve us, whatever will be the end of this!

ACT II.

The same scene as in previous act. A lighted lamp is on the table; it is night. The Doctor *and* Laura *are discovered at rise of curtain.*

DOCTOR: From what I gathered during my conversation with him the case is not fully proved to me. In the first place you made a mistake in saying that he had arrived at these astonishing results about other heavenly bodies by means of a microscope. Now that I have learned that it was a spectroscope, he is not only cleared of any suspicion of insanity, but has rendered a great service to science.

LAURA: Yes, but I never said that.

DOCTOR: Madam, I made careful notes of our conversation, and I remember that I asked about this very point because I thought I had misunderstood you. One must be very careful in making such accusations when a certificate in lunacy is in question.

LAURA: A certificate in lunacy?

DOCTOR: Yes, you must surely know that an insane person loses both civil and family rights.

LAURA: No, I did not know that.

DOCTOR: There was another matter that seemed to me suspicious. He spoke of his communications to his booksellers not being answered. Permit me to ask if you, through motives of mistaken kindness, have intercepted them?

LAURA: Yes, I have. It was my duty to guard the interests of the family, and I could not let him ruin us all without some intervention.

DOCTOR: Pardon me, but I think you cannot have considered the consequences of such an act. If he discovers your secret interference in his affairs, he will have grounds for suspicions, and they will grow like an avalanche. And besides, in doing this you have thwarted his will and irritated him still more. You must have felt yourself how the mind rebels when one's deepest desires are thwarted and one's will is crossed.

LAURA: Haven't I felt that!

DOCTOR: Think, then, what he must have gone through.

LAURA: [*Rising*] It is midnight and he hasn't come home. Now we may fear the worst.

DOCTOR: But tell me what actually happened this evening after I left. I must know everything.

LAURA: He raved in the wildest way and had the strangest ideas. For instance, that he is not the father of his child.

DOCTOR: That is strange. How did such an idea come into his head?

LAURA: I really can't imagine, unless it was because he had to question one of the men about supporting a child, and when I tried to defend the girl, he grew excited and said no one could tell who was the father of the child. God knows I did everything to calm him, but now I believe there is no help for him. [*Cries*]

DOCTOR: But this cannot go on. Something must be done here without, of course, arousing his suspicions. Tell me, has the Captain ever had such delusions before?

LAURA: Six years ago things were in the same state, and then he, himself, confessed in his own letter to the doctor that he feared for his reason.

DOCTOR: Yes, yes, yes, this is a story that has deep roots and the sanctity of the family life—and so on—of course I cannot ask about everything, but must limit myself to appearances. What is done can't be undone, more's the pity, yet the remedy should be based upon all the past.—Where do you think he is now?

LAURA: I have no idea, he has such wild streaks.

DOCTOR: Would you like to have me stay until he returns? To avoid suspicion, I could say that I had come to see your mother who is not well.

LAURA: Yes, that will do very nicely. Don't leave us, Doctor; if you only knew how troubled I am! But wouldn't it be better to tell him outright what you think of his condition?

DOCTOR: We never do that unless the patient mentions the subject himself, and very seldom even then. It depends entirely on the case. But we mustn't sit here; perhaps I had better go into the next room; it will look more natural.

LAURA: Yes, that will be better, and Margret can sit here. She always waits up when he is out, and she is the only one who has any power over him. [*Goes to the door left*] Margret, Margret!

NURSE: Yes, Ma'am. Has the master come home?

LAURA: No; but you are to sit here and wait for him, and when he does come you are to say my mother is ill and that's why the doctor is here.

NURSE: Yes, yes. I'll see that everything is all right.

LAURA: [*Opens the door to inner rooms*] Will you come in here, Doctor?

DOCTOR: Thank you.

[Nurse *seats herself at the table and takes up a hymn book and spectacles and reads*]

NURSE: Ah, yes, ah, yes! [*Reads half aloud*]
    Ah woe is me, how sad a thing
    Is life within this vale of tears,
    Death's angel triumphs like a king,
    And calls aloud to all the spheres—
      Vanity, all is vanity.
Yes, yes! Yes, yes!
[*Reads again*]
    All that on earth hath life and breath
    To earth must fall before his spear,
    And sorrow, saved alone from death,
    Inscribes above the mighty bier.
      Vanity, all is vanity.
Yes, Yes.

BERTHA: [*Comes in with a coffee-pot and some embroidery. She speaks in a low voice*] Margret, may I sit with you? It is so frightfully lonely up there.

NURSE: For goodness sake, are you still up, Bertha?

BERTHA: You see I want to finish Father's Christmas present. And here's something that you'll like.

NURSE: But bless my soul, this won't do. You must be up in the morning, and it's after midnight now.

BERTHA: What does it matter? I don't dare sit up there alone. I believe the spirits are at work.

NURSE: You see, just what I've said. Mark my words, this house was not built on a lucky spot. What did you hear?

BERTHA: Think of it, I heard some one singing up in the attic!

NURSE: In the attic? At this hour?

BERTHA: Yes, it was such a sorrowful, melancholy song! I never heard anything like it. It sounded as if it came from the store-room, where the cradle stands, you know, to the left——

NURSE: Dear me, dear me! And such a fearful night. It seems as if the chimneys would blow down. "Ah, what is then this earthly life. But grief, affliction and great strife? E'en when fairest it has seemed, Nought but pain it can be deemed." Ah, dear child, may God give us a good Christmas!

BERTHA: Margret, is it true that Father is ill?

NURSE: Yes, I'm afraid he is.

BERTHA: Then we can't keep Christmas Eve? But how can he be up and around if he is ill?

NURSE: You see, my child, the kind of illness he has doesn't keep him from being up. Hush, there's some one out in the hall. Go to bed now and take the coffeepot away or the master will be angry.

BERTHA: [*Going out with tray*] Good night, Margret.

NURSE: Good night, my child. God bless you.
[Captain *comes in, takes off his overcoat*]

CAPTAIN: Are you still up? Go to bed.

NURSE: I was only waiting till——
[Captain *lights a candle, opens his desk, sits down at it and takes letters and newspapers out of his pocket*]

NURSE: Mr. Adolf.

CAPTAIN: What do you want?

NURSE: Old mistress is ill and the doctor is here.

CAPTAIN: Is it anything dangerous?

NURSE: No, I don't think so. Just a cold.

CAPTAIN: [*Gets up*] Margret, who was the father of your child?

NURSE: Oh, I've told you many and many a time; it was that scamp Johansson.

CAPTAIN: Are you sure that it was he?

NURSE: How childish you are; of course I'm sure when he was the only one.

CAPTAIN: Yes, but was he sure that he was the only one? No, he could not be, but you could be sure of it. There is a difference, you see.

NURSE: Well, I can't see any difference.

CAPTAIN: No, you cannot see it, but the difference exists, nevertheless. [*Turns over the pages of a photograph album which is on the table*] Do you think Bertha looks like me?

NURSE: Of course! Why, you are as like as two peas.

CAPTAIN: Did Johansson confess that he was the father?

NURSE: He was forced to!

CAPTAIN: How terrible! Here is the Doctor. [Doctor *comes in*] Good evening, Doctor. How is my mother-in-law?

DOCTOR: Oh, it's nothing serious; merely a slight sprain of the left ankle.

CAPTAIN: I thought Margret said it was a cold.

There seem to be different opinions about the same case. Go to bed, Margret.

[Nurse *goes. A pause*]

CAPTAIN: Sit down, Doctor.

DOCTOR: [*Sits*] Thanks.

CAPTAIN: Is it true that you obtain striped foals if you cross a zebra and a mare?

DOCTOR: [*Astonished*] Perfectly true.

CAPTAIN: Is it true that the foals continue to be striped if the breed is continued with a stallion?

DOCTOR: Yes, that is true, too.

CAPTAIN: That is to say, under certain conditions a stallion can be sire to striped foals or the opposite?

DOCTOR: Yes, so it seems.

CAPTAIN: Therefore an offspring's likeness to the father proves nothing?

DOCTOR: Well——

CAPTAIN: That is to say, paternity cannot be proven.

DOCTOR: H'm——well——

CAPTAIN: You are a widower, aren't you, and have had children?

DOCTOR: Ye-es.

CAPTAIN: Didn't you ever feel ridiculous as a father? I know of nothing so ludicrous as to see a father leading his children by the hand around the streets, or to hear a father talk about his children. "My wife's children," he ought to say. Did you ever feel how false your position was? Weren't you ever afflicted with doubts, I won't say suspicions, for, as a gentleman, I assume that your wife was above suspicion.

DOCTOR: No, really, I never was; but, Captain, I believe Goethe says a man must take his children on good faith.

CAPTAIN: It's risky to take anything on good faith where a woman is concerned.

DOCTOR: Oh, there are so many kinds of women.

CAPTAIN: Modern investigations have pronounced that there is only one kind! Lately I have recalled two instances in my life that make me believe this. When I was young I was strong and, if I may boast, handsome. Once when I was making a trip on a steamer and sitting with a few friends in the saloon, the young stewardess came and flung herself down by me, burst into tears, and told us that her sweetheart was drowned. We sympathized with her, and I ordered some champagne. After the second glass I touched her foot; after the fourth her knee, and before morning I had consoled her.

DOCTOR: That was just a winter fly.

CAPTAIN: Now comes the second instance—and that was a real summer fly. I was at Lysekil. There was a young married woman stopping there with her children, but her husband was in town. She was religious, had extremely strict principles, preached morals to me, and was, I believe, entirely honorable. I lent her a book, two books, and when she was leaving, she returned them, strange to say! Three months later, in those very books I found her card with a declaration on it. It was innocent, as innocent as a declaration of love can be from a married woman to a strange man who never made any advances. Now comes the moral. Just don't have too much faith.

DOCTOR: Don't have too little faith, either.

CAPTAIN: No, but just enough. But, you see, Doctor, that woman was so unconsciously dishonest that she talked to her husband about the fancy she had taken to me. That's what makes it dangerous, this very unconsciousness of their instinctive dishonesty. That is a mitigating circumstance, I admit, but it cannot nullify judgment, only soften it.

DOCTOR: Captain, your thoughts are taking a morbid turn, and you ought to control them.

CAPTAIN: You must not use the word morbid. Steam boilers, as you know, explode at a certain pressure, but the same pressure is not needed for all boiler explosions. You understand? However, you are here to watch me. If I were not a man I should have the right to make accusations or complaints, as they are so cleverly called, and perhaps I should be able to give you the whole diagnosis, and, what is more, the history of my disease. But unfortunately, I am a man, and there is nothing for me to do but, like a Roman, fold my arms across my breast and hold my breath till I die.

DOCTOR: Captain, if you are ill, it will not reflect upon your honor as a man to tell me all. In fact, I ought to hear the other side.

CAPTAIN: You have had enough in hearing the one, I imagine. Do you know when I heard Mrs. Alving eulogizing her dead husband, I thought to myself what a damned pity it was the fellow was dead. Do you suppose that he would have spoken if he had been alive? And do you suppose that if any of the dead husbands came back they would be believed? Good night, Doctor. You see that I am calm, and you can retire without fear.

DOCTOR: Good night, then, Captain. I'm afraid I can be of no further use in this case.

CAPTAIN: Are we enemies?

DOCTOR: Far from it. But it is too bad we cannot be friends. Good night.

[*Goes. The* Captain *follows the* Doctor *to the door at back and then goes to the door at left and opens it slightly*]

CAPTAIN: Come in, and we'll talk. I heard you out there listening. [Laura, *embarrassed*. Captain *sits at desk*] It is late, but we must come to some decision. Sit down. [*Pause*] I have been at the post office tonight to get my letters. From these it appears that you have been keeping back my mail, both coming and going. The consequence of which is that the loss of time has as good as destroyed the result I expected from my work.

LAURA: It was an act of kindness on my part, as you neglected the service for this other work.

CAPTAIN: It was hardly kindness, for you were quite sure that some day I should win more honor from that than from the service; but you were particularly anxious that I should not win such honors, for fear your own insignificance would be emphasized by it. In consequence of all this I have intercepted letters addressed to you.

LAURA: That was a noble act.

CAPTAIN: You see, you have, as you might say, a high opinion of me. It appears from these letters that for some time past you have been arraying my old friends against me by spreading reports about my mental condition. And you have succeeded in your efforts, for now not more than one person exists from the Colonel down to the cook, who believes that I am sane. Now these are the facts about my illness; my mind is sound, as you know, so that I can take care of my duties in the service as well as my responsibilities as a father; my feelings are more or less under my control, as my will has not been completely undermined; but you have gnawed and nibbled at it so that it will soon slip the cogs, and then the whole mechanism will slip and go to smash. I will not appeal to your feelings, for you have none; that is your strength; but I will appeal to your interests.

LAURA: Let me hear.

CAPTAIN: You have succeeded to such an extent that my judgment is no longer clear, and my thoughts begin to wander. This is the approaching insanity that you are waiting for, which may come at any time now. So you are face to face with the question whether it is more to your interest that I should be sane or insane. Consider. If I go under I shall lose the service, and where will you be then? If I die, my life insurance will fall to you. But if I take my own life, you will get nothing. Consequently, it is to your interest that I should live out my life.

LAURA: Is this a trap?

CAPTAIN: To be sure. But it rests with you whether you will run around it or stick your head into it.

LAURA: You say that you will kill yourself! You won't do that!

CAPTAIN: Are you sure? Do you think a man can live when he has nothing and no one to live for?

LAURA: You surrender, then?

CAPTAIN: No, I offer peace.

LAURA: The conditions?

CAPTAIN: That I may keep my reason. Free me from my suspicions and I give up the conflict.

LAURA: What suspicions?

CAPTAIN: About Bertha's origin.

LAURA: Are there any doubts about that?

CAPTAIN: Yes, I have doubts, and you have awakened them.

LAURA: I?

CAPTAIN: Yes, you have dropped them like henbane in my ears, and circumstances have strengthened them. Free me from the uncertainty; tell me outright that it is true and I will forgive you beforehand.

LAURA: How can I acknowledge a sin that I have not committed?

CAPTAIN: What does it matter when you know that I shall not divulge it? Do you think a man would go and spread his own shame broadcast?

LAURA: If I say it isn't true, you won't be convinced; but if I say it is, then you will be convinced. You seem to hope it is true!

CAPTAIN: Yes, strangely enough; it must be, because the first supposition can't be proved; the latter can be.

LAURA: Have you any ground for your suspicions?

CAPTAIN: Yes, and no.

LAURA: I believe you want to prove me guilty, so that you can get rid of me and then have absolute control over the child. But you won't catch me in any such snare.

CAPTAIN: Do you think that I would want to be responsible for another man's child, if I were convinced of your guilt?

LAURA: No, I'm sure you wouldn't, and that's what makes me know you lied just now when you said that you would forgive me beforehand.

CAPTAIN: [Rises] Laura, save me and my reason. You don't seem to understand what I say. If the child is not mine I have no control over her and don't want to have any, and that is precisely what you do want, isn't it? But perhaps you want even more—to have power over the child, but still have me to support you.

LAURA: Power, yes! What has this whole life and death struggle been for but power?

CAPTAIN: To me it has meant more. I do not believe in a hereafter; the child was my future life. That was my conception of immortality, and perhaps the only one that has any analogy in reality. If you take that away from me, you cut off my life.

LAURA: Why didn't we separate in time?

CAPTAIN: Because the child bound us together, but the link became a chain. And how did it happen, how? I have never thought about this, but now memories rise up accusingly, condemningly perhaps. We had been married two years, and had no children; you know why. I fell ill and lay at the point of death. During a conscious interval of the fever I heard voices out in the drawing-room. It was you and the lawyer talking about the fortune that I still possessed. He explained that you could inherit nothing because we had no children, and he asked you if you were expecting to become a mother. I did not hear you reply. I recovered and we had a child. Who is its father?

LAURA: You.

CAPTAIN: No, I am not. Here is a buried crime that begins to stench, and what a hellish crime! You women have been compassionate enough to free the black slaves, but you have kept the white ones. I have worked and slaved for you, your child, your mother, your servants; I have sacrificed promotion and career; I have endured torture, flagellation, sleeplessness, worry for your sake, until my hair has grown gray; and all that you might enjoy a life without care, and when you grew old, enjoy life over again in your child. I have borne everything without complaint, because I thought myself the father of your child. This is the commonest kind of theft, the most brutal slavery. I have had seventeen years of penal servitude and have been innocent. What can you give me in return for that?

LAURA: Now you are quite mad.

CAPTAIN: That is your hope!—And I see how you have labored to conceal your crime. I sympathized with you because I did not understand your grief. I have often lulled your evil conscience to rest when I thought I was driving away morbid thoughts. I have heard you cry out in your sleep and not wanted to listen. I remember now night before last—Bertha's birthday—it was between two and three in the morning, and I was sitting up reading; you shrieked, "Don't, don't!" as if someone were strangling you; I knocked on the wall—I didn't want to hear any more. I have had my suspicions for a long time but I did not dare to hear them confirmed. All this I have suffered for you. What will you do for me?

LAURA: What can I do? I will swear by God and all I hold sacred that you are Bertha's father.

CAPTAIN: What use is that when you have often said that a mother can and ought to commit any crime for her child? I implore you as a wounded man begs for a death-blow, to tell me all. Don't you see I'm as helpless as a child? Don't you hear me complaining as to a mother? Won't you forget that I am a man, that I am a soldier who can tame men and beasts with a word? Like a sick man I only ask for compassion. I lay down the tokens of my power and implore you to have mercy on my life.

[Laura *approaches him and lays her hand on his brow*]

LAURA: What! You are crying, man!

CAPTAIN: Yes, I am crying although I am a man. But has not a man eyes? Has not a man hands, limbs, senses, thoughts, passions? Is he not fed with the same food, hurt by the same weapons, warmed and cooled by the same summer and winter as a woman? If you prick us do we not bleed? If you tickle us do we not laugh? And if you poison us, do we not die? Why shouldn't a man complain, a soldier weep? Because it is unmanly? Why is it unmanly?

LAURA: Weep then, my child, as if you were with your mother once more. Do you remember when I first came into your life, I was like a second mother? Your great strong body needed nerves; you were a giant child that had either come too early into the world, or perhaps was not wanted at all.

CAPTAIN: Yes, that's how it was. My father's and my mother's will was against my coming into the world, and consequently I was born without a will. I thought I was completing myself when you and I became one, and therefore you were allowed to rule, and I, the commander at the barracks and before the troops, became obedient to you, grew through you, looked up to you as to a more highly-gifted being, listened to you as if I had been your undeveloped child.

LAURA: Yes, that's the way it was, and therefore I loved you as my child. But you know, you must have seen, when the nature of your feelings changed and you appeared as my lover that I blushed, and your embraces were joy that was followed by a remorseful conscience as if my blood were ashamed. The mother became the mistress. Ugh!

CAPTAIN: I saw it, but I did not understand. I believed you despised me for my unmanliness, and I wanted to win you as a woman by being a man.

LAURA: Yes, but there was the mistake. The mother was your friend, you see, but the woman was your enemy, and love between the sexes is strife. Do not think that I gave myself; I did not give, but I took—what I wanted. But you had one advantage. I felt that, and I wanted you to feel it.

CAPTAIN: You always had the advantage. You could hypnotize me when I was wide awake, so that I neither saw nor heard, but merely obeyed; you could give me a raw potato and make me imagine it was a peach; you could force me to admire your foolish caprices as though they were strokes of genius. You could have influenced me to crime, yes, even to mean, paltry deeds. Because you lacked intelligence, instead of carrying out my ideas you acted on your own judgment. But when at last I awoke, I realized that my honor had been corrupted and I wanted to blot out the memory by a great deed, an achievement, a discovery, or an honorable suicide. I wanted to go to war, but was not permitted. It was then that I threw myself into science. And now when I was about to reach out my hand to gather in its fruits, you chop off my arm. Now I am dishonored and can live no longer, for a man cannot live without honor.

LAURA: But a woman?

CAPTAIN: Yes, for she has her children, which he has not. But, like the rest of mankind, we lived our lives unconscious as children, full of imagination, ideals, and illusions, and then we awoke; it was all over. But we awoke with our feet on the pillow, and he who waked us was himself a sleep-walker. When women grow old and cease to be women, they get beards on their chins; I wonder what men get when they grow old and cease to be men. Those who crowed were no longer cocks, but capons, and the pullets answered their call, so that when we thought the sun was about to rise we found ourselves in the bright moonlight amid ruins, just as in the good old times. It had only been a little morning slumber with wild dreams, and there was no awakening.

LAURA: Do you know, you should have been a poet!

CAPTAIN: Who knows.

LAURA: Now I am sleepy, so if you have any more fantastic visions keep them till tomorrow.

CAPTAIN: First, a word more about realities. Do you hate me?

LAURA: Yes, sometimes, when you are a man.

CAPTAIN: This is like race hatred. If it is true that we are descended from monkeys, at least it must be from two separate species. We are certainly not like one another, are we?

LAURA: What do you mean to say by all this?

CAPTAIN: I feel that one of us must go under in this struggle.

LAURA: Which?

CAPTAIN: The weaker, of course.

LAURA: And the stronger will be in the right?

CAPTAIN: Always, since he has the power.

LAURA: Then I am in the right.

CAPTAIN: Have you the power already, then?

LAURA: Yes, and a legal power with which I shall put you under the control of a guardian.

CAPTAIN: Under a guardian?

LAURA: And then I shall educate my child without listening to your fantastic notions.

CAPTAIN: And who will pay for the education when I am no longer here?

LAURA: Your pension will pay for it.

CAPTAIN: [Threateningly] How can you have me put under a guardian?

LAURA: [Takes out a letter] With this letter of which an attested copy is in the hands of the board of lunacy.

CAPTAIN: What letter?

LAURA: [Moving backward toward the door left] Yours! Your declaration to the doctor that you are insane. [The Captain stares at her in silence] Now you have fulfilled your function as an unfortunately necessary father and breadwinner, you are not needed any longer and you must go. You must go, since you have realized that my intellect is as strong as my will, and since you will not stay and acknowledge it.

[The Captain goes to the table, seizes the lighted lamp and hurls it at Laura, who disappears backward through the door]

CURTAIN DROP.

ACT III.

Same Scene. Another lamp on the table. The private door is barricaded with a chair.

LAURA: [To Nurse] Did he give you the keys?

NURSE: Give them to me, no! God help me, but I took them from the master's clothes that Nöjd had out to brush.

LAURA: Oh, Nöjd is on duty today?

NURSE: Yes, Nöjd.

LAURA: Give me the keys.

NURSE: Yes, but this seems like downright stealing. Do you hear him walking up there, Ma'am? Back and forth, back and forth.

LAURA: Is the door well barred?

NURSE: Oh, yes, it's barred well enough!

LAURA: Control your feelings, Margret. We must be calm if we are to be saved. [Knock] Who is it?

NURSE: [Opens door to hall] It is Nöjd.

LAURA: Let him come in.

NÖJD: [Comes in] A message from the Colonel.

LAURA: Give it to me. [Reads] Ah!—Nöjd, have you taken all the cartridges out of the guns and pouches?

NÖJD: Yes, Ma'am.

LAURA: Good, wait outside while I answer the Colonel's letter.

[Nöjd goes. Laura writes]

NURSE: Listen. What in the world is he doing up there now?

LAURA: Be quiet while I write.

[The sound of sawing is heard]

NURSE: [Half to herself] Oh, God have mercy on us all! Where will this end!

LAURA: Here, give this to Nöjd. And my mother must not know anything about all this. Do you hear?

[Nurse goes out, Laura opens drawers in desk and takes out papers. The Pastor comes in, he takes a chair and sits near Laura by the desk]

PASTOR: Good evening, sister. I have been away all day, as you know, and only just got back. Terrible things have been happening here.

LAURA: Yes, brother, never have I gone through such a night and such a day.

PASTOR: I see that you are none the worse for it all.

LAURA: No, God be praised, but think what might have happened!

PASTOR: Tell me one thing, how did it begin? I have heard so many different versions.

LAURA: It began with his wild idea of not being Bertha's father, and ended with his throwing the lighted lamp in my face.

PASTOR: But this is dreadful! It is fully developed insanity. And what is to be done now?

LAURA: We must try to prevent further violence and the doctor has sent to the hospital for a strait-jacket. In the meantime I have sent a message to the Colonel, and I am now trying to straighten out the affairs of the household, which he has carried on in a most reprehensible manner.

PASTOR: This is a deplorable story, but I have always expected something of the sort. Fire and powder must end in an explosion. What have you got in the drawer there?

LAURA: [Has pulled out a drawer in the desk] Look, he has hidden everything here.

PASTOR: [Looking into drawer] Good Heavens, here is your doll and here is your christening cap and Bertha's rattle; and your letters; and the locket [Wipes his eyes] After all he must have loved you very dearly, Laura. I never kept such things!

LAURA: I believe he used to love me, but time—time changes so many things.

PASTOR: What is that big paper? The receipt for a grave! Yes, better the grave than the lunatic asylum! Laura, tell me, are you blameless in all this?

LAURA: I? Why should I be to blame because a man goes out of his mind?

PASTOR: Well, well, I shan't say anything. After all, blood is thicker than water.

LAURA: What do you dare to intimate?

PASTOR: [*Looking at her penetratingly*] Now, listen!

LAURA: Yes?

PASTOR: You can hardly deny that it suits you pretty well to be able to educate your child as you wish?

LAURA: I don't understand.

PASTOR: How I admire you!

LAURA: Me? H'm!

PASTOR: And I am to become the guardian of that free-thinker! Do you know I have always looked on him as a weed in our garden.

[Laura *gives a short laugh, and then becomes suddenly serious*]

LAURA: And you dare say that to me—his wife?

PASTOR: You are strong, Laura, incredibly strong. You are like a fox in a trap, you would rather gnaw off your own leg than let yourself be caught! Like a master thief—no accomplice, not even your own conscience. Look at yourself in the glass! You dare not!

LAURA: I never use a looking glass!

PASTOR: No, you dare not! Let me look at your hand. Not a tell-tale blood stain, not a trace of insidious poison! A little innocent murder that the law cannot reach, an unconscious crime—unconscious! What a splendid idea! Do you hear how he is working up there? Take care! If that man gets loose he will make short work of you.

LAURA: You talk so much, you must have a bad conscience. Accuse me if you can!

PASTOR: I cannot.

LAURA: You see! You cannot, and therefore I am innocent. You take care of your ward, and I will take care of mine! Here's the doctor.

[Doctor *comes in*]

LAURA: [*Rising*] Good evening, Doctor. You at least will help me, won't you? But unfortunately there is not much that can be done. Do you hear how he is carrying on up there? Are you convinced now?

DOCTOR: I am convinced that an act of violence has been committed, but the question now is whether that act of violence can be considered an outbreak of passion or madness.

PASTOR: But apart from the actual outbreak, you must acknowledge that he has "fixed ideas."

DOCTOR: I think that your ideas, Pastor, are much more fixed.

PASTOR: My settled views about the highest things are——

DOCTOR: We'll leave settled views out of this. Madam, it rests with you to decide whether your husband is guilty to the extent of imprisonment and fine or should be put in an asylum! How do you class his behavior?

LAURA: I cannot answer that now.

DOCTOR: That is to say you have no decided opinion as to what will be most advantageous to the interests of the family? What do you say, Pastor?

PASTOR: Well, there will be a scandal in either case. It is not easy to say.

LAURA: But if he is only sentenced to a fine for violence, he will be able to repeat the violence.

DOCTOR: And if he is sent to prison he will soon be out again. Therefore we consider it most advantageous for all parties that he should be immediately treated as insane. Where is the nurse?

LAURA: Why?

DOCTOR: She must put the straitjacket on the patient when I have talked to him and given the order! But not before. I have—the garment out here. [*Goes out into the hall and returns with a large bundle*] Please ask the nurse to come in here.

[Laura *rings*]

PASTOR: Dreadful! Dreadful!

[Nurse *comes in*]

DOCTOR: [*Takes out the straitjacket*] I want you to pay attention to this. We want you to slip this jacket on the Captain, from behind, you understand, when I find it necessary to prevent another outbreak of violence. You notice it has very long sleeves to prevent his moving and they are to be tied at the back. Here are two straps that go through buckles which are afterwards fastened to the arm of a chair or the sofa or whatever is convenient. Will you do it?

NURSE: No, Doctor, I can't do that; I can't.

LAURA: Why don't you do it yourself, Doctor?

DOCTOR: Because the patient distrusts me. You, Madam, would seem to be the one to do it, but I fear he distrusts even you.

[Laura's *face changes for an instant*]

DOCTOR: Perhaps you, Pastor——

PASTOR: No, I must ask to be excused.

[Nöjd *comes in*]

LAURA: Have you delivered the message already?

NÖJD: Yes, Madam.

DOCTOR: Oh, is it you, Nöjd? You know the circumstances here, you know that the Captain is out of his mind and you must help us to take care of him.

NÖJD: If there is anything I can do for the Captain, you may be sure I will do it.

DOCTOR: You must put this jacket on him——

NURSE: No, he shan't touch him. Nöjd might hurt him. I would rather do it myself, very, very gently. But Nöjd can wait outside and help me if necessary. He can do that.

[*There is loud knocking on the private door*]

DOCTOR: There he is! Put the jacket under your shawl on the chair, and you must all go out for the time being and the Pastor and I will receive him, for that door will not hold out many minutes. Now go.

NURSE: [*Going out left*] The Lord help us!

[Laura *locks desk, then goes out left. Nöjd goes out back. After a moment the private door is forced open, with such violence that the lock is broken and the chair is thrown into the middle of the room. The* Captain *comes in with a pile of books under his arm, which he puts on the table*]

CAPTAIN: The whole thing is to be read here, in every book. So I wasn't out of my mind after all! Here it is in the *Odyssey,* book first, verse 215, page 6, of the Upsala translation. It is Telemachus speaking to Athene. "My mother indeed maintains that he, Odysseus, is my father, but I myself know it not, for no man yet hath known his own origin." And this suspicion is harbored by Telemachus about Penelope, the most virtuous of women! Beautiful, eh? And here we have the prophet Ezekiel: "The fool saith; behold here is my father, but who can tell whose loins engendered him." That's quite clear! And what have we here? The *History of Russian Literature* by Mersläkow. Alexander Pushkin, Russia's greatest poet, died of torture from the reports circulated about his wife's unfaithfulness rather than by the bullet in his breast from a duel. On his death-bed he swore she was innocent. Ass, ass! How could he swear to it! You see, I read my books. Ah, Jonas, are you here? and the doctor, naturally. Have you heard what I answered when an English lady complained about Irishmen who used to throw lighted lamps in their wives' faces? "God, what women," I cried. "Women," she gasped. "Yes, of course," I answered. "When things go so far that a man, a man who loved and worshipped a woman, takes a lighted lamp and throws it in her face, then one may know."

PASTOR: Know what?

CAPTAIN: Nothing. One never knows anything. One only believes. Isn't that true, Jonas? One believes and then one is saved! Yes, to be sure. No, I know that one can be damned by his faith. I know that.

DOCTOR: Captain!

CAPTAIN: Silence! I don't want to talk to you; I won't listen to you repeating their chatter in there, like a telephone! In there! You know! Look here, Jonas; do you believe that you are the father of your children? I remember that you had a tutor in your house who had a handsome face, and the people gossiped about him.

PASTOR: Adolf, take care!

CAPTAIN: Grope under your toupee and feel if there are not two bumps there. By my soul, I believe he turns pale! Yes, yes, they will talk; but, good Lord, they talk so much. Still we are a lot of ridiculous dupes, we married men. Isn't that true, Doctor? How was it with your marriage bed? Didn't you have a lieutenant in the house, eh? Wait a moment and I will make a guess—his name was— [*Whispers in the* Doctor's *ear*] You see he turns pale, too! Don't be disturbed. She is dead and buried and what is done can't be undone. I knew him well, by the way, and he is now—look at me, Doctor— No, straight in my eyes—a major in the cavalry!

By God, if I don't believe he has horns, too.

DOCTOR: [*Tortured*] Captain, won't you talk about something else?

CAPTAIN: Do you see? He immediately wants to talk of something else when I mention horns.

PASTOR: Do you know, Adolf, that you are insane?

CAPTAIN: Yes; I know that well enough. But if I only had the handling of your illustrious brains for awhile I'd soon have you shut up, too! I am mad, but how did I become so? That doesn't concern you, and it doesn't concern anyone. But you want to talk of something else now. [*Takes a photograph album from the table*] Good Lord, that is my child! Mine? We can never know. Do you know what we would have to do to make sure? First, one should marry to get the respect of society, then be divorced soon after and become lovers, and finally adopt the children. Then one would at least be sure that they were one's adopted children. Isn't that right? But how can all that help us now? What can keep me now that you have taken my conception of immortality from me, what use is science and philosophy to me when I have nothing to live for, what can I do with life when I am dishonored? I grafted my right arm, half my brain, half my marrow on another trunk, for I believed they would knit themselves together and grow into a more perfect tree, and then someone came with a knife and cut below the graft, and now I am only half a tree. But the other half goes on growing with my arm and half my brain, while I wither and die, for they were the best parts I gave away. Now I want to die. Do with me as you will. I am no more.

[*Buries his head on his arms on table. The* Doctor *whispers to the* Pastor, *and they go out through the door left. Soon after* Bertha *comes in*]

BERTHA: [*Goes up to* Captain] Are you ill, Father?

CAPTAIN: [*Looks up dazed*] I?

BERTHA: Do you know what you have done? Do you know that you threw the lamp at Mother?

CAPTAIN: Did I?

BERTHA: Yes, you did. Just think if she had been hurt.

CAPTAIN: What would that have mattered?

BERTHA: You are not my father when you talk like that.

CAPTAIN: What do you say? Am I not your father? How do you know that? Who told you that? And who is your father, then? Who?

BERTHA: Not you at any rate.

CAPTAIN: Still not I? Who, then? Who? You seem to be well informed. Who told you? That I should live to see my child come and tell me to my face that I am not her father! But don't you know that you disgrace your mother when you say that? Don't you know that it is to her shame if it is so?

BERTHA: Don't say anything bad about Mother; do you hear?

CAPTAIN: No; you hold together, every one of

you, against me! and you have always done so.

BERTHA: Father!

CAPTAIN: Don't use that word again!

BERTHA: Father, father!

CAPTAIN: [Draws her to him] Bertha, dear, dear child, you are my child! Yes. Yes; it cannot be otherwise. It is so. The other was only sickly thoughts that come with the wind like pestilence and fever. Look at me that I may see my soul in your eyes!— But I see her soul, too! You have two souls and you love me with one and hate me with the other. But you must only love me! You must have only one soul, or you will never have peace, nor I either. You must have only one mind, which is the child of my mind and one will, which is my will.

BERTHA: But I don't want to, I want to be myself.

CAPTAIN: You must not. You see, I am a cannibal, and I want to eat you. Your mother wanted to eat me, but she was not allowed to. I am Saturn who ate his children because it had been prophesied that they would eat him. To eat or be eaten! That is the question. If I do not eat you, you will eat me, and you have already shown your teeth! But don't be frightened, my dear child; I won't harm you. [Goes and takes a revolver from the wall]

BERTHA: [Trying to escape] Help, Mother, help, he wants to kill me.

NURSE: [Comes in] Mr. Adolf, what is it?

CAPTAIN: [Examining revolver] Have you taken out the cartridges?

NURSE: Yes, I put them away when I was tidying up, but sit down and be quiet and I'll get them out again!

[She takes the Captain by the arm and gets him into a chair, into which he sinks feebly. Then she takes out the straitjacket and goes behind the chair. Bertha slips out left]

NURSE: Mr. Adolf, do you remember when you were my dear little boy and I tucked you in at night and used to repeat: "God who holds his children dear" to you, and do you remember how I used to get up in the night and give you a drink, how I would light the candle and tell you stories when you had bad dreams and couldn't sleep? Do you remember all that?

CAPTAIN: Go on talking, Margret, it soothes my head so. Tell me some more.

NURSE: O yes, but you must listen then! Do you remember when you took the big kitchen knife and wanted to cut out boats with it, and how I came in and had to get the knife away by fooling you? You were just a little child who didn't understand, so I had to fool you, for you didn't know that it was for your own good. "Give me that snake," I said, "or it will bite you!" and then you let go of the knife. [Takes the revolver out of the Captain's hand] And then when you had to be dressed and didn't want to, I had to coax you and say that you should have a coat of gold and be dressed like a prince. And then I took your little blouse that was just made of green wool and held it in front of you

and said: "In with both arms," and then I said, "Now sit nice and still while I button it down the back," [She puts the straitjacket on] and then I said, "Get up now, and walk across the floor like a good boy so I can see how it fits." [She leads him to the sofa] And then I said, "Now you must go to bed."

CAPTAIN: What did you say? Was I to go to bed when I was dressed—damnation! what have you done to me? [Tries to get free] Ah! you cunning devil of a woman! Who would have thought you had so much wit. [Lies down on sofa] Trapped, shorn, outwitted, and not to be able to die!

NURSE: Forgive me, Mr. Adolf, forgive me, but I wanted to keep you from killing your child.

CAPTAIN: Why didn't you let me? You say life is hell and death the kingdom of heaven, and children belong to heaven.

NURSE: How do you know what comes after death?

CAPTAIN: That is the only thing we do know, but of life we know nothing! Oh, if one had only known from the beginning.

NURSE: Mr. Adolf, humble your hard heart and cry to God for mercy; it is not yet too late. It was not too late for the thief on the cross, when the Saviour said, "Today shalt thou be with me in Paradise."

CAPTAIN: Are you croaking for a corpse already, you old crow?

[Nurse takes a hymn book out of her pocket]

CAPTAIN: [Calls] Nöjd, is Nöjd out there?

[Nöjd comes in]

CAPTAIN: Throw this woman out! She wants to suffocate me with her hymnbook. Throw her out of the window, or up the chimney, or anywhere.

NÖJD: [Looks at Nurse] Heaven help you, Captain, but I can't do that, I can't. If it were only six men, but a woman!

CAPTAIN: Can't you manage one woman, eh?

NÖJD: Of course I can—but—well, you see, it's queer, but one never wants to lay hands on a woman.

CAPTAIN: Why not? Haven't they laid hands on me?

NÖJD: Yes, but I can't, Captain. It's just as if you asked me to strike the Pastor. It's second nature, like religion, I can't!

[Laura comes in, she motions Nöjd to go]

CAPTAIN: Omphale, Omphale! Now you play with the club while Hercules spins your wool.

LAURA: [Goes to sofa] Adolf, look at me. Do you believe that I am your enemy?

CAPTAIN: Yes, I do. I believe that you are all my enemies! My mother was my enemy when she did not want to bring me into the world because I was to be born with pain, and she robbed my embryonic life of its nourishment, and made a weakling of me. My sister was my enemy when she taught me that I must be submissive to her. The first woman I embraced was my enemy, for she gave me ten years of illness in return for the love I gave her. My daughter became my enemy when she had to choose between me and you. And you, my wife, you have been my arch enemy, because you never let up on me till I lay here lifeless.

LAURA: I don't know that I ever thought or even intended what you think I did. It may be that a dim desire to get rid of you as an obstacle lay at the bottom of it, and if you see any design in my behavior, it is possible that it existed, although I was unconscious of it. I have never thought how it all came about, but it is the result of the course you yourself laid out, and before God and my conscience I feel that I am innocent, even if I am not. Your existence has lain like a stone on my heart—lain so heavily that I tried to shake off the oppressive burden. This is the truth, and if I have unconsciously struck you down, I ask your forgiveness.

CAPTAIN: All that sounds plausible. But how does it help me? And whose fault is it? Perhaps spiritual marriages! Formerly one married a wife, now, one enters into partnership with a business woman, or goes to live with a friend—and then one ruins the partner, and dishonors the friend!—What has become of love, healthy sensuous love? It died in the transaction. And what is the result of this love in shares, payable to the bearer without joint liability? Who is the bearer when the crash comes? Who is the fleshly father of the spiritual child?

LAURA: And as for your suspicions about the child, they are absolutely groundless.

CAPTAIN: That's just what makes it so horrible. If at least there were any grounds for them, it would be something to get hold of, to cling to. Now there are only shadows that hide themselves in the bushes, and stick out their heads and grin; it is like fighting with the air, or firing blank cartridges in a sham fight. A fatal reality would have called forth resistance, stirred life and soul to action; but now my thoughts dissolve into air, and my brain grinds a void until it is on fire.—Put a pillow under my head, and throw something over me, I am cold. I am terribly cold!

[Laura *takes her shawl and spreads it over him. Nurse goes to get a pillow*]

LAURA: Give you your hand, friend.

CAPTAIN: My hand! The hand that you have bound! Omphale! Omphale!—But I feel your shawl against my mouth; it is as warm and soft as your arm, and it smells of vanilla, like your hair when you were young. Laura, when you were young, and we walked in the birch woods, with the primroses and the thrushes—glorious, glorious! Think how beautiful life was, and what it is now. You didn't want to have it like this, nor did I, and yet it happened. Who then rules over life?

LAURA: God alone rules——

CAPTAIN: The God of strife then! Or the Goddess perhaps, nowadays.—Take away the cat that is lying on me! Take it away!

[Nurse *brings in a pillow and takes the shawl away*]

CAPTAIN: Give me my army coat!—Throw it over me! [Nurse *gets the coat and puts it over him*] Ah, my rough lion skin that you wanted to take away from me! Omphale! Omphale! You cunning woman, champion of peace and contriver of man's disarmament. Wake, Hercules, before they take your club away from you! You would wile our armor from us too, and make believe that it is nothing but glittering finery. No, it was iron, let me tell you, before it ever glittered. In olden days the smith made the armor, now it is the needle woman. Omphale! Omphale! Rude strength has fallen before treacherous weakness.—Out on you infernal woman, and damnation on your sex. [He raises himself to spit but falls back on the sofa] What have you given me for a pillow, Margret? It is so hard, and so cold, so cold. Come and sit near me. There. May I put my head on your knee? So!—This is warm! Bend over me so that I can feel your breast! Oh, it is sweet to sleep against a woman's breast, a mother's or a mistress', but the mother's is sweetest.

LAURA: Would you like to see your child, Adolf?

CAPTAIN: My child? A man has no children, it is only woman who has children, and therefore the future is hers when we die childless. Oh, God, who holds his children dear!

NURSE: Listen, he is praying to God.

CAPTAIN: No, to you to put me to sleep, for I am tired, so tired. Good night, Margret, and blessed be you among women.

[He raises himself, but falls with a cry on the Nurse's lap. Laura goes to the left and calls the Doctor, who comes in with the Pastor]

LAURA: Help us, Doctor, if it isn't too late. Look, he has stopped breathing.

DOCTOR: [Feels the Captain's pulse] It is a stroke.

PASTOR: Is he dead?

DOCTOR: No, he may yet come back to life, but to what an awakening we cannot tell.

PASTOR: "First death, and then the judgment."

DOCTOR: No judgment, and no accusations. You who believe that a God shapes man's destiny must go to him about this.

NURSE: Ah, Pastor, with his last breath he prayed to God.

PASTOR: [To Laura] Is that true?

LAURA: It is.

DOCTOR: In that case, which I can understand as little as the cause of his illness, my skill is at an end. You try yours now, Pastor.

LAURA: Is that all you have to say at this deathbed, Doctor?

DOCTOR: That is all! I know no more. Let him speak who knows more.

[Bertha comes in from left and runs to her mother]

BERTHA: Mother, Mother!

LAURA: My child, my own child!

PASTOR: Amen.

CURTAIN.

Henry Becque

(1837–1899)

It was Henry Becque's ironic destiny to be neglected while he was laying the foundations of dramatic realism in France and to be unable to complete a single long play once the theatre recognized his merit and was eager to do him justice. In the eighteen-seventies, Emile Zola was thundering precepts for a new dramatic art and searching for saviors of the French stage. His eyes lighted readily enough on the De Goncourt brothers, fellow novelists who shared his credo of naturalism and whose wretched play *Henriette Maréchal* had been hissed off the stage. He also glanced appreciatively at himself while writing some half-dozen plays which he hoped would serve as good examples to a new generation. Zola, indeed, looked in every direction except that of Becque, who was then making desperate efforts to win a place for himself in the theatre and was developing an irascible temper in the process. When the long-frustrated dramatist came to write his memoirs in *Souvenirs d'un auteur dramatique* (1885), he remarked glumly that Zola was "an excellent lawmaker who wrote superb programmes and miserable plays." No love was lost between the two men even after they came to be regarded as the twin deities of the naturalistic theatre.

Upon graduation from the Lycée Bonaparte, Henry-François Becque, the son of a lowly government clerk in Paris, first found employment in a railroad office. But encouraged by a maternal uncle who had collaborated on a comedy with the successful playwright Labiche and wrote short farces, the young man turned eagerly to the theatre. Bored by his humdrum work in the railroad company, he took a minor position in the chancellery of the Legion of Honor, and from there graduated to the household of the influential Polish diplomat Count Potoczki, doubling as tutor and private secretary. Here he found his first opportunity to emerge as a writer when the Count introduced him to a young composer, Victorien Joncières. A collaboration ensued, with Becque contributing the libretto to Joncières' opera *Sardanapale* in 1865. In the same year, Becque started writing dramatic criticism for the newspaper *Le Peuple,* and in 1866 he had the good fortune of seeing his little farce *The Prodigal Son* produced successfully.

Encouraged by this first taste of success, the young author resolved to rely solely on his literary labors for a livelihood. The rash decision was to cost him a lifetime of struggle with producers and critics. He staged his first full-length serious play, *Michel Pauper,* at his own expense in 1870 only to encounter a crushing failure, and his next attempt, *The Elopement,* fared no better in 1871, although it was a problem play composed in the popular didactic vein of Dumas *fils.* Seven years were to elapse before another play of his was to appear on the stage. Twice defeated, the financially depleted author returned to the chancellery of the Legion of Honor, and, from there, moved to the more practical world of a stockbroker's office. He remained in the stockmarket for several years before venturing once more upon the insecure career of a playwright and free-lance journalist. Some measure of success did come to Becque in 1878 with the production of a short play, *The Shuttle,* and in 1880 with *The Virtuous Women,* which was ultimately included in the repertory of the Comédie Française. But neither play greatly improved his financial condition, and his temper was sorely tried by failure to obtain a production for his masterpiece *The Vultures (Les Corbeaux),* written in 1877. It took him five years to win a hearing, and its acceptance by the Comédie Française was only the beginning of a protracted struggle with the directors of the theatre.

Stubbornly rejecting all their demands for changes in the text, Becque finally saw *The Vultures* on the stage in 1882 exactly as he had written it. The artificial style of staging then in vogue brought only a qualified success, and the hisses that greeted his unpleasant picture of middle-class life were as loud as the applause of the progressives who welcomed his realism. The *première* threatened to become another pitched battle in the theatre, like the "battle of *Hernani*" half a century earlier when romanticists had fought classicists on behalf of Hugo's romantic melodrama. Nor did Becque gain enough prestige at the time to be able to place his next work, *The Parisian Woman (La Parisienne),* without encountering many rejections. The first production (1885) proved a sensation but failed to attract large audiences, and when the Comédie Française finally condescended to revive this candid description of Parisian immorality five years later, it nearly turned a masterpiece into a complete fiasco with its inept staging methods.

Becque needed a theatre capable of conveying his detached art of representing reality. The entire point of both *The Vultures* and *The Parisian Woman* lay in their revelation of moral turpitude through the natural behavior of his characters. They were drawn by Becque as people who consider their questionable morals beyond reproach and regard themselves as proper men and women. Their conduct and sentiments are norms of the social level on which they live and thrive—or so they believe. Becque's masterpieces derive their sharp humor, as well as their implicit indictment, entirely from the discrepancy between what the characters think of themselves and our judgment of them. The "little foxes" of Becque's picture of the middle class (and Lillian Hellman's *The Little Foxes* strongly recalls *The Vultures* with its portraits of predatory people) call themselves realistic businessmen when they cheat a widow and three orphaned daughters of their inheritance. They are only acting sensibly in conformity with the law of the survival of the fittest! It is regrettable that the weak and helpless must become their prey, they believe, but that is how the world is ordered and the spoils belong to the strong. They are "social Darwinists," so to speak. The family's lawyer in *The Vultures* is, indeed, so great a believer in the doctrine that whoever has the upper hand should take advantage of the opportunity that he urges the daughter Marie to compel Teissier to settle half his estate on her before she marries him. Previously the advocate was on the side of Teissier; but since the elderly Teissier hankers for a young girl, the advantage has passed into Marie's hands and it is only proper that she make full use of it!

Becque's characters condemn themselves in our eyes even when they are consistent, but it is their inconsistency that completely annihilates them. The adulterous Clotilde in *The Parisian Woman*, for example, believes herself to be a loyal wife when she wins political advancement for her husband with her infidelity. She possesses so strong a sense of propriety and so little sense of morality that she can seriously reprove her lover for his lack of religion: "You even pass for a freethinker," she declares, "and no doubt you would get along famously with a mistress who had no religion at all, perish the thought!" The lover Lafont, whose squabble with her in the first scene would pass for a quarrel between husband and wife, is equally self-righteous. "Remember one thing," he warns her, "that a folly once committed can never be undone. . . . Remain loyal to me, and keep your honor and self-respect." In *The Vultures* the despoilers of the weak are extremely alert to the villainies of others and voice their indignation in no uncertain terms. Irony can go no further than the conclusion, when Teissier, the worst of the birds of prey, who has married the daughter of the family he has impoverished, proceeds to drive off the other vultures, remarking to the girl that her family has been surrounded by a pack of scoundrels ever since her father's death.

The effectiveness of such writing depends entirely on the objectivity of the playwright, and the proper staging of such plays must be equally objective. To allow the actor to play to the audience and address his remarks to it instead of to other characters, to declaim his lines as in the classic drama, and to solicit applause from the spectators with well-timed pauses—these were the unpardonable sins that the old-fashioned theatre committed against Becque's plays. A major revolution in theatrical art was needed to make the revolution in playwriting effective, and this did not materialize until after Antoine founded the Théâtre Libre in 1887. It was as natural that Becque should rally to its support as it was that Antoine should cherish Becque's merits as a playwright. It was Antoine who gave *The Parisian Woman* its first satisfactory production at the Théâtre Antoine, a theatre he founded in 1897, two years before the author's death.

With the triumph of the new naturalistic stagecraft Becque finally came into his own, without being able, however, to profit from his opportunities. He wrote nothing of significance after 1885 except the two short pieces *The Start* and *Widowed*, both in 1897. The former was a naturalistic sketch of a shopgirl's induction into vice by a "respectable" employer who discharges her for refusing to yield to his son. *Widowed* was a sequel to *The Parisian Woman* which presented Clotilde widowed at last but otherwise unchanged. A few other one-acters were only slight sketches; a promising full-length drama, *The Puppets*, an exposé of the world of finance, was left unfinished at Becque's death. Although he was admitted to the Legion of Honor in 1886, lionized in society for his acrid wit, and invited to lecture in Italy, where his plays had won appreciation, he remained a poor and unsociable man. His admirers racked their brains for ways of stimulating him to create more masterpieces, and Antoine even lured him to Brittany for a summer vacation in order to induce him to write again. A fire that the solitary man started in his bedroom with a lighted cigar caused him a severe shock, and he had to be placed in a sanatorium by his friends. He never recovered. His death on May 15, 1899, was a deep blow to the men of the theatre who gratefully remembered his struggle to modernize the French drama.

Writing about Becque in 1905, James Huneker declared that *The Vultures* was "the bible of the dramatic realists." The statement is substantially correct if we remember to distinguish between the surface realism of the contrived "well-made plays" and the slice-of-life technique of Becque to which his contemporaries applied the term "naturalism." By no means a theorist of naturalism like Zola, Becque offered no program for playwrights. He did not even evince any enthusiasm for Ibsen, and the only realist who affected him was Tolstoy, whose peasant tragedy *The Power of Darkness* impressed him greatly. With curious inconsistency, apparently for reasons of personal gratitude, he maintained a lifelong admiration for Victorien Sardou, the playwright who was scorned by all confirmed naturalists and whose extreme theatricality was dismissed by the young Bernard Shaw as "Sardoodledom." In writing a preface to *The Vultures,* Becque disassociated himself from the naturalists' fondness for sordid drama and from their pet doctrine that man should be studied scientifically in terms of conditioning and heredity. He wrote: "I have never entertained much liking for assassins, hysterical and alcoholic characters, or for the martyrs of heredity and victims of evolution." Concerning his own encounters with conservative critics and managers, he maintained only that there were no conventions that originality could not destroy or displace, and that "the history of art is nothing but a struggle between original talents and routine-bound minds."

All that Becque intended to do was to set down reality as he saw it without comment or preachment. "Make what you will of it," he seemed to say, "but this is how people behave in our time and place, this is how they think, and this is how they speak." He tried, moreover, to create a natural flow of life instead of chopping up a play with mechanical calculation into "exposition," "climax" or "crisis," and "dénouement" or "resolution." Nor would he cater to the audiences of his time with tricks of the trade by composing high-flown declamatory passages for which the actor could be applauded, building "big" scenes with which to stun the spectators, or writing act endings calculated to bring the curtain down with a dramatic flourish. Theatrical expediency, which was honored in Becque's time as it too often still is in our own, was anathema to his uncompromising and formidable spirit. In such a play as *The Vultures,* as well as in the more brilliantly executed but also more narrowly Parisian comedy *The Parisian Woman,* it is not a naturalistic formula, scientific or sociological, that thrusts itself forward. The power of the play, still undiminished for all its occasional prolixity, lies in the hard integrity of the writing and the structure. It is this virtue, for which there has never been sufficient regard in the practical theatre, which accounts for the influence that *The Vultures* exerted on the formative modern drama.

BIBLIOGRAPHY: James Huneker, *Iconoclasts,* 1905; Matthew Josephson, *Zola and His Time,* 1928; Edmond Sée, *Henry Becque,* 1920; Adolphe Thalasso, *Le Théâtre Libre,* 1909; Samuel Montefiore Waxman, *Antoine and the Théâtre Libre,* 1926. See also Becque's nondramatic writings: *Querelles littéraires, Notes d'album,* and *Souvenirs d'un auteur dramatique.*

THE VULTURES

By Henry Becque

TRANSLATED FROM THE FRENCH BY FREEMAN TILDEN

CHARACTERS

VIGNERON, *a manufacturer*
MRS. VIGNERON
MRS. DE SAINT-GENIS
MARIE
BLANCHE } *the Vignerons' daughters*
JUDITH

TEISSIER, *formerly a small banker,*
now Vigneron's partner
BOURDON, *a lawyer*
MERCKENS, *a music-teacher*
LEFORT, *an architect*
DUPUIS, *a dealer in house furnishings*
GASTON, *the Vignerons' son*

AUGUSTE, *the Vignerons' butler*
A DOCTOR
GEORGE DE SAINT-GENIS
LENORMAND
GENERAL FROMENTIN
ROSALIE, *the Vignerons' old servant*

The action takes place at Paris in our own day.[1]

ACT I.

A luxuriously furnished drawing-room. There are three double doors at the rear, and double doors on the sides. At the right, in the foreground, there is a piano; and at the left, against the wall, a writing-table. Behind this writing-table is a fireplace. At the rear, on the right, a table; at the left, in the foreground, a couch. Other furniture, mirrors, flowers, etc.

When the curtain rises, Vigneron *is seen asleep on the couch. He is in a dressing-gown, and has a newspaper in his hands.* Marie, *seated near him, is engaged in needle-work.* Judith *is at the piano.* Blanche *is writing at the table.*

MRS. VIGNERON: Don't play any more, Judith; your father is asleep. [*Going over to the table*] Blanche.

BLANCHE: Yes, Mama.

MRS. VIGNERON: Is it finished?

BLANCHE: Just one minute.

MRS. VIGNERON: Have you gone over them? How many will there be at table?

BLANCHE: Sixteen.

MRS. VIGNERON: That's good.

[*She brings a chair and sits down beside* Blanche]

BLANCHE: Do you think the dinner will be any better for putting a menu at each plate?

MRS. VIGNERON: It won't be any the worse for it, anyhow.

BLANCHE: What a queer custom! But are you quite sure it is the proper thing?

MRS. VIGNERON: Absolutely sure. I saw it in the *Ladies' Home Companion.*

BLANCHE: Shall we run over the places together?

[1] The time would be any year between 1877 and 1882.

MRS. VIGNERON: Let's go over the list first. Mrs. de Saint-Genis?

BLANCHE: I've got her down.

MRS. VIGNERON: Her son?

BLANCHE: You needn't be afraid of my forgetting him.

MRS. VIGNERON: Father Mouton?

BLANCHE: The dear old man! He baptized me, and confirmed me—and now he is going to marry me.

MRS. VIGNERON: If you are going to gossip about every name we come to, we won't be through by next week. Mr. Teissier?

BLANCHE: I've got him down. I could get along very well without him, though.

VIGNERON: [*Waking*] What's that I hear? Is Miss Blanche giving orders in my house?

BLANCHE: Goodness, yes, Papa; it's little Blanche.

VIGNERON: And may we know what Mr. Teissier has done to you, miss?

BLANCHE: To me? Nothing. But he is old, and ugly, and boorish, and a miser. And he never looks anybody in the face; that's reason enough why I don't like him around me.

VIGNERON: Fine! Bully! I'll fix things all right. Mrs. Vigneron, you needn't save a place at the table for this young lady. She is going to have dinner in her room.

BLANCHE: You'll be saying soon that the wedding will go ahead without me.

VIGNERON: If you say another word, you shan't be married—— Oh!

[*A pause*]

MARIE: [*Rising*] Listen, Daddy dear, and give me a serious answer—which you never do when anybody speaks to you about your health. How do you feel?

VIGNERON: Oh, not bad.

MARIE: But your face is red.

VIGNERON: Red! That'll go away as soon as I get outdoors.

MARIE: If your dizziness comes back, we shall have to call in a doctor.

VIGNERON: A doctor! Do you want me to die?

MARIE: You know that kind of joking hurts me. We won't talk any more about it.

[*She starts away, and he catches her by the bottom of her gown and pulls her down into his arms*]

VIGNERON: Does she love her old daddy?

MARIE: I love you so, so, so much . . . but you don't do a thing I want you to, or a thing you should do. Why don't you work less, get some fun out of your money, and look out for yourself when you are sick?

VIGNERON: But I am not sick, little girl. I know what's the matter with me. I'm a bit tired, and there's too much blood in my head. It's just the same every year about this time, after I have finished taking inventory. The inventory of the house of Teissier, Vigneron, and Company! Do you know what Teissier and I were offered for our factory, only a week ago? Six hundred thousand francs!

MARIE: Well, sell it.

VIGNERON: Ten years from now, I am going to sell for a million. And in the meantime it will bring us in that much.

MARIE: How old will you be then?

VIGNERON: How old? Ten years from now? I shall be just the age of my grandchildren; and we shall have fine times together. [Auguste *enters*] What is it, Auguste?

AUGUSTE: Your architect, sir. He wants only a word with you.

VIGNERON: Tell Mr. Lefort if he wants to speak to me he should see me at the factory.

AUGUSTE: He has just come from there, sir.

VIGNERON: Let him go back there. I am at home here, with my wife and children, and I shan't be bothered by my contractors. [Auguste *goes out*] Let me get up.

[Marie *steps aside;* Vigneron *rises with an effort; then he is seized with dizziness and walks a few steps unsteadily*]

MARIE: [*Returning to him*] Why won't you see a doctor?

VIGNERON: Isn't that question settled?

MARIE: No; it is not settled. There's no use talking—you are not well, and it makes me uneasy. Take care of yourself; do something; perhaps a little dieting for seven or eight days would make you all right again.

VIGNERON: Sly puss! I see through you and your little dieting. I eat too much, eh? Come, speak right out; I don't mind. I eat too much. Well, little girl, what do you expect? I haven't always had a table full of good things. Ask your mother; she will tell you that when we began keeping house I went to bed many a time without my supper. Now I'm mak-

ing up for it. It's stupid, beastly, it hurts me, but I can't resist the temptation. [*Leaving* Marie] And then, I suppose I shouldn't read the newspaper after luncheon; it hurts my digestion. [*He crumples up the newspaper and going back to the couch throws himself upon it; then his glance falls upon* Judith, *who, seated at the piano, her back turned to her father, is in a brown study; he tiptoes over to her and shouts in her ear*] Judith!

JUDITH: Oh, Father, you know I don't like such jokes!

VIGNERON: Don't be angry, missy, I won't do it again. Judith, tell me something about what's going on—in the moon.

JUDITH: Now make fun of me.

VIGNERON: How do you make that out? I have a daughter named Judith. Is she here? Is she somewhere else? How can I know? We never hear from her.

JUDITH: I haven't anything to say.

VIGNERON: That doesn't bother most people.

JUDITH: What fun is there in teasing me all the time about it? I see you, hear you, love you, and I am happy.

VIGNERON: Are you happy?

JUDITH: Quite.

VIGNERON: Well, then, little girl, you're right and I'm wrong. Have you got a kiss for me?

JUDITH: [*Rising*] Have I? A hundred of them, Daddy.

[*They embrace;* Auguste *enters*]

VIGNERON: Now what is it? I don't seem to be able to kiss my children in peace, nowadays.

AUGUSTE: Mr. Dupuis, sir.

VIGNERON: Dupuis? Dupuis, the house furnisher? What does he want? I settled his bill long ago.

AUGUSTE: Mr. Dupuis stopped in to see if you wished anything, sir.

VIGNERON: Tell Mr. Dupuis for me that I don't buy twice of a swindler like him. Go ahead. [Auguste *goes out;* Vigneron *walks over to the table*] Well, what have you got your heads together about?

MRS. VIGNERON: Let us alone, that's a dear. We're busy with this evening's dinner.

VIGNERON: Oh!—Come and let me whisper just a few words in your ear. [Mrs. Vigneron *rises and joins her husband at the front of the stage*] So it's all settled that we are going to marry our daughter to that popinjay?

MRS. VIGNERON: Did you interrupt me just to say that?

VIGNERON: Now listen: I haven't any prejudice against this marriage. Mrs. de Saint-Genis impresses me as a first-rate woman. It isn't her fault if she hasn't a cent. Her son is a lovely little boy, very pleasant and polite, and he certainly does curl his hair nicely. For a long while, now, I've hardly been able to keep from telling him that he uses too much hair-oil. His government job carries a good salary with it, for a chap of his age. But at the last moment, I can't help wondering whether this marriage is well-advised, and whether Blanche will be really happy with that young fellow, even if he does belong to one of the oldest families.

MRS. VIGNERON: But Blanche is crazy about him.

VIGNERON: Blanche is only a child. It's easy to see that the first young fellow she met turned her head.

MRS. VIGNERON: What have you got up your sleeve? What's the use of talking that way about a marriage which is done and over with, one might say? You aren't reproaching me, are you, with Mrs. de Saint-Genis' financial position? Ours wasn't always what it is now. Then what are you complaining of? Because George is a good-looking young fellow, well-brought-up, and of a good family? If he comes from one of the best families, so much the better for him.

VIGNERON: It flatters you to have a son-in-law from one of the oldest families.

MRS. VIGNERON: Yes, I admit it does flatter me; but I wouldn't sacrifice one of my girls to mere vanity. [Coming nearer and speaking in a lower tone] Do you want me to tell you the whole truth? It is true that Blanche is a child, as modest and innocent—the dear little girl—as can be; but her feelings are unusually powerful for a girl of her age, and we shan't regret having her married early. And then, our friend, Father Mouton, who has known us twenty years, wouldn't interest himself in the marriage if it were not for the best all around.

VIGNERON: Who said he would? But no matter, we are going ahead too fast. In the first place, it isn't a priest's business to make matches. And then, I'd like to have you tell me how it is that Mrs. de Saint-Genis—who hasn't a cent, I repeat—has such good connections. I thought that her son's witnesses would be common-place people; gracious, she's found some smarter than our own! A high government official and a general! The government official I can account for—George works in his office—but the general!

MRS. VIGNERON: What's that? Oh, the general? Surely, you know that Mr. de Saint-Genis was a captain in the army. Run along to your work, dear. [She turns away from him] Blanche, give your father his coat.

[She goes out at the right, leaving the door open behind her]

VIGNERON: [Taking off his dressing-gown and putting on the coat brought by Blanche] So here you are, you ingrate!

BLANCHE: Ingrate! Why do you call me that?

VIGNERON: Why? Now that we are rich, and are going to let you be married, and give you a dowry, why shouldn't we marry you to Mr. Teissier?

BLANCHE: No, Papa.

VIGNERON: "No, Papa." Why not? I reckon it's Teissier and his factory that have made me what I am.

BLANCHE: You mean that you have made Mr.

Teissier's factory what it is. Without you, it would have cost him money enough; with you, heaven only knows how much money it has brought him in. Now see here, Papa, if Mr. Teissier were anybody else—if he were a fair man—here is what he would say, after all the work you have done and the pains you have taken: "This factory first belonged to me; then it belonged to both of us; now it belongs to you."

VIGNERON: Her kind little heart puts sentiment into everything. It's a good thing to have sentiment, but not to count too much on other people's having it. [He kisses her]

MRS. VIGNERON: [Entering] What, are you still here?

VIGNERON: Answer this question: Am I under obligation to Teissier, or is Teissier under obligations to me?

MRS. VIGNERON: Neither.

VIGNERON: How is that?

MRS. VIGNERON: Do you really want me to go all over that story again?

VIGNERON: Yes.

MRS. VIGNERON: Well, children, Mr. Teissier was a banker in a small way, on the street where we used to live. We knew him, and yet we didn't. We had been under obligations to him at certain times when we were in need, and he had taken our note without much hesitation, because our reputation was good. Later on, in the course of his business, he found that he had a factory on his hands. He remembered your father and offered him the management, but with a salary. At that time we were getting along pretty well because your father had a good position with a good business house, and the wisest thing to do was to keep it. Fifteen months passed. We had thought nothing more of it for a long time, when one evening at exactly half-past nine—I remember the hour—when your father and I were looking through the door that led into your room, and watching you as you lay asleep, somebody rang. It was Mr. Teissier, and it was the first time he had ever climbed the five flights to our floor. He had made up his mind at last. The truth was his works were not working, and he came to ask your father to come to his assistance by joining forces with him. Your father thanked him politely and asked him to wait till the following day for an answer. As soon as Mr. Teissier had gone, your father said to me—now listen to this—your father said to me: "Here is an opportunity, my dear. It comes rather late, and just when we are beginning to take things easy. It's going to be a lot of work for me, and you will always be in a state of terror until I make a go of it—if I do make a go of it. But we have four children, and perhaps this is their chance." [She weeps and clutches her husband's hand; the children gather around them, amid general emotion] To come back to the question you asked it seems to me easily answered. Mr. Teissier and Mr. Vigneron went into business together. It was a good thing for both of them, and they owe each other nothing.

VIGNERON: There, children, is a model woman! Pattern after this woman, measure up to her standard, and nothing more can be expected of you. [*He kisses his wife*]

MRS. VIGNERON: You do it beautifully, but it isn't natural to you, my dear. Do you feel ill?

VIGNERON: No, sweetheart; on the contrary, I feel better. I believe I have wholly recovered. Now I am going to ask Miss Judith, the g-r-r-reat musician of the family, to play me something, and then I'll relieve you of my company.

JUDITH: What do you want me to play? *Il Trovatore?*

VIGNERON: Find *Il Trovatore*. [*To* Blanche] That's fine, that *Trovatore* piece. Is it by Rossini?

BLANCHE: No; Verdi.

VIGNERON: Oh, Verdi, the author of the *Huguenots*.

BLANCHE: No; the *Huguenots* was written by Meyerbeer.

VIGNERON: That's so. The great Meyerbeer. How old is Meyerbeer, now?

BLANCHE: He's dead.

VIGNERON: What? My goodness, did he die without my knowing it? [*To* Judith] Can't you find *Il Trovatore?* Never mind, don't take the trouble to look for it. Listen: play me—just play me—*La Dame Blanche*.

JUDITH: I don't know it.

VIGNERON: You don't know *La Dame Blanche?* Say that again. You don't know——? What's the good, then, of the lessons I'm having you take at ten francs an hour? What *does* your music-teacher teach you? Tell me, now, what *does* he teach you?

JUDITH: He teaches me music.

VIGNERON: Well? Isn't *La Dame Blanche* music?

MARIE: [*Leading* Judith *to the piano*] Come, big sister, play Daddy what he wants to hear. [*Judith seats herself at the piano and begins the famous selection*]

> "From here behold that fair domain
> Whose lofty turrets touch the sky;
> A strange and spectral chatelaine
> Guards that old castle ceaselessly.
> Perfidious and faithless knight
> Weaving your plots of shame and spite,
>   Take care!
> *La Dame Blanche* sees you there,
> She hears—the woman in white!" [2]

[Vigneron *begins to sing, then his wife joins him, then his daughters follow suit; half-way through the verse* Gaston *enters, having first stuck his head in at one of the rear doors. Then* Gaston *goes to the fireplace, takes the shovel and tongs, and contributes to the hubbub*]

VIGNERON: [*Going toward his son, when the verse*

2 Translated by Allan Updegraff.

is sung] Where did you come from, you young rascal? Why weren't you at luncheon with us?

GASTON: I lunched with one of my friends.

VIGNERON: What's that friend's name?

GASTON: You don't know him.

VIGNERON: I know well enough that I don't know him. Stand there while I have a look at you. [*He draws off a few steps, the better to survey his son.* Gaston *still has the shovel and tongs in his hands.* Vigneron *takes them away and puts them back in their place; then he goes back toward his son and regards him tenderly*] Stand up straight! [*He goes over to him and strokes his hair*] Show me your tongue! Good! Put it out a little farther. Farther than that. That's all right. [*In a low tone*] I hope you're not tiring yourself out too much.

GASTON: Doing what, Dad? I haven't been doing anything.

VIGNERON: Now you're talking nonsense. When I said, "You're not tiring yourself out too much," I knew what I meant, and so did you, you scamp. Do you need any money?

GASTON: No.

VIGNERON: Open your hand.

GASTON: What's the use?

VIGNERON: [*Speaking louder*] Open your hand.

GASTON: I don't want to.

VIGNERON: Papa Vigneron brought this boy up, so he did! Here, put this money in your pocket, and be quick about it! Have a good time, son—I want you to have the best kind of a time. Cut loose and raise the dickens. But remember—away from here you are your own boss—but here, among your sisters, mind how you act! Be careful what you say; and above all, no mushy letters! If you want to confide in anybody, I'm the one.

JUDITH: We're waiting for you to join in the second verse, Dad.

VIGNERON: [*Looking at his watch*] You'll have to sing the second verse without me. [*He takes his hat and goes toward the door. Then, pausing and looking around at his family, he comes back like a man who is happy where he is, and does not want to go away*] Come here a minute, old lady! [Mrs. Vigneron *comes over to him, and he puts one arm under hers*] Judith, get up! [*He does the same to* Judith] Come here, you other girls! If I had my own way, dearies, I'd get back into my dressing-gown and stay here until dinner time. But unfortunately my work won't do itself; and I haven't money enough yet to live without working. Perhaps I shall have some day, when I am the owner of the factory. But I must wait for two things—till my new buildings are finished, and until my children are provided for. Who could have thought that this little minx Blanche, the youngest of you, would be the first to get married? Whose turn is it next? Judith? Oh, Judith is a young lady hard to please. Unless she meets a prince, she'll die an old maid. Well, then, let some prince come along, and I'll buy him for her. As for you, you young scamp, standing over there laughing while I am talking—you can have your fling, but it won't be for long. Some fine day I'm going to take you to work with me, and you are going to start in by sweeping the factory, from top to bottom—until I make an errand boy of you. After that we'll see whether you are good for anything. Of you all, I'm the least worried about Marie. She isn't a dreamer [*Looking at* Judith] like you; nor a sentimentalist [*Looking at* Blanche] like you. She'll marry some good fellow, some healthy chap, a hard worker and tough as a knot, who will make you think of your father when he's not here any more. [*To his wife*] I haven't mentioned you, sweetheart, because at our age, we don't have any great longings or needs. We're happy if the kids are happy. I don't think these children of ours would have been any happier anywhere else. Well, and what next? Just let the old man put in a few more years to ensure the future of this little family, and then he'll have earned the right to take a rest. Now, then, I'm off!

THE CHILDREN: Good-by, Papa. Kiss me. Good-by.

[Vigneron *escapes from them and goes out quickly*]

MRS. VIGNERON: Now, girls, get yourselves ready. [*To* Blanche] I want you to wait a minute; I've got something to say to you. [*To* Marie] Look in at the kitchen, dear, and tell Rosalie to be sure not to keep us waiting; hurry her up a little. Rosalie is very fond of us, but she's always late with dinner. Gaston, let your sister go to her room—you can take your music lesson some other time. [*There is a hustle and bustle as all the children except* Blanche *go out*] Now pay attention, dearie; I haven't time to talk much. I want you to make use of what I'm going to tell you; and don't interrupt me. I don't like the way you conduct yourself when your future husband is here. You look at him too much; when he gets up, you get up; you get into little corners to do your talking. I don't like those things; and to-day, when we have visitors, I should like it less than ever. If you admire George, and if you love each other, so much the better, since you are going to be married—but you are not married yet. Until you are, I want you to be more careful, and I want you to keep your feelings to yourself, as a nice girl should do. There's no sense in crying about it! It's all said and done. Now dry your eyes, give me a kiss, and go and get yourself ready. [Blanche *leaves her mother and is going out at the door when* Auguste *enters at the rear and announces* Mrs. de Saint-Genis; Blanche *pauses*] Go and get ready!

MRS. DE SAINT-GENIS: How do you do, dear. Come, kiss me. It's not only the style, it's a perfect mania now, for people to kiss every five minutes. I'm here early, but don't let me disturb you. If I bother you the least bit, just say so. I'll stay or go, just as you please.

MRS. VIGNERON: Oh, stay. by all means.

MRS. DE SAINT-GENIS: Perhaps you have calls to make?

MRS. VIGNERON: Not one.

MRS. DE SAINT-GENIS: Then maybe you expect to receive some?

MRS. VIGNERON: No.

MRS. DE SAINT-GENIS: Shall I take off my hat?

MRS. VIGNERON: If you don't I'll put mine on.

MRS. DE SAINT-GENIS: It isn't often nowadays, Mrs. Vigneron, that one finds a woman like you—a woman who can be seen any time. I wouldn't want to risk such a thing with some of my most intimate friends.

MRS. VIGNERON: Sit down and tell me: how are you?

MRS. DE SAINT-GENIS: I'm well; quite well. I don't remember ever feeling better. I was saying this morning, at my toilet, that I had got back my color and figure.

MRS. VIGNERON: There is a question I've been wanting to ask you, ever so long. It shouldn't make any difference between us. How old are you?

MRS. DE SAINT-GENIS: Why, Mrs. Vigneron, I never try to hide my age. Even if I wanted to, I couldn't; on account of my son. He will be twenty-three years old in a few days; I was seventeen when he was born; you can figure it out.

MRS. VIGNERON: Then you don't mind my curiosity?

MRS. DE SAINT-GENIS: It is quite natural, between two old women.

MRS. VIGNERON: You know we are two rash mothers—you, in letting your son marry so young, at twenty-three, and I, in letting my daughter marry him!

MRS. DE SAINT-GENIS: Don't worry about that, my dear. George has obeyed me so far, and I certainly count on keeping him straight after he is married. I have brought up my son very strictly, as I think I have already told you, and there are few children like him. He has never gone into debt; and what is just as unusual, he has never frittered away his time with women. All the same, I know some women who wouldn't have asked anything better. My son has had a very thorough education; he speaks three languages, he plays, he bears a good name, has good manners and religious principles. So, with all that, he won't go far wrong, unless the world changes a good deal. [*Changing her tone*] Tell me, now that we are talking about George, and since I am looking out for his interest, does your husband know that I asked my lawyer to rectify an omission in the marriage contract?

MRS. VIGNERON: I can't say as to that.

MRS. DE SAINT-GENIS: You remember that Mr. Vigneron, after having fixed Blanche's marriage portion at two hundred thousand francs, asked us to let him pay it in the form of an annuity.

MRS. VIGNERON: That's not so, Mrs. de Saint-Genis. From the very first my husband said that he wanted time to settle his daughter's dowry. It was then that you spoke of some guarantee, a mortgage on the buildings under construction; and he refused to do that. Finally, the amount and the time of payment was fully agreed upon.

MRS. DE SAINT-GENIS: Very well. It seemed to me only natural and fair that until the young couple come into the whole sum, it should pay them interest of five or six per cent—say, six per cent. However, in making out the contract Mr. Vigneron showed such kind spirit toward all my little whims, that there will be no trouble between us. Let us talk about something else. Your dinner, for instance. Are you going to have many here?

MRS. VIGNERON: There are your witnesses, and ours, and my eldest daughter's music-teacher——

MRS. DE SAINT-GENIS: Oh, you have invited him——

MRS. VIGNERON: Yes; we invited the young fellow. He is a musician, I know; but really we didn't want to make him feel his position.

MRS. DE SAINT-GENIS: Well, Mrs. Vigneron, perhaps you will think I am meddling with what doesn't concern me, but if I were in your place I'd let him come this once, and then see no more of him.

MRS. VIGNERON: Why, Mrs. de Saint-Genis? My daughter has never had reason to complain either of him or his work.

MRS. DE SAINT-GENIS: Well, never mind. Who else is there?

MRS. VIGNERON: Mr. Teissier—that's all.

MRS. DE SAINT-GENIS: So I am going to meet this Mr. Teissier, whom I have heard so much of, but whom I have never yet seen! [*She rises and goes over to* Mrs. Vigneron, *taking her by the hand in a friendly way*] Why is it, Mrs. Vigneron, we have never seen your husband's partner?

MRS. VIGNERON: My daughters don't like him.

MRS. DE SAINT-GENIS: Surely your daughters do not lay down the law in your house? I should think Mr. Vigneron would have his partner come here regardless of childish whims.

MRS. VIGNERON: But the men see each other every day at the factory, and when they have talked over their business affairs, they have nothing more to say to each other.

MRS. DE SAINT-GENIS: Now see here, Mrs. Vigneron, I am not the kind of a woman to betray anybody's confidence; but if I guessed a secret, that would be different. Now own up—for some reason or other, it's you who have kept Mr. Teissier from coming here.

MRS. VIGNERON: I? You are entirely wrong about that. In the first place I do whatever my family wishes; besides, if I don't exactly like Mr. Teissier, at least I don't absolutely dislike him.

MRS. DE SAINT-GENIS: You—just feel indifferent toward him?

MRS. VIGNERON: That's exactly it—indifferent.

MRS. DE SAINT-GENIS: Then I must say that you are either very shortsighted, or altogether too unselfish. Isn't Mr. Teissier extremely wealthy?

MRS. VIGNERON: Yes.

MRS. DE SAINT-GENIS: And past sixty?

MRS. VIGNERON: Long past.

MRS. DE SAINT-GENIS: He has no wife or children.

MRS. VIGNERON: That's right.

MRS. DE SAINT-GENIS: It isn't known that he has a mistress?

MRS. VIGNERON: A mistress! Mr. Teissier! Good Lord, what would he be doing with a mistress?

MRS. DE SAINT-GENIS: Now listen; it's no laughing matter. Here you have, right in your grasp, a big unclaimed legacy which may come any day. It could fall to you without making talk and without underhanded means. Doesn't such a legacy mean anything to you? Either you don't care for money, or you think that it would be buying it too dearly if you showed some semblance of affection for an old man.

MRS. VIGNERON: What you say is true enough, Mrs. de Saint-Genis, and you are not the first one who has said as much. I'll explain my position. If we should be indebted to a stranger, our home wouldn't be quite the same; my husband couldn't hold up his head, and we shouldn't be as happy. But this reason doesn't apply to you. There's nothing to keep you from trying your luck with Mr. Teissier, after the children are married. If he takes an interest in this marriage, so much the better. I would be only too glad if Blanche and her husband could benefit in that way. Well, I'm drifting away from the point. If Mr. Teissier, who must be tired of living alone at his age, should succumb to your charms, I should be quite pleased to see you married to him. Of course, there would be certain disadvantages on your side, but the compensations would be great.

MRS. DE SAINT-GENIS: You don't know men, Mrs. Vigneron, and you're talking nonsense. In a pinch, Mr. Teissier wouldn't be too old for me; the trouble is I'm not young enough for him.

AUGUSTE: [*Entering*] Mr. Merckens has just come, ma'am. Shall I show him into the other parlor?

MRS. VIGNERON: Which would you rather do, Mrs. de Saint-Genis—stay here and talk with Mr. Merckens or come and help me dress?

MRS. DE SAINT-GENIS: Just as you please.

MRS. VIGNERON: Then come with me. I'll show you some things I have bought, and you must tell me whether they are the latest style.

MRS. DE SAINT-GENIS: With pleasure.

MRS. VIGNERON: Bring Mr. Merckens in and ask him to wait a few moments.

[*They go out at the left*]

AUGUSTE: Come in and have a chair, Mr. Merckens; I'm the only one here just at the moment.

MERCKENS: All right; go ahead with your work, Auguste, don't let me disturb you. [*Going down the* stage] The servant is a good fellow, but this treatment is intolerable.

AUGUSTE: [Coming back again] No lessons today, Mr. Merckens. You're here to have a good time.

MERCKENS: Is Miss Judith dressing?

AUGUSTE: Probably. But you know, with her it's one, two, three—done!

MERCKENS: Please tell Miss Judith that I'm here and have brought the music she wanted.

[At this moment Judith enters]

AUGUSTE: Now what did I tell you! [To Judith] You weren't long dressing, miss, but you put in your time pretty well.

JUDITH: Thank you, Auguste.

[Auguste takes up Vigneron's dressing-gown and goes out]

MERCKENS: Your servant took that compliment out of my mouth; and I don't know what to say.

JUDITH: Well, it isn't worth bothering about.

MERCKENS: [Unrolling some sheets of music] Here is your composition, Miss Judith.

JUDITH: Let me have it.

MERCKENS: The name of the composer isn't on it, but I can have it put on.

JUDITH: You must keep it to yourself.

MERCKENS: Are you satisfied?

JUDITH: I don't know what to do. I know so well that the family, and particularly Mama, wouldn't like our little conspiracy.

MERCKENS: I repeat what I told you about this little piece. It is distinctive and interesting. It's a little bit melancholy; perhaps you had a cold in the head that day. We had it printed because it was worth it; that's all there is to it.

JUDITH: Now understand, Mr. Merckens, I reserve the right to show my composition or to say nothing about it, just as I please.

MERCKENS: Why?

JUDITH: Because a girl of my age must live very quietly, without letting herself indulge in unbecoming fancies.

MERCKENS: The young ladies I know are not so particular.

JUDITH: All the more reason. [She opens the music and reads the title tenderly] "Farewell to the Bride and Groom." I'm not surprised that this piece is sad. I felt deeply while I was writing it. I was thinking of my little sister whom we all love so much and who is so soon to leave us. Who knows what she is giving up, and what fate awaits her!

MERCKENS: To tell the truth, wasn't there something underhanded about this marriage?

JUDITH: No. Why do you ask?

MERCKENS: Mrs. de Saint-Genis had her pick. She could have asked for the oldest rather than the youngest.

JUDITH: That would have been too bad. He and my sister make a fine couple, and that wouldn't have been the case—otherwise.

MERCKENS: Don't be impatient; your turn will come.

JUDITH: I don't let that worry me.

MERCKENS: Yet you do wish a little that you were married?

JUDITH: As late as possible. I'm getting along first-rate, and I don't care to make any change.

MERCKENS: Composing satisfies you?

JUDITH: You are right, it does.

MERCKENS: It seems too bad that such a delightful young women, so gifted, should lack just a little something which would make her work worth while.

JUDITH: What is that something?

MERCKENS: [In a low tone] A little of the devil.

JUDITH: Mama wouldn't be pleased if she heard you say that; she'd think I was already running wild.

MERCKENS: Does your mother scold you sometimes?

JUDITH: Yes, sometimes. But worse than that, when she is angry she locks up my piano; and she has told father not to take us to the Opera.

MERCKENS: Where do you go, then?

JUDITH: To the Circus. I don't blame Mama, though. She thinks the Opera is bad for me; and perhaps she is right. It's true; the wonders of the scenery, the allurement of the acting, and the splendid singing—why, it's a week before I am myself again.

MERCKENS: These great singers get high prices, you know.

JUDITH: They are all great to me.

MERCKENS: Perhaps you envy them?

JUDITH: I'm wild about them.

MERCKENS: Why don't you be one?

JUDITH: What! I go on the stage?

MERCKENS: Why not? You have a good contralto voice, and there are very few contraltos. You have the presence, and vivacity, and, above all, you have feeling—a great deal of it. The world will never miss one housekeeper, and it will rejoice in one more artist.

JUDITH: Hush! don't say any more about it. I am going to stick to your lessons. They seem to me better than your advice. Have you an engagement for this evening? Will you stay a little while after dinner?

MERCKENS: A little while. I still count on hearing your composition.

JUDITH: And you will play something for us, too?

MERCKENS: Don't ask that. I don't stand on ceremony with you; you and I speak right out. When I am talking I can be witty and amusing; but my music doesn't resemble my conversation the least bit.

JUDITH: We're going to dance.

MERCKENS: Nonsense!

JUDITH: Yes, we are. Blanche wanted to. The least she can do is to dance once or twice with her future husband before she is married. And then

Gaston has a surprise for us. He insists he is going to dance a quadrille with his father, and that we won't be able to tell them apart.

MERCKENS: How so?

JUDITH: You'll see. You don't know how my brother can imitate Papa to the very life. It's wonderful how much like him he seems at those times —his voice, his gestures, his way of joking.

MERCKENS: I can see you are going to have a good time. Thank you for asking me to be here.

JUDITH: Now you're making fun of me, Mr. Artist. I don't want to be too severe, but I fancy that many of your parties aren't worth all the fuss you make about them. Our folks would consider them ridiculous, too, to say the least. There's one thing we can say, anyway; here you will be among respectable people.

[Mrs. Vigneron, *and* Mrs. de Saint-Genis *re-enter*]

MRS. DE SAINT-GENIS: [*Aside*] I knew we'd find them together.

[Judith *goes over to her and they greet each other affectionately*]

MRS. VIGNERON: [*Dressed loudly and covered with jewelry*] Pardon me, Mr. Merckens, for making you wait. Women never do get dressed. Do you think I look well?

MERCKENS: Dazzling!

MRS. VIGNERON: Perhaps I have too much jewelry on. Mrs. de Saint-Genis advised me to take off some of it.

MERCKENS: Why, Mrs. Vigneron? Princess Limperani wore three hundred thousand francs' worth at the dinner she gave yesterday.

MRS. VIGNERON: Three hundred thousand francs! Then I can keep on what I have.

[Marie *and* Blanche *enter*]

MRS. VIGNERON: [*Going to* Judith] Your father is late. He won't be here to receive his guests.

BLANCHE: [*To* Mrs. de Saint-Genis] Why didn't your son come with you?

MRS. DE SAINT-GENIS: George is working, dear. You mustn't expect me to keep him from his duties.

BLANCHE: He has more than one kind of duty now. He must love me as much as I love him.

MRS. DE SAINT-GENIS: That's easy. He won't have to forget his other duties to do that. I warn you we are going to pull hair if you begin to spoil my boy.

MRS. VIGNERON: [*To* Mrs. de Saint-Genis] I suppose George's witnesses will arrive together.

MRS. DE SAINT-GENIS: No. Mr. Lenormand and my son will leave the office and come here together; the general will come alone. The general and Mr. Lenormand know each other, because they have met at our house, but I have never tried to bring about any closer relationship between them.

AUGUSTE: [*Announcing*] Mr. Teissier!

TEISSIER: [*Entering*] How do you do, Mrs. Vigneron?

MRS. VIGNERON: Let me take your hat, Mr. Teissier.

TEISSIER: Never mind. I'll put it somewhere myself, so as to be sure of finding it again.

MRS. VIGNERON: Just as you like. Won't you sit here, in this armchair?

TEISSIER: I will in a few minutes. It's so cold outdoors and so warm in here that I'm going to stay on my feet until I get used to the temperature of the room.

MRS. VIGNERON: I hope you are not ill?

TEISSIER: I try to keep from being ill.

MRS. VIGNERON: How do you think my husband has been lately?

TEISSIER: Very well. Vigneron takes better care of himself, now that he's got some money ahead. He's right, too. A man's life is worth more when he's got something laid by. You can attend to your guests, Mrs. Vigneron; I'll sit in the corner until dinner time. [*He leaves her*]

MRS. VIGNERON: [*Going over to* Mrs. de Saint-Genis] Well, that's Mr. Teissier! What do you think of him?

MRS. DE SAINT-GENIS: He has the eyes of a fox and the face of a monkey.

AUGUSTE: [*Announcing*] Mr. Bourdon!

MRS. VIGNERON: I forgot to tell you that our lawyer will dine with us.

BOURDON: How do you do, ladies—young people—— [*Greetings*]

MRS. VIGNERON: [*Presenting* Bourdon] Mrs. de Saint-Genis; Mr. Merckens, my eldest daughter's music-teacher. You are one of the first to come, Mr. Bourdon; that's very nice of you.

[Bourdon *bows*]

MRS. DE SAINT-GENIS: Mr. Bourdon is setting a good example for his brother lawyers. They don't usually pride themselves on their punctuality.

BOURDON: Yes, we do sometimes keep people waiting—but never at dinner. [*Going over to* Mrs. de Saint-Genis] I have been asked to congratulate you, Mrs. de Saint-Genis.

MRS. DE SAINT-GENIS: Mr. Testelin?

BOURDON: Yes. We were talking about your son's marriage to Miss Vigneron, and I happened to say that I was going to have dinner with you. "There will be a delightful woman there," he said. "Give her my best regards."

MRS. DE SAINT-GENIS: Mr. Testelin has been my lawyer for twenty years.

BOURDON: So he said. [*In a lower tone, coming nearer to her*] Testelin is a courteous fellow, with considerable weakness for pretty women.

MRS. DE SAINT-GENIS: [*Dryly*] It's the first time I ever heard that. [*She leaves him, smiling*]

BOURDON: [*To* Mrs. Vigneron] Is Teissier dining here?

MRS. VIGNERON: [*Pointing out* Teissier *to him*] There he is, if you want to talk to him.

BOURDON: How are you, Teissier?

TEISSIER: Oh, it's you, Bourdon! Come here a minute; I want to tell you something. [*In a low tone*] I was at the Lawyer's Club to-day on business. I was speaking to the President about my long acquaintance with you, and he got rather confidential about you. "I know Bourdon," he said. "He's got brains enough; he's as shrewd as they make them; but sometimes he overplays his hand. We've got to squelch him."

BOURDON: What do I care for the Lawyer's Club? They're a crowd of stiff-necks who want to give the Club a goody-goody tone. The Club is meant to be a protection for us—not for the public.

TEISSIER: Now listen, Bourdon: I haven't repeated this conversation to keep you from doing business. I just thought I would be doing you a favor by letting you know.

BOURDON: So I take it, friend Teissier. I'm much obliged.

AUGUSTE: [*Announcing*] Mr. Lenormand and Mr. George de Saint-Genis!

MRS. DE SAINT-GENIS: [*To* Mrs. Vigneron] I want you to meet Mr. Lenormand.

[*This presentation and those following take place at the rear.* George *alone goes to the front of the stage*]

BLANCHE: [*Speaking in a low tone to* George] Don't say anything to me, and don't come too near me. Mama has given me a dressing down. I was terribly afraid; I didn't know just what she was going to say.

AUGUSTE: [*Announcing*] General Fromentin!

BOURDON: [*To* Merckens] You are a pianist?

MERCKENS: A composer.

BOURDON: A musician—that's what I should have said. Do you like to go into society?

MERCKENS: I can't help myself; I'm dragged into it.

BOURDON: You might remember my name and address, "Mr. Bourdon, lawyer, 22 St. Anne Street." We have a few friends with us every Sunday evening. I ought to warn you there's nothing fancy about it. The people come at nine o'clock, we have a little music, sing a few songs, have a cup of tea, and by midnight everybody is in bed.

MERCKENS: I couldn't promise to come every Sunday.

BOURDON: Come when you can; we'll be glad to see you any time.

AUGUSTE: [*Announcing*] Mr. Vigneron!

MRS. DE SAINT-GENIS: [*To* Mrs. Vigneron] What! Is your husband in the habit of announcing his arrival?

MRS. VIGNERON: The servant has made a mistake, of course.

[Gaston *enters, with his father's dressing-gown on. He imitates his father's voice and walk*]

GASTON: [*Approaching* Mrs. de Saint-Genis] How is the lovely Mrs. de Saint-Genis?

MRS. DE SAINT-GENIS: [*Taking the joke in good part*] I'm very well, thank you, Mr. Vigneron.

GASTON: Mr. Bourdon, I am your humble servant. [*To* Merckens] How do you do, young man. [*To* Lenormand *and the* General] Delighted to meet you, gentlemen.

MRS. VIGNERON: That's what we get for spoiling children! This young rascal is caricaturing his father.

GASTON: [*To* Mrs. Vigneron] Well, old lady, is dinner ready? By heavens, we haven't spared any expense to give you a good time; we don't have a marriage in the family every day. [*To his sisters*] Which one of you is it? I don't remember. It strikes me that while we are waiting for dinner Miss Judith ought to play us something—*La Dame Blanche*, for instance.

MRS. VIGNERON: Come, Gaston, that's enough. Take off that dressing-gown and act properly.

GASTON: Yes, old lady.

[*The sisters help him off with the gown, amid general laughter*]

AUGUSTE: [*Approaching* Mrs. Vigneron] There's a gentleman here who wasn't invited to dinner and wants to speak with you.

MRS. VIGNERON: What gentleman, Auguste? Is this some new joke of my sons's?

AUGUSTE: If you order me to admit him you will see whether it is or not.

MRS. VIGNERON: Don't admit any one. Tell the gentleman I can't see him.

AUGUSTE: If he insists, ma'am?

MRS. VIGNERON: Then send him about his business.

AUGUSTE: [*Returning*] Here he is, ma'am.

THE DOCTOR: [*Coming forward*] Mrs. Vigneron!

MRS. VIGNERON: Yes, sir.

THE DOCTOR: [*Coming close to her and speaking in a very low voice*] Have you children here, Mrs. Vigneron?

MRS. VIGNERON: Yes, sir.

THE DOCTOR: Send them out of the room. Please do it at once.

MRS. VIGNERON: [*Disturbed, and speaking quickly*] Go into the other parlor, girls. Run along, now; do as I tell you; go into the other parlor. Gaston, you go along with your sisters. Mrs. de Saint-Genis, will you please take the girls in?

[*She opens the door at the right, and the children pass out*]

THE DOCTOR: [*Speaking to the men, who have risen*] You can stay, gentlemen. Are you relatives of Mr. Vigneron?

BOURDON: No, just his friends.

THE DOCTOR: Well, gentlemen, your friend has just had a stroke of apoplexy.

[Vigneron *is brought in at the rear.* Mrs. Vigneron *cries out and throws herself upon her husband's body*]

CURTAIN

ACT II.

The scene is the same as in the preceding act.

MRS. VIGNERON: [*Weeping with handkerchief in hand*] Do forgive me, Mrs. de Saint-Genis; I'm ashamed to weep like this before you, but I can't help it. To think that only one month ago he was sitting there right where you are now, and that I shall never see him again! You knew him; he was so good, so happy; he was too happy, and so were we all; it couldn't last. Do talk to me; it will give me a chance to control myself. I know I ought to make the best of it. He had to die sometime. But many a time I used to ask God to let me be the first to go. Don't you think men as good as my husband go to heaven?

MRS. DE SAINT-GENIS: There's no doubt about it, Mrs. Vigneron.

MRS. VIGNERON: Tell me about your son. I have scarcely laid eyes on him since our misfortune. He's good, too; Blanche told me he wept.

MRS. DE SAINT-GENIS: George is well, thank you.

MRS. VIGNERON: What a setback it is for the poor dears! And they love each other so much!

MRS. DE SAINT-GENIS: This marriage is exactly what I should have talked of if I had found you composed. You are not sensible or courageous, my dear. I know what it is to lose a husband. I've been all through it. Only I had more reason to complain than you. When Mr. de Saint-Genis died he left me nothing but debts and a four-year-old child on my hands. Your daughters are old enough to be a consolation to you; they are grown up; and you don't have to worry about their future or your own. [*Changing her tone*] I suppose now, in the condition you are in, you haven't given thought to your business affairs?

MRS. VIGNERON: What business affairs?

MRS. DE SAINT-GENIS: You ought to know that Mr. Vigneron's estate won't settle itself. You will have to have the apportionment settled, and perhaps there will be some difficulties to meet.

MRS. VIGNERON: Oh, no, Mrs. de Saint-Genis, no difficulties. My husband was too honest a man ever to have business difficulties.

MRS. DE SAINT-GENIS: They could arise after his death. Now listen to me. It isn't Mr. Vigneron's uprightness I'm questioning; it's that of the other people. Have you seen Mr. Teissier yet?

MRS. VIGNERON: Mr. Teissier has stayed at home as usual. I needed money, and he sent it to me after a little urging; that is the extent of our dealings.

MRS. DE SAINT-GENIS: Now listen to what I tell you, Mrs. Vigneron. Even if my advice should be wrong in this case, adopt it as a general rule: Keep an eye on Mr. Teissier.

MRS. VIGNERON: All right, I will keep an eye on him. But just suppose he should have bad intentions: it's my lawyer, not I, who should bring him to terms.

MRS. DE SAINT-GENIS: Keep an eye on your lawyer.

MRS. VIGNERON: Oh, Mrs. de Saint-Genis!

MRS. DE SAINT-GENIS: There's no use saying "Oh!" I know these lawyers, Mrs. Vigneron. You never know whether they are going to save you or be the undoing of you; and according to their ideas you are always in the wrong.

MRS. VIGNERON: What would you say if I should tell you that my lawyer, Mr. Bourdon, is also Mr. Teissier's lawyer?

MRS. DE SAINT-GENIS: I would advise you to get another.

MRS. VIGNERON: No; I have a blind confidence in Mr. Bourdon, and I shan't get rid of him till I lose it.

MRS. DE SAINT-GENIS: It will be too late then.

AUGUSTE: [*Entering and speaking to* Mrs. Vigneron] Mr. Lefort sends his regards and wants to know if you have looked over his memorandum.

MRS. VIGNERON: His memorandum! Did he give me one?

AUGUSTE: Yes, ma'am.

MRS. VIGNERON: Where did I put it? I don't know anything about it.

AUGUSTE: Mr. Lefort will call sometime during the day.

MRS. VIGNERON: Very well, tell him I will see him. [Auguste *goes out*] Mr. Lefort is our architect.

MRS. DE SAINT-GENIS: Keep an eye on your architect!

MRS. VIGNERON: I don't know where you got such a bad opinion of other people, Mrs. de Saint-Genis; but if I were you, I shouldn't display it.

MRS. DE SAINT-GENIS: It's the least I can do to put you on your guard. Everybody looks honest to you.

MRS. VIGNERON: And nobody looks honest to you.

MRS. DE SAINT-GENIS: [*Rising*] I don't wish you any harm, Mrs. Vigneron, and I hope with all my heart, for your sake and the sake of your daughters, who are really delightful girls, that everything goes smoothly in settling Mr. Vigneron's estate. But in business nothing goes smoothly. What seems simple is complicated, and what seems complicated is beyond understanding. Take my word for it, you will be wise to stop thinking a little while of him who is gone, in order to think of yourself and your children instead. Unfortunately I don't know whether Mr. Vigneron left you an annuity or government bonds. He didn't, did he? I dare say his fortune was in that factory, owned by him and Mr. Teissier together? He had land, true enough; but he had bought most of it with borrowed money and on mortgage. I tell you all this with the best of feeling. Women ought to warn and help each other. As for self-interest, it looks as though I no longer had any. We had a very nice plan, to marry our children. I must say it is not merely postponed, but really in danger. It doesn't seem possible for you to fulfill the financial obligations you undertook, and I wouldn't let **my son** make a poor marriage for anything—and have him blame me for it afterwards.

MRS. VIGNERON: Just as you please, Mrs. de Saint-Genis.

[*A pause and embarrassed silence*]

MRS. DE SAINT-GENIS: [*Speaking quickly*] Good-by, Mrs. Vigneron. Do as I tell you; look out for your interests, and we can talk about our children some other time. But for heaven's sake, Mrs. Vigneron, get this into your head—it is the most useful and the friendliest advice I can give you: Keep an eye on everybody—*everybody!* [*She goes toward the door at the rear,* Mrs. Vigneron *coldly escorting her. The door opens and* Teissier *enters*] Stay here; you needn't go to the door with me. [*She goes out*]

MRS. VIGNERON: [*Weeping, handkerchief in hand*] What a terrible thing this is, Mr. Teissier! My poor husband! It was work that killed him! Why did he work so hard? He didn't care for money; he spent nothing on himself. Oh, he wanted to see his children happy while he was living, and to leave them rich!

[*A silence*]

TEISSIER: Mrs. Vigneron, did you authorize Mrs. de Saint-Genis to come to my house to find out how things stand in regard to your husband's estate?

MRS. VIGNERON: I know nothing about it, and I should not have sanctioned it.

TEISSIER: I did my duty on the double-quick. I took the lady by the arm and showed her the door.

MRS. VIGNERON: That's all she deserved. Mrs. de Saint-Genis was here when you came, Mr. Teissier, and was talking about my husband's affairs. You know all about them and understand them better than anybody else. Won't you enlighten me?

TEISSIER: When I have a few minutes of leisure, I'll take pleasure in drawing up a statement of your husband's estate. What do you want most to know? Whether it will be settled at a loss or profit? [Mrs. Vigneron *waves her hand deprecatingly*] From off-hand calculations I have made, the situation in general looks something like this—now pay attention: when the factory is sold——

MRS. VIGNERON: Why sell it?

TEISSIER: We shall have to. When your real estate and the unfinished buildings, also, are sold——

MRS. VIGNERON: I'm going to keep my real estate.

TEISSIER: You can't. When your current debts are liquidated——

MRS. VIGNERON: But I have no debts.

TEISSIER: I figure them at about forty thousand francs. In that sum I haven't included your architect, who will have to be paid after your real estate is sold. Let me go on. After the registry tax is paid——

MRS. VIGNERON: What! Does a person have to pay for inheriting money?

TEISSIER: Certainly you have to pay, Mrs. Vigneron. Now, when the usual expenses have been met—I include under the head of "usual expenses" such things as the lawyers' fees, and those of his associates, unforeseen bills, carriage hire, postage, *etc*. In

a word, when you have closed the account which you must open under the head of "Settlement of the estate of the late Mr. Vigneron, my husband," there will be left about fifty thousand francs.

MRS. VIGNERON: Fifty thousand francs a year income.

TEISSIER: What, income? Don't you hear what I'm telling you? How do you see in what Vigneron left the capital necessary to provide an income of fifty thousand francs?

MRS. VIGNERON: [*Leaves him abruptly, and, having rung, opens the writing-desk in a hurry and writes*] "My dear Mr. Bourdon. Please come and see me as soon as you can. I shall not rest till I have seen you. Mrs. Vigneron." Fifty thousand francs! [*To* Auguste, *who has just come in*] Deliver this letter at once.

TEISSIER: [*Having taken out a pocketbook cram-full of papers*] Now if you will pay better attention while I am reading——

MRS. VIGNERON: Fifty thousand francs! [*Turning to* Teissier *and making him stuff the papers back into his pocketbook*] Keep your papers, Mr. Teissier; I want nothing more to do with you. [*She goes out at the left hurriedly*]

TEISSIER: [*Stuffing the papers back*] Ignorance, incompetence, impulsiveness—that's a woman, all over. What's she thinking of, I'd like to know? She wants to keep her lands. Well, she can't. Bourdon will have to make her understand that. If Bourdon can handle this case as he promised me he could—quickly and quietly—I can get my hands on real estate worth twice what it will cost me. But we can't lose a minute's time. Delay will bring around a crowd of prospective buyers, and that puts prices up. When Bourdon finds out that I have struck the first blow, he'll do the rest in a hurry.

[*He is going out when* Marie *enters at the left*]

MARIE: Don't go away, Mr. Teissier, before making up with my mother. She has cried so much, poor thing, that she doesn't know which end her head is on.

TEISSIER: [*Coming back*] You stopped me just in time, young woman. I was going to have your mother summoned into court, in order to recover the money I have advanced to her. For my part, I'd rather not leave your mother in this mess. [*He takes out his pocketbook again and selects a different paper from it*] Please give your mother this little bill. She can verify it easily enough: "On the seventh of January, advanced to Mrs. Vigneron 4,000 francs to pay the expenses of your father's funeral; on the fifteenth of January, advanced to Mrs. Vigneron 5,000 francs for household expenses" (at least that's what she said it was for); "on the same day"—the fifteenth, understand?—"paid out, in taking up a bill of exchange signed by your brother and drawn to the order of a money-lender named Lefébure, 10,000 francs." Your brother being under age, his signature was worthless. But your mother, knowing that your brother deceived the man about his age and personal resources, didn't want the money-lender to be cheated. [*He folds up the paper and puts it back in the pocketbook*] Now, what can I do for you?

MARIE: Please stay awhile, Mr. Teissier. It wasn't this bill that upset my mother and made her lose her temper with you. On the contrary, she would have thanked you for honoring my brother's signature. She put the blame on him, where it belongs.

TEISSIER: [*Surprised, and smiling*] Then you know what a signature is?

MARIE: My father told me.

TEISSIER: He would have done better by telling your brother.

MARIE: Sit down, Mr. Teissier. Perhaps I am rather young to talk business with you.

TEISSIER: [*Remaining standing, smiling all the while*] Go ahead, talk; I'm listening.

MARIE: Speaking for myself, I am looking for a great change in our social condition, but I don't think that we shall lose everything. In any case, Mr. Teissier, you would not advise us to be either too yielding or too rash, would you? Then what are we to do? Why, we must find out just where we stand, ask for advice, and not take a single step without knowing the why and wherefore of our condition.

TEISSIER: Ah!—Leaving aside the real estate, which doesn't concern me, what would you do with the factory, while you are waiting?

MARIE: What will happen, Mr. Teissier, if we want to keep it, and you want to sell it?

TEISSIER: It will be sold. The law provides for such a case.

MARIE: There is a law about it?

TEISSIER: [*Smiling all the while*] Yes, miss, there is a law on the subject. Article 815 of the Statutes authorizes either one of two partners to dissolve a partnership that has been broken by the death of one of them. I can prove it to you on the spot. [*Taking a book from his pocket*] You see the title of this book: "Collected Laws and Regulations in Force throughout French Territory." I always carry a copy with me. I advise you to do the same. [*He passes her the book with a certain page indicated. While she is reading he watches her with a look in which are mingled interest, pleasure, and mockery*] Do you understand it?

MARIE: Perfectly.

[*A pause*]

TEISSIER: Your name is Marie, and you are the second daughter?

MARIE: Yes, Mr. Teissier. Why?

TEISSIER: Your father had a marked preference for you.

MARIE: My father loved all his children alike.

TEISSIER: Nevertheless, he considered you cleverer than your sisters.

MARIE: He used to say so sometimes, to console me for not being as good-looking as they are.

TEISSIER: What's the matter with you? You have pretty eyes, rosy cheeks, a well-rounded figure, everything that goes to indicate a healthy woman.

MARIE: I am not worried about my appearance. All I ask is not to be noticed.

TEISSIER: Of course, you are the one that helps your mother run the house. In a pinch you would make a good private secretary.

MARIE: There has never been any necessity for it so far.

TEISSIER: Now is the time. I don't believe your mother is capable of disentangling herself alone. You will be a great help to her. Have you any taste for business?

MARIE: I understand as much of it as I have to.

TEISSIER: You're not afraid to take care of correspondence?

MARIE: No; I know what has to be said.

TEISSIER: Are you good at figures? Come, yes or no? You don't want to tell? [*Leaving her*] She ought to be a wonder at figures.

MARIE: Mr. Teissier, what do you think our real estate is worth?

TEISSIER: Your lawyer can tell you that better than I can. [*Going back toward her, after taking up his hat*] I must get back to business now, miss. I know what you are thinking of; that the factory is a fine property, and you can keep a hold on it. Who is going to assure me that it won't fall down some night? Who is going to convince me that you yourselves, by some slick trick, might not sell it so that you could buy it up at half price?

MARIE: Why should you anticipate that, Mr. Teissier?

TEISSIER: I anticipate only what I would do myself, if I were forty years old instead of sixty odd. To sum up, your need of money on the one hand, and on the other hand my knowledge of where my best interests lie, are going to end in the sale of the factory. Its condition is very prosperous. The death of its manager is a good excuse, and one that doesn't often happen along, to sell out at a profit. Have you got anything else to say to me?

MARIE: Don't go away, Mr. Teissier, without seeing my mother again. She is calmer now, and will listen to you very willingly.

TEISSIER: It's no use. I told your mother what I had to say. You are intelligent enough to explain the rest to her.

MARIE: [*Having rung*] Do what I ask, Mr. Teissier. My mother could not help losing her temper; by going in to see her, you will give her a chance to apologize.

TEISSIER: Well, just as you say. So you want us to be on good terms? I'll tell you right now, you can't gain anything by it. How old are you, Miss Marie? Scarcely turned twenty! And already a modest, sensible little woman, who is able to express herself very clearly. [*Leaving her*] And what her father did not tell me, a very tempting creature.

[Auguste *enters*]

MARIE: Go with Auguste, please; he will take you in to my mother.

TEISSIER: My best wishes for you, miss.

[*He goes out at the left, at a signal from Auguste to follow him*]

MARIE: [*Bursting into tears*] Oh, Father, Father!

BLANCHE: [*Entering and going slowly over to her sister*] What's the matter, dear?

MARIE: Mr. Teissier.

BLANCHE: Is it that scoundrel you've been with such a long while?

MARIE: Hush, dear, hush! We must be careful now and not talk indiscreetly.

BLANCHE: Why?

MARIE: Why? I don't want to tell you; but whether you know to-day or to-morrow, it will be just as hard for you.

BLANCHE: What do you mean by that?

MARIE: We may be ruined.

BLANCHE: Ruined!

[Marie *lowers her head.* Blanche *bursts into tears, and the two girls put their arms around each other. Then they separate, but* Blanche *continues to weep, and is greatly affected*]

MARIE: I shouldn't have told you about a misfortune that may not happen. Here is the whole truth: I don't yet see very clearly into our situation, but it doesn't look promising. Nevertheless, it may all come out right, on one condition: that we are reasonable, prudent, careful in our dealings with everybody, and make up our minds from this moment to overlook many distasteful things.

BLANCHE: You can do as you please, Mama, Judith and you; but I shall have nothing to do with it. I should like to sleep until after I am married.

MARIE: Until after your marriage, dear!

BLANCHE: Now what have you on your mind?

MARIE: I'm sorry to think that this marriage, which means so much to you, may not take place, after all.

BLANCHE: You are wrong, if you think Mr. de Saint-Genis thinks more about a dowry than he does about a loving heart.

MARIE: Men want both when they marry. But even if Mr. de Saint-Genis were the most disinterested man in the world, he has a mother who will do the calculating for him.

BLANCHE: His mother is his mother. If she has faults, I don't want to see them. But she has been married, and she would not want her son to be disloyal to another woman.

MARIE: Let's not be unreasonable and unjust in our misfortune, dear. Both families have promised certain things; if we cannot keep ours, Mr. de Saint-Genis will be released from his.

BLANCHE: You are wrong, you are wrong, I am sure of it. If I should say the word to-morrow, or a year from now, or ten years from now, George would marry me, just as he ought to do, if I wished

it. You see, dear, my marriage is not like so many others, which can take place or not, without doing harm. You don't know how you are hurting me by having the least doubt about its taking place. [*Pause*] Tell me something about how we are ruined.

MARIE: Later on; I don't know myself, yet.

BLANCHE: Who told you about it?

MARIE: Mr. Teissier. I must tell you again to be careful. Mr. Teissier is in the other room with Mama. I have just made it up between them.

BLANCHE: Were they angry with each other?

MARIE: Yes, they were. Mama lost her temper and told him to get out.

BLANCHE: She did right.

MARIE: She did wrong; and she knew it right away. Our situation is bad enough without making it worse by hasty and thoughtless actions. Bear in mind, Blanche, the very existence of all of us, you as well as the rest of us, is at stake. No matter how sure you may feel of Mr. de Saint-Genis, a man looks twice before marrying a woman who hasn't a cent. You are the sweetest little woman in the world; you are all heart and feelings; for you money doesn't exist; but you will find it exists for other people. You will find that out wherever you go. In business, for instance; and we are engaged in business with Mr. Teissier. In marriages, too, as perhaps you are going to learn to your cost. Money certainly has its price. Otherwise there would not be so many misfortunes coming from the lack of it, or so many vile deeds committed because of it.

BLANCHE: [*Aside*] Is it possible that a young man like him, loving and beloved as he is, would stoop to such a base act rather than sacrifice his money interests?

MARIE: You know what I would like, don't you, dear? You know I want this marriage to take place, because you see happiness in it. But if I were in your place, I should be prepared for anything. I should be in raptures if it took place; and if it didn't I should be resigned.

BLANCHE: Resigned! If I thought that Mr. de Saint-Genis had sought me out for my money, I shouldn't be able to hold up my head again. And if he refused to marry me because I had lost my money, I should either go crazy or I should die.

MARIE: Then you do love him a great deal?

BLANCHE: Yes, I do. If you want to know, I worship him! He is kind and loving, and childlike, just as I am. I am positive he has a big heart and couldn't bring himself to do a wrong thing. You can see, can't you, how much I want to marry him? But even if I should be deceived in him; if I should find out that he was not worthy of either love or respect; if he should prove to be the vilest creature in the world, I should still have to marry him——

MARIE: [*Aside*] The poor girl is suffering so much she doesn't know what she is saying.

BLANCHE: [*Aside*] Oh, what a mistake! What a mistake!—You know me, sister dear. We have lived ogether for twenty years without any secrets from each other. Haven't I been a good girl? I have been very affectionate, I know; but haven't I been good, oo? I have never had a single thought that I couldn't ell. If I had met Mr. de Saint-Genis in the street, I shouldn't have even looked at him. But he came here arm in arm with my father. We liked each other immediately, and so we were engaged. Mama old me to keep an eye on the future, but I couldn't see any great harm or wrong in trusting him.

MARIE: Come, don't go on that way; you are exaggerating, as you always do. You told Mr. de Saint-Genis that you loved him, I suppose? Well, you are going to marry him, so that's excusable. You held hands sometimes? Perhaps you let him kiss you? You shouldn't have done that; but it doesn't call for all the reproaches you are heaping on yourself.

BLANCHE: [*After a little hesitation*] I am his wife, do you hear? I am his wife!

MARIE: [*Very innocently*] I don't see what you mean.

BLANCHE: [*At first overcome with amazement*] Oh, forgive me, dearie. You are as pure as an angel. I shouldn't have spoken to you that way. Forget what I have just said; don't try to understand it; and please don't say anything about it to Mama or Judith.

MARIE: Either you are slightly out of your head or I am rather stupid.

BLANCHE: Yes, that's it; I am out of my head. And you are the dearest and sweetest sister any one ever had. [*She kisses her passionately*]

BOURDON: [*Entering*] How do you do? Your mother is in, isn't she? Will you please tell her that I am here?

MARIE: You go, dear.

[Blanche *goes out at the left*]

BOURDON: Your mother just wrote me that she was very eager to see me; and I can readily believe it. I have been at my office every day, waiting for her to call me.

MARIE: My mother has been so afflicted, Mr. Bourdon, and has suffered so much——

BOURDON: I understand perfectly, my dear young lady, that a woman who has had such a blow as your mother can't enjoy paying visits or going shopping. But it is no more than proper to see your lawyer, or at least to ask him to drop in. Fortunately, your father's estate does not offer very great difficulties. Nevertheless, your father left considerable real estate which ought to be inspected at once and turned into cash as soon as possible. Understand me, as soon as possible.

MARIE: Here's Mother.

MRS. VIGNERON: [*Weeping, handkerchief in hand*] What a terrible blow, Mr. Bourdon! What a dreadful thing! My poor husband! I don't seem to be able to weep enough. I just know I shall never live through it.

[*A silence*]

BOURDON: Tell me, Mrs. Vigneron, while I happen to think of it: did you give Mrs. de Saint-Genis permission to call on me to learn how things stand in regard to your husband's estate?

MRS. VIGNERON: She had no permission from me. And so Mrs. de Saint-Genis paid you a visit too——!

BOURDON: Don't worry about that. The way I treated her she won't want to come again. You wanted to see me, Mrs. Vigneron. Please speak quickly and clearly, and make it brief.

MRS. VIGNERON: I won't detain you long, Mr. Bourdon. I have only one question to ask you. Is it true—is it possible that my husband left all told only fifty thousand francs?

BOURDON: Who told you that?

MRS. VIGNERON: Mr. Teissier.

BOURDON: Fifty thousand francs! Teissier was too quick about it. You know him; he isn't a bad man, but he is brutal when it comes to a matter of money. I hope you will get more than that out of it, Mrs. Vigneron, and I will do all I can, you may be sure. [Mrs. Vigneron *bursts into tears and sinks upon the couch;* Bourdon *goes over to her*] So, you were hoping that Mr. Vigneron's estate would amount to a great deal? What was your estimate?

MRS. VIGNERON: I don't know, Mr. Bourdon.

BOURDON: But you should have figured up what your husband left. When a woman loses her husband, that's the first thing she should think of. [*He walks away*] However, it was none the less wrong on Teissier's part—and I'll tell him so, too—to name an amount at random. Business isn't conducted that way. In a settlement, the way to begin is at the beginning, taking up the most urgent matters: then advancing step by step until the end is reached —and then you have what you have. [*Returning to* Mrs. Vigneron] Have you made any decision, Mrs. Vigneron, about your real estate? There your necessity is manifest; it must be sold.

MARIE: How much do you think it would bring us?

BOURDON: [*Going over to* Marie] How much? Nothing. You can't count on anything.

MRS. VIGNERON: [*Rising*] Then what is the advantage of getting rid of it?

BOURDON: [*Returning to* Mrs. Vigneron] What advantage, Mrs. Vigneron? By doing so you remove the shackles from your feet. Believe me, I am not usually so downright in my advice as I am at this moment. Each day's delay is filled with grave consequences for you. While you are deliberating, Catiline is at the gates of Rome; Catiline being, in this case, the mortgages that are eating you up, your architect with his bill, and the civil authorities, with their taxes and fees.

[Teissier *reenters at the left;* Blanche *comes in behind him*]

TEISSIER: How are you, Bourdon?

BOURDON: How do you do, Teissier? I was just

explaining to Mrs. Vigneron and her daughter the impossibility of their holding on to their real estate.

TEISSIER: I have nothing to say as to that. The ladies couldn't find a better adviser than you. They are in good hands.

BOURDON: Mrs. Vigneron, please look at the thing from my point of view, so that we won't misunderstand each other. I don't want to be reproached later on for what wasn't my fault. I restrict myself to this principle: the *status quo* being deadly against you, you must get rid of the *status quo*. I can't say that your real estate is well situated, or that this is the best time to put it up at auction. Far from it. But, by having the sale at the most favorable time—and I'll look out for that—and getting rid of certain obstacles, together with some smooth work and clever advertising, we may get something good out of it.

TEISSIER: [*Aside*] What's that? What's that? [*In a low voice to* Bourdon] Then we're not working together in this?

BOURDON: [*In a low tone to* Teissier] Let me go ahead. [*Going over to* Mrs. Vigneron] Now, then, Mrs. Vigneron, think it over; but think it over quickly, I urge you. When you have made up your mind, please let me know. [*He makes a move as if to go*]

TEISSIER: Don't go, Bourdon, without saying something about the factory.

BOURDON: The factory can wait, friend Teissier. I want to help Mrs. Vigneron get rid of her real estate before we do anything else. We see here a widow and four children who are growing poorer every day. That's a mighty important state of things; we mustn't forget that.

[Teissier *smiles*]

AUGUSTE: [*Entering, and in a low voice to* Mrs. Vigneron] Mr. Lefort is here, ma'am.

MRS. VIGNERON: Please wait for a minute, Mr. Bourdon. After hearing what our architect has to say you may change your mind.

BOURDON: Just as you say, madam.

MRS. VIGNERON: [*To* Auguste] Bring Mr. Lefort in, and ask Judith to come here.

[Lefort *enters*]

MRS. VIGNERON: [*Weeping, her handkerchief in her hand*] What a terrible blow, Mr. Lefort! What a dreadful thing! My poor husband! I shall never get over his loss.

LEFORT: [*Has vulgar manners and a powerful voice*] Come, madam, don't cry like that. With a little nerve and perseverance you can fill your husband's boots. [*He goes up stage*]

TEISSIER: Hello, Lefort!

LEFORT: Glad to see you, Teissier.

[Judith *enters*]

MARIE: [*To* Lefort] Were you very much interested, Mr. Lefort, in the buildings entrusted to you?

LEFORT: Yes, miss. Vigneron was more like a brother than a client.

MARIE: We are on the eve of making an important decision——

LEFORT: Ask me anything you want to. My time is yours, my money is at your service. Vigneron's children are my children.

MARIE: If you had some explanations, or even some project, to let us hear, please tell us in the presence of these gentlemen.

LEFORT: I am ready, miss. These gentlemen don't scare me. It's a way of mine to stand right up to everybody.

MRS. VIGNERON: Sit there, Mr. Lefort.

LEFORT: [*Seated*] Have you looked at my memorandum, madam? No? That's bad. It contained a little account of Mr. Vigneron's real estate, showing the whole business from A to Z. If I had that account right here before me, I could be briefer and make you understand better.

MARIE: I can give it to you, Mr. Lefort. I put it away myself.

LEFORT: If you please.

[Marie *goes to the writing-desk, passing in front of her mother and* Teissier, *who are seated side by side*]

TEISSIER: [*To* Mrs. Vigneron] Is your daughter methodical?

MRS. VIGNERON: Very.

TEISSIER: She's likely to grow up to be a clever woman, isn't she?

MRS. VIGNERON: Yes, I think so.

TEISSIER: Is she good at figures?

[*No reply*]

BOURDON: [*Having taken the memorandum from* Marie, *detaches part of it and hands it to* Lefort] That's what you want, undoubtedly. If you don't mind, I'll run over your memorandum while I'm listening to you.

[*The two exchange hostile glances*]

LEFORT: [*Stressing each phrase*] In the first place, Mr. Vigneron's real estate, situated on the outskirts of Paris near a railway station, and on that account under a thousand disadvantages, was, at the price he paid for it, a sorry bargain. To speak plainly, he was a sucker.

BOURDON: Stop! Nobody had any reason to deceive Mr. Vigneron. He bought this land hoping it would be taken by eminent domain.

LEFORT: By whom?

BOURDON: By the railroad.

LEFORT: Great joke, that is! It was the railroad that sold it to him.

BOURDON: Are you sure of that?

LEFORT: Absolutely sure.

BOURDON: Well, even so. Then he must have supposed that the city, which had undertaken some big work in the neighborhood, would need that land. I remember, now; he expected to do business with the city.

LEFORT: Huh! With the city or with the Turks! You can't tell me anything about real estate. I know the lay of Paris land from A to Z. Well, I'll go on. Mr. Vigneron having been caught for a sucker—I say it again—very quickly realized his foolishness and wanted to dodge the consequences. How could he do it? By building on the land. Then he sent for me. He knew of old that I was square and straightforward, and before I left him he had given me the work of making plans. Unfortunately, I had scarcely begun the work, and the foundations had hardly been laid [*He accompanies his words with a comical pantomime*] when Vigneron moved on to the next world.

BOURDON: We know all these details, my dear fellow. You are wasting our time in telling them over again.

LEFORT: The heirs are in a bad fix; but they can get out of it and make something, too. They can command the services of a man who is faithful, intelligent and highly esteemed throughout the building profession in Paris. That man is the architect who served the deceased. He is now their architect. Will they listen to him? If they ignore his advice and management [*Another comical pantomime*] their goose is cooked.

BOURDON: Now, sir, cutting out phraseology, what's your plan?

LEFORT: Let's reason it out from the least favorable hypothesis. Leave Lefort out of it. He put in an honest bill, without quibbling over each item. He asked for nothing more for himself. Now what's going to become of the real estate? I repeat that it is situated far from the center of the city, and I add that it suffers from numerous other defects. It is encumbered with mortgages. These are just so many points which some unknown purchaser could turn against the owners. [*Volubly*] It would be like this: somebody would depreciate the property, precipitate a public sale, get rid of any honest prospective buyers, fool the courts into granting a judgment at some miserably small sum, pack the auction [*More pantomime*] and there you have a property reduced to nothing.

BOURDON: I demand, sir, that you be more precise. You say somebody would do this, that, and the other. Who would do it, pray? Do you know that only one person could do it, and that you are slandering the lawyer who has charge of the settlement of the estate?

LEFORT: That's you, ain't it?

BOURDON: I am not speaking for myself, sir, but for all my brother lawyers, whom you are libelling. You are attacking, offhand, the most respectable body of men I know of. You are bringing under suspicion the Law itself, in the persons of the officers sworn to execute it. Sir, you are doing worse, if it be possible. You are disturbing the security of families. Really, now, it's rather stiff to make an accusation like this, and then bring in a bill of thirty-seven thousand francs!

LEFORT: I should like to be present when you present *your* bill.

BOURDON: Enough, sir! Now, briefly, what do you propose?

LEFORT: I'm coming to my proposal. I propose that the Vigneron heirs carry out the building——

BOURDON: Well, now, that's what I thought you were getting at. You are the architect, and you propose to continue the building operations.

LEFORT: Let me go on, sir.

BOURDON: It isn't worth while. If Mrs. Vigneron wants to listen to you, she may; but I can't bear such rambling talk any longer. How much money can you sink in it? Mrs. Vigneron has no money; of that I warn you. Where is yours? In three months we should be back at the same point, with this difference—that your bill, now thirty-seven thousand francs, would be doubled, at the rate you are going. Don't force me to say any more. I take your offers in the spirit they are made. I don't want to witness any such shady transaction, which would hand the ownership over to you for a song.

LEFORT: Do you know what you are saying, sir? Look me in the eye. Do I look like a man who would indulge in shady transactions? Upon my soul, I never saw such a clown as you in my life.

BOURDON: [*Restraining himself, and speaking just above a whisper*] What did you call me? You humbug!

[Mrs. Vigneron *rises to intervene*]

TEISSIER: Let 'em go on, madam; don't say anything. Never interrupt a business conversation.

LEFORT: [*To* Mrs. Vigneron] I give in, madam. If you want to know my plan and the resources at my disposal, you can call me again. In the other event, you will please settle my bill as soon as possible. I have to advance money to my clients; while lawyers juggle with their clients' money. [*He goes out*]

TEISSIER: Wait for me, Lefort. We'll go up street together. [*To* Mrs. Vigneron] I leave you in Bourdon's hands, Mrs. Vigneron. Profit by his advice.

LEFORT: [*Returning*] I forgot to say, madam— was it with your permission that Mrs. de Saint-Genis came to my place——?

MRS. VIGNERON: She has been everywhere! I gave nobody permission to go to see you, Mr. Lefort; nobody. And if she comes again——

LEFORT: She won't. She went down the stairs quicker than she came up.

TEISSIER: [*To* Marie] Good-by, Miss Marie, and good health to you. [*He leaves her, and then comes back*] Stay as you are. You won't lack lovers. If I were not so old, I'd get in line.

[*He and* Lefort *go out together*]

BOURDON: Well, madam?

MRS. VIGNERON: What have I done, Mr. Bourdon to have such a scene?

BOURDON: I shall not regret that discussion, madam, if it shows you where your interests lie.

MRS. VIGNERON: Putting aside what has just passed, let's look at things as they are. I agree that Mr. Lefort is a man who lacks good breeding, but he has a good deal of common sense and a knack of getting things done. After all, what he proposes is nothing more than what my husband would have done, if he had lived.

BOURDON: Are you serious, madam, in what you are saying? Haven't you learned to appraise that architect's offers at their real value?

MRS. VIGNERON: By taking somebody else we could——

BOURDON: You are not satisfied yet? [*A pause*] Come here, young ladies; you are not in the way. Your mother is wandering in cloudland; help me get her back on earth. Mrs. Vigneron, I am not going to present the matter in its best light. Admitting, for the sake of argument, that the real estate belongs to you—forgetting the creditors and mortgagees who have claims on it—do you know what it would cost to finish those buildings of yours, of which the foundations have hardly been put in? Four to five hundred thousand francs! You know well that Mr. Lefort hasn't that amount. You cannot count on me to get it for you. And then, even if you could get it through me or any one else, would it look well for a woman, I ask, to place herself at the head of a large establishment and throw herself into an enterprise that nobody could see the end of? This question that I am asking you is so serious that if it were brought up before the civil authorities, whose duty it is to help you bring up your minor children, it could be opposed on the ground that the children's inheritances—what little they have—were being risked in mere speculation. [*Speaking solemnly*] As a member of that civil board, pledged to look out for the best interest of minor children—the greatest duty in existence—I should oppose it myself. [*Silence*] Take heed, madam. I will not overstep the bounds of my duty by saying anything more. You know where my office is; I will await further orders there. [*He goes out*]

MRS. VIGNERON: Let's talk awhile, children. Don't all speak at once, and try to listen. Mr. Lefort——

JUDITH: [*Interrupting*] Oh, Mr. Lefort!

MRS. VIGNERON: You don't know yet what I was going to say. Perhaps Mr. Lefort did express himself very clumsily, but I believe he has a good and loyal heart.

JUDITH: I don't believe so.

MRS. VIGNERON: Why?

JUDITH: I think he has the manner of a swindler.

MRS. VIGNERON: Oh! And you, Blanche; do you think Mr. Lefort has a swindler's manner?

BLANCHE: Yes, somewhat. I agree with Judith.

MRS. VIGNERON: So! Anyhow, his advice seems better to me than Mr. Bourdon's. All Mr. Bourdon's amounts to is that we shall sell our property. What do you think, Marie?

MARIE: I haven't anything to say just yet.

MRS. VIGNERON: We're making a splendid headway, are we not?—Well, then, what do you think about Mr. Teissier?

MARIE: It seems to me that if we don't offend him, but show him a little regard, we may get help from Mr. Teissier.

BLANCHE: What's that, Marie? Mr. Teissier is the most treacherous and dangerous man in the world.

MRS. VIGNERON: Judith?

JUDITH: I don't know who is right, Marie or Blanche; but the way I look at it, we can't count on getting help from any one but Mr. Bourdon.

MRS. VIGNERON: I don't agree with you, dear. Mr. Bourdon! Mr. Bourdon! There is one question that Mr. Bourdon should have asked me right off, and he never seemed once to think of it. Then I noticed something obscure about his words. What did he mean by saying: "Catiline is at the gates of Rome"? [*To* Marie] Did you understand that?

MARIE: Yes, I understood it.

MRS. VIGNERON: You did? Is that so? We won't talk about it any more; you are wiser than I am. But Mr. Bourdon could have spoken to me about Catiline some other time. Why didn't he ask if we needed money? Now listen, children. If we must sell the real estate, we must. What we shall lose, we shall lose. But remember what your mother says; once and forever, as long as I live: they shall *not* touch the factory.

MARIE: You are wrong there, Mama.

MRS. VIGNERON: As long as I live they shan't touch the factory!

MARIE: Mr. Teissier could sell it to-day. He has a legal right to do it.

MRS. VIGNERON: As long as I live——

MARIE: There is a law——

BLANCHE AND JUDITH: If there is a law!

MRS. VIGNERON: Come, don't bother me about your law. If I should go through many days like this, I couldn't stand it; you would soon be without either father or mother. [*She falls upon the couch, weeping*]

AUGUSTE: [*Entering*] Here are some letters for you, ma'am.

MRS. VIGNERON: [*To* Marie] Take these and read them, dear.

MARIE: This one is a letter from your dressmaker: "Dear Madam: We take the liberty of sending you your bill, and beg to remind you that it has passed the ordinary credit limit. Our cashier will call upon you to-day. Believe us, madam, yours very truly. P.S. May we call your attention to a brand new dress-goods called 'short-term mourning,' which looks well on young women, and can be worn by misses with equally good effect." [*She opens and reads another letter:*] "Dear Madam: Mr. Dubois hereby gives you permission to sub-let your apartment, which will not be difficult, provided you make a small sacrifice. Mr. Dubois would like to do more, but he cannot. If he should permit you to break a lease on account of the death of the lessee, he would be establishing a precedent which would cause him much trouble." [*Third letter:*] "Dear Madam: I sent to your house last week concerning my bill against you, and my young lady representative was rudely treated by your servants, and could not make collection. Not being able to reach you, I do not know how to understand a delay which must not be further prolonged. I do not run after business, and as you know, madam, I do not advertise in the papers; I leave that to the big Parisian houses that charge you more on that account. If I am able to make hats at a surprisingly low price, at the same time showing originality and superior workmanship, it is merely because of my large business and regular collections."

[Marie *prepares to read a fourth letter.* Mrs. Vigneron *stops her and begins to weep. The young girls look on without a word, with bowed heads, saddened and frightened*]

CURTAIN

ACT III.

The scene is the same as in the first and second acts.

ROSALIE: Sit down, ma'am.

MRS. DE SAINT-GENIS: [*Hesitating and annoyed*] I don't know.

ROSALIE: Do as I tell you, ma'am. Sit down there and be comfortable, with your pretty little feet on this hassock.

MRS. DE SAINT-GENIS: Don't urge me, Rosalie. I am wondering whether it would be wiser to wait or to come again.

ROSALIE: Do as I say, ma'am. Wait. You'll get me in trouble with Blanchy if I let you go away without seeing her.

MRS. DE SAINT-GENIS: Blanche will see me a little later. She is just the one I came to see, and I want to talk to her about a very serious matter. I didn't think Mrs. Vigneron would have company at luncheon.

ROSALIE: Not company; no, there's no company.

MRS. DE SAINT-GENIS: The ladies of the house are at luncheon; is that what you mean?

ROSALIE: Yes.

MRS. DE SAINT-GENIS: They are not alone, are they?

ROSALIE: No.

MRS. DE SAINT-GENIS: Then there is somebody with them?

ROSALIE: Yes. [*In a low voice*] Mr. Teissier.

MRS. DE SAINT-GENIS: Oh, Mr. Teissier! [*Coming close to* Rosalie] He comes here now, does he?

ROSALIE: Oftener than folks like to have him.

MRS. DE SAINT-GENIS: But they give him a welcome?

ROSALIE: They have to. The young ladies are right in not liking him, but the need of being on good terms with him overcomes that feeling.

MRS. DE SAINT-GENIS: On good terms with him? What for?

ROSALIE: For the sake of their fortune.

MRS. DE SAINT-GENIS: Yes, Rosalie, for the sake of their fortune [*Moving away*] or his.

ROSALIE: You're going to stay, aren't you, ma'am?

MRS. DE SAINT-GENIS: No, I'm going. I've made up my mind. Mr. Teissier is here, and the ladies have business with him. What business? I don't want to embarrass anybody, or pry into any secrets. [*She goes toward the door*]

ROSALIE: Will you call again, ma'am?

MRS. DE SAINT-GENIS: I'll call again.

ROSALIE: Surely?

MRS. DE SAINT-GENIS: Surely. Listen, Rosalie. If Mrs. Vigneron and her daughters—except Blanche, you understand—wish to go out, let them go; don't let them put themselves out for me. Blanche is the only one who need wait in for me. I want to speak with her once and for all. You are her old nurse; so you tell her to keep calm—to think it all over—to make up her mind to the inevitable—that it isn't my fault that her father is dead—that she must take into account her financial condition—and my son can't be responsible—that he can't—not by any means—— Now, Rosalie, do you understand what I'm asking you to say?

ROSALIE: Certainly I understand, ma'am. But you mustn't expect me to say anything that would distress my little Blanchy.

MRS. DE SAINT-GENIS: There, that's your bell. See what's wanted, and I'll find my own way out. [*She leaves*]

ROSALIE: She gives me the creeps, that woman does. I cross myself every time she comes in and goes out.

[*The third door at the rear opens.* Teissier *comes in with* Marie *on his arm, and* Mrs. Vigneron *behind them. Then come* Judith, *and finally* Blanche. Rosalie *steps aside to let them pass; she stops* Blanche, *arranges her dress and embraces her, then goes out through the open door, closing it behind her*]

TEISSIER: Do you mind if I lean on you a little? I'm not used to eating so much at luncheon, and with such nice people. [*Stopping*] What did I say at the table?

MARIE: Different things.

TEISSIER: What about?

MARIE: About life in general.

TEISSIER: Did we say anything about your affairs?

MARIE: The subject didn't come up.

[*They proceed, going toward the right; then* Marie *disengages herself and walks away*]

TEISSIER: [*Following her*] Your sisters are nice;

the oldest one, especially, is well built. Yet I prefer you. I haven't always been old. I can still tell a blonde from a brunette. I'm very much pleased with you, understand?

MARIE: Pay a little attention to my mother.

TEISSIER: Why is it, Mrs. Vigneron, that Gaston, the boy that writes such fine I. O. U.'s, didn't have luncheon with us?

MRS. VIGNERON: [With some emotion] My son is engaged.

TEISSIER: He's gone soldiering. That's the best thing he could do. A soldier is lodged, fed, and warmed at the expense of the government. What risk does he take? None but being killed. And then he doesn't need anything.

MRS. VIGNERON: My son did what he wished; but he will be sorry for it later. I wanted to arrange with you, Mr. Teissier, to put him in the factory; and if the factory, as I believe, doesn't go out of your hands or ours, Gaston would take his father's place in a few years.

[Silence]

TEISSIER: Have you seen Bourdon?

MRS. VIGNERON: No. Should we see him?

TEISSIER: [Embarrassed and making no reply, but turning to Marie] Your sisters are nice; but they are city women. You can see that at a glance. No color. Looking at you, nobody would ever say that you had been brought up with them. In the summer I have roses in my garden, but they haven't the bloom your cheeks have. You and your mother and sisters must come and visit my country house. You are no longer children, so you won't hurt anything. You can have luncheon at home before you start, and be back in time for dinner. You haven't many diversions; that will be one for us.

MARIE: You mustn't expect us to come to see you, Mr. Teissier, before our position is easier. You know we haven't progressed a bit, just got more tangled up, that's all. We are being tormented now by our old tradesmen. They have become very impatient creditors.

TEISSIER: [Embarrassed, and making no reply, but turning to Mrs. Vigneron] If you want to go on with your work, madam, don't bother about me. Your girls will keep me company until I go.

MRS. VIGNERON: Stay as long as you please; we shan't send you away. [Going over to Marie] Have you spoken to Mr. Teissier?

MARIE: No, not yet.

MRS. VIGNERON: Are you ashamed to?

MARIE: Yes, I am ashamed to. Twelve thousand francs is a big sum to ask for.

MRS. VIGNERON: Let's not ask for it.

MARIE: And where shall we be to-morrow if that dressmaker puts her bill in the hands of a sheriff? She will do just as she said.

MRS. VIGNERON: Do you want me to take Mr. Teissier aside and save you from doing it?

MARIE: No. This is the time to show courage, and I am going to show it.

TEISSIER: [Seated on the couch beside Judith] Do you get along well with your sisters?

JUDITH: Very well.

TEISSIER: Who is the cleverest of you three?

JUDITH: Marie.

TEISSIER: Miss Marie. [He looks at her] Does she think very much about getting married?

JUDITH: She never says anything about it.

TEISSIER: Yet people think she is pretty.

JUDITH: She is more than pretty; she is charming.

TEISSIER: Exactly. [He looks again at Marie] She isn't a living skeleton, like so many of the young girls, and she isn't a heavyweight, either. Has she a firm character?

JUDITH: Very.

TEISSIER: Simple tastes?

JUDITH: Very simple.

TEISSIER: Is she the kind of woman who would stay at home and like to take care of an old person?

JUDITH: Maybe.

TEISSIER: Could a person give her the keys of a house, without being uneasy about it? [Judith looks at him in astonishment] Then what's she thinking of? Why doesn't she have a talk with me? [Rising and speaking to Judith] I don't want to keep you, miss. Go over there [Pointing at Blanche] where your sister is sitting, looking as though she were doing penance. [Marie approaches him. He joins her and they come out to the front of the stage] What do you call that little thing you have there?

MARIE: Just a purse.

TEISSIER: What for?

MARIE: A charity bazaar.

TEISSIER: For the poor? I see. You're working for them while they are loafing.

MARIE: Mr. Teissier, my mother wants me to ask something of you that she herself doesn't dare to ask.

TEISSIER: What is it?

MARIE: As I was telling you just now, it seems that our tradesmen have got their heads together. Where we once couldn't get them to send in their bills, now it is a question of which can get his money first.

TEISSIER: These people are within their rights in claiming their due.

MARIE: Unfortunately we haven't the amount necessary to settle with them. A pretty round sum. Twelve thousand francs. Mr. Teissier, please lend us this much more; you will be relieving us of many little embarrassments, which are sometimes worse than big ones.

[A pause]

TEISSIER: Have you seen Bourdon?

MARIE: No. Do we have to see Bourdon?

TEISSIER: You know well that this state of things can't last, either for you or for me. Twelve thousand francs that you want and twenty thousand that you owe me make thirty-two thousand francs that have come out of my pocket. I am not risking anything, of course. I know where to get back that money. But it certainly must come back to me. You won't be surprised to learn that I have taken steps toward that end. Don't cry; don't cry. You have time enough ahead of you to get sunken eyes and hollow cheeks. Keep your twenty-year-old advantages; a little girl of your age, blooming and flourishing, is unhappy only when she wants to be. Understand me? Only when she wants to be. [*He quits her suddenly, takes his hat and goes over to* Mrs. Vigneron] Your second daughter has just told me that you need twelve thousand francs. You needn't add anything to what she said; it isn't necessary. Just you wait while I go and get the money. [*He goes out abruptly*]

MRS. VIGNERON: Thanks, Marie dear. It makes one feel so silly and shamefaced to have to take money from that old codger! At the last minute I really came near deciding not to ask him for it.

MARIE: It's done.

MRS. VIGNERON: Judith—where are you going, child?

JUDITH: I'm going to leave you; I need sleep.

MRS. VIGNERON: Stay here, please do.

JUDITH: But, Mama——

MRS. VIGNERON: [*Commandingly*] Stay here! [*Judith obeys, and goes over to her mother*] Isn't our situation serious? Doesn't it interest you? We can't talk about it half enough.

JUDITH: What's the use talking about it? We are always saying over the same things without making the slightest decision. Don't you see it requires a different kind of woman than you to get us out of the scrape we are in?

MRS. VIGNERON: Soon you'll be saying that I am not doing my duty.

JUDITH: I don't say that. It isn't your fault that you don't understand anything about business.

MRS. VIGNERON: Then why don't you take charge of our business affairs?

JUDITH: Excuse me! I can't add a column of figures.

MRS. VIGNERON: Nobody is asking you to add a column of figures. We are asking you to be here, to take part in the discussion, and give us your opinion when you have any.

JUDITH: You know what my opinion is; and it won't change. We can't do anything, and there is nothing to do.

MRS. VIGNERON: But suppose they are robbing us?

JUDITH: Well, then they'll rob us. You can't stop them and I can't. Neither can Marie. She ought to see plainly that we must wait for something to turn up. As for me, I should like a thousand times better —yes, a thousand times—to settle the whole thing to-day and take what they leave us, because they really *are* willing to leave us something. Then, when we no longer had to think about the past, we could think about the future.

MRS. VIGNERON: You talk very glibly about the future, Judith.

JUDITH: It worries me, but it doesn't frighten me. I think Blanche is by far the most unfortunate of us. She is going to lose the man she loves.

MARIE: Nobody said she was going to lose him.

JUDITH: On the contrary, everybody says so. It's as clear as daylight that Blanche won't be married. If I were in her place, I shouldn't wait for Mr. de Saint-Genis to ask for his release; I'd throw him over myself.

MRS. VIGNERON: Now just see, Judith, what silly things you've been saying in the last five minutes. First you hurt me, and now you have discouraged one of your sisters and made the other one cry.

JUDITH: [*Going over to* Blanche] Are you angry with me?

BLANCHE: No, I'm not angry with you. You don't know Mr. de Saint-Genis, or you wouldn't say such things. I was very glad to be able to bring him a dowry, but he won't love me less because I have lost it, and he will have just the same desire to marry me. All the trouble comes from his mother. But sooner or later mothers have to give in, and Mrs. de Saint-Genis will do just as the rest. She will find that the wisest thing is to give her consent, when she sees that we would marry without it. You are right, Judith, when you say that we are not defending ourselves very well. But though we may lack decision in dealing with our business affairs, I don't lack any in regard to my marriage.

MRS. VIGNERON: Oh, dear! I don't understand you, girls. You are always talking about decision: we lack decision; we must have decision. You don't say anything else. And when I propose some real idea, you are the first ones to throw cold water on it. Come now, yes or no: do you want me to dismiss Mr. Bourdon and get another lawyer?

MARIE: Who?

MRS. VIGNERON: Who? The first one that comes along. [*To* Judith] That man, for instance, who sent us his card.

JUDITH: Take him; I'd just as lief.

MARIE: I'm opposed to it.

MRS. VIGNERON: Well, children, I'll have to settle it. If Mr. Bourdon says one more word to me—just one more word—that seems out of place to me, I'll get rid of him and send for this other man. But first of all, where is this man's card? [*Silence*] Look in the desk for it, Judith, and look carefully. Marie, you look on the piano, perhaps it's over there. Blanche, you look, too. Do something! Look on the shelf over the fireplace. [*Another silence*] You needn't look any more, children. I have it in my pocket. [*To* Judith] What are you laughing about?

JUDITH: I had to laugh. I was thinking that our enemies know what they do with *their* things.

MRS. VIGNERON: [*Sadly*] Are you going to begin again?

JUDITH: No; I'm not going to, and I'm sorry for

what I said. If I said anything wrong, I didn't mean to. I wish this whole business was over with. It makes us irritable and sour-tempered; and instead of fighting our enemies we quarrel with one another. One might think that we should have loved each other more when we were happier; but the contrary is true.

[*She kisses her mother.* Marie *and* Blanche *make up. All are greatly affected*]

ROSALIE: [*Entering*] Mr. Bourdon, ma'am.

JUDITH: This time I *am* going.

MRS. VIGNERON: Go to bed, children. I'll talk with Mr. Bourdon.

[*The three girls leave*]

BOURDON: [*Entering*] Seeing how useless my previous advice proved, Mrs. Vigneron, I had intended to let matters take their course and not come to see you until you were ready for me. Believe me, I have no hand in the bad news I have been asked to bring you.

MRS. VIGNERON: I am beginning to get used to bad news, Mr. Bourdon.

BOURDON: You must, madam, you must. In your position, courage and resignation are of prime necessity.

MRS. VIGNERON: It strikes me, Mr. Bourdon, that my affairs give you a good deal of trouble, considering the little you get out of them. I have just heard of a man, very upright and intelligent, who will take charge of them.

BOURDON: Very well, madam, very well. Perhaps it would have been a little more seemly to have saved me this visit by letting me know of your decision earlier. Never mind. Shall I send all your papers here, or will they call at my office for them?

MRS. VIGNERON: [*Disconcerted*] But I haven't made any arrangements with this man yet. Wait awhile; there's no hurry.

BOURDON: On the contrary, madam, there is hurry. And since you have found, as you say, a capable, true and tried man, he shouldn't lose any time getting acquainted with the details of your estate—a matter of which he knows absolutely nothing. He is a business man, I suppose?

MRS. VIGNERON: Who told you he was a business man?

BOURDON: I guessed as much. Would it be indiscreet of me to ask who this man is? [Mrs. Vigneron, *after some hesitation, takes the card from her pocket and hands it to him; he returns it, smiling*] One last piece of advice, Mrs. Vigneron, which you may take or not, as you please. Duhamel, whose card this is, is an old lawyer who was debarred for embezzlement. Perhaps you do not know that in the legal profession black sheep are summarily expelled. After that setback, Duhamel set up a business office near the Court Buildings. It isn't my business to tell you what goes on in his office; but you will come to me with news about it before long.

MRS. VIGNERON: Tear up that card, Mr. Bourdon, and tell me what you came to see me about.

BOURDON: Mrs. Vigneron, you really deserve to be left in this man Duhamel's clutches. All he would have to do would be to come to an understanding with another scoundrel like himself—Lefort, for instance—and that would be the last of Mr. Vigneron's estate. You are angry with me because I spoil your illusions. Am I wrong to do so? Judge for yourself. In the face of your obstinate resolve to keep your real estate—a resolve I do not favor—I had to make an accurate survey of the situation. Well, in going over the bundle of mortgages, I found that one of them had fallen due. I wrote immediately to ask for a renewal. This request was refused. We need sixty-odd thousand francs to take up this mortgage, and we need it right now.

MRS. VIGNERON: What are we going to do?

BOURDON: That's what I am asking you. And that isn't all. Time is passing; are you ready to pay the inheritance taxes?

MRS. VIGNERON: But, Mr. Bourdon, according to you, our real estate is worth nothing; and where there is nothing, the authorities can't claim anything.

BOURDON: You are wrong. The authorities, in dealing with an estate, chase no wild geese. They collect taxes where they see the chance, regardless of who ought to be paying them.

MRS. VIGNERON: Are you sure of that?

BOURDON: What a question, Mrs. Vigneron! Why my office-boy, a twelve-year-old boy, knows those things as well as I do. Now you can just see what a hard time we have with clients like you—entirely respectable, of course, but also entirely ignorant. If by some inadvertence we had not taken up this point together, and then, later on—in going over the accounts after the inevitable sale of your real estate—you had found set down "Inheritance tax: so much," who knows but you might have said: "Mr. Bourdon put that money in his own pocket."

MRS. VIGNERON: Such an idea never would have occurred to me.

BOURDON: Well, Mrs. Vigneron, you are a little suspicious that I am not fulfilling my duty toward you in all respects; and that accusation is grave enough. But let it go. While you are floundering about, doing nothing, waiting for something or other to turn up, that won't turn up, Teissier, like the business man he is, has gone right ahead. He has put experts into the factory. They have finished their report. In short, Teissier has just sent me instructions to put your factory up for sale.

MRS. VIGNERON: I don't believe you.

BOURDON: What, madam, you don't believe me? [*He takes a letter from his pocket and hands it to her*] Teissier's letter is clear enough; right to the point, just as he always writes.

MRS. VIGNERON: Will you leave that letter with me, Mr. Bourdon?

BOURDON: I don't see what you could do with it, and it ought to remain in my files.

MRS. VIGNERON: I'll return it to you to-morrow, if Mr. Teissier persists in his determination.

BOURDON: As you please.

MRS. VIGNERON: You don't know, Mr. Bourdon, that our dealings with Mr. Teissier have become very friendly.

BOURDON: Why shouldn't they be?

MRS. VIGNERON: He likes my daughters.

BOURDON: That's fine, Mrs. Vigneron, that's very fine.

MRS. VIGNERON: Why, he even took luncheon with us to-day.

BOURDON: I should be more surprised if you had taken luncheon with him.

MRS. VIGNERON: Well, we have let Mr. Teissier know about our straitened circumstances, and he has consented to lend us a pretty round sum of money; and it isn't the first, either.

BOURDON: Why do you ask Teissier for money? Am I not here? I told you, Mrs. Vigneron, that you could not look to me for four or five hundred thousand francs for imaginary building operations. Teissier wouldn't let you have it either, I'm dead sure of that. But it is I, your lawyer, who ought to provide for your everyday needs, and you would have pleased me if you had not waited for me to tell you so.

MRS. VIGNERON: I beg your pardon, Mr. Bourdon; I did doubt you for a moment. You mustn't be angry with me; my head is whirling in the midst of these complications; and you were right when you said that I am ignorant. If I could do as I wished, I would stay in my bedroom and mourn for my husband; but what would people say of a mother who did not defend her children as best she could? [She sobs and throws herself down on the couch]

BOURDON: [Going over to her, and speaking softly] I will try hard to get Teissier to put off the sale of the factory, but on one condition: that you give up your real estate. [She looks at him fixedly] You certainly must understand why I suggest this condition, which is wholly to your advantage. I can't think of spending useless energy and serving your interests on one point only to have you getting me in hot water on another.

[Silence]

MRS. VIGNERON: [To Rosalie, who comes in] What is it, Rosalie?

ROSALIE: Mr. Merckens wishes to see you, ma'am.

MRS. VIGNERON: [Rising] Very well. Show him in. [To Bourdon] Do you mind having Mr. Merckens with you a moment, while I talk this over with my daughters?

BOURDON: Go ahead, Mrs. Vigneron; go and talk it over with your daughters.

[She goes out at the left]

MERCKENS: [Entering] How d'ye do, Mr. Bourdon?

BOURDON: How are you, young man? How have you been since that unlucky dinner when I saw you last?

MERCKENS: The dinner wasn't bad, but unfortunately we had to eat it on top of a rather nasty spectacle.

BOURDON: Right you are. Poor Vigneron was brought in right under our noses. . . .

MERCKENS: What did you have in mind when you took me to the restaurant that day?

BOURDON: That was your idea. You said to me, as we were coming out of the house: "I don't like the idea of going home with a white necktie and an empty stomach." I said: "Let's dine somewhere, and then think up something to do during the rest of the evening." Well, we had a half-hearted meal, and the only thing we wanted to do was to go to bed. You see, people are always more sensitive to the death of others than they imagine, and it is particularly the case with a violent death. In spite of yourself you can't help thinking that the same thing might happen to you the very next day; and you don't feel much like laughing about it.

MERCKENS: Are you waiting to see Mrs. Vigneron?

BOURDON: Yes. I ought not to wait, but Mrs. Vigneron is no ordinary client of mine, and I spoil her. You don't give lessons here any more, I suppose?

MERCKENS: Miss Judith hasn't taken any since her father died.

BOURDON: If you'll take my advice, you won't count on having her for a pupil any more, and you'll look somewhere else.

MERCKENS: Why?

BOURDON: I know what I'm talking about. This family's new circumstances are going to force them to economize.

MERCKENS: No?

BOURDON: Yes.

MERCKENS: Really?

BOURDON: Really.

[A pause]

MERCKENS: But Mr. Vigneron was wealthy.

BOURDON: He wasn't wealthy; he made a lot of money, that's all.

MERCKENS: He didn't spend it on himself.

BOURDON: He speculated with it, and that's often worse.

MERCKENS: I thought that husky chap was going to leave his wife and children a fortune.

BOURDON: A fortune! You'll do me a favor if you'll show me where it is. Any minute, now, the Vigneron family are likely to find themselves in a bad predicament; and I can tell you, without shouting about my devotion to their interests, that they'll owe it to me if they save a loaf of bread.

MERCKENS: Impossible!

BOURDON: That's just where it stands, young man. Keep this news confidential, and make what use you can of it.

[*A pause*]

MERCKEN: [*In a low voice*] What do they say about it here?

BOURDON: What would you expect them to say?

MERCKENS: These women can't be in very good spirits.

BOURDON: Well, what has happened to them hasn't been any cause for rejoicing.

MERCKENS: Tears?

BOURDON: Tears!

MERCKENS: [*Going over to him with a smile*] Do me a slight favor, will you? Be good enough to tell Mrs. Vigneron that I only had a minute to spare, that I didn't want to bother her, and that I'll call again shortly.

BOURDON: You *will* call again?

MERCKENS: Not very likely.

BOURDON: Stay awhile, then, now that you are here, young man. You'll be repaid in listening to the poor woman, and she'll be thankful for a little kindness. She is really beginning to doubt whether any one is interested in her misfortunes.

MERCKENS: It's certain that Miss Judith won't continue with her lessons?

BOURDON: That's very certain.

MERCKENS: You don't see anything ahead which could put Mrs. Vigneron and her daughters on their feet?

BOURDON: I do not.

MERCKENS: Then you bet I'm off. That suits me better. No jabbering nonsense such as I could talk to Mrs. Vigneron would make her feel any better. I know myself too well. I should probably make some awful break; while you, with your great command of language, can find some excuse for me. How's that?

BOURDON: Just as you say.

MERCKENS: Thanks. Good-by, Mr. Bourdon.

BOURDON: Good-by.

MERCKENS: [*Returning*] Up to what time are you at your office?

BOURDON: Till seven o'clock.

MERCKENS: I'm coming after you one of these days, and we'll go to the theater together. Is that all right?

BOURDON: Indeed it is.

MERCKENS: Which do you like best, grand opera or musical comedy?

BOURDON: Musical comedy.

MERCKENS: Musical comedy! You want something light. All right, we'll see that kind of a show. Say, I hope this time we shan't have our evening spoiled by an apoplectic fit. So long!

BOURDON: So long, young man.

[Merckens *goes out at the rear while* Mrs. Vigneron *is coming in at the left*]

MRS. VIGNERON: Why did Mr. Merckens go away without waiting for me?

BOURDON: The young man was very much embarrassed, Mrs. Vigneron. When he saw me here, he understood that you were already occupied, and he thought best to postpone his visit until some more convenient time.

MRS. VIGNERON: He shouldn't have gone. I just told my daughters he was here, and they were going to entertain him.

BOURDON: Well, Mrs. Vigneron, what is the result of your conference with your daughters?

MRS. VIGNERON: Nothing, Mr. Bourdon.

BOURDON: What are you going to wait for now?

MRS. VIGNERON: We shan't do anything until we have seen Mr. Teissier.

BOURDON: And what do you expect he will say to you?

MRS. VIGNERON: There is no doubt about his intentions, that's true. He wants to sell our factory as much as he did yesterday. But this move would be so disastrous for us that he wouldn't dare to have a finger in it. We are going to have a straight talk with Mr. Teissier and we shan't hide the fact from him that he isn't treating us square.

BOURDON: Not square? That's rather strong talk. I doubt very much, Mrs. Vigneron, whether you can change his mind by using that kind of language to him.

MRS. VIGNERON: I'm not going to do the talking to Mr. Teissier. I lost my temper the first time, and could easily do so again. Besides, considering the turn our affairs have taken, I would let them go as they please now, were it not for the fact that one of my daughters shows more perseverance than the rest of us—her sisters and myself. Mr. Teissier really seems to be well disposed toward her; so perhaps she can succeed in making him change his mind.

BOURDON: Excuse me—you say Teissier has taken a liking to one of your daughters?

MRS. VIGNERON: At least, we think so.

BOURDON: Which one?

MRS. VIGNERON: My second daughter, Marie.

BOURDON: And does Miss Marie reciprocate the kindly feeling shown by Mr. Teissier?

MRS. VIGNERON: What in the world are you thinking about, Mr. Bourdon? You're not figuring on making a match, are you?

BOURDON: Wait a minute, Mrs. Vigneron. If Teissier were disposed to marry this young lady, she wouldn't do a bad stroke of business in accepting him; but I had something else in mind. You know Teissier is no longer young; he has reached an age where the slightest sickness might carry him off. this very sudden affection he is showing toward your daughter should lead him, later on, to make some provisions for her, perhaps it would be just as well if you didn't antagonize the old man at this point.

MRS. VIGNERON: We expect nothing from Mr. Teissier. Let him live as long as he can and do what he pleases with his money. But this factory he wants to sell belongs to both of us, and not to him alone. To do as he pleases with my husband's work and my children's property would be to abuse the rights given him by the law.

BOURDON: I won't argue further.

ROSALIE: [Entering] Mr. Teissier is here, ma'am.

MRS. VIGNERON: Just a minute, Rosalie. [To Bourdon] Is it necessary for you to meet?

BOURDON: Yes; I should prefer it. Please understand perfectly, Mrs. Vigneron, that I am working for Teissier as well as you. I make no difference between you. All I want is for you to come to some decision, so that I may know what to do.

MRS. VIGNERON: Very well. I'll send my daughter in.

[She goes out at the left, gesturing to Rosalie to have Teissier come in. Teissier enters]

BOURDON: You here—you?

TEISSIER: Yes, I'm here.

BOURDON: What's this I've been hearing? Nobody sees you anywhere else but here.

TEISSIER: I have been here several times. What of it?

BOURDON: You are hostile to the interests of this family, and yet you sit at their table?

TEISSIER: What are you kicking about, as long as what I do doesn't interfere with you?

BOURDON: My position isn't an easy one as it is. You are making it more difficult.

TEISSIER: Go right ahead as we agreed, Bourdon —do you understand? Don't bother yourself about my doings.

BOURDON: Miss Marie will get what she wants out of you.

TEISSIER: Miss Marie will get nothing.

BOURDON: It seems you have a weakness for this young lady.

TEISSIER: Who told you so?

BOURDON: Her mother.

TEISSIER: What is she meddling for?

BOURDON: You had better get ready for a carefully planned siege on the part of your simple maiden. I warn you they are looking to her to bring you to terms.

TEISSIER: Take your hat, Bourdon, and go back to your office.

BOURDON: All right; just as you say. [Returning to Teissier] I needn't wait any longer, eh? Shall I start the thing going?

TEISSIER: Sure! [Calling Bourdon back] Listen, Bourdon! I told you about my talk with Lefort, didn't I? He's an ugly customer, and he's right after us. The wise thing will be to go easy with him, don't you think? He is still in charge of the building operations.

BOURDON: What? Have you had dealings with Lefort, after that wretched scene when he insulted both of us?

TEISSIER: Still thinking about that, are you? If we should refuse to see people just because a few strong words had passed between us, then we couldn't see anybody at all.

BOURDON: Well, it's your business, after all. I don't know why I should mix into it. I promised you should get the real estate, and you shall. The rest doesn't worry me. [Marie enters, he goes over to her and speaks in a low tone] I leave you with Teissier, my dear young lady. Try to convince him; a woman sometimes succeeds where we fail. If you get anything out of him, you will be more fortunate and cleverer than I am. [He goes out]

TEISSIER: Here is the money you asked me for. You told me it was intended for your tradespeople. Meet them yourself. Look sharp at the bills they render; don't be afraid to beat them down as much as you can; and, above all, take good care not to pay the same bill twice. [Detaining her] Where is my receipt?

MARIE: I'll give it to you by and by.

TEISSIER: I ought to take it in one hand while I am handing over the money with the other. Just this minute I am flustered. [She goes to the writing-desk and puts the banknotes in a drawer; then she comes back. There is a moment of silence] You have something to tell me, and I have something to tell you, too. Come sit beside me, won't you, and have a nice friendly talk. [They sit down] What do you figure on doing?

MARIE: I don't understand your question.

TEISSIER: My question is simple enough, nevertheless. I told you before that there would be fifty thousand francs coming to you; no more. You can't think of holding on to this apartment and keeping open house until your last cent is gone. What do you figure on doing?

MARIE: A relative of my mother's who lives in the country has invited us to come and settle near him.

TEISSIER: Your mother's relative is like all relatives. He made that suggestion thinking to get an invitation in return; he won't cling to the idea when it will be his turn to carry out the suggestion.

MARIE: Then we'll stay in Paris.

TEISSIER: What are you going to do in Paris?

MARIE: My oldest sister is ready to give music lessons, when the time comes.

TEISSIER: Good. Your oldest sister, if she carries out that idea, will promptly let the rest of the family support themselves. She will want her money herself, and she will be right.

MARIE: But I count on getting something to do, too.

TEISSIER: What?

MARIE: That's it, what? I don't know yet. It's so hard for a woman to find work, and she gets so little for it.

TEISSIER: That brings us to what I wanted to say. [A pause; he continues with some hesitation and embarrassment] I know of a house where, if you want to, you can come to live. You will get your room and board there, and every month a small sum which you can save up for a rainy day. You will not have to look any further for a place.

MARIE: Whose house? Yours?

TEISSIER: [With an equivocal half-smile] Mine.

MARIE: [After a display of emotion; not knowing how she ought to interpret his words, nor how she ought to reply] What you propose is impossible. In the first place, my mother would not let me leave her.

TEISSIER: Yes; I had an idea your mother might interpose some opposition. But you are of age now and can consider your best interests without consulting anybody.

MARIE: I told you no, Mr. Teissier; no!

TEISSIER: Wouldn't you be mighty glad to let your family stay in the ditch and go out and do something on your own account? That's the way I should feel, if I were in your place.

MARIE: That isn't the way I feel.

TEISSIER: What good do you see in all scrambling around together, instead of going your separate ways?

MARIE: Just the advantage of not being separated. [Leaving him] Sometimes it is good to have consolation nearby. That way you are not troubled so much with certain events that would otherwise be disconcerting.

[A pause]

TEISSIER: It is some time now since I began coming here. I don't stay away from my business without a good reason. You aren't stupid—you have a quick wit. You ought to be able to see through it.

MARIE: I was thinking of something else.

TEISSIER: What?

MARIE: I was thinking only of my family. I can think only of the fate that awaits them, now that they have lost everything.

TEISSIER: [With a smile] So you are trying to get the best of me and worm something out of me for them?

MARIE: Oh, Mr. Teissier! I have enough sorrow without your adding anything to it. You want to know what I thought; I will tell you. I was thinking that you are no longer young, that you live a very dreary and lonely life, that you have no children, and so you like the company of other people—those were my thoughts. Yet you were right, I admit. We did not have you coming here before my father died; and we shouldn't have begun afterward. We shall have to take things as they come, meeting our difficulties courageously, and telling ourselves that after all women are never unhappy when they love each other, and are brave, and stand by one another.

[A pause]

TEISSIER: How many are there of you? You, your mother and your two sisters?

MARIE: And Rosalie.

TEISSIER: Where does Rosalie come in?

MARIE: She is a saint. She brought us all up.

TEISSIER: What do you do to keep your servants? I could never get one attached to me. There are four of you—Rosalie doesn't count. Unfortunately, four is too many; that you can understand that. Even to please a little friend I want to have with me, I can't be responsible for a whole family. They would bore me to death.

MARIE: Nobody asked you to; and nobody dreamed of such a thing.

TEISSIER: I didn't want to tell you, but you guessed it. A fellow doesn't complain of being alone as long as he is young; but at my age it is tiresome and unsafe.

MARIE: If you are alone, it's because you prefer to be.

TEISSIER: I ought to get married?

MARIE: It isn't necessary to get married to have people around you. You still have your parents.

TEISSIER: I don't see them any more, because I wanted to get out of reach of their demands for money; they are starving. I want very much to get hold of a little woman of simple tastes, kind and trustworthy, who will conduct herself decently in my house, and who won't steal everything in sight. Perhaps later on I'll see whether I ought to marry her. But you women are all lambs before marriage, and God knows what afterward. I would regulate my conduct according to hers; she would not be badly off while I was living, and she'd have no cause to complain after I died. Married or not, it would be just the same for her.

MARIE: Take your hat, Mr. Teissier, and go away. I don't want to have you near me another minute. I believe you are unhappy, and I pity you. I believe your proposal was an honest and proper one, and I thank you for it. But it could have another meaning, a meaning so loathsome that my heart trembles at the very thought of it. Go away.

TEISSIER: [Standing, embarrassed, blubbering] Just stop and think of what you are saying to me.

MARIE: No more! Not a word! I ought to be ashamed of having spoken to you about my family; I ought to be ashamed for them as well as for myself. Think it over. Consider what kind of man my father was, and what you owe to his honesty, to his work, to his memory. [She goes hurriedly to the desk, takes out the banknotes and hands them back to him] Take your money. Don't be embarrassed; take it. Mr. Bourdon has just offered to help us, and we shall get from him what we could not have asked of you. Go now! Go, before I call Rosalie to show you out. [A pause; Rosalie enters] Here she is now. What is it, Rosalie?

ROSALIE: Mrs. de Saint-Genis is here.

MARIE: Very well, show her in.

ROSALIE: What's the matter, dearie; you are blushing? [Looking alternately from Marie to Teissier] I hope nobody has said anything to you they shouldn't?

MARIE: Show Mrs. de Saint-Genis in.

TEISSIER: I'll go. I'll stop in and see Bourdon on my way, as to whether there is still a way to fix things up; but don't count too much on it. Good-by!

ROSALIE: It isn't wise to leave such a child with a man of his age!

[Mrs. de Saint-Genis, *entering, encounters* Teissier *on his way out*]

MRS. DE SAINT-GENIS: How do you do, Miss Vigneron? I never come here these days without meeting Mr. Teissier. Is that a good sign? Are you going to come to terms with him?

MARIE: No, Mrs. de Saint-Genis.

MRS. DE SAINT-GENIS: Pshaw! I thought you were.

MARIE: Why?

MRS. DE SAINT-GENIS: An old man ought to find it pleasant to be in a house like yours.

MARIE: Mr. Teissier came to-day for the last time.

MRS. DE SAINT-GENIS: Then I can sincerely say I am sorry for you. Is your sister at home?

MARIE: Yes.

MRS. DE SAINT-GENIS: Please have her come here. Don't bother your mother; it isn't necessary; I can see her another time. I want to talk with Blanche.

MARIE: She'll be right in. [*Goes out*]

MRS. DE SAINT-GENIS: It is decidedly better to have a talk with this young woman and tell her straight out that the marriage is not postponed, but broken off. It is better for her to know where she stands, and it will clear my own mind, too. For the first time in his life George was going contrary to my wishes. He clung to his sweetheart, and wanted to marry her. Fortunately another good match came along, and I gave him his choice—to obey me or never see me again. He gave in. But what a brigand a young man twenty-three years old can be! And as for this giddy miss, who couldn't wait until she was married—well, so much the worse for her.

BLANCHE: [*Entering*] Oh, I am so glad to see you, Mrs. de Saint-Genis!

MRS. DE SAINT-GENIS: How do you do, child; how do you do?

BLANCHE: Give me a good hug!

MRS. DE SAINT-GENIS: Of course I will.

BLANCHE: You know I love you so much.

MRS. DE SAINT-GENIS: Come, Blanche, dear, don't get so excited. I have come to-day to talk seriously with you; so listen to me like the great big woman you are. It is time, at your age, to use a little reason. [*She sits down*] My son loves you, child; I tell you very frankly, he loves you a great deal. Don't interrupt me. I know, too, that you feel somewhat the same toward him—a light, thoughtless affection such as young girls often have when they meet a nice young man.

BLANCHE: Oh, Mrs. de Saint-Genis, you are disparaging a feeling which goes very much deeper than that.

MRS. DE SAINT-GENIS: Well, I was wrong, then. Love is a very fine thing, very vague and poetic; but a passion, however great it may be, never lasts very long, and never gets anywhere. I know what I am talking about. You can't pay the rent and the baker's bill with that kind of currency. You know I am not rich; my son's position is not yet assured; and certain deplorable circumstances have endangered your domestic situation, and perhaps will ruin you. Now, my child, I want to ask you if under these circumstances it would be very discreet to go on with a marriage which promises so unfavorably?

BLANCHE: [*Quickly*] We ought to be married, Mrs. de Saint-Genis, and we are going to be.

MRS. DE SAINT-GENIS: [*Sweetly*] You are, if I say so.

BLANCHE: You will give your consent.

MRS. DE SAINT-GENIS: I don't think so.

BLANCHE: Yes, Mrs. de Saint-Genis; yes, you will! There are affections so sincere that even a mother has no right to come between them. There are promises so sacred that a man is dishonored if he does not fulfil them.

MRS. DE SAINT-GENIS: What promises are you talking about? [*Silence*] I admit, if that suits you, that a marriage was planned between you and my son; but it was subject to certain conditions, and it is not my fault if you cannot live up to them. I was hoping, child, you would think of that yourself. I was hoping you would bow in submission before a changed situation which is nobody's fault, but which necessarily alters the expectations of you both.

BLANCHE: George does not talk that way, Mrs. de Saint-Genis. His expectations are the same as ever. The loss of our money hasn't affected him in the least bit, and I think he is only more eager to marry me.

MRS. DE SAINT-GENIS: Leave my son out of the matter, won't you? I tell him every day he is too young yet to know what he does or says.

BLANCHE: George is twenty-three.

MRS. DE SAINT-GENIS: Twenty-three! Indeed!

BLANCHE: At that age, Mrs. de Saint-Genis, a man has passions, and will-power, and certain rights.

MRS. DE SAINT-GENIS: You insist on talking about my son—very well, we'll talk about him. Are you so sure of his feelings? I don't see them in the same light as you. Placed, as he is, between an affection which is dear to him and a future in which he is interested, the poor boy is uncertain, hesitating.

BLANCHE: [*Rising suddenly*] You are deceiving me, Mrs. de Saint-Genis.

MRS. DE SAINT-GENIS: No, child, I am not deceiving you—no, indeed! I have given my son the benefit of my serious reflection, and I should be sorry for him if he did not make good use of it. Another thing: do we ever know what is going on in a man's brain? George is no more sincere than the next man. Perhaps he is only waiting for my order to get out of an embarrassing situation.

BLANCHE: Well, give him that order.

MRS. DE SAINT-GENIS: He would obey it.

BLANCHE: No, Mrs. de Saint-Genis.

MRS. DE SAINT-GENIS: I assure you he would, even if reluctantly.

BLANCHE: If it comes to that, Mrs. de Saint-Genis, your son would decide to confess to you something he has withheld out of respect for me.

MRS. DE SAINT-GENIS: What confession? [*Silence*] So! I thought you would be the first one to break the reserve on that subject. You may spare yourself any delicate confidence. I know all about it. [Blanche, *confused and blushing, runs to* Mrs. de Saint-Genis *and throws herself at her feet, with her head on the older woman's knees;* Mrs. de Saint-Genis *rebukes her, caressing her all the while*] I don't care to inquire, child, whether you or George was responsible. It is your mother and I who are at fault, for leaving you two children together when you should have been watched. You see, I do not attach any undue importance to the result of a moment of forgetfulness, justified by your youth, and all the surrounding circumstances. You ought to want your fault to remain a secret; my son is an honorable man who would never betray you. So much said, the next question is: is it necessary for both of you to sacrifice your whole lives for the sake of a slip? Wouldn't it be better to forget it?

BLANCHE: [*Rising*] Never.

[*A pause*]

MRS. DE SAINT-GENIS: [*Has risen and her tone changes*] You will not be surprised, Blanche, if my son doesn't come here any more.

BLANCHE: I want to hear that from *him*.

MRS. DE SAINT-GENIS: Are you hoping he will disobey his mother?

BLANCHE: Yes; to do his duty.

MRS. DE SAINT-GENIS: You should not have forgotten yours, in the first place.

BLANCHE: Go ahead, wound me, humiliate me; I know I deserve it.

MRS. DE SAINT-GENIS: I feel more like pitying you, Blanche, than hurting you. But it seems to me that a young girl, after a misfortune like yours, should bow her head and submit.

BLANCHE: You shall see, Mrs. de Saint-Genis, what a young girl can do toward getting the reparation due her.

MRS. DE SAINT-GENIS: Well, what will you do?

BLANCHE: I'll find out first whether your son has two kinds of talk, one for you and another for me. I don't say yet that he has. He knows what you want, and so he conceals his own thoughts from you. But if I am dealing with a coward who hides behind his mother's skirts, he needn't think he can get rid of me so easily. Everywhere, everywhere he goes, I shall injure him. I'll ruin his standing, and spoil his future.

MRS. DE SAINT-GENIS: You'll get yourself talked about that way; that's all. Perhaps that's what you want to do. Fortunately, your mother will stop that. She'll think a stain on the family's name is enough without adding a scandal to it. Good day, Blanche.

BLANCHE: [*Holding her*] Don't go, Mrs. de Saint-Genis.

MRS. DE SAINT-GENIS: [*Sweetly*] We have nothing more to say.

BLANCHE: Stay here. See, I am weeping! I am suffering! Feel my hand; I am burning up with fever.

MRS. DE SAINT-GENIS: Yes; I understand the frame of mind you are in; but that will pass. Whereas, if you should be married to my son, your regrets and his would last forever.

BLANCHE: We love each other.

MRS. DE SAINT-GENIS: To-day, yes—but to-morrow?

BLANCHE: Give us your consent, I implore you.

MRS. DE SAINT-GENIS: Must I repeat that word you just said to me? Never!

[Blanche *leaves her and walks back and forth across the stage in a state of great emotion and violent grief; then she drops into an armchair*]

MRS. DE SAINT-GENIS: [*Going up to* Blanche] I am very sorry, child, to seem so cruel and to leave you in this condition. But I am right; absolutely right. A woman of my age and experience, who has seen all there is to see in this world, knows the true value of things and doesn't exaggerate one thing at the expense of another.

BLANCHE: [*Throwing herself on her knees*] Listen, Mrs. de Saint-Genis. What will become of me if your son does not marry me? It is his duty. There is nothing nobler or kinder in a man than to cling to the woman he loves. Believe me, if it were an ordinary engagement, I shouldn't humiliate myself to the extent of holding him back. Yes, I should break my heart rather than offer it to one who disdained it, or was unworthy of it. But your son must marry me; I say again it is his duty. Everything gives way before that fact. You speak about the future. The future will be as he pleases. I am thinking only of the past. I should die of shame and sorrow.

MRS. DE SAINT-GENIS: Child that you are, to speak of dying at your age! Come, get up and listen to me now. I see that you really do love my son more than I thought, if you still cling to a boy who is almost poverty-stricken. But if I should consent to this marriage, in a year—yes, in six months, you would bitterly reproach me for my weakness. Love would pass, but you would have a household still. What do you think would be your lot then? Shabby, worried, vulgar, nursing your children yourself, while your discontented husband would be reproaching you all the time on account of the sacrifice he had made for you. Do what I ask. Make the sacrifice yourself instead. Can't you see how different all will be then? George will not have abandoned you; it will be you who have dismissed him generously. He will be under obligation to you. You will hold forever a place way down deep in his heart. Men always remain sensitive to the memory of a woman they have truly loved, even for an hour. It is so rare! And what will happen to you after that? I'll tell you. Little by little the love for my son, which seems so tremendous to you just now, will disappear. Yes; quicker than you think. You are young, pretty, full of charm for young men. Ten, yes, twenty, young fellows will come along. You will choose, not the most attractive, but the one who is best off. And on your wedding day you will think of me and say to yourself: "Mrs. de Saint-Genis was right."

BLANCHE: What kind of a woman are you, Mrs. de Saint-Genis, to give me such advice as that? What would your son say if he knew it? I would rather be his mistress than the wife of another man.

MRS. DE SAINT-GENIS: His mistress! Pretty words to come from you! My son shall know what you have just said. It's one more sign of your waywardness.

BLANCHE: No, no, Mrs. de Saint-Genis; don't repeat that awful word. I blushed when I said it.

MRS. DE SAINT-GENIS: His mistress! Evidently you can stand anything; so I am going to tell you all. I should never have broken off your marriage for a matter of dollars and cents. But I want my son to have a wife whose past is above suspicion, and who will give him no anxiety for the future. [*She goes toward the door*]

BLANCHE: Oh, oh, oh! You insult me, Mrs. de Saint-Genis, without any reason—without pity!

MRS. DE SAINT-GENIS: Let me go, young woman. His mistress! Why, that's the talk of a fallen woman!

[*She repulses* Blanche *gently and goes out*]

BLANCHE: A fallen woman! She dares to call me—— Oh, God! [*She bursts into tears*] Oh, it's all over now! George is weak, his mother controls him . . . he will obey her. A fallen woman! [*She weeps increasingly*] A fine fellow like him! Not at all like that woman! And yet under her thumb! . . . I can't stand it. A little while ago my hands were burning hot; now they are cold as ice. [*She rings and comes to the front of the stage; she speaks in a broken voice*] He is young . . . barely twenty-three . . . gentle, refined, charming . . . some other woman will love him and marry him.

ROSALIE: [*Entering*] Is it you, dearie, who rang for me?

BLANCHE: [*Going to her sadly*] I'm cold, nursey. Throw something over me.

ROSALIE: [*Having scrutinized her*] I'm going to put you to bed; that'll be much better.

BLANCHE: No.

ROSALIE: Do as I tell you, if you don't want to be sick.

BLANCHE: Oh, yes; I am going to be sick.

ROSALIE: Come, Rosalie is going to undress you. It won't be the first time.

BLANCHE: Call Mama.

ROSALIE: You don't need your mother; I'm here.

BLANCHE: I'm not going to be married, Rosalie.

ROSALIE: Well, it's an ill wind that blows no good!

We've spoiled you; but not enough to make you prefer that she-devil and her monkey. That's what they are. That marriage, I tell you, wasn't the right kind for you. If they had listened to your father and me, it wouldn't have been considered a minute.

BLANCHE: [*Out of her head*] My father! I see my father now! He's reaching out his arms to me and beckoning me to come with him.

ROSALIE: Come and lie down, Blanchy.

BLANCHE: Your Blanchy is a fallen woman! You didn't know it. I'm a fallen woman!

ROSALIE: Don't talk that way, dearie; it isn't nice. Come, come with your old nursey.

BLANCHE: Oh, I can't bear it! [*She cries out*] Marie! Marie! Marie!

[*She grows weak in* Rosalie's *arms and slips little by little to the floor*]

MARIE: [*Entering and throwing herself down by her sister*] Blanche! Blanche!

ROSALIE: Keep still, girlie; it's no use, she can't hear. Take her up gently, poor lamb, and we'll put her to bed.

BLANCHE: [*Murmuring*] Fallen woman!

MRS. VIGNERON: [*Appearing*] What's the matter? [*She throws herself down by* Blanche]

ROSALIE: Come away from her, ma'am; you'll bother us more than you'll help.

[Judith *appears*]

MRS. VIGNERON: Judith, come here. [*They walk aside together*] You were right, Judith. We've got nothing in the world. They're putting your sister to bed; to-morrow it will be your turn, and the next day mine. You still think the best way is to settle everything?

JUDITH: Yes; I still think so.

MRS. VIGNERON: Good. Take Rosalie with you and go to see Mr. Bourdon. Tell him I accept everything, approve everything, and all I want now is to have it over with. You can add that we are just as much in a hurry as he is. That's your idea, too?

JUDITH: That's my idea.

MRS. VIGNERON: Go ahead then. [*They separate*] I should like to keep what belongs to me; but the first thing is to save my children.

CURTAIN

ACT IV.

A cheaply furnished dining-room, with a shabby-genteel look. Here and there a few chairs; in one place everything is reminiscent of the furniture of the previous acts, and plainly not fitting these new surroundings. There are two single doors, one at the left and the other at the back. At the rear, to the right, a mahogany table covered with red oil-

cloth stands against the wall; on this table appears
a loaf of bread; also cups and other dishes.

ROSALIE: Come in, Mr. Merckens. They'll be glad to see somebody they know.

MERCKENS: [*Having looked about him*] Well, well! The lawyer wasn't lying to me. This is poverty, sure enough!

ROSALIE: You're looking at our new home? Yes, it isn't very much! Oh, Lord; yesterday and to-day are two different things.

MERCKENS: What's happened to the family?

ROSALIE: Ruined, Mr. Merckens. My poor missus and the girls have lost everything. I'm not saying how it happened, but I've got my opinion, and I'll keep it, too. You see, when business men get into a house where a person has just died, you may as well say: "Here come the vultures." They don't leave anything they can carry away.

MERCKENS: It isn't a pleasant place any more, eh, Rosalie?

ROSALIE: Not for anybody, Mr. Merckens, not for anybody.

MERCKENS: Why don't you find another place?

ROSALIE: How can the girls get along without me, any more than I can without them? I'm one more mouth to be fed, true enough; but you bet I earn what I eat. You mustn't think you can stay to luncheon with us, Mr. Merckens. In the old days, when I saw you coming at this hour, I didn't need any orders to know what to do; you'd find your place ready at the table; but things are different now. I'll go and tell Mrs. Vigneron you are here.

MERCKENS: No; don't bother Mrs. Vigneron. Just tell Miss Judith I am here.

[Judith *enters*]

ROSALIE: Here she is now.

JUDITH: How do you do, Mr. Merckens?

[Merckens *bows*]

ROSALIE: But of course, if a good cup of coffee will do you, we can still offer you that.

JUDITH: Leave us, Rosalie——

[Rosalie *goes out*]

JUDITH: [*To* Merckens] First of all, I've a little bone to pick with you, and then that'll be out of the way. I wrote to you twice asking you to come and see me. Once ought to be enough.

MERCKENS: [*Awkwardly*] Are you sure you wrote me twice?

JUDITH: You know well I did.

MERCKENS: No, really; your first letter didn't reach me.

JUDITH: Well, never mind. I don't need to tell you the conditions we are reduced to; you saw the moment you came in.

MERCKENS: [*Half serious, half joking*] Tell me about it.

JUDITH: It's a story you wouldn't be interested in, and it wouldn't be pleasant for me to tell. In a word, we didn't have money enough to fight for our rights; we had to have a hundred thousand francs in cash.

MERCKENS: Why didn't you tell me? I would have found the money.

JUDITH: It's too late now. Please sit down. Mr. Merckens, you have seen, and you remember, our family life. We were very happy; very fond of one another; we knew very few people outside, and cared to know none. We didn't think that some day we should have need of acquaintances, and that then we shouldn't have any. [Merckens *looks at his watch*] Are you in a hurry?

MERCKENS: Yes; I am. Will you please cut the story short? You wanted to see me; here I am. You want to ask me something. What is it? Perhaps it would be just as well for me to tell you that I am not a very obliging person.

JUDITH: Shall I go on?

MERCKENS: Yes, certainly; go ahead.

JUDITH: Here is what I first thought of; I'll start with the simplest and surest thing. I am thinking of turning to account the fine lessons you have given me, by giving lessons myself.

MERCKENS: [*Touching her knee*] What, poor child—you've got down to that?

JUDITH: Come, come, Mr. Merckens; please call me "Miss," as you have been used to do, and answer me seriously.

MERCKENS: Lessons! In the first place, are you capable of giving lessons? I'm not so sure of it. But let's suppose you are. Would you do what is necessary to get pupils? To get them, you have to play the part of a beggar. You don't get any by being dignified and putting on airs. But it is possible that people might take pity on you, and in four or five years—not before—you might have enough pupils. Your pupils would as often as not be disagreeable; their parents would nearly always be brutes. What is a poor little music teacher to a lot of Philistines that don't even know what C major is? You needn't look any farther, for instance, than your dad. . . .

JUDITH: We won't speak of my father.

MERCKENS: Surely a fellow can laugh a little—he didn't leave you anything.

[*A pause*]

JUDITH: Let's put aside the question of music lessons a minute; we can come back to that. Now in what I am going to say to you, Mr. Merckens, please don't think I am prompted by vanity or presumption; I am just trying to make use of what talent I have for music. I have composed a good deal; you know that. With the little things I've already written, and others I can produce, can't I get a living for my family?

MERCKENS: [*After laughing*] Look at me. [*He laughs again*] Never, never say that again; understand? I mean what you have just said to me. You'd be the laughing-stock of the whole world. [*He laughs again*] Earn a living! Is that all?

JUDITH: No, it isn't. We were talking once about a profession that didn't strike me favorably then, and still doesn't more than half appeal to me. But the way my family is fixed, I ought not to hesitate at anything to help them out. The stage?

MERCKENS: Too late.

JUDITH: Why can't I do as others have—women who felt undecided at first, but summoned up their courage and went into it?

MERCKENS: Too late.

JUDITH: Perhaps I have natural qualities—and lack only work and experience?

MERCKENS: Too late. It's no use thinking of the stage without preparing for it a long time. You'll never be an artist. It isn't in you. As you are now, all you'd find on the stage would be disillusionment . . . or adventures; and that isn't what you are after, is it?

JUDITH: But what can I do, then?

MERCKENS: Nothing. I see the fix you are in. You're not the first one I've seen in the same situation, and made the same reply to. There are no resources for a woman; or, at least, only one. Now I'll tell you the whole truth in one sentence. If you are good, people will respect you without doing anything for you; and if you're not, they'll do things for you without respecting you. There's no other way about it. Are you going to take up the subject of giving lessons again?

JUDITH: It's no use. I'm sorry to have bothered you.

MERCKENS: You want me to go?

JUDITH: I shan't stop you.

MERCKENS: Good-by, Miss Judith.

JUDITH: Good-by, Mr. Merckens.

MERCKENS: [At the door] There was nothing else to tell her.

MARIE: [Entering] Well?

JUDITH: Well, if Mr. Merckens is right, and if things are as he says, we aren't out of our difficulties yet. Meanwhile, here are all my plans upset; those you know of, and another one I had kept to myself.

MARIE: What other?

JUDITH: What's the use telling you?

MARIE: Tell me, anyway.

JUDITH: I did think, for a while, of making use of my voice, by going on the stage.

MARIE: You, sister, on the stage!

JUDITH: Well, why not? We must be doing something, and we've got to take what comes. We can't wait till we have got down to our last cent. Mama isn't able to go to work, and furthermore we don't want her to. Who knows whether poor Blanche will ever recover her reason? Well, then, there's just you and me; and what is there you can do, dearie? You would have to work twelve hours a day to earn a franc and a half.

MARIE: Tell me, really and truly, what you think of Blanche's condition? How do you find her?

JUDITH: One day better and the next day worse. We expect her to recognize us any moment; but as yet she doesn't seem to see any one or hear anything. I've been thinking over this misfortune; and perhaps we have escaped a worse one. If Blanche, in that condition, had heard of the marriage of Mr. de Saint-Genis, might it not have killed her? She is alive. That's the main thing. We have her still with us. If we must always take care of her, we will. If we must go hungry for her, we'll do that, too. She isn't our sister now—she's our little girl.

MARIE: How good you are, sister; I love you so much!

[They embrace]

JUDITH: I love you, too. At times I am blunt; but I always have you here, in my heart. It seems to me that I, the eldest sister—"big sister," as you call me —I am the one who should find a way out of our troubles. I don't know how to do it. I've looked, and I can't find a way. If the only thing needed were to go through fire and water for the rest of you, I should have done that before now.

[A pause]

MARIE: Has Mama said anything about a visit from Mr. Bourdon?

JUDITH: No. What was he doing here?

MARIE: Mr. Teissier sent him to ask me to be his wife.

JUDITH: I'm not surprised. It was easy enough to see that Mr. Teissier took a liking to you, and sooner or later the idea of marriage was bound to come to him.

MARIE: Would you advise me to accept him?

JUDITH: You mustn't ask my advice on that point. You are the one concerned; it is for you to decide. Think it over well, look at it from all sides, but by all means think only of yourself. If you are frightened at our situation, and you look back regretfully to the times when we had plenty of money, marry Mr. Teissier. He will make you pay dearly enough for your comfort and security. But if I understand you, and the way you love your mother and sisters, and how you could do for them what would be repulsive if you alone were concerned, we should be very wrong—all the guiltier—to advise you to make the greatest sacrifice a woman can make.

MARIE: What you say is right from the heart; kiss me again.

[Rosalie enters at the rear; in one hand she carries a coffee-pot, in the other a casserole full of milk; she places them on the table, and then draws near the two sisters and watches them, sighing; Marie and Judith separate]

JUDITH: Is luncheon ready?

ROSALIE: Yes, miss. I'll serve it whenever you wish.

MARIE: Judith is going to help you with the table, Rosalie.

[Judith and Rosalie carry the table to the front of the stage, placing it at the right; Rosalie arranges the cups and serves the coffee while Judith places the chairs. Marie meanwhile, goes to the door at the left and opens it. Blanche *comes in, followed by her mother.* Blanche *is pale, limp, and stares stupidly, her attitude being that of a harmless insane person.* Mrs. Vigneron *is aged and whitened.* Marie *helps* Blanche *to a place, and then they sit down one by one, except* Rosalie, *who takes her coffee standing. There is a prolonged silence, and an atmosphere of utter desolation*]

MRS. VIGNERON: [*Suddenly bursting out*] Oh, children; if your father could see us!

[*Tears and sobbing. At that moment* Bourdon *steps quietly into the room*]

ROSALIE: [*To* Bourdon] How did you get in?

BOURDON: By the open door. You ought not leave your outside door open. Thieves could steal everything you've got.

ROSALIE: [*Speaking directly at him*] No fear of that. That job has been done—and done brown.

BOURDON: [*To* Mrs. Vigneron, *who has risen*] Don't let me disturb you, madam; I'll wait until you have finished luncheon.

MRS. VIGNERON: [*Going to him*] What have you got to say to me, Mr. Bourdon?

BOURDON: [*In a low tone*] This time, madam, I've come for Teissier, regarding a matter very dear to him. I assume you have let your daughter know about the offer I spoke about?

MRS. VIGNERON: Certainly.

BOURDON: Do I have your permission to renew the offer to her, in your presence?

MRS. VIGNERON: Very well, you have my consent. Judith, dear, take your sister away. Marie, Mr. Bourdon wishes to speak with us.

[Judith *leads* Blanche *out*]

BOURDON: [*To* Marie] You mother has told you, young lady, of the desire expressed by Mr. Teissier?

MARIE: Yes, sir.

BOURDON: Of your own free will you have declined this proposal of marriage?

MARIE: Of my own free will.

BOURDON: Good! Good! I'm glad it's that way. For a moment, I was afraid, when you refused such a handsome offer, that your mother and sisters had conspired to keep you with them—not out of jealousy, but in a spirit of misdirected affection. If you have come to a definite, unalterable decision, of your own accord, I don't see any use in going further into the matter.

[*A silence*]

MRS. VIGNERON: Don't be afraid, dear; answer frankly just what you think. [*Another silence*]

BOURDON: In case you regret your first decision, young lady—and that's easy to explain—I am offering you a chance to change your mind. You had better take advantage of it.

MARIE: You must tell Mr. Teissier for me that I like him better for his persistence, but that I still wish some time to think it over.

BOURDON: Well! That's a reasonable answer, madam—very sensible, indeed.—That doesn't look like the categorical refusal you gave me.

MRS. VIGNERON: My daughter may have changed her mind. But she should know that I don't approve of it.

BOURDON: Say no more, madam. Leave the young lady to her own devices. Later on she might reproach you because she followed your wishes. [*Returning to* Marie] I understand perfectly, young lady, why this marriage must present some objectionable features to you, and why you have been in no hurry to enter it. Unfortunately, Teissier is not twenty years old, like yourself—indeed, that is your greatest cause for complaint—and at his age, a man isn't willing to have things delayed.

MARIE: Mr. Bourdon, I want to know, and I beg you will tell me sincerely, whether Mr. Teissier is an honest man.

BOURDON: An honest man! What do you mean by that? In case you should marry Mr. Teissier, I should not advise you to place implicit confidence in a simple promise; but there are lawyers to draw up contracts establishing the rights of the parties concerned. Have I answered your question?

MARIE: No; you didn't understand me. When a young woman says "an honest man," she thinks of a good many things.

BOURDON: Do you want to know whether Teissier has made his money in an honorable way?

MARIE: Yes; I want to be assured on that point, as well as some others.

BOURDON: Why should that worry you? If you were to look into all the fortunes in France, there aren't a hundred—no, not fifty—that would stand a close examination. I speak as a man who has been through the mill. Teissier has been in business all his life; he has amassed a considerable sum, and nobody would dream of attacking his right to it. That's all you need to know.

MARIE: What is Mr. Teissier's ordinary conduct? What are his tastes and his habits?

BOURDON: Just the tastes and habits of any man of his age. I don't think you have anything to fear on that score. I see now what you are driving at. Believe me, as a husband Teissier will have rather too much than too little virtue. I leave it to your mother.

MRS. VIGNERON: It occurs to me to ask what interest you have in this marriage, Mr. Bourdon?

BOURDON: What interest, madam? Only the welfare of this young lady, and yours, at the same time.

MRS. VIGNERON: It's rather late, isn't it, to show such devotion for us?

BOURDON: Madam, you are still thinking of that wretched business. I know everything went about as badly as it could. But was it my fault that you were unable to fight for your husband's estate? You had to give way to the law of the strongest, that's all. To-day, this law has shifted in your favor. It happens that your daughter has made a conquest of **an** old man, who will grant anything to be able to spend his remaining days with her. The whole situation favors you. You've got the trumps. Play 'em. Do I need to tell you, madam, that we lawyers know neither the weak nor the strong; that absolute impartiality is a duty we never depart from? Nevertheless, I don't think I do wrong, even though I am Teissier's attorney, to stipulate for your daughter all the advantages she is in a position to demand. [*Returning to* Marie] You heard what I have just said to your mother, miss. Put whatever questions you wish to me; but particularly the question which is really the most important—the question of money. I'm listening.

MARIE: No; you speak.

BOURDON: [*With a half-smile*] I'm here to listen to you, and advise you.

MARIE: It would be painful for me to talk about it.

BOURDON: [*Smiling*] Nonsense! What you want to know is what Mr. Teissier is worth, down to a cent, isn't it?

MARIE: It's enough, I know, without being told.

BOURDON: Right you are. Teissier is rich, very rich. Why, he's richer, the old fox, than he himself knows. Come, now, miss, I'm waiting for you.

MARIE: Of course Mr. Teissier has told you of his intentions?

BOURDON: Yes; but I must know yours, too. It's always fun for us lawyers to see the parties fighting tooth and nail over the terms.

MARIE: Please don't add to my embarrassment. If this marriage must take place, I had rather run my chances than make the conditions.

BOURDON: [*Smiling continually*] Really! [Marie *looks at him fixedly*] I don't doubt your scruples, miss. When they are so plainly shown, we are forced to believe them sincere. But Teissier doesn't think you are marrying him for his beauty. So he is already willing to make a settlement on you. But this settlement, I hasten to tell you, is not sufficient. You are making a bargain, are you not? Or, if that word hurts you, at any rate a speculation. And you ought to reap all the benefits of it. So it is only just—and you can insist—that when Teissier marries you, he shall make you half-owner of all he possesses, irrevocably and incontestably, so that you will receive one-half after he dies. Then all you would have to do would be to pray that the time would not be too long deferred. [*Turning to* Mrs. Vigneron] You heard what I have just told your daughter, madam?

MRS. VIGNERON: I heard.

BOURDON: What do you think?

MRS. VIGNERON: If you want to know, Mr. Bourdon, I think instead of promising my daughter half Mr. Teissier's fortune, you would have done better to have saved her father's for her.

BOURDON: Can't get away from that subject, eh, madam? [*Returning to* Marie] Well, miss, now you know the great advantages in store for you in the near future. I am wondering what objections you can find now. I can't think of any. Sentimental objections? I am speaking, I think, to a sensible young woman, well brought up, without foolish notions. You ought to know there is no such thing as love. I never met with it. This world is made up of businesses. Marriage is a business, just like the rest, and the chances offered you to-day will never come your way again.

MARIE: In the conversations you have had with Mr. Teissier, has he said anything about my family?

BOURDON: About your family? No. [*In a low tone*] Do they want something, too?

MARIE: Mr. Teissier ought to know that I would never consent to separate from them.

BOURDON: Why should you? Your sisters are nice girls, and your mother is very agreeable. Besides, Teissier has every reason not to want to leave a young wife with idle moments on her hands. Now, miss, be ready for what remains for me to tell you. Teissier came here with me. He is outside. He is waiting for a reply, and this time it must be a definite answer. You will take long chances in doing otherwise. So it is a "yes" or "no" that I am asking for.

MRS. VIGNERON: That's enough of that, Mr. Bourdon. I was willing enough for you to tell my daughter whatever propositions were made to her. Whether she accepts them or not, is her business. But I don't intend that she shall be surprised into acceptance, or do anything in a moment of weakness or emotion. Moreover, you must know that I reserve the right to have a talk with her and tell her certain things which would be out of place with you here—things a mother can tell her child, and must tell, when they are alone. One thing I can tell you: I haven't brought up a girl to be twenty—a girl full of health and fine spirit—only to hand her over to an old man.

BOURDON: To whom are you going to give her? To hear you talk, madam, anyone might think you had your pockets full of sons-in-law, and that your daughters' only trouble was to choose between them. Why was it that the marriage of one of them—a marriage that seemed practically settled—fell through? Lack of money. And lack of money, madam, is just what will keep every one of your daughters an old maid.

MRS. VIGNERON: You're wrong. I had nothing, and neither did my husband. He married me all the same, and we have been very happy.

BOURDON: It is true you have had four children. But if your husband were still in this world, madam, he would disagree with you—perhaps for the first time. When he saw the situation of his daughters, he would be frightened—for, whatever you may think of it, it is perplexing and dangerous. He would put a true value on Mr. Teissier's proposal. To be sure, it is not perfect; but it is more than acceptable. It is reassuring for the present and

[*Looking at* Marie] full of dazzling prospects for the future. I know well enough that it's easy to say what dead people might or mightn't do, but this young lady's father, whose heart was just as big as yours, had all the experience that you lack. He knew life. He knew that you pay for what you get in this world. And, in the end, his thoughts to-day would be something like this: "I have lived for my family; I died for them; surely my daughter can sacrifice a few years for them."

MARIE: [*With her eyes full of tears*] Tell Mr. Teissier I accept.

BOURDON: Come now, young lady, you're giving yourself a great deal of trouble over making your fortune. Here is your contract. I drew it up in advance, without knowing whether I should be paid for my trouble. Read it over carefully and soberly. All it needs is Teissier's signature; and I'll attend to that. I was your father's lawyer, and I'm hoping to be yours. I'll go find Teissier and bring him here. [*He goes out*]

MARIE: [*To her mother*] Kiss me—but don't say anything. Don't take away my courage. I've no more than I need, as it is. You must see that Mr. Bourdon is right. This marriage is our salvation. I'm ashamed —oh, so ashamed!—to do it; but I should always feel guilty if I did not. Mother dear, could you, at your age, begin to live another life of misery and privation? Yes, yes, I know—you are full of courage! But Blanche—Blanche, the poor child—we can't ask her to have courage—not her. What remorse I should have to suffer later, if her health were to demand care that we couldn't give her! And Judith! Oh, I'm thinking of Judith, too. Who knows what would become of a young girl, the best, the highest-minded girl in the world, if she should be driven to extremes, and should lose her fear—of things. Come, I feel a weight off my shoulders now that it's done. It will be just as he wishes—a dishonest, self-seeking marriage—and a sad one, too. But still I prefer a little shame and regret that I know about to a host of terrors of all kinds that might end in a terrible misfortune. Don't cry any more; don't let them see that you have been crying.

[Bourdon *comes in, followed by* Teissier. Teissier, *smiling, goes toward* Marie; *but* Bourdon *stops him and motions that he must first speak to* Mrs. Vigneron]

TEISSIER: How do you do, madam? [*Going to* Marie] Is it really true, what Bourdon just told me —that you will be my wife?

MARIE: It is true.

TEISSIER: A mighty good decision—you won't change your mind by to-morrow, will you? [*She offers him her hand; he kisses her on both cheeks*] Don't blush. That's the way we do in the village I came from. A man kisses his bride-to-be first on the right cheek, saying, "Here's one for the Mayor"; and then one on the left cheek, saying, "Here's one for the priest." [Marie *smiles:* Teissier *goes over to*

Mrs. Vigneron] If you are willing, madam, we'll publish the banns to-morrow. Bourdon will make us a little contract—won't you, Bourdon? [Bourdon *replies with a significant gesture*] And three weeks from now your second daughter will be Mrs. Teissier.

[Rosalie *enters*]

MRS. VIGNERON: What is it, Rosalie?

ROSALIE: Will you see Mr. Dupuis, ma'am?

MRS. VIGNERON: Mr. Dupuis? The house-furnisher?

ROSALIE: Yes, ma'am.

MRS. VIGNERON: What does he want of us?

ROSALIE: You owe him money, ma'am. At least, he says so. Another vulture, sure as you live!

MRS. VIGNERON: We owe Mr. Dupuis nothing—do you hear?—nothing! Tell him I don't want to see him.

TEISSIER: Yes, madam, yes; you must see Mr. Dupuis. Either there is really something due him, in spite of what you think, or Mr. Dupuis is mistaken, in which case it won't be out of place to show him his error. You are not alone; you have a man with you now. Show Mr. Dupuis in. Miss Marie is going to receive him. She will soon be mistress of a house, and I want to see how she will act. Come, Bourdon. Let's leave your daughter with Mr. Dupuis.

[Mrs. Vigneron *and* Bourdon *go out at the left*]

TEISSIER: [*To* Marie] I'll be here, behind this door; I won't miss a word. [*He hides behind the door*]

DUPUIS: [*Entering*] How do you do, Miss Marie?

MARIE: How do you do, Mr. Dupuis?

DUPUIS: Is your mother well?

MARIE: Pretty well, thank you.

DUPUIS: Your sisters are well?

MARIE: Yes.

DUPUIS: I don't need to ask how you are; you're as fresh and rosy as a new-born babe.

MARIE: My mother told me to receive you for her, Mr. Dupuis. Tell me as soon as possible what brings you here.

DUPUIS: Can't you make a little guess as to what brings me here?

MARIE: No, really.

DUPUIS: Is that so? Don't you say to yourself, that if I come here, after so long a time has passed, it must be that I need money?

MARIE: Explain yourself.

DUPUIS: I would have given a whole lot—yes, I would, young lady—not to have to make this visit. When I heard of your father's death, I said to my wife: "I believe Mr. Vigneron still owes us something—but what of it?—it isn't much, and we won't die if we set it down to profit and loss." That's the way I do with my good customers. Mr. Vigneron was a good customer; never had the least trouble with him; that's the way things ought to be between honest folks. Unfortunately, you know how business is—up one day and down the next; well, it isn't good just now. Understand?

MARIE: I'm pretty certain, Mr. Dupuis, that my father settled everything with you.

DUPUIS: Don't say that—you hurt me.

MARIE: Nevertheless, I'm as sure as any one can be that my father squared his account with you.

DUPUIS: Be careful; you'll get me angry. It's only a matter of two thousand francs. The amount isn't worth the trouble. Perhaps you are embarrassed at this moment. Then say so. I haven't come to take your last cent. Just let your mother give me a note for two thousand francs, at three months. Her signature is the same as ready money to me.

MARIE: I'll tell my mother you are here to collect two thousand francs. But I tell you again you are mistaken. I'm certain we don't owe it.

DUPUIS: Well, young lady, I don't leave here till I get it. I came politely, with my hat in my hand [*He puts it on*] and you seem to be treating me like a robber. Those ways don't go with me. You'd better find your mother and make her give me two thousand francs—or a note—I'm still willing to take her note—or Mr. Dupuis will have a fit of anger that will shake the house.

[Teissier *enters;* Dupuis, *surprised and quickly intimidated by his appearance, takes off his hat again*]

TEISSIER: Keep your hat on. There's no ceremony in business. You've got your bill with you?

DUPUIS: Certainly, sir, I have my bill.

TEISSIER: Let's have it.

DUPUIS: Shall I give my bill to this gentleman, miss?

MARIE: Do as he says.

TEISSIER: [*Reading the bill*] "Received of Mrs. Vigneron, two thousand francs to settle her account in full." What kind of bill is this? Don't you usually give an itemized account?

DUPUIS: We can't make out the same bill five or six times, sir. The first one I rendered to Mr. Vigneron contained all the necessary specifications.

TEISSIER: All right. I'm going to pay you. I'll verify the bill when I get home.

DUPUIS: Go ahead, sir, and verify it. Mr. Vigneron should have left his papers in order.

TEISSIER: Yes, he did. [*Holding the bill close to his eyes*] Dupuis is the name, eh? Is this signature yours? You are Mr. Dupuis?

DUPUIS: Yes, sir.

TEISSIER: I am going to give you your two thousand francs.

DUPUIS: Verify it, sir, if you can. I'll wait till then.

TEISSIER: You're very sure that when Mr. Vigneron died, he still owed you two thousand francs?

DUPUIS: Yes, sir—yes, sir. My wife may have made a mistake in her figures; but I don't think so.

TEISSIER: Your wife has nothing to do with it. It's you who would be liable if you received the same amount twice.

DUPUIS: I don't demand it, sir, if it isn't due me I am an honest man.

TEISSIER: [*Offering him the money*] Here's your two thousand francs.

DUPUIS: No; verify it first. I'd rather you would.

TEISSIER: Get out of here! And don't let me see you inside these doors again. Do you hear?

DUPUIS: What's that, sir?

TEISSIER: I tell you not to come back here. Don't be fresh, or you'll regret it.

DUPUIS: Give me back my bill, anyway.

TEISSIER: Look out, or you'll see it again in a courtroom.

DUPUIS: Now that's too much! How dare you—I don't even know who you are—how dare you talk to me like that! I'm going, miss; but you'll hear from me again—and soon! [*He puts on his hat and goes out*]

TEISSIER: Child, since your father died you've been surrounded by a lot of scoundrels. . . . Let's go and join your family.

CURTAIN

Gerhart Hauptmann

(1862–1946)

The career of Hauptmann, long considered Germany's greatest modern playwright, is a record of many successes and distinctions, including the Nobel Prize in 1912 and honorary degrees from the universities of Oxford, Leipzig, Prague, and Columbia. But there is also a history of fluctuations in his work that has made us suspect the quality of his talent; if anything, we have tended to underrate this writer who was for many years overrated. One sharp critic accused him of having no more constancy than a weather vane, and the charge was vigorously maintained against the man himself, as well as the artist, when, after 1933, Hauptmann allowed his reputation to serve as window dressing for the Hitler regime. No particular importance can be attached to the plays written during the last twenty-five years of his life, and today even the bulk of his work before 1921 rings hollow outside, and apparently also inside, Germany. Hauptmann, nevertheless, went as far in the direction of international importance between 1889 and 1912 as a writer can be carried by keen responsiveness to literary and social currents and by virtuosity.

Hauptmann was largely responsible for giving the naturalist style its high estate in Central Europe for a decade or longer. And more than that, he enlarged the scope of dramatic naturalism in the Western world, directing it into the channels of class-conflict drama with *The Weavers* and of comedy of peasant and proletarian life with such plays as *The Beaver Coat* and *The Conflagration*. Social drama, which came to the fore earlier and was made impressive by Ibsen, was led into the unexplored world of working-class problems by the example of *The Weavers,* Hauptmann's account of an uprising of the Silesian weavers in the eighteen-forties. Since the writing of *The Weavers* in 1892, the modern theatre has represented conflicts between capital and labor with great frequency, and the plays have run the gamut from such moderate studies as Galsworthy's *Strife* to such inflammatory documents as Odets' *Waiting for Lefty*.

Hauptmann, the son of a prosperous innkeeper, was born in the village of Obersalzbrunn in Silesia, and was exposed early in life to the mystical pietism of the Moravian sect. He was in delicate health for many years, and it took him some time to find himself as a young man. After failing in preparatory studies for the university, he turned to science, pursued agronomy for a time on an uncle's estate, and then veered toward the arts. He attended the Art School of Breslau and studied sculpture in Rome,

evidently with no great success, before turning to literature. Marriage to a wealthy girl, who supported him during the four years of their engagement, gave him the leisure to unfold as a writer, to experiment with various types of writing, and to make careful notations on dialect which were to prove useful when he adopted naturalism. His marriage at twenty-three, which lasted ten years, was unhappy, and Hauptmann remarried in 1905.

Hauptmann was attracted as early as 1885 to the scientific realism of the liberal "youngest Germany" group and the Social-Democratic movement. He was also one of many young Germans to feel the attraction of Ibsen and Zola. In Berlin, a literary club called "Through" made strides, and Hauptmann was active in its membership, which included scientists, liberal theologians, and journalists. Finally, he aligned himself with the Freie Bühne, or Free Stage, founded in Berlin by Otto Brahm.

Hauptmann's *Before Sunrise* was produced during the new theatre's first season in 1889. It created a sensation with its study of degeneracy among the Silesian peasants who had been enriched but not improved by the discovery of coal in the area. The style was severely naturalistic in its frankness and its use of dialogue appropriate to the characters. The educated people spoke high German, one character from the German capital talked in the Berlin dialect, and the peasants used the Silesian patois. In content and point of view the play observed Zolaist tenets. Hauptmann placed such great importance on the role of heredity that he made his young hero refuse to marry the heroine whose germ plasm carried a tendency toward alcoholism. Next between 1890 and 1892, came such plays as *The Reconciliation* and *Lonely Lives,* middle-class studies of domestic misery that recalled Ibsen's social plays just as *Before Sunrise* recalled Tolstoy's peasant tragedy *The Power of Darkness*. Then Hauptmann struck out in a new direction with *The Weavers* (1892), which won him world-wide fame; and in still another direction with *The Beaver Coat* (1893) a picaresque comedy noteworthy for its satire on Prussian bureaucracy and for the character of Mrs Wolff, a Falstaff among women.

As though he had not yet displayed all the virtuosity of which he was capable, he started on a new romantic-symbolist track with *The Assumption of Hannele* (1893). This drama of a poor girl's suicide and delirious fantasy was a transitional work. Starting with a grossly naturalistic picture of life in the poorhouse, Hauptmann proceeded to make rich use of the symbolism that was beginning to be favored in literary circles under the influence of French poetry. The child's dying delirium, rendered in terms of her reading of fairy tales and the Bible, was an unusual innovation for a playwright hitherto considered Germany's chief exponent of naturalism.

The poetic plays that followed ranged from *The Sunken Bell,* an allegory on the artist's struggle between commonplace duty and desire for freedom, to legendary or historical dramas such as *Schluck und Jau* (1899), *Poor Henry* (1902), and *The White Savior* (1920). In between, moreover, Hauptmann returned to naturalism with works of varying quality, the best of which are *Drayman Henschel* (1898) and *Rose Bernd* (1903), the tragedy of a girl in the grip of the sexual instinct; and, finally, in *The Rats* (1911), Hauptmann added a half-humorous, half-tragic justification of naturalistic art.

Of the great number of plays—he wrote continuously—*The Weavers* is undoubtedly his most significant. Hauptmann attempted to achieve an air of detachment in his treatment of the starving weavers who go berserk, wreck their employer's home, and then proceed to destroy the newly introduced machines upon which they blame their misfortunes. But in *The Weavers,* perhaps by identification with a grandfather who had been one of the weavers, as well as with the insurgent German Social-Democratic movement, Hauptmann managed to make naturalism not only exciting but compassionate. James Huneker, one of its many admirers, correctly described the play as "a symphony in five movements with one grim, leading motive—hunger."

It is to be regretted that Hauptmann did not find it to his purpose to round out his characters and that his slice-of-life chronicle presents the miseries of the people three times (in the first, second, and fifth acts) and the weavers' revolt twice. It is also true that the play falls back upon the past and that the weavers' course of action contributes nothing to an intelligent treatment of modern realities. Hauptmann, however, could justify his brutish representation of the people on the ground that starvation is not conducive to the development of rich personalities, and that the Silesian workers of the eighteen-forties had too limited an understanding of the Industrial Revolution to resort to anything but elemental revenge and destruction of the machines. As for the repetitiveness of the drama, it could be argued that the grievances of the unfortunates had to be represented as pervasive and as cumulative in effect.

Historically, *The Weavers* is memorable for Hauptmann's use of a collective hero of some seventy characters. Here we find the drama of a group rather than of an individual. Ibsen and the other precursors dealt with the single person, Hauptmann with the mass. In this play, moreover, the group is moved by economic forces, and these are primary in the drama, although they translate themselves into emotion through the characters' suffering and protest. We may well wonder whether Hauptmann himself realized when he wrote *The Weavers* what important innovations he was making; how many subsequent plays would represent the working class; and how many would present the group rather than the individual hero. "If Hauptmann had died after writing *The Weavers,*" wrote Huneker, "he would have been acclaimed a great dramatist."

Staged at the Freie Bühne on February 26, 1893, after a year's litigation with the authorities, the play took the theatre by storm. Shortly thereafter the large Berlin Deutsches Theater signalized its conversion to naturalism by reviving the work with a famous ensemble. Kaiser Wilhelm II removed his imperial arms from the theatre in protest. But the *première* was the occasion of one of the greatest demonstrations ever accorded a play. The audience, led by the Socialist leader August Bebel, punctuated the performance with cheers for the weavers and sang their song "Bloody Justice" with them. The production became a rallying ground for the partisans of labor, even if it would appear that Hauptmann's own convictions were neither strong nor long lasting. The play was also produced with great success at the Théâtre Libre on May 29, 1893. The entire Parisian audience in the orchestra stood up in the fourth act when the weavers entered the manufacturer Dreissiger's house. Antoine was so enthusiastic over his production that he acclaimed the play "the masterpiece of a social drama which is still in its infancy."

BIBLIOGRAPHY: Anita Block, *The Changing World in Plays and Theatre* (pp. 33–39), 1939; Frank W. Chandler, *Modern Continental Writers* (pp. 268–298), 1931; Barrett Clark and George Freedley, *A History of Modern Drama* (pp. 78–85), 1947; John Gassner, *Masters of the Drama* (pp. 446–466), 1945; *Columbia Dictionary of Modern European Literature* (pp. 369–371), 1947; James Huneker, *Iconoclasts* (pp. 182–210); Ludwig Lewisohn, *The Modern Drama* (pp. 110–128), 1921.

THE WEAVERS

By Gerhart Hauptmann
TRANSLATED FROM THE GERMAN BY MARY MORISON

COMPLETE LIST OF CHARACTERS

DREISSIGER, *fustian manufacturer*
MRS. DREISSIGER
PFEIFER, *manager*
NEUMANN, *cashier*
AN APPRENTICE
JOHN, *coachman*
A MAID
WEINHOLD, *tutor to* DREISSIGER'S sons

in DREISSIGER'S *employment*

PASTOR KITTELHAUS
MRS. KITTELHAUS
HEiDE, *Police Superintendent*
KUTSCHE, *policeman*
WELZEL, *publican*
MRS. WELZEL
ANNA WELZEL
WIEGAND, *joiner*

A COMMERCIAL TRAVELER
A PEASANT
A FORESTER
SCHMIDT, *surgeon*
HORNIG, *rag-dealer*
WITTIG, *smith*

WEAVERS

BECKER
MORITZ JAEGER
OLD BAUMERT
MOTHER BAUMERT
BERTHA
EMMA
} BAUMERT
FRITZ, EMMA'S *son (four years old)*

AUGUST BAUMERT
OLD ANSORGE
MRS. HEINRICH
OLD HILSE
MOTHER HILSE
GOTTLIEB HILSE
LUISE, GOTTLIEB'S *wife*

MIELCHEN, *their daughter (six years old)*
REIMANN, *weaver*
HEIBER, *weaver*
A WEAVER'S WIFE
A number of weavers, young and old, of both sexes

The action passes in the forties, at Kaschbach, Peterswaldau and Langenbielau, in the Eulengebirge.

ACT I.

A large whitewashed room on the ground floor of Dreissiger's *house at Peterswaldau, where the weavers deliver their finished webs and the fustian is stored. To the left are uncurtained windows, in the back wall there is a glass door, and to the right another glass door, through which weavers, male and female, and children are passing in and out. All three walls are lined with shelves for the storing of the fustian. Against the right wall stands a long bench, on which a number of weavers have already spread out their cloth. In the order of arrival each presents his piece to be examined by* Pfeifer, *Dreissiger's manager, who stands, with compass and magnifying-glass, behind a large table, on which the web to be inspected is laid. When* Pfeifer *has satisfied himself, the weaver lays the fustian on the scale, and an office apprentice tests its weight. The same boy stores the accepted pieces on the shelves.* Pfeifer *calls out the payment due in each case to* Neumann, *the cashier, who is seated at a small table.*

It is a sultry day toward the end of May. The clock is on the stroke of twelve. Most of the waiting work-people have the air of standing before the bar of justice in torturing expectation of a decision that means life or death to them. They are marked, too, by the anxious timidity characteristic of the receiver of charity, who has suffered many humiliations, and, conscious that he is barely tolerated, has acquired the habit of self-effacement. Add to this an expression on every face that tells of constant, fruitless brooding. There is a general resemblance among the men. They have something about them of the dwarf, something of the schoolmaster. The majority are flat-breasted, short-winded, sallow, and poor-looking—creatures of the loom, their knees bent with much sitting. At a first glance the women show fewer typical traits. They look over-driven, worried, reckless, whereas the men still make some show of a pitiful self-respect; and their clothes are ragged, while the men's are patched and mended. Some of the young girls are not without a certain charm, consisting in a wax-like pallor, a slender figure, and large, projecting, melancholy eyes.

NEUMANN: [*Counting out money*] Comes to one and sevenpence halfpenny.

WEAVER'S WIFE: [*About thirty, emaciated, takes up the money with trembling fingers*] Thank you, sir.

NEUMANN: [*Seeing that she does not move on*] Well, something wrong this time, too?

WEAVER'S WIFE: [*Agitated, imploringly*] Do you think I might have a few pence in advance, sir? I need it that bad.

NEUMANN: And I need a few pounds. If it was only a question of needing it—! [*Already occupied in counting out another weaver's money, shortly*] It's Mr. Dreissiger who settles about pay in advance.

WEAVER'S WIFE: Couldn't I speak to Mr. Dreissiger himself, then, sir?

PFEIFER: [*Now manager, formerly weaver. The type is unmistakable, only he is well fed, well dressed, clean-shaven; also takes snuff copiously. He calls out roughly*] Mr. Dreissiger would have enough to do if he had to attend to every trifle himself. That's what we are here for. [*He measures, and then examines through the magnifying-glass*] Mercy on us! what a draught! [*Puts a thick muffler round his neck*] Shut the door, whoever comes in.

APPRENTICE: [*Loudly to Pfeifer*] You might as well talk to stocks and stones.

PFEIFER: That's done—Weigh! [*The weaver places his web on the scales*] If you only understood your business a little better! Full of lumps again. . . . I hardly need to look at the cloth to see them. Call yourself a weaver, and "draw as long a bow" as you've done there!

[Becker *has entered. A young, exceptionally powerfully-built weaver; off-hand, almost bold in manner.* Pfeifer, Neumann, *and the* Apprentice *exchange looks of mutual understanding as he comes in*]

BECKER: Devil take it! This is a sweating job, and no mistake.

FIRST WEAVER: [*In a low voice*] This blazing heat means rain.

[Old Baumert *forces his way in at the glass door on the right, through which the crowd of weavers can be seen, standing shoulder to shoulder, waiting their turn. The old man stumbles forward and lays his bundle on the bench, beside* Becker's. *He sits down by it, and wipes the sweat from his face*]

OLD BAUMERT: A man has a right to a rest after that.

BECKER: Rest's better than money.

OLD BAUMERT: Yes, but we needs the money, too. Good-mornin' to you, Becker!

BECKER: Morning, Father Baumert! Goodness knows how long we'll have to stand here again.

FIRST WEAVER: And what does that matter? What's to hinder a weaver waitin' for an hour, or for a day if need be? What else is he there for?

PFEIFER: Silence there! We can't hear our own voices.

BECKER: [*In a low voice*] This is one of his bad days.

PFEIFER: [*To the weaver standing before him*] How often have I told you that you must bring cleaner cloth? What sort of mess is this? Knots, and straw, and all kinds of dirt.

REIMANN: It's for want of a new picker, sir.

APPRENTICE: [*Has weighed the piece*] Short weight, too.

PFEIFER: I never saw such weavers. I hate to give out the yarn to them. It was another story in my day! I'd have caught it finely from my master for work like that. The business was carried on in different style then. A man had to know his trade—that's the last thing that's thought of nowadays. Reimann, one shilling.

REIMANN: But there's always a pound allowed for waste.

PFEIFER: I've no time. Next man!—What have you to show?

HEIBER: [*Lays his web on the table. While* Pfeifer *is examining it, he goes close up to him; eagerly in a low tone*] Beg pardon, Mr. Pfeifer, but I wanted to ask you, sir, if you would perhaps be so very kind as do me the favor an' not take my advance money off this week's pay.

PFEIFER: [*Measuring and examining the texture; jeeringly*] Well! What next, I wonder? This looks very much as if half the weft had stuck to the bobbins again.

HEIBER: [*Continues*] I'll be sure to make it all right next week, sir. But this last week I've had to put in two days' work on the estate. And my missus is ill in bed. . . .

PFEIFER: [*Giving the web to be weighed*] Another piece of real slop-work. [*Already examining a new web*] What a selvage! Here it's broad, there it's narrow; here it's drawn in by the wefts goodness knows how tight, and there it's torn out again by the temples. And hardly seventy threads weft to the inch. What's come of the rest? Do you call this honest work? I never saw anything like it.

[Heiber, *repressing tears, stands humiliated and helpless*]

BECKER: [*In a low voice to* Baumert] To please that brute you would have to pay for extra yarn out of your own pocket.

[*The* Weaver's Wife, *who has remained standing near the cashier's table, from time to time looking around appealingly, takes courage and once more comes forward*]

WEAVER'S WIFE: [*To cashier imploringly*] I don't know what's to come of me, sir, if you won't give me a little advance this time—O Lord, O Lord!

PFEIFER: [*Calls across*] It's no good whining, or dragging the Lord's name into the matter. You're not so anxious about Him at other times. You look after your husband and see that he's not to be found so often lounging in the public house. We can give no pay in advance. We have to account for every penny. It's not our money. People that are industrious, and understand their work, and do it in the fear of God, never need their pay in advance. So now you know.

NEUMANN: If a Bielau weaver got four times as much pay, he would squander it four times over and be in debt into the bargain.

WEAVER'S WIFE: [*In a loud voice, as if appealing to the general sense of justice*] No one can't call me idle, but I'm not fit now for what I once was. I've twice had a miscarriage. And as to John, he's but a poor creature. He's been to the shepherd at Zerlau, but he couldn't do him no good, and . . . you can't do more than you've strength for. . . . We works as hard as ever we can. This many a week I've been at it till far on into the night. An' we'll keep our heads above water right enough if I can just get a bit of strength into me. But you must have pity on us, Mr. Pfeifer, sir. [*Eagerly, coaxingly*] You'll please be so very kind as to let me have a few pence on the next job, sir?

PFEIFER: [*Paying no attention*] Fiedler, one and twopence.

WEAVER'S WIFE: Only a few pence, to buy bread with. We can't get no more credit. We've a lot of little ones.

NEUMANN: [*Half aside to the* Apprentice, *in a serio-comic tone*] "Every year brings a child to the linen-weaver's wife, heigh-ho, heigh-ho, heigh."

APPRENTICE: [*Takes up the rhyme, half singing*] "And the little brat it's blind the first weeks of its life, heigh-ho, heigh-ho, heigh."

REIMANN: [*Not touching the money which the cashier has counted out to him*] We've always got one and fourpence for the web.

PFEIFER: [*Calls across*] If our terms don't suit you, Reimann, you have only to say so. There's no scarcity of weavers—especially of your sort. For full weight we give full pay.

REIMANN: How anything can be wrong with the weight is past . . .

PFEIFER: You bring a piece of fustian with no faults in it, and there will be no fault in the pay.

REIMANN: It's not possible that there's too many knots in this web.

PFEIFER: [*Examining*] If you want to live well, then be sure you weave well.

HEIBER: [*Has remained standing near* Pfeifer, *so as to seize any favorable opportunity. He laughs at* Pfeifer's *little witticism, then steps forward and again addresses him*] I wanted to ask you, sir, if you would perhaps have the great kindness not to take my advance of six-pence off to-day's pay? My missus has been bedridden since February. She can't do a hand's turn for me, and I've to pay a bobbin girl. And so . . .

PFEIFER: [*Takes a pinch of snuff*] Heiber, do you think I have no one to attend to but you? The others must have their turn.

REIMANN: As the warp was given me I took it home and fastened it to the beam. I can't bring back better yarn than I get.

PFEIFER: If you are not satisfied, you need come for no more. There are plenty ready to tramp the soles off their shoes to get it.

NEUMANN: [*To* Reimann] Do you not want your money?

REIMANN: I can't bring myself to take such pay.

NEUMANN: [*Paying no further attention to* Reimann] Heiber, one shilling. Deduct sixpence for pay in advance. Leave sixpence.

HEIBER: [*Goes up to the table, looks at the money, stands shaking his head as if unable to believe his eyes, then slowly takes it up*] Well, I never!—[*Sighing*] Oh, dear, oh, dear!

OLD BAUMERT: [*Looking into* Heiber's *face*] Yes, Franz, that's so. There's matter enough for sighing.

HEIBER: [*Speaking with difficulty*] I've a girl lying sick at home, too, an' she needs a bottle of medicine.

OLD BAUMERT: What's wrong with her?

HEIBER: Well, you see, she's always been a sickly bit of a thing. I don't know. . . . I needn't mind tellin' you—she brought her trouble with her. It's in her blood, and it breaks out here, there, and everywhere.

OLD BAUMERT: It's always the way. Let folks be poor, and one trouble comes to them on the top of another. There's no help for it and there's no end to it.

HEIBER: What are you carryin' in that cloth, Father Baumert?

OLD BAUMERT: We haven't so much as a bite in the house, and so I've had the little dog killed. There's not much on him, for the poor beast was half starved. A nice little dog he was! I couldn't kill him myself. I hadn't the heart to do it.

PFEIFER: [*Has inspected* Becker's *web—calls*] Becker, one and threepence.

BECKER: That's what you might give to a beggar: it's not pay.

PFEIFER: Every one who has been attended to must clear out. We haven't room to turn round in.

BECKER: [*To those standing near, without lowering his voice*] It's a beggarly pittance, nothing else. A man works his treadle from early morning till late at night, an' when he has bent over his loom for days an' days, tired to death every evening, sick with the dust and the heat, he finds he's made a beggarly one and threepence!

PFEIFER: No impudence allowed here.

BECKER: If you think I'll hold my tongue for your telling, you're much mistaken.

PFEIFER: [*Exclaims*] We'll see about that! [*Rushes to the glass door and calls into the office*] Mr. Dreissiger, Mr. Dreissiger, will you be good enough to come here?

[*Enter* Dreissiger. *About forty, full-bodied, asthmatic. Looks severe*]

DREISSIGER: What is it, Pfeifer?

PFEIFER: [*Spitefully*] Becker says he won't be told to hold his tongue.

DREISSIGER: [*Draws himself up, throws back his head, stares at* Becker; *his nostrils tremble*] Oh, indeed!—Becker. [*To* Pfeifer] Is he the man? . . . [*The clerks nod*]

BECKER: [*Insolently*] Yes, Mr. Dreissiger, yes! [*Pointing to himself*] This is the man. [*Pointing to* Dreissiger] And that's a man, too!

DREISSIGER: [*Angrily*] Fellow, how dare you?

PFEIFER: He's too well off. He'll go dancing on the ice once too often, though.

BECKER: [*Recklessly*] You shut up, you Jack-in-the-box. Your mother must have gone dancing once too often with Satan to have got such a devil for a son.

DREISSIGER: [*Now in a violent passion, roars*] Hold your tongue this moment, sir, or . . .

[*He trembles and takes a few steps forward*]

BECKER: [*Holding his ground steadily*] I'm not deaf. My hearing's quite good yet.

DREISSIGER: [*Controls himself, asks in an apparently cool business tone*] Was this fellow not one of the pack? . . .

PFEIFER: He's a Bielau weaver. When there's any mischief going, they are sure to be in it.

DREISSIGER: [*Trembling*] Well, I give you all warning: if the same thing happens again as last night—a troop of half-drunken cubs, marching past my windows singing that low song . . .

BECKER: Is it "Bloody Justice" you mean?

DREISSIGER: You know well enough what I mean. I tell you that if I hear it again I'll get hold of one of you, and—mind, I'm not joking—before the justice he shall go. And if I can find out who it was that made up that vile doggerel . . .

BECKER: It's a beautiful song, that's what it is!

DREISSIGER: Another word and I send for the police on the spot, without more ado. I'll make short work with you young fellows. I've got the better of very different men before now.

BECKER: I believe you there. A real thoroughbred manufacturer will get the better of two or three hundred weavers in the time it takes you to turn round—swallow them up, and not leave as much as a bone. He's got four stomachs like a cow, and teeth like a wolf. That's nothing to him at all!

DREISSIGER: [*To his clerks*] That man gets no more work from us.

BECKER: It's all the same to me whether I starve at my loom or by the roadside.

DREISSIGER: Out you go, then, this moment! . . .

BECKER: [*Determinedly*] Not without my pay.

DREISSIGER: How much is owing to the fellow, Neumann?

NEUMANN: One and threepence.

DREISSIGER: [*Takes the money hurriedly out of the cashier's hand, and flings it on the table, so that some of the coins roll off on the floor*] There you are, then; and now, out of my sight with you!

BECKER: Not without my pay.

DREISSIGER: Do you not see it lying there? If you don't take it and go . . . It's exactly twelve now . . . The dyers are coming out for their dinner. . . .

BECKER: I get my pay into my hand—here. [*Points with the fingers of his right hand at the palm of his left*]

DREISSIGER: [*To the* Apprentice] Pick up the money, Tilgner.

[*The* Apprentice *lifts the money and puts it into* Becker's *hand*]

BECKER: Everything in proper order.

[*Deliberately takes an old purse out of his pocket and puts the money into it*]

DREISSIGER: [*As* Becker *still does not move away*] Well? Do you want me to come and help you?

[*Signs of agitation are observable among the crowd of weavers. A long, loud sigh is heard, and then a fall. General interest is at once diverted to this new event*]

DREISSIGER: What's the matter there?

CHORUS OF WEAVERS AND WOMEN: "Some one's fainted."—"It's a little sickly boy." —"Is it a fit, or what?"

DREISSIGER: What do you say? Fainted?

[*He goes nearer*]

OLD WEAVER: There he lies, any way.

[*They make room. A boy of about eight is seen lying on the floor as if dead*]

DREISSIGER: Does any one know the boy?

OLD WEAVER: He's not from our village.

OLD BAUMERT: He's like one of Weaver Heinrich's boys. [*Looks at him more closely*] Yes, that's Heinrich's little Philip.

DREISSIGER: Where do they live?

OLD BAUMERT: Up near us in Kaschbach, sir. He goes round playin' music in the evenings, and all day he's at the loom. They've nine children an' a tenth a-coming.

CHORUS OF WEAVERS AND WOMEN: "They're terrible put to it."—"The rain comes through their roof."—"The woman hasn't two shirts among the nine."

OLD BAUMERT: [*Taking the boy by the arm*] Now then, lad, what's wrong with you? Wake up, lad.

DREISSIGER: Some of you help me, and we'll get him up. It's disgraceful to send a sickly child this distance. Bring some water, Pfeifer.

WOMAN: [*Helping to lift the boy*] Surely you're not going to die, lad!

DREISSIGER: Brandy, Pfeifer, brandy will be better.

BECKER: [*Forgotten by all, has stood looking on. With his hand on the door-latch, he now calls loudly and tauntingly*] Give him something to eat, an' he'll soon be all right.

[*Goes out*]

DREISSIGER: That fellow will come to a bad end.—Take him under the arm, Neumann. Easy now, easy; we'll get him into my room. What?

NEUMANN: He said something, Mr. Dreissiger. His lips are moving.

DREISSIGER: What—what is it, boy?

BOY: [*Whispers*] I'm h—hungry.

WOMAN: I think he says . . .

DREISSIGER: We'll find out. Don't stop. Let us get him into my room. He can lie on the sofa there. We'll hear what the doctor says.

[Dreissiger, Neumann, *and the woman lead the boy into the office. The weavers begin to behave like school-children when their master has left the classroom. They stretch themselves, whisper, move from one foot to the other, and in the course of a few moments are conversing loudly*]

OLD BAUMERT: I believe as how Becker was right.

CHORUS OF WOMEN AND WEAVERS: "He did say something like that."—"It's nothing new here to fall down from hunger."—"God knows what's to come of them in winter if this cutting down of wages goes on."—"An' this winter the potatoes aren't no good at all."—"Things'll get worse and worse till we're all done for together."

OLD BAUMERT: The best thing a man could do would be to put a rope round his neck and hang hisself on his own loom, like Weaver Nentwich. [*To another old weaver*] Here, take a pinch. I was at Neurode yesterday. My brother-in-law, he works in the snuff factory there, and he gave me a grain or two. Have you anything good in your handkercher?

OLD WEAVER: Only a little pearl barley. I was coming along behind Ulbrich the miller's cart, and there was a slit in one of the sacks. I can tell you we'll be glad of it.

OLD BAUMERT: There's twenty-two mills in Peterswaldau, but of all they grind, there's never nothing comes our way.

OLD WEAVER: We must keep up heart. There's always something comes to help us on again.

HEIBER: Yes, when we're hungry, we can pray to all the saints to help us, and if that don't fill our bellies we can put a pebble in our mouths and suck it. Eh, Baumert?

[*Reënter* Dreissiger, Pfeifer, *and* Neumann]

DREISSIGER: It was nothing serious. The boy is all right again. [*Walks about excitedly, panting*] But all the same it's a disgrace. The child's so weak that a puff of wind would blow him over. How people, how any parents can be so thoughtless is what passes my comprehension. Loading him with two heavy pieces of fustian to carry a good six miles! No one would believe it that hadn't seen it. It simply means that I shall have to make a rule that no goods brought by children will be taken over. [*He walks up and down silently for a few moments*] I sincerely trust such a thing will not occur again.—Who gets all the blame for it? Why, of course the manufacturer. It's entirely our fault. If some poor little fellow sticks in the snow in winter and goes to sleep, a special correspondent arrives posthaste, and in two days we have a blood-curdling story served up in all the papers. Is any blame laid on the father, the parents, that send such a child?—Not a bit of it. How should they be to blame? It's all the manufacturer's fault—he's made the scapegoat. They flatter the weaver, and give the manufacturer nothing but abuse—he's a cruel man, with a heart like a stone, a wicked fellow, at whose calves every cur of a journalist may take a bite. He lives on the fat of the land, and pays the poor weavers starvation wages. In the flow of his eloquence the writer forgets to mention that such a man has his cares too and his sleepless nights; that he runs risks of which the workman never dreams; that he is often driven distracted by all the calculations he has to make, and all the different things he has to take into account; that he has to struggle for his very life against competition; and that no day passes without some annoyance or some loss. And think of the manufacturer's responsibilities, think of the numbers that depend on him, that look to him for their daily bread. No, no! none of you need wish yourselves in my shoes—you would soon have enough of it. [*After a moment's reflection*] You all saw how that fellow, that scoundrel Becker, behaved. Now he'll go and spread about all sorts of tales of my hard-heartedness, of how my weavers are turned off for a mere trifle, without a moment's notice. Is that true? Am I so very unmerciful?

CHORUS OF VOICES: No, sir.

DREISSIGER: It doesn't seem to me that I am. And yet these ne'er-do-wells come round singing low songs about us manufacturers—prating about hunger, with enough in their pockets to pay for quarts of bad brandy. If they would like to know what want is, let them go and ask the linen-weavers: they can tell something about it. But you here, you fustian-weavers, have every reason to thank God that things are no worse than they are. And I put it to all the old, industrious weavers present: Is a good workman able to gain a living in my employment, or is he not?

MANY VOICES: Yes, sir; he is, sir.

DREISSIGER: There now! You see! Of course such a fellow as that Becker can't. I advise you to keep these young lads in check. If there's much more of this sort of thing, I'll shut up shop—give up the business altogether, and then you can shift for yourselves, get work where you like—perhaps Mr. Becker will provide it.

FIRST WEAVER'S WIFE: [*Has come close to* Dreissiger, *obsequiously removes a little dust from his coat*] You've been an' rubbed ag'in' something, sir.

DREISSIGER: Business is as bad as it can be just now, you know that yourselves. Instead of making money, I am losing it every day. If, in spite of this, I take care that my weavers are kept in work, I look for some little gratitude from them. I have thousands of pieces of cloth in stock, and don't know if I'll ever be able to sell them. Well, now, I've heard how many weavers hereabouts are out of work, and—I'll leave Pfeifer to give the particulars —but this much I'll tell you, just to show you my good will. . . . I can't deal out charity all round;

I'm not rich enough for that; but I can give the people who are out of work the chance of earning at any rate a little. It's a great business risk I run by doing it, but that's my affair. I say to myself: Better that a man should work for a bite of bread than that he should starve altogether. Am I not right?

CHORUS OF VOICES: Yes, yes, sir.

DREISSIGER: And therefore I am ready to give employment to two hundred more weavers. Pfeifer will tell you on what conditions.

[He turns to go]

FIRST WEAVER'S WIFE: [Comes between him and the door, speaks hurriedly, eagerly, imploringly] Oh, if you please, sir, will you let me ask you if you'll be so good . . . I've been twice laid up for . . .

DREISSIGER: [Hastily] Speak to Pfeifer, good woman. I'm too late as it is.

[Passes on, leaving her standing]

REIMANN: [Stops him again. In an injured, complaining tone] I have a complaint to make, if you please, sir. Mr. Pfeifer refuses to . . . I've always got one and two-pence for a web . . .

DREISSIGER: [Interrupts him] Mr. Pfeifer's my manager. There he is. Apply to him.

HEIBER: [Detaining Dreissiger; hurriedly and confusedly] O sir, I wanted to ask if you would p'r'aps, if I might p'r'aps . . . if Mr. Pfeifer might . . . might . . .

DREISSIGER: What is it you want?

HEIBER: That advance pay I had last time, sir; I thought p'r'aps you would kindly . . .

DREISSIGER: I have no idea what you are talking about.

HEIBER: I'm awful hard up, sir, because . . .

DREISSIGER: These are things Pfeifer must look into—I really have not the time. Arrange the matter with Pfeifer.

[He escapes into the office. The supplicants look helplessly at one another, sigh, and take their places again among the others]

PFEIFER: [Resuming his task of inspection] Well, Annie, let us see what yours is like.

OLD BAUMERT: How much are we to get for the web, then, Mr. Pfeifer?

HEIBER: One shilling a web.

OLD BAUMERT: Has it come to that!

[Excited whispering and murmuring among the weavers]

ACT II.

A small room in the house of Wilhelm Ansorge, weaver and house-owner in the village of Kaschbach, in the Eulengebirge.

In this room, which does not measure six feet from the dilapidated wooden floor to the smoke-blackened rafters, sit four people. Two young girls, Emma and Bertha Baumert, are working at their looms; Mother Baumert, a decrepit old woman, sits on a stool beside the bed, with a winding-wheel in front of her; her idiot son August sits on a footstool, also winding. He is twenty, has a small body and head, and long, spider-like legs and arms.

Faint, rosy evening light makes its way through two small windows in the right wall, which have their broken panes pasted over with paper or stuffed with straw. It lights up the flaxen hair of the girls, which falls loose on their slender white necks and thin bare shoulders, and their coarse chemises. These, with a short petticoat of the roughest linen, form their whole attire. The warm glow falls on the old woman's face, neck, and breast—a face worn away to a skeleton, with shriveled skin and sunken eyes, red and watery with smoke, dust, and working by lamplight; a long goitre neck, wrinkled and sinewy; a hollow breast covered with faded, ragged shawls.

Part of the right wall is also lighted up, with stove, stove-bench, bedstead, and one or two gaudily colored sacred prints. On the stove-rail rags are hanging to dry, and behind the stove is a collection of worthless lumber. On the bench stand some old pots and cooking-utensils, and potato-parings are laid out on it, on paper, to dry. Hanks of yarn and reels hang from the rafters; baskets of bobbins stand beside the looms. In the backwall there is a low door without fastening. Beside it a bundle of willow wands is set up against the wall, and beyond them lie some damaged quarter-bushel baskets.

The room is full of sound—the rhythmic thud of the looms, shaking floor and walls, the click and rattle of the shuttles passing back and forward, and the steady whirr of the winding-wheels, like the hum of gigantic bees.

MOTHER BAUMERT: [In a querulous, feeble voice, as the girls stop weaving and bend over their webs] Got to make knots again already, have you?

EMMA: [The elder of the two girls, about twenty-two, tying a broken thread] It's the plaguyest web, this!

BERTHA: [Fifteen] Yes, it's real bad yarn they've given us this time.

EMMA: What can have happened to father? He's been away since nine.

MOTHER BAUMERT: You may well ask. Where in the wide world can he be?

BERTHA: Don't you worry yourself, mother.

MOTHER BAUMERT: I can't help it, Bertha lass.

[Emma begins to weave again]

BERTHA: Stop a minute, Emma!

EMMA: What is it!

BERTHA: I thought I heard some one.

EMMA: It'll be Ansorge coming home.

[Enter Fritz, a little, barefooted, ragged boy of four]

FRITZ: [Whimpering] I'm hungry, mother.

EMMA: Wait, Fritzel, wait a bit! Gran'father will

be here very soon, an' he's bringin' bread along with him, an' coffee, too.

FRITZ: But I'm awful hungry, mother.

EMMA: Be a good boy now, Fritz. Listen to what I'm tellin' you. He'll be here this minute. He's bringin' nice bread au' nice corn-coffee; an' when we stop working mother'll take the tater peelin's and carry them to the farmer, and the farmer'll give her a drop o' good skim milk for her little boy.

FRITZ: Where's grandfather gone?

EMMA: To the manufacturer, Fritz, with a web.

FRITZ: To the manufacturer?

EMMA: Yes, yes, Fritz; down to Dreissiger's at Peterswaldau.

FRITZ: Is it there he gets the bread?

EMMA: Yes; Dreissiger gives him money, and then he buys the bread.

FRITZ: Does he give him a heap of money?

EMMA: [*Impatiently*] Oh, stop that chatter, boy.

[*She and Bertha go on weaving for a time, and then both stop again*]

BERTHA: August, go and ask Ansorge if he'll give us a light.

[August *goes out accompanied by* Fritz]

MOTHER BAUMERT: [*Overcome by her childish apprehension, whimpers*] Emma! Bertha! where can father be?

BERTHA: He'll have looked in to see Hauffen.

MOTHER BAUMERT: [*Crying*] What if he's sittin' drinkin' in the public house?

EMMA: Don't cry, mother! You know well enough father's not the man to do that.

MOTHER BAUMERT: [*Half distracted by a multitude of gloomy forebodings*] What . . . what . . . what's to become of us if he doesn't come home? —if he drink the money, and brings us nothin' at all? There's not so much as a handful of salt in the house—not a bite o' bread, nor a bit o' wood for the fire.

BERTHA: Wait a bit, mother! It's moonlight just now. We'll take August with us and go into the wood and get some sticks.

MOTHER BAUMERT: Yes, an' be caught by the forester.

[Ansorge, *an old weaver of gigantic stature, who has to bend down to get into the room, puts his head and shoulders in at the door. Long, unkempt hair and beard*]

ANSORGE: What's wanted?

BERTHA: Light, if you please.

ANSORGE: [*In a muffled voice, as if speaking in a sick-room*] There's good daylight yet.

MOTHER BAUMERT: Are we to sit in the dark next?

ANSORGE: I've to do the same myself. [*Goes out*]

BERTHA: It's easy to see that he's a miser.

EMMA: Well, there's nothin' for it but to sit an' wait his pleasure.

[*Enter* Mrs. Heinrich, *a woman of thirty, enceinte; an expression of torturing anxiety and apprehension on her worn face*]

MRS. HEINRICH: Good-evenin' t' you all.

MOTHER BAUMERT: Well, Jenny, and what's your news?

MRS. HEINRICH: [*Who limps*] I've got a piece o' glass into my foot.

BERTHA: Come an' sit down, then, an' I'll see if I can get it out.

[Mrs. Heinrich *seats herself.* Bertha *kneels down in front of her, and examines her foot*]

MOTHER BAUMERT: How are you all at home, Jenny?

MRS. HEINRICH: [*Breaks out despairingly*] Things is in a terrible way with us! [*She struggles in vain against a rush of tears; then weeps silently*]

MOTHER BAUMERT: The best thing as could happen to the likes of us, Jenny, would be if God had pity on us an' took us away out o' this weary world.

MRS. HEINRICH: [*No longer able to control herself, screams, still crying*] My children's starvin'. [*Sobs and moans*] I'm at my wits' ends. Let me work till I fall down—I'm more dead than alive—it's all no use. Am I able to fill nine hungry mouths? We got a bit o' bread last night, but it wasn't enough even for the two smallest ones. Who was I to give it to, eh? They all cried: Me, me, mother! give it to me! . . . An' if it's like this while I'm still on my feet, what'll it be when I've to take to bed? Our few taters was washed away. We haven't a thing to put in our mouths.

BERTHA: [*Has removed the bit of glass and washed the wound*] We'll put a rag around. Emma, see if you can find one.

MOTHER BAUMERT: We're no better off than you, Jenny.

MRS. HEINRICH: You have your girls, anyway. You've a husband as can work. Mine was taken with one of his fits last week again—so bad that I didn't know what to do with him, and was half out o' my mind with fright. And when he's had a turn like that. he can't stir out of bed under a week.

MOTHER BAUMERT: Mine's no better. His breathin 's bad now as well as his back. An' there's not a farthin' nor a farthin's worth in the house. If he don't bring a few pence with him to-day, I don't know what we're to do.

EMMA: It's the truth she's tellin' you, Jenny. We had to let father take the little dog with him to-day, to have him killed, that we might get a bite into our stomachs again!

MRS. HEINRICH: Have you not got as much as a handful of flour to spare?

MOTHER BAUMERT: And that we have not, Jenny There's not as much as a grain of salt in the house.

MRS. HEINRICH: Oh, whatever am I to do? [*Rises; stands still, brooding*] I don't know what'll be the end of this! It's more nor I can bear. [*Screams in rage and despair*] I would be contented if it was nothin' but pigs' food!—But I can't go home again empty-handed—that I can't. God forgive me, I see no other way out of it. [*She limps quickly out*]

MOTHER BAUMERT: [*Calls after her in a warning voice*] Jenny, Jenny! don't you be doin' anything foolish, now!

BERTHA: She'll do herself no harm, mother. You needn't be afraid.

EMMA: That's the way she always goes on. [*Seats herself at the loom and weaves for a few seconds*]

[August *enters, carrying a tallow candle, and lighting his father,* Old Baumert, *who follows close behind him, staggering under a heavy bundle of yarn*]

MOTHER BAUMERT: Oh, father, where have you been all this long time? Where have you been?

OLD BAUMERT: Come now, mother, don't fall on a man like that. Give me time to get my breath first. An' look who I've brought with me.

[Moritz Jaeger *comes stooping in at the low door. Reserve soldier, newly discharged. Middle height, rosy-cheeked, military carriage. His cap on the side of his head, hussar fashion, whole clothes and shoes, a clean shirt without collar. Draws himself up and salutes*]

JAEGER: [*In a hearty voice*] Good-evening, Auntie Baumert!

MOTHER BAUMERT: Well, well, now! And to think you've got back! An' you've not forgotten us? Take a chair, then, lad.

EMMA: [*Wiping a wooden chair with her apron, and pushing it toward* Moritz] An' so you've come to see what poor folks are like again, Moritz?

JAEGER: I say, Emma, is it true that you've got a boy nearly old enough to be a soldier? Where did you get hold of him, eh?

[Bertha, *having taken the small supply of provisions which her father has brought, puts meat into a saucepan, and shoves it into the oven, while* August *lights the fire*]

BERTHA: You knew Weaver Finger, didn't you?

MOTHER BAUMERT: We had him here in the house with us. He was ready enough to marry her; but he was too far gone in consumption; he was as good as a dead man. It didn't happen for want of warning from me. But do you think she would listen? Not she. Now he's dead an' forgotten long ago, an' she's left with the boy to provide for as best she can. But now tell us how you've been gettin' on, Moritz.

OLD BAUMERT: You've only to look at him, mother, to know that. He's had luck. It'll be about as much as he can do to speak to the likes of us. He's got clothes like a prince, an' a silver watch, an' thirty shillings in his pocket into the bargain.

JAEGER: [*Stretching himself consequentially, a knowing smile on his face*] I can't complain. I didn't get on at all badly in the regiment.

OLD BAUMERT: He was the major's own servant. Just listen to him—he speaks like a gentleman.

JAEGER: I've got so accustomed to it that I can't help it.

MOTHER BAUMERT: Well, now, to think that such a good-for-nothing as you were should have come to be a rich man. For there wasn't nothing to be made of you. You would never sit still to wind more than a hank of yarn at a time, that you wouldn't. Off you went to your tom-tit boxes an' your robin redbreast snares—they was all you cared about. Is it not the truth I'm telling?

JAEGER: Yes, yes, auntie, it's true enough. It wasn't only redbreasts. I went after swallows, too.

EMMA: Though we were always tellin' you that swallows were poison.

JAEGER: What did I care?—But how have you all been getting on, Auntie Baumert?

MOTHER BAUMERT: Oh, badly, lad, badly these last four years. I've had the rheumatics—just look at them hands. And it's more than likely as I've had a stroke o' some kind, too, I'm that helpless. I can hardly move a limb, an' nobody knows the pains I suffers.

OLD BAUMERT: She's in a bad way, she is. She'll not hold out long.

BERTHA: We've to dress her in the mornin' an' undress her at night, an' to feed her like a baby.

MOTHER BAUMERT: [*Speaking in a complaining, tearful voice*] Not a thing can I do for myself. It's far worse than bein' ill. For it's not only a burden to myself I am, but to every one else. Often and often do I pray to God to take me. For oh! mine's a weary life. I don't know . . . p'r'aps they think . . . but I'm one that's been a hard worker all my days. An' I've always been able to do my turn, too; but now, all at once, [*She vainly attempts to rise*] I can't do nothing.—I've a good husband an' good children, but to have to sit here and see them! . . . Look at the girls! There's hardly any blood left in them—faces the color of a sheet. But on they must work at these weary looms whether they earn enough to keep theirselves or not. What sort o' life is it they lead? Their feet never off the treadle from year's end to year's end. An' with it all they can't scrape together as much as'll buy them clothes that they can let theirselves be seen in; never a step can they go to church, to hear a word of comfort. They're liker scarecrows than young girls of fifteen and twenty.

BERTHA: [*At the stove*] It's beginnin' to smoke again!

OLD BAUMERT: There now; look at that smoke. And we can't do nothin' for it. The whole stove's goin' to pieces. We must let it fall, and swallow the soot. We're coughin' already, one worse than the other. We may cough till we choke, or till we cough our lungs up—nobody cares.

JAEGER: But this here is Ansorge's business; he must see to the stove.

BERTHA: He'll see us out of the house first; he has plenty against us without that.

MOTHER BAUMERT: We've only been in his way this long time past.

OLD BAUMERT: One word of complaint an' out we go. He's had no rent from us this last half-year.

MOTHER BAUMERT: A well-off man like him needn't be so hard.

OLD BAUMERT: He's no better off than we are, mother. He's hard put to it, too, for all he holds his tongue about it.

MOTHER BAUMERT: He's got his house.

OLD BAUMERT: What are you talkin' about, mother? Not one stone in the wall is the man's own.

JAEGER: [*Has seated himself, and taken a short pipe with gay tassels out of one coat-pocket, and a quart bottle of brandy out of another*] Things can't go on like this. I'm dumbfoundered when I see the life the people live here. The very dogs in the towns live better.

OLD BAUMERT: [*Eagerly*] That's what I say! Eh? eh? You know it, too! But if you say that here, they'll tell you that it's only bad times.

[*Enter* Ansorge, *an earthenware pan with soup in one hand, in the other a half-finished quarter-bushel basket*]

ANSORGE: Glad to see you again, Moritz!

JAEGER: Thank you, Father Ansorge—same to you!

ANSORGE: [*Shoving his pan into the oven*] Why, lad, you look like a duke!

OLD BAUMERT: Show him your watch, Moritz! An' he's got a new suit of clothes besides them he's on, an' thirty shillings in his purse.

ANSORGE: [*Shaking his head*] Is that so? Well, well!

EMMA: [*Puts the potato-parings into a bag*] I must be off; I'll maybe get a drop o' skim milk for these. [*Goes out*]

JAEGER: [*The others hanging on his words*] You know how you all used to be down on me. It was always: Wait, Moritz, till your soldiering time comes —you'll catch it then. But you see how well I've got on. At the end of the first half-year I had got my good conduct stripes. You've got to be willing —that's where the secret lies. I brushed the sergeant's boots; I groomed his horse; I fetched his beer. I was as sharp as a needle. Always ready, accoutrements clean and shining—first at stables, first at roll-call, first in the saddle. And when the bugle sounded to the assault—why, then, blood and thunder, and ride to the devil with you!! I was as keen as a pointer. Says I to myself: There's no help for it now, my boy, it's got to be done; and I set my mind to it and did it. Till at last the major said before the whole squadron: There's a hussar now that shows you what a hussar should be!

[*Silence. He lights his pipe*]

ANSORGE: [*Shaking his head*] Well, well, well! You had luck with you, Moritz. [*Sits down on the floor, with his willow twigs beside him, and continues mending the basket, which he holds between his legs*]

OLD BAUMERT: Let's hope you've brought some of it to us.—Are we to have a drop to drink your health in?

JAEGER: Of course you are, Father Baumert. And when this bottle's done, we'll send for more. [*He flings a coin on the table*]

ANSORGE: [*Open-mouthed with amazement*] Oh, my! Oh, my! What goings on to be sure! Roast meat frizzlin' in the oven! A bottle o' brandy on the table! [*He drinks out of the bottle*] Here's to you, Moritz!—Well, well, well!

[*The bottle circulates freely after this*]

OLD BAUMERT: If we could anyway have a bit o' meat on Sundays and holidays, instead of never seein' the sight of it from year's end to year's end! Now we'll have to wait till another poor little dog finds its way into the house like this one did four weeks gone by—an' that's not likely to happen soon again.

ANSORGE: Have you killed the little dog?

OLD BAUMERT: We had to do that or starve.

ANSORGE: Well, well!

MOTHER BAUMERT: A nice, kind little beast he was, too!

JAEGER: Are you as keen as ever on roast dog hereabouts?

OLD BAUMERT: My word, if we could only get enough of it!

MOTHER BAUMERT: A nice little bit o' meat like that does you a lot o' good.

OLD BAUMERT: Have you lost the taste for it, Moritz? Stay with us a bit, and it'll soon come back to you.

ANSORGE: [*Sniffing*] Yes, yes! That will be a tasty bite—what a good smell it has!

OLD BAUMERT: [*Sniffing*] Splendid!

ANSORGE: Come, then, Moritz, tell us your opinion, you that's been out and seen the world. Are things at all like improving for us weavers, eh?

JAEGER: They would need to.

ANSORGE: We're in an awful state here. It's not livin' an' it's not dyin'. A man fights to the bitter end, but he's bound to be beat at last—to be left without a roof over his head, you may say without ground under his feet. As long as he can work at the loom he can earn some sort o' poor, miserable livin'. But it's many a day since I've been able to get that sort o' job. Now I tries to put a bite into my mouth with this here basket-makin'. I sits at it late into the night, and by the time I tumbles into bed I've earned three-halfpence. I put it to you if a man can live on that, when everything's so dear? Nine shillin' goes in one lump for house tax, three shillin' for land tax, nine shillin' for mortgage interest— that makes one pound one. I may reckon my year's earnin' at just double that money, and that leaves me twenty-one shillin' for a whole year's food, an' fire, an' clothes, an' shoes; and I've got to keep up some sort of a place to live in. Is it any wonder if I'm behind-hand with my interest payments?

OLD BAUMERT: Some one would need to go to Berlin an' tell the King how hard put to it we are.

JAEGER: Little good that would do, Father Baumert. There's been plenty written about it in the newspapers. But the rich people, they can turn and twist things round . . . as cunning as the devil himself.

OLD BAUMERT: [*Shaking his head*] To think they've no more sense than that in Berlin!

ANSORGE: And is it really true, Moritz? Is there no law to help us? If a man hasn't been able to scrape together enough to pay his mortgage interest, though he's worked the very skin off his hands, must his house be taken from him? The peasant that's lent the money on it, he wants his rights—what else can you look for from him? But what's to be the end of it all, I don't know.—If I'm put out o' the house. . . . [*In a voice choked by tears*] I was born here, and here my father sat at his loom for more than forty year. Many was the time he said to mother: Mother, when I'm gone, the house'll still be here. I've worked hard for it. Every nail means a night's weaving, every plank a year's dry bread. A man would think that . . .

JAEGER: They're quite fit to take the last bite out of your mouth—that's what they are.

ANSORGE: Well, well, well! I would rather be carried out than have to walk out now in my old days. Who minds dyin'? My father, he was glad to die. At the very end he got frightened, but I crept into bed beside him, an' he quieted down again. I was a lad of thirteen then. I was tired and fell asleep beside him—I knew no better—and when I woke he was quite cold.

MOTHER BAUMERT: [*After a pause*] Give Ansorge his soup out o' the oven, Bertha.

BERTHA: Here, Father Ansorge, it'll do you good.

ANSORGE: [*Eating and shedding tears*] Well, well, well!

[Old Baumert *has begun to eat the meat out of the saucepan*]

MOTHER BAUMERT: Father, father, can't you have patience an' let Bertha serve it up properly?

OLD BAUMERT: [*Chewing*] It's two years now since I took the Sacrament. I went straight after that an' sold my Sunday coat, an' we bought a good bit o' pork, an' since then never a mouthful of meat has passed my lips till to-night.

JAEGER: How should *we* need meat? The manufacturers eat it for us. It's the fat of the land *they* live on. Whoever doesn't believe that has only to go down to Bielau and Peterswaldau. He'll see fine things there—palace upon palace, with towers and iron railings and plate-glass windows. Who do they all belong to? Why, of course, the manufacturers! No signs of bad times there! Baked and boiled and fried—horses and carriages and governesses—they've money to pay for all that and goodness knows how much more. They're swelled out to bursting with pride and good living.

ANSORGE: Things was different in my young days. Then the manufacturers let the weaver have his share. Now they keep everything to theirselves. An'

would you like to know what's at the bottom of it all? It's that the fine folks nowadays believes neither in God nor devil. What do they care about commandments or punishments? And so they steal our last scrap of bread, an' leave us no chance of earnin' the barest living. For it's their fault. If our manufacturers was good men, there would be no bad times for us.

JAEGER: Listen, then, and I'll read you something that will please you. [*He takes one or two loose papers from his pocket*] I say, August, run and fetch another quart from the public-house. Eh, boy, do you laugh all day long?

MOTHER BAUMERT: No one knows why, but our August's always happy—grins an' laughs, come what may. Off with you, then, quick! [*Exit* August *with the empty brandy-bottle*] You've got something good now, eh, father?

OLD BAUMERT: [*Still chewing; spirits rising from the effect of food and drink*] Moritz, you're the very man we want. You can read an' write. You understand the weavin' trade, and you've a heart to feel for the poor weavers' sufferin's. You should stand up for us here.

JAEGER: I'd do that quick enough! There's nothing I'd like better than to give the manufacturers round here a bit of a fright—dogs that they are! I'm an easygoing fellow, but let me once get worked up into a real rage, and I'll take Dreissiger in the one hand and Dittrich in the other, and knock their heads together till the sparks fly out of their eyes.— If we could only arrange all to join together, we'd soon give the manufacturers a proper lesson . . . without help from King or Government . . . all we'd have to do would be to say: We want this and that, and we don't want the other thing. There would be a change of days then. As soon as they see that there's some pluck in us, they'll cave in. I know the rascals; they're a pack of cowardly hounds.

MOTHER BAUMERT: There's some truth in what you say. I'm not an ill-natured woman. I've always been the one to say as how there must be rich folks as well as poor. But when things come to such a pass as this. . . .

JAEGER: The devil may take them all, for what I care. It would be no more than they deserve.

[Old Baumert *has quietly gone out*]

BERTHA: Where's father?

MOTHER BAUMERT: I don't know where he can have gone.

BERTHA: Do you think he's not been able to stomach the meat, with not gettin' none for so long?

MOTHER BAUMERT: [*In distress, crying*] There, now, there! He's not even able to keep it down when he's got it. Up it comes again, the only bite o' good food as he's tasted this many a day.

[*Reënter* Old Baumert, *crying with rage*]

OLD BAUMERT: It's no good! I'm too far gone! Now that I've at last got hold of somethin' with a taste in it, my stomach won't keep it. [*He sits down on the bench by the stove crying*]

JAEGER: [*With a sudden violent ebullition of rage*] And yet there are people not far from here, justices they call themselves too, over-fed brutes, that have nothing to do all the year round but invent new ways of wasting their time. And these people say that the weavers would be quite well off if only they weren't so lazy.

ANSORGE: The men as say that are no men at all, they're monsters.

JAEGER: Never mind, Father Ansorge; we're making the place hot for 'em. Becker and I have been and given Dreissiger a piece of our mind, and before we came away we sang him "Bloody Justice."

ANSORGE: Good Lord! Is that the song?

JAEGER: Yes; I have it here.

ANSORGE: They call it Dreissiger's song, don't they?

JAEGER: I'll read it to you.

MOTHER BAUMERT: Who wrote it?

JAEGER: That's what nobody knows. Now listen. [*He reads, hesitating like a schoolboy, with incorrect accentuation, but unmistakably strong feeling. Despair, suffering, rage, hatred, thirst for revenge, all find utterance*]

The justice to us weavers dealt
   Is bloody, cruel, and hateful;
Our life's one torture, long drawn out:
   For Lynch law we'd be grateful.
Stretched on the rack day after day,
   Hearts sick and bodies aching,
Our heavy sighs their witness bear
   To spirits slowly breaking.

[*The words of the song make a strong impression on* Old Baumert. *Deeply agitated, he struggles against the temptation to interrupt* Jaeger. *At last he can keep quiet no longer*]

OLD BAUMERT: [*To his wife, half laughing, half crying, stammering*] Stretched on the rack day after day. Whoever wrote that, mother, wrote the truth. You can bear witness . . . eh, how does it go? "Our heavy sighs their witness bear" . . . what's the rest?

JAEGER: "To spirits slowly breaking."

OLD BAUMERT: You know the way we sigh, mother, day and night, sleepin' and wakin'.

[Ansorge *has stopped working, and cowers on the floor, strongly agitated.* Mother Baumert *and* Bertha *wipe their eyes frequently during the course of the reading*]

JAEGER: [*Continues to read*]

The Dreissigers true hangmen are,
   Servants no whit behind them;
Masters and men with one accord
   Set on the poor to grind them.
You villains all, you brood of hell . . .

OLD BAUMERT: [*Trembling with rage, stamping on the floor*] Yes, brood of hell!!!

JAEGER: [*Reads*]

You fiends in fashion human,
A curse will fall on all like you,
   Who prey on man and woman.

ANSORGE: Yes, yes, a curse upon them!

OLD BAUMERT: [*Clenching his fist threateningly*] You prey on man and woman.

JAEGER: [*Reads*]

The suppliant knows he asks in vain,
   Vain every word that's spoken.
"If not content, then go and starve—
   Our rules cannot be broken."

OLD BAUMERT: What is it? "The suppliant knows he asks in vain"? Every word of it's true . . . every word . . . as true as the Bible. He knows he asks in vain.

ANSORGE: Yes, yes! It's all no good.

JAEGER: [*Reads*]

Then think of all our woe and want,
   O ye who hear this ditty!
Our struggle vain for daily bread
   Hard hearts would move to pity.
But pity's what *you've* never known,—
   You'd take both skin and clothing,
You cannibals, whose cruel deeds
   Fill all good men with loathing.

OLD BAUMERT: [*Jumps up, beside himself with excitement*] Both skin and clothing. It's true, it's all true! Here I stand, Robert Baumert, master-weaver of Kaschbach. Who can bring up anything against me? I've been an honest, hard-working man all my life long, an' look at me now! What have I to show for it? Look at me! See what they've made of me. Stretched on the rack day after day. [*He holds out his arms*] Feel that! Skin and bone! "You villains all, you brood of hell!!" [*He sinks down on a chair weeping with rage and despair*]

ANSORGE: [*Flings his basket from him into a corner, rises, his whole body trembling with rage, gasps*] And the time's come now for a change, I say. We'll stand it no longer! We'll stand it no longer! Come what may!

ACT III.

The common room of the principal public house in Peterswaldau. A large room with a raftered roof supported by a central wooden pillar, round which a table runs. In the back wall, a little to the right of the pillar, is the entrance door, through the opening of which the spacious lobby or outer room is seen with barrels and brewing utensils. To the right of this door, in the corner, is the bar—a high wooden counter with receptacles for beermugs, glasses, etc., a cupboard with rows of brandy and liqueur bottles on the wall behind, and between counter and cupboard a narrow space for the barkeeper. In front of the bar stands a table with a gay-colored cover, a pretty lamp hanging above it, and several cane chairs placed around it. Not far off, in the right wall, is a door with the inscription: Bar Parlor. Nearer the front on the same side an old eight-day clock stands ticking. At the back, to the left of the entrance door, is a table with bottles and glasses, and beyond this, in the corner, is the great stove. In the left wall there are three small windows. Below them runs a long bench; and in front of each stands a large oblong wooden table, with the end towards the wall. There are benches with backs along the sides of these tables, and at the end of each facing the window stands a wooden chair. The walls are washed blue and decorated with advertisements, colored prints and oleographs, among the latter a portrait of Frederick William III.

Welzel, the publican, a good-natured giant, upwards of fifty, stands behind the counter, letting beer run from a barrel into a glass.

Mrs. Welzel is ironing by the stove. She is a handsome, tidily dressed woman in her thirty-fifth year.

Anna Welzel, a good-looking girl of seventeen, with a quantity of beautiful, fair, reddish hair, sits, nicely dressed, with her embroidery, at the table with the colored cover. She looks up from her work for a moment and listens, as the sound of a funeral hymn sung by school-children is heard in the distance.

Wiegand, the joiner, in his working clothes, is sitting at the same table, with a glass of Bavarian beer before him. His face shows that he understands what the world requires of a man if he is to attain his ends—namely, craftiness, sharpness, and relentless determination.

A Commercial Traveler is seated at the pillar-table, vigorously masticating a beefsteak. He is of middle height, stout and thriving-looking, inclined to jocosity, lively, and impudent. He is dressed in the fashion of the day, and his portmanteau, pattern-case, umbrella, overcoat, and traveling-rug lie on chairs beside him.

WELZEL: [*Carrying a glass of beer to the* Traveler, *but addressing* Wiegand] The devil's loose in Peterswaldau to-day.

WIEGAND: [*In a sharp, shrill voice*] That's because it's delivery day at Dreissiger's.

MRS. WELZEL: But they don't generally make such an awful row.

WIEGAND: It's maybe because of the two hundred new weavers that he's going to take on.

MRS. WELZEL: [*At her ironing*] Yes, yes, that'll be it. If he wants two hundred, six hundred's sure to have come. There's no lack of *them*.

WIEGAND: You may well say that. There's no fear of their dying out, let them be ever so badly off. They bring more children into the world than we know what to do with. [*The strains of the funeral hymn are suddenly heard more distinctly*] There's a funeral to-day, too. Weaver Nentwich is dead, as no doubt you know.

WELZEL: He's been long enough about it. He's been goin' about like a livin' ghost this many a long day.

WIEGAND: You never saw such a little coffin, Welzel; it was the tiniest, miserablest little thing I ever glued together. And what a corpse! It didn't weigh ninety pounds.

TRAVELER: [*His mouth full*] What I don't understand's this. . . . Take up whatever paper you like and you'll find the most heartrending accounts of the destitution among the weavers. You get the impression that three-quarters of the people in this neighborhood are starving. Then you come and see a funeral like what's going on just now. I met it as I came into the village. Brass band, schoolmaster, school-children, pastor, and such a procession behind them that you would think it was the Emperor of China that was getting buried. If the people have money to spend on this sort of thing, well! . . . [*He takes a drink of beer; puts down the glass; suddenly and jocosely*] What do you say to it, miss? Don't you agree with me?

[Anna *gives an embarrassed laugh, and goes on working busily*]

TRAVELER: Now, I'll take a bet that these are slippers for papa.

WELZEL: You're wrong, then; I wouldn't put such things on my feet.

TRAVELER: You don't say so! Now, I would give half of what I'm worth if these slippers were for me.

MRS. WELZEL: Oh, you don't know nothing about such things.

WIEGAND: [*Has coughed once or twice, moved his chair, and prepared himself to speak*] You were saying, sir, that you wondered to see such a funeral as this. I tell you, and Mrs. Welzel here will bear me out, that it's quite a small funeral.

TRAVELER: But, my good man . . . what a monstrous lot of money it must cost! Where does that all come from?

WIEGAND: If you'll excuse me for saying so, sir, there's a deal of foolishness among the poorer working-people hereabouts. They have a kind of inordinate idea, if I may say so, of the respect an' duty an' honor they're bound to show to such as are taken from their midst. And when it comes to be a case of parents, then there's no bounds whatever to their superstitiousness. The children and the nearest family scrapes together every farthing they can call their own, an' what's still wanting, that they borrow from some rich man. They run themselves into debt over head and ears; they're owing money to the pastor, to the sexton, and to all concerned. Then there's the victuals an' the drink, an' such like. No, sir, I'm far from speaking against dutifulness to parents; but it's too much when it goes the length of the mourners having to bear the weight of it for the rest of their lives.

TRAVELER: But surely the pastor might reason them out of such foolishness.

WIEGAND: Begging your pardon, sir, but I must mention that every little place hereabouts has its church an' its respected pastor to support. These honorable gentlemen has their advantages from big funerals. The larger the attendance is, the larger the offertory is bound to be. Whoever knows the circumstances connected with the working classes here, sir, will assure you that the pastors are strong against quiet funerals.

[*Enter* Hornig, *the rag-dealer, a little bandy-legged old man, with a strap round his chest*]

HORNIG: Good-mornin', ladies and gentlemen! A glass of schnapps, if you please, Mr. Welzel. Has the young mistress anything for me to-day? I've got beautiful ribbons in my cart, Miss Anna, an' tapes, an' garters, an' the very best of pins an' hairpins an' hooks an' eyes. An' all in exchange for a few rags. [*He changes his voice*] An' out of them rags fine white paper's to be made, for your sweetheart to write you a letter on.

ANNA: Thank you, but I've nothing to do with sweethearts.

MRS. WELZEL: [*Putting a bolt into her iron*] No, she's not that kind. She'll not hear of marrying.

TRAVELER: [*Jumps up, affecting delighted surprise, goes forward to* Anna's *table, and holds out his hand to her across it*] That's right, miss. You and I think alike in this matter. Give me your hand on it. We'll both remain single.

ANNA: [*Blushing scarlet, gives him her hand*] But you are married already!

TRAVELER: Not a bit of it. I only pretend to be. You think so because I wear a ring. I only have it on my finger to protect my charms against shameless attacks. I'm not afraid of you, though. [*He puts the ring into his pocket*] But tell me, truly, miss, are you quite determined never, never, never, to marry?

ANNA: [*Shakes her head*] Oh, get along with you!

MRS. WELZEL: You may trust her to remain single unless something very extra good turns up.

TRAVELER: And why should it not? I know of a rich Silesian proprietor who married his mother's lady's maid. And there's Dreissiger, the rich manufacturer, his wife is an innkeeper's daughter, too, and not half so pretty as you, miss, though she rides in her carriage now, with servants in livery. And why not? [*He marches about, stretching himself, and stamping his feet*] Let me have a cup of coffee, please.

[*Enter* Ansorge *and* Old Baumert, *each with a bundle. They seat themselves meekly and silently beside* Hornig, *at the front table to the left*]

WELZEL: How are you, Father Ansorge? Glad to see you once again.

HORNIG: Yes, it's not often as you crawl down from that smoky old nest.

ANSORGE: [*Visibly embarrassed, mumbles*] I've been fetchin' myself a web again.

BAUMERT: He's going to work at a shilling the web.

ANSORGE: I wouldn't have it, but there's no more to be made now by basket-weavin'.

WIEGAND: It's always better than nothing. He does it only to give you employment. I know Dreissiger very well. When I was up there taking out his double windows last week we were talking about it, him and me. It's out of pity that he does it.

ANSORGE: Well, well, well! That may be so.

WELZEL: [*Setting a glass of schnapps on the table before each of the weavers*] Here you are, then. I say, Ansorge, how long is it since you had a shave? The gentleman over there would like to know.

TRAVELER: [*Calls across*] Now, Mr. Welzel, you know I didn't say that. I was only struck by the venerable appearance of the master-weaver. It isn't often one sees such a gigantic figure.

ANSORGE: [*Scratching his head, embarrassed*] Well, well!

TRAVELER: Such specimens of primitive strength are rare nowadays. We're all rubbed smooth by civilization . . . but I can still take pleasure in nature untampered with. . . . These bushy eyebrows! That tangled length of beard!

HORNIG: Let me tell you, sir, that these people haven't the money to pay a barber, and as to a razor for themselves, that's altogether beyond them. What grows, grows. They haven't nothing to throw away on their outsides.

TRAVELER: My good friend, you surely don't imagine that I would. . . . [*Aside to* Welzel] Do you think I might offer the hairy one a glass of beer?

WELZEL: No, no; you mustn't do that. He wouldn't take it. He's got some queer ideas in that head of his.

TRAVELER: All right, then, I won't. With your permission, miss. [*He seats himself at* Anna's *table*] I declare, miss, that I've not been able to take my eyes off your hair since I came in—such glossy softness, such a splendid quantity! [*Ecstatically kisses his finger-tips*] And what a color! . . . like ripe wheat. Come to Berlin with that hair and you'll create no end of a sensation. On my honor, with hair like that you may go to Court. . . . [*Leans back, looking at it*] Glorious, simply glorious!

WIEGAND: They've given her a name because of it.

TRAVELER: And what may that be?

HORNIG: The chestnut filly, isn't it?

WELZEL: Come, now, we've had enough o' this. I'm not goin' to have the girl's head turned altogether. She's had a-plenty of silly notions put into it already. She'll hear of nothing under a count to-day, and to-morrow it'll be a prince.

MRS. WELZEL: You let her alone, father. There's no harm in wantin' to rise in the world. It's as well that people don't all think as you do, or nobody would get on at all. If Dreissiger's grandfather had been of your way of thinkin', they would be poor weavers still. And now they're rollin' in wealth. An look at old Tromtra. He was nothing but a weaver, too, and now he owns twelve estates, an' he's been made a nobleman into the bargain.

WIEGAND: Yes, Welzel, you must look at the thing fairly. Your wife's in the right this time. I can answer for that. I'd never be where I am, with seven workmen under me, if I had thought like you.

HORNIG: Yes, you understand the way to get on; that your worst enemy must allow. Before the weaver has taken to bed, you're gettin' his coffin ready.

WIEGAND: A man must attend to his business if he's to make anything of it.

HORNIG: No fear of you for that. You know before the doctor when death's on the way to knock at a weaver's door.

WIEGAND: [Attempting to laugh, suddenly furious] And you know better than the police where the thieves are among the weavers, that keep back two or three bobbins full every week. It's rags you ask for, but you don't say No, if there's a little yarn among them.

HORNIG: An' your corn grows in the churchyard. The more that are bedded on the sawdust, the better for you. When you see the rows of little children's graves, you pats yourself on the belly, and says you: This has been a good year; the little brats have fallen like cockchafers off the trees. I can allow myself a quart extra in the week again.

WIEGAND: And supposing this is all true, it still doesn't make me a receiver of stolen goods.

HORNIG: No; perhaps the worst you do is to send in an account twice to the rich fustian manufacturers, or to help yourself to a plank or two at Dreissiger's when there's building goin' on and the moon happens not to be shinin'.

WIEGAND: [Turning his back] Talk to any one you like, but not to me. [Then suddenly] Hornig the liar!

HORNIG: Wiegand the coffin-jobber!

WIEGAND: [To the rest of the company] He knows charms for bewitching cattle.

HORNIG: If you don't look out, I'll try one of 'em on you.

[Wiegand turns pale]

MRS. WELZEL: [Had gone out; now returns with the Traveler's coffee; in the act of putting it on the table] Perhaps you would rather have it in the parlor, sir?

TRAVELER: Most certainly not! [With a languishing look at Anna] I could sit here till I die.

[Enter a Young Forester and a Peasant, the latter carrying a whip. They wish the others "Good-Morning," and remain standing at the counter]

PEASANT: Two brandies, if you please.

WELZEL: Good-morning to you, gentlemen. [He pours out their beverage; the two touch glasses, take a mouthful, and then set the glasses down on the counter]

TRAVELER: [To Forester] Come far this morning, sir?

FORESTER: From Steinseiffersdorf—that's a good step.

[Two old Weavers enter, and seat themselves beside Ansorge, Baumert, and Hornig]

TRAVELER: Excuse me asking, but are you in Count Hochheim's service?

FORESTER: No. I'm in Count Keil's.

TRAVELER: Yes, yes, of course—that was what I meant. One gets confused here among all the counts and barons and other gentlemen. It would take a giant's memory to remember them all. Why do you carry an ax, if I may ask?

FORESTER: I've just taken this one from a man who was stealing wood.

OLD BAUMERT: Yes, their lordships are mighty strict with us about a few sticks for the fire.

TRAVELER: You must allow that if every one were to help himself to what he wanted. . . .

OLD BAUMERT: By your leave, sir, but there's a difference made here as elsewhere between the big an' the little thieves. There's some here as deals in stolen wood wholesale, and grows rich on it. But if a poor weaver . . .

FIRST OLD WEAVER: [Interrupts Baumert] We're forbid to take a single branch; but their lordships, they take the very skin off of us—we've assurance money to pay, an' spinning money, an' charges in kind—we must go here an' go there, an' do so an' so much field work, all willy-nilly.

ANSORGE: That's just how it is—what the manufacturer leaves us, their lordships takes from us.

SECOND OLD WEAVER: [Has taken a seat at the next table] I've said it to his lordship himself. By your leave, my lord, says I, it's not possible for me to work on the estate so many days this year. For why—my own bit of ground, my lord, it's been next to carried away by the rains. I've to work both night and day if I'm to live at all. For oh, what a flood that was! . . . There I stood an' wrung my hands, an' watched the good soil come pourin' down the hill, into the very house! And all that dear, fine seed! . . . I could do nothing but roar an' cry until I couldn't see out o' my eyes for a week. And then I had to start an' wheel eighty heavy barrowloads of earth up that hill, till my back was all but broken.

PEASANT: [Roughly] You weavers here make such an awful outcry. As if we hadn't all to put up with what Heaven sends us. An' if you are badly off just now, whose fault is it but your own? What did you do when trade was good? Drank an' squandered all you made. If you had saved a bit then, you'd have it to fall back on now when times is bad, and not need to be goin' stealin' yarn and wood.

FIRST YOUNG WEAVER: [Standing with several comrades in the lobby or outer room, calls in at the door] What's a peasant but a peasant, though he lies in bed till nine?

FIRST OLD WEAVER: The peasant an' the count, it's the same story with 'em both. Says the peasant when a weaver wants a house: I'll give you a little bit of a hole to live in, an' you'll pay me so much rent in money, an' the rest of it you'll make up by helpin' me to get in my hay an' my corn—an' if that doesn't please you, why, then you may go elsewhere. He tries another, and the second he says the same as the first.

BAUMERT: [Angrily] The weaver's like a bone that every dog takes a gnaw at.

PEASANT: [Furious] You starving curs, you're no good for anything. Can you yoke a plough? Can you draw a straight furrow or throw a bundle of sheaves on to a cart? You're fit for nothing but to idle about an' go after the women. A pack of scoundrelly ne'er-do-wells!

[He has paid and now goes out. The Forester follows, laughing. Welzel, the Joiner, and Mrs. Welzel laugh aloud; the Traveler laughs to himself. Then there is a moment's silence]

HORNIG: A peasant like that's as stupid as his own ox. As if I didn't know all about the distress in the villages round here. Sad sights I've seen! Four and five lyin' naked on one sack of straw.

TRAVELER: [In a mildly remonstrative tone] Allow me to remark, my good man, that there's a great difference of opinion as to the amount of distress here in the Eulengebirge. If you can read . . .

HORNIG: I can read straight off, as well as you. An' I know what I've seen with my own eyes. It would be queer if a man that's traveled the country with a pack on his back these forty years an' more didn't know something about it. There was Fullern, now. You saw the children scraping about among the dung-heaps with the peasants' geese. The people up there died naked, on the bare stone floors. In their sore need they ate the stinking weavers' glue. Hunger carried them off by the hundred.

TRAVELER: You must be aware, since you are able to read, that strict investigation has been made by the Government, and that . . .

HORNIG: Yes, yes, we all know what that means. They send a gentleman that knows all about it already better nor if he had seen it, an' he goes about a bit in the village, at the lower end, where the best houses are. He doesn't want to dirty his shining boots. Thinks he to himself: All the rest'll be the same as this. An' so he steps into his carriage, an' drives away home again, an' then writes to Berlin that there's no distress in the place at all. If he had but taken the trouble to go higher up into a village like that, to where the stream comes in, or across the stream on to the narrow side—or, better still, if he'd gone up to the little out-o'-the-way hovels on the hill above, some of 'em that black an' tumble-down as it would be the waste of a good match to set fire to 'em—it's another kind of report he'd have sent to Berlin. They should have come to me, these government gentlemen that wouldn't believe there was no distress here. I would have shown them something. I'd have opened their eyes for 'em in some of these starvation holes.

[The strains of the Weavers' Song are heard, sung outside]

WELZEL: There they are, roaring at that devil's song again.

WIEGAND: They're turning the whole place upside down.

MRS. WELZEL: You'd think there was something in the air.

[Jaeger and Becker arm in arm, at the head of a troop of young weavers, march noisily through the outer room and enter the bar]

JAEGER: Halt! To your places!

[The new arrivals sit down at the various tables, and begin to talk to other weavers already seated there]

HORNIG: [Calls out to Becker] What's up now, Becker, that you've got together a crowd like this?

BECKER: [Significantly] Who knows but something may be going to happen? Eh, Moritz?

HORNIG: Come, come, lads. Don't you be a-gettin' of yourselves into mischief.

BECKER: Blood's flowed already. Would you like to see it? [He pulls up his sleeve and shows bleeding tattoo-marks on the upper part of his arm. Many of the other young weavers do the same]

BECKER: We've been at Father Schmidt's gettin' ourselves vaccinated.

HORNIG: Now the thing's explained. Little wonder there's such an uproar in the place, with a band of young rapscallions like you paradin' round.

JAEGER: [Consequentially, in a loud voice] You may bring two quarts at once, Welzel! I pay. Perhaps you think I haven't got the needful. You're wrong, then. If we wanted we could sit an' drink your best brandy an' swill coffee till to-morrow morning with any bagman in the land.

[Laughter among the young weavers]

TRAVELER: [Affecting comic surprise] Is the young gentleman kind enough to take notice of me?

[Host, hostess, and their daughter, Wiegand, and the Traveler all laugh]

JAEGER: If the cap fits wear it.

TRAVELER: Your affairs seem to be in a thriving condition, young man, if I may be allowed to say so.

JAEGER: I can't complain. I'm a traveler in made-up goods. I go shares with the manufacturers. The nearer starvation the weaver is, the better I fare. His want butters my bread.

BECKER: Well done, Moritz! You gave it to him that time. Here's to you!

[Welzel has brought the corn-brandy. On his way back to the counter he stops, turns round slowly, and stands, an embodiment of phlegmatic strength, facing the weavers]

WELZEL: [Calmly but emphatically] You let the gentleman alone. He's done you no harm.

YOUNG WEAVERS: And we're doing him no harm.

[Mrs. Welzel *has exchanged a few words with the* Traveler. *She takes the cup with the remains of his coffee and carries it into the parlor. The* Traveler *follows her amidst the laughter of the weavers*]

YOUNG WEAVERS: [*Singing*]

"The Dreissigers the hangmen are,
Servants no whit behind them."

WELZEL: Hush-sh! Sing that song anywhere else you like, but not in my house.

FIRST OLD WEAVER: He's quite right. Stop that singin', lads.

BECKER: [*Roars*] But we must march past Dreissiger's boys, and let them hear it once more.

WIEGAND: You'd better take care—you may march once too often.

[*Laughter and cries of Ho, ho!*]

[Wittig *has entered; a gray-haired old smith, bareheaded, with leather apron and wooden shoes, sooty from the smithy. He is standing at the counter waiting for his schnapps*]

YOUNG WEAVER: Wittig, Wittig!

WITTIG: Here he is. What do you want with him?

YOUNG WEAVERS: "It's Wittig!"—"Wittig, Wittig!" —"Come here, Wittig."—"Sit beside us, Wittig."

WITTIG: Do you think I would sit beside a set of rascals like you?

JAEGER: Come and take a glass with us.

WITTIG: Keep your brandy to yourselves. I pay for my own drink. [*Takes his glass and sits down beside* Baumert *and* Ansorge. *Clapping the latter on the stomach*] What's the weavers' food so nice? Sauerkraut and roasted lice!

OLD BAUMERT: [*Excitedly*] But what would you say now if they'd made up their minds as how they would put up with it no longer.

WITTIG: [*With pretended astonishment, staring open-mouthed at the old weaver*] Heinerle! you don't mean to tell me that that's you? [*Laughs immoderately*] O Lord, O Lord! I could laugh myself to death. Old Baumert risin' in rebellion! We'll have the tailors at it next, and then there'll be a rebellion among the baa-lambs, and the rats and the mice. Damn it all, but we'll see some sport. [*He nearly spits with laughter*]

OLD BAUMERT: You needn't go on like that, Wittig. I'm the same man I've always been. I still say 't would be better if things could be put right peaceably.

WITTIG: Peaceably! How could it be done peaceably? Did they do it peaceably in France? Did Robespeer tickle the rich men's palms? No! It was: Away with them, everyone! To the gilyoteen with them! Allongs onfong! You've got your work before you. The geese'll not fly ready roasted into your mouths.

OLD BAUMERT: If I could make even half a livin'—

FIRST OLD WEAVER: The water's up to our chins now, Wittig.

SECOND OLD WEAVER: We're afraid to go home.

It's all the same whether we works or whether we lies abed; it's starvation both ways.

FIRST OLD WEAVER: A man's like to go mad at home.

OLD ANSORGE: It's that length with me now that I don't care how things go.

OLD WEAVERS: [*With increasing excitement*] "We've no peace anywhere."—"We've no spirit left to work."—"Up with us in Steenkunzendorf you can see a weaver sittin' by the stream washin' hisself the whole day long, naked as God made him. It's driven him clean out of his mind."

THIRD OLD WEAVER: [*Moved by the spirit, stands up and begins to "speak with tongues," stretching out his hand threateningly*] Judgment is at hand! Have no dealings with the rich and the great! Judgment is at hand! The Lord God of Sabaoth . . .

[*Some of the weavers laugh. He is pulled down on his seat*]

WELZEL: That's a chap that can't stand a simple glass—he gets wild at once.

THIRD OLD WEAVER: [*Jumps up again*] But they— they believe not in God, not in hell, not in heaven. They mock at religion . . .

FIRST OLD WEAVER: Come, come now, that's enough!

BECKER: You let him do his little bit o' preaching. There's many a one would be the better for taking it to heart.

VOICES: [*In excited confusion*] "Let him alone!"— "Let him speak!"

THIRD OLD WEAVER: [*Raising his voice*] But hell is opened, saith the Lord; its jaws are gaping wide, to swallow up all those that oppress the afflicted and pervert judgment in the cause of the poor. [*Wild excitement*]

THIRD OLD WEAVER: [*Suddenly declaiming, school-boy fashion*]

When one has thought upon it well,
It's still more difficult to tell
Why they the linen-weaver's work despise.

BECKER: But we're fustian-weavers, man.

[*Laughter*]

HORNIG: The linen-weavers is ever so much worse off than you. They're wandering about among the hills like ghosts. You people here have still got the pluck left in you to kick up a row.

WITTIG: Do you suppose the worst's over here? It won't be long till the manufacturers drain away that little bit of strength they still have left in their bodies.

BECKER: You know what he said: It will come to the weavers working for a bit of bread.

[*Uproar*]

SEVERAL OLD AND YOUNG WEAVERS: Who said that?

BECKER: Dreissiger said it.

A YOUNG WEAVER: The damned rascal should be hung up by the heels.

JAEGER: Look here, Wittig. You've always jawed

such a lot about the French revolution, and a good deal too about your own doings. A time may be coming, and that before long, when every one will have a chance to show whether he's a braggart or a true man.

WITTIG: [*Flaring up angrily*] Say another word if you dare! Have you heard the whistle of bullets? Have you done outpost duty in an enemy's country?

JAEGER: You needn't get angry about it. We're comrades. I meant no harm.

WITTIG: None of your comradeship for me, you impudent young fool.

[*Enter Kutsche, the policeman*]

SEVERAL VOICES: Hush—sh! Police!

[*This calling goes on for some time, till at last there is complete silence, amidst which* Kutsche *takes his place at the central pillar-table*]

KUTSCHE: A small brandy, please.

[*Again complete silence*]

WITTIG: I suppose you've come to see if we're all behaving ourselves, Kutsche?

KUTSCHE: [*Paying no attention to* Wittig] Good-morning, Mr. Wiegand.

WIEGAND: [*Still in the corner in front of the counter*] Good-morning t' you, sir.

KUTSCHE: How's trade?

WIEGAND: Thank you, much as usual.

BECKER: The chief constable's sent him to see if we're spoiling our stomach on these big wages we're getting.

[*Laughter*]

JAEGER: I say, Welzel, you will tell him how we've been feasting on roast pork an' sauce an' dumplings and sauerkraut, and now we're sitting at our champagne wine.

[*Laughter*]

WELZEL: The world's upside down with them to-day.

KUTSCHE: An' even if you had the champagne wine and the roast meat, you wouldn't be satisfied. I've to get on without champagne wine as well as you.

BECKER: [*Referring to* Kutsche's *nose*] He waters his beet-root with brandy and gin. An' it thrives upon it, too.

[*Laughter*]

WITTIG: A p'liceman like that has a hard life. Now it's a starving beggar boy he has to lock up, then it's a pretty weaver girl he has to lead astray; then he has to get roarin' drunk an' beat his wife till she goes screamin' to the neighbors for help; and there's the ridin' about on horseback and the lyin' in bed till nine—nay, faith, but it's no easy job!

KUTSCHE: Jaw away; you'll jaw a rope round your neck in time. It's long been known what sort of a fellow you are. The magistrates know all about that dangerous tongue of yours. I know who'll drink wife and child into the poorhouse an' himself into jail before long, who it is that'll go on agitatin' and

agitatin' till he brings down judgment on himself and all concerned.

WITTIG: [*Laughs bitterly*] It's true enough—no one knows what'll be the end of it. You may be right yet. [*Bursts out in fury*] But if it does come to that, I know who I've got to thank for it, who it is that's blabbed to the manufacturers an' all the gentlemen round, an' blackened my character to that extent that they never give me a hand's turn of work to do—an' set the peasants an' the millers against me, so that I'm often a whole week without a horse to shoe or a wheel to put a tire on. I know who's done it. I once pulled the damned brute off his horse, because he was givin' a little stupid boy the most awful flogging for stealin' a few unripe pears. But I tell you this, Kutsche, and you know me—if you get me put into prison, you may make your own will. If I hear as much as a whisper of it, I'll take the first thing as comes handy, whether it's a horseshoe or a hammer, a wheel-spoke or a pail; I'll get hold of you if I've to drag you out of bed from beside your wife, and I'll beat in your brains, as sure as my name's Wittig. [*He has jumped up and is going to rush at* Kutsche]

OLD AND YOUNG WEAVERS: [*Holding him back*] Wittig, Wittig! Don't lose your head!

KUTSCHE: [*Has risen involuntarily, his face pale. He backs toward the door while speaking. The nearer the door the higher his courage rises. He speaks the last words on the threshold, and then instantly disappears*] What are you goin' on at me about? I didn't meddle with you. I came to say something to the weavers. My business is with them an' not with you, and I've done nothing to you. But I've this to say to you weavers: The Superintendent of Police herewith forbids the singing of that song—Dreissiger's song, or whatever it is you call it. And if the yelling of it on the streets isn't stopped at once, he'll provide you with plenty of time and leisure for going on with it in jail. You may sing there, on bread and water, to your hearts' content. [*Goes out*]

WITTIG: [*Roars after him*] He's no right to forbid it—not if we were to roar till the windows shook an' they could hear us at Reichenbach—not if we sang till the manufacturers' houses tumbled about their ears an' all the Superintendents' helmets danced on the top of their heads. It's nobody's business but our own.

[Becker *has in the meantime got up, made a signal for singing, and now leads off, the others joining in*]

The justice to us weavers dealt
    Is bloody, cruel, and hateful;
Our life's one torture, long drawn out;
    For Lynch law we'd be grateful.

[Welzel *attempts to quiet them but they pay no attention to him.* Wiegand *puts his hands to his ears and rushes off. During the singing of the next verse the weavers rise and form into* procession behind Becker *and* Wittig, *who have given pantomimic signs for a general break-up*]

Stretched on the rack, day after day,
  Hearts sick and bodies aching,
Our heavy sighs their witness bear
  To spirit slowly breaking.

[*Most of the weavers sing the following verse out on the street, only a few young fellows, who are paying, being still in the bar. At the conclusion of the verse no one is left in the room except* Welzel *and his wife and daughter,* Hornig, *and* Old Baumert]

You villains, all you brood of hell,
  You fiends in fashion human,
A curse will fall on all like you
  Who prey on man and woman.

WELZEL: [*Phlegmatically collecting the glasses*] Their backs are up to-day, and no mistake.

HORNIG: [*To* Old Baumert, *who is preparing to go*] What in the name of Heaven are they up to, Baumert?

BAUMERT: They're goin' to Dreissiger's to make him add something on to the pay.

WELZEL: And are you joining in these foolish on-goings?

OLD BAUMERT: I've no choice, Welzel. The young men may an' the old men must. [*Goes out rather shamefacedly*]

HORNIG: It'll not surprise me if this ends badly.

WELZEL: To think that even old fellows like him are goin' right off their heads!

HORNIG: We all set our hearts on something!

ACT IV.

Peterswaldau. *Private room of* Dreissiger, *the fustian manufacturer—luxuriously furnished in the chilly taste of the first half of this century. Ceiling, doors, and stove are white, and the wall paper with its small, straight-lined floral pattern, is dull and cold in tone. The furniture is mahogany, richly-carved, and upholstered in red. On the right, between two windows with crimson damask curtains, stands the writing-table, a high bureau with falling flap. Directly opposite to this is the sofa, with the strong-box beside it; in front of the sofa a table, with chairs and easy-chairs arranged about it. Against the back wall is a gun-cupboard. All three walls are decorated with bad pictures in gilt frames. Above the sofa is a mirror with a heavily gilt rococo frame. On the left an ordinary door leads into the hall. An open folding-door at the back shows the drawing-room, over-furnished in the same style of comfortless splendor. Two ladies,* Mrs. Dreissiger *and* Mrs. Kittelhaus, *the Pastor's wife, are seen in the drawing-room, looking at pictures.* Pastor Kittelhaus *is there too, engaged in conversation with* Weinhold, *the tutor, a theological graduate.*

KITTELHAUS: [*A kindly little elderly man, enters the front room, smoking and talking to the tutor, who is also smoking; he looks round and shakes his head in surprise at finding the room empty*] You are young, Mr. Weinhold, which explains everything. At your age we old fellows held—well, I won't say the same opinions—but certainly opinions of the same tendency. And there's something fine about youth—youth with its grand ideals. But unfortunately, Mr. Weinhold, they don't last; they are as fleeting as April sunshine. Wait till you are my age. When a man has said his say from the pulpit for thirty years—fifty-two times every year, not including saints' days—he has inevitably calmed down. Think of me, Mr. Weinhold, when you come that length.

WEINHOLD: [*Nineteen, pale, thin, tall, with lanky fair hair; restless and nervous in his movements*] With all due respect, Mr. Kittelhaus—I can't think —people have such different natures.

KITTELHAUS: My dear Mr. Weinhold, however restless-minded and unsettled a man may be—[*in a tone of reproof*]—and you are a case in point—however violently and wantonly he may attack the existing order of things, he calms down in the end. I grant you, certainly, that among our professional brethren individuals are to be found, who, at a fairly advanced age, still play youthful pranks. One preaches against the drink evil and founds temperance societies, another publishes appeals which undoubtedly read most effectively. But what good do they do? The distress among the weavers, where it does exist, is in no way lessened—but the peace of society is undermined. No, no; one feels inclined in such cases to say: Cobbler, stick to your last; don't take to caring for the belly, you who have the care of souls. Preach the pure Word of God, and leave all else to Him who provides shelter and food for the birds, and clothes the lilies of the field. But I should like to know where our good host, Mr. Dreissiger, has suddenly disappeared to.

[Mrs. Dreissiger, *followed by* Mrs. Kittelhaus, *now comes forward. She is a pretty woman of thirty, of a healthy, florid type. A certain discordance is noticeable between her deportment and way of expressing herself and her rich, elegant toilette*]

MRS. DREISSIGER: That's what I want to know, too, Mr. Kittelhaus. But it's what William always does. No sooner does a thing come into his head than off he goes and leaves me in the lurch. I've said enough about it, but it does no good.

KITTELHAUS: It's always the way with business men, my dear Mrs. Dreissiger.

WEINHOLD: I'm almost certain that something has happened downstairs.

[Dreissiger *enters, hot and excited*]

DREISSIGER: Well, Rosa, is coffee served?

MRS. DREISSIGER: [*Sulkily*] Fancy your needing to run away again!

DREISSIGER: [*Carelessly*] Ah! these are things you don't understand.

KITTELHAUS: Excuse me—has anything happened to annoy you, Mr. Dreissiger?

DREISSIGER: Never a day passes without that, my dear sir. I am accustomed to it. What about that coffee, Rosa?

[Mrs. Dreissiger *goes ill-humoredly and gives one or two violent tugs at the broad embroidered bell-pull*]

DREISSIGER: I wish you had been down stairs just now, Mr. Weinhold. You'd have gained a little experience. Besides . . . But now let us have our game of whist.

KITTELHAUS: By all means, sir. Shake off the dust and burden of the day, Mr. Dreissiger; forget it in our company.

DREISSIGER: [*Has gone to the window, pushed aside a curtain, and is looking out*] Vile rabble!! Come here, Rosa! [*She goes to the window*] Look . . . that tall red-haired fellow there! . . .

KITTELHAUS: That's the man they call Red Becker.

DREISSIGER: Is he the man that insulted you the day before yesterday? You remember what you told me—when John was helping you into the carriage?

MRS. DREISSIGER: [*Pouting, carelessly*] I'm sure I don't know.

DREISSIGER: Come now, what's the use of being cross? I must know. If he's the man, I mean to have him arrested. [*The strains of the Weavers' Song are heard*] Listen to that! Just listen!

KITTELHAUS: [*Highly incensed*] Is there to be no end to this nuisance? I must acknowledge now that it is time for the police to interfere. Permit me. [*He goes forward to the window*] See, see, Mr. Weinhold! These are not only young people. There are numbers of steady-going old weavers among them, men whom I have known for years and looked upon as most deserving and God-fearing. There they are, taking part in this intolerable uproar, trampling God's law under foot. Do you mean to tell me that you still defend these people?

WEINHOLD: Certainly not, Mr. Kittelhaus. That is, sir . . . *cum grano salis*. For after all, they are hungry and they are ignorant. They are giving expression to their dissatisfaction in the only way they understand. I don't expect that such people . . .

MRS. KITTELHAUS: [*Short, thin, faded, more like an old maid than a married woman*] Mr. Weinhold, Mr. Weinhold, how can you?

DREISSIGER: Mr. Weinhold, I am sorry to be obliged to . . . I didn't bring you into my house to give me lectures on philanthropy, and I must request that you will confine yourself to the education of my boys, and leave my other affairs entirely to me— entirely! Do you understand?

WEINHOLD: [*Stands for a moment rigid and deathly pale, then bows, with a strained smile. In a low voice*] Certainly, of course I understand. I have seen this coming. It is my wish too. [*Goes out*]

DREISSIGER: [*Rudely*] As soon as possible then, please. We require the room.

MRS. DREISSIGER: William, William!

DREISSIGER: Have you lost your senses, Rosa, that you're taking the part of a man who defends a low, blackguardly libel like that song?

MRS. DREISSIGER: But, William, he didn't defend it.

DREISSIGER: Mr. Kittelhaus, did he defend it or did he not?

KITTELHAUS: His youth must be his excuse, Mr. Dreissiger.

MRS. KITTELHAUS: I can't understand it. The young man comes of such a good, respectable family. His father held a public appointment for forty years, without a breath on his reputation. His mother was overjoyed at his getting this good situation here. And now . . . he himself shows so little appreciation of it.

PFEIFER: [*Suddenly opens the door leading from the hall and shouts in*] Mr. Dreissiger, Mr. Dreissiger! they've got him! Will you come, please? They've caught one of them.

DREISSIGER: [*Hastily*] Has some one gone for the police?

PFEIFER: The Superintendent's on his way upstairs.

DREISSIGER: [*At the door*] Glad to see you, sir. We want you here.

[Kittelhaus *makes signs to the ladies that it will be better for them to retire. He, his wife, and* Mrs. Dreissiger *disappear into the drawing-room*]

DREISSIGER: [*Exasperated, to the* Police Superintendent, *who has now entered*] I have at last had one of the ringleaders seized by my dyers. I could stand it no longer—their insolence was beyond all bounds —quite unbearable. I have visitors in my house, and these blackguards dare to . . . They insult my wife whenever she shows herself; my boys' lives are not safe. My visitors run the risk of being jostled and cuffed. Is it possible that in a well-ordered community incessant public insult offered to unoffending people like myself and my family should pass unpunished? If so . . . then . . . then I must confess that I have other ideas of law and order.

SUPERINTENDENT: [*A man of fifty, middle height, corpulent, full-blooded. He wears cavalry uniform with a long sword and spurs*] No, no, Mr. Dreissiger . . . certainly not! I am entirely at your disposal. Make your mind easy on the subject. Dispose of me as you will. What you have done is quite right. I am delighted that you have had one of the ringleaders arrested. I am very glad indeed that a settling day has come. There are a few disturbers of the peace here whom I have long had my eye on.

DREISSIGER: Yes, one or two raw lads, lazy vagabonds, that shirk every kind of work, and lead a life of low dissipation, hanging about the public-houses until they've sent their last halfpenny down their throats. But I'm determined to put a stop to the trade of these professional blackguards once and for all. It's in the public interest to do so, not only my private interest.

SUPERINTENDENT: Of course it is! Most undoubtedly, Mr. Dreissiger! No one can possibly blame you. And everything that lies in my power . . .

DREISSIGER: The cat-o'-nine tails is what should be taken to the beggarly pack.

SUPERINTENDENT: You're right, quite right. We must make an example.

[Kutsche, *the policeman, enters and salutes. The door is open, and the sound of heavy steps stumbling up the stair is heard*]

KUTSCHE: I have to inform you, sir, that we have arrested a man.

DREISSIGER: [*To* Superintendent] Do you wish to see the fellow?

SUPERINTENDENT: Certainly, most certainly. We must begin by having a look at him at close quarters. Oblige me, Mr. Dreissiger, by not speaking to him at present. I'll see to it that you get complete satisfaction, or my name's not Heide.

DREISSIGER: That's not enough for me, though. He goes before the magistrates. My mind's made up.

[Jaeger *is led in by five dyers, who have come straight from their work—faces, hands, and clothes stained with dye. The prisoner, his cap set jauntily on the side of his head, presents an appearance of impudent gayety; he is excited by the brandy he has just drunk*]

JAEGER: Hounds that you are!—Call yourselves workingmen!—Pretend to be comrades! Before I would do such a thing as lay my hands on a mate, I'd see my hand rot off my arm!

[*At a sign from the* Superintendent, Kutsche *orders the dyers to let go their victim. Jaeger straightens himself up, quite free and easy. Both doors are guarded*]

SUPERINTENDENT: [*Shouts to* Jaeger] Off with your cap, sir. [Jaeger *takes it off, but very slowly, still with an impudent grin on his face*] What's your name!

JAEGER: What's yours? I'm not your swineherd.
[*Great excitement is produced among the audience by this reply*]

DREISSIGER: This is too much of a good thing.

SUPERINTENDENT: [*Changes color, is on the point of breaking out furiously, but controls his rage*] We'll see about this afterwards.—Once more, what's your name? [*Receiving no answer, furiously*] If you don't answer at once, fellow, I'll have you flogged on the spot.

JAEGER: [*Perfectly cheerful, not showing by so much as the twitch of an eyelid that he has heard the* Superintendent's *angry words, calls over the heads of those around him to a pretty servant girl,* who *has brought in the coffee and is standing open-mouthed with astonishment at the unexpected sight*] Hullo, Emmy, do you belong to this company now? The sooner you find your way out of it, then, the better. A wind may begin to blow here, an' blow everything away overnight.

[*The girl stares at Jaeger,* and *as soon as she comprehends that it is to her he is speaking, blushes with shame, covers her eyes with her hands, and rushes out, leaving the coffee things in confusion on the table. Renewed excitement among those present*]

SUPERINTENDENT: [*Half beside himself, to* Dreissiger] Never in all my long service . . . such a case of shameless effrontery . . .

[Jaeger *spits on the floor*]

DREISSIGER: I'll thank you to remember that this is not a stable.

SUPERINTENDENT: My patience is at an end now. For the last time: What's your name?

[Kittelhaus, *who has been peering out at the partly opened drawing-room door, listening to what has been going on, can no longer refrain from coming forward to interfere. He is trembling with excitement*]

KITTELHAUS: His name is Jaeger, sir. Moritz . . . is it not? Moritz Jaeger. [*To* Jaeger] And, Jaeger, you know me.

JAEGER: [*Seriously*] You are Pastor Kittelhaus.

KITTELHAUS: Yes, I am your pastor, Jaeger! It was I who received you, a babe in swaddling clothes, into the Church of Christ. From my hands you took for the first time the body of the Lord. Do you remember that, and how I toiled and strove to bring God's Word home to your heart? Is this your gratitude?

JAEGER: [*Like a scolded schoolboy, in a surly voice*] I paid my half-crown like the rest.

KITTELHAUS: Money, money . . . Do you imagine that the miserable little bit of money . . . Such utter nonsense! I'd much rather you kept your money. Be a good man, be a Christian! Think of what you promised. Keep God's law. Money, money! . . .

JAEGER: I'm a Quaker now, sir. I don't believe in anything.

KITTELHAUS: Quaker! What are you talking about? Try to behave yourself, and don't use words you don't understand. Quaker, indeed! They are good Christian people, and not heathens like you.

SUPERINTENDENT: Mr. Kittelhaus, I must ask you . . . [*He comes between the* Pastor *and* Jaeger] Kutsche! tie his hands!

[*Wild yelling outside: "Jaeger, Jaeger! come out!"*]

DREISSIGER: [*Like the others, slightly startled, goes instinctively to the window*] What's the meaning of this next?

SUPERINTENDENT: Oh, I understand well enough. It means that they want to have the blackguard out among them again. But we're not going to oblige them. Kutsche, you have your orders. He goes to the lock-up.

KUTSCHE: [*With the rope in his hand, hesitating*] By your leave, sir, but it'll not be an easy job. There's a confounded big crowd out there—a pack of raging devils. They've got Becker with them, and the smith . . .

KITTELHAUS: Allow me one more word!—So as not to rouse still worse feeling, would it not be better if we tried to arrange things peaceably? Perhaps Jaeger will give his word to go with us quietly, or . . .

SUPERINTENDENT: Quite impossible! Think of my responsibility. I couldn't allow such a thing. Come, Kutsche! lose no more time.

JAEGER: [*Putting his hands together, and holding them out*] Tight, tight, as tight as ever you can! It's not for long.

[Kutsche, *assisted by the workmen, ties his hands*]

SUPERINTENDENT: Now, off with you, march [*To* Dreissiger] If you feel anxious, let six of the weavers go with him. They can walk on each side of him, I'll ride in front, and Kutsche will bring up the rear. Whoever blocks the way will be cut down.

[*Cries from below: "Cock-a-doodle-doo-oo-oo! ow, wow, wow!"*]

SUPERINTENDENT: [*With a threatening gesture in the direction of the window*] You rascals, I'll cock-a-doodle-doo and bow-wow you! Forward! March! [*He marches out first, with drawn sword; the others, with* Jaeger, *follow*]

JAEGER: [*Shouts as he goes*] An' Mrs. Dreissiger there may play the lady as proud as she likes, but for all tha, she's no better than us. Many a hundred times she's served my father with a half penny-worth of schnapps. Left wheel—march! [*Exit laughing*]

DREISSIGER: [*After a pause, with apparent calmness*] Well, Mr. Kittelhaus, shall we have our game now? I think there will be no further interruption. [*He lights a cigar, giving short laughs as he does so; when it is lighted, bursts into a regular fit of laughing*] I'm beginning now to think the whole thing very funny. That fellow! [*Still laughing nervously*] It really is too comical: first came the dispute at dinner with Weinhold—five minutes after that he takes leave—off to the other end of the world; then this affair crops up—and now we'll proceed with our whist.

KITTELHAUS: Yes, but . . . [*Roaring is heard outside*] Yes, but . . . that's a terrible uproar they're making outside.

DREISSIGER: All we have to do is to go into the other room; it won't disturb us in the least there.

KITTELHAUS: [*Shaking his head*] I wish I knew what has come over these people. In so far I must agree with Mr. Weinhold, or at least till quite lately I was of his opinion, that the weavers were a patient, humble, easily-led class. Was it not your idea of them, too, Mr. Dreissiger?

DREISSIGER: Most certainly that is what they used to be—patient, easily managed, peaceable people. They were that as long as these so-called humanitarians let them alone. But for ever so long now they've had the awful misery of their condition held up to them. Think of all the societies and associations for the alleviation of the distress among the weavers. At last the weaver believes in it himself, and his head's turned. Some of them had better come and turn it back again, for now he's fairly set a-going there's no end to his complaining. This doesn't please him, and that doesn't please him. He must have everything of the best.

[*A loud roar of "Hurrah!" is heard from the crowd*]

KITTELHAUS: So that with all their humanitarianism they have only succeeded in almost literally turning lambs into wolves.

DREISSIGER: I won't say that, sir. When you take time to think of the matter coolly, it's possible that some good may come of it yet. Such occurrences as this will not pass unnoticed by those in authority, and may lead them to see that things can't be allowed to go on as they are doing—that means must be taken to prevent the utter ruin of our home industries.

KITTELHAUS: Possibly. But what is the cause, then, of this terrible falling off of trade?

DREISSIGER: Our best markets have been closed to us by the heavy import duties foreign countries have laid on our goods. At home the competition is terrible, for we have no protection, none whatever.

PFEIFER: [*Staggers in, pale and breathless*] Mr. Dreissiger, Mr. Dreissiger!

DREISSIGER: [*In the act of walking into the drawing-room, turns round, annoyed*] Well, Pfeifer, what now?

PFEIFER: Oh, sir! Oh, sir! . . . It's worse than ever!

DREISSIGER: What are they up to next?

KITTELHAUS: You're really alarming us—what is it?

PFEIFER: [*Still confused*] I never saw the like. Good Lord!—The Superintendent himself . . . they'll catch it for this yet.

DREISSIGER: What's the matter with you, in the devil's name? Is any one's neck broken?

PFEIFER: [*Almost crying with fear, screams*] They've set Moritz Jaeger free—they've thrashed the Superintendent and driven him away—they've thrashed the policeman and sent him off too—without his helmet . . . his sword broken . . . Oh dear, oh dear!

DREISSIGER: I think you've gone crazy, Pfeifer.

KITTELHAUS: This is actual riot.

PFEIFER: [*Sitting on a chair, his whole body trembling*] It's turning serious, Mr. Dreissiger! Mr. Dreissiger, it's serious now!

DREISSIGER: Well, if that's all the police . . .

PFEIFER: Mr. Dreissiger, it's serious now!

DREISSIGER: Damn it all, Pfeifer, will you hold your tongue?

MRS. DREISSIGER: [*Coming out of the drawing-room with* Mrs. Kittelhaus] This is really too bad, William. Our whole evening's being spoiled. Here's Mrs. Kittelhaus saying that she'd better go home.

KITTELHAUS: You mustn't take it amiss, dear Mrs. Dreissiger, but perhaps, under the circumstances, it *would* be better . . .

MRS. DREISSIGER: But, William, why in the world don't you go out and put a stop to it?

DREISSIGER: Go you and try if you can do it. Try! Go and speak to them! [*Standing helplessly in front of the* Pastor] Am I such a tyrant? Am I a cruel master?

[*Enter* John *the coachman*]

JOHN: If you please, m'm, I've put to the horses. Mr. Weinhold's put Georgie and Charlie into the carriage. If it comes to the worst, we're ready to be off.

MRS. DREISSIGER: If what comes to the worst?

JOHN: I'm sure I don't know, m'm. But the crowd's gettin' bigger and bigger, an' they've sent the Superintendent an' the p'liceman to the right-about.

PFEIFER: It's serious now, Mr. Dreissiger! It's serious!

MRS. DREISSIGER: [*With increasing alarm*] What's going to happen?—What do the people want?—They're never going to attack us, John?

JOHN: There's some rascally hounds among 'em, ma'am.

PFEIFER: It's serious now! serious!

DREISSIGER: Hold your tongue, fool!—Are the doors barred?

KITTELHAUS: I ask you as a favor, Mr. Dreissiger . . . as a favor . . . I am determined to . . . I ask you as a favor . . . [*To* John] What demands are the people making?

JOHN: [*Awkwardly*] It's higher wages they're after, the blackguards.

KITTELHAUS: Good, good!—I shall go out and do my duty. I shall speak seriously to these people.

JOHN: Oh, sir, please, sir, don't do any such thing. Words is quite useless.

KITTELHAUS: One little favor, Mr. Dreissiger. May I ask you to post men behind the door, and to have it closed at once after me?

MRS. KITTELHAUS: Oh Joseph, Joseph! you're not really going out?

KITTELHAUS: I am. Indeed I am. I know what I'm doing. Don't be afraid. God will protect me.

[Mrs. Kittelhaus *presses his hand, draws back, and wipes tears from her eyes*]

KITTELHAUS: [*While the murmur of a great, excited crowd is heard uninterruptedly outside*] I'll go . . . I'll go out as if I were simply on my way home. I shall see if my sacred office . . . if the

people have not sufficient respect for me left to . . . I shall try . . . [*He takes his hat and stick*] Forward, then, in God's name!

[*Goes out accompanied by* Dreissiger, Pfeifer, *and* John]

MRS. KITTELHAUS: Oh, dear Mrs. Dreissiger! [*She bursts into tears and embraces her*] I do trust nothing will happen to him.

MRS. DREISSIGER: [*Absently*] I don't know how it is, Mrs. Kittelhaus, but I . . . I can't tell you how I feel. I didn't think such a thing was possible. It's . . . it's as if it was a sin to be rich. If I had been told about all this beforehand, Mrs. Kittelhaus, I don't know but what I would rather have been left in my own humble position.

MRS. KITTELHAUS: There are troubles and disappointments in every condition of life, Mrs. Dreissiger.

MRS. DREISSIGER: True, true, I can well believe that. And suppose we have more than other people . . . goodness me! we didn't steal it. It's been honestly got, every penny of it. It's not possible that the people can be going to attack us! If trade's bad, that's not William's fault, is it?

[*Loud, confused yelling is heard outside. While the two women stand gazing at each other, pale and startled,* Dreissiger *rushes in*]

DREISSIGER: Quick, Rosa—put on something, and get into the carriage. I'll be after you this moment. [*He rushes to the strong box, and takes out papers and various articles of value*]

[*Enter* John]

JOHN: We're ready to start. But come quickly, before they get round to the back door.

MRS. DREISSIGER: [*In a transport of fear, throwing her arms around* John's *neck*] John, John, dear, good John! Save us, John. Save my boys! Oh, what is to become of us?

DREISSIGER: Rosa, try to keep your head. Let John go.

JOHN: Yes, yes, ma'am! Don't you be frightened. Our good horses'll soon leave them all behind; an' whoever doesn't get out of the way'll be driven over.

MRS. KITTELHAUS: [*In helpless anxiety*] But my husband . . . my husband? But, Mr. Dreissiger, my husband?

DREISSIGER: He's in safety now, Mrs. Kittelhaus. Don't alarm yourself; he's all right.

MRS. KITTELHAUS: Something dreadful has happened to him. I know it. You needn't try to keep it from me.

DREISSIGER: You mustn't take it to heart—they'll be sorry for it yet. I know exactly whose fault it was. Such a detestable, shameful outrage will not go unpunished. A community laying hands on its own pastor and maltreating him—abominable! Mad dogs they are—raging brutes—and they'll be treated as such. [*To his wife who still stands petrified*] Go, for my sake, Rosa, go quickly! [*The clatter of window panes being smashed on the ground floor is heard*] They've gone quite mad. There's nothing for it but to get away as fast as we can.

[*Cries of "Pfeifer, come out!"—"We want Pfeifer!"—"Pfeifer, come out!" are heard*]

MRS. DREISSIGER: Pfeifer, Pfeifer, they want Pfeifer!

PFEIFER: [*Dashes in*] Mr. Dreissiger, there are people at the back gate already, and the house door won't hold much longer. The smith's battering it in with a stable pail.

[*The cry sounds louder and clearer: "Pfeifer! Pfeifer! Pfeifer! come out!" Mrs. Dreissiger rushes off as if pursued. Mrs. Kittelhaus follows. Pfeifer listens, and changes color as he hears what the cry is. A perfect panic of fear seizes him; he weeps, entreats, whimpers, writhes, all at the same moment. He overwhelms Dreissiger with childish caresses, strokes his cheeks and arms, kisses his hands, and at last, like a drowning man, throws his arms round him and prevents him moving*]

PFEIFER: Dear, good, kind Mr. Dreissiger, don't leave me behind. I've always served you faithfully. I've always treated the people well. I couldn't give them more wages than the fixed rate. Don't leave me here—they'll do for me. If they find me, they'll kill me. O God! O God! My wife, my children!

DREISSIGER: [*Making his way out, vainly endeavoring to free himself from Pfeifer's clutch*] Can't you let me go, fellow? It'll be all right; it'll be all right.

[*For a few seconds the room is empty. Windows are broken in the drawing-room. A loud crash resounds through the house, followed by shouts of "Hurrah!" For an instant there is silence. Then gentle, cautious steps are heard on the stair, then timid, hushed ejaculations: "To the left!"—"Up with you!"—"Hush!"—"Slow, slow!"—"Don't shove like that!"—"It's a wedding we're goin' to!"—"Stop that crowding"—"You go first!"—"No, you go!"*]

[*Young weavers and weaver girls appear at the door leading from the hall, not daring to enter, but each trying to shove the other in. In the course of a few moments their timidity is overcome, and the poor, thin, ragged or patched figures, many of them sickly-looking, disperse themselves through Dreissiger's room and the drawing-room, first gazing timidly and curiously at everything, then beginning to touch things. Girls sit down on the sofas, whole groups admire themselves in the mirrors, men stand up on chairs, examine the pictures and take them down. There is a steady influx of miserable-looking creatures from the hall*]

FIRST OLD WEAVER: [*Entering*] No, no, this is carryin' it too far. They've started smashing things downstairs. There's no sense nor reason in that. There'll be a bad end to it. No man in his wits would do that. I'll keep clear of such ongoings.

[*Jaeger, Becker, Wittig carrying a wooden pail, Baumert, and a number of other old and young weavers, rush in as if in pursuit of something, shouting hoarsely*]

JAEGER: Where has he gone?

BECKER: Where's the cruel brute?

BAUMERT: If we can eat grass, he may eat sawdust.

WITTIG: We'll hang him whenever we catch him.

FIRST YOUNG WEAVER: We'll take him by the legs and fling him out at the window, onto the stones. He'll never get up again.

SECOND YOUNG WEAVER: [*Enters*] He's off!

ALL: Who?

SECOND YOUNG WEAVER: Dreissiger.

BECKER: Pfeifer too?

VOICES: Let's get hold of Pfeifer. Look for Pfeifer!

BAUMERT: Yes, yes! Pfeifer! Tell him there's a weaver here for him to starve.

[*Laughter*]

JAEGER: If we can't lay hands on that brute Dreissiger himself . . . we'll at any rate make a poor man of him.

BAUMERT: As poor as a church mouse . . . we'll see to that!

[*All, bent on the work of destruction, rush towards the drawing-room door*]

BECKER: [*Who is leading, turns round and stops the others*] Halt! Listen to me! This is nothing but a beginning. When we're done here, we'll go straight to Bielau, to Dittrich's, where the steam power-looms are. The whole mischief's done by these factories.

OLD ANSORGE: [*Enters from hall. Takes a few steps, then stops and looks round, bewildered; shakes his head, taps his forehead*] Who am I? Weaver Anton Ansorge. Has he gone mad, Old Ansorge? My head's goin' round like a humming-top, sure enough. What's he doing here? He'll do whatever he's a mind to. Where is Ansorge? [*He taps his forehead repeatedly*] Something's wrong! I'm not answerable! I'm off my head! Off with you, off with you, rioters that you are! Heads off, legs off, hands off! If you take my house, I take your house. Forward, forward!

[*Goes yelling into the drawing-room, followed by a yelling, laughing mob*]

ACT V.

Langenbielau. Old Weaver Hilse's work-room. On the left a small window, in front of which stands the loom. On the right a bed, with a table pushed close to it. Stove, with stove-bench, in the right-hand corner. Family worship is going on. Hilse, his old, blind, and almost deaf wife, his son Gottlieb, and Luise, Gottlieb's wife, are sitting at the table, on the bed and wooden stools. A winding-wheel and bob-

bins on the floor between table and loom. Old spin-
ning, weaving, and winding implements are disposed
of on the smoky rafters; hanks of yarn are hang-
ing down. There is much useless lumber in the low
narrow room. The door, which is in the back wall,
and leads into the big outer passage, or entry-room
of the house, stands open. Through another open
door on the opposite side of the passage, a second,
in most respects similar weaver's room is seen. The
large passage, or entry-room of the house, is paved
with stone, has damaged plaster, and a tumble-down
wooden staircase leading to the attics; a washing-
tub on a stool is partly visible; dirty linen of the most
miserable description and poor household utensils
lie about untidily. The light falls from the left into
all three apartments.

Old Hilse *is a bearded man of strong build, but*
bent and wasted with age, toil, sickness, and hard-
ship. He is an old soldier, and has lost an arm. His
nose is sharp, his complexion ashen-gray, and he
shakes; he is nothing but skin and bone, and has the
deep-set, sore weaver's eyes.

OLD HILSE: [*Stands up, as do his son and daughter-*
in-law; prays] O Lord, we know not how to be
thankful enough to Thee, for that Thou hast spared
us this night again in thy goodness . . . an' hast
had pity on us . . . an' hast suffered us to take no
harm. Thou art the All-Merciful, an' we are poor,
sinful children of men—that bad that we are not
worthy to be trampled under thy feet. Yet Thou art
our loving Father, an' Thou will look upon us an'
accept us for the sake of thy dear Son, our Lord and
Saviour Jesus Christ. "Jesus' blood and righteousness,
Our covering is and glorious dress." An' if we're
sometimes too sore cast down under thy chastening
—when the fire of thy purification burns too raging
hot—oh, lay it not to our charge; forgive us our sin.
Give us patience, heavenly Father, that after all
these sufferin's we may be made partakers of thy
eternal blessedness. Amen.

MOTHER HILSE: [*Who has been bending forward,*
trying hard to hear] What a beautiful prayer you
do say, father!

[Luise *goes off to the wash-tub*, Gottlieb *to the*
room on the other side of the passage]

OLD HILSE: Where's the little lass?

LUISE: She's gone to Peterswaldau, to Dreissiger's.
She finished all she had to wind last night.

OLD HILSE: [*Speaking very loud*] You'd like the
wheel now, mother, eh?

MOTHER HILSE: Yes, father, I'm quite ready.

OLD HILSE: [*Setting it down before her*] I wish I
could do the work for you.

MOTHER HILSE: An' what would be the good of
that, father? There would I be, sittin' not knowin'
what to do.

OLD HILSE: I'll give your fingers a wipe, then,
so that they'll not grease the yarn. [*He wipes her*
hands with a rag]

LUISE: [*At her tub*] If there's grease on her hands,
it's not from what she's eaten.

OLD HILSE: If we've no butter, we can eat dry
bread—when we've no bread, we can eat potatoes
—when there's no potatoes left, we can eat bran.

LUISE: [*Saucily*] An' when that's all eaten, we'll
do as the Wenglers did—we'll find out where the
skinner's buried some stinking old horse, an' we'll
dig it up an' live for a week or two on rotten carrion
—how nice that'll be!

GOTTLIEB: [*From the other room*] There you are,
letting that tongue of yours run away with you again.

OLD HILSE: You should think twice, lass, before
you talk that godless way. [*He goes to his loom,*
calls] Can you give me a hand, Gottlieb?—there's a
few threads to pull through.

LUISE: [*From her tub*] Gottlieb, you're wanted to
help father.

[Gottlieb *comes in, and he and his father set*
themselves to the troublesome task of "draw-
ing and slaying," that is, pulling the strands of
the warp through the "heddles" and "reed" of
the loom. They have hardly begun to do this
when Hornig *appears in the outer room*]

HORNIG: [*At the door*] Good luck to your work!

HILSE AND HIS SON: Thank you, Hornig.

GOTTLIEB: I say, Hornig, when do you take your
sleep? You're on your rounds all day, and on watch
all night.

HORNIG: Sleep's gone from me nowadays.

LUISE: Glad to see you, Hornig!

OLD HILSE: And what's the news?

HORNIG: It's queer news this mornin'. The weavers
at Peterswaldau have taken the law into their own
hands, an' chased Dreissiger an' his whole family out
of the place.

LUISE: [*Perceptibly agitated*] Hornig's at his lies
again.

HORNIG: No, missus, not this time, not to-day.—
I've some beautiful pinafores in my cart.—No, it's
God's truth I'm telling you. They've sent him to the
right-about. He came down to Reichenbach last
night, but, Lord love you! they daren't take him in
there, for fear of the weavers—off he had to go
again, all the way to Schweidnitz.

OLD HILSE: [*Has been carefully lifting threads of*
the web and approaching them to the holes, through
which, from the other side, Gottlieb *pushes a wire*
hook, with which he catches them and draws them
through] It's about time you were stopping now,
Hornig!

HORNIG: It's as sure as I'm a livin' man. Every
child in the place'll soon tell you the same story.

OLD HILSE: Either your wits are a-wool-gatherin'
or mine are.

HORNIG: Not mine. What I'm telling you's as true
as the Bible. I wouldn't believe it myself if I hadn't
stood there an' seen it with my own eyes—as I see
you now, Gottlieb. They've wrecked his house from
the cellar to the roof. The good china came flyin'

out at the garret windows, rattlin' down the roof. God only knows how many pieces of fustian are lying soakin' in the river! The water can't get away for them—it's running over the banks, the color of washin'-blue with all the indigo they've poured out at the window—it was flyin' like clouds of sky-blue dust. Oh, it's a terrible destruction they've worked! And it's not only the house—it's the dyeworks, too —an' the stores! They've broken the stair rails, they've torn up the fine flooring—smashed the lookin'-glasses—cut an' hacked an' torn an' smashed the sofas an' the chairs.—It's awful—it's worse than war.

OLD HILSE: An' you would have me believe that my fellow weavers did all that? [*He shakes his head incredulously. Other tenants of the house have collected at the door and are listening eagerly*]

HORNIG: Who else, I'd like to know? I could put names to every one of 'em. It was me took the sheriff through the house, an' I spoke to a whole lot of 'em, an' they answered me back quite friendly like. They did their business with little noise, but my word! they did it well. The sheriff spoke to them, and they answered him mannerly, as they always do. But there wasn't no stoppin' of them. They hacked on at the beautiful furniture as if they were workin' for wages.

OLD HILSE: *You* took the sheriff through the house?

HORNIG: An' what would I be frightened of? Every one knows me. I'm always turning up, like a bad penny. But no one has anything agin' me. They're all glad to see me. Yes, I went the rounds with him, as sure as my name's Hornig. An' you may believe me or not as you like, but my heart's sore yet from the sight—an' I could see by the sheriff's face that he felt queer enough, too. Not a living word did we hear—they were doin' their work and holdin' their tongues. It was a solemn an' a woeful sight to see the poor starving creatures for once in a way takin' their revenge.

LUISE: [*With irrepressible excitement, trembling, wiping her eyes with her apron*] An' right they are! It's only what should be!

VOICES AMONG THE CROWD AT THE DOOR: "There's some of the same sort here."—"There's one no farther away than across the river."—"He's got four horses in his stable an' six carriages, an' he starves his weavers to keep them."

OLD HILSE: [*Still incredulous*] What was it set them off?

HORNIG: Who knows? Who knows? One says this, another says that.

OLD HILSE: What do they say?

HORNIG: The story as most of them tells is that it began with Dreissiger sayin' that if the weavers were hungry they might eat grass.

[*Excitement at the door, as one person repeats this to the other, with signs of indignation*]

OLD HILSE: Well, now, Hornig—if you was to say

to me: Father Hilse, says you, you'll die to-morrow, I would answer back: That may be—an' why not? You might even go to the length of saying: You'll have a visit to-morrow from the King of Prussia. But to tell me that weavers, men like me an' my son, have done such things as that—never! I'll never in this world believe it.

MIELCHEN: [*A pretty girl of seven, with long, loose flaxen hair, carrying a basket on her arm, comes running in, holding out a silver spoon to her mother*] Mammy, mammy! look what I've got! An' you're to buy me a new frock with it.

LUISE: What d'you come tearing in like that for, girl? [*With increased excitement and curiosity*] An' what's that you've got hold of now? You've been runnin' yourself out o' breath, an' there—if the bobbins aren't in her basket yet? What's all this about?

OLD HILSE: Mielchen, where did that spoon come from?

LUISE: She found it, maybe.

HORNIG: It's worth its seven or eight shillin's at least.

OLD HILSE: [*In distressed excitement*] Off with you, lass—out of the house this moment—unless you want a lickin'! Take that spoon back where you got it from. Out you go! Do you want to make thieves of us all, eh? I'll soon drive that out of you. [*He looks round for something to beat her with*]

MIELCHEN: [*Clinging to her mother's skirts, crying*] No, grandfather, no! don't lick me! We—we did find them. All the other bob—bobbin . . . girls has . . . has them too.

LUISE: [*Half frightened, half excited*] I was right, you see. She found it. Where did you find it, Mielchen?

MIELCHEN: [*Sobbing*] At—at—Peterswaldau. We —we found them in front of—in front of Drei—Dreissiger's house.

OLD HILSE: This is worse an' worse! Get off with you this moment, unless you would like me to help you.

MOTHER HILSE: What's all the to-do about?

HORNIG: I'll tell you what, Father Hilse. The best way'll be for Gottlieb to put on his coat an' take the spoon to the police office.

OLD HILSE: Gottlieb, put on your coat.

GOTTLIEB: [*Pulling it on, eagerly*] Yes, an' I'll go right in to the office an' say they're not to blame us for it, for what can a child like that understand about it? an' I brought the spoon back at once. Stop your crying now, Mielchen!

[*The crying child is taken into the opposite room by her mother, who shuts her in and comes back*]

HORNIG: I believe it's worth as much as nine shillin's.

GOTTLIEB: Give us a cloth to wrap it in, Luise, so that it'll take no harm. To think of the thing bein' worth all that money. [*Tears come into his eyes while he is wrapping up the spoon*]

LUISE: If it was only ours, we could live on it for many a day.

OLD HILSE: Hurry up, now! Look sharp! As quick as ever you can. A fine state o' matters, this! Get that devil's spoon out o' the house.

[Gottlieb *goes off with the spoon*]

HORNIG: I must be off now, too. [*He goes, is seen talking to the people in the entry-room before he leaves the house*]

SURGEON SCHMIDT: [*A jerky little ball of a man, with a red, knowing face, comes into the entry-room*] Good-morning, all! These are fine goings on! Take care! Take care! [*Threatening with his finger*] You're a sly lot—that's what you are. [*At Hilse's door without coming in*] Morning, Father Hilse. [*To a woman in the outer room*] And how are the pains, mother? Better, eh? Well, well. And how's all with you, Father Hilse? [*Enters*] Why the deuce! what's the matter with mother?

LUISE: It's the eye veins, sir—they've dried up, so as she can't see at all now.

SURGEON SCHMIDT: That's from the dust and weaving by candle-light. Will you tell me what it means that all Peterswaldau's on the way here? I set off on my rounds this morning as usual, thinking no harm; but it wasn't long till I had my eyes opened. Strange doings, these! What in the devil's name has taken possession of them, Hilse? They're like a pack of raging wolves. Riot—why, it's revolution! they're plundering and laying waste right and left . . . Mielchen! where's Mielchen? [Mielchen, *her face red with crying, is pushed in by her mother*] Here, Mielchen, put your hand into my coat pocket. [Mielchen *does so*] The ginger-bread nuts are for you. Not all at once, though, you baggage! And a song first! The fox jumped up on a . . . come, now . . . The fox jumped up . . . on a moonlight . . . Mind, I've heard what you did. You called the sparrows on the churchyard hedge a nasty name, and they're gone and told the pastor. Did any one ever hear the like? Fifteen hundred of them agog—men, women, and children. [*Distant bells are heard*] That's at Reichenbach—alarm-bells! Fifteen hundred people! Uncomfortably like the world coming to an end!

OLD HILSE: An' is it true that they're on their way to Bielau?

SURGEON SCHMIDT: That's just what I'm telling you. I've driven through the middle of the whole crowd. What I'd have liked to do would have been to get down and give each of them a pill there and then. They were following on each other's heels like grim death, and their singing was more than enough to turn a man's stomach. I was nearly sick, and Friedrich was shaking on the box like an old woman. We had to take a stiff glass at the first opportunity. I wouldn't be a manufacturer, not though I could drive my carriage and pair. [*Distant singing*] Listen to that! It's for all the world as if they were beating at some broken old boiler. We'll have them here in five minutes, friends. Good-bye! Don't you be foolish. The troops will be upon them in no time. Keep your wits about you. The Peterswaldau people have lost theirs. [*Bells ring close at hand*] Good gracious! There are our bells ringing too! Every one's going mad. [*He goes upstairs*]

GOTTLIEB: [*Comes back. In the entry-room, out of breath*] I've seen them, I've seen them! [*To a woman*] They're here, auntie, they're here! [*At the door*] They're here, father, they're here! They've got bean-poles, an' ox-goads, an' axes. They're standin' outside the upper Dittrich's kickin' up an awful row. I think he's payin' them money. O Lord! whatever's goin' to happen? What a crowd! Oh, you never saw such a crowd! Dash it all—if once they make a rush, our manufacturers'll be hard put to it.

OLD HILSE: What have you been runnin' like that for? You'll go racin' till you bring on your old trouble, and then we'll have you on your back again, strugglin' for breath.

GOTTLIEB: [*Almost joyously excited*] I had to run, or they would have caught me an' kept me. They were all roarin' to me to join them. Father Baumert was there too, and says he to me: You come an' get your sixpence with the rest—you're a poor starving weaver, too. An' I was to tell you, father, from him, that you were to come an' help to pay out the manufacturers for their grindin' of us down. Other times is coming, he says. There's going to be a change of days for us weavers. An' we're all to come an' help to bring it about. We're to have our half-pound of meat on Sundays, and now and again on a holiday sausage with our cabbage. Yes, things is to be quite different, by what he tells me.

OLD HILSE: [*With repressed indignation*] An' that man calls himself your godfather! and he bids you take part in such works of wickedness? Have nothing to do with them, Gottlieb. They've let themselves be tempted by Satan, an' it's his works they're doin'.

LUISE: [*No longer able to restrain her passionate excitement, vehemently*] Yes, Gottlieb, get into the chimney corner, an' take a spoon in your hand, an' a dish of skim milk on your knee, an' put on a petticoat an' say your prayers, an' then father'll be pleased with you. And *he* sets up to be a man!

[*Laughter from the people in the entry-room*]

OLD HILSE: [*Quivering with suppressed rage*] An' you set up to be a good wife, eh? You call yourself a mother, an' let your evil tongue run away with you like that? You think yourself fit to teach your girl, you that would egg on your husband to crime an' wickedness?

LUISE: [*Has lost all control of herself*] You an your piety an' religion—did they serve to keep the life in my poor children? In rags an' dirt they lay, all the four—it didn't as much as keep them dry.

Yes! I set up to be a mother, that's what I do—an' if you'd like to know it, that's why I would send all the manufacturers to hell—because I'm a mother!—Not one of the four could I keep in life! It was cryin' more than breathin' with me from the time each poor little thing came into the world till death took pity on it. The devil a bit you cared! You sat there prayin' and singin', and let me run about till my feet bled, tryin' to get one little drop o' skim milk. How many hundred nights have I lain an' racked my head to think what I could do to cheat the churchyard of my little one? What harm has a baby like that done that it must come to such a miserable end—eh? An' over there at Dittrich's they're bathed in wine an' washed in milk. No! you may talk as you like, but if you begin here, ten horses won't hold me back. An' what's more—if there's a rush on Dittrich's, you'll see me in the forefront of it—an' pity the man as tries to prevent me—I've stood it long enough, so now you know it.

OLD HILSE: You're a lost soul—there's no help for you.

LUISE: [Frenzied] It's you that there's no help for! Tater-breeched scarecrows—that's what you are—an' not men at all. Whey-faced gutter-scrapers that take to your heels at the sound of a child's rattle. Fellows that say "thank you" to the man as gives you a hidin'. They've not left that much blood in you as that you can turn red in the face. You should have the whip taken to you, an' a little pluck flogged into your rotten bones. [She goes out quickly]

[Embarrassed pause]

MOTHER HILSE: What's the matter with Liesl, father?

OLD HILSE: Nothin', mother! What should be the matter with her?

MOTHER HILSE: Father, is it only me that's thinkin' it, or are the bells ringin'?

OLD HILSE: It'll be a funeral, mother.

MOTHER HILSE: An' I've got to sit waitin' here yet. Why must I be so long a-dyin', father?

[Pause]

OLD HILSE: [Leaves his work, holds himself up straight; solemnly] Gottlieb!—you heard all your wife said to us. Look here, Gottlieb! [He bares his breast] Here they cut out a bullet as big as a thimble. The King knows where I lost my arm. It wasn't the mice as ate it. [He walks up and down] Before that wife of yours was ever thought of, I had spilled my blood by the quart for King an' country. So let her call what names she likes—an' welcome! It does me no harm.—Frightened? Me frightened? What would I be frightened of, will you tell me that? Of the few soldiers, maybe, that'll be comin' after the rioters? Good gracious me! That would be a lot to be frightened at! No, no, lad; I may be a bit stiff in the back, but there's some strength left in the old bones; I've got the stuff in me yet to make a stand against a few rubbishin' bay'nets.—An' if it came to the worst! Willin', willin' would I be to say good-bye to this weary world. Death would be welcome—welcomer to me to-day than to-morrow. For what is it we leave behind? That old bundle of aches an' pains we call our body, the care an' the oppression we call by the name of life. We may be glad to get away from it.—But there's something to come after, Gottlieb!—an' if we've done ourselves out of that too—why, then it's all over with us!

GOTTLIEB: Who knows what's to come after? Nobody's seen it.

OLD HILSE: Gottlieb! don't you be throwin' doubts on the one comfort us poor people have. Why have I sat here an' worked my treadle like a slave this forty year an' more?—sat still an' looked on at him over yonder livin' in pride an' wastefulness—why? Because I have a better hope, something as supports me in all my troubles. [Points out at the window] You have your good things in this world—I'll have mine in the next. That's been my thought. An' I'm that certain of it—I'd let myself be torn in pieces. Have we not His promise? There's a Day of Judgment coming; but it's not us as are the judges—no: vengeance is mine, saith the Lord.

[A cry of "Weavers, come out!" is heard outside the window]

OLD HILSE: Do what you will for me. [He seats himself at his loom] I stay here.

GOTTLIEB: [After a short struggle] I'm going to work, too—come what may. [Goes out]

[The Weavers' Song is heard, sung by hundreds of voices quite close at hand; it sounds like a dull monotonous wail]

INMATES OF THE HOUSE: [In the entry-room] "Oh, mercy on us! there they come swarmin' like ants!"—"Where can all these weavers be from?"—"Don't shove like that, I want to see too."—"Look at that great maypole of a woman leadin' on in front!"—"Gracious! they're comin' thicker an' thicker."

HORNIG: [Comes into the entry-room from outside] There's a theayter play for you now! That's what you don't see every day. But you should go up to the other Dittrich's an' look what they've done there. It's been no half work. He's got no house now, nor no factory, nor no wine-cellar, nor nothing. They're drinkin' out of the bottles—not so much as takin' the time to get out the corks. One, two, three, an' off with the neck, an' no matter whether they cut their mouths or not. There's some of them runnin' about bleedin' like stuck pigs.—Now they're goin' to do for this Dittrich.

[The singing has stopped]

INMATES OF THE HOUSE: There's nothin' so very wicked-like about them.

HORNIG: You wait a bit! you'll soon see! All they're doin' just now is makin' up their minds where they'll begin. Look, they're inspectin' the palace from every side. Do you see that little stout man there, him with the stable pail? That's the smith from Peterswaldau—an' a dangerous little chap he is. He batters in the thickest doors as if they were made o' pie-crust. If a manufacturer was to fall into his hands it would be all over with him!

INMATES OF THE HOUSE: "That was a crack!"— "There went a stone through the window!"— "There's old Dittrich, shakin' with fright."—"He's hangin' out a board."—"Hangin' out a board?"— "What's written on it?"—"Can you not read?"—"It would be a bad job for me if I couldn't read!"— "Well, read it, then!"—"'You—shall have—full— satisfaction! You—shall have full satisfaction.'"

HORNIG: He might ha' spared himself the trouble —*that* won't help him. It's something else they've set their minds on here. It's the factories. They're goin' to smash up the power-looms. For it's them that are ruinin' the hand-loom weaver. Even a blind man might see that. No! the good folks know what they're after, an' no sheriff an' no p'lice superintendent'll bring them to reason—much less a bit of a board. Him as has seen them at work already knows what's comin'.

INMATES OF THE HOUSE: "Did any one ever see such a crowd?"—"What can these ones be wantin'?" —[*Hastily*] "They're crossin' the bridge!"—[*Anxiously*] "They're never comin' over on this side, are they?"—[*In excitement and terror*] "It's to us they're comin'!"—"They're comin' to us!"—"They're comin' to fetch the weavers out of their houses!'

[*General flight. The entry-room is empty. A crowd of dirty, dusty rioters rush in, their faces scarlet with brandy and excitement; tattered, untidy-looking, as if they had been up all night. With the shout: "Weavers, come out!" they disperse themselves through the house.* Becker *and several other young weavers, armed with cudgels and poles, come into* Old Hilse's *room. When they see the old man at his loom they start, and cool down a little*]

BECKER: Come, Father Hilse, stop that. Leave your work to them as wants to work. There's no need now for you to be doin' yourself harm. You'll be well taken care of.

FIRST YOUNG WEAVER: You'll never need to go hungry to bed again.

SECOND YOUNG WEAVER: The weaver's goin' to have a roof over his head and a shirt on his back once more.

OLD HILSE: An' what's the devil sendin' you to do now, with your poles an' axes?

BECKER: These are what we're goin' to break on Dittrich's back.

SECOND YOUNG WEAVER: We'll beat them red hot an' stick them down the manufacturers' throats, so as they'll feel for once what burnin' hunger tastes like.

THIRD YOUNG WEAVER: Come along, Father Hilse! We'll give no quarter.

SECOND YOUNG WEAVER: No one had mercy on us—neither God nor man. Now we're standin' up for our rights ourselves.

[Old Baumert *enters, somewhat shaky on the legs, a newly killed cock under his arm*]

OLD BAUMERT: [*Stretching out his arms*] My brothers—we're all brothers! Come to my arms, brothers!

[*Laughter*]

OLD HILSE: And that's the state you're in, Willem?

OLD BAUMERT: Gustav, is it you? My poor starvin' friend! Come to my arms, Gustav!

OLD HILSE: [*Mutters*] Let me alone.

OLD BAUMERT: I'll tell you what, Gustav. It's nothin' but luck that's wanted. You look at me. What do I look like? Luck's what's wanted. Do I not look like a lord? [*Pats his stomach*] Guess what's in there! There's food fit for a prince in that belly. When luck's with him a man gets roast hare to eat an' champagne wine to drink.—I'll tell you somethin': We've made a big mistake—we must help ourselves.

ALL: [*Speaking at once*] We must help ourselves, hurrah!

OLD BAUMERT: As soon as we get the first good bite inside us we're different men. Damn it all! but you feel the power comin' into you till you're like an ox, an' that wild with strength that you hit out right an' left without as much as takin' time to look. Dash it, but it's grand!

JAEGER: [*At the door, armed with an old cavalry sword*] We've made one or two first-rate attacks.

BECKER: We know how to set about it now. One, two, three, an' we're inside the house. Then, at it like lightning—bang, crack, shiver! till the sparks are flyin' as if it was a smithy.

FIRST YOUNG WEAVER: It wouldn't be half bad to light a bit o' fire.

SECOND YOUNG WEAVER: Let's march to Reichenbach an' burn the rich folks' houses over their heads!

JAEGER: That would be nothing but butterin' their bread. Think of all the insurance money they'd get.

[*Laughter*]

BECKER: No, from here we'll go to Freiburg, to Tromtra's.

JAEGER: What would you say to givin' all them as holds Government appointments a lesson? I've read somewhere as how all our troubles come from them birocrats, as they call them.

SECOND YOUNG WEAVER: Before long we'll go to Breslau, for more an' more'll be joining us.

OLD BAUMERT: [*To* Hilse] Won't you take a drop, Gustav?

OLD HILSE: I never touches it.

OLD BAUMERT: That was in the old world; we're in a new world to-day, Gustav.

FIRST YOUNG WEAVER: Christmas comes but once a year.

[*Laughter*]

OLD HILSE: [*Impatiently*] What is it you want in my house, you limbs of Satan?

OLD BAUMERT: [*A little intimidated, coaxingly*]

I was bringin' you a chicken, Gustav. I thought it would make a drop o' soup for mother.

OLD HILSE: [*Embarrassed, almost friendly*] Well, you can tell mother yourself.

MOTHER HILSE: [*Who has been making efforts to hear, her hand at her ear, motions them off*] Let me alone. I don't want no chicken soup.

OLD HILSE: That's right, mother. An' I want none, an' least of all that sort. An' let me say this much to you, Baumert: The devil stands on his head for joy when he hears the old ones jabberin' and talkin' as if they was infants. An' to you all I say—to every one of you: Me and you, we've got nothing to do with each other. It's not with my will that you're here. In law an' justice you've no right to be in my house.

A VOICE: Him that's not with us is against us.

JAEGER: [*Roughly and threateningly*] You're a cross-grained old chap, and I'd have you remember that we're not thieves.

A VOICE: We're hungry men, that's all.

FIRST YOUNG WEAVER: We want to *live*—that's all. An' so we've cut the rope we were hung up with.

JAEGER: And we were in our right! [*Holding his fist in front of the old man's face*] Say another word, and I'll give you one between the eyes.

BECKER: Come now, Jaeger, be quiet. Let the old man alone.—What we say to ourselves, Father Hilse, is this: Better dead than begin the old life again.

OLD HILSE: Have I not lived that life for sixty years an' more?

BECKER: That doesn't help us—there's got to be a change.

OLD HILSE: On the Judgment Day.

BECKER: What they'll not give us willingly we're going to take by force.

OLD HILSE: By force. [*Laughs*] You may as well go an' dig your graves at once. They'll not be long showin' you where the force lies. Wait a bit, lad!

JAEGER: Is it the soldiers you're meaning? We've been soldiers, too. We'll soon do for a company or two of them.

OLD HILSE: With your tongues, maybe. But supposin' you did—for two that you'd beat off, ten'll come back.

VOICES: [*Call through the window*] The soldiers are comin'! Look out!

[*General, sudden silence. For a moment a faint sound of fifes and drums is heard; in the ensuing silence a short, involuntary exclamation, "The devil! I'm off!" followed by general laughter*]

BECKER: Who was that? Who speaks of running away?

JAEGER: Which of you is it that's afraid of a few paltry helmets? You have me to command you, and I've been in the trade. I know their tricks.

OLD HILSE: An' what are you goin' to shoot with? Your sticks, eh?

FIRST YOUNG WEAVER: Never mind that old chap; he's wrong in the upper story.

SECOND YOUNG WEAVER: Yes, he's a bit off his head.

GOTTLIEB: [*Has made his way unnoticed among the rioters; catches hold of the speaker*] Would you give your impudence to an old man like him?

SECOND YOUNG WEAVER: Let me alone. 'Twasn't anything bad I said.

OLD HILSE: [*Interfering*] Let him jaw, Gottlieb. What would you be meddlin' with him for? He'll soon see who it is that's been off his head to-day, him or me.

BECKER: Are you comin', Gottlieb?

OLD HILSE: No, he's goin' to do no such thing.

LUISE: [*Comes into the entry-room, calls*] What are you puttin' off your time with prayin' hypocrites like them for? Come quick to where you're wanted! Quick! Father Baumert, run all you can! The Major's speakin' to the crowd from horseback. They're to go home. If you don't hurry up, it'll be all over.

JAEGER: [*As he goes out*] That's a brave husband of yours.

LUISE: Where is he? I've got no husband!

[*Some of the people in the entry-room sing*]
> Once on a time a man so small,
>   Heigh-ho, heigh!
> Set his heart on a wife so tall,
>   Heigh diddle-di-dum-di!

WITTIG, THE SMITH: [*Comes downstairs, still carrying the stable pail; stops on his way through the entry-room*] Come on! all of you that are not cowardly scoundrels!—hurrah! [*He dashes out, followed by* Luise, Jaeger, *and others, all shouting "Hurrah!"*]

BECKER: Good-bye, then, Father Hilse; we'll see each other again. [*Is going*]

OLD HILSE: I doubt that. I've not five years to live, and that'll be the soonest you'll get out.

BECKER: [*Stops, not understanding*] Out o' what, Father Hilse?

OLD HILSE: Out of prison—where else?

BECKER: [*Laughs wildly*] Do you think I would mind that? There's bread to be had there anyhow! [*Goes out*]

OLD BAUMERT: [*Has been cowering on a low stool, painfully beating his brains; he now gets up*] It's true, Gustav, as I've had a drop too much. But for all that I know what I'm about. You think one way in this here matter; I think another. I say Becker's right: even if it ends in chains an' ropes—we'll be better off in prison than at home. You're cared for there, an' you don't need to starve. I wouldn't have joined them, Gustav, if I could have let it be; but once in a lifetime a man's got to show what he feels. [*Goes slowly toward the door*] Good-bye, Gustav. If anything happens, mind you put in a word for me in your prayers. [*Goes out*]

[*The rioters are now all gone. The entry-room gradually fills again with curious onlookers from the different rooms of the house.* Old Hilse *knots at his web.* Gottlieb *has taken an ax from behind the stove and is unconsciously feeling its edge. He and the old man are silently agitated. The hum and roar of a great crowd penetrate into the room*]

MOTHER HILSE: The very boards is shakin', father—what's goin' on? What's goin' to happen to us?

[*Pause*]

OLD HILSE: Gottlieb!

GOTTLIEB: What is it?

OLD HILSE: Let that ax alone.

GOTTLIEB: Who's to split the wood, then? [*He leans the ax against the stove*]

[*Pause*]

MOTHER HILSE: Gottlieb, you listen to what father says to you.

[*Some one sings outside the window*]

Our little man does all that he can,
    Heigh-ho, heigh!
At home he cleans the pots an' the pan,
    Heigh-diddle-di-dum-di!

[*Passes on*]

GOTTLIEB: [*Jumps up, shakes his clenched fist at the window*] Brute that you are, would you drive me crazy?

[*A volley of musketry is heard*]

MOTHER HILSE: [*Starts and trembles*] Good Lord! is that thunder again?

OLD HILSE: [*Instinctively folding his hands*] Oh, our Father in heaven! defend the poor weavers, protect my poor brothers!

[*A short pause ensues*]

OLD HILSE: [*To himself, painfully agitated*] There's blood flowing now.

GOTTLIEB: [*Had started up and grasped the ax when the shooting was heard; deathly pale, almost beside himself with excitement*] And am I to lie to heel like a dog still?

A GIRL: [*Calls from the entry-room*] Father Hilse, Father Hilse! get away from the window. A bullet's just flown in at ours upstairs. [*Disappears*]

MIELCHEN: [*Puts her head in at the window, laughing*] Gran'father, gran'father, they've shot with their guns. Two or three's been knocked down, an' one of them's turnin' round and round like a top, an' one's twistin' himself like a sparrow when its head's bein' pulled of. An' oh, if you saw all the blood that came pourin'—! [*Disappears*]

A WEAVER'S WIFE: Yes, there's two or three'll never get up again.

AN OLD WEAVER: [*In the entry-room*] Look out! They're goin' to make a rush on the soldiers.

A SECOND WEAVER: [*Wildly*] Look, look, look at the women!—skirts up, an' spittin' in the soldiers' faces already!

A WEAVER'S WIFE: [*Calls in*] Gottlieb, look at your wife. She's more pluck in her than you. She's jumpin' about in front o' the bay'nets as if she was dancin' to music.

[*Four men carry a wounded rioter through the entry-room. Silence, which is broken by some one saying in a distinct voice, "It's Weaver Ulbrich." Once more silence for a few seconds, when the same voice is heard again: "It's all over with him; he's got a bullet in his ear." The men are heard climbing the wooden stair. Sudden shouting outside: "Hurrah, hurrah!"*]

VOICES IN THE ENTRY-ROOM: "Where did they get the stones from?"—"Yes, it's time you were off!"—"From the new road."—"Ta-ta, soldiers!"—"It's raining paving-stones."

[*Shrieks of terror and loud roaring outside, taken up by those in the entry-room. There is a cry of fear, and the house door is shut with a bang*]

VOICES IN THE ENTRY-ROOM: "They're loading again."—"They'll fire another volley this minute."—"Father Hilse, get away from that window."

GOTTLIEB: [*Clutches the ax*] What! are we mad dogs? Are we to eat powder an' shot now instead of bread? [*Hesitating an instant: to the old man*] Would you have me sit here an' see my wife shot? Never! [*As he rushes out*] Look out! I'm coming!

OLD HILSE: Gottlieb, Gottlieb!

MOTHER HILSE: Where's Gottlieb gone?

OLD HILSE: He's gone to the devil.

VOICES FROM THE ENTRY-ROOM: Go away from the window, Father Hilse.

OLD HILSE: Not I! Not if you all go crazy together! [*To* Mother Hilse, *with rapt excitement*] My heavenly Father has placed me here. Isn't that so, mother? Here we'll sit, an' do our bounden duty—ay, though the snow was to go on fire. [*He begins to weave*]

[*Rattle of another volley.* Old Hilse, *mortally wounded, starts to his feet and then falls over the loom. At the same moment loud shouting of "Hurrah!" is heard. The people who till now have been standing in the entry-room dash out, joining in the cry. The old woman repeatedly asks: "Father, father, what's wrong with you?" The continued shouting dies away gradually in the distance.* Mielchen *comes rushing in*]

MIELCHEN: Gran'father, gran'father, they're drivin' the soldiers out of the village; they've got into Dittrich's house, an' they're doin' what they did at Dreissiger's. Gran'father!

[*The child grows frightened, notices that something has happened, puts her finger in her mouth, and goes up cautiously to the dead man*]

Gran'father!

MOTHER HILSE: Come now, father, can't you say something? You're frightenin' me.

Frank Wedekind

(1864–1918)

Frank Wedekind, christened Benjamin Franklin, was born in the city of Hanover, shortly after his parents returned to Germany from the United States. It is ironical that but for chance he might have been born on American soil, since few important writers of the European stage are less known to the American public. For an actor-playwright who rebelled against convention and combined romantic and scientific attitudes in his work, Wedekind, we may add, was introduced to the world by an "appropriate" set of parents. His mother was a young German actress sojourning in San Francisco when she met the considerably older man who became her husband. He was a physician, an adventurer who left Germany and moved from Turkey to California, and a passionate democrat who detested Bismarck as intensely as he revered Washington and Franklin. The father's political convictions apparently descended to the son. Wedekind was imprisoned in 1899 for publishing certain political poems in the satirical periodical *Simplicissimus*.

It was mostly with plays, however, that Wedekind stirred the hornet's nest of the old German monarchy, its bureaucracy, and its conservative adherents. He was a strong admirer of Ibsen and, upon turning actor, toured Germany giving effective professional readings from Ibsen's works. By the time he reached his twenty-fifth birthday, the naturalistic movement was in full swing in Munich and Berlin, and it was intensified in the German empire by the political agitation of the Social-Democratic movement, which Germany's "iron chancellor" Bismarck tried vainly to suppress. The young writer aligned himself with the naturalists to the extent of concerning himself with the operations of the sexual instinct and exhibiting it in situations extremely shocking to the sensibilities of staid citizens. He started his career of iconoclasm in 1890 with *The World of Youth*, a picture of conditions in a girls' boarding school, and became increasingly devastating in *The Awakening of Spring* (1892), *Earth Spirit* (1894), and *Pandora's Box* (1903). He continued to write variations on erotic subjects long after they ceased to be novel, and he did so with decreasing effectiveness. As a lyricist of the flesh, Wedekind placed himself in the vanguard of the anti-Philistine progressives. He also came to be regarded as one of the progenitors of nudism and eurythmics, both of which enjoyed a great vogue in Germany. Wedekind knew that slavery to eroticism results in enervation and depression, and declared it in his work; hence it is an error to consider him a simple-minded propagandist for free love. But it was inevitable that he should be alternately denounced as a mere pornographer and acclaimed as a liberator.

Hauptmann and other naturalists were tame by comparison with Wedekind in his excursions into the tabooed field of sexual problems. Yet Wedekind was not a consistent naturalist. An original artist who was not apt to follow fashions, he helped himself to much naturalistic detail to support his personal crusade for frankness about the elemental power of the sexual instinct. Absolute candor, which the English-speaking world still finds too strong for its stomach, was an essential quality of his talent. As a result, some of his work gives the impression of having been written expressly according to Zola's formula for naturalistic "scientism"—"to see the beast [animal] in man, and only the beast." No prurience, but a primal amorality, characterizes his studies of Lulu, the heroine of *Earth Spirit* and *Pandora's Box*, who destroys man after man, only to be destroyed herself by a male counterpart. And sexual awakening in adolescence has a melancholy and hypnotic quality in *The Awakening of Spring*, the play that first brought its author international renown.

Because he was an overintense and highly imaginative person (and partly, no doubt, because his subject lay beneath surface reality) Wedekind also followed antirealistic directions. In *The Awakening of Spring* he even added a spectral fantasy to his story of the inner torments and suicide of his adolescents, who find themselves in the grip of the sexual instinct without proper guidance from their convention-bound, obtuse elders. Wedekind wrote the play in short, jerky scenes, and he shifted the background frequently—a procedure not favored in realistic circles. The weird—now and then macabre—and explosive dramaturgy and style of much of his work made Wedekind, indeed, a precursor of "expressionism." He brought the naturalistic tendencies of the theatre to their logical conclusion with his subjects and his uncompromising treatment, but he also introduced us to a nervous, subjective style of drama. When Hauptmann and other contemporaries of Wedekind departed from naturalism they turned toward a somewhat effete romanticism. Although himself impatient with the commonplace and leisurely spirit of standard naturalistic plays, Wedekind was too explosive to content himself with lyricism, legend, and gentle allegories such as Max Reinhardt's spectacle *The Miracle*.

Like other writers, Wedekind was, of course, not always at his best; and never a particularly disciplined person, in many ill-conceived and disordered plays he failed to do justice to his talent. But his importance in the modern theatre cannot be underestimated. Nor is it based entirely on his studies of "the tyranny of sex," the title of the only collection of his plays in English. He was also a master of a wry kind of comedy dedicated to characters who live outside the pale of middle-class life either as swindlers, like the hero of his tantalizing masterpiece *The Marquis of Keith* (1901), or as artists, like the singer Gerardo in *The Tenor* (1899). Wedekind himself stood outside the pale, unable to remain at peace with the secure world of respectability, which he tended to bait on the grounds that it was stupid, smug, and hypocritical. He was therefore strongly attracted to characters who would not or could not lead easy, conventional lives. Since he was a penetrative artist, however, his approach to his subject tended to be antiheroic, quizzical, and a trifle blighting.

The Tenor was Wedekind's most popular work. It is also frequently regarded as his best. Although it does not represent the full scope of his talent and lacks the profundity of several of his longer pieces, it is his most thoroughly integrated play. If its technique is in no respect expressionistic, its picture of the life of the singer who is slave to his profession is curiously unreal. That, indeed, is the point of this ironic little comedy, and Wedekind is all the more realistic in presenting the unreality of this public idol. Gerardo dreads yielding to real emotions because he belongs to the Philistines he is paid to entertain. Wedekind's powers of incisive observation and style are all impacted here. His play would have been welcomed as an ultranaturalistic masterpiece by the playwrights who began to supply Antoine's Théâtre Libre in 1887 with cynical one-acters known as *comédies rosses*. Since *The Tenor* happens to be better than anything of the kind they wrote in the service of naturalism, Wedekind's mordant masterpiece can be allowed to represent their *avant-garde* shockers, as well as its author's often uneven but always striking work.

BIBLIOGRAPHY: Eric Bentley, *The Playwright as Thinker* (pp. 64–67, 318–321), 1946; Anita Block, *The Changing World in Plays and Theatre* (pp. 39–45), 1939; Samuel Eliot, *Tragedies of Sex*, 1923; Arthur Kutscher, *Frank Wedekind, sein Leben und seine Werke*, 1931; Raimund Pissin, *Frank Wedekind*, volume 53 of *Moderne Essays*, 1905(?).

THE TENOR

By Frank Wedekind

TRANSLATED FROM THE GERMAN BY ANDRÉ TRIDON

CHARACTERS

GERARDO, *Wagnerian tenor, thirty-six years old*
HELEN MAROVA, *a beautiful dark-haired woman of twenty-five*
PROFESSOR DUHRING, *sixty, the typical "misunderstood genius"*
MISS ISABEL CŒURNE, *a blond English girl of sixteen*
MULLER, *hotel manager*
A VALET   A BELL BOY   AN UNKNOWN WOMAN

TIME: *The present.*   PLACE: *A city in Austria.*

SCENE: *A large hotel room. There are doors at the right and in the center, and at the left a window with heavy portières. Behind a grand piano at the right stands a Japanese screen which conceals the fireplace. There are several large trunks, open; bunches of flowers are all over the room; many bouquets are piled up on the piano.*

VALET: [*Entering from the adjoining room carrying an armful of clothes which he proceeds to pack in one of the trunks. There is a knock at the door*] Come in.

BELL BOY: There is a lady who wants to know if the Maestro is in.

VALET: He isn't in. [*Exit Bell Boy. The* Valet *goes into the adjoining room and returns with another armful of clothes. There is another knock at the door. He puts the clothes on a chair and goes to the door*] What's this again? [*He opens the door and some one hands him several large bunches of flowers, which he places carefully on the piano; then he goes back to his packing. There is another knock. He opens the door and takes a handful of letters. He glances at the addresses and reads aloud:*] "Mister Gerardo. Monsieur Gerardo. Gerardo Esquire. Signor Gerardo." [*He drops the letters on a tray and resumes his packing*]

[*Enter* Gerardo]

GERARDO: Haven't you finished packing yet? How much longer will it take you?

VALET: I'll be through in a minute, sir.

GERARDO: Hurry! I still have things to do. Let me see. [*He reaches for something in a trunk*] God Almighty! Don't you know how to fold a pair of trousers? [*Taking the trousers out*] This is what you call packing! Look here! You still have something to learn from me, after all. You take the trousers like this. . . . You lock this up here. . . . Then you take hold of these buttons. Watch these buttons here, that's the important thing. Then—you pull them straight. . . . There. . . . There. . . . Then you fold them here. . . . See. . . . Now these trousers would keep their shape for a hundred years.

VALET: [*Respectfully, with downcast eyes*] You must have been a tailor once, sir.

GERARDO: What! Well, not exactly. . . . [*He gives the trousers to the* Valet] Pack those up, but be quick about it. Now about that train. You are sure this is the last one we can take?

VALET: It is the only one that gets you there in time, sir. The next train does not reach Brussels until ten o'clock.

GERARDO: Well, then, we must catch this one. I will just have time to go over the second act. Unless I go over that. . . . Now don't let anybody. . . . I am out to everybody.

VALET: All right, sir. There are some letters for you, sir.

GERARDO: I have seen them.

VALET: And flowers!

GERARDO: Yes, all right. [*He takes the letters from the tray and throws them on a chair before the piano. Then he opens the letters, glances over them with beaming eyes, crumples them up and throws them under the chair*] Remember! I am out to everybody.

VALET: I know, sir. [*He locks the trunks*]

GERARDO: To everybody.

VALET: You needn't worry, sir. [*Giving him the trunk keys*] Here are the keys, sir.

GERARDO: [*Pocketing the keys*] To everybody!

VALET: The trunks will be taken down at once [*He goes out*]

GERARDO: [*Looking at his watch*] Forty minutes [*He pulls the score of "Tristan" from underneath the flowers on the piano and walks up and down humming*] "Isolde! Geliebte! Bist du mein? Hab' ich dich wieder? Darf ich dich fassen?" [*He clears his throat, strikes a chord on the piano and starts again*] "Isolde! Geliebte! Bist du mein? Hab' ich dich wieder? . . ." [*He clears his throat*] The air is dead

166

here. [*He sings*] *"Isolde! Geliebte. . . ."* It's oppressive here. Let's have a little fresh air. [*He goes to the window at the left and fumbles for the curtain cord*] Where is the thing? On the other side! Here! [*He pulls the cord and throws his head back with an annoyed expression when he sees* Miss Cœurne]

MISS CŒURNE: [*In three-quarter length skirt, her blonde hair down her back, holding a bunch of red roses; she speaks with an English accent and looks straight at* Gerardo] Oh, please don't send me away.

GERARDO: What else can I do? God knows, I haven't asked you to come here. Do not take it badly, dear young lady, but I have to sing to-morrow night in Brussels. I must confess, I hoped I would have this half-hour to myself. I had just given positive orders not to let any one, whoever it might be, come up to my rooms.

MISS CŒURNE: [*Coming down stage*] Don't send me away. I heard you yesterday in "Tannhäuser," and I was just bringing you these roses, and—

GERARDO: And—and what?

MISS CŒURNE: And myself. . . . I don't know whether you understand me.

GERARDO: [*Holding the back of a chair; he hesitates, then shakes his head*] Who are you?

MISS CŒURNE: My name is Miss Cœurne.

GERARDO: Yes. . . . Well?

MISS CŒURNE: I am very silly.

GERARDO: I know. Come here, my dear girl. [*He sits down in an armchair and she stands before him*] Let's have a good earnest talk, such as you have never had in your life—and seem to need. An artist like myself—don't misunderstand me; you are—how old are you?

MISS CŒURNE: Twenty-two.

GERARDO: You are sixteen or perhaps seventeen. You make yourself a little older so as to appear more—tempting. Well? Yes, you are very silly. It is really none of my business, as an artist, to cure you of your silliness. . . . Don't take this badly. . . . Now then! Why are you staring away like this?

MISS CŒURNE: I said I was very silly, because I thought you Germans liked that in a young girl.

GERARDO: I am not a German, but just the same. . . .

MISS CŒURNE: What! I am not as silly as all that.

GERARDO: Now look here, my dear girl—you have your tennis court, your skating club; you have your riding class, your dances; you have all a young girl can wish for. What on earth made you come to me?

MISS CŒURNE: Because all those things are awful, and they bore me to death.

GERARDO: I will not dispute that. Personally, I must tell you, I know life from an entirely different side. But, my child, I am a man; I am thirty-six. The time will come when you, too, will claim a fuller existence. Wait another two years and there will be some one for you, and then you won't need to—hide yourself behind curtains, in my room, in the room

of a man who—never asked you, and whom you don't know any better than—the whole continent of Europe knows him—in order to look at life from his—wonderful point of view. [*Miss Cœurne sighs deeply*] Now then. . . . Many thanks from the bottom of my heart for your roses. [*He presses her hand*] Will this do for to-day?

MISS CŒURNE: I had never in all my life thought of a man, until I saw you on the stage last night in "Tannhäuser." And I promise you—

GERARDO: Oh, don't promise me anything, my child. What good could your promise do me? The burden of it would all fall upon you. You see, I am talking to you as lovingly as the most loving father could. Be thankful to God that with your recklessness you haven't fallen into the hands of another artist. [*He presses her hand again*] Let this be a lesson to you and never try it again.

MISS CŒURNE: [*Holding her handkerchief to her face but shedding no tears*] Am I so homely?

GERARDO: Homely! Not homely, but young and indiscreet. [*He rises nervously, goes to the right, comes back, puts his arm around her waist and takes her hand*] Listen to me, child. You are not homely because I have to be a singer, because I have to be an artist. Don't misunderstand me, but I can't see why I should simply, because I am an artist, have to assure you that I appreciate your youthful freshness and beauty. It is a question of time. Two hundred, maybe three hundred, nice, lovely girls of your age saw me last night in the rôle of Tannhäuser. Now if every one of those girls made the same demands upon me which you are making— what would become of my singing? What would become of my voice? What would become of my art?

[*Miss Cœurne sinks into a seat, covers her face and weeps*]

GERARDO: [*Leaning over the back of her chair, in a friendly tone*] It is a crime for you, child, to weep over the fact that you are still so young. Your whole life is ahead of you. Is it my fault if you fell in love with me? They all do. That is what I am for. Now won't you be a good girl and let me, for the few minutes I have left, prepare myself for to-morrow's appearance?

MISS CŒURNE: [*Rising and drying her tears*] I can't believe that any other girl would have acted the way I have.

GERARDO: [*Leading her to the door*] No, dear child.

MISS CŒURNE: [*With sobs in her voice*] At least, not if—

GERARDO: If my valet had stood before the door.

MISS CŒURNE: If—

GERARDO: If the girl had been as beautiful and youthfully fresh as you.

MISS CŒURNE: If—

GERARDO: If she had heard me only once in "Tannhäuser."

MISS CŒURNE: [*Indignant*] If she were as respectable as I am!

GERARDO: [*Pointing to the piano*] Before saying good-by to me, child, have a look at all those flowers. May this be a warning to you in case you feel tempted again to fall in love with a singer. See how fresh they all are. And I have to let them wither, dry up, or I give them to the porter. And look at those letters. [*He takes a handful of them from a tray*] I don't know any of these women. Don't worry; I leave them all to their fate. What else could I do? But I'll wager with you that every one of your lovely young friends sent in her little note.

MISS CŒURNE: Well, I promise not to do it again, not to hide myself behind your curtains. But don't send me away.

GERARDO: My time, my time, dear child. If I were not on the point of taking a train! I have already told you, I am very sorry for you. But my train leaves in twenty-five minutes. What do you expect?

MISS CŒURNE: A kiss.

GERARDO: [*Stiffening up*] From me?

MISS CŒURNE: Yes.

GERARDO: [*Holding her around the waist and looking very serious*] You rob Art of its dignity, my child. I do not wish to appear an unfeeling brute, and I am going to give you my picture. Give me your word that after that you will leave me.

MISS CŒURNE: Yes.

GERARDO: Good. [*He sits at the table and autographs one of his pictures*] You should try to become interested in the operas themselves instead of the men who sing them. You would probably derive much greater enjoyment.

MISS CŒURNE: [*To herself*] I am too young yet.

GERARDO: Sacrifice yourself to music. [*He comes down stage and gives her the picture*] Don't see in me a famous tenor but a mere tool in the hands of a noble master. Look at all the married women among your acquaintances. All Wagnerians. Study Wagner's works; learn to understand his *leit motifs*. That will save you from further foolishness.

MISS CŒURNE: I thank you.

[Gerardo *leads her out and rings the bell. He takes up his piano score again. There is a knock at the door*]

VALET: [*Coming in out of breath*] Yes, sir.

GERARDO: Are you standing at the door?

VALET: Not just now, sir.

GERARDO: Of course not! Be sure not to let anybody come up here.

VALET: There were three ladies who asked for you, sir.

GERARDO: Don't you dare to let any one of them come up, whatever she may tell you.

VALET: And then here are some more letters.

GERARDO: Oh, all right. [*The* Valet *places the letters on a tray*] And don't you dare to let any one come up.

VALET: [*At the door*] No, sir.

GERARDO: Even if she offers to settle a fortune upon you.

VALET: No, sir. [*He goes out*]

GERARDO: [*Singing*] "Isolde! Geliebte! Bist du . . ." Well, if women don't get tired of me— Only the world is so full of them; and I am only one man. Every one has his burden to carry. [*He strikes a chord on the piano*]

[Prof. Duhring, *dressed all in black, with a long white beard, a red hooked nose, gold spectacles, Prince Albert coat and silk hat, an opera score under his arm, enters without knocking*]

GERARDO: What do you want?

DUHRING: Maestro—I—I—have—an opera.

GERARDO: How did you get in?

DUHRING: I have been watching for two hours for a chance to run up the stairs unnoticed.

GERARDO: But, my dear good man, I have no time.

DUHRING: Oh, I will not play the whole opera for you.

GERARDO: I haven't the time. My train leaves in forty minutes.

DUHRING: You haven't the time! What should I say? You are thirty and successful. You have your whole life to live yet. Just listen to your part in my opera. You promised to listen to it when you came to this city.

GERARDO: What is the use? I am not a free agent—

DUHRING: Please! Please! Please! Maestro! I stand before you an old man, ready to fall on my knees before you; an old man who has never cared for anything in the world but his art. For fifty years I have been a willing victim to the tyranny of art—

GERARDO: [*Interrupting him*] Yes, I understand; I understand, but—

DUHRING: [*Excitedly*] No, you don't understand. You could not understand. How could you, the favorite of fortune, you understand what fifty years of bootless work means? But I will try to make you understand it. You see, I am too old to take my own life. People who do that do it at twenty-five, and I let the time pass by. I must now drag along to the end of my days. Please, sir, please don't let these moments pass in vain for me, even if you have to lose a day thereby, a week even. This is in your own interest. A week ago, when you first came for your special appearances, you promised to let me play my opera for you. I have come here every day since; either you had a rehearsal or a woman caller. And now you are on the point of going away. You have only to say one word: I will sing the part of Hermann—and they will produce my opera. You will then thank God for my insistence. . . . Of course you sing Siegfried, you sing Florestan—but you have no rôle like Hermann in your repertoire, no rôle better suited to your middle register.

[Gerardo *leans against the mantelpiece; while drumming on the top with his right hand, he discovers something behind the screen; he suddenly stretches out his arm and pulls out a woman in a gray gown, whom he leads out of the room through the middle door; after closing the door, he turns to* Duhring]

GERARDO: Oh, are you still there?

DUHRING: [Undisturbed] This opera is good; it is dramatic; it is a financial success. I can show you letters from Liszt, from Wagner, from Rubinstein, in which they consider me as a superior man. And why hasn't my opera ever been produced? Because I am not crying wares on the market-place. And then you know our directors: they will revive ten dead men before they give a live man a chance. Their walls are well guarded. At thirty you are in. At sixty I am still out. One word from you and I shall be in, too. This is why I have come, and [Raising his voice] if you are not an unfeeling brute, if success has not killed in you the last spark of artistic sympathy, you will not refuse to hear my work.

GERARDO: I will give you an answer in a week. I will go over your opera. Let me have it.

DUHRING: No, I am too old, Maestro. In a week, in what you call a week, I shall be dead and buried. In a week—that is what they all say; and then they keep it for years.

GERARDO: I am very sorry but—

DUHRING: To-morrow perhaps you will be on your knees before me; you will boast of knowing me . . . and today, in your sordid lust for gold, you cannot even spare the half-hour which would mean the breaking of my fetters.

GERARDO: No, really, I have only thirty-five minutes left, and unless I go over a few passages . . . . You know I sing Tristan in Brussels to-morrow night. [He pulls out his watch] I haven't even half an hour. . . .

DUHRING: Half an hour. . . . Oh, then, let me play to you your big aria at the end of the first act. [He attempts to sit down on the piano bench. Gerardo restrains him]

GERARDO: Now, frankly, my dear sir . . . I am a singer; I am not a critic. If you wish to have your opera produced, address yourself to those gentlemen who are paid to know what is good and what is not. People scorn and ignore my opinions in such matters as completely as they appreciate and admire my singing.

DUHRING: My dear Maestro, you may take it from me that I myself attach no importance whatever to your judgment. What do I care about your opinions? I know you tenors; I would like to play my score for you so that you could say: "I would like to sing the rôle of Hermann."

GERARDO: If you only knew how many things I would like to do and which I have to renounce, and how many things I must do for which I do not care in the least! Half a million a year does not repay me for the many joys of life which I must sacrifice for the sake of my profession. I am not a free man. But you were a free man all your life. Why didn't you go to the market-place and cry your wares?

DUHRING: Oh, the vulgarity of it. . . . I have tried it a hundred times. I am a composer, Maestro, and nothing more.

GERARDO: By which you mean that you have exhausted all your strength in the writing of your operas and kept none of it to secure their production.

DUHRING: That is true.

GERARDO: The composers I know reverse the process. They get their operas written somehow and then spend all their strength in an effort to get them produced.

DUHRING: That is the type of artist I despise.

GERARDO: Well, I despise the type of man that wastes his life in useless endeavor. What have you done in those fifty years of struggle, for yourself or for the world? Fifty years of useless struggle! That should convince the worst blockhead of the impracticability of his dreams. What have you done with your life? You have wasted it shamefully. If I had wasted my life as you have wasted yours—of course I am only speaking for myself—I don't think I should have the courage to look any one in the face.

DUHRING: I am not doing it for myself; I am doing it for my art.

GERARDO: [Scornfully] Art, my dear man! Let me tell you that art is quite different from what the papers tell us it is.

DUHRING: To me it is the highest thing in the world.

GERARDO: You may believe that, but nobody else does. We artists are merely a luxury for the use of the bourgeoisie. When I stand there on the stage I feel absolutely certain that not one solitary human being in the audience takes the slightest interest in what we, the artists, are doing. If they did, how could they listen to "Die Walküre," for instance? Why, it is an indecent story which could not be mentioned anywhere in polite society. And yet, when I sing Siegmund, the most puritanical mothers bring their fourteen-year-old daughters to hear me. This, you see, is the meaning of whatever you call art. This is what you have sacrificed fifty years of your life to. Find out how many people came to hear me sing and how many came to gape at me as they would at the Emperor of China if he should turn up here to-morrow. Do you know what the artistic wants of the public consist in? To applaud, to send flowers, to have a subject for conversation, to see and be seen. They pay me half a million, but then I make business for hundreds of cabbies, writers, dressmakers, restaurant keepers. It keeps money circulat-ing; it keeps blood running. It gets girls engaged, spinsters married, wives tempted, old cronies supplied with gossip; a woman loses her pocketbook in the crowd, a fellow becomes insane during the performance. Doctors, lawyers made. . . . [He coughs] And with this I must sing Tristan in Brussels to-morrow night! I tell you all this, not out of vanity, but to cure you of your delusions. The measure of a man's worth is the world's opinion of him, not the inner belief which one finally adopts after brooding over it for years. Don't imagine that you are a misunderstood genius. There are no misunderstood geniuses.

DUHRING: Let me just play to you the first scene of the second act. A park landscape as in the painting, "Embarkation for the Isle of Cythera."

GERARDO: I repeat to you I have no time. And furthermore, since Wagner's death the need for new operas has never been felt by any one. If you come with new music, you set against yourself all the music schools, the artists, the public. If you want to succeed just steal enough out of Wagner's works to make up a whole opera. Why should I cudgel my brains with your new music when I have cudgeled them cruelly with the old?

DUHRING: [*Holding out his trembling hand*] I am afraid I am too old to learn how to steal. Unless one begins very young, one can never learn it.

GERARDO: Don't feel hurt. My dear sir—if I could. . . . The thought of how you have to struggle. . . . I happen to have received some five hundred marks more than my fee. . . .

DUHRING: [*Turning to the door*] Don't! Please don't! Do not say that. I did not try to show you my opera in order to work a touch. No, I think too much of this child of my brain. . . . No, Maestro.

[*He goes out through the center door*]

GERARDO: [*Following him to the door*] I beg your pardon. . . . Pleased to have met you.

[*He closes the door and sinks into an armchair. A voice is heard outside: "I will not let that man step in my way."* Helen *rushes into the room followed by the* Valet. *She is an unusually beautiful young woman in street dress*]

HELEN: That man stood there to prevent me from seeing you!

GERARDO: Helen!

HELEN: You knew that I would come to see you.

VALET: [*Rubbing his cheek*] I did all I could, sir, but this lady actually—

HELEN: Yes, I slapped his face.

GERARDO: Helen!

HELEN: Should I have let him insult me?

GERARDO: [*To the* Valet] Please leave us.

[*The* Valet *goes out*]

HELEN: [*Placing her muff on a chair*] I can no longer live without you. Either you take me with you or I will kill myself.

GERARDO: Helen!

HELEN: Yes, kill myself. A day like yesterday, without even seeing you—no, I could not live through that again. I am not strong enough. I beseech you, Oscar, take me with you.

GERARDO: I couldn't.

HELEN: You could if you wanted to. You can't leave me without killing me. These are not mere words. This isn't a threat. It is a fact: I will die if I can no longer have you. You must take me with you—it is your duty—if only for a short time.

GERARDO: I give you my word of honor, Helen, I can't—I give you my word.

HELEN: You must, Oscar. Whether you can or not, you must bear the consequences of your acts. I love life, but to me life and you are one and the same thing. Take me with you, Oscar, if you don't want to have my blood on your hands.

GERARDO: Do you remember what I said to you the first day we were together here?

HELEN: I remember, but what good does that do me?

GERARDO: I said that there couldn't be any question of love between us.

HELEN: I can't help that. I didn't know you then. I never knew what a man could be to me until I met you. You knew very well that it would come to this, otherwise you wouldn't have obliged me to promise not to make you a parting scene.

GERARDO: I simply cannot take you with me.

HELEN: Oh, God! I knew you would say that! I knew it when I came here. That's what you say to every woman. And I am just one of a hundred. I know it. But, Oscar, I am lovesick; I am dying of love. This is your work, and you can save me without any sacrifice on your part, without assuming any burden. Why can't you do it?

GERARDO: [*Very slowly*] Because my contract forbids me to marry or to travel in the company of a woman.

HELEN: [*Disturbed*] What can prevent you?

GERARDO: My contract.

HELEN: You cannot . . .

GERARDO: I cannot marry until my contract expires.

HELEN: And you cannot . . .

GERARDO: I cannot travel in the company of a woman.

HELEN: That is incredible. And whom in the world should it concern?

GERARDO: My manager.

HELEN: Your manager! What business is it of his?

GERARDO: It is precisely his business.

HELEN: Is it perhaps because it might—affect your voice?

GERARDO: Yes.

HELEN: That is preposterous. Does it affect your voice?

[Gerardo *chuckles*]

HELEN: Does your manager believe that nonsense?

GERARDO: No, he doesn't.

HELEN: This is beyond me. I can't understand how a decent man could sign such a contract.

GERARDO: I am an artist first and a man next.

HELEN: Yes, that's what you are—a great artist—an eminent artist. Can't you understand how much I must love you? You are the first man whose superiority I have felt and whom I desired to please, and you despise me for it. I have bitten my lips many a time not to let you suspect how much you meant to me; I was so afraid I might bore you. Yesterday, however, put me in a state of mind which no woman can endure. If I didn't love you so insanely, Oscar, you would think more of me. That is the terrible thing about you—that you must scorn a woman who thinks the world of you.

GERARDO: Helen!

HELEN: Your contract! Don't use your contract as a weapon to murder me with. Let me go with you, Oscar. You will see if your manager ever mentions a breach of contract. He would not do such a thing. I know men. And if he says a word, it will be time then for me to die.

GERARDO: We have no right to do that, Helen. You are just as little free to follow me, as I am to shoulder such a responsibility. I don't belong to myself; I belong to my art.

HELEN: Oh, leave your art alone. What do I care about your art? Has God created a man like you to make a puppet of himself every night? You should be ashamed of it instead of boasting of it. You see, I overlooked the fact that you were merely an artist. What wouldn't I overlook for a god like you? Even if you were a convict, Oscar, my feelings would be the same. I would lie in the dust at your feet and beg for your pity. I would face death as I am facing it now.

GERARDO: [Laughing] Facing death, Helen! Women who are endowed with your gifts for enjoying life don't make away with themselves. You know even better than I do the value of life.

HELEN: [Dreamily] Oscar, I didn't say that I would shoot myself. When did I say that? Where would I find the courage to do that? I only said that I will die, if you don't take me with you. I will die as I would of an illness, for I only live when I am with you. I can live without my home, without my children, but not without you, Oscar. I cannot live without you.

GERARDO: Helen, if you don't calm yourself. . . . You put me in an awful position. . . . I have only ten minutes left. . . . I can't explain in court that your excitement made me break my contract. . . . I can only give you ten minutes. . . . If you don't calm yourself in that time . . . I can't leave you alone in this condition. Think all you have at stake!

HELEN: As though I had anything else at stake!

GERARDO: You can lose your position in society.

HELEN: I can lose you!

GERARDO: And your family

HELEN: I care for no one but you.

GERARDO: But I cannot be yours.

HELEN: Then I have nothing to lose but my life.

GERARDO: Your children!

HELEN: Who has taken me from them, Oscar? Who has taken me from my children?

GERARDO: Did I make any advances to you?

HELEN: [Passionately] No, no. I have thrown myself at you, and would throw myself at you again. Neither my husband nor my children could keep me back. When I die, at least I will have lived:

thanks to you, Oscar! I thank you, Oscar, for revealing me to myself. I thank you for that.

GERARDO: Helen, calm yourself and listen to me.

HELEN: Yes, yes, for ten minutes.

GERARDO: Listen to me. [Both sit down on the divan]

HELEN: [Staring at him] Yes, I thank you for it.

GERARDO: Helen!

HELEN: I don't even ask you to love me. Let me only breathe the air you breathe.

GERARDO: [Trying to be calm] Helen—a man of my type cannot be swayed by any of the bourgeois ideas. I have known society women in every country of the world. Some made parting scenes to me, but at least they all knew what they owed to their position. This is the first time in my life that I have witnessed such an outburst of passion. . . . Helen, the temptation comes to me daily to step with some woman into an idyllic Arcadia. But every human being has his duties; you have your duties as I have mine, and the call of duty is the highest thing in the world. . . .

HELEN: I know better than you do what the highest duty is.

GERARDO: What, then? Your love for me? That's what they all say. Whatever a woman has set her heart on winning is to her good; whatever crosses her plans is evil. It is the fault of our playwrights. To draw full houses they set the world upside down, and when a woman abandons her children and her family to follow her instincts they call that—oh, broad-mindedness. I personally wouldn't mind living the way turtle doves live. But since I am a part of this world I must obey my duty first. Then whenever the opportunity arises I quaff of the cup of joy. Whoever refuses to do his duty has no right to make any demands upon another fellow being.

HELEN: [Staring absent-mindedly] That does not bring the dead back to life.

GERARDO: [Nervously] Helen, I will give you back your life. I will give you back what you have sacrificed for me. For God's sake take it. What does it come to, after all? Helen, how can a woman lower herself to that point? Where is your pride? What am I in the eyes of the world? A man who makes a puppet of himself every night! Helen, are you going to kill yourself for a man whom hundreds of women loved before you, whom hundreds of women will love after you without letting their feelings disturb their life one second? Will you, by shedding your warm blood, make yourself ridiculous before God and the world?

HELEN: [Looking away from him] I know I am asking a good deal, but—what else can I do?

GERARDO: Helen, you said I should bear the consequences of my acts. Will you reproach me for not refusing to receive you when you first came here, ostensibly to ask me to try your voice? What can a man do in such a case? You are the beauty of this town. Either I would be known as the bear among artists who denies himself to all women callers, or I might have received you and pretended that I didn't understand what you meant and then pass for a fool. Or the very first day I might have talked to you as frankly as I am talking now. Dangerous business. You would have called me a conceited idiot. Tell me, Helen—what else could I do?

HELEN: [*Staring at him with imploring eyes, shuddering and making an effort to speak*] O God! O God! Oscar, what would you say if to-morrow I should go and be as happy with another man as I have been with you? Oscar—what would you say?

GERARDO: [*After a silence*] Nothing. [*He looks at his watch*] Helen—

HELEN: Oscar! [*She kneels before him*] For the last time, I implore you. . . . You don't know what you are doing. . . . It isn't your fault—but don't let me die. . . . Save me—save me!

GERARDO: [*Raising her up*] Helen, I am not such a wonderful man. How many men have you known? The more men you come to know, the lower all men will fall in your estimation. When you know men better you will not take your life for any one of them. You will not think any more of them than I do of women.

HELEN: I am not like you in that respect.

GERARDO: I speak earnestly, Helen. We don't fall in love with one person or another; we fall in love with our type, which we find everywhere in the world if we only look sharply enough.

HELEN: And when we meet our type, are we sure then of being loved again?

GERARDO: [*Angrily*] You have no right to complain of your husband. Was any girl ever compelled to marry against her will? That is all rot. It is only the women who have sold themselves for certain material advantages and then try to dodge their obligations who try to make us believe that nonsense.

HELEN: [*Smiling*] They break their contracts.

GERARDO: [*Pounding his chest*] When I sell myself at least I am honest about it.

HELEN: Isn't love honest?

GERARDO: No! Love is a beastly bourgeois virtue. Love is the last refuge of the mollycoddle, of the coward. In my world every man has his actual value, and when two human beings make up a pact they know exactly what to expect from each other. Love has nothing to do with it, either.

HELEN: Won't you lead me into your world, then?

GERARDO: Helen, will you compromise the happiness of your life and the happiness of your dear ones for just a few days' pleasure?

HELEN: No.

GERARDO: [*Much relieved*] Will you promise me to go home quietly now?

HELEN: Yes.

GERARDO: And will you promise me that you will not die. . . .

HELEN: Yes.

GERARDO: You promise me that?

HELEN: Yes.

GERARDO: And you promise me to fulfill your duties as mother and—as wife?

HELEN: Yes.

GERARDO: Helen!

HELEN: Yes. What else do you want? I will promise anything.

GERARDO: And now may I go away in peace?

HELEN: [*Rising*] Yes.

GERARDO: A last kiss?

HELEN: Yes, yes, yes. [*They kiss passionately*]

GERARDO: In a year I am booked again to sing here, Helen.

HELEN: In a year! Oh, I am glad!

GERARDO: [*Tenderly*] Helen!

[Helen *presses his hand, takes a revolver out of her muff, shoots herself and falls*]

GERARDO: Helen! [*He totters and collapses in an armchair*]

BELL BOY: [*Rushing in*] My God! Mr. Gerardo! [Gerardo *remains motionless; the* Bell Boy *rushes toward* Helen]

GERARDO: [*Jumping up, running to the door and colliding with the manager of the hotel*] Send for the police! I must be arrested! If I went away now I should be a brute, and if I stay I break my contract. I still have [*Looking at his watch*] One minute and ten seconds.

MANAGER: Fred, run and get a policeman.

BELL BOY: All right, sir.

MANAGER: Be quick about it. [*To Gerardo*] Don't take it too hard, sir. Those things happen once in a while.

GERARDO: [*Kneeling before* Helen's *body and taking her hand*] Helen! . . . She still lives—she still lives! If I am arrested I am not wilfully breaking my contract. . . . And my trunks? Is the carriage at the door?

MANAGER: It has been waiting twenty minutes, Mr. Gerardo. [*He opens the door for the porter, who takes down one of the trunks*]

GERARDO: [*Bending over her*] Helen! [*To himself*] Well, after all. . . . [*To Muller*] Have you called a doctor?

MANAGER: Yes, we had the doctor called at once. He will be here at any minute.

GERARDO: [*Holding her under the arms*] Helen! Don't you know me any more? Helen! The doctor will be here right away, Helen. This is your Oscar.

BELL BOY: [*Appearing in the door at the center*] Can't find any policeman, sir.

GERARDO: [*Letting* Helen's *body drop back*] Well, if I can't get arrested, that settles it. I must catch that train and sing in Brussels to-morrow night. [*He takes up his score and runs out through the center door, bumping against several chairs*]

CURTAIN

Leo Nikolayevich Tolstoy

(1828–1910)

Although Tolstoy is best known to the world as a novelist, his genius can also be legitimately claimed by the theatre, for the author of *War and Peace* and *Anna Karenina* is the dramatist of *The Power of Darkness* and of other more or less distinguished works for the stage. It was with the 1888 production of *The Power of Darkness* that the Théâtre Libre and its director Antoine had their epoch-making debut as an international influence instead of remaining a local phenomenon in Paris. The French saw this peasant tragedy even before *Ghosts,* and it made a deeper impression than Ibsen's play on France's pioneer in dramatic realism, Henry Becque. Since Otto Brahm also staged the play a year later in his Freie Bühne in Berlin, Tolstoy's drama was quickly established as a classic of the progressive naturalistic movement in Western Europe. The greater part of the author's lifetime lay behind the composition of *The Power of Darkness.* Tolstoy was able to fill it with all the understanding of the peasantry that he had amassed in the course of a varied career as a landowner, writer, and social reformer.

Tolstoy's restless spirit carried him through a period of wayward university studies, furious dissipations, experiments in scientific farming, and military adventures in the Caucasus Mountains before he became a professional writer with the publication of his first book, *Childhood* (1852). Two years later, he enlarged his reputation with his realistic *Sevastopol* sketches inspired by the Crimean war, during which he had commanded an exposed bastion at the siege of Sevastopol. Disillusioned with war and his military career, he retired to private life, published the second and third parts of his autobiographical novel *Childhood, Boyhood, and Youth,* traveled extensively in Europe, and finally settled down on his estate, Yasnaya Polyana (1860). Here he devoted himself to educating the children of the peasantry with modern methods, and he made an unsuccessful attempt to convert his serfs into free farmers. Upon marrying the eighteen-year-old daughter of a physician in 1862, he threw himself wholeheartedly into domestic life, rearing a large family of sons and daughters. For a period of some sixteen years Tolstoy led a life that any man of letters could have envied—a useful and essentially unclouded life, during which he turned out such masterpieces as *War and Peace* (1865–1869) and *Anna Karenina* (1875–1877).

In 1876, however, Tolstoy lost his confidence in the values that had brought him gratifications as a family man and artist. Shocked by the death of a brother into reviewing the meaning of his life, he began to search for spiritual comfort and moral direction. He embraced religion with such fervor that before long he found himself excommunicated by the Greek Orthodox Church for propounding heretical doctrines, and he became an apostle of a highly idealistic faith that brought him into conflict with the state and his own family as well as with the Russian Church. Resolved to communicate his views to the common man, he began to write instructive stories for the peasantry and tracts for the educated classes, such as *What Then Must We Do?*, in which he condemned war, private property, and the economic exploitation of man by man. The stories were beautiful folk tales, although there is no evidence that they made much impression on the largely illiterate public for which they were intended; but the tracts brought Tolstoy a horde of disciples, among them Romain Rolland and Gandhi. "Tolstoyism," with its doctrine of pacifism and passive resistance, absorbed much of its author's time and energy. His creative faculties, however, were not materially diminished by his crusading activities, and it is to this reformist period, which lasted until his death, that we owe the great novelist's contributions to the theatre.

Tolstoy wrote *The Power of Darkness* in 1886, mastering a new medium. Playwriting continued to be one of his strong interests in close to two and a half decades of writing, of attempting to pattern his life after unworldly Christian principles, and of quarreling with a hysterical wife embittered by his effort to divest himself of earthly possessions and well-earned royalties. When he died on November 8, 1910, after running away from home in his eighty-second year, he left a collection of dramatic work which is impressive even if it ranks below his greatest novels. In 1889 appeared his satirical comedy about the bumbling aristocracy, *The Fruits of Enlightenment,* which Bernard Shaw, writing in 1921, called "the first of the Heartbreak Houses." It anticipated by a decade Chekhov's obituaries on the Russian upper classes.

The rest of Tolstoy's dramatic work awaited posthumous publication. *The Cause of It All,* a short drama with which he had hoped to wean the peasantry from vodka, is considerably more poignant than most problem dramas, and the Enoch Arden play *The Living Corpse* has had many successful productions under a variety of titles. (It is better known in America as *Redemption,* the title under which it was produced in 1919 with John Barrymore in the role of the ne'er-do-well who pretends to be dead in order to relieve his wife of his presence.) Finally, Tolstoy left an uncompleted masterpiece patterned after his own idealistic efforts and inner contradictions, *The Light That Shines in Darkness,* the last act of which exists only in outline.

The Power of Darkness contains all the vibrancy of humanization that makes Tolstoy one of the major writers of all time. He brought to bear on the drama all the heavy artillery we associate with "naturalism"—the raw passions, the sordid life and action, and the authentic colloquial speech upon which the naturalists prided themselves. Tolstoy, however, did not write according to any of their practices, or, for that matter, according to the practices of any of his predecessors in the modern theatre. Dramatic technique was not even a practical calculation in his case, as he had never had an opportunity to see his earlier plays on the stage. He did not, for example, pay any particular attention to the art of concentration that Ibsen started refining with *A Doll's House; The Power of Darkness* starts fully two acts before the "point of attack" that the Norwegian dramatist would have chosen. (Tolstoy, indeed, expressed no particular fondness for Ibsen; he liked neither Ibsen's *An Enemy of the People* nor *When We Dead Awaken,* according to the Moscow Art Theatre's codirector, Dantchenko.) Nor did he seem aware of the "fourth-wall convention," which would have made him avoid soliloquies. Scene after scene in *The Power of Darkness* is a triumph of dramatic art without the least exertion of theatrical virtuosity, because here, as in Tolstoy's best fiction, the thing felt is also the thing plainly spoken and clearly seen. Drama in *The Power of Darkness* was only a specialization of the qualities of genius present in his narrative writing. In one important respect, moreover, he could have no traffic with the theorists and practitioners of naturalism: he was constitutionally, as well as in principle, incapable of viewing men as animalcules conveniently placed under the lens of a microscope. For all the lusts of the flesh, man for Tolstoy was a spiritual entity in a universe ruled by spirit. Like all true tragedy, his great play affirms the distinctive humanity of the species.

Nevertheless, *The Power of Darkness* is no more an exercise in easy optimism than it is a preachment pure and simple. It is "the power of darkness" that constitutes the basis of the play, and the light of redemption with which it glows in the last act not only needs the "darkness" to set it off but would have been dramatically ineffective without it. Whereas the naturalistic scientism, for which Zola proselytized so zealously, produced mostly cold-storage passions, Tolstoy's natural energy infused his drama with burning life.

It is not farfetched to believe that had Russia developed a free theatre early enough to attract Tolstoy's allegiance, the world would have been the richer by several dramatic masterpieces. In his most creative years, he could hope at most for amateur productions, for even the representation of mild intellectual revolt and feminism in *The Progressives,* which he read to friends in 1865, was enough to prevent its production in Russia. Tolstoy had no stage to write for until the advent of the Moscow Art Theatre, by which time he was already an aged man, a harassed zealot, and an institution.

Stanislavsky and Dantchenko produced *The Power of Darkness* at their Art Theatre in their fifth season, on November 5, 1902, after some remarkable experiences when they brought a peasant woman from the provinces to help them stage the play with maximum authenticity. (She proved to be so realistic in every role she was given that she made the rest of the great Moscow cast seem woefully unauthentic.) Some seven years earlier, Tolstoy had said to Stanislavsky, who had given an amateur production of *The Fruits of Enlightenment,* "Make an old man happy; free *The Power of Darkness* from censorship and play it," and he proceeded to discuss revisions for the stage production. But when the Art Theatre's production eventuated, it had too much surface naturalism. Stanislavsky himself expressed dissatisfaction with the staging of the drama in later years because it failed to fuse the detailed village realism "with the more important line of the intuition of feelings." It was only with the staging of *The Living Corpse* that the Art Theatre did justice to Tolstoy's genius, and this took place on September 23, 1911, after the author's death.

In conclusion, it should be noted that after *The Power of Darkness* had been sent to press, Tolstoy wrote variant scenes for the end of Act IV upon being informed that the original ending would be too gruesome in the theatre. Candidly confessing to ignorance of the practical theatre, he even requested the young Stanislavsky to assist him in combining the two variants to the greatest advantage. These scenes appear on pages 196–199, and it will be apparent to the reader that Tolstoy, in the hope of seeing his play staged, effected a compromise without the least sacrifice of artistic integrity and dramatic force. The scene which merely reports the murder of the infant is the one which has been used in most productions.

BIBLIOGRAPHY: Vladimir Nemirovitch-Dantchenko, *My Life in the Russian Theatre* (English translation, 1936), pp. 338–340, 343–441; Aylmer Maude, *Life of Tolstoy,* 1910; George R. Noyes, *Tolstoy,* 1918; Ernest J. Simmons, *Leo Tolstoy,* 1946; Constantin Stanislavsky, *My Life in Art* (English translation, 1924), pp. 217–225, 400–403.

THE POWER OF DARKNESS

By Leo Nikolayevich Tolstoy

TRANSLATED FROM THE RUSSIAN BY
GEORGE RAPALL NOYES AND GEORGE Z. PATRICK

CHARACTERS

PETR, *a rich peasant, forty-two years old, married for a second time, in poor health*

ANISYA, *his wife, thirty-two years old, smartly dressed (in Acts I and II)*

AKULINA, *daughter of* Petr *by his first marriage, sixteen years old, hard of hearing and feeble-minded*

ANYUTKA, *daughter of* Petr *and* Anisya, *ten years old*

NIKITA, *their workman, twenty-five years old, smartly dressed*

AKIM, *father of* Nikita, *fifty years old, a pious peasant, unattractive in external appearance*

MATRENA, *his wife, fifty years old*

MARINA, *an orphan girl, twenty-two years old*

FRIEND *of* Anisya

MARFA, *sister of* Petr

MITRICH, *an old laborer, a soldier retired because of age*

NEIGHBOR *(woman)*

MATCHMAKER *(man). a glum peasant*

HUSBAND *of* Marina

FIRST GIRL

SECOND GIRL

POLICEMAN

COACHMAN

MATCHMAKER *(woman)*

BRIDEGROOM *of* Akulina

BEST MAN *(at wedding)*

VILLAGE ELDER

Peasants: men, women, and girls

ACT I.

The action takes place in autumn in a large peasant village. The stage represents Petr's *spacious cottage.* Petr *is seated on a bench, repairing a horse-collar.* Anisya *and* Akulina *are spinning and singing together.*

PETR: [*Glancing out of the window*] The horses have got loose again. They'll kill the colt before you know it. Nikita! Hey, Nikita! He's deaf! [*Listens for a moment. To the women*] Keep still, will you! I can't hear anything.

NIKITA: [*From the yard, off stage*] What?

PETR: Drive in the horses.

NIKITA: [*Same*] I'll drive 'em in. Give me time.

PETR: [*Shaking his head*] Drat these hired men! If I was well, I'd never think of keeping one. They do nothing but make trouble. [*Rises and sits down again*] Nikita! I can't make him hear.— One of you go, will you? Akulina, go and drive 'em in.

AKULINA: The horses?

PETR: What do you suppose?

AKULINA: Right away. [*Goes out*]

PETR: The fellow's a loafer, no good on the farm. If he'd only stir himself!

ANISYA: You're mighty spry yourself—just crawl from the stove to the bench. All you do is boss the rest of us.

PETR: If I didn't boss you, the whole farm'd be ruined in a year. Oh, what a lot you are!

ANISYA: You give us a dozen jobs and then growl. It's easy to lie on the stove and give orders.

PETR: [*Sighing*] Oh, if this sickness didn't have hold of me, I wouldn't keep him for a day.

AKULINA: [*Off stage*] Shoo! shoo! shoo! [*One can hear the colt whinny and the horses run into the yard. The gate creaks*]

PETR: Fancy talk is all he's good for. Honest, I wouldn't keep him.

ANISYA: [*Mimicking him*] "I won't keep him." If you'd only get a move on yourself, you might talk.

AKULINA: [*Coming in*] I had hard work to drive 'em in. The roan kept—

PETR: Where's that Nikita?

AKULINA: Nikita? He's standing in the street.

PETR: What's he standing there for?

AKULINA: What for? He's standing round the corner and chatting.

PETR: Can't get sense out of her! Who's he chatting with?

AKULINA: [*Not catching his words*] What?

[Petr *brandishes his arm at* Akulina; *she sits down at her spinning*]

ANYUTKA: [*Running in. To her mother*] Nikita's father and mother have come to see him. They're taking him home to marry him—just think!

ANISYA: Aren't you lying?

ANYUTKA: Honest and true, may I die if it ain't! [*Laughs*] I was going by, and Nikita says to me: "Now good-by, young lady," he says; "come and have some fun at my wedding. I'm leaving you," he says. And then he just laughed.

ANISYA: [*To her husband*] Folks haven't much need of you. You see he was getting ready to leave himself. And you were saying: "I'll turn him out"!

PETR: Let him go; can't I find other men?

175

ANISYA: But haven't you paid him in advance?

[Anyutka *goes toward the door, listens to their words for a moment, and goes out*]

PETR: [*Frowning*] He can work off the money next summer if necessary.

ANISYA: Yes, you're glad to let him go—one less mouth to feed. But during the winter I'll have to tend to things all alone, like a work horse. The girl ain't awful eager to work, and you'll just lie on the stove. I know you!

PETR: What's the use of wagging your tongue for nothing when you ain't heard anything yet?

ANISYA: The place is crowded with the animals. You haven't sold the cow and you've taken in all the sheep for the winter—it'll be hard enough to store up feed for all of 'em, and to water 'em. And now you want to let the hired man go. I won't do a man's work! I'll lie down on the stove just like you and let things go to smash—and you can do what you please about it.

PETR: [*To* Akulina] Go for the fodder, will you? It's time.

AKULINA: For the fodder? All right. [*Puts on her coat and takes a rope*]

ANISYA: I won't work for you. I've had enough of it—I won't! Work for yourself.

PETR: Shut up! What are you mad about? You're like a wet hen.

ANISYA: You're a mad dog yourself! There's no work or joy to be got out of you. You're just sucking the life out of me. A mad dog, that's what you are.

PETR: [*Spits and puts on his coat*] Plague take you—Lord forgive me! I'll go and find out how things are. [*Goes out*]

ANISYA: [*Shouts after him*] Rotten, long-nosed devil!

AKULINA: What are you scolding dad for?

ANISYA: Shut up, you fool!

AKULINA: [*Going toward the door*] I know what you're scolding him for. You're a fool yourself, you cur. I ain't afraid of you.

ANISYA: What's that? [*Jumps up and looks for something with which to strike her*] Look out or I'll take the poker to you.

AKULINA: [*Opening the door*] You're a cur, you're a devil; that's what you are. Devil, cur, cur, devil! [*Runs out*]

ANISYA: [*Meditates*] "Come to the wedding," says he. So that's what they're up to—marrying him? Look out, Nikita, if that's your doings, I'll have my say too. . . . I can't live without him. I won't let him go.

NIKITA: [*Comes in and glances about. Seeing that* Anisya *is alone, he approaches her quickly. Whispers*] Well, my girl, I'm in trouble! My father's come and wants to take me away—tells me I must go home. "We're marrying you off for good and all," says he, "and you'll have to stay at home."

ANISYA: Well then, marry. What do I care?

NIKITA: Oh, re-ally! I thought it'd be better to talk things over; but this is what he says: he tells me I must marry. What does this mean? [*Winks*] Have you forgotten?

ANISYA: Go ahead and marry. You needn't—

NIKITA: What are you snorting at? You won't even let me pet you a bit.—Well, what's wrong with you?

ANISYA: I think you want to desert me. And if you do want to desert me, then I've no use for you either. That's the whole story!

NIKITA: Oh, stop, Anisya. Do you think I want to forget you?—Not so long as I live. So I won't leave you for good and all. This is the way I figure it; let 'em marry me, but then I'll come back to you—if only they don't make me stay at home.

ANISYA: Much I'll care for you if you're married.

NIKITA: But remember, my dear girl: I simply can't go against my father's will.

ANISYA: You put the blame on your father, but the scheme's your own. You've been plotting for a long time with your sweetheart, with Marina. She put you up to this. She didn't run over here the other day for nothing.

NIKITA: Marina? Much I care for her! . . . Many of her kind fall for me!

ANISYA: Why did your father come? You told him to! You've been deceiving me! [*Weeps*]

NIKITA: Anisya, do you believe in God or not? I never even dreamed of any such thing. Honestly I never thought of it. My old man made the plan out of his own head.

ANISYA: If you don't want to get married your self, can any one pull you to it like a jackass?

NIKITA: All the same, I figure a fellow can't oppose his father. And I don't want to.

ANISYA: Just say you won't, and stick to it.

NIKITA: One fellow refused, and they thrashed him in the village jail. Then he understood. I don't want to go through that. I tell you, it's ticklish.

ANISYA: Quit your fooling. Listen, Nikita: if you're going to marry Marina, I don't know what I'll do to myself. . . . I'll kill myself! I've sinned and broken the law, but now I can't turn back. Just as soon as you leave me, I'll do it.

NIKITA: Why should I leave? If I wanted to leave I'd have gone long ago. The other day Ivan Semenych offered me a job as coachman . . . and what an easy life! Yet I didn't take it. I think that everybody likes me. If you didn't love me, I'd act differently.

ANISYA: Just remember this. The old man may die any day; then I think we can cover up all our sins. I've planned to marry you; then you'll be the master of the house.

NIKITA: No use guessing. What do I care? I do the work as if it was for my own self. The master likes me, and his wife—well, she's in love with me. And if women love me, I'm not to blame; it's a simple matter.

ANISYA: Will you love me?

NIKITA: [*Embracing her*] Just this way! You've always been in my heart.

[Matrena *comes in and for some time stands before the ikon in the corner of the room, crossing herself.* Nikita *and* Anisya *move away from each other*]

MATRENA: Oh, what I've seen, I didn't see; what I've heard, I didn't hear. Been having fun with a nice little woman, have you? What of it? Even calves have their fun, you know. Why shouldn't you? You're still young. But the master is asking for you in the yard, my son.

NIKITA: I came in to get the ax.

MATRENA: I know, my boy; I know what sort of an ax you came for. You're likely to find that kind near a woman.

NIKITA: [*Bends down and picks up an ax*] Well, mother, are you really going to marry me? I think there's no reason for that at all. And then I don't want to marry.

MATRENA: Oh, my darling, why should we marry you? You're living and having a good time; it's only the old man's plan. Go ahead, my boy; we'll settle the whole business without your help.

NIKITA: This is queer: first you want to marry me, and then you say there's no need of it. I can't understand things at all. [*Goes out*]

ANISYA: Well, Auntie Matrena, do you really want to marry him?

MATRENA: Why should we marry him, my precious? You know what our family's like. My old man keeps mumbling foolish stuff: "Marry him, must marry him." But he hasn't enough sense to judge. Horses don't run away from oats, you know, men don't quit one good thing for another: that's the way to look at it. Don't I see [*Winks*] the turn things are taking?

ANISYA: It's no use for me to hide from you, Auntie Matrena. You know everything. I have sinned; I have fallen in love with your son.

MATRENA: Well, this is news! And Auntie Matrena didn't know! Oh, girlie, Auntie Matrena is an old bird, a sly old bird. Auntie Matrena, I can tell you, darling, can see a yard underground. I know everything, precious! I know why young wives need sleeping powders. I've brought some. [*Unties a corner of her kerchief and takes out a packet of powders*] What I need to, I see; and what I don't need to, I don't know and don't want to know. That's the way. Auntie Matrena was young once herself. I've had to find out how to live with my own fool, you see. I know the whole seventy-seven tricks. I see your old man's withering away, darling, withering away. What sort of life can you have? Stick a pitchfork into him and the blood won't flow. I tell you: you'll be burying him next spring!

You must get some one else to be the boss. And ain't my son up to the job? He's no worse than others. So what use would it be for me to pull my son away from a good soft place? Am I my own child's enemy?

ANISYA: If only he don't leave us!

MATRENA: He won't leave you, birdie. That's all nonsense. You know my old man. His wits are all gone by now; but sometimes, when he gets a notion into his noodle, you can't knock it out with a mallet.

ANISYA: But how did the business start?

MATRENA: You see, darling; you know yourself the lad is daft on women; and he's handsome too, I must say. Well, he was living on the railroad, you know, and there they had an orphan girl as cook. Well, that hussy began to chase after him.

ANISYA: Marina?

MATRENA: Yes, plague take her! Well, whether anything happened or not, my old man only knows. Whether people talked, or whether the girl herself got round him—

ANISYA: What impudence, the bold thing!

MATRENA: So my silly old fool got on his ear and kept saying: "We must marry him, marry him to cover up the sin. Let's take the lad home," says he, "and marry him." I argued all I could, but it was no use. "All right," thinks I, "I'll play another game." You have to know how to manage those fools, darling. Just pretend to agree, but when the time comes you can turn things your own way. You know a woman can fly up in the air and think seven and seventy thoughts, and how's a man to guess 'em! "Well, old man," says I, "it's a good plan, but we must think it over. Let's go call on our son," says I, "and ask the advice of Petr Ignatych. Let's see what he'll say." So we've come.

ANISYA: Oh, auntie, how's this? What if his father orders him?

MATRENA: Orders him? Stick his orders under a dog's tail! Don't you worry: this thing won't come off. I'll talk over the whole business with your old man right away; I'll sift it so there won't be anything left of it. I came along just to fix it up. Think of it: my son's living in happiness and expecting more—and I'm to marry him off to a vagabond girl! Do you think I'm a fool?

ANISYA: She's even been running over here to see him, that Marina.—Will you believe it, auntie: when they told me he was to be married, I felt a knife run through my heart? I thought that his heart was with her.

MATRENA: Eh, darling! Do you think he's a fool? He's not the man to love a homeless trollop. Nikita, you know, is a lad of some sense. He knows whom it's worth while to love. And don't you worry, darling. We'll never take him away as long as he lives. And we won't marry him. Just hand us a little money, and we'll let him stay here.

ANISYA: If Nikita left, I think I'd die.

MATRENA: Yes, you're young. Hard lines! For a

woman like you, fresh and rosy, to live with that old scarecrow—

ANISYA: Believe me, auntie, I'm sick to death of that man of mine, that long-nosed cur; I don't want ever to see him again.

MATRENA: Yes, such is your lot. But look here. [*In a whisper, glancing around*] I went to that old man for powders, you know, and he gave me two different kinds. Just look here. "This is a sleeping powder," says he. "Give him one of 'em," says he, "and he'll fall asleep so sound you could walk on him. And this," says he "is a sort that she must have him drink—there's no smell to it, but it's awful strong. Give it seven times over," says he, "one pinch at a time. Give it to him seven times. And then," says he, "she'll soon be free from him."

ANISYA: Oh ho ho! What's that!

MATRENA: "It won't leave any traces," says he. He charged a whole ruble. "Can't let you have 'em for less," says he, "for it's hard to get 'em, you know." I paid my own money for 'em, darling. I thought you could use 'em; if you can't, I'll take 'em to Mikhaylovna.

ANISYA: Oh! oh! But maybe there's something bad about 'em.

MATRENA: What's bad about it, darling? It'd be different if your man was in strong health, but now he just makes a bluff at being alive. He don't belong to the living, he don't. There are a lot of men like him.

ANISYA: Oh! oh! poor me! Auntie, I'm afraid it may be sinful. Oh, what have I come to!

MATRENA: I can take 'em back.

ANISYA: Do you dissolve the second sort in water, like the others?

MATRENA: It's better in tea, he says. "You don't notice 'em at all," he says, "there's no smell to 'em, not a bit." He's a clever man.

ANISYA: [*Taking the powders*] Oh! oh! poor me! I'd never meddle with such things if my life wasn't a torment worse than prison.

MATRENA: And don't forget the ruble; I promised to take it to the old man. He has troubles of his own.

ANISYA: Sure! [*Goes to the chest and hides the powders*]

MATRENA: And keep 'em tight, darling, so that people won't know. And if he finds 'em—God forbid!—say that they're for cockroaches. [*Takes the ruble*] They're good for cockroaches too. . . . [*Stops suddenly*]

[Akim *comes in and crosses himself before the ikon;* Petr *comes in and sits down*]

PETR: Well, how goes it, Uncle Akim?

AKIM: A bit better, Ignatych, a bit better, y'see; a bit better. Because I was afraid that there might— Foolery, you know. I'd like, y'see, I'd like to get the lad down to business. And if you'd agree, y'see, then we might. It'd be better if—

PETR: All right, all right. Sit down and let's talk.

[Akim *sits down*] Well then? So you want to marry him?

MATRENA: We can wait about marrying him, Petr Ignatych. You know how hard up we are, Ignatych. If we marry him, we can't make a living ourselves. How can we marry him!

PETR: Decide for yourselves what's better.

MATRENA: Well, there's no haste about the marrying. It'll wait. She's no raspberry; she won't fall off the bush.

PETR: Of course, it'd be a good thing if you married him.

AKIM: I'd like to, y'see. Because, y'see, I've some work in town; I struck a good job, y'see.

MATRENA: Fine job! Cleaning cesspools. When he came home the other day, I puked and puked. Ugh!

AKIM: That's true; at first it just knocks you over, y'see, the smell of it. But when you get used to it, it's no worse than malt dregs, and after all it suits me. And about the smell, y'see— Men like me needn't mind it. And then we can change our clothes.— I wanted to have Nikita at home, you know; he can tend to things there. He can tend to things at home, and I'll make some money in town, y'see.

PETR: You want to keep your son at home: very well then. But how about the pay he took in advance?

AKIM: That's right, Ignatych, that's right; you told the truth there, y'see. He's hired himself out and sold himself, so let the bargain stand. But we must just marry him, y'see; so you just let him off for a while.

PETR: Well, that's possible.

MATRENA: But we two don't agree about it. Petr Ignatych, I'll tell you the truth as I'd tell it to God. You judge between me and my old man. He keeps saying, "Marry him, marry him." But marry him to whom, may I ask? If she was a decent girl, I'd not stand in my boy's way, but she's a low-lived hussy.

AKIM: That's all wrong. You're wrong in slandering the girl, y'see; you're wrong. Because she— that girl, I say—has been injured by my son; she's been injured, I tell you. The girl has, you know.

PETR: What was the injury?

AKIM: She got mixed up with my son, Nikita, y'see. With Nikita, you know.

MATRENA: Don't you speak of it; my tongue's softer, I'll tell the story. Before he came to you, you know, our lad was living on the railroad. And there a girl got hold of him; you know, a stupid hussy named Marina—she was cook for the railroad gang. So she accused him, that hussy did, our own son, and said that it was he, Nikita, that deceived her.

PETR: That's a bad business.

MATRENA: But she's a low-lived creature herself, runs after the men. She's just a streetwalker.

AKIM: Old woman, you're telling wrong stories again, y'see; it ain't a bit so. I tell you it ain't, y'see.

MATRENA: All my old boy can say is, "y'see,

y'see"; but what he means by it he don't know himself. Don't ask me about the hussy, Petr Ignatych, ask other folks; anybody'll tell you. She's just a homeless vagrant.

PETR: [*To Akim*] Well, Uncle Akim, if that's the case, then there's no use marrying him. The business ain't an old shoe that you can kick off by making him marry her.

AKIM: [*Getting excited*] It's an injury to the girl, y'see, old woman, an injury, y'see. Because the girl is a very decent sort, y'see, a very decent sort; and I'm sorry for her, sorry for the girl, you know.

MATRENA: You're just like a silly old woman; you waste your sorrow on the whole world, while your own folks go hungry. You're sorry for the girl, but you ain't sorry for your son. Tie her round your own neck and walk with her! Quit talking nonsense!

AKIM: No, it ain't nonsense.

MATRENA: Don't you get on your ear: I'll say my say.

AKIM: [*Interrupting*] No, it ain't nonsense. You turn things your own way—maybe about the girl, maybe about yourself—you turn things your own way, as it's best for you; but, y'see, God will turn 'em his way. That's how it stands.

MATRENA: Bah! No use wasting words on you.

AKIM: The girl's a hard worker, a decent sort, and she knows how to look out for herself, y'see. And we're poor, and she'll be an extra hand, y'see; and the wedding won't cost much. But the main thing's the injury done the girl, you know; she's an orphan, y'see, the girl is. And she's been injured.

MATRENA: Any girl'd say that.

ANISYA: Just you listen to us women, Uncle Akim. We can tell you things.

AKIM: But God, I tell you, God! Ain't she a human being, that girl? So, y'see, God cares for her. What do you think about that?

MATRENA: Oh, he's off again!

PETR: See here, Uncle Akim, you can't much believe those hussies either. And the lad's alive. He's close by! Let's send and ask him straight out whether it's true. He won't perjure his soul. Call the lad here! [*Anisya rises*] Tell him his father's calling for him. [*Anisya goes out*]

MATRENA: You've settled the business, my dear, you've cleaned it up: let the lad speak for himself. And these times you can't marry off a lad by force. We must ask him what he thinks. He'll never want to marry her and shame himself. What I think is: he'd better stay with you and work for his master. Even in summer we won't need to take him; we can hire somebody. Just give us ten rubles and he can stay here.

PETR: We'll talk about that later: take things in order. Finish one job before you start another.

AKIM: I'm talking this way, Petr Ignatych, you know, because such things happen sometimes, y'see. You keep trying to better yourself, and you forget about God, y'see; you think it'd be better—you go

your own gait, and find the load's on your own shoulders. We think it'll be better for us, you know; and then it's much worse, for we've left out God.

PETR: Of course! We must remember God.

AKIM: All of a sudden it's worse. But if you act according to the law, and as God wills, then, y'see, somehow everything makes you happy. So that's how you want to do. So I struck the idea, you know: I'll marry the lad and keep him out of sin. He'll be at home, y'see, just as he should be by rights; and I'll just go to work in the town, y'see. It's a pleasant job. Suits me. Do as God wills, y'see, and things are better. And then she's an orphan. For instance, last summer they stole some wood from the clerk—what a trick! They thought they'd fool him. They did fool the clerk, but y'see, they didn't fool God: so, y'see—

[*Enter* Nikita *and* Anyutka]

NIKITA: Did you ask for me? [*Sits down and takes out his tobacco*]

PETR: [*In a low voice, reproachfully*] Look here, don't you know how to behave? Your father is going to ask you questions, and you're fooling with your tobacco, and you've sat down. Get up and come over here.

[Nikita *takes his stand by the table, jauntily leaning against it, and smiling*]

AKIM: Well, y'see, there's a complaint against you, Nikita; a complaint, y'see.

NIKITA: Who complained?

AKIM: Who complained? A girl, an orphan complained. It was she, that same Marina, who complained on you, y'see.

NIKITA: [*Grinning*] Mighty queer. What's the complaint? Who told you about it? Was it she?

AKIM: Now I'm asking you questions, y'see, and you've got to answer, you know. Did you get mixed up with the girl? Did you get mixed up with her, I say?

NIKITA: I simply don't understand what you're talking about.

AKIM: I mean, was there any foolery, y'see, between you and her? Foolery, foolery, you know.

NIKITA: Of course there was. You have fun with the cook to pass the time away; you play the accordion and she dances. What more foolery do you want?

PETR: Nikita, don't shuffle around: answer straight out what your father's asking you.

AKIM: [*Solemnly*] Nikita, you can hide things from men, but you can't hide 'em from God. Nikita, just think it over, y'see; don't you tell me lies! She's an orphan, y'see; it's easy to injure her. An orphan, you know. Tell me plain how it was.

NIKITA: But there's nothing to tell. I'm telling you the whole story, because there's nothing to tell. [*Getting excited*] She'll say anything. She can spread all the stories she wants, as if a man was dead. What stories didn't she tell of Fedka Mikishkin? So I suppose nowadays you can't have any fun! Let her talk!

AKIM: Eh, Nikita, look out! The truth will be known. Was there something or wasn't there?

NIKITA: [*Aside*] They're pressing me hard. [*To Akim*] I tell you there wasn't anything. There was nothing between me and her. [*Angrily*] I swear to Christ, may I die on the spot if there was! [*Crosses himself*] I don't know anything about the business. [*Silence. Nikita continues still more excitedly*] How did you get the idea of marrying me to her! What's all this anyhow? It's an outrage. Nowadays you've no right to marry a man by force. It's simple enough. I've just sworn to you—I don't know a thing about it.

MATRENA: [*To her husband*] That's it, you silly old fool: whatever rubbish they tell you, you believe it all. You've just put the lad to shame for nothing. And he'd better just stay on living here with the master. Now the master will give us ten rubles to help us out. And when the time comes—

PETR: Well then, Uncle Akim?

AKIM: [*Clucks with his tongue. To his son*] Look out, Nikita; the tear of an injured girl don't flow in vain, y'see; it drops on a man's head. Look out for what's coming.

NIKITA: What's there to look out for? Look out yourself. [*Sits down*]

ANYUTKA: I'll go tell mama. [*Goes out*]

MATRENA: [*To Petr*] That's how it always is, Petr Ignatych. My old man just makes trouble with his talk; when he gets a notion in his nut, you can't knock it out. We've just bothered you for nothing. Let the lad stay on living here as he has done. Keep the lad—he's your servant.

PETR: How about it, Uncle Akim?

AKIM: Well, y'see, I didn't want to force the lad— I was just afraid—Y'see, I'd like to have—

MATRENA: You don't know yourself what you're meddling with. Let him live here just as he has. The lad himself don't want to leave. And what use have we for him? We'll manage alone.

PETR: Just one thing, Uncle Akim: if you're going to take him in the summer, I don't want him this winter. If he's to say here, it must be for a year.

MATRENA: He'll promise for the whole year. At home, when the working time comes, if we need anybody we'll hire him; and let the lad stay here. And now you give us ten rubles.

PETR: Well then, for a year more?

AKIM: [*Sighing*] Well, seems like, y'see; I suppose it's so.

MATRENA: One year more, from the feast of St. Dmitry. You won't beat us down on the price—and now give us ten rubles. You'll do us that favor. [*Rises and bows*]

[*Anisya comes in with* Anyutka *and sits down at one side*]

PETR: Well? If that's all right, then—then let's go

to the tavern and wet down the bargain. Come on, Uncle Akim, and have a drink of vodka.

AKIM: I don't drink vodka, I don't.

PETR: Well, you'll have some tea.

AKIM: Tea's my sin. Tea, sure.

PETR: The women will have some tea too. Nikita, see that you don't drive the sheep too fast—and rake up the straw.

NIKITA: All right.

[*All go out except* Nikita. *Darkness is falling*]

NIKITA: [*Lights a cigarette*] They nagged and nagged me to tell about my doings with the girls. Those'd make a long story. He told me to marry her. If I married 'em all, I'd have a lot of wives No use of my marrying; I'm as well off now as a married man: people envy me. And how lucky it was that something or other just put me up to go and cross myself before the ikon. That way I cut the whole business short. They say it's scary to swear to what ain't true. That's all bosh. Nothing but words anyhow. It's simple enough.

AKULINA: [*Comes in, lays down the rope, takes off her coat, and goes to the storeroom*] You might give us a light, anyhow.

NIKITA: To look at you? I can see you without it.

AKULINA: Drat you!

ANYUTKA: [*Runs in and whispers to* Nikita] Nikita, hurry up; somebody's asking for you. Can you imagine!

NIKITA: Who is it?

ANYUTKA: Marina from the railroad. She's standing round the corner.

NIKITA: You lie.

ANYUTKA: Honest!

NIKITA: What's she want?

ANYUTKA: Wants you to come. "I just need to speak one word to Nikita," she says. I began to ask questions, but she won't tell. She just asked if it was true that you're leaving us. "It ain't true," says I, "his father wanted to take him away and marry him, but he refused and he's going to stay another year with us." And she says: "Just send him to me, for Christ's sake. I just must say one word to him," she says. She's been waiting a long time. You go to her.

NIKITA: Plague take her! Why should I go?

ANYUTKA: "If he don't come," she says, "I'll come into the cottage for him. Honest I'll come," she says.

NIKITA: Don't worry: she'll stand there a while and then go away.

ANYUTKA: "Do they want to marry him to Akulina?" she says.

AKULINA: [*Still spinning, goes up to* Nikita] Marry whom to Akulina?

ANYUTKA: Nikita.

AKULINA: Really? Who says so?

NIKITA: Some people say so. [*Looks at her and laughs*] Akulina, will you marry me?

AKULINA: You? Maybe I'd have married you a little while ago, but now I won't.

NIKITA: Why won't you now?

AKULINA: 'Cause you won't love me.

NIKITA: Why won't I?

AKULINA: They won't let you. [Laughs]

NIKITA: Who won't?

AKULINA: Stepmother, of course. She keeps scolding; she watches you all the time.

NIKITA: [Laughing] Bright girl! What sharp eyes you have!

AKULINA: I? Course I see. Am I blind? She blew up dad sky-high to-day. She's a witch with a big snout. [Goes into the storeroom]

ANYUTKA: Nikita, just look! [She looks out of the window] She's coming. Honest, it's she. I'll clear out. [Goes out]

MARINA: [Coming in] What's this you're doing to me?

NIKITA: What am I doing? I'm not doing anything.

MARINA: You're going to desert me.

NIKITA: [Rising angrily] Well, what do you mean by coming here?

MARINA: Oh, Nikita!

NIKITA: You girls are a queer lot. . . . What have you come for?

MARINA: Nikita!

NIKITA: Nikita, you say? I'm Nikita. What do you want? Get out, I tell you.

MARINA: I see you mean to desert me, to forget me.

NIKITA: Why should I remember you? You don't know yourself. You were standing round the corner and sent Anyutka to me, and I didn't come to you. So I haven't any use for you; that's all. Now get out.

MARINA: No use for me! You've no use for me now. I believed you when you said you'd love me. And now you've done this with me and haven't any use for me.

NIKITA: This talk of yours is all no use, don't amount to anything. You even blabbed to my father. Clear out, please!

MARINA: You know yourself that I never loved anybody but you. You might marry me or not, as you please; I shouldn't care. Have I done you any wrong that you've stopped loving me? Why did you?

NIKITA: There's no use of our wasting time talking. Clear out! . . . These senseless girls!

MARINA: What hurts ain't that you deceived me and promised to marry me, but that you don't love me any more. And it don't hurt that you don't love me, but that you've changed me off for another woman. For whom? I know!

NIKITA: [Steps towards her angrily] No use talking with girls like you; they won't listen to reason. Clear out, I tell you, or you'll make me do something bad.

MARINA: Something bad? Well, are you going to beat me? Go on, do! What are you turning away your mug for? Oh, Nikita!

NIKITA: Of course, it won't do; people'd come. But talking's no use.

MARINA: Well, this is the end; what's done is done. You tell me to forget it all! Well, Nikita, remember this. I guarded my honor more than my very eyes. You just ruined me and deceived me. You had no pity for an orphan [Weeps]; you deserted me. You've killed me, but I don't bear you any grudge. Good-by; I don't care. If you find a better one, you'll forget me; if you find a worse one, you'll remember. You'll remember, Nikita! Good-by, if I must go. But how I loved you! Good-by for the last time! [Tries to embrace him and clasp his head]

NIKITA: [Tearing himself free] Bah! I'm sick of talking with you. If you won't go, I'll go myself and you can stay here.

MARINA: [Screams] You're a beast! [In the doorway] God won't give you happiness! [Goes out, weeping]

AKULINA: [Coming out of the storeroom] You're a cur, Nikita!

NIKITA: Well?

AKULINA: How she yelled! [Weeps]

NIKITA: What's the matter with you?

AKULINA: What? You wronged her. You'll wrong me the same way—you cur! [Goes out into the store-room]

NIKITA: [After an interval of silence] It's all a puzzle to me. I love those women like sugar; but if a man sins with them—there's trouble!

ACT II.

The stage represents a street and Petr's *cottage. On the spectators' left, a cottage with a porch in the center, and on each side of this a living room; on the right, the yard fence, with a gate. Near the fence* Anisya *is stripping hemp. Six months have passed since the first act.*

ANISYA: [Stopping and listening] He's growling once more. Most likely he's got off the stove.[1]

[Akulina *comes in, carrying pails on a yoke*]

ANISYA: He's calling. Go and see what he wants. Hear him yell!

AKULINA: Why don't you go yourself?

ANISYA: Go along, I tell you!

[Akulina *goes into the cottage*]

ANISYA: He's worn me out: he won't tell where the money is; that's all there is to it. The other day he was in the entry way; most likely he'd hid it there. Now I don't know myself where it is. It's lucky he's afraid to part with it. It's still in the house. If I could only find it! It wasn't on him yesterday. Now I don't know where it is myself. He's clean worn me out.

[Akulina *comes out, tying on her kerchief*]

[1] In a Russian peasant cottage the best couch is on top of the oven. It is generally reserved for the old or infirm.

ANISYA: Where are you going?

AKULINA: Where? He told me to call Auntie Marfa. "Send for my sister," he says. "I'm dying," he says, "and I need to tell her something."

ANISYA: [To herself] Sending for his sister! Oh, poor me! Oh! oh! Most likely he wants to give it to her. What shall I do? Oh! [To Akulina] Don't you go! Where are you going?

AKULINA: For auntie.

ANISYA: Don't you go, I tell you; I'll go myself. And you go to the brook with the wash. Otherwise you won't finish it before night.

AKULINA: But he told me to.

ANISYA: Go where I'm sending you. I'll go for Marfa myself, I tell you. Take the shirts off the fence.

AKULINA: The shirts? But I'm afraid you won't go. He told me to.

ANISYA: I've told you I'll go. Where's Anyutka?

AKULINA: Anyutka? She's herding the calves.

ANISYA: Send her here; they won't stray.

[Akulina gathers up the clothes and goes out]

ANISYA: If I don't go, he'll scold at me. If I go, he'll give his sister the money. All my toil will go for nothing. I don't know myself what to do. My head's all mixed up. [Continues her work]

[Matrena comes in with a staff and a small bundle, equipped for traveling on foot]

MATRENA: God help you, darling.

ANISYA: [Looks around, drops her work, and claps her hands for joy] Well, I never expected you, auntie. God has sent me such a guest just in time.

MATRENA: Well then?

ANISYA: I was just going crazy. Trouble!

MATRENA: Well, he's still alive, they tell me?

ANISYA: Don't speak of it. He's half alive and half dead.

MATRENA: Has he given the money to anybody?

ANISYA: He's just sending for Marfa, his own sister. Must be about the money.

MATRENA: Sure thing. But ain't he given it to somebody without your knowing it?

ANISYA: Not much! I've been watching him like a hawk.

MATRENA: But where is it?

ANISYA: He won't tell. And I can't find out anyhow. He hides it first one place and then another. And Akulina hampers me. She's only a silly fool, but she too keeps spying round and watching. Oh, poor me! I'm all worn out.

MATRENA: Eh, darling, if he gives the money to some one without your knowing it, you'll weep forever. They'll turn you out of the house emptyhanded. You've worn yourself out, my precious, worn yourself out all your life with a man you don't love, and when you're a widow you'll have to go begging.

ANISYA: Don't speak of it, auntie. My heart aches and I don't know what to do and I've nobody to advise me. I told Nikita. But he's afraid to meddle

with the business. He just told me yesterday that it was under the floor.

MATRENA: Well, did you look to see?

ANISYA: I couldn't; he was there himself. I notice sometimes he carries it on him, sometimes he hides it.

MATRENA: Just remember, girlie: if you slip up once, you'll never get straight again. [In a whisper] Well, have you given him the strong tea?

ANISYA: O-oh! [Is about to reply, but sees her friend, and stops short]

[Another housewife, a friend of Anisya, walks past the cottage, and stops to listen to the shouts from within it]

FRIEND: [To Anisya] Hey, friend! Anisya, Anisya, I say! Your man seems to be calling you.

ANISYA: He keeps coughing that way, and it sounds as if he was calling. He's pretty low by now.

FRIEND: [Coming up to Matrena] Good day, old woman, where in the world did you come from?

MATRENA: From home, of course, my dear. I came to see my son. I've brought him some shirts. He's my boy, you know, and I'm sorry for him.

FRIEND: That's natural. [To Anisya] I was going to bleach my linen, friend, but I think it's too soon. People haven't begun yet.

ANISYA: No use of hurrying.

MATRENA: Well, have they given him the Communion?

ANISYA: Sure; the priest was here yesterday.

FRIEND: [To Matrena] I had a look at him yesterday myself, my dear; and he seemed hardly alive. He'd just wasted away. And the other day, my friend, he seemed on the point of death; they laid him out under the holy ikons. They were already wailing for him, and getting ready to wash the body.

ANISYA: He's come to life again—got out of bed; now he's walking again.

MATRENA: Well, will you give him extreme unction?

ANISYA: People are urging me to. If he's alive we're going to send for the priest to-morrow.

FRIEND: Eh, it must be pretty hard for you, Anisya dear. It's a true saying: The bed's soft for the sick man, but hard for those that tend him.

ANISYA: That's so, but there's more to it.

FRIEND: Of course, he's been dying for most a year. He's tied you hand and foot.

MATRENA: A widow's lot is hard too. It's all right when you're young, but when you're old nobody will pity you. Old age is no joy. Take me for instance. I haven't walked far; but I'm tired out—my legs are numb.— Where's my son?

ANISYA: Plowing.— But come in, we'll start the samovar. The tea'll refresh you.

MATRENA: [Sitting down] I'm certainly tired, my dears. But you simply must give him the unction. People say that it's good for the soul.

ANISYA: Yes, we'll send to-morrow.

MATRENA: That's right.— But we're having a wedding down our way, girlie.

FRIEND: What, in the spring?

MATRENA: It's a good old proverb: "A poor man hurries to marry before the night's over." Semyon Matveyevich is going to take Marina.

ANISYA: She's in great luck!

FRIEND: He must be a widower; she'll have to look out for the children.

MATRENA: There are four of 'em. What decent girl would marry him? Well, he took her. And she's glad enough. They were drinking, you know, and the glass was cracked—they spilled the wine.

FRIEND: Just think! Was there gossip? And has the man some property?

MATRENA: They get along pretty well.

FRIEND: It's true, hardly any girl will marry a man with children. . . . Just take our Mikhaylo. My dear, he's a man who—

PEASANT: [Off stage] Hey, Mavra, what the devil are you up to? Go and drive home the cow.

[Friend goes out]

MATRENA: [While the Friend is going out, she speaks in a calm voice] They've got her out of harm's way, girlie; at any rate my old fool won't think any more about Nikita. [Suddenly changes her voice to a whisper] She's gone! [Whispers] Well, I say, did you give him the tea?

ANISYA: Don't speak of it. He'd better die all by himself. He's not dying anyhow; I've just got the sin of it on my conscience. O-oh, poor me! Why did you give me those powders?

MATRENA: Powders? They were sleeping powders, girlie; why shouldn't I give 'em to you? They won't do any harm.

ANISYA: I don't mean the sleeping powders; I mean the others, the white ones.

MATRENA: Well, darling, those powders were medicine.

ANISYA: [Sighs] I know, but I'm afraid. He's worn me out.

MATRENA: Have you used much of it?

ANISYA: I gave it to him twice.

MATRENA: Well, he didn't notice?

ANISYA: I tasted it a bit in the tea, myself; it's a trifle bitter. And he drank it with the tea and said: "I can't stand that tea." And says I, "Everything's bitter to a sick man." And I felt my heart sink, auntie.

MATRENA: Don't think about it; thinking makes things worse.

ANISYA: I wish you hadn't given 'em to me and led me into sin. When I remember it, it makes me shiver. And why did you give 'em to me?

MATRENA: Eh, what do you mean, darling! Lord help you! Why do you throw the blame on me? Look out, girlie, don't shift the blame to some one else's shoulders. If any questions are asked, I'm not concerned; I don't know a thing about it: I'll kiss the cross and say I never gave her powders, never

saw any, never even heard that there were such powders. Just think for yourself, girlie. We were talking about you the other day, saying how the precious woman was just tormented to death. Her step-daughter's a fool, and her husband's no good, just skin and bones. Such a life'd make a woman do anything.

ANISYA: Well, I don't deny it. My life'd make me do worse things than these; I'm ready to hang myself or strangle him. 'Tain't being alive.

MATRENA: That's just the point. No time to stand and yawn. Somehow you must find the money and give him some more tea.

ANISYA: O-oh! Poor me! What to do now I don't know myself; it makes me shiver. I wish he'd die all by himself. I don't want to have the guilt on my soul.

MATRENA: [Angrily] But why don't he tell where the money is? Does he expect to take it with him and not let anybody have it? Is that right and proper? God forbid that such a lot of money should be wasted. Ain't that a sin? What's he doing? May I have a look at him?

ANISYA: I don't know myself. He's worn me out.

MATRENA: What don't you know? It's a clear case. If you make a slip now, you'll repent of it forever. He'll give the money to his sister, and you'll be left out.

ANISYA: O-oh, he was sending for her—I must go.

MATRENA: Don't go yet awhile: we'll start the samovar first thing. We'll give him the tea and between us we'll find where the money is—we'll manage to get it.

ANISYA: O-oh! Something may happen.

MATRENA: What's the matter? What are you staring at? Are you just going to roll your eyes at the money and not get it in your hands? Get to work.

ANISYA: Then I'll go and start the samovar.

MATRENA: Go on, darling; do the business right, so that you won't be sorry afterwards. That's the way. [Anisya moves away, Matrena urging her] Be sure and not tell Nikita about all this business. He's sort of silly. God forbid he find out about the powders. God knows what he'd do. He's very tenderhearted. You know, he never would kill a chicken for me. Don't you tell him. Trouble is, he won't understand it. [She stops in horror; Petr makes his appearance on the threshold]

[Petr, holding to the wall, crawls out on the porch and calls in a weak voice]

PETR: Why can't I make you hear? O-oh! Anisya, who's here? [Falls on the bench]

ANISYA: [Coming in from around the corner] What have you come out for? You ought to lie where you were.

PETR: Well, has the girl gone for Marfa? . . . I feel bad. . . . Oh, if death would only hurry up!

ANISYA: She's busy; I sent her to the brook. Give me time and I'll attend to it. I'll go myself.

PETR: Send Anyutka. Where is she? Oh, I feel bad! Oh, my death!

ANISYA: I've sent for her already.

PETR: O-oh! Where is she?

ANISYA: Where can she be? Plague take her!

PETR: O-oh, I can't stand it! My inside is burning. Seems like an auger was boring me. Why have you deserted me like a dog? . . . There's no one even to give me a drink. . . . O-oh! . . . Send Anyutka to me.

ANISYA: Here she is.—Anyutka, go to your father.

[Anyutka *runs in and* Anisya *retires around the corner*]

PETR: Go and tell—o-oh!—your Aunt Marfa that your father wants to see her; tell her to come here.

ANYUTKA: Is that all?

PETR: Wait. Tell her to hurry up. Tell her I'm almost dead. O-oh!

ANYUTKA: I'll just get my kerchief and go right away. [*Runs out*]

MATRENA: [*Winking*] Now girlie, get down to work. Go into the cottage and rummage everywhere. Look for it like a dog looks for fleas; turn over everything, and I'll search him right away.

ANISYA: [*To* Matrena] With you seems like I have more courage. [*Goes towards the porch. To* Petr] Shan't I start a samovar for you? Auntie Matrena's come to see her son; you'll have tea with her.

PETR: Go ahead and start it. [Anisya *goes into the cottage.* Matrena *comes towards the porch*]

PETR: Hello!

MATRENA: Good day, my benefactor! Good day, my precious! I see you're still sick. And my old man is so sorry for you. "Go and inquire," says he. He sent his regards. [*Bows once more*]

PETR: I'm dying.

MATRENA: Well, when I look at you, Ignatych, I can see that trouble haunts men and not the forest. You've wasted away, my precious, all wasted away; I can see that. Sickness don't bring beauty, I suppose?

PETR: My death's near.

MATRENA: Well, Petr Ignatych, it's God's will. They've given you the Communion, and now, God willing, they'll give the unction. Thank God, your wife's a sensible woman; she'll bury you and have prayers said, all as is proper. And my son too, while he's needed, he'll tend to things about the house.

PETR: There's no one that I can give orders to! The woman's heedless and spends her time on foolery; I know all about it—I know. The girl's half-witted, and young at that. I've gathered a good property, and there's nobody to attend to it. It's too bad. [*Snivels*]

MATRENA: Well, if it's money or anything like that, you can give directions.

PETR: [*Calls into the house, to* Anisya] Has Anyutka gone yet?

MATRENA: [*Aside*] Oh my, he still remembers!

ANISYA: [*From indoors*] She went right off. Come into the house; I'll help you.

PETR: Let me sit here for the last time. It's close in there. I feel bad. . . . Oh, my heart's burning . . . If only death would come!

MATRENA: When God won't take a soul, the soul won't leave of itself. God's the judge of life and death, Petr Ignatych. You can never tell when death will come. Sometimes you recover. For instance in our village a peasant was just on the point of death—

PETR: No! I feel that I'll die to-day; I feel it. [*Leans against the wall and closes his eyes*]

ANISYA: [*Coming out of the cottage*] Well, are you coming in or not? Don't keep me waiting. Petr! Petr, I say!

MATRENA: [*Walking away and beckoning to* Anisya] Well, how about it?

ANISYA: [*Coming down from the porch, to* Matrena] Not there.

MATRENA: But did you look everywhere? Under the floor?

ANISYA: Not there either. Maybe in the shed. He went there yesterday.

MATRENA: Search, search, I tell you. Lick things clean. And it's my notion he'll die to-day anyhow; his nails are blue and his face like earth. Is the samovar ready?

ANISYA: It'll boil right off.

[Nikita *comes in from the other side of the stage—if possible on horseback, he comes up to the gate without seeing* Petr]

NIKITA: [*To his mother*] Hello, mother; are you all well at home?

MATRENA: Thanks to the Lord God, we're still alive; we can still eat.

NIKITA: Well, how's the boss?

MATRENA: Shh—he's sitting there. [*Points to the porch*]

NIKITA: Well, let him sit. What do I care?

PETR: [*Opening his eyes*] Nikita; hey, Nikita, come here!

[Nikita *goes to him.* Anisya *and* Matrena *whisper*]

PETR: Why have you come home so early?

NIKITA: I finished the plowing.

PETR: Did you plow the strip beyond the bridge?

NIKITA: It was too far to go there.

PETR: Too far? It's still farther from the house. You'll have to go there specially. You ought to have finished it at the same time.

[Anisya *listens to the conversation without showing herself*]

MATRENA: [*Approaching them*] Oh, sonny, why don't you try to please the master? The master is ill and relies on you; you ought to work for him as for your own father. Just stir yourself and work hard for him as I've told you to so often.

PETR: Then—ugh!—haul out the potatoes; the women—o-oh!—will sort them over.

ANISYA: [*To herself*] Well, I won't budge. He's

rying to send everybody away from him once more;
most likely he has the money on him. He wants to
hide it somewhere.

PETR: Otherwise—o-oh!— It'll be time to plant
em, and they'll have sweated. O-oh, I'm exhausted.
Rises]

MATRENA: *[Runs up on the porch and supports
Petr]* Shall I take you into the room?

PETR: Yes. *[Stops]* Nikita!

NIKITA: *[Angrily]* What next?

PETR: I shan't see you again. . . . I shall die to-
day. . . . Forgive me for Christ's sake if I've sinned
against you. . . . Whether in word or deed . . . if I
ever sinned. There were many times. Forgive me.

NIKITA: No need to forgive; I'm a sinner myself.

MATRENA: Oh, sonny, take this to heart!

PETR: Forgive me, for Christ's sake! . . . *[Weeps]*

NIKITA: *[In a choked voice]* God will forgive you,
Uncle Petr. I've no cause to bear you a grudge.
I've never been ill treated by you. You forgive me;
maybe I've sinned more against you. *[Weeps]*

 [Petr goes out, sniffling, supported by Matrena]

ANISYA: Oh, poor me! He didn't think of that for
nothing; it's clear that— *[Goes up to Nikita]* Well,
you said that the money was under the floor.— It
ain't there.

NIKITA: *[Sobs, without replying]* He was always
fair and square to me—and see what I've done!

ANISYA: Well, stop it. Where's the money?

NIKITA: *[Angrily]* How should I know? Look for
yourself.

ANISYA: You seem to be awful sorry for him?

NIKITA: Yes, I am sorry for him, mighty sorry.
How he wept! O-oh!

ANISYA: How kind you are—found somebody to
pity! He treated you like a dog, like a dog. Just now
he was telling us to turn you out. You might be
sorry for me instead.

NIKITA: Why should I be sorry for you?

ANISYA: He'll die and hide the money. . . .

NIKITA: Maybe he won't hide it. . . .

ANISYA: Oh, Nikita dear! He's sent for his sister
and wants to give it to her. Bad luck for us! How
can we live if he gives away the money? They'll
drive me out of the house. You might do something
about it. Didn't you tell me he went to the shed last
evening?

NIKITA: I saw him coming out of there, but nobody knows where he hid it.

ANISYA: Oh, poor me, I'll go and look there.
[Nikita walks away]

 *[Matrena comes out of the cottage and goes
 over to Anisya and Nikita]*

MATRENA: *[Whispers]* You needn't go anywhere.
The money's on him: I felt it; it's on a string around
his neck.

ANISYA: Oh, poor me!

MATRENA: If you let it out of your sight now, you
can look for it next door to nowhere. His sister'll
come and you're done for.

ANISYA: She'll come and he'll give it to her. What
shall we do? Oh, poor me!

MATRENA: What shall you do? See here: the samovar's boiling; go make the tea and pour it out for
him, and *[In a whisper]* sprinkle in all the powder
out of the paper and make him drink it. When he's
drunk a cupful, just pull the string. Don't worry;
he'll never tell about it.

ANISYA: Oh, I'm afraid!

MATRENA: Don't argue, hurry up about it; and
I'll take care of the sister if she comes. Don't make
a slip. Pull out the money and bring it here, and
Nikita will hide it.

ANISYA: Oh, poor me! How can I ever dare to . . .
and . . . and . . .

MATRENA: Don't argue, I tell you; do as I say.
Nikita!

NIKITA: What?

MATRENA: Stay here; sit down on the bench close
to the house, in case—you're needed.

NIKITA: *[With a wave of his hand]* Those women
are crafty. They make a man dizzy. Plague take
you! I'll go haul out the potatoes.

MATRENA: *[Clutching his arm]* Stay here, I tell
you.

 [Anyutka *comes in*]

ANISYA: *[To Anyutka]* Well?

ANYUTKA: She was at her daughter's in the garden;
she'll come right away.

ANISYA: If she comes, what'll we do?

MATRENA: *[To Anisya]* Don't bother about her
now; do as I tell you.

ANISYA: I don't know myself—I don't know anything; my head's all mixed up. Anyutka, girlie, run
off for the calves; they must have strayed away. Oh,
I'll never dare!

 [Anyutka *runs out*]

MATRENA: Go along; the samovar's boiling over,
most likely.

ANISYA: Oh, poor me! *[Goes out]*

MATRENA: *[Going up to her son]* Well, sonny!
*[Sits down beside him on the earth bench around
the house]* Now we must think over your business,
not just let it drift.

NIKITA: What business?

MATRENA: Why, how you're going to get along
and make your living.

NIKITA: Get along? Other people do, and so can I.

MATRENA: The old man's sure to die to-day.

NIKITA: If he dies, let him go to heaven! What do
I care?

MATRENA: *[During her speech she keeps glancing
at the porch]* Eh, sonny! The living must think of
life. Here you need a lot of sense, my precious. Just
think, for your sake I've run around everywhere;
I've trotted my legs off working for you. And mind
you: don't forget me later.

NIKITA: What sort of work were you doing?

MATRENA: For your sake, for your future. If you
don't take pains in time, nothing ever succeeds. You

know Ivan Moseich? I called on him too. I went over the other day, you know, and told him about a certain matter; I sat there and we got to talking. "Ivan Moseich," says I, "how could a case like this be fixed up? Suppose," says I, "a peasant is a widower, and suppose he takes another wife; and just suppose," says I, "he has children, one daughter by his first wife and one by the second. Well," says I, "if that peasant dies, is it possible," says I, "for another peasant to marry the widow and get the farm? Is it possible," says I, "for that peasant to marry off the daughters and stay on the farm himself?" "It's possible," says he, "only you need to take a lot of pains; and," says he, "you need to use money to fix things up. Without money," says he, "there's no use meddling with it."

NIKITA: [*Laughing*] You needn't tell me that; just give 'em money. Everybody needs money.

MATRENA: Well, darling, I explained everything to him. "First of all," says he, "your son must get himself enrolled legally as a member of that village commune: for this he'll need money, to give a drink to the old men of the village. Then they'll agree to it and sign the paper. Only," says he, "you must do everything with some sense." Look here [*Takes a paper from her kerchief*] he wrote out a paper. Read it—you're smart.

[Nikita *reads, and* Matrena *listens*]

NIKITA: The paper is a legal order, of course. No great amount of sense needed here.

MATRENA: But just hear what Ivan Moseich had to say. "The main thing is, auntie," says he, "look out and don't let the money slip past you. If she don't grab the money," says he, "they won't let her marry off her daughter. The money's the root of the whole matter," says he. So look out. The time's coming to act, sonny.

NIKITA: What do I care: the money's hers, let her worry about it.

MATRENA: Is that what you think, sonny! Can a woman make plans? Even if she gets the money, she won't know how to manage it. She's nothing but a woman, and you're a man. So you can hide it and do anything you choose. Anyhow, you have more sense if any hitch comes.

NIKITA: Oh, you women don't understand anything!

MATRENA: Don't we though? You get hold of the money. Then the woman will be in your hands. If she ever happens to growl or grumble, then you can take her down.

NIKITA: Oh, you make me tired! I'm going.

[Anisya *runs out of the cottage, all pale, and goes around the corner to* Matrena]

ANISYA: It was on him. There it is. [*Points under her apron*]

MATRENA: Give it to Nikita; he'll hide it. Nikita, take it and hide it somewhere.

NIKITA: Well, give it here!

ANISYA: O-oh, poor me! Maybe I'd better do it myself. [*Goes towards the gate*]

MATRENA: [*Clutching her by the arm*] Where are you going? They'll miss it; his sister's coming. Give it to him; he knows what to do. How silly you are!

ANISYA: [*Stops, undecided*] Oh, poor me!

NIKITA: Well, give it here; I'll hide it somewhere.

ANISYA: Where'll you hide it?

NIKITA: Are you afraid? [*Laughs*]

[Akulina *comes in with the clothes*]

ANISYA: O-oh, poor me, poor me! [*Hands him the money*] Look out, Nikita!

NIKITA: What're you afraid of? I'll tuck it away where I can't find it myself. [*Goes out*]

ANISYA: [*Stands terrified*] O-oh, what if he—

MATRENA: Well, is he dead?

ANISYA: Yes, seems dead. I pulled it out, and he didn't feel it.

MATRENA: Go inside; there's Akulina coming.

ANISYA: Well, I've sinned—and now he's got the money.—

MATRENA: That'll do; go inside: there's Marfa coming.

ANISYA: Well, I trusted him. What'll come of it? [*Goes out*]

[Marfa *comes in from one side;* Akulina *approaches from the other*]

MARFA: [*To* Akulina] I'd have come long ago, but I'd gone to my daughter's.— Well, how's the old man? Is he dying?

AKULINA: [*Sorting out the clothes*] How should I know? I've been at the brook.

MARFA: [*Pointing to* Matrena] Where's she from?

MATRENA: I'm from Zuyev; I'm Nikita's mother from Zuyev, dearie. Good day to you! Your dear brother is very sick, very sick. He came out here himself. "Send for my sister," says he, "because," says he— Oh! Maybe he's dead already?

[Anisya *runs out of the cottage with a cry, clutches the post of the porch, and begins to wail*]

ANISYA: O-o-oh! O-o-oh! Why have you left— o-o-oh!—and why have you deserted—o-o-oh!—your wretched widow?— Forever and ever, he has closed his bright eyes!—

[Friend *comes in. The* Friend *and* Matrena *support* Anisya *under the arms.* Akulina *and* Marfa *go into the cottage. Peasants, both men and women, come in*]

VOICE FROM THE CROWD: Call the old women, they must lay him out.

MATRENA: [*Rolling up her sleeves*] Is there any water in the kettle? And I don't believe the samovar's been emptied. I'll help in the work myself.

ACT III.

Petr's *cottage. Winter. Nine months have passed since Act II.* Anisya, *dressed in shabby workaday clothes, is seated at the loom, weaving.* Anyutka *is perched on the stove.* Mitrich, *an old laborer, comes in.*

MITRICH: Oh, the Lord be with you! Well, hasn't the master come home?

ANISYA: What?

MITRICH: Hasn't Nikita come home from town?

ANISYA: No.

MITRICH: Seems like he's been on a spree. Oh, Lord!

ANISYA: Have you fixed up the threshing floor?

MITRICH: Sure. I fixed it all up proper, covered it with straw. I don't like a halfway job. Oh, Lord! Gracious St. Nicholas! [*Pecks at his callouses*] Yes, it's high time for him to be here.

ANISYA: Why should he hurry? He has money; I suppose he's on a spree with some hussy.

MITRICH: He has money; so why shouldn't he go on a spree? What did Akulina go to town for?

ANISYA: Ask her why the devil took her there!

MITRICH: Why should she go to town? There are all kinds of things in town, if you only have the money. Oh, Lord!

ANYUTKA: Mama, I heard why. "I'll buy you a little shawl," says he, just think; "you can pick it out yourself," says he. And she dressed up just fine; put on her plush wrap and a French kerchief.

ANISYA: That's just it: maiden's modesty as far as the threshold; but when she's crossed it she forgets everything. She's a shameless hussy.

MITRICH: Really! Why be modest? If you have money, go on a spree! Oh, Lord! Is it too soon for supper? [Anisya *is silent*] I'll go warm myself meanwhile. [*Climbs on the stove*] Oh, Lord! Holy Virgin Mother! St. Nicholas the Martyr!

FRIEND: [*Coming in*] I see your man ain't back yet?

ANISYA: No.

FRIEND: Time for him. Hasn't he gone to our tavern? Sister Fekla said, my dear, that a lot of sleighs from town were standing there.

ANISYA: Anyutka! Hey, Anyutka!

ANYUTKA: What?

ANISYA: Run over to the tavern, Anyutka, and take a look. See if he's got drunk and gone there.

ANYUTKA: [*Jumping down from the stove and putting on her coat*] Right away.

FRIEND: Did he take Akulina with him?

ANISYA: Otherwise he'd have no reason to go. It's he who keeps him busy in town. "I must go to the bank," says he, "there's some money due me"—but he's really the cause of all this mess.

FRIEND: [*Shaking her head*] You don't say! [*Silence*]

ANYUTKA: [*At the door*] If he's there, what shall I say!

ANISYA: Just see if he's there.

ANYUTKA: All right, I'll fly like a bird. [*Goes out. A long silence*]

MITRICH: [*Bellows*] Oh, Lord! Gracious St. Nicholas!

FRIEND: [*Starts from fright*] Oh, he scared me! Who's that?

ANISYA: Mitrich, our laborer.

FRIEND: O-oh, how he frightened me! I forgot about him. Well, friend, they say people have made proposals for Akulina?

ANISYA: [*Coming out from behind the loom and sitting down at the table*] People from Dedlov hinted about it, but they must have heard something—they hinted and then shut up, so the matter dropped. Who wants her?

FRIEND: How about the Lizunovs from Zuyev?

ANISYA: They sent to inquire. But that too came to nothing. He wouldn't receive them.

FRIEND: But you ought to marry her off.

ANISYA: We sure ought. I can hardly wait to get her out of the house, friend, but I've no luck. He don't want to, nor she either. You see he's not had fun enough yet with that beauty of his.

FRIEND: Eh-eh-eh! Sins! The idea of it! Why, he's her stepfather.

ANISYA: Ah, friend! They tied me hand and foot too cleverly for words. Fool that I was, I didn't notice anything, didn't even think of it—and so I married him. I didn't guess one single thing, but they already had an understanding.

FRIEND: O-oh, how sad things are!

ANISYA: More and more, I see, they're hiding things from me. Oh, friend, my life has been miserable, just miserable. It'd be all right if I only didn't love him.

FRIEND: You needn't tell me!

ANISYA: And it hurts me, friend, it hurts me to suffer such an insult from him. Oh, how it hurts!

FRIEND: Well, they say he's even getting rough with his hands. Is that so?

ANISYA: Rough every kind of way. When he was drunk he used to be gentle; even in old times he used to take a drop, but it never made him turn against me. But now, when he gets liquor in him, he just flies at me and wants to trample on me. The other day he got his hands into my hair, and I had hard work to break loose. And the hussy is worse than a snake; I wonder how the earth can bear such spiteful creatures.

FRIEND: O-o-oh! You're in hard luck, friend, the more I think of it! How can you stand it? You took in a beggar, and now he's going to make sport of you like that. Why don't you take him down a bit?

ANISYA: Oh, my dear friend, with a heart like mine what can I do! My dead husband was mighty severe, but all the same I could manage him whatever way I wanted to; but here I can't, friend. When

I see him, my heart just melts. Against him I haven't any courage; he makes me feel like a wet hen.

FRIEND: O-oh, friend, I can see that somebody's bewitched you. That Matrena—they say she practices such things. Must be she.

ANISYA: I think so myself, friend. Sometimes I'm fairly ashamed of myself. I feel as if I'd like to tear him in pieces. But when I see him, no, my heart won't rise against him.

FRIEND: There must be a spell on you. It's easy enough to ruin a person, my precious. When I look at you, I can see that something's happened.

ANISYA: My legs are thin as bean poles. But look at that fool Akulina. She was a frowsy, sluttish hussy, and now look at her! What's the reason of this change? He's given her finery. She's swelled up and puffed up like a bubble on water. And then, no matter if she is a fool, she's got notions into her head. "I'm the mistress here," she says, "the house is mine. Dad wanted to marry me to him." And what a temper! God save us! When she gets mad, she fairly tears the straw off the roof.

FRIEND: O-oh, I see what a life you have, friend! And yet people envy you! "They're rich," they say; but, my dear, tears flow even through gold, you know.

ANISYA: Much there is to envy! And even the wealth will scatter like dust. He squanders money something awful.

FRIEND: But haven't you given him a pretty free rein, friend? The money's yours.

ANISYA: If you only knew the whole story! I made one big mistake.

FRIEND: In your place, friend, I'd go straight to the chief of police. The money's yours. How can he squander it? He's no right to.

ANISYA: Nowadays rights don't matter.

FRIEND: Oh, friend, I can see that you've grown weak.

ANISYA: Yes, darling, weak as a rag. He's bound me hand and foot. And I can't see any way out of it. O-oh, poor me!

FRIEND: Isn't somebody coming? [*She listens. The door opens and* Akim *comes in*]

AKIM: [*Crossing himself, knocking the snow off his bast shoes, and taking off his coat*] Peace to this house! Are you all well? Good evening, auntie.

ANISYA: Good evening, daddy. Have you come from home?

AKIM: I thought, y'see, I'd come see my son, y'see; I'd call on my son, you know. I didn't start early, had my dinner, you know; I started and it was deep snow, y'see, hard going, hard going; and so, y'see, I'm pretty late, you know. But is sonny at home? Is he home?

ANISYA: No, in town.

AKIM: [*Sitting down on the bench*] I have some business with him, y'see; a bit of business. I was telling him the other day, you know; telling him about our needs, y'see: the old horse has given out,

you know, the old horse. So we must get some sor of nag, y'see; some kind of nag. And so, y'see, I'v come.

ANISYA: Nikita told me: when he comes, you car talk with him. [*Rises and goes to the oven*] Hav supper, and he'll come. Mitrich, hey, Mitrich, com and have supper.

MITRICH: Oh, Lord, merciful St. Nicholas!

ANISYA: Come and have supper.

FRIEND: I'll be going; good-by. [*Goes out*]

MITRICH: [*Climbing down*] I never noticed hov I went to sleep. Oh, Lord, St. Nicholas the Martyr!— Good evening, Uncle Akim.

AKIM: Huh! Mitrich! What're you doing here?

MITRICH: I'm working for Nikita now; I'm livin with your son.

AKIM: Do say! So, y'see, you're working for my son. Do say!

MITRICH: I was living with a merchant in town but I ruined myself by drink there. So I came to th country. I'd no home to go to, so I hired myself out [*Yawns*] Oh, Lord!

AKIM: Well, y'see, well, what's Nikita doing him self? Is he so fixed, y'see, that he has to hire a work man, you know?

ANISYA: How's he fixed? First he managed b himself, but now he don't want to: so he's hired laborer.

MITRICH: He has money, so what does he care?

AKIM: That's wrong, y'see; that's all wrong, y'see It's wrong. He's just lazy.

ANISYA: Yes, he's got lazy, got lazy: that's th trouble.

AKIM: That's it, y'see; you think it'll be better and, y'see, it turns out worse. When a man' wealthy, he gets lazy, gets lazy.

MITRICH: Fat makes a dog go mad, so why shouldn't fat make a man lazy! Fat was what was th ruin of me. I drank for three weeks without stop ping. I drank up my last pair of pants. When I' nothing more, I just quit. Now I've sworn off Plague take the stuff!

AKIM: And where's your old woman now, y'see?

MITRICH: My old woman, friend, has found place of her own. She's in town; sits in the tavern and begs. She's a beauty, too: one eye pulled ou and the other knocked in and her mouth twistec sidewise. And—may she always have cakes and pie —she's never sober.

AKIM: Oh ho! What's that?

MITRICH: But where's there a place for a soldier' wife? She's found her job. [*Silence*]

AKIM: [*To* Anisya] What did Nikita go to towr for? Did he take something, y'see? Did he take something to sell, you know?

ANISYA: [*Setting the table and passing the food* He went empty-handed. He went for money, to ge some money in the bank.

AKIM: [*Eating*] What do you want the money for y'see? Are you going to make some new use of it?

ANISYA: No, we don't spend much. Only twenty or thirty rubles. We ran short, so we had to get some.

AKIM: Had to get some? What's the use of taking it, y'see, that money? To-day you take some, you know; to-morrow you take some, y'see: that way you'll use it all up, you know.

ANISYA: This was just extra. But the money's all there.

AKIM: All there? How can it be all there, y'see? You take it and still it's all there? See here: if you pour meal, y'see, or something, you know, into a chest, y'see, or a storehouse, and then go take the meal out of there—will it still be all there, y'see? That means something is wrong, you know; they're cheating you. You see to it, or they'll cheat you. Much it's all there! You keep on taking it, and it's all there.

ANISYA: I don't know about such things. Ivan Moseich gave us some advice then. "Put your money in the bank," says he, "and the money'll be safer, and you'll get interest."

MITRICH: [Finishing his meal] That's right. I lived with a merchant. They all do that way. Put your money in and lie on the stove and earn more.

AKIM: That's queer talk of yours, y'see. You say, "earn more," y'see, "earn more," but how do they earn that money, you know; who do they earn it from?

ANISYA: They give 'em the money from the bank.

MITRICH: What a notion! Women can't understand things. Look here and I'll explain the whole thing to you. You pay attention. You, for instance, have money; and I, for instance, when spring comes, have an empty field and nothing to sow on it, or I can't pay my taxes, maybe. So I just come to you, you know: "Akim," says I, "give me ten rubles; and when I harvest my crop, I'll return it to you on St. Mary's Day in October, and I'll help you to harvest your field for your kindness." You, for instance, see that I have something to use as security, a horse or a cow, maybe, and you say: "Give me two or three rubles extra for my kindness and let it go at that." I have the halter round my neck and can't help myself. "All right," says I, "I'll take the ten rubles." In the autumn I make a turnover and bring you the money, and you skin me of those three rubles extra.

AKIM: That means, y'see, those peasants are acting crooked, y'see; that's how it is when a man forgets God, y'see; 'tain't right, you know.

MITRICH: Wait a bit. It'll work out the same way over again. Remember now, that's what you've done, skinned me, you know: well, Anisya too, for instance, has some money on hand. She's nowhere to put it; and, just like a woman, you know, don't know what to do with it. She comes to you and says: "Can't you make some use of my money too?" she says. "Sure I can," says you. And you just wait. Then I come again next spring. "Give me another ten," says I, "and I'll pay you for it." So you just

look and see if the skin ain't all peeled off of me, maybe you can tear off a bit more, and you give me Anisya's money. But if, for instance, I haven't a rag left, nothing to seize on, you just know it at a glance, and see that there's nothing to squeeze out of me, and you say right away, "Go somewhere else, my dear man, and may God help you!" and you look for some other fellow: then you lend him your own money once more and Anisya's too, and so you skin him. That's what a bank amounts to. It just goes round and round. It's a clever scheme, friend.

AKIM: [Getting excited] What's that? That's just nasty work, y'see. Peasants do that way; but the peasants, y'see, they feel it's sinful. That ain't lawful, y'see; it ain't lawful. It's nasty work. How do those learned men, y'see—?

MITRICH: That's just what they like best, my friend. Just remember this. If there's a man stupider than the rest of us, or a woman, and he can't make any use of the money himself, he just takes it to the bank; and they—it's fine bread and butter for them—just grab at it; and with that money they skin the people. It's a clever scheme.

AKIM: [Sighing] Eh, I see, it's hard not to have money, y'see; and it's twice as hard if you have it, y'see. Anyhow God bids us toil. But you, y'see, just put your money in the bank and go to sleep; and the money, y'see, will feed you while you lie idle. That's nasty work, you know; 'tain't lawful.

MITRICH: Not lawful? That ain't what folks think nowadays, my friend. And how they do strip a man bare. That's the point.

AKIM: [Sighing] That's the kind of times we're coming to, y'see. I've seen privies in town, you know. The new kind, y'see. All polished and polished, you know; made fine as a tavern. But it's no use, no use at all. Oh, they've forgotten God! They've forgotten him, you know! We've forgotten God, forgotten God!— Thank you, friend Anisya, I'm full; I've had enough. [Gets up and leaves the table; Mitrich climbs on the stove]

ANISYA: [Putting away the dishes and eating] If only his father would make him repent of his sins —but I'm ashamed to tell him.

AKIM: What?

ANISYA: I was just talking to myself.

[Anyutka comes in]

AKIM: [To Anyutka] Hello, girlie! Always busy? Got chilled, didn't you?

ANYUTKA: Just awful chilled. Hello, grandpa!

ANISYA: Well? Is he there?

ANYUTKA: No. Only Andrian was there, just come from town; he said he'd seen 'em in town, in a tavern. He said dad was drunk, drunk as a fish.

ANISYA: Are you hungry? There's something for you.

ANYUTKA: [Going to the stove] I'm so cold. My hands are numb.

[Akim takes off his bast shoes, Anisya washes the dishes]

ANISYA: Daddy!

AKIM: What do you want?

ANISYA: Tell me: is Marina getting on well?

AKIM: All right. She's getting on. She's a sensible, quiet little woman, y'see; she gets on, y'see; she tries hard. She's a good sort of woman, you know; clever and hard-working and patient, y'see. She's a good sort of little woman, you know.

ANISYA: Well, people from your village tell me, the kinsfolk of Marina's husband want to ask for our Akulina in marriage. Have you heard of it?

AKIM: The Mironovs? The women were saying something about it. But I didn't pay attention, you know. I don't know whether it's true, y'see. The old women were talking about it. But I've a poor memory, poor memory, y'see. Well, the Mironovs, y'see, are decent sort of folks, y'see.

ANISYA: I wish that we could marry her off in a hurry.

AKIM: Why so?

ANYUTKA: [Listening] They've come.

ANISYA: Well, let 'em alone. [Continues to wash the dishes, without turning her head. Enter Nikita]

NIKITA: Anisya, wife, who's come?

[Anisya glances at him and turns away in silence]

NIKITA: [Threateningly] Who's come? Have you forgotten?

ANISYA: Quit your bullying. Come in.

NIKITA: [Still more threateningly] Who's come?

ANISYA: [Going to him and taking his arm] Well, my husband's come. Come into the room.

NIKITA: [Resisting] So that's it! Your husband. And what's your husband's name? Say it right.

ANISYA: Confound you: Nikita.

NIKITA: So that's it! Booby! Say the full name.

ANISYA: Akimych. Well!

NIKITA: [Still in the doorway] So that's it! No, tell me what's the last name.

ANISYA: [Laughing and pulling at his arm] Chilikin. How drunk you are!

NIKITA: That's so! [Holds to the door jam] No, tell me what foot Chilikin puts into the room first.

ANISYA: Oh, stop, you'll cool off the room.

NIKITA: Say what foot he puts into the room first. You must tell me.

ANISYA: [To herself] I'm sick of this. [Aloud] Well, the left. Come in, will you?

NIKITA: So that's it!

ANISYA: Just see who's in the room.

NLKITA: Father? Well, I don't despise my father. I can show respect to my father. Good evening, daddy. [Bows to him and offers his hand] My respects to you!

AKIM: [Not replying to him] Liquor, liquor, that's what it does. Nasty business.

NIKITA: Liquor? Have I had a drink? I'm certainly guilty; I had a drink with a friend—drank his health.

ANISYA: You'd better go lie down.

NIKITA: Wife, where am I standing? Tell me!

ANISYA: Oh, that's all right. Go lie down.

NIKITA: I'm going to have some tea with my father. Start the samovar. Akulina, come in, will you?

[Akulina, gayly dressed, comes in with packages she has bought and goes to Nikita]

AKULINA: You've mislaid everything. Where's the yarn?

NIKITA: The yarn? The yarn's over there.— Hey. Mitrich, what're you doing there? Gone to sleep? Go and unharness the horse.

AKIM: [Without noticing Akulina, looks at his son] Just see how he's acting. The old man's tired out, y'see; been thrashing, you know; and he's showing his authority, you know. "Unharness the horse!" Bah! nasty!

MITRICH: [Climbs down from the stove and puts on his felt boots] Oh, merciful Lord! Is the horse in the yard? It sure must be tired. How drunk he is, confound him! Beats all! Oh, Lord! St. Nicholas the Martyr! [Puts on his sheepskin and goes outdoors]

NIKITA: [Sitting down] Forgive me, daddy. I had a drink, that's true; but how can a man help it? Even a hen drinks. Ain't that so? And you forgive me? What about Mitrich? He don't take it ill; he'll unharness.

ANISYA: Shall I really start the samovar?

NIKITA: Yes. My father's come, I want to talk with him; I'll have tea. [To Akulina] Have you brought in all the packages?

AKULINA: Packages? I took my own, but there are some left in the sleigh.— Here, this ain't mine. [She tosses a bundle on the table and puts away the rest of the packages in the chest. Anyutka watches her do so. Akim, without looking at his son, sets his leg wrappers and bast shoes on the stove]

ANISYA: [Going out with the samovar] The chest was full already, and he's bought more.

NIKITA: [Assuming a sober air] Don't be cross with me, dad. You think I'm drunk? I'm equal to anything whatever, because I can drink and not lose my senses. I can talk things over with you this very minute, dad. I remember the whole business. You gave directions about money; the horse was worn out —I remember. I can do the whole thing. I have it right on hand. If you needed a huge sum of money, then you might have to wait a bit; but I can attend to all this! Here it is!

AKIM: [Continues to fuss with the leg wrappers] Eh, my boy, y'see, spring's coming on, y'see; bad traveling.

NIKITA: What're you saying that for? There's no talking with a man that's drunk. But don't you worry; we'll have some tea. And I can do everything; I can fix up absolutely the whole business.

AKIM: [Shaking his head] Eh-eh-eh!

NIKITA: Here's the money. [Puts his hand in his pocket and takes out his purse; he turns over the bills and pulls out a ten-ruble note] Take that for the horse. Take it for the horse; I can't neglect my father. I certainly won't desert you, for you're my father. Here, take it. It's easy enough; I don't grudge it.

[*He comes up and thrusts the money at* Akim; Akim *does not take the money*]

NIKITA: [*Clutching his hand*] Take it, I say, when I give it to you—I don't grudge it.

AKIM: I can't take it, my boy, y'see; and I can't talk with you, you know, because there's no decency in you, y'see.

NIKITA: I won't let you off. Take it. [*Stuffs the money into* Akim's *hands*]

ANISYA: [*Comes in and stops suddenly*] Go ahead and take it. He won't let up, you know.

AKIM: [*Taking the money and shaking his head*] Oh, that liquor! A drunkard's not a man, you know.

NIKITA: There, that's better. If you return it, all right; and if you don't return it, I don't care. That's my way! [*Sees* Akulina] Akulina, show 'em your presents.

AKULINA: What?

NIKITA: Show 'em your presents.

AKULINA: Presents? Why should I show 'em? I've put 'em away already.

NIKITA: Get 'em out, I tell you; Anyutka'll like to see 'em. Show 'em to Anyutka, I tell you. Untie that little shawl. Give it here.

AKIM: O-oh, makes me sick to watch! [*Climbs on the stove*]

AKULINA: [*Getting her presents and laying them on the table*] There! What's the use of looking at 'em?

ANYUTKA: That's pretty! Good as Stepanida's.

AKULINA: Stepanida's? Stepanida's is nothing to this. [*Becoming animated and spreading out the things*] Look here at the quality! It's French.

ANYUTKA: And what gay chintz! Mashutka has one like it, only hers is lighter-colored, with a blue background. That's awful pretty.

NIKITA: That's right.

[Anisya *goes angrily into the storeroom, comes back with the tablecloth and the chimney for the samovar, and goes to the table*]

ANISYA: Confound you! You've covered up all the table.

NIKITA: Just look here!

ANISYA: Why should I look! Haven't I seen 'em? Take 'em away. [*Brushes off the shawl on the floor with her hand*]

AKULINA: What are you slinging round? Sling round your own things. [*Picks it up*]

NIKITA: Anisya! Look out!

ANISYA: What should I look out for?

NIKITA: Do you think I forgot you? Look here! [*Shows her the roll and sits down on it*] There's a present for you. Only you must earn it. Wife, where am I sitting?

ANISYA: Quit your bullying. I'm not afraid of you.

Whose money have you spent on your spree, and on your presents for your fat hussy? Mine.

AKULINA: Much it's yours! You wanted to steal it and couldn't. Get out of my way. [*Tries to pass by her and bumps into her*]

ANISYA: Who are you shoving? I'll give you a push.

AKULINA: A push? Come on now! [*Pushes against her*]

NIKITA: Here, women, women! Stop it! [*Stands between them*]

AKULINA: She picks on me. She'd better shut up and remember what she did. Do you think people don't know?

ANISYA: What do they know? Tell us, tell us what they know.

AKULINA: They know something about you.

ANISYA: You're a slut; you're living with another woman's husband.

AKULINA: And you put yours out of the way.

ANISYA: [*Rushes at* Akulina] You lie!

NIKITA: [*Holding her back*] Anisya! Have you forgotten?

ANISYA: Are you trying to scare me? I'm not afraid of you.

NIKITA: Get out! [*Turns* Anisya *around and starts to push her out*]

ANISYA: Where'll I go? I won't leave my own house.

NIKITA: Get out, I tell you! And don't you dare come back!

ANISYA: I won't go. [Nikita *pushes her;* Anisya *weeps and shrieks, clutching at the door*] What, are you going to kick me out of my own house? What are you doing, you villain? Do you think there's no law for you? You just wait!

NIKITA: Come, come!

ANISYA: I'll go to the village elder, to the policeman.

NIKITA: Get out, I tell you. [*Pushes her out*]

ANISYA: [*Outside*] I'll hang myself!

NIKITA: Don't worry!

ANYUTKA: Oh, oh, oh! Dear, darling mother. [*Weeps*]

NIKITA: Well, I was awful scared of her. What are you crying for? She'll come home all right! Go and see to the samovar. [Anyutka *goes out*]

AKULINA: [*Gathing up and folding the presents*] Nasty woman, how she dirtied it! Just you wait, I'll slit her frock for her. I sure will.

NIKITA: I've turned her out. What more do you want?

AKULINA: She's soiled my new shawl. The bitch— if she hadn't left I'd sure have clawed her eyes out.

NIKITA: Just calm down. What's there for you to be angry at? Think I love her?

AKULINA: Love her? Could anybody love **that** broad mug? If you'd only quit her then, nothing'd have happened. You ought to have sent her to **the** devil. But the house is mine anyhow and the **money's** mine. And then she says she's the mistress. Mistress! She was a fine mistress for her husband! She's a murderess; that's what she is. She'll do the same to you!

NIKITA: Oh, you can't stop up a woman's throat. Do you know yourself what you're talking about?

AKULINA: Yes, I know. I won't live with her. I'll turn her off the place. She can't live with me. She the mistress! She ain't the mistress; she's a prison rat.

NIKITA: Stop it. You needn't meddle with her. Don't even look at her. Look at me. I'm the master. What I wish, I do. I don't love her any more; I love you. I love whoever I want to. I'm the boss. And she'll have to mind. That's where I've got her. [*Points under his feet*] Oh, I haven't my accordion! [*Sings*]

> On the stove are buns,
> Porridge in the oven;
> Now we'll live gaily,
> We'll take our pleasure.
> And then when death comes,
> Then we'll just be dying.
> On the stove are buns,
> Porridge in the oven.

[Mitrich *comes in, takes off his coat, and climbs on the stove*]

MITRICH: I see the women have been fighting again! Another quarrel! Oh, Lord! Gracious St. Nicholas!

AKIM: [*Sits up on the edge of the stove, gets his leg wrappers and bast shoes, and puts them on*] Crawl in, crawl into the corner there.

MITRICH: [*Crawls in*] I see they're still arguing over their property. Oh, Lord!

NIKITA: Get out the brandy; we'll drink it with the tea.

ANYUTKA: [*Coming in, to* Akulina] Sister, the samovar's going to boil over.

NIKITA: Where's your mother?

ANYUTKA: She's standing in the hall, crying.

NIKITA: All right: call her in, tell her to bring the samovar. And give us the dishes, Akulina.

AKULINA: Dishes? Well, all right. [*Takes out the dishes*]

NIKITA: [*Brings brandy, biscuits, and salt herring*] This is for me, this is yarn for the woman, the kerosene's there in the hall. And here's the money. Wait. [*Takes the counting frame*] I'll reckon it up right away. [*Moves the counters on the frame*] Wheat flour eighty kopecks, vegetable oil . . . Ten rubles for dad. Dad, come and have tea.

[*Silence.* Akim *sits on the stove and puts on his leg wrappers*]

ANISYA: [*Bringing in the samovar*] Where shall I put it?

NIKITA: Put it on the table. Well, did you go to the village elder? Now, then, talk ahead and have a bit to eat. Just quit being cross. Sit down and drink. [*He pours her out a glass of brandy*] And

here I've brought a present for you. [*Hands her the roll on which he has been sitting.* Anisya *takes it in silence, shaking her head*]

AKIM: [*Climbs down and puts on his coat. Goes to the table and puts the ten-ruble note on it*] Here, that's your money. Take it.

NIKITA: [*Not seeing the note*] Where're you going to now you're all dressed?

AKIM: I'm going, I'm going, y'see. Bid me goodby, for Christ's sake. [*Takes his hat and girdle*]

NIKITA: Do say! Where are you going by night?

AKIM: I can't stay in your house, y'see; I can't stay, you know. Bid me good-by.

NIKITA: But you are running away from tea?

AKIM: [*Tying on his girdle*] I'm going, y'see, because it ain't good in your house, you know; it ain't good in your house, Nikita, you know. Your life is bad, Nikita, y'see; it's bad. I'm going.

NIKITA: Come, quit your talk; sit down and have tea.

ANISYA: Why, daddy, we'll be ashamed to face folks. What're you taking offense at?

AKIM: I'm not offended at all, y'see, not at all; but I can just see, you know, that my son's going to ruin, you know, going to ruin.

NIKITA: What ruin? Show me.

AKIM: To ruin, to ruin, you're ruined now. What did I tell you last summer?

NIKITA: You told me a lot of stuff.

AKIM: I told you, y'see, about the orphan; that you injured the orphan: you injured Marina, you know.

NIKITA: The old story! Don't talk twice about last year's snow: that thing's past and gone.

AKIM: Past and gone? No, my boy, it ain't gone. One sin brings another, you know; it brings more; and you're stuck fast in sin, Nikita boy. You're stuck fast in sin, I see. You're stuck fast, deep in it, you know.

NIKITA: Sit down and drink tea; that's all I have to say.

AKIM: I can't drink tea, y'see. Because your wicked ways make me sick, you know, awful sick. I can't drink tea with you, y'see.

NIKITA: Oh! . . . He's just talking silly. Sit down at the table.

AKIM: Your wealth, y'see, has caught you in a net; in a net, you know. Ah, Nikita, you need a soul.

NIKITA: What sort of right have you to reproach me in my own house? And what are you bothering me for anyhow? Am I just a kid for you to pull my hair? The time for such things has past.

AKIM: That's true; I've heard that nowadays, y'see, men pull their fathers' beards, you know; and that brings ruin, you know, brings ruin.

NIKITA: [*Angrily*] We make our living and don't beg of you, and you come to us in distress.

AKIM: Money? There's your money. I'll go begging, you know; but that money I won't take, y'see.

NIKITA: Stop that. What are you cross for, breaking up the party? [*Holds him back by the arm*]

AKIM: [*Screaming*] Let me go; I won't stay. I'd rather spend the night under a fence than in this filth of yours. Bah, God forgive me! [*Goes out*]

NIKITA: Well, well!

AKIM: [*Opening the door*] Come to your senses, Nikita! You need a soul. [*Goes out*]

AKULINA: [*Taking the cups*] Well, shall I pour the tea? [*All are silent*]

MITRICH: [*Bellows*] O Lord, be merciful to me a sinner! [*All start with terror*]

NIKITA: [*Lying down on the bench*] Oh, life is hard, hard! Akulina! Where's my accordion?

AKULINA: Your accordion? Don't you know that you took it to be fixed? I've poured the tea. Drink it.

NIKITA: I don't want it. Put out the light. . . . Oh, life is hard for me, awful hard! [*Weeps*]

ACT IV.

A moonlight evening in autumn. The yard behind the cottage. In the center of the stage is the hall, to the right the warm side of the house and a gate, to the left the cold side of the house and the cellar. From within the house can be heard talking and drunken shouts. A Neighbor comes out of the house and beckons to her Anisya's Friend.

NEIGHBOR: Why hasn't Akulina joined the company?

FRIEND: Why not? She'd have been glad to, but it was no time for her, believe me. The matchmakers have come to look at the bride; and she, my dear woman, just lies in the cold room and don't show herself at all, the darling.

NEIGHBOR: Why so?

FRIEND: They say the evil eye has lighted on her belly.

NEIGHBOR: Really!

FRIEND: And you know— [*Whispers in her ear*]

NEIGHBOR: What? That's a sin. But the matchmakers will find out.

FRIEND: How can they find out? They're all drunk. And they're mostly concerned with the dowry. It's no small amount, my dear, they're giving with the hussy: two coats, six silk gowns, a French shawl, and then a whole lot of linen, and—so they say—two hundred in cash.

NEIGHBOR: Well, in a case like this even money won't make a man happy. Such a disgrace!

FRIEND: Sh! There's the matchmaker. [*They stop talking and withdraw into the vestibule of the cottage*]

MATCHMAKER: (*man*) [*Coming out of the vestibule, alone, hiccuping*] I'm all in a sweat. Awful hot! I want to cool off a bit. [*Stands and catches his breath*] And the Lord knows—! Something's wrong.

It don't make me happy. Well, here's the old woman.

[Matrena *comes out of the vestibule*]

MATRENA: And I was gazing round! "Where's the matchmaker? Where's the matchmaker?" says I. So here's where you are, my man. Well, friend, thank the Lord, all's going fine. Wooing's not boasting. And I never learned how to boast. But as you came on a good errand, so, God grant, you'll always be grateful. And the bride, you know, is a marvel. Hard to find such a girl in the district.

MATCHMAKER: That's all right, but we mustn't forget about the money.

MATRENA: Don't you worry about the money. All her parents ever gave her, she still has. By now it must amount to a hundred and fifty.

MATCHMAKER: We're well enough satisfied; but he's our own child, you know. We must do the best we can for him.

MATRENA: I'm telling you the truth, friend: if it wasn't for me, you'd never have found the girl. There was a party from the Kormilins that wanted to get her, but I held out against it. And as for the money I can tell you true and honest: When the deceased—heaven's peace be with him!—was dying, he gave directions that his widow should take Nikita into the house—I know all this through my son— but that the money should be Akulina's. Another man would have made his profit out of the thing, but Nikita is giving them up, every kopek. Just think what a lot of money!

MATCHMAKER: Folks say she was left more money. He's a sly fellow.

MATRENA: Oh, fiddle-faddle! The other man's slice always looks big: they're giving you all there was. I tell you: quit your reckonings. Make it a firm bargain. The girl's pretty as a spring cherry.

MATCHMAKER: That's so. My old woman and I were wondering about one thing in the girl: Why didn't she show herself? We think she may be sickly.

MATRENA: Huh? She sickly? There ain't her like in the district. The girl's so plump you can't pinch her. You saw her the other day yourself. And she's a marvel at working. She's a bit deaf, that's true. Well, one little wormhole don't spoil a red apple. And the reason she didn't show herself, you know, was because of the evil eye. There's a spell on her. I know what bitch contrived it. They knew a charm, you see, and worked it on her. But I know a cure for it. The girl will get up to-morrow. Don't you worry about the girl.

MATCHMAKER: Well, the bargain's made.

MATRENA: That's right—and now don't go back on it. And don't forget me. I worked hard on it too. Don't you leave me out.

[*The voice of a woman is heard from the vestibule:* "We must be going: come along, Ivan."]

MATCHMAKER: Right away. [*Goes out. Peasants throng the vestibule and take their departure. As*

yutka *runs out of the vestibule and beckons* Anisya
to follow her]

ANYUTKA: Mama!

ANISYA: [*From the vestibule*] What?

ANYUTKA: Mama, come here, or they'll hear us.
[*Goes off with her to the side of the cart shed*]

ANISYA: Well, what? Where's Akulina?

ANYUTKA: She's gone into the grain shed. It's awful what she's doing there! Just think, "No," says
she, "I can't stand it. I'll scream with all my might,"
she says. Just think!

ANISYA: She can wait. We must see the guests off,
you know.

ANYUTKA: Oh, mama! It's so hard for her. And
she's cross. "They needn't drink me out of the
house," she says. "I won't marry," she says. "I'm
going to die," she says. Mama, what if she died?
It's awful! I'm afraid!

ANISYA: It ain't likely she'll die; don't you go near
her. Get along.

[*Anisya and* Anyutka *go out.* Mitrich *comes in
from the gate and sets to raking up the hay
that is strewn about*]

MITRICH: Oh, Lord! Merciful St. Nicholas! What
a lot of liquor they put down! And they did raise
a smell. Stinks even out of doors. No, I won't—I
won't touch it. See how they've scattered the hay!
They're like a dog in the manger. Just look at this
bundle! What a smell! Right under your nose.
Plague take it! [*Yawns*] Time to go to sleep! But
I don't want to go into the room. It fills up a man's
nose. How it smells, damn it! [*One can hear the
guests driving away*] Well, they've gone. Oh, Lord!
Merciful St. Nicholas! They hug each other and
make fools of each other. But it don't amount to
nothing.

NIKITA: [*Coming in*] Mitrich! Go lie down on the
stove; I'll rake it up.

MITRICH: All right; give some to the sheep.—
Well, did you see 'em off?

NIKITA: We saw 'em off, but things didn't go
well. I don't know what'll happen.

MITRICH: Rotten business! Too bad we have it
here; that's what the Foundling Asylum's for. There
you can spill anything you like, they'll pick it up.
Give 'em anything; they ask no questions. And they
give money too. But the girl has to turn wet nurse.
It's simple nowadays.

NIKITA: Look out, Mitrich: if anything happens,
don't blab.

MITRICH: What do I care? Cover your tracks as
you like. Eh, how you stink of liquor! I'll go in the
house. [*Goes out, yawning*] Oh, Lord!

NIKITA: [*After a long silence, sitting down on a
sleigh*] What a life!

ANISYA: [*Coming out of the house*] Where are
you?

NIKITA: Here!

ANISYA: What are you sitting still for? There's no
time to wait. You must take it away right off.

NIKITA: What are we going to do?

ANISYA: I'll tell you what—and you do it.

NIKITA: You women might take it to the Foundling Asylum, maybe.

ANISYA: Take it and carry it, if you want to.
You're ready enough to do anything nasty, but you
don't know how to get rid of it. I can see that.

NIKITA: Well, what's to be done?

ANISYA: Go in the cellar, I tell you, and dig a
hole.

NIKITA: But you women might manage somehow.

ANISYA: [*Mimicking*] Yes, "somehow." You can't
let things just slide. You ought to have thought of
it in time. Go where you're sent.

NIKITA: Oh, what a life! What a life!

[*Enter* Anyutka]

ANYUTKA: Mama! Grandma's calling you. Sister
must have a baby; just think—it cried.

ANISYA: What lies are you telling, plague take
you! The kittens are squealing in there. Go into the
house and go to sleep. Or I'll thrash you!

ANYUTKA: Mama dear, honest to God!

ANISYA: [*Brandishing her arm at her*] I'll give it
to you. Get out of here and don't show yourself
again. [Anyutka *runs out*] Go and do what you're
told. Otherwise, look out! [*Goes out*]

NIKITA: [*After a long silence*] What a life! Oh,
those women! What a mess! "Ought to have thought
of it in time," she says. How could I have thought
of it in time? When could I have thought of it?
Well, last summer, when that Anisya began to nag
me about it. What of it? Am I a monk? The master
died, and so then I covered up the sin as was proper.
I wasn't to blame for that. Such things often happen. And then those powders. Did I set her up to
that? If I'd known of it, I'd have killed her on the
spot, the bitch. I'd sure have killed her! She made
me her partner in that dirty work, the good-for-
nothing! And from that time on she was hateful to
me. When my mother told me of it at the time, I
began to hate her, to hate her; I didn't want to look
at her. Well, how could I live with her? And then
this thing started! . . . That hussy began to make
up to me. What did I care? If it hadn't been me,
it'd been somebody else. And this business now!
Again I'm not to blame for it a bit. Oh, what a
life! [*He sits down and reflects*] Those women are
nervy—see what they've thought of! But I won't
join in.

[Matrena *comes in out of breath, with a lantern
and spade*]

MATRENA: What're you sitting here for like a hen
on a perch? What did your wife tell you? Get down
to work.

NIKITA: What're you women going to do?

MATRENA: We know what to do. You just attend
to your share.

NIKITA: You're getting me mixed up in it.

MATRENA: What's that? Do you think of backing
out? So it's come to this: you're trying to back out!

NIKITA: But think what this means! It's a living soul.

MATRENA: Eh, a living soul! Anyhow, it's barely alive. And what can we do with it? If you go and carry it to the Foundling Asylum, it'll die all the same, and there'll be talk; they'll spread the news and that girl'll be left on our hands.

NIKITA: But what if they find out?

MATRENA: We can do what we like in our own house. We'll do it so there won't be a trace. Just do what I tell you. It's our woman's work, but we can't manage it without a man. Here's the spade: now climb down and attend to things there. I'll hold the lantern.

NIKITA: What shall I do?

MATRENA: [Whispers] Dig a hole. And then we'll bring it out and stuff it in there quick. There she is calling again. Go on, will you! And I'll be going.

NIKITA: Well, is it dead?

MATRENA: Of course it's dead. Only you must hurry up. Folks haven't gone to bed yet. They may hear and see; the scoundrels meddle with everything. And the policeman passed by this evening. This is for you. [Hands him the spade] Get down into the cellar. Dig a hole there in the corner, the earth's soft, and you can even it off again. Mother earth won't tell any one; she'll lick it clean as a cow with her tongue. Go on, go on, my boy.

NIKITA: You're getting me mixed up in it. Plague take you! I'm going off. Do the thing alone, as you please.

ANISYA: [From the door] Well, has he dug the hole?

MATRENA: What've you come out for? Where did you put it?

ANISYA: Covered it with some burlap. Nobody'll hear it. Well, has he dug it?

MATRENA: He don't want to!

ANISYA: [Pushing out in a rage] Don't want to! Does he want to feed lice in prison? . . . I'll go right away and tell the whole thing to the policeman. We can go to ruin together. I'll tell it all right off!

NIKITA: [Panic-stricken] What'll you tell?

ANISYA: What? I'll tell everything! Who took the money? You! [Nikita is silent] And who gave him the poison? I gave it to him! But you knew it, knew I was in conspiracy with you!

MATRENA: Oh, stop it! Nikita, why are you so stubborn? See here, what's to be done? You must set to work. Come on, darling.

ANISYA: Look what an innocent you are! Don't want to! You've been abusing me long enough. You've been riding over me, but my turn's come now. Go along, I tell you, or I'll do what I said! . Here's the spade: take it! Get along!

NIKITA: Well, what are you nagging me for? [Takes the spade, but falters] If I don't want to, I won't go.

ANISYA: Won't go? [Begins to shout] Hey. folks!

MATRENA: [Stopping her mouth] What are you doing? Are you daft! He'll go. . . . Go along, sonny; go along, my dear boy.

ANISYA: I'll cry for help right off.

NIKITA: Stop it! Oh, what a lot you women are! But you'd better hurry up. The sooner the better. [Goes toward the cellar]

MATRENA: Yes, that's the way it is, darling; if you've had your fun, you must know how to cover up your tracks.

ANISYA: [Still agitated] He and his hussy have been taking out their spite on me, and I've had enough of it! I'm not going to be the only one. Let him be a murderer too. He'll find out how it feels.

MATRENA: Well, well, you're excited. Now, girlie, don't be cross: take it slow and easy, and it'll be better. You go in to the hussy. He'll do the work. [She follows Nikita with the lantern; he climbs down into the cellar]

ANISYA: I'll tell him to strangle his dirty brat. [Still excited] I had my torture all alone, pulling Petr's bones. Let him find out, too. I'll do my best to make him; I tell you, I will.

NIKITA: [From the cellar] Give me a light, will you!

MATRENA: [Holding the light, to Anisya] He's digging; go and bring it.

ANISYA: You just watch him. Otherwise he'll run away, the wretch. And I'll go bring it out.

MATRENA: See that you don't forget to put a cross on it. Or I'll attend to that. Is there a cross for it?

ANISYA: I'll find one; I know about that. [Goes out] [2]

MATRENA: How the woman did get worked up! And I must say, it was rough on her. Well, thank God, we'll just hush up this business and hide the traces. We'll get rid of the girl without scandal. My son will rest easy now. The house, thank God, is rich and well-stocked. He won't forget me either. They couldn't get along without Matrena. They couldn't attend to things. [Calls into the cellar] All ready, sonny?

NIKITA: [Climbs up; only his head can be seen] What are you doing there? Bring it, will you! What are you dawdling for? If you're going to do it, go ahead.

[Matrena goes towards the house door and meets Anisya. Anisya comes out with the baby, wrapped in rags]

MATRENA: Well, did you put the cross on?

ANISYA: Sure! I had hard work to get the brat; she wouldn't give it to me. [Comes up and holds out the baby to Nikita]

NIKITA: [Not taking it] Bring it down here yourself.

ANISYA: Here, take it, I tell you. [Throws the baby to him]

NIKITA: [Picking it up] It's alive! Darling mother, it's moving! It's alive! What shall I do with it?

[2] For variant ending of Act IV, see p. 196.

ANISYA: [*Snatching the baby out of his hands and throwing it into the cellar*] Hurry up and strangle it and it won't be alive. [*Pushing* Nikita *down*] It's your business; you finish it.

MATRENA: He's too kind-hearted. It's hard for him, the dear boy. Well, no help for it! It's his sin too. [Anisya *stands over the cellar.* Matrena *sits down on the house step, watches her, and reflects*] Eh, eh, eh! How scared he was! Well, even if it is hard, you couldn't do anything else. No way out. And then just think how sometimes people beg for children! And then, y'see, God don't give 'em; they're all born dead. Take the priest's wife for instance. . . . But here it wasn't wanted, and it's alive. [*Looks toward the cellar*] He must have finished. [*To* Anisya] Well?

ANISYA: [*Looking into the cellar*] He's covered it with a board and sat down on the board. Must've finished.

MATRENA: O-oh! He'd be glad not to sin, but what can you do?

NIKITA: [*Climbing out, shaking all over*] It's still alive! I can't! It's alive!

ANISYA: If it's alive, where are you going? [*Tries to stop him*]

NIKITA: [*Rushing at her*] Get out; I'll kill you! [*He clutches her by the arm, she tears herself free; he runs after her with the spade.* Matrena *rushes toward him and stops him.* Anisya *runs off to the house.* Matrena *tries to take away the spade from* Nikita]

NIKITA: [*To* Matrena] I'll kill you; I'll kill you too! Get out! [Matrena *runs to the house, to* Anisya. Nikita *stops*] I'll kill you; I'll kill you all!

MATRENA: That's because he's scared. Never mind; it'll pass off!

NIKITA: What's this they've done? What have they done to me? How it wailed! . . . How it cracked underneath me! What have they done to me! And it's still alive, alive sure enough! [*Is silent and listens*] It's wailing! . . . Hear it wail! [*He runs towards the cellar*]

MATRENA: [*To* Anisya] He's going; he must mean to bury it. Nikita, you need a lantern.

NIKITA: [*Listens at the cellar, without answering her*] I can't hear it. I just fancied. [*Walks away and stops*] And how the little bones cracked underneath me! . . . Krr . . . krr. . . . What have they done to me? [*Listens once more*] It's wailing again; it's sure wailing. What's this? Mother! Mother, I say! [*Goes up to her*]

MATRENA: What, sonny?

NIKITA: Mother, darling, I can't do any more. I can't do anything. Mother, darling, have pity on me!

MATRENA: Oh, you're frightened, my dear boy. Come, come, drink a drop to give you courage.

NIKITA: Mother, darling, my time must have come. What have you done to me? How those little bones cracked, and how it wailed! Mother, darling,

what have you done to me! [*Goes off and sits down on a sleigh*]

MATRENA: Go have a drink, my lad. It's true enough, nighttime makes you shiver. But just wait the dawn will come; and then, you know, a day or two will pass, and you'll forget to think about it. Just wait, we'll get rid of the girl and forget to think about it. But you have a drink, go have a drink. I'll attend to things in the cellar myself.

NIKITA: [*Shaking himself*] Is any liquor left in there? Can't I drink this down! [*He goes out.* Anisya *who has been standing by the door all this time silently stands aside to let him pass*]

MATRENA: Come, come, darling, I'll get to work myself; I'll climb down and bury it. Where did he throw the spade? [*She finds the spade and descends half way into the cellar*] Anisya, come here; give me a light.

ANISYA: But what's the matter with him?

MATRENA: He got awful scared. You gave it to him pretty hard. Don't meddle with him; he'll come to himself. Let him alone; I'll get to work myself. Set the lantern here. Then I can see. [Matrena *disappears into the cellar*]

ANISYA: [*Shouts at the door by which* Nikita *had departed*] Well, is your fun over? You've had your fling: now just wait, you'll find out yourself how it feels. You won't be so lofty.

[Nikita *rushes out of the house towards the cellar*]

NIKITA: Mother! Hey, mother!

MATRENA: [*Emerging from the cellar*] What, sonny?

NIKITA: [*Listening*] Don't bury it; it's alive! Don't you hear it? It's alive! There, it's wailing! . . . There . . . plainly. . . .

MATRENA: How could it wail? You squashed it into a pancake. You crushed all its head.

NIKITA: What's that? [*Stops his ears*] It's still wailing! I've ruined my life, ruined it! What have they done to me? . . . Where shall I go! . . . [*Sits down on the steps*]

VARIANT ENDING FOR ACT IV

The same scene as in Act I.

Anyutka, *undressed, is lying on a bench with a coat spread over her.* Mitrich *is sitting on a bunk at the head of the room, smoking.*

MITRICH: Pah! They've raised a smell, good luck to 'em for it! They spilled the goods. You can drown it with tobacco. It gets into a man's nose. Oh, Lord! I'd better go to sleep. [*Goes to the lamp and is about to turn it out*]

ANYUTKA: [*Sitting up with a start*] Granddad, dear, don't put it out.

MITRICH: Why not put it out?

ANYUTKA: They're up to something in the yard.

[*Listens*] Do you hear? They've gone into the grain shed again.

MITRICH: What do you care? They aren't asking you about it. Lie down and go to sleep. And I'll turn down the light. [*Turns it down*]

ANYUTKA: Granddad, precious! Don't put it way out. Leave just a tiny bit, or I'll feel creepy.

MITRICH: [*Laughing*] All right, all right. [*Sits down beside her*] What makes you creepy?

ANYUTKA: I can't help feeling creepy, granddad! How sister struggled. She kept knocking her head against the chest. [*Whispers*] I know—she's going to have a baby. . . . Maybe it's born already.

MITRICH: What a little imp, confound you! You want to know everything. Lie down and go to sleep. [Anyutka *lies down*] That's the way. [*Covers her up*] That's the way. If you know too much, you'll grow old too soon.

ANYUTKA: Are you going up on the stove?

MITRICH: Of course I am. . . . You're a silly little girl, I see. You want to know everything. [*Covers her up and rises to go*] Just lie there like that and go to sleep. [*Goes to the stove*]

ANYUTKA: It cried just once, but now I can't hear it.

MITRICH: Oh, Lord! Merciful St. Nicholas! . . . What can't you hear?

ANYUTKA: The baby.

MITRICH: There isn't any, so you can't hear it.

ANYUTKA: But I heard it; just think, I heard it. A little shrill voice.

MITRICH: You heard a lot. Did you hear how the bogy-man put a naughty little girl like you in a sack and carried her off?

ANYUTKA: What's the bogy-man?

MITRICH: Just the bogy-man. [*Climbs on the stove*] The stove's fine and warm now. Nice! Oh, Lord! Merciful St. Nicholas!

ANYUTKA: Granddad! Are you going to sleep?

MITRICH: What do you think? That I'm going to sing songs? [*Silence*]

ANYUTKA: Granddad! Oh, granddad! They're digging! Honest to God they're digging! Do you hear? Just think, they're digging!

MITRICH: What notions you have! Digging? Digging at night? Who's digging? It's the cow scratching herself. And you say, digging! Go to sleep, I tell you, or I'll put out the light right away.

ANYUTKA: Granddad, darling, don't put it out. I'll stop. Honest to God, I'll stop. It scares me.

MITRICH: Scares you? Don't you be afraid of anything, and then you won't be scared. Now you just feel afraid and you say that it scares you. Of course it scares you when you're afraid. What a silly little girl!

[*Silence. The cricket chirps*]

ANYUTKA: [*Whispers*] Granddad! Hey, granddad! Are you asleep?

MITRICH: Well, what do you want?

ANYUTKA: What's the bogy-man like?

MITRICH: I'll tell you what he's like. Whenever there's any little girl, like you, who won't go to sleep, he comes along with his sack, and he pops the little girl into the sack; and then he pops his own head in and lifts up her little shirtie, and he gives her a spanking.

ANYUTKA: What does he spank her with?

MITRICH: He takes a broom.

ANYUTKA: But he can't see, himself, can he, in the sack?

MITRICH: He'll see all right.

ANYUTKA: But I'll bite him.

MITRICH: No, girlie, you won't bite him.

ANYUTKA: Granddad, somebody's coming! Who is it? Oh, holy saints, who is it?

MITRICH: If somebody's coming, let him come. What do you care? . . . I think it's your mother coming.

[Anisya *comes in*]

ANISYA: Anyutka! [Anyutka *pretends to be asleep*] Mitrich!

MITRICH: What?

ANISYA: What have you a light burning for? We'll go to bed in the cold half.

MITRICH: I've just finished my work. I'll put it out.

ANISYA: [*Searching in the chest and grumbling*] When you want something, you can't find it.

MITRICH: What are you looking for?

ANISYA: I'm looking for a cross, I must put one on him. He'll die unchristened, God have mercy on him! Without a cross! It's a sin, you know!

MITRICH: Of course, you must do things properly. . . . Well, have you found it?

ANISYA: Yes. [*Goes out*]

MITRICH: That's lucky—otherwise I'd have given her my own. Oh, Lord!

ANYUTKA: [*Jumps up, trembling*] O-oh, granddad! Don't go to sleep, for Christ's sake! I'm so scared!

MITRICH: What are you scared of?

ANYUTKA: Won't the baby die, most likely? Grandma put a cross on Auntie Arina's too—and it died.

MITRICH: If it dies, they'll bury it.

ANYUTKA: But maybe it wouldn't die if Grandma Matrena wasn't here. You know I heard what grandma was saying; just think, I heard it.

MITRICH: What did you hear? Go to sleep, I tell you. Pull things over your head: that's all.

ANYUTKA: But if it was alive, I'd nurse it.

MITRICH: [*Bellows*] Oh, Lord!

ANYUTKA: Where'll they put it?

MITRICH: They'll put it where it's proper. It's not your business. Go to sleep, I tell you. Your mother'll come—she'll give it to you! [*Silence*]

ANYUTKA: Granddad! That little girl you were telling about—they didn't kill her?

MITRICH: That one? Oh, that girl came out all right.

ANYUTKA: How was it you were telling me they found her, granddad?

MITRICH: They just found her.

ANYUTKA: But where did they find her? Tell me.

MITRICH: They found her in a house over there. The soldiers came to a village and began to search the house; and there that same little girl was lying on her belly. They were going to smash her. But I just felt lonesome and I took her in my arms—she struggled. She was as heavy as if she had two hundred pounds inside her; and she clutched at everything with her hands—you could hardly tear her away. Well, I took her and stroked her head, stroked her head. And she was bristly as a hedgehog. I stroked her and stroked her, and she quieted down. I soaked a biscuit and gave it to her. She caught on. She chewed it. What could we do with her? We took her with us. We took her and just fed her and fed her; and she got so used to us we took her with us on the march: she just went with us. She was a nice little girl.

ANYUTKA: Well, she wasn't christened, was she?

MITRICH: Nobody knows. Not altogether, they said. For her people weren't ours.

ANYUTKA: Germans?

MITRICH: "Germans," you say? Not Germans, but Asiatics. They are just the same as Jews, but they aren't Jews either. They're Poles, but they're Asiatics. They're called Krudly or Krugly: I've forgotten the name.— We called the little girl Sashka. Sashka—and she was pretty. I've forgotten everything else, you see; but that little girl—Lord bless her!—I can see before my eyes right now. That's all I remember of life in the army. I recollect how they flogged me, and then I remember that little girl. She used to hang round your neck when you carried her. You couldn't have found a nicer little girl nowhere. Later we gave her away. The sergeant's wife adopted her as her daughter. And she came out all right. How sorry the soldiers were!

ANYUTKA: See here, granddad, I remember how daddy died too. You hadn't come to live with us then. He called Nikita and says to him: "Forgive me, Nikita," he says—and he began to cry himself. [Sighs] That made me sad too.

MITRICH: Well, that's the way things go.

ANYUTKA: Granddad; oh, granddad! They're making a noise again in the cellar. Oh, dearie me, holy saints! Oh, granddad, they'll do something to him. They'll destroy him. He's just a little thing.—Oh! oh! [Pulls the clothes over her head and weeps]

MITRICH: [Listening] They really are up to something nasty—curse 'em! Those women are a nasty lot. The men ain't much to boast of, but the women —they're like beasts of the woods. They ain't afraid of anything.

ANYUTKA: [Getting up] Granddad! Hey, granddad!

MITRICH: Well, what next?

ANYUTKA: The other day, a passer-by spent the night here. He was saying that when a child dies its soul goes straight to heaven. Is that true?

MITRICH: How should I know? Most likely. What of it?

ANYUTKA: Why, then I'd like to die too. [Whimpers]

MITRICH: If you die, nobody'll miss you.

ANYUTKA: Till you're ten years old you're still a child, and maybe your soul'll still go to God. After that you get spoiled, you know.

MITRICH: You certainly do get spoiled! How can girls like you help getting spoiled? Who teaches you anything? What do you ever see? What do you hear? Nothing but nastiness. I'm not very learned, but still I know something; not very well, but anyhow better than a village woman.— What is a village woman? Just mud. There's huge millions of your sort in Russia, and you're all like blind moles—don't know anything. How to keep cows safe from the evil eye— all kinds of charms—how to cure children by putting 'em under the hen roost—that's what women know how to do.

ANYUTKA: Mama used to put 'em there.

MITRICH: That's just it. How many millions of you women and girls there are, and you're all like beasts of the forest. You grow up and then you die. You don't see anything and don't hear anything. A man—even if it's in a tavern, or maybe in a fortress, accidentally, or in the army, like me—he learns something or other. But what about a woman? Don't ask her about God and what's right! She don't even know sensibly what Good Friday is. Friday's Friday, but ask her anything about it and she don't know. They crawl round just like blind pups and stick their noses in the manure.— All they know is their silly songs: "Ho, ho! Ho, ho!" And they don't know themselves what "Ho, ho!" means.

ANYUTKA: But, granddad, I know "Our Father" halfway through.

MITRICH: You know a lot! But then one can't expect much of you. Who teaches you? Only a drunken peasant teaches you now and then with a strap. That's all your training. I don't know who'll ever answer for you. They put a sergeant in charge of recruits and hold him responsible for 'em. But nobody's responsible for you girls. So you women are just like a herd of cattle—without a herdsman— that run wild; your kind is the stupidest that's made. Your kind is just hopeless.

ANYUTKA: But what can you do about it?

MITRICH: Not much. . . . Now pull the clothes over your head and go to sleep. Oh, Lord! [Silence. The cricket chirps]

ANYUTKA: [Jumping up] Granddad! Somebody's shouting, somebody's just yelling! Honest to God, he's shouting. Granddad, dear, he's coming this way.

MITRICH: I tell you, pull the clothes over your head.

NIKITA: [Coming in] What have they done to me? What have they done to me!

MATRENA: Have a drink, have a drink, darling. What's the matter? [*Gets liquor and sets it before him*]

NIKITA: Give it here: I guess I'd better take some.

MATRENA: Shh! They aren't asleep, you know. Here, drink it.

NIKITA: What does this mean? Why did you want to act that way? You might have carried it off.

MATRENA: [*In a whisper*] Sit here, sit here; have another drink, and then smoke a bit. That'll divert your thoughts.

NIKITA: Mother darling, my time must have come. When it wailed, and when those little bones cracked, krr . . . krr . . . my strength gave out.

MATRENA: E-eh! You're just talking silly stuff. It's true enough, nighttime makes you shiver. But just wait till the day comes; a day or two will pass and you'll forget to think about it. [*Goes to* Nikita *and puts her hand on his shoulder*]

NIKITA: Get away from me! What have you done to me?

MATRENA: What do you mean, sonny, anyhow? [*Takes him by the hand*]

NIKITA: Get away from me! I'll kill you! I don't care for anything now. I'll kill you!

MATRENA: Oh, oh, how scared you are! Now go away and go to bed.

NIKITA: I've nowhere to go to. I'm a lost man.

MATRENA: [*Shaking her head*] Oh! oh! I'd better go fix things up myself; and let him sit here for a while till he gets rid of all this. [*Goes out*]

[Nikita *sits still, covering his face with his hands.* Mitrich *and* Anyutka *are stiff with terror*]

NIKITA: It's wailing, it's sure wailing: hark, hark, you can hear it. . . . She'll bury it, she'll bury it! [*Runs to the door*] Mother, don't bury it, it's alive! . . .

MATRENA: [*Returning, in a whisper*] What do you mean, Christ help you! What fancies you have! How can it be alive! All its bones are crushed.

NIKITA: Give me some more liquor! [*Drinks*]

MATRENA: Go along, sonny. Now you'll go to sleep and it'll be all right.

NIKITA: [*Standing and listening*] It's still alive. . . . Hark! . . . It's wailing. Don't you hear it? Hark!

MATRENA: [*In a whisper*] Not a bit of it!

NIKITA: Mother dear! I've ruined my life. What have you done to me? Where shall I go? [*Runs out of the house,* Matrena *following him*]

ANYUTKA: Granddad, dear, darling, they've strangled him!

MITRICH: [*Angrily*] Go to sleep, I tell you! Bother you, confound you! I'll take a broom to you! Go to sleep, I tell you.

ANYUTKA: Granddad, precious. Somebody's grabbing me by the shoulders, somebody's grabbing me, grabbing me with his paws. Dear granddad, just think: I'll be gone right away. Granddad, precious, let me up on the stove! Let me up for Christ's sake! . . . He's grabbing me . . . grabbing. . . . O-o-oh! [*Runs to the stove*]

MITRICH: See how they've scared the poor little girl—those nasty women, confound 'em! Well, come up if you want to.

ANYUTKA: [*Climbing on the stove*] And don't you go away.

MITRICH: Where should I go to? Climb up, climb up! Oh, Lord! St. Nicholas the Martyr! Holy Virgin Mother of Kazan! . . . How they scared the little girl! [*Covers her up*] You're a little fool, just a little fool. . . . They sure scared you, those nasty women, much good may it do 'em!

ACT V. SCENE I.

In the foreground, on the left, a threshing floor, and near it a stack of straw; on the right, a cart shed. The doors of the shed are open; straw is scattered about in the doorway. In the background farm buildings can be seen; songs and the tinkling of tambourines are heard. Two peasant girls come walking along the path past the shed towards the farm buildings.

FIRST GIRL: You see how well we got across, we didn't even soil our boots; but on the road it was awful, so dirty! [*They stop and wipe their feet with straw*]

FIRST GIRL: [*Looks at the straw and sees something*] What's that there?

SECOND GIRL: [*Taking a look*] It's Mitrich, their workman. He's dead drunk.

FIRST GIRL: But he didn't use to drink at all, did he?

SECOND GIRL: Not till to-day, so it seems.

FIRST GIRL: Just look: he must have come here for straw. You see he has a rope in his hands, but he just went to sleep.

SECOND GIRL: [*Listening*] They're still singing the wedding songs. Most likely they haven't given 'em the blessing yet. They say Akulina didn't wail a bit.

FIRST GIRL: Mama told me she didn't want to be married. Her stepfather threatened her; otherwise she'd never have consented. You know what talk there was about her!

MARINA: [*Overtaking the girls*] Hello, girls!

GIRLS: Hello, auntie!

MARINA: Going to the wedding, darlings?

FIRST GIRL: It must be over by now. We just came to look around.

MARINA: Call my old man for me, Semyon of Zuyev. You know him, don't you?

FIRST GIRL: Of course we know him. He's some relative of the bridegroom, it seems.

MARINA: Sure: the bridegroom is a nephew of my boss.

SECOND GIRL: Why don't you go yourself? How can you miss the wedding!

MARINA: I don't feel like going, girlie; and then I haven't the time. I must be riding off. We weren't on our way to the wedding. We were carting oats to town. We stopped to feed the horses, and they called in my old man.

FIRST GIRL: Whose house did you stop at? Fedorych's?

MARINA: Yes. So I'll stand here a bit, and you go call my old man, darling. Make him come, precious. Say: "Your wife Marina says you must be going; the fellows are harnessing already."

FIRST GIRL: All right, very well, if you won't go yourself.

[*The girls go out along the path towards the farm buildings. Songs and the tinkling of tambourines are heard*]

MARINA: [*Muses*] It'd be all right to go, but I don't want to, for I haven't seen him since the very time that he refused me. That's more than a year ago. But I'd like to peep in and see how he gets along with his Anisya. Folks say they don't agree. She's a coarse, ill-tempered woman. He's remembered me many a time, I'll warrant. He must have had a liking for an easy life. He gave me the go-by. Well, God help him, I bear no grudge. It hurt then. Oh, how it pained me! But now it's worn off and I've forgotten. But I'd like to see him. . . . [*Looks towards the house and sees* Nikita] Just look! What's he coming here for? Did the girls tell him? Why's he left the guests? I'll be going.

[Nikita *comes in, at first hanging his head, waving his arms, and muttering to himself*]

MARINA: How gloomy he looks!

NIKITA: [*Seeing* Marina *and recognizing her*] Marina! My dear, darling Marina! What are you here for?

MARINA: I've come for my old man.

NIKITA: Why didn't you come to the wedding? You'd have looked on and laughed at me.

MARINA: What do I want to laugh for? I've come for my boss.

NIKITA: Oh Marina dear! [*Tries to embrace her*]

MARINA: [*Turning away angrily*] Nikita, you quit those tricks. That's been and gone. I've come for my boss. Is he at your house?

NIKITA: So we can't call to mind old times? You won't let me?

MARINA: No use remembering old times. That's been and gone.

NIKITA: So you can't bring it back?

MARINA: It won't come back. But what have you strayed off for? You're the master, and you've deserted the wedding.

NIKITA: [*Sitting down on the straw*] Why have I strayed off? Oh, if you only knew and understood! . . . My life's hard, Marina, so hard that I don't want to look at it. I got up from the table and came away, came away from people so that I needn't see anybody.

MARINA: [*Coming nearer to him*] How's that?

NIKITA: Well, it's that I have no joy in food or drink, no rest in sleep. Oh, I'm sick of life, just sick of it! And what makes me sickest of all, Marina dear, is that I'm all alone, and have nobody that I can share my grief with.

MARINA: You can't live without grief, Nikita. I cried over mine and now it's gone.

NIKITA: You're talking about old, old times. Just think, dear! You've done crying over yours, and now it's come my turn.

MARINA: But how's that?

NIKITA: It's that I loathe my whole life. I loathe myself. Ah, Marina, you could not hold me fast, and so you ruined me and yourself too! Well, is this a life worth living?

MARINA: [*Stands by the shed, weeps, but restrains herself*] I don't complain of my own life, Nikita. God grant that everybody had as good as mine! I don't complain. I confessed right off to my old man. He forgave me. And he don't reproach me. I'm satisfied with my own life. He's a gentle old man. And I like him; I wash and dress his children! And he's kind to me too. I've no reason to complain. It must be what God intended for me.— But what about your life? You're a rich man.

NIKITA: My life! . . . I just don't want to break up the wedding, or I'd take a rope—this one [*Takes up a rope from the straw*], and I'd throw it right over that crossbeam. And I'd fix up a nice noose, and I'd climb on the crossbeam and put my head in it. That's what my life is like!

MARINA: Stop, Christ help you!

NIKITA: You think I'm joking? You think I'm drunk? I'm not drunk. Nowadays even liquor don't affect me. But I'm sick of life, sick to death of it! I'm done for, in such misery that I care for nothing! Oh, Marina dear, do you remember how we lived together, how we spent happy nights on the railroad?

MARINA: Nikita, don't rub my sore spot. I'm married now and you are too. My sin's forgiven; don't bring back the past.

NIKITA: What can I do with my heart? To whom can I give it?

MARINA: What should you do? You have a wife: don't lust after other women, but care for your own. You loved Anisya; keep on loving her.

NIKITA: Ah, that Anisya is bitter wormwood to me. She's just tangled up my legs like witchgrass.

MARINA: Whatever she is, she's your wife.— But it's no use talking! You'd better go to the guests and call my husband.

NIKITA: Oh, if you knew everything!— But why talk about it!

HUSBAND: [*Coming in from the farm buildings, red-faced and drunken, accompanied by* Anyutka] Marina! Wife! Old lady! Are you here?

NIKITA: Here's your boss coming and calling for you. Go along!

MARINA: And what'll you do?

NIKITA: I? I'll lie down here. [*Lies down in the straw*]

HUSBAND: Where is she?

ANYUTKA: There she is, uncle, close to the shed.

HUSBAND: What are you standing here for? Come to the wedding! The hosts want you to come and pay your respects. The marriage party will soon start out: then we'll go.

MARINA: [*Coming to meet her husband*] But I didn't want to.

HUSBAND: Come on, I tell you. We'll have a glass; you'll congratulate that rogue Petrunka. The hosts are taking offense—and we'll have time enough for everything.

[Marina's Husband *embraces her and goes out with her, staggering*]

NIKITA: [*Sitting up on the straw*] Oh, when I saw her, I felt sicker than ever. The only real life I ever had was with her. I've wasted my days for nothing at all; I've ruined my happiness! [*Lies down*] What shall I do with myself? Oh, if only damp mother earth would open!

ANYUTKA: [*Sees Nikita and runs to him*] Daddy! Oh, daddy! They're looking for you. Godfather and everybody have given their blessing. Just think, they've given their blessing; they're cross.

NIKITA: [*To himself*] What shall I do with myself?

ANYUTKA: What's that? What are you saying?

NIKITA: I'm not saying anything. Don't bother me!

ANYUTKA: Daddy! Come on, will you! [Nikita *is silent;* Anyutka *pulls at his arm*] Daddy, go and give your blessing! Honest, they're cross; they're scolding.

NIKITA: [*Pulls away his arm*] Let me alone!

ANYUTKA: Come on!

NIKITA: [*Threatening her with the rope*] Get out, I tell you. I'll give it to you!

ANYUTKA: Then I'll send mother. [*Runs out*]

NIKITA: [*Sitting up*] How can I go in there? How can I take the holy ikon in my hands? How can I look her in the eyes? [*Lies down again*] Oh, if there were a hole in the earth, I'd crawl into it. People wouldn't see me; I'd see nobody. [*Sits up again*] But I won't go. . . . Let 'em go to thunder. I won't go. [*Removes his boots and takes up the rope; he makes a noose and puts it around his neck*] That's the way.

[Matrena *comes in hurriedly.* Nikita *sees her, takes the rope off his neck, and again lies down on the straw*]

MATRENA: Nikita! Hey, Nikita! There you are, and you won't answer. Nikita, what's the matter with you? Are you drunk? Come on, Nikita dear; come on, my precious! Folks are tired of waiting.

NIKITA: Oh, what have you done to me? I'm no longer a man.

MATRENA: What do you mean? Come on, my boy; give the blessing as is proper, and then it'll all be over. Folks are waiting for you.

NIKITA: How can I give a blessing?

MATRENA: Just as usual. Don't you know how?

NIKITA: I know, I know. But who am I going to bless? What have I done to her?

MATRENA: What have you done? The idea of remembering that! Nobody knows: not the cat, nor the mouse, nor the louse in the house. And then the girl herself is willing to marry.

NIKITA: But how is she willing?

MATRENA: Of course, she's doing it out of fear. But she's willing all the same. What else can she do? She ought to have thought of it then. But now she has no other choice. And the matchmakers feel satisfied. They've seen the girl twice, and the money goes with her. All's covered up clean.

NIKITA: But what's in the cellar?

MATRENA: [*Laughing*] What's in the cellar? Cabbage, mushrooms, and potatoes, I suppose. Let bygones be bygones.

NIKITA: I'd be glad to, but I can't. Whenever you make me think, I can hear things. Oh, what have you women done to me?

MATRENA: What are you acting so queer for anyhow?

NIKITA: [*Turning over flat on his face*] Mother, don't torture me! I can't stand it any longer.

MATRENA: But you must, all the same. There's talk among the people anyhow—and then all of a sudden the father goes off and won't come back, don't dare give his blessing. They'll put two and two together right away. If you shrink from it, they'll guess what's up right away. If you walk the beaten path, nobody thinks you a thief. But if you run away from a wolf, you run into a bear. Above all, don't betray yourself; don't be timid, my boy, or they'll think worse of it.

NIKITA: Oh, you've tied me tight!

MATRENA: Stop it, come along. Come into the company and give your blessing; everything must be as is proper and usual, and then the thing's over.

NIKITA: [*Still lying on his face*] I can't.

MATRENA: [*To herself*] What's happened? Everything was all right, all right, and all of a sudden it struck him. There must be a spell on him.— Nikita, get up! Look, there's Anisya coming; she's left the guests.

[Anisya *comes in gayly dressed and flushed with drink*]

ANISYA: Ain't this fine, mother! So fine and proper! And how happy folks are over it! . . . Where is he?

MATRENA: Here, darling, here. He lay down in the straw and there he lies. He won't come.

NIKITA: [*Looking at his wife*] Huh, she's drunk too. When I see her, it makes my heart sick. How can I live with her? [*Turns over on his face*] I'll kill her some day. It'll be still worse!

ANISYA: Look where he is, buried in the straw!

Has he got over his drunk? [*Laughs*] I'd like to lie down there with you, but I haven't the time. Come on; I'll lead you. And it's so nice in the house! It's a pleasure to see 'em. And the accordion! The women are singing songs, just splendid. Everybody's drunk; all's fine and proper!

NIKITA: What's fine?

ANISYA: The wedding, the merry wedding. Everybody says that it's just a marvel of a wedding. Everything's so fine and lovely. Come on! We'll go together. . . . I've had a drink, but I can lead you. [*Takes his arm*]

NIKITA: [*Pulling away from her, with revulsion*] Go on alone. I'll come later.

ANISYA: What're you in such a temper for! All our troubles are over, we've got rid of the girl that stood between us, we can just live and enjoy ourselves. All's nice and proper, according to the law. I'm so happy over it that I can't tell you. It's just as if I was marrying you a second time. Ha ha! Folks are so pleased! They'll all thank us. And the guests are all nice people. Ivan Moseich is there too, and the policeman. They joined in on the songs.

NIKITA: Well, go sit with them. What did you come out here for?

ANISYA: But you must come along. Otherwise it ain't decent: the hosts have left and deserted the guests. And the guests are all nice people.

NIKITA: [*Rising and brushing off the straw*] Go on; I'll come directly.

MATRENA: The night cuckoo sings louder than the day bird. He wouldn't heed me, but he followed his wife right away.

[Matrena *and* Anisya *move away*]

MATRENA: Are you coming?

NIKITA: I'll come right away. You go along, and I'll follow. I'll come and give my blessing. . . . [*The women pause*] Go on, and—I'll follow. Go along.

[*The women go out.* Nikita *gazes after them, musing*]

NIKITA: [*Sitting down and taking off his boots*] Not much I won't go! No indeed! No, you'd better look for me on the crossbeam. I'll straighten the noose and jump from the crossbeam, and then you can look for me. And here are some rope reins, that's lucky. [*Meditates*] I'd get over my grief, however heavy it was; I'd get over it. But it's right here, it's in my heart; I can't drive it out. [*Looks towards the house*] Looks like she was coming again. [*Mimics* Anisya] "Fine, just fine! I'll lie down with you!" Ugh! the nasty hag! Wait a bit: embrace me when they take me off the beam! That's all that's left. [*Seizes the rope and pulls it*]

MITRICH: [*Drunken, sits up, but does not let go of the rope*] I won't let you have it. I won't let anybody have it. I'll bring it myself. I said I'd bring the straw, and I'll bring it. Is that you, Nikita? [*Laughs*] Oh, the devil! Did you come for straw?

NIKITA: Give me the rope.

MITRICH: No, you wait. The folks sent me. I'll bring it. . . . [*He rises to his feet and begins to rake up the straw, but staggers, recovers himself, and finally falls down*] The liquor's got the best of me. Too much for me!

NIKITA: Give me the reins.

MITRICH: I told you I wouldn't. Oh, Nikita, you're stupid as a blind jackass. [*Laughs*] I like you, but you're stupid. You think I've been drinking. To hell with you! You think I need you. . . . Just look at me! I'm a corporal! You fool, you can't even say it, "Corporal of Her Majesty's very First Regiment of Grenadiers." I served tsar and country with faith and truth. But who am I? You think I'm a soldier? No, I'm not a soldier, but the very least of men; I'm an orphan, a vagrant. I swore off drinking. And now I've started in again! . . . Well, do you think I'm afraid of you? Not much! I ain't afraid of nobody. When I start to drink, I drink! Now I'll swill for two weeks and raise the devil. I'll drink away everything down to my cross, I'll drink away my hat, I'll pawn my passport—and I ain't afraid of nobody! They flogged me in the regiment to keep me from drinking! They laid it on and laid it on. "Well," says they, "will you drink any more?" "Yes," says I. Why should I be afraid of 'em: that's the kind of man I am! I'm the way God made me. I swore off drinking, and I didn't drink. Now I've started again, and I drink! And I ain't afraid of nobody. I'm not lying; that's the way it is. . . . Why should I be afraid of 'em, such rot! "There," says I, "that's the kind of man I am!" A priest was telling me: "The devil is the worst boaster. As soon as you begin to boast," says he, "then you'll feel afraid right away. And when you begin to be afraid of people, then the devil, with his cloven hoof, will snatch you up right away and stick you wherever he wants to." But seeing I'm not afraid of people, it's easy for me. I spit on his beard, the lame cuss, the son of a swine. He won't harm me. "Does my fist taste good?" says I.

NIKITA: [*Crossing himself*] But what's this I'm doing, anyhow? [*Throws away the rope*]

MITRICH: What?

NIKITA: [*Getting up*] You say not to be afraid of people?

MITRICH: Much you need to be afraid of 'em, such rot! Just you look at 'em in the bath. They're all of the same dough. One has a fatter belly, and the other a thinner; that's all the difference between 'em. They're a fine lot to be afraid of, good luck to 'em!

[Matrena *approaches from the house*]

MATRENA: [*Shouts*] Well, are you coming?

NIKITA: Ugh! It *is* better that way. I'm coming! [*Goes off towards the house*]

CHANGE OF SCENE

The cottage of Act I, filled with people, some sitting at tables, others standing. In the front corner are Akulina *and the* Bridegroom. *On the table are the ikons and bread. Among the guests are* Marina, *her* Husband, *and the* Policeman. *The women are singing songs.* Anisya *is passing wine. The songs subside.*

Anisya, Marina *and her* Husband, Akulina, *the* Bridegroom, Coachman, Policeman, Matchmaker (*woman*), *Bridegroom's* Best Man, Matrena, Guests, Peasants.

COACHMAN: It's high time we were going; the church is a long way off.

BEST MAN: Just wait a while; the stepfather will give his blessing. But where is he?

ANISYA: He's coming, he's coming directly, my dears. Have another glass all round; don't hurt our feelings.

MATCHMAKER: (*woman*) What makes him so slow? We've been waiting a long time already.

ANISYA: He's coming. He's coming directly. He'll be here in two shakes of a lamb's tail. Have some more, my dears. [*Passes wine*] He'll be here, directly. Sing some more, my beauties, while you wait.

COACHMAN: They've sung all their songs while we've been waiting.

[*The women sing; in the middle of the song* Nikita *and* Akim *come in*]

NIKITA: [*Holding* Akim *by the arm and pushing him in front of him*] Go on, daddy; I can't do it without you.

AKIM: I don't like it, y'see.

NIKITA: [*To the women*] That's enough; keep still. [*Looks around at everybody in the room*] Marina, are you here?

MATCHMAKER: (*woman*) Come, take the ikon and give us your blessing.

NIKITA: Wait a while, give me time. [*Looking around*] Akulina, are you here?

MATCHMAKER: (*woman*) What are you calling the roll for? Where should she be?— What a freak he is!

ANISYA: Holy saints! Why's he taken off his boots?

NIKITA: Daddy! Are you here? Look at me! Orthodox people, you are here, and I'm here! Here I am! [*Falls on his knees*]

ANISYA: Nikita dear, what are you up to? Oh, poor me!

MATCHMAKER: (*woman*) Well, well!

MATRENA: I'll tell you what: he's had too much of that French wine. Come to your senses, will you? [*She tries to raise him up. He pays no attention to anybody, but looks straight ahead*]

NIKITA: Orthodox people! I am guilty; I wish to repent.

MATRENA: [*Pulling him by the shoulder*] What's the matter with you? Have you gone crazy? Friends, his head's turned; we must take him away.

NIKITA: [*Shoving her aside with his shoulder*] Let me alone! And you, daddy, listen to me. To begin with! Marina, look here! [*He bows down to her feet and rises again*] I did you wrong; I promised to marry you, I seduced you. I deceived you, I cast you off: forgive me for Christ's sake! [*Bows down to her feet once more*]

ANISYA: What are you prating about? This ain't decent. Nobody's questioning you. Get up: what are you making a row for?

MATRENA: O-oh, he's bewitched! How did it happen? He's out of his head.— Get up, what are you talking nonsense for? [*Pulls at him*]

NIKITA: [*Shaking his head*] Don't touch me! Forgive me, Marina! Forgive my sins against you for Christ's sake!

[Marina *covers her face with her hands and is silent*]

ANISYA: Get up, I tell you: what are you making a row for? No use mentioning bygones. Stop your foolery. Shame on you! Oh, poor me! He's gone clean daft.

NIKITA: [*Pushing away his wife and turning to* Akulina] Akulina, I'll talk to you now. Listen, orthodox people! I am an accursed man. Akulina, I did you wrong! Your father did not die a natural death. He was poisoned.

ANISYA: [*Shrieks*] Poor me! What does he mean?

MATRENA: The man's out of his head. Take him away, will you! [*Several men approach and are about to seize him*]

AKIM: [*Shielding him with his arms*] Wait! Here, fellows, wait, y'see; wait, I tell you!

NIKITA: Akulina, I poisoned him. Forgive me, for Christ's sake!

AKULINA: [*Jumping up*] He lies! I know who did it.

MATCHMAKER: (*woman*) What are you doing? Sit still.

AKIM: Oh, Lord! What a sin! What a sin!

POLICEMAN: Seize him! And send for the village elder, and witnesses. We must draw up the document. Get up and come here.

AKIM: [*To the* Policeman] But you, you know— Brass Buttons, y'see—just wait a bit, you know. Just let him tell the story, y'see.

POLICEMAN: [*To* Akim] Look out, old man; don't meddle. I must draw up the document.

AKIM: What a fellow you are, y'see. Wait, I tell you. Don't fuss about the document, y'see. God's work's going on here, you know. A man is repenting, y'see; and you talk about a document, you know.

POLICEMAN: Call the elder!

AKIM: Let God's work go on, you know; when it's over, y'see, then you do your business, y'see.

NIKITA: I did you another great wrong, Akulina; I seduced you. Forgive me for Christ's sake! [*Bows down to her feet*]

AKULINA: [*Coming out from behind the table*] Let me go; I won't get married. He told me to, but now I won't.

POLICEMAN: Repeat what you have said.

NIKITA: Wait, please, policeman; let me finish.

AKIM: [*In ecstasy*] Speak on, my lad; tell it all; it'll be easier for you. Repent in the sight of God; do not fear men. God! God! This is His work!

NIKITA: I poisoned the father; I ruined, cur that *I* am, the daughter. I had power over her; I ruined her and her baby.

AKULINA: It's true, it's true.

NIKITA: I crushed her child in the cellar with a plank. I sat on it. . . . I crushed it . . . and the little bones in it cracked. [*Weeps*] And I buried it in the earth. I did it, nobody but me!

AKULINA: He lies! I told him to. . . .

NIKITA: Don't shield me! I'm not afraid of anybody now! Forgive me, orthodox people! [*Bows down to the earth. Silence*]

POLICEMAN: Bind him. Your marriage is broken up, that's plain.

[*Men approach* Nikita *with sashes*]

NIKITA: Wait, you'll have time. . . . [*Bows down to his father's feet*] Dearest father! Forgive me, accursed sinner that I am—you also! You said to me in the very beginning, when I began to meddle with this nasty whoredom, you said to me: "If a claw is caught, the whole bird is lost." I did not listen to you, cur that I was, and it has come out as you said. Forgive me, for Christ's sake!

AKIM: [*In ecstasy*] God will forgive you, my beloved child! [*Embraces him*] You have not spared yourself, He will spare you. God! God! This is His work!

ELDER: [*Coming in*] There are plenty of witnesses here already.

POLICEMAN: We'll have the examination right away. [*They bind* Nikita]

AKULINA: [*Coming up and standing beside him*] I'll tell the truth. Question me too.

NIKITA: [*Bound*] No use questioning. I did it all by myself. I planned it and I did it. Lead me wherever you want to. I shall say nothing more.

Anton Chekhov

(1860–1904)

Anyone familiar only with the short stories that first made Chekhov famous would find it difficult to believe that the author was, or could ever have become, one of the greatest playwrights of the modern world. Certainly few of the thousand and more stories reveal any interest in action and plot. At times, in fact, Chekhov himself found it difficult to believe that he could have any serious traffic with the stage. He had a retiring disposition, and detested all self-dramatization and exhibitionism. He declared once that he regarded the narrative form as "a lawful wife" and the drama as "a showy, noisy, impertinent, and tiresome mistress." He advised a friend, "Don't write a single line for the theatre unless it is a thousand miles away from you." Nevertheless, Chekhov was enchanted with the stage from boyhood on, became the Moscow Art Theatre's favorite dramatist, fell in love with its ablest actress, Olga Knipper, and married her about two years before his untimely death.

The son of an ex-serf who attained some prosperity for a time and then lost it, Anton Chekhov knew enough about common life to be able to write numerous tales about the country and small town with memorable realism. His knowledge grew materially when he became a physician, practiced medicine among the peasantry, often without charging a fee, and went to eastern Siberia to investigate conditions in the convict camps on Sakhalin. But possibly because of his delicate health (the result of having contracted tuberculosis while studying at the University of Moscow) he acquired a gentleness quite unusual among writers who presented reality as candidly as he did. Most remarkable of all, however, was his almost disconcerting simplicity. It gained him the love of the elderly but still tempestuous Tolstoy, who treated him with a tenderness reserved for women, and it won the admiration of the rugged Gorki, who wrote in his *Reminiscences,* "I think that in Anton Chekhov's presence everyone involuntarily felt in himself a desire to be simple, more truthful, more one's self."

On receiving his medical degree in 1884, Chekhov decided to refrain from practice, because he found story writing a lucrative profession. He published his first collection two years later and won the coveted Pushkin Prize. But it was as early as the year of his graduation that he wrote his first, and only serious, one-act play, *On the High Road,* a poignant scene of devastated souls which could have served as a preliminary sketch for just the sort of play that Gorki wrote in *The Lower Depths* and

O'Neill in *The Iceman Cometh.* In 1887, he composed his first full-length drama, *Ivanov,* the tragedy of a Hamlet of the provinces whose unconventional marriage proved a failure. (The play failed dismally at first in a provincial performance, but was later carried to success by a popular actor at the St. Petersburg Imperial Theatre.) Next Chekhov worked an entire year (1888–1889) on a play unsuccessfully produced under the title of *The Wood Demon* and later published in revised form under the title of *Uncle Vanya.* Putting the manuscript aside as a failure, he continued to write only one-acters of the farcical variety, then called vaudevilles, several of which—*The Boor* (1888), *The Proposal,* and *The Wedding* (1889)—are still played by amateur and professional companies. Except for an unfinished melodrama about a provincial Don Juan *(That Worthless Fellow Platonov),* Chekhov refrained from serious playwriting for some six years. Then the disastrous fate of *The Sea Gull* at the St. Petersburg Alexandrinsky Theatre in 1896 threatened to divorce him permanently from the theatre. Chekhov left the Alexandrinsky before the curtain fell, vowing to leave playwriting alone forever, a resolution that could be applauded only by those who considered his muted artistry ill adapted to the stage. "Never will I write these plays or try to produce them," he wrote, "not if I live to be 700 years old."

Fortunately the Moscow Art Theatre was able to induce him to reconsider his decision, and he allowed Stanislavsky and Dantchenko to revive *The Sea Gull.* Both Chekhov and the new actors' company were saved for the theatre by the *première* of the revival on December 17, 1898. Congratulatory telegrams were showered on the author, then living in Yalta for his health, and in a postscript to a letter describing the triumph Dantchenko asked him for *Uncle Vanya.* After some difficulties when a rival company got hold of the play, the group produced this absorbing tragicomedy with great success on October 26, 1899, and thereafter Chekhov and the Art Theatre never parted. He wrote *The Three Sisters* for the company, with special attention to the talents of certain of its members, and the production on January 31, 1901, was, in Dantchenko's opinion, the best ever given by the Art Theatre. Then, on January 17, 1904, came *The Cherry Orchard,* Chekhov's last as well as most notable play, for Chekhov succumbed to his malady at a German health resort in July of the same year. From *Ivanov* to *The Cherry Orchard,* Chekhov's development as a dramatist was a steady ascent. In the melancholy *Ivanov,* he dramatized the failure of a morbid individual with considerable feeling and insight. In the sensitive tragedy *The Sea Gull,* he added a lyric component, using evocative atmosphere, the device of a play within a play, and delicate symbolism to present the failures of a girl with theatrical ambitions and of a young author who strives to create literature out of his unhappiness as a son and lover. In *Uncle Vanya,* Chekhov succeeded in writing a touching antiheroic drama of wasted lives. The search for happiness was next dramatized with enriched vitality in *The Three Sisters,* and here Chekhov's writing not only deepened but became affirmative through the resolve of his unhappy characters to dedicate themselves to a fruitful way of life even if they themselves were not to enjoy any of the fruits. Finally, in *The Cherry Orchard,* Chekhov broke the impasse of his customary social situation of upper-class decadence by representing a change in society and giving his play a forward direction.

If *The Cherry Orchard* may be construed as an augury of a new order in Russia, at that time on the eve of the Revolution of 1905, the play is also a universal drama of destiny. It speaks for all orders that are fated to pass away, for the humanity that suffers in the course of a transition from an old way of life to a new one, and for all individuals in whom the capacity for adaptation to new conditions is undeveloped—for all "victims of history," so to speak. Gorki's *Yegor Bulychov,* the Soviet playwright Bulgakov's *Days of the Turbins,* Denis Johnston's *The Moon in the Yellow River,* Paul Green's *The House of Connelly,* and Shaw's *Heartbreak House*—these are only a few of the many modern plays that represent a society in the process of transition. Among these studies *The Cherry Orchard* stands out as the most affecting drama and the one most firmly rooted in the life that people hold in common regardless of the interests of contending classes. Chekhov maintained a sensitive equilibrium between regret for the loss of old values and jubilation over the dawn of a new day. And it is the quality of detachment that also enabled him to equalize pathos and humor, and to render a probing account of the contradictions of human character.

The Cherry Orchard holds in solution all of the stylistic and technical attributes of Chekhov's dramatic artistry. Here we find his artful artlessness in presenting the flow and commingling of lives. The characters are often so absorbed in themselves that they are unaware of the trend of a conversation or a situation. Being largely directionless, they fly off at a tangent from their own and other characters' action or thoughts. Chekhov manages to make drama of this very trait and to shape a complete play out of scattered fragments of human reality. It is for this quality that his technique has been designated as "centrifugal." And since people's lives meet only to fly apart or fly apart only to meet, since they cross and recross one another's orbits, Chekhov's method of creating dramatic experience has been aptly called "contrapuntal." As this method of writing is a fascinating problem for playwrights, it has been attempted by others since his day, but rarely with his effectiveness. Only a master can sustain counterpoint interestingly for any length of time in drama, as in music.

It may also be noted that, by creating a new kind of catastrophe, Chekhov, almost alone, introduced into the theatre a new kind of tragedy, a tragedy of attrition. Instead of showing noble people as eventfully destroyed, he generally represented them as being eroded. His characters are seen rusting away in disuse, eventlessly stalemated, or permanently dislocated. Although *Uncle Vanya* and *The Three Sisters* provide the supreme examples, attrition is also the fate of the gentry of *The Cherry Orchard.* The dispersed family has no future, for there is no reason to believe that its members will make a successful adaptation to reality.

If, nevertheless, the effect is not actually depressing, this is due not only to the bountiful humanity of the play but to the realization that if the old order must pass it will not leave a vacuum. The axes that fell the trees of the cherry orchard are clearing the ground for more vital, if less refined, men and women. The summer bungalows will accommodate adults who make a civilization instead of living parasitically on it, and they will probably teem with the common man's brood of children, among whom will be the heroes, saints, scientists, and poets of tomorrow. Stanislavsky, who must have understood Chekhov's plays better than anyone else, found them fundamentally "positive" and rejected the view that they were the elegies of a world-weary man.

BIBLIOGRAPHY: Anton Chekhov, *Note-Book of Anton Chekhov,* 1921; Chekhov, *Letters of A. Tchekov to His Family and Friends,* translated by Constance Garnett, 1920; Chekhov, *The Life and Letters of A. Tchekhov,* translated by S. S. Koteliansky and Philip Tomlinson, 1925; Chekhov, *The Personal Papers of Anton Chekhov, 1948;* Vladimir Nemirovitch-Dantchenko, *My Life in the Russian Theatre* (pp. 139–142, 161–164, 165–167), 1931; John Gassner, *Masters of the Drama,* (pp. 508–520), 1945; William Gerhardi, *Anton Chekhov; A Critical Study,* 1923; Maxim Gorki, *Reminiscences of Tolstoy, Chekhov and Andreyev* (Dover Publications, 1946 edition); Constantin Stanislavsky, *My Life in Art* (pp. 345–375, 415–419), 1924, 1928; Leo Wiener, *The Contemporary Drama of Russia,* 1924.

THE CHERRY ORCHARD

By Anton Chekhov

TRANSLATED FROM THE RUSSIAN BY CONSTANCE GARNETT

CHARACTERS IN THE PLAY

MADAME RANEVSKY (LYUBOV AN-
DREYEVNA), *the owner of the
Cherry Orchard*
ANYA, *her daughter, aged 17*
VARYA, *her adopted daughter, aged
24*
GAEV (LEONID ANDREYEVITCH),
brother of Madame Ranevsky

LOPAHIN (YERMOLAY ALEXEYE-
VITCH), *a merchant*
TROFIMOV (PYOTR SERGEYEVITCH),
a student
SEMYONOV-PISHTCHIK, *a landowner*
CHARLOTTA IVANOVNA, *a governess*
EPIHODOV (SEMYON PANTALEYE-
VITCH), *a clerk*

DUNYASHA, *a maid*
FIRS, *an old valet, aged 87*
YASHA, *a young valet*
A WAYFARER
THE STATION MASTER
A POST-OFFICE CLERK
VISITORS, SERVANTS

The action takes place on the estate of Madame
Ranevsky.

ACT I.

*A room, which has always been called the nur-
sery. One of the doors leads into Anya's room.
Dawn, sun rises during the scene. May, the cherry
trees in flower, but it is cold in the garden with
the frost of early morning. Windows closed.
Enter Dunyasha with a candle and Lopahin with
a book in his hand.*

LOPAHIN: The train's in, thank God. What time
is it?

DUNYASHA: Nearly two o'clock. [*Puts out the
candle*] It's daylight already.

LOPAHIN: The train's late! Two hours, at least.
[*Yawns and stretches*] I'm a pretty one; what a
fool I've been. Came here on purpose to meet them
at the station and dropped asleep. . . . Dozed off
as I sat in the chair. It's annoying. . . . You might
have waked me.

DUNYASHA: I thought you had gone. [*Listens*]
There, I do believe they're coming!

LOPAHIN: [*Listens*] No, what with the luggage and
one thing and another. [*A pause*] Lyubov Andreyevna has been abroad five years; I don't know what
she is like now. . . . She's a splendid woman. A
good-natured, kind-hearted woman. I remember
when I was a lad of fifteen, my poor father—he used
to keep a little shop here in the village in those days
—gave me a punch in the face with his fist and
made my nose bleed. We were in the yard here, I
forget what we'd come about—he had had a drop.
Lyubov Andreyevna—I can see her now—she was
a slim young girl then—took me to wash my face,
and then brought me into this very room, into the
nursery. "Don't cry, little peasant," says she, "it

will be well in time for your wedding day." . . .
[*A pause*] Little peasant. . . . My father was a
peasant, it's true, but here am I in a white waistcoat
and brown shoes, like a pig in a bun shop. Yes, I'm
a rich man, but for all my money, come to think, a
peasant I was, and a peasant I am. [*Turns over the
pages of the book*] I've been reading this book and I
can't make head or tail of it. I fell asleep over it.
[*A pause*]

DUNYASHA: The dogs have been awake all night,
they feel that the mistress is coming.

LOPAHIN: Why, what's the matter with you, Dunyasha?

DUNYASHA: My hands are all of a tremble. I feel
as though I should faint.

LOPAHIN: You're a spoilt soft creature, Dunyasha.
And dressed like a lady too, and your hair done up.
That's not the thing. One must know one's place.

[*Enter* Epihodov *with a nosegay; he wears a
pea-jacket and highly polished creaking top-
boots; he drops the nosegay as he comes in*]

EPIHODOV: [*Picking up the nosegay*] Here! the
gardener's sent this, says you're to put it in the
dining-room. [*Gives* Dunyasha *the nosegay*]

LOPAHIN: And bring me some kvass.

DUNYASHA: I will. [*Goes out*]

EPIHODOV: It's chilly this morning, three degrees
of frost, though the cherries are all in flower. I
can't say much for our climate. [*Sighs*] I can't. Our
climate is not often propitious to the occasion. Yermolay Alexeyevitch, permit me to call your attention to the fact that I purchased myself a pair of
boots the day before yesterday, and they creak, I
venture to assure you, so that there's no tolerating
them. What ought I to grease them with?

LOPAHIN: Oh, shut up! Don't bother me.

EPIHODOV: Every day some misfortune befalls
me. I don't complain, I'm used to it, and I wear
a smiling face.

[Dunyasha *comes in, hands* Lopahin *the kvass*]

EPIHODOV: I am going. [*Stumbles against a chair.*

which *falls over*] There! [*As though triumphant*] There you see now, excuse the expression, an accident like that among others. . . . It's positively remarkable. [*Goes out*]

DUNYASHA: Do you know, Yermolay Alexeyevitch, I must confess, Epihodov has made me a proposal.

LOPAHIN: Ah!

DUNYASHA: I'm sure I don't know. . . . He's a harmless fellow, but sometimes when he begins talking, there's no making anything of it. It's all very fine and expressive, only there's no understanding it. I've a sort of liking for him too. He loves me to distraction. He's an unfortunate man; every day there's something. They tease him about it—two and twenty misfortunes they call him.

LOPAHIN: [*Listening*] There! I do believe they're coming.

DUNYASHA: They are coming! What's the matter with me? . . . I'm cold all over.

LOPAHIN: They really are coming. Let's go and meet them. Will she know me? It's five years since I saw her.

DUNYASHA: [*In a flutter*] I shall drop this very minute. . . . Ah, I shall drop.

[*There is a sound of two carriages driving up to the house.* Lopahin *and* Dunyasha *go out quickly. The stage is left empty. A noise is heard in the adjoining rooms.* Firs, *who has driven to meet Madame Ranevsky, crosses the stage hurriedly leaning on a stick. He is wearing old-fashioned livery and a high hat. He says something to himself, but not a word can be distinguished. The noise behind the scenes goes on increasing. A voice: "Come, let's go in here." Enter* Lyubov Andreyevna, Anya, *and* Charlotta Ivanovna *with a pet dog on a chain, all in traveling dresses.* Varya *in an out-door coat with a kerchief over her head,* Gaev, Semyonov-Pishtchik, Lopahin, Dunyasha *with bag and parasol, servants with other articles. All walk across the room*]

ANYA: Let's come in here. Do you remember what room this is, mamma?

LYUBOV: [*Joyfully, through her tears*] The nursery!

VARYA: How cold it is, my hands are numb [*To* Lyubov Andreyevna] Your rooms, the white room and the lavender one, are just the same as ever, mamma.

LYUBOV: My nursery, dear delightful room. . . . I used to sleep here when I was little. . . . [*Cries*] And here I am, like a little child. . . . [*Kisses her brother and* Varya, *and then her brother again*] Varya's just the same as ever, like a nun. And I knew Dunyasha. [*Kisses* Dunyasha]

GAEV: The train was two hours late. What do you think of that? Is that the way to do things?

CHARLOTTA: [*To* Pishtchik] My dog eats nuts, too.

PISHTCHIK: [*Wonderingly*] Fancy that!

[*They all go out except* Anya *and* Dunyasha]

DUNYASHA: We've been expecting you so long [*Takes* Anya's *hat and coat*]

ANYA: I haven't slept for four nights on the journey. I feel dreadfully cold.

DUNYASHA: You set out in Lent, there was snow and frost, and now? My darling! [*Laughs and kisses her*] I *have* missed you, my precious, my joy. I must tell you . . . I can't put it off a minute. . . .

ANYA: [*Wearily*] What now?

DUNYASHA: Epihodov, the clerk, made me a proposal just after Easter.

ANYA: It's always the same thing with you. . . [*Straightening her hair*] I've lost all my hairpins. [*She is staggering from exhaustion*]

DUNYASHA: I don't know what to think, really. He does love me, he does love me so!

ANYA: [*Looking towards her door, tenderly*] My own room, my windows just as though I had never gone away. I'm home! To-morrow morning I shall get up and run into the garden. . . . Oh, if I could get to sleep! I haven't slept all the journey, I was so anxious and worried.

DUNYASHA: Pyotr Sergeyevitch came the day before yesterday.

ANYA: [*Joyfully*] Petya!

DUNYASHA: He's asleep in the bath house, he has settled in there. I'm afraid of being in their way, says he. [*Glancing at her watch*] I was to have waked him, but Varvara Mihalovna told me not to. Don't you wake him, says she.

[*Enter* Varya *with a bunch of keys at her waist*]

VARYA: Dunyasha, coffee and make haste. . . Mamma's asking for coffee.

DUNYASHA: This very minute. [*Goes out*]

VARYA: Well, thank God, you've come. You're home again. [*Petting her*] My little darling has come back! My precious beauty has come back again!

ANYA: I have had a time of it!

VARYA: I can fancy.

ANYA: We set off in Holy Week—it was so cold then, and all the way Charlotta would talk and show off her tricks. What did you want to burden me with Charlotta for?

VARYA: You couldn't have traveled all alone, darling. At seventeen!

ANYA: We got to Paris at last, it was cold there, snow. I speak French shockingly. Mamma lives on the fifth floor, I went up to her and there were a lot of French people, ladies, an old priest with a book. The place smelt of tobacco and so comfortless. I felt sorry, oh! so sorry for mamma all at once, I put my arms round her neck, and hugged her and wouldn't let her go. Mamma was as kind as she could be, and she cried. . . .

VARYA: [*Through her tears*] Don't speak of it, don't speak of it!

ANYA: She had sold her villa at Mentone, she had nothing left, nothing. I hadn't a farthing left either, we only just had enough to get here. And mamma doesn't understand! When we had dinner at the stations, she always ordered the most expensive things and gave the waiters a whole rouble. Charlotta's just the same. Yasha too must have the same as we do; it's simply awful. You know Yasha is mamma's valet now, we brought him here with us.

VARYA: Yes, I've seen the young rascal.

ANYA: Well, tell me—have you paid the arrears on the mortgage?

VARYA: How could we get the money?

ANYA: Oh, dear! Oh, dear!

VARYA: In August the place will be sold.

ANYA: My goodness!

LOPAHIN: [Peeps in at the door and moos like a cow] Moo! [Disappears]

VARYA: [Weeping] There, that's what I could do to him. [Shakes her fist]

ANYA: [Embracing Varya, softly] Varya, has he made you an offer? [Varya shakes her head] Why, but he loves you. Why is it you don't come to an understanding? What are you waiting for?

VARYA: I believe that there never will be anything between us. He has a lot to do, he has no time for me . . . and takes no notice of me. Bless the man, it makes me miserable to see him. . . . Everyone's talking of our being married, everyone's congratulating me, and all the while there's really nothing in it; it's all like a dream. [In another tone] You have a new brooch like a bee.

ANYA: [Mournfully] Mamma bought it. [Goes into her own room and in a light-hearted childish tone] And you know, in Paris I went up in a balloon!

VARYA: My darling's home again! My pretty is home again!

[Dunyasha returns with the coffee-pot and is making the coffee]

VARYA: [Standing at the door] All day long, darling, as I go about looking after the house, I keep dreaming all the time. If only we could marry you to a rich man, then I should feel more at rest. Then I would go off by myself on a pilgrimage to Kiev, to Moscow . . . and so I would spend my life going from one holy place to another. . . . I would go on and on. . . . What bliss!

ANYA: The birds are singing in the garden. What time is it?

VARYA: It must be nearly three. It's time you were asleep, darling. [Going into Anya's room] What bliss!

[Yasha enters with a rug and a traveling bag]

YASHA: [Crosses the stage, mincingly] May one come in here, pray?

DUNYASHA: I shouldn't have known you, Yasha. How you have changed abroad.

YASHA: H'm! . . . And who are you?

DUNYASHA: When you went away, I was that high. [Shows distance from floor] Dunyasha, Fyodor's daughter. . . . You don't remember me!

YASHA: H'm! . . . You're a peach! [Looks round and embraces her: she shrieks and drops a saucer. Yasha goes out hastily]

VARYA: [In the doorway, in a tone of vexation] What now?

DUNYASHA: [Through her tears] I have broken a saucer.

VARYA: Well, that brings good luck.

ANYA: [Coming out of her room] We ought to prepare mamma: Petya is here.

VARYA: I told them not to wake him.

ANYA: [Dreamily] It's six years since father died. Then only a month later little brother Grisha was drowned in the river, such a pretty boy he was, only seven. It was more than mamma could bear, so she went away, went away without looking back. [Shuddering] . . . How well I understand her, if only she knew! [A pause] And Petya Trofimov was Grisha's tutor, he may remind her.

[Enter Firs: he is wearing a pea-jacket and a white waistcoat]

FIRS: [Goes up to the coffee-pot, anxiously] The mistress will be served here. [Puts on white gloves] Is the coffee ready? [Sternly to Dunyasha] Girl! Where's the cream?

DUNYASHA: Ah, mercy on us! [Goes out quickly]

FIRS: [Fussing round the coffee-pot] Ech! you good-for-nothing! [Muttering to himself] Come back from Paris. And the old master used to go to Paris too . . . horses all the way. [Laughs]

VARYA: What is it, Firs?

FIRS: What is your pleasure? [Gleefully] My lady has come home! I have lived to see her again! Now I can die. [Weeps with joy]

[Enter Lyubov Andreyevna, Gaev and Semyonov-Pishtchik; the latter is in a short-waisted full coat of fine cloth, and full trousers. Gaev, as he comes in, makes a gesture with his arms and his whole body, as though he were playing billiards]

LYUBOV: How does it go? Let me remember Cannon off the red!

GAEV: That's it—in off the white! Why, once, sister, we used to sleep together in this very room, and now I'm fifty-one, strange as it seems.

LOPAHIN: Yes, time flies.

GAEV: What do you say?

LOPAHIN: Time, I say, flies.

GAEV: What a smell of patchouli!

ANYA: I'm going to bed. Good-night, mamma. [Kisses her mother]

LYUBOV: My precious darling. [Kisses her hands] Are you glad to be home? I can't believe it.

ANYA: Good-night, uncle.

GAEV: [Kissing her face and hands] God bless you! How like you are to your mother! [To his sister] At her age you were just the same, Lyuba.

[Anya shakes hands with Lopahin and Pishtchik, then goes out, shutting the door after her]

LYUBOV: She's quite worn out.

PISHTCHIK: Aye, it's a long journey, to be sure.

VARYA: [*To* Lopahin *and* Pishtchik] Well, gentlemen? It's three o'clock and time to say good-bye.

LYUBOV: [*Laughs*] You're just the same as ever, Varya. [*Draws her to her and kisses her*] I'll just drink my coffee and then we will all go and rest. [Firs *puts a cushion under her feet*] Thanks, friend. I am so fond of coffee, I drink it day and night. Thanks, dear old man. [*Kisses* Firs]

VARYA: I'll just see whether all the things have been brought in. [*Goes out*]

LYUBOV: Can it really be me sitting here? [*Laughs*] I want to dance about and clap my hands. [*Covers her face with her hands*] And I could drop asleep in a moment! God knows I love my country, I love it tenderly; I couldn't look out of the window in the train, I kept crying so. [*Through her tears*] But I must drink my coffee, though. Thank you, Firs, thanks, dear old man. I'm so glad to find you still alive.

FIRS: The day before yesterday.

GAEV: He's rather deaf.

LOPAHIN: I have to set off for Harkov directly, at five o'clock. . . . It is annoying! I wanted to have a look at you, and a little talk. . . . You are just as splendid as ever.

PISHTCHIK: [*Breathing heavily*] Handsomer, indeed. . . . Dressed in Parisian style . . . completely bowled me over.

LOPAHIN: Your brother, Leonid Andreyevitch here, is always saying that I'm a low-born knave, that I'm a money-grubber, but I don't care one straw for that. Let him talk. Only I do want you to believe in me as you used to. I do want your wonderful tender eyes to look at me as they used to in the old days. Merciful God! My father was a serf of your father and of your grandfather, but you—you—did so much for me once, that I've forgotten all that; I love you as though you were my kin . . . more than my kin.

LYUBOV: I can't sit still, I simply can't. . . .

[*Jumps up and walks about in violent agitation*] This happiness is too much for me. . . . You may laugh at me, I know I'm silly. . . . My own bookcase. [*Kisses the bookcase*] My little table.

GAEV: Nurse died while you were away.

LYUBOV: [*Sits down and drinks coffee*] Yes, the Kingdom of Heaven be hers! You wrote me of her death.

GAEV: And Anastasy is dead. Squinting Petruchka has left me and is in service now with the police captain in the town.

[*Takes a box of caramels out of his pocket and sucks one*]

PISHTCHIK: My daughter, Dashenka, wishes to be remembered to you.

LOPAHIN: I want to tell you something very pleasant and cheering. [*Glancing at his watch*] I'm going directly . . . there's no time to say much . . . well, I can say it in a couple of words. I needn't tell you your cherry orchard is to be sold to pay your debts; the 22nd of August is the date fixed for the sale; but don't you worry, dearest lady, you may sleep in peace, there is a way of saving it. . . . This is what I propose. I beg your attention! Your estate is not twenty miles from the town, the railway runs close by it, and if the cherry orchard and the land along the river bank were cut up into building plots and then let on lease for summer villas, you would make an income of at least 25,000 roubles a year out of it.

GAEV: That's all rot, if you'll excuse me.

LYUBOV: I don't quite understand you, Yermolay Alexeyevitch.

LOPAHIN: You will get a rent of at least 25 roubles a year for a three-acre plot from summer visitors, and if you say the word now, I'll bet you what you like there won't be one square foot of ground vacant by the autumn, all the plots will be taken up. I congratulate you; in fact, you are saved. It's a perfect situation with that deep river. Only, of course, it must be cleared—all the old buildings, for example, must be removed, this house too, which is really good for nothing and the old cherry orchard must be cut down.

LYUBOV: Cut down? My dear fellow, forgive me, but you don't know what you are talking about. If there is one thing interesting—remarkable indeed—in the whole province, it's just our cherry orchard.

LOPAHIN: The only thing remarkable about the orchard is that it's a very large one. There's a crop of cherries every alternate year, and then there's nothing to be done with them, no one buys them.

GAEV: This orchard is mentioned in the *Encyclopædia*.

LOPAHIN: [*Glancing at his watch*] If we don't decide on something and don't take some steps, on the 22nd of August the cherry orchard and the whole estate too will be sold by auction. Make up your minds! There is no other way of saving it, I'll take my oath on that. No, No!

FIRS: In old days, forty or fifty years ago, they used to dry the cherries, soak them, pickle them, make jam too, and they used——

GAEV: Be quiet, Firs.

FIRS: And they used to send the preserved cherries to Moscow and to Harkov by the wagon-load. That brought the money in! And the preserved cherries in those days were soft and juicy, sweet and fragrant . . . They knew the way to do them then. . . .

LYUBOV: And where is the recipe now?

FIRS: It's forgotten. Nobody remembers it.

PISHTCHIK: [*To* Lyubov Andreyevna] What's it like in Paris? Did you eat frogs there?

LYUBOV: Oh, I ate crocodiles.

PISHTCHIK: Fancy that now!

LOPAHIN: There used to be only the gentlefolks and the peasants in the country, but now there are these summer visitors. All the towns, even the small ones, are surrounded, nowadays by these summer villas. And one may say for sure, that in another twenty years there'll be many more of these people and that they'll be everywhere. At present the summer visitor only drinks tea in his verandah, but maybe he'll take to working his bit of land too, and then your cherry orchard would become happy, rich and prosperous. . . .

GAEV: [Indignant] What rot!

[Enter Varya and Yasha]

VARYA: There are two telegrams for you, mamma [Takes out keys and opens an old-fashioned bookcase with a loud crack] Here they are.

LYUBOV: From Paris [Tears the telegrams, without reading them] I have done with Paris.

GAEV: Do you know, Lyuba, how old that bookcase is? Last week I pulled out the bottom drawer and there I found the date branded on it. The bookcase was made just a hundred years ago. What do you say to that? We might have celebrated its jubilee. Though it's an inanimate object, still it is a book case.

PISHTCHIK: [Amazed] A hundred years! Fancy that now.

GAEV: Yes. . . . It is a thing. . . . [Feeling the bookcase] Dear, honored, bookcase! Hail to thee who for more than a hundred years hast served the pure ideals of good and justice; thy silent call to fruitful labor has never flagged in those hundred years, maintaining [in tears] in the generations of man, courage and faith in a brighter future and fostering in us ideals of good and social consciousness [A pause]

LOPAHIN: Yes. . . .

LYUBOV: You are just the same as ever, Leonid.

GAEV: [A little embarrassed] Cannon off the right into the pocket!

LOPAHIN: [Looking at his watch] Well, it's time I was off.

YASHA: [Handing Lyubov Andreyevna medicine] Perhaps you will take your pills now.

PISHTCHIK: You shouldn't take medicines, my dear madam . . . they do no harm and no good. Give them here . . . honored lady [Takes the pillbox, pours the pills into the hollow of his hand, blows on them, puts them in his mouth and drinks off some kvass] There!

LYUBOV: [In alarm] Why, you must be out of your mind!

PISHTCHIK: I have taken all the pills.

LOPAHIN: What a glutton! [All laugh]

FIRS: His honor stayed with us in Easter week, ate a gallon and a half of cucumbers. . . . [Mutters]

LYUBOV: What is he saying?

VARYA: He has taken to muttering like that for the last three years. We are used to it.

YASHA: His declining years!

[Charlotta Ivanovna, a very thin, lanky figure in a white dress with a lorgnette in her belt, walks across the stage]

LOPAHIN: I beg your pardon, Charlotta Ivanovna, I have not had time to greet you. [Tries to kiss her hand]

CHARLOTTA: [Pulling away her hand] If I let you kiss my hand, you'll be wanting to kiss my elbow, and then my shoulder.

LOPAHIN: I've no luck to-day! [All laugh] Charlotta Ivanovna, show us some tricks!

LYUBOV: Charlotta, do show us some tricks!

CHARLOTTA: I don't want to. I'm sleepy. [Goes out]

LOPAHIN: In three weeks' time we shall meet again. [Kisses Lyubov Andreyevna's hand] Good-bye till then—I must go. [To Gaev] Good-bye. [Kisses Pishtchik] Good-bye. [Gives his hand to Varya, then to Firs and Yasha] I don't want to go. [To Lyubov Andreyevna] If you think over my plan for the villas and make up your mind, then let me know; I will lend you 50,000 roubles. Think of it seriously.

VARYA: [Angrily] Well, do go, for goodness sake.

LOPAHIN: I'm going, I'm going. [Goes out]

GAEV: Low-born knave! I beg pardon, though . . . Varya is going to marry him, he's Varya's fiancé.

VARYA: Don't talk nonsense, uncle.

LYUBOV: Well, Varya, I shall be delighted. He's a good man.

PISHTCHIK: He is, one must acknowledge, a most worthy man. And my Dashenka . . . says too that . . . she says . . . various things. [Snores, but at once wakes up] But all the same, honored lady, could you oblige me . . . with a loan of 240 roubles . . . to pay the interest on my mortgage to-morrow?

VARYA: [Dismayed] No, no.

LYUBOV: I really haven't any money.

PISHTCHIK: It will turn up. [Laughs] I never lose hope. I thought everything was over, I was a ruined man, and lo and behold—the railway passed through my land and . . . they paid me for it. And something else will turn up again, if not to-day, then to-morrow . . . Dashenka'll win two hundred thousand . . . she's got a lottery ticket.

LYUBOV: Well, we've finished our coffee, we can go to bed.

FIRS: [Brushes Gaev, reprovingly] You have got on the wrong trousers again! What am I to do with you?

VARYA: [Softly] Anya's asleep. [Softly opens the window] Now the sun's risen, it's not a bit cold. Look, mamma, what exquisite trees! My goodness! And the air! The starlings are singing!

GAEV: [Opens another window] The orchard is all white. You've not forgotten it, Lyuba? That long avenue that runs straight, straight as an arrow, how it shines on a moonlight night. You remember? You've not forgotten?

LYUBOV: [Looking out of the window into the garden] Oh, my childhood, my innocence! It was in this nursery I used to sleep, from here I looked out into the orchard, happiness waked with me every morning and in those days the orchard was just the same, nothing has changed. [*Laughs with delight*] All, all white! Oh, my orchard! After the dark gloomy autumn, and the cold winter; you are young again, and full of happiness, the heavenly angels have never left you. . . . If I could cast off the burden that weighs on my heart, if I could forget the past!

GAEV: H'm! and the orchard will be sold to pay our debts; it seems strange. . . .

LYUBOV: See, our mother walking . . . all in white, down the avenue! [*Laughs with delight*] It is she!

GAEV: Where?

VARYA: Oh, don't, mamma!

LYUBOV: There is no one. It was my fancy. On the right there, by the path to the arbor, there is a white tree bending like a woman. . . .

[*Enter* Trofimov *wearing a shabby student's uniform and spectacles*]

LYUBOV: What a ravishing orchard! White masses of blossom, blue sky. . . .

TROFIMOV: Lyubov Andreyevna! [*She looks round at him*] I will just pay my respects to you and then leave you at once. [*Kisses her hand warmly*] I was told to wait until morning, but I hadn't the patience to wait any longer. . . .

[*Lyubov Andreyevna looks at him in perplexity*]

VARYA: [*Through her tears*] This is Petya Trofimov.

TROFIMOV: Petya Trofimov, who was your Grisha's tutor. . . . Can I have changed so much?

[*Lyubov Andreyevna embraces him and weeps quietly*]

GAEV: [*In confusion*] There, there, Lyuba.

VARYA: [*Crying*] I told you, Petya, to wait till to-morrow.

LYUBOV: My Grisha . . . my boy . . . Grisha . . . my son!

VARYA: We can't help it, mamma, it is God's will.

TROFIMOV: [*Softly through his tears*] There . . . there.

LYUBOV: [*Weeping quietly*] My boy was lost . . . drowned. Why? Oh, why, dear Petya? [*More quietly*] Anya is asleep in there, and I'm talking loudly . . . making this noise. . . . But, Petya? Why have you grown so ugly? Why do you look so old?

TROFIMOV: A peasant-woman in the train called me a mangy-looking gentleman.

LYUBOV: You were quite a boy then, a pretty little student, and now your hair's thin—and spectacles. Are you really a student still? [*Goes towards the door*]

TROFIMOV: I seem likely to be a perpetual student.

LYUBOV: [*Kisses her brother, then* Varya] Well, go to bed. . . . You are older too, Leonid.

PISHTCHIK: [*Follows her*] I suppose it's time we were asleep. . . . Ugh! my gout. I'm staying the night! Lyubov Andreyevna, my dear soul, if you could . . . to-morrow morning . . . 240 roubles.

GAEV: That's always his story.

PISHTCHIK: 240 roubles . . . to pay the interest on my mortgage.

LYUBOV: My dear man, I have no money.

PISHTCHIK: I'll pay it back, my dear . . . a trifling sum.

LYUBOV: Oh, well, Leonid will give it you. . . . You give him the money, Leonid.

GAEV: Me give it him! Let him wait till he gets it!

LYUBOV: It can't be helped, give it him. He needs it. He'll pay it back.

[Lyubov Andreyevna, Trofimov, Pishtchik *and* Firs *go out*. Gaev, Varya *and* Yasha *remain*]

GAEV: Sister hasn't got out of the habit of flinging away her money. [*To* Yasha] Get away, my good fellow, you smell of the hen-house.

YASHA: [*With a grin*] And you, Leonid Andreyevitch, are just the same as ever.

GAEV: What's that? [*To* Varya] What did he say?

VARYA: [*To* Yasha] Your mother has come from the village; she has been sitting in the servants' room since yesterday, waiting to see you.

YASHA: Oh, bother her!

VARYA: For shame!

YASHA: What's the hurry? She might just as well have come to-morrow. [*Goes out*]

VARYA: Mamma's just the same as ever, she hasn't changed a bit. If she had her own way, she'd give away everything.

GAEV: Yes. [*A pause*] If a great many remedies are suggested for some disease, it means that the disease is incurable. I keep thinking and racking my brains; I have many schemes, a great many, and that really means none. If we could only come in for a legacy from somebody, or marry our Anya to a very rich man, or we might go to Yaroslav and try our luck with our old aunt, the Countess. She's very, very rich, you know.

VARYA: [*Weeps*] If God would help us.

GAEV: Don't blubber. Aunt's very rich, but she doesn't like us. First, sister married a lawyer instead of a nobleman. . . .

[Anya *appears in the doorway*]

GAEV: And then her conduct, one can't call virtuous. She is good, and kind, and nice, and I love her, but, however one allows for extenuating circumstances, there's no denying that she's an immoral woman. One feels it in her slightest gesture.

VARYA: [*In a whisper*] Anya's in the doorway.

GAEV: What do you say? [*A pause*] It's queer, there seems to be something wrong with my right eye. I don't see as well as I did. And on Thursday when I was in the district Court . . .

[*Enter* Anya]

VARYA: Why aren't you asleep, Anya?

ANYA: I can't get to sleep.

GAEV: My pet. [*Kisses* Anya's *face and hands*] My child. [*Weeps*] You are not my niece, you are my angel, you are everything to me. Believe me, believe. . . .

ANYA: I believe you, uncle. Everyone loves you and respects you . . . but, uncle dear, you must be silent . . . simply be silent. What were you saying just now about my mother, about your own sister? What made you say that?

GAEV: Yes, yes. . . . [*Puts his hand over his face*] Really, that was awful! My God, save me! And to-day I made a speech to the bookcase . . . so stupid! And only when I had finished, I saw how stupid it was.

VARYA: It's true, uncle, you ought to keep quiet. Don't talk, that's all.

ANYA: If you could keep from talking, it would make things easier for you, too.

GAEV: I won't speak. [*Kisses* Anya's *and* Varya's *hands*] I'll be silent. Only this is about business. On Thursday I was in the district Court; well, there was a large party of us there and we began talking of one thing and another, and this and that, and do you know, I believe that it will be possible to raise a loan on an I.O.U. to pay the arrears on the mortgage.

VARYA: If the Lord would help us!

GAEV: I'm going on Tuesday; I'll talk of it again. [*To* Varya] Don't blubber. [*To* Anya] Your mamma will talk to Lopahin; of course, he won't refuse her. And as soon as you're rested you shall go to Yaroslavl to the Countess, your great-aunt. So we shall all set to work in three directions at once, and the business is done. We shall pay off arrears, I'm convinced of it. [*Puts a caramel in his mouth*] I swear on my honor, I swear by anything you like, the estate shan't be sold. [*Excitedly*] By my own happiness, I swear it! Here's my hand on it, call me the basest, vilest of men, if I let it come to an auction! Upon my soul I swear it!

ANYA: [*Her equanimity has returned, she is quite happy*] How good you are, uncle, and how clever! [*Embraces her uncle*] I'm at peace now! Quite at peace! I'm happy!

[*Enter* Firs]

FIRS: [*Reproachfully*] Leonid Andreyevitch, have you no fear of God? When are you going to bed?

GAEV: Directly, directly. You can go, Firs. I'll . . . yes, I will undress myself. Come, children, bye-bye. We'll go into details to-morrow, but now go to bed. [*Kisses* Anya *and* Varya] I'm a man of the eighties. They run down that period, but still I can say I have had to suffer not a little for my convictions in my life, it's not for nothing that the peasant loves me. One must know the peasant! One must know how. . . .

ANYA: At it again, uncle!

VARYA: Uncle dear, you'd better be quiet!

FIRS: [*Angrily*] Leonid Andreyevitch!

GAEV: I'm coming. I'm coming. Go to bed. Potted the shot—there's a shot for you! A beauty! [*Goes out,* Firs *hobbling after him*]

ANYA: My mind's at rest now. I don't want to go to Yaroslavl, I don't like my great-aunt, but still my mind's at rest. Thanks to uncle. [*Sits down*]

VARYA: We must go to bed. I'm going. Something unpleasant happened while you were away. In the old servants' quarters there are only the old servants, as you know—Efimyushka, Polya and Yevstigney—and Karp too. They began letting stray people in to spend the night—I said nothing. But all at once I heard they had been spreading a report that I gave them nothing but pease pudding to eat. Out of stinginess, you know. . . . And it was all Yevstigney's doing. . . .Very well, I said to myself. . . . If that's how it is, I thought, wait a bit. I sent for Yevstigney. . . . [*Yawns*] He comes. . . . "How's this, Yevstigney," I said, "you could be such a fool as to? . . ." [*Looking at* Anya] Anitchka! [*A pause*] She's asleep. [*Puts her arm around* Anya] Come to bed . . . come along! [*Leads her*] My darling has fallen asleep! Come . . . [*They go*]

[*Far away beyond the orchard a shepherd plays on a pipe.* Trofimov *crosses the stage and, seeing* Varya *and* Anya, *stands still*]

VARYA: 'Sh! asleep, asleep. Come, my own.

ANYA: [*Softly, half asleep*] I'm so tired. Still those bells. Uncle . . . dear . . . mamma and uncle. . . .

VARYA: Come, my own, come along.

[*They go into* Anya's *room*]

TROFIMOV: [*Tenderly*] My sunshine! My spring.

CURTAIN.

ACT II.

The open country. An old shrine, long abandoned and fallen out of the perpendicular; near it a well, large stones that have apparently once been tombstones, and an old garden seat. The road to Gaev's *house is seen. On one side rise dark poplars; and there the cherry orchard begins. In the distance a row of telegraph poles and far, far away on the horizon there is faintly outlined a great town, only visible in very fine clear weather. It is near sunset.* Charlotta, Yasha *and* Dunyasha *are sitting on the seat.* Epihodov *is standing near, playing something mournful on a guitar. All sit plunged in thought.* Charlotta *wears an old forage cap; she has taken a gun from her shoulder and is tightening the buckle on the strap.*

CHARLOTTA: [*Musingly*] I haven't a real passport of my own, and I don't know how old I am, and I always feel that I'm a young thing. When I was a little girl, my father and mother used to travel about to fairs and give performances—very good ones. And I used to dance *salto mortale* and all sorts of things. And when papa and mamma died, a German lady took me and had me educated. And so I grew up and became a governess. But where I came from, and who I am, I don't know. . . . Who my parents were, very likely they weren't married. . . . I don't know. [*Takes a cucumber out of her pocket and eats*] I know nothing at all. [*A pause*] One wants to talk and has no one to talk to. . . . I have nobody.

EPIHODOV: [*Plays on the guitar and sings*] "What care I for the noisy world! What care I for friends or foes!" How agreeable it is to play on the mandoline!

DUNYASHA: That's a guitar, not a mandoline. [*Looks in a hand-mirror and powders herself*]

EPIHODOV: To a man mad with love, it's a mandoline. [*Sings*] "Were her heart but aglow with love's mutual flame."

[Yasha *joins in*]

CHARLOTTA: How shockingly these people sing! Foo! Like jackals!

DUNYASHA: [*To* Yasha] What happiness, though, to visit foreign lands.

YASHA: Ah, yes! I rather agree with you there. [*Yawns, then lights a cigar*]

EPIHODOV: That's comprehensible. In foreign lands everything has long since reached full complexion.

YASHA: That's so, of course.

EPIHODOV: I'm a cultivated man, I read remarkable books of all sorts, but I can never make out the tendency I am myself precisely inclined for, whether to live or to shoot myself, speaking precisely, but nevertheless I always carry a revolver. Here it is. . . . [*Shows revolver*]

CHARLOTTA: I've had enough, and now I'm going. [*Puts on the gun*] Epihodov, you're a very clever fellow, and a very terrible one too, all the women must be wild about you. Br-r-r! [*Goes*] These clever fellows are all so stupid; there's not a creature for me to speak to. . . . Always alone, alone, nobody belonging to me . . . and who I am, and why I'm on earth, I don't know. [*Walks away slowly*]

EPIHODOV: Speaking precisely, not touching upon other subjects, I'm bound to admit about myself, that destiny behaves mercilessly to me, as a storm to a little boat. If, let us suppose, I am mistaken, then why did I wake up this morning, to quote an example, and look round, and there on my chest was a spider of fearful magnitude . . . like this. [*Shows with both hands*] And then I take up a jug of kvass, to quench my thirst, and in it there is something in the highest degree unseemly of the nature of a cockroach. [*A pause*] Have you read Buckle? [*A pause*] I am desirous of troubling you, Dunyasha, with a couple of words.

DUNYASHA: Well, speak.

EPIHODOV: I should be desirous to speak with you alone. [*Sighs*]

DUNYASHA: [*Embarrassed*] Well—only bring me my mantle first. It's by the cupboard. It's rather damp here.

EPIHODOV: Certainly. I will fetch it. Now I know what I must do with my revolver. [*Takes guitar and goes off playing on it*]

YASHA: Two and twenty misfortunes! Between ourselves, he's a fool. [*Yawns*]

DUNYASHA: God grant he doesn't shoot himself! [*A pause*] I am so nervous, I'm always in a flutter. I was a little girl when I was taken into our lady's house, and now I have quite grown out of peasant ways, and my hands are white, as white as a lady's. I'm such a delicate, sensitive creature, I'm afraid of everything. I'm so frightened. And if you deceive me, Yasha, I don't know what will become of my nerves.

YASHA: [*Kisses her*] You're a peach! Of course a girl must never forget herself; what I dislike more than anything is a girl being flighty in her behavior.

DUNYASHA: I'm passionately in love with you, Yasha; you are a man of culture—you can give your opinion about anything. [*A pause*]

YASHA: [*Yawns*] Yes, that's so. My opinion is this: if a girl loves anyone, that means that she has no principles. [*A pause*] It's pleasant smoking a cigar in the open air. [*Listens*] Someone's coming this way . . . it's the gentlefolk. [Dunyasha *embraces him impulsively*] Go home, as though you had been to the river to bathe; go by that path, or else they'll meet you and suppose I have made an appointment with you here. That I can't endure.

DUNYASHA: [*Coughing softly*] The cigar has made my head ache. . . . [*Goes off*]

[Yasha *remains sitting near the shrine. Enter* Lyubov Andreyevna, Gaev *and* Lopahin]

LOPAHIN: You must make up your mind once for all—there's no time to lose. It's quite a simple question, you know. Will you consent to letting the land for building or not? One word in answer: Yes or no? Only one word!

LYUBOV: Who is smoking such horrible cigars here? [*Sits down*]

GAEV: Now the railway line has been brought near, it's made things very convenient. [*Sits down*] Here we have been over and lunched in town. Cannon off the white! I should like to go home and have a game.

LYUBOV: You have plenty of time.

LOPAHIN: Only one word! [*Beseechingly*] Give me an answer!

GAEV: [*Yawning*] What do you say?

LYUBOV: [*Looks in her purse*] I had quite a lot of money here yesterday, and there's scarcely any left to-day. My poor Varya feeds us all on milk soup for the sake of economy; the old folks in the kitchen get nothing but pease pudding, while I waste my money in a senseless way. [*Drops purse, scattering gold pieces*] There, they have all fallen out! [*Annoyed*]

YASHA: Allow me, I'll soon pick them up. [*Collects the coins*]

LYUBOV: Pray do, Yasha. And what did I go off to the town to lunch for? Your restaurant's a wretched place with its music and the tablecloth smelling of soap. . . . Why drink so much, Leonid? And eat so much? And talk so much? To-day you talked a great deal again in the restaurant, and all so inappropriately. About the era of the seventies, about the decadents. And to whom? Talking to waiters about decadents!

LOPAHIN: Yes.

GAEV: [*Waving his hand*] I'm incorrigible; that's evident. [*Irritably to* Yasha] Why is it you keep fidgeting about in front of us!

YASHA: [*Laughs*] I can't help laughing when I hear your voice.

GAEV: [*To his sister*] Either I or he. . . .

LYUBOV: Get along! Go away, Yasha.

YASHA: [*Gives* Lyubov Andreyevna *her purse*] Directly. [*Hardly able to suppress his laughter*] This minute. . . . [*Goes off*]

LOPAHIN: Deriganov, the millionaire, means to buy your estate. They say he is coming to the sale himself.

LYUBOV: Where did you hear that?

LOPAHIN: That's what they say in town.

GAEV: Our aunt in Yaroslavl has promised to send help; but when, and how much she will send, we don't know.

LOPAHIN: How much will she send? A hundred thousand? Two hundred?

LYUBOV: Oh, well! . . . Ten or fifteen thousand, and we must be thankful to get that.

LOPAHIN: Forgive me, but such reckless people as you are—such queer, unbusiness-like people—I never met in my life. One tells you in plain Russian your estate is going to be sold, and you seem not to understand it.

LYUBOV: What are we to do? Tell us what to do.

LOPAHIN: I do tell you every day. Every day I say the same thing. You absolutely must let the cherry orchard and the land on building leases; and do it at once, as quick as may be—the auction's close upon us! Do understand! Once make up your mind to build villas, and you can raise as much money as you like, and then you are saved.

LYUBOV: Villas and summer visitors—forgive me saying so—it's so vulgar.

GAEV: There I perfectly agree with you.

LOPAHIN: I shall sob, or scream, or fall into a fit. I can't stand it! You drive me mad! [*To* Gaev] You're an old woman!

GAEV: What do you say?

LOPAHIN: An old woman! [*Gets up to go*]

LYUBOV: [*In dismay*] No, don't go! Do stay, my dear friend! Perhaps we shall think of something.

LOPAHIN: What is there to think of?

LYUBOV: Don't go, I entreat you! With you here it's more cheerful, anyway. [*A pause*] I keep expecting something, as though the house were going to fall about our ears.

GAEV: [*In profound dejection*] Potted the white! It fails—a kiss.

LYUBOV: We have been great sinners. . . .

LOPAHIN: You have no sins to repent of.

GAEV: [*Puts a caramel in his mouth*] They say I've eaten up my property in caramels. [*Laughs*]

LYUBOV: Oh, my sins! I've always thrown my money away recklessly like a lunatic. I married a man who made nothing but debts. My husband died of champagne—he drank dreadfully. To my misery I loved another man, and immediately—it was my first punishment—the blow fell upon me, here, in the river . . . my boy was drowned and I went abroad—went away for ever, never to return, not to see that river again . . . I shut my eyes, and fled, distracted, and *he* after me . . . pitilessly, brutally. I bought a villa at Mentone, for *he* fell ill there, and for three years I had no rest day or night. His illness wore me out, my soul was dried up. And last year, when my villa was sold to pay my debts, I went to Paris and there he robbed me of everything and abandoned me for another woman; and I tried to poison myself. . . . So stupid, so shameful! . . . And suddenly I felt a yearning for Russia, for my country, for my little girl. . . . [*Dries her tears*] Lord, Lord, be merciful! Forgive my sins! Do not chastise me more! [*Takes a telegram out of her pocket*] I got this to-day from Paris. He implores forgiveness, entreats me to return. [*Tears up the telegram*] I fancy there is music somewhere. [*Listens*]

GAEV: That's our famous Jewish orchestra. You remember, four violins, a flute and a double bass.

LYUBOV: That still in existence? We ought to send for them one evening, and give a dance.

LOPAHIN: [*Listens*] I can't hear. . . . [*Hums softly*] "For money the Germans will turn a Russian into a Frenchman." [*Laughs*] I did see such a piece at the theater yesterday! It was funny!

LYUBOV: And most likely there was nothing funny in it. You shouldn't look at plays, you should look at yourselves a little oftener. How gray your lives are! How much nonsense you talk.

LOPAHIN: That's true. One may say honestly, we live a fool's life. [*Pause*] My father was a peasant, an idiot; he knew nothing and taught me nothing, only beat me when he was drunk, and always with his stick. In reality I am just such another blockhead and idiot. I've learnt nothing properly. I write a wretched hand. I write so that I feel ashamed before folks, like a pig.

LYUBOV: You ought to get married, my dear fellow.

LOPAHIN: Yes . . . that's true.

LYUBOV: You should marry our Varya, she's a good girl.

LOPAHIN: Yes.

LYUBOV: She's a good-natured girl, she's busy all day long, and what's more, she loves you. And you have liked her for ever so long.

LOPAHIN: Well? I'm not against it. . . . She's a good girl. [Pause]

GAEV: I've been offered a place in the bank: 6,000 roubles a year. Did you know?

LYUBOV: You would never do for that! You must stay as you are.

[Enter Firs with overcoat]

FIRS: Put it on, sir, it's damp.

GAEV: [Putting it on] You bother me, old fellow.

FIRS: You can't go on like this. You went away in the morning without leaving word. [Looks him over]

LYUBOV: You look older, Firs!

FIRS: What is your pleasure?

LOPAHIN: You look older, she said.

FIRS: I've had a long life. They were arranging my wedding before your papa was born. . . . [Laughs] I was the head footman before the emancipation came. I wouldn't consent to be set free then; I stayed on with the old master. . . . [A pause] I remember what rejoicings they made and didn't know themselves what they were rejoicing over.

LOPAHIN: Those were fine old times. There was flogging anyway.

FIRS: [Not hearing] To be sure! The peasants knew their place, and the masters knew theirs; but now they're all at sixes and sevens, there's no making it out.

GAEV: Hold your tongue, Firs. I must go to town to-morrow. I have been promised an introduction to a general, who might let us have a loan.

LOPAHIN: You won't bring that off. And you won't pay your arrears, you may rest assured of that.

LYUBOV: That's all his nonsense. There is no such general.

[Enter Trofimov, Anya and Varya]

GAEV: Here come our girls.

ANYA: There's mamma on the seat.

LYUBOV: [Tenderly] Come here, come along. My darlings! [Embraces Anya and Varya] If you only knew how I love you both. Sit beside me, there, like that. [All sit down]

LOPAHIN: Our perpetual student is always with the young ladies.

TROFIMOV: That's not your business.

LOPAHIN: He'll soon be fifty, and he's still a student.

TROFIMOV: Drop your idiotic jokes.

LOPAHIN: Why are you so cross, you queer fish?

TROFIMOV: Oh, don't persist!

LOPAHIN: [Laughs] Allow me to ask you what's your idea of me?

TROFIMOV: I'll tell you my idea of you. Yermolay Alexeyevitch: you are a rich man, you'll soon be a millionaire. Well, just as in the economy of nature a wild beast is of use, who devours everything that comes in his way, so you too have your use.

[All laugh]

VARYA: Better tell us something about the planets, Petya.

LYUBOV: No, let us go on with the conversation we had yesterday.

TROFIMOV: What was it about?

GAEV: About pride.

TROFIMOV: We had a long conversation yesterday, but we came to no conclusion. In pride, in your sense of it, there is something mystical. Perhaps you are right from your point of view; but if one looks at it simply, without subtlety, what sort of pride can there be, what sense is there in it, if man in his physiological formation is very imperfect, if in the immense majority of cases he is coarse, dull-witted, profoundly unhappy? One must give up glorification of self. One should work, and nothing else.

GAEV: One must die in any case.

TROFIMOV: Who knows? And what does it mean —dying? Perhaps man has a hundred senses, and only the five we know are lost at death, while the other ninety-five remain alive.

LYUBOV: How clever you are, Petya!

LOPAHIN: [Ironically] Fearfully clever!

TROFIMOV: Humanity progresses, perfecting its powers. Everything that is beyond its ken now will one day become familiar and comprehensible; only we must work, we must with all our powers aid the seeker after truth. Here among us in Russia the workers are few in number as yet. The vast majority of the intellectual people I know, seek nothing, do nothing, are not fit as yet for work of any kind. They call themselves intellectual, but they treat their servants as inferiors, behave to the peasants as though they were animals, learn little, read nothing seriously, do practically nothing, only talk about science and know very little about art. They are all serious people, they all have severe faces, they all talk of weighty matters and air their theories, and yet the vast majority of us—ninety-nine per cent.— live like savages, at the least thing fly to blows and abuse, eat piggishly, sleep in filth and stuffiness, bugs everywhere, stench and damp and moral impurity. And it's clear all our fine talk is only to divert our attention and other people's. Show me where to find the crèches there's so much talk about, and the reading-rooms? They only exist in novels: in real life there are none of them. There is nothing but filth and vulgarity and Asiatic apathy. I fear and dislike very serious faces. I'm afraid of serious conversation. We should do better to be silent.

LOPAHIN: You know, I get up at five o'clock in the morning, and I work from morning to night; and I've money, my own and other people's, always passing through my hands, and I see what people are made of all round me. One has only to begin to do anything to see how few honest decent peop there are. Sometimes when I lie awake at night, I think: "Oh! Lord, thou hast given us immense forests, boundless plains, the widest horizons, and living here we ourselves ought really to be giants."

LYUBOV: You ask for giants! They are no good except in story-books; in real life they frighten us.

[Epihodov *advances in the background, playing on the guitar*]

LYUBOV: [*Dreamily*] There goes Epihodov.

ANYA: [*Dreamily*] There goes Epihodov.

GAEV: The sun has set, my friends.

TROFIMOV: Yes.

GAEV: [*Not loudly, but, as it were, declaiming*] O nature, divine nature, thou art bright with eternal luster, beautiful and indifferent! Thou, whom we call mother, thou dost unite within thee life and death! Thou dost give life and dost destroy!

VARYA: [*In a tone of supplication*] Uncle!

ANYA: Uncle, you are at it again!

TROFIMOV: You'd much better be cannoning off the red!

GAEV: I'll hold my tongue, I will.

[*All sit plunged in thought. Perfect stillness. The only thing audible is the muttering of* Firs. *Suddenly there is a sound in the distance, as it were from the sky—the sound of a breaking harp-string, mournfully dying away*]

LYUBOV: What is that?

LOPAHIN: I don't know. Somewhere far away a bucket fallen and broken in the pits. But somewhere very far away.

GAEV: It might be a bird of some sort—such as a heron.

TROFIMOV: Or an owl.

LYUBOV: [*Shudders*] I don't know why, but it's horrid. [*A pause*]

FIRS: It was the same before the calamity—the owl hooted and the samovar hissed all the time.

GAEV: Before what calamity?

FIRS: Before the emancipation. [*A pause*]

LYUBOV: Come, my friends, let us be going; evening is falling. [*To* Anya] There are tears in your eyes. What is it, darling? [*Embraces her*]

ANYA: Nothing, mamma; it's nothing.

TROFIMOV: There is somebody coming.

[*The* Wayfarer *appears in a shabby white forage cap and an overcoat; he is slightly drunk*]

WAYFARER: Allow me to inquire, can I get to the station this way?

GAEV: Yes. Go along that road.

WAYFARER: I thank you most feelingly. [*Coughing*] The weather is superb. [*Declaims*] My brother, my suffering brother! . . . Come out to the Volga! Whose groan do you hear? . . . [*To* Varya] Mademoiselle, vouchsafe a hungry Russian thirty kopecks.

[Varya *utters a shriek of alarm*]

LOPAHIN: [*Angrily*] There's a right and a wrong way of doing everything!

LYUBOV: [*Hurriedly*] Here, take this. [*Looks in her purse*] I've no silver. No matter—here's gold for you.

WAYFARER: I thank you most feelingly! [*Goes off*] [*Laughter*]

VARYA: [*Frightened*] I'm going home—I'm going. . . . Oh, mamma, the servants have nothing to eat, and you gave him gold!

LYUBOV: There's no doing anything with me. I'm so silly! When we get home, I'll give you all I possess. Yermolay Alexeyevitch, you will lend me some more! . . .

LOPAHIN: I will.

LYUBOV: Come, friends, it's time to be going. And Varya, we have made a match of it for you. I congratulate you.

VARYA: [*Through her tears*] Mamma, that's not a joking matter.

LOPAHIN: "Ophelia, get thee to a nunnery!"

GAEV: My hands are trembling; it's a long while since I had a game of billiards.

LOPAHIN: "Ophelia! Nymph, in thy orisons be all my sins remember'd."

LYUBOV: Come, it will soon be supper-time.

VARYA: How he frightened me! My heart's simply throbbing.

LOPAHIN: Let me remind you, ladies and gentlemen: on the 22nd of August the cherry orchard will be sold. Think about that! Think about it!

[*All go off, except* Trofimov *and* Anya]

ANYA: [*Laughing*] I'm grateful to the wayfarer! He frightened Varya and we are left alone.

TROFIMOV: Varya's afraid we shall fall in love with each other, and for days together she won't leave us. With her narrow brain she can't grasp that we are above love. To eliminate the petty and transitory which hinder us from being free and happy—that is the aim and meaning of our life. Forward! We go forward irresistibly towards the bright star that shines yonder in the distance. Forward! Do not lag behind, friends.

ANYA: [*Claps her hands*] How well you speak! [*A pause*] It is divine here to-day.

TROFIMOV: Yes, it's glorious weather.

ANYA: Somehow, Petya, you've made me so that I don't love the cherry orchard as I used to. I used to love it so dearly. I used to think that there was no spot on earth like our garden.

TROFIMOV: All Russia is our garden. The earth is great and beautiful—there are many beautiful places in it. [*A pause*] Think only, Anya, your grandfather, and great-grandfather, and all your ancestors were slave-owners—the owners of living souls—and from every cherry in the orchard, from every leaf, from every trunk there are human creatures looking at you. Cannot you hear their voices? Oh, it is awful! Your orchard is a fearful thing, and when in the evening or at night one walks about the orchard, the old bark on the trees glimmers dimly in the dusk, and the old cherry trees seem to be dreaming of centuries gone by and tortured by fearful visions. Yes! We are at least two hundred years behind, we have really gained nothing yet, we have no definite attitude to the past, we do nothing but theorize or complain of depression or drink vodka. It is clear that to begin to live in the present, we must first expiate our past; we must break with it; and we can expiate it only by suffering, by extraordinary unceasing labor. Understand that, Anya.

ANYA: The house we live in has long ceased to be our own, and I shall leave it, I give you my word.

TROFIMOV: If you have the house keys, fling them into the well and go away. Be free as the wind.

ANYA: [*In ecstasy*] How beautifully you said that!

TROFIMOV: Believe me, Anya, believe me! I am not thirty yet, I am young, I am still a student, but I have gone through so much already! As soon as winter comes I am hungry, sick, careworn, poor as a beggar, and what ups and downs of fortune have I not known! And my soul was always, every minute, day and night, full of inexplicable forebodings. I have a foreboding of happiness, Anya. I see glimpses of it already.

ANYA: [*Pensively*] The moon is rising.

[*Epihodov is heard playing still the same mournful song on the guitar. The moon rises. Somewhere near the poplars Varya is looking for Anya and calling "Anya! where are you?"*]

TROFIMOV: Yes, the moon is rising. [*A pause*] Here is happiness—here it comes! It is coming nearer and nearer; already I can hear its footsteps. And if we never see it—if we may never know it— what does it matter? Others will see it after us.

VARYA'S VOICE: Anya! Where are you?

TROFIMOV: That Varya again! [*Angrily*] It's revolting!

ANYA: Well, let's go down to the river. It's lovely there.

TROFIMOV: Yes, let's go. [*They go*]

VARYA'S VOICE: Anya! Anya!

CURTAIN.

ACT III.

A drawing-room divided by an arch from a larger drawing-room. A chandelier burning. The Jewish orchestra, the same that was mentioned in Act II, is heard playing in the ante-room. It is evening. In the larger drawing-room they are dancing the grand chain. The voice of Semyonov-Pishtchik: "*Promenade à une paire!*" *Then enter the drawing-room in couples first* Pishtchik *and* Charlotta Ivanova, *then* Trofimov *and* Lyubov Andreyevna, *thirdly* Anya *with the* Post-Office Clerk, *fourthly* Varya *with the* Station Master, *and other guests.* Varya *is quietly weeping and wiping away her tears as she dances. In the last couple is* Dunyasha. *They move across the*

drawing-room. Pishtchik *shouts:* "Grand rond, balancez!" *and* "Les Cavaliers à genou et remerciez vos dames."

Firs *in a swallow-tail coat brings in seltzer water on a tray.* Pishtchik *and* Trofimov *enter the drawing-room.*

PISHTCHIK: I am a full-blooded man; I have already had two strokes. Dancing's hard work for me, but as they say, if you're in the pack, you must bark with the rest. I'm as strong, I may say, as a horse. My parent, who would have his joke—may the Kingdom of Heaven be his!—used to say about our origin that the ancient stock of the Semyonov-Pishtchiks was derived from the very horse that Caligula made a member of the senate. [*Sits down*] But I've no money, that's where the mischief is. A hungry dog believes in nothing but meat. [*Snores, but at once wakes up*] That's like me . . . I can think of nothing but money.

TROFIMOV: There really is something horsy about your appearance.

PISHTCHIK: Well . . . a horse is a fine beast . . . a horse can be sold.

[*There is the sound of billiards being played in an adjoining room.* Varya *appears in the arch leading to the larger drawing-room*]

TROFIMOV: [*Teasing*] Madame Lopahin! Madame Lopahin!

VARYA: [*Angrily*] Mangy-looking gentleman!

TROFIMOV: Yes, I am a mangy-looking gentleman, and I'm proud of it!

VARYA: [*Pondering bitterly*] Here we have hired musicians and nothing to pay them! [*Goes out*]

TROFIMOV: [*To Pishtchik*] If the energy you have wasted during your lifetime in trying to find the money to pay your interest had gone to something else, you might in the end have turned the world upside down.

PISHTCHIK: Nietzsche, the philosopher, a very great and celebrated man . . . of enormous intellect . . . says in his works, that one can make forged bank-notes.

TROFIMOV: Why, have you read Nietzsche?

PISHTCHIK: What next . . . Dashenka told me. . . . And now I am in such a position, I might just as well forge banknotes. The day after to-morrow I must pay 310 roubles—130 I have procured. [*Feels in his pockets, in alarm*] The money's gone! I have lost my money! [*Through his tears*] Where's the money? [*Gleefully*] Why, here it is behind the lining. . . . It has made me hot all over.

[*Enter* Lyubov Andreyevna *and* Charlotta Ivanova]

LYUBOV: [*Hums the* Lezginka] Why is Leonid so long? What can he be doing in town? [*To Dunyasha*] Offer the musicians some tea.

TROFIMOV: The sale hasn't taken place, most likely.

LYUBOV: It's the wrong time to have the orchestra, and the wrong time to give a dance. Well, never mind. [*Sits down and hums softly*]

CHARLOTTA: [*Gives* Pishtchik *a pack of cards*] Here's a pack of cards. Think of any card you like.

PISHTCHIK: I've thought of one.

CHARLOTTA: Shuffle the pack now. That's right. Give it here, my dear Mr. Pishtchik. *Ein, zwei, drei*—now look, it's in your breast pocket.

PISHTCHIK: [*Taking a card out of his breast pocket*] The eight of spades! Perfectly right! [*Wonderingly*] Fancy that now!

CHARLOTTA: [*Holding pack of cards in her hands, to* Trofimov] Tell me quickly which is the top card.

TROFIMOV: Well, the queen of spades.

CHARLOTTA: It is! [*To* Pishtchik] Well, which card is uppermost?

PISHTCHIK: The ace of hearts.

CHARLOTTA: It is! [*Claps her hands, pack of cards disappears*] Ah! what lovely weather it is to-day!

[*A mysterious feminine voice which seems coming out of the floor answers her.* "Oh, yes, it's magnificent weather, madam"]

CHARLOTTA: You are my perfect ideal.

VOICE: And I greatly admire you too, madam.

STATION MASTER: [*Applauding*] The lady ventriloquist—bravo!

PISHTCHIK: [*Wonderingly*] Fancy that now! Most enchanting Charlotta Ivanovna. I'm simply in love with you.

CHARLOTTA: In love? [*Shrugging shoulders*] What do you know of love, *guter Mensch, aber schlechter Musikant*.

TROFIMOV: [*Pats* Pishtchik *on the shoulder*] You dear old horse. . . .

CHARLOTTA: Attention, please! Another trick! [*Takes a traveling rug from a chair*] Here's a very good rug; I want to sell it. [*Shaking it out*] Doesn't anyone want to buy it?

PISHTCHIK: [*Wonderingly*] Fancy that!

CHARLOTTA: *Ein, zwei, drei!* [*Quickly picks up rug she has dropped; behind the rug stands* Anya; *she makes a curtsey, runs to her mother, embraces her and runs back into the larger drawing-room amidst general enthusiasm*]

LYUBOV: [*Applauds*] Bravo! Bravo!

CHARLOTTA: Now again! *Ein, zwei, drei!* [*Lifts up the rug; behind the rug stands* Varya, *bowing*]

ᵖISHTCHIK: [*Wonderingly*] Fancy that now!

CHARLOTTA: That's the end. [*Throws the rug at* Pishtchik, *makes a curtsey, runs into the larger drawing-room*]

PISHTCHIK: [*Hurries after her*] Mischievous creature! Fancy! [*Goes out*]

LYUBOV: And still Leonid doesn't come. I can't understand what he's doing in the town so long! Why, everything must be over by now. The estate is sold, or the sale has not taken place. Why keep us so long in suspense?

VARYA: [*Trying to console her*] Uncle's bought it. I feel sure of that.

TROFIMOV: [*Ironically*] Oh, yes!

VARYA: Great-aunt sent him an authorization to buy it in her name, and transfer the debt. She's doing it for Anya's sake, and I'm sure God will be merciful. Uncle will buy it.

LYUBOV: My aunt in Yaroslavl sent fifteen thousand to buy the estate in her name, she doesn't trust us—but that's not enough even to pay the arrears. [*Hides her face in her hands*] My fate is being sealed to-day, my fate. . . .

TROFIMOV: [*Teasing* Varya] Madame Lopahin.

VARYA: [*Angrily*] Perpetual student! Twice already you've been sent down from the University.

LYUBOV: Why are you angry, Varya? He's teasing you about Lopahin. Well, what of that? Marry Lopahin if you like, he's a good man, and interesting; if you don't want to, don't! Nobody compels you, darling.

VARYA: I must tell you plainly, mamma, I look at the matter seriously; he's a good man, I like him.

LYUBOV: Well, marry him. I can't see what you're waiting for.

VARYA: Mamma. I can't make him an offer myself. For the last two years, everyone's been talking to me about him. Everyone talks; but he says nothing or else makes a joke. I see what it means. He's growing rich, he's absorbed in business, he has no thoughts for me. If I had money, were it ever so little, if I had only a hundred roubles, I'd throw everything up and go far away. I would go into a nunnery.

TROFIMOV: What bliss!

VARYA: [*To* Trofimov] A student ought to have sense! [*In a soft tone with tears*] How ugly you've grown, Petya! How old you look! [*To* Lyubov Andreyevna, *no longer crying*] But I can't do without work, mamma; I must have something to do every minute.

[*Enter* Yasha]

YASHA: [*Hardly restraining his laughter*] Epihodov has broken a billiard cue! [*Goes out*]

VARYA: What is Epihodov doing here? Who gave him leave to play billiards? I can't make these people out. [*Goes out*]

LYUBOV: Don't tease her, Petya. You see she has grief enough without that.

TROFIMOV: She is so very officious, meddling in what's not her business. All the summer she's given Anya and me no peace. She's afraid of a love affair between us. What's it to do with her? Besides, I have given no grounds for it. Such triviality is not in my line. We are above love!

LYUBOV: And I suppose I am beneath love. [*Very uneasily*] Why is it Leonid's not here? If only I could know whether the estate is sold or not! It seems such an incredible calamity that I really don't know what to think. I am distracted . . . I shall scream in a minute . . . I shall do something stupid. Save me, Petya, tell me something, talk to me!

TROFIMOV: What does it matter whether the estate

is sold to-day or not? That's all done with long ago. There's no turning back, the path is overgrown. Don't worry yourself, dear Lyubov Andreyevna. You mustn't deceive yourself; for once in your life you must face the truth!

LYUBOV: What truth? You see where the truth lies, but I seem to have lost my sight, I see nothing. You settle every great problem so boldly, but tell me, my dear boy, isn't it because you're young— because you haven't yet understood one of your problems through suffering? You look forward boldly, and isn't it that you don't see and don't expect anything dreadful because life is still hidden from your young eyes? You're bolder, more honest, deeper than we are, but think, be just a little magnanimous, have pity on me. I was born here, you know, my father and mother lived here, my grandfather lived here, I love this house. I can't conceive of life without the cherry orchard, and if it really must be sold, then sell me with the orchard. [*Embraces* Trofimov, *kisses him on the forehead*] My boy was drowned here. [*Weeps*] Pity me, my dear kind fellow.

TROFIMOV: You know I feel for you with all my heart.

LYUBOV: But that should have been said differently, so differently. [*Takes out her handkerchief, telegram falls on the floor*] My heart is so heavy to-day. It's so noisy here, my soul is quivering at every sound, I'm shuddering all over, but I can't go away; I'm afraid to be quiet and alone. Don't be hard on me, Petya . . . I love you as though you were one of ourselves. I would gladly let you marry Anya—I swear I would—only, my dear boy, you must take your degree, you do nothing—you're simply tossed by fate from place to place. That's so strange. It is, isn't it? And you must do something with your beard to make it grow somehow. [*Laughs*] You look so funny!

TROFIMOV: [*Picks up the telegram*] I've no wish to be a beauty.

LYUBOV: That's a telegram from Paris. I get one every day. One yesterday and one to-day. That savage creature is ill again, he's in trouble again. He begs forgiveness, beseeches me to go, and really I ought to go to Paris to see him. You look shocked, Petya. What am I to do, my dear boy, what am I to do? He is ill, he is alone and unhappy, and who'll look after him, who'll keep him from doing the wrong thing, who'll give him his medicine at the right time? And why hide it or be silent? I love him, that's clear. I love him! I love him! He's a millstone about my neck, I'm going to the bottom with him, but I love that stone and can't live without it. [*Presses* Trofimov's *hand*] Don't think ill of me, Petya, don't tell me anything, don't tell me. . . .

TROFIMOV: [*Through his tears*] For God's sake forgive my frankness: why, he robbed you!

LYUBOV: No! No! No! You mustn't speak like that. [*Covers her ears*]

TROFIMOV: He is a wretch! You're the only person that doesn't know it! He's a worthless creature! A despicable wretch!

LYUBOV: [*Getting angry, but speaking with restraint*] You're twenty-six or twenty-seven years old, but you're still a schoolboy.

TROFIMOV: Possibly.

LYUBOV: You should be a man at your age! You should understand what love means! And you ought to be in love yourself. You ought to fall in love! [*Angrily*] Yes, yes, and it's not purity in you, you're simply a prude, a comic fool, a freak.

TROFIMOV: [*In horror*] The things she's saying!

LYUBOV: I am above love! You're not above love, but simply as our Firs here says, "You are a good-for-nothing." At your age not to have a mistress!

TROFIMOV: [*In horror*] This is awful! The things she is saying! [*Goes rapidly into the larger drawing-room clutching his head*] This is awful! I can't stand it! I'm going. [*Goes off, but at once returns*] All is over between us! [*Goes off into the ante-room*]

LYUBOV: [*Shouts after him*] Petya! Wait a minute! You funny creature! I was joking! Petya! [*There is a sound of somebody running quickly downstairs and suddenly falling with a crash.* Anya *and* Varya *scream, but there is a sound of laughter at once*]

LYUBOV: What has happened?

[Anya *runs in*]

ANYA: [*Laughing*] Petya's fallen downstairs! [*Runs out*]

LYUBOV: What a queer fellow that Petya is!

[*The* Station Master *stands in the middle of the larger room and reads* The Magdalene, *by Alexey Tolstoy. They listen to him, but before he has recited many lines strains of a waltz are heard from the ante-room and the reading is broken off. All dance.* Trofimov, Anya, Varya *and* Lyubov Andreyevna *come in from the ante-room*]

LYUBOV: Come, Petya—come, pure heart! I beg your pardon. Let's have a dance! [*Dances with* Petya]

[Anya *and* Varya *dance.* Firs *comes in, puts his stick down near the side door.* Yasha *also comes into the drawing-room and looks on at the dancing*]

YASHA: What is it, old man?

FIRS: I don't feel well. In old days we used to have generals, barons and admirals dancing at our balls, and now we send for the post-office clerk and the station master and even they're not overanxious to come. I am getting feeble. The old master, the grandfather, used to give sealing-wax for all complaints. I have been taking sealing-wax for twenty years or more. Perhaps that's what's kept me alive.

YASHA: You bore me, old man! [*Yawns*] It's time you were done with.

FIRS: Ach, you're a good-for-nothing! [*Mutters*]

[Trofimov *and* Lyubov Andreyevna *dance in larger room and then on to the stage*]

LYUBOV: *Merci.* I'll sit down a little. [*Sits down*] I'm tired.

[*Enter* Anya]

ANYA: [*Excitedly*] There's a man in the kitchen has been saying that the cherry orchard's been sold to-day.

LYUBOV: Sold to whom?

ANYA: He didn't say to whom. He's gone away.

[*She dances with* Trofimov, *and they go off into the larger room*]

YASHA: There was an old man gossiping there, a stranger.

FIRS: Leonid Andreyevitch isn't here yet, he hasn't come back. He has his light overcoat on, *demi-saison,* he'll catch cold for sure. *Ach!* Foolish young things!

LYUBOV: I feel as though I should die. Go, Yasha, find out to whom it has been sold.

YASHA: But he went away long ago, the old chap. [*Laughs*]

LYUBOV: [*With slight vexation*] What are you laughing at? What are you pleased at?

YASHA: Epihodov is so funny. He's a silly fellow, two and twenty misfortunes.

LYUBOV: Firs, if the estate is sold, where will you go?

FIRS: Where you bid me, there I'll go.

LYUBOV: Why do you look like that? Are you ill? You ought to be in bed.

FIRS: Yes. [*Ironically*] Me go to bed and who's to wait here? Who's to see to things without me? I'm the only one in all the house.

YASHA: [*To Lyubov Andreyevna*] Lyubov Andreyevna, permit me to make a request of you; if you go back to Paris again, be so kind as to take me with you. It's positively impossible for me to stay here. [*Looking about him; in an undertone*] There's no need to say it, you see for yourself—an uncivilized country, the people have no morals, and then the dullness! The food in the kitchen's abominable, and then Firs runs after one muttering all sorts of unsuitable words. Take me with you, please do!

[*Enter* Pishtchik]

PISHTCHIK: Allow me to ask you for a waltz, my dear lady. [Lyubov Andreyevna *goes with him*] Enchanting lady, I really must borrow of you just 180 roubles, [*dances*] only 180 roubles. [*They pass into the larger room*]

[*In the larger drawing-room, a figure in a gray top hat and in check trousers is gesticulating and jumping about. Shouts of "Bravo, Charlotta Ivanovna"*]

DUNYASHA: [*She has stopped to powder herself*] My young lady tells me to dance. There are plenty of gentlemen, and too few ladies, but dancing makes me giddy and makes my heart beat. Firs, the post-office clerk said something to me just now that quite took my breath away.

[*Music becomes more subdued*]

FIRS: What did he say to you?

DUNYASHA: He said I was like a flower.

YASHA: [*Yawns*] What ignorance! [*Goes out*]

DUNYASHA: Like a flower. I am a girl of such delicate feelings, I am awfully fond of soft speeches.

FIRS: Your head's being turned.

[*Enter* Epihodov]

EPIHODOV: You have no desire to see me. Dunyasha. I might be an insect. [*Sighs*] Ah! life!

DUNYASHA: What is it you want?

EPIHODOV: Undoubtedly you may be right. [*Sighs*] But, of course, if one looks at it from that point of view, if I may so express myself, you have, excuse my plain speaking, reduced me to a complete state of mind. I know my destiny. Every day some misfortune befalls me and I have long ago grown accustomed to it, so that I look upon my fate with a smile. You gave me your word, and though I——

DUNYASHA: Let us have a talk later, I entreat you, but now leave me in peace, for I am lost in reverie. [*Plays with her fan*]

EPIHODOV: I have a misfortune every day, and if I may venture to express myself, I merely smile at it, I even laugh.

[Varya *enters from the larger drawing-room*]

VARYA: You still have not gone, Epihodov. What a disrespectful creature you are, really! [*To* Dunyasha] Go along, Dunyasha! [*To* Epihodov] First you play billiards and break the cue, then you go wandering about the drawing-room like a visitor!

EPIHODOV: You really cannot, if I may so express myself, call me to account like this.

VARYA: I'm not calling you to account, I'm speaking to you. You do nothing but wander from place to place and don't do your work. We keep you as a counting-house clerk, but what use you are I can't say.

EPIHODOV: [*Offended*] Whether I work or whether I walk, whether I eat or whether I play billiards, is a matter to be judged by persons of understanding and my elders.

VARYA: You dare to tell me that! [*Firing up*] You dare! You mean to say I've no understanding. Begone from here! This minute!

EPIHODOV: [*Intimidated*] I beg you to express yourself with delicacy.

VARYA: [*Beside herself with anger*] This moment! get out! away! [*He goes towards the door, she following him*] Two and twenty misfortunes! Take yourself off! Don't let me set eyes on you! [Epihodov *has gone out, behind the door his voice,* "I shall lodge a complaint against you"] What! You're coming back? [*Snatches up the stick* Firs *has put down near the door*] Come! Come! Come! I'll show you! What! you're coming? Then take that! [*She swings the stick, at the very moment that* Lopahin *comes in*]

LOPAHIN: Very much obliged to you!

VARYA: [*Angrily and ironically*] I beg your pardon!

LOPAHIN: Not at all! I humbly thank you for your kind reception!

VARYA: No need of thanks for it. [*Moves away, then looks round and asks softly*] I haven't hurt you?

LOPAHIN: Oh, no! Not at all! There's an immense bump coming up, though!

VOICES FROM LARGER ROOM: Lopahin has come! Yermolay Alexeyevitch!

PISHTCHIK: What do I see and hear? [*Kisses Lopahin*] There's a whiff of cognac about you, my dear soul, and we're making merry here too!

[*Enter Lyubov Andreyevna*]

LYUBOV: Is it you, Yermolay Alexeyevitch? Why have you been so long? Where's Leonid?

LOPAHIN: Leonid Andreyevitch arrived with me. He is coming.

LYUBOV: [*In agitation*] Well! Well! Was there a sale? Speak!

LOPAHIN: [*Embarrassed, afraid of betraying his joy*] The sale was over at four o'clock. We missed our train—had to wait till half-past nine. [*Sighing heavily*] Ugh! I feel a little giddy.

[*Enter Gaev. In his right hand he has purchases, with his left hand he is wiping away his tears*]

LYUBOV: Well, Leonid? What news? [*Impatiently, with tears*] Make haste, for God's sake!

GAEV: [*Makes her no answer, simply waves his hand. To Firs, weeping*] Here, take them; there's anchovies, Kertch herrings. I have eaten nothing all day. What I have been through! [*Door into the billiard room is open. There is heard a knocking of balls and the voice of* Yasha *saying* "Eighty-seven." Gaev's *expression changes, he leaves off weeping*] I am fearfully tired. Firs, come and help me change my things. [*Goes to his own room across the larger drawing-room*]

PISHTCHIK: How about the sale? Tell us, do!

LYUBOV: Is the cherry orchard sold?

LOPAHIN: It is sold.

LYUBOV: Who has bought it?

LOPAHIN: I have bought it. [*A pause. Lyubov is crushed; she would fall down if she were not standing near a chair and table*]

[*Varya takes keys from her waistband, flings them on the floor in middle of drawing-room and goes out*]

LOPAHIN: I have bought it! Wait a bit, ladies and gentlemen, pray. My head's a bit muddled, I can't speak. [*Laughs*] We came to the auction. Deriganov was there already. Leonid Andreyevitch only had 15,000 and Deriganov bid 30,000, besides the arrears, straight off. I saw how the land lay. I bid against him. I bid 40,000, he bid 45,000, I said 55, and so he went on, adding 5 thousands and I adding 10. Well . . . So it ended. I bid 90, and it was knocked down to me. Now the cherry orchard's mine! Mine! [*Chuckles*] My God, the cherry or-

chard's mine! Tell me that I'm drunk, that I'm out of my mind, that it's all a dream. [*Stamps with his feet*] Don't laugh at me! If my father and my grandfather could rise from their graves and see all that has happened! How their Yermolay, ignorant, beaten Yermolay, who used to run about barefoot in winter, how that very Yermolay has bought the finest estate in the world! I have bought the estate where my father and grandfather were slaves, where they weren't even admitted into the kitchen. I am asleep, I am dreaming! It is all fancy, it is the work of your imagination plunged in the darkness of ignorance. [*Picks up keys, smiling fondly*] She threw away the keys; she means to show she's not the housewife now. [*Jingles the keys*] Well, no matter. [*The orchestra is heard tuning up*] Hey, musicians! Play! I want to hear you. Come, all of you, and look how Yermolay Lopahin will take the ax to the cherry orchard, how the trees will fall to the ground! We will build houses on it and our grandsons and great-grandsons will see a new life springing up there. Music! Play up!

[*Music begins to play.* Lyubov Andreyevna *has sunk into a chair and is weeping bitterly*]

LOPAHIN: [*Reproachfully*] Why, why didn't you listen to me? My poor friend! Dear lady, there's no turning back now. [*With tears*] Oh, if all this could be over, oh, if our miserable disjointed life could somehow soon be changed!

PISHTCHIK: [*Takes him by the arm, in an undertone*] She's weeping, let us go and leave her alone. Come. [*Takes him by the arm and leads him into the larger drawing-room*]

LOPAHIN: What's that? Musicians, play up! All must be as I wish it. [*With irony*] Here comes the new master, the owner of the cherry orchard! [*Accidentally tips over a little table, almost upsetting the candelabra*] I can pay for everything! [*Goes out with* Pishtchik. *No one remains on the stage or in the larger drawing-room except* Lyubov, *who sits huddled up, weeping bitterly. The music plays softly.* Anya *and* Trofimov *come in quickly.* Anya *goes up to her mother and falls on her knees before her.* Trofimov *stands at the entrance to the larger drawing-room*]

ANYA: Mamma! Mamma, you're crying, dear, kind, good mamma! My precious! I love you! I bless you! The cherry orchard is sold, it is gone, that's true, that's true! But don't weep, mamma! Life is still before you, you have still your good, pure heart! Let us go, let us go, darling, away from here! We will make a new garden, more splendid than this one; you will see it, you will understand. And joy, quiet, deep joy, will sink into your soul like the sun at evening! And you will smile, mamma! Come, darling, let us go!

CURTAIN.

ACT IV.

SCENE: *Same as in First Act. There are neither curtains on the windows nor pictures on the walls: only a little furniture remains piled up in a corner as if for sale. There is a sense of desolation; near the outer door and in the background of the scene are packed trunks, traveling bags, etc. On the left the door is open, and from here the voices of* Varya *and* Anya *are audible. Lopahin is standing waiting. Yasha is holding a tray with glasses full of champagne. In front of the stage Epihodov is tying up a box. In the background behind the scene a hum of talk from the peasants who have come to say good-bye. The voice of* Gaev: "Thanks, brothers, thanks!"*

YASHA: The peasants have come to say good-bye. In my opinion, Yermolay Alexeyevitch, the peasants are good-natured, but they don't know much about things.

[*The hum of talk dies away. Enter across front of stage* Lyubov Andreyevna *and* Gaev. *She is not weeping, but is pale; her face is quivering—she cannot speak*]

GAEV: You gave them your purse, Lyuba. That won't do—that won't do!

LYUBOV: I couldn't help it! I couldn't help it!

[*Both go out*]

LOPAHIN: [*In the doorway, calls after them*] You will take a glass at parting? Please do. I didn't think to bring any from the town, and at the station I could only get one bottle. Please take a glass [*A pause*] What? You don't care for any? [*Comes away from the door*] If I'd known, I wouldn't have bought it. Well, and I'm not going to drink it. [Yasha *carefully sets the tray down on a chair*] You have a glass, Yasha, anyway.

YASHA: Good luck to the travelers, and luck to those that stay behind! [*Drinks*] This champagne isn't the real thing, I can assure you.

LOPAHIN: It cost eight roubles the bottle. [*A pause*] It's devilish cold here.

YASHA: They haven't heated the stove to-day—it's all the same since we're going. [*Laughs*]

LOPAHIN: What are you laughing for?

YASHA: For pleasure.

LOPAHIN: Though it's October, it's as still and sunny as though it were summer. It's just right for building! [*Looks at his watch; says in doorway*] Take note, ladies and gentlemen, the train goes in forty-seven minutes; so you ought to start for the station in twenty minutes. You must hurry up!

[Trofimov *comes in from out of doors wearing a great-coat*]

TROFIMOV: I think it must be time to start, the horses are ready. The devil only knows what's become of my goloshes; they're lost. [*In the doorway*] Anya! My goloshes aren't here. I can't find them.

LOPAHIN: And I'm getting off to Harkov. I am going in the same train with you. I'm spending all the winter at Harkov. I've been wasting all my time gossiping with you and fretting with no work to do. I can't get on without work. I don't know what to do with my hands, they flap about so queerly, as if they didn't belong to me.

TROFIMOV: Well, we're just going away, and you will take up your profitable labors again.

LOPAHIN: Do take a glass.

TROFIMOV: No, thanks.

LOPAHIN: Then you're going to Moscow now?

TROFIMOV: Yes. I shall see them as far as the town, and to-morrow I shall go on to Moscow.

LOPAHIN: Yes, I daresay, the professors aren't giving any lectures, they're waiting for your arrival.

TROFIMOV: That's not your business.

LOPAHIN: How many years have you been at the University?

TROFIMOV: Do think of something newer than that—that's stale and flat. [*Hunts for goloshes*] You know we shall most likely never see each other again, so let me give you one piece of advice at parting: don't wave your arms about—get out of the habit. And another thing, building villas, reckoning up that the summer visitors will in time become independent farmers—reckoning like that, that's not the thing to do either. After all, I am fond of you: you have fine delicate fingers like an artist, you've a fine delicate soul.

LOPAHIN: [*Embraces him*] Good-bye, my dear fellow. Thanks for everything. Let me give you money for the journey, if you need it.

TROFIMOV: What for? I don't need it.

LOPAHIN: Why, you haven't got a half-penny.

TROFIMOV: Yes, I have, thank you. I got some money for a translation. Here it is in my pocket, [*anxiously*] but where can my goloshes be!

VARYA: [*From the next room*] Take the nasty things! [*Flings a pair of goloshes on to the stage*]

TROFIMOV: Why are you so cross, Varya? h'm! . . . but those aren't my goloshes.

LOPAHIN: I sowed three thousand acres with poppies in the spring, and now I have cleared forty thousand profit. And when my poppies were in flower, wasn't it a picture! So here, as I say, I made forty thousand, and I'm offering you a loan because I can afford to. Why turn up your nose? I am a peasant—I speak bluntly.

TROFIMOV: Your father was a peasant, mine was a chemist—and that proves absolutely nothing whatever. [Lopahin *takes out his pocket-book*] Stop that—stop that. If you were to offer me two hundred thousand I wouldn't take it. I am an independent man, and everything that all of you, rich and poor alike, prize so highly and hold so dear, hasn't the slightest power over me—it's like so much fluff fluttering in the air. I can get on without you. I can pass by you. I am strong and proud. Humanity is advancing towards the highest truth, the highest happiness, which is possible on earth, and I am in the front ranks.

LOPAHIN: Will you get there?

TROFIMOV: I shall get there. [*A pause*] I shall get there, or I shall show others the way to get there.

[*In the distance is heard the stroke of an ax on a tree*]

LOPAHIN: Good-bye, my dear fellow; it's time to be off. We turn up our noses at one another, but life is passing all the while. When I am working hard without resting, then my mind is more at ease, and it seems to me as though I too know what I exist for; but how many people are in Russia, my dear boy, who exist, one doesn't know what for. Well, it doesn't matter. That's not what keeps things spinning. They tell me Leonid Andreyevitch has taken a situation. He is going to be a clerk at the bank—6,000 roubles a year. Only, of course, he won't stick to it—he's too lazy.

ANYA: [*In the doorway*] Mamma begs you not to let them chop down the orchard until she's gone.

TROFIMOV: Yes, really, you might have the tact. [*Walks out across the front of the stage*]

LOPAHIN: I'll see to it! I'll see to it! Stupid fellows! [*Goes out after him*]

ANYA: Has Firs been taken to the hospital?

YASHA: I told them this morning. No doubt they have taken him.

ANYA: [*To Epihodov, who passes across the drawing-room*] Semyon Pantaleyevitch, inquire, please, if Firs has been taken to the hospital.

YASHA: [*In a tone of offence*] I told Yegor this morning—why ask a dozen times?

EPIHODOV: Firs is advanced in years. It's my conclusive opinion no treatment would do him good; it's time he was gathered to his fathers. And I can only envy him. [*Puts a trunk down on a cardboard hat-box and crushes it*] There, now, of course—I knew it would be so.

YASHA: [*Jeeringly*] Two and twenty misfortunes!

VARYA: [*Through the door*] Has Firs been taken to the hospital?

ANYA: Yes.

VARYA: Why wasn't the note for the doctor taken too?

ANYA: Oh, then, we must send it after them. [*Goes out*]

VARYA: [*From the adjoining room*] Where's Yasha? Tell him his mother's come to say good-bye to him.

YASHA: [*Waves his hand*] They put me out of all patience! [Dunyasha *has all this time been busy about the luggage. Now, when* Yasha *is left alone, she goes up to him*]

DUNYASHA: You might just give me one look, Yasha. You're going away. You're leaving me. [*Weeps and throws herself on his neck*]

YASHA: What are you crying for? [*Drinks the champagne*] In six days I shall be in Paris again. To-morrow we shall get into the express train and roll away in a flash. I can scarcely believe it! *Vive la France!* It doesn't suit me here—it's not the life for me; there's no doing anything. I have seen enough of the ignorance here. I have had enough of it. [*Drinks champagne*] What are you crying for? Behave yourself properly, and then you won't cry.

DUNYASHA: [*Powders her face, looking in a pocket-mirror*] Do send me a letter from Paris. You know how I loved you, Yasha—how I loved you! I am a tender creature, Yasha.

YASHA: Here they are coming!

[*Busies himself about the trunks, humming softly. Enter* Lyubov Andreyevna, Gaev, Anya *and* Charlotta Ivanovna]

GAEV: We ought to be off. There's not much time now. [*Looking at* Yasha] What a smell of herrings!

LYUBOV: In ten minutes we must get into the carriage. [*Casts a look about the room*] Farewell, dear house, dear old home of our fathers! Winter will pass and spring will come, and then you will be no more; they will tear you down! How much those walls have seen! [*Kisses her daughter passionately*] My treasure, how bright you look! Your eyes are sparkling like diamonds! Are you glad? Very glad?

ANYA: Very glad! A new life is beginning, mamma.

GAEV: Yes, really, everything is all right now. Before the cherry orchard was sold, we were all worried and wretched, but afterwards, when once the question was settled conclusively, irrevocably, we all felt calm and even cheerful. I am a bank clerk now—I am a financier—cannon off the red. And you, Lyuba, after all, you are looking better; there's no question of that.

LYUBOV: Yes. My nerves are better, that's true. [*Her hat and coat are handed to her*] I'm sleeping well. Carry out my things, Yasha. It's time. [*To* Anya] My darling, we shall soon see each other again. I am going to Paris. I can live there on the money your Yaroslavl auntie sent us to buy the estate with—hurrah for auntie!—but that money won't last long.

ANYA: You'll come back soon, mamma, won't you? I'll be working up for my examination in the high school, and when I have passed that, I shall set to work and be a help to you. We will read all sorts of things together, mamma, won't we? [*Kisses her mother's hands*] We will read in the autumn evenings. We'll read lots of books, and a new wonderful world will open out before us. [*Dreamily*] Mamma, come soon.

LYUBOV: I shall come, my precious treasure. [*Embraces her*]

[*Enter* Lopahin. Charlotta *softly hums a song*]

GAEV: Charlotta's happy; she's singing!

CHARLOTTA: [*Picks up a bundle like a swaddled baby*] Bye, bye, my baby. [*A baby is heard crying: "Ooah! ooah!"*] Hush, hush, my pretty boy! [*Ooah! ooah!*] Poor little thing! [*Throws the bundle back*]

You must please find me a situation. I can't go on like this.

LOPAHIN: We'll find you one, Charlotta Ivanovna. Don't you worry yourself.

GAEV: Everyone's leaving us. Varya's going away. We have become of no use all at once.

CHARLOTTA: There's nowhere for me to be in the town. I must go away. [Hums] What care I . . .

[Enter Pishtchik]

LOPAHIN: The freak of nature.

PISHTCHIK: [Gasping] Oh . . . let me get my breath. . . . I'm worn out . . . my most honored . . . Give me some water.

GAEV: Want some money, I suppose? Your humble servant! I'll go out of the way of temptation. [Goes out]

PISHTCHIK: It's a long while since I have been to see you . . . dearest lady. [To Lopahin] You are here . . . glad to see you . . . a man of immense intellect . . . take . . . here [gives Lopahin] 400 roubles. That leaves me owing 840.

LOPAHIN: [Shrugging his shoulders in amazement] It's like a dream. Where did you get it?

PISHTCHIK: Wait a bit . . . I'm hot . . . a most extraordinary occurrence! Some Englishmen came along and found in my land some sort of white clay. [To Lyubov Andreyevna] And 400 for you . . . most lovely . . . wonderful. [Gives money] The rest later. [Sips water] A young man in the train was telling me just now that a great philosopher advises jumping off a house-top. "Jump!" says he; "the whole gist of the problem lies in that." [Wonderingly] Fancy that, now! Water, please!

LOPAHIN: What Englishmen?

PISHTCHIK: I have made over to them the rights to dig the clay for twenty-four years . . . and now, excuse me . . . I can't stay . . . I must be trotting on. I'm going to Znoikovo . . . to Kardamanovo. . . . I'm in debt all round. [Sips] . . . To your very good health! . . . I'll come in on Thursday.

LYUBOV: We are just off to the town, and to-morrow I start for abroad.

PISHTCHIK: What! [In agitation] Why to the town? Oh, I see the furniture . . . the boxes. No matter . . . [Through his tears] . . . no matter . . . men of enormous intellect . . . these Englishmen. . . . Never mind . . . be happy. God will succor you . . . no matter . . . everything in this world must have an end. [Kisses Lyubov Andreyevna's hand] If the rumor reaches you that my end has come, think of this . . . old horse, and say: "There once was such a man in the world . . . Semyonov-Pishtchik . . . the Kingdom of Heaven be his!" . . . most extraordinary weather . . . yes. [Goes out in violent agitation, but at once returns and says in the doorway] Dashenka wishes to be remembered to you. [Goes out]

LYUBOV: Now we can start. I leave with two cares in my heart. The first is leaving Firs ill. [Looking at her watch] We have still five minutes.

ANYA: Mamma, Firs has been taken to the hospital. Yasha sent him off this morning.

LYUBOV: My other anxiety is Varya. She is used to getting up early and working; and now, without work, she's like a fish out of water. She is thin and pale, and she's crying, poor dear! [A pause] You are well aware, Yermolay Alexeyevitch, I dreamed of marrying her to you, and everything seemed to show that you would get married. [Whispers to Anya and motions to Charlotta and both go out] She loves you—she suits you. And I don't know—I don't know why it is you seem, as it were, to avoid each other. I can't understand it!

LOPAHIN: I don't understand it myself, I confess. It's queer somehow, altogether. If there's still time, I'm ready now at once. Let's settle it straight off, and go ahead; but without you, I feel I shan't make her an offer.

LYUBOV: That's excellent. Why, a single moment's all that's necessary. I'll call her at once.

LOPAHIN: And there's champagne all ready too. [Looking into the glasses] Empty! Someone's emptied them already. [Yasha coughs] I call that greedy.

LYUBOV: [Eagerly] Capital! We will go out. Yasha, allez! I'll call her in. [At the door] Varya, leave all that; come here. Come along! [Goes out with Yasha]

LOPAHIN: [Looking at his watch] Yes.

[A pause. Behind the door, smothered laughter and whispering, and, at last, enter Varya]

VARYA: [Looking a long while over the things] It is strange, I can't find it anywhere.

LOPAHIN: What are you looking for?

VARYA: I packed it myself, and I can't remember. [A pause]

LOPAHIN: Where are you going now, Varvara Mihailova?

VARYA: I? To the Ragulins. I have arranged to go to them to look after the house—as a housekeeper.

LOPAHIN: That's in Yashnovo? It'll be seventy miles away. [A pause] So this is the end of life in this house!

VARYA: [Looking among the things] Where is it? Perhaps I put it in the trunk. Yes, life in this house is over—there will be no more of it.

LOPAHIN: And I'm just off to Harkov—by this next train. I've a lot of business there. I'm leaving Epihodov here, and I've taken him on.

VARYA: Really!

LOPAHIN: This time last year we had snow already, if you remember; but now it's so fine and sunny. Though it's cold, to be sure—three degrees of frost.

VARYA: I haven't looked. [A pause] And besides, our thermometer's broken. [A pause]

[Voice at the door from the yard: "Yermolay Alexeyevitch!"]

LOPAHIN: [As though he had long been expecting this summons] This minute!

[Lopahin goes out quickly. Varya sitting on the floor and laying her head on a bag full of *clothes, sobs quietly. The door opens.* Lyubov Andreyevna *comes in cautiously*]

LYUBOV: Well? [*A pause*] We must be going.

VARYA: [*Has wiped her eyes and is no longer crying*] Yes, mamma, it's time to start. I shall have time to get to the Ragulins to-day, if only you're not late for the train.

LYUBOV: [*In the doorway*] Anya, put your things on.

[*Enter* Anya, *then* Gaev *and* Charlotta Ivanovna. Gaev *has on a warm coat with a hood. Servants and cabmen come in.* Epihodov *bustles about the luggage*]

LYUBOV: Now we can start on our travels.

ANYA: [*Joyfully*] On our travels!

GAEV: My friends—my dear, my precious friends! Leaving this house for ever, can I be silent? Can I refrain from giving utterance at leave-taking to those emotions which now flood all my being?

ANYA: [*Supplicatingly*] Uncle!

VARYA: Uncle, you mustn't!

GAEV: [*Dejectedly*] Cannon and into the pocket . . . I'll be quiet. . . .

[*Enter* Trofimov *and afterwards* Lopahin]

TROFIMOV: Well, ladies and gentlemen, we must start.

LOPAHIN: Epihodov, my coat!

LYUBOV: I'll stay just one minute. It seems as though I have never seen before what the walls, what the ceilings in this house were like, and now I look at them with greediness, with such tender love.

GAEV: I remember when I was six years old sitting in that window on Trinity Day watching my father going to church.

LYUBOV: Have all the things been taken?

LOPAHIN: I think all. [*Putting on overcoat, to* Epihodov] You, Epihodov, mind you see everything is right.

EPIHODOV: [*In a husky voice*] Don't you trouble, Yermolay Alexeyevitch.

LOPAHIN: Why, what's wrong with your voice?

EPIHODOV: I've just had a drink of water, and I choked over something.

YASHA: [*Contemptuously*] The ignorance!

LYUBOV: We are going—and not a soul will be left here.

LOPAHIN: Not till the spring.

VARYA: [*Pulls a parasol out of a bundle, as though about to hit someone with it.* Lopahin *makes a gesture as though alarmed*] What is it? I didn't mean anything.

TROFIMOV: Ladies and gentlemen, let us get into the carriage. It's time. The train will be in directly.

VARYA: Petya, here they are, your goloshes, by that box. [*With tears*] And what dirty old things they are!

TROFIMOV: [*Putting on his goloshes*] Let us go, friends!

GAEV: [*Greatly agitated, afraid of weeping*] The train—the station! Double baulk, ah!

LYUBOV: Let us go!

LOPAHIN: Are we all here? [*Locks the sidedoor on left*] The things are all here. We must lock up. Let us go!

ANYA: Good-bye, home! Good-bye to the old life!

TROFIMOV: Welcome to the new life!

[Trofimov *goes out with* Anya. Varya *looks round the room and goes out slowly.* Yasha *and* Charlotta Ivanovna, *with her dog, go out*]

LOPAHIN: Till the spring, then! Come, friends, till we meet! [*Goes out*]

[Lyubov Andreyevna *and* Gaev *remain alone. As though they had been waiting for this, they throw themselves on each other's necks, and break into subdued smothered sobbing, afraid of being overheard*]

GAEV: [*In despair*] Sister, my sister!

LYUBOV: Oh, my orchard!—my sweet, beautiful orchard! My life, my youth, my happiness, good-bye! good-bye!

VOICE OF ANYA: [*Calling gaily*] Mamma!

VOICE OF TROFIMOV: [*Gaily, excitedly*] Aa—oo!

LYUBOV: One last look at the walls, at the windows. My dear mother loved to walk about this room.

GAEV: Sister, sister!

VOICE OF ANYA: Mamma!

VOICE OF TROFIMOV: Aa—oo!

LYUBOV: We are coming. [*They go out*]

[*The stage is empty. There is the sound of the doors being locked up, then of the carriages driving away. There is silence. In the stillness there is the dull stroke of an ax in a tree, clanging with a mournful lonely sound. Footsteps are heard.* Firs *appears in the doorway on the right. He is dressed as always—in a pea-jacket and white waistcoat, with slippers on his feet. He is ill*]

FIRS: [*Goes up to the doors, and tries the handles*] Locked! They have gone . . . [*Sits down on sofa*] They have forgotten me. . . . Never mind . . . I'll sit here a bit. . . . I'll be bound Leonid Andreyevitch hasn't put his fur coat on and has gone off in his thin overcoat. [*Sighs anxiously*] I didn't see after him. . . . These young people . . . [*Mutters something that can't be distinguished*] Life has slipped by as though I hadn't lived. [*Lies down*] I'll lie down a bit. . . . There's no strength in you, nothing left you—all gone! Ech! I'm good for nothing. [*Lies motionless*]

[*A sound is heard that seems to come from the sky, like a breaking harp-string, dying away mournfully. All is still again, and there is heard nothing but the strokes of the ax far away in the orchard*]

CURTAIN.

Maxim Gorki

(1868–1936)

Paying tribute to the man whose pen-name means "Maxim the Bitter," Romain Rolland called Gorki "the man who, like Dante, emerged from hell, but not alone, and brought with him his companions in torment, his comrades in salvation." Gorki did precisely this in *The Lower Depths,* for which James Huneker found an apt description in the quotation from the Vulgate *"de profundis ad te clamavi."* "Out of the depths I cry unto Thee" might have been accepted by the playwright himself as a definition of his intent in much of his work, especially if the "Thee" is allowed to stand for the spirit of humanity instead of some supernatural agency. His humanitarianism early took the form of social protest and led him in time to engage in revolutionary activities that made him a fugitive from his country until the Russian Revolution turned him into the grand old man of Soviet letters. Today both his birthplace, the renamed industrial city of Nizhni-Novgorod, and the Moscow Art Theatre "in the Name of Gorki" bear witness to the esteem in which he came to be held in his homeland.

Alexei Maximovitch Pyeshkov, as he was called before he began to sign himself Maxim Gorki, knew the worst about humanity by the time he attracted attention as a writer of unusual powers. Orphaned in childhood, he grew up in the household of a tyrannical grandfather who bullied him and apprenticed him to unpleasant trades. Escaping from a detestable employer, he wandered over the steppes, a frequently starving young tramp in the company of pilgrims, thieves, and all the flotsam and jetsam of Russian society. With knowledge came pity, and it is the combination of grime-stained realism and compassion that made him the spokesman of the outcasts he called "the creatures that once were men." In his writings he was to remember, for example, the bruised harlot who forgot her own desperation to mother him when a storm drove him to take shelter under an overturned boat; the half-wit he met during his wanderings who was "more hunted than an animal"; the madwoman he found rearing seven subnormal children; and the peasant woman he impetuously defended from her husband. (His intervention resulted in his having to be taken to a hospital by a good Samaritan who found him lying half-dead in the bushes.) In his eighth year, he had hurled himself at his stepfather with a breadknife when he found him beating his consumptive mother. Ever since that childhood episode Gorki had raged against injustice. He became one of the seekers after salvation with which the Russia of the eighteen-nineties teemed, and he needed only an introduction to literature to find an outlet for his social passion.

Introduced to the mysteries of the alphabet by a philosophical cook whose helper he had been on a Volga steamboat, Gorki began educating himself with the aid of members of the provincial intelligentsia who were then attempting to enlighten the masses. His first short story, written in 1892, attracted the attention of a prominent literary figure, Korolenko, who sent it to a periodical. Its publication aroused interest in literary circles, and soon Gorki's sketches of workers and outcasts were hailed as the ultimate in realism. They introduced fresh material into Russian literature, which was already well acquainted, if not surfeited, with the middle classes and the peasantry but had yet to discover the proletariat. As a result, his stories and novels were, if anything, overrated. It was none other than Tolstoy who told the young author that he had serious limitations as an artist because he was apt to become "literary" and to sentimentalize reality. It is the Gorki of a series of candid autobiographies (*My Childhood, In the World, My University Days,* and various *Reminiscences*) and of *The Lower Depths* who is likely to weather time.

Chekhov attracted Gorki to the theatre by introducing him to members of the Moscow Art Theatre, and the actors promptly wrung the promise of a play from him. At first suspicious of them because they were "middle class" people, the laureate of the common man obliged with his first drama, *The Smug Citizen,* and the Art Theatre produced it in a strained atmosphere. As the radical author's election to the Imperial Academy of Russian Artists had just been annulled by the government, a squadron of Cossacks surrounded the playhouse to suppress an expected demonstration. There was no demonstration within the theatre itself only because the management requested self-control from the public "in order that Gorki may continue to write for the theatre," although one enthusiast did climax the last performance with a stentorian "Down with the Grand Duke!" Censorship had also compelled the deletion of such passages in *The Smug Citizen* as "He who works is the master" and "In Russia it is more comfortable to be a drunkard or a tramp than to be a sober and hard-working man." The play, a highly charged account of decadence and rebellion in middle-class life, was an explosive commodity for the then politically neutral theatre, whose program had moved no further left than a production of Ibsen's *An Enemy of the People.* Nevertheless, the actors busied themselves preparing a second Gorki play for production while the first was still running.

The new work was *The Lower Depths,* also known in English as *A Night's Lodging* as well as by other titles. Under the author's expert guidance, the company made trips to the disreputable Khitrov marketplace to acquaint itself with the life presented in a drama so uncompromisingly naturalistic that James Huneker was hardly exaggerating when he wrote that Zola "might have gone to school to learn the alphabet of his art at the knees of the young man from Nizhni-Novgorod." Gorki even naïvely offered to bring a streetwalker to stay with the Art Theatre's leading actress, Olga Knipper (Chekhov's wife), who played Nastya. On December 18, 1902, as a result of such scrupulous realism, *The Lower Depths* became one of the Art Theatre's most triumphant productions. Never before had the company thrown itself so wholeheartedly into a play whose matter was so foreign to its own experience. The actors performed as if they walked through a world of half-lights interrupted by sudden flashes of lightning. For a long time the play remained one of the Moscow Art Theatre's most inspired productions.

Gorki provided a rare dramatic experience by taking as sordid a slice of life as it was possible to find and electrifying it with pity rather than revulsion and with hope rather than despair. And to these qualities the author, here not unaided by the memorable first production, added a natural fluidity well described by the historian of the Art Theatre Oliver Sayler when he wrote that Gorki's work is "not so much a matter of utterable line and recountable gesture as it is of the intangible flow of human souls in endlessly shifting contact with one another."

Although it does not appear that *The Lower Depths* was ever again presented on the stage as effectively as in the Moscow company's performances, its unique quality attracted attention throughout the Western world. The Stage Society of London produced it less than a year after its *première* and again in 1911, and Arthur Hopkins gave it for the first time in English on Broadway in 1919, while performances in German and other European languages multiplied over the years. Its great success in Russia, moreover, encouraged Gorki to write a number of other plays, such as *Summer Folk, Children of the Sun,* and *Enemies,* before the Russian Revolution, and afterward two parts of an intended trilogy, *Dostigaev and Others* (1933) and *Yegor Bulychov* (1932). Most of these plays were uneven in quality and owed their importance largely to the social protest imbedded in them. In *Summer Folk* and *Children of the Sun,* for example, Gorki denounced the "intelligentsia" for failing to range itself on the side of social reform, and in *Enemies* he proclaimed that there could be no meeting ground between even well-intentioned employers and workers. *Yegor Bulychov* presented the end of middle-class society through the lingering death of a merchant who reviews the failure of his life on the eve of the Russian Revolution. But even this play, his best after *The Lower Depths,* failed to equal its author's achievement in his memorable picture of "creatures that once were men."

Gorki was himself aware of his shortcomings as a dramatist, and regretted that he tended to become didactic. Admitting that characters should be permitted to act independently of the author's will in accordance with their individuality and environment, he declared himself incapable of abiding by this principle in practice. Nor did he believe that any other European playwright had done so, which is a debatable conclusion. *The Lower Depths* did, however, bring him as close to the ideal of objectivity as a man of his convictions could come. Although the faith-healer Luka constantly preaches in the first three acts, it is plain that Gorki was not using him as his mouthpiece. The climactic action actually demonstrates the futility of Luka's illusion-peddling. Even the tribute to truth by Satine in the last act, which may be taken to express the author's own views, is presented as the wisdom of a tipsy failure whose only regret when the alcoholic actor hangs himself is that he has spoiled the singing.

A national hero after throwing his influence on the side of Lenin, Gorki tried to mitigate the rigors of the Bolshevik terror in the early years of the revolution. He devoted his last years to encouraging and guiding young Russian writers. He also wrote a series of turgid, if vivid, novels reviewing Russian life from 1880 to 1924 and celebrating the rise of an insurgent spirit.

Gorki died after an illness in 1936, under the aura of revolutionary sanctity. He was allegedly murdered by an anti-Stalinist physician who was subsequently executed in the purge of the Trotsky faction. In essence, however, Gorki belongs to no party. His compassion for mankind, his hopes for its ultimate freedom, and his faith have been expressed in an essay in which he wrote that the "true Shekinah"—the "Holy of Holies"—is Man. For all his readiness to present the squalor into which men could sink, he was possessed of romantic fervor. He insisted only on drawing a distinction between the "passive romanticism" that reconciles men to reality by disguising it and the "active romanticism" which strengthens men's will to live and rouses them to action.

BIBLIOGRAPHY: Vladimir Nemirovitch-Dantchenko, *My Life in the Russian Theatre* (pp. 241–243, 237–241, etc.), 1936; John Gassner, *Masters of the Drama* (pp. 526–533), 1945; Maxim Gorky *Reminiscences of Tolstoy, Chekhov, and Andreyev* (Dover Publications, 1946 edition); Alexander Kaun, *Maxim Gorki and His Russia,* 1931; Constantin Stanislavsky, *My Life in Art* (pp. 367–369, 390–399), 1924, 1938; Leo Wiener, *The Contemporary Drama of Russia,* 1924.

THE LOWER DEPTHS

By Maxim Gorki

TRANSLATED FROM THE RUSSIAN BY JENNY COVAN

CAST OF CHARACTERS

MIKHAIL IVANOFF KOSTILYOFF, *keeper of a night lodging*
VASSILISA KARPOVNA, *his wife*
NATASHA, *her sister*
MIEDVIEDIEFF, *her uncle, a policeman*
VASKA PEPEL, *a young thief*

ANDREI MITRITCH KLESHTCH, *a locksmith*
ANNA, *his wife*
NASTYA, *a street-walker*
KVASHNYA, *a vendor of meat-pies*
BUBNOFF, *a cap-maker*
THE BARON

SATINE
THE ACTOR
LUKA, *a pilgrim*
ALYOSHKA, *a shoemaker*
KRIVOY ZOB ⎱ *Porters*
THE TARTAR ⎰
NIGHT LODGERS, TRAMPS AND OTHERS

The action takes place in a Night Lodging and in "The Waste," an area in its rear.

ACT I.

A cellar resembling a cave. The ceiling, which merges into stone walls, is low and grimy, and the plaster and paint are peeling off. There is a window, high up on the right wall, from which comes the light. The right corner, which constitutes Pepel's room, is partitioned off by thin boards. Close to the corner of this room is Bubnoff's wooden bunk. In the left corner stands a large Russian stove. In the stone wall, left, is a door leading to the kitchen where live Kvashnya, the Baron, and Nastya. Against the wall, between the stove and the door, is a large bed covered with dirty chintz. Bunks line the walls. In the foreground, by the left wall, is a block of wood with a vise and a small anvil fastened to it, and another smaller block of wood somewhat further towards the back. Kleshtch is seated on the smaller block, trying keys into old locks. At his feet are two large bundles of various keys, wired together, also a battered tin samovar, a hammer, and pincers. In the center are a large table, two benches, and a stool, all of which are of dirty, unpainted wood. Behind the table Kvashnya is busying herself with the samovar. The Baron sits chewing a piece of black bread, and Nastya occupies the stool, leans her elbows on the table, and reads a tattered book. In the bed, behind curtains, Anna lies coughing. Bubnoff is seated on his bunk, attempting to shape a pair of old trousers with the help of an ancient hat shape which he holds between his knees. Scattered about him are pieces of buckram, oilcloth, and rags. Satine, just awakened, lies in his bunk, grunting. On top of the stove, the Actor, invisible to the audience, tosses about and coughs.

It is an early spring morning.

THE BARON: And then?

KVASHNYA: No, my dear, said I, keep away from me with such proposals. I've been through it all, you see—and not for a hundred baked lobsters would I marry again!

BUBNOFF: [*To* Satine] What are you grunting about? [Satine *keeps on grunting*]

KVASHNYA: Why should I, said I, a free woman, my own mistress, enter my name into somebody else's passport and sell myself into slavery—no! Why —I wouldn't marry a man even if he were an American prince!

KLESHTCH: You lie!

KVASHNYA: Wha-at?

KLESHTCH: You lie! You're going to marry Abramka. . . .

THE BARON: [*Snatching the book out of* Nastya's *hand and reading the title*] "Fatal Love". . . [*Laughs*]

NASTYA: [*Stretching out her hand*] Give it back— give it back! Stop fooling!

[The Baron *looks at her and waves the book in the air*]

KVASHNYA: [*To* Kleshtch] You crimson goat, you —calling me a liar! How dare you be so rude to me?

THE BARON: [*Hitting* Nastya *on the head with the book*] Nastya, you little fool!

NASTYA: [*Reaching for the book*] Give it back!

KLESHTCH: Oh—what a great lady . . . but you'll marry Abramka just the same—that's all you're waiting for . . .

KVASHNYA: Sure! Anything else? You nearly beat your wife to death!

KLESHTCH: Shut up, you old bitch! It's none of your business!

KVASHNYA: Ho-ho! can't stand the truth, can you?

THE BARON: They're off again! Nastya, where are you?

NASTYA: [*Without lifting her head*] Hey—go away!

ANNA: [*Putting her head through the curtains*]

229

The day has started. For God's sake, don't row!

KLESHTCH: Whining again!

ANNA: Every blessed day . . . let me die in peace, can't you?

BUBNOFF: Noise won't keep you from dying.

KVASHNYA: [Walking up to Anna] Little mother, how did you ever manage to live with this wretch?

ANNA: Leave me alone—get away from me. . . .

KVASHNYA: Well, well! You poor soul . . . how's the pain in the chest—any better?

THE BARON: Kvashnya! Time to go to market. . . .

KVASHNYA: We'll go presently. [To Anna] Like some hot dumplings?

ANNA: No, thanks. Why should I eat?

KVASHNYA: You must eat. Hot food—good for you! I'll leave you some in a cup. Eat them when you feel like it. Come on, sir! [To Kleshtch] You evil spirit!

[Goes into kitchen]

ANNA: [Coughing] Lord, Lord . . .

THE BARON: [Painfully pushing forward Nastya's head] Throw it away—little fool!

NASTYA: [Muttering] Leave me alone—I don't bother you . . .

[The Baron follows Kvashnya, whistling]

SATINE: [Sitting up in his bunk] Who beat me up yesterday?

BUBNOFF: Does it make any difference who?

SATINE: Suppose they did—but why did they?

BUBNOFF: Were you playing cards?

SATINE: Yes!

BUBNOFF: That's why they beat you.

SATINE: Scoundrels!

THE ACTOR: [Raising his head from the top of the stove] One of these days they'll beat you to death!

SATINE: You're a jackass!

THE ACTOR: Why?

SATINE: Because a man can die only once!

THE ACTOR: [After a silence] I don't understand—

KLESHTCH: Say! You crawl from that stove—and start cleaning house! Don't play the delicate primrose!

THE ACTOR: None of your business!

KLESHTCH: Wait till Vassilisa comes—she'll show you whose business it is!

THE ACTOR: To hell with Vassilisa! To-day is the Baron's turn to clean. . . . Baron!

[The Baron comes from the kitchen]

THE BARON: I've no time to clean . . . I'm going to market with Kvashnya.

THE ACTOR: That doesn't concern me. Go to the gallows if you like. It's your turn to sweep the floor just the same—I'm not going to do other people's work . . .

THE BARON: Go to blazes! Nastya will do it. Hey there—fatal love! Wake up! [Takes the book away from Nastya]

NASTYA: [Getting up] What do you want? Give it

back to me! You scoundrel! And that's a nobleman for you!

THE BARON: [Returning the book to her] Nastya! Sweep the floor for me—will you?

NASTYA: [Goes to kitchen] Not so's you'll notice it!

KVASHNYA: [To the Baron through kitchen door] Come on—you! They don't need you! Actor! You were asked to do it, and now you go ahead and attend to it—it won't kill you . . .

THE ACTOR: It's always I . . . I don't understand why. . . .

[The Baron comes from the kitchen, across his shoulders a wooden beam from which hang earthen pots covered with rags]

THE BARON: Heavier than ever!

SATINE: It paid you to be born a Baron, eh?

KVASHNYA: [To Actor] See to it that you sweep up! [Crosses to outer door, letting the Baron pass ahead]

THE ACTOR: [Climbing down from the stove] It's bad for me to inhale dust. [With pride] My organism is poisoned with alcohol. [Sits down on a bunk meditating]

SATINE: Organism—organon. . . .

ANNA: Andrei Mitritch. . . .

KLESHTCH: What now?

ANNA: Kvashnya left me some dumplings over there—you eat them.

KLESHTCH: [Coming over to her] And you—don't you want any?

ANNA: No. Why should I eat? You're a workman—you need it.

KLESHTCH: Frightened, are you? Don't be! You'll get all right!

ANNA: Go and eat! It's hard on me. . . . I suppose very soon . . .

KLESHTCH: [Walking away] Never mind—maybe you'll get well—you can never tell! [Goes into kitchen]

THE ACTOR: [Loud, as if he had suddenly awakened] Yesterday the doctor in the hospital said to me: "Your organism," he said, "is entirely poisoned with alcohol . . ."

SATINE: [Smiling] Organon . . .

THE ACTOR: [Stubbornly] Not organon—organism

SATINE: Sibylline. . . .

THE ACTOR: [Shaking his fist at him] Nonsense! I'm telling you seriously . . . if the organism is poisoned . . . that means it's bad for me to sweep the floor—to inhale the dust . . .

SATINE: Macrobistic . . . hah!

BUBNOFF: What are you muttering?

SATINE: Words—and here's another one for you —transcendentalistic . . .

BUBNOFF: What does it mean?

SATINE: Don't know—I forgot . . .

BUBNOFF: Then why did you say it?

SATINE: Just so! I'm bored, brother, with human

words—all our words. Bored! I've heard each one of them a thousand times surely.

THE ACTOR: In Hamlet they say: "Words, words, words!" It's a good play. I played the grave-digger in it once. . . .

[Kleshtch *comes from the kitchen*]

KLESHTCH: Will you start playing with the broom?

THE ACTOR: None of your business. [*Striking his chest*] Ophelia! O—remember me in thy prayers!

[*Back stage is heard a dull murmur, cries, and a police whistle. Kleshtch sits down to work, filing screechily*]

SATINE: I love unintelligible, obsolete words. When I was a youngster—and worked as a telegraph operator—I read heaps of books. . . .

BUBNOFF: Were you really a telegrapher?

SATINE: I was. There are some excellent books— and lots of curious words . . . Once I was an educated man, do you know?

BUBNOFF: I've heard it a hundred times. Well, so you were! That isn't very important! Me—well— once I was a furrier. I had my own shop—what with dyeing the fur all day long, my arms were yellow up to the elbows, brother. I thought I'd never be able ever to get clean again—that I'd go to my grave, all yellow! But look at my hands now—they're plain dirty—that's what!

SATINE: Well, and what then?

BUBNOFF: That's all!

SATINE: What are you trying to prove?

BUBNOFF: Oh, well—just matching thoughts—no matter how much dye you get on yourself, it all comes off in the end—yes, yes—

SATINE: Oh—my bones ache!

THE ACTOR: [*Sits, nursing his knees*] Education is all rot. Talent is the thing. I knew an actor—who read his parts by heart, syllable by syllable—but he played heroes in a way that . . . why—the whole theater would rock with ecstasy!

SATINE: Bubnoff, give me five kopecks.

BUBNOFF: I only have two—

THE ACTOR: I say—talent, that's what you need to play heroes. And talent is nothing but faith in yourself, in your own powers—

SATINE: Give me five kopecks and I'll have faith that you're a hero, a crocodile, or a police inspector —Kleshtch, give me five kopecks.

KLESHTCH: Go to hell! All of you!

SATINE: What are you cursing for? I know you haven't a kopeck in the world!

ANNA: Andrei Mitritch—I'm suffocating—I can't breathe—

KLESHTCH: What shall I do?

BUBNOFF: Open the door into the hall.

KLESHTCH: All right. You're sitting on the bunk, I on the floor. You change places with me, and I'll let you open the door. I have a cold as it is.

BUBNOFF: [*Unconcernedly*] I don't care if you open the door—it's your wife who's asking—

KLESHTCH: [*Morosely*] I don't care who's asking—

SATINE: My head buzzes—ah—why do people have to hit each other over the heads?

BUBNOFF: They don't only hit you over the head, but over the rest of the body as well. [*Rises*] I must go and buy some thread—our bosses are late to-day —seems as if they've croaked. [*Exit*]

[Anna *coughs*; Satine *is lying down motionless, his hands folded behind his head*]

THE ACTOR: [*Looks about him morosely, then goes to* Anna] Feeling bad, eh?

ANNA: I'm choking—

THE ACTOR: If you wish, I'll take you into the hallway. Get up, then, come! [*He helps her to rise, wraps some sort of a rag about her shoulders, and supports her toward the hall*] It isn't easy. I'm sick myself—poisoned with alcohol . . .

[Kostilyoff *appears in the doorway*]

KOSTILYOFF: Going for a stroll? What a nice couple—the gallant cavalier and the lady fair!

THE ACTOR: Step aside, you—don't you see that we're invalids?

KOSTILYOFF: Pass on, please! [*Hums a religious tune, glances about him suspiciously, and bends his head to the left as if listening to what is happening in* Pepel's *room*. Kleshtch *is jangling his keys and scraping away with his file, and looks askance at the other*] Filing?

KLESHTCH: What?

KOSTILYOFF: I say, are you filing? [*Pause*] What did I want to ask? [*Quick and low*] Hasn't my wife been here?

KLESHTCH: I didn't see her.

KOSTILYOFF: [*Carefully moving toward* Pepel's *room*] You take up a whole lot of room for your two rubles a month. The bed—and your bench— yes—you take up five rubles' worth of space, so help me God! I'll have to put another half ruble to your rent—

KLESHTCH: You'll put a noose around my neck and choke me . . . you'll croak soon enough, and still all you think of is half rubles—

KOSTILYOFF: Why should I choke you? What would be the use? God be with you—live and prosper! But I'll have to raise you half a ruble—I'll buy oil for the ikon lamp, and my offering will atone for my sins, and for yours as well. You don't think much of your sins—not much! Oh, Andrushka, you're a wicked man! Your wife is dying because of your wickedness—no one loves you, no one respects you—your work is squeaky, jarring on every one.

KLESHTCH: [*Shouts*] What do you come here for —just to annoy me?

[Satine *grunts loudly*]

KOSTILYOFF: [*With a start*] God, what a noise!

[The Actor *enters*]

THE ACTOR: I've put her down in the hall and wrapped her up.

KOSTILYOFF: You're a kindly fellow. That's good. Some day you'll be rewarded for it.

THE ACTOR: When?

KOSTILYOFF: In the Beyond, little brother—there all our deeds will be reckoned up.

THE ACTOR: Suppose you reward me right now?

KOSTILYOFF: How can I do that?

THE ACTOR: Wipe out half my debt.

KOSTILYOFF: He-ho! You're always jesting, darling—always poking fun . . . can kindliness of heart be repaid with gold? Kindliness—it's above all other qualities. But your debt to me—remains a debt. And so you'll have to pay me back. You ought to be kind to me, an old man, without seeking for reward!

THE ACTOR: You're a swindler, old man! [*Goes into kitchen*]

[Kleshtch *rises and goes into the hall*]

KOSTILYOFF: [*To* Satine] See that squeaker—? He ran away—he doesn't like me!

SATINE: Does anybody like you besides the Devil.

KOSTILYOFF: [*Laughing*] Oh—you're so quarrelsome! But I like you all—I understand you all, my unfortunate downtrodden, useless brethren . . . [*Suddenly, rapidly*] Is Vaska home?

SATINE: See for yourself—

KOSTILYOFF: [*Goes to the door and knocks*] Vaska!

[The Actor *appears at the kitchen door, chewing something*]

PEPEL: Who is it?

KOSTILYOFF: It's I—I, Vaska!

PEPEL: What do you want?

KOSTILYOFF: [*Stepping aside*] Open!

SATINE: [*Without looking at* Kostilyoff] He'll open—and she's there—

[The Actor *makes a grimace*]

KOSTILYOFF: [*In a low, anxious tone*] Eh? Who's there? What?

SATINE: Speaking to me?

KOSTILYOFF: What did you say?

SATINE: Oh—nothing—I was just talking to myself—

KOSTILYOFF: Take care, brother. Don't carry your joking too far! [*Knocks loudly at door*] Vassily!

PEPEL: [*Opening door*] Well? What are you disturbing me for?

KOSTILYOFF: [*Peering into room*] I—you see—

PEPEL: Did you bring the money?

KOSTILYOFF: I've something to tell you—

PEPEL: Did you bring the money?

KOSTILYOFF: What money? Wait—

PEPEL: Why—the seven rubles for the watch—well?

KOSTILYOFF: What watch, Vaska? Oh, you—

PEPEL: Look here. Yesterday, before witnesses, I sold you a watch for ten rubles, you gave me three—now let me have the other seven. What are you blinking for? You hang around here—you disturb people—and don't seem to know yourself what you're after.

KOSTILYOFF: Sh-sh! Don't be angry, Vaska. The watch—it is—

SATINE: Stolen!

KOSTILYOFF: [*Sternly*] I do not accept stolen goods—how can you imagine—

PEPEL: [*Taking him by the shoulder*] What did you disturb me for? What do you want?

KOSTILYOFF: I don't want—anything. I'll go—if you're in such a state—

PEPEL: Be off, and bring the money!

KOSTILYOFF: What ruffians! I—I—[*Exit*]

THE ACTOR: What a farce!

SATINE: That's fine—I like it.

PEPEL: What did he come here for?

SATINE: [*Laughing*] Don't you understand? He's looking for his wife. Why don't you beat him up once and for all, Vaska?

PEPEL: Why should I let such trash interfere with my life?

SATINE: Show some brains! And then you can marry Vassilisa—and become our boss—

PEPEL: Heavenly bliss! And you'd smash up my household and, because I'm a soft-hearted fool, you'll drink up everything I possess. [*Sits on a bunk*] Old devil—woke me up—I was having such a pleasant dream. I dreamed I was fishing—and I caught an enormous trout—such a trout as you only see in dreams! I was playing him—and I was so afraid the line would snap. I had just got out the gaff—and I thought to myself—in a moment—

SATINE: It wasn't a trout, it was Vassilisa—

THE ACTOR: He caught Vassilisa a long time ago.

PEPEL: [*Angrily*] You can all go to the devil—and Vassilisa with you—

[Kleshtch *comes from the hall*]

KLESHTCH: Devilishly cold!

THE ACTOR: Why didn't you bring Anna back? She'll freeze, out there—

KLESHTCH: Natasha took her into the kitchen—

THE ACTOR: The old man will kick her out—

KLESHTCH: [*Sitting down to his work*] Well—Natasha will bring her in here—

SATINE: Vassily—give me five kopecks!

THE ACTOR: [*To* Satine] Oh, you—always five kopecks—Vassya—give us twenty kopecks—

PEPEL: I'd better give it to them now before they ask for a ruble. Here you are!

SATINE: Gibraltar! There are no kindlier people in the world than thieves!

KLESHTCH: [*Morosely*] They earn their money easily—they don't work—

SATINE: Many earn it easily, but not many part with it so easily. Work? Make work pleasant—and maybe I'll work too. Yes—maybe. When work's a pleasure, life's, too. When it's toil, then life is a drudge. [*To the* Actor] You, Sardanapalus! Come on!

THE ACTOR: Let's go, Nebuchadnezzar! I'll get as drunk as forty thousand topers! [*They leave*]

PEPEL: [*Yawning*] Well, how's your wife?

KLESHTCH: It seems as if soon—[*Pause*]

PEPEL: Now I look at you—seems to me all that filing and scraping of yours is useless.

KLESHTCH: Well—what else can I do?

PEPEL: Nothing.

KLESHTCH: How can I live?

PEPEL: People manage, somehow.

KLESHTCH: Them? Call them people? Muck and dregs—that's what they are! I'm a workman—I'm ashamed even to look at them. I've slaved since I was a child. . . . D'you think I shan't be able to tear myself away from here? I'll crawl out of here, even if I have to leave my skin behind—but crawl out I will! Just wait . . . my wife'll die . . . I've lived here six months, and it seems like six years.

PEPEL: Nobody here's any worse off than you . . . say what you like . . .

KLESHTCH: No worse is right. They've neither honor nor conscience.

PEPEL: [Indifferently] What good does it do— honor or conscience? Can you get them on their feet instead of on their uppers—through honor and conscience? Honor and conscience are needed only by those who have power and energy . . .

BUBNOFF: [Coming back] Oh—I'm frozen.

PEPEL: Bubnoff! Got a conscience?

BUBNOFF: What? A conscience?

PEPEL: Exactly!

BUBNOFF: What do I need a conscience for? I'm not rich.

PEPEL: Just what I said: honor and conscience are for the rich—right! And Kleshtch is upbraiding us because we haven't any!

BUBNOFF: Why—did he want to borrow some of it?

PEPEL: No—he has plenty of his own . . .

BUBNOFF: Oh—are you selling it? You won't sell much around here. But if you had some old boxes, I'd buy them—on credit . . .

PEPEL: [Didactically] You're a jackass, Andrushka! On the subject of conscience you ought to hear Satine—or the Baron . . .

KLESHTCH: I've nothing to talk to them about!

PEPEL: They have more brains than you—even if they're drunkards . . .

BUBNOFF: He who can be drunk and wise at the same time is doubly blessed . . .

PEPEL: Satine says every man expects his neighbor to have a conscience, but—you see—it isn't to any one's advantage to have one—that's a fact.

[Natasha enters, followed by Luka who carries a stick in his hand, a bundle on his back, a kettle and a teapot slung from his belt]

LUKA: How are you, honest folks?

PEPEL: [Twisting his mustache] Aha—Natasha!

BUBNOFF: [To Luka] I was honest—up to spring before last.

NATASHA: Here's a new lodger . . .

LUKA: Oh, it's all the same to me. Crooks—I don't mind them, either. For my part there's no bad flea— they're all black—and they all jump— . . . Well, dearie, show me where I can stow myself.

NATASHA: [Pointing to kitchen door] Go in there, grand-dad.

LUKA: Thanks, girlie. One place is like another— as long as an old fellow keeps warm, he keeps happy . . .

PEPEL: What an amusing old codger you brought in, Natasha!

NATASHA: A hanged sight more interesting than you! . . . Andrei, your wife's in the kitchen with us—come and fetch her after a while. . . .

KLESHTCH: All right—I will . . .

NATASHA: And be a little more kind to her— you know she won't last much longer.

KLESHTCH: I know . . .

NATASHA: Knowing won't do any good—it's terrible—dying—don't you understand?

PEPEL: Well—look at me—I'm not afraid . . .

NATASHA: Oh—you're a wonder, aren't you?

BUBNOFF: [Whistling] Oh—this thread's rotten . . .

PEPEL: Honestly, I'm not afraid! I'm ready to die right now. Knife me to the heart—and I'll die without making a sound . . . even gladly—from such a pure hand . . .

NATASHA: [Going out] Spin that yarn for some one else!

BUBNOFF: Oh—that thread is rotten—rotten—

NATASHA: [At hallway door] Don't forget your wife, Andrei!

KLESHTCH: All right.

PEPEL: She's a wonderful girl!

BUBNOFF: She's all right.

PEPEL: What makes her so curt with me? Anyway—she'll come to no good here . . .

BUBNOFF: Through you—sure!

PEPEL: Why through me? I feel sorry for her . . .

BUBNOFF: As the wolf for the lamb!

PEPEL: You lie! I feel very sorry for her . . . very . . . very sorry! She has a tough life here—I can see that . . .

KLESHTCH: Just wait till Vassilisa catches you talking to her!

BUBNOFF: Vassilisa? She won't give up so easily what belongs to her—she's a cruel woman!

PEPEL: [Stretching himself on the bunk] You two prophets can go to hell!

KLESHTCH: Just wait—you'll see!

LUKA: [Singing in the kitchen] "In the dark of the night the way is black . . ."

KLESHTCH: Another one who yelps!

PEPEL: It's dreary! Why do I feel so dreary? You live—and everything seems all right. But suddenly a cold chill goes through you—and then everything gets dreary . . .

BUBNOFF: Dreary? Hm-hm—

PEPEL: Yes—yes—

LUKA: [Sings] "The way is black . . ."

PEPEL: Old fellow! Hey there!

LUKA: [*Looking from kitchen door*] You call me?

PEPEL: Yes. Don't sing!

LUKA: [*Coming in*] You don't like it?

PEPEL: When people sing well I like it—

LUKA: In other words—I don't sing well?

PEPEL: Evidently!

LUKA: Well, well—and I thought I sang well. That's always the way: a man imagines there's one thing he can do well, and suddenly he finds out that other people don't think so . . .

PEPEL: [*Laughs*] That's right . . .

BUBNOFF: First you say you feel dreary—and then you laugh!

PEPEL: None of your business, raven!

LUKA: Who do they say feels dreary?

PEPEL: I do.

[The Baron *enters*]

LUKA: Well, well—out there in the kitchen there's a girl reading and crying! That's so! Her eyes are wet with tears . . . I say to her: "What's the matter, darling?" And she says: "It's so sad!" "What's so sad?" say I. "The book!" says she.—And that's how people spend their time. Just because they're bored . . .

THE BARON: She's a fool!

PEPEL: Have you had tea, Baron?

THE BARON: Yes. Go on!

PEPEL: Well—want me to open a bottle?

THE BARON: Of course. Go on!

PEPEL: Drop on all fours, and bark like a dog!

THE BARON: Fool! What's the matter with you? Are you drunk?

PEPEL: Go on—bark a little! It'll amuse me. You're an aristocrat. You didn't even consider us human formerly, did you?

THE BARON: Go on!

PEPEL: Well—and now I am making you bark like a dog—and you will bark, won't you?

THE BARON: All right. I will. You jackass! What pleasure can you derive from it, since I myself know that I have sunk almost lower than you. You should have made me drop on all fours in the days when I was still above you.

BUBNOFF: That's right . . .

LUKA: I say so, too!

BUBNOFF: What's over, is over. Remain only trivialities. We know no class distinctions here. We've shed all pride and self-respect. Blood and bone—man—just plain man—that's what we are!

LUKA: In other words, we're all equal . . . and you, friend, were you really a Baron?

THE BARON: Who are you? A ghost?

LUKA: [*Laughing*] I've seen counts and princes in my day—this is the first time I meet a baron—and one who's decaying—at that!

PEPEL: [*Laughing*] Baron, I blush for you!

THE BARON: It's time you knew better, Vassily . . .

LUKA: Hey-hey—I look at you, brothers—the life you're leading . . .

BUBNOFF: Such a life! As soon as the sun rises, our voices rise, too—in quarrels!

THE BARON: We've all seen better days—yes! I used to wake up in the morning and drink my coffee in bed—coffee—with cream! Yes—

LUKA: And yet we're all human beings. Pretend all you want to, put on all the airs you wish, but man you were born, and man you must die. And as I watch I see that the wiser people get, the busier they get—and though from bad to worse, they still strive to improve—stubbornly—

THE BARON: Who are you, old fellow? Where do you come from?

LUKA: I?

THE BARON: Are you a tramp?

LUKA: We're all of us tramps—why—I've heard said that the very earth we walk on is nothing but a tramp in the universe.

THE BARON: [*Severely*] Perhaps. But have you a passport?

LUKA: [*After a short pause*] And what are you—a police inspector?

PEPEL: [*Delighted*] You scored, old fellow! Well, Barosha, you got it this time!

BUBNOFF: Yes—our little aristocrat got his!

THE BARON: [*Embarrassed*] What's the matter? I was only joking, old man. Why, brother, I haven't a passport, either.

BUBNOFF: You lie!

THE BARON: Oh—well—I have some sort of papers—but they have no value—

LUKA: They're papers just the same—and no papers are any good—

PEPEL: Baron—come on to the saloon with me—

THE BARON: I'm ready. Good-bye, old man—you old scamp—

LUKA: Maybe I am one, brother—

PEPEL: [*Near doorway*] Come on—come on!

[*Leaves*, Baron *following him quickly*]

LUKA: Was he really once a Baron?

BUBNOFF: Who knows? A gentleman—? Yes. That much he's even now. Occasionally it sticks out. He never got rid of the habit.

LUKA: Nobility is like small-pox. A man may get over it—but it leaves marks . . .

BUBNOFF: He's all right all the same—occasionally he kicks—as he did about your passport . . .

[Alyoshka *comes in, slightly drunk, with a concertina in his hand, whistling*]

ALYOSHKA: Hey there, lodgers!

BUBNOFF: What are you yelling for?

ALYOSHKA: Excuse me—I beg your pardon! I'm a well-bred man—

BUBNOFF: On a spree again?

ALYOSHKA: Right you are! A moment ago Medyakin, the precinct captain, threw me out of the police station and said: "Look here—I don't want as much as a smell of you to stay in the streets—d'you hear?" I'm a man of principles, and the boss croaks at me—and what's a boss anyway—pah!—

t's all bosh—the boss is a drunkard. I don't make
any demands on life. I want nothing—that's all.
Offer me one ruble, offer me twenty—it doesn't
affect me. [Nastya *comes from the kitchen*] Offer
me a million—I won't take it! And to think that I,
a respectable man, should be ordered about by a
pal of mine—and he a drunkard! I won't have it—
I won't!

[Nastya *stands in the doorway, shaking her
head at* Alyoshka]

LUKA: [*Good-naturedly*] Well, boy, you're a bit
confused—

BUBNOFF: Aren't men fools!

ALYOSHKA: [*Stretches out on the floor*] Here,
eat me up alive—and I don't want anything. I'm a
desperate man. Show me one better! Why am I
worse than others? There! Medyakin said: "If you
show yourself on the streets I smash your face!"
And yet I shall go out—I'll go—and stretch out
in the middle of the street—let them choke me—
I don't want a thing!

NASTYA: Poor fellow—only a boy—and he's already putting on such airs—

ALYOSHKA: [*Kneeling before her*] Lady! Mademoiselle! *Parlez français—? Prix courrant?* I'm on a
spree—

NASTYA: [*In a loud whisper*] Vassilisa!

VASSILISA: [*Opens door quickly; to* Alyoshka] You
here again?

ALYOSHKA: How do you do—? Come in—you're
welcome—

VASSILISA: I told you, young puppy, that not a
shadow of you should stick around here—and you're
back—eh?

ALYOSHKA: Vassilisa Karpovna . . . shall I tune
up a funeral march for you?

VASSILISA: [*Seizing him by the shoulders*] Get out!

ALYOSHKA: [*Moving towards the door*] Wait—you
can't put me out this way! I learned this funeral
march a little while ago! It's refreshing music . . .
wait—you can't put me out like that!

VASSILISA: I'll show whether I can or not. I'll rouse
the whole street against you—you foul-mouthed
creature—you're too young to bark about me—

ALYOSHKA: [*Running out*] All right—I'll go—

VASSILISA: Look out—I'll get you yet!

ALYOSHKA: [*Opens the door and shouts*] Vassilisa
Karpovna—I'm not afraid of you—[*Hides*]

[Luka *laughs*]

VASSILISA: Who are you?

LUKA: A passer-by—a traveler . . .

VASSILISA: Stopping for the night or going to stay
here?

LUKA: I'll see.

VASSILISA: Have you a passport?

LUKA: Yes.

VASSILISA: Give it to me.

LUKA: I'll bring it over to your house—

VASSILISA: Call yourself a traveler? If you'd say
a tramp—that would be nearer the truth—

LUKA: [*Sighing*] You're not very kindly, mother!
[Vassilisa *goes to door that leads to* Pepel's
room. Alyoshka *pokes his head through the
kitchen door*]

ALYOSHKA: Has she left?

VASSILISA: [*Turning around*] Are you still here?
[Alyoshka *disappears, whistling.* Nastya *and*
Luka *laugh*]

BUBNOFF: [*To* Vassilisa] He isn't here—

VASSILISA: Who?

BUBNOFF: Vaska.

VASSILISA: Did I ask you about him?

BUBNOFF: I noticed you were looking around—

VASSILISA: I am looking to see if things are in
order, you see? Why aren't the floors swept yet?
How often did I give orders to keep the house
clean?

BUBNOFF: It's the actor's turn to sweep—

VASSILISA: Never mind whose turn it is! If the
health inspector comes and fines me, I'll throw out
the lot of you—

BUBNOFF: [*Calmly*] Then how are you going to
earn your living?

VASSILISA: I don't want a speck of dirt! [*Goes to
kitchen; to* Nastya] What are you hanging round
here for? Why's your face all swollen up? Why are
you standing there like a dummy? Go on—sweep the
floor! Did you see Natalia? Was she here?

NASTYA: I don't know—I haven't seen her . . .

VASSILISA: Bubnoff! Was my sister here?

BUBNOFF: She brought him along.

VASSILISA: That one—was he home?

BUBNOFF: Vassily? Yes—Natalia was here talking
to Kleshtch—

VASSILISA: I'm not asking you whom she talked
to. Dirt everywhere—filth—oh, you swine! Mop it
all up—do you hear? [*Exit rapidly*]

BUBNOFF: What a savage beast she is!

LUKA: She's a lady that means business!

NASTYA: You grow to be an animal, leading such
a life—any human being tied to such a husband as
hers . . .

BUBNOFF: Well—that tie isn't worrying her any—

LUKA: Does she always have these fits?

BUBNOFF: Always. You see, she came to find her
lover—but he isn't home—

LUKA: I guess she was hurt. Oh-ho! Everybody is
trying to be boss—and is threatening everybody else
with all kinds of punishment—and still there's no
order in life . . . and no cleanliness—

BUBNOFF: All the world likes order—but some
people's brains aren't fit for it. All the same—the
room should be swept—Nastya—you ought to get
busy!

NASTYA: Oh, certainly? Anything else? Think I'm
your servant? [*Silence*] I'm going to get drunk to-
night—dead-drunk!

BUBNOFF: Fine business!

LUKA: Why do you want to get drunk, girlie? A

while ago you were crying—and now you say you'll get drunk—

NASTYA: [*Defiantly*] I'll drink—then I cry again—that's all there's to it!

BUBNOFF: That's nothing!

LUKA: But for what reason—tell me. Every pimple has a cause! [Nastya *remains silent, shaking her head*] Oh—you men—what's to become of you? All right—I'll sweep the place. Where's your broom?

BUBNOFF: Behind the door—in the hall—
[Luka *goes into the hall*]
Nastinka!

NASTYA: Yes?

BUBNOFF: Why did Vassilisa jump on Alyoshka?

NASTYA: He told her that Vaska was tired of her and was going to get rid of her—and that he's going to make up to Natasha—I'll go away from here—I'll find another lodging-house—

BUBNOFF: Why? Where?

NASTYA: I'm sick of this—I'm not wanted here!

BUBNOFF: [*Calmly*] You're not wanted anywhere —and, anyway, all people on earth are superfluous—
[Nastya *shakes her head. Rises and slowly, quietly, leaves the cellar. Miedviedieff comes in.* Luka, *with the broom, follows him*]

MIEDVIEDIEFF: I don't think I know you—

LUKA: How about the others—d'you know them all?

MIEDVIEDIEFF: I must know everybody in my precinct. But I don't know you.

LUKA: That's because, uncle, the whole world can't stow itself away in your precinct—some of it was bound to remain outside . . . [*Goes into kitchen*]

MIEDVIEDIEFF: [*Crosses to* Bubnoff] It's true—my precinct is rather small—yet it's worse than any of the very largest. Just now, before getting off duty, I had to bring Alyoshka, the shoemaker, to the station house. Just imagine—there he was, stretched right in the middle of the street, playing his concertina and yelping: "I want nothing, nothing!" Horses going past all the time—and with all the traffic going on, he could easily have been run over —and so on! He's a wild youngster—so I just collared him—he likes to make mischief—

BUBNOFF: Coming to play checkers to-night?

MIEDVIEDIEFF: Yes—I'll come—how's Vaska?

BUBNOFF: Same as ever—

MIEDVIEDIEFF: Meaning—he's getting along—?

BUBNOFF: Why shouldn't he? He's able to get along all right.

MIEDVIEDIEFF: [*Doubtfully*] Why shouldn't he? [Luka *goes into hallway, carrying a pail*] M-yes—there's a lot of talk about Vaska. Haven't you heard?

BUBNOFF: I hear all sorts of gossip . . .

MIEDVIEDIEFF: There seems to have been some sort of talk concerning Vassilisa. Haven't you heard about it?

BUBNOFF: What?

MIEDVIEDIEFF: Oh—why—generally speaking.

Perhaps you know—and lie. Everybody knows— [*Severely*] You mustn't lie, brother!

BUBNOFF: Why should I lie?

MIEDVIEDIEFF: That's right. Dogs! They say that Vaska and Vassilisa . . . but what's that to me? I'm not her father. I'm her uncle. Why should they ridicule me? [Kvashnya *comes in*] What are people coming to? They laugh at everything. Aha—you here?

KVASHNYA: Well—my love-sick garrison—? Bubnoff! He came up to me again on the marketplace and started pestering me about marrying him . . .

BUBNOFF: Go to it! Why not? He has money and he's still a husky fellow.

MIEDVIEDIEFF: Me—? I should say so!

KVASHNYA: You ruffian! Don't you dare touch my sore spot! I've gone through it once already, darling. Marriage to a woman is just like jumping through a hole in the ice in winter. You do it once, and you remember it the rest of your life . . .

MIEDVIEDIEFF: Wait! There are different breeds of husbands . . .

KVASHNYA: But there's only one of me! When my beloved husband kicked the bucket, I spent the whole day all by my lonely—just bursting with joy. I sat and simply couldn't believe it was true. . . .

MIEDVIEDIEFF: If your husband beat you without cause, you should have complained to the police.

KVASHNYA: I complained to God for eight years—and he didn't help.

MIEDVIEDIEFF: Nowadays the law forbids to beat your wife . . . all is very strict these days—there's law and order everywhere. You can't beat up people without due cause. If you beat them to maintain discipline—all right . . .

LUKA: [*Comes in with* Anna] Well—we finally managed to get here after all. Oh, you! Why do you, weak as you are, walk about alone? Where's your bunk?

ANNA: [*Pointing*] Thank you, grand-dad.

KVASHNYA: There—she's married—look at her!

LUKA: The little woman is in very bad shape . . . she was creeping along the hallway, clinging to the wall and moaning—why do you leave her by herself?

KVASHNYA: Oh, pure carelessness on our part, little father—forgive us! Her maid, it appears, went out for a walk . . .

LUKA: Go on—poke fun at me . . . but, all the same, how can you neglect a human being like that? No matter who or what, every human life has its worth . . .

MIEDVIEDIEFF: There should be supervision! Suppose she died suddenly—? That would cause a lot of bother . . . we must look after her!

LUKA: True, sergeant!

MIEDVIEDIEFF: Well—yes—though I'm not a sergeant—ah—yet!

LUKA: No! But you carry yourself most martially!

[*Noise of shuffling feet is heard in the hallway. Muffled cries*]

MIEDVIEDIEFF: What now—a row?

BUBNOFF: Sounds like it?

KVASHNYA: I'll go and see . . .

MIEDVIEDIEFF: I'll go, too. It is my duty! Why separate people when they fight? They'll stop sooner or later of their own accord. One gets tired of fighting. Why not let them fight all they want to—freely? They wouldn't fight half as often—if they'd remember former beatings . . .

BUBNOFF: [*Climbing down from his bunk*] Why don't you speak to your superiors about it?

KOSTILYOFF: [*Throws open the door and shouts*] Abram! Come quick—Vassilisa is killing Natasha—come quick.

[*Kvashnya, Miedviedieff, and Bubnoff rush into hallway; Luka looks after them, shaking his head*]

ANNA: Oh God—poor little Natasha . . .

LUKA: Who's fighting out there?

ANNA: Our landladies—they're sisters . . .

LUKA: [*Crossing to Anna*] Why?

ANNA: Oh—for no reason—except that they're both fat and healthy . . .

LUKA: What's your name?

ANNA: Anna . . . I look at you . . . you're like my father—my dear father . . . you're as gentle as he was—and as soft. . . .

LUKA: Soft! Yes! They pounded me till I got soft! [*Laughs tremulously*]

CURTAIN

ACT II.

Same as Act I—Night.

On the bunks near the stove Satine, *the* Baron, Krivoy Zob, *and the* Tartar *play cards.* Kleshtch *and the* Actor *watch them.* Bubnoff, *on his bunk, is playing checkers with* Miedviedieff. Luka *sits on a stool by* Anna's *bedside. The place is lit by two lamps, one on the wall near the card players, the other is on* Bubnoff's *bunk.*

THE TARTAR: I'll play one more game—then I'll stop . . .

BUBNOFF: Zob! Sing! [*He sings*]
"The sun rises and sets . . ."

ZOB: [*Joining in*]
"But my prison is dark, dark . . ."

THE TARTAR: [*To* Satine] Shuffle the cards—and shuffle them well. We know your kind—

ZOB AND BUBNOFF: [*Together*]
"Day and night the wardens
  Watch beneath my window . . ."

ANNA: Blows—insults—I've had nothing but that all my life long . . .

LUKA: Don't worry, little mother!

MIEDVIEDIEFF: Look where you're moving!

BUBNOFF: Oh, yes—that's right . . .

THE TARTAR: [*Threatening* Satine *with his fist*] You're trying to palm a card? I've seen you—you scoundrel . . .

ZOB: Stop it, Hassan! They'll skin us anyway . . . come on, Bubnoff!

ANNA: I can't remember a single day when I didn't go hungry . . . I've been afraid, waking, eating, and sleeping . . . all my life I've trembled—afraid I wouldn't get another bite . . . all my life I've been in rags—all through my wretched life—and why . . . ?

LUKA: Yes, yes, child—you're tired—never you mind!

THE ACTOR: [*To* Zob] Play the Jack—the Jack, devil take you!

THE BARON: And we play the King!

KLESHTCH: They always win.

SATINE: Such is our habit.

MIEDVIEDIEFF: I have the Queen!

BUBNOFF: And so have I!

ANNA: I'm dying . . .

KLESHTCH: Look, look! Prince, throw up the game—throw it up, I tell you!

THE ACTOR: Can't he play without your assistance?

THE BARON: Look out, Andrushka, or I'll beat the life out of you!

THE TARTAR: Deal once more—the pitcher went after water—and got broke—and so did I!

[Kleshtch *shakes his head and crosses to* Bubnoff]

ANNA: I keep on thinking—is it possible that I'll suffer in the other world as I did in this—is it possible? There, too?

LUKA: Nothing of the sort! Don't you disturb yourself! You'll rest there . . . be patient. We all suffer, dear, each in our own way. . . . [*Rises and goes quickly into kitchen*]

BUBNOFF: [*Sings*]
"Watch as long as you please . . ."

ZOB: "I shan't run away . . ."

BOTH: [*Together*]
"I long to be free, free—
  Alas! I cannot break my chains. . . ."

THE TARTAR: [*Yells*] That card was up his sleeve!

THE BARON: [*Embarrassed*] Do you want me to shove it up your nose?

THE ACTOR: [*Emphatically*] Prince! You're mistaken—nobody—ever . . .

THE TARTAR: I saw it! You cheat! I won't play!

SATINE: [*Gathering up the cards*] Leave us alone, Hassan . . . you knew right along that we're cheats—why did you play with us?

THE BARON: He lost forty kopecks and he yelps as if he had lost a fortune! And a Prince at that!

THE TARTAR: [*Excitedly*] Then play honest!

SATINE: What for?

THE TARTAR: What do you mean "what for"?

SATINE: Exactly. What for?

THE TARTAR: Don't you know?

SATINE: I don't. Do you?

[The Tartar *spits out, furiously; the others laugh at him*]

ZOB: [*Good-naturedly*] You're a funny fellow, Hassan! Try to understand this! If they should begin to live honestly, they'd die of starvation inside of three days.

THE TARTAR: That's none of my business. You must live honestly!

ZOB: They did you brown! Come and let's have tea. . . . [*Sings*]

"O my chains, my heavy chains . . ."

BUBNOFF: [*Sings*]

"You're my steely, clanking wardens . . ."

ZOB: Come on, Hassanka! [*Leaves the room, singing*]

"I cannot tear you, cannot break you . . ."

[The Tartar *shakes his fist threateningly at the Baron, and follows the other out of the room*]

SATINE: [*To Baron, laughing*] Well, Your Imperial Highness, you've again sat down magnificently in a mud puddle! You've learned a lot—but you're an ignoramus when it comes to palming a card.

THE BARON: [*Spreading his hands*] The Devil knows how it happened. . . .

THE ACTOR: You're not gifted—you've no faith in yourself—and without that you can never accomplish anything . . .

MIEDVIEDIEFF: I've one Queen—and you've two—oh, well . . .

BUBNOFF: One's enough if she has brains—play!

KLESHTCH: You lost, Abram Ivanovitch?

MIEDVIEDIEFF: None of your business—see? Shut up!

SATINE: I've won fifty-three kopecks.

THE ACTOR: Give me three of them . . . though, what'll I do with them?

LUKA: [*Coming from kitchen*] Well—the Tartar was fleeced all right, eh? Going to have some vodka?

THE BARON: Come with us.

SATINE: I wonder what you'll be like when you're drunk.

LUKA: Same as when I'm sober.

THE ACTOR: Come on, old man—I'll recite verses for you . . .

LUKA: What?

THE ACTOR: Verses. Don't you understand?

LUKA: Verses? And what do I want with verses?

THE ACTOR: Sometimes they're funny—sometimes sad.

SATINE: Well, poet, are you coming? [*Exit with the* Baron]

THE ACTOR: I'm coming. I'll join you. For instance, old man, here's a bit of verse—I forget how it begins—I forget . . . [*Brushes his hand across his forehead*]

BUBNOFF: There! Your Queen is lost—go on, play!

MIEDVIEDIEFF: I made the wrong move.

THE ACTOR: Formerly, before my organism was poisoned with alcohol, old man, I had a good memory. But now it's all over with me, brother. I used to declaim these verses with tremendous success—thunders of applause . . . you have no idea what applause means . . . it goes to your head like vodka! I'd step out on the stage—stand this way—[*Strikes a pose*]—I'd stand there and . . . [*Pause*] I can't remember a word—I can't remember! My favorite verses—isn't it ghastly, old man?

LUKA: Yes—is there anything worse than forgetting what you loved? Your very soul is in the thing you love!

THE ACTOR: I've drunk my soul away, old man—brother, I'm lost . . . and why? Because I had no faith . . . I'm done with . . .

LUKA: Well—then—cure yourself! Nowadays they have a cure for drunkards. They treat you free of charge, brother. There's a hospital for drunkards—where they're treated for nothing. They've owned up, you see, that even a drunkard is a human being, and they're only too glad to help him get well. Well—then—go to it!

THE ACTOR: [*Thoughtfully*] Where? Where is it?

LUKA: Oh—in some town or other . . . what do they call it—? I'll tell you the name presently—only, in the meanwhile, get ready. Don't drink so much! Take yourself in hand—and bear up! And then, when you're cured, you'll begin life all over again. Sounds good, brother, doesn't it, to begin all over again? Well—make up your mind!

THE ACTOR: [*Smiling*] All over again—from the very beginning—that's fine . . . yes . . . all over again . . . [*Laughs*] Well—then—I can, can't I?

LUKA: Why not? A human being can do anything—if he only makes up his mind.

THE ACTOR: [*Suddenly, as if coming out of a trance*] You're a queer bird! See you anon! [*Whistles*] Old man—au revoir! [*Exit*]

ANNA: Grand-dad!

LUKA: Yes, little mother?

ANNA: Talk to me.

LUKA: [*Close to her*] Come on—let's chat . . . [Kleshtch, *glancing around, silently walks over to his wife, looks at her, and makes queer gestures with his hands, as though he wanted to say something*]

LUKA: What is it, brother?

KLESHTCH: [*Quietly*] Nothing . . . [*Crosses slowly to hallway door, stands on the threshold for a few seconds, and exit*]

LUKA: [*Looking after him*] Hard on your man, isn't it?

ANNA: He doesn't concern me much . . .

LUKA: Did he beat you?

ANNA: Worse than that—it's he who's killed me—

BUBNOFF: My wife used to have a lover—the scoundrel—how clever he was at checkers!

MIEDVIEDIEFF: Hm-hm—

ANNA: Grand-dad! Talk to me, darling—I feel so sick . . .

LUKA: Never mind—it's always like this before you die, little dove—never mind, dear! Just have faith! Once you're dead, you'll have peace—always. There's nothing to be afraid of—nothing. Quiet! Peace! Lie quietly! Death wipes out everything. Death is kindly. You die—and you rest—that's what they say. It is true, dear! Because—where can we find rest on this earth?

[Pepel enters. He is slightly drunk, dishevelled, and sullen. Sits down on bunk near door, and remains silent and motionless]

ANNA: And how is it—there? More suffering?

LUKA: Nothing of the kind! No suffering! Trust me! Rest—nothing else! They'll lead you into God's presence, and they'll say: "Dear God! Behold! Here is Anna, Thy servant!"

MIEDVIEDIEFF: [Sternly] How do you know what they'll say up there? Oh, you . . .

[Pepel, on hearing Miedviedieff's voice, raises his head and listens]

LUKA: Apparently I do know, Mr. Sergeant!

MIEDVIEDIEFF: [Conciliatory] Yes—it's your own affair—though I'm not exactly a sergeant—yet—

BUBNOFF: I jump two!

MIEDVIEDIEFF: Damn—play!

LUKA: And the Lord will look at you gently and tenderly and He'll say: "I know this Anna!" Then He'll say: "Take Anna into Paradise. Let her have peace. I know. Her life on earth was hard. She is very weary. Let Anna rest in peace!"

ANNA: [Choking] Grandfather—if it were only so —if there were only rest and peace . . .

LUKA: There won't be anything else! Trust me! Die in joy and not in grief. Death is to us like a mother to small children . . .

ANNA: But—perhaps—perhaps I get well . . .?

LUKA: [Laughing] Why—? Just to suffer more?

ANNA: But—just to live a little longer . . . just a little longer! Since there'll be no suffering hereafter, I could bear it a little longer down here . . .

LUKA: There'll be nothing in the hereafter . . . but only . . .

PEPEL: [Rising] Maybe yes—maybe no!

ANNA: [Frightened] Oh—God!

LUKA: Hey—Adonis!

MIEDVIEDIEFF: Who's that yelping?

PEPEL: [Crossing over to him] I! What of it?

MIEDVIEDIEFF: You yelp needlessly—that's what! People ought to have some dignity!

PEPEL: Block-head! And that's an uncle for you— ho-ho!

LUKA: [To Pepel, in an undertone] Look here— don't shout—this woman's dying—her lips are already grey—don't disturb her!

PEPEL: I've respect for you, grand-dad. You're all right, you are! You lie well, and you spin pleasant yarns. Go on lying, brother—there's little fun in this world . . .

BUBNOFF: Is the woman really dying?

LUKA: You think I'm joking?

BUBNOFF: That means she'll stop coughing. Her cough was very disturbing. I jump two!

MIEDVIEDIEFF: I'd like to murder you!

PEPEL: Abramka!

MIEDVIEDIEFF: I'm not Abramka to you!

PEPEL: Abrashka! Is Natasha ill?

MIEDVIEDIEFF: None of your business!

PEPEL: Come—tell me! Did Vassilisa beat her up very badly?

MIEDVIEDIEFF: That's none of your business, either! It's a family affair! Who are you anyway?

PEPEL: Whoever I am, you'll never see Natashka again if I choose!

MIEDVIEDIEFF: [Throwing up the game] What's that? Who are you alluding to? My niece by any chance? You thief!

PEPEL: A thief whom you were never able to catch!

MIEDVIEDIEFF: Wait—I'll catch you yet—you'll see—sooner than you think!

PEPEL: If you catch me, God help your whole nest! Do you think I'll keep quiet before the examining magistrate? Every wolf howls! They'll ask me: "Who made you steal and showed you where?" "Mishka Kostilyoff and his wife!" "Who was your fence?" "Mishka Kostilyoff and his wife!"

MIEDVIEDIEFF: You lie! No one will believe you!

PEPEL: They'll believe me all right—because it's the truth! And I'll drag you into it, too. Ha! I'll ruin the lot of you—devils—just watch!

MIEDVIEDIEFF: [Confused] You lie! You lie! And what harm did I do to you, you mad dog?

PEPEL: And what good did you ever do me?

LUKA: That's right!

MIEDVIEDIEFF: [To Luka] Well—what are you croaking about? Is it any of your business? This is a family matter!

BUBNOFF: [To Luka] Leave them alone! What do we care if they twist each other's tails?

LUKA: [Peacefully] I meant no harm. All I said was that if a man isn't good to you, then he's acting wrong. . . .

MIEDVIEDIEFF: [Uncomprehending] Now then— we all of us here know each other—but you—who are you? [Frowns and exit]

LUKA: The cavalier is peeved! Oh-ho, brothers, I see your affairs are a bit tangled up!

PEPEL: He'll run to complain about us to Vassilisa . . .

BUBNOFF: You're a fool, Vassily. You're very bold these days, aren't you? Watch out! It's all right to be bold when you go gathering mushrooms, but what good is it here? They'll break your neck before you know it!

PEPEL: Well—not as fast as all that! You don't catch us Yaroslavl boys napping! If it's going to be war, we'll fight . . .

LUKA: Look here, boy, you really ought to go away from here—

PEPEL: Where? Please tell me!

LUKA: Go to Siberia!

PEPEL: If I go to Siberia, it'll be at the Tsar's expense!

LUKA: Listen! You go just the same! You can make your own way there. They need your kind out there . . .

PEPEL: My way is clear. My father spent all his life in prison, and I inherited the trait. Even when I was a small child, they called me thief—thief's son.

LUKA: But Siberia is a fine country—a land of gold. Any one who has health and strength and brains can live there like a cucumber in a hot-house.

PEPEL: Old man, why do you always tell lies?

LUKA: What?

PEPEL: Are you deaf? I ask—why do you always lie?

LUKA: What do I lie about?

PEPEL: About everything. According to you, life's wonderful everywhere—but you lie . . . why?

LUKA: Try to believe me. Go and see for yourself. And some day you'll thank me for it. What are you hanging round here for? And, besides, why is truth so important to you? Just think! Truth may spell death to you!

PEPEL: It's all one to me! If that—let it be that!

LUKA: Oh—what a madman! Why should you kill yourself?

BUBNOFF: What are you two jawing about, anyway? I don't understand. What kind of truth do you want, Vaska? And what for? You know the truth about yourself—and so does everybody else . . .

PEPEL: Just a moment! Don't crow! Let him tell me! Listen, old man! Is there a God?

[Luka smiles silently]

BUBNOFF: People just drift along—like shavings on a stream. When a house is built—the shavings are thrown away!

PEPEL: Well? Is there a God? Tell me.

LUKA: [In a low voice] If you have faith, there is; if you haven't, there isn't . . . whatever you believe in, exists . . .

[Pepel looks at Luka in staring surprise]

BUBNOFF: I'm going to have tea—come on over to the restaurant!

LUKA: [To Pepel] What are you staring at?

PEPEL: Oh—just because! Wait now—you mean to say . . .

BUBNOFF: Well—I'm off.

[Goes to door and runs into Vassilisa]

PEPEL: So—you . . .

VASSILISA: [To Bubnoff] Is Natasya home?

BUBNOFF: No. [Exit]

PEPEL: Oh—you've come—?

VASSILISA: [Crossing to Anna] Is she alive yet?

LUKA: Don't disturb her!

VASSILISA: What are you loafing around here for?

LUKA: I'll go—if you want me to . . .

VASSILISA: [Turning towards Pepel's room] Vassily! I've some business with you . . .

[Luka goes to hallway door, opens it, and shuts it loudly, then warily climbs into a bunk, and from there to the top of the stove]

VASSILISA: [Calling from Pepel's room] Vaska—come here!

PEPEL: I won't come—I don't want to . . .

VASSILISA: Why? What are you angry about?

PEPEL: I'm sick of the whole thing . . .

VASSILISA: Sick of me, too?

PEPEL: Yes! Of you, too!

[Vassilisa draws her shawl about her, pressing her hands over her breast. Crosses to Anna, looks carefully through the bed curtains, and returns to Pepel]

Well—out with it!

VASSILISA: What do you want me to say? I can't force you to be loving, and I'm not the sort to beg for kindness. Thank you for telling me the truth.

PEPEL: What truth?

VASSILISA: That you're sick of me—or isn't it the truth? [Pepel looks at her silently. She turns to him] What are you staring at? Don't you recognize me?

PEPEL: [Sighing] You're beautiful, Vassilisa! [She puts her arm about his neck, but he shakes it off] But I never gave my heart to you. . . . I've lived with you and all that—But I never really liked you . . .

VASSILISA: [Quietly] That so? Well—?

PEPEL: What is there to talk about? Nothing. Go away from me!

VASSILISA: Taken a fancy to some one else?

PEPEL: None of your business! Suppose I have—I wouldn't ask you to be my match-maker!

VASSILISA: [Significantly] That's too bad . . perhaps I might arrange a match . . .

PEPEL: [Suspiciously] Who with?

VASSILISA: You know—why do you pretend? Vassily—let me be frank [With lower voice] I won't deny it—you've offended me . . . it was like a bolt from the blue . . . you said you loved me—and then all of a sudden . . .

PEPEL: It wasn't sudden at all. It's been a long time since I . . . woman, you've no soul! A woman must have a soul . . . we men are beasts—we must be taught—and you, what have you taught me—?

VASSILISA: Never mind the past! I know—no man owns his own heart—you don't love me any longer . . . well and good, it can't be helped!

PEPEL: So that's over. We part peaceably, without a row—as it should be!

VASSILISA: Just a moment! All the same, when I lived with you, I hoped you'd help me out of this swamp—I thought you'd free me from my husband and my uncle—from all this life—and perhaps, Vassya, it wasn't you whom I loved—but my hope—do you understand? I waited for you to drag me out of this mire . . .

PEPEL: You aren't a nail—and I'm not a pair of pincers! I thought you had brains—you are so clever—so crafty . . .

VASSILISA: [*Leaning closely towards him*] Vassa— Let's help each other!

PEPEL: How?

VASSILISA: [*Low and forcibly*] My sister—I know you've fallen for her . . .

PEPEL: And that's why you beat her up, like the beast you are! Look out, Vassilisa! Don't you touch her!

VASSILISA: Wait. Don't get excited. We can do everything quietly and pleasantly. You want to marry her. I'll give you money . . . three hundred rubles—even more than . . .

PEPEL: [*Moving away from her*] Stop! What do you mean?

VASSILISA: Rid me of my husband! Take that noose from around my neck . . .

PEPEL: [*Whistling softly*] So that's the way the land lies! You certainly planned it cleverly . . . in other words, the grave for the husband, the gallows for the lover, and as for yourself . . .

VASSILISA: Vassya! Why the gallows? It doesn't have to be yourself—but one of your pals! And supposing it were yourself—who'd know? Natalia—just think—and you'll have money—you go away somewhere . . . you free me forever—and it'll be very good for my sister to be away from me—the sight of her enrages me. . . . I get furious with her on account of you, and I can't control myself. I tortured the girl—I beat her up—beat her up so that I myself cried with pity for her—but I'll beat her—and I'll go on beating her!

PEPEL: Beast! Bragging about your beastliness?

VASSILISA: I'm not bragging—I speak the truth. Think now, Vassa. You've been to prison twice because of my husband—through his greed. He clings to me like a bed-bug—he's been sucking the life out of me for the last four years—and what sort of a husband is he to me? He's forever abusing Natasha—calls her a beggar—he's just poison, plain poison, to every one . . .

PEPEL: You spin your yarn cleverly . . .

VASSILISA: Everything I say is true. Only a fool could be as blind as you. . . .

[*Kostilyoff enters stealthily and comes forward noisily*]

PEPEL: [*To* Vassilisa] Oh—go away!

VASSILISA: Think it over! [*Sees her husband*] What? You? Following me?

[Pepel *leaps up and stares at* Kostilyoff *savagely*]

KOSTILYOFF: It's I, I! So the two of you were here alone—you were—ah—conversing? [*Suddenly stamps his feet and screams*] Vassilisa—you bitch! You beggar! You damned hag! [*Frightened by his own screams which are met by silence and indifference on the part of the others*] Forgive me, O Lord . . . Vassilisa—again you've led me into the path

of sin. . . . I've been looking for you everywhere. It's time to go to bed. You forgot to fill the lamps—oh, you . . . beggar! Swine! [*Shakes his trembling fist at her, while* Vassilisa *slowly goes to door, glancing at* Pepel *over her shoulder*]

PEPEL: [*To* Kostilyoff] Go away—clear out of here—

KOSTILYOFF: [*Yelling*] What? I? The Boss? I get out? You thief!

PEPEL: [*Sullenly*] Go away, Mishka!

KOSTILYOFF: Don't you dare—I—I'll show you.

[Pepel *seizes him by the collar and shakes him. From the stove comes loud noises and yawns.* Pepel *releases* Kostilyoff *who runs into the hallway, screaming*]

PEPEL: [*Jumping on a bunk*] Who is it? Who's on the stove?

LUKA: [*Raising his head*] Eh?

PEPEL: You?

LUKA: [*Undisturbed*] I—I myself—oh, dear Jesus!

PEPEL: [*Shuts hallway door, looks for the wooden closing bar, but can't find it*] The devil! Come down, old man!

LUKA: I'm climbing down—all right . . .

PEPEL: [*Roughly*] What did you climb on that stove for?

LUKA: Where was I to go?

PEPEL: Why—didn't you go out into the hall?

LUKA: The hall's too cold for an old fellow like myself, brother.

PEPEL: You overheard?

LUKA: Yes—I did. How could I help it? Am I deaf? Well, my boy, happiness is coming your way. Real, good fortune I call it!

PEPEL: [*Suspiciously*] What good fortune—?

LUKA: In so far as I was lying on the stove . . .

PEPEL: Why did you make all that noise?

LUKA: Because I was getting warm . . . it was your good luck . . . I thought if only the boy wouldn't make a mistake and choke the old man . . .

PEPEL: Yes—I might have done it . . . how terrible . . .

LUKA: Small wonder! It isn't difficult to make a mistake of that sort.

PEPEL: [*Smiling*] What's the matter? Did you make the same sort of mistake once upon a time?

LUKA: Boy, listen to me. Send that woman out of your life. Don't let her near you! Her husband—she'll get rid of him herself—and in a shrewder way than you could—yes! Don't you listen to that devil! Look at me! I am bald-headed—know why? Because of all these women. . . . Perhaps I knew more women than I had hair on the top of my head—but this Vassilisa—she's worse than the plague. . . .

PEPEL: I don't understand . . . I don't know whether to thank you—or—well . . .

LUKA: Don't say a word! You won't improve on what I said. Listen: take the one you like by the arm, and march out of here—get out of here—clean out . . .

PEPEL: [*Sadly*] I can't understand people. Who is kind and who isn't? It's all a mystery to me . . .

LUKA: What's there to understand? There's all breeds of men . . . they all live as their hearts tell them . . . good to-day, bad to-morrow! But if you really care for that girl . . . take her away from here and that's all there is to it. Otherwise go away alone . . . you're young—you're in no hurry for a wife . . .

PEPEL: [*Taking him by the shoulder*] Tell me! Why do you say all this?

LUKA: Wait. Let me go. I want a look at Anna . . . she was coughing so terribly . . . [*Goes to Anna's bed, pulls the curtains, looks, touches her.* Pepel, *thoughtfully and distraught, follows him with his eyes*] Merciful Jesus Christ! Take into Thy keeping the soul of this woman Anna, new-comer amongst the blessed!

PEPEL: [*Softly*] Is she dead?

[*Without approaching, he stretches himself and looks at the bed*]

LUKA: [*Gently*] Her sufferings are over! Where's her husband?

PEPEL: In the saloon, most likely . . .

LUKA: Well—he'll have to be told . . .

PEPEL: [*Shuddering*] I don't like corpses!

LUKA: [*Going to door*] Why should you like them? It's the living who demand our love—the living . . .

PEPEL: I'm coming with you . . .

LUKA: Are you afraid?

PEPEL: I don't like it . . .

[*They go out quickly. The stage is empty and silent for a few moments. Behind the door is heard a dull, staccato, incomprehensible noise. Then the* Actor *enters*]

THE ACTOR: [*Stands at the open door, supporting himself against the jamb, and shouts*] Hey, old man —where are you—? I just remembered—listen . . . [*Takes two staggering steps forward and, striking a pose, recites*]

"Good people! If the world cannot find
A path to holy truth,
Glory be to the madman who will enfold all humanity
In a golden dream . . ."

[Natasha *appears in the doorway behind the* Actor]

Old man! [*Recites*]

"If to-morrow the sun were to forget
To light our earth,
To-morrow then some madman's thought
Would bathe the world in sunshine. . . ."

NATASHA: [*Laughing*] Scarecrow! You're drunk!

THE ACTOR: [*Turns to her*] Oh—it's you? Where's the old man, the dear old man? Not a soul here, seems to me . . . Natasha, farewell—right—farewell!

NATASHA: [*Entering*] Don't wish me farewell, before you've wished me how-d'you-do!

THE ACTOR: [*Barring her way*] I am going. Spring will come—and I'll be here no longer—

NATASHA: Wait a moment! Where do you propose going?

THE ACTOR: In search of a town—to be cured— And you, Ophelia, must go away! Take the veil! Just imagine—there's a hospital to cure—ah—organisms for drunkards—a wonderful hospital— built of marble—with marble floors . . . light— clean—food—and all gratis! And a marble floor— yes! I'll find it—I'll get cured—and then I shall start life anew. . . . I'm on my way to regeneration, as King Lear said. Natasha, my stage name is . . . Svertchkoff—Zavoloushski . . . do you realize how painful it is to lose one's name? Even dogs have their names . . .

[Natasha *carefully passes the* Actor, *stops at* Anna's *bed and looks*]

To be nameless—is not to exist!

NATASHA: Look, my dear—why—she's dead. . .

THE ACTOR: [*Shakes his head*] Impossible . . .

NATASHA: [*Stepping back*] So help me God— look . . .

BUBNOFF: [*Appearing in doorway*] What is there to look at?

NATASHA: Anna—she's dead!

BUBNOFF: That means—she's stopped coughing! [*Goes to* Anna's *bed, looks, and returns to his bunk*] We must tell Kleshtch—it's his business to know . . .

THE ACTOR: I'll go—I'll say to him—she lost her name—[*Exit*]

NATASHA: [*In centre of room*] I, too—some day— I'll be found in the cellar—dead. . . .

BUBNOFF: [*Spreading out some rags on his bunk*] What's that? What are you muttering?

NATASHA: Nothing much . . .

BUBNOFF: Waiting for Vaska, eh? Take care— Vassilisa'll break your head!

NATASHA: Isn't it the same who breaks it? I'd much rather he'd do it!

BUBNOFF: [*Lying down*] Well—that's your own affair . . .

NATASHA: It's best for her to be dead—yet it's a pity . . . oh, Lord—why do we live?

BUBNOFF: It's so with all . . . we're born, live and die—and I'll die, too—and so'll you—what's there to be gloomy about?

[*Enter* Luka, *the* Tartar, Zob, *and* Kleshtch. *The latter comes after the others, slowly, shrunk up*]

NATASHA: Sh-sh! Anna!

ZOB: We've heard—God rest her soul . . .

THE TARTAR: [*To* Kleshtch] We must take her out of here. Out into the hall! This is no place for corpses—but for the living . . .

KLESHTCH: [*Quietly*] We'll take her out—

[*Everybody goes to the bed*, Kleshtch *looks at his wife over the others' shoulders*]

ZOB: [*To* The Tartar] You think she'll smell? I don't think she will—she dried up while she was still alive . . .

NATASHA: God! If they'd only a little pity . . . if only some one would say a kindly word—oh, you . . .

LUKA: Don't be hurt, girl—never mind! Why and how should we pity the dead? Come, dear! We don't pity the living—we can't even pity our own selves—how can we?

BUBNOFF: [*Yawning*] And, besides, when you're dead, no word will help you—when you're still alive, even sick, it may. . . .

THE TARTAR: [*Stepping aside*] The police must be notified . . .

ZOB: The police—must be done! Kleshtch! Did you notify the police?

KLESHTCH: No—she's got to be buried—and all I have is forty kopecks—

ZOB: Well—you'll have to borrow then—otherwise we'll take up a collection . . . one'll give five kopecks, others as much as they can. But the police must be notified at once—or they'll think you killed her or God knows what not . . .

[*Crosses to* The Tartar's *bunk and prepares to lie down by his side*]

NATASHA: [*Going to* Bubnoff's *bunk*] Now—I'll dream of her . . . I always dream of the dead . . . I'm afraid to go out into the hall by myself—it's dark there . . .

LUKA: [*Following her*] You better fear the living—I'm telling you . . .

NATASHA: Take me across the hall, grandfather.

LUKA: Come on—come on—I'll take you across—

[*They go away. Pause*]

ZOB: [*To* The Tartar] Oh-ho! Spring will soon be here, little brother, and it'll be quite warm. In the villages the peasants are already making ready their ploughs and harrows, preparing to till . . . and we . . . Hassan? Snoring already? Damned Mohammedan!

BUBNOFF: Tartars love sleep!

KLESHTCH: [*In centre of room, staring in front of him*] What am I to do now?

ZOB: Lie down and sleep—that's all . . .

KLESHTCH: [*Softly*] But—she . . . how about . . .

[*No one answers him.* Satine *and* The Actor *enter*]

THE ACTOR: [*Yelling*] Old man! Come here, my trusted Duke of Kent!

SATINE: Miklookha-Maklai is coming—ho-ho!

THE ACTOR: It has been decided upon! Old man, where's the town—where are you?

SATINE: Fata Morgana, the old man bilked you from top to bottom! There's nothing—no towns—no people—nothing at all!

THE ACTOR: You lie!

THE TARTAR: [*Jumping up*] Where's the boss? I'm

going to the boss. If I can't sleep, I won't pay! Corpses—drunkards . . . [*Exit quickly*]

[Satine *looks after him and whistles*]

BUBNOFF: [*In a sleepy voice*] Go to bed, boys—be quiet . . . night is for sleep.

THE ACTOR: Yes—so—there's a corpse here. . . . "Our net fished up a corpse. . . ." Verses by Béranger. . . .

SATINE: [*Screams*] The dead can't hear . . . the dead do not feel—Scream!—Roar! . . . the deaf don't hear!

[*In the doorway appears* Luka]

CURTAIN

ACT III.

"The Waste," a yard strewn with rubbish and overgrown with weeds. Back, a high brick wall which shuts out the sight of the sky. Near it are elder-bushes. Right, the dark, wooden wall of some sort of house, barn or stable. Left, the grey tumbledown wall of Kostilyoff's *night asylum. It is built at an angle so that the further corner reaches almost to the centre of the yard. Between it and the wall runs a narrow passage. In the grey, plastered wall are two windows, one on a level with the ground, the other about six feet higher up and closer to the brick wall. Near the latter wall is a big sledge turned upside down and a beam about twelve feet long. Right of the wall is a heap of old planks. Evening. The sun is setting, throwing a crimson light on the brick wall. Early spring, the snow having only recently melted. The elder-bushes are not yet in bud.*

Natasha *and* Nastya *are sitting side by side on the beam.* Luka *and the* Baron *are on the sledge.* Kleshtch *is stretched on the pile of planks to the right.* Bubnoff's *face is at the ground floor window*

NASTYA: [*With closed eyes, nodding her head in rhythm to the tale she is telling in a sing-song voice*] So then at night he came into the garden. I had been waiting for him quite a while. I trembled with fear and grief—he trembled, too . . . he was as white as chalk—and he had the pistol in his hand . . .

NATASHA: [*Chewing sun-flower seeds*] Oh—are these students really such desperate fellows? . . .

NASTYA: And he says to me in a dreadful voice: "My precious darling . . ."

BUBNOFF: Ho-ho! Precious—?

THE BARON: Shut up! If you don't like it, you can lump it! But don't interrupt her. . . . Go on . . .

NASTYA: "My one and only love," he says, "my parents," he says, "refuse to give their consent to our wedding—and threaten to disown me because of my love for you. Therefore," he says, "I must take my life." And his pistol was huge—and loaded with ten bullets . . . "Farewell," he says, "beloved comrade! I have made up my mind for good and all . . . I can't live without you . . ." and I replied: "My unforgettable friend—my Raoul. . . ."

BUBNOFF: [Surprised] What? What? Krawl—did you call him—?

THE BARON: Nastka! But last time his name was Gaston. . . .

NASTYA: [Jumping up] Shut up, you bastards! Ah —you lousy mongrels! You think for a moment that you can understand love—true love? My love was real honest-to-God love! [To the Baron] You good-for-nothing! . . . educated, you call yourself— drinking coffee in bed, did you?

LUKA: Now, now! Wait, people! Don't interfere! Show a little respect to your neighbors . . . it isn't the word that matters, but what's in back of the word. That's what matters! Go on, girl! It's all right!

BUBNOFF: Go on, crow! See if you can make your feathers white!

THE BARON: Well—continue!

NATASHA: Pay no attention to them . . . what are they? They're just jealous . . . they've nothing to tell about themselves . . .

NASTYA: [Sits down again] I'm going to say no more! If they don't believe me they'll laugh. [Stops suddenly, is silent for a few seconds, then, shutting her eyes, continues in a loud and intense voice, swaying her hands as if to the rhythm of far music] And then I replied to him: "Joy of my life! My bright moon! And I, too, I can't live without you— because I love you madly, so madly—and I shall keep on loving you as long as my heart beats in my bosom. But—" I say—"don't take your young life! Think how necessary it is to your dear parents whose only happiness you are. Leave me! Better that I should perish from longing for you, my life! I alone! I—ah—as such, such! Better that I should die—it doesn't matter . . . I am of no use to the world—and I have nothing, nothing at all—" [Covers her face with her hand and weeps gently]

NATASHA: [In a low voice] Don't cry—don't!

[Luka, smiling, strokes Nastya's head]

BUBNOFF: [Laughs] Ah—you limb of Satan!

THE BARON: [Also laughs] Hey, old man? Do you think it's true? It's all from that book, Fatal Love . . . it's all nonsense! Let her alone!

NATASHA: And what's it to you? Shut up—or God'll punish you!

NASTYA: [Bitterly] God damn your soul! You worthless pig! Soul—bah!—you haven't got one!

LUKA: [Takes Nastya's hand] Come, dear! It's nothing! Don't be angry—I know—I believe you! You're right, not they! If you believe you had a real love affair, then you did—yes! And as for him —don't be angry with a fellow-lodger . . . maybe he's really jealous, and that's why he's laughing. Maybe he never had any real love—maybe not— come on—let's go!

NASTYA: [Pressing her hand against her breast] Grandfather! So help me God—it happened! It happened! He was a student, a Frenchman—Gastotcha was his name—he had a little black beard— and patent leathers—may God strike me dead if I'm lying! And he loved me so—My God, how he loved me!

LUKA: Yes, yes, it's all right. I believe you! Patent leathers, you said? Well, well, well—and you loved him, did you? [Disappears with her around the corner]

THE BARON: God—isn't she a fool, though? She's good-hearted—but such a fool—it's past belief!

BUBNOFF: And why are people so fond of lying —just as if they were up before the judge—really!

NATASHA: I guess lying is more fun than speaking the truth—I, too . . .

THE BARON: What—you, too? Go on!

NATASHA: Oh—I imagine things—invent them— and I wait—

THE BARON: For what?

NATASHA: [Smiling confusedly] Oh—I think that perhaps—well—to-morrow somebody will really appear—some one—oh—out of the ordinary—or something'll happen—also out of the ordinary. . . . I've been waiting for it—oh—always . . . But, really, what is there to wait for?

[Pause]

THE BARON: [With a slight smile] Nothing—I expect nothing! What is past, is past! Through! Over with! And then what?

NATASHA: And then—well—to-morrow I imagine suddenly that I'll die—and I get frightened . . . in summer it's all right to dream of death—then there are thunder storms—one might get struck by lightning . . .

THE BARON: You've a hard life . . . your sister's a wicked-tempered devil!

NATASHA: Tell me—does anybody live happily? It's hard for all of us—I can see that . . .

KLESHTCH: [Who until this moment has sat motionless and indifferent, jumps up suddenly] For all? You lie! Not for all! If it were so—all right! Then it wouldn't hurt—yes!

BUBNOFF: What in hell's bit you? Just listen to him yelping!

[Kleshtch lies down again and grunts]

THE BARON: Well—I'd better go and make my peace with Nastinka—if I don't, she won't treat me to vodka . . .

BUBNOFF: Hm—people love to lie . . . with Nastka—I can see the reason why. She's used to painting that mutt of hers—and now she wants to paint her soul as well . . . put rouge on her soul, eh? But the others—why do they? Take Luka for instance—he lies a lot . . . and what does he get out of it? He's an old fellow, too—why does he do it?

THE BARON: [Smiling and walking away] All people have drab-colored souls—and they like to brighten them up a bit . . .

LUKA: [*Appearing from round the corner*] You, sir, why do you tease the girl? Leave her alone—let her cry if it amuses her . . . she weeps for her own pleasure—what harm is it to you?

THE BARON: Nonsense, old man! She's a nuisance. Raoul to-day, Gaston to-morrow—always the same old yarn, though! Still—I'll go and make up with her. [*Leaves*]

LUKA: That's right—go—and be nice to her. Being nice to people never does them any harm . . .

NATASHA: You're so good, little father—why are you so good?

LUKA: Good, did you say? Well—call it that! [*Behind the brick wall is heard soft singing and the sounds of a concertina*] Some one has to be kind, girl—some one must pity people! Christ pitied everybody—and he said to us: "Go and do likewise!" I tell you—if you pity a man when he most needs it, good comes of it. Why—I used to be a watchman on the estate of an engineer near Tomsk—all right—the house was right in the middle of a forest—lonely place—winter came—and I remained all by myself. Well—one night I heard a noise—

NATASHA: Thieves?

LUKA: Exactly! Thieves creeping in! I took my gun—I went out. I looked and saw two of them opening a window—and so busy that they didn't even see me. I yell: "Hey there—get out of here!" And they turn on me with their axes—I warn them to stand back, or I'd shoot—and as I speak, I keep on covering them with my gun, first the one, then the other—they go down on their knees, as if to implore me for mercy. And by that time I was furious—because of those axes, you see—and so I say to them: "I was chasing you, you scoundrels—and you didn't go. Now you go and break off some stout branches!"—and they did so—and I say: "Now—one of you lie down and let the other one flog him!" So they obey me and flog each other—and then they begin to implore me again. "Grandfather," they say, "for God's sake give us some bread! We're hungry!" There's thieves for you, my dear! [*Laughs*] And with an ax, too! Yes—honest peasants, both of them! And I say to them, "You should have asked for bread straight away!" And they say: "We got tired of asking—you beg and beg—and nobody gives you a crumb—it hurts!" So they stayed with me all that winter—one of them, Stepan, would take my gun and go shooting in the forest—and the other, Yakoff, was ill most of the time—he coughed a lot . . . and so the three of us together looked after the house . . . then spring came . . . "Good-bye, grandfather," they said—and they went away—back home to Russia . . .

NATASHA: Were they escaped convicts?

LUKA: That's just what they were—escaped convicts—from a Siberian prison camp . . . honest peasants! If I hadn't felt sorry for them—they might have killed me—or maybe worse—and then there would have been trial and prison and afterwards Siberia—what's the sense of it? Prison teaches no good—and Siberia doesn't either—but another human being can . . . yes, a human being can teach another one kindness—very simply! [*Pause*]

BUBNOFF: Hm—yes—I, for instance, don't know how to lie . . . why—as far as I'm concerned, I believe in coming out with the whole truth and putting it on thick . . . why fuss about it?

KLESHTCH: [*Again jumps up as if his clothes were on fire, and screams*] What truth? Where is there truth? [*Tearing at his ragged clothes*] Here's truth for you! No work! No strength! That's the only truth! Shelter—there's no shelter! You die—that's the truth! Hell! What do I want with the truth? Let me breathe! Why should I be blamed? What do I want with truth? To live—Christ Almighty!—they won't let you live—and that's another truth!

BUBNOFF: He's mad!

LUKA: Dear Lord . . . listen to me, brother—

KLESHTCH: [*Trembling with excitement*] They say: there's truth! You, old man, try to console every one . . . I tell you—I hate every one! And there's your truth—God curse it—understand? I tell you—God curse it!

[*Rushes away round the corner, turning as he goes*]

LUKA: Ah—how excited he got! Where did he run off to?

NATASHA: He's off his head . . .

BUBNOFF: God—didn't he say a whole lot, though? As if he was playing drama—he gets those fits often . . . he isn't used to life yet . . .

PEPEL: [*Comes slowly round the corner*] Peace on all this honest gathering! Well, Luka, you wily old fellow—still telling them stories?

LUKA: You should have heard how that fellow carried on!

PEPEL: Kleshtch—wasn't it? What's wrong with him? He was running like one possessed!

LUKA: You'd do the same if your own heart were breaking!

PEPEL: [*Sitting down*] I don't like him . . . he's got such a nasty, bad temper—and so proud! [*Imitating* Kleshtch] "I'm a workman!" And he thinks everyone's beneath him. Go on working if you feel like it—nothing to be so damned haughty about! If work is the standard—a horse can give us points—pulls like hell and says nothing! Natasha—are your folks at home?

NATASHA: They went to the cemetery—then to night service . . .

PEPEL: So that's why you're free for once—quite a novelty.

LUKA: [*To Bubnoff, thoughtfully*] There—you say—truth! Truth doesn't always heal a wounded soul. For instance, I knew of a man who believed in a land of righteousness . . .

BUBNOFF: In what?

LUKA: In a land of righteousness. He said: "Somewhere on this earth there must be a righteous land—

and wonderful people live there—good people! They respect each other, help each other, and everything is peaceful and good!" And so that man—who was always searching for this land of righteousness—he was poor and lived miserably—and when things got to be so bad with him that it seemed there was nothing else for him to do except lie down and die —even then he never lost heart—but he'd just smile and say: "Never mind! I can stand it! A little while longer—and I'll have done with this life—and I'll go in search of the righteous land!"—it was his one happiness—the thought of that land . . .

PEPEL: Well? Did he go there?

BUBNOFF: Where? Ho-ho!

LUKA: And then to this place—in Siberia, by the way—there came a convict—a learned man with books and maps—yes, a learned man who knew all sorts of things—and the other man said to him: "Do me a favor—show me where is the land of righteousness and how I can get there." At once the learned man opened his books, spread out his maps, and looked and looked and he said—no—he couldn't find this land anywhere . . . everything was correct—all the lands on earth were marked—but not this land of righteousness . . .

PEPEL: [In a low voice] Well? Wasn't there a trace of it?

[Bubnoff roars with laughter]

NATASHA: Wait . . . well, little father?

LUKA: The man wouldn't believe it. . . . "It must exist," he said, "look carefully. Otherwise," he says, "your books and maps are of no use if there's no land of righteousness." The learned man was offended. "My plans," he said, "are correct. But there exists no land of righteousness anywhere." Well, then the other man got angry. He'd lived and lived and suffered and suffered, and had believed all the time in the existence of this land—and now, according to the plans, it didn't exist at all. He felt robbed! And he said to the learned man: "Ah—you scum of the earth! You're not a learned man at all—but just a damned cheat!"—and he gave him a good wallop in the eye—then another one . . . [After a moment's silence] And then he went home and hanged himself!

[All are silent. Luka, smiling, looks at Pepel and Natasha]

PEPEL: [Low-voiced] To hell with this story—it isn't very cheerful . . .

NATASHA: He couldn't stand the disappointment . . .

BUBNOFF: [Sullen] Ah—it's nothing but a fairy-tale . . .

PEPEL: Well—there is the righteous land for you —doesn't exist, it seems . . .

NATASHA: I'm sorry for that man . . .

BUBNOFF: All a story—ho-ho!—land of righteous-ness—what an idea! [Exit through window]

LUKA: [Pointing to window] He's laughing!

[Pause] Well, children, God be with you! I'll leave you soon . . .

PEPEL: Where are you going to?

LUKA: To the Ukraine—I heard they discovered a new religion there—I want to see—yes! People are always seeking—they always want something better—God grant them patience!

PEPEL: You think they'll find it?

LUKA: The people? They will find it! He who seeks, will find! He who desires strongly, will find!

NATASHA: If only they could find something better —invent something better . . .

LUKA: They're trying to! But we must help them, girl—we must respect them . . .

NATASHA: How can I help them? I am helpless myself!

PEPEL: [Determined] Again—listen—I'll speak to you again, Natasha—here—before him—he knows everything . . . run away with me?

NATASHA: Where? From one prison to another?

PEPEL: I told you—I'm through with being a thief, so help me God! I'll quit! If I say so, I'll do it! I can read and write—I'll work—He's been telling me to go to Siberia on my own hook—let's go there together, what do you say? Do you think I'm not disgusted with my life? Oh—Natasha—I know . . . I see . . . I console myself with the thought that there are lots of people who are honored and re-spected—and who are bigger thieves than I! But what good is that to me? It isn't that I repent . . . I've no conscience . . . but I do feel one thing: One must live differently. One must live a better life . . . one must be able to respect one's own self . . .

LUKA: That's right, friend! May God help you! It's true! A man must respect himself!

PEPEL: I've been a thief from childhood on! Everybody always called me "Vaska—the thief—the son of a thief!" Oh—very well then—I am a thief— . . . just imagine—now, perhaps, I'm a thief out of spite—perhaps I'm a thief because no one ever called me anything different. . . . Well, Natasha—

NATASHA: [Sadly] Somehow I don't believe in words—and I'm restless to-day—my heart is heavy . . . as if I were expecting something . . . it's a pity, Vassily, that you talked to me to-day . . .

PEPEL: When should I? It isn't the first time I speak to you . . .

NATASHA: And why should I go with you? I don't love you so very much—sometimes I like you—and other times the mere sight of you makes me sick . . . it seems—no—I don't really love you . . . when one really loves, one sees no fault. . . . But I do see . . .

PEPEL: Never mind—you'll love me after a while! I'll make you care for me . . . if you'll just say yes! For over a year I've watched you . . . you're a decent girl . . . you're kind—you're reliable—I'm very much in love with you . . .

[Vassilisa, *in her best dress, appears at window and listens*]

NATASHA: Yes—you love me—but how about my sister? . . .

PEPEL: [*Confused*] Well, what of her? There are plenty like her . . .

LUKA: You'll be all right, girl! If there's no bread, you have to eat weeds . . .

PEPEL: [*Gloomily*] Please—feel a little sorry for me! My life isn't all roses—it's a hell of a life . . . little happiness in it . . . I feel as if a swamp were sucking me under . . . and whatever I try to catch and hold on to, is rotten . . . it breaks . . . Your sister—oh—I thought she was different . . . if she weren't so greedy after money . . . I'd have done anything for her sake, if she were only all mine . . . but she must have someone else . . . and she has to have money—and freedom . . . because she doesn't like the straight and narrow . . . she can't help me. But you're like a young fir-tree . . . you bend, but you don't break . . .

LUKA: Yes—go with him, girl, go! He's a good lad—he's all right! Only tell him every now and then that he's a good lad so that he won't forget it—and he'll believe you. Just you keep on telling him "Vasya, you're a good man—don't you forget it!" Just think, dear, where else could you go except with him? Your sister is a savage beast . . . and as for her husband, there's little to say of him? He's rotten beyond words . . . and all this life here, where will it get you? But this lad is strong . . .

NATASHA: Nowhere to go—I know—I thought of it. The only thing is—I've no faith in anybody—and there's no place for me to turn to . . .

PEPEL: Yes, there is! But I won't let you go that way—I'd rather cut your throat!

NATASHA: [*Smiling*] There—I'm not his wife yet—and he talks already of killing me!

PEPEL: [*Puts his arms around her*] Come, Natasha! Say yes!

NATASHA: [*Holding him close*] But I'll tell you one thing, Vassily—I swear it before God . . . the first time you strike me or hurt me any other way, I'll have no pity on myself . . . I'll either hang myself . . . or . . .

PEPEL: May my hand wither if ever I touch you!

LUKA: Don't doubt him, dear! He needs you more than you need him!

VASSILISA: [*From the window*] So now they're engaged! Love and advice!

NATASHA: They've come back—oh, God—they saw—oh, Vassily . . .

PEPEL: Why are you frightened? Nobody'll dare touch you now!

VASSILISA: Don't be afraid, Natalia! He won't beat you . . . he don't know how to love or how to beat . . . I know!

LUKA: [*In a low voice*] Rotten old hag—like a snake in the grass . . .

VASSILISA: He dares only with the word!

KOSTILYOFF: [*Enters*] Natashka! What are you doing here, you parasite? Gossiping? Kicking about your family? And the samovar not ready? And the table not cleared?

NATASHA: [*Going out*] I thought you were going to church . . .?

KOSTILYOFF: None of your business what we intended doing! Mind your own affairs—and do what you're told!

PEPEL: Shut up, you! She's no longer your servant! Don't go, Natalia—don't do a thing!

NATASHA: Stop ordering me about—you're commencing too soon! [*Leaves*]

PEPEL: [*To* Kostilyoff] That's enough. You've used her long enough—now she's mine!

KOSTILYOFF: Yours? When did you buy her—and for how much?

[Vassilisa *roars with laughter*]

LUKA: Go away, Vasya!

PEPEL: Don't laugh, you fools—or first thing you know I'll make you cry!

VASSILISA: Oh, how terrible! Oh—how you frighten me!

LUKA: Vassily—go away! Don't you see—she's goading you on . . . ridiculing you, don't you understand? . . .

PEPEL: Yes . . . You lie, lie! You won't get what you want!

VASSILISA: Nor will I get what I don't want, Vasya!

PEPEL: [*Shaking his fist at her*] We'll see . . . [*Exit*]

VASSILISA: [*Disappearing through window*] I'll arrange some wedding for you . . .

KOSTILYOFF: [*Crossing to* Luka] Well, old man, how's everything?

LUKA: All right!

KOSTILYOFF: You're going away, they say—?

LUKA: Soon.

KOSTILYOFF: Where to?

LUKA: I'll follow my nose . . .

KOSTILYOFF: Tramping, eh? Don't like stopping in one place all the time, do you?

LUKA: Even water won't pass beneath a stone that's sunk too firmly in the ground, they say . . .

KOSTILYOFF: That's true for a stone. But man must settle in one place. Men can't live like cockroaches, crawling about wherever they want. . . . A man must stick to one place—and not wander about aimlessly . . .

LUKA: But suppose his home is wherever he hangs his hat?

KOSTILYOFF: Why, then—he's a vagabond—useless . . . a human being must be of some sort of use—he must work . . .

LUKA: That's what you think, eh?

KOSTILYOFF: Yes—sure . . . just look! What's a vagabond? A strange fellow . . . unlike all others. If he's a real pilgrim then he's some good in the world . . . perhaps he discovered a new truth. Well

—but not every truth is worth while. Let him keep it to himself and shut up about it! Or else—let him speak in a way which no one can understand . . . don't let him interfere . . . don't let him stir up people without cause! It's none of his business how other people live! Let him follow his own righteous path . . . in the woods—or in a monastery—away from everybody! He mustn't interfere—nor condemn other people—but pray—pray for all of us—for all the world's sins—for mine—for yours—for everybody's. To pray—that's why he forsakes the world's turmoil! That's so! [*Pause*] But you—what sort of pilgrim are you—? An honest person must have a passport . . . all honest people have passports . . . yes! . . .

LUKA: In this world there are people—and also just plain men . . .

KOSTILYOFF: Don't coin wise sayings! Don't give me riddles! I'm as clever as you . . . what's the difference—people and men?

LUKA: What riddle is there? I say—there's sterile and there's fertile ground . . . whatever you sow in it, grows . . . that's all . . .

KOSTILYOFF: What do you mean?

LUKA: Take yourself for instance . . . if the Lord God himself said to you: "Mikhailo, be a man!"— it would be useless—nothing would come of it— you're doomed to remain just as you are . . .

KOSTILYOFF: Oh—but do you realize that my wife's uncle is a policeman, and that if I . . .

VASSILISA: [*Coming in*] Mikhail Ivanitch—come and have your tea . . .

KOSTILYOFF: [*To* Luka] You listen! Get out! You leave this place—hear?

VASSILISA: Yes—get out, old man! Your tongue's too long! And—who knows—you may be an escaped convict . . .

KOSTILYOFF: If I ever see sign of you again after to-day—well—I've warned you!

LUKA: You'll call your uncle, eh? Go on—call him! Tell him you've caught an escaped convict— and maybe uncle'll get a reward—perhaps all of three kopecks . . .

BUBNOFF: [*In the window*] What are you bargaining about? Three kopecks—for what?

LUKA: They're threatening to sell me . . .

VASSILISA: [*To her husband*] Come . . .

BUBNOFF: For three kopecks? Well—look out, old man—they may even do it for one!

KOSTILYOFF: [*To* Bubnoff] You have a habit of jumping up like a jack-in-the-box!

VASSILISA: The world is full of shady people and crooks—

LUKA: Hope you'll enjoy your tea!

VASSILISA: [*Turning*] Shut up! You rotten toadstool!

[*Leaves with her husband*]

LUKA: I'm off to-night.

BUBNOFF: That's right. Don't outstay your welcome!

LUKA: True enough.

BUBNOFF: I know. Perhaps I've escaped the gallows by getting away in time . . .

LUKA: Well?

BUBNOFF: That's true. It was this way. My wife took up with my boss. He was great at his trade— could dye a dog's skin so that it looked like a raccoon's—could change cat's skin into kangaroo—muskrats, all sorts of things. Well—my wife took up with him—and they were so mad about each other that I got afraid they might poison me or something like that—so I commenced beating up my wife—and the boss beat me . . . we fought savagely! Once he tore off half my whiskers—and broke one of my ribs . . . well, then I, too, got enraged. . . . I cracked my wife over the head with an iron yard-measure—well—and altogether it was like an honest-to-God war! And then I saw that nothing really could come of it . . . they were planning to get the best of me! So I started planning—how to kill my wife—I thought of it a whole lot . . . but I thought better of it just in time . . . and got away . . .

LUKA: That was best! Let them go on changing dogs into raccoons!

BUBNOFF: Only—the shop was in my wife's name . . . and so I did myself out of it, you see? Although, to tell the truth, I would have drunk it away . . . I'm a hard drinker, you know . . .

LUKA: A hard drinker—oh . . .

BUBNOFF: The worst you ever met! Once I start drinking, I drink, everything in sight, I'll spend every bit of money I have—everything except my bones and my skin . . . what's more, I'm lazy . . . it's terrible how I hate work!

[*Enter* Satine *and the* Actor, *quarreling*]

SATINE: Nonsense! You'll go nowhere—it's all a damned lie! Old man, what did you stuff him with all those fairy-tales for?

THE ACTOR: You lie! Grandfather! Tell him that he lies!—I am going away. I worked to-day— swept the streets . . . and I didn't have a drop of vodka. What do you think of that? Here they are—two fifteen-kopeck pieces—and I'm sober!

SATINE: Why—that's absurd! Give it to me—I'll either drink it up—or lose it at cards . . .

THE ACTOR: Get out—this is for my journey . .

LUKA: [*To* Satine] And you—why are you trying to lead him astray?

SATINE: Tell me, soothsayer, beloved by the gods, what's my future going to be? I've gone to pieces, brother—but everything isn't lost yet, grandfather . . . there are sharks in this world who got more brains than I!

LUKA: You're cheerful, Constantine—and very agreeable!

BUBNOFF: Actor, come over here! [*The Actor crosses to window, sits down on the sill before* Bubnoff, *and speaks in a low voice with him*]

SATINE: You know, brother, I used to be a clever

youngster. It's nice to think of it. I was a devil of a fellow . . . danced splendidly, played on the stage, loved to amuse people . . . it was awfully gay . . .

LUKA: How did you get to be what you are?

SATINE: You're inquisitive, old man! You want to know everything? What for?

LUKA: I want to understand the ways of men—I look at you, and I don't understand. You're a bold lad, Constantine, and you're no fool . . . yet, all of a sudden . . .

SATINE: It's prison, grandfather—I spent four years and seven months in prison . . . afterwards —where could I go?

LUKA: Aha! What were you there for?

SATINE: On account of a scoundrel—whom I killed in a fit of rage . . . and despair . . . and in prison I learned to play cards. . . .

LUKA: You killed—because of a woman?

SATINE: Because of my own sister. . . . But look here—leave me alone! I don't care for these cross-examinations—and all this happened a long time ago. It's already nine years since my sister's death. . . . Brother, she was a wonderful girl . . .

LUKA: You take life easily! And only a while ago that locksmith was here—and how he did yell!

SATINE: Kleshtch?

LUKA: Yes—"There's no work," he shouted, "there isn't anything . . ."

SATINE: He'll get used to it. What could I do?

LUKA: [Softly] Look—here he comes!

[Kleshtch walks in slowly, his head bowed low]

SATINE: Hey, widower! Why are you so down in the mouth? What are you thinking?

KLESHTCH: I'm thinking—what'll I do? I've no food—nothing—the funeral ate up all . . .

SATINE: I'll give you a bit of advice . . . do nothing! Just be a burden to the world at large!

KLESHTCH: Go on—talk—I'd be ashamed of myself . . .

SATINE: Why—people aren't ashamed to let you live worse than a dog. Just think . . . you stop work—so do I—so do hundreds, thousands of others —everybody—understand?—everybody'll quit working . . . nobody'll do a damned thing—and then what'll happen?

KLESHTCH: They'll all starve to death . . .

LUKA: [To Satine] If those are your notions, you ought to join the order of Béguines—you know—there's some such organization . . .

SATINE: I know—grandfather—and they're no fools . . .

[Natasha is heard screaming behind Kostilyoff's window: "What for? Stop! What have I done?"]

LUKA: [Worried] Natasha! That was she crying— oh, God . . .

[From Kostilyoff's room is heard noise, shuffling, breaking of crockery, and Kostilyoff's shrill cry: "Ah! Heretic! Bitch!"]

VASSILISA: Wait, wait—I'll teach her—there, there!

NATASHA: They're beating me—killing me . . .

SATINE: [Shouts through the window] Hey—you there— . . .

LUKA: [Trembling] Where's Vassily—? Call Vaska —oh, God—listen, brothers . . .

THE ACTOR: [Running out] I'll find him at once!

BUBNOFF: They beat her a lot these days . . .

SATINE: Come on, old man—we'll be witnesses . . .

LUKA: [Following Satine] Oh—witnesses—what for? Vassily—he should be called at once!

NATASHA: Sister—sister dear! Va-a-a . . .

BUBNOFF: They've gagged her—I'll go and see . . .

[The noise in Kostilyoff's room dies down gradually as if they had gone into the hallway. The old man's cry: "Stop!" is heard. A door is slammed noisily, and the latter sound cuts off all the other noises sharply. Quiet on the stage. Twilight]

KLESHTCH: [Seated on the sledge, indifferently, rubbing his hands; mutters at first indistinguishably, then:] What then? One must live. [Louder] Must have shelter—well? There's no shelter, no roof— nothing . . . there's only man—man alone—no hope . . . no help . . .

[Exit slowly, his head bent. A few moments of ominous silence, then somewhere in the hallway a mass of sounds, which grows in volume and comes nearer. Individual voices are heard]

VASSILISA: I'm her sister—let go . . .

KOSTILYOFF: What right have you . . .?

VASSILISA: Jail-bird!

SATINE: Call Vaska—quickly! Zob—hit him!

[A police whistle. The Tartar runs in, his right hand in a sling]

THE TARTAR: There's a new law for you—kill only in daytime!

[Enter Zob, followed by Miedviedieff]

ZOB: I handed him a good one!

MIEDVIEDIEFF: You—how dare you fight?

THE TARTAR: What about yourself? What's your duty?

MIEDVIEDIEFF: [Running after] Stop—give back my whistle!

KOSTILYOFF: [Runs in] Abram! Stop him! Hold him! He's a murderer—he . . .

[Enter Kvashnya and Nastya supporting Natasha who is disheveled. Satine backs away, pushing away Vassilisa who is trying to attack her sister, while, near her, Alyoshka jumps up and down like a madman, whistles into her ear, shrieking, roaring. Also other ragged men and women]

SATINE: [To Vassilisa] Well—you damned bitch!

VASSILISA: Let go, you jail-bird! I'll tear you to pieces—if I have to pay for it with my own life!

KVASHNYA: [Leading Natasha aside] You—Karpovna—that's enough—stand back—aren't you ashamed? Or are you crazy?

MIEDVIEDIEFF: [*Seizes* Satine] Aha—caught at last!

SATINE: Zob—beat them up! Vaska—Vaska . . . [*They all, in a chaotic mass, struggle near the brick wall. They lead* Natasha *to the right, and set her on a pile of wood.* Pepel *rushes in from the hallway and, silently, with powerful movements, pushes the crowd aside*]

PEPEL: Natalia, where are you . . . you . . .

KOSTILYOFF: [*Disappearing behind a corner*] Abram! Seize Vaska! Comrades—help us get him! The thief! The robber!

PEPEL: You—you old bastard! [*Aiming a terrific blow at* Kostilyoff. Kostilyoff *falls so that only the upper part of his body is seen.* Pepel *rushes to* Natasha]

VASSILISA: Beat Vaska! Brothers! Beat the thief!

MIEDVIEDIEFF: [*Yells to* Satine] Keep out of this—it's a family affair . . . they're relatives—and who are you? . . .

PEPEL: [*To* Natasha] What did she do to you? She used a knife?

KVASHNYA: God—what beasts! They've scalded the child's feet with boiling water!

NASTYA: They overturned the samovar . . .

THE TARTAR: Maybe an accident—you must make sure—you can't exactly tell . . .

NATASHA: [*Half fainting*] Vassily—take me away—

VASSILISA: Good people! Come! Look! He's dead! Murdered!

[*All crowd into the hallway near* Kostilyoff. Bubnoff *leaves the crowd and crosses to* Pepel]

BUBNOFF: [*In a low voice, to* Pepel] Vaska—the old man is done for!

PEPEL: [*Looks at him, as though he does not understand*] Go—for help—she must be taken to the hospital . . . I'll settle with them . . .

BUBNOFF: I say—the old man—somebody's killed him . . .

[*The noise on the stage dies out like a fire under water. Distinct, whispered exclamations: "Not really?" "Well—let's go away, brothers!" "The devil!" "Hold on now!" "Let's get away before the police comes!" The crowd disappears.* Bubnoff, *the* Tartar, Nastya, *and* Kvashnya, *rush up to* Kostilyoff's *body*]

VASSILISA: [*Rises and cries out triumphantly*] Killed—my husband's killed! Vaska killed him! I saw him! Brothers, I saw him! Well—Vasya—the police!

PEPEL: [*Moves away from* Natasha] Let me alone. [*Looks at* Kostilyoff; *to* Vassilisa] Well—are you glad? [*Touches the corpse with his foot*] The old bastard is dead! Your wish has been granted! Why not do the same to you? [*Throws himself at her*]

[Satine *and* Zob *quickly overpower him, and* Vassilisa *disappears in the passage*]

SATINE: Come to your senses!

ZOB: Hold on! Not so fast!

VASSILISA: [*Appearing*] Well, Vaska, dear friend? You can't escape your fate. . . . police—Abram—whistle!

MIEDVIEDIEFF: Those devils tore my whistle off!

ALYOSHKA: Here it is! [*Whistles*, Miedviedieff *runs after him*]

SATINE: [*Leading* Pepel *to* Natasha] Don't be afraid, Vaska! Killed in a row! That's nonsense—only manslaughter—you won't have to serve a long term . . .

VASSILISA: Hold Vaska—he killed him—I saw it!

SATINE: I, too, gave the old man a couple of blows—he was easily fixed . . . you call me as witness, Vaska!

PEPEL: I don't need to defend myself . . . I want to drag Vassilisa into this mess—and I'll do it—she was the one who wanted it . . . she was the one who urged me to kill him—she goaded me on . . .

NATASHA: [*Sudden and loud*] Oh—I understand—so that's it, Vassily? Good people! They're both guilty—my sister and he—they're both guilty! They had it all planned! So, Vassily, that's why you spoke to me a while ago—so that she should overhear everything—? Good people! She's his mistress—you know it—everybody knows it—they're both guilty! She—she urged him to kill her husband—he was in their way—and so was I! And now they've maimed me . . .

PEPEL: Natalia! What's the matter with you? What are you saying?

SATINE: Oh—hell!

VASSILISA: You lie. She lies. He—Vaska killed him . . .

NATASHA: They're both guilty! God damn you both!

SATINE: What a mix-up! Hold on, Vassily—or they'll ruin you between them!

ZOB: I can't understand it—oh—what a mess!

PEPEL: Natalia! It can't be true! Surely you don't believe that I—with her—

SATINE: So help me God, Natasha! Just think . . .

VASSILISA: [*In the passage*] They've killed my husband—Your Excellency! Vaska Pepel, the thief, killed him, Captain! I saw it—everybody saw it . . .

NATASHA: [*Tossing about in agony; her mind wandering*] Good people—my sister and Vaska killed him! The police—listen—this sister of mine—here—she urged, coaxed her lover—there he stands—the scoundrel! They both killed him! Put them in jail! Bring them before the judge! Take me along, too! To prison! Christ Almighty—take me to prison, too!

CURTAIN

ACT IV.

Same as Act I. But Pepel's *room is no longer there, and the partition has been removed. Furthermore, there is no anvil at the place where* Kleshtch *used to sit and work. In the corner, where* Pepel's *room used to be, the* Tartar *lies stretched out, rather restless, and groaning from time to time.* Kleshtch *sits at one end of the table, repairing a concertina and now and then testing the stops. At the other end of the table sit* Satine, *the* Baron, *and* Nastya. *In front of them stand a bottle of vodka, three bottles of beer, and a large loaf of black bread. The* Actor *lies on top of the stove, shifting about and coughing. It is night. The stage is lit by a lamp in the middle of the table. Outside the wind howls.*

KLESHTCH: Yes . . . he disappeared during the confusion and noise . . .

THE BARON: He vanished under the very eyes of the police—just like a puff of smoke . . .

SATINE: That's how sinners flee from the company of the righteous!

NASTYA: He was a dear old soul! But you—you aren't men—you're just—oh—like rust on iron!

THE BARON: [*Drinks*] Here's to you, my lady!

SATINE: He was an inquisitive old fellow—yes! Nastenka here fell in love with him . . .

NASTYA: Yes! I did! Madly! It's true! He saw everything—understood everything . . .

SATINE: [*Laughing*] Yes, generally speaking, I would say that he was—oh—like mush to those who can't chew. . . .

THE BARON: [*Laughing*] Right! Like plaster on a boil!

KLESHTCH: He was merciful—you people don't know what pity means . . .

SATINE: What good can I do you by pitying you?

KLESHTCH: You needn't have pity—but you needn't harm or offend your fellow-beings, either!

THE TARTAR: [*Sits up on his bunk, nursing his wounded hand carefully*] He was a fine old man. The law of life was the law of his heart . . . and he who obeys this law, is good, while he who disregards it, perishes. . . .

THE BARON: What law, Prince?

THE TARTAR: There are a number—different ones —you know . . .

THE BARON: Proceed!

THE TARTAR: Do not do harm unto others—such is the law!

SATINE: Oh—you mean the Penal Code, criminal and correctional, eh?

THE BARON: And also the Code of Penalties inflicted by Justices of the Peace!

THE TARTAR: No. I mean the Koran. It is the supreme law—and your own soul ought to be the Koran—yes!

KLESHTCH: [*Testing his concertina*] It wheezes like all hell! But the Prince speaks the truth—one must live abiding by the law—by the teachings of the Gospels . . .

SATINE: Well—go ahead and do it!

THE BARON: Just try it!

THE TARTAR: The Prophet Mohammed gave to us the law. He said: "Here is the law! Do as it is written therein!" Later on a time will arrive when the Koran will have outlived its purpose—and time will bring forth its own laws—every generation will create its own . . .

SATINE: To be sure! Time passed on—and gave us the Criminal Code . . . It's a strong law, brother— it won't wear off so very soon!

NASTYA: [*Banging her glass on the table*] Why— why do I stay here—with you? I'll go away somewhere—to the ends of the world!

THE BARON: Without any shoes, my lady?

NASTYA: I'll go—naked, if must be—creeping on all fours!

THE BARON: That'll be rather picturesque, my lady —on all fours!

NASTYA: Yes—and I'll crawl if I have to—anything at all—as long as I don't have to see your faces any longer—oh, I'm so sick of it all—the life— the people—everything!

SATINE: When you go, please take the actor along —he's preparing to go to the very same place—he has learned that within a half mile's distance of the end of the world there's a hospital for diseased organons . . .

THE ACTOR: [*Raising his head over the top of the stove*] A hospital for organisms—you fool!

SATINE: For organons—poisoned with vodka!

THE ACTOR: Yes! He will go! He will indeed! You'll see!

THE BARON: Who is he, sir?

THE ACTOR: I!

THE BARON: Thanks, servant of the goddess— what's her name—? The goddess of drama—tragedy —whatever is her name—?

THE ACTOR: The muse, idiot! Not the goddess— the muse!

SATINE: Lachesis—Hera—Aphrodite—Atropos— oh! To hell with them all! You see—Baron—it was the old man who stuffed the actor's head full with this rot . . .

THE BARON: That old man's a fool . . .

THE ACTOR: Ignoramuses! Beasts! Melpomene— that's her name! Heartless brutes! Bastards! You'll see! He'll go! "On with the orgy, dismal spirits!"— poem—ah—by Béranger! Yes—he'll find some spot where there's no—no . . .

THE BARON: Where there's nothing, sir?

THE ACTOR: Right! Nothing! "This hole shall be my grave—I am dying—ill and exhausted . . ." Why do you exist? Why?

THE BARON: You! God or genius or orgy—or whatever you are—don't roar so loud!

THE ACTOR: You lie! I'll roar all I want to!

NASTYA: [*Lifting her head from the table and throwing up her hands*] Go on! Yell! Let them listen to you!

THE BARON: Where is the sense, my lady?

SATINE: Leave them alone, Baron! To hell with the lot! Let them yell—let them knock their damned heads off if they feel like it! There's a method in their madness! Don't you go and interfere with people as that old fellow did! Yes—it's he—the damned old fool—he bewitched the whole gang of us!

KLESHTCH: He persuaded them to go away—but failed to show them the road . . .

THE BARON: That old man was a humbug!

NASTYA: Liar! You're a humbug yourself!

THE BARON: Shut up, my lady!

KLESHTCH: The old man didn't like truth very much—as a matter of fact he strongly resented it—and wasn't he right, though? Just look—where is there any truth? And yet, without it, you can't breathe! For instance, our Tartar Prince over there, crushed his hand at his work—and now he'll have to have his arm amputated—and there's the truth for you!

SATINE: [*Striking the table with his clenched fist*] Shut up! You sons of bitches! Fools! Not another word about that old fellow! [*To the* Baron] You, Baron, are the worst of the lot! You don't understand a thing, and you lie like the devil! The old man's no humbug! What's the truth? Man! Man—that's the truth! He understood man—you don't! You're all as dumb as stones! I understand the old man—yes! He lied—but lied out of sheer pity for you . . . God damn you! Lots of people lie out of pity for their fellow-beings! I know! I've read about it! They lie—oh—beautifully, inspiringly, stirringly! Some lies bring comfort, and others bring peace—a lie alone can justify the burden which crushed a workman's hand and condemns those who are starving! I know what lying means! The weakling and the one who is a parasite through his very weakness—they both need lies—lies are their support, their shield, their armor! But the man who is strong, who is his own master, who is free and does not have to suck his neighbors' blood—he needs no lies! To lie—it's the creed of slaves and masters of slaves! Truth is the religion of the free man!

THE BARON: Bravo! Well spoken! Hear, hear! I agree! You speak like an honest man!

SATINE: And why can't a crook at times speak the truth—since honest people at times speak like crooks? Yes—I've forgotten a lot—but I still know a thing or two! The old man? Oh—he's wise! He affected me as acid affects a dirty old silver coin! Let's drink to his health! Fill the glasses . . . [*Nastya* fills a glass with beer and hands it to Satine, *who laughs*] The old man lives within himself . . . he looks upon all the world from his own angle. Once I asked him: "Grand-dad, why do people live?" [*Tries to imitate* Luka's *voice and gestures*] And he replied: "Why, my dear fellow, people live

in the hope of something better! For example—let's say there are carpenters in this world, and all sorts of trash . . . people . . . and they give birth to a carpenter the like of which has never been seen upon the face of the earth . . . he's way above everybody else, and has no equal among carpenters! The brilliancy of his personality was reflected on all his trade, on all the other carpenters, so that they advanced twenty years in one day! This applies to all other trades—blacksmiths and shoemakers and other workmen—and all the peasants—and even the aristocrats live in the hopes of a higher life! Each individual thinks that he's living for his own self, but in reality he lives in the hope of something better. A hundred years—sometimes longer—do we expect, live for the finer, higher life . . ." [*Nastya* stares *intently into* Satine's *face.* Kleshtch *stops working and listens.* The Baron *bows his head very low, drumming softly on the table with his fingers. The* Actor, *peering down from the stove, tries to climb noiselessly into the bunk*] "Every one, brothers, every one lives in the hope of something better. That's why we must respect each and every human being! How do we know who he is, why he was born, and what he is capable of accomplishing? Perhaps his coming into the world will prove to be our good fortune . . . Especially must we respect little children! Children—need freedom! Don't interfere with their lives! Respect children!" [*Pause*]

THE BARON: [*Thoughtfully*] Hm—yes—something better?—That reminds me of my family . . . an old family dating back to the time of Catherine . . . all noblemen, soldiers, originally French—they served their country and gradually rose higher and higher. In the days of Nicholas the First my grandfather, Gustave DeBille, held a high post—riches—hundreds of serfs . . . horses—cooks—

NASTYA: You liar! It isn't true!

THE BARON: [*Jumping up*] What? Well—go on—

NASTYA: It isn't true.

THE BARON: [*Screams*] A house in Moscow! A house in Petersburg! Carriages! Carriages with coats of arms!

[Kleshtch *takes his concertina and goes to one side, watching the scene with interest*]

NASTYA: You lie!

THE BARON: Shut up!—I say—dozens of footmen . . .

NASTYA: [*Delighted*] You lie!

THE BARON: I'll kill you!

NASTYA: [*Ready to run away*] There were no carriages!

SATINE: Stop, Nastenka! Don't infuriate him!

THE BARON: Wait—you bitch! My grandfather . . .

NASTYA: There was no grandfather! There was nothing!

[Satine *roars with laughter*]

THE BARON: [*Worn out with rage, sits down on bench*] Satine! Tell that slut—what—? You, too, are laughing? You—don't believe me either? [*Cries out in despair, pounding the table with his fists*] It's true —damn the whole lot of you!

NASTYA: [*Triumphantly*] So—you're crying? Understand now what a human being feels like when nobody believes him?

KLESHTCH: [*Returning to the table*] I thought there'd be a fight . . .

THE TARTAR: Oh—people are fools! It's too bad . . .

THE BARON: I shall not permit any one to ridicule me! I have proofs—documents—damn you!

SATINE: Forget it! Forget about your grandfather's carriages! You can't drive anywhere in a carriage of the past!

THE BARON: How dare she—just the same—?

NASTYA: Just imagine! How dare I—?

SATINE: You see—she does dare! How is she any worse than you are? Although, surely, in her past there wasn't even a father and mother, let alone carriages and a grandfather . . .

THE BARON: [*Quieting down*] Devil take you—you do know how to argue dispassionately—and I, it seems—I've no will-power . . .

SATINE: Acquire some—it's useful . . . [*Pause*] Nastya! Are you going to the hospital?

NASTYA: What for?

SATINE: To see Natashka.

NASTYA: Oh—just woke up, did you? She's been out of the hospital for some time—and they can't find a trace of her . . .

SATINE: Oh—that woman's a goner!

KLESHTCH: It's interesting to see whether Vaska will get the best of Vassilisa, or the other way around—?

NASTYA: Vassilisa will win out! She's shrewd! And Vaska will go to the gallows!

SATINE: For manslaughter? No—only to jail . . .

NASTYA: Too bad—the gallows would have been better . . . that's where all of you should be sent . . . swept off into a hole—like filth . . .

SATINE: [*Astonished*] What's the matter? Are you crazy?

THE BARON: Oh—give her a wallop—that'll teach her to be less impertinent . . .

NASTYA: Just you try to touch me!

THE BARON: I shall!

SATINE: Stop! Don't insult her! I can't get the thought of the old man out of my head! [*Roars with laughter*] Don't offend your fellow-beings! Suppose I were offended once in such a way that I'd remember it for the rest of my life? What then? Should I forgive? No, no!

THE BARON: [*To* Nastya] You must understand that I'm not your sort . . . you—ah—you piece of dirt!

NASTYA: You bastard! Why—you live off me like a worm off an apple!

[*The men laugh amusedly*]

KLESHTCH: Fool! An apple—?

THE BARON: You can't be angry with her—she's just an ass—

NASTYA: You laugh! Liars? Don't strike you as funny, eh?

THE ACTOR: [*Morosely*] Give them a good beating!

NASTYA: If I only could! [*Takes a cup from the table and throws it on the floor*] That's what I'd like to do to you all!

THE TARTAR: Why break dishes—eh—silly girl?

THE BARON: [*Rising*] That'll do! I'll teach her manners in half a second!

NASTYA: [*Running toward the door*] Go to hell!

SATINE: [*Calling after her*] Hey! That's enough! Whom are you trying to frighten? What's all the row about, anyway?

NASTYA: Dogs! I hope you'll croak! Dogs! [*Runs out*]

THE ACTOR: [*Morosely*] Amen!

THE TARTAR: Allah! Mad women, these Russians! They're bold, wilful; Tartar women aren't like that! They know the law and abide by it. . . .

KLESHTCH: She ought to be given a sound hiding!

THE BARON: The slut!

KLESHTCH: [*Testing the concertina*] It's ready! But its owner isn't here yet—that young fellow is burning his life away . . .

SATINE: Care for a drink—now?

KLESHTCH: Thanks . . . it's time to go to bed . . .

SATINE: Getting used to us?

KLESHTCH: [*Drinks, then goes to his bunk*] It's all right . . . there are people everywhere—at first you don't notice it . . . but after a while you don't mind. . . .

[*The* Tartar *spreads some rags over his bunk, then kneels on them and prays*]

THE BARON: [*To* Satine, *pointing at the* Tartar] Look!

SATINE: Stop! He's a good fellow! Leave him alone! [*Roars with laughter*] I feel kindly to-day —the devil alone knows the reason why . . .

THE BARON: You always feel kindly when you're drunk—you're even wiser at such times . . .

SATINE: When I'm drunk? Yes—then I like everything—right—He prays? That's fine! A man may believe or not—that's his own affair—a man is free —he pays for everything himself—belief or unbelief —love—wisdom . . . a man pays for everything— and that's just why he's free! Man is—truth! And what is man? It's neither you nor I nor they—oh, no —it's you and they and I and the old man—and Napoleon—Mohammed—all in one! [*Outlines vaguely in the air the contour of a human being*] Do you understand? It's tremendous! It contains the beginning and the end of everything—everything is in man—and everything exists for him! Man alone exists—everything else is the creation of his hands and his brain! Man! It is glorious! It sounds—oh— so big! Man must be respected—not degraded with pity—but respected, respected! Let us drink to man,

Baron! [*Rises*] It is good to feel that you are a man! I'm a convict, a murderer, a crook—granted!—When I'm out on the street people stare at me as if I were a scoundrel—they draw away from me—they look after me and often they say: "You dog! You humbug! Work!" Work? And what for? to fill my belly? [*Roars with laughter*] I've always despised people who worry too much about their bellies. It isn't right, Baron! It isn't! Man is loftier than that! Man stands above hunger!

THE BARON: You—reason things out. . . . Well and good—it brings you a certain amount of consolation. . . . Personally I'm incapable of it . . . I don't know how. [*Glances around him and then, softly, guardedly*] Brother—I am afraid—at times. Do you understand? Afraid!—Because—what next?

SATINE: Rot! What's a man to be afraid of?

THE BARON: [*Pacing up and down*] You know—as far back as I can remember, there's been a sort of fog in my brain. I was never able to understand anything. Somehow I feel embarrassed—it seems to me that all my life I've done nothing but change clothes—and why? I don't understand! I studied—I wore the uniform of the Institute for the Sons of the Nobility . . . but what have I learned? I don't remember! I married—I wore a frock-coat—then a dressing-gown . . . but I chose a disagreeable wife . . . and why? I don't understand. I squandered everything that I possessed—I wore some sort of a grey jacket and brick-colored trousers—but how did I happen to ruin myself? I haven't the slightest idea. . . . I had a position in the Department of State. . . . I wore a uniform and a cap with insignia of rank. . . . I embezzled government funds . . . so they dressed me in a convict's garb—and later on I got into these clothes here—and it all happened as in a dream—it's funny . . .

SATINE: Not very! It's rather—silly!

THE BARON: Yes—silly! I think so, too. Still—wasn't I born for some sort of purpose?

SATINE: [*Laughing*] Probably—a man is born to conceive a better man. [*Shaking his head*]—It's all right!

THE BARON: That she-devil Nastka! Where did she run to? I'll go and see—after all, she . . . [*Exit; pause*]

THE ACTOR: Tartar! [*Pause*] Prince! [*The Tartar looks round*] Say a prayer for me . . .

THE TARTAR: What?

THE ACTOR: [*Softly*] Pray—for me!

THE TARTAR: [*After a silence*] Pray for your own self!

THE ACTOR: [*Quickly crawls off the stove and goes to the table, pours out a drink with shaking hands, drinks, then almost runs to passage*] All over!

SATINE: Hey, proud Sicambrian! Where are you going?

[*Satine whistles. Miedviedieff enters, dressed in a woman's flannel shirtwaist; followed by Bubnoff. Both are slightly drunk. Bubnoff carries a bunch of pretzels in one hand, a couple of smoked fish in the other, a bottle of vodka under one arm, another bottle in his coat pocket*]

MIEDVIEDIEFF: A camel is something like a donkey—only it has no ears. . . .

BUBNOFF: Shut up! You're a variety of donkey yourself!

MIEDVIEDIEFF: A camel has no ears at all, at all—it hears through its nostrils . . .

BUBNOFF: [*To* Satine] Friend! I've looked for you in all the saloons and all the cabarets! Take this bottle—my hands are full . . .

SATINE: Put the pretzels on the table—then you'll have one hand free—

BUBNOFF: Right! Hey—you donkey—look! Isn't he a clever fellow?

MIEDVIEDIEFF: All crooks are clever—I know! They couldn't do a thing without brains. An honest man is all right even if he's an idiot . . . but a crook must have brains. But, speaking about camels, you're wrong . . . you can ride them—they have no horns . . . and no teeth either . . .

BUBNOFF: Where's everybody? Why is there no one here? Come on out . . . I treat! Who's in the corner?

SATINE: How soon will you drink up everything you have? Scarecrow!

BUBNOFF: Very soon! I've very little this time. Zob—where's Zob?

KLESHTCH: [*Crossing to table*] He isn't here . . .

BUBNOFF: Waughrr! Bull-dog! Br-zz-zz—Turkey-cock! Don't bark and don't growl! Drink—make merry—and don't be sullen!—I treat everybody—Brother, I love to treat—if I were rich, I'd run a free saloon! So help me God, I would! With an orchestra and a lot of singers! Come, every one! Drink and eat—listen to the music—and rest in peace! Beggars—come, all you beggars—and enter my saloon free of charge! Satine—you can have my capital—just like that!

SATINE: You better give me all you have straight away!

BUBNOFF: All my capital? Right now? Well—here's a ruble—here's twenty kopecks—five kopecks—sun-flower seeds—and that's all!

SATINE: That's splendid! It'll be safer with me—I'll gamble with it . . .

MIEDVIEDIEFF: I'm a witness—the money was given you for safe-keeping. How much is it?

BUBNOFF: You? You're a camel—we don't need witnesses . . .

ALYOSHKA: [*Comes in barefoot*] Brothers, I got my feet wet!

BUBNOFF: Go on and get your throat wet—and nothing'll happen—you're a fine fellow—you sing and you play—that's all right! But it's too bad you drink—drink, little brother, is harmful. very harmful . . .

ALYOSHKA: I judge by you! Only when you're drunk do you resemble a human being . . . Kleshtch! Is my concertina fixed? [*Sings and dances*]
    "If my mug were not so attractive,
      My sweetheart wouldn't love me at all . . ."
Boys, I'm frozen—it's cold . . .

MIEDVIEDIEFF: Hm—and may I ask who's this sweetheart?

BUBNOFF: Shut up! From now on, brother, you are neither a policeman nor an uncle!

ALYOSHKA: Just auntie's husband!

BUBNOFF: One of your nieces is in jail—the other one's dying . . .

MIEDVIEDIEFF: [*Proudly*] You lie! She's not dying —she disappeared—without trace . . .
    [Satine *roars*]

BUBNOFF: All the same, brothers—a man without nieces isn't an uncle!

ALYOSHKA: Your Excellency! Listen to the drummer of the retired billygoats' brigade! [*Sings*]
    "My sweetheart has money,
      I haven't a cent.
      But I'm a cheerful,
      Merry lad!"
Oh—isn't it cold!
    [*Enter Zob. From now until the final curtain men and women drift in, undress, and stretch out on the bunks, grumbling*]

ZOB: Bubnoff! Why did you run off?

BUBNOFF: Come here—sit down—brother, let's sing my favorite ditty, eh?

THE TARTAR: Night was made for sleep! Sing your songs in the daytime!

SATINE: Well—never mind, Prince—come here!

THE TARTAR: What do you mean—never mind? There's going to be a noise—there always is when people sing!

BUBNOFF: [*Crossing to the* Tartar] Count—ah— I mean Prince—how's your hand? Did they cut it off?

THE TARTAR: What for? We'll wait and see—perhaps it won't be necessary . . . a hand isn't made of iron—it won't take long to cut it off . . .

ZOB: It's your own affair, Hassanka! You'll be good for nothing without your hand. We're judged by our hands and backs—without the pride of your hand, you're no longer a human being. Tobacco-carting—that's your business! Come on—have a drink of vodka—and stop worrying!

KVASHNYA: [*Comes in*] Ah, my beloved fellow-lodgers! It's horrible outside—snow and slush . . . is my policeman here?

MIEDVIEDIEFF: Right here!

KVASHNYA: Wearing my blouse again? And drunk, eh? What's the idea?

MIEDVIEDIEFF: In celebration of Bubnoff's birthday . . . besides, it's cold . . .

KVASHNYA: Better look out—stop fooling about and go to sleep!

MIEDVIEDIEFF: [*Goes to kitchen*] Sleep? I can—I want to—it's time—[*Exit*]

SATINE: What's the matter? Why are you so strict with him?

KVASHNYA: You can't be otherwise, friend. You have to be strict with his sort. I took him as a partner. I thought he'd be of some benefit to me— because he's a military man—and you're a rough lot . . . and I am a woman—and now he's turned drunkard—that won't do at all!

SATINE: You picked a good one for partner!

KVASHNYA: Couldn't get a better one. You wouldn't want to live with me . . . you think you're too fine! And even if you did it wouldn't last more than a week . . . you'd gamble me and all I own away at cards!

SATINE: [*Roars with laughter*] That's true, land-lady—I'd gamble . . .

KVASHNYA: Yes, yes. Alyoshka!

ALYOSHKA: Here he is—I, myself!

KVASHNYA: What do you mean by gossiping about me?

ALYOSHKA: I? Speak out everything—whatever my conscience tells me. There, I say, is a wonderful woman! Splendid meat, fat, bones—over four hundred pounds! But brains—? Not an ounce!

KVASHNYA: You're a liar! I've a lot of brains! What do you mean by saying I beat my policeman?

ALYOSHKA: I thought you did—when you pulled him by the hair!

KVASHNYA: [*Laughs*] You fool! You aren't blind are you? Why wash dirty linen in public? And—it hurts his feelings—that's why he took to drink . . .

ALYOSHKA: It's true, evidently, that even a chicken likes vodka . . .
    [Satine *and* Kleshtch *roar with laughter*]

KVASHNYA: Go on—show your teeth! What sort of a man are you anyway, Alyoshka?

ALYOSHKA: Oh—I am first-rate! Master of all trades! I follow my nose!

BUBNOFF: [*Near the* Tartar's *bunk*] Come on! At all events—we won't let you sleep! We'll sing all night. Zob!

ZOB: Sing—? All right . . .

ALYOSHKA: And I'll play . . .

SATINE: We'll listen!

THE TARTAR: [*Smiling*] Well—Bubnoff—you devil —bring the vodka—we'll drink—we'll have a hell of a good time! The end will come soon enough—and then we'll be dead!

BUBNOFF: Fill his glass, Satine! Zob—sit down! Ah—brothers—what does a man need after all? There, for instance, I've had a drink—and I'm happy! Zob! Start my favorite song! I'll sing—and then I'll cry. . . .

ZOB: [*Begins to sing*]
    "The sun rises and sets . . ."

BUBNOFF: [*Joining in*]
    "But my prison is all dark . . ."

THE BARON: [*On the threshold; yells*] Hey—you —come—come here! Out in the waste—in the yard , . . over there . . . The actor—he's hanged himself. . . .

[*Silence. All stare at the* Baron. *Behind him appears* Nastya, *and slowly, her eyes wide with horror, she walks to the table*]

SATINE: [*In a matter-of-fact voice*] Damned fool —he ruined the song . . . !

CURTAIN.

Departures from Realism

Departures from Realism

There was a time when a particular style of theatre had the opportunity to develop its optimal possibilities. Actors from Betterton to Coquelin could refine their art and make it as personal a possession as an old habit. Such playwrights as Sophocles, Shakespeare, and Molière could grow steadily into greatness. But opportunities for arriving at maturity in a particular style have been meager in the modern theatre. It has adopted and abandoned styles with great celerity, and there has been little stability on the stage since 1890.

No sooner had naturalistic art triumphed after the eighteen-eighties than it was challenged by new romantic playwrights such as Maeterlinck and Rostand. Scene designers such as Gordon Craig and Appia denounced the realistic stage picture and became oracles of imaginative stagecraft. Producers and stage directors such as Lugné-Poë and Max Reinhardt abandoned the peepshow theatre of realism. Then followed the vogues of "expressionism," "formalism," "theatricalism," "constructivism," "futurism," "surrealism," "epic realism," and other antinaturalistic styles, although none of these ever quite displaced realism as the dominant mode of the theatre. The least extreme changes in dramatic style occurred when naturalism was modified and writers, scene designers, and directors achieved verisimilitude with selective realism. But mere modifications did not satisfy the demand for poetry and imagination in dramatic art. A passion for stylization has characterized the modern stage ever since 1890.

EXPERIMENT IN THE THEATRE

The effect of experimentation in poetic and generally nonrealistic drama can be seen in the European section which follows, as well as in the English and American parts of this anthology. We can observe the obvious effects of a return to romanticism, for example, in *Cyrano de Bergerac* and *Elizabeth the Queen*, both based on romantic careers of the past. A "symbolism" of poetic overtones and suggestiveness is strongly marked in Maeterlinck's *The Intruder*, and is realistically fortified in Synge's *Riders to the Sea*. If labels are of convenience to us, we may also find elements of symbolism in the tenderly wry extravaganza of Saroyan's *My Heart's in the Highlands* and in the delicate mood of reminiscence that enfolds Williams' *The Glass Menagerie*, not to mention the more conspicuous symbolization in Strindberg's *There Are Crimes and Crimes*, Molnár's *Liliom*, and Lorca's *Blood Wedding*. The technique of Arthur Miller's *Death of a Salesman* represents a departure from naturalism in spite of its realistic content. Vivacious fantastication characterizes *Blithe Spirit*, which Noel Coward candidly subtitled "An Improbable Farce," and *Liliom* becomes a fantastic drama after the fourth scene. Folk fantasy is celebrated in *The Green Pastures*, and myth forms the groundwork of Sartre's "existentialist" fable *The Flies*. Lorca's *Blood Wedding* is a poetic drama that contains even traditional allegorical figures of the "Moon" and "Death." Capek's *R. U. R.* is a fantasy with some of the depersonalization and telegraphic style that the expressionistic movement popularized in Central Europe after the First World War, and O'Neill's *The Hairy Ape* is both symbolic and expressionistic. Brecht's play *The Private Life of the Master Race* typifies so-called epic realism. Pirandello's *Six Characters in Search of an Author* is representative of a "grotesque" school of theatre in Italy and of frank "theatricalism." It cuts the realistic theatre into shreds, presenting a play in rehearsal and then showing the author's characters asserting their independence by enacting scenes not as he wrote them but as they experienced them in "real life." Thornton Wilder not only combines a real and, in the last part, fantasied world in *Our Town* but adopts Chinese theatricalism for his account of ordinary life in a New England town. There is much overlapping of styles in these and other plays that exemplify a reaction against naturalism. Playgoers and critics have had to adjust their sights continually in trying to make sense of the progressive modern theatre as it has moved from style to style, often with a set of well-publicized if not always clearly defined or conclusively demonstrated principles.

The restlessness of the modern spirit was especially marked in the art of stage production, and the acting profession in particular could report on some bewildering experiences as it submitted to the transmutations of theatrical style. Actors had no sooner adapted themselves to one style of performance than they were expected to adopt a different one. After 1890, many a performer who had just learned to present a fully realized, concrete personality on the realistic stage had to dissolve himself in a mist of poetic implication and become an essence instead of a person—a figment of dream rather than a multidimensional character. When the symbolist *Blue Bird* and *Pelléas and Mélisande* vogue died down and realism proved more tenacious than some enthusiasts of poetic drama had expected, the actor found it necessary to serve reality again. But not for long! Between 1919 and 1925, when expressionism became fashionable, he had to transform himself into a self-charging dynamo by order of such expressionist directors as Leopold Jessner and Jürgen Fehling. In Germany, he was expected to shriek his lines, negotiate flights of stairs at breakneck speed, and strike passionate poses; had he sizzled out of a witches' cauldron he could not have sputtered more than he did in some of the stage productions that eventuated in Central Europe. V. E. Meyerhold, the apostle of "constructivism" in Soviet Russia, made still other demands, and the actor had to become a "biodynamic" automaton swinging from trapeze bars and performing acrobatic stunts on settings that looked like bricklayers' scaffolds or catwalks in an industrial plant. The Russian director Alexander Tairov turned acting into a form of choreography. Still another director, Erwin Piscator, asked the actor to be a character, a lecturer, a harlequin, and a symbol, all in the same body. Even the well-trained actors of the Moscow Art Theatre and the New York Group Theatre could not always respond successfully to the flexibility required of them.

Many a stage production got out of hand while the director displayed his virtuosity. Playwrights, of course, followed suit, impelled by a dissatisfaction with naturalism that affected even its pioneers, Ibsen and Strindberg. Too many of the plays proved distressingly chaotic or pretentious. It is not altogether surprising that there were reactions against so much experimentation and that cautious theatre people clung to the life-belt of simple realism.

There was, nevertheless, often method in the madness of the theatre. In adopting various styles, dramatists responded to insistent social or political pressures and to the new penetrations of psychological science or psychoanalysis, while directors and scenic artists stimulated their creative faculties with the theatrical possibilities of the electric switchboard, the Linnebach projector, the motion picture, the revolving stage, and other technical advances. If the modern theatre brought forth few unassailable dramatic masterpieces, it nevertheless gave us many creditable plays and a great many beautiful and sometimes fascinating stage productions. The modern theatre has been exciting largely because it evolved a succession of experiments and endeavored to find stylized expression on the stage.

SYMBOLIST DRAMA AND THEATRE

The first departures from realism took the form of revived romanticism and of symbolism. Romanticism, which had actually never vanished from the stage, began to reassert its claims with much fanfare after 1890 in scattered works such as *Cyrano de Bergerac* and Sem Benelli's *The Jest,* one of John Barrymore's most popular successes. When romanticism returned creditably it tended, however, to be more disciplined and temperate than in the work of early nineteenth-century romanticists such as Hugo and Schiller, not to mention more erratic writers. The idiom was more brittle, gusty, or colloquial, or the tone was more or less ironic, as in *Cyrano de Bergerac* or in Edwin Justin Mayer's unjustly neglected

tragicomedy *The Children of Darkness.* We may observe the difference of style by turning from the operatic plays of Victor Hugo to Maxwell Anderson's verse dramas *Elizabeth the Queen, Mary of Scotland,* and *Anne of the Thousand Days.* (A meretricious, vulgar romanticism has, besides, been present everywhere in our century, as in other times. It masquerades as prose realism and tries to cheat with false notions. *Abie's Irish Rose* is generally singled out as the prime American example, but only because it won unusual popularity. The world's most hospitable haven for degenerate romanticism has, of course, been Hollywood.) Symbolism was a variant form of romanticism. It arose as a poetic and somewhat vaguely defined movement, strongly influenced by the philosophical idealism of Bergson, the poetry of Baudelaire, Rimbaud, and Verlaine, the painting style of the impressionists, and the music of Wagner.

For a symbolist playwright such as Maeterlinck, Andreyev, or Yeats, the world was full of wonders, and "correspondences" could be found between actual reality and an indefinable spiritual undercurrent. Portentous atmosphere and strange nuances appeared in the symbolist plays of Maeterlinck after 1889. Little was stated and presented directly or plainly. Much was suggested and implied. In many instances, the playwright also told a fanciful story or a fable, as Maeterlinck did in his once very popular *Blue Bird,* Hauptmann in *The Sunken Bell,* James M. Barrie in *Peter Pan,* and Karl Vollmöller in the famous Reinhardt-staged spectacle *The Miracle.* Or the playwright wrote more or less allegorically, like the Austrian poet Hugo von Hofmannsthal in his *Jedermann* (a version of the medieval morality play *Everyman*) and the Russian creator of dreams Leonid Andreyev in *The Life of Man, The Black Maskers,* and *King Hunger.* In some plays, the symbolism was simply an extended and elusive metaphor; in others the symbol was obtrusive, with figures like Death or Hunger appearing on the stage—as in Andreyev's plays. The personification of abstractions, indeed, has persisted to some degree ever since the vogue of symbolism between 1890 and 1914. We may cite such later examples as Alberto Casella's *Death Takes a Holiday,* Paul Osborn's *On Borrowed Time,* in which Death, or Mr. Brink, wears a bowler hat, and Philip Barry's *Here Come the Clowns* in which the Devil is a vaudeville illusionist.

The best and most lasting effect of symbolism, and not only on the nonrealistic but on the realistic theatre of all gradations, came from the efforts of scene designers and stage directors. Artists of the theatre became aware of the illogicality and wastefulness of too much literal procedure in a medium that is essentially make-believe. After all, the "fourth wall" is only empty space. Foreign characters in a play do not speak their own tongue but that of the country in which the production takes place. And even the most natural acting violates actual reality in order to convey an orderly impression of reality. In time, naturalism was supplanted by a "selective realism," and this is the prevailing style today.

The reaction to naturalism in the nineties went much further, however, than mere selectivity in stage design. The word "theatricality," which had been buried with so much opprobrium by the naturalists, was restored to good standing. Opposed to Antoine's Théâtre Libre there arose little "art" theatres which strove to swing the tide back to theatricalism in the name of beauty and spiritual truth. As early as 1890, the French poet Paul Fort established his Théâtre d'Art and dedicated it to the discovery of "the miracle of daily life, the sense of the mysterious." Three years later, Lugné-Poë produced Maeterlinck's penumbral *Pelléas and Mélisande* there, and then founded the Théâtre de l'Oeuvre, where he gave imaginative productions of Ibsen's romantic tale *Peer Gynt,* Hauptmann's symbolist play *The Sunken Bell,* Maeterlinck's *Monna Vanna,* and the French poet Paul Claudel's *The Tidings Brought to Mary.* The art theatres soon spread over Europe, sometimes founded or supervised by the playwrights themselves—by Strindberg and Pirandello, for example.

Efforts to depart from realism led to simplifications and formalizations of the stage. There was even a return to Elizabethan platform staging in Jocza Savits' Shakespeare Theatre in Munich and William Poel's Elizabethan Stage Society in England. Especially effective were the simplifications achieved by Jacques Copeau in his Théâtre du Vieux Colombier, established in Paris in 1913. Here the forestage was lengthened into an "apron" in the Elizabethan manner and the practically bare stage was backed by a permanent set. Other departures brought the nonrealistic painter into the theatre. Just as the Duke of Meiningen had used settings by realistic painters, French producers employed Picasso, Matisse, Derain, Braque, and Léger.

These and many other efforts to "retheatricalize" the theatre were directly or indirectly inspired by the work of the two poets of the physical theatre Adolphe Appia and Gordon Craig. And significantly the first impetus came from music, the least representational of the arts.

Early nineteenth-century romanticists had long ago held the doctrine that music was the ideal of all art and that the theatre could reach its apotheosis only in music. The philosopher Nietzsche stressed the same doctrine in *The Birth of Tragedy,* and his friend Wagner's significant innovations in opera, which he called music-drama, served the romantic ideal of fusing the arts into a single overwhelming theatrical experience. Wagner's formula, "Music is the soul of drama, drama is the body of music."

announced a synthesis of the arts to which all his major operas were devoted. The great composer regarded himself as primarily a theatrician.

Wagner's far-flung dreams for stagecraft were translated into theatrical design by his Swiss disciple, Adolphe Appia (1862–1928), who had worked with him at Bayreuth. In 1895 appeared Appia's *La mise en scène du drame Wagnérien,* with eighteen superb designs for the Wagnerian operas; in 1899 appeared *Die Musik und die Inszenierung* (translated from a French text); this was followed by a series of shorter studies. Antipathetic to the naturalism that had gained a foothold in Paris a dozen years before, Appia wanted to endow scenic representation with the fluid and suggestive quality of music—that "loftiest expression of the eternal in art," as he called it. The elements of scenic design were to be the scenery, the floor, the moving actor, and the lighted space. The theatre that projects the dramatist's script was to present a perfect synthesis, a single effect. And the unifying element was to be light, which was no longer to provide a blank visibility but was to blend the scene and the actors, thereby creating a unified mood and conveying the "essence" of a dramatic production. Only light, Appia declared, can express "the inner nature of all appearance." Light, with its "infinite capacity for varying nuance," is the "counterpart of a musical score," and it must play as directly upon the emotions as music.

Appia's influence after 1900, especially on Max Reinhardt and on the later expressionists, was to prove tremendous, even though the Wagnerian opera house in Bayreuth did not use his designs and few of them were seen anywhere on the stage. If excesses of grandiosity and pretentious spirituality may be laid at Appia's door, owing to his advocacy of penumbral masses on the stage, his lessons were reflected in the best productions of the present century. Ellen Terry's impulsive son, Gordon Craig, was his spiritual brother, and, being a much more strident pamphleteer, he succeeded in popularizing the doctrine of theatricality. He, too, considered the ideal production of a play to be a single effect that would engage all the senses simultaneously and would address itself directly to the spirit; he convinced stage designers and directors that suggestion is the supreme law of the theatre. "Actuality, accuracy of detail, is useless upon the stage," he declared. But by means of suggestion "you may bring to the stage a sense of all things." The main instrument of suggestion, moreover, is organization, or design, and every production needs a pattern. So concerned was Craig with the inviolability of "design" that at one time he even wanted to banish the living actor as an unreliable agent too easily disturbed by accidental factors like the emotions; the "ideal and tentative solution" proposed by Craig was a "super-marionette." With his magazine *The Mask* and a series of pamphlets and books, the first of which, *The Art of the Theatre,* appeared in 1905, Craig took the theatre by storm.

If Craig was impractical, he nevertheless set up an ideal of production and scenic design. The practical directors and designers who followed parallel paths or caught fire from his ideas at least discarded literal realism. From Appia, moreover, the scenic artists took the basic principle of their art—the use of light as an expressive medium. If Appia the Wagnerian romanticist affected theatrical art only slightly, Appia the practical forerunner of contemporary lighting technique still dominates the theatre, even when this theatre continues to express realism.

The leaders of modern scenic design, however, would have been considerably less influential if they had not found able support from stage directors, and among these Max Reinhardt (1873–1943) assumed undisputed leadership. In starting many projects of imaginative theatre in Germany and Austria before and after the First World War, and in bringing some of his productions as far west as America, Reinhardt became a major influence. He developed a delicate production style in 1922 at the tiny Redoutensaal in Vienna, where he placed a platform at one end of an eighteenth-century ballroom and used nothing but a beautiful rococo screen as a permanent scenic background. He also went to the other extreme, staging great pageants such as *The Miracle* in 1912. (His last spectacle, staged in 1937 in New York, was Franz Werfel's chronicle of the Jewish people *The Eternal Road,* with settings by Norman Bel Geddes.) He gave poetic productions to the romantic plays that were supplanting naturalism at the beginning of his career in 1902. In addition to giving modern poets a hearing by staging poetic works of Maeterlinck and Hofmannsthal, he dusted off Goethe's and Schiller's youthful plays in some spectacular productions. The symbolists won a major victory when Reinhardt was appointed to succeed the naturalist Otto Brahm as director of Berlin's Deutsches Theater in 1905.

Reinhardt brought back the theatricality of the theatre by departing from the peepshow, fourth-wall stage of realism. He renewed the lost connection between the audience and the stage. In producing *Sumurûn,* in 1910, for example, he employed a runway that extended in Japanese theatrical style from the stage well into the audience. For *The Miracle,* two years later, he redesigned the entire theatre building as a cathedral in order to make the public participate in the religious experience of the play. He was not averse, it is true, to employing realism when it served his purposes, but he was willing to resort to any device or to any degree of stylization. An eclectic artist, he did not hesitate to help himself to any older style of theatrical production that suited his taste and his interpretation of a play or to combine a variety of styles. The circus ring or "mass theatre" suited him on some occasions just as well as the most intimate type of staging in a small room. He was adept at employing the simplest devices on the one hand, and the most complicated stage machinery, such as revolving stages, on the other. In his work, the misty impressionism advocated by Appia and Gordon Craig won spectacular victories. Other artists of the stage, especially Jacques Copeau in Paris at his Théâtre du Vieux Colombier, labored with tact and penetration, with grace and understanding. Reinhardt triumphed with effects that publicized the art theatre with Germanic thoroughness and *éclat.*

EXPRESSIONISM AND ITS SEQUELS

Notable after the poetic and spectacular ventures of the symbolists and of Reinhardt the showman was the work of the expressionists. Expressionism was foreshadowed by the dramatic experiments of Strindberg and Wedekind and became full blown after the First World War, especially in Central Europe. Between 1919 and 1925, in fact, the new style promised to effect a challenging transvaluation of dramatic and theatrical values.

Expressionistic techniques were employed not only by undisciplined exhibitionists but by playwrights whose motives were anything but superficial. Writers such as Strindberg and O'Neill endeavored to express personal tensions and problems they considered representative of modern man's alienation in materialistic society. Believing that poetic feeling alone was ineffectual and that realism could project neither inner experience nor the external world as it presented itself to the troubled spirit, they resorted to a fragmentary, constantly dissolving picture. They regarded the inner self not as a fairly orderly organism that moved more or less clearly toward well-defined, attainable ends such as winning a girl in marriage or getting on in business, but as a highly unstable compound of promptings and confusions. The concept of a unified self was a product of eighteenth-century rationalism and nineteenth-century materialism and mechanistic science. Its ideal representatives were the settled people and the career men of the bourgeois world. The rebels against this society were actually no different in spirit or outlook since they too had settled convictions, clear aims, and simple goals realizable by the application of common sense and well-directed efforts. But what if a career or an attainable program of reform was no longer considered a desirable objective? What if it could not be pursued or even entertained by a divided and bedeviled personality? What if the individual's major difficulty was precisely his lack of a unified self that could look out through a clear pane of perceptions at a plainly outlined world?

Such dramatists as Strindberg and O'Neill concerned themselves with the inner fact of psychological division. The form of plays such as *The Dream Play, The Spook Sonata, Emperor Jones,* and *The Hairy Ape* therefore became a whirl of fragmentary events in short scenes. And since the external world is the world formed by the perceiver, it fragmented itself, too. It appeared dislocated, turned out of shape, and exaggerated by the character's state of mind, as well as, of course, by the author, who intended to give us his view of the world as distressingly disordered and of the times as wholly out of joint. Strindberg, for example, made life on this planet look like a nightmare in *The Dream Play,* in support of his more or less Buddhist view in the play that all life was a delusion and a meaningless suffering. Supplementary characters changed their identity again and again or acquired abnormal attributes in Strindberg's expressionist plays. O'Neill's burly stoker in *The Hairy Ape* hurls himself at well-dressed citizens coming out of church only to rebound from them because they represent a society to which he cannot belong.

Making a subjective world out of an objective one ordered by conventional perceptions, playwrights even abolished the conventions of time and place. The Officer in *The Dream Play* changes from youth to middle age to old age with uncanny rapidity. Past and present time mingled freely in expressionist drama; memory scenes intruded into a present situation and not only dominated but altered it. Strindberg's Officer goes back to his childhood school as a teacher only to find himself a pupil again, unable to do simple arithmetic. O'Neill's Emperor Jones is assailed by memories of his past as he tries to escape from his enemies—memories of life on the chain gang in the United States, which he had experienced personally, and "racial" fears of ghosts and of the auction blocks of the slave traffic.

Expressionists, then, found uses not merely for conventional fantasy as old as the theatre but for dream formations and for explosions of the Freudian and Jungian "unconscious." The playwrights' inventions appeared not in the context of stable, everyday consciousness like the story of *A Midsummer Night's Dream* (which lent itself ideally to a romantic Reinhardt production) but in the elusive context of an altered field of consciousness. The significant element in expressionism was the "psychological," by which is meant neither the ordinary probing into the motivations of characters in realistic drama nor the simple, mechanistic psychology of the nineteenth century before the work of Charcot and other forerunners of Freud. Expressionism presented processes of exaggeration, condensation, and distortion that defy Aristotelian logic or have a subconscious logic of their own. The theatre began to play host to the phenomena of "free association," the "stream of consciousness," depersonalization, strange recurrences, "split" personality, schizophrenic

behavior, and mental telepathy. By comparison with the explorations undertaken by expressionist playwrights, Arthur Miller's imaginative treatment of Willy Loman in *Death of a Salesman* is elementary.

Expressionism, however, was applied, not only to psychologically unique experience; both Strindberg and O'Neill, whose primary concerns were psychological and spiritual, employed the expressionist technique for social commentary as well. *The Dream Play* clearly points a finger at the failure of society as well as of individuals, and *The Hairy Ape* is less important as the drama of an individual stoker who went berserk after being snubbed than as the story of humanity's disorientation. Indeed, the application of expressionism to social drama gave us many challenging plays, from Wedekind's first assault on sexual taboos in his tragedy of adolescence *The Awakening of Spring* (1898) to the dramas of social conflict with which the theatre abounded after 1918. To dramas of antiwar protest and social revolt, especially after the First World War, expressionist playwrights brought hortatory and nervous dialogue, high-strung characters, and a general explosiveness. They were also greatly concerned with the theme of modern mechanization, and writers like Georg Kaiser (in *The Coral* and *Gas I* and *II*) and Karel Capek (in *R. U. R.*) foretold disaster for an over-industrialized, overmechanized world, using an appropriate style of stenographic dialogue and depersonalization of characters. For social satire, moreover, the expressionistic style proved particularly effective insofar as extravaganza is more lively and pointed than humdrum slices of life and pedestrian problem plays. Before 1920, the German playwright Carl Sternheim cultivated an acrid antibourgeois satire in comedies such as *Burgher Schippel* and *The Snob,* and Georg Kaiser exposed the shams of society under the Hohenzollern monarchy in animated nightmares when he wrote *From Morn to Midnight* (1916). After 1920, expressionistic satire was adopted even by playwrights in America, and the results were gratifying in Elmer Rice's *The Adding Machine,* Kaufman and Connelly's *Beggar on Horseback,* and John Howard Lawson's *Processional.* Expressionism made the social theatre theatrical; it is not surprising, therefore, that it should have lingered on long after the follies of its enthusiasts cast discredit on the expressionist movement and ushered in a reaction against its excesses of hysteria, irrationality, and confusion.

Expressionism was never given enough time to simmer down to the viable substance of art and become a well-established style of drama. Consequently, after 1925 expressionistic drama was no longer written with much frequency, although its devices have cropped up again and again, and its tone has been borrowed by playwrights more often than is realized. But the antinaturalistic style has continued to challenge the conventional theatre. It has exploded in a variety of exotic movements such as futurism and surrealism, producing oddities, such as the totally incomprehensible but entrancing *tour de force* by Virgil Thomson and Gertrude Stein, *Four Saints in Three Acts.* It has turned somersaults in the work of Jean Cocteau and has displayed an ingratiating madness in the plays of Saroyan. It has found a vital form in epic realism, impressively represented by a number of plays by Bertolt Brecht and by the Federal Theatre's living newspapers, *Power* and *One-Third of a Nation,* in the nineteen-thirties. Lyric drama flared up in the work of Federico García Lorca until his flame was extinguished by a fascist band, and other poets less endowed with theatrical talent, among them T. S. Eliot and W. H. Auden, have tried to create a modern poetic theatre. And it is significant that even in pragmatic America, playwrights such as Tennessee Williams and Arthur Miller have been applauded for combining realistic with imaginative writing. As for stagecraft, efforts to introduce expressive theatricalism continued to be made with singular success long after expressionism ceased to be a force in the theatre, and it is unlikely that imaginative artists will ever allow themselves to be suppressed by considerations of caution—or of money. The theatre of the twentieth century, facing the crossfire of political struggles and war of unprecedented magnitude and destructiveness, continued, and is likely to continue, to serve the spirit of poetry and imaginative truth.

Maurice Maeterlinck

(1862–1949)

At the beginning of the present century, Maurice Maeterlinck, according to James Huneker, signified to most Americans "a crazy crow masquerading in tail feathers plucked from the Swan of Avon." The scales were more than balanced, however, by the weight of critical opinion in Europe, where he was regarded as the promulgator and creator of a "new drama." Heralded as the messiah of the anti-naturalistic symbolist theatre, he was expected to free dramatic art from bondage to concrete but superficial fact and lead it by the hand into the wonderland of the imagination. By following his guidance, the drama would find itself—and not merely in Poe's misty midregions of Weir but in the forest of symbols where life is a high mystery of the soul and where the truths of life and death are finally revealed to the knight-errant! And there would be related rewards for any stage that would follow his pure vision. It would exfoliate itself from the sordid rags that naturalism had forced it to wear, as well as from the business suits of ordinary, bourgeois realism. The theatre would put on robes of gold and the glowing jewelry of poetry. It would also wear the noble mask of tragedy, and through the mask would be seen the soulful eyes of the Muse that looks upon eternal mystery and universal sorrow. The high art of tragedy would return again to a theatre demeaned by encounters in the cold glare of the workaday world.

Even that irascible genius of naturalism Strindberg, who was not often given to idolatry, became reverential toward Maeterlinck, acclaimed him a master, and paid him the tribute of imitation for a time. And the citadel of naturalistic stagecraft, the Moscow Art Theatre, also succumbed to Maeterlinck's spell, producing his one-act plays *The Blind* and *Interior* on October 2, 1904 (some nine months after presenting the realistic masterpiece *The Cherry Orchard*), and staging *The Blue Bird* on September 30, 1908. Poet, essayist, mystic, entomologist, and philosopher as well as dramatist, Maeterlinck was a potent figure in European culture until after 1910, when the tide of "Maeterlinckism" began to recede.

Maeterlinck was a Belgian, born in Ghent and educated at its university, although his name is linked chiefly with French letters and theatre. After practising law in a desultory fashion, he went to Paris in 1886 and joined the circle of symbolist poets there, publishing in 1889 a collection of dreamful, loosely organized poems, *Serres chaudes,* comparable to the hallucinatory poetry of Arthur Rimbaud. That year he also produced a bizarre tragedy of fear and fate, *La Princesse Maleine,* reminiscent in its violence and moodiness of the plays of Elizabethans such as John Webster and Cyril Tourneur. Its melancholy and its assault on the nervous system with eerie atmosphere and haunting dialogue created a strong impression. The naturalistic writer Octave Mirbeau, writing in the columns of *Figaro* in 1890, called the play the most inspired work of the times and lauded it as "more tragic" than *Macbeth* and superior in meaningfulness to *Hamlet.* These extraordinary overstatements about an overwrought drama of hatred and murder made the twenty-eight-year-old author the most talked-of new playwright in Europe.

This undeserved reputation was soon made more deserving in 1890 by two symbolic short mood pieces, *The Intruder* and *The Blind.* These were followed by *The Seven Princesses* in 1891; the full-length variant of Dante's Paolo and Francesca story, *Pelléas and Mélisande,* in 1892; the affecting one-acter *Interior* and *The Death of Tintagiles,* both in 1894. Their effect communicated itself easily as a dramatic tension and as poetry. The plays also lent themselves admirably to an atmospheric type of staging widely divergent from the precision of realistic stagecraft. And Maeterlinck himself translated his practice into a widely noticed dramatic theory in *The Treasure of the Humble,* published in 1896. In addition to paying tribute to the mysticism and transcendentalism of the men he admired (among whom were the German romanticist Novalis and Ralph Waldo Emerson), Maeterlinck set down thoughts on art that impressed an entire generation with the possibility of creating a new style of dramatic composition.

A play, according to one essay in *The Treasure of the Humble,* should penetrate beneath the surface of reality. Everything concrete and definable is unimportant by comparison with the inner life of man and the universe, and this life is a mystery. Indeed, Maeterlinck believed that ideally his early plays should be acted by marionettes. The human actor would spoil the effect of plays in which atmosphere and vague intimations were intended to convey a universal and largely unutterable experience. The drama should deal with the ultimate reality of the soul rather than with transparent physical reality. For this purpose, moreover, action was to be supplanted by states of feeling. Truth would be served not only to the degree that there is more reality in spirit than in matter, as Plato and Plotinus had taught long ago, but to the degree that much of life is uneventful.

For Maeterlinck there was supreme drama in an externally inactive presentation of an old man sitting in his armchair at night with a lamp beside him, "giving unconscious ear to all the eternal laws that reign about his house, interpreting, without comprehending, the silence of doors and windows and the quivering voice of the light, submitting with bent head to the presence of his soul and his destiny." Such a man, although motionless, lived in reality "a deeper, more human, and more universal life" than the usual characters of the drama—"than the lover who strangles his mistress, the captain who conquers in battle, or the husband who avenges his honor."

From the contemplation of uneventful life, no matter how humble, the dramatist would acquire a high, dignified art and convey a tragic sense of life much more true to fact than the tragedies of violent struggle. Conflict was unnecessary in the drama, and there was no need for showing us the human will constantly engaged in battle. Even dialogue, as normally written for the theatre, was apt to be false because it was always definite and always eloquent. Maeterlinck chose for his slogan an old medieval inscription on a door in Bruges: "Within me there is more." Unspoken dialogue was often more eloquent and significant. There are pregnant silences that teem with inexpressible feeling and thought, and the best modern drama would use silence to good tragic and metaphysical effect. Also, dialogue should be used not only to promote the situation but, as in all great tragedies, to reveal soul states. In great art, it is the dialogue superfluous to the action that draws us closest to beauty and the lofty truths of the spirit. The dialogue that implies rather than states, the mood, or atmosphere, the profound suggestion, and the overtone were to be the most valuable ingredients of dramatic composition. It was not only desirable, then, but possible to create a "static drama" different from the time-honored theatre of primitive violence and brutal passion. Maeterlinck cited the superiority of *Hamlet* to *Othello* as an example, writing that "Othello does not appear to live the august daily life of Hamlet, who has the time to live, inasmuch as he does not act." He added that it was an ancient error to assume that we live our truest lives when we are possessed by some passion. The ideal of dramatic art should be the representation of a "stasis."

One may question all of Maeterlinck's premises, and Maeterlinck himself departed from them, mingling mood and action in *Pelléas and Mélisande* and launching into violently active drama with the romantic Renaissance story of *Monna Vanna* (1902). He came to realize that it was impossible to write long plays effectively without recourse to active events, and years later told his correspondent Barrett Clark not to attach too much weight to his theory of static drama: it was a theory of his youth, "worth what most literary theories are worth—that

is, almost nothing. Maeterlinck, indeed, wrote a good many plays which did not adhere to his pristine notions of a new kind of dramatic poetry. He also began to abandon his pessimistic view of life in 1901, when he made the heroine of his *Ariane and Blue-Beard* free Blue-Beard's prisoners, and when he composed a tribute to triumphant love in *Joyzelle* (1903). In this play, the magician Merlin subjects a girl to every conceivable trial only to find her invincibly devoted in love. Maeterlinck came, indeed, to be regarded as a leader of spiritual "uplift" when he wrote a series of semiscientific, philosophically affirmative books. His search for a ruling spirit led him to engage in occult studies and to write a good deal of pabulum for the popular press.

It must also be admitted that many of his stage pieces were exceedingly tenuous. His *Sister Beatrice* (1900) and *Ariane and Blue-Beard* (1901) are little more than libretti. His medieval cast of mind often caused him to play with horror in an artificially romantic and decorative style, as in *The Seven Princesses*. He cultivated disingenuousness a trifle too strenuously in plays such as *The Seven Princesses* (1891) and *Alladine and Palomides* (1894); the naïveté of *The Blue Bird* (1908), combined with its banal idea that happiness is to be found at home, leaves this once extravagantly esteemed fantasy shelterless except in children's theatres. He often promised more with the portentousness of his atmosphere, as in the theatrically effective *Death of Tintagiles* (1894), than he actually delivered. And even the comparatively active drama *Pelléas and Mélisande,* produced in many countries, is now better known through the Claude Debussy opera of the same title, because the slender story is supersaturated with poetic mood and attenuated by the elfin character of the heroine. It may be accurately said of Maeterlinck's dramatic work in general that there is less in it than meets the eye. Nor would such criticism have troubled Maeterlinck, because he tried to make his plays approximate the state of music and it was the point of his argument that what meets the eye is the least important part of reality. On the whole, his plays had more manner than they had matter.

Nevertheless, during the early part of his career Maeterlinck achieved a pervasive importance in the theatre which was officially acknowledged in 1911 with the Nobel Prize for literature. As a critic of other men's work he drew attention to the presence of poetry even in such masterpieces of naturalism as Ibsen's *Ghosts* and Tolstoy's *The Power of Darkness,* reminding his contemporaries that there was more in these plays than their demonstration of a problem. (He was, indeed, a better critic than many of Ibsen's champions when he wrote in 1901 that in *Ghosts,* "in a stuffy middle-class drawing-room, unbearable, maddening to the characters, there breaks forth one of the most terrible mysteries of human destiny," which took the form of "a law of justice or injustice, formidable and only recently suspected—the law of heredity.") His emphasis on the value of dramatizing inner experience exerted a long-lasting influence which many an expressionistic or simply psychological drama reflected after 1900. His idea of static drama bore fruit in at least one masterpiece, John Millington Synge's *Riders to the Sea*, and his depreciation of the role of violent action in plays was vindicated in realistic, rather than romantic, art when Chekhov wrote his masterly dramas *The Three Sisters* and *The Cherry Orchard*. The ideal of stasis was echoed in many quarters at the beginning of the century, and James Joyce was to recall it memorably (and more sensibly than Maeterlinck) in his autobiographical novel *Portrait of the Artist as a Young Man* (1914–1915) when he made the young hero elaborate a theory of tragedy to a schoolmate. About the same time, Leonid Andreyev, Maeterlinck's ardent Russian disciple, asserted in his *Letter on the Theatre* (1914) that action was unnecessary because in modern times "life has gone within," having become "psychological." The true contemporary hero, Andreyev maintained and demonstrated in his own plays, was a character in whom we are interested because he represents "human thought, with all its sufferings, joys and struggles." These adumbrations of Maeterlinckian theory bring us a step nearer to the inner agonies of O'Neill's plays and to the psychological complications represented by Pirandello.

It is in the early plays, *The Intruder, The Blind,* and *Interior* that Maeterlinck's artistry is most successful. Among these, *The Intruder* is the purest expression of his aims. If the play has no external conflict and approaches a condition of stasis, it nevertheless progresses from point to point in representing the growing apprehension of the characters. Although they obviously cannot cope with anything so intangible as death, their plight does represent the oldest and most universal of all conflicts. Conflict moreover, has its equivalent here in tension; and tension may be essentially more dynamic than mere melodramatic excitation. The grandfather makes an impressive central figure in the penumbral world of the play, and death, as sensed largely through his apprehensiveness, is an intensely dramatic reality. *The Intruder* also involves the actuality of a woman dying in another room after giving birth to a child, and the playwright presents his characters in an atmospheric setting without the customary trappings of medieval romance. There is no pretentious and anachronistic romanticism in this play. Fortunately, moreover, Maeterlinck had the good sense not to overextend and enfeeble his poetic effects. Like *The Blind* and *Interior, The Intruder* is short enough to be sustained by its tension. Nor does Maeterlinck overstrain the mystery he invokes by means of half-uttered thoughts, haunting repetitions, and still more haunting silences. Except in *Pelléas and Mélisande,* Maeterlinck's most impressive triumphs entailed a short, exquisite flight.

BIBLIOGRAPHY: A. Bailly, *Maeterlinck,* 1931; Eric Bentley, *The Playwright as Thinker* (pp. 90–94, 96–97, 325–328), 1946; Jethro Bithell, *Life and Writings of Maurice Maeterlinck,* 1913; *Columbia Dictionary of Modern European Literature* (p. 501), 1947; James Huneker, *Iconoclasts* (pp. 367–429), 1905; Maurice Maeterlinck, "The Tragical in Daily Life," in *The Treasure of the Humble,* 1907, and in Barrett H. Clark, *Chief European Theories of the Drama* (pp. 411–413), 1918, 1945; Maeterlinck, "Silence," in *The Treasure of the Humble;* Maeterlinck, "Preface to the Plays," 1901, in Clark, *Chief European Theories of the Drama* (pp. 414–416).

THE INTRUDER

By Maurice Maeterlinck

TRANSLATED FROM THE FRENCH

CHARACTERS

THE GRANDFATHER [*blind*]   THE THREE DAUGHTERS   THE SERVANT
THE FATHER   THE UNCLE

A sombre room in an old Château. A door on the right, a door on the left, and a small concealed door in a corner. At the back, stained-glass windows, in which green is the dominant color, and a glass door giving on to a terrace. A big Dutch clock in one corner. A lighted lamp.

THE THREE DAUGHTERS: Come here, grandfather. Sit down under the lamp.

THE GRANDFATHER: There does not seem to me to be much light here.

THE FATHER: Shall we go out on the terrace, or stay in this room?

THE UNCLE: Would it not be better to stay here? It has rained the whole week, and the nights are damp and cold.

THE ELDEST DAUGHTER: But the stars are shining.

THE UNCLE: Oh the stars—that's nothing.

THE GRANDFATHER: We had better stay here. One never knows what may happen.

THE FATHER: There is no longer any cause for anxiety. The danger is over, and she is saved. . . .

THE GRANDFATHER: I believe she is not doing so well. . . .

THE FATHER: Why do you say that?

THE GRANDFATHER: I have heard her voice.

THE FATHER: But since the doctors assure us we may be easy. . . .

THE UNCLE: You know quite well that your father-in-law likes to alarm us needlessly.

THE GRANDFATHER: I don't see things as you do.

THE UNCLE: You ought to rely on us, then, who can see. She looked very well this afternoon. She is sleeping quietly now; and we are not going to mar, needlessly, the first pleasant evening that chance has put in our way. . . . It seems to me we have a perfect right to peace, and even to laugh a little, this evening, without fear.

THE FATHER: That's true; this is the first time I have felt at home with my family since this terrible confinement.

THE UNCLE: When once illness has come into a house, it is as though a stranger had forced himself into the family circle.

THE FATHER: And then you understand, too, that you can count on no one outside the family.

THE UNCLE: You are quite right.

THE GRANDFATHER: Why couldn't I see my poor daughter to-day?

THE UNCLE: You know quite well—the doctor forbade it.

THE GRANDFATHER: I do not know what to think. . . .

THE UNCLE: It is useless to worry.

THE GRANDFATHER: [*Pointing to the door on the left*] She cannot hear us?

THE FATHER: We will not talk too loud; besides, the door is very thick, and the Sister of Mercy is with her, and she is sure to warn us if we are making too much noise.

THE GRANDFATHER: [*Pointing to the door on the right*] He cannot hear us?

THE FATHER: No, no.

THE GRANDFATHER: He is asleep?

THE FATHER: I suppose so.

THE GRANDFATHER: Some one had better go and see.

THE UNCLE: The little one would cause *me* more anxiety than your wife. It is now several weeks since he was born, and he has scarcely stirred. He has not cried once all the time! He is like a wax doll.

THE GRANDFATHER: I think he will be deaf—dumb too, perhaps—the usual result of a marriage between cousins. . . . [*A reproving silence*]

THE FATHER: I could almost wish him ill for the suffering he has caused his mother.

THE UNCLE: Do be reasonable; it is not the poor little thing's fault. He is quite alone in the room?

THE FATHER: Yes; the doctor does not wish him to stay in his mother's room any longer.

THE UNCLE: But the nurse is with him?

THE FATHER: No; she has gone to rest a little; she has well deserved it these last few days. Ursula, just go and see if he is asleep.

THE ELDEST DAUGHTER: Yes, father. [The Three Sisters *get up, and go into the room on the right, hand in hand*]

THE FATHER: When will your sister come?

THE UNCLE: I think she will come about nine.

THE FATHER: It is past nine. I hope she will come this evening, my wife is so anxious to see her.

THE UNCLE: She is sure to come. This will be the first time she has been here?

THE FATHER: She has never been in the house.

THE UNCLE: It is very difficult for her to leave her convent.

THE FATHER: Will she be alone?

THE UNCLE: I expect one of the nuns will come with her. They are not allowed to go out alone.

THE FATHER: But she is the Superior.

THE UNCLE: The rule is the same for all.

THE GRANDFATHER: Do you not feel anxious?

THE UNCLE: Why should we feel anxious? What's the good of harping on that? There is nothing more to fear.

THE GRANDFATHER: Your sister is older than you?

THE UNCLE: She is the eldest.

THE GRANDFATHER: I do not know what ails me; I feel uneasy. I wish your sister were here.

THE UNCLE: She will come; she promised to.

THE GRANDFATHER: Ah, if this evening were only over!

[The Three Daughters *come in again*]

THE FATHER: He is asleep?

THE ELDEST DAUGHTER: Yes, father; he is sleeping soundly.

THE UNCLE: What shall we do while we are waiting?

THE GRANDFATHER: Waiting for what?

THE UNCLE: Waiting for our sister.

THE FATHER: You see nothing coming, Ursula?

THE ELDEST DAUGHTER: [*At the window*] Nothing, father.

THE FATHER: Not in the avenue? Can you see the avenue?

THE DAUGHTER: Yes, father; it is moonlight, and I can see the avenue as far as the cypress wood.

THE GRANDFATHER: And you do not see any one?

THE DAUGHTER: No one, grandfather.

THE UNCLE: What sort of a night is it?

THE DAUGHTER: Very fine. Do you hear the nightingales?

THE UNCLE: Yes, yes.

THE DAUGHTER: A little wind is rising in the avenue.

THE GRANDFATHER: A little wind in the avenue?

THE DAUGHTER: Yes; the trees are trembling a little.

THE UNCLE: I am surprised that my sister is not here yet.

THE GRANDFATHER: I cannot hear the nightingales any longer.

THE DAUGHTER: I think some one has come into the garden, grandfather.

THE GRANDFATHER: Who is it?

THE DAUGHTER: I do not know: I can see no one.

THE UNCLE: Because there is no one there.

THE DAUGHTER: There must be some one in the garden; the nightingales have suddenly ceased singing.

THE GRANDFATHER: But I do not hear any one coming.

THE DAUGHTER: Some one must be passing by the pond, because the swans are ruffled.

ANOTHER DAUGHTER: All the fishes in the pond are diving suddenly.

THE FATHER: You cannot see any one.

THE DAUGHTER: No one, father.

THE FATHER: But the pond lies in the moonlight. . . .

THE DAUGHTER: Yes; I can see that the swans are ruffled.

THE UNCLE: I am sure it is my sister who is scaring them. She must have come in by the little gate.

THE FATHER: I cannot understand why the dogs do not bark.

THE DAUGHTER: I can see the watch-dog right at the back of his kennel. The swans are crossing to the other bank! . . .

THE UNCLE: They are afraid of my sister. I will go and see. [*He calls*] Sister! sister! Is that you? . . . There is no one there.

THE DAUGHTER: I am sure that some one has come into the garden. You will see.

THE UNCLE: But she would answer me!

THE GRANDFATHER: Are not the nightingales beginning to sing again, Ursula?

THE DAUGHTER: I cannot hear one anywhere.

THE GRANDFATHER: But there is no noise.

THE FATHER: There is a silence of the grave.

THE GRANDFATHER: It must be a stranger that is frightening them, for if it were one of the family they would not be silent.

THE UNCLE: How much longer are you going to discuss these nightingales?

THE GRANDFATHER: Are all the windows open, Ursula?

THE DAUGHTER: The glass door is open, grandfather.

THE GRANDFATHER: It seems to be that the cold is penetrating into the room.

THE DAUGHTER: There is a little wind in the garden, grandfather, and the rose-leaves are falling.

THE FATHER: Well, shut the door. It is late.

THE DAUGHTER: Yes, father. . . . I cannot shut the door.

THE TWO OTHER DAUGHTERS: We cannot shut the door.

THE GRANDFATHER: Why, what is the matter with the door, my children?

THE UNCLE: You need not say that in such an extraordinary voice. I will go and help them.

THE ELDEST DAUGHTER: We cannot manage to shut it quite.

THE UNCLE: It is because of the damp. Let us all push together. There must be something in the way.

THE FATHER: The carpenter will set it right tomorrow.

THE GRANDFATHER: Is the carpenter coming to-morrow?

THE DAUGHTER: Yes, grandfather; he is coming to do some work in the cellar.

THE GRANDFATHER: He will make a noise in the house.

THE DAUGHTER: I will tell him to work quietly.

[*Suddenly the sound of a scythe being sharpened is heard outside*]

THE GRANDFATHER: [*With a shudder*] Oh!

THE UNCLE: What is that?

THE DAUGHTER: I don't quite know; I think it is the gardener. I cannot quite see; he is in the shadow of the house.

THE FATHER: It is the gardener going to mow.

THE UNCLE: He mows by night?

THE FATHER: Is not to-morrow Sunday?—Yes.—I noticed that the grass was very long round the house.

THE GRANDFATHER: It seems to me that his scythe makes as much noise. . . .

THE DAUGHTER: He is mowing near the house.

THE GRANDFATHER: Can you see him, Ursula?

THE DAUGHTER: No, grandfather. He is standing in the dark.

THE GRANDFATHER: I am afraid he will wake my daughter.

THE UNCLE: We can scarcely hear him.

THE GRANDFATHER: It sounds as if he were mowing inside the house.

THE UNCLE: The invalid will not hear it! There is no danger.

THE FATHER: It seems to me that the lamp is not burning well this evening.

THE UNCLE: It wants filling.

THE FATHER: I saw it filled this morning. It has burnt badly since the window was shut.

THE UNCLE: I fancy the chimney is dirty.

THE FATHER: It will burn better presently.

THE DAUGHTER: Grandfather is asleep. He has not slept for three nights.

THE FATHER: He has been so much worried.

THE UNCLE: He always worries too much. At times he will not listen to reason.

THE FATHER: It is quite excusable at his age.

THE UNCLE: God knows what we shall be like at his age!

THE FATHER: He is nearly eighty.

THE UNCLE: Then he has a right to be strange.

THE FATHER: He is like all blind people.

THE UNCLE: They think too much.

THE FATHER: They have too much time to spare.

THE UNCLE: They have nothing else to do.

THE FATHER: And, besides, they have no distractions.

THE UNCLE: That must be terrible.

THE FATHER: Apparently one gets used to it.

THE UNCLE: I cannot imagine it.

THE FATHER: They are certainly to be pitied.

THE UNCLE: Not to know where one is, not to know where one has come from, not to know whither one is going, not to be able to distinguish midday from midnight, or summer from winter—and always darkness, darkness! I would rather not live. Is it absolutely incurable?

THE FATHER: Apparently so.

THE UNCLE: But he is not absolutely blind?

THE FATHER: He can perceive a strong light.

THE UNCLE: Let us take care of our poor eyes.

THE FATHER: He often has strange ideas.

THE UNCLE: At times he is not at all amusing.

THE FATHER: He says absolutely everything he thinks.

THE UNCLE: But he was not always like this?

THE FATHER: No; once he was as rational as we are; he never said anything extraordinary. I am afraid Ursula encourages him a little too much; she answers all his questions. . . .

THE UNCLE: It would be better not to answer them. It's a mistaken kindness to him.

[*Ten o'clock strikes*]

THE GRANDFATHER: [*Waking up*] Am I facing the glass door?

THE DAUGHTER: You have had a nice sleep, grandfather?

THE GRANDFATHER: Am I facing the glass door?

THE DAUGHTER: Yes, grandfather.

THE GRANDFATHER: There is nobody at the glass door?

THE DAUGHTER: No, grandfather; I do not see any one.

THE GRANDFATHER: I thought some one was waiting. No one has come?

THE DAUGHTER: No one, grandfather.

THE GRANDFATHER: [*To the* Uncle *and* Father] And your sister has not come?

THE UNCLE: It is too late; she will not come now. It is not nice of her.

THE FATHER: I'm beginning to be anxious about her. [*A noise, as of some one coming into the house*]

THE UNCLE: She is here! Did you hear?

THE FATHER: Yes; some one has come in at the basement.

THE UNCLE: It must be our sister. I recognized her step.

THE GRANDFATHER: I heard slow footsteps.

THE FATHER: She came in very quietly.

THE UNCLE: She knows there is an invalid.

THE GRANDFATHER: I hear nothing now.

THE UNCLE: She will come up directly; they will tell her we are here.

THE FATHER: I am glad she has come.

THE UNCLE: I was sure she would come this evening.

THE GRANDFATHER: She is a very long time coming up.

THE UNCLE: It must be she.

THE FATHER: We are not expecting any other visitors.

THE GRANDFATHER: I cannot hear any noise in the basement.

THE FATHER: I will call the servant. We shall know how things stand. [*He pulls a bell-rope*]

THE GRANDFATHER: I can hear a noise on the stairs already.

THE FATHER: It is the servant coming up.

THE GRANDFATHER: To me it sounds as if she were not alone.

THE FATHER: She is coming up slowly. . . .

THE GRANDFATHER: I hear your sister's step!

THE FATHER: I can only hear the servant.

THE GRANDFATHER: It is your sister! It is your sister!

[*There is a knock at the little door*]

THE UNCLE: She is knocking at the door of the back stairs.

THE FATHER: I will go and open it myself. [*He opens the little door partly; the* Servant *remains outside in the opening*] Where are you?

THE SERVANT: Here, sir.

THE GRANDFATHER: Your sister is at the door?

THE UNCLE: I can only see the servant.

THE FATHER: It is only the servant. [*To the* Servant] Who was that, that came into the house?

THE SERVANT: Came into the house?

THE FATHER: Yes; some one came in just now?

THE SERVANT: No one came in, sir.

THE GRANDFATHER: Who is it sighing like that?

THE UNCLE: It is the servant; she is out of breath.

THE GRANDFATHER: Is she crying?

THE UNCLE: No; why should she be crying?

THE FATHER: [*To the* Servant] No one came in just now?

THE SERVANT: No, sir.

THE FATHER: But we heard some one open the door!

THE SERVANT: It was I shutting the door.

THE FATHER: It was open?

THE SERVANT: Yes, sir.

THE FATHER: Why was it open at this time of night?

THE SERVANT: I do not know, sir. I had shut it myself.

THE FATHER: Then who was it that opened it?

THE SERVANT: I do not know, sir. Some one must have gone out after me, sir. . . .

THE FATHER: You must be careful.—Don't push the door; you know what a noise it makes!

THE SERVANT: But, sir, I am not touching the door.

THE FATHER: But you are. You are pushing as if you were trying to get into the room.

THE SERVANT: But, sir, I am three yards away from the door.

THE FATHER: Don't talk so loud. . . .

THE GRANDFATHER: Are they putting out the light?

THE ELDEST DAUGHTER: No, grandfather.

THE GRANDFATHER: It seems to me it has grown pitch dark all at once.

THE FATHER: [*To the* Servant] You can go down again now; but do not make so much noise on the stairs.

THE SERVANT: I did not make any noise on the stairs.

THE FATHER: I tell you that you did make a noise. Go down quietly; you will wake your mistress. And if any one comes now, say that we are not at home.

THE UNCLE: Yes; say that we are not at home.

THE GRANDFATHER: [*Shuddering*] You must not say that!

THE FATHER: . . . Except to my sister and the doctor.

THE UNCLE: When will the doctor come?

THE FATHER: He will not be able to come before midnight. [*He shuts the door. A clock is heard striking eleven*]

THE GRANDFATHER: She has come in?

THE FATHER: Who?

THE GRANDFATHER: The servant.

THE FATHER: No, she has gone downstairs.

THE GRANDFATHER: I thought that she was sitting at the table.

THE UNCLE: The servant?

THE GRANDFATHER: Yes.

THE UNCLE: That would complete one's happiness!

THE GRANDFATHER: No one has come into the room?

THE FATHER: No; no one has come in.

THE GRANDFATHER: And your sister is not here?

THE UNCLE: Our sister has not come.

THE GRANDFATHER: You want to deceive me.

THE UNCLE: Deceive you?

THE GRANDFATHER: Ursula, tell me the truth, for the love of God!

THE ELDEST DAUGHTER: Grandfather! Grandfather! what is the matter with you?

THE GRANDFATHER: Something has happened! I am sure my daughter is worse! . . .

THE UNCLE: Are you dreaming?

THE GRANDFATHER: You do not want to tell me! . . . I can see quite well there is something. . . .

THE UNCLE: In that case you can see better than we can.

THE GRANDFATHER: Ursula, tell me the truth!

THE DAUGHTER: But we have told you the truth, grandfather!

THE GRANDFATHER: You do not speak in your ordinary voice.

THE FATHER: That is because you frighten her.

THE GRANDFATHER: Your voice is changed, too.

THE FATHER: You are going mad! [*He and the* Uncle *make signs to each other to signify the* Grandfather *has lost his reason*]

THE GRANDFATHER: I can hear quite well that you are afraid.

THE FATHER: But what should we be afraid of?

THE GRANDFATHER: Why do you want to deceive me?

THE UNCLE: Who is thinking of deceiving you?

THE GRANDFATHER: Why have you put out the light?

THE UNCLE: But the light has not been put out; there is as much light as there was before.

THE DAUGHTER: It seems to me that the lamp has gone down.

THE FATHER: I see as well now as ever.

THE GRANDFATHER: I have millstones on my eyes! Tell me, girls, what is going on here! Tell me, for the love of God, you who can see! I am here, all alone, in darkness without end! I do not know who seats himself beside me! I do not know what is happening a yard from me! . . . Why were you talking under your breath just now?

THE FATHER: No one was talking under his breath.

THE GRANDFATHER: You did talk in a low voice at the door.

THE FATHER: You heard all I said.

THE GRANDFATHER: You brought some one into the room! . . .

THE FATHER: But I tell you no one has come in!

THE GRANDFATHER: Is it your sister or a priest?— You should not try to deceive me.—Ursula, who was it that came in?

THE DAUGHTER: No one, grandfather.

THE GRANDFATHER: You must not try to deceive me; I know what I know.—How many of us are there here?

THE DAUGHTER: There are six of us round the table, grandfather.

THE GRANDFATHER: You are all round the table?

THE DAUGHTER: Yes, grandfather.

THE GRANDFATHER: You are there, Paul?

THE FATHER: Yes.

THE GRANDFATHER: You are there, Oliver?

THE UNCLE: Yes, of course I am here, in my usual place. That's not alarming, is it?

THE GRANDFATHER: You are there, Geneviève?

ONE OF THE DAUGHTERS: Yes, grandfather.

THE GRANDFATHER: You are there, Gertrude?

ANOTHER DAUGHTER: Yes, grandfather.

THE GRANDFATHER: You are here, Ursula?

THE ELDEST DAUGHTER: Yes, grandfather; next to you.

THE GRANDFATHER: And who is that sitting there?

THE DAUGHTER: Where do you mean, grandfather? —There is no one.

THE GRANDFATHER: There, there—in the midst of us!

THE DAUGHTER: But there is no one, grandfather!

THE FATHER: We tell you there is no one!

THE GRANDFATHER: But you cannot see—any of you!

THE UNCLE: Pshaw! You are joking.

THE GRANDFATHER: I do not feel inclined for joking, I can assure you.

THE UNCLE: Then believe those who can see.

THE GRANDFATHER: [Undecidedly] I thought there was some one . . . I believe I shall not live long. . . .

THE UNCLE: Why should we deceive you? What use would there be in that?

THE FATHER: It would be our duty to tell you the truth . . .

THE UNCLE: What would be the good of deceiving each other?

THE FATHER: You could not live in error long.

THE GRANDFATHER: [Trying to rise] I should like to pierce this darkness! . . .

THE FATHER: Where do you want to go?

THE GRANDFATHER: Over there. . . .

THE FATHER: Don't be so anxious.

THE UNCLE: You are strange this evening.

THE GRANDFATHER: It is all of you who seem to me to be strange!

THE FATHER: Do you want anything?

THE GRANDFATHER: I do not know what ails me.

THE ELDEST DAUGHTER: Grandfather! grandfather! What do you want, grandfather?

THE GRANDFATHER: Give me your little hands, my children.

THE THREE DAUGHTERS: Yes, grandfather.

THE GRANDFATHER: Why are you all three trembling, girls?

THE ELDEST DAUGHTER: We are scarcely trembling at all, grandfather.

THE GRANDFATHER: I fancy you are all three pale.

THE ELDEST DAUGHTER: It is late, grandfather, and we are tired.

THE FATHER: You must go to bed, and grandfather himself would do well to take a little rest.

THE GRANDFATHER: I could not sleep to-night!

THE UNCLE: We will wait for the doctor.

THE GRANDFATHER: Prepare for the truth.

THE UNCLE: But there is no truth!

THE GRANDFATHER: Then I do not know what there is!

THE UNCLE: I tell you there is nothing at all!

THE GRANDFATHER: I wish I could see my poor daughter!

THE FATHER: But you know quite well it is impossible; she must not be awakened unnecessarily.

THE UNCLE: You will see her to-morrow.

THE GRANDFATHER: There is no sound in her room.

THE UNCLE: I should be uneasy if I heard any sound.

THE GRANDFATHER: It is a very long time since I saw my daughter! . . . I took her hands yesterday evening, but I could not see her! . . . I do not know what has become of her. . . . I do not know how she is. . . . I do not know what her face is like now. . . . She must have changed these weeks! . . . I felt the little bones of her cheeks under my hands. . . . There is nothing but the darkness between her and me, and the rest of you! . . . I cannot go on living like this . . . this is not living. . . . You sit there, all of you, looking with open eyes at

my dead eyes, and not one of you has pity on me!
. . . I do not know what ails me. . . . No one tells
me what ought to be told me . . . And everything is
terrifying when one's dreams dwell upon it. . . .
But why are you not speaking?

THE UNCLE: What should we say, since you will
not believe us?

THE GRANDFATHER: You are afraid of betraying
yourselves!

THE FATHER: Come now, be rational!

THE GRANDFATHER: You have been hiding something from me for a long time! . . . Something has
happened in the house. . . . But I am beginning to
understand now. . . . You have been deceiving me
too long!—You fancy that I shall never know anything?—There are moments when I am less blind
than you, you know! . . . Do you think I have not
heard you whispering—for days and days—as if you
were in the house of some one who had been
hanged—I dare not say what I know this evening.
. . . But I shall know the truth! . . . I shall wait
for you to tell me the truth; but I have known it
for a long time, in spite of you!—And now, I feel
that you are all paler than the dead!

THE THREE DAUGHTERS: Grandfather! grandfather!
What is the matter, grandfather?

THE GRANDFATHER: It is not you that I am speaking of, girls. No; it is not you that I am speaking of.
. . . I know quite well you would tell me the truth
—if they were not by! . . . And besides, I feel
sure that they are deceiving you as well. . . . You
will see, children—you will see! . . . Do not I hear
you all sobbing?

THE FATHER: Is my wife really so ill?

THE GRANDFATHER: It is no good trying to deceive
me any longer; it is too late now, and I know the
truth better than you! . . .

THE UNCLE: But we are not blind; we are not.

THE FATHER: Would you like to go into your
daughter's room? This misunderstanding must be
put an end to.—Would you?

THE GRANDFATHER: [Becoming suddenly unde-
cided] No, no, not now—not yet.

THE UNCLE: You see, you are not reasonable.

THE GRANDFATHER: One never knows how much
a man has been unable to express in his life! . . .
Who made that noise?

THE ELDEST DAUGHTER: It is the lamp flickering,
grandfather.

THE GRANDFATHER: It seems to me to be very
unsteady—very!

THE DAUGHTER: It is the cold wind troubling
it. . . .

THE UNCLE: There is no cold wind, the windows
are shut.

THE DAUGHTER: I think it is going out.

THE FATHER: There is no more oil.

THE DAUGHTER: It has gone right out.

THE FATHER: We cannot stay like this in the dark.

THE UNCLE: Why not?—I am quite accustomed
to it.

THE FATHER: There is a light in my wife's room.

THE UNCLE: We will take it from there presently,
when the doctor has been.

THE FATHER: Well, we can see enough here; there
is the light from outside.

THE GRANDFATHER: Is it light outside?

THE FATHER: Lighter than here.

THE UNCLE: For my part, I would as soon talk
in the dark.

THE FATHER: So would I. [Silence]

THE GRANDFATHER: It seems to me the clock
makes a great deal of noise . . .

THE ELDEST DAUGHTER: That is because we are
not talking any more, grandfather.

THE GRANDFATHER: But why are you all silent?

THE UNCLE: What do you want us to talk about?
—You are really very peculiar to-night.

THE GRANDFATHER: Is it very dark in this room?

THE UNCLE: There is not much light. [Silence]

THE GRANDFATHER: I do not feel well, Ursula;
open the window a little.

THE FATHER: Yes, child; open the window a little.
I begin to feel the want of air myself. [The girl
opens the window]

THE UNCLE: I really believe we have stayed shut
up too long.

THE GRANDFATHER: Is the window open?

THE DAUGHTER: Yes, grandfather; it is wide open.

THE GRANDFATHER: One would not have thought
it was open, there was not a sound outside.

THE DAUGHTER: No, grandfather; there is not
the slightest sound.

THE FATHER: The silence is extraordinary!

THE DAUGHTER: One could hear an angel tread!

THE UNCLE: That is why I do not like the country.

THE GRANDFATHER: I wish I could hear some
sound. What o'clock is it, Ursula?

THE DAUGHTER: It will soon be midnight, grandfather. [Here the Uncle begins to pace up and down
the room]

THE GRANDFATHER: Who is that walking round us
like that?

THE UNCLE: Only I! only I! Do not be frightened!
I want to walk about a little. [Silence]—But I am
going to sit down again;—I cannot see where I am
going. [Silence]

THE GRANDFATHER: I wish I were out of this place.

THE DAUGHTER: Where would you like to go,
grandfather?

THE GRANDFATHER: I do not know where—into
another room, no matter where! no matter where!

THE FATHER: Where could we go?

THE UNCLE: It is too late to go anywhere else.

[Silence. They are sitting, motionless, round the
table]

THE GRANDFATHER: What is that I hear, Ursula?

THE DAUGHTER: Nothing, grandfather: it is the

leaves falling.—Yes, it is the leaves falling on the terrace.

THE GRANDFATHER: Go and shut the window, Ursula.

THE DAUGHTER: Yes, grandfather. [*She shuts the window, comes back, and sits down*]

THE GRANDFATHER: I am cold. [*Silence. The Three Sisters kiss each other*] What is that I hear now?

THE FATHER: It is the three sisters kissing each other.

THE UNCLE: It seems to me they are very pale this evening. [*Silence*]

THE GRANDFATHER: What is that I hear now, Ursula?

THE DAUGHTER: Nothing, grandfather; it is the clasping of my hands. [*Silence*]

THE GRANDFATHER: And that? . . .

THE DAUGHTER: I do not know, grandfather . . . perhaps my sisters are trembling a little? . . .

THE GRANDFATHER: I am afraid, too, my children.

[*Here a ray of moonlight penetrates through a corner of the stained glass, and throws strange gleams here and there in the room. A clock strikes midnight; at the last stroke there is a very vague sound, as of some one rising in haste*]

THE GRANDFATHER: [*Shuddering with peculiar horror*] Who is that who got up?

THE UNCLE: No one got up!

THE FATHER: I did not get up!

THE THREE DAUGHTERS: Nor I!—Nor I!—Nor I!

THE GRANDFATHER: Some one got up from the table!

THE UNCLE: Light the lamp! . . .

[*Cries of terror are suddenly heard from the child's room, on the right; these cries continue, with gradations of horror, until the end of the scene*]

THE FATHER: Listen to the child!

THE UNCLE: He has never cried before!

THE FATHER: Let us go and see him!

THE UNCLE: The light! The light!

[*At this moment, quick and heavy steps are heard in the room on the left.—Then a deathly silence.—They listen in mute terror, until the door of the room opens slowly; the light from it is cast into the room where they are sitting, and the Sister of Mercy appears on the threshold, in her black garments, and bows as she makes the sign of the cross, to announce the death of the wife. They understand, and, after a moment of hesitation and fright, silently enter the chamber of death, while the Uncle politely steps aside on the threshold to let the three girls pass. The blind man, left alone, gets up, agitated, and feels his way round the table in the darkness*]

THE GRANDFATHER: Where are you going?—Where are you going?—The girls have left me all alone!

CURTAIN

Edmond Rostand

(1868–1918)

Rostand's masterpiece, *Cyrano de Bergerac*, is subtitled a "Heroic Comedy," and the combination of the adjective and the noun is descriptive not only of this play but of its author's unique power in the theatre. To compose romantic drama successfully in the machine age requires unusual endowment and considerable tact. Rostand was able to blend romantic action and lyricism with humor, and the result was a brief renewal of romanticism on the European continent.

A talent for lyric delight and heroic exaltation appears to have come naturally to this poet. Born in Marseilles to wealthy and distinguished parents who cherished memories of French glory (his mother was the granddaughter of one of Napoleon's marshals), Rostand turned to the writing of poetry and plays at an early age, almost as though a romantic career were his birthright. When he married the poetess Rosemonde Gérard in his twenty-second year, he was able to present his bride with a published volume of verse. Settling in Paris after his marriage in 1890, he quickly made himself at home in theatrical circles, and won the friendship of the superb romantic actor Constant Coquelin, for whom he later wrote the role of Cyrano. It was, in fact, Rostand's good fortune to attract distinguished performers throughout his career.

Rostand's first play to reach the stage, *The Romantics* (1894) proved captivating by virtue of its charming lyricism and its refreshingly frank theatricality. The young hero and heroine, who fall in love lyrically, are first found reading *Romeo and Juliet*. The play was presented as a trifle without apology, and romantic feeling was gaily affirmed by the information that the scene could be laid "wherever you please, provided the costumes are pretty." The action concluded with the actors facing the audience and singing a rondel which lauds the brief tale of "parents, lovers, walled and flowery ways," the rustic "scenes by Watteau," and the poetry as a relief from "all these bitter plays"—presumably, the bleak pictures of life provided by the Zolaist disciples. A year later came *The Faraway Princess,* Rostand's tribute to the Provençal poet Rudel. The play was a celebration of love beyond reason and logic. It bordered on silliness, but there was an engagingly youthful enthusiasm in its story and ecstatic verses. Next, Rostand made an unsuccessful effort to weave a romantic pattern out of Biblical matter in *The Woman of Samaria*. But this failure was quickly followed in the same year of 1897 by the triumphant production of *Cyrano de Bergerac;* and its author won a second resounding success in 1900 when Sarah Bernhardt, then at the peak of her career, played Napoleon's frail son in the pathetic drama of the eaglet with clipped wings, *L'Aiglon.*

Ill health caused Rostand to retire to the south at the height of his glory and it was there, in the romantic setting of Cambon, at the foot of the Pyrenees, that he made a valiant effort to live up to the high expectations entertained for his next drama. He did, indeed, create a frequently delightful, if uneven, play in *Chantecler.* Mixed with satire on French foibles, it was essentially another affirmation of the heroic spirit that feeds upon intoxicating illusions—such as the rooster's belief that his crowing makes the sun rise—but that can reach new heights when reality brings disenchantment. Having wrested a romantic victory from the facts of life, including the fact of his own illness and retirement, Rostand evidently expected much from his animal fable. *Chantecler,* however, failed on the stage in 1910 and did not attract the French public until 1928, a decade after the playwright's death, when the play received a modernistic production. Deeply disappointed, Rostand remained at Cambon for the rest of his days, writing only the trifle *The Sacred Wood* and an unfinished play about the collapse of Don Juan's amatory career, *The Last Night of Don Juan,* which, published posthumously (1921), came closer to disillusionment than Rostand would have brought himself in the days when he confidently tried to make romance prevail on the modern stage.

Only with *Cyrano de Bergerac,* which had its stirring *première* in Paris on December 28, 1897, when its author was only twenty-nine years old, did Rostand achieve an instantaneous romantic triumph that has not been tarnished by time and the troubled life of the twentieth century. *L'Aiglon* became outmoded because it was compounded of too much pathos and sentimentality, and *Chantecler* presented difficult problems for a stage production, among which the necessity of playing under rooster feathers is not the least. *Cyrano* never fails to exert its spell when performed with tasteful gusto. It has survived translation into English, and it has served American actors extremely well ever since Richard Mansfield, the foremost American actor at the turn of the century, played Rostand's hero to New York audiences in the fall of 1898. Walter Hampden, using the Brian Hooker version, reached the pinnacle of his career with the play in November 1923, and his production was on view for a long time in New

York and other cities. More than two decades later, the play proved just as attractive when it was revived by the young actor-manager José Ferrer.

The secret of *Cyrano's* charm on the stage is an open one. It is one of the most playable of plays, almost superabundant in color and movement, and altogether a work of pure theatre. With his fondness for magnificent gestures, Cyrano is a figure ready-made for the stage in all respects. Yet Rostand's swashbuckling hero also emerges as a human being out of the vividly realized background of the age of Louis XIII. His physical appearance contradicts his spirit and drives him to put on the armor of wit and defiance. The man's triumph of pose and posturing (his "panache") project and compensate an underlying defeat in fact (for he never possesses his Roxane) and in self-esteem (for he never dares to propose to her in his own behalf). Behind his pose lies his pathos, as Cyrano himself well knows. Upon being informed before his death that Molière has stolen a scene from him, he declares that his destiny was always to prompt others. The ironic gods respected by modern man are well served by Rostand, and Cyrano is all the more human, as well as theatrically attractive, for being victimized by them.

Temperament and a love of the theatre helped Rostand escape the pitfalls of the romantic "Wagnerism" that Maeterlinck and the scenic artists Appia and Craig postulated for the theatre. They strove to dissolve dramatic matter into nuances, whereas he accentuated and highlighted drama. They tried to transmute action into elusive music, whereas he translated music—the music of his hero worship and poetry—into exciting action. "With Rostand," as T. S. Eliot noted, "the centre of gravity is in the expression of the emotion, not as with Maeterlinck in the emotion which cannot be expressed." Emotions for Rostand were always significant and strong enough to be exposed on the stage. They were even important enough to carry the full weight of the rhetoric with which he invested them. Few writers have been endurably rhetorical since the seventeenth century. Cyrano's speech on noses is one of the rare acceptable purple patches of the modern drama.

Rostand understood the art of making emotionalism tolerable to the modern world. He made a tragicomedy out of a story that Hugo, sixty years earlier, would have turned into a melodrama masquerading as a tragedy. Hugo, having made the use of grotesque elements a canon of romantic art, lost ironic force by being indiscriminately grandiose. When Rostand selected a grotesque hero, however, he took full advantage of the possibilities of deriving an ironic view of life from grotesqueness, and employed grandiloquence only to characterize Cyrano and to underscore effects. The pyrotechnics of Cyrano's dying speech, for example, can be received all the more gratefully because Rostand heaped the ignominy of a commonplace death on his hero.

It will always be questionable whether the heroic fanfare of *Cyrano de Bergerac* is any more attractive than its antiheroic counterpoint. It is the conjunction of opposites that most absorbs the reader and playgoer, whether he knows it or not. The romanticism of the play Rostand wrote is comparable to Cyrano's "plume." When, as he expects to do, this French Don Quixote sweeps it across the threshold of God's house with a gallant gesture, it is doubtful whether God will regard the feather rather than the man.

The famous Brian Hooker version of *Cyrano de Bergerac* was made especially for Walter Hampden. It was instantly acclaimed as the best, and indeed the only entirely satisfactory, English translation for the stage—the only one that conveyed the brisk theatricality, wit, and rapturous eloquence of the original French. Hooker preserved the meters and rhyme schemes of the incidental lyrics but turned Rostand's Alexandrine couplets into blank verse, which is a more congenial meter in English than the classic French hexameter. Without adding or subtracting lines, the translator took a few liberties in paraphrasing expressions (such as "elegant like Celadon") that would have lacked point for the American public. He also substituted a celebrated quotation from *Dr. Faustus* for a French quotation less known to Americans in Cyrano's tirade on noses.

BIBLIOGRAPHY: Frank W. Chandler, *Modern Continental Playwrights* (pp. 229–236), 1931; T. S. Eliot, *Selected Essays*, 1932; Rosemonde Gérard, *Edmond Rostand*, 1935; Ludwig Lewisohn, *The Modern Drama* (pp. 236–247), 1921.

CYRANO DE BERGERAC

By Edmond Rostand

A NEW VERSION IN ENGLISH VERSE BY BRIAN HOOKER

THE PERSONS

CYRANO DE BERGERAC	CUIGY	TWO MUSICIANS
CHRISTIAN DE NEUVILLETTE	BRISSAILLE	THE POETS
COMTE DE GUICHE	A MEDDLER	THE PASTRYCOOKS
RAGUENEAU	A MUSKETEER	THE PAGES
LE BRET	ANOTHER MUSKETEER	ROXANE
CARBON DE CASTEL-JALOUX	A SPANISH OFFICER	HER DUENNA
THE CADETS	A CAVALIER	LISE
LIGNIÈRE	THE PORTER	THE ORANGE GIRL
VICOMTE DE VALVERT	A CITIZEN	MCTHER MARGUÉRITE DE JÉSUS
A MARQUIS	HIS SON	SISTER MARTHE
SECOND MARQUIS	A CUT-PURSE	SISTER CLAIRE
THIRD MARQUIS	A SPECTATOR	AN ACTRESS
MONTFLEURY	A SENTRY	A SOUBRETTE
BELLEROSE	BERTRANDOU THE FIFER	THE FLOWER GIRL
JODELET	A CAPUCHIN	

The Crowd, Citizens, Marquis, Musketeers, Thieves, Pastrycooks, Poets, Cadets of Gascoyne, Actors, Violins, Pages, Children, Spanish Soldiers, Spectators, Intellectuals, Academicians, Nuns, etc.

[*The first four Acts in 1640; the fifth in 1655*]

FIRST ACT: *A Performance at the Hôtel de Bourgogne.*
SECOND ACT: *The Bakery of the Poets.*
THIRD ACT: *Roxane's Kiss.*
FOURTH ACT: *The Cadets of Gascoyne.*
FIFTH ACT: *Cyrano's Gazette.*

ACT I.

A Performance at the Hôtel de Bourgogne.

The hall of the Hôtel de Bourgogne in 1640. A sort of tennis court, arranged and decorated for theatrical productions. The hall is a long rectangle; we see it diagonally, in such a way that one side of it forms the back scene, which begins at the first entrance on the right and runs up to the last entrance on the left where it makes a right angle with the stage which is seen obliquely. The stage is provided on either hand with benches placed along the wings. The curtain is formed by two lengths of tapestry which can be drawn apart. Above a Harlequin cloak, the royal arms. Broad steps lead from the stage down to the floor of the hall. On either side of these steps, a place for the musicians. A row of candles serving as footlights. Two tiers of galleries along the side of the hall; the upper one divided into boxes. There are no seats upon the floor, which the actual stage of our theatre; but toward the bac of the hall, on the right, a few benches are arranged and underneath a stairway on the extreme righ which leads up to the galleries, and of which on the lower portion is visible, there is a sort of sid board, decorated with little tapers, vases of flower bottles and glasses, plates of cake, et cetera. Farthe along, toward the centre of our stage is the entranc to the hall; a great double door which opens on slightly to admit the audience. On one of the pane of this door, as also in other places about the ha and in particular just over the sideboard, are pla bills in red, upon which we may read the title "I Clorise."

As the curtain rises, the hall is dimly lighted ar still empty. The chandeliers are lowered to the floc in the middle of the hall, ready for lighting. Soun of voices outside the door. Then a Cavalier ente abruptly.

THE PORTER: [*Follows him*] Halloa there!—Fifteen sols!

THE CAVALIER: I enter free.

THE PORTER: Why?

THE CAVALIER: Soldier of the Household of the King!

THE PORTER: [*Turns to another* Cavalier *who has just entered*] You?

SECOND CAVALIER: I pay nothing.

THE PORTER: Why not?

SECOND CAVALIER: Musketeer!

FIRST CAVALIER: [*To the second*]
The play begins at two. Plenty of time—
And here's the whole floor empty. Shall we try
Our exercise?
[*They fence with the foils which they have brought*]

A LACKEY: [*Enters*]—Pst! . . . Flanquin! . . .

ANOTHER: [*Already on stage*] What, champagne?

FIRST LACKEY: [*Showing games which he takes out of his doublet*] Cards. Dice. Come on. [*Sits on the floor*]

SECOND LACKEY: [*Same action*] Come on, old cock!

FIRST LACKEY: [*Takes from his pocket a bit of candle, lights it, sets it on the floor*] I have stolen
A little of my master's fire.

A GUARDSMAN: [*To a* Flower Girl *who comes forward*] How sweet
Of you, to come before they light the hall.
[*Puts his arm around her*]

FIRST CAVALIER: [*Receives a thrust of the foil*] A hit!

SECOND LACKEY: A club!

THE GUARDSMAN: [*Pursuing the girl*] A kiss!

THE FLOWER GIRL: [*Pushing away from him*] They'll see us!—

THE GUARDSMAN: [*Draws her into a dark corner*] No danger!

A MAN: [*Sits on the floor, together with several others who have brought packages of food*] When we come early, we have time to eat.

A CITIZEN: [*Escorting his son, a boy of sixteen*] Sit here, my son.

FIRST LACKEY: Mark the Ace!

ANOTHER MAN: [*Draws a bottle from under his cloak and sits down with the others*] Here's the spot
For a jolly old sot to suck his Burgundy—
[*Drinks*]
Here—in the house of the Burgundians!

THE CITIZEN: [*To his son*] Would you not think you were in some den of vice?
[*Points with his cane at the drunkard*]
Drunkards—[*In stepping back, one of the cavaliers trips him up*] Bullies!—[*He falls between the lackeys*] Gamblers!—

THE GUARDSMAN: [*Behind him as he rises, still struggling with the* Flower Girl] One kiss—

THE CITIZEN: Good God!—[*Draws his son quickly away*]

Here!—And to think, my son, that in this hall
They play Rotrou!

THE BOY: Yes father—and Corneille!

THE PAGES: [*Dance in, holding hands and singing*]
Tra-la-la-la-la-la-la-la-la-lère . . .

THE PORTER: You pages there—no nonsense!

FIRST PAGE: [*With wounded dignity*] Oh, monsieur!
Really! How could you?
[*To the* Second, *the moment the* Porter *turns his back*] Pst!—a bit of string?

SECOND PAGE: [*Shows fishline with hook*] Yes—and a hook.

FIRST PAGE: Up in the gallery,
And fish for wigs!

A CUT-PURSE: [*Gathers around him several evil-looking young fellows*] Now then, you picaroons.
Perk up, and hear me mutter. Here's your bout—
Bustle around some cull, and bite his bung . . .

SECOND PAGE: [*Calls to other pages already in the gallery*]
Hey! Brought your pea-shooters?

THIRD PAGE: [*From above*] And our peas, too!
[*Blows, and showers them with peas*]

THE BOY: What is the play this afternoon?

THE CITIZEN: "Clorise."

THE BOY: Who wrote that?

THE CITIZEN: Balthasar Baro.
What a play! . . .
[*He takes the* Boy's *arms and leads him upstage*]

THE CUT-PURSE: [*To his pupils*] Lace now, on those long sleeves, you cut it off—
[*Gesture with thumb and finger, as if using scissors*]

A SPECTATOR: [*To another, pointing upward toward the gallery*] Ah, *Le Cid!*—Yes, the first night,
I sat there—

THE CUT-PURSE: Watches—[*Gesture as of picking a pocket*]

THE CITIZEN: [*Coming down with his son*] Great actors we shall see to-day—

THE CUT-PURSE: Handkerchiefs—[*Gesture of holding the pocket with left hand, and drawing out handkerchief with right*]

THE CITIZEN: Montfleury—

A VOICE: [*In the gallery*] Lights! Light the lights!

THE CITIZEN: Bellerose, l'Épy, Beaupré, Jodelet—

A PAGE: [*On the floor*] Here comes the orange girl.

THE ORANGE GIRL: Oranges, milk,
Raspberry syrup, lemonade—
[*Noise at the door*]

A FALSETTO VOICE: [*Outside*] Make way, Brutes!

FIRST LACKEY: What, the Marquis—on the floor?
[*The* Marquis *enter in a little group*]

SECOND LACKEY: Not long—
Only a few moments; they'll go and sit
On the stage presently.

FIRST MARQUIS: [*Seeing the hall half empty*] How now! We enter

Like tradespeople—no crowding, no disturbance!—
No treading on the toes of citizens?
Oh fie! Oh fie!

> [*He encounters two gentlemen who have al-
> ready arrived*] Cuigy! Brissaille!
> [*Great embracings*]

CUIGY: The faithful!

> [*Looks around him*]

We are here before the candles.

FIRST MARQUIS: Ah, be still!
You put me in a temper.

SECOND MARQUIS: Console yourself,
Marquis—The lamplighter!

THE CROWD: [*Applauding the appearance of the
lamplighter*] Ah! . . .

> [*A group gathers around the chandelier while
> he lights it. A few people have already taken
> their place in the gallery.* Lignière *enters the
> hall, arm in arm with* Christian de Neuvillette.
> Lignière *is a slightly disheveled figure, dissi-
> pated and yet distinguished looking.* Christian,
> *elegantly but rather unfashionably dressed, ap-
> pears preoccupied and keeps looking up at the
> boxes*]

CUIGY: Lignière!—

BRISSAILLE: [*Laughing*] Still sober—at this hour?

LIGNIÈRE: [*To* Christian] May I present you?

> [Christian *assents*]

Baron Christian de Neuvillette. [*They salute*]

THE CROWD: [*Applauding as the lighted chandelier
is hoisted into place*]   Ah!—

CUIGY: [*Aside to* Brissaille, *looking at* Christian]
Rather a fine head, is it not? The profile . . .

FIRST MARQUIS: [*Who has overheard*]   Peuh!

LIGNIÈRE: [*Presenting them to* Christian]
Messieurs de Cuigy . . . de Brissaille . . .

CHRISTIAN: [*Bows*]   Enchanted!

FIRST MARQUIS: [*To the second*] He is not ill-
looking; possibly a shade
Behind the fashion.

LIGNIÈRE: [*To* Cuigy] Monsieur is recently
From the Touraine.

CHRISTIAN: Yes, I have been in Paris
Two or three weeks only. I join the Guards
To-morrow.

FIRST MARQUIS: [*Watching the people who come
into the boxes*] Look—Madame la Présidente
Aubry!

THE ORANGE GIRL: Oranges, milk—

THE VIOLINS: [*Tuning up*] La . . . la . . .

CUIGY: [*To* Christian, *calling his attention to the
increasing crowd*]   We have
An audience to-day!

CHRISTIAN: A brilliant one.

FIRST MARQUIS: Oh yes, all our own people—the
gay world!

> [*They name the ladies who enter the boxes
> elaborately dressed. Bows and smiles are ex-
> changed*]

SECOND MARQUIS: Madame de Guéméné . . .

CUIGY: De
Bois-Dauphin . . .

FIRST MARQUIS: Whom we adore—

BRISSAILLE: Madame
de Chavigny . . .

SECOND MARQUIS: Who plays with all our hearts—

LIGNIÈRE: Why, there's Corneille returned from
Rouen!

THE BOY: [*To his father*] Are the Academy
All here?

THE CITIZEN: I see some of them . . . there's
Boudu—Boissat—Cureau—Porchères—Colomby—
Bourzeys—Bourdon—Arbaut—
                    Ah, those great names,
Never to be forgotten!

FIRST MARQUIS: Look—at last!
Our Intellectuals! Barthénoide,
Urimédonte, Félixérie . . .

SECOND MARQUIS: [*Languishing*] Sweet heaven!
How exquisite their surnames are! Marquis,
You know them all?

FIRST MARQUIS: I know them all, Marquis!

LIGNIÈRE: [*Draws* Christian *aside*] My dear boy,
I came here to serve you—   Well,
But where's the lady? I'll be going.

CHRISTIAN: Not yet—
A little longer! She is always here.
Please! I must find some way of meeting her.
I am dying of love! And you—you know
Everyone, the whole court and the whole town,
And put them all into your songs—at least
You can tell me her name!

THE FIRST VIOLIN: [*Raps on his desk with his bow*]
Pst— Gentlemen!

> [*Raises his bow*]

THE ORANGE GIRL: Macaroons, lemonade—

CHRISTIAN: Then she may be
One of those æsthetes . . . Intellectuals,
You call them— How can I talk to a woman
In that style? I have no wit. This fine manner
Of speaking and of writing nowadays—
Not for me! I am a soldier—and afraid.
That's her box, on the right—the empty one.

LIGNIÈRE: [*Starts for the door*] I am going.

CHRISTIAN: [*Restrains him*] No—wait!

LIGNIÈRE: Not I.
There's a tavern not far away—
And I am dying of thirst.

THE ORANGE GIRL: [*Passes with her tray*] Orange
    juice?

LIGNIÈRE: No!

THE ORANGE GIRL: Milk?

LIGNIÈRE: Pouah!

THE ORANGE GIRL: Muscatel?

LIGNIÈRE: Here! Stop! [*To* Christian] I'll stay a
little.

> [*To the* Girl] Let me see
Your Muscatel.

> [*He sits down by the sideboard. The* Girl *pours
> out wine for him*]

VOICES: [*In the crowd about the door, upon the entrance of a spruce little man, rather fat, with a beaming smile*] Ragueneau!

LIGNIÈRE: [*To* Christian] Ragueneau,
Poet and pastry-cook—a character!

RAGUENEAU: [*Dressed like a confectioner in his Sunday clothes, advances quickly to* Lignière]
Sir, have you seen Monsieur de Cyrano?

LIGNIÈRE: [*Presents him to* Christian] Permit me
. . . Ragueneau, confectioner,
The chief support of modern poetry.

RAGUENEAU: [*Bridling*] Oh—too much honor!

LIGNIÈRE: Patron of the Arts—
Mæcenas! Yes, you are—

RAGUENEAU: Undoubtedly,
The poets gather round my hearth.

LIGNIÈRE: On credit—
Himself a poet—

RAGUENEAU: So they say—

LIGNIÈRE: Maintains
The Muses.

RAGUENEAU: It is true that for an ode—

LIGNIÈRE: You
Give a tart—

RAGUENEAU: A tartlet—

LIGNIÈRE: Modesty!
And for a triolet you give—

RAGUENEAU: Plain bread.

LIGNIÈRE: [*Severely*] Bread and milk!
And you love the theatre?

RAGUENEAU: I adore it!

LIGNIÈRE: Well, pastry pays for all.
Your place to-day now—Come, between ourselves,
What did it cost you?

RAGUENEAU: Four pies; fourteen cakes.
[*Looking about*] But— Cyrano not here?
Astonishing!

LIGNIÈRE: Why so?

RAGUENEAU: Why— Montfleury plays!

LIGNIÈRE: Yes, I hear
That hippopotamus assumes the rôle
Of Phédon. What is that to Cyrano?

RAGUENEAU: Have you not heard? Monsieur de
     Bergerac
So hates Montfleury, he has forbidden him
For three weeks to appear upon the stage.

LIGNIÈRE: [*Who is, by this time, at his fourth glass*] Well?

RAGUENEAU: Montfleury plays!—

CUIGY: [*Strolls over to them*]   Yes—what then?

RAGUENEAU: Ah! That is what I came to see.

FIRST MARQUIS: This Cyrano—
Who is he?

CUIGY: Oh, he is the lad with the long sword.

SECOND MARQUIS: Noble?

CUIGY: Sufficiently; he is in
the Guards. [*Points to a gentleman who comes and goes about the hall as though seeking for someone*]
His friend Le Bret can tell you more. [*Calls to him*]

Le Bret! [Le Bret *comes down to them*] Looking for
Bergerac?

LE BRET: Yes. And for trouble.

CUIGY: Is he not an extraordinary man?

LE BRET: The best friend and the bravest soul
alive!

RAGUENEAU: Poet—

CUIGY: Swordsman—

LE BRET: Musician—

BRISSAILLE: Philosopher—

LIGNIÈRE: Such a remarkable appearance, too!

RAGUENEAU: Truly, I should not look to find his
portrait
By the grave hand of Philippe de Champagne.
He might have been a model for Callot—
One of those wild swashbucklers in a masque—
Hat with three plumes, and a doublet with six
     points—
His cloak behind him over his long sword
Cocked, like the tail of strutting Chanticleer—
Prouder than all the swaggering Tamburlaines
Hatched out of Gascony. And to complete
This Punchinello figure—such a nose!—
My lords, there is no such nose as that nose—
You cannot look upon it without crying: "Oh no,
Impossible! Exaggerated!" Then
You smile, and say: "Of course— I might have
     known;
Presently he will take it off." But that
Monsieur de Bergerac will never do.

LIGNIÈRE: [*Grimly*] He keeps it—and God help
The man who smiles!

RAGUENEAU: His sword is one half of the
Shears of Fate!

FIRST MARQUIS: [*Shrugs*] He will not come.

RAGUENEAU: Will he not? Sir, I'll lay you
A pullet à la Ragueneau!

FIRST MARQUIS: [*Laughing*] Done!

[*Murmurs of admiration;* Roxane *has just appeared in her box. She sits at the front of the box, and her* Duenna *takes a seat toward the rear.* Christian, *busy paying the* Orange Girl, *does not see her at first*]

SECOND MARQUIS: [*With little excited cries*] Ah!
Oh! Oh! Sweet sirs, look yonder! Is she not
Frightfully ravishing?

FIRST MARQUIS: Bloom of the peach—
Blush of the strawberry—

SECOND MARQUIS: So fresh—so cool,
That our hearts, grown all warm with loving her,
May catch their death of cold!

CHRISTIAN: [*Looks up, sees* Roxane, *and seizes* Lignière *by the arm*] There! Quick—up there—
In the box! Look!—

LIGNIÈRE: [*Coolly*] Herself?

CHRISTIAN: Quickly— Her name?

LIGNIÈRE: [*Sipping his wine, and speaking between sips*] Madeleine Robin, called Roxane . . . refined
. . .
Intellectual . . .

CHRISTIAN: Ah!—

LIGNIÈRE: Unmarried . . .

CHRISTIAN: Oh!—

LIGNIÈRE: No title . . . rich enough . . . an orphan . . . cousin

To Cyrano . . . of whom we spoke just now . . .
[*At this point, a very distinguished looking gentleman, the Cordon Bleu around his neck, enters the box, and stands a moment talking with* Roxane]

CHRISTIAN: [*Starts*] And the man? . . .

LIGNIÈRE: [*Beginning to feel his wine a little; cocks his eye at them*] Oho! That man? . . . Comte de Guiche . . .

In love with her . . . married himself, however,
To the niece of the Cardinal—Richelieu . . .
Wishes Roxane, therefore, to marry one
Monsieur de Valvert . . . Vicomte . . . friend of his . . .
A somewhat melancholy gentleman . . .
But . . . well, accommodating! . . . She says No . . .
Nevertheless, de Guiche is powerful . . .
Not above persecuting . . .
[*He rises, swaying a little, and very happy*] I have written
A little song about his little game . . .
Good little song, too . . . Here, I'll sing it for you . . .
Make de Guiche furious . . . naughty little song . . .
Not so bad, either— Listen! . . .
[*He stands with his glass held aloft, ready to sing*]

CHRISTIAN: No. Adieu.

LIGNIÈRE: Whither away?

CHRISTIAN: To Monsieur de Valvert!

LIGNIÈRE: Careful! The man's a swordsman . . .
[*Nods toward* Roxane, *who is watching* Christian]
                              Wait! Someone
Looking at you—

CHRISTIAN: Roxane! . . .
[*He forgets everything, and stands spellbound, gazing toward* Roxane. *The* Cut-Purse *and his crew, observing him transfixed, his eyes raised and his mouth half open, begin edging in his direction*]

LIGNIÈRE: Oh! Very well,
Then I'll be leaving you . . . Good day . . . Good day! . . .
[*Christian remains motionless*]
Everywhere else, they like to hear me sing!—
Also, I am thirsty.
[*He goes out, navigating carefully. Le Bret, having made the circuit of the hall, returns to* Ragueneau, *somewhat reassured*]

LE BRET: No sign anywhere
Of Cyrano!

RAGUENEAU: [*Incredulous*] Wait and see!

LE BRET: Humph! I hope
He has not seen the bill.

THE CROWD: The play!—The play!—

FIRST MARQUIS: [*Observing* de Guiche, *as he descends from* Roxane's *box and crosses the floor, followed by a knot of obsequious gentlemen, the* Vicomte de Valvert *among them*] This man de Guiche—what ostentation!

SECOND MARQUIS: Bah!—
Another Gascon!

FIRST MARQUIS: Gascon, yes—but cold
And calculating—certain to suceed—
My word for it. Come, shall we make our bow?
We shall be none the worse, I promise you . . .
[*They go toward* de Guiche]

SECOND MARQUIS: Beautiful ribbons, Count! That color, now,
What is it—"Kiss-me-Dear" or "Startled-Fawn"?

DE GUICHE: I call that shade "The Dying Spaniard."

FIRST MARQUIS: Ha!
And no false colors either—thanks to you
And your brave troops, in Flanders before long
The Spaniard will die daily.

DE GUICHE: Shall we go
And sit upon the stage? Come, Valvert.

CHRISTIAN: [*Starts at the name*] Valvert!—
The Vicomte— Ah, that scoundrel! Quick—my glove—
I'll throw it in his face—
[*Reaching into his pocket for his glove, he catches the hand of the* Cut-Purse]

THE CUT-PURSE: Oh!—

CHRISTIAN: [*Holding fast to the man's wrist*] Who are you?
I was looking for a glove—

THE CUT-PURSE: [*Cringing*] You found a hand
[*Hurriedly*] Let me go—I can tell you something—

CHRISTIAN: [*Still holding him*] Well?

THE CUT-PURSE: Lignière—that friends of yours—

CHRISTIAN: [*Same business*] Well?

THE CUT-PURSE: Good as dead—
Understand? Ambuscaded. Wrote a song
About—no matter. There's a hundred men
Waiting for him to-night—I'm one of them.

CHRISTIAN: A hundred! Who arranged this?

THE CUT-PURSE: Secret

CHRISTIAN: Oh!

THE CUT-PURSE: [*With dignity*] Professional secret

CHRISTIAN: Where are they to be?

THE CUT-PURSE: Port de Nesle. On his way home
Tell him so. Save his life.

CHRISTIAN: [*Releases the man*] Yes, but where am I to find him?

THE CUT-PURSE: Go round the taverns. There's the Golden Grape,
The Pineapple, the Bursting Belt, the Two
Torches, the Three Funnels—in every one
You leave a line of writing—understand?
To warn him.

CHRISTIAN: [*Starts for the door*] I'll go! God, what swine—a hundred
Against one man! . . . [*Stops and looks longingly at* Roxane]   Leave *her* here!

[*Savagely, turning toward* Valvert] And leave *him!*— [*Decidedly*] I must save Lignière! [*Exit.* De Guiche, Valvert, *and all the* Marquis *have disappeared through the curtains, to take their seats upon the stage. The floor is entirely filled; not a vacant seat remains in the gallery or in the boxes*]

THE CROWD: The play! The play! Begin the play!

A CITIZEN: [*As his wig is hoisted into the air on the end of a fishline, in the hands of a page in the gallery*] My wig!!

CRIES OF JOY: He's bald! Bravo, You pages! Ha ha ha!

THE CITIZEN: [*Furious, shakes his fist at the boy*] Here, you young villain!

CRIES AND LAUGHTER: [*Beginning very loud, then suddenly repressed*] HA HA! Ha Ha! ha ha. . . . [*Complete silence*]

LE BRET: [*Surprised*] That sudden hush? . . . [*A* Spectator *whispers in his ear*] Yes?

THE SPECTATOR: I was told on good authority . . .

MURMURS: [*Here and there*] What? . . . Here? . . . No . . . Yes . . . Look—in the latticed box— The Cardinal! . . . The Cardinal! . . .

A PAGE: The Devil!— Now we shall all have to behave ourselves! [*Three raps on the stage. The audience becomes motionless. Silence*]

THE VOICE OF A MARQUIS: [*From the stage, behind the curtains*] Snuff that candle!

ANOTHER MARQUIS: [*Puts his head out through the curtains*] A chair! . . . [*A chair is passed from hand to hand over the heads of the crowd. He takes it, and disappears behind the curtains, not without having blown a few kisses to the occupants of the boxes*]

A SPECTATOR: Silence!

VOICES: Hssh! . . . Hssh! . . . [*Again the three raps on the stage. The curtains part. Tableau. The* Marquis *seated on their chairs to right and left of the stage, insolently posed. Back drop representing a pastoral scene, bluish in tone. Four little crystal chandeliers light up the stage. The violins play softly*]

LE BRET: [*In a low tone, to* Ragueneau] Montfleury *enters now?*

RAGUENEAU: [*Nods*] Opens the play.

LE BRET: [*Much relieved*] Then Cyrano is not here!

RAGUENEAU: I lose . . .

LE BRET: Humph!— So much the better! [*The melody of a musette is heard.* Montfleury *appears upon the scene, a ponderous figure in the costume of a rustic shepherd, a hat garlanded with roses tilted over one ear, playing upon a beribboned pastoral pipe*]

THE CROWD: [*Applauds*] Montfleury! . . . Bravo! . . .

MONTFLEURY: [*After bowing to the applause, begins the rôle of* Phédon] "Thrice happy he who hides from pomp and power In sylvan shade or solitary bower; Where balmy zephyrs fan his burning cheeks—"

A VOICE: [*From the midst of the hall*] Wretch! Have I not forbade you these three weeks? [*Sensation. Every one turns to look. Murmurs*]

SEVERAL VOICES: What? . . . Where? . . . Who is it? . . .

CUIGY: Cyrano!

LE BRET: [*In alarm*] Himself!

THE VOICE: King of clowns! Leave the stage— at once!

THE CROWD: Oh!—

MONTFLEURY: Now, Now, now—

THE VOICE: You disobey me?

SEVERAL VOICES: [*From the floor, from the boxes*] Hsh! Go on— Quiet!—Go on, Montfleury!—Who's afraid?—

MONTFLEURY: [*In a voice of no great assurance*] "Thrice happy he who hides from . . ."

THE VOICE: [*More menacingly*] Well? Well? Well? . . . Monarch of montebanks! Must I come and plant A forest on your shoulders? [*A cane at the end of a long arm shakes above the heads of the crowd*]

MONTFLEURY: [*In a voice increasingly feeble*] "Thrice hap—" [*The cane is violently agitated*]

THE VOICE: GO!!!

THE CROWD: Ah!—

CYRANO: [*Arises in the center of the floor, erect upon a chair, his arms folded, his hat cocked ferociously, his moustache bristling, his nose terrible*] Presently I shall grow angry! [*Sensation at his appearance*]

MONTFLEURY: [*To the* Marquis] Messieurs, If you protect me—

A MARQUIS: [*Nonchalantly*] Well—proceed!

CYRANO: Fat swine! If you dare breathe one balmy zephyr more, I'll fan your cheeks for you!

THE MARQUIS: Quiet down there!

CYRANO: Unless these gentlemen retain their seats, My cane may bite their ribbons!

ALL THE MARQUIS: [*On their feet*] That will do!— Montfleury—

CYRANO: Fly, goose! Shoo! Take to your wings, Before I pluck your plumes, and draw your gorge!

A VOICE: See here!—

CYRANO: Off stage!!

ANOTHER VOICE: One moment—

CYRANO: What—still there? [*Turns back his cuffs deliberately*] Very good—then I enter—*Left—with knife—* To carve this large Italian sausage.

MONTFLEURY: [*Desperately attempting dignity*] Sir,
When you insult me, you insult the Muse!
  CYRANO: [*With great politeness*]
Sir, if the Muse, who never knew your name,
Had the honor to meet you—then be sure
That after one glance at that face of yours,
That figure of a mortuary urn—
She would apply her buskin—toward the rear!
  THE CROWD: Montfleury! . . . Montfleury! . . .
    The play! The play!
  CYRANO: [*To those who are shouting and crowding about him*]
Pray you, be gentle with my scabbard here—
She'll put her tongue out at you presently—
    [*The circle enlarges*]
  THE CROWD: [*Recoiling*] Keep back—
  CYRANO: [*To* Montfleury] Begone!
  THE CROWD: [*Pushing in closer, and growling*]
    Ahr! . . . ahr! . . .
  CYRANO: [*Turns upon them*] Did someone speak?
    [*They recoil again*]
  A VOICE: [*In the back of the hall, sings*]
        Monsieur de Cyrano
          Must be another Caesar—
        Let Brutus lay him low,
          And play us "La Clorise"!
  ALL THE CROWD: [*Singing*] "La Clorise!" "La Clorise!"
  CYRANO: Let me hear one more word of that same song,
And I destroy you all!
  A CITIZEN: Who might you be?
Samson?—
  CYRANO: Precisely. Would you kindly lend me
Your jawbone?
  A LADY: [*In one of the boxes*] What an outrage!
  A NOBLE: Scandalous!
  A CITIZEN: Annoying!
  A PAGE: What a game!
  THE CROWD: Kss!
Montfleury! Cyrano!
  CYRANO: Silence!
  THE CROWD: [*Delirious*] Woof! Woof! Baa!
    Cockadoo!
  CYRANO: I—
  A PAGE: Meow!
  CYRANO: I say be silent!—
    [*His voice dominates the uproar. Momentary hush*]
                            And I offer
One universal challenge to you all!
Approach, young heroes—I will take your names.
Each in his turn—no crowding! One, two, three—
Come, get your numbers—who will head the list—
You sir? No— You? Ah, no. To the first man
Who falls I'll build a monument! . . . Not one?
Will all who wish to die, please raise their hands? . . .
I see. You are so modest, you might blush
Before a sword naked. Sweet innocence! . . .

Not one name? Not one finger? . . . Very well,
Then I go on:
    [*Turning back towards the stage, where Montfleury waits in despair*]
            I'd have our theatre cured
Of this carbuncle. Or if not, why then—
    [*His hand on his sword hilt*]
The lancet!
  MONTFLEURY: I—
  CYRANO: [*Descends from his chair, seats himself comfortably in the center of the circle which has formed around him, and makes himself quite at home*]   Attend to me—full moon!
I clap my hands, three times—thus. At the third
You will eclipse yourself.
  THE CROWD: [*Amused*] Ah!
  CYRANO: Ready? One!
  MONTFLEURY: I—
  A VOICE: [*From the boxes*] No!
  THE CROWD: He'll go— He'll stay—
  MONTFLEURY: I really think,
Gentlemen—
  CYRANO: Two!
  MONTFLEURY: Perhaps I had better—
  CYRANO: Three!
    [*Montfleury disappears, as if through a trap-door. Tempest of laughter, hoots and hisses*]
  THE CROWD: Yah!—Coward— Come back—
  CYRANO: [*Beaming, drops back in his chair and crosses his legs*] Let him—if he dare!
  A CITIZEN: The Manager! Speech! Speech!
    [*Bellerose advances and bows*]
  THE BOXES: Ah! Bellerose!
  BELLEROSE: [*With elegance*] Most noble—most fair—
  THE CROWD: No! The Comedian—
Jodelet!—
  JODELET: [*Advances, and speaks through his nose*]
    Lewd fellows of the baser sort—
  THE CROWD: Ha! ha! Not bad! Bravo!
  JODELET: No Bravos here!
Our heavy tragedian with the voluptuous bust
Was taken suddenly—
  THE CROWD: Yah! Coward!
  JODELET: I mean . . .
He had to be excused—
  THE CROWD: Call him back— No!—
Yes!—
  THE BOY: [*To* Cyrano] After all, Monsieur, what reason have you
To hate this Montfleury?
  CYRANO: [*Graciously, still seated*] My dear young man,
I have two reasons, either one alone
Conclusive. *Primo:* A lamentable actor,
Who mouths his verse and moans his tragedy,
And heaves up— Ugh!—like a hod-carrier, lines
That ought to soar on their own wings. *Secundo:*—
Well—that's my secret.

THE OLD CITIZEN: [*Behind him*] But you close the
play—
"La Clorise"—by Baro! Are we to miss
Our entertainment, merely—
CYRANO: [*Respectfully, turns his chair towards
the old man*] My dear old boy,
The poetry of Baro being worth
Zero, or less, I feel that I have done
Poetic justice!
THE INTELLECTUALS: [*In the boxes*] Really!—our
Baro!—
My dear!—Who ever?—Ah, dieu! The idea!—
CYRANO: [*Gallantly, turns his chair toward the
boxes*]
Fair ladies—shine upon us like the sun,
Blossom like flowers around us—be our songs,
Heard in a dream— Make sweet the hour of death,
Smiling upon us as you close our eyes—
Inspire, but do not try to criticise!
BELLEROSE: Quite so!—and the mere money—
possibly
You would like that returned— Yes?
CYRANO: Bellerose,
You speak the first word of intelligence!
I will not wound the mantle of the Muse—
Here, catch!—
        [*Throws him a purse*] And hold your tongue.
THE CROWD: [*Astonished*] Ah! Ah!
JODELET: [*Deftly catches the purse, weighs it in
his hand*] Monsieur,
You are hereby authorized to close our play
Every night, on the same terms.
THE CROWD: Boo!
JODELET: And welcome!
Let us be booed together, you and I!
BELLEROSE: Kindly pass out quietly . . .
JODELET: [*Burlesquing* Bellerose] Quietly . . .
        [*They begin to go out, while* Cyrano *looks
        about him with satisfaction. But the exodus
        ceases presently during the ensuing scene. The
        ladies in the boxes who have already risen and
        put on their wraps, stop to listen, and finally sit
        down again*]
LE BRET: [*To* Cyrano] Idiot!
A MEDDLER: [*Hurries up to* Cyrano] But what a
scandal! Montfleury—
The great Montfleury! Did you know the Duc De
Candale was his patron? Who is yours?
CYRANO: No one.
THE MEDDLER: No one—no patron?
CYRANO: I said no.
THE MEDDLER: What, no great lord, to cover with
his name—
CYRANO: [*With visible annoyance*] No, I have
told you twice. Must I repeat?
No sir, no patron—
        [*His hand on his sword*] But a patroness!
THE MEDDLER: And when do you leave Paris?
CYRANO: That's as may be.

THE MEDDLER: The Duc de Candale has a long
arm.
CYRANO: Mine
Is longer,
        [*Drawing his sword*] by three feet of steel.
THE MEDDLER: Yes, yes.
But do you dream of daring—
CYRANO: I do dream
Of daring . . .
THE MEDDLER: But—
CYRANO: You may go now.
THE MEDDLER: But—
CYRANO: You may go—
Or tell me why are you staring at my nose!
THE MEDDLER: [*In confusion*] No—I—
CYRANO: [*Stepping up to him*] Does it astonish
you?
THE MEDDLER: [*Drawing back*] Your grace
Misunderstands my—
CYRANO: Is it long and soft
And dangling, like a trunk?
THE MEDDLER: [*Same business*] I never said—
CYRANO: Or crooked, like an owl's beak?
THE MEDDLER: I—
CYRANO: Perhaps
A pimple ornaments the end of it?
THE MEDDLER: No—
CYRANO: Or a fly parading up and down?
What is this portent?
THE MEDDLER: Oh!—
CYRANO: This phenomenon?
THE MEDDLER: But I have been careful not to
look—
CYRANO: And why
Not, if you please?
THE MEDDLER: Why—
CYRANO: It disgusts you, then?
THE MEDDLER: My dear sir—
CYRANO: Does its color appear to you
Unwholesome?
THE MEDDLER: Oh, by no means!
CYRANO: Or its form
Obscene?
THE MEDDLER: Not in the least—
CYRANO: Then why assume
This deprecating manner? Possibly
You find it just a trifle large?
THE MEDDLER: [*Babbling*] Oh no!—
Small, very small, infinitesimal—
CYRANO: [*Roars*] What!
How? You accuse me of absurdity?
Small—*my nose?* Why—
THE MEDDLER: [*Breathless*] My God!—
CYRANO: Magnificent,
My nose! . . . You pug, you knob, you button-
head,
Know that I glory in this nose of mine,
For a great nose indicates a great man—
Genial, courteous, intellectual,
Virile, courageous—as I am—and such

As you—poor wretch—will never dare to be
Even in imagination. For that face—
That blank, inglorious concavity
Which my right hand finds—
    [*He strikes him*]
    THE MEDDLER: Ow!
    CYRANO: —on top of you,
Is as devoid of pride, of poetry,
Of soul, of picturesqueness, of contour,
Of character, of NOSE in short—as that
    [*Takes him by the shoulders and turns him
    around, suiting the action to the word*]
Which at the end of that limp spine of yours
My left foot—
    THE MEDDLER: [*Escaping*] Help! The Guard!
    CYRANO: Take notice, all
Who find this feature of my countenance
A theme for comedy! When the humorist
Is noble, then my custom is to show
Appreciation proper to his rank—
More heartfelt . . . and more pointed. . . .
    DE GUICHE: [*Who has come down from the stage,
surrounded by the* Marquis] Presently
This fellow will grow tiresome.
    VALVERT: [*Shrugs*] Oh, he blows
His trumpet!
    DE GUICHE: Well—will no one interfere?
    VALVERT: No one? [*Looks round*] Observe. I my-
self will proceed
To put him in his place.
    [*He walks up to* Cyrano, *who has been watch-
ing him, and stands there, looking him over
with an affected air*] Ah . . . your nose . . .
hem! . . .
Your nose is . . . rather large!
    CYRANO: [*Gravely*] Rather.
    VALVERT: [*Simpering*] Oh well—
    CYRANO: [*Coolly*] Is that all?
    VALVERT: [*Turns away, with a shrug*] Well, of
course—
    CYRANO: Ah, no, young sir!
You are too simple. Why, you might have said—
Oh, a great many things! Mon dieu, why waste
Your opportunity? For example, thus:—
Aggressive: I, sir, if that nose were mine,
I'd have it amputated—on the spot!
Friendly: How do you drink with such a nose?
You ought to have a cup made specially.
Descriptive: 'Tis a rock—a crag—a cape—
A cape? say rather, a peninsula!
Inquisitive: What is that receptacle —
A razor-case or a portfolio?
Kindly: Ah, do you love the little birds
So much that when they come and sing to you,
You give them this to perch on? Insolent:
Sir, when you smoke, the neighbors must suppose
Your chimney is on fire. Cautious: Take care—
A weight like that might make you topheavy.
Thoughtful: Somebody fetch my parasol—
Those delicate colors fade so in the sun!

Pedantic: Does not Aristophanes
Mention a mythologic monster called
Hippocampelephantocamelos?
Surely we have here the original!
Familiar: Well, old torchlight! Hang your hat
Over that chandelier—it hurts my eyes.
Eloquent: When it blows, the typhoon howls,
And the clouds darken. Dramatic: When it bleeds—
The Red Sea! Enterprising: What a sign
For some perfumer! Lyric: Hark—the horn
Of Roland calls to summon Charlemagne!—
Simple: When do they unveil the monument?
Respectful: Sir, I recognize in you
A man of parts, a man of prominence—
Rustic: Hey? What? Call that a nose? Na, na—
I be no fool like what you think I be—
That there's a blue cucumber! Military:
Point against cavalry! Practical: Why not
A lottery with this for the grand prize?
Or—parodying Faustus in the play—
"Was this the nose that launched a thousand ships
And burned the topless towers of Ilium?"
These, my dear sir, are things you might have said
Had you some tinge of letters, or of wit
To color your discourse. But wit,—not so,
You never had an atom—and of letters,
You need but three to write you down—an Ass.
Moreover,—if you had the invention, here
Before these folk to make a jest of me—
Be sure you would not then articulate
The twentieth part of half a syllable
Of the beginning! For I say these things
Lightly enough myself, about myself,
But I allow none else to utter them.
    DE GUICHE: [*Tries to lead away the amazed* Val-
vert] Vicomte—come.
    VALVERT: [*Choking*] Oh— These arrogant grand
airs!—
A clown who—look at him—not even gloves!
No ribbons—no lace—no buckles on his shoes—
    CYRANO: I carry my adornments on my soul.
I do not dress up like a popinjay;
But inwardly, I keep my daintiness.
I do not bear with me, by any chance,
An insult not yet washed away—a conscience
Yellow with unpurged bile—an honor frayed
To rags, a set of scruples badly worn.
I go caparisoned in gems unseen,
Trailing white plumes of freedom, garlanded
With my good name—no figure of a man,
But a soul clothed in shining armor, hung
With deeds for decorations, twirling—thus—
A bristling wit, and swinging at my side
Courage, and on the stones of this old town
Making the sharp truth ring, like golden spurs!
    VALVERT: But—
    CYRANO: But I have no gloves! A pity too!
I had one—the last one of an old pair—
And lost that. Very careless of me. Some

Gentleman offered me an impertinence.
I left it—in his face.

VALVERT: Dolt, bumpkin, fool,
Insolent puppy, jobbernowl!

CYRANO: [*Removes his hat and bows*] Ah, yes?
And I—Cyrano-Savinien-Hercule
De Bergerac!

VALVERT: [*Turns away*] Buffoon!

CYRANO: [*Cries out as if suddenly taken with a
cramp*] Oh!

VALVERT: [*Turns back*] Well, what now?

CYRANO: [*With grimaces of anguish*]
I must do something to relieve these cramps—
This is what comes of lack of exercise—
Ah!—

VALVERT: What is all this?

CYRANO: My sword has gone to sleep!

VALVERT: [*Draws*] So be it!

CYRANO: You shall die exquisitely.

VALVERT: [*Contemptuously*] Poet!

CYRANO: Why yes, a poet, if you will;
So while we fence, I'll make you a Ballade
Extempore.

VALVERT: A Ballade?

CYRANO: Yes. You know
What that is?

VALVERT: I—

CYRANO: The Ballade, sir, is formed
Of three stanzas of eight lines each—

VALVERT: Oh, come!

CYRANO: And a refrain of four.

VALVERT: You—

CYRANO: I'll compose
One, while I fight with you; and at the end
Of the last line—thrust home!

VALVERT: Will you?

CYRANO: I will.
   [*Declaims*]
"Ballade of the duel at the Hôtel de Bourgogne
  Between de Bergerac and a Boeotian."

VALVERT: [*Sneering*] What do you mean by that?

CYRANO: Oh, that? The title.

THE CROWD: [*Excited*] Come on—-

                              A circle—
                                   Quiet—
Down in front!
      [*Tableau. A ring of interested spectators in the
      centre of the floor, the* Marquis *and the* Officers
      mingling with the citizens and common folk.
      Pages *swarming up on men's shoulders to see
      better; the* Ladies *in the boxes standing and
      leaning over. To the right,* De Guiche *and his
      following; to the left,* Le Bret, Cuigy, Rague-
      neau, *and others of* Cyrano's *friends*]

CYRANO: [*Closes his eyes for an instant*]
Stop . . . Let me choose my rimes. . . . Now!
   Here we go—[*He suits the action to the word,
      throughout the following*]
Lightly I toss my hat away,

Languidly over my arm let fall
The cloak that covers my bright array—
   Then out swords, and to work withal!
   A Launcelot, in his Lady's hall . . .
A Spartacus, at the Hippodrome! . . .
   I dally awhile with you, dear jackal,
Then, as I end the refrain, thrust home!
      [*The swords cross—the fight is on*]
Where shall I skewer my peacock? . . . Nay,
   Better for you to have shunned this brawl!—
Here, in the heart, thro' your ribbons gay?
   —In the belly, under your silken shawl?
   Hark, how the steel rings musical!
Mark how my point floats, light as the foam,
   Ready to drive you back to the wall,
Then, as I end the refrain, thrust home!

Ho, for a rime! . . . You are white as whey—
   You break, you cower, you cringe, you . . . crawl!
Tac!—and I parry your last essay:
   So may the turn of a hand forestall
Life with its honey, death with its gall;
   So may the turn of my fancy roam
Free, for a time, till the rimes recall,
Then, as I end the refrain, thrust home!
      [*He announces solemnly*]
Refrain:
   Prince! Pray God, that is Lord of all,
Pardon your soul, for your time has come!
   Beat—pass—fling you aslant, asprawl—
Then, as I end the refrain . . .
      [*He lunges;* Valvert *staggers back and falls into
      the arms of his friends.* Cyrano *recovers, and
      salutes*]—Thrust home!
      [*Shouts. Applause from the boxes. Flowers and
      handkerchiefs come fluttering down. The* Offi-
      cers *surround* Cyrano *and congratulate him.*
      Ragueneau *dances for joy.* Le Bret *is unable to
      conceal his enthusiasm. The friends of* Valvert
      hold him up and help him away]

THE CROWD: [*In one long cry*] Ah-h!

A CAVALIER: Superb!

A WOMAN: Simply sweet!

RAGUENEAU: Magnelephant!

A MARQUIS: A novelty!

LE BRET: Bah!

THE CROWD: [*Thronging around* Cyrano] Compli-
   ments—regards—
Bravo!—

A WOMAN'S VOICE: Why, he's a hero!

A MUSKETEER: [*Advances quickly to* Cyrano, *with
outstretched hands*] Monsieur, will you
Permit me?—It was altogether fine!
I think I may appreciate these things—
Moreover, I have been stamping for pure joy!
   [*He retires quickly*]

CYRANO: [*To* Cuigy] What was that gentleman's
name?

CUIGY: Oh . . . D'Artagnan.

LE BRET: [*Takes* Cyrano's *arm*] Come here and
  tell me—
CYRANO: Let this crowd go first—[*To* Bellerose]
May we stay?
  BELLEROSE: [*With great respect*] Certainly!
    [*Cries and cat-calls off stage*]
  JODELET: [*Comes down from the door where he
has been looking out*] Hark!—Montfleury—
They are hooting him.
  BELLEROSE: [*Solemnly*] "Sic transit gloria!"
[*Changes his tone and shouts to the* Porter *and the*
Lamplighter]—Strike! . . . Close the house! . . .
  Leave the lights— We rehearse
The new farce after dinner.
    [Jodelet *and* Bellerose *go out after elaborately
    saluting* Cyrano]
  THE PORTER: [*To* Cyrano] You do not dine?
  CYRANO: I?—No! [*The* Porter *turns away*]
  LE BRET: Why not?
  CYRANO: [*Haughtily*] Because—
    [*Changing his tone when he sees the* Porter
    has gone] Because I have
No money.
  LE BRET: [*Gesture of tossing*] But—the purse of
  gold?
  CYRANO: Farewell,
Paternal pension!
  LE BRET: So you have, until
The first of next month—?
  CYRANO: Nothing.
  LE BRET: What a fool!—
  CYRANO: But—what a gesture!
  THE ORANGE GIRL: [*Behind her little counter;
coughs*] Hem!
    [Cyrano *and* Le Bret *look around; she advances
    timidly*] Pardon, monsieur . . .
'A man ought never to go hungry . . .
    [*Indicating the sideboard*] See,
I have everything here . . . [*Eagerly*] Please!—
  CYRANO: [*Uncovers*] My dear child,
I cannot bend this Gascon pride of mine
To accept such a kindness— Yet, for fear
That I may give you pain if I refuse,
I will take . . .
    [*He goes to the sideboard and makes his selec-
    tion*] Oh, not very much! A grape . . .
    [*She gives him the bunch; he removes a single
    grape*] One only! And a glass of water . . .
    [*She starts to pour wine into it; he stops her*]
    Clear!
And . . . half a macaroon!
    [*He gravely returns the other half*]
  LE BRET: Old idiot!
  THE ORANGE GIRL: Please!—Nothing more?
  CYRANO: Why yes— Your hand to kiss. [*He kisses
the hand which she holds out, as he would the hand
of a princess*]
  THE ORANGE GIRL: Thank you, sir. [*She curtseys*]
Good-night. [*She goes out*]
  CYRANO: Now, I am listening.

    [*Plants himself before the sideboard and ar-
    ranges thereon—*] Dinner!—[—*the macaroon*]
Drink!—[—*the glass of water*]
            Dessert!—[—*the grape*]
                    There—now I'll sit down
[*Seats himself*]
Lord, I was hungry! Abominably! [*Eating*] Well?
  LE BRET: These fatheads with the bellicose grand
    airs
Will have you ruined if you listen to them;
Talk to a man of sense and hear how all
Your swagger impresses him.
  CYRANO: [*Finishes his macaroon*] Enormously.
  LE BRET: The Cardinal—
  CYRANO: [*Beaming*] Was he there?
  LE BRET: He must have thought you—
  CYRANO: Original.
  LE BRET: Well, but—
  CYRANO: He is himself
A playwright. He will not be too displeased
That I have closed another author's play.
  LE BRET: But look at all the enemies you have
    made!
  CYRANO: [*Begins on the grape*] How many—do
  you think?
  LE BRET: Just forty-eight
Without the women.
  CYRANO: Count them.
  LE BRET: Montfleury,
Baro, de Guiche, the Vicomte, the Old Man,
All the Academy—
  CYRANO: Enough! You make me
Happy!
  LE BRET: But where is all this leading you?
What is your plan?
  CYRANO: I have been wandering—
Wasting my force upon too many plans.
Now I have chosen one.
  LE BRET: What one?
  CYRANO: The simplest—
To make myself in all things admirable!
  LE BRET: Hmph!—Well, then, the real reason
    why you hate
Montfleury— Come, the truth, now!
  CYRANO: [*Rises*] That Silenus,
Who cannot hold his belly in his arms,
Still dreams of being sweetly dangerous
Among the women—sighs and languishes,
Making sheeps' eyes out of his great frog's face—
I hate him ever since one day he dared
Smile upon—
            Oh, my friend, I seemed to see
Over some flower a great snail crawling!
  LE BRET: [*Amazed*] How,
What? Is it possible?—
  CYRANO: [*With a bitter smile*] For me to love? . . .
    [*Changing his tone; seriously*] I love.
  LE BRET: May I know? You have never said—
  CYRANO: Whom I love? Think a moment Think
  of me—

Me, whom the plainest woman would despise—
Me, with this nose of mine that marches on
Before me by a quarter of an hour!
Whom should I love? Why—of course—it must be
The woman in the world most beautiful.
    LE BRET: Most beautiful?
    CYRANO: In all this world—most sweet;
Also most wise; most witty; and most fair!
    LE BRET: Who and what is this woman?
    CYRANO: Dangerous
Mortally, without meaning; exquisite
Without imagining. Nature's own snare
To allure manhood. A white rose wherein
Love lies in ambush for his natural prey.
Who knows her smile has known a perfect thing.
She creates grace in her own image, brings
Heaven to earth in one movement of her hand—
Nor thou, O Venus! balancing thy shell
Over the Mediterranean blue, nor thou,
Diana! marching through broad, blossoming woods,
Art so divine as when she mounts her chair,
And goes abroad through Paris!
    LE BRET: Oh, well—of course,
That makes everything clear!
    CYRANO: Transparently.
    LE BRET: Madeleine Robin—your cousin?
    CYRANO: Yes; Roxane.
    LE BRET: And why not? If you love her, tell her
      so!
You have covered yourself with glory in her eyes
This very day.
    CYRANO: My old friend—look at me,
And tell me how much hope remains for me
With this protuberance! Oh I have no more
Illusions! Now and then—bah! I may grow
Tender, walking alone in the blue cool
Of evening, through some garden fresh with flowers
After the benediction of the rain;
My poor big devil of a nose inhales
April . . . and so I follow with my eyes
Where some boy, with a girl upon his arm,
Passes a patch of silver . . . and I feel
Somehow, I wish I had a woman too,
Walking with little steps under the moon,
And holding my arm so, and smiling. Then
I dream—and I forget. . . .
                 And then I see
The shadow of my profile on the wall!
    LE BRET: My friend! . . .
    CYRANO: My friend, I have my bitter days,
Knowing myself so ugly, so alone.
Sometimes—
    LE BRET: You weep?
    CYRANO: [Quickly] Oh, not that ever! No,
That would be too grotesque—tears trickling down
All the long way along this nose of mine?
I will not so profane the dignity
Of sorrow. Never any tears for me!
Why, there is nothing more sublime than tears,

Nothing!—Shall I make them ridiculous
In my poor person?
    LE BRET: Love's no more than chance!
    CYRANO: [Shakes his head]
No. I love Cleopatra; do I appear
Cæsar? I adore Beatrice; have I
The look of Dante?
    LE BRET: But your wit—your courage—
Why, that poor child who offered you just now
Your dinner! She—you saw with your own eyes,
Her eyes did not avoid you.
    CYRANO: [Thoughtful] That is true . . .
    LE BRET: Well then! Roxane herself, watching
      your duel,
Paler than—
    CYRANO: Pale?—
    LE BRET: Her lips parted, her hand
Thus, at her breast—I saw it! Speak to her
Speak, man!
    CYRANO: Through my nose? She might laugh at
      me;
That is the one thing in this world I fear!
    THE PORTER: [Followed by the Duenna, ap-
proaches Cyrano respectfully] A lady asking for
Monsieur.
    CYRANO: Mon dieu . . .
Her Duenna!—
    THE DUENNA: [A sweeping curtsey] Monsieur . . .
A message for you:
From our good cousin we desire to know
When and where we may see him privately.
    CYRANO: [Amazed] To see me?
    THE DUENNA: [An elaborate reverence] To see
      you. We have certain things
To tell you.
    CYRANO: Certain—
    THE DUENNA: Things.
    CYRANO: [Trembling] Mon dieu! . . .
    THE DUENNA: We go
To-morrow, at the first flush of the dawn,
To hear Mass at St. Roch. Then afterwards,
Where can we meet and talk a little?
    CYRANO: [Catching Le Bret's arm] Where?—
I— Ah, mon dieu! . . . mon dieu! . . .
    THE DUENNA: Well?
    CYRANO: I am thinking . . .
    THE DUENNA: And you think?
    CYRANO: I . . . The shop of Ragueneau . . .
Ragueneau—pastrycook . . .
    THE DUENNA: Who dwells?—
    CYRANO: Mon dieu! . . .
Oh, yes . . . Ah, mon dieu! . . . Rue St.-Honoré.
    THE DUENNA: We are agreed. Remember—seven
      o'clock. [Reverence]
Until then—
    CYRANO: I'll be there. [The Duenna goes out]
    CYRANO: [Falls into the arms of Le Bret] Me . . .
      to see me! . . .
    LE BRET: You are not quite so gloomy.

CYRANO: After all,
She knows that I exist—no matter why!
LE BRET: So now, you are going to be happy.
CYRANO: Now! . . . [*Beside himself*]
I—I am going to be a storm—a flame—
I need to fight whole armies all alone;
I have ten hearts; I have a hundred arms; I feel
Too strong to war with mortals—
       [*He shouts at the top of his voice*] Bring me
       giants!
       [*A moment since, the shadows of the comedians
       have been visible moving and posturing upon
       the stage. The violins have taken their places*]
A VOICE: [*From the stage*] Hey—pst—less noise!
       We are rehearsing here!
CYRANO: [*Laughs*] We are going.
       [*He turns up stage. Through the street door
       enter* Cuigy, Brissaille, *and a number of offi-
       cers, supporting* Lignière, *who is now thor-
       oughly drunk*]
CUIGY: Cyrano!
CYRANO: What is it?
CUIGY: Here—
Here's your stray lamb!
       CYRANO: [*Recognizes* Lignière] Lignière—What's
       wrong with him?
CUIGY: He wants you.
BRISSAILLE: He's afraid to go home.
CYRANO: Why?
LIGNIÈRE: [*Showing a crumpled scrap of paper
and speaking with the elaborate logic of profound
intoxication*]
This letter—hundred against one—that's me—
I'm the one—all because of little song—
Good song— Hundred men, waiting, understand?
Porte de Nesle—way home— Might be dangerous—
Would you permit me spend the night with you?
       CYRANO: A hundred—is that all? You are going
       home!
       LIGNIÈRE: [*Astonished*] Why—
CYRANO: [*In a voice of thunder, indicating the
lighted lantern which the* Porter *holds up curiously
as he regards the scene*] Take that lantern!
       [Lignière *precipitately seizes the lantern*] For-
       ward march! I say
I'll be the man to-night that sees you home.
       [*To the officers*]
You others follow—I want an audience!
       CUIGY: A hundred against one—
CYRANO: Those are the odds
To-night!
       [*The* Comedians *in their costumes are descend-
       ing from the stage and joining the group*]
       LE BRET: But why help this—
CYRANO: There goes Le Bret
Growling!
       LE BRET: —This drunkard here?
       CYRANO: [*His hand on* Le Bret's *shoulder*] Be-
       cause this drunkard—
This tun of sack, this butt of Burgundy—

Once in his life has done one lovely thing:
After the Mass, according to the form,
He saw, one day, the lady of his heart
Take holy water for a blessing. So
This one, who shudders at a drop of rain,
This fellow here—runs headlong to the font
Bends down and drinks it dry!
       A SOUBRETTE: I say that was
A pretty thought!
       CYRANO: Ah, was it not?
       THE SOUBRETTE: [*To the others*] But why
Against one poor poet, a hundred men?
       CYRANO: March!
       [*To the officers*] And you gentlemen, remember
       now,
No rescue— Let me fight alone.
       A COMEDIENNE: [*Jumps down from the stage*]
       Come on!
I'm going to watch—
       CYRANO: Come along!
       ANOTHER COMEDIENNE: [*Jumps down, speaks to a*
Comedian *costumed as an old man*] You, Cassandre?
       CYRANO: Come all of you—the Doctor, Isabelle,
Léandre—the whole company—a swarm
Of murmuring, golden bees—we'll parody
Italian farce and Tragedy-of-Blood;
Ribbons for banners, masks for blazonry,
And tambourines to be our rolling drums!
       ALL THE WOMEN: [*Jumping for joy*] Bravo!—My
       hood— My cloak— Hurry!
       JODELET: [*Mock heroic*] Lead on!—
       CYRANO: [*To the violins*] You violins—play us an
       overture—
       [*The violins join the procession which is form-
       ing. The lighted candles are snatched from
       the stage and distributed; it becomes a torch-
       light procession*]
Bravo!—Officers— Ladies in costume—
And twenty paces in advance. . . .
       [*He takes his station as he speaks*] Myself,
Alone, with glory fluttering over me,
Alone as Lucifer at war with heaven!
Remember—no one lifts a hand to help—
Ready there? One . . . two . . . three! Porter, the
       doors! . . .
       [*The* Porter *flings wide the great doors. We
       see in the dim moonlight a corner of old Paris,
       purple and picturesque*]
Look—Paris dreams—nocturnal, nebulous.
Under blue moonbeams hung from wall to wall—
Nature's own setting for the scene we play!—
Yonder, behind her veil of mist, the Seine,
Like a mysterious and magic mirror
Trembles—
                    And you shall see what you shall see!
       ALL: To the Porte de Nesle!
       CYRANO: [*Erect upon the threshold*] To the Porte
       de Nesle!
       [*He turns back for a moment to the* Soubrette]

Did you not ask, my dear, why against one
Singer they send a hundred swords?

    [*Quietly, drawing his own sword*]

                           Because
They know this one man for a friend of mine!

    [*He goes out. The procession follows:* Lignière
    zigzagging at its head, then the Comediennes
    on the arms of the Officers, *then the* Come-
    dians, *leaping and dancing as they go. It van-
    ishes into the night to the music of the violins,
    illuminated by the flickering glimmer of the
    candles*]

                CURTAIN

ACT II.
The Bakery of the Poets

The shop of Ragueneau, *baker and pastrycook:
a spacious affair at the corner of the Rue St.-Honoré
and the Rue de l'Arbre Sec. The street, seen vaguely
through the glass panes in the door at the back,
is gray in the first light of dawn. In the foreground,
at the left, a counter is surmounted by a canopy
of wrought iron from which are hanging ducks,
geese, and white peacocks. Great crockery jars hold
bouquets of common flowers, yellow sunflowers in
particular. On the same side farther back, a huge
fireplace; in front of it, between great andirons, of
which each one supports a little saucepan, roast
fowls revolve and weep into their dripping-pans.
To the right at the first entrance, a door. Beyond
it, second entrance, a staircase leads up to a little
dining-room under the eaves, its interior visible
through open shutters. A table is set there and a
tiny Flemish candlestick is lighted; there one may
retire to eat and drink in private. A wooden gallery,
extending from the head of the stairway, seems to
lead to other little dining rooms. In the center of
the shop, an iron ring hangs by a rope over a
pulley so that it can be raised or lowered; adorned
with game of various kinds hung from it by hooks,
it has the appearance of a sort of gastronomic chandelier. In the shadow under the staircase, ovens are
glowing. The spits revolve; the copper pots and
pans gleam ruddily. Pastries in pyramids. Hams
hanging from the rafters. The morning baking is in
progress: a bustle of tall cooks and timid scullions
and scurrying apprentices; a blossoming of white
caps adorned with cock's feathers or the wings of
guinea fowl. On wicker trays or on great metal
platters they bring in rows of pastries and fancy
dishes of various kinds. Tables are covered with
trays of cakes and rolls; others with chairs placed
about them are set for guests. One little table in a
corner disappears under a heap of papers. At the
curtain rise* Ragueneau *is seated there. He is writing
poetry.*

A PASTRYCOOK: [*Brings in a dish*] Fruits en gelée!

SECOND PASTRYCOOK: [*Brings dish*] Custard!

THIRD PASTRYCOOK: [*Brings roast peacock ornamented with feathers*] Peacock rôti!

FOURTH PASTRYCOOK: [*Brings tray of cakes*] Cakes
and confections!

FIFTH PASTRYCOOK: [*Brings earthen dish*] Beef en
casserole!

RAGUENEAU: [*Raises his head; returns to mere
earth*]
Over the coppers of my kitchen flows
The frosted-silver dawn. Silence awhile
The god who sings within thee, Ragueneau!
Lay down the lute—the oven calls for thee!
    [*Rises; goes to one of the cooks*]
Here's a hiatus in your sauce; fill up
The measure.

    THE COOK: How much?

    RAGUENEAU: [*Measures on his finger*] One more
    dactyl.

    THE COOK: Huh?

    FIRST PASTRYCOOK: Rolls!

    SECOND PASTRYCOOK: Roulades!

    RAGUENEAU: [*Before the fireplace*] Veil, O Muse,
thy virgin eyes
From the lewd gleam of these terrestrial fires!
    [*To First Pastrycook*]
Your rolls lack balance. Here's the proper form—
An equal hemistich on either side,
And the caesura in between.
    [*To another, pointing out an unfinished pie*]
                       Your house
Of crust should have a roof upon it.
    [*To another, who is seated on the hearth, plac-
    ing poultry on a spit*]
                       And you—
Along the interminable spit, arrange
The modest pullet and the lordly Turk
Alternately, my son—as great Malherbe
Alternates male and female rimes. Remember,
A couplet, or a roast, should be well turned.

AN APPRENTICE: [*Advances with a dish covered
by a napkin*]
Master, I thought of you when I designed
This, hoping it might please you.

    RAGUENEAU: Ah! A lyre—

    THE APPRENTICE: In puff-paste—

    RAGUENEAU: And the jewels—candied fruit!

    THE APPRENTICE: And the strings, barley-sugar!

    RAGUENEAU: [*Gives him money*] Go and drink
My health.
    [Lise *enters*]
              St!—My wife— Circulate, and hide
That money!
    [*Shows the lyre to* Lise, *with languid air*]
             Graceful—yes?

    LISE: Ridiculous! [*She places on the counter a
pile of paper bags*]

    RAGUENEAU: Paper bags? Thank you . . .
    [*He looks at them*] Ciel! My manuscripts!

The sacred verses of my poets—rent
Asunder, limb from limb—butchered to make
Base packages of pastry! Ah, you are one
Of those insane Bacchantes who destroyed
Orpheus!

LISE: Your dirty poets left them here
To pay for eating half our stock-in-trade:
We ought to make some profit out of them!

RAGUENEAU: Ant! Would you blame the locust for
his song?

LISE: I blame the locust for his appetite!
There used to be a time—before you had
Your hungry friends—you never called me Ants—
No, nor Bacchantes!

RAGUENEAU: What a way to use
Poetry!

LISE: Well, what is the use of it?

RAGUENEAU: But, my dear girl, what would you
    do with prose?
    [*Two children enter*] Well, dears?

A CHILD: Three little patties.

RAGUENEAU: [*Serves them*] There we are!
All hot and brown.

THE CHILD: Would you mind wrapping them?

RAGUENEAU: One of my paper bags! . . . Oh,
    certainly.
    [*Reads from the bag, as he is about to wrap the
    patties in it*]
"Ulysses, when he left Penelope"—
Not that one!
    [*Takes another bag; reads*]
'Phoebus, golden-crowned"—Not that one.

LISE: Well? They are waiting!

RAGUENEAU: Very well, very well!—
The Sonnet to Phyllis . . .

                Yet—it does seem hard . . .

LISE: Made up your mind—at last! Mph!—Jack-
    o'-Dreams!

RAGUENEAU: [*As her back is turned, calls back
the children, who are already at the door*]
Pst!—Children— Give me back the bag. Instead
Of three patties, you shall have six of them!
    [*Makes the exchange. The children go out. He
    reads from the bag, as he smooths it out ten-
    derly*]
"Phyllis"—A spot of butter on her name!—
"Phyllis"—

CYRANO: [*Enters hurriedly*] What is the time?

RAGUENEAU: Six o'clock.

CYRANO: One
Hour more . . .

RAGUENEAU: Felicitations!

CYRANO: And for what?

RAGUENEAU: Your victory! I saw it all—

CYRANO: Which one?

RAGUENEAU: At the Hôtel de Bourgogne.

CYRANO: Oh—the duel!

RAGUENEAU: The duel in Rime!

LISE: He talks of nothing else.

CYRANO: Nonsense!

RAGUENEAU: [*Fencing and foining with a spit,
which he snatches up from the hearth*]
    "Then, as I end the refrain, thrust home!"
"Then, as I end the refrain"—

                Gods! What a line!
"Then, as I end"—

CYRANO: What time now, Ragueneau?

RAGUENEAU: [*Petrified at the full extent of a
lunge, while he looks at the clock*] Five after six—
    [*Recovers*]
"—thrust home!"

                A Ballade, too!

LISE: [*To* Cyrano, *who in passing has mechanically shaken hands with her*] Your hand—what
have you done?

CYRANO: Oh, my hand?—Nothing.

RAGUENEAU: What danger now—

CYRANO: No danger.

LISE: I believe
He is lying.

CYRANO: Why? Was I looking down my nose?
That must have been a devil of a lie!
    [*Changing his tone; to* Ragueneau]
I expect someone. Leave us here alone,
When the time comes.

RAGUENEAU: How can I? In a moment,
My poets will be here.

LISE: To break their . . . fast!

CYRANO: Take them away, then, when I give the
    sign.
—What time?

RAGUENEAU: Ten minutes after.

CYRANO: Have you a pen?

RAGUENEAU: [*Offers him a pen*] An eagle's
    feather!

A MUSKETEER: [*Enters, and speaks to* Lise *in a
stentorian voice*] Greeting!

CYRANO: [*To* Ragueneau] Who is this?

RAGUENEAU: My wife's friend. A terrific warrior.
So he says.

CYRANO: Ah—I see. [*Takes up the pen,
waves* Ragueneau *away*]

                Only to write—
To fold— To give it to her—and to go . . .
    [*Throws down the pen*]
Coward! And yet—the Devil take my soul
If I dare speak one word to her . . .
    [*To* Ragueneau] What time now?

RAGUENEAU: A quarter after six.

CYRANO: [*Striking his breast*]—One little word
Of all the many thousand I have here!
Whereas in writing . . .
    [*Takes up the pen*] Come, I'll write to her
That letter I have written on my heart,
Torn up, and written over many times—
So many times . . . that all I have to do
Is to remember, and to write it down.
    [*He writes. Through the glass of the door ap-
    pear vague and hesitating shadows. The* Poets

enter, clothed in rusty black and spotted with mud]

LISE: [*To* Ragueneau] Here come your scarecrows!

FIRST POET: Comrade!

SECOND POET: [*Takes both* Ragueneau's *hands*] My dear brother!

THIRD POET: [*Sniffing*]
O Lord of Roasts, how sweet thy dwellings are!

FOURTH POET: Phoebus Apollo of the Silver Spoon!

FIFTH POET: Cupid of Cookery!

RAGUENEAU: [*Surrounded, embraced, beaten on the back*] These geniuses,
They put one at one's ease!

FIRST POET: We were delayed
By the crowd at the Porte de Nesle.

SECOND POET: Dead men
All scarred and gory, scattered on the stones,
Villainous-looking scoundrels—eight of them.

CYRANO: [*Looks up an instant*] Eight? I thought only seven—

RAGUENEAU: Do you know
The hero of this hecatomb?

CYRANO: I? . . . No.

LISE: [*To the* Musketeer] Do you?

THE MUSKETEER: Hmm—perhaps!

FIRST POET: They say one man alone
Put to flight all this crowd.

SECOND POET: Everywhere lay
Swords, daggers, pikes, bludgeons—

CYRANO: [*Writing*] "Your eyes . . ."

THIRD POET: As far
As the Quai des Orfèvres, hats and cloaks—

FIRST POET: Why, that man must have been the devil!

CYRANO: "Your lips . . ."

FIRST POET: Some savage monster might have done this thing!

CYRANO: "Looking upon you, I grow faint with fear . . ."

SECOND POET: What have you written lately, Ragueneau?

CYRANO: "Your Friend—Who loves you . . ."
       So. No signature;
I'll give it to her myself.

RAGUENEAU: A Recipe
In Rime.

THIRD POET: Read us your rimes!

FOURTH POET: Here's a brioche
Cocking its hat at me.
       [*He bites off the top of it*]

FIRST POET: Look how those buns
Follow the hungry poet with their eyes—
Those almond eyes!

SECOND POET: We are listening—

THIRD POET: See this cream-puff—
Fat little baby, drooling while it smiles!

SECOND POET: [*Nibbling at the pastry lyre*]
For the first time, the lyre is my support.

RAGUENEAU: [*Coughs, adjusts his cap, strikes an attitude*]
A Recipe in Rime—

SECOND POET: [*Gives* First Poet *a dig with his elbow*] Your breakfast?

FIRST POET: Dinner!

RAGUENEAU: [*Declaims*]
       A Recipe for Making Almond Tarts

Beat your egg, the yolk and white,
       Very light;
Mingle with their creamy fluff
       Drops of lime-juice, cool and green;
       Then pour in
Milk of Almonds, just enough.

Dainty patty-pans, embraced
       In puff-paste—
Have these ready within reach;
       With your thumb and finger, pinch
       Half an inch
Up around the edge of each—

Into these, a score or more,
       Slowly pour
All your store of custard; so
       Take them, bake them golden-brown—
       Now sit down! . . .
Almond tartlets, Ragueneau!

THE POETS: Delicious! Melting!

A POET: [*Chokes*] Humph!

CYRANO: [*To* Ragueneau] Do you not see
Those fellows fattening themselves?—

RAGUENEAU: I know.
I would not look—it might embarrass them—
You see, I love a friendly audience.
Besides—another vanity—I am pleased
When they enjoy my cooking.

CYRANO: [*Slaps him on the back*] Be off with you!—
       [Ragueneau *goes upstage*]
Good little soul! [*Calls to* Lise] Madame!—
       [*She leaves the* Musketeer *and comes down to him*]   This musketeer—
He is making love to you?

LISE: [*Haughtily*] If any man
Offends my virtue—all I have to do
Is look at him—once!

CYRANO: [*Looks at her gravely; she drops her eyes*] I do not find
Those eyes of yours unconquerable.

LISE: [*Panting*]—Ah!

CYRANO: [*Raising his voice a little*]
Now listen—I am fond of Ragueneau;
I allow no one—do you understand?—
To . . . take his name in vain!

LISE: You think—

CYRANO: [*Ironic emphasis*] I think
I interrupt you.
       [*He salutes the* Musketeer, *who has heard with-*

out uaring to resent the warning. Lise *goes to the* Musketeer *as he returns* Cyrano's *salute*]

LISE: You—you swallow that?—
You ought to have pulled his nose!

THE MUSKETEER: His nose?—His nose! . . .
[*He goes out hurriedly.* Roxane *and the* Duenna *appear outside the door*]

CYRANO: [*Nods to* Ragueneau] Pst!—

RAGUENEAU: [*To the* Poets] Come inside—

CYRANO: [*Impatient*] Pst! . . . Pst! . . .

RAGUENEAU: We shall be more
Comfortable . . .
[*He leads the* Poets *into inner room*]

FIRST POET: The cakes!

SECOND POET: Bring them along!
[*They go out*]

CYRANO: If I can see the faintest spark of hope,
Then—[*Throws door open—bows*] Welcome!
[Roxane *enters, followed by the* Duenna, *whom* Cyrano *detains*]
Pardon me—one word—

THE DUENNA: Take two.

CYRANO: Have you a good digestion?

THE DUENNA: Wonderful!

CYRANO: Good. Here are two sonnets, by Ben-
serade—

THE DUENNA: Euh?

CYRANO: Which I fill for you with éclairs.

THE DUENNA: Ooo!

CYRANO: Do you like cream-puffs?

THE DUENNA: Only with whipped cream.

CYRANO: Here are three . . . six—embosomed in
a poem
By Saint-Amant. This ode of Chapelin
Looks deep enough to hold—a jelly roll.
—Do you love Nature?

THE DUENNA: Mad about it.

CYRANO: Then
Go out and eat these in the street. Do not
Return—

THE DUENNA: Oh, but—

CYRANO: Until you finish them.
[*Down to* Roxane]
Blessed above all others be the hour
When you remembered to remember me,
And came to tell me . . . what?

ROXANE: [*Takes off her mask*] First let me thank
you
Because . . . That man . . . that creature, whom
your sword
Made sport of yesterday— His patron, one—

CYRANO: De Guiche?—

ROXANE: —who thinks himself in love with me
Would have forced that man upon me for—
a husband—

CYRANO: I understand—so much the better then!
I fought, not for my nose, but your bright eyes.

ROXANE: And then, to tell you—but before I can
Tell you— Are you, I wonder still the same
Big Brother—almost—that you used to be

When we were children, playing by the pond
In the old garden down there—

CYRANO: I remember—
Every summer you came to Bergerac! . . .

ROXANE: You used to make swords out of bul-
rushes—

CYRANO: Your dandelion-dolls with golden hair—

ROXANE: And those green plums—

CYRANO: And those black mulberries—

ROXANE: In those days, you did everything I
wished!

CYRANO: Roxane, in short skirts, was called Madeleine.

ROXANE: Was I pretty?

CYRANO: Oh—not too plain!

ROXANE: Sometimes
When you had hurt your hand you used to come
Running to me—and I would be your mother,
And say— Oh, in a very grown-up voice:
[*She takes his hand*]
"Now, what have you been doing to yourself?
Let me see—"
[*She sees the hand—starts*] Oh! Wait— I said,
"Let me see!"
Still—at your age! How did you do that?

CYRANO: Playing
With the big boys, down by the Porte de Nesle.

ROXANE: [*Sits at a table and wets her handkerchief in a glass of water*] Come here to me.

CYRANO: —Such a wise little mother!

ROXANE: And tell me, while I wash this blood
away,
How many you—played with?

CYRANO: Oh, about a hundred.

ROXANE: Tell me.

CYRANO: No. Let me go. Tell me what you
Were going to tell me—if you dared?

ROXANE: [*Still holding his hand*] I think
I do dare—now. It seems like long ago
When I could tell you things. Yes—I dare . . .
Listen:
I . . . love someone.

CYRANO: Ah! . . .

ROXANE: Someone who does not know.

CYRANO: Ah! . . .

ROXANE: At least—not yet.

CYRANO: Ah! . . .

ROXANE: But he will know
Some day.

CYRANO: Ah! . . .

ROXANE: A big boy who loves me too,
And is afraid of me, and keeps away,
And never says one word.

CYRANO: Ah! . . .

ROXANE: Let me have
Your hand a moment—why how hot it is!—
I know. I see him trying . . .

CYRANO: Ah! . . .

ROXANE: There now!

Is that better?—[*She finishes bandaging the hand
with her handkerchief*]
                    Besides—only to think—
(This is a secret.) He is a soldier too,
In your own regiment—
    CYRANO: Ah! . . .
    ROXANE: Yes, in the Guards,
Your company too.
    CYRANO: Ah! . . .
    ROXANE: And such a man!—
He is proud—noble—young—brave—beautiful—
    CYRANO: [*Turns pale; rises*] Beautiful!—
    ROXANE: What's the matter?
    CYRANO: [*Smiling*] Nothing—this—
My sore hand!
    ROXANE: Well, I love him. That is all.
Oh—and I never saw him anywhere
Except the *Comédie.*
    CYRANO: You have never spoken?—
    ROXANE: Only our eyes . . .
    CYRANO: Why, then— How do you know?—
    ROXANE: People talk about people; and I hear
Things . . . and I know.
    CYRANO: You say he is in the Guards:
His name?
    ROXANE: Baron Christian de Neuvillette.
    CYRANO: He is not in the Guards.
    ROXANE: Yes. Since this morning.
Captain Carbon de Castel-Jaloux.
    CYRANO: So soon! . . .
So soon we lose our hearts!—
                    But, my dear child,—
    THE DUENNA: [*Opens the door*]
I have eaten the cakes, Monsieur de Bergerac!
    CYRANO: Good! Now go out and read the poetry!
    [*The Duenna disappears*]
—But, my dear child! You, who love only words,
Wit, the grand manner— Why, for all you know,
The man may be a savage, or a fool.
    ROXANE: His curls are like a hero from D'Urfé.
    CYRANO: His mind may be as curly as his hair.
    ROXANE: Not with such eyes. I read his soul in
      them.
    CYRANO: Yes, all our souls are written in our eyes!
But—if he be a bungler?
    ROXANE: Then I shall die—
There!
    CYRANO: [*After a pause*] And you brought me here
      to tell me this?
I do not yet quite understand, Madame,
The reason for your confidence.
    ROXANE: They say
That in your company— It frightens me—
You are all Gascons . . .
    CYRANO: And we pick a quarrel
With any flat-foot who intrudes himself.
Whose blood is not pure Gascon like our own?
Is this what you have heard?
    ROXANE: I am so afraid
For him!

    CYRANO: [*Between his teeth*] Not without rea-
      son!—
    ROXANE: And I thought
You . . . You were so brave, so invincible
Yesterday, against all those brutes!—If you,
Whom they all fear—
    CYRANO: Oh well— I will defend
Your little Baron.
    ROXANE: Will you? Just for me?
Because I have always been—your friend!
    CYRANO: Of course . . .
    ROXANE: Will you be *his* friend?
    CYRANO: I will be his friend.
    ROXANE: And never let him fight a duel?
    CYRANO: No—never.
    ROXANE: Oh, but you are a darling!—I must go—
You never told me about last night— Why,
You must have been a hero! Have him write
And tell me all about it—will you?
    CYRANO: Of course . . .
    ROXANE: [*Kisses her hand*]
I always did love you!—A hundred men
Against one— Well. . . . Adieu. We are great
    friends,
Are we not?
    CYRANO: Of course . . .
    ROXANE: He *must* write to me—
A hundred— You shall tell me the whole story
Some day, when I have time. A hundred men—
What courage!
    CYRANO: [*Salutes as she goes out*] Oh . . . I have
      done better since!
    [*The door closes after her.* Cyrano *remains mo-
      tionless, his eyes on the ground. Pause. The
      other door opens;* Ragueneau *puts in his head*]
    RAGUENEAU: May I come in?
    CYRANO: [*Without moving*] Yes . . .
    [Ragueneau *and his friends re-enter. At the
      same time,* Carbon de Castel-Jaloux *appears
      at the street door in uniform as Captain of the
      Guards; recognizes* Cyrano *with a sweeping
      gesture*]
    CARBON: Here he is!—Our hero!
    CYRANO: [*Raises his head and salutes*] Our Cap-
      tain!
    CARBON: We know! All our company
Are here—
    CYRANO: [*Recoils*] No—
    CARBON: Come! They are waiting for you.
    CYRANO: No!
    CARBON: [*Tries to lead him out*] Only across the
      street— Come!
    CYRANO: Please—
    CARBON: [*Goes to the door and shouts in a voice
of thunder*] Our champion
Refuses! He is not feeling well to-day!
    A VOICE OUTSIDE: Ah! Sandious!
    [*Noise outside of swords and trampling feet
      approaching*]
    CARBON: Here they come now!

THE CADETS: [*Entering the shop*] Mille dious!—
Mordious!—Capdedious!—Pocapdedious!

RAGUENEAU: [*In astonishment*] Gentlemen—
You are all Gascons?

THE CADETS: All!

FIRST CADET: [*To* Cyrano] Bravo!

CYRANO: Baron!

ANOTHER CADET: [*Takes both his hands*] Vivat!

CYRANO: Baron!

THIRD CADET: Come to my arms!

CYRANO: Baron!

OTHERS: To mine!—To mine!—

CYRANO: Baron . . . Baron . . . Have mercy—

RAGUENEAU: You are all Barons too?

THE CADETS: *Are* we?

RAGUENEAU: Are they? . . .

FIRST CADET: Our coronets would star the midnight sky!

LE BRET: [*Enters; hurries to* Cyrano] The whole
town's looking for you! Raving mad—
A triumph! Those who saw the fight—

CYRANO: I hope
You have not told them where I—

LE BRET: [*Rubbing his hands*] Certainly
I told them!

CITIZEN: [*Enters, followed by a group*] Listen!
Shut the door!—Here comes
All Paris!
[*The street outside fills with a shouting crowd.
Chairs and carriages stop at the door*]

LE BRET: [*Aside to* Cyrano, *smiling*] And Roxane?

CYRANO: [*Quickly*] Hush!

THE CROWD OUTSIDE: Cyrano!
[*A mob bursts into the shop. Shouts, acclama-
tions, general disturbance*]

RAGUENEAU: [*Standing on a table*]
My shop invaded— They'll break everything—
Glorious!

SEVERAL MEN: [*Crowding about* Cyrano] My
friend! . . . My friend! . . .

CYRANO: Why, yesterday
I did not have so many friends!

LE BRET: Success
At last!

A MARQUIS: [*Runs to* Cyrano, *with outstretched
hands*] My dear—really!—

CYRANO: [*Coldly*] So? And how long
Have I been dear to you?

ANOTHER MARQUIS: One moment—pray!
I have two ladies in my carriage here;
Let me present you—

CYRANO: Certainly! And first,
Who will present you, sir,—to me?

LE BRET: [*Astounded*] Why, what
The devil?—

CYRANO: Hush!

A MAN OF LETTERS: [*With a portfolio*] May I have
the details? . . .

CYRANO: You may not.

LE BRET: [*Plucking* Cyrano's *sleeve*] Theophrast
Renaudot!—Editor
Of the *Gazette*—your reputation! . . .

CYRANO: No.

A POET: [*Advances*] Monsieur—

CYRANO: Well?

THE POET: Your full name? I will compos
A pentacrostic—

ANOTHER: Monsieur—

CYRANO: That will do!
[*Movement. The crowd arranges itself. D
Guiche appears, escorted by* Cuigy, Brissaill
and the other officers who were with Cyran
at the close of the first act]

CUIGY: [*Goes to* Cyrano] Monsieur de Guiche!—
[*Murmur. Everyone moves*]
                          A message from the Marsha
De Gassion—

DE GUICHE: [*Saluting* Cyrano] Who wishes to ex
press
Through me his admiration. He has heard
Of your affair—

THE CROWD: Bravo!

CYRANO: [*Bowing*] The Marshal speaks
As an authority.

DE GUICHE: He said just now
The story would have been incredible
Were it not for the witness—

CUIGY: Of our eyes!

LE BRET: [*Aside to* Cyrano] What is it?

CYRANO: Hush!—

LE BRET: Something is wrong with you
Are you in pain?

CYRANO: [*Recovering himself*] In pain? Before thi
crowd?
[*His moustache bristles. He throws out h
chest*]
I? In pain? You shall see!

DE GUICHE: [*To whom* Cuigy *has been whispering
Your name is known
Already as a soldier. You are one
Of those wild Gascons, are you not?

CYRANO: The Guard
Yes. A Cadet.

A CADET: [*In a voice of thunder*] One of ourselves

DE GUICHE: Ah! So—
Then all these gentlemen with the haughty air,
These are the famous—

CARBON: Cyrano!

CYRANO: Captain?

CARBON: Our troop being all present, be so kind
As to present them to the Comte de Guiche!

CYRANO: [*With a gesture presenting the* Cadets
De Guiche, *declaims:*]
The Cadets of Gascoyne—the defenders
Of Carbon de Castel-Jaloux:
Free fighters, free lovers, free spenders—
The Cadets of Gascoyne—the defenders
Of old homes, old names, and old splendors—

A proud and a pestilent crew!
The Cadets of Gascoyne, the defenders
    Of Carbon de Castel-Jaloux.

Hawk-eyed, they stare down all contenders—
    The wolf bares his fangs as they do—
Make way there, you fat money-lenders!
(Hawk-eyed, they stare down all contenders)
Old boots that have been to the menders,
    Old cloaks that are worn through and through—
Hawk-eyed, they stare down all contenders—
    The wolf bares his fangs as they do!

Skull-breakers they are, and sword-benders;
    Red blood is their favorite brew;
Hot haters and loyal befrienders,
Skull-breakers they are, and sword-benders.
Wherever a quarrel engenders,
    They're ready and waiting for you!
Skull-breakers they are, and sword-benders;
    Red blood is their favorite brew!

Behold them, our Gascon defenders
    Who win every woman they woo!
There's never a dame but surrenders—
Behold them, our Gascon defenders!
Young wives who are clever pretenders—
    Old husbands who house the cuckoo—
Behold them—our Gascon defenders
    Who win every woman they woo!
    DE GUICHE: [Languidly, sitting in a chair]
Poets are fashionable nowadays
To have about one. Would you care to join
My following?
    CYRANO: No, sir. I do not follow.
    DU GUICHE: Your duel yesterday amused my uncle
The Cardinal. I might help you there.
    LE BRET: Grand Dieu!
    DE GUICHE: I suppose you have written a
        tragedy—
They all have.
    LE BRET: [Aside to Cyrano] Now at last you'll
        have it played—
Your "Agrippine!"
    DE GUICHE: Why not? Take it to him.
    CYRANO: [Tempted] Really—
    DE GUICHE: He is himself a dramatist;
Let him rewrite a few lines here and there,
And he'll approve the rest.
    CYRANO: [His face falls again] Impossible.
My blood curdles to think of altering
One comma.
    DE GUICHE: Ah, but when he likes a thing
He pays well.
    CYRANO: Yes—but not so well as I—
When I have made a line that sings itself
So that I love the sound of it—I pay
Myself a hundred times.
    DE GUICHE: You are proud, my friend.
    CYRANO: You have observed that?

    A CADET: [Enters with a drawn sword, along the
whole blade of which is transfixed a collection of
disreputable hats, their plumes draggled, their crowns
cut and torn] Cyrano! See here—
Look what we found this morning in the street—
The plumes dropped in their flight by those fine
    birds
Who showed the white feather!
                              Spoils of the hunt—
Well mounted!
    THE CROWD: Ha-ha-ha!
    CUIGY: Whoever hired
Those rascals, he must be an angry man
To-day!
    BRISSAILLE: Who was it? Do you know?
    DE GUICHE: Myself!—
    [The laughter ceases]
I hired them to do the sort of work
We do not soil our hands with—punishing
A drunken poet. . . .
    [Uncomfortable silence]
    THE CADET: [To Cyrano] What shall we do with
        them?
They ought to be preserved before they spoil—
    CYRANO: [Takes the sword, and in the gesture of
saluting De Guiche with it, makes all the hats slide
off at his feet]
Sir, will you not return these to your friends?
    DE GUICHE: My chair—my porters here—imme-
        diately! [To Cyrano violently]
—As for you, sir!—
    A VOICE: [In the street] The chair of Monseigneur
Le Comte de Guiche!—
    DE GUICHE: [Who has recovered his self-control;
smiling] Have you read Don Quixote?
    CYRANO: I have—and found myself the hero.
    A PORTER: [Appears at the door] Chair
Ready!
    DE GUICHE: Be so good as to read once more
The chapter of the windmills.
    CYRANO: [Gravely] Chapter Thirteen.
    DE GUICHE: Windmills, remember, if you fight
        with them—
    CYRANO: My enemies change, then, with every
        wind?
    DE GUICHE:—May swing round their huge arms
        and cast you down
Into the mire.
    CYRANO: Or up—among the stars!
    [De Guiche goes out. We see him get into the
        chair. The Officers follow murmuring among
        themselves. Le Bret goes up with them. The
        crowd goes out]
    CYRANO: [Saluting with burlesque politeness, those
who go out without daring to take leave of him]
Gentlemen. . . . Gentlemen. . . .
    LE BRET: [As the door closes, comes down, shak-
ing his clenched hands to heaven] You have done it
    now—
You have made your fortune!

CYRANO: There you go again,
Growling!—
LE BRET: At least this latest pose of yours—
Ruining every chance that comes your way—
Becomes exaggerated—
CYRANO: Very well,
Then I exaggerate!
LE BRET: [*Triumphantly*] Oh, you do!
CYRANO: Yes.
On principle. There are things in this world
A man does well to carry to extremes.
    LE BRET: Stop trying to be Three Musketeers in
        one!
Fortune and glory—
    CYRANO: What would you have me do?
Seek for the patronage of some great man,
And like a creeping vine on a tall tree
Crawl upward, where I cannot stand alone?
No thank you! Dedicate, as others do,
Poems to pawnbrokers? Be a buffoon
In the vile hope of teasing out a smile
On some cold face? No thank you! Eat a toad
For breakfast every morning? Make my knees
Callous, and cultivate a supple spine,—
Wear out my belly grovelling in the dust?
No thank you! Scratch the back of any swine
That roots up gold for me? Tickle the horns
Of Mammon with my left hand, while my right
Too proud to know his partner's business,
Takes in the fee? No thank you! Use the fire
God gave me to burn incense all day long
Under the nose of wood and stone? No thank you!
Shall I go leaping into ladies' laps
And licking fingers?—or—to change the form—
Navigating with madrigals for oars,
My sails full of sighs of dowagers?
No thank you! Publish verses at my own
Expense? No thank you! Be the patron saint
Of a small group of literary souls
Who dine together every Tuesday? No
I thank you! Shall I labor night and day
To build a reputation on one song,
And never write another? Shall I find
True genius only among Geniuses,
Palpitate over little paragraphs,
And struggle to insinuate my name
Into the columns of the *Mercury?*
No thank you! Calculate, scheme, be afraid,
Love more to make a visit than a poem,
Seek introductions, favors, influences?—
No thank you! No, I thank you! And again
I thank you!—But . . .
                    To sing, to laugh, to dream,
To walk in my own way and be alone,
Free, with an eye to see things as they are,
A voice that means manhood—to cock my hat
Where I choose— At a word, a *Yes*, a *No*,
To fight—or write. To travel any road
Under the sun, under the stars, nor doubt
If fame or fortune lie beyond the bourne—

Never to make a line I have not heard
In my own heart; yet, with all modesty
To say: "My soul, be satisfied with flowers,
With fruit, with weeds even; but gather them
In the one garden you may call your own."
So, when I win some triumph, by some chance,
Render no share to Cæsar—in a word,
I am too proud to be a parasite,
And if my nature wants the germ that grows
Towering to heaven like the mountain pine,
Or like the oak, sheltering multitudes—
I stand, not high it may be—but alone!
    LE BRET: Alone, yes!—But why stand against the
        world?
What devil has possessed you now, to go
Everywhere making yourself enemies?
    CYRANO: Watching you other people making friends
Everywhere—as a dog makes friends! I mark
The manner of these canine courtesies
And think: "My friends are of a cleaner breed;
Here comes—thank God!—another enemy!"
    LE BRET: But this is madness!
    CYRANO: Method, let us say.
It is my pleasure to displease. I love
Hatred. Imagine how it feels to face
The volley of a thousand angry eyes—
The bile of envy and the froth of fear
Spattering little drops about me— You—
Good nature all around you, soft and warm—
You are like those Italians, in great cowls
Comfortable and loose— Your chin sinks down
Into the folds, your shoulders droop. But I—
The Spanish ruff I wear around my throat
Is like a ring of enemies; hard, proud,
Each point another pride, another thorn—
So that I hold myself erect perforce.
Wearing the hatred of the common herd
Haughtily, the harsh collar of Old Spain,
At once a fetter and—a halo!
    LE BRET: Yes . . .
    [*After a silence, draws* Cyrano's *arm through
        his own*]
Tell this to all the world— And then to me
Say very softly that . . . She loves you not.
    CYRANO: [*Quickly*] Hush!
    [*A moment since,* Christian *has entered and
        mingled with the* Cadets, *who do not offer to
        speak to him. Finally, he sits down alone at a
        small table, where he is served by* Lise]
    A CADET: [*Rises from a table up stage, his glass
in his hand*] Cyrano!—Your story!
    CYRANO: Presently . .
    [*He goes up, on the arm of* Le Bret, *talking to
        him. The* Cadet *comes down stage*]
    THE CADET: The story of the combat! An example
For—
    [*He stops by the table where* Christian *is sit-
        ting*]
    —this young tadpole here.

CHRISTIAN: [*Looks up*] Tadpole?

ANOTHER CADET: Yes, you!—
You narrow-gutted Northerner!

CHRISTIAN: Sir?

FIRST CADET: Hark ye,
Monsieur de Neuvillette: You are to know
There is a certain subject—I would say,
A certain object—never to be named
Among us: utterly unmentionable!

CHRISTIAN: And that is?

THIRD CADET: [*In an awful voice*] Look at me! . . .
   [*He strikes his nose three times with his finger,
   mysteriously*]
                                   You understand?

CHRISTIAN: Why, yes; the—

FOURTH CADET: Sh! . . . We never speak that
   word—
   [*Indicating Cyrano by a gesture*]
To breathe it is to have to do with HIM!

FIFTH CADET: [*Speaks through his nose*] He has
   exterminated several
Whose tone of voice suggested . . .

SIXTH CADET: [*In a hollow tone; rising from
   under the table on all fours*] Would you die
Before your time! Just mention anything
Convex . . . or cartilaginous . . .

SEVENTH CADET: [*His hand on* Christian's
   shoulder*] One word—
One syllable—one gesture—nay, one sneeze—
Your handkerchief becomes your winding-sheet!
   [*Silence. In a circle around* Christian, *arms
   crossed, they regard him expectantly*]

CHRISTIAN: [*Rises and goes to* Carbon, *who is
   conversing with an officer, and pretending not to
   see what is taking place*] Captain!

CARBON: [*Turns, and looks him over*] Sir?

CHRISTIAN: What is the proper thing to do
When Gascons grow too boastful?

CARBON: Prove to them
That one may be a Norman, and have courage.
   [*Turns his back*]

CHRISTIAN: I thank you.

FIRST CADET: [*To* Cyrano] Come—the story!

ALL: The story!

CYRANO: [*Comes down*]   Oh,
My story? Well . . .
   [*They all draw up their stools and group them-
   selves around him, eagerly.* Christian *places
   himself astride of a chair, his arms on the
   back of it*]
                         I marched on, all alone
To meet those devils. Overhead, the moon
Hung like a gold watch at the fob of heaven,
Till suddenly some Angel rubbed a cloud,
As it might be his handkerchief, across
The shining crystal, and—the night came down.
No lamps in those back streets— It was so dark—
Mordious! You could not see beyond—

CHRISTIAN: Your nose.

[*Silence. Every man slowly rises to his feet.
They look at* Cyrano *almost with terror. He
has stopped short, utterly astonished. Pause*]

CYRANO: Who is that man there?

A CADET: [*In a low voice*] A recruit—arrived
This morning.

CYRANO: [*Takes a step toward* Christian] A recruit—

CARBON: [*In a low voice*]
                         His name is Christian
De Neuvil—

CYRANO: [*Suddenly motionless*] Oh . . .
   [*He turns pale, flushes, makes a movement as
   if to throw himself upon* Christian]
I—[*Controls himself, and goes on in a choking voice*]
   I see. Very well,
As I was saying—
   [*With a sudden burst of rage*]
                         Mordious! . . .
   [*He goes on in a natural tone*]
                                   It grew dark,
You could not see your hand before your eyes.
I marched on, thinking how, all for the sake
Of one old souse
   [*They slowly sit down, watching him*]
                         who wrote a bawdy song
Whenever he took—

CHRISTIAN: A noseful—
   [*Everyone rises.* Christian *balances himself on
   two legs of his chair*]

CYRANO: [*Half strangled*] —Took a notion . . .
Whenever he took a notion— For his sake,
I might antagonize some dangerous man,
One powerful enough to make me pay—

CHRISTIAN: Through the nose—

CYRANO: [*Wipes the sweat from his forehead*]
                         —Pay the Piper. After all,
I thought, why am I putting in my—

CHRISTIAN: Nose—

CYRANO:—My oar . . . Why am I putting in my
oar?
The quarrel's none of mine. However—now
I am here, I may as well go through with it.
Come Gascon—do your duty!—Suddenly
A sword flashed in the dark. I caught it fair—

CHRISTIAN: On the nose—

CYRANO: On my blade. Before I knew it,
There I was—

CHRISTIAN: Rubbing noses—

CYRANO: [*Pale and smiling*] Crossing swords
With half a score at once. I handed one—

CHRISTIAN: A nosegay—

CYRANO: [*Leaping at him*] Ventre-Saint-Gris! . . .
   [*The Gascons tumble over each other to get a
   good view. Arrived in front of* Christian, *who
   has not moved an inch,* Cyrano *masters himself again, and continues*] He went down;
The rest gave way; I charged—

CHRISTIAN: Nose in the air—

CYRANO: I skewered two of them—disarmed a
third—
Another lunged— Paf! And I countered—
CHRISTIAN: Pif!
CYRANO: [*Bellowing*] *Tonnerre!* Out of here!—All
of you!
[*All the* Cadets *rush for the door*]
FIRST CADET: At last—
The old lion wakes!
CYRANO: All of you! Leave me here
Alone with that man!
[*The lines following are heard brokenly, in the
confusion of getting through the door*]
SECOND CADET: Bigre! He'll have the fellow
Chopped into sausage—
RAGUENEAU: Sausage?—
THIRD CADET: Mince-meat, then—
One of your pies!—
RAGUENEAU: Am I pale? You look white
As a fresh napkin—
CARBON: [*At the door*] Come!
FOURTH CADET: He'll never leave
Enough of him to—
FIFTH CADET: Why, it frightens *me*. . . .
To think of what will—
SIXTH CADET: [*Closing the door*] Something hor-
rible
Beyond imagination . . .
[*They are all gone: some through the street
door, some by the inner doors to right and left.
A few disappear up the staircase.* Cyrano *and*
Christian *stand face to face a moment, and
look at each other*]
CYRANO: To my arms!
CHRISTIAN: Sir? . . .
CYRANO: You have courage!
CHRISTIAN: Oh, that! . . .
CYRANO: You are brave—
That pleases me.
CHRISTIAN: You mean? . . .
CYRANO: Do you not know
I am her brother? Come!
CHRISTIAN: Whose?—
CYRANO: Hers—Roxane!
CHRISTIAN: Her . . . brother? You? [*Hurries to
him*]
CYRANO: Her cousin. Much the same.
CHRISTIAN: And she has told you? . . .
CYRANO: Everything.
CHRISTIAN: She loves me?
CYRANO: Perhaps.
CHRISTIAN: [*Takes both his hands*] My dear sir—
more than I can say,
I am honored—
CYRANO: This is rather sudden.
CHRISTIAN: Please
Forgive me—
CYRANO: [*Holds him at arms length, looking at
him*] Why, he is a handsome devil,
This fellow!

CHRISTIAN: On my honor—if you knew
How much I have admired—
CYRANO: Yes, yes—and all
Those Noses which—
CHRISTIAN: Please! I apologize.
CYRANO: [*Change of tone*] Roxane expects a
letter—
CHRISTIAN: Not from me?—
CYRANO: Yes. Why not?
CHRISTIAN: Once I write, that ruins all!
CYRANO: And why?
CHRISTIAN: Because . . . because I am a fool,
Stupid enough to hang myself!
CYRANO: But no—
You are no fool; you call yourself a fool,
There's proof enough in that. Besides, you did not
Attack me like a fool.
CHRISTIAN: Bah! Any one
Can pick a quarrel. Yes, I have a sort
Of rough and ready soldier's tongue. I know
That. But with any woman—paralyzed,
Speechless, dumb. I can only look at them.
Yet sometimes, when I go away, their eyes . . .
CYRANO: Why not their hearts, if you should wait
and see?
CHRISTIAN: No. I am one of those— I know—
those men
Who never can make love.
CYRANO: Strange. . . . Now it seems
I, if I gave my mind to it, I might
Perhaps make love well.
CHRISTIAN: Oh, if I had words
To say what I have here!
CYRANO: If I could be
A handsome little Musketeer with eyes!—
CHRISTIAN: Besides—you know Roxane—how sen-
sitive—
One rough word, and the sweet illusion—gone!
CYRANO: I wish you might be my interpreter.
CHRISTIAN: I wish I had your wit—
CYRANO: Borrow it, then!—
Your beautiful young manhood—lend me that,
And we two make one hero of romance!
CHRISTIAN: What?
CYRANO: Would you dare repeat to
her the words
I gave you, day by day?
CHRISTIAN: You mean?
CYRANO: I mean
Roxane shall have no disillusionment!
Come, shall we win her both together? Take
The soul within this leathern jack of mine,
And breathe it into you?
[*Touches him on the breast*]
So—there's my heart
Under your velvet, now!
CHRISTIAN: But— Cyrano!—
CYRANO: But— Christian, why not?
CHRISTIAN: I am afraid—
CYRANO: I know—

Afraid that when you have her all alone,
You lose all. Have no fear. It is yourself
She loves—give her yourself put into words—
My words, upon your lips!

CHRISTIAN: But . . . but your eyes! . . .
They burn like—

CYRANO: Will you? . . . Will you?

CHRISTIAN: Does it mean
So much to you?

CYRANO: [*Beside himself*] It means—
     [*Recovers, changes tone*]   A comedy,
A situation for a poet! Come,
Shall we collaborate? I'll be your cloak
Of darkness, your enchanted sword, your ring
To charm the fairy Princess!

CHRISTIAN: But the letter—
I cannot write—

CYRANO: Oh yes, the letter.
     [*He takes from his pocket the letter which he
     has written*] Here.

CHRISTIAN: What is this?

CYRANO: All there; all but the address.

CHRISTIAN: I—

CYRANO: Oh, you may send it. It will serve.

CHRISTIAN: But why

Have you done this?

CYRANO: I have amused myself
As we all do, we poets—writing vows
To Chloris, Phyllis—any pretty name—
You might have had a pocketful of them!
Take it, and turn to facts my fantasies—
I loosed these loves like doves into the air;
Give them a habitation and a home.
Here, take it— You will find me all the more
Eloquent, being insincere! Come!

CHRISTIAN: First,
There must be a few changes here and there—
Written at random, can it fit Roxane?

CYRANO: Like her own glove.

CHRISTIAN: No, but—

CYRANO: My son, have faith—
Faith in the love of women for themselves—
Roxane will know this letter for her own!

CHRISTIAN: [*Throws himself into the arms of
Cyrano. They stand embraced*] My friend!
     [*The door up stage opens a little. A* Cadet *steals
     in*]

THE CADET: Nothing. A silence like the tomb . . .
I hardly dare look—
     [*He sees the two*]
                    Wha-at?
     [*The other* Cadets *crowd in behind him and see*]

THE CADET: No!—No!

SECOND CADET: Mon dieu!

THE MUSKETEER: [*Slaps his knee*] Well, well, well!

CARBON: Here's our devil . . . Christianized!
Offend one nostril, and he turns the other.

THE MUSKETEER: Now we are allowed to talk
     about his nose!
     [*Calls*]

Hey, Lise! Come here—
     [*Affectedly*] Snf! What a horrid smell!
What is it? . . .
     [*Plants himself in front of* Cyrano, *and looks
     at his nose in an impolite manner*]
                    You ought to know about such things;
What seems to have died around here?

CYRANO: [*Knocks him backward over a bench*]
     Cabbage-heads!
     [*Joy. The* Cadets *have found their old* Cyrano
     again. General disturbance]

CURTAIN

ACT III.

Roxane's Kiss

A little square in the old Marais: old houses, and
a glimpse of narrow streets. On the right, the house
of Roxane and her garden wall, overhung with tall
shrubbery. Over the door of the house a balcony
and a tall window; to one side of the door, a
bench. Ivy clings to the wall; jasmine embraces the
balcony, trembles, and falls away. By the bench and
the jutting stonework of the wall one might easily
climb up to the balcony. Opposite, an ancient house
of the like character, brick and stone, whose front
door forms an entrance. The knocker on this door is
tied up in linen like an injured thumb. At the curtain
rise the Duenna is seated on the bench beside the
door. The window is wide open on Roxane's balcony;
a light within suggests that it is early evening. By the
Duenna stands Ragueneau dressed in what might be
the livery of one attached to the household. He is
by way of telling her something, and wiping his eyes
meanwhile.

RAGUENEAU: —And so she ran off with a Muske-
     teer!
I was ruined— I was alone— Remained
Nothing for me to do but hang myself,
So I did that. Presently along comes
Monsieur de Bergerac, and cuts me down,
And makes me steward to his cousin.

THE DUENNA: Ruined?—
I thought your pastry was a great success!

RAGUENEAU: [*Shakes his head*] Lise loved the sol-
     diers, and I loved the poets—
Mars ate up all the cakes Apollo left;
It did not take long. . . .

THE DUENNA: [*Calls up to window*] Roxane! Are
     you ready?
We are late!

VOICE OF ROXANE: [*Within*] Putting on my cape—

THE DUENNA: [*To* Ragueneau, *indicating the house
opposite*]   Clomire
Across the way receives on Thursday nights—

We are to have a psycho-colloquy
Upon the Tender Passion.
 RAGUENEAU: Ah—the Tender . . .
 THE DUENNA: [*Sighs*]—Passion! . . .
  [*Calls up to window*]
      Roxane!—Hurry, dear—we shall miss
The Tender Passion!
 ROXANE: Coming!—
  [*Music of stringed instruments off-stage approaching*]
 THE VOICE OF CYRANO: [*Singing*] La, la, la!—
 THE DUENNA: A serenade?—How pleasant—
 CYRANO: No, no, no!—
F natural, you natural born fool!
  [*Enters, followed by two pages, carrying theorbos*]
 FIRST PAGE: [*Ironically*]
No doubt your honor knows F natural
When he hears—
 CYRANO: I am a musician, infant!—
A pupil of Gassendi.
 THE PAGE: [*Plays and sings*] La, la,—
 CYRANO: Here—
Give me that—
  [*He snatches the instrument from the* Page *and continues the tune*] La, la, la, la—
 ROXANE: [*Appears on the balcony*] Is that you,
Cyrano?
 CYRANO: [*Singing*] I, who praise your lilies fair,
But long to love your ro . . . ses!
 ROXANE: I'll be down—
Wait—[*Goes in through window*]
 THE DUENNA: Did you train these virtuosi?
 CYRANO: No—
I won them on a bet from D'Assoucy.
We were debating a fine point of grammar
When, pointing out these two young nightingales
Dressed up like peacocks, with their instruments,
He cries: "No, but I KNOW! I'll wager you
A day of music." Well, of course he lost;
And so until to-morrow they are mine,
My private orchestra. Pleasant at first,
But they become a trifle—
  [*To the* Pages] Here! Go play
A minuet to Montfleury—and tell him
I sent you!
  [*The* Pages *go up to the exit.* Cyrano *turns to the* Duenna]
     I came here as usual
To inquire after our friend—
  [*To* Pages]
      Play out of tune.
And keep on playing!
  [*The* Pages *go out. He turns to the* Duenna]
    —Our friend with the great soul.
 ROXANE: [*Enters in time to hear the last words*]
He is beautiful and brilliant—and I love him!
 CYRANO: Do you find Christian . . . intellectual?
 ROXANE: More so than you, even.
 CYRANO: I am glad.

 ROXANE: No man
Ever so beautifully said those things—
Those pretty nothings that are everything.
Sometimes he falls into a reverie;
His inspiration fails—then all at once,
He will say something absolutely . . . Oh! . . .
 CYRANO: Really!
 ROXANE: How like a man! You think a man
Who has a handsome face must be a fool.
 CYRANO: He talks well about . . . matters of the
  heart?
 ROXANE: He does not talk; he rhapsodizes . . .
  dreams . . .
 CYRANO: [*Twisting his moustache*] He . . . writes
well?
 ROXANE: Wonderfully. Listen now:
  [*Reciting as from memory*]
"Take my heart; I shall have it all the more;
Plucking the flowers, we keep the plant in bloom—"
Well?
 CYRANO: Pooh!
 ROXANE: And this:
      "Knowing you have in store
More heart to give than I to find heart-room—"
 CYRANO: First he has too much, then too little; just
How much heart does he need?
 ROXANE: [*Tapping her foot*] You are teasing me!
You are jealous!
 CYRANO: [*Startled*] Jealous?
 ROXANE: Of his poetry—
You poets are like that . . .
      And these last lines
Are they not the last word in tenderness?—
"There is no more to say: only believe
That unto you my whole heart gives one cry,
And writing, writes down more than you receive;
Sending you kisses through my finger-tips—
Lady, O read my letter with your lips!"
 CYRANO: H'm, yes—those last lines . . . but he
  overwrites!
 ROXANE: Listen to this—
 CYRANO: You know them all by heart?
 ROXANE: Every one!
 CYRANO: [*Twisting his moustache*] I may call that
flattering . . .
 ROXANE: He is a master!
 CYRANO: Oh—come.
 ROXANE: Yes—a master!
 CYRANO: [*Bowing*] A master—if you will!
 THE DUENNA: [*Comes down stage quickly*] Monsieur de Guiche!—
  [*To* Cyrano, *pushing him toward the house*]
Go inside— If he does not find you here,
It may be just as well. He may suspect —
 ROXANE: —My secret! Yes; he is in love with me
And he is powerful. Let him not know—
One look would frost my roses before bloom.
 CYRANO: [*Going into house*] Very well, very well!
 ROXANE: [*To* De Guiche, *as he enters*] We were
  just going—

DE GUICHE: I came only to say farewell.

ROXANE: You leave
Paris?

DE GUICHE: Yes—for the front.

ROXANE: Ah!

DE GUICHE: And to-night!

ROXANE: Ah!

DE GUICHE: We have orders to besiege Arras.

ROXANE: Arras?

DE GUICHE: Yes. My departure leaves you . . .
cold?

ROXANE: [*Politely*] Oh! Not that.

DE GUICHE: It has left me desolate—
When shall I see you? Ever? Did you know
I was made Colonel?

ROXANE: [*Indifferent*] Bravo.

DE GUICHE: Regiment
Of the Guards.

ROXANE: [*Catching her breath*] Of the Guards?—

DE GUICHE: *His* regiment.
Your cousin, the mighty man of words!—
[*Grimly*]

           Down there
We may have an accounting!

ROXANE: [*Suffocating*] Are you sure
The Guards are ordered?

DE GUICHE: Under my command!

ROXANE: [*Sinks down, breathless, on the bench;
aside*] Christian!—

DE GUICHE: What is it?

ROXANE: [*Losing control of herself*] To the war—
perhaps
Never again to— When a woman cares,
Is that nothing?

DE GUICHE: [*Surprised and delighted*] You say this
now—to me—
Now, at the very moment?—

ROXANE: [*Recovers—changes her tone*]
           Tell me something:
My cousin— You say you mean to be revenged
On him. Do you mean that?

DE GUICHE: [*Smiles*] Why? Would you care?

ROXANE: Not for him.

DE GUICHE: Do you see him?

ROXANE: Now and then.

DE GUICHE: He goes about everywhere nowadays
With one of the Cadets—de Neuve—Neuville—
Neuvillers—

ROXANE: [*Coolly*] A tall man?—

DE GUICHE: Blond—

ROXANE: Rosy cheeks?—

DE GUICHE: Handsome!—

ROXANE: Pooh!—

DE GUICHE: And a fool.

ROXANE: [*Languidly*] So he appears . . .
[*Animated*]
But Cyrano? What will you do to him?
Order him into danger? He loves that!
I know what *I* should do.

DE GUICHE: What?

ROXANE: Leave him here
With his Cadets, while all the regiment
Goes on to glory! That would torture him—
To sit all through the war with folded arms—
I know his nature. If you hate that man,
Strike at his self-esteem.

DE GUICHE: Oh woman—woman!
Who but a woman would have thought of this?

ROXANE: He'll eat his heart out, while his Gascon
friends
Bite their nails all day long in Paris here.
And you will be avenged!

DE GUICHE: You love me then,
A little? . . .
[*She smiles*]
        Making my enemies your own,
Hating them—I should like to see in that
A sign of love, Roxane.

ROXANE: Perhaps it is one . . .

DE GUICHE: [*Shows a number of folded despatches*]
Here are the orders—for each company—
Ready to send . . .
[*Selects one*]
        So— This is for the Guards—
I'll keep that. Aha, Cyrano!
[*To* Roxane]
        You too,
You play your little games, do you?

ROXANE: [*Watching him*] Sometimes . . .

DE GUICHE: [*Close to her, speaking hurriedly*]
And you!—Oh, I am mad over you!—Listen—
I leave to-night—but—let you through my hands
Now, when I feel you trembling?—Listen— Close
by,
In the Rue d'Orléans, the Capuchins
Have their new convent. By their law, no layman
May pass inside those walls. I'll see to that—
Their sleeves are wide enough to cover me—
The servants of my Uncle Cardinal
Will fear his nephew. So—I'll come to you
Masked, after everyone knows I have gone—
Oh, let me wait one day!—

ROXANE: If this be known,
Your honor—

DE GUICHE: Bah!

ROXANE: The war—your duty—

DE GUICHE: [*Blows away an imaginary feather*]
Phoo!—
Only say yes!

ROXANE: No!

DE GUICHE: Whisper . . .

ROXANE: [*Tenderly*] I ought not
To let you . . .

DE GUICHE: Ah! . . .

ROXANE: [*Pretends to break down*] Ah, go!
[*Aside*]
        —Christian remains—
[*Aloud—heroically*]
I must have you a hero—Antoine . . .

DE GUICHE: Heaven! . . .

So you can love—

ROXANE: One for whose sake I fear.

DE GUICHE: [*Triumphant*]

I go!

Will that content you?

[*Kisses her hand*]

ROXANE: Yes—my friend!

[*He goes out*]

THE DUENNA: [*As* De Guiche *disappears, making a deep curtsey behind his back, and imitating* Roxane's *intense tone*] Yes—my friend!

ROXANE: [*Quickly, close to her*]

Not a word to Cyrano—

He would never forgive me if he knew

I stole his war!

[*She calls toward the house*] Cousin!

[Cyrano *comes out of the house; she turns to him, indicating the house opposite*]

We are going over—

Alcandre speaks to-night—and Lysimon.

THE DUENNA: [*Puts finger in her ear*]

My little finger says we shall not hear

Everything.

CYRANO: Never mind me—

THE DUENNA: [*Across the street*] Look— Oh, look!

The knocker tied up in a napkin—Yes,

They muzzled you because you bark too loud

And interrupt the lecture—little beast!

ROXANE: [*As the door opens*] Enter . . .

[*To* Cyrano]

If Christian comes, tell him to wait.

CYRANO: Oh—

[Roxane *returns*]

When he comes, what will you talk about?

You always know beforehand.

ROXANE: About . . .

CYRANO: Well?

ROXANE: You will not tell him, will you?

CYRANO: I am dumb.

ROXANE: About nothing! Or about everything—

I shall say: "Speak of love in your own words—

Improvise! Rhapsodize! Be eloquent!"

CYRANO: [*Smiling*] Good!

ROXANE: Sh!—

CYRANO: Sh!—

ROXANE: Not a word!

[*She goes in; the door closes*]

CYRANO: [*Bowing*] Thank you so much—

ROXANE: [*Opens door and puts out her head*]

He must be unprepared—

CYRANO: Of course!

ROXANE: Sh!—

[*Goes in again*]

CYRANO: [*Calls*] Christian!

[Christian *enters*]

I have your theme—bring on your memory!—

Here is your chance now to surpass yourself,

No time to lose— Come! Look intelligent—

Come home and learn your lines.

CHRISTIAN: No.

CYRANO: What?

CHRISTIAN: I'll wait

Here for Roxane.

CYRANO: What lunacy is this?

Come quickly!

CHRISTIAN: No, I say! I have had enough—

Taking my words, my letters, all from you—

Making our love a little comedy!

It was a game at first; but now—she cares . . .

Thanks to you. I am not afraid. I'll speak

For myself now.

CYRANO: Undoubtedly!

CHRISTIAN: I will!

Why not? I am no such fool—you shall see!

Besides—my dear friend—you have taught me much:

I ought to know something . . . By God, I know

Enough to take a woman in my arms!

[Roxane *appears in the doorway, opposite*]

There she is now . . . Cyrano, wait! Stay here!

CYRANO: [*Bows*] Speak for yourself, my friend!

[*He goes out*]

ROXANE: [*Taking leave of the company*]—Barthé-noide!

Alcandre! . . . Grémione! . . .

THE DUENNA: I told you so—

We missed the Tender Passion!

[*She goes into* Roxane's *house*]

ROXANE: Urimédonte!—

Adieu!

[*As the guests disappear down the street, she turns to* Christian]

Is that you, Christian? Let us stay

Here, in the twilight. They are gone. The air

Is fragrant. We shall be alone. Sit down

There—so . . .

[*They sit on the bench*]

Now tell me things.

CHRISTIAN: [*After a silence*] I love you.

ROXANE: [*Closes her eyes*] Yes,

Speak to me about love . . .

CHRISTIAN: I love you.

ROXANE: Now

Be eloquent! . . .

CHRISTIAN: I love—

ROXANE: [*Opens her eyes*] You have your theme—

Improvise! Rhapsodize!

CHRISTIAN: I love you so!

ROXANE: Of course. And then? . . .

CHRISTIAN: And then . . . Oh, I should be

So happy if you loved me too! Roxane,

Say that you love me too!

ROXANE: [*Making a face*] I ask for cream—

You give me milk and water. Tell me first

A little, how you love me.

CHRISTIAN: Very much.

ROXANE: Oh—tell me how you *feel*!

CHRISTIAN: [*Coming nearer, and devouring her with his eyes*] Your throat . . . If only

I might . . . kiss it—

ROXANE: Christian!

CHRISTIAN: I love you so!

ROXANE: [*Makes as if to rise*] Again?

CHRISTIAN: [*Desperately, restraining her*] No, not again— I do not love you—

ROXANE: [*Settles back*] That is better . . .

CHRISTIAN: I adore you!

ROXANE: Oh!— [*Rises and moves away*]

CHRISTIAN: I know;
I grow absurd.

ROXANE: [*Coldly*] And that displeases me
As much as if you had grown ugly.

CHRISTIAN: I—

ROXANE: Gather your dreams together into words!

CHRISTIAN: I love—

ROXANE: I know; you love me. Adieu.
[*She goes to the house*]

CHRISTIAN: No,
But wait—please—let me— I was going to say—

ROXANE: [*Pushes the door open*]
That you adore me. Yes; I know that too.
No! . . . Go away! . . .
[*She goes in and shuts the door in his face*]

CHRISTIAN: I . . . I . . .

CYRANO: [*Enters*] A great success!

CHRISTIAN: Help me!

CYRANO: Not I.

CHRISTIAN: I cannot live unless
She loves me—now, this moment!

CYRANO: How the devil
Am I to teach you now—this moment?

CHRISTIAN: [*Catches him by the arm*]—Wait!—
Look! Up there!—Quick—
[*The light shows in* Roxane's *window*]

CYRANO: Her window—

CHRISTIAN: [*Wailing*] I shall die!—

CYRANO: Less noise!

CHRISTIAN: Oh, I—

CYRANO: It does seem fairly dark—

CHRISTIAN: [*Excitedly*] Well?—Well?—Well?—

CYRANO: Let us try what can be done;
It is more than you deserve—stand over there,
Idiot—there!—before the balcony—
Let me stand underneath. I'll whisper you
What to say.

CHRISTIAN: She may hear—she may—

CYRANO: Less noise!
[*The* Pages *appear up stage*]

FIRST PAGE: Hep!—

CYRANO: [*Finger to lips*] Sh!—

FIRST PAGE: [*Low voice*] We serenaded Montfleury!—
What next?

CYRANO: Down to the corner of the street—
One this way—and the other over there—
If anybody passes, play a tune!

PAGE: What tune, O musical Philosopher?

CYRANO: Sad for a man, or merry for a woman—
Now go!
[*The* Pages *disappear, one toward each corner of the street*]

CYRANO: [*To* Christian] Call her!

CHRISTIAN: Roxane!

CYRANO: Wait . . . [*Gathers up a handful of pebbles*] Gravel . . . [*Throws it at the window*]
There!—

ROXANE: [*Opens the window*] Who is calling?

CHRISTIAN: I—

ROXANE: Who?

CHRISTIAN: Christian.

ROXANE: You again?

CHRISTIAN: I had to tell you—

CYRANO: [*Under the balcony*] Good— Keep your voice down.

ROXANE: No. Go away. You tell me nothing.

CHRISTIAN: Please!—

ROXANE: You do not love me any more—

CHRISTIAN: [*To whom* Cyrano *whispers his words*]
No—no—
Not any more— I love you . . . evermore . . .
And ever . . . more and more!

ROXANE: [*About to close the window—pauses*] A
little better . . .

CHRISTIAN: [*Same business*]
Love grows and struggles like . . . an angry child . . .
Breaking my heart . . . his cradle . . .

ROXANE: [*Coming out on the balcony*] Better still—
But . . . such a babe is dangerous; why not
Have smothered it new-born?

CHRISTIAN: [*Same business*] And so I do . . .
And yet he lives . . . I found . . . as you shall find . . .
This new-born babe . . . an infant . . . Hercules!

ROXANE: [*Further forward*] Good!—

CHRISTIAN: [*Same business*] Strong enough . . .
at birth . . . to strangle those
Two serpents—Doubt and . . . Pride.

ROXANE: [*Leans over balcony*] Why, very well!
Tell me now why you speak so haltingly—
Has your imagination gone lame?

CYRANO: [*Thrusts* Christian *under the balcony, and stands in his place*] Here—
This grows too difficult!

ROXANE: Your words to-night
Hesitate. Why?

CYRANO: [*In a low tone, imitating* Christian]
Through the warm summer gloom
They grope in darkness toward the light of you.

ROXANE: My words, well aimed, find you more readily.

CYRANO: My heart is open wide and waits for them—
Too large a mark to miss! My words fly home,
Heavy with honey like returning bees,
To your small secret ear. Moreover—yours
Fall to me swiftly. Mine more slowly rise.

ROXANE: Yet not so slowly as they did at first.

CYRANO: They have learned the way, and you have welcomed them.

ROXANE: [*Softly*] Am I so far above you now?

CYRANO: So far—
If you let fall upon me one hard word,
Out of that height—you crush me!
   ROXANE: [*Turns*] I'll come down—
   CYRANO: [*Quickly*] No!
   ROXANE: [*Points out the bench under the balcony*] Stand you on the bench. Come nearer!
   CYRANO: [*Recoils into the shadow*] No!—
   ROXANE: And why—so great a *No?*
   CYRANO: [*More and more overcome by emotion*]
                                 Let me enjoy
The one moment I ever—my one chance
To speak to you . . . unseen!
   ROXANE: Unseen?—
   CYRANO: Yes!—yes . . .
Night, making all things dimly beautiful,
One veil over us both— You only see
The darkness of a long cloak in the gloom,
And I the whiteness of a summer gown—
You are all light— I am all shadow! . . . How
Can you know what this moment means to me?
If I was ever eloquent—
   ROXANE: You were
Eloquent—
   CYRANO: —You have never heard till now
My own heart speaking!
   ROXANE: Why not?
   CYRANO: Until now,
I spoke through . . .
   ROXANE: Yes?—
   CYRANO: —through that sweet drunkenness
You pour into the world out of your eyes!
But to-night . . . but to-night, I indeed speak
For the first time!
   ROXANE: For the first time— Your voice,
Even, is not the same.
   CYRANO: [*Passionately; moves nearer*] How should
    it be?
I have another voice to-night—my own,
Myself, daring—
   [*He stops, confused; then tries to recover himself*]
                    Where was I? . . . I forget! . . .
Forgive me. This is all sweet like a dream . . .
Strange—like a dream . . .
   ROXANE: How, strange?
   CYRANO: Is it not so
To be myself to you, and have no fear
Of moving you to laughter?
   ROXANE: Laughter—why?
   CYRANO: [*Struggling for an explanation*]
Because . . . What am I . . . What is any man,
That he dare ask for you? Therefore my heart
Hides behind phrases. There's a modesty
In these things too— I come here to pluck down
Out of the sky the evening star—then smile,
And stoop to gather little flowers.
   ROXANE: Are they
Not sweet, those little flowers?

CYRANO: Not enough sweet
For you and me, to-night!
   ROXANE: [*Breathless*] You never spoke
To me like this . . .
   CYRANO: Little things, pretty things—
Arrows and hearts and torches—roses red,
And violets blue—are these all? Come away,
And breathe fresh air! Must we keep on and on
Sipping stale honey out of tiny cups
Decorated with golden tracery,
Drop by drop, all day long? We are alive;
We thirst— Come away, plunge, and drink, and drown
In the great river flowing to the sea!
   ROXANE: But . . . Poetry?
   CYRANO: I have made rimes for you—
Not now— Shall we insult Nature, this night,
These flowers, this moment—shall we set all these
To phrases from a letter by Voiture?
Look once at the high stars that shine in heaven,
And put off artificiality!
Have you not seen great gaudy hothouse flowers,
Barren, without fragrance?—Souls are like that:
Forced to show all, they soon become all show—
The means to Nature's end ends meaningless!
   ROXANE: But . . . Poetry?
   CYRANO: Love hates that game of words!
It is a crime to fence with life— I tell you,
There comes one moment, once—and God help those
Who pass that moment by!—when Beauty stands
Looking into the soul with grave, sweet eyes
That sicken at pretty words!
   ROXANE: If that be true—
And when that moment comes to you and me—
What words will you? . . .
   CYRANO: All those, all those, all those
That blossom in my heart, I'll fling to you—
Armfuls of loose bloom! Love, I love beyond
Breath, beyond reason, beyond love's own power
Of loving! Your name is like a golden bell
Hung in my heart; and when I think of you.
I tremble, and the bell swings and rings—
                              "Roxane!" . . .
"Roxane!" . . . along my veins, "Roxane!" . . .
                                             I know
All small forgotten things that once meant You—
I remember last year, the First of May,
A little before noon, you had your hair
Drawn low, that one time only. Is that strange?
You know how, after looking at the sun,
One sees red suns everywhere—so, for hours
After the flood of sunshine that you are,
My eyes are blinded by your burning hair!
   ROXANE: [*Very low*] Yes . . . that is . . .
Love—
   CYRANO: Yes, that is Love—that wind
Of terrible and jealous beauty, blowing
Over me—that dark fire, that music . . .
                                             Ye?

Love seeketh not his own! Dear, you may take
My happiness to make you happier,
Even though you never know I gave it you—
Only let me hear sometimes, all alone,
The distant laughter of your joy! . . .
                             I never
Look at you, but there's some new virtue born
In me, some new courage. Do you begin
To understand, a little? Can you feel
My soul, there in the darkness, breathe on you?
—Oh, but to-night, now, I dare say these things—
I . . . to you . . . and you hear them! . . . It is
    too much!
In my most sweet unreasonable dreams,
I have not hoped for this! Now let me die,
Having lived. It is my voice, mine, my own,
That makes you tremble there in the green gloom
Above me—for you do tremble, as a blossom
Among the leaves— You tremble, and I can feel,
All the way down along these jasmine branches,
Whether you will or no, the passion of you
Trembling . . .
    [*He kisses wildly the end of a drooping spray
      of jasmine*]
    ROXANE: Yes, I do tremble . . . and I
    weep . . .
And I love you . . . and I am yours . . . and you
Have made me thus!
    CYRANO: [*After a pause; quietly*] What is death
    like, I wonder?
I know everything else now . . .
                        I have done
This, to you—I, myself . . .
                   Only let me
Ask one thing more—
    CHRISTIAN: [*Under the balcony*] One kiss!
    ROXANE: [*Startled*] One?—
    CYRANO: [*To* Christian] You! . . .
    ROXANE: You ask me
For—
    CYRANO: I . . . Yes, but—I mean—
    [*To* Christian] You go too far!
    CHRISTIAN: She is willing!—Why not make the
    most of it?
    CYRANO: [*To* Roxane] I did ask . . . but I know
    I ask too much . . .
    ROXANE: Only one— Is that all?
    CYRANO: All!—How much more
Than all!—I know—I frighten you—I ask . . .
I ask you to refuse—
    CHRISTIAN: [*To* Cyrano] But why? Why? Why?
    CYRANO: Christian, be quiet!
    ROXANE: [*Leaning over*] What is that you say
To yourself?
    CYRANO: I am angry with myself
Because I go too far, and so I say
To myself: "Christian, be quiet!"—
    [*The theorbos begin to play*]
                      Hark—someone
Is coming—

    [Roxane *closes her window.* Cyrano *listens to
    the theorbos, one of which plays a gay melody,
    the other a mournful one*]
                 A sad tune, a merry tune—
Man, woman—what do they mean?—
    [*A* Capuchin *enters; he carries a lantern, and
    goes from house to house, looking at the doors*]
                   Aha!—a priest!
    [*To the* Capuchin]
What is this new game of Diogenes?
    THE CAPUCHIN: I am looking for the house of
Madame—
    CHRISTIAN: [*Impatient*] Bah!—
    THE CAPUCHIN: Madeleine Robin—
    CHRISTIAN: What does he want?
    CYRANO: [*To the* Capuchin; *points out a street*]
    This way—
To the right—keep to the right—
    THE CAPUCHIN: I thank you, sir!—
I'll say my beads for you to the last grain.
    CYRANO: Good fortune, father, and my service to
    you!
    [*The* Capuchin *goes out*]
    CHRISTIAN: Win me that kiss!
    CYRANO: No.
    CHRISTIAN: Sooner or later—
    CYRANO: True . . .
That is true . . . Soon or late, it will be so
Because you are young and she is beautiful—
    [*To himself*]
Since it must be, I had rather be myself
    [*The window re-opens.* Christian *hides under
    the balcony*]
The cause of . . . what must be.
    ROXANE: [*Out on the balcony*] Are you still there?
We were speaking of—
    CYRANO: A kiss. The word is sweet—
What will the deed be? Are your lips afraid
Even of its burning name? Not much afraid—
Not too much! Have you not unwittingly
Laid aside laughter, slipping beyond speech
Insensibly, already, without fear,
From words to smiles . . . from smiles to sighs . . .
    from sighing,
Even to tears? One step more—only one—
From a tear to a kiss—one step, one thrill!
    ROXANE: Hush!—
    CYRANO: And what is a kiss, when all is done?
A promise given under seal—a vow
Taken before the shrine of memory—
A signature acknowledged—a rosy dot
Over the *i* of Loving—a secret whispered
To listening lips apart—a moment made
Immortal, with a rush of wings unseen—
A sacrament of blossoms, a new song
Sung by two hearts to an old simple tune—
The ring of one horizon around two souls
Together, all alone!
    ROXANE: Hush! . . .
    CYRANO: Why, what shame?

There was a Queen of France, not long ago,
And a great lord of England—a queen's gift,
A crown jewel!—
    ROXANE: Indeed!
    CYRANO: Indeed, like him,
I have my sorrows and my silences;
Like her, you are the queen I dare adore;
Like him I am faithful and forlorn—
    ROXANE: Like him,
Beautiful—
    CYRANO: [*Aside*] So I am—I forgot that!
    ROXANE: Then— Come! . . . Gather your sacred
    blossom . . .
    CYRANO: [*To* Christian] Go!—
    ROXANE: Your crown jewel . . .
    CYRANO: Go on!—
    ROXANE: Your old new song . . .
    CYRANO: Climb!—
    CHRISTIAN: [*Hesitates*] No— Would you?—not
    yet—
    ROXANE: Your moment made
Immortal . . .
    CYRANO: [*Pushing him*] Climb up, animal!
    [Christian *springs on the bench, and climbs by
    the pillars, the branches, the vines, until he
    bestrides the balcony railing*]
    CHRISTIAN: Roxane! . . .
    [*He takes her in his arms and bends over her*]
    CYRANO: [*Very low*] Ah! . . . Roxane! . . .
        I have won what I have won—
The feast of love—and I am Lazarus!
Yet . . . I have something here that is mine now
And was not mine before I spoke the words
That won her—not for me! . . . Kissing my words
My words, upon your lips!
    [*The theorbos begin to play*]
        A merry tune—
A sad tune— So! The Capuchin!
    [*He pretends to be running, as if he had arrived
    from a distance; then calls up to the balcony*]
        Hola!
    ROXANE: Who is it?
    CYRANO: I. Is Christian there with you?
    CHRISTIAN: [*Astonished*] Cyrano!
    ROXANE: Good morrow, Cousin!
    CYRANO: Cousin, . . . good
    morrow!
    ROXANE: I am coming down.
    [*She disappears into the house. The* Capuchin
    enters up stage]
    CHRISTIAN: [*Sees him*] Oh—again!
    THE CAPUCHIN: [*To* Cyrano] She lives *here*, Made-
    leine Robin!
    CYRANO: You said RO-LIN.
    THE CAPUCHIN: No—
R-O-B-I-N
    ROXANE: [*Appears on the threshold of the house,
followed by* Ragueneau *with a lantern, and by* Chris-
tian] What is it?

    THE CAPUCHIN: A letter.
    CHRISTIAN: Oh! . . .
    THE CAPUCHIN: [*To* Roxane]
Some matter profitable to the soul—
A very noble lord gave it to me!
    ROXANE: [*To* Christian] De Guiche!
    CHRISTIAN: He dares?—
    ROXANE: It will not be for long;
When he learns that I love you . . .
    [*By the light of the lantern which* Ragueneau
    *holds, she reads the letter in a low tone, as if to
    herself*]
        "Mademoiselle
The drums are beating, and the regiment
Arms for the march. Secretly I remain
Here, in the Convent. I have disobeyed;
I shall be with you soon. I send this first
By an old monk, as simple as a sheep,
Who understands nothing of this. Your smile
Is more than I can bear, and seek no more.
Be alone to-night, waiting for one who dares
To hope you will forgive . . .—" etcetera—
    [*To the* Capuchin]
Father, this letter concerns you . . .
    [*To* Christian]
        —and you.
Listen:
    [*The others gather around her. She pretends to
    read from the letter, aloud*]
        "Mademoiselle:
            The Cardinal
Will have his way, although against your will;
That is why I am sending this to you
By a most holy man, intelligent,
Discreet. You will communicate to him
Our order to perform, here and at once
The rite of . . .
    [*Turns the page*]
        —Holy Matrimony. You
And Christian will be married privately
In your house. I have sent him to you. I know
You hesitate. Be resigned, nevertheless,
To the Cardinal's command, who sends herewith
His blessing. Be assured, also of my own
Respect and high consideration—*signed,*
Your very humble and—etcetera—"
    THE CAPUCHIN: A noble lord! I said so—never
    fear—
A worthy lord!—a very worthy lord!—
    ROXANE: [*To* Christian] Am I a good reader of
    letters?
    CHRISTIAN: [*Motions toward the* Capuchin] Care-
    ful!—
    ROXANE: [*In a tragic tone*] Oh, this is terrible!
    THE CAPUCHIN: [*Turns the light of his lantern on*
Cyrano] You are to be—
    CHRISTIAN: *I* am the bridegroom!
    THE CAPUCHIN: [*Turns his lantern upon* Christian;
then, as if some suspicion crossed his mind, upon

seeing the young man so handsome] Oh—why,
you . . .

ROXANE: [*Quickly*] Look here—
"Postscript: Give to the Convent in my name
One hundred and twenty pistoles"—

THE CAPUCHIN: Think of it!
A worthy lord—a very worthy lord! . . .
      [*To* Roxane, *solemnly*]
Daughter, resign yourself!

ROXANE: [*With an air of martyrdom*] I am re-
signed . . .
      [*While* Ragueneau *opens the door for the*
      Capuchin *and* Christian *invites him to enter,*
      she turns to Cyrano]
De Guiche may come. Keep him out here with you
Do not let him—

CYRANO: I understand! [*To the* Capuchin] How
long
Will you be?—

THE CAPUCHIN: Oh, a quarter of an hour.

CYRANO: [*Hurrying them into the house*] Hurry—
I'll wait here—

ROXANE: [*To* Christian] Come!
      [*They go into the house*]

CYRANO: Now then, to make
His Grace delay that quarter of an hour . . .
I have it!—up here—
      [*He steps on the bench, and climbs up the*
      wall toward the balcony. The theorbos begin
      to play a mournful melody]
           Sad music— Ah, a man! . . .
      [*The music pauses on a sinister tremolo*]
Oh—very much a man!
      [*He sits astride of the railing and, drawing*
      toward him a long branch of one of the trees
      which border the garden wall, he grasps it with
      both hands, ready to swing himself down]
            So—not too high—
      [*He peers down at the ground*]
I must float gently through the atmosphere—

DE GUICHE: [*Enters masked, groping in the dark*
toward the house] Where is that cursed, bleating
Capuchin?

CYRANO: What if he knows my voice?—the devil!
—Tic-tac,
Bergerac—we unlock our Gascon tongue;
A good strong accent—

DE GUICHE: Here is the house—all dark—
Damn this mask!—
      [*As he is about to enter the house,* Cyrano
      leaps from the balcony, still holding fast to
      the branch, which bends and swings him be-
      tween De Guiche *and the door; then he re-*
      leases the branch and pretends to fall heavily
      as though from a height. He lands flatly on the
      ground, where he lies motionless, as if stunned.
      De Guiche *leaps back*]
           What is that?
      [*When he lifts his eyes, the branch has sprung*

back into place. He can see nothing but the
sky; he does not understand]
           Why . . . where did this man
Fall from?

CYRANO: [*Sits up, and speaks with a strong ac-*
cent]—The moon!

DE GUICHE: You—

CYRANO: From the moon, the moon!
I fell out of the moon!

DE GUICHE: The fellow is mad—

CYRANO: [*Dreamily*] Where am I?

DE GUICHE: Why—

CYRANO: What time is it? What place
Is this? What day? What season?

DE GUICHE: You—

CYRANO: I am stunned!

DE GUICHE: My dear sir—

CYRANO: Like a bomb—a bomb—I fell
From the moon!

DE GUICHE: Now, see here—

CYRANO: [*Rising to his feet, and speaking in a*
terrible voice] I say, the moon!

DE GUICHE: [*Recoils*] Very well—if you say so—
      [*Aside*]
            Raving mad!—

CYRANO: [*Advancing upon him*] I am not speaking metaphorically!

DE GUICHE: Pardon.

CYRANO: A hundred years—an hour ago—
I really cannot say how long I fell—
I was in yonder shining sphere—

DE GUICHE: [*Shrugs*] Quite so.
Please let me pass.

CYRANO: [*Interposes himself*] Where am I? Tell the
truth—
I can bear it. In what quarter of the globe
Have I descended like a meteorite?

DE GUICHE: Morbleu!

CYRANO: I could not choose my place to fall—
The earth spun round so fast— Was it the Earth,
I wonder?—Or is this another world?
Another moon? Whither have I been drawn
By the dead weight of my posterior?

DE GUICHE: Sir, I repeat—

CYRANO: [*With a sudden cry, which causes* De
Guiche *to recoil again*] His face! My God—black!

DE GUICHE: [*Carries his hand to his mask*] Oh!—

CYRANO: [*Terrified*] Are you a native? Is this
Africa?

DE GUICHE: —This mask!

CYRANO: [*Somewhat reassured*] Are we in Venice?
Genoa?

DE GUICHE: [*Tries to pass him*] A lady is waiting
for me.

CYRANO: [*Quite happy again*] So this is Paris!

DE GUICHE: [*Smiling in spite of himself*] This fool
becomes amusing.

CYRANO: Ah! You smile?

DE GUICHE: I do. Kindly permit me—

CYRANO: [*Delighted*] Dear old Paris—
Well, well!—
    [*Wholly at his ease, smiles, bows, arranges his dress*]
              Excuse my appearance. I arrive
By the last thunderbolt—a trifle singed
As I came through the ether. These long journeys—
You know! There are so few conveniences!
My eyes are full of star-dust. On my spurs,
Some sort of fur . . . Planet's apparently . . .
    [*Plucks something from his sleeve*]
Look—on my doublet— That's a Comet's hair!
    [*He blows something from the back of his hand*]
Phoo!
    DE GUICHE: [*Grows angry*] Monsieur—
    CYRANO: [*As* De Guiche *is about to push past, thrusts his leg in the way*] Here's a tooth, stuck in my boot,
From the Great Bear. Trying to get away,
I tripped over the Scorpion and came down
Slap, into one scale of the Balances—
The pointer marks my weight this moment . . .
    [*Pointing upward*]   See?
    [*De Guiche makes a sudden movement. Cyrano catches his arm*]
Be careful! If you struck me on the nose,
It would drip milk!
    DE GUICHE: Milk?
    CYRANO: From the Milky Way!
    DE GUICHE: Hell!
    CYRANO: No, no—Heaven.
    [*Crossing his arms*] Curious place up there—
Did you know Sirius wore a nightcap? True!
    [*Confidentially*]
The Little Bear is still too young to bite.
    [*Laughing*]
My foot caught in the Lyre, and broke a string.
    [*Proudly*]
Well—when I write my book, and tell the tale
Of my adventures—all these little stars
That shake out of my cloak—I must save those
To use for asterisks!
    DE GUICHE: That will do now—
I wish—
    CYRANO: Yes, yes—I know—
    DE GUICHE: Sir—
    CYRANO: You desire
To learn from my own lips the character
Of the moon's surface—its inhabitants
If any—
    DE GUICHE: [*Loses patience and shouts*] I desire no such thing! I—
    CYRANO: [*Rapidly*] You wish to know by what mysterious means
I reached the moon?—well—confidentially—
It was a new invention of my own.
    DE GUICHE: [*Discouraged*] Drunk too—as well as mad!
    CYRANO: I scorned the eagle

Of Regiomontanus, and the dove
Of Archytas!
    DE GUICHE: A learned lunatic!—
    CYRANO: I imitated no one. I myself
Discovered not one scheme merely, but six—
Six ways to violate the virgin sky!
    [*De Guiche has succeeded in passing him, and moves toward the door of* Roxane's *house. Cyrano follows, ready to use violence if necessary*]
    DE GUICHE: [*Looks around*] Six?
    CYRANO: [*With increasing volubility*] As for instance—Having stripped myself
Bare as a wax candle, adorn my form
With crystal vials filled with morning dew,
And so be drawn aloft, as the sun rises
Drinking the mist of dawn!
    DE GUICHE: [*Takes a step toward* Cyrano] Yes—that makes one.
    CYRANO: [*Draws back to lead him away from the door; speaks faster and faster*]
Or, sealing up the air in a cedar chest,
Rarefy it by means of mirrors, placed
In an icosahedron.
    DE GUICHE: [*Takes another step*] Two.
    CYRANO: [*Still retreating*] Again,
I might construct a rocket, in the form
Of a huge locust, driven by impulses
Of villainous saltpetre from the rear,
Upward, by leaps and bounds.
    DE GUICHE: [*Interested in spite of himself, and counting on his fingers*] Three.
    CYRANO: [*Same business*] Or again,
Smoke having a natural tendency to rise,
Blow in a globe enough to raise me.
    DE GUICHE: [*Same business, more and more astonished*] Four!
    CYRANO: Or since Diana, as old fables tell,
Draws forth to fill her crescent horn, the marrow
Of bulls and goats—to annoint myself therewith.
    DE GUICHE: [*Hypnotized*] Five!—
    CYRANO: [*Has by this time led him all the way across the street, close to a bench*] Finally—seated on an iron plate,
To hurl a magnet in the air—the iron
Follows— I catch the magnet—throw again—
And so proceed indefinitely.
    DE GUICHE: Six!—
All excellent,—and which did you adopt?
    CYRANO: [*Coolly*] Why, none of them. . . . A seventh.
    DE GUICHE: Which was?—
    CYRANO: Guess!—
    DE GUICHE: An interesting idiot, this!
    CYRANO: [*Imitates the sound of waves with his voice, and their movement by large, vague gestures*]
Hoo! . . . Hoo! . . .
    DE GUICHE: Well?
    CYRANO: Have you guessed it yet?
    DE GUICHE: Why, no.

CYRANO: [*Grandiloquent*] The ocean! . . .
What hour its rising tide seeks the full moon,
I laid me on the strand, fresh from the spray,
My head fronting the moonbeams, since the hair
Retains moisture—and so I slowly rose
As upon angels' wings, effortlessly,
Upward—then suddenly I felt a shock!—
And then . . .

    DE GUICHE: [*Overcome by curiosity, sits down on the bench*] And then?

    CYRANO: And then—
    [*Changes abruptly to his natural voice*]
                   The time is up!—
Fifteen minutes, your Grace!—You are now free;
And—they are bound—in wedlock.

    DE GUICHE: [*Leaping up*] Am *I* drunk?
That voice . . .
    [*The door of* Roxane's *house opens; lackeys appear, bearing lighted candles. Lights up.* Cyrano *removes his hat*]
            And that nose!—Cyrano!

    CYRANO: [*Saluting*] Cyrano! . . .
This very moment, they have exchanged rings.

    DE GUICHE: Who?
    [*He turns up stage. Tableau: between the lackeys,* Roxane *and* Christian *appear, hand in hand. The* Capuchin *follows them, smiling.* Ragueneau *holds aloft a torch. The* Duenna *brings up the rear, in a negligée, and a pleasant flutter of emotion*]
          Zounds!
    [*To* Roxane]
             You?—[*Recognizes* Christian]
He?—
    [*Saluting* Roxane] My sincere compliments!
    [*To* Cyrano]
You also, my inventor of machines!
Your rigmarole would have detained a saint
Entering Paradise—decidedly
You must not fail to write that book some day!

    CYRANO: [*Bowing*] Sir, I engage myself to do so.
    [*Leads the bridal pair down to* De Guiche *and strokes with great satisfaction his long white beard*]
                  My lord,
The handsome couple you—and God—have joined
Together!

    DE GUICHE: [*Regarding him with a frosty eye*]
Quite so.
    [*Turns to* Roxane]
              Madame, kindly bid
Your . . . husband farewell.

    ROXANE: Oh!—

    DE GUICHE: [*To* Christian] Your regiment
Leaves to-night, sir. Report at once!

    ROXANE: You mean
For the front? The war?

    DE GUICHE: Certainly!

    ROXANE: I thought
The Cadets were not going—

    DE GUICHE: Oh yes, they *are*!
    [*Taking out the despatch from his pocket*]
Here is the order—
    [*To* Christian] Baron! Deliver this.

    ROXANE: [*Throws herself into* Christian's *arms*]
Christian!

    DE GUICHE: [*To* Cyrano, *sneering*] The bridal night
is not so near!

    CYRANO: [*Aside*] Somehow that news fails to disquiet me.

    CHRISTIAN: [*To* Roxane] Your lips again . . .

    CYRANO: There . . . That will do now— Come!

    CHRISTIAN: [*Still holding* Roxane] You do not
know how hard it is—

    CYRANO: [*Tries to drag him away*] I know!
    [*The beating of drums is heard in the distance*]

    DE GUICHE: [*Up stage*] The regiment—on the
march!

    ROXANE: [*As* Cyrano *tries to lead* Christian *away, follows, and detains them*] Take care of him
For me—[*Appealingly*] Promise me never to let him
do
Anything dangerous!

    CYRANO: I'll do my best—
I cannot promise—

    ROXANE: [*Same business*] Make him be careful!

    CYRANO: Yes—
I'll try—

    ROXANE: [*Same business*] Be sure you keep him
dry and warm!

    CYRANO: Yes, yes—if possible—

    ROXANE: [*Same business; confidentially, in his ear*] See that he remains
Faithful!—

    CYRANO: Of course! If—

    ROXANE: [*Same business*] And have him write to
me
Every single day!

    CYRANO: [*Stops*] That, I promise you!

                 CURTAIN

ACT IV.

The Cadets of Gascoyne
The post occupied by the company of Carbon De
Castel-Jaloux *at the Siege of Arras. In the background, a rampart traversing the entire scene; beyond this, and apparently below, a plain stretches away to the horizon. The country is cut up with earthworks and other suggestions of the siege. In the distance, against the sky-line, the houses and the walls of Arras. Tents; scattered weapons; drums, et cetera. It is near daybreak, and the east is yellow with approaching dawn. Sentries at intervals. Campfires. Curtain rise discovers the* Cadets *asleep, rolled in their cloaks.* Carbon De Castel-Jaloux *and* Le Bret *keep watch. They are both very thin and pale.*

Christian *is asleep among the others, wrapped in his cloak, in the foreground, his face lighted by the flickering fire. Silence.*

LE BRET: Horrible!

CARBON: Why, yes. All of that.

LE BRET: Mordious!

CARBON: [*Gesture toward the sleeping* Cadets] Swear gently— You might wake them.
[*To* Cadets]
Go to sleep—
Hush! [*To* Le Bret] Who sleeps dines.

LE BRET: I have insomnia.
God! What a famine.
[*Firing off stage*]

CARBON: Curse that musketry!
They'll wake my babies.
[*To the men*] Go to sleep!—

A CADET: [*Rouses*] Diantre!
Again?

CARBON: No—only Cyrano coming home.
[*The heads which have been raised sink back again*]

A SENTRY: [*Off stage*] Halt! Who goes there?

VOICE OF CYRANO: Bergerac!

THE SENTRY ON THE PARAPET: Halt! Who goes?—

CYRANO: [*Appears on the parapet*] Bergerac, idiot!

LE BRET: [*Goes to meet him*] Thank God again!

CYRANO: [*Signs to him not to wake anyone*] Hush!

LE BRET: Wounded?—

CYRANO: No— They always miss me—quite
A habit by this time!

LE BRET: Yes— Go right on—
Risk your life every morning before breakfast
To send a letter!

CYRANO: [*Stops near* Christian] I promised he
should write
Every single day . . .
[*Looks down at him*]
Hm— The boy looks pale
When he is asleep—thin too—starving to death—
If that poor child knew! Handsome, none the less . . .

LE BRET: Go and get some sleep!

CYRANO: [*Affectionately*] Now, now—you old bear,
No growling!—I am careful—you know I am—
Every night, when I cross the Spanish lines
I wait till they are all drunk.

LE BRET: You might bring
Something with you.

CYRANO: I have to travel light
To pass through— By the way, there will be news
For you to-day: the French will eat or die,
If what I saw means anything.

LE BRET: Tell us!

CYRANO: No—
I am not sure—we shall see!

CARBON: What a war,
When the besieger starves to death!

LE BRET: Fine war—
Fine situation! We besiege Arras—

The Cardinal Prince of Spain besieges us—
And—here we are!

CYRANO: Someone might besiege *him*.

CARBON: A hungry joke!

CYRANO: Ho, ho!

LE BRET: Yes, you can laugh—
Risking a life like yours to carry letters—
Where are you going now?

CYRANO: [*At the tent door*] To write another.
[*Goes into tent*]
[*A little more daylight. The clouds redden. The town of Arras shows on the horizon. A cannon shot is heard, followed immediately by a roll of drums, far away to the left. Other drums beat a little nearer. The drums go on answering each other here and there, approach, beat loudly almost on the stage, and die away toward the right, across the camp. The camp awakes. Voices of officers in the distance*]

CARBON: [*Sighs*] Those drums!—another good
nourishing sleep
Gone to the devil.
[*The* Cadets *rouse themselves*]
Now then!—

FIRST CADET: [*Sits up, yawns*] God! I'm hungry!

SECOND CADET: Starving!

ALL: [*Groan*] Aoh!

CARBON: Up with you!

THIRD CADET: Not another step!

FOURTH CADET: Not another movement!

FIRST CADET: Look at my tongue—
I said this air was indigestible!

FIFTH CADET: My coronet for half a pound of
cheese!

SIXTH CADET: I have no stomach for this war—
I'll stay
In my tent—like Achilles.

ANOTHER: Yes—no bread,
No fighting—

CARBON: Cyrano!

OTHERS: May as well die—

CARBON: Come out here!—You know how to talk
to them.
Get them laughing—

SECOND CADET: [*Rushes up to* First Cadet *who is eating something*] What are you gnawing there?

FIRST CADET: Gun wads and axle-grease. Fat country
try this
Around Arras.

ANOTHER: [*Enters*] I have been out hunting!

ANOTHER: [*Enters*] I
Went fishing, in the Scarpe!

ALL: [*Leaping up and surrounding the newcomers*]
Find anything?
Any fish? Any game? Perch? Partridges?
Let me look!

THE FISHERMAN: Yes—one gudgeon.
[*Shows it*]

THE HUNTER: One fat . . . sparrow.
[*Shows it*]

ALL: Ah!—See here, this—mutiny!—

CARBON: Cyrano!
Come and help!

CYRANO: [*Enters from tent*] Well?
[*Silence. To the* First Cadet *who is walking away, with his chin on his chest*]
                    You there, with the long face?

FIRST CADET: I have something on my mind that troubles me.

CYRANO: What is that?

FIRST CADET: My stomach.

CYRANO: So have I.

FIRST CADET: No doubt
You enjoy this!

CYRANO: [*Tightens his belt*] It keeps me looking young.

SECOND CADET: My teeth are growing rusty.

CYRANO: Sharpen them!

THIRD CADET: My belly sounds as hollow as a drum.

CYRANO: Beat the long roll on it!

FOURTH CADET: My ears are ringing.

CYRANO: Liar! A hungry belly has no ears.

FIFTH CADET: Oh for a barrel of good wine!

CYRANO: [*Offers him his own helmet*] Your casque.

SIXTH CADET: I'll swallow anything!

CYRANO: [*Throws him the book which he has in his hand*] Try the "Iliad."

SEVENTH CADET: The Cardinal, he has four meals a day—
What does he care!

CYRANO: Ask him; he really ought
To send you . . . a spring lamb out of his flock,
Roasted whole—

THE CADET: Yes, and a bottle—

CYRANO: [*Exaggerates the manner of one speaking to a servant*] If you please,
Richelieu—a little more of the Red Seal . . .
Ah, thank you!

THE CADET: And the salad—

CYRANO: Of course—Romaine!

ANOTHER: [*Shivering*] I am as hungry as a wolf.

CYRANO: [*Tosses him a cloak*] Put on
Your sheep's clothing.

FIRST CADET: [*With a shrug*] Always the clever answer!

CYRANO: Always the answer—yes! Let me die
so—
Under some rosy-golden sunset, saying
A good thing, for a good cause! By the sword,
The point of honor—by the hand of one
Worthy to be my foeman, let me fall—
Steel in my heart, and laughter on my lips!

VOICES HERE AND THERE: All very well— We are hungry!

CYRANO: Bah! You think
Of nothing but yourselves.
[*His eye singles out the old fifer in the background*]
                    Here, Bertrandou,

You were a shepherd once— Your pipe now! **Come,**
Breathe, blow,— Play to these belly-worshippers
The old airs of the South—
                    "Airs with a smile in **them,**
Airs with a sigh in them, airs with the breeze
And the blue of the sky in them—"
                                        Small, demure tunes
Whose every note is like a little sister—
Songs heard only in some long silent voice
Not quite forgotten— Mountain melodies
Like thin smoke rising from brown cottages
In the still noon, slowly— Quaint lullabies,
Whose very music has a Southern tongue—
            [*The old man sits down and prepares his fife*]
Now let the fife, that dry old warrior,
Dream, while over the stops your fingers dance
A minuet of little birds—let him
Dream beyond ebony and ivory;
Let him remember he was once a reed
Out of the river, and recall the spirit
Of innocent, untroubled country days . . .
            [*The fifer begins to play a Provençal melody*]
Listen, you Gascons! Now it is no more
The shrill fife— It is the flute, through **woodlands** far
Away, calling—no longer the hot battle-cry,
But the cool, quiet pipe our goatherds play!
Listen—the forest glens . . . the hills . . . the downs . . .
The green sweetness of night on the Dordogne . . .
Listen, you Gascons! It is all Gascoyne! . . .
            [*Every head is bowed; every eye cast down. Here and there a tear is furtively brushed away with the back of a hand, the corner of a cloak*]

CARBON: [*Softly to* Cyrano] You make them weep—

CYRANO: For homesickness—a hunger
More noble than that hunger of the flesh;
It is their hearts now that are starving.

CARBON: Yes,
But you melt down their manhood.

CYRANO: [*Motions the drummer to approach*] You think so?
Let them be. There is iron in their blood
Not easily dissolved in tears. You need
Only—
            [*He makes a gesture; the drum beats*]

ALL: [*Spring up and rush toward their weapons*]
What's that? Where is it?—What?—

CYRANO: [*Smiles*] You see—
Let Mars snore in his sleep once—and farewell
Venus—sweet dreams—regrets—dear thoughts of home—
All the fife lulls to rest wakes at the drums!

A CADET: [*Looks up stage*] Aha— Monsieur de Guiche!

THE CADETS: [*Mutter among themselves*] Ugh! . . .

CYRANO: [*Smiles*] Flattering murmur!

A CADET: He makes me weary!

ANOTHER: With his collar
Of lace over his corselet—
ANOTHER: Like a ribbon
Tied round a sword!
ANOTHER: Bandages for a boil
On the back of his neck—
SECOND CADET: A courtier always!
ANOTHER: The Cardinal's nephew!
CARBON: None the less—a Gascon.
FIRST CADET: A counterfeit! Never you trust that
man—
Because we Gascons, look you, are all mad—
But this fellow is reasonable—nothing more
Dangerous than a reasonable Gascon!
LE BRET: He looks pale.
ANOTHER: Oh, he can be hungry too,
Like any other poor devil—but he wears
So many jewels on that belt of his
That his cramps glitter in the sun!
CYRANO: [*Quickly*] Is he
To see us looking miserable? Quick—
Pipes!—Cards!—Dice!—
> [*They all hurriedly begin to play, on their
> stools, on the drums, or on their cloaks spread
> on the ground, lighting their long pipes mean-
> while*]
As for me, I read Descartes.
> [*He walks up and down, reading a small book
> which he takes from his pocket. Tableau: De
> Guiche enters, looking pale and haggard. All
> are absorbed in their games. General air of
> contentment. De Guiche goes to Carbon.
> They look at each other askance, each observ-
> ing with satisfaction the condition of the other*]
DE GUICHE: Good morning!
> [*Aside*] He looks yellow.
CARBON: [*Same business*] He is all eyes.
DE GUICHE: [*Looks at the Cadets*]
What have we here? Black looks? Yes, gentlemen—
I am informed I am not popular;
The hill-nobility, barons of Béarn,
The pomp and pride of Périgord—I learn
They disapprove their colonel; call him courtier,
Politician—they take it ill that I
Cover my steel with lace of Genoa.
It is a great offense to be a Gascon
And not to be a beggar!
> [*Silence. They smoke. They play*]
Well— Shall I have
Your captain punish you? . . . No.
CARBON: As to that,
It would be impossible.
DE GUICHE: Oh?
CARBON: I am free;
I pay my company; it is my own;
I obey military orders.
DE GUICHE: Oh!
That will be quite enough.
> [*To the* Cadets] I can afford
Your little hates. My conduct under fire

Is well known. It was only yesterday
I drove the Count de Bucquoi from Bapaume,
Pouring my men down like an avalanche,
I myself led the charge—
CYRANO: [*Without looking up from his book*] And
your white scarf?
DE GUICHE: [*Surprised and gratified*]
You heard that episode? Yes—rallying
My men for the third time, I found myself
Carried among a crowd of fugitives
Into the enemy's lines. I was in danger
Of being shot or captured; but I thought
Quickly—took off and flung away the scarf
That marked my military rank—and so
Being inconspicuous, escaped among
My own force, rallied them, returned again
And won the day! . . .
> [*The* Cadets *do not appear to be listening, but
> here and there the cards and the dice boxes re-
> main motionless, the smoke is retained in their
> cheeks*]
What do you say to that?
Presence of mind—yes?
CYRANO: Henry of Navarre
Being outnumbered, never flung away
His white plume.
> [*Silent enjoyment. The cards flutter, the dice
> roll, the smoke puffs out*]
DE GUICHE: My device was a success,
However!
> [*Some attentive pause, interrupting the games
> and the smoking*]
CYRANO: Possibly . . . An officer
Does not lightly resign the privilege
Of being a target.
> [*Cards, dice, and smoke fall, roll, and float
> away with increasing satisfaction*]
Now, if I had been there—
Your courage and my own differ in this—
When your scarf fell, I should have put it on.
DE GUICHE: Boasting again!
CYRANO: Boasting? Lend it to me
To-night; I'll lead the first charge, with your scarf
Over my shoulder!
DE GUICHE: Gasconnade once more!
You are safe making that offer, and you know it—
My scarf lies on the river bank between
The lines, a spot swept by artillery
Impossible to reach alive!
CYRANO: [*Produces the scarf from his pocket*]
Yes. Here . . .
> [*Silence. The* Cadets *stifle their laughter behind
> their cards and their dice boxes. De Guiche
> turns to look at them. Immediately they resume
> their gravity and their game. One of them
> whistles carelessly the mountain air which the
> fifer was playing*]
DE GUICHE: [*Takes the scarf*]
Thank you! That bit of white is what I need

To make a signal. I was hesitating—
You have decided me.
> [*He goes up to the parapet, climbs upon it, and waves the scarf at arm's length several times*]

ALL: What is he doing?—
What?—

THE SENTRY ON THE PARAPET: There's a man down there running away!

DE GUICHE: [*Descending*] A Spaniard. Very useful as a spy
To both sides. He informs the enemy
As I instruct him. By his influence
I can arrange their dispositions.

CYRANO: Traitor!

DE GUICHE: [*Folding the scarf*] A traitor, yes; but useful . . .

> We were saying? . . .

Oh, yes— Here is a bit of news for you:
Last night we had hopes of reprovisioning
The army. Under cover of the dark,
The Marshal moved to Dourlens. Our supplies
Are there. He may reach them. But to return
Safely, he needs a large force—at least half
Our entire strength. At present, we have here
Merely a skeleton.

CARBON: Fortunately,
The Spaniards do not know that.

DE GUICHE: Oh, yes; they know.
They will attack.

CARBON: Ah!

DE GUICHE: From that spy of mine
I learned of their intention. His report
Will determine the point of their advance.
The fellow asked me what to say! I told him:
"Go out between the lines; watch for my signal;
Where you see that, let them attack there."

CARBON: [*To the* Cadets] Well,
Gentlemen!

> [*All rise. Noise of sword belts and breastplates being buckled on*]

DE GUICHE: You may have perhaps an hour.

FIRST CADET: Oh— An hour!

> [*They all sit down and resume their games once more*]

DE GUICHE: [*To* Carbon] The great thing is to gain time.
Any moment the Marshal may return.

CARBON: And to gain time?

DE GUICHE: You will all be so kind
As to lay down your lives!

CYRANO: Ah! Your revenge?

DE GUICHE: I make no great pretence of loving you!
But—since you gentlemen esteem yourselves
Invincible, the bravest of the brave,
And all that—why need we be personal?
I serve the king in choosing . . . as I choose!

CYRANO: [*Salutes*] Sir, permit me to offer—all our thanks.

DE GUICHE: [*Returns the salute*] You love to fight
a hundred against one;
Here is your opportunity!

> [*He goes up stage with* Carbon]

CYRANO: [*To the* Cadets] My friends,
We shall add now to our old Gascon arms
With their six chevrons, blue and gold, a seventh—
Blood-red!

> [*De Guiche talks in a low tone to* Carbon *up stage. Orders are given. The defense is arranged.* Cyrano *goes to* Christian *who has remained motionless with folded arms*]

> Christian? [*Lays a hand on his shoulder*]

CHRISTIAN: [*Shakes his head*] Roxane . . .

CYRANO: Yes.

CHRISTIAN: I should like
To say farewell to her, with my whole heart
Written for her to keep.

CYRANO: I thought of that—
> [*Takes a letter from his doublet*]

I have written your farewell.

CHRISTIAN: Show me!

CYRANO: You wish
To read it?

CHRISTIAN: Of course!

> [*He takes the letter; begins to read, looks up suddenly*] What?—

CYRANO: What is it?

CHRISTIAN: Look—
This little circle—

CYRANO: [*Takes back the letter quickly, and looks innocent*] Circle?—

CHRISTIAN: Yes—a tear!

CYRANO: So it is! . . . Well—a poet while he writes
Is like a lover in his lady's arms,
Believing his imagination—all
Seems true—you understand? There's half the charm
Of writing— Now, this letter as you see
I have made so pathetic that I wept
While I was writing it!

CHRISTIAN: You—wept?

CYRANO: Why, yes—
Because . . . it is a little thing to die,
But—not to see her . . . that is terrible!
And I shall never—
> [Christian *looks at him*]

We shall never—[*Quickly*] You
Will never—

CHRISTIAN: [*Snatches the letter*] Give me that!
> [*Noise in the distance on the outskirts of the camp*]

VOICE OF A SENTRY: Halt—who goes there?
> [*Shots, shouting, jingle of harness*]

CARBON: What is it?—

THE SENTRY ON THE WATCH: Why, a coach.
> [*They rush to look*]

CONFUSED VOICES: What? In the Camp?
A coach? Coming this way— It must have driven

Through the Spanish lines—what the devil— Fire!—
No— Hark! The driver shouting—what does he say?
Wait— He said: "On the service of the King!"
　　　[*They are all on the parapet looking over. The
　　　jingling comes nearer*]
DE GUICHE: Of the King?
　　　[*They come down and fall into line*]
CARBON:　　　　　　　　　Hats off, all!
DE GUICHE: [*Speaks off stage*] The King! Fall in,
Rascals!—
　　　[*The coach enters at full trot. It is covered with
　　　mud and dust. The curtains are drawn. Two
　　　footmen are seated behind. It stops suddenly*]
CARBON: [*Shouts*] Beat the assembly—
　　　[*Roll of drums. All the* Cadets *uncover*]
DE GUICHE:　　　　　　　　　Two of you,
Lower the steps—open the door—
　　　[*Two men rush to the coach. The door opens*]
ROXANE: [*Comes out of the coach*] Good morning!
　　　[*At the sound of a woman's voice, every head
　　　is raised. Sensation*]
DE GUICHE: On the King's service— You?
ROXANE:　　　　　　　Yes—my own king—
Love!
CYRANO: [*Aside*] God is merciful . . .
CHRISTIAN: [*Hastens to her*] You! Why have you—
ROXANE: Your war lasted so long!
CHRISTIAN:　　　　　　　　　But why?—
ROXANE: Not now—
CYRANO: [*Aside*] I wonder if I dare to look at
her . . .
DE GUICHE: You cannot remain here!
ROXANE:　　　　　　　　Why, certainly!
Roll that drum here, somebody. . . .
　　　[*She sits on the drum, which is brought to
　　　her*]
　　　　　　　　　　　Thank you— There!
　　　[*She laughs*]
Would you believe—they fired upon us?
　　　　　　　　　　　—My coach
Looks like the pumpkin in the fairy tale,
Does it not? And my footmen—
　　　[*She throws a kiss to* Christian]
　　　　　　　　　　　How do you do?
　　　[*She looks about*]
How serious you all are! Do you know,
It is a long drive here—from Arras?
　　　[*Sees* Cyrano]
　　　　　　　　　　　　Cousin,
I am glad to see you!
CYRANO: [*Advances*] Oh— How did you come?
ROXANE: How did I find you? Very easily—
I followed where the country was laid waste
—Oh, but I saw such things! I had to see
To believe. Gentlemen, is that the service
Of your King? I prefer my own!
CYRANO:　　　　　　　　But how
Did you come through?
ROXANE:　　　　　Why, through the Spanish lines
Of course!

FIRST CADET: They let you pass?—
DE GUICHE:　　　　　　　What did you say?
How did you manage?
LE BRET:　　　　Yes, that must have been
Difficult!
ROXANE: No— I simply drove along.
Now and then some hidalgo scowled at me
And I smiled back—my best smile; whereupon,
The Spaniards being (without prejudice
To the French) the most polished gentlemen
In the world—I passed!
CARBON:　　　　　Certainly that smile
Should be a passport! Did they never ask
Your errand or your destination?
ROXANE:　　　　　　　　Oh,
Frequently! Then I drooped my eyes and said:
"I have a lover . . ." Whereupon, the Spaniard
With an air of ferocious dignity
Would close the carriage door—with such a gesture
As any king might envy, wave aside
The muskets that were levelled at my breast,
Fall back three paces, equally superb
In grace and gloom, draw himself up, thrust forth
A spur under his cloak, sweeping the air
With his long plumes, bow very low, and say:
"Pass, Senorita!"
CHRISTIAN:　　　　　But Roxane—
ROXANE:　　　　　　　　I know—
I said "a lover"—but you understand—
Forgive me!—If I said "I am going to meet
My husband," no one would believe me!
CHRISTIAN:　　　　　　　　　Yes,
But—
ROXANE: What then?
DE GUICHE:　　　You must leave this place.
CYRANO:　　　　　　　　At once.
ROXANE: I?
LE BRET: Yes—immediately.
ROXANE:　　　　　　　　And why?
CHRISTIAN: [*Embarrassed*] Because . . .
CYRANO: [*Same*] In half an hour . . .
DE GUICHE: [*Same*] Or three quarters . . .
CARBON: [*Same*] Perhaps
It might be better . . .
LE BRET:　　　　If you . . .
ROXANE:　　　　　　　Oh— I see!
You are going to fight. I remain here.
ALL:　　　　　　　　　No—no!
ROXANE: He is my husband—
　　　[*Throws herself in* Christian's *arms*]
　　　　　　　　　　　I will die with you!
CHRISTIAN: Your eyes! . . . Why do you?—
ROXANE:　　　　　　You know why . . .
DE GUICHE: [*Desperate*] This post
Is dangerous—
ROXANE: [*Turns*] How—dangerous?
CYRANO:　　　　　　　　The proof
Is, we are ordered—
ROXANE: [*To De Guiche*] Oh—you wish to make
A widow of me?

DE GUICHE: On my word of honor—

ROXANE: No matter. I am just a little mad—
I will stay. It may be amusing.

CYRANO: What,
A heroine—our intellectual?

ROXANE: Monsieur de Bergerac, I am your cousin!

A CADET: We'll fight now! Hurrah!

ROXANE: [More and more excited] I am safe with
    you—my friends!

ANOTHER: [Carried away] The whole camp
    breathes of lilies!—

ROXANE: And I think,
This hat would look well on the battlefield! . . .
But perhaps—
    [Looks at De Guiche]
            The Count ought to leave us. Any moment
Now, there may be danger.

DE GUICHE: This is too much!
I must inspect my guns. I shall return—
You may change your mind— There will yet be
    time—

ROXANE: Never! [De Guiche goes out]

CHRISTIAN: [Imploring] Roxane! . . .

ROXANE: No!

FIRST CADET: [To the rest] She stays here!

ALL: [Rushing about, elbowing each other, brush-
ing off their clothes] A comb!—
Soap!—Here's a hole in my— A needle!—Who
Has a ribbon?—Your mirror, quick!—My cuffs—
A razor—

ROXANE: [To Cyrano, who is still urging her] No!
    I shall not stir one step!

CARBON: [Having, like the others, tightened his
    belt, dusted himself, brushed off his hat,
    smoothed out his plume and put on his lace
    cuffs, advances to Roxane ceremoniously]
In that case, may I not present to you
Some of these gentlemen who are to have
The honor of dying in your presence?

ROXANE: [Bows] Please!—
    [She waits, standing, on the arm of Christian,
    while]

CARBON: [—presents] Baron de Peyrescous de
    Colignac!

THE CADET: [Salutes] Madame . . .

ROXANE: Monsieur . . .

CARBON: [Continues] Baron de Casterac
De Cahuzac— Vidame de Malgouyre
Estressac Lesbas d'Escarabiot—

THE VIDAME: Madame . . .

CARBON: Chevalier d'Antignac-Juzet—
Baron Hillot de Blagnac-Saléchan
De Castel-Crabioules—

THE BARON: Madame . . .

ROXANE: How many
Names you all have!

THE BARON: Hundreds!

CARBON: [To Roxane] Open the hand
That holds your handkerchief.

ROXANE: [Opens her hand; the handkerchief falls]
    Why?
    [The whole company makes a movement to-
    ward it]

CARBON: [Picks it up quickly] My company
Was in want of a banner. We have now
The fairest in the army!

ROXANE: [Smiling] Rather small—

CARBON: [Fastens the handkerchief to his lance]
Lace—and embroidered!

A CADET: [To the others] With her smiling on me,
I could die happy, if I only had
Something in my—

CARBON: [Turns upon him] Shame on you! Feast
    your eyes
And forget your—

ROXANE: [Quickly] It must be this fresh air—
I am starving! Let me see . . .
                              Cold partridges,
Pastry, a little white wine—that would do.
Will some one bring that to me?

A CADET: [Aside] Will some one!—

ANOTHER: Where the devil are we to find—

ROXANE: [Overhears; sweetly] Why, there—
In my carriage.

ALL: Wha-at?

ROXANE: All you have to do
Is to unpack, and carve, and serve things.
                                        Oh,
Notice my coachman; you may recognize
An old friend.

THE CADETS: [Rush to the coach] Ragueneau!

ROXANE: [Follows them with her eyes] Poor fel-
    lows . . .

THE CADETS: [Acclamations] Ah!
Ah!

CYRANO: [Kisses her hand] Our good fairy!

RAGUENEAU: [Standing on his box, like a monte-
bank before a crowd] Gentlemen!—[Enthusiasm]

THE CADETS: Bravo!
Bravo!

RAGUENEAU: The Spaniards, basking in our smiles,
Smiled on our baskets!
    [Applause]

CYRANO: [Aside, to Christian] Christian!—

RAGUENEAU: They adored
The Fair, and missed—
    [He takes from under the seat a dish, which he
    holds aloft]
                              the Fowl!
    [Applause. The dish is passed from hand to
    hand]

CYRANO: [As before, to Christian] One moment—

RAGUENEAU: Venus
Charmed their eyes, while Adonis quietly
    [Brandishing a ham]
Brought home the Boar!
    [Applause; the ham is seized by a score of
    hands outstretched]

CYRANO: [As before] Pst— Let me speak to you—

ROXANE: [*As the* Cadets *return, their arms full of provisions*] Spread them out on the ground.
[*Calls*]
Christian! Come here;
Make yourself useful.
[Christian *turns to her, at the moment when* Cyrano *was leading him aside. She arranges the food, with his aid and that of the two imperturbable footmen*]
RAGUENEAU: Peacock, aux truffes!
FIRST CADET: [*Comes down, cutting a huge slice of the ham*] Tonnerre!
We are not going to die without a gorge—
[*Sees* Roxane; *corrects himself hastily*]
Pardon—a banquet!
RAGUENEAU: [*Tossing out the cushions of the carriage*] Open these— they are full
Of ortolans!
[*Tumult; laughter; the cushions are eviscerated*]
THIRD CADET: Lucullus!
RAGUENEAU: [*Throws out bottles of red wine*]
Flasks of ruby—[*And of white*]
Flasks of topaz—
ROXANE: [*Throws a tablecloth at the head of* Cyrano] Come back out of your dreams!
Unfold this cloth—
RAGUENEAU: [*Takes off one of the lanterns of the carriage, and flourishes it*] Our lamps are bonbonnières!
CYRANO: [*To* Christian] I must see you before you speak with her—
RAGUENEAU: [*More and more lyrical*] My whip-handle is one long sausage!
ROXANE: [*Pouring wine; passing the food*] We
Being about to die, first let us dine!
Never mind the others—all for Gascoyne!
And if De Guiche comes, he is not invited!
[*Going from one to another*]
Plenty of time—you need not eat so fast—
Hold your cup—[*To another*] What's the matter?
THE CADET: [*Sobbing*] You are so good
To us . . .
ROXANE: There, there! Red or white wine?
—Some bread
For Monsieur de Carbon!—Napkins— A knife—
Pass your plate— Some of the crust? A little more—
Light or dark?—Burgundy?—
CYRANO: [*Follows her with an armful of dishes, helping to serve*] Adorable!
ROXANE: [*Goes to* Christian] What would you like?
CHRISTIAN: Nothing.
ROXANE: Oh, but you must!—
A little wine? A biscuit?
CHRISTIAN: Tell me first
Why you came—
ROXANE: By and by. I must take care
Of these poor boys—
LE BRET: [*Who has gone up stage to pass up food to the sentry on the parapet, on the end of a lance*]

De Guiche!—
CYRANO: Hide everything
Quick!—Dishes, bottles, tablecloth—
Now look
Hungry again—
[*To* Ragueneau]
You there! Up on your box—
—Everything out of sight?—
[*In a twinkling, everything has been pushed inside the tents, hidden in their hats or under their cloaks. De Guiche enters quickly, then stops, sniffing the air. Silence*]
DE GUICHE: It smells good here.
A CADET: [*Humming with an air of great unconcern*] Sing ha-ha-ha and ho-ho-ho—
DE GUICHE: [*Stares at him; he grows embarrassed*]
You there—
What are you blushing for?
THE CADET: Nothing—my blood
Stirs at the thought of battle.
ANOTHER: Pom . . . pom . . . pom! . . .
DE GUICHE: [*Turns upon him*] What is that?
THE CADET: [*Slightly stimulated*] Only song—only little song—
DE GUICHE: You appear happy!
THE CADET: Oh yes—always happy
Before a fight—
DE GUICHE: [*Calls to* Carbon, *for the purpose of giving him an order*] Captain! I—
[*Stops and looks at him*]
What the devil—
You are looking happy too!—
CARBON: [*Pulls a long face and hides a bottle behind his back*] No!
DE GUICHE: Here—I had
One gun remaining. I have had it placed
[*He points off stage*]
There—in that corner—for your men.
A CADET: [*Simpering*] So kind!—
Charming attention!
ANOTHER: [*Same business; burlesque*] Sweet solicitude!—
DE GUICHE: [*Contemptuous*] I believe you are both drunk—
[*Coldly*]
Being unaccustomed
To guns—take care of the recoil!
FIRST CADET: [*Gesture*] Ah-h . . . Pfft!
DE GUICHE: [*Goes up to him, furious*] How dare you?
FIRST CADET: A Gascon's gun never recoils!
DE GUICHE: [*Shakes him by the arm*] You *are* drunk—
FIRST CADET: [*Superbly*] With the smell of powder!
DE GUICHE: [*Turns away with a shrug*] Bah!
[*To* Roxane]
Madame, have you decided?
ROXANE: I stay here.
DE GUICHE: You have time to escape—

ROXANE: No!

DE GUICHE: Very well—
Someone give me a musket!

CARBON: What?

DE GUICHE: I stay
Here also.

CYRANO: [Formally] Sir, you show courage!

FIRST CADET: A Gascon
In spite of all that lace!

ROXANE: Why—

DE GUICHE: Must I run
Away, and leave a woman?

SECOND CADET: [To First Cadet] We might give
him
Something to eat—what do you say?
[All the food re-appears, as if by magic]

DE GUICHE: [His face lights up] A feast!

THIRD CADET: Here a little, there a little—

DE GUICHE: [Recovers his self-control; haughtily]
Do you think
I want your leavings?

CYRANO: [Saluting] Colonel—you improve!

DE GUICHE: I can fight as I am!

FIRST CADET: [Delighted] Listen to him—
He has an accent!

DE GUICHE: [Laughs] Have I so?

FIRST CADET: A Gascon!—
A Gascon, after all!
[They all begin to dance]

CARBON: [Who has disappeared for a moment behind the parapet, reappears on top of it] I have
placed my pikemen
Here.
[Indicates a row of pikes showing above the
parapet]

DE GUICHE: [Bows to Roxane] We'll review them;
will you take my arm?
[She takes his arm; they go up on the parapet.
The rest uncover, and follow them up stage]

CHRISTIAN: [Goes hurriedly to Cyrano] Speak
quickly!
[At the moment when Roxane appears on the
parapet the pikes are lowered in salute, and
a cheer is heard. She bows]

THE PIKEMEN: [Off stage] Hurrah!

CHRISTIAN: What is it?

CYRANO: If Roxane . . .

CHRISTIAN: Well?

CYRANO: Speaks about your letters . . .

CHRISTIAN: Yes—I know!

CYRANO: Do not make the mistake of showing . . .

CHRISTIAN: What?

CYRANO: Showing surprise.

CHRISTIAN: Surprise—why?

CYRANO: I must tell you! . . .
It is quite simple—I had forgotten it
Until just now. You have . . .

CHRISTIAN: Speak quickly!—

CYRANO: You
Have written oftener than you think.

CHRISTIAN: Oh—have I!

CYRANO: I took upon me to interpret you;
And wrote—sometimes . . . without . . .

CHRISTIAN: My knowing. Well?

CYRANO: Perfectly simple!

CHRISTIAN: Oh yes, perfectly!—
For a month, we have been blockaded here!—
How did you send all these letters?

CYRANO: Before
Daylight, I managed—

CHRISTIAN: I see. That was also
Perfectly simple!
—So I wrote to her,
How many times a week? Twice? Three times?
Four?

CYRANO: Oftener.

CHRISTIAN: Every day?

CYRANO: Yes—every day . . .
Every single day . . .

CHRISTIAN: [Violently] And that wrought you up
Into such a flame that you faced death—

CYRANO: [Sees Roxane returning] Hush—
Not before her!
[He goes quickly into the tent. Roxane comes
up to Christian]

ROXANE: Now—Christian!

CHRISTIAN: [Takes her hands] Tell me now
Why you came here—over these ruined roads—
Why you made your way among mosstroopers
And ruffians—you—to join me here?

ROXANE: Because—
Your letters . . .

CHRISTIAN: Meaning?

ROXANE: It was your own fault
If I ran into danger; I went mad—
Mad with you! Think what you have written me,
How many times, each one more wonderful
Than the last!

CHRISTIAN: All this for a few absurd
Love-letters—

ROXANE: Hush—absurd! How can you know?
I thought I loved you, ever since one night
When a voice that I never would have known
Under my window breathed your soul to me . . .
But—all this time, your letters—every one
Was like hearing your voice there in the dark,
All around me, like your arms around me . . .
[More lightly]
At last,
I came. Anyone would! Do you suppose
The prim Penelope had stayed at home
Embroidering,—if Ulysses wrote like you?
She would have fallen like another Helen—
Tucked up those linen petticoats of hers
And followed him to Troy!

CHRISTIAN: But you—

ROXANE: I read them
Over and over. I grew faint reading them.
I belonged to you. Every page of them
Was like a petal fallen from your soul—

Like the light and the fire of a great love,
Sweet and strong and true—
    CHRISTIAN: Sweet . . . and strong . . . and true
    . . .
You felt that, Roxane?—
    ROXANE: You know how I feel! . . .
    CHRISTIAN: So—you came . . .
    ROXANE: Oh my Christian, oh my king,—
Lift me up if I fall upon my knees—
It is the heart of me that kneels to you,
And will remain forever at your feet—
You cannot lift that!—
                I came here to say
'Forgive me'—(It is time to be forgiven
Now, when we may die presently)—forgive me
For being light and vain and loving you
Only because you were beautiful.
    CHRISTIAN: [*Astonished*] Roxane! . . .
    ROXANE: Afterwards I knew better. Afterwards
(I had to learn to use my wings) I loved you
For yourself too—knowing you more, and loving
More of you. And now—
    CHRISTIAN: Now? . . .
    ROXANE: It is yourself
I love now: your own self.
    CHRISTIAN: [*Taken aback*] Roxane!
    ROXANE: [*Gravely*] Be happy!—
You must have suffered; for you must have seen
How frivolous I was; and to be loved
For the mere costume, the poor casual body
You went about in—to a soul like yours,
That must have been torture! Therefore with words
You revealed your heart. Now that image of you
Which filled my eyes first—I see better now,
And I see it no more!
    CHRISTIAN: Oh!—
    ROXANE: You still doubt
Your victory?
    CHRISTIAN: [*Miserably*] Roxane!—
    ROXANE: I understand:
You cannot perfectly believe in me—
A love like this—
    CHRISTIAN: I want no love like this!
I want love only for—
    ROXANE: Only for what
Every woman sees in you? I can do
Better than that!
    CHRISTIAN: No—it was best before!
    ROXANE: You do not altogether know me . . .
    Dear,
There is more of me than there was—with this,
I can love more of you—more of what makes
You your own self—Truly! . . . If you were less
Lovable—
    CHRISTIAN: No!
    ROXANE: —Less charming—ugly even—
I should love you still.
    CHRISTIAN: You mean that?
    ROXANE: I do
Mean that!

    CHRISTIAN: Ugly? . . .
    ROXANE: Yes. Even then!
    CHRISTIAN: [*Agonized*] Oh . . . God! . . .
    ROXANE: Now are you happy?
    CHRISTIAN: [*Choking*] Yes . . .
    ROXANE: What is it?
    CHRISTIAN: [*Pushes her away gently*] Only . . .
Nothing . . . one moment . . .
    ROXANE: But—
    CHRISTIAN: [*Gesture toward the* Cadets] I am
    keeping you
From those poor fellows—Go and smile at them;
They are going to die!
    ROXANE: [*Softly*] Dear Christian!
    CHRISTIAN: Go—
    [*She goes up among the* Gascons *who gather
    round her respectfully*]
Cyrano!
    CYRANO: [*Comes out of the tent, armed for the
battle*] What is wrong? You look—
    CHRISTIAN: She does not
Love me any more.
    CYRANO: [*Smiles*] You think not?
    CHRISTIAN: She loves
You.
    CYRANO: No!—
    CHRISTIAN: [*Bitterly*] She loves only my soul.
    CYRANO: No!
    CHRISTIAN: Yes—
That means you. And you love her.
    CYRANO: I?
    CHRISTIAN: I see—
I know!
    CYRANO: That is true . . .
    CHRISTIAN: More than—
    CYRANO: [*Quietly*] More than that.
    CHRISTIAN: Tell her so!
    CYRANO: No.
    CHRISTIAN: Why not?
    CYRANO: Why—look at me!
    CHRISTIAN: She would love me if I were ugly,
    CYRANO: [*Startled*] She—
Said that?
    CHRISTIAN: Yes. Now then!
    CYRANO: [*Half to himself*] It was good of her
To tell you that . . .
    [*Change of tone*]
             Nonsense! Do not believe
Any such madness—
          It was good of her
To tell you. . . .
          Do not take her at her word!
Go on—you never will be ugly— Go!
She would never forgive me.
    CHRISTIAN: That is what
We shall see.
    CYRANO: No, no—
    CHRISTIAN: Let her choose between us!—
Tell her everything!
    CYRANO: No—you torture me—

CHRISTIAN: Shall I ruin your happiness, because
I have a cursed pretty face? That seems
Too unfair!

CYRANO: And am I to ruin yours
Because I happen to be born with power
To say what you—perhaps—feel?

CHRISTIAN: Tell her!

CYRANO: Man—
Do not try me too far!

CHRISTIAN: I am tired of being
My own rival!

CYRANO: Christian!—

CHRISTIAN: Our secret marriage—
No witnesses—fraudulent—that can be
Annulled—

CYRANO: Do not try me—

CHRISTIAN: I want her love
For the poor fool I am—or not at all!
Oh, I am going through with this! I'll know,
One way or the other. Now I shall walk down
To the end of the post. Go tell her. Let her choose
One of us.

CYRANO: It will be you.

CHRISTIAN: God—I hope so!
    [He turns and calls]
Roxane!

CYRANO: No—no—

ROXANE: [Hurries down to him] Yes, Christian?

CHRISTIAN: Cyrano
Has news for you—important.
    [She turns to Cyrano. Christian goes out]

ROXANE: [Lightly] Oh—important?

CYRANO: He is gone . . .
    [To Roxane]
           Nothing—only Christian thinks
You ought to know—

ROXANE: I do know. He still doubts
What I told him just now. I saw that.

CYRANO: [Takes her hand] Was it
True—what you told him just now?

ROXANE: It was true!
I said that I should love him even . . .

CYRANO: [Smiling sadly] The word
Comes hard—before me?

ROXANE: Even if he were . . .

CYRANO: Say it—
I shall not be hurt!—Ugly?

ROXANE: Even then
I should love him.
    [A few shots, off stage, in the direction in
     which Christian disappeared]
           Hark! The guns—

CYRANO: Hideous?

ROXANE: Hideous.

CYRANO: Disfigured?

ROXANE: Or disfigured.

CYRANO: Even
Grotesque?

ROXANE: How could he ever be grotesque—
Ever—to me!

CYRANO: But you could love him so,
As much as?—

ROXANE: Yes—and more!

CYRANO: [Aside, excitedly] It is true!—true!—
Perhaps—God! This is too much happiness . . .
    [To Roxane]
I—Roxane—listen—

LE BRET: [Enters quickly; calls to Cyrano in a
low tone] Cyrano—

CYRANO: [Turns] Yes?

LE BRET: Hush! . . .
    [Whispers a few words to him]

CYRANO: [Lets fall Roxane's hand] Ah!

ROXANE: What is it?

CYRANO: [Half stunned, and aside] All gone . . .

ROXANE: [More shots] What is it? Oh,
They are fighting!—
    [She goes up to look off stage]

CYRANO: All gone. I cannot ever
Tell her, now . . . ever . . .

ROXANE: [Starts to rush away] What has happened?

CYRANO: [Restrains her] Nothing.
    [Several Cadets enter. They conceal something
     which they are carrying, and form a group so
     as to prevent Roxane from seeing their burden]

ROXANE: These men—

CYRANO: Come away . . .
    [He leads her away from the group]

ROXANE: You were telling me
Something—

CYRANO: Oh, that? Nothing. . . .
    [Gravely]
           I swear to you
That the spirit of Christian—that his soul
Was—[Corrects himself quickly] That his soul is no
less great—

ROXANE: [Catches at the word] Was?
    [Crying out]
          Oh!—
    [She rushes among the men, and scatters them]

CYRANO: All gone . . .

ROXANE: [Sees Christian lying upon his cloak]
Christian!

LE BRET: [To Cyrano] At the first volley.
    [Roxane throws herself upon the body of Chris-
     tian. Shots; at first scattered, then increasing.
     Drums. Voices shouting]

CARBON: [Sword in hand] Here
They come!—Ready!—
    [Followed by the Cadets, he climbs over the
     parapet and disappears]

ROXANE: Christian!

CARBON: [Off stage] Come on, there, You!

ROXANE: Christian!

CARBON: Fall in!

ROXANE: Christian!

CARBON: Measure your fuse!
    [Ragueneau hurries up, carrying a helmet full
     of water]

CHRISTIAN: [*Faintly*] Roxane! . . .

CYRANO: [*Low and quick, in* Christian's *ear, while* Roxane *is dipping into the water a strip of linen torn from her dress*] I have told her; she loves you.

[Christian *closes his eyes*]

ROXANE: [*Turns to* Christian] Yes, My darling?

CARBON: Draw your ramrods!

ROXANE: [*To* Cyrano] He is not dead? . . .

CARBON: Open your charges!

ROXANE: I can feel his cheek Growing cold against mine—

CARBON: Take aim!

ROXANE: A letter— Over his heart—

    [*She opens it*]
                    For me.

CYRANO: [*Aside*] My letter . . .

CARBON: Fire!
    [*Musketry, cries and groans. Din of battle*]

CYRANO: [*Trying to withdraw his hand, which* Roxane, *still upon her knees, is holding*] But Roxane —they are fighting—

ROXANE: Wait a little . . . He is dead. No one else knew him but you . . .
    [*She weeps quietly*]
Was he not a great lover, a great man, A hero?

CYRANO: [*Standing, bareheaded*] Yes, Roxane.

ROXANE: A poet, unknown, Adorable?

CYRANO: Yes, Roxane.

ROXANE: A fine mind?

CYRANO: Yes, Roxane.

ROXANE: A heart deeper than we knew— A soul magnificently tender?

CYRANO: [*Firmly*] Yes, Roxane!

ROXANE: [*Sinks down upon the breast of* Christian] He is dead now . . .

CYRANO: [*Aside; draws his sword*] Why, so am I— For I am dead, and my love mourns for me And does not know . . .
    [*Trumpets in distance*]

DE GUICHE: [*Appears on the parapet, disheveled, wounded on the forehead, shouting*] The signal— hark—the trumpets! The army has returned— Hold them now!—Hold them! The army! —

ROXANE: On his letter—blood . . . and tears.

A VOICE: [*Off stage*] Surrender!

THE CADETS: No!

RAGUENEAU: This place is dangerous!—

CYRANO: [*To* De Guiche] Take her away—I am going—

ROXANE: [*Kisses the letter; faintly*] His blood . . . his tears . . .

RAGUENEAU: [*Leaps down from the coach and runs to her*] She has fainted—

DE GUICHE: [*On the parapet; savagely, to the* Cadets] Hold them!

VOICE OFF STAGE: Lay down your arms!

VOICES: No! No!

CYRANO: [*To* De Guiche] Sir, you have proved yourself— Take care of her.

DE GUICHE: [*Hurries to* Roxane *and takes her up in his arms*] As you will—we can win, if you hold on A little longer—

CYRANO: Good!
    [*Calls out to* Roxane, *as she is carried away, fainting, by* De Guiche *and* Ragueneau]
                    Adieu, Roxane!
    [*Tumult, outcries. Several* Cadets *come back wounded and fall on the stage.* Cyrano *rushing to the fight, is stopped on the crest of the parapet by* Carbon, *covered with blood*]

CARBON: We are breaking—I am twice wounded—

CYRANO: [*Shouts to* Gascons] Hardi! Reculez pas, Drollos!
    [*To* Carbon, *holding him up*]
                    So—never fear! I have two deaths to avenge now—Christian's And my own!
    [*They come down.* Cyrano *takes from him the lance with* Roxane's *handkerchief still fastened to it*]
                    Float, little banner, with her name!
    [*He plants it on the parapet; then shouts to the* Cadets]
Toumbé dessus! Escrasas lous!
    [*To the fifer*]
                         Your fife! Music!
    [*Fife plays. The wounded drag themselves to their feet. Other* Cadets *scramble over the parapet and group themselves around* Cyrano *and his tiny flag. The coach is filled and covered with men, bristling with muskets, transformed into a redoubt*]

A CADET: [*Reels backward over the wall, still fighting. Shouts*] They are climbing over! [*And falls dead*]

CYRANO: Very good— Let them come!— A salute now—
    [*The parapet is crowned for an instant with a rank of enemies. The imperial banner of Spain is raised aloft*]
                              Fire!
    [*General volley*]

VOICE: [*Among the ranks of the enemy*] Fire!
    [*Murderous counter-fire; the* Cadets *fall on every side*]

A SPANISH OFFICER: [*Uncovers*] Who are these men who are so fond of death?

CYRANO: [*Erect amid the hail of bullets, declaims*] The Cadets of Gascoyne, the defenders Of Carbon de Castel-Jaloux— Free fighters, free lovers, free spenders—

[*He rushes forward, followed by a few survivors*]
The Cadets of Gascoyne . . .
[*The rest is lost in the din of battle*]

CURTAIN

ACT V.

Cyrano's Gazette

Fifteen years later, in 1565. The park of the convent occupied by the Ladies of the Cross, at Paris. Magnificent foliage. To the left, the house upon a broad terrace at the head of a flight of steps, with several doors opening upon the terrace. In the center of the scene an enormous tree alone in the center of a little open space. Toward the right, in the foreground, among boxwood bushes, a semicircular bench of stone. All the way across the background of the scene, an avenue overarched by the chestnut trees, leading to the door of a chapel on the right, just visible among the branches of the trees. Beyond the double curtain of the trees, we catch a glimpse of bright lawns and shaded walks, masses of shrubbery; the perspective of the park; the sky. A little side door of the chapel opens upon a colonnade, garlanded with autumnal vines, and disappearing on the right behind the box-trees. It is late October. Above the still living green of the turf all the foliage is red and yellow and brown. The evergreen masses of box and yew stand out darkly against this autumnal coloring. A heap of dead leaves under every tree. The leaves are falling everywhere. They rustle underfoot along the walks; the terrace and the bench are half covered with them. Before the bench on the right, on the side toward the tree, is placed a tall embroidery frame and beside it a little chair. Baskets filled with skeins and many-colored silks and balls of wool. Tapestry unfinished on the frame. At the curtain rise the nuns are coming and going across the Park; several of them are seated on the Bench around Mother Marguérite de Jésus. *The leaves are falling.*

SISTER MARTHE: [*To* Mother Marguérite]
Sister Claire has been looking in the glass
At her new cap; twice!

    MOTHER MARGUÉRITE: [*To* Sister Claire] It is
      very plain;
Very.

    SISTER CLAIRE: And Sister Marthe stole a plum
Out of the tart this morning!

    MOTHER MARGUÉRITE: [*To* Sister Marthe] That
      was wrong;
Very wrong.

    SISTER CLAIRE: Oh, but such a little look!
    SISTER MARTHE: Such a little plum!

MOTHER MARGUÉRITE: [*Severely*] I shall tell Monsieur
De Cyrano, this evening.

    SISTER CLAIRE: No! Oh, no!—
He will make fun of us.

    SISTER MARTHE: He will say nuns
Are so gay!

    SISTER CLAIRE: And so greedy!

    MOTHER MARGUÉRITE: [*Smiling*] And so good . . .

    SISTER CLAIRE: It must be ten years, Mother
      Marguérite,
That he has come here every Saturday,
Is it not?

    MOTHER MARGUÉRITE: More than ten years; ever
      since
His cousin came to live among us here—
Her worldly weeds among our linen veils,
Her widowhood and our virginity—
Like a black dove among white doves.

    SISTER MARTHE: No one
Else ever turns that happy sorrow of hers
Into a smile.

    ALL THE NUNS: He is such fun!—He makes us
Almost laugh!—And he teases everyone—
And pleases everyone— And we all love him—
And he likes our cake, too—

    SISTER MARTHE: I am afraid
He is not a good Catholic.

    SISTER CLAIRE: Some day
We shall convert him.

    THE NUNS: Yes—yes!

    MOTHER MARGUÉRITE: Let him be;
I forbid you to worry him. Perhaps
He might stop coming here.

    SISTER MARTHE: But . . . God?

    MOTHER MARGUÉRITE: You need not
Be afraid. God knows all about him.

    SISTER MARTHE: Yes . . .
But every Saturday he says to me,
Just as if he were proud of it: "Well, Sister,
I ate meat yesterday!"

    MOTHER MARGUÉRITE: He tells you so?
The last time he said that, he had not eaten
Anything, for two days.

    SISTER MARTHE: Mother!—

    MOTHER MARGUÉRITE: He is poor;
Very poor.

    SISTER MARTHE: Who said so?

    MOTHER MARGUÉRITE: Monsieur Le Bret.

    SISTER MARTHE: Why does not someone help him?

    MOTHER MARGUÉRITE: He would be
Angry; very angry . . .
    [*Between the trees up stage,* Roxane *appears, all in black, with a widow's cap and long veils.* De Guiche, *magnificently grown old, walks beside her. They move slowly.* Mother Marguérite *rises*]
               Let us go in—
Madame Madeleine has a visitor.

SISTER MARTHE: [*To* Sister Claire] The Duc de
Grammont, is it not? The Marshal?

SISTER CLAIRE: [*Looks toward* De Guiche] I think
so—yes.

SISTER MARTHE: He has not been to see her
For months—

THE NUNS: He is busy—the Court!—the Camp!—

SISTER CLAIRE: The world! . . .

[*They go out.* De Guiche *and* Roxane *come
down in silence, and stop near the embroidery
frame. Pause*]

DE GUICHE: And you remain here, wasting all that
gold—
For ever in mourning?

ROXANE: For ever.

DE GUICHE: And still faithful?

ROXANE: And still faithful . . .

DE GUICHE: [*After a pause*] Have you forgiven me?

ROXANE: [*Simply, looking up at the cross of the
Convent*] I am here.

[*Another pause*]

DE GUICHE: Was Christian . . . all that?

ROXANE: If you knew him.

DE GUICHE: Ah? We were not precisely . . .
intimate . . .
And his last letter—always at your heart?

ROXANE: It hangs here, like a holy reliquary.

DE GUICHE: Dead—and you love him still!

ROXANE: Sometimes I think
He has not altogether died; our hearts
Meet, and his love flows all around me, living.

DE GUICHE: [*After another pause*]
You see Cyrano often?

ROXANE: Every week.
My old friend takes the place of my Gazette,
Brings me all the news. Every Saturday,
Under that tree where you are now, his chair
Stands, if the day be fine. I wait for him,
Embroidering; the hour strikes; then I hear,
(I need not turn to look!) at the last stroke,
His cane tapping the steps. He laughs at me
For my eternal needlework. He tells
The story of the past week—

[Le Bret *appears on the steps*]

                          There's Le Bret!—

[Le Bret *approaches*]

How is it with our friend?

LE BRET: Badly.

DE GUICHE: Indeed?

ROXANE: [*To* De Guiche] Oh, he exaggerates!

LE BRET: Just as I said—
Loneliness, misery—I told him so!—
His satires make a host of enemies—
He attacks the false nobles, the false saints,
The false heroes, the false artists—in short,
Everyone!

ROXANE: But they fear that sword of his—
No one dare touch him!

DE GUICHE: [*With a shrug*] H'm—that may be so.

LE BRET: It is not violence I fear for him,
But solitude—poverty—old gray December,
Stealing on wolf's feet, with a wolf's green eyes,
Into his darkening room. Those bravoes yet
May strike our Swordsman down! Every day now,
He draws his belt up one hole; his poor nose
Looks like old ivory; he has one coat
Left—his old black serge.

DE GUICHE: That is nothing strange
In this world! No, you need not pity him
Overmuch.

LE BRET: [*With a bitter smile*] My lord Marshal! . . .

DE GUICHE: I say, do not
Pity him overmuch. He lives his life,
His own life, his own way—thought, word, and deed
Free!

LE BRET: [*As before*] My lord Duke! . . .

DE GUICHE: [*Haughtily*] Yes, I know—I have all;
He has nothing. Nevertheless, to-day
I should be proud to shake his hand . . .

[*Saluting* Roxane]

                          Adieu.

ROXANE: I will go with you.

[De Guiche *salutes* Le Bret, *and turns with*
Roxane *toward the steps*]

DE GUICHE: [*Pauses on the steps, as she climbs*]
                          Yes— I envy him
Now and then . . .
                 Do you know, when a man wins
Everything in this world, when he succeeds
Too much—he feels, having done nothing wrong
Especially, Heaven knows!—he feels somehow
A thousand small displeasures with himself,
Whose whole sum is not quite Remorse, but rather
A sort of vague disgust . . . The ducal robes
Mounting up, step by step, to pride and power,
Somewhere among their folds draw after them
A rustle of dry illusions, vain regrets,
As your veil, up the stairs here, draws along
The whisper of dead leaves.

ROXANE: [*Ironical*] The sentiment
Does you honor.

DE GUICHE: Oh, yes . . .

[*Pausing suddenly*] Monsieur Le Bret!—

[*To* Roxane]

You pardon us?—

[*He goes to* Le Bret, *and speaks in a low tone*]
                 One moment— It is true
That no one dares attack your friend. Some people
Dislike him, none the less. The other day
At Court, such a one said to me: "This man
Cyrano may die—accidentally."

LE BRET: [*Coldly*] Thank you.

DE GUICHE: You may thank me. Keep him at
home
All you can. Tell him to be careful.

LE BRET: [*Shaking his hands to heaven*] Careful!—
He is coming here. I'll warn him—yes, but! . . .

ROXANE: [*Still on the steps, to a* Nun *who approaches her*]

                                            Here

I am—what is it?

THE NUN: Madame, Ragueneau
Wishes to see you.

ROXANE: Bring him here.
    [*To* Le Bret *and* De Guiche]

                            He comes

For sympathy—having been first of all
A Poet, he became since then, in turn,
A Singer—

LE BRET: Bath-house keeper—

ROXANE: Sacristan—

LE BRET: Actor—

ROXANE: Hairdresser—

LE BRET: Music-master—

ROXANE: Now,
To-day—

RAGUENEAU: [*Enters hurriedly*] Madame!—
    [*He sees* Le Bret] Monsieur!—

ROXANE: [*Smiling*] First tell your troubles
To Le Bret for a moment.

RAGUENEAU: But Madame—
    [*She goes out, with* De Guiche, *not hearing
       him.* Ragueneau *comes to* Le Bret]

After all, I had rather— You are here—
She need not know so soon— I went to see him
Just now— Our friend— As I came near his door,
I saw him coming out. I hurried on
To join him. At the corner of the street,
As he passed— Could it be an accident?—
I wonder!—At the window overhead,
A lackey with a heavy log of wood
Let it fall—

LE BRET: Cyrano!

RAGUENEAU: I ran to him—

LE BRET: God! The cowards!

RAGUENEAU: I found him lying there—
A great hole in his head—

LE BRET: Is he alive?

RAGUENEAU: Alive—yes. But . . . I had to carry
    him
Up to his room—Dieu! Have you seen his room?—

LE BRET: Is he suffering?

RAGUENEAU: No; unconscious.

LE BRET: Did you
Call a doctor?

RAGUENEAU: One came—for charity.

LE BRET: Poor Cyrano!—We must not tell Roxane
All at once . . . Did the doctor say?—

RAGUENEAU: He said
Fever, and lesions of the— I forget
Those long names— Ah, if you had seen him there,
His head all white bandages!—Let us go
Quickly—there is no one to care for him—
All alone— If he tries to raise his head,
He may die!

LE BRET: [*Draws him away to the right*] This
way— It is shorter—through
The Chapel—

ROXANE: [*Appears on the stairway, and calls to*
Le Bret *as he is going out by the colonnade which
leads to the small door of the Chapel*] Monsieur Le
    Bret!—
    [Le Bret *and* Ragueneau *rush off without hear-
      ing*] Running away
When I call to him? Poor dear Ragueneau
Must have been very tragic!
    [*She comes slowly down the stair, toward the
      tree*]

                            What a day! . . .

Something in these bright Autumn afternoons
Happy and yet regretful—an old sorrow
Smiling . . . as though poor little April dried
Her tears long ago—and remembered . . .
    [*She sits down at her work. Two* Nuns *come
      out of the house carrying a great chair and
      set it under the tree*]

                                Ah—

The old chair, for my old friend!—

SISTER MARTHE: The best one
In our best parlor!—

ROXANE: Thank you, Sister—[*The
    Nuns *withdraw*] There—
    [*She begins embroidering. The clock strikes*]
The hour!—He will be coming now—my silks—
All done striking? He never was so late
Before! The sister at the door—my thimble . . .
Here it is—she must be exhorting him
To repent all his sins . . . [*A pause*]
                      He ought to be
Converted, by this time— Another leaf—
    [*A dead leaf falls on her work; she brushes it
      away*]
Certainly nothing could—my scissors—ever
Keep him away—

A NUN: [*Appears on the steps*] Monsieur de Bergerac.

ROXANE: [*Without turning*]
What was I saying? . . . Hard, sometimes, to match
These faded colors! . . .
    [*While she goes on working,* Cyrano *appears
      at the top of the steps, very pale, his hat
      drawn over his eyes. The Nun who has brought
      him in goes away. He begins to descend the
      steps leaning on his cane, and holding himself
      on his feet only by an evident effort. Roxane
      turns to him, with a tone of friendly banter*]
                     After fourteen years,
Late—for the first time!

CYRANO: [*Reaches the chair, and sinks into it; his
gay tone contrasting with his tortured face*]
                  Yes, yes—maddening!
I was detained by—

ROXANE: Well?

CYRANO: A visitor,
Most unexpected.

ROXANE: [*Carelessly, still sewing*] Was your visitor
Tiresome?

CYRANO: Why, hardly that—inopportune,
Let us say—an old friend of mine—at least
A very old acquaintance.

ROXANE: Did you tell him
To go away?

CYRANO: For the time being, yes.
I said: "Excuse me—this is Saturday—
I have a previous engagement, one
I cannot miss, even for you— Come back
An hour from now."

ROXANE: Your friend will have to wait;
I shall not let you go till dark.

CYRANO: [*Very gently*] Perhaps
A little before dark, I must go . . .

    [*He leans back in the chair, and closes his eyes.
    Sister Marthe crosses above the stairway. Rox-
    ane sees her, motions her to wait, then turns to
    Cyrano*]

ROXANE: Look—
Somebody waiting to be teased.

CYRANO: [*Quickly, opens his eyes*] Of course!
    [*In a big, comic voice*] Sister, approach!
    [*Sister Marthe glides toward him*] Beautiful
    downcast eyes!—
So shy—

SISTER MARTHE: [*Looks up, smiling*] You— [*She
sees his face*] Oh!—

CYRANO: [*Indicates Roxane*] Sh!—Careful!
    [*Resumes his burlesque tone*]
          Yesterday,
I ate meat again!

SISTER MARTHE: Yes, I know. [*Aside*] That is
    why
He looks so pale . . .
    [*To him: low and quickly*]
          In the refectory,
Before you go—come to me there—
          I'll make you
A great bowl of hot soup—will you come?

CYRANO: [*Boisterously*] Ah—
Will I come!

SISTER MARTHE: You are quite reasonable
To-day!

ROXANE: Has she converted you?

SISTER MARTHE: Oh, no—
Not for the world!—

CYRANO: Why, now I think of it,
That is so— You, bursting with holiness,
And yet you never preach! Astonishing
I call it. . . .
    [*With burlesque ferocity*]
        Ah—now I'll astonish you—
I am going to—
    [*With the air of seeking for a good joke and
    finding it*]
        —let you pray for me
To-night, at vespers!

ROXANE: Aha!

CYRANO: Look at her—
Absolutely struck dumb!

SISTER MARTHE: [*Gently*] I did not wait
For you to say I might.
    [*She goes out*]

CYRANO: [*Returns to Roxane, who is bending over
her work*]
        Now, may the devil
Admire me, if I ever hope to see
The end of that embroidery!

ROXANE: [*Smiling*] I thought
It was time you said that.
    [*A breath of wind causes a few leaves to fall*]

CYRANO: The leaves—

ROXANE: [*Raises her head and looks away through
the trees*]
        What color—
Perfect Venetian red! Look at them fall.

CYRANO: Yes—they know how to die. A little way
From the branch to the earth, a little fear
Of mingling with the common dust—and yet
They go down gracefully—a fall that seems
Like flying!

ROXANE: Melancholy—you?

CYRANO: Why, no,
Roxane!

ROXANE: Then let the leaves fall. Tell me now
The Court news—my gazette!

CYRANO: Let me see—

ROXANE: Ah

CYRANO: [*More and more pale, struggling against
pain*]
Saturday, the nineteenth: The King fell ill,
After eight helpings of grape marmalade.
His malady was brought before the court,
Found guilty of high treason; whereupon
His Majesty revived. The royal pulse
Is now normal. Sunday, the twentieth:
The Queen gave a grand ball, at which they burne
Seven hundred and sixty-three wax candles. Note:
They say our troops have been victorious
In Austria. Later: Three sorcerers
Have been hung. Special post: The little dog
Of Madame d'Athis was obliged to take
Four pills before—

ROXANE: Monsieur de Bergerac,
Will you kindly be quiet!

CYRANO: Monday . . . nothing
Lygdamire has a new lover.

ROXANE: Oh!

CYRANO: [*His face more and more altered*] Tue
    day,
The Twenty-second: All the court has gone
To Fontainebleau. Wednesday: The Comte de Fiesqu
Spoke to Madame de Montglat; she said No.
Thursday: Mancini was the Queen of France
Or—very nearly! Friday: La Montglat
Said Yes. Saturday, twenty-sixth. . . .
    [*His eyes close; his head sinks back; silence*]

ROXANE: [*Surprised at not hearing any more,
turns, looks at him, and rises, frightened*]
He has fainted—[*She runs to him, crying out*]
Cyrano?
  CYRANO: [*Opens his eyes*] What . . . What is
     it? . . .
     [*He sees* Roxane *leaning over him, and quickly
     pulls his hat down over his head and leans back
     away from her in the chair*]
                    No—oh no—
It is nothing—truly!
  ROXANE: But—
  CYRANO: My old wound—
At Arras—sometimes—you know. . . .
  ROXANE: My poor friend!
  CYRANO: Oh it is nothing; it will soon be
gone. . . .
     [*Forcing a smile*]
There! It is gone!
  ROXANE: [*Standing close to him*] We all have our
     old wounds—
I have mine—here . . . [*Her hand at her breast*]
     under this faded scrap
Of writing. . . . It is hard to read now—all
But the blood—and the tears. . . .
     [*Twilight begins to fall*]
  CYRANO: His letter! . . . Did you
Not promise me that some day . . . that some
     day. . . .
You would let me read it?
  ROXANE: His letter?—You . . .
You wish—
  CYRANO: I do wish it—to-day.
  ROXANE: [*Gives him the little silken bag from
around her neck*] Here. . . .
  CYRANO: May I . . . open it?
  ROXANE: Open it, and read.
     [*She goes back to her work, folds it again, re-
     arranges her silks*]
  CYRANO: [*Unfolds the letter; reads*]
"Farewell Roxane, because to-day I die—"
  ROXANE: [*Looks up, surprised*] Aloud?
  CYRANO: [*Reads*]
                    "I know that it will be to-day
My own dearly beloved—and my heart
Still so heavy with love I have not told,
And I die without telling you! No more
Shall my eyes drink the sight of you like wine,
Never more, with a look that is a kiss,
Follow the sweet grace of you—"
  ROXANE: How you read it—
His letter!
  CYRANO: [*Continues*]
     "I remember now the way
You have, of pushing back a lock of hair
With one hand, from your forehead—and my heart
Cries out—"
  ROXANE: His letter . . . and you read it
     so . . .
     [*The darkness increases imperceptibly*]

CYRANO: "Cries out and keeps crying: 'Farewell,
     my dear,
My dearest—' "
  ROXANE: In a voice. . . .
  CYRANO: "—My own heart's own,
My own treasure—"
  ROXANE: [*Dreamily*] In such a voice. . . .
  CYRANO: —"My love—"
  ROXANE: —As I remember hearing . . .
     [*She trembles*]
                    —long ago. . . .
     [*She comes near him, softly, without his seeing
     her; passes the chair, leans over silently, look-
     ing at the letter. The darkness increases*]
  CYRANO: "—I am never away from you. Even
     now,
I shall not leave you. In another world,
I shall be still that one who loves you, loves you
Beyond measure, beyond—"
  ROXANE: [*Lays her hand on his shoulder*]
                    How can you read
Now? It is dark. . . .
     [*He starts, turns, and sees her there close to
     him. A little movement of surprise, almost of
     fear; then he bows his head. A long pause;
     then in the twilight now completely fallen, she
     says very softly, clasping her hands*]
                    And all these fourteen years,
He has been the old friend, who came to me
To be amusing.
  CYRANO: Roxane!—
  ROXANE: It was you.
  CYRANO: No, no, Roxane, no!
  ROXANE: And I might have known
Every time that I heard you speak my name! . . .
  CYRANO: No— It was not I—
  ROXANE: It was . . . you!
  CYRANO: I swear—
  ROXANE: I understand everything now: The let-
     ters—
That was you . . .
  CYRANO: No!
  ROXANE: And the dear, foolish words—
That was you. . . .
  CYRANO: No!
  ROXANE: And the voice . . . in
     the dark. . . .
That was . . . you!
  CYRANO: On my honor—
  ROXANE: And . . . the Soul!—
That was all you.
  CYRANO: I never loved you—
  ROXANE: Yes,
You loved me.
  CYRANO: [*Desperately*] No— He loved you—
  ROXANE: Even now,
You love me!
  CYRANO: [*His voice weakens*] No!
  ROXANE: [*Smiling*] And why . . . so great a
     "No"?

CYRANO: No, no, my own dear love, I love you
not! . . .
[Pause]

ROXANE: How many things have died . . . and
are newborn! . . .
Why were you silent for so many years,
All the while, every night and every day,
He gave me nothing—you knew that— You knew
Here, in this letter lying on my breast,
Your tears— You knew they were your tears—

CYRANO: [Holds the letter out to her] The blood
Was his.

ROXANE: Why do you break that silence now,
To-day?

CYRANO: Why? Oh, because—
[Le Bret and Ragueneau enter, running]

LE BRET: What recklessness—
I knew it! He is here!

CYRANO: [Smiling, and trying to rise] Well? Here
I am!

RAGUENEAU: He has killed himself, Madame,
coming here!

ROXANE: He— Oh, God. . . . And that faintness
. . . was that?—

CYRANO: No,
Nothing! I did not finish my Gazette—
Saturday, twenty-sixth: An hour or so
Before dinner, Monsieur de Bergerac
Died, foully murdered.
[He uncovers his head, and shows it swathed
in bandages]

ROXANE: Oh, what does he mean?—
Cyrano!—What have they done to you?—

CYRANO: "Struck down
By the sword of a hero, let me fall—
Steel in my heart, and laughter on my lips!"
Yes, I said that once. How Fate loves a jest!—
Behold me ambushed—taken in the rear—
My battlefield a gutter—my noble foe
A lackey, with a log of wood! . . .

It seems
Too logical— I have missed everything,
Even my death!

RAGUENEAU: [Breaks down] Ah, monsieur!—

CYRANO: Ragueneau,
Stop blubbering! [Takes his hand]
What are you writing nowadays,
Old poet?

RAGUENEAU: [Through his tears] I am not a poet
now;
I snuff the—light the candles—for Molière!

CYRANO: Oh—Molière!

RAGUENEAU: Yes, but I am leaving him
To-morrow. Yesterday they played "Scapin"—
He has stolen your scene—

LE BRET: The whole scene—word for word!

RAGUENEAU: Yes: "What the devil was he doing
there"—
That one!

LE BRET: [Furious] And Molière stole it all from
you—
Bodily!—

CYRANO: Bah— He showed good taste. . . .
[To Ragueneau] The scene
Went well? . . .

RAGUENEAU: Ah, monsieur, they laughed—and
laughed—
How they did laugh!

CYRANO: Yes—that has been my life. . . .
Do you remember that night Christian spoke
Under your window? It was always so!
While I stood in the darkness underneath,
Others climbed up to win the applause—the kiss!—
Well—that seems only justice— I still say,
Even now, on the threshold of my tomb—
"Molière has genius—Christian had good looks—"
[The chapel bell is ringing. Along the avenue
of trees above the stairway, the Nuns pass in
procession to their prayers]
They are going to pray now; there is the bell.

ROXANE: [Raises herself and calls to them] Sister!
—Sister!—

CYRANO: [Holding on to her hand] No.—do not
go away—
I may not still be here when you return. . . .
[The Nuns have gone into the chapel. The or-
gan begins to play]
A little harmony is all I need—
Listen. . . .

ROXANE: You shall not die! I love you—

CYRANO: No—
That is not in the story! You remember
When Beauty said "I love you" to the Beast
That was a fairy prince, his ugliness
Changed and dissolved, like magic. . . . But you
see
I am still the same.

ROXANE: And I—I have done
This to you! All my fault—mine!

CYRANO: You? Why no.
On the contrary! I had never known
Womanhood and its sweetness but for you.
My mother did not love to look at me—
I never had a sister— Later on,
I feared the mistress with a mockery
Behind her smile. But you—because of you
I have had one friend not quite all a friend—
Across my life, one whispering silken gown! . . .

LE BRET: [Points to the rising moon which begins
to shine down between the trees]
Your other friend is looking at you.

CYRANO: [Smiling at the moon] I see. . . .

ROXANE: I never loved but one man in my life,
And I have lost him—twice. . . .

CYRANO: Le Bret—I shall be up there presently
In the moon—without having to invent
Any flying machines!

ROXANE: What are you saying? . . .

CYRANO: The moon—yes, that would be the place
for me—
My kind of paradise! I shall find there
Those other souls who should be friends of mine—
Socrates—Galileo—
LE BRET: [*Revolting*] No! No! No!
It is too idiotic—too unfair—
Such a friend—such a poet—such a man
To die so—to die so!—
CYRANO: [*Affectionately*] There goes Le Bret,
Growling!
LE BRET: [*Breaks down*] My friend!—
CYRANO: [*Half raises himself, his eye wanders*]
The Cadets of Gascoyne,
The Defenders. . . . The elementary mass—
Ah—there's the point! Now, then . . .
LE BRET: Delirious—
And all that learning—
CYRANO: On the other hand,
We have Copernicus—
ROXANE: Oh!
CYRANO: [*More and more delirious*] "Very well,
But what the devil was he doing there?—
What the devil was he doing there, up there?". . .
[*He declaims*]
Philosopher and scientist,
Poet, musician, duellist—
He flew high, and fell back again!
A pretty wit—whose like we lack—
A lover . . . not like other men. . . .
Here lies Hercule-Savinien
De Cyrano de Bergerac—
Who was all things—and all in vain!
Well, I must go—pardon— I cannot stay!
My moonbeam comes to carry me away. . . .
[*He falls back into the chair, half fainting. The
sobbing of* Roxane *recalls him to reality.
Gradually his mind comes back to him. He
looks at her, stroking the veil that hides her
hair*]
I would not have you mourn any the less
That good, brave, noble Christian; but perhaps—
I ask you only this—when the great cold
Gathers around my bones, that you may give
A double meaning to your widow's weeds
And the tears you let fall for him may be
For a little—my tears. . . .
ROXANE: [*Sobbing*] Oh, my love! . . .
CYRANO: [*Suddenly shaken as with a fever fit,
he raises himself erect and pushes her away*]
— Not here!—
Not lying down! . . .

[*They spring forward to help him; he motions
them back*]
Let no one help me—no one!—
Only the tree. . . .
[*He sets his back against the trunk. Pause*]
It is coming . . . I feel
Already shod with marble . . . gloved with lead . .
[*Joyously*]
Let the old fellow come now! He shall find me
On my feet—sword in hand—
[*Draws his sword*]
LE BRET: Cyrano!—
ROXANE: [*Half fainting*] Oh,
Cyrano!
CYRANO: I can see him there—he grins—
He is looking at my nose—that skeleton
—What's that you say? Hopeless?—Why, very
well!—
But a man does not fight merely to win!
No—no—better to know one fights in vain! . . .
You there— Who are you? A hundred against one—
I know them now, my ancient enemies—
[*He lunges at the empty air*]
Falsehood! . . . There! There! Prejudice—Compro-
mise—
Cowardice—
[*Thrusting*] What's that? No! Surrender? No!
Never—never! . . .
Ah, you too, Vanity!
I knew you would overthrow me in the end—
No! I fight on! I fight on! I fight on!
[*He swings the blade in great circles, then
pauses, gasping. When he speaks again, it is in
another tone*]
Yes, all my laurels you have riven away
And all my roses; yet in spite of you,
There is one crown I bear away with me,
And to-night, when I enter before God,
My salute shall sweep all the stars away
From the blue threshold! One thing without stain,
Unspotted from the world, in spite of doom
Mine own!—
[*He springs forward, his sword aloft*]
And that is . . .
[*The sword escapes from his hand; he totters,
and falls into the arms of* Le Bret *and* Rag-
ueneau]
ROXANE: [*Bends over him and kisses him on the
forehead*]
—That is . . .
CYRANO: [*Opens his eyes and smiles up at her*]
My white plume. . . .
CURTAIN

August Strindberg

(1849–1912)

We left Strindberg (pp. 75–94) as a vastly influential realist in *The Father*. We must now also consider him as one of the major playwrights who carried the drama beyond realism or naturalism, for Strindberg straddled the two main currents of modern theatre. He was not, of course, the only dramatist to restore imagination to the stage before the turn of the century and to bring back atmosphere and suggestiveness; but he was surely one of the most potent pioneers in imaginative drama, as well as the playwright who could least be charged with mental flabbiness and mere theatricality, or "artiness." He did not depart from realism because he was intent on following a new fashion or because he thought it would be clever of him to show how ingenious he could be. He adopted a new style because he felt compelled to express the ineffable and to dramatize personal stresses which the limited scope of dramatic realism could neither encompass nor project. This view is substantiated by the fact that during the period of his subjective dramas he also wrote a series of realistic historical plays (*Gustavus Vasa, Erik XIV,* and *Queen Christina,* for example, after 1899), as well as the inexorably naturalistic drama *The Dance of Death* (1901). The combination of inner compulsion and original talent in his experiments had an important effect on the theatre. He inaugurated a new dramatic style that superseded merely poetic and symbolist styles. It eventuated in Central European expressionism after 1916. It also stimulated the imagination of Eugene O'Neill to create *Emperor Jones* and *The Hairy Ape* before he acquired any familiarity with the German expressionist theatre or any interest in its plays.

In 1893 Strindberg married an Austrian writer, Frida Uhl, and became a father for the fourth time. But this second marriage ended quickly and his troubled mind led him to seek refuge in Swedenborgian mysticism and to make fantastic chemical experiments. (He believed he could make gold and suspected that America cheated him of his invention.) He began to dread a mental collapse even earlier, when, after a weird correspondence with Nietzsche toward the end of 1888, he learned that the philosopher had gone mad. (Nietzsche's last letter to him was signed "The Crucified One.") Fearing that his own state of mind was open to question after his stormy conflict with his first wife, Strindberg had tried to get a certificate of sanity for himself—without success, since he had refused to remain under observation. During and especially after his second marriage, he developed hallucinations and delusions of persecution, and felt tormented by invisible spirits. He believed that his food was being poisoned, that gas was being piped into his room, and that an electric girdle was suffocating him. He reached his mental crisis in Paris in 1895–1896. When Swedenborgian mysticism failed to heal him and his nervous crisis became intolerable, Strindberg finally took the precaution of entering a private sanatorium.

He recovered quickly, but never quite shook off his peculiar psychic tendencies, including a belief in rare telepathic powers and a conviction that servants were avenging themselves on their masters by draining their food of nourishing ingredients. A number of his plays reflected both his crisis and its aftereffects. When he dealt with objective material as in his dramatic chronicles of Swedish history, his mind was crystal clear and gave no indication of aberrant thinking or feeling. In other work (as in the graceful little fairy drama *Swanwhite,* the powerful folk tale *The Bridal Crown,* and the beautiful drama of reconciliation *Easter*), he developed a gentle mysticism tinged at most with melancholia. "One gets more and more humble," wrote the man whose vindictiveness had known no bounds. In some of these plays he also acknowledged the influence of Maeterlinck. He interested himself in a practical theatrical venture, helping a young producer to create an Intimate Theatre for an audience of two hundred. Here he reformed the art of staging, abolishing footlights and using only draperies for the background, and for the small stage of this theatre he wrote a number of simplified works he called "chamber plays," analogous to chamber music as compared with symphonies. In these concentrated dramas, the best of which was *The Spook Sonata* (1907), he sought to strip all pretense from people's lives and expose everything hidden. Along with *The Spook Sonata,* finally, Strindberg wrote several long plays which are among the most original and experimental in the history of Western drama: *To Damascus,* a trilogy on the search for mystic salvation, written between 1898 and 1904; *The Dream Play* (1902), a Buddhistic allegory and fantasy on the misery and failure of life; and *The Great Highway* (1909). To these may be added *There Are Crimes and Crimes* (1898), perhaps the most curious comedy in the modern repertory. Along with equally subjective books like *Inferno* (1897) and *Legends* (1898), with which their author anticipated expressionistic fiction of the stream-of-consciousness variety, these dramas made Strindberg the chief precursor of ultramodernism.

With his "dream plays"—a term that applies with variable appropriateness to the nonrealistic works—Strindberg helped to liberate modern drama from the prosiness to which naturalism had dedicated the theatre. Indeed, his dream plays come to mind whenever we think of the plays of Pirandello, Toller, Kaiser, the Capek brothers, Cocteau, Saroyan, Wilder, and many other contemporary experimentalists, although it is questionable that any later playwright has approximated the compressed passion and anguish that Strindberg had at his command. If the bedlam dance in his expressionistic work often proves confusing, it is largely because Strindberg followed the shifting forms of the dream. He frequently telescoped time and place, made characters undergo numerous changes of identity, allowed symbols to manifest themselves elusively, and presented supersensory and nonrational experience. Above all, he abolished the boundaries between the real and the unreal, and between the objective and the subjective worlds, so that the one blends into the other without warning. In truth, some of this writing was not so much expressionistic as surrealistic. And its ultimate justification was that Strindberg viewed man in modern life as devoid of integration. The world Strindberg placed on the stage had no consistency; it continually disintegrated because he saw it as the nightmare of the divided and bedeviled modern soul.

Representative of the playwright's essays in subjective and symbolic dramaturgy, but less extreme in style and structure than some of the other plays, is *There Are Crimes and Crimes*. Here Strindberg retains considerable realism throughout but allows scope for invisible and indefinable agencies in the dramatic development—agencies malign, sardonic, and moral. The spirit world is present as a functional element, but it is not materialized on the stage; it is left to both the characters and the reader as a matter for wonder and speculation. Perhaps it is unwise, however, to speculate too closely on the identity of these agents of calumny and punishment in this grimly humorous exposé of human egotism and frailty. The excoriation of weakness in the character of his hero, Maurice, needs no explanation. The playwright has merely given the wishes and the "guilt" of Maurice an external dramatic manifestation in the death of Maurice's child and his persecution for a crime he did not commit except "in thought." A clue for the reader was provided by Strindberg himself when he published *There Are Crimes and Crimes* together with the short "mystery" play *Advent*, under the inclusive title *In a Higher Court*. Since the crimes of Maurice are "not mentioned in the criminal code" because they are crimes against the spirit, he can be tried only "in the higher court" of the spirit. It is enough to follow the play *as if* certain things could happen. With a final *coup de grâce* Strindberg returns us to reality in as sardonic a resolution as any we may conceive, when Maurice makes a final adjustment between conscience and egotism. After noting in one of his autobiographical books, *The Author* (1909), that his mental crisis at the age of fifty had been "revolutions in the life of the soul, desert wanderings, Swedenborgian Heavens and Hells," Strindberg added that this play had been "light after darkness" and productivity with restored certitude, hope, and love. *There Are Crimes and Crimes* was also productivity with "lightness," for it is executed with skillful fantastication and with an air of playfulness, as if both Strindberg and the spirit world were making sport of Maurice and of frail mankind. The conclusion, after the weirdly shattering complications, makes the play technically a comedy. But it certainly provides cold comfort for both moralists and optimists. It is a grim jest with strange overtones, and its mood is no happier than that darkest of Shakespeare's "dark" comedies *Measure for Measure*. It can also remind us of the sultry comedies of Ben Jonson and Henry Becque.

BIBLIOGRAPHY: Eric Bentley, *The Playwright as Thinker* (pp. 60–64, 94–99, 193–221, 316–318, 351–353), 1946; Edwin Bjorkman, Introductions to *Plays by August Strindberg* (4 volumes, 1912–1916); G. A. Campbell, *Strindberg*, 1933; Barrett H. Clark and George Freedley, *A History of the Modern Drama*, (pp. 20–44), 1947; John Gassner, *Masters of the Drama* (pp. 388–395), 1945; John Gassner, "Strindberg in America," in *Theatre Arts*, May 1949 (pp. 49–52); A. Jolivet, *Le Théâtre de Strindberg*, 1931; V. J McGill, *August Strindberg, the Bedeviled Viking*, 1930; Elizabeth Sprigge, *The Strange Life of August Strindberg*, 1949.

For additional commentary, see pages 75–77.

THERE ARE CRIMES AND CRIMES

By *August Strindberg*

TRANSLATED FROM THE SWEDISH BY EDWIN BJÖRKMAN

CHARACTERS

MAURICE, *a playwright*
JEANNE, *his mistress*
MARION, *their daughter, five years
old*
ADOLPHE, *a painter*
HENRIETTE, *his mistress*

EMILE, *a workman, brother of
Jeanne*
MADAME CATHERINE
THE ABBÉ
A WATCHMAN
A HEAD WAITER

A COMMISSAIRE
TWO DETECTIVES
A WAITER
A GUARD
A SERVANT GIRL

All the scenes are laid in Paris.

ACT I. SCENE I.

The upper avenue of cypresses in the Montparnasse Cemetery at Paris. The background shows mortuary chapels, stone crosses on which are inscribed "O Crux! Ave Spes Unica!" and the ruins of a windmill covered with ivy. A well-dressed woman in widow's weeds is kneeling and muttering prayers in front of a grave decorated with flowers. Jeanne is walking back and forth as if expecting somebody. Marion is playing with some withered flowers picked from a rubbish heap on the ground. The Abbé is reading his breviary while walking along the farther end of the avenue.

WATCHMAN: [*Enters and goes up to* Jeanne] Look here, this is no playground.

JEANNE: [*Submissively*] I am only waiting for somebody who'll soon be here—

WATCHMAN: All right, but you're not allowed to pick any flowers.

JEANNE: [*To* Marion] Drop the flowers, dear.

ABBÉ: [*Comes forward and is saluted by the* Watchman] Can't the child play with the flowers that have been thrown away?

WATCHMAN: The regulations don't permit anybody to touch even the flowers that have been thrown

away, because it's believed they may spread infection—which I don't know if it's true.

ABBÉ: [*To* Marion] In that case we have to obey, of course. What's your name, my little girl?

MARION: My name is Marion.

ABBÉ: And who is your father?

[Marion *begins to bite one of her fingers and does not answer*]

ABBÉ: Pardon my question, madame. I had no intention—I was just talking to keep the little one quiet.

[*The* Watchman *has gone out*]

JEANNE: I understand it, Reverend Father, and I wish you would say something to quiet me also. I feel very much disturbed after having waited here two hours.

ABBÉ: Two hours—for him! How these human beings torture each other! O Crux! Ave spes unica!

JEANNE: What do they mean, these words you read all around here?

ABBÉ: They mean: O cross, our only hope!

JEANNE: Is it the only one?

ABBÉ: The only certain one.

JEANNE: I shall soon believe that you are right, Father.

ABBÉ: May I ask why?

JEANNE: You have already guessed it. When he

lets the woman and the child wait two hours in a cemetery, then the end is not far off.

ABBÉ: And when he has left you, what then?

JEANNE: Then we have to go into the river.

ABBÉ: Oh, no, no!

JEANNE: Yes, yes!

MARION: Mamma, I want to go home, for I am hungry.

JEANNE: Just a little longer, dear, and we'll go home.

ABBÉ: Woe unto those who call evil good and good evil.

JEANNE: What is that woman doing at the grave over there?

ABBÉ: She seems to be talking to the dead.

JEANNE: But you cannot do that?

ABBÉ: She seems to know how.

JEANNE: This would mean that the end of life is not the end of our misery?

ABBÉ: And you don't know it?

JEANNE: Where can I find out?

ABBÉ: Hm! The next time you feel as if you wanted to learn about this well-known matter, you can look me up in Our Lady's Chapel at the Church of St. Germain— Here comes the one you are waiting for, I guess.

JEANNE: [Embarrassed] No, he is not the one, but I know him.

ABBÉ: [To Marion] Good-bye, little Marion! May God take care of you! [Kisses the child and goes out] At St. Germain des Prés.

EMILE: [Enters] Good morning, sister. What are you doing here?

JEANNE: I am waiting for Maurice.

EMILE: Then I guess you'll have a lot of waiting to do, for I saw him on the boulevard an hour ago, taking breakfast with some friends. [Kissing the child] Good morning, Marion.

JEANNE: Ladies also?

EMILE: Of course. But that doesn't mean anything. He writes plays, and his latest one has its first performance to-night. I suppose he had with him some of the actresses.

JEANNE: Did he recognize you?

EMILE: No, he doesn't know who I am, and it is just as well. I know my place as a workman, and I don't care for any condescension from those that are above me.

JEANNE: But if he leaves us without anything to live on?

EMILE: Well, you see, when it gets that far, then I suppose I shall have to introduce myself. But you don't expect anything of the kind, do you—seeing that he is fond of you and very much attached to the child?

JEANNE: I don't know, but I have a feeling that something dreadful is in store for me.

EMILE: Has he promised to marry you?

JEANNE: No, not promised exactly, but he has held out hopes.

EMILE: Hopes, yes! Do you remember my words at the start: don't hope for anything, for those above us don't marry downward.

JEANNE: But such things have happened.

EMILE: Yes, they have happened. But would you feel at home in his world? I can't believe it, for you wouldn't even understand what they were talking of. Now and then I take my meals where he is eating— out in the kitchen is my place, of course—and I don't make out a word of what they say.

JEANNE: So you take your meals at that place?

EMILE: Yes, in the kitchen.

JEANNE: And think of it, he has never asked me to come with him.

EMILE: Well, that's rather to his credit, and it shows he has some respect for the mother of his child. The women over there are a queer lot.

JEANNE: Is that so?

EMILE: But Maurice never pays any attention to the women. There is something *square* about that fellow.

JEANNE: That's what I feel about him, too, but as soon as there is a woman in it, a man isn't himself any longer.

EMILE: [Smiling] You don't tell me! But listen: are you hard up for money?

JEANNE: No, nothing of that kind.

EMILE: Well, then, the worst hasn't come yet— Look! Over there! There he comes. And I'll leave you. Good-bye, little girl.

JEANNE: Is he coming? Yes, that's him.

EMILE: Don't make him mad now—with your jealousy, Jeanne!

[Goes out]

JEANNE: No, I won't.

[Maurice enters]

MARION: [Runs up to him and is lifted up into his arms] Papa, papa!

MAURICE: My little girl! [Greets Jeanne] Can you forgive me, Jeanne, that I have kept you waiting so long?

JEANNE: Of course I can.

MAURICE: But say it in such a way that I can hear that you are forgiving me.

JEANNE: Come here and let me whisper it to you. [Maurice goes up close to her. Jeanne kisses him on the cheek]

MAURICE: I didn't hear.

[Jeanne kisses him on the mouth]

MAURICE: Now I heard! Well—you know, I suppose that this is the day that will settle my fate? My play is on for to-night, and there is every chance that it will succeed—or fail.

JEANNE: I'll make sure of success by praying for you.

MAURICE: Thank you. If it doesn't help, it can at least do no harm— Look over there, down there in the valley, where the haze is thickest: there lies Paris. To-day Paris doesn't know who Maurice is, but it is going to know within twenty-four hours.

The haze, which has kept me obscured for thirty years, will vanish before my breath, and I shall become visible, I shall assume definite shape and begin to be somebody. My enemies—which means all who would like to do what I have done—will be writhing in pains that shall be my pleasures, for they will be suffering all that I have suffered.

JEANNE: Don't talk that way, don't!

MAURICE: But that's the way it is.

JEANNE: Yes, but don't speak of it— And then?

MAURICE: Then we are on firm ground, and then you and Marion will bear the name I have made famous.

JEANNE: You love me then?

MAURICE: I love both of you, equally much, or perhaps Marion a little more.

JEANNE: I am glad of it, for you can grow tired of me, but not of her.

MAURICE: Have you no confidence in my feelings towards you?

JEANNE: I don't know, but I am afraid of something, afraid of something terrible—

MAURICE: You are tired out and depressed by your long wait, which once more I ask you to forgive. What have you to be afraid of?

JEANNE: The unexpected: that which you may foresee without having any particular reason to do so.

MAURICE: But I foresee only success, and I have particular reasons for doing so: the keen instincts of the management and their knowledge of the public, not to speak of their personal acquaintance with the critics. So now you must be in good spirits—

JEANNE: I can't, I can't. Do you know, there was an Abbé here a while ago, who talked so beautifully to us. My faith—which you haven't destroyed, but just covered up, as when you put chalk on a window to clean it—I couldn't lay hold on it for that reason, but this old man just passed his hand over the chalk, and the light came through, and it was possible again to see that the people within were at home— To-night I will pray for you at St. Germain.

MAURICE: Now I am getting scared.

JEANNE: Fear of God is the beginning of wisdom.

MAURICE: God? What is that? Who is he?

JEANNE: It was he who gave joy to your youth, and strength to your manhood. And it is he who will carry us through the terrors that lie ahead of us.

MAURICE: What is lying ahead of us? What do you know? Where have you learned of this? This thing that I don't know?

JEANNE: I can't tell. I have dreamt nothing, seen nothing, heard nothing. But during these two dreadful hours I have experienced such an infinity of pain that I am ready for the worst.

MARION: Now I want to go home, mamma, for I am hungry.

MAURICE: Yes, you'll go home now, my little darling.

[*Takes her into his arms*]

MARION: [*Shrinking*] Oh, you hurt me, papa!

JEANNE: Yes, we must get home for dinner. Good-bye then, Maurice. And good luck to you!

MAURICE: [*To* Marion] How did I hurt you? Doesn't my little girl know that I always want to be nice to her?

MARION: If you are nice, you'll come home with us.

MAURICE: [*To* Jeanne] When I hear the child talk like that, you know, I feel as if I ought to do what she says. But then reason and duty protest— Good-bye, my dear little girl!

[*He kisses the child, who puts her arms around his neck*]

JEANNE: When do we meet again?

MAURICE: We'll meet to-morrow, dear. And then we'll never part again.

JEANNE: [*Embraces him*] Never, never to part again! [*She makes the sign of the cross on his forhead*] May God protect you!

MAURICE: [*Moved against his own will*] My dear, beloved Jeanne!

[Jeanne *and* Marion *go towards the right;* Maurice *towards the left. Both turn around simultaneously and throw kisses at each other*]

MAURICE: [*Comes back*] Jeanne, I am ashamed of myself. I am always forgetting you, and you are the last one to remind me of it. Here are the tickets for to-night.

JEANNE: Thank you, dear, but—you have to take up your post of duty alone, and so I have to take up mine—with Marion.

MAURICE: Your wisdom is as great as the goodness of your heart. Yes, I am sure no other woman would have sacrificed a pleasure to serve her husband— I must have my hands free to-night, and there is no place for women and children on the battlefield—and this you understand!

JEANNE: Don't think too highly of a poor woman like myself, and then you'll have no illusions to lose. And now you'll see that I can be as forgetful as you —I have bought you a tie and a pair of gloves which I thought you might wear for my sake on your day of honour.

MAURICE: [*Kissing her hand*] Thank you, dear.

JEANNE: And then, Maurice, don't forget to have your hair fixed, as you do all the time. I want you to be good-looking, so that others will like you, too.

MAURICE: There is no jealousy in *you!*

JEANNE: Don't mention that word, for **evil** thoughts spring from it.

MAURICE: Just now I feel as if I could **give up** this evening's victory—for I am going to win—

JEANNE: Hush, hush!

MAURICE: And go home with you instead.

JEANNE: But you mustn't do that! Go now: your destiny is waiting for you.

MAURICE: Good-bye then! And may that happen which must happen! [*Goes out*]

JEANNE: [*Alone with* Marion] O Crux! Ave spes unica!

SCENE II.

The Crêmerie. On the right stands a buffet, on which are placed an aquarium with goldfish and dishes containing vegetables, fruit, preserves, etc. In the background is a door leading to the kitchen, where workmen are taking their meals. At the other end of the kitchen can be seen a door leading out to a garden. On the left, in the background, stands a counter on a raised platform, and back of it are shelves containing all sorts of bottles. On the right, a long table with a marble top is placed along the wall, and another table is placed parallel to the first farther out on the floor. Straw-bottomed chairs stand around the tables. The walls are covered with oil-paintings. Mme. Catherine *is sitting at the counter.* Maurice *stands leaning against it. He has his hat on and is smoking a cigarette.*

MME. CATHERINE: So it's to-night the great event comes off, Monsieur Maurice?

MAURICE: Yes, to-night.

MME. CATHERINE: Do you feel upset?

MAURICE: Cool as a cucumber.

MME. CATHERINE: Well, I wish you luck anyhow, and you have deserved it, Monsieur Maurice, after having had to fight against such difficulties as yours.

MAURICE: Thank you, Madame Catherine. You have been very kind to me, and without your help I should probably have been down and out by this time.

MME. CATHERINE: Don't let us talk of that now. I help along where I see hard work and the right kind of will, but I don't want to be exploited— Can we trust you to come back here after the play and let us drink a glass with you?

MAURICE: Yes, you can—of course, you can, as I have already promised you.

[Henriette *enters from the right.* Maurice *turns around, raises his hat, and stares at* Henriette, *who looks him over carefully*]

HENRIETTE: Monsieur Adolphe is not here yet?

MME. CATHERINE: No, madame. But he'll soon be here now. Won't you sit down?

HENRIETTE: No, thank you, I'd rather wait for him outside.

[*Goes out*]

MAURICE: Who—was—that?

MME. CATHERINE: Why, that's Monsieur Adolphe's friend.

MAURICE: Was—that—her?

MME. CATHERINE: Have you never seen her before?

MAURICE: No, he has been hiding her from me, just as if he was afraid I might take her away from him.

MME. CATHERINE: Ha-ha!— Well, how did you think she looked?

MAURICE: How she looked? Let me see: I can't tell—I didn't see her, for it was as if she had rushed straight into my arms at once and come so close to me that I couldn't make out her features at all. And she left her impression on the air behind her. I can still see her standing there. [*He goes towards the door and makes a gesture as if putting his arm around somebody*] Whew! [*He makes a gesture as if he had pricked his finger*] There are pins in her waist. She is of the kind that stings!

MME. CATHERINE: Oh, you are crazy, you with your ladies!

MAURICE: Yes, it's craziness, that's what it is. But do you know, Madame Catherine, I am going before she comes back, or else, or else— Oh, that woman is horrible!

MME. CATHERINE: Are you afraid?

MAURICE: Yes, I am afraid for myself, and also for some others.

MME. CATHERINE: Well, go then.

MAURICE: She seemed to suck herself out through the door, and in her wake rose a little whirlwind that dragged me along— Yes, you may laugh, but can't you see that the palm over there on the buffet is still shaking? She's the very devil of a woman!

MME. CATHERINE: Oh, get out of here, man, before you lose all your reason.

MAURICE: I want to go, but I cannot— Do you believe in fate, Madame Catherine?

MME. CATHERINE: No, I believe in a good God, who protects us against evil powers if we ask him in the right way.

MAURICE: So there are evil powers after all! I think I can hear them in the hallway now.

MME. CATHERINE: Yes, her clothes rustle as when the clerk tears off a piece of linen for you. Get away now—through the kitchen.

[Maurice *rushes towards the kitchen door, where he bumps into* Emile]

EMILE: I beg your pardon. [*He retires the way he came*]

ADOLPHE: [*Comes in first; after him* Henriette] Why, there's Maurice. How are you? Let me introduce this lady here to my oldest and best friend. Mademoiselle Henriette—Monsieur Maurice.

MAURICE: [*Saluting stiffly*] Pleased to meet you.

HENRIETTE: We have seen each other before.

ADOLPHE: Is that so? When, if I may ask?

MAURICE: A moment ago. Right here.

ADOLPHE: O-oh!— But now you must stay and have a chat with us.

MAURICE: [*After a glance at* Mme. Catherine] If I only had time.

ADOLPHE: Take the time. And we won't be sitting here very long.

HENRIETTE: I won't interrupt, if you have to talk business.

MAURICE: The only business we have is so bad that we don't want to talk of it.

HENRIETTE: Then we'll talk of something else. [*Takes the hat away from* Maurice *and hangs it up*] Now be nice, and let me become acquainted with the great author.

[Mme. Catherine *signals to* Maurice, *who doesn't notice her*]

ADOLPHE: That's right, Henriette, you take charge of him.

[*They seat themselves at one of the tables*]

HENRIETTE: [*To* Maurice] You certainly have a good friend in Adolphe, Monsieur Maurice. He never talks of anything but you, and in such a way that I feel myself rather thrown in the background.

ADOLPHE: You don't say so! Well, Henriette on her side never leaves me in peace about you, Maurice. She has read your works, and she is always wanting to know where you got this and where that. She has been questioning me about your looks, your age, your tastes. I have, in a word, had you for breakfast, dinner, and supper. It has almost seemed as if the three of us were living together.

MAURICE: [*To* Henriette] Heavens, why didn't you come over here and have a look at this wonder of wonders? Then your curiosity could have been satisfied in a trice.

HENRIETTE: Adolphe didn't want it.

[Adolphe *looks embarrassed*]

HENRIETTE: Not that he was jealous—

MAURICE: And why should he be, when he knows that my feelings are tied up elsewhere?

HENRIETTE: Perhaps he didn't trust the stability of your feelings.

MAURICE: I can't understand that, seeing that I am notorious for my constancy.

ADOLPHE: Well, it wasn't that—

HENRIETTE: [*Interrupting him*] Perhaps that is because you have not faced the fiery ordeal—

ADOLPHE: Oh, you don't know—

HENRIETTE: [*Interrupting*]—for the world has not yet beheld a faithful man.

MAURICE: Then it's going to behold one.

HENRIETTE: Where?

MAURICE: Here.

[Henriette *laughs*]

ADOLPHE: Well, that's going it—

HENRIETTE: [*Interrupting him and directing herself continuously to* Maurice] Do you think I ever trust my dear Adolphe more than a month at a time?

MAURICE: I have no right to question your lack of confidence, but I can guarantee that Adolphe is faithful.

HENRIETTE: You don't need to do so—my tongue is just running away with me, and I have to take back a lot—not only for fear of feeling less generous than you, but because it is the truth. It is a bad habit I have of only seeing the ugly side of things,

and I keep it up although I know better. But if I had a chance to be with you two for some time, then your company would make me good once more. Pardon me, Adolphe! [*She puts her hand against his cheek*]

ADOLPHE: You are always wrong in your talk and right in your actions. What you really think—that I don't know.

HENRIETTE: Who does know that kind of thing?

MAURICE: Well, if we had to answer for our thoughts, who could then clear himself?

HENRIETTE: Do you also have evil thoughts?

MAURICE: Certainly; just as I commit the worst kind of cruelties in my dreams.

HENRIETTE: Oh, when you are dreaming, of course— Just think of it— No, I am ashamed of telling—

MAURICE: Go on, go on!

HENRIETTE: Last night I dreamt that I was coolly dissecting the muscles on Adolphe's breast—you see, I am a sculptor—and he, with his usual kindness, made no resistance, but helped me instead with the worst places, as he knows more anatomy than I.

MAURICE: Was he dead?

HENRIETTE: No, he was living.

MAURICE: But that's horrible! And didn't it make you suffer?

HENRIETTE: Not at all, and that astonished me most, for I am rather sensitive to other people's sufferings. Isn't that so, Adolphe?

ADOLPHE: That's right. Rather abnormally so, in fact, and not the least when animals are concerned.

MAURICE: And I, on the other hand, am rather callous towards the sufferings both of myself and others.

ADOLPHE: Now he is not telling the truth about himself. Or what do you say, Madame Catherine?

MME. CATHERINE: I don't know of anybody with a softer heart than Monsieur Maurice. He came near calling in the police because I didn't give the goldfish fresh water—those over there on the buffet. Just look at them: it is as if they could hear what I am saying.

MAURICE: Yes, here we are making ourselves out as white as angels, and yet we are, taking it all in all, capable of any kind of polite atrocity the moment glory, gold, or women are concerned— So you are a sculptor, Mademoiselle Henriette?

HENRIETTE: A bit of one. Enough to do a bust. And to do one of you—which has long been my cherished dream—I hold myself quite capable.

MAURICE: Go ahead! That dream at least need not be long in coming true.

HENRIETTE: But I don't want to fix your features in my mind until this evening's success is over. Not until then will you have become what you should be.

MAURICE: How sure you are of victory!

HENRIETTE: Yes, it is written on your face that you are going to win this battle, and I think you must feel that yourself.

MAURICE: Why do you think so?

HENRIETTE: Because I can feel it. This morning I was ill, you know, and now I am well.

[Adolphe *begins to look depressed*]

MAURICE: [*Embarrassed*] Listen, I have a single ticket left—only one. I place it at your disposal, Adolphe.

ADOLPHE: Thank you, but I surrender it to Henriette.

HENRIETTE: But that wouldn't do!

ADOLPHE: Why not? And I never go to the theatre anyhow, as I cannot stand the heat.

HENRIETTE: But you will come and take us home at least after the show is over.

ADOLPHE: If you insist on it. Otherwise Maurice has to come back here, where we shall all be waiting for him.

MAURICE: You can just as well take the trouble of meeting us. In fact, I ask, I beg you to do so— And if you don't want to wait outside the theatre, you can meet us at the Auberge des Adrets— That's settled then, isn't it?

ADOLPHE: Wait a little. You have a way of settling things to suit yourself, before other people have a chance to consider them.

MAURICE: What is there to consider—whether you are to see your lady home or not?

ADOLPHE: You never know what may be involved in a simple act like that, but I have a sort of premonition.

HENRIETTE: Hush, hush, hush! Don't talk of spooks while the sun is shining. Let him come or not, as it pleases him. We can always find our way back here.

ADOLPHE: [*Rising*] Well, now I have to leave you —model, you know. Good-bye, both of you. And good luck to you, Maurice. To-morrow you will be out on the right side. Good-bye, Henriette.

HENRIETTE: Do you really have to go?

ADOLPHE: I must.

MAURICE: Good-bye then. We'll meet later.

[Adolphe *goes out, saluting* Mme. Catherine *in passing*]

HENRIETTE: Think of it, that we should meet at last!

MAURICE: Do you find anything remarkable in that?

HENRIETTE: It looks as if it had to happen, for Adolphe has done his best to prevent it.

MAURICE: Has he?

HENRIETTE: Oh, you must have noticed it.

MAURICE: I have noticed it, but why should you mention it?

HENRIETTE: I had to.

MAURICE: No, and I don't have to tell you that I wanted to run away through the kitchen in order to avoid meeting you and was stopped by a guest who closed the door in front of me.

HENRIETTE: Why do you tell me about it now?

MAURICE: I don't know.

[Mme. Catherine *upsets a number of glasses and bottles*]

MAURICE: That's all right, Madame Catherine. There's nothing to be afraid of.

HENRIETTE: Was that meant as a signal or a warning?

MAURICE: Probably both.

HENRIETTE: Do they take me for a locomotive that has to have flagmen ahead of it?

MAURICE: And switchmen! The danger is always greatest at the switches.

HENRIETTE: How nasty you can be!

MME. CATHERINE: Monsieur Maurice isn't nasty at all. So far nobody has been kinder than he to those that love him and trust in him.

MAURICE: Sh, sh, sh!

HENRIETTE: [*To* Maurice] The old lady is rather impertinent.

MAURICE: We can walk over to the boulevard, if you care to do so.

HENRIETTE: With pleasure. This is not the place for me. I can just feel their hatred clawing at me. [*Goes out*]

MAURICE: [*Starts after her*] Good-bye, Madame Catherine.

MME. CATHERINE: A moment! May I speak a word to you, Monsieur Maurice?

MAURICE: [*Stops unwillingly*] What is it?

MME. CATHERINE: Don't do it! Don't do it!

MAURICE: What?

MME. CATHERINE: Don't do it!

MAURICE: Don't be scared. This lady is not my kind, but she interests me. Or hardly that even.

MME. CATHERINE: Don't trust yourself!

MAURICE: Yes, I do trust myself. Good-bye. [*Goes out*]

CURTAIN

ACT II. SCENE I.

The Auberge des Adrets: a café in sixteenth-century style, with a suggestion of stage effect. Tables and easy-chairs are scattered in corners and nooks. The walls are decorated with armour and weapons. Along the ledge of the wainscoting stand glasses and jugs. Maurice and Henriette are in evening dress and sit facing each other at a table on which stands a bottle of champagne and three filled glasses. The third glass is placed at that side of the table which is nearest the background, and there an easy-chair is kept ready for the still missing "third man."

MAURICE: [*Puts his watch in front of himself on the table*] If he doesn't get here within the next five minutes, he isn't coming at all. And suppose in the meantime we drink with his ghost.

[*Touches the third glass with the rim of his own*]

HENRIETTE: [*Doing the same*] Here's to you, Adolphe!

MAURICE: He won't come.

HENRIETTE: He will come.

MAURICE: He won't.

HENRIETTE: He will.

MAURICE: What an evening! What a wonderful day! I can hardly grasp that a new life has begun. Think only: the manager believes that I may count on no less than one hundred thousand francs. I'll spend twenty thousand on a villa outside the city. That leaves me eighty thousand. I won't be able to take it all in until to-morrow, for I am tired, tired, tired. [*Sinks back into the chair*] Have you ever felt really happy?

HENRIETTE: Never. How does it feel?

MAURICE: I don't quite know how to put it. I cannot express it, but I seem chiefly to be thinking of the chagrin of my enemies. It isn't nice, but that's the way it is.

HENRIETTE: Is it happiness to be thinking of one's enemies?

MAURICE: Why, the victor has to count his killed and wounded enemies in order to gauge the extent of his victory.

HENRIETTE: Are you as bloodthirsty as all that?

MAURICE: Perhaps not. But when you have felt the pressure of other people's heels on your chest for years, it must be pleasant to shake off the enemy and draw a full breath at last.

HENRIETTE: Don't you find it strange that you are sitting here, alone with me, an insignificant girl practically unknown to you—and on an evening like this, when you ought to have a craving to show yourself like a triumphant hero to all the people, on the boulevards, in the big restaurants?

MAURICE: Of course, it's rather funny, but it feels good to be here, and your company is all I care for.

HENRIETTE: You don't look very hilarious.

MAURICE: No, I feel rather sad, and I should like to weep a little.

HENRIETTE: What is the meaning of that?

MAURICE: It is fortune conscious of its own nothingness and waiting for misfortune to appear.

HENRIETTE: Oh my, how sad! What is it you are missing anyhow?

MAURICE: I miss the only thing that gives value to life.

HENRIETTE: So you love her no longer then?

MAURICE: Not in the way I understand love. Do you think she has read my play, or that she wants to see it? Oh, she is so good, so self-sacrificing and considerate, but to go out with me for a night's fun she would regard as sinful. Once I treated her to champagne, you know, and instead of feeling happy over it, she picked up the wine list to see what it cost. And when she read the price, she wept—wept because Marion was in need of new stockings. It is beautiful, of course: it is touching, if you please. But I can get no pleasure out of it. And I do want

a little pleasure before life runs out. So far I have had nothing but privation, but now, now—life is beginning for me. [*The clock strikes twelve*] Now begins a new day, a new era!

HENRIETTE: Adolphe is not coming.

MAURICE: No, now he won't come. And now it is too late to go back to the Crêmerie.

HENRIETTE: But they are waiting for you.

MAURICE: Let them wait. They have made me promise to come, and I take back my promise. Are you longing to go there?

HENRIETTE: On the contrary!

MAURICE: Will you keep me company then?

HENRIETTE: With pleasure, if you care to have me.

MAURICE: Otherwise I shouldn't be asking you. It is strange, you know, that the victor's wreath seems worthless if you can't place it at the feet of some woman—that everything seems worthless when you have not a woman.

HENRIETTE: You don't need to be without a woman—you?

MAURICE: Well, that's the question.

HENRIETTE: Don't you know that a man is irresistible in his hour of success and fame?

MAURICE: No, I don't know, for I have had no experience of it.

HENRIETTE: You are a queer sort! At this moment, when you are the most envied man in Paris, you sit here and brood. Perhaps your conscience is troubling you because you have neglected that invitation to drink chicory coffee with the old lady over at the milk shop?

MAURICE: Yes, my conscience is troubling me on that score, and even here I am aware of their resentment, their hurt feelings, their well-grounded anger. My comrades in distress had the right to demand my presence this evening. The good Madame Catherine had a privileged claim on my success, from which a glimmer of hope was to spread over the poor fellows who have not yet succeeded. And I have robbed them of their faith in me. I can hear the vows they have been making: "Maurice will come, for he is a good fellow; he doesn't despise us, and he never fails to keep his word." Now I have made them forswear themselves.

[*While he is still speaking, somebody in the next room has begun to play the finale of Beethoven's Sonata in D-minor (Op. 31, No. 2). The allegretto is first played piano, then more forte, and at last passionately, violently, with complete abandon*]

MAURICE: Who can be playing at this time of the night?

HENRIETTE: Probably some nightbirds of the same kind as we. But listen! Your presentation of the case is not correct. Remember that Adolphe promised to meet us here. We waited for him, and he failed to keep his promise. So that you are not to blame——

MAURICE: You think so? While you are speaking,

I believe you, but when you stop, my conscience begins again. What have you in that package?

HENRIETTE: Oh, it is only a laurel wreath that I meant to send up to the stage, but I had no chance to do so. Let me give it to you now—it is said to have a cooling effect on burning foreheads. [*She rises and crowns him with the wreath; then she kisses him on the forehead*] Hail to the victor!

MAURICE: Don't.

HENRIETTE: [*Kneeling*] Hail to the King!

MAURICE: [*Rising*] No, now you scare me.

HENRIETTE: You timid man! You of little faith who are afraid of fortune even! Who robbed you of your self-assurance and turned you into a dwarf?

MAURICE: A dwarf? Yes, you are right. I am not working up in the clouds, like a giant, with crashing and roaring, but I forge my weapons deep down in the silent heart of the mountain. You think that my modesty shrinks before the victor's wreath. On the contrary, I despise it: it is not enough for me. You think I am afraid of that ghost with its jealous green eyes which sits over there and keeps watch on my feelings—the strength of which you don't suspect. Away, ghost! [*He brushes the third, untouched glass off the table*] Away with you, you superfluous third person—you absent one who has lost your rights, if you ever had any. You stayed away from the field of battle because you knew myself already beaten. As I crush this glass under my foot, so I will crush the image of yourself which you have reared in a temple no longer yours.

HENRIETTE: Good! That's the way! Well spoken, my hero!

MAURICE: Now I have sacrificed my best friend, my most faithful helper, on your altar, Astarte! Are you satisfied?

HENRIETTE: Astarte is a pretty name, and I'll keep it—I think you love me, Maurice.

MAURICE: Of course I do— Woman of evil omen, you who stir up man's courage with your scent of blood, whence do you come and where do you lead me? I loved you before I saw you, for I trembled when I heard them speak of you. And when I saw you in the doorway, your soul poured itself into mine. And when you left, I could still feel your presence in my arms. I wanted to flee from you, but something held me back, and this evening we have been driven together as the prey is driven into the hunter's net. Whose is the fault? Your friend's, who pandered for us!

HENRIETTE: Fault or no fault: what does it matter, and what does it mean?— Adolphe has been at fault in not bringing us together before. He is guilty of having stolen from us two weeks of bliss, to which he had no right himself. I am jealous of him on your behalf. I hate him because he has cheated you out of your mistress. I should like to blot him from the host of the living, and his memory with him—wipe him out of the past even, make him unmade, unborn!

MAURICE: Well, we'll bury him beneath our own memories. We'll cover him with leaves and branches far out in the wild woods, and then we'll pile stone on top of the mound so that he will never look up again. [*Raising his glass*] Our fate is sealed. Woe unto us! What will come next?

HENRIETTE: Next comes the new era— What have you in that package?

MAURICE: I cannot remember.

HENRIETTE: [*Opens the package and takes out a tie and a pair of gloves*] That tie is a fright! It must have cost at least fifty centimes.

MAURICE: [*Snatching the things away from her*] Don't you touch them!

HENRIETTE: They are from her?

MAURICE: Yes, they are.

HENRIETTE: Give them to me.

MAURICE: No, she's better than we, better than everybody else.

HENRIETTE: I don't believe it. She is simply stupider and stingier. One who weeps because you order champagne——

MAURICE: When the child was without stockings. Yes, she is a good woman.

HENRIETTE: Philistine! You'll never be an artist. But I am an artist, and I'll make a bust of you with a shopkeeper's cap instead of the laurel wreath!— Her name is Jeanne?

MAURICE: How did you know?

HENRIETTE: Why, that's the name of all housekeepers.

MAURICE: Henriette!

[Henriette *takes the tie and the gloves and throws them into the fireplace*]

MAURICE: [*Weakly*] Astarte, now you demand the sacrifice of women. You shall have them, but if you ask for innocent children, too, then I'll send you packing.

HENRIETTE: Can you tell me what it is that binds you to me?

MAURICE: If I only knew, I should be able to tear myself away. But I believe it must be those qualities which you have and I lack. I believe that the evil within you draws me with the irresistible lure of novelty.

HENRIETTE: Have you ever committed a crime?

MAURICE: No real one. Have you?

HENRIETTE: Yes.

MAURICE: Well, how did you find it?

HENRIETTE: It was greater than to perform a good deed, for by that we are placed on equality with others; it was greater than to perform some act of heroism, for by that we are raised above others and rewarded. That crime placed me outside and beyond life, society, and my fellow-beings. Since then I am living only a partial life, a sort of dream life, and that's why reality never gets a hold on me.

MAURICE: What was it you did?

HENRIETTE: I won't tell, for then you would **get** scared again.

MAURICE: Can you ever be found out?

HENRIETTE: Never. But that does not prevent me from seeing, frequently, the five stones at the Place de Roquette, where the scaffold used to stand; and for this reason I never dare to open a pack of cards, as I always turn up the five of diamonds.

MAURICE: Was it that kind of a crime?

HENRIETTE: Yes, it was that kind.

MAURICE: Of course, it's horrible, but it is interesting. Have you no conscience?

HENRIETTE: None, but I should be grateful if you would talk of something else.

MAURICE: Suppose we talk of—love?

HENRIETTE: Of that you don't talk until it is over.

MAURICE: Have you been in love with Adolphe?

HENRIETTE: I don't know. The goodness of his nature drew me like some beautiful, all-but-vanished memory of childhood. Yet there was much about his person that offended my eye, so that I had to spend a long time retouching, altering, adding, subtracting, before I could make a presentable figure of him. When he talked, I could notice that he had learned from you, and the lesson was often badly digested and awkwardly applied. You can imagine then how miserable the copy must appear now, when I am permitted to study the original. That's why he was afraid of having us two meet; and when it did happen, he understood at once that his time was up.

MAURICE: Poor Adolphe!

HENRIETTE: I feel sorry for him, too, as I know he must be suffering beyond all bounds——

MAURICE: Sh! Somebody is coming.

HENRIETTE: I wonder if it could be he?

MAURICE: That would be unbearable.

HENRIETTE: No, it isn't he, but if it had been, how do you think the situation would have shaped itself?

MAURICE: At first he would have been a little sore at you because he had made a mistake in regard to the meeting-place—and tried to find us in several other cafés—but his soreness would have changed into pleasure at finding us—and seeing that we had not deceived him. And in the joy at having wronged us by his suspicions, he would love both of us. And so it would make him happy to notice that we had become such good friends. It had always been his dream—hm! he is making the speech now—his dream that the three of us should form a triumvirate that could set the world a great example of friendship asking for nothing— "Yes, I trust you, Maurice, partly because you are my friend, and partly because your feelings are tied up elsewhere."

HENRIETTE: Bravo! You must have been in a similar situation before, or you couldn't give such a lifelike picture of it. Do you know that Adolphe is just that kind of a third person who cannot enjoy his mistress without having his friend along?

MAURICE: That's why I had to be called in to entertain you— Hush! There is somebody outside— It must be he.

HENRIETTE: No, don't you know these are the hours when ghosts walk, and then you can see so many things, and hear them also. To keep awake at night, when you ought to be sleeping, has for me the same charm as a crime: it is to place oneself above and beyond the laws of nature.

MAURICE: But the punishment is fearful—I am shivering or quivering, with cold or with fear.

HENRIETTE: [Wraps her opera cloak about him] Put this on. It will make you warm.

MAURICE: That's nice. It is as if I were inside of your skin, as if my body had been melted up by lack of sleep and were being remoulded in your shape. I can feel the moulding process going on. But I am also growing a new soul, new thoughts, and here, where your bosom has left an impression, I can feel my own beginning to bulge.

[During this entire scene, the pianist in the next room has been practising the Sonata in D-minor, sometimes pianissimo, sometimes wildly fortissimo; now and then he has kept silent for a little while, and at other times nothing has been heard but a part of the finale: bars 96 to 107]

MAURICE: What a monster, to sit there all night practising on the piano. It gives me a sick feeling. Do you know what I propose? Let us drive out to the Bois de Boulogne and take breakfast in the Pavilion, and see the sun rise over the lakes.

HENRIETTE: Bully!

MAURICE: But first of all I must arrange to have my mail and the morning papers sent out by messenger to the Pavilion. Tell me Henriette: shall we invite Adolphe?

HENRIETTE: Oh, that's going too far! But why not? The ass can also be harnessed to the triumphal chariot. Let him come.

[They get up]

MAURICE: [Taking off the cloak] Then I'll ring.

HENRIETTE: Wait a moment! [Throws herself into his arms]

CURTAIN

SCENE II.

A large, splendidly furnished restaurant room in the Bois de Boulogne. It is richly carpeted and full of mirrors, easy-chairs, and divans. There are glass doors in the background, and beside them windows overlooking the lakes. In the foreground a table is spread, with flowers in the centre, bowls full of fruit, wine in decanters, oysters on platters, many different kinds of wine, glasses, and two lighted candelabra. On the right there is a round table full of newspapers and telegrams. Maurice and Henriette are sitting opposite each other at this small table. The sun is just rising outside.

MAURICE: There is no longer any doubt about it. The newspapers tell me it is so, and these telegrams congratulate me on my success. This is the beginning of a new life, and my fate is wedded to yours by this night, when you were the only one to share my hopes and my triumph. From your hand I received the laurel, and it seems to me as if everything had come from you.

HENRIETTE: What a wonderful night! Have we been dreaming, or is this something we have really lived through?

MAURICE: [*Rising*] And what a morning after such a night! I feel as if it were the world's first day that is now being illumined by the rising sun. Only this minute was the earth created and stripped of those white films that are now floating off into space. There lies the Garden of Eden in the rosy light of dawn, and here is the first human couple— Do you know, I am so happy I could cry at the thought that all mankind is not equally happy— Do you hear that distant murmur as of ocean waves beating against a rocky shore, as of winds sweeping through a forest? Do you know what it is? It is Paris whispering my name. Do you see the columns of smoke that rise skyward in thousand and tens of thousands? They are the fires burning on my altars, and if that be not so, then it must become so, for I will it. At this moment all the telegraph instruments of Europe are clicking out my name. The Oriental Express is carrying the newspapers to the Far East, towards the rising sun; and the ocean steamers are carrying them to the utmost West. The earth is mine, and for that reason it is beautiful. Now I should like to have wings for us two, so that we might rise from here and fly far, far away, before anybody can soil my happiness, before envy has chance to wake me out of my dream—for it is probably a dream!

HENRIETTE: [*Holding out her hand to him*] Here you can feel that you are not dreaming.

MAURICE: It is not a dream, but it has been one. As a poor young man, you know, when I was walking in the woods down there, and looked up to this Pavilion, it looked to me like a fairy castle, and always my thoughts carried me up to this room, with the balcony outside and the heavy curtains, as to a place of supreme bliss. To be sitting here in company with a beloved woman and see the sun rise while the candles were still burning in the candelabra: that was the most audacious dream of my youth. Now it has come true, and now I have no more to ask of life— Do you want to die now, together with me?

HENRIETTE: No, you fool! Now I want to begin living.

MAURICE: [*Rising*] To live; that is to suffer! Now comes reality. I can hear his steps on the stairs. He is panting with alarm, and his heart is beating with dread of having lost what it holds most precious. Can you believe me if I tell you that Adolphe is under this roof? Within a minute he will be standing in the middle of this floor.

HENRIETTE: [*Alarmed*] It was a stupid trick to ask him to come here, and I am already regretting it— Well, we shall see anyhow if your forecast of the situation proves correct.

MAURICE: Oh, it is easy to be mistaken about a person's feelings.

[*The* Head Waiter *enters with a card*]

MAURICE: Ask the gentleman to step in. [*To* Henriette] I am afraid we'll regret this.

HENRIETTE: Too late to think of that now— Hush!

[Adolphe *enters, pale and hollow-eyed*]

MAURICE: [*Trying to speak unconcernedly*] There you are! What became of you last night?

ADOLPHE: I looked for you at the Hôtel des Arrêts and waited a whole hour.

MAURICE: So you went to the wrong place. We were waiting several hours for you at the Auberge des Adrets, and we are still waiting for you, as you see.

ADOLPHE: [*Relieved*] Thank heaven!

HENRIETTE: Good morning, Adolphe. You are always expecting the worst and worrying yourself needlessly. I suppose you imagined that we wanted to avoid your company. And though you see that we sent for you, you are still thinking yourself superfluous.

ADOLPHE: Pardon me: I was wrong, but the night was dreadful.

[*They sit down. Embarrassed silence follows*]

HENRIETTE: [*To* Adolphe] Well, are you not going to congratulate Maurice on his great success?

ADOLPHE: Oh, yes! Your success is the real thing, and envy itself cannot deny it. Everything is giving way before you, and even I have a sense of my own smallness in your presence.

MAURICE: Nonsense!— Henriette, are you not going to offer Adolphe a glass of wine?

ADOLPHE: Thank you, not for me—nothing at all!

HENRIETTE: [*To* Adolphe] What's the matter with you? Are you ill?

ADOLPHE: Not yet, but——

HENRIETTE: Your eyes——

ADOLPHE: What of them?

MAURICE: What happened at the Crêmerie last night? I suppose they are angry with me?

ADOLPHE: Nobody is angry with you, but your absence caused a depression which it hurt me to watch. But nobody was angry with you, believe me. Your friends understood, and they regarded your failure to come with sympathetic forbearance. Madame Catherine herself defended you and proposed your health. We all rejoiced in your success as if it had been our own.

HENRIETTE: Well, those are nice people! What good friends you have, Maurice.

MAURICE: Yes, better than I deserve.

ADOLPHE: Nobody has better friends than he deserves, and you are a man greatly blessed in his friends— Can't you feel how the air is softened today by all the kind thoughts and wishes that stream toward you from a thousand breasts?

[Maurice *rises in order to hide his emotion*]

ADOLPHE: From a thousand breasts that you have rid of the nightmare that had been crushing them during a life-time. Humanity had been slandered— and you have exonerated it: that's why men feel grateful towards you. To-day they are once more holding their heads high and saying: You see, we are a little better than our reputation after all. And that thought *makes* them better.

[Henriette *tries to hide her emotion*]

ADOLPHE: Am I in the way? Just let me warm myself a little in your sunshine, Maurice, and then I'll go.

MAURICE: Why should you go when you have only just arrived?

ADOLPHE: Why? Because I have seen what I need not have seen; because I know now that my hour is past. [*Pause*] That you sent for me, I take as an expression of thoughtfulness, a notice of what has happened, a frankness that hurts less than deceit. You hear that I think well of my fellow-beings, and this I have learned from you, Maurice. [*Pause*] But, my friend, a few moments ago I passed through the Church of St. Germain, and there I saw a woman and a child. I am not wishing that you had seen them, for what has happened cannot be altered, but if you gave a thought or a word to them before you set them adrift on the waters of the great city, then you could enjoy your happiness undisturbed. And now I bid you good-bye.

HENRIETTE: Why must you go?

ADOLPHE: And you ask that? Do you want me to tell you?

HENRIETTE: No, I don't.

ADOLPHE: Good-bye then. [*Goes out*]

MAURICE: The Fall: and lo! "they knew that they were naked."

HENRIETTE: What a difference between this scene and the one we imagined! He is better than we.

MAURICE: It seems to me now as if all the rest were better than we.

HENRIETTE: Do you see that the sun has vanished behind a cloud, and the woods have lost their rose colour?

MAURICE: Yes, I see, and the blue lake has turned to black. Let us flee to some place where the sky is always blue and the trees are always green.

HENRIETTE: Yes, let us—but without any farewells.

MAURICE: No, with farewells.

HENRIETTE: We were to fly. You spoke of wings —and your feet are of lead. I am not jealous, but if you go to say farewell and get two pairs of arms around your neck—then you can't tear yourself away.

MAURICE: Perhaps you are right, but only one pair of little arms is needed to hold me fast.

HENRIETTE: It is the child that holds you then, and not the woman?

MAURICE: It is the child.

HENRIETTE: The child! Another woman's child! And for the sake of it I am to suffer. Why must that child block the way where I want to pass, and must pass?

MAURICE: Yes, why? It would be better if it had never existed.

HENRIETTE: [*Walks excitedly back and forth*] Indeed! But now it does exist. Like a rock on the road, a rock set firmly in the ground, immovable, so that it upsets the carriage.

MAURICE: The triumphal chariot!— The ass is driven to death, but the rock remains. Curse it!

[*Pause*]

HENRIETTE: There is nothing to do.

MAURICE: Yes, we must get married, and then *our* child will make us forget the other one.

HENRIETTE: This will kill this!

MAURICE: Kill! What kind of word is that?

HENRIETTE: [*Changing tone*] Your child will kill our love.

MAURICE: No, girl, our love will kill whatever stands in its way, but it will not be killed.

HENRIETTE: [*Opens a deck of cards lying on the mantelpiece*] Look at it! The five of diamonds—the scaffold! Can it be possible that our fates are determined in advance? That our thoughts are guided as if through pipes to the spot for which they are bound, without chance for us to stop them? But I don't want it, I don't want it!— Do you realise that I must go to the scaffold if my crime should be discovered?

MAURICE: Tell me about your crime. Now is the time for it.

HENRIETTE: No, I should regret it afterwards, and you would despise me—no, no, no!— Have you ever heard that a person could be hated to death? Well, my father incurred the hatred of my mother and my sisters, and he melted away like wax before a fire. Ugh! Let us talk of something else. And, above all, let us get away. The air is poisoned here. To-morrow your laurels will be withered, the triumph will be forgotten, and in a week another triumphant hero will hold the public attention. Away from here, to work for new victories! But first of all, Maurice, you must embrace your child and provide for its immediate future. You don't have to see the mother at all.

MAURICE: Thank you! Your good heart does you honour, and I love you doubly when you show the kindness you generally hide.

HENRIETTE: And then you go to the Crêmerie and say good-bye to the old lady and your friends. Leave no unsettled business behind to make your mind heavy on our trip.

MAURICE: I'll clear up everything, and to-night we meet at the railroad station.

HENRIETTE: Agreed! And then: away from here —away towards the sea and the sun!

CURTAIN

ACT III. SCENE I.

In the Crêmerie. The gas is lit. Mme. Catherine *is seated at the counter,* Adolphe *at a table.*

MME. CATHERINE: Such is life, Monsieur Adolphe. But you young ones are always demanding too much, and then you come here and blubber over it afterwards.

ADOLPHE: No, it isn't that. I reproach nobody, and am as fond as ever of both of them. But there is one thing that makes me sick at heart. You see, I thought more of Maurice than of anybody else; so much that I wouldn't have grudged him anything that could give him pleasure—but now I have lost him, and it hurts me worse than the loss of her. I have lost both of them, and so my loneliness is made doubly painful. And then there is still something else which I have not yet been able to clear up.

MME. CATHERINE: Don't brood so much. Work and divert yourself. Now, for instance, do you ever go to church?

ADOLPHE: What should I do there?

MME. CATHERINE: Oh, there's so much to look at, and then there is the music. There is nothing commonplace about it, at least.

ADOLPHE: Perhaps not. But I don't belong to that fold, I guess, for it never stirs me to any devotion. And then, Madame Catherine, faith is a gift, they tell me, and I haven't got it yet.

MME. CATHERINE: Well, wait till you get it— But what is this I heard a while ago? Is it true that you have sold a picture in London for a high price, and that you have got a medal?

ADOLPHE: Yes, it's true.

MME. CATHERINE: Merciful heavens!—and not a word do you say about it?

ADOLPHE: I am afraid of fortune, and besides it seems almost worthless to me at this moment. I am afraid of it as of a spectre: it brings disaster to speak of having seen it.

MME. CATHERINE: You're a queer fellow, and that's what you have always been.

ADOLPHE: Not queer at all, but I have seen so much misfortune come in the wake of fortune, and I have seen how adversity brings out true friends, while none but false ones appear in the hour of success— You asked me if I ever went to church, and I answered evasively. This morning I stepped into the Church of St. Germain without really knowing why I did so. It seemed as if I were looking for somebody in there—somebody to whom I could silently offer my gratitude. But I found nobody. Then I dropped a gold coin in the poor-box. It was all I could get out of my church-going, and that was rather commonplace, I should say.

MME. CATHERINE: It was always something; and then it was fine to think of the poor after having heard good news.

ADOLPHE: It was neither fine nor anything else: it was something I did because I couldn't help myself. But something more occurred while I was in the church. I saw Maurice's girl friend, Jeanne, and her child. Struck down, crushed by his triumphal chariot, they seemed aware of the full extent of their misfortune.

MME. CATHERINE: Well, children, I don't know in what kind of shape you keep your consciences. But how a decent fellow, a careful and considerate man like Monsieur Maurice, can all of a sudden desert a woman and her child, that is something I cannot explain.

ADOLPHE: Nor can I explain it, and he doesn't seem to understand it himself. I met them this morning, and everything appeared quite natural to them, quite proper, as if they couldn't imagine anything else. It was as if they had been enjoying the satisfaction of a good deed or the fulfilment of a sacred duty. There are things, Madame Catherine, that we cannot explain, and for this reason it is not for us to judge. And besides, you saw how it happened. Maurice felt the danger in the air. I foresaw it and tried to prevent their meeting. Maurice wanted to run away from it, but nothing helped. Why, it was as if a plot had been laid by some invisible power, and as if they had been driven by guile into each other's arms. Of course, I am disqualified in this case, but I wouldn't hesitate to pronounce a verdict of "not guilty."

MME. CATHERINE: Well, now, to be able to forgive as you do, that's what I call religion.

ADOLPHE: Heavens, could it be that I am religious without knowing it.

MME. CATHERINE: But then, to *let* oneself be driven or tempted into evil, as Monsieur Maurice has done, means weakness or bad character. And if you feel your strength failing you, then you ask for help, and then you get it. But he was too conceited to do that— Who is this coming? The Abbé, I think.

ADOLPHE: What does he want here?

ABBÉ: [*Enters*] Good evening, madame. Good evening, monsieur.

MME. CATHERINE: Can I be of any service?

ABBÉ: Has Monsieur Maurice, the author, been here to-day?

MME. CATHERINE: Not to-day. His play has just been put on, and that is probably keeping him busy.

ABBÉ: I have—sad news to bring him. Sad in several respects.

MME. CATHERINE: May I ask of what kind?

ABBÉ: Yes, it's no secret. The daughter he had with that girl, Jeanne, is dead.

MME. CATHERINE: Dead!

ADOLPHE: Marion dead!

ABBÉ: Yes, she died suddenly this morning without any previous illness.

MME. CATHERINE: O Lord, who can tell Thy ways!

ABBÉ: The mother's grief makes it necessary that Monsieur Maurice look after her, so we must try to find him. But first a question in confidence: do you know whether Monsieur Maurice was fond of the child, or was indifferent to it?

MME. CATHERINE: If he was fond of Marion? Why, all of us know how he loved her.

ADOLPHE: There's no doubt about that.

ABBÉ: I am glad to hear it, and it settles the matter so far as I am concerned.

MME. CATHERINE: Has there been any doubt about it?

ABBÉ: Yes, unfortunately. It has even been rumoured in the neighbourhood that he had abandoned the child and its mother in order to go away with a strange woman. In a few hours this rumour has grown into definite accusations, and at the same time the feeling against him has risen to such a point that his life is threatened and he is being called a murderer.

MME. CATHERINE: Good God, what is *this?* What does it mean?

ABBÉ: Now I'll tell you my opinion— I am convinced that the man is innocent on this score, and the mother feels as certain about it as I do. But appearances are against Monsieur Maurice, and I think he will find it rather hard to clear himself when the police come to question him.

ADOLPHE: Have the police got hold of the matter?

ABBÉ: Yes, the police have had to step in to protect him against all those ugly rumours and the rage of the people. Probably the Commissaire will be here soon.

MME. CATHERINE: [*To* Adolphe] There, you see what happens when a man cannot tell the difference between good and evil, and when he trifles with vice. God will punish!

ADOLPHE: Then he is more merciless than man.

ABBÉ: What do you know about that?

ADOLPHE: Not very much, but I keep an eye on what happens——

ABBÉ: And you understand it also?

ADOLPHE: Not yet perhaps.

ABBÉ: Let us look more closely at the matter— Oh, here comes the Commissaire.

COMMISSAIRE: [*Enters*] Gentlemen—Madame Catherine—I have to trouble you for a moment with a few questions concerning Monsieur Maurice. As you have probably heard, he has become the object of a hideous rumour, which, by the by, I don't believe in.

MME. CATHERINE: None of us believes in it either.

COMMISSAIRE: That strengthens my own opinion, but for his own sake I must give him a chance to defend himself.

ABBÉ: That's right, and I guess he will find justice, although it may come hard.

COMMISSAIRE: Appearances are very much against him, but I have seen guiltless people reach the scaffold before their innocence was discovered. Let me tell you what there is against him. The little girl, Marion, being left alone by her mother, was secretly visited by the father, who seems to have made sure of the time when the child was to be found alone. Fifteen minutes after his visit the mother returned home and found the child dead. All this makes the position of the accused man very unpleasant— The post-mortem examination brought out no signs of violence or of poison, but the physicians admit the existence of new poisons that leave no traces behind them. To me all this is mere coincidence of the kind I frequently come across. But here's something that looks worse. Last night Monsieur Maurice was seen at the Auberge des Adrets in company with a strange lady. According to the waiter, they were talking about crimes. The Place de Roquette and the scaffold were both mentioned. A queer topic of conversation for a pair of lovers of good breeding and good social position! But even this may be passed over, as we know by experience that people who have been drinking and losing a lot of sleep seem inclined to dig up all the worst that lies at the bottom of their souls. Far more serious is the evidence given by the head waiter as to their champagne breakfast in the Bois de Boulogne this morning. He says that he heard them wish the life out of a child. The man is said to have remarked that, "It would be better if it had never existed." To which the woman replied: "Indeed! But now it does exist." And as they went on talking, these words occurred: "This will kill this!" And the answer was: "Kill! What kind of word is that?" And also: "The five of diamonds—the scaffold, the Place de Roquette." All this, you see, will be hard to get out of, and so will the foreign journey planned for this evening. These are serious matters.

ADOLPHE: He is lost!

MME. CATHERINE: That's a dreadful story. One doesn't know what to believe.

ABBÉ: This is not the work of man. God have mercy on him!

ADOLPHE: He is in the net, and he will never get out of it.

MME. CATHERINE: He had no business to get in.

ADOLPHE: Do you begin to suspect him also, Madame Catherine?

MME. CATHERINE: Yes and no. I have got beyond having an opinion in this matter. Have you not seen angels turn into devils just as you turn your hand, and then become angels again?

COMMISSAIRE: It certainly does look queer. However, we'll have to wait and hear what explanations he can give. No one will be judged unheard. Good evening, gentlemen. Good evening, Madame Catherine. [*Goes out*]

ABBÉ: This is not the work of man.

ADOLPHE: No, it looks as if demons had been at work for the undoing of man.

ABBÉ: It is either a punishment for secret misdeeds, or it is a terrible test.

JEANNE: [*Enters, dressed in mourning*] Good evening. Pardon me for asking, but have you seen Monsieur Maurice?

MME. CATHERINE: No, madame, but I think he may be here any minute. You haven't met him then since——

JEANNE: Not since this morning.

MME. CATHERINE: Let me tell you that I share in your great sorrow.

JEANNE: Thank you, madame. [*To the* Abbé] So you are here, Father.

ABBÉ: Yes, my child. I thought I might be of some use to you. And it was fortunate, as it gave me a chance to speak to the Commissaire.

JEANNE: The Commissaire! He doesn't suspect Maurice also, does he?

ABBÉ: No, he doesn't, and none of us here do. But appearances are against him in a most appalling manner.

JEANNE: You mean on account of the talk the waiters overheard—it means nothing to me, who has heard such things before when Maurice had had a few drinks. Then it is his custom to speculate on crimes and their punishment. Besides it seems to have been the woman in his company who dropped the most dangerous remarks. I should like to have a look into that woman's eyes.

ADOLPHE: My dear Jeanne, no matter how much harm that woman may have done you, she did nothing with evil intention—in fact, she had no intention whatever, but just followed the promptings of her nature. I know her to be a good soul and one who can very well bear being looked straight in the eye.

JEANNE: Your judgment in this matter, Adolphe, has great value to me, and I believe what you say. It means that I cannot hold anybody but myself responsible for what has happened. It is my carelessness that is now being punished. [*She begins to cry*]

ABBÉ: Don't accuse yourself unjustly! I know you, and the serious spirit in which you have regarded your motherhood. That your assumption of this responsibility had not been sanctioned by religion and the civil law was not your fault. No, we are here facing something quite different.

ADOLPHE: What then?

ABBÉ: Who can tell?

[Henriette *enters, dressed in travelling suit*]

ADOLPHE: [*Rises with an air of determination and goes to meet* Henriette] You here?

HENRIETTE: Yes, where is Maurice?

ADOLPHE: Do you know—or don't you?

HENRIETTE: I know everything. Excuse me, Madame Catherine, but I was ready to start and absolutely had to step in here a moment. [*To* Adolphe] Who is that woman?—Oh!

[Henriette *and* Jeanne *stare at each other.* Emile *appears in the kitchen door*]

HENRIETTE: [*To* Jeanne] I ought to say something, but it matters very little, for anything I can say must sound like an insult or a mockery. But if I ask you simply to believe that I share your deep sorrow as much as anybody standing closer to you, then you must not turn away from me. You mustn't, for I deserve your pity if not your forbearance. [*Holds out her hand*]

JEANNE: [*Looks hard at her*] I believe you now—and in the next moment I don't. [*Takes* Henriette's *hand*]

HENRIETTE: [*Kisses* Jeanne's *hand*] Thank you!

JEANNE: [*Drawing back her hand*] Oh, don't! I don't deserve it! I don't deserve it!

ABBÉ: Pardon me, but while we are gathered here and peace seems to prevail temporarily at least, won't you, Mademoiselle Henriette, shed some light into all the uncertainty and darkness surrounding the main point of accusation? I ask you, as a friend among friends, to tell us what you meant with all that talk about killing, and crime, and the Place de Roquette. That your words had no connection with the death of the child, we have reason to believe, but it would give us added assurance to hear what you were really talking about. Won't you tell us?

HENRIETTE: [*After a pause*] That I cannot tell! No, I cannot!

ADOLPHE: Henriette, do tell! Give us the word that will relieve us all.

HENRIETTE: I cannot! Don't ask me!

ABBÉ: This is not the work of man!

HENRIETTE: Oh, that this moment had to come! And in this manner! [*To* Jeanne] Madame, I swear that I am not guilty of your child's death. Is that enough?

JEANNE: Enough for us, but not for Justice.

HENRIETTE: Justice! If you knew how true your words are!

ABBÉ: [*To* Henriette] And if you knew what you were saying just now!

HENRIETTE: Do you know that better than I?

ABBÉ: Yes, I do.

[Henriette *looks fixedly at the* Abbé]

ABBÉ: Have no fear, for even if I guess your secret, it will not be exposed. Besides, I have nothing to do with human justice, but a great deal with divine mercy.

MAURICE: [*Enters, hastily, dressed for travelling. He doesn't look at the others, who are standing in the background, but goes straight up to the counter, where* Mme. Catherine *is sitting*] You are not angry at me, Madame Catherine, because I didn't show up? I have come now to apologise to you before I start for the South at eight o'clock this evening.

[Mme. Catherine *is too startled to say a word*]

MAURICE: Then you are angry at me? [*Looks around*] What does all this mean? Is it a dream, or what is it? Of course, I can see that it is all real, but it looks like a wax cabinet— There is Jeanne, looking like a statue and dressed in black— And Henriette looking like a corpse— What does it mean?

[*All remain silent*]

MAURICE: Nobody answers. It must mean something dreadful. [*Silence*] But speak, please! Adolphe, you are my friend, what is it? [*Pointing to* Emile] And there is a detective!

ADOLPHE: [*Comes forward*] You don't know then?

MAURICE: Nothing at all. But I must know!

ADOLPHE: Well, then—Marion is dead.

MAURICE: Marion—dead?

ADOLPHE: Yes, she died this morning.

MAURICE: [*To* Jeanne] So that's why you are in mourning. Jeanne, Jeanne, who has done this to us?

JEANNE: He who holds life and death in his hand.

MAURICE: But I saw her looking well and happy this morning. How did it happen? Who did it? Somebody must have done it? [*His eyes seek* Henriette]

ADOLPHE: Don't look for the guilty one here, for there is none to be found. Unfortunately, the police have turned their suspicion in a direction where none ought to exist.

MAURICE: What direction is that?

ADOLPHE: Well—you may as well know that your reckless talk last night and this morning has placed you in a light that is anything but favorable.

MAURICE: So they were listening to us. Let me see, what were we saying—I remember!— Then I am lost!

ADOLPHE: But if you explain your thoughtless words we will believe you.

MAURICE: I cannot! And I will not! I shall be sent to prison, but it doesn't matter. Marion is dead! Dead! And I have killed her!

[*General consternation*]

ADOLPHE: Think of what you are saying! Weigh your words! Do you realise what you said just now?

MAURICE: What did I say?

ADOLPHE: You said that you had killed Marion.

MAURICE: Is there a human being here who could believe me a murderer, and who could hold me capable of taking my own child's life? You who know me, Madame Catherine, tell me; do you believe, can you believe——

MME. CATHERINE: I don't know any longer what to believe. What the heart thinketh the tongue speaketh. And your tongue has spoken evil words.

MAURICE: She doesn't believe me!

ADOLPHE: But explain your words, man! Explain what you meant by saying that "your love would kill everything that stood in its way".

MAURICE: So they know that too— Are you willing to explain it, Henriette?

HENRIETTE: No, I cannot do that.

ABBÉ: There is something wrong behind all this and you have lost our sympathy, my friend. A while

ago I could have sworn that you were innocent, and I wouldn't do that now.

MAURICE: [*To* Jeanne] What you have to say means more to me than anything else.

JEANNE: [*Coldly*] Answer a question first: who was it you cursed during that orgy out there?

MAURICE: Have I done that, too? Maybe. Yes, I am guilty, and yet I am guiltless. Let me go away from here, for I am ashamed of myself, and I have done more wrong than I can forgive myself.

HENRIETTE: [*To* Adolphe] Go with him and see that he doesn't do himself any harm.

ADOLPHE: Shall I——?

HENRIETTE: Who else?

ADOLPHE: [*Without bitterness*] You are nearest to it— Sh! A carriage is stopping outside.

MME. CATHERINE: It's the Commissaire. Well, much as I have seen of life, I could never have believed that success and fame were such short-lived things.

MAURICE: [*To* Henriette] From the triumphal chariot to the patrol wagon!

JEANNE: [*Simply*] And the ass—who was that?

ADOLPHE: Oh, that must have been me.

COMMISSAIRE: [*Enters with a paper in his hands*] A summons to Police Headquarters—to-night, at once—for Monsieur Maurice Gérard—and for Mademoiselle Henriette Mauclerc—both here?

MAURICE *and* HENRIETTE: Yes.

MAURICE: Is this an arrest?

COMMISSAIRE: Not yet. Only a summons.

MAURICE: And then?

COMMISSAIRE: We don't know yet.

[Maurice *and* Henriette *go towards the door*]

MAURICE: Good-bye to all!

[*Everybody shows emotion. The* Commissaire, Maurice, *and* Henriette *go out*]

EMILE: [*Enters and goes up to* Jeanne] Now I'll take you home, sister.

JEANNE: And what do you think of all this?

EMILE: The man is innocent.

ABBÉ: But as I see it, it is, and must always be, something despicable to break one's promise, and it becomes unpardonable when a woman and her child are involved.

EMILE: Well, I should rather feel that way, too, now when it concerns my own sister, but, unfortunately, I am prevented from throwing the first stone because I have done the same thing myself.

ABBÉ: Although I am free from blame in that respect, I am not throwing any stones either, but the act condemns itself and is punished by its consequences.

JEANNE: Pray for him! For both of them!

ABBÉ: No, I'll do nothing of the kind, for it is an impertinence to want to change the counsels of the Lord. And what has happened here is, indeed, not the work of man.

CURTAIN

SCENE II.

The Auberge des Adrets. Adolphe *and* Henriette *are seated at the same table where* Maurice *and* Henriette *were sitting in the second act. A cup of coffee stands in front of* Adolphe. Henriette *has ordered nothing.*

ADOLPHE: You believe then that he will come here?

HENRIETTE: I am sure. He was released this noon for lack of evidence, but he didn't want to show himself in the streets before it was dark.

ADOLPHE: Poor fellow! Oh, I tell you, life seems horrible to me since yesterday.

HENRIETTE: And what about me? I am afraid to live, dare hardly breathe, dare hardly think even, since I know that somebody is spying not only on my words but on my thoughts.

ADOLPHE: So it was here you sat that night when I couldn't find you?

HENRIETTE: Yes, but don't talk of it. I could die from shame when I think of it. Adolphe, you are made of a different, a better, stuff than he or I—

ADOLPHE: Sh, sh, sh!

HENRIETTE: Yes, indeed! And what was it that made me stay here? I was lazy; I was tired; his success intoxicated me and bewitched me—I cannot explain it. But if you had come it would never have happened. And to-day you are great, and he is small —less than the least of all. Yesterday he had one hundred thousand francs. To-day he has nothing, because his play has been withdrawn. And public opinion will never excuse him, for his lack of faith will be judged as harshly as if he were the murderer, and those that see farthest hold that the child died from sorrow, so that he was responsible for it anyhow.

ADOLPHE: You know what my thoughts are in this matter, Henriette, but I should like to know that both of you are spotless. Won't you tell me what those dreadful words of yours meant? It cannot be a chance that your talk in a festive moment like that dealt so largely with killing and the scaffold.

HENRIETTE: It was no chance. It was something that had to be said, something I cannot tell you— probably because I have no right to appear spotless in your eyes, seeing that I am not spotless.

ADOLPHE: All this is beyond me.

HENRIETTE: Let us talk of something else— Do you believe there are many unpunished criminals at large among us, some of whom may even be our intimate friends?

ADOLPHE: [*Nervously*] Why? What do you mean?

HENRIETTE: Don't you believe that every human being at some time or another has been guilty of some kind of act which would fall under the law if it were discovered?

ADOLPHE: Yes, I believe that is true, but no evil act escapes being punished by one's own conscience at least. [*Rises and unbuttons his coat*] And—nobody is really good who has not erred. [*Breathing heavily*] For in order to know how to forgive, one must have been in need of forgiveness—I had a friend whom we used to regard as a model man. He never spoke a hard word to anybody; he forgave everything and everybody; and he suffered insults with a strange satisfaction that we couldn't explain. At last, late in life, he gave me his secret in a single word: I am a penitent! [*He sits down again*]

[Henriette *remains silent, looking at him with surprise*]

ADOLPHE: [*As if speaking to himself*] There are crimes not mentioned in the Criminal Code, and these are the worse ones, for they have to be punished by ourselves, and no judge could be more severe than we are against our own selves.

HENRIETTE: [*After a pause*] Well, that friend of yours, did he find peace?

ADOLPHE: After endless self-torture he reached a certain degree of composure, but life had never any real pleasures to offer him. He never dared to accept any kind of distinction; he never dared to feel himself entitled to a kind word or even well-earned praise: in a word, he could never quite forgive himself.

HENRIETTE: Never? What had he done then?

ADOLPHE: He had wished the life out of his father. And when his father suddenly died, the son imagined himself to have killed him. Those imaginations were regarded as signs of some mental disease, and he was sent to an asylum. From this he was discharged after a time as wholly recovered—as they put it. But the sense of guilt remained with him, and so he continued to punish himself for his evil thoughts.

HENRIETTE: Are you sure the evil will cannot kill?

ADOLPHE: You mean in some mystic way?

HENRIETTE: As you please. Let it go at mystic. In my own family—I am sure that my mother and my sisters killed my father with their hatred. You see, he had the awful idea that he must oppose all our tastes and inclinations. Wherever he discovered a natural gift, he tried to root it out. In that way he aroused a resistance that accumulated until it became like an electrical battery charged with hatred. At last it grew so powerful that he languished away, became depolarised, lost his will-power, and, in the end, came to wish himself dead.

ADOLPHE: And your conscience never troubled you?

HENRIETTE: No, and furthermore, I don't know what conscience is.

ADOLPHE: You don't? Well, then you'll soon learn. [*Pause*] How do you believe Maurice will look when he gets here? What do you think he will say?

HENRIETTE: Yesterday morning, you know, he and I tried to make the same kind of guess about you while we were waiting for you.

ADOLPHE: Well?

HENRIETTE: We guessed entirely wrong.

ADOLPHE: Can you tell me why you sent for me?

HENRIETTE: Malice, arrogance, outright cruelty!

ADOLPHE: How strange it is that you can admit your faults and yet not repent of them.

HENRIETTE: It must be because I don't feel quite responsible for them. They are like the dirt left behind by things handled during the day and washed off at night. But tell me one thing: do you really think so highly of humanity as you profess to do?

ADOLPHE: Yes, we are a little better than our reputation—and a little worse.

HENRIETTE: That is not a straightforward answer.

ADOLPHE: No, it isn't. But are you willing to answer me frankly when I ask you: do you still love Maurice?

HENRIETTE: I cannot tell until I see him. But at this moment I feel no longing for him, and it seems as if I could very well live without him.

ADOLPHE: It's likely you could, but I fear you have become chained to his fate—Sh! Here he comes.

HENRIETTE: How everything repeats itself. The situation is the same, the very words are the same, as when we were expecting you yesterday.

MAURICE: [Enters, pale as death, hollow-eyed, unshaven] Here I am, my dear friends, if this be me. For that last night in a cell changed me into a new sort of being.

[Notices Henriette and Adolphe]

ADOLPHE: Sit down and pull yourself together, and then we can talk things over.

MAURICE: [To Henriette] Perhaps I am in the way?

ADOLPHE: Now don't get bitter.

MAURICE: I have grown bad in these twenty-four hours, and suspicious also, so I guess I'll soon be left to myself. And who wants to keep company with a murderer?

HENRIETTE: But you have been cleared of the charge.

MAURICE: [Picks up a newspaper] By the police, yes, but not by public opinion. Here you see the murderer Maurice Gérard, once a playwright, and his mistress, Henriette Mauclerc——

HENRIETTE: O my mother and my sisters—my mother! Jesus, have mercy!

MAURICE: And can you see that I actually look like a murderer? And then it is suggested that my play was stolen. So there isn't a vestige left of the victorious hero from yesterday. In place of my own, the name of Octave, my enemy, appears on the bill-boards, and he is going to collect my one hundred thousand francs. O Solon, Solon! Such is fortune, and such is fame! You are fortunate, Adolphe, because you have not yet succeeded.

HENRIETTE: So you don't know that Adolphe has made a great success in London and carried off the first prize?

MAURICE: [Darkly] No, I didn't know that. Is it true, Adolphe?

ADOLPHE: It is true, but I have returned the prize.

HENRIETTE: [With emphasis] That I didn't know! So you are also prevented from accepting any distinction—like your friend?

ADOLPHE: My friend? [Embarrassed] Oh, yes, yes!

MAURICE: Your success gives me pleasure, but it puts us still farther apart.

ADOLPHE: That's what I expected, and I suppose I'll be as lonely with my success as you with your adversity. Think of it—that people feel hurt by your fortune! Oh, it's ghastly to be alive!

MAURICE: You say that! What am I then to say? It is as if my eyes had been covered with a black veil, and as if the colour and shape of all life had been changed by it. This room looks like the room I saw yesterday, and yet it is quite different. I recognise both of you, of course, but your faces are new to me. I sit here and search for words because I don't know what to say to you. I ought to defend myself, but I cannot. And I almost miss the cell, for it protected me, at least, against the curious glances that pass right through me. The murderer Maurice and his mistress. You don't love me any longer, Henriette, and no more do I care for you. To-day you are ugly, clumsy, insipid, repulsive.

[Two men in civilian clothes have quietly seated themselves at a table in the background]

ADOLPHE: Wait a little and get your thoughts together. That you have been discharged and cleared of all suspicion must appear in some of the evening papers. And that puts an end to the whole matter. Your play will be put on again, and if it comes to the worst, you can write a new one. Leave Paris for a year and let everything become forgotten. You who have exonerated mankind will be exonerated yourself.

MAURICE: Ha-ha! Mankind! Ha-ha!

ADOLPHE: You have ceased to believe in goodness!

MAURICE: Yes, if I ever did believe in it. Perhaps it was only a mood, a manner of looking at things, a way of being polite to the wild beasts. When I, who was held among the best, can be so rotten to the core, what must then be the wretchedness of the rest?

ADOLPHE: Now I'll go out and get all the evening papers, and then we'll undoubtedly have reason to look at things in a different way.

MAURICE: [Turning towards the background] Two detectives!—It means that I am released under surveillance, so that I can give myself away by careless talking.

ADOLPHE: Those are not detectives. That's only your imagination. I recognise both of them. [Goes towards the door]

MAURICE: Don't leave us alone, Adolphe. I fear that Henriette and I may come to open explanations.

ADOLPHE: Oh, be sensible, Maurice, and think of your future. Try to keep him quiet, Henriette. I'll be back in a moment. [Goes out]

HENRIETTE: Well, Maurice, what do you think now of our guilt or guiltlessness?

MAURICE: I have killed nobody. All I did was to talk a lot of nonsense while I was drunk. But it is your crime that comes back, and that crime you have grafted on to me.

HENRIETTE: Oh, that's the tone you talk now!— Was it not you who cursed your own child, and wished the life out of it, and wanted to go away without saying good-bye to anybody? And was it not I who made you visit Marion and show yourself to Madame Catherine?

MAURICE: Yes, you are right. Forgive me! You proved yourself more human than I, and the guilt is wholly my own. Forgive me! But all the same I am without guilt. Who has tied this net from which I can never free myself? Guilty and guiltless: guiltless and yet guilty! Oh, it is driving me mad— Look, now they sit over there and listen to us— And no waiter comes to take our order. I'll go out and order a cup of tea. Do you want anything?

HENRIETTE: Nothing.

[Maurice goes out]

FIRST DETECTIVE: [Goes up to Henriette] Let me look at your papers.

HENRIETTE: How dare you speak to me?

DETECTIVE: Dare? I'll show you!

HENRIETTE: What do you mean?

DETECTIVE: It's my job to keep an eye on street-walkers. Yesterday you came here with one man, and to-day with another. That's as good as walking the streets. And unescorted ladies don't get anything here. So you'd better get out and come along with me.

HENRIETTE: My escort will be back in a moment.

DETECTIVE: Yes, and a pretty kind of escort you've got—the kind that doesn't help a girl a bit!

HENRIETTE: O God! My mother, my sisters!— I am of good family, I tell you.

DETECTIVE: Yes, first-rate family, I am sure. But you are too well known through the papers. Come along!

HENRIETTE: Where? What do you mean?

DETECTIVE: Oh, to the Bureau, of course. There you'll get a nice little card and a license that brings you free medical care.

HENRIETTE: O Lord Jesus, you don't mean it!

DETECTIVE: [Grabbing Henriette by the arm] Don't I mean it?

HENRIETTE: [Falling on her knees] Save me, Maurice! Help!

DETECTIVE: Shut up, you fool!

[Maurice enters, followed by Waiter]

WAITER: Gentlemen of that kind are not served here. You just pay and get out! And take the girl along!

MAURICE: [Crushed, searches his pocket-book for money] Henriette, pay for me, and let us get away from this place. I haven't a sou left.

WAITER: So the lady has to put up for her Alphonse! Alphonse! Do you know what that is?

HENRIETTE: [Looking through her pocket-book] Oh, merciful heavens! I have no money either!— Why doesn't Adolphe come back?

DETECTIVE: Well, did you ever see such rotters! Get out of here, and put up something as security. That kind of ladies generally have their fingers full of rings.

MAURICE: Can it be possible that we have sunk so low?

HENRIETTE: [Takes off a ring and hands it to the Waiter] The Abbé was right: this is not the work of man.

MAURICE: No, it's the devil's!— But if we leave before Adolphe returns, he will think that we have deceived him and run away.

HENRIETTE: That would be in keeping with the rest— But we'll go into the river now, won't we?

MAURICE: [Takes Henriette by the hand as they walk out together] Into the river—yes!

CURTAIN

ACT IV. SCENE I.

In the Luxembourg Gardens, at the group of Adam and Eve. The wind is shaking the trees and stirring up dead leaves, straws, and pieces of paper from the ground. Maurice and Henriette are seated on a bench.

HENRIETTE: So you don't want to die?

MAURICE: No, I am afraid. I imagine that I am going to be very cold down there in the grave, with only a sheet to cover me and a few shavings to lie on. And besides that, it seems to me as if there were still some task waiting for me, but I cannot make out what it is.

HENRIETTE: But I can guess what it is.

MAURICE: Tell me.

HENRIETTE: It is revenge. You, like me, must have suspected Jeanne and Emile of sending the detectives after me yesterday. Such a revenge on a rival none but a woman could devise.

MAURICE: Exactly what I was thinking. But let me tell you that my suspicions go even further. It seems as if my sufferings during these last few days had sharpened my wits. Can you explain, for instance, why the waiter from the Auberge des Adrets and the head waiter from the Pavilion were not called to testify at the hearing?

HENRIETTE: I never thought of it before. But now I know why. They had nothing to tell, because they had not been listening.

MAURICE: But how could the Commissaire then know what we had been saying?

HENRIETTE: He didn't know, but he figured it out.

He was guessing, and he guessed right. Perhaps he had had to deal with some similar case before.

MAURICE: Or else he concluded from our looks what we had been saying. There are those who can read other people's thoughts— Adolphe being the dupe, it seemed quite natural that we should have called him an ass. It's the rule, I understand, although it's varied at times by the use of "idiot" instead. But ass was nearer at hand in this case, as we had been talking of carriages and triumphal chariots. It is quite simple to figure out a fourth fact, when you have three known ones to start from.

HENRIETTE: Just think that we have let ourselves be taken in so completely.

MAURICE: That's the result of thinking too well of one's fellow beings. This is all you get out of it. But do you know, I suspect somebody else behind the Commissaire, who, by the by, must be a full-fledged scoundrel.

HENRIETTE: You mean the Abbé, who was taking the part of a private detective.

MAURICE: That's what I mean. That man has to receive all kinds of confessions. And note you: Adolphe himself told us he had been at the Church of St. Germain that morning. What was he doing there? He was blabbing, of course, and bewailing his fate. And then the priest put the questions together for the Commissaire.

HENRIETTE: Tell me something: do you trust Adolphe?

MAURICE: I trust no human being any longer.

HENRIETTE: Not even Adolphe?

MAURICE: Him least of all. How could I trust an enemy—a man from whom I have taken away his mistress?

HENRIETTE: Well, as you were the first one to speak of this, I'll give you some data about our friend. You heard he had returned that medal from London. Do you know his reason for doing so?

MAURICE: No.

HENRIETTE: He thinks himself unworthy of it, and he has taken a penitential vow never to receive any kind of distinction.

MAURICE: Can that be possible? But what has he done?

HENRIETTE: He has committed a crime of the kind that is not punishable under the law. That's what he gave me to understand indirectly.

MAURICE: He, too! He, the best one of all, the model man, who never speaks a hard word of anybody and who forgives everything.

HENRIETTE: Well, there you can see that we are no worse than others. And yet we are being hounded day and night as if devils were after us.

MAURICE: He, also! Then mankind has not been slandered— But if he has been capable of *one* crime, then you may expect anything of him. Perhaps it was he who sent the police after you yesterday. Coming to think of it now, it was he who sneaked away from us when he saw that we were in the papers, and he lied when he insisted that those fellows were not detectives. But, of course, you may expect anything from a deceived lover.

HENRIETTE: Could he be as mean as that? No, it is impossible, impossible!

MAURICE: Why so? If he is a scoundrel?— What were you two talking of yesterday, before I came?

HENRIETTE: He had nothing but good to say of you.

MAURICE: That's a lie!

HENRIETTE: [*Controlling herself and changing her tone*] Listen. There is one person on whom you have cast no suspicion whatever—for what reason, I don't know. Have you thought of Madame Catherine's wavering attitude in this matter? Didn't she say finally that she believed you capable of anything?

MAURICE: Yes, she did, and that shows what kind of person she is. To think evil of other people without reason, you must be a villain yourself.

[Henriette *looks hard at him. Pause*]

HENRIETTE: To think evil of others, you must be a villain yourself.

MAURICE: What do you mean?

HENRIETTE: What I said.

MAURICE: Do you mean that I——?

HENRIETTE: Yes, that's what I mean now! Look here! Did you meet anybody but Marion when you called there yesterday morning?

MAURICE: Why do you ask?

HENRIETTE: Guess!

MAURICE: Well, as you seem to know—I met Jeanne, too.

HENRIETTE: Why did you lie to me?

MAURICE: I wanted to spare you.

HENRIETTE: And now you want me to believe in one who has been lying to me? No, my boy, now I believe you guilty of that murder.

MAURICE: Wait a moment! We have now reached the place for which my thoughts have been heading all the time, though I resisted as long as possible. It's queer that what lies next to one is seen last of all, and what one doesn't *want* to believe cannot be believed— Tell me something: where did you go yesterday, after we parted in the Bois?

HENRIETTE: [*Alarmed*] Why?

MAURICE: You went either to Adolphe—which you couldn't do, as he was attending a lesson—or you went to—Marion!

HENRIETTE: Now I am convinced that you are the murderer.

MAURICE: And I, that you are the murderess! You alone had an interest in getting the child out of the way—to get rid of the rock on the road, as you so aptly put it.

HENRIETTE: It was you who said that.

MAURICE: And the one who had an interest in it must have committed the crime.

HENRIETTE: Now, Maurice, we have been running around and around in this tread-mill, scourging each other. Let us quit before we get to the point of sheer madness.

MAURICE: You have reached that point already.

HENRIETTE: Don't you think it's time for us to part, before we drive each other insane?

MAURICE: Yes, I think so.

HENRIETTE: [*Rising*] Good-bye then!

[*Two men in civilian clothes become visible in the background*]

HENRIETTE: [*Turns and comes back to* Maurice] There they are again!

MAURICE: The dark angels that want to drive us out of the garden.

HENRIETTE: And force us back upon each other as if we were chained together.

MAURICE: Or as if we were condemned to lifelong marriage. Are we really to marry? To settle down in the same place? To be able to close the door behind us and perhaps get peace at last?

HENRIETTE: And shut ourselves up in order to torture each other to death; get behind locks and bolts, with a ghost for marriage portion; you torturing me with the memory of Adolphe, and I getting back at you with Jeanne—and Marion.

MAURICE: Never mention the name of Marion again! Don't you know that she was to be buried to-day—at this very moment perhaps?

HENRIETTE: And you are not there? What does that mean?

MAURICE: It means that both Jeanne and the police have warned me against the rage of the people.

HENRIETTE: A coward, too?

MAURICE: All the vices! How could you ever have cared for me?

HENRIETTE: Because two days ago you were another person, well worthy of being loved——

MAURICE: And now sunk to such a depth!

HENRIETTE: It isn't that. But you are beginning to flaunt bad qualities which are not your own.

MAURICE: But yours?

HENRIETTE: Perhaps, for when you appear a little worse I feel at once a little better.

MAURICE: It's like passing on a disease to save one's self-respect.

HENRIETTE: And how vulgar you have become, too!

MAURICE: Yes, I notice it myself, and I hardly recognise myself since that night in the cell. They put in one person and let out another through that gate which separates us from the rest of society. And now I feel myself the enemy of all mankind: I should like to set fire to the earth and dry up the oceans, for nothing less than a universal conflagration can wipe out my dishonour.

HENRIETTE: I had a letter from my mother to-day. She is the widow of a major in the army, well educated, with old-fashioned ideas of honour and that kind of thing. Do you want to read the letter? No, you don't!— Do you know that I am an outcast? My respectable acquaintances will have noth-

ing to do with me, and if I show myself on the streets alone the police will take me. Do you realise now that we have to get married?

MAURICE: We despise each other, and yet we have to marry: that is hell pure and simple! But, Henriette, before we unite our destinies you must tell me your secret, so that we may be on more equal terms.

HENRIETTE: All right, I'll tell you. I had a friend who got into trouble—you understand. I wanted to help her, as her whole future was at stake—and she died!

MAURICE: That was reckless, but one might almost call it noble, too.

HENRIETTE: You say so now, but the next time you lose your temper you will accuse me of it.

MAURICE: No, I won't. But I cannot deny that it has shaken my faith in you and that it makes me afraid of you. Tell me, is her lover still alive, and does he know to what extent you were responsible?

HENRIETTE: He was as guilty as I.

MAURICE: And if his conscience should begin to trouble him—such things do happen—and if he should feel inclined to confess: then you would be lost.

HENRIETTE: I know it, and it is this constant dread which has made me rush from one dissipation to another—so that I should never have time to wake up to full consciousness.

MAURICE: And now you want me to take my marriage portion out of your dread. That's asking a little too much.

HENRIETTE: But when I shared the shame of Maurice the murderer——

MAURICE: Oh, let's come to an end with it!

HENRIETTE: No, the end is not yet, and I'll not let go my hold until I have put you where you belong. For you can't go around thinking yourself better than I am.

MAURICE: So you want to fight me then? All right, as you please!

HENRIETTE: A fight of life and death!

[*The rolling of drums is heard in the distance*]

MAURICE: The garden is to be closed. "Cursed is the ground for thy sake; thorns and thistles shall it bring forth to thee."

HENRIETTE: "And the Lord God said unto the woman——"

A GUARD: [*In uniform, speaking very politely*] Sorry, but the garden has to be closed.

CURTAIN

SCENE II.

The Crêmerie. Mme. Catherine *is sitting at the counter making entries into an account book.* Adolphe *and* Henriette *are seated at a table.*

ADOLPHE: [*Calmly and kindly*] But if I give you my final assurance that I didn't run away, but that, on the contrary, I thought you had played me false, this ought to convince you.

HENRIETTE: But why did you fool us by saying that those fellows were not policemen?

ADOLPHE: I didn't think myself that they were, and then I wanted to reassure you.

HENRIETTE: When you say it, I believe you. But then you must also believe me, if I reveal my innermost thoughts to you.

ADOLPHE: Go on.

HENRIETTE: But you mustn't come back with your usual talk of fancies and delusions.

ADOLPHE: You seem to have reason to fear that I may.

HENRIETTE: I fear nothing, but I know you and your scepticism— Well, and then you mustn't tell this to anybody—promise me!

ADOLPHE: I promise.

HENRIETTE: Now think of it, although I must say it's something terrible: I have partial evidence that Maurice is guilty, or at least, I have reasonable suspicions——

ADOLPHE: You don't mean it!

HENRIETTE: Listen, and judge for yourself. When Maurice left me in the Bois, he said he was going to see Marion alone, as the mother was out. And now I have discovered afterwards that he did meet the mother. So that he has been lying to me.

ADOLPHE: That's possible, and his motive for doing so may have been the best, but how can anybody conclude from it that he is guilty of a murder?

HENRIETTE: Can't you see that?— Don't you understand?

ADOLPHE: Not at all.

HENRIETTE: Because you don't want to!— Then there is nothing left for me but to report him, and we'll see whether he can prove an alibi.

ADOLPHE: Henriette, let me tell you the grim truth. You, like he, have reached the border-line of —insanity. The demons of distrust have got hold of you, and each of you is using his own sense of partial guilt to wound the other with. Let me see if I can make a straight guess: he has also come to suspect you of killing his child?

HENRIETTE: Yes, he's mad enough to do so.

ADOLPHE: You call his suspicions mad, but not your own.

HENRIETTE: You have first to prove the contrary, or that I suspect him unjustly.

ADOLPHE: Yes, that's easy. A new autopsy has proved that Marion died of a well-known disease, the queer name of which I cannot recall just now.

HENRIETTE: Is it true?

ADOLPHE: The official report is printed in to-day's paper.

HENRIETTE: I don't take any stock of it. They can make up that kind of thing.

ADOLPHE: Beware, Henriette—or you may, without knowing it, pass across that border line. Beware especially of throwing out accusations that may put you into prison. Beware! [*He places his hand on her head*] You hate Maurice?

HENRIETTE: Beyond all bounds!

ADOLPHE: When love turns into hatred, it means that it was tainted from the start.

HENRIETTE: [*In a quieter mood*] What am I to do? Tell me, you who are the only one that understands me.

ADOLPHE: But you don't want any sermons.

HENRIETTE: Have you nothing else to offer me?

ADOLPHE: Nothing else. But they have helped me.

HENRIETTE: Preach away then!

ADOLPHE: Try to turn your hatred against yourself. Put the knife to the evil spot in yourself, for it is there that *your* trouble roots.

HENRIETTE: Explain yourself.

ADOLPHE: Part from Maurice first of all, so that you cannot nurse your qualms of conscience together. Break off your career as an artist, for the only thing that led you into it was a craving for freedom and fun—as they call it. And you have seen how much fun there is in it. Then go home to your mother.

HENRIETTE: Never!

ADOLPHE: Some other place then.

HENRIETTE: I suppose you know, Adolphe, that I have guessed your secret and why you wouldn't accept the prize?

ADOLPHE: Oh, I assumed that you would understand a half-told story.

HENRIETTE: Well—what did you do to get peace?

ADOLPHE: What I have suggested: I became conscious of my guilt, repented, decided to turn over a new leaf, and arranged my life like that of a penitent.

HENRIETTE: How can you repent when, like me, you have no conscience? Is repentance an act of grace bestowed on you as faith is?

ADOLPHE: Everything is a grace, but it isn't granted unless you seek it— Seek!

[Henriette *remains silent*]

ADOLPHE: But don't wait beyond the allotted time, or you may harden yourself until you tumble down into the irretrievable.

HENRIETTE: [*After a pause*] Is conscience fear of punishment?

ADOLPHE: No, it is the horror inspired in our better selves by the misdeeds of our lower selves.

HENRIETTE: Then I must have a conscience also?

ADOLPHE: Of course you have, but——

HENRIETTE: Tell me, Adolphe, are you what they call religious?

ADOLPHE: Not the least bit.

HENRIETTE: It's all so queer— What is religion?

ADOLPHE: Frankly speaking, I don't know! And I don't think anybody else can tell you. Sometimes it appears to me like a punishment, for nobody becomes religious without having a bad conscience.

HENRIETTE: Yes, it is a punishment. Now I know what to do. Good-bye, Adolphe!

ADOLPHE: You'll go away from here?

HENRIETTE: Yes, I am going—to where you said. Good-bye my friend! Good-bye, Madame Catherine!

MME. CATHERINE: Have you to go in such a hurry?

HENRIETTE: Yes.

ADOLPHE: Do you want me to go with you?

HENRIETTE: No, it wouldn't do. I am going alone, alone as I came here, one day in Spring, thinking that I belonged where I don't belong, and believing there was something called freedom, which does not exist. Good-bye! [*Goes out*]

MME. CATHERINE: I hope that lady never comes back, and I wish she had never come here at all!

ADOLPHE: Who knows but that she may have had some mission to fill here? And at any rate she deserves pity, endless pity.

MME. CATHERINE: I don't deny it, for all of us deserve that.

ADOLPHE: And she has even done less wrong than the rest of us.

MME. CATHERINE: That's possible, but not probable.

ADOLPHE: You are always so severe, Madame Catherine. Tell me: have you never done anything wrong?

MME. CATHERINE: [*Startled*] Of course, as I am a sinful human creature. But if you have been on thin ice and fallen in, you have a right to tell others to keep away. And you may do so without being held severe or uncharitable. Didn't I say to Monsieur Maurice the moment that lady entered here: Look out! Keep away! And he didn't, and so he fell in. Just like a naughty, self-willed child. And when a man acts like that he has to have a spanking, like any disobedient youngster.

ADOLPHE: Well, hasn't he had his spanking?

MME. CATHERINE: Yes, but it does not seem to have been enough, as he is still going around complaining.

ADOLPHE: That's a very popular interpretation of the whole intricate question.

MME. CATHERINE: Oh, pish! You do nothing but philosophise about your vices, and while you are still at it the police come along and solve the riddle. Now please leave me alone with my accounts!

ADOLPHE: There's Maurice now.

MME. CATHERINE: Yes, God bless him!

MAURICE: [*Enters, his face very flushed, and takes a seat near* Adolphe] Good evening.

[Mme. Catherine *nods and goes on figuring*]

ADOLPHE: Well, how's everything with you?

MAURICE: Oh, beginning to clear up.

ADOLPHE: [*Hands him a newspaper, which* Maurice *does not take*] So you have read the paper?

MAURICE: No, I don't read the papers any longer. There's nothing but infamies in them.

ADOLPHE: But you had better read it first——

MAURICE: No, I don't! It's nothing but lies— But listen: I have found a new clue. Can you guess who committed that murder?

ADOLPHE: Nobody, nobody!

MAURICE: Do you know where Henriette was during that quarter hour when the child was left alone?— She was *there!* And it is she who has done it!

ADOLPHE: You are crazy, man.

MAURICE: Not I, but Henriette, is crazy. She suspects me and has threatened to report me.

ADOLPHE: Henriette was here a while ago, and she used the self-same words as you. Both of you are crazy, for it has been proved by a second autopsy that the child died from a well-known disease, the name of which I have forgotten.

MAURICE: It isn't true!

ADOLPHE: That's what she said also. But the official report is printed in the paper.

MAURICE: A report? Then they have made it up!

ADOLPHE: And that's also what she said. The two of you are suffering from the same mental trouble. But with her I got far enough to make her realise her own condition.

MAURICE: Where did she go?

ADOLPHE: She went far away from here to begin a new life.

MAURICE: Hm, hm!— Did you go to the funeral?

ADOLPHE: I did.

MAURICE: Well?

ADOLPHE: Well, Jeanne seemed resigned and didn't have a hard word to say about you.

MAURICE: She is a good woman.

ADOLPHE: Why did you desert her then?

MAURICE: Because I *was* crazy—blown up with pride especially—and then we had been drinking champagne——

ADOLPHE: Can you understand now why Jeanne wept when you drank champagne?

MAURICE: Yes, I understand now— And for that reason I have already written to her and asked her to forgive me— Do you think she will forgive me?

ADOLPHE: I think so, for it's not like her to hate anybody.

MAURICE: Do you think she will forgive me completely, so that she will come back to me?

ADOLPHE: Well, I don't know about *that*. You have shown yourself so poor in keeping faith that it is doubtful whether she will trust her fate to you any longer.

MAURICE: But I can feel that her fondness for me has not ceased, and I know she will come back to me.

ADOLPHE: How can you know that? How can you believe it? Didn't you even suspect her and that decent brother of hers of having sent the police after Henriette out of revenge?

MAURICE: But I don't believe it any longer—that is to say, I guess that fellow Emile is a pretty slick customer.

MME. CATHERINE: Now look here! What are you saying of Monsieur Emile? Of course, he is nothing but a workman, but if everybody kept as straight as he— There is no flaw in him, but a lot of sense and tact.

EMILE: [*Enters*] Monsieur Gérard?

MAURICE: That's me.

EMILE: Pardon me, but I have something to say to you in private.

MAURICE: Go right on. We are all friends here.

[*The* Abbé *enters and sits down*]

EMILE: [*With a glance at the* Abbé] Perhaps after——

MAURICE: Never mind. The Abbé is also a friend, although he and I differ.

EMILE: You know who I am, Monsieur Gérard? My sister has asked me to give you this package as an answer to your letter.

[Maurice *takes the package and opens it*]

EMILE: And now I have only to add, seeing as I am in a way my sister's guardian, that, on her behalf as well as my own, I acknowledge you free of all obligations, now when the natural tie between you does not exist any longer.

MAURICE: But you must have a grudge against me?

EMILE: Must I? I can't see why. On the other hand, I should like to have a declaration from you, here in the presence of your friends, that you don't think either me or my sister capable of such a meanness as to send the police after Mademoiselle Henriette.

MAURICE: I wish to take back what I said, and I offer you my apology, if you will accept it.

EMILE: It is accepted. And I wish all of you a good evening. [*Goes out*]

EVERYBODY: Good evening!

MAURICE: The tie and the gloves which Jeanne gave me for the opening night of my play, and which I let Henriette throw into the fireplace. Who can have picked them up? Everything is dug up; everything comes back!— And when she gave them to me in the cemetery, she said she wanted me to look fine and handsome, so that other people would like me also— And she herself stayed at home— This hurt her too deeply, and well it might. I have no right to keep company with decent human beings. Oh, have I done this? Scoffed at a gift coming from a good heart; scorned a sacrifice offered to my own welfare. This was what I threw away in order to get —a laurel that is lying on the rubbish heap, and a bust that would have belonged in the pillory—Abbé, now I come over to you.

ABBÉ: Welcome!

MAURICE: Give me the word that I need.

ABBÉ: Do you expect me to contradict your self-accusations and inform you that you have done nothing wrong?

MAURICE: Speak the right word!

ABBÉ: With your leave, I'll say then that I have found your behaviour just as abominable as you have found it yourself.

MAURICE: What can I do, what can I do, to get out of this?

ABBÉ: You know as well as I do.

MAURICE: No, I only know that I am lost, that my life is spoiled, my career cut off, my reputation in this world ruined for ever.

ABBÉ: And so you are looking for a new existence in some better world, which you are now beginning to believe in?

MAURICE: Yes, that's it.

ABBÉ: You have been living in the flesh and you want now to live in the spirit. Are you then so sure that this world has no more attractions for you?

MAURICE: None whatever! Honour is a phantom; gold, nothing but dry leaves; women, mere intoxicants. Let me hide myself behind your consecrated walls and forget this horrible dream that has filled two days and lasted two eternities.

ABBÉ: All right! But this is not the place to go into the matter more closely. Let us make an appointment for this evening at nine o'clock in the Church of St. Germain. For I am going to preach to the inmates of St. Lazare, and that may be your first step along the hard road of penitence.

MAURICE: Penitence?

ABBÉ: Well, didn't you wish——

MAURICE: Yes, yes!

ABBÉ: Then we have vigils between midnight and two o'clock.

MAURICE: That will be splendid!

ABBÉ: Give me your hand that you will not look back.

MAURICE: [*Rising, holds out his hand*] Here is my hand, and my will goes with it.

SERVANT GIRL: [*Enters from the kitchen*] A telephone call for Monsieur Maurice.

MAURICE: From whom?

SERVANT GIRL: From the theatre.

[Maurice *tries to get away, but the* Abbé *holds on to his hand*]

ABBÉ: [*To the* Servant Girl] Find out what it is.

SERVANT GIRL: They want to know if Monsieur Maurice is going to attend the performance to-night.

ABBÉ: [*To* Maurice, *who is trying to get away*] No, I won't let you go.

MAURICE: What performance is that?

ADOLPHE: Why don't you read the paper?

MME. CATHERINE AND THE ABBÉ: He hasn't read the paper?

MAURICE: It's all lies and slander. [*To the* Servant Girl] Tell them that I am engaged for this evening: I am going to church.

[*The* Servant Girl *goes out into the kitchen*]

ADOLPHE: As you don't want to read the paper, I shall have to tell you that your play has been put on again, now when you are exonerated. And your literary friends have planned a demonstration for this evening in recognition of your indisputable talent.

MAURICE: It isn't true.

EVERYBODY: It is true.

MAURICE: [*After a pause*] I have not deserved it!

ABBÉ: Good!

ADOLPHE: And, furthermore, Maurice——

MAURICE: [*Hiding his face in his hands*] Furthermore!

MME. CATHERINE: One hundred thousand francs! Do you see now that they come back to you? And the villa outside the city. Everything is coming back except Mademoiselle Henriette.

ABBÉ: [*Smiling*] You ought to take this matter a little more seriously, Madame Catherine.

MME. CATHERINE: Oh, I cannot—I just can't keep serious any longer! [*She breaks into open laughter, which she vainly tries to smother with her handkerchief*]

ADOLPHE: Say, Maurice, the play begins at eight.

ABBÉ: But the church services are at nine.

ADOLPHE: Maurice!

MME. CATHERINE: Let us hear what the end is going to be, Monsieur Maurice.

[*Maurice drops his head on the table, in his arms*]

ADOLPHE: Loose him, Abbé.

ABBÉ: No, it is not for me to loose or bind. He must do that himself.

MAURICE: [*Rising*] Well, I go with the Abbé.

ABBÉ: No, my young friend. I have nothing to give you but a scolding, which you can give yourself. And you owe a duty to yourself and to your good name. That you have got through with this as quickly as you have is to me a sign that you have suffered your punishment as intensely as if it had lasted an eternity. And when Providence absolves you there is nothing for me to add.

MAURICE: But why did the punishment have to be so hard when I was innocent?

ABBÉ: Hard? Only two days! And you were not innocent. For we have to stand responsible for our thoughts and words and desires also. And in your thought you became a murderer when your evil self wished the life out of your child.

MAURICE: You are right. But my decision is made. To-night I will meet you at the church in order to have a reckoning with myself—but to-morrow evening I go to the theatre.

MME. CATHERINE: A good solution, Monsieur Maurice.

ADOLPHE: Yes, that is the solution. Whew!

ABBÉ: Yes, so it is!

CURTAIN

Ferenc Molnar

(1878–)

During the last two decades of its existence, the Austrian-Hungarian Empire teemed with theatrical activity, and Vienna and Budapest were the Mecca and Medina toward which Americans turned their faces whenever they longed for gay times and even gayer plays. The old Empire was tottering in a gavotte that was extremely attractive to those who fancied themselves connoisseurs of good living. In Vienna were to be found facile poet laureates of the gay life. In Vienna, too, resided Arthur Schnitzler (1862–1931), a playwright and novelist of great penetration who brought a physician's mind to bear on the perpetual Mardi gras of the capital of the Hapsburgs. The sister capital, Budapest, even brighter and more colorful, harbored a great number of playwrights (Biro, Lengyel, Herczeg, Vajda, Fodor, and others) who distilled the elixir of *amour* for well-edified audiences. One man of letters and man of the world, however, led all the rest in cunning and theatrical virtuosity, Ferenc Molnár. Celebrated as a *bon vivant* of the old continental school and as a blithe contriver of plays, he became the symbol of "sophistication," if not indeed the culture hero of the Austro-Hungarian upper classes and intellectuals.

Molnár, a native of Budapest, was the son of an affluent merchant family and enjoyed every advantage that wealth and social position could provide. Well educated, handsome, witty, and charming, he quickly drew attention to himself when, abandoning the legal profession for which he had been trained, he turned to journalism and began to publish stories and novels. A number of these were merely entertaining, but one novel, *The Paul Street Boys* (1907), was a simple and warm study of adolescence in Budapest. Its author's facility for drama, however, soon overshadowed his talent for fiction; and his private life, celebrated for its numerous affairs of the heart, was as exciting and entertaining as fiction for his contemporaries. His many social accomplishments, witty conversation, romantic encounters, and pranks furnished Budapest with much of its gossip for more than two decades. He continued to entrance his countrymen even after the First World War had dampened their spirits. When he settled in America just before the outbreak of the Second World War, he could also count on many American admirers. His reputation had preceded him. Better still, his plays had preceded him. A number of them —especially, *The Guardsman, The Play's the Thing, The Glass Slipper,* and, above all, *Liliom*—had made him one of New York's most successful and highly regarded playwrights by adoption. And in the country that welcomed him he could console himself for the failure of his new plays with the successful revival of *The Play's the Thing* and the attractive musical-comedy transmutation of *Liliom* by Rodgers and Hammerstein into *Carousel.*

Molnár's ability to treat upper- and lower-class life with equal charm made his career as a playwright an almost continuous triumph before 1920. Some of his plays were intentionally frothy. Others mingled realism with generous doses of sentimentality and romanticism. In some plays, Molnár played at fantasy, generally with a view to making a piquant situation still more piquant, as when he brought Mephistopheles into his first successful play, *The Devil* (1907), in order to facilitate some fashionable adultery. He flavored intrigue with much worldly shrewdness and breezy cynicism, as in his ingenious comedy *The Guardsman* (1910), which Alfred Lunt and Lynn Fontanne turned into a sparkling article for Broadway and the screen.

Molnár's flair for comedy of manners seemed inexhaustible. It was no less in evidence when he treated royalty, as in *The Swan* (1920), than when he bestowed his interest on the artists, professional and business classes, and the common folk of the Hungarian capital. Nor could he be charged with deficient sympathy in spite of his wit and his fondness for exploiting the foibles of men and women. Goodness and innocence of heart attracted him immensely, even though he made it look like an idiosyncrasy in a world not remarkable for saintliness. Naïveté and the dreams of little people received a ready, if not altogether unpatronizing, sympathy from him in a work like *The Glass Slipper* (1924), which recounts the adventures of a boarding-house drudge who plays Cinderella to a cabinetmaker elevated in her imagination to the role of Prince Charming. Molnár was, indeed, both the Noel Coward and James M. Barrie of the Central European stage. And he filled both roles with equal ingenuity, a dash of irony, considerable skepticism, and an inexhaustibly sanguine temperament. Theatre for him was not life itself—merely its bouquet.

Molnár will be remembered mainly for his *Liliom,* a work of no great profundity, it is true, but his one successful play that is permeated with a serious view of life. (Another serious drama, *The Miracle in the Mountain,* was unsuccessful.) It was written in 1909 after his divorce from his first wife, who made the proceedings painful by charging that he had struck their little girl in a fit of anger. He was apparently bent upon dramatizing the contradictions of human nature as a way of discharging unhappy memories. Even in *Liliom,* however, Molnár did not suppress the theatrician in himself. His story of the good-for-nothing merry-go-round barker Liliom ("Lily" or worthless fellow in Hungarian) is a thoroughly theatricalized drama from the moment it opens with its "amusement-park pantomime." It settles down into a naturalistic drama, it is true, with the first scene, but it turns into a romantic fantasy. We may regard this part of the play as watered-down expressionism, if we wish, because its serio-comic heaven is conceived in terms suitable to the mentality of Liliom. But it is not Liliom's dream, since he is dead. It is a tour de force, a symbolic contrivance, invented to advance the author's thesis that behavior often contradicts intention. Liliom's fate after his death has the pathos of Molnár's wisdom which takes note of the failure of men to correct their errors, although he also purveys romantic exaltation through the devotion of Liliom's Julie. The fantasy also serves the purposes of characterization; it is the hypothesis by means of which Molnár reminds us that Liliom's behavior is rooted in his character. If he had a second chance to express the love and tenderness he feels, he would make a mess of life again. If he wanted to do good to his child, he would steal again, even if he had to steal a star from heaven. His love would be inarticulate and gauche even if the emissaries of the Lord were making it the final test of his character and were watching him.

Liliom confused its first audiences in Budapest; it was set down as a failure when produced in 1909. But when it was revived ten years later it was enthusiastically acclaimed and its fame spread rapidly thereafter. The play was produced in London (first under the title of *The Daisy*) in 1920 and 1926, and Paris saw it first in 1923. In New York, it had a memorable Theatre Guild production in 1920, with Joseph Schildkraut and Eva Le Gallienne in the roles of the shiftless Liliom and the faithful Julie. It was revived less successfully on Broadway in the spring of 1940, with Burgess Meredith and Ingrid Bergman in the leading parts, and it was reincarnated in *Carousel* in 1945.

BIBLIOGRAPHY: Frank W. Chandler, *Modern Continental Playwrights* (pp. 438–453), 1931; John Gassner, *Masters of the Drama* (pp. 478–481), 1940, 1945.

LILIOM

By Ferenc Molnár

TRANSLATED FROM THE HUNGARIAN BY BENJAMIN GLAZER

CHARACTERS

LILIOM	YOUNG HOLLUNDER	TWO PLAINCLOTHES POLICEMEN
JULIE	WOLF BEIFELD	TWO HEAVENLY POLICEMEN
MARIE	THE CARPENTER	THE RICHLY DRESSED MAN
MRS. MUSKAT	LINZMAN	THE POORLY DRESSED MAN
LOUISE	THE DOCTOR	THE GUARD
MRS. HOLLUNDER	THE MAGISTRATE	A SUBURBAN POLICEMAN
FICSUR	TWO MOUNTED POLICEMEN	

THE PROLOGUE

An amusement park on the outskirts of Budapest on a late afternoon in Spring. Barkers stand before the booths of the sideshows haranguing the passing crowd. The strident music of a calliope is heard; laughter, shouts, the scuffle of feet, the signal bells of a merry-go-round.

The merry-go-round is at center. Liliom *stands at the entrance, a cigarette in his mouth, coaxing the people in. The girls regard him with idolizing glances and screech with pleasure as he playfully pushes them through entrance. Now and then some girl's escort resents the familiarity, whereupon* Liliom's *demeanor becomes ugly and menacing, and the cowed escort slinks through the entrance behind his girl or contents himself with a muttered resentful comment.*

One girl hands Liliom *a red carnation; he rewards her with a bow and a smile. When the soldier who accompanies her protests,* Liliom *cows him with a fierce glance and a threatening gesture.* Marie *and* Julie *come out of the crowd and* Liliom *favors them with particular notice as they pass into the merry-go-round.*

Mrs. Muskat *comes out of the merry-go-round, bringing* Liliom *coffee and rolls.* Liliom *mounts the barker's stand at the entrance, where he is elevated over every one on the stage. Here he begins his harangue. Everybody turns toward him. The other booths are gradually deserted. The tumult makes it impossible for the audience to hear what he is saying, but every now and then some witticism of his provokes a storm of laughter which is audible above the din. Many people enter the merry-go-round. Here and there one catches a phrase "Room for one more on the zebra's back," "Which of you ladies?" "Ten heller for adults, five for children," "Step right up——"*

It is growing darker. A lamplighter crosses the stage, and begins unperturbedly lighting the colored gas-lamps. The whistle of a distant locomotive is heard. Suddenly the tumult ceases, the lights go out, and the curtain falls in darkness.

END OF PROLOGUE

SCENE I.

A lonely place in the park, half hidden by trees and shrubbery. Under a flowering acacia tree stands a painted wooden bench. From the distance, faintly, comes the tumult of the amusement park. It is the sunset of the same day.

When the curtain rises the stage is empty.

[Marie *enters quickly, pauses at center, and looks back*]

MARIE: Julie, Julie! [*There is no answer*] Do you hear me, Julie? Let her be! Come on. Let her be. [*Starts to go back*]

[Julie *enters, looks back angrily*]

JULIE: Did you ever hear of such a thing? What's the matter with the woman anyway?

MARIE: [*Looking back again*] Here she comes again.

JULIE: Let her come. I didn't do anything to her. All of a sudden she comes up to me and begins to raise a row.

MARIE: Here she is. Come on, let's run.

[*Tries to urge her off*]

JULIE: Run? I should say not. What would I want to run for? I'm not afraid of her.

MARIE: Oh, come on. She'll only start a fight.

JULIE: I'm going to stay right here. Let her *start* a fight.

MRS. MUSKAT: [*Entering*] What do you want to run away for? [*To* Julie] Don't worry. I won't eat you. But there's one thing I want to tell you, my dear. Don't let me catch you in my carousel again. I stand for a whole lot, I have to in my business. It makes no difference to me whether my customers are ladies or the likes of you—as long as they pay their money. But when a girl misbehaves herself on my carousel—out she goes. Do you understand?

JULIE: Are you talking to me?

MRS. MUSKAT: Yes, you! You—chambermaid, you! In my carousel——

JULIE: Who did anything in your old carousel? I paid my fare and took my seat and never said a word, except to my friend here.

MARIE: No, she never opened her mouth. Liliom came over to her of his own accord.

MRS. MUSKAT: It's all the same. I'm not going to get in trouble with the police, and lose my license on account of you—you shabby kitchen maid!

JULIE: Shabby yourself.

MRS. MUSKAT: You stay out of my carousel! Letting my barker fool with you! Aren't you ashamed of yourself?

JULIE: What did you say?

MRS. MUSKAT: I suppose you think I have no eyes in my head. I see everything that goes on in my carousel. During the whole ride she let Liliom fool with her—the shameless hussy!

JULIE: He did not fool with me! I don't let any man fool with me!

MRS. MUSKAT: He leaned against you all through the ride!

JULIE: He leaned against the panther. He always leans against something, doesn't he? Everybody leans where he wants. I couldn't tell him not to lean, if he always leans, could I? But he didn't lay a hand on me.

MRS. MUSKAT: Oh, didn't he? And I suppose he didn't put his hand around your waist, either?

MARIE: And if he did? What of it?

MRS. MUSKAT: You hold your tongue! No one's asking you—just you keep out of it.

JULIE: He put his arm around my waist—just the same as he does to all the girls. He always does that.

MRS. MUSKAT: I'll teach him not to do it any more, my dear. No carryings on in my carousel! If you are looking for that sort of thing, you'd better go to the circus! You'll find lots of soldiers there to carry on with!

JULIE: You keep your soldiers for yourself!

MARIE: Soldiers! As if we wanted soldiers!

MRS. MUSKAT: Well, I only want to tell you this, my dear, so that we understand each other perfectly. If you ever stick your nose in my carousel again, you'll wish you hadn't! I'm not going to lose my license on account of the likes of you! People who don't know how to behave, have got to stay out!

JULIE: You're wasting your breath. If I feel like riding on your carousel I'll pay my ten heller and I'll ride. I'd like to see any one try to stop me!

MRS. MUSKAT: Just come and try it, my dear—just come and try it.

MARIE: We'll see what'll happen.

MRS. MUSKAT: Yes, you will see something happen that never happened before in this park.

JULIE: Perhaps you think you could throw me out!

MRS. MUSKAT: I'm sure of it, my dear.

JULIE: And suppose I'm stronger than you?

MRS. MUSKAT: I'd think twice before I'd dirty my hands on a common servant girl. I'll have Liliom throw you out. He knows how to handle your kind.

JULIE: You think Liliom would throw me out.

MRS. MUSKAT: Yes, my dear, so fast that you won't know what happened to you!

JULIE: He'd throw me——

[Stops suddenly, for Mrs. Muskat has turned away. Both look off stage until Liliom enters, surrounded by four giggling servant girls]

LILIOM: Go away! Stop following me, or I'll smack your face!

A LITTLE SERVANT GIRL: Well, give me back my handkerchief.

LILIOM: Go on now——

THE FOUR SERVANT GIRLS: [Simultaneously] What do you think of him?—My handkerchief!—Give it back to her!—That's a nice thing to do!

THE LITTLE SERVANT GIRL: [To Mrs. Muskat] Please, lady, make him——

MRS. MUSKAT: Oh, shut up!

LILIOM: Will you get out of here?

[Makes a threatening gesture—the Four Servant Girls exit in voluble but fearful haste]

MRS. MUSKAT: What have you been doing now?

LILIOM: None of your business. [Glances at Julie] Have you been starting with her again?

JULIE: Mister Liliom, please——

LILIOM: [Steps threateningly toward her] Don't yell!

JULIE: [Timidly] I didn't yell.

LILIOM: Well, don't. [To Mrs. Muskat] What's the matter? What has she done to you?

MRS. MUSKAT: What has she done? She's been impudent to me. Just as impudent as she could be! I put her out of the carousel. Take a good look at this innocent thing, Liliom. She's never to be allowed in my carousel again!

LILIOM: [To Julie] You heard that. Run home, now.

MARIE: Come on. Don't waste your time with such people.

[Tries to lead Julie away]

JULIE: No, I won't——

MRS. MUSKAT: If she ever comes again, you're not to let her in. And if she gets in before you see her, throw her out. Understand?

LILIOM: What has she done, anyhow?

JULIE: [Agitated and very earnest] Mister Liliom —tell me please—honest and truly—if I come into the carousel, will you throw me out?

MRS. MUSKAT: Of course he'll throw you out.

MARIE: She wasn't talking to you.

JULIE: Tell me straight to my face, Mister Liliom, would you throw me out?

[They face each other. There is a brief pause]

LILIOM: Yes, little girl, if there was a reason—but if there was no reason, why should I throw you out?

MARIE: [*To* Mrs. Muskat] There, you see!

JULIE: Thank you, Mister Liliom.

MRS. MUSKAT: And I tell you again, if this little slut dares to set her foot in my carousel, she's to be thrown out! I'll stand for no indecency in my establishment.

LILIOM: What do you mean—indecency?

MRS. MUSKAT: I saw it all. There's no use denying it.

JULIE: She says you put your arm around my waist.

LILIOM: Me?

MRS. MUSKAT: Yes, you! I saw you. Don't play the innocent.

LILIOM: Here's something new! I'm not to put my arm around a girl's waist any more! I suppose I'm to ask your permission before I touch another girl!

MRS. MUSKAT: You can touch as many girls as you want and as often as you want—for my part you can go as far as you like with any of them—but not this one—I permit no indecency in my carousel.

[*There is a long pause*]

LILIOM: [*To* Mrs. Muskat] And now I'll ask you please to shut your mouth.

MRS. MUSKAT: What?

LILIOM: Shut your mouth quick, and go back to your carousel.

MRS. MUSKAT: What?

LILIOM: What did she do to you, anyhow? Tryin' to start a fight with a little pigeon like that . . . just because I touched her?—You come to the carousel as often as you want, little girl. Come every afternoon, and sit on the panther's back, and if you haven't got the price, Liliom will pay for you. And if any one dares to bother you, you come and tell *me*.

MRS. MUSKAT: You reprobate!

LILIOM: Old witch!

JULIE: Thank you, Mister Liliom.

MRS. MUSKAT: You seem to think that I can't throw you out, too. What's the reason I can't? Because you are the best barker in the park? Well, you are very much mistaken. In fact, you can consider yourself thrown out already. You're discharged!

LILIOM: Very good.

MRS. MUSKAT: [*Weakening a little*] I can discharge you any time I feel like it.

LILIOM: Very good, you feel like discharging me. I'm discharged. That settles it.

MRS. MUSKAT: Playing the high and mighty, are you? Conceited pig! Good-for-nothing!

LILIOM: You said you'd throw me out, didn't you? Well, that suits me; I'm thrown out.

MRS. MUSKAT: [*Softening*] Do you have to take up every word I say?

LILIOM: It's all right; it's all settled. I'm a good-for-nothing. And a conceited pig. And I'm discharged.

MRS. MUSKAT: Do you want to ruin my business?

LILIOM: A good-for-nothing? Now I know! And I'm discharged! Very good.

MRS. MUSKAT: You're a devil, you are . . . and that woman——

LILIOM: Keep away from her!

MRS. MUSKAT: I'll get Hollinger to give you such a beating that you'll hear all the angels sing . . . and it won't be the first time, either.

LILIOM: Get out of here. I'm discharged. And you get out of here.

JULIE: [*Timidly*] Mister Liliom, if she's willing to say that she hasn't discharged you——

LILIOM: You keep out of this.

JULIE: [*Timidly*] I don't want this to happen on account of me.

LILIOM: [*To* Mrs. Muskat, *pointing to* Julie] Apologize to her!

MARIE: A-ha!

MRS. MUSKAT: Apologize? To who?

LILIOM: To this little pigeon. Well—are you going to do it?

MRS. MUSKAT: If you give me this whole park on a silver plate, and all the gold of the Rothschilds on top of it—I'd—I'd—— Let her dare to come into my carousel again and she'll get thrown out so hard that she'll see stars in daylight!

LILIOM: In that case, dear lady [*Takes off his cap with a flourish*] you are respectfully requested to get out o' here as fast as your legs will carry you—I never beat up a woman yet—except that Holzer woman who I sent to the hospital for three weeks—but—if you don't get out o' here this minute, and let this little squab be, I'll give you the prettiest slap in the jaw you ever had in your life.

MRS MUSKAT: Very good, my son. Now you *can* go to the devil. Good-bye. You're discharged, and you needn't try to come back, either.

[*She exits. It is beginning to grow dark*]

MARIE: [*With grave concern*] Mister Liliom——

LILIOM: Don't you pity me or I'll give *you* a slap in the jaw. [*To* Julie] And don't you pity me, either.

JULIE: [*In alarm*] I don't pity you, Mister Liliom.

LILIOM: You're a liar, you *are* pitying me. I can see it in your face. You're thinking, now that Madame Muskat has thrown him out, Liliom will have to go begging. Huh! Look at me. I'm big enough to get along without a Madame Muskat. I have been thrown out of better jobs than hers.

JULIE: What will you do now, Mister Liliom?

LILIOM: Now? First of all, I'll go and get myself—a glass of beer. You see, when something happens to annoy me, I always drink a glass of beer.

JULIE: Then you are annoyed about losing your job.

LILIOM: No, only about where I'm going to get the beer.

MARIE: Well—eh——

LILIOM: Well—eh—what?

MARIE: Well—eh—are you going to stay with us, Mister Liliom?

LILIOM: Will you pay for the beer? [Marie *looks doubtful; he turns to* Julie] Will you? [*She does not answer*] How much money have you got?

JULIE: [*Bashfully*] Eight heller.

LILIOM: And you? [Marie *casts down her eyes and does not reply.* Liliom *continues sternly*] I asked you how much you've got? [Marie *begins to weep softly*] I understand. Well, you needn't cry about it. You girls stay here, while I go back to the carousel and get my clothes and things. And when I come back, we'll go to the Hungarian beer-garden. It's all right, I'll pay. Keep your money.

> [*He exits.* Marie *and* Julie *stand silent, watching him until he has gone*]

MARIE: Are you sorry for him?

JULIE: Are you?

MARIE: Yes, a little. Why are you looking after him in that funny way?

JULIE: [*Sits down*] Nothing—except I'm sorry he lost his job.

MARIE: [*With a touch of pride*] It was on our account he lost his job. Because he's fallen in love with you.

JULIE: He hasn't at all.

MARIE: [*Confidently*] Oh, yes! he is in love with you. [*Hesitantly, romantically*] There is some one in love with me, too.

JULIE: There is? Who?

MARIE: I—I never mentioned it before, because you hadn't a lover of your own—but now you have —and I'm free to speak. [*Very grandiloquently*] My heart has found its mate.

JULIE: You're only making it up.

MARIE: No, it's true—my heart's true love——

JULIE: Who? Who is he?

MARIE: A soldier.

JULIE: What kind of a soldier?

MARIE: I don't know. Just a soldier. Are there different kinds?

JULIE: Many different kinds. There are hussars, artillerymen, engineers, infantry—that's the kind that walks—and——

MARIE: How can you tell which is which?

JULIE: By their uniforms.

MARIE: [*After trying to puzzle it out*] The conductors on the street cars—are they soldiers?

JULIE: Certainly not. They're conductors.

MARIE: Well, they have uniforms.

JULIE: But they don't carry swords or guns.

MARIE: Oh! [*Thinks it over again; then*] Well, policemen—are they?

JULIE: [*With a touch of exasperation*] Are they what?

MARIE: Soldiers.

JULIE: Certainly not. They're just policemen.

MARIE: [*Triumphantly*] But they have uniforms— and they carry weapons, too.

JULIE: You're just as dumb as you can be. You don't go by their uniforms.

MARIE: But you said——

JULIE: No, I didn't. A letter-carrier wears a uniform, too, but that doesn't make him a soldier.

MARIE: But if he carried a gun or a sword, would he be——

JULIE: No, he'd still be a letter-carrier. You can't go by guns or swords, either.

MARIE: Well, if you don't go by the uniforms or the weapons, what *do* you go by?

JULIE: By—— [*Tries to put it into words; fails; then breaks off suddenly*] Oh, you'll get to know when you've lived in the city long enough. You're nothing but a country girl. When you've lived in the city a year, like I have, you'll know all about it.

MARIE: [*Half angrily*] Well, how *do* you know when *you* see a real soldier?

JULIE: By one thing.

MARIE: What?

JULIE: One thing——[*She pauses.* Marie *starts to cry*] Oh, what are you crying about?

MARIE: Because you're making fun of me . . . You're a city girl, and I'm just fresh from the country . . . and how am I expected to know a soldier when I see one? . . . You, you ought to tell me, instead of making fun of me——

JULIE: All right. Listen then, cry-baby. There's only one way to tell a soldier: by his salute! That's the only way.

MARIE: [*Joyfully; with a sigh of relief*] Ah—that's good.

JULIE: What?

MARIE: I say—it's all right then—because Wolf —Wolf——[Julie *laughs derisively*] Wolf—that's his name.

> [*She weeps again*]

JULIE: Crying again? What now?

MARIE: You're making fun of me again.

JULIE: I'm not. But when you say, "Wolf— Wolf—" like that, I have to laugh, don't I? [*Archly*] What's his name again?

MARIE: I won't tell you.

JULIE: All right. If you won't say it, then he's no soldier.

MARIE: I'll say it.

JULIE: Go on.

MARIE: No, I won't. [*She weeps again*]

JULIE: Then he's not a soldier. I guess he's a letter-carrier——

MARIE: No—no—I'd rather say it.

JULIE: Well, then.

MARIE: [*Giggling*] But you mustn't look at me. You look the other way, and I'll say it. [Julie *looks away.* Marie *can hardly restrain her own laughter*] Wolf! [*She laughs*] That's his real name. Wolf, Wolf, Soldier—Wolf!

JULIE: What kind of a uniform does he wear?

MARIE: Red.

JULIE: Red trousers?

MARIE: No.

JULIE: Red coat?

MARIE: No.

JULIE: What then?

MARIE: [*Triumphantly*] His cap!

JULIE: [*After a long pause*] He's just a porter, you dunce. Red cap . . . that's a porter—and he doesn't carry a gun or a sword, either.

MARIE: [*Triumphantly*] But he salutes. You said yourself that was the only way to tell a soldier——

JULIE: He doesn't salute at all. He only greets people——

MARIE: He salutes me. . . . And if his name *is* Wolf, that doesn't prove he ain't a soldier—he salutes, and he wears a red cap and he stands on guard all day long outside a big building——

JULIE: What does he do there?

MARIE: [*Seriously*] He spits.

JULIE: [*With contempt*] He's nothing—nothing but a common porter.

MARIE: What's Liliom?

JULIE: [*Indignantly*] Why speak of him? What has he to do with me?

MARIE: The same as Wolf has to do with me. If you can talk to me like that about Wolf, I can talk to you about Liliom.

JULIE: He's nothing to me. He put his arm around me in the carousel. I couldn't tell him not to put his arm around me after he had done it, could I?

MARIE: I suppose you didn't like him to do it?

JULIE: No.

MARIE: Then why are you waiting for him? Why don't you go home?

JULIE: Why—eh—he *said* we were to wait for him.

[Liliom *enters. There is a long silence*]

LILIOM: Are you still here? What are you waiting for?

MARIE: You told us to wait.

LILIOM: Must you always interfere? No one is talking to you.

MARIE: You asked us—why we——

LILIOM: Will you keep your mouth shut? What do you suppose I want with two of you? I meant that one of you was to wait. The other can go home.

MARIE: All right.

JULIE: All right. [*Neither starts to go*]

LILIOM: One of you goes home. [*To* Marie] Where do you work?

MARIE: At the Breiers', Damjanovitsch Street, Number Twenty.

LILIOM: And you?

JULIE: I work there, too.

LILIOM: Well, one of you goes home. Which of you wants to stay? [*There is no answer*] Come on, speak up, which of you stays?

MARIE: [*Officiously*] She'll lose her job if she stays.

LILIOM: Who will?

MARIE: Julie. She has to be back by seven o'clock.

LILIOM: Is that true? Will they discharge you if you're not back on time?

JULIE: Yes.

LILIOM: Well, wasn't I discharged?

JULIE: Yes—you were discharged, too.

MARIE: Julie, shall I go?

JULIE: I—can't tell you what to do.

MARIE: All right—stay if you like.

LILIOM: You'll be discharged if you do?

MARIE: Shall I go, Julie?

JULIE: [*Embarrassed*] Why do you keep asking me that?

MARIE: You know best what to do.

JULIE: [*Profoundly moved; slowly*] It's all right, Marie, you can go home.

MARIE: [*Exits reluctantly, but comes back, and says uncertainly*] Good-night.

[*She waits a moment to see if* Julie *will follow her.* Julie *does not move.* Marie *exits. Meantime it has grown quite dark. During the following scene the gas-lamps far in the distance are lighted one by one.* Liliom *and* Julie *sit on the bench. From afar, very faintly, comes the music of a calliope. But the music is intermittently heard; now it breaks off, now it resumes again, as if it came down on a fitful wind. Blending with it are the sounds of human voices, now loud, now soft; the blare of a toy trumpet; the confused noises of the show booths. It grows progressively darker until the end of the scene. There is no moonlight. The spring iridescence glows in the deep blue sky*]

LILIOM: Now we're both discharged. [*She does not answer. From now on they speak gradually lower and lower until the end of the scene, which is played almost in whispers. Whistles softly, then*] Have you had your supper?

JULIE: No.

LILIOM: Want to go eat something at the Garden?

JULIE: No.

LILIOM: Anywhere else?

JULIE: No.

LILIOM: [*Whistles softly, then*] You don't come to this park very often, do you? I've only seen you three times. Been here oftener than that?

JULIE: Oh, yes.

LILIOM: Did you see me?

JULIE: Yes.

LILIOM: And did you know I was Liliom?

JULIE: They told me.

LILIOM: [*Whistles softly, then*] Have you got a sweetheart?

JULIE: No.

LILIOM: Don't lie to me.

JULIE: I haven't. If I had, I'd tell you. I've never had one.

LILIOM: What an awful liar you are. I've got a good mind to go away and leave you here.

JULIE: I've never had one.

LILIOM: Tell that to some one else.

JULIE: [*Reproachfully*] Why do you insist I have?

LILIOM: Because you stayed here with me the first time I asked you to. You know your way around, you do.

JULIE: No, I don't, Mister Liliom.

LILIOM: I suppose you'll tell me you don't know why you're sitting here—like this, in the dark, alone with me—— You wouldn't 'a' stayed so quick, if you hadn't done it before—with some soldier, maybe. This isn't the first time. You wouldn't have been so ready to stay if it was—what *did* you stay for, anyhow?

JULIE: So you wouldn't be left alone.

LILIOM: Alone! God, you're dumb! I don't need to be alone. I can have all the girls I want. Not only servant girls like you, but cooks and governesses, even French girls, I could have twenty of them if I wanted to.

JULIE: I know, Mister Liliom.

LILIOM: What do you know?

JULIE: That all the girls are in love with you. But that's not why *I* stayed. I stayed because you've been so good to me.

LILIOM: Well, then you can go home.

JULIE: I don't want to go home now.

LILIOM: And what if I go away and leave you sitting here?

JULIE: If you did, I wouldn't go home.

LILIOM: Do you know what you remind me of? A sweetheart I had once—I'll tell you how I met her—— One night, at closing time we had put out the lights in the carousel, and just as I was——

[*He is interrupted by the entrance of two* Plainclothes Policemen. *They take their stations on either side of the bench. They are police, searching the park for vagabonds*]

FIRST POLICEMAN: What are you doing there?

LILIOM: Me?

SECOND POLICEMAN: Stand up when you're spoken to!

[*He taps* Liliom *imperatively on the shoulder*]

FIRST POLICEMAN: What's your name?

LILIOM: Andreas Zavocki.

[Julie *begins to weep softly*]

SECOND POLICEMAN: Stop your bawling. We're not goin' to eat you. We are only making our rounds.

FIRST POLICEMAN: See that he doesn't get away. [*The* Second Policeman *steps closer to* Liliom] What's your business?

LILIOM: Barker and bouncer.

SECOND POLICEMAN: They call him Liliom, Chief. We've had him up a couple of times.

FIRST POLICEMAN: So that's who you are! Who do you work for now?

LILIOM: I work for the widow Muskat.

FIRST POLICEMAN: What are you hanging around here for?

LILIOM: We're just sitting here—me and this girl.

FIRST POLICEMAN: Your sweetheart?

LILIOM: No.

FIRST POLICEMAN: [*To* Julie] And who are you?

JULIE: Julie Zeller.

FIRST POLICEMAN: Servant girl?

JULIE: Maid of all work for Mister Georg Breier, Number Twenty Damjanovitsch Street.

FIRST POLICEMAN: Show your hands.

SECOND POLICEMAN: [*After examining* Julie's *hand*] Servant girl.

FIRST POLICEMAN: Why aren't you at home? What are you doing out here with him?

JULIE: This is my day out, sir.

FIRST POLICEMAN: It would be better for you if you didn't spend it sitting around with a fellow like this.

SECOND POLICEMAN: They'll be disappearing in the bushes as soon as we turn our backs.

FIRST POLICEMAN: He's only after your money. We know this fine fellow. He picks up you silly servant girls and takes what money you have. To-morrow you'll probably be coming around to report him. If you do, I'll throw you out.

JULIE: I haven't any money, sir.

FIRST POLICEMAN: Do you hear that, Liliom?

LILIOM: I'm not looking for her money.

SECOND POLICEMAN: [*Nudging him warningly*] Keep your mouth shut.

FIRST POLICEMAN: It is my duty to warn you, my child, what kind of company you're in. He makes a specialty of servant girls. That's why he works in a carousel. He gets hold of a girl, promises to marry her, then he takes her money and her ring.

JULIE: But I haven't got a ring.

SECOND POLICEMAN: You're not to talk unless you're asked a question.

FIRST POLICEMAN: You be thankful that I'm warning you. It's nothing to me what you do. I'm not your father, thank God. But I'm telling you what kind of a fellow he is. By to-morrow morning you'll be coming around to us to report him. Now you be sensible and go home. You needn't be afraid of him. This officer will take you home if you're afraid.

JULIE: Do I *have* to go?

FIRST POLICEMAN: No, you don't *have* to go.

JULIE: Then I'll stay, sir.

FIRST POLICEMAN: Well, you've been warned.

JULIE: Yes, sir. Thank you, sir.

FIRST POLICEMAN: Come on, Berkovics.

[*The* Policemen *exit.* Julie *and* Liliom *sit on the bench again. There is a brief pause*]

JULIE: Well, and what then?

LILIOM: [*Fails to understand*] Huh?

JULIE: You were beginning to tell me a story.

LILIOM: Me?

JULIE: Yes, about a sweetheart. You said, one night, just as they were putting out the lights of the carousel—— That's as far as you got.

LILIOM: Oh, yes, yes, just as the lights were going out, some one came along—a little girl with a big shawl—you know—— She came—eh—from——

Say—tell me—ain't you—that is, ain't you at all—afraid of me? The officer told you what kind of a fellow I am—and that I'd take your money away from you——

JULIE: You couldn't take it away—I haven't got any. But if I had—I'd—I'd give it to you—I'd give it all to you.

LILIOM: You would?

JULIE: If you asked me for it.

LILIOM: Have you ever had a fellow you gave money to?

JULIE: No.

LILIOM: Haven't you ever had a sweetheart?

JULIE: No.

LILIOM: Some one you used to go walking with. You've had one like that?

JULIE: Yes.

LILIOM: A soldier?

JULIE: He came from the same village I did.

LILIOM: That's what all the soldiers say. Where *do* you come from, anyway?

JULIE: Not far from here.

[*There is a pause*]

LILIOM: Were you in love with him?

JULIE: Why do you keep asking me that all the time, Mister Liliom? I wasn't in love with him. We only went walking together.

LILIOM: Where did you walk?

JULIE: In the park.

LILIOM: And your virtue? Where did you lose that?

JULIE: I haven't got any virtue.

LILIOM: Well, you had once.

JULIE: No, I never had. I'm a respectable girl.

LILIOM: Yes, but you gave the soldier something.

JULIE: Why do you question me like that, Mister Liliom?

LILIOM: Did you give him something?

JULIE: You have to. But I didn't love him.

LILIOM: Do you love me?

JULIE: No, Mister Liliom.

LILIOM: Then why do you stay here with me?

JULIE: Um—nothing.

[*There is a pause. The music from afar is plainly heard*]

LILIOM: Want to dance?

JULIE: No. I have to be very careful.

LILIOM: Of what?

JULIE: My—character.

LILIOM: Why?

JULIE: Because I'm never going to marry. If I was going to marry, it would be different. Then I wouldn't need to worry so much about my character. It doesn't make any difference if you're married. But I shan't marry—and that's why I've got to take care to be a respectable girl.

LILIOM: Suppose I were to say to you—I'll marry you.

JULIE: You?

LILIOM: That frightens you, doesn't it? You're thinking of what the officer said and you're afraid.

JULIE: No, I'm not, Mister Liliom. I don't pay any attention to what he said.

LILIOM: But you wouldn't dare to marry any one like me, would you?

JULIE: I know that—that—if I loved any one—it wouldn't make any difference to me what he—even if I died for it.

LILIOM: But you wouldn't marry a rough guy like me—that is—eh—if you loved me——

JULIE: Yes, I would—if I loved you, Mister Liliom.

[*There is a pause*]

LILIOM: [*Whispers*] Well—you just said—didn't you?—that you don't love me. Well, why don't you go home then?

JULIE: It's too late now, they'd all be asleep.

LILIOM: Locked out?

JULIE: Certainly.

[*They are silent awhile*]

LILIOM: I think—that even a low-down good-for-nothing—can make a man of himself.

JULIE: Certainly.

[*They are silent again. A lamp-lighter crosses the stage, lights the lamp over the bench, and exits*]

LILIOM: Are you hungry?

JULIE: No.

[*Another pause*]

LILIOM: Suppose—you had some money—and I took it from you?

JULIE: Then you could take it, that's all.

LILIOM: [*After another brief silence*] All ⅰ ⅿave to do—is go back to her—that Muskat woman—she'll be glad to get me back—then I'd be earning my wages again.

[*She is silent. The twilight folds darker about them*]

JULIE: [*Very softly*] Don't go back—to her——

[*Pause*]

LILIOM: There are a lot of acacia trees around here.

[*Pause*]

JULIE: Don't go back to her——

[*Pause*]

LILIOM: She'd take me back the minute I asked her. I know why—she knows, too——

[*Pause*]

JULIE: I can smell them, too—acacia blos-soms——

[*There is a pause. Some blossoms drift down from the tree-top to the bench. Liliom picks one up and smells it*]

LILIOM: White acacias!

JULIE: [*After a brief pause*] The wind brings them down.

[*They are silent. There is a long pause before*

THE CURTAIN FALLS

SCENE II.

A photographer's "studio," operated by the Hollunders, *on the fringe of the park. It is a dilapidated hovel. The general entrance is back left. Back right there is a window with a sofa before it. The outlook is on the amusement park with perhaps a small Ferris wheel or the scaffolding of a "scenic-railway" in the background.*

The door to the kitchen is up left and a black-curtained entrance to the dark-room is down left. Just in front of the dark-room stands the camera on its tripod. Against the back wall, between the door and window, stands the inevitable photographer's background-screen, ready to be wheeled into place.

It is forenoon. When the curtain rises, Marie *and* Julie *are discovered.*

MARIE: And *he* beat up Hollinger?

JULIE: Yes, he gave him an awful licking.

MARIE: But Hollinger is bigger than he is.

JULIE: He licked him just the same. It isn't size that counts, you know, it's cleverness. And Liliom's awful quick.

MARIE: And then he was arrested?

JULIE: Yes, they arrested him, but they let him go the next day. That makes twice in the two months we've been living here that Liliom's been arrested and let go again.

MARIE: Why do they let him go?

JULIE: Because he is innocent.

[Mother Hollunder, *a very old woman, sharp-tongued, but in reality quite warm-hearted beneath her formidable exterior, enters at back carrying a few sticks of firewood, and scolding, half to herself*]

MOTHER HOLLUNDER: Always wanting something, but never willing to work for it. He won't work, and he won't steal, but he'll use up a poor old widow's last bit of firewood. He'll do that cheerfully enough! A big, strong lout like that lying around all day resting his lazy bones! He ought to be ashamed to look decent people in the face.

JULIE: I'm sorry, Mother Hollunder. . . .

MOTHER HOLLUNDER: Sorry! Better be sorry the lazy good-for-nothing ain't in jail where he belongs instead of in the way of honest, hard-working people.

[*She exits into the kitchen*]

MARIE: Who's that?

JULIE: Mrs. Hollunder—my aunt. This is her [*with a sweeping gesture that takes in the camera, dark-room and screen*] studio. She lets us live here for nothing.

MARIE: What's she fetching the wood for?

JULIE: She brings us everything we need. If it weren't for her I don't know what would become of us. She's a good-hearted soul even if her tongue is sharp.

[*There is a pause*]

MARIE: [*Shyly*] Do you know—I've found out. He's not a soldier.

JULIE: Do you still see him?

MARIE: Oh, yes.

JULIE: Often?

MARIE: Very often. He's asked me——

JULIE: To marry you?

MARIE: To marry me.

JULIE: You see—that proves he isn't a soldier.

[*There is another pause*]

MARIE: [*Abashed, yet a bit boastfully*] Do you know what I'm doing—I'm flirting with him.

JULIE: Flirting?

MARIE: Yes. He asks me to go to the park—and I say I can't go. Then he coaxes me, and promises me a new scarf for my head if I go. But I don't go—even then. . . . So then he walks all the way home with me—and I bid him good-night at the door.

JULIE: Is that what you call flirting?

MARIE: Um-hm! It's sinful, but it's so *thrilling.*

JULIE: Do you ever quarrel?

MARIE: [*Grandly*] Only when our Passionate Love surges up.

JULIE: Your passionate love?

MARIE: Yes. . . . He takes my hand and we walk along together. Then he wants to swing hands, but I won't let him. I say: "Don't swing my hand"; and he says, "Don't be so stubborn." And then he tries to swing my hand again, but still I don't let him. And for a long time I don't let him—until in the end I let him. Then we walk along swinging hands—up and down, up and down—just like this. *That* is Passionate Love. It's sinful, but it's awfully *thrilling.*

JULIE: You're happy, aren't you?

MARIE: Happier than—anything—— But the most beautiful thing on earth is Ideal Love.

JULIE: What kind is that?

MARIE: Daylight comes about three in the morning this time of the year. When we've been up that long we're all through with flirting and Passionate Love—and then our Ideal Love comes to the surface. It comes like this: I'll be sitting on the bench and Wolf, he holds my hand tight—and he puts his cheek against my cheek and we don't talk . . . we just sit there very quiet. . . . And after a while he gets sleepy, and his head sinks down, and he falls asleep . . . but even in his sleep he holds tight to my hand. And I—I sit perfectly still just looking around me and taking long, deep breaths—for by that time it's morning and the trees and flowers are fresh with dew. But Wolf doesn't smell anything because he's so fast asleep. And I get awfully sleepy myself, but I don't sleep. And we sit like that for a long time. That is Ideal Love——

[*There is a long pause*]

JULIE: [*Regretfully; uneasily*] He went out last night and he hasn't come home yet.

MARIE: Here are sixteen kreuzer. It was supposed

to be carfare to take my young lady to the conservatory—eight there and eight back—but I made her walk. Here—save it with the rest.

JULIE: This makes three gulden, forty-six.

MARIE: Three gulden, forty-six.

JULIE: He won't work at all.

MARIE: Too lazy?

JULIE: No. He never learned a trade, you see, and he can't just go and be a day-laborer—so he just does nothing.

MARIE: That ain't right.

JULIE: No. Have the Breiers got a new maid yet?

MARIE: They've had three since you left. You know, Wolf's going to take a new job. He's going to work for the city. He'll get rent free, too.

JULIE: He won't go back to work at the carousel, either. I ask him why, but he won't tell me——Last Monday he hit me.

MARIE: Did you hit him back?

JULIE: No.

MARIE: Why don't you leave him?

JULIE: I don't want to.

MARIE: I would. I'd leave him.

[*There is a strained silence*]

MOTHER HOLLUNDER: [*Enters, carrying a pot of water; muttering aloud*] He can play cards, all right. He can fight, too; and take money from poor servant girls. And the police turn their heads the other way——The carpenter was here.

JULIE: Is that water for the soup?

MOTHER HOLLUNDER: The carpenter was here. There's a *man* for you! Dark, handsome, lots of hair, a respectable widower with two children—and money, and a good paying business.

JULIE: [*To* Marie] It's three gulden, sixty-six, not forty-six.

MARIE: Yes, that's what I make it—sixty-six.

MOTHER HOLLUNDER: He wants to take her out of this and marry her. This is the fifth time he's been here. He has two children, but——

JULIE: Please don't bother, Aunt Hollunder, I'll get the water myself.

MOTHER HOLLUNDER: He's waiting outside now.

JULIE: Send him away.

MOTHER HOLLUNDER: He'll only come back again —and first thing you know that vagabond will get jealous and there'll be a fight. [*Goes out, muttering*] Oh, he's ready enough to fight, he is. Strike a poor little girl like that! Ought to be ashamed of himself! And the police just let him go on doing as he pleases.

[*Still scolding, she exits at back*]

MARIE: A carpenter wants to marry you?

JULIE: Yes.

MARIE: Why don't you?

JULIE: Because——

MARIE: Liliom doesn't support you, and he beats you—he thinks he can do whatever he likes just because he's Liliom. He's a bad one.

JULIE: He's not really bad.

MARIE: That night you sat on the bench together —he was gentle then.

JULIE: Yes, he was gentle.

MARIE: And afterwards he got wild again.

JULIE: Afterwards he got wild—sometimes. But that night on the bench . . . he was gentle. He's gentle now, sometimes, very gentle. After supper, when he stands there and listens to the music of the carousel, something comes over him—and he is gentle.

MARIE: Does he say anything?

JULIE: He doesn't say anything. He gets thoughtful and very quiet, and his big eyes stare straight ahead of him.

MARIE: Into your eyes?

JULIE: Not exactly. He's unhappy because he isn't working. That's really why he hit me on Monday.

MARIE: That's a fine reason for hitting you! Beats his wife because he isn't working, the ruffian!

JULIE: It preys on his mind——

MARIE: Did he hurt you?

JULIE: [*Very eagerly*] Oh, no.

MRS. MUSKAT: [*Enters haughtily*] Good-morning. Is Liliom home?

JULIE: No.

MRS. MUSKAT: Gone out?

JULIE: He hasn't come home yet.

MRS. MUSKAT: I'll wait for him.

[*She sits down*]

MARIE: You've got a lot of gall—to come here.

MRS. MUSKAT: Are you the lady of the house, my dear? Better look out or you'll get a slap in the mouth.

MARIE: How dare you set foot in Julie's house?

MRS. MUSKAT: [*To* Julie] Pay no attention to her, my child. You know what brings me here. That vagabond, that good-for-nothing, I've come to give him his bread and butter back.

MARIE: He's not dependent on you for his bread.

MRS. MUSKAT: [*To* Julie] Just ignore her, my child. She's just ignorant.

MARIE: [*Going*] Good-bye.

JULIE: Good-bye.

MARIE: [*In the doorway, calling back*] Sixty-six.

JULIE: Yes, sixty-six.

MARIE: Good-bye.

[*She exits. Julie* starts to go toward the kitchen]

MRS. MUSKAT: I paid him a krone a day, and on Sunday a gulden. And he got all the beer and cigars he wanted from the customers. [Julie *pauses on the threshold, but does not answer*] And he'd rather starve than beg my pardon. Well, I don't insist on that. I'll take him back without it. [Julie *does not answer*] The fact is the people ask for him—and, you see, I've got to consider business first. It's nothing to me if he starves. I wouldn't be here at all, if it wasn't for business——

[*She pauses, for* Liliom *and* Ficsur *have entered*]

JULIE: Mrs. Muskat is here.

LILIOM: I see she is.

JULIE: You might say good-morning.

LILIOM: What for? And what do *you* want, anyhow?

JULIE: I don't want anything.

LILIOM: Then keep your mouth shut. Next thing you'll be starting to nag again about my being out all night and out of work and living on your relations——

JULIE: I'm not saying anything.

LILIOM: But it's all on the tip of your tongue—I know you—now don't start or you'll get another.

[*He paces angrily up and down. They are all a bit afraid of him, and shrink and look away as he passes them.* Ficsur *shambles from place to place, his eyes cast down as if he were searching for something on the floor*]

MRS. MUSKAT: [*Suddenly, to* Ficsur] You're always dragging him out to play cards and drink with you. I'll have you locked up, I will.

FICSUR: I don't want to talk to you. You're too common.

[*He goes out by the door at back and lingers there in plain view. There is a pause*]

JULIE: Mrs. Muskat is here.

LILIOM: Well, why doesn't she open her mouth, if she has anything to say?

MRS. MUSKAT: Why do you go around with this man, Ficsur? He'll get you mixed up in one of his robberies first thing you know.

LILIOM: What's it to you who I go with? I do what I please. What do you want?

MRS. MUSKAT: You know what I want.

LILIOM: No, I don't.

MRS. MUSKAT: What do you suppose I want? Think I've come just to pay a social call?

LILIOM: Do I owe you anything?

MRS. MUSKAT: Yes, you do—but that's not what I came for. You're a fine one to come to for money! You earn so much these days! You know very well what I'm here for.

LILIOM: You've got Hollinger at the carousel, haven't you?

MRS. MUSKAT: Sure I have.

LILIOM: Well, what else do you want? He's as good as I am.

MRS. MUSKAT: You're quite right, my boy. He's every bit as good as you are. I'd not dream of letting him go. But one isn't enough any more. There's work enough for two——

LILIOM: One was enough when *I* was there.

MRS. MUSKAT: Well, I might let Hollinger go——

LILIOM: Why let him go, if he's so good?

MRS. MUSKAT: [*Shrugs her shoulders*] Yes, he's good.

[*Not once until now has she looked at* Liliom]

LILIOM: [*To* Julie] Ask your aunt if I can have a cup of coffee. [Julie *exits into the kitchen*] So Hollinger is good, is he?

MRS. MUSKAT: [*Crosses to him and looks him in the face*] Why don't you stay home and sleep at night? You're a sight to look at.

LILIOM: He's good, is he?

MRS. MUSKAT: Push your hair back from your forehead.

LILIOM: Let my hair be. It's nothing to you.

MRS. MUSKAT: All right. But if I'd told you to let it hang down over your eyes you'd have pushed it back—I hear you've been beating her, this—this——

LILIOM: None of your business.

MRS. MUSKAT: You're a fine fellow! Beating a skinny little thing like that! If you're tired of her, leave her, but there's no use beating the poor——

LILIOM: Leave her, eh? You'd like that, wouldn't you?

MRS. MUSKAT: Don't flatter yourself. [*Quite embarrassed*] Serves me right, too. If I had any sense I wouldn't have run after you—— My God, the things one must do for the sake of business! If I could only sell the carousel I wouldn't be sitting here. . . . Come, Liliom, if you have any sense, you'll come back. I'll pay you well.

LILIOM: The carousel is crowded just the same . . . *without me*?

MRS. MUSKAT: Crowded, yes—but it's not the same.

LILIOM: Then you admit that you *do* miss me.

MRS. MUSKAT: Miss you? Not I. But the silly girls miss you. They're always asking for you. Well, are you going to be sensible and come back?

LILIOM: And leave—her?

MRS. MUSKAT: You beat her, don't you?

LILIOM: No, I don't beat her. What's all this damn fool talk about beating her? I hit her once—that was all—and now the whole city seems to be talking about it. You don't call that beating her, do you?

MRS. MUSKAT: All right, all right. I take it back. I don't want to get mixed up in it.

LILIOM: Beating her! As if I'd beat her——

MRS. MUSKAT: I can't make out why you're so concerned about her. You've been married to her two months—it's plain to see that you're sick of it—and out there is the carousel—and the show booths—and money—and you'd throw it all away. For what? Heavens, how can any one be such a fool? [*Looks at him appraisingly*] Where have you been all night? You look awful.

LILIOM: It's no business of yours.

MRS. MUSKAT: You never used to look like that. This life is telling on you. [*Pauses*] Do you know—I've got a new organ.

LILIOM: [*Softly*] I know.

MRS. MUSKAT: How did you know?

LILIOM: You can hear it—from here.

MRS. MUSKAT: It's a good one, eh?

LILIOM: [*Wistfully*] Very good. Fine. It roars and snorts—so fine.

MRS. MUSKAT: You should hear it close by—it's heavenly. Even the carousel seems to know . . . it goes quicker. I got rid of those two horses—you know, the ones with the broken ears?

LILIOM: What have you put in their place?

MRS. MUSKAT: Guess.

LILIOM: Zebras?

MRS. MUSKAT: No—an automobile.

LILIOM: [*Transported*] An automobile——

MRS. MUSKAT: Yes. If you've got any sense you'll come back. What good are you doing here? Out there is your *art*, the only thing you're fit for. You are an artist, not a respectable married man.

LILIOM: *Leave* her—this little——

MRS. MUSKAT: She'll be better off. She'll go back and be a servant girl again. As for you—you're an artist and you belong among artists. All the beer you want, cigars, a krone a day and a gulden on Sunday, and the girls, Liliom, the girls—I've always treated you right, haven't I? I bought you a watch, and——

LILIOM: She's not that kind. She'd never be a servant girl again.

MRS. MUSKAT: I suppose you think she'd kill herself. Don't worry. Heavens, if every girl was to commit suicide just because her—— [*Finishes with a gesture*]

LILIOM: [*Stares at her a moment, considering, then with sudden, smiling animation*] So the people don't like Hollinger?

MRS. MUSKAT: You know very well they don't, you rascal.

LILIOM: Well——

MRS. MUSKAT: You've always been happy at the carousel. It's a great life—pretty girls and beer and cigars and music—a great life and an easy one. I'll tell you what—come back and I'll give you a ring that used to belong to my dear departed husband. Well, will you come?

LILIOM: She's not that kind. She'd never be a servant girl again. But—but—for my part—if I decide—that needn't make any difference. I can go on living with her even if I do go back to my art——

MRS. MUSKAT: My God!

LILIOM: What's the matter?

MRS. MUSKAT: Who ever heard of a married man—I suppose you think all girls would be pleased to know that you were running home to your wife every night. It's ridiculous! When the people found out they'd laugh themselves sick——

LILIOM: I know what you want.

MRS. MUSKAT: [*Refuses to meet his gaze*] You flatter yourself.

LILIOM: You'll give me that ring, too?

MRS. MUSKAT: [*Pushes the hair back from his forehead*] Yes.

LILIOM: I'm not happy in this house.

MRS. MUSKAT: [*Still stroking his hair*] Nobody takes care of you.

[*They are silent.* Julie *enters, carrying a cup of* coffee. Mrs. Muskat *removes her hand from* Liliom's *head. There is a pause*]

LILIOM: Do you want anything?

JULIE: No.

[*There is a pause. She exits slowly into the kitchen*]

MRS. MUSKAT: The old woman says there is a carpenter, a widower, who——

LILIOM: I know—I know——

JULIE: [*Reëntering*] Liliom, before I forget, I have something to tell you.

LILIOM: All right.

JULIE: I've been wanting to tell you—in fact, I was going to tell you yesterday——

LILIOM: Go ahead.

JULIE: But I must tell you alone—if you'll come in—it will only take a minute.

LILIOM: Don't you see I'm busy now? Here I am talking business and you interrupt with——

JULIE: It'll only take a minute.

LILIOM: Get out of here, or——

JULIE: But I tell you it will only take a minute——

LILIOM: Will you get out of here?

JULIE: [*Courageously*] No.

LILIOM: [*Rising*] What's that!

JULIE: No.

MRS. MUSKAT: [*Rises, too*] Now don't start fighting. I'll go out and look at the photographs in the show case a while and come back later for your answer.

[*She exits at back*]

JULIE: You can hit me again if you like—don't look at me like that. I'm not afraid of you. . . . I'm not afraid of any one. I told you I had something to tell you.

LILIOM: Well, out with it—quick.

JULIE: I can't tell you so quick. Why don't you drink your coffee?

LILIOM: Is that what you wanted to tell me?

JULIE: No. By the time you've drunk your coffee I'll have told you.

LILIOM: [*Gets the coffee and sips it*] Well?

JULIE: Yesterday my head ached—and you asked me——

LILIOM: Yes——

JULIE: Well—you see—that's what it is——

LILIOM: Are you sick?

JULIE: No. . . . But you wanted to know what my headaches came from—and you said I seemed —changed.

LILIOM: Did I? I guess I meant the carpenter.

JULIE: I've been—what? The carpenter? No. It's something entirely different—it's awful hard to tell —but you'll have to know sooner or later—I'm not a bit—scared—because it's a perfectly natural thing——

LILIOM: [*Puts the coffee cup on the table*] What?

JULIE: When—when a man and woman—live together——

LILIOM: Yes.

JULIE: I'm going to have a baby.

[*She exits swiftly at back. There is a pause. Ficsur appears at the open window and looks in*]

LILIOM: Ficsur! [Ficsur *sticks his head in*] Say, Ficsur—Julie is going to have a baby.

FICSUR: Yes? What of it?

LILIOM: Nothing. [*Suddenly*] Get out of here.

[Ficsur's *head is quickly withdrawn. Mrs. Muskat reënters*]

MRS. MUSKAT: Has she gone?

LILIOM: Yes.

MRS. MUSKAT: I might as well give you ten kronen in advance. [*Opens her purse. Liliom takes up his coffee cup*] Here you are. [*She proffers some coins. Liliom ignores her*] Why don't you take it?

LILIOM: [*Very nonchalantly, his cup poised ready to drink*] Go home, Mrs. Muskat.

MRS. MUSKAT: What's the matter with you?

LILIOM: Go home [*Sips his coffee*] and let me finish my coffee in peace. Don't you see I'm at breakfast?

MRS MUSKAT: Have you gone crazy?

LILIOM: Will you get out of here?

[*Turns to her threateningly*]

MRS. MUSKAT: [*Restoring the coins to her purse*] I'll never speak to you again as long as you live.

LILIOM: That worries me a lot.

MRS. MUSKAT: Good-bye!

LILIOM: Good-bye. [*As she exits, he calls*] Ficsur! [Ficsur *enters*] Tell me, Ficsur. You said you knew a way to get a whole lot of money——

FICSUR: Sure I do.

LILIOM: How much?

FICSUR: More than you ever had in your life before. You leave it to an old hand like me.

MOTHER HOLLUNDER: [*Enters from the kitchen*] In the morning he must have his coffee, and at noon his soup, and in the evening coffee again—and plenty of firewood—and I'm expected to furnish it all. Give me back my cup and saucer.

[*The show booths of the amusement park have opened for business. The familiar noises begin to sound; clear above them all, but far in the distance, sounds the organ of the carousel*]

LILIOM: Now, Aunt Hollunder.

[*From now until the fall of the curtain it is apparent that the sound of the organ makes him more and more uneasy*]

MOTHER HOLLUNDER: And you, you vagabond, get out of here this minute or I'll call my son——

FICSUR: I have nothing to do with the likes of him. He's too common.

[*But he slinks out at back*]

LILIOM: Aunt Hollunder!

MOTHER HOLLUNDER: What now?

LILIOM: When your son was born—when you brought him into the world——

MOTHER HOLLUNDER: Well?

LILIOM: Nothing.

MOTHER HOLLUNDER: [*Muttering as she exits*] Sleep it off, you good-for-nothing lout. Drink and play cards all night long—that's all you know how to do—and take the bread out of poor people's mouths—you can do that, too.

[*She exits*]

LILIOM: Ficsur!

FICSUR: [*At the window*] Julie's going to have a baby. You told me before.

LILIOM: This scheme—about the cashier of the leather factory—there's money in it——

FICSUR: Lots of money—but—it takes two to pull it off.

LILIOM: [*Meditatively*] Yes. [*Uneasily*] All right, Ficsur. Go away—and come back later.

[Ficsur *vanishes. The organ in the distant carousel drones incessantly. Liliom listens awhile, then goes to the door and calls*]

LILIOM: Aunt Hollunder! [*With naïve joy*] Julie's going to have a baby. [*Then he goes to the window, jumps on the sofa, looks out. Suddenly, in a voice that overtops the droning of the organ, he shouts as if addressing the far-off carousel*] I'm going to be a father.

JULIE: [*Enters from the kitchen*] Liliom! What's the matter? What's happened?

LILIOM: [*Coming down from the sofa*] Nothing. [*Throws himself on the sofa, buries his face in the cushion. Julie watches him a moment, comes over to him and covers him with a shawl. Then she goes on tiptoe to the door at back and remains standing in the doorway, looking out and listening to the droning of the organ*]

THE CURTAIN FALLS

SCENE III.

The setting is the same, later that afternoon. Liliom is sitting opposite Ficsur, who is teaching him a song. Julie hovers in the background, engaged in some household task.

FICSUR: Listen now. Here's the third verse.

[*Sings hoarsely*]

"*Look out, look out, my pretty lad,
The damn police are on your trail;
The nicest girl you ever had
Has now commenced to weep and wail:
Look out here comes the damn police,
The damn police,
The damn police,
Look out here comes the damn police,
They'll get you every time.*"

LILIOM: [*Sings*]

"*Look out, look out, my pretty lad,
The damn police——*"

FICSUR, LILIOM: [*Sing together*]
        "are on your trail;
The nicest girl you ever had
Has now commenced to weep and wail."
        LILIOM: [*Alone*]
"Look out here comes the damn police,
The damn police,
The damn police———"
        [Julie, *troubled and uneasy, looks from one to the other, then exits into the kitchen*]
        FICSUR: [*When she has gone, comes quickly over to* Liliom *and speaks furtively*] As you go down Franzen Street you come to the railroad embankment. Beyond that—all the way to the leather factory—there's not a thing in sight, not even a watchman's hut.
        LILIOM: And does he always come that way?
        FICSUR: Yes. Not along the embankment, but down below along the path across the fields. Since last year he's been going alone. Before that he always used to have some one with him.
        LILIOM: Every Saturday?
        FICSUR: Every Saturday.
        LILIOM: And the money? Where does he keep it?
        FICSUR: In a leather bag. The whole week's pay for the workmen at the factory.
        LILIOM: Much?
        FICSUR: Sixteen thousand kronen. Quite a haul, what?
        LILIOM: What's his name?
        FICSUR: Linzman. He's a Jew.
        LILIOM: The cashier?
        FICSUR: Yes—but when he gets a knife between his ribs—or if I smash his skull for him—he won't be a cashier any more.
        LILIOM: Does he have to be killed?
        FICSUR: No, he doesn't *have* to be. He can give up the money *without* being killed—but most of these cashiers are peculiar—they'd rather be killed.
        [Julie *reënters, pretends to get something on the other side of the room, then exits at back. During the ensuing dialogue she keeps coming in and out in the same way, showing plainly that she is suspicious and anxious. She attempts to overhear what they are saying and, in spite of their caution, does catch a word here and there, which adds to her disquiet.* Ficsur, *catching sight of her, abruptly changes the conversation*]
        FICSUR: And the next verse is:
"And when you're in the prison cell
They'll feed you bread and water."
        FICSUR AND LILIOM: [*Sing together*]
"They'll make your little sweetheart tell
Them all the things you brought her.
Look out here comes the damn police,
The damn police,
The damn police,
Look out here comes the damn police,
They'll get you every time."

        LILIOM: [*Sings alone*]
"And when you're in the prison cell
They'll feed you bread and water———"
        [*Breaks off, as* Julie *exits*]
And when it's done, do we start right off for America?
        FICSUR: No.
        LILIOM: What then?
        FICSUR: We bury the money for six months. That's the usual time. And after the sixth month we dig it up again.
        LILIOM: And then?
        FICSUR: Then you go on living just as usual for six months more—you don't touch a heller of the money.
        LILIOM: In six months the baby will be born.
        FICSUR: Then we'll take the baby with us, too. Three months before the time you'll go to work so as to be able to say you saved up your wages to get to America.
        LILIOM: Which of us goes up and talks to him.
        FICSUR: One of us talks to him with his mouth and the other talks with his knife. Depends on which you'd rather do. I'll tell you what—you talk to him with your mouth.
        LILIOM: Do you hear that?
        FICSUR: What?
        LILIOM: Outside . . . like the rattle of swords. [Ficsur *listens. After a pause,* Liliom *continues*] What do I say to him?
        FICSUR: You say good-evening to him and: "Excuse me, sir; can you tell me the time?"
        LILIOM: And then what?
        FICSUR: By that time I'll have stuck him—and then you take *your knife*———
        [*He stops as a* Policeman *enters at back*]
        POLICEMAN: Good-day!
        FICSUR, LILIOM: [*In unison*] Good-day!
        FICSUR: [*Calling toward the kitchen*] Hey, photographer, come out. . . . Here's a customer.
        [*There is a pause. The* Policeman *waits.* Ficsur *sings softly*]
"And when you're in the prison cell
They'll feed you bread and water
They'll make your little sweetheart tell"
        LILIOM, FICSUR: [*Sing together, low*]
"Them all the things you brought her.
Look out here comes the———"
        [*They hum the rest so as not to let the* Policeman *hear the words "the damn police." As they sing,* Mrs. Hollunder *and her* Son *enter*]
        POLICEMAN: Do you make cabinet photographs?
        YOUNG HOLLUNDER: Certainly, sir. [*Points to a rack of photographs on the wall*] Take your choice, sir. Would you like one full length?
        POLICEMAN: Yes, full length.
        [Mother Hollunder *pushes out the camera while her* Son *poses the* Policeman, *runs from him to the camera and back again, now altering the pose, now ducking under the black cloth*

and pushing the camera nearer. Meanwhile Mother Hollunder *has fetched a plate from the dark-room and thrust it in the camera. While this is going on,* Liliom *and* Ficsur, *their heads together, speak in very low tones*]

LILIOM: Belong around here?

FICSUR: Not around here.

LILIOM: Where, then?

FICSUR: Suburban. [*There is a pause*]

LILIOM: [*Bursts out suddenly in a rather grotesquely childish and overstrained lament*] O God, what a dirty life I'm leading—God, God!

FICSUR: [*Reassuring him benevolently*] Over in America it will be better, all right.

LILIOM: What's over there?

FICSUR: [*Virtuously*] Factories . . . industries—

YOUNG HOLLUNDER: [*To the* Policeman] Now, quite still, please. One, two, three. [*Deftly removes the cover of the lens and in a few seconds restores it*] Thank you.

MOTHER HOLLUNDER: The picture will be ready in five minutes.

POLICEMAN: Good. I'll come back in five minutes. How much do I owe you?

YOUNG HOLLUNDER: [*With exaggerated deference*] You don't need to pay in advance, Mr. Commissioner.

[*The* Policeman *salutes condescendingly and exits at back.* Mother Hollunder *carries the plate into the dark-room.* Young Hollunder, *after pushing the camera back in place, follows her*]

MOTHER HOLLUNDER: [*Muttering angrily at she passes* Ficsur *and* Liliom] You hang around and dirty the whole place up! Why don't you go take a walk? Things are going so well with you that you have to sing, eh? [*Confronting* Ficsur *suddenly*] Weren't you frightened sick when you saw the policeman?

FICSUR: [*With loathing*] Go 'way, or I'll step on you. [*She exits into the dark-room*]

LILIOM: They like Hollinger at the carousel?

FICSUR: I should say they do.

LILIOM: Did you see the Muskat woman, too?

FICSUR: Sure. She takes care of Hollinger's hair.

LILIOM: Combs his hair?

FICSUR: She fixes him all up.

LILIOM: Let her fix him all she likes.

FICSUR: [*Urging him toward the kitchen door*] Go on. Now's your chance.

LILIOM: What for?

FICSUR: To get the knife.

LILIOM: What knife?

FICSUR: The kitchen knife. I've got a pocket-knife, but if he shows fight, we'll let him have the big knife.

LILIOM: What for? If he gets ugly, I'll bat him one over the head that'll make him squint for the rest of his life.

FICSUR: You've got to have something on you. You can't slit his throat with a bat over the head.

LILIOM: Must his throat be slit?

FICSUR: No, it *mustn't*. But if he asks for it. [*There is a pause*] You'd like to sail on the big steamer, wouldn't you? And you want to see the factories over there, don't you? But you're not willing to inconvenience yourself a little for them.

LILIOM: If I take the knife, Julie will see me.

FICSUR: Take it so she won't see you.

LILIOM: [*Advances a few paces toward the kitchen. The* Policeman *enters at back.* Liliom *knocks on the door of the dark-room*] Here's the policeman!

MOTHER HOLLUNDER: [*Coming out*] One minute more, please. Just a minute.

[*She reënters the dark-room.* Liliom *hesitates a moment, then exits into the kitchen. The* Policeman *scrutinizes* Ficsur *mockingly*]

FICSUR: [*Returns his stare, walks a few paces toward him, then deliberately turns his back. Suddenly he wheels around, points at the* Policeman *and addresses him in a teasing, childish tone*] Christiana Street at the corner of Retti!

POLICEMAN: [*Amazed, self-conscious*] How do you know that?

FICSUR: I used to practice my profession in that neighborhood.

POLICEMAN: What is your profession?

FICSUR: Professor of pianola——

[*The* Policeman *glares, aware that the man is joking with him, twirls his moustache indignantly.* Young Hollunder *comes out of the dark-room and gives him the finished pictures*]

YOUNG HOLLUNDER: Here you are, sir.

[*The* Policeman *examines the photographs, pays for them, starts to go, stops, glares at* Ficsur *and exits. When he is gone,* Ficsur *goes to the doorway and looks out after him.* Young Hollunder *exits.* Liliom *reënters, buttoning his coat*]

FICSUR: [*Turns, sees* Liliom] What are you staring at?

LILIOM: I'm not staring.

FICSUR: What then are you doing?

LILIOM: I'm thinking it over.

FICSUR: [*Comes very close to him*] Tell me then— what will you say to him?

LILIOM: [*Unsteadily*] I'll say—"Good-evening— Excuse me, sir—Can you tell me the time?" And suppose he answers me, what do I say to him?

FICSUR: He won't answer you.

LILIOM: Don't you think so?

FICSUR: No. [*Feeling for the knife under* Liliom's *coat*] Where is it? Where did you put it?

LILIOM: [*Stonily*] Left side.

FICSUR: That's right—over your heart. [*Feels it*] Ah—there it is—there—there's the blade—quite a big fellow, isn't it—ah, here it begins to get narrower. [*Reaches the tip of the knife*] And here is its eye—that's what it sees with. [Julie *enters from the kitchen, passes them slowly, watching them in silent terror, then stops.* Ficsur *nudges* Liliom] Sing, come on, sing!

LILIOM: [*In a quavering voice*]
"Look out for the damn police."

FICSUR: [*Joining in, cheerily, loudly, marking time with the swaying of his body*] "Look out, look out, my pretty lad."

LILIOM:
"—look out, my pretty lad."

[Julie *goes out at back.* Liliom's *glance follows her. When she has gone, he turns to* Ficsur] At night—in my dreams—if his ghost comes back—what will I do then?

FICSUR: His ghost won't never come back.

LILIOM: Why not?

FICSUR: A Jew's ghost don't come back.

LILIOM: Well then—afterwards——

FICSUR: [*Impatiently*] What do you mean—afterwards?

LILIOM: In the next world—when I come up before the Lord God—what'll I say then?

FICSUR: The likes of you will never come up before Him.

LILIOM: Why not?

FICSUR: Have you ever come up before the high court?

LILIOM: No.

FICSUR: Our kind comes up before the police magistrate—and the highest we *ever* get is the criminal court.

LILIOM: Will it be the same in the next world?

FICSUR: Just the same. We'll come up before a police magistrate, same as we did in this world.

LILIOM: A police magistrate?

FICSUR: Sure. For the rich folks—the Heavenly Court. For us poor people—only a police magistrate. For the rich folks—fine music and angels—For us——

LILIOM: For us?

FICSUR: For us, my son, there's only justice. In the next world there'll be lots of justice, yes, nothing but justice. And where there's justice, there must be police magistrates; and where they're police magistrates, people like us get——

LILIOM: [*Interrupting*] Good-evening. Excuse me, sir, can you tell me the time?

[*Lays his hand over his heart*]

FICSUR: What do you put your hand there for?

LILIOM: My heart is jumping—under the knife.

FICSUR: Put it on the other side then. [*Looks out at the sky*] It's time we started—we'll walk slow——

LILIOM: It's too early.

FICSUR: Come on.

[*As they are about to go,* Julie *appears in the doorway at back, obstructing the way*]

JULIE: Where are you going with him?

LILIOM: Where am I going with him?

JULIE: Stay home.

LILIOM: No.

JULIE: Stay home. It's going to rain soon, and you'll get wet.

FICSUR: It won't rain.

JULIE: How do you know?

FICSUR: I always get notice in advance.

JULIE: Stay home. This evening the carpenter's coming. I've asked him to give you work.

LILIOM: I'm not a carpenter.

JULIE: [*More and more anxious, though she tries to conceal it*] Stay home. Marie's coming with her intended to have their picture taken. She wants to introduce us to her intended husband.

LILIOM: I've seen enough intended husbands——

JULIE: Stay home. Marie's bringing some money, and I'll give it all to you.

LILIOM: [*Approaching the door*] I'm going—for a walk—with Ficsur. We'll be right back.

JULIE: [*Forcing a smile to keep back her tears*] If you stay home, I'll get you a glass of beer—or wine, if you prefer.

FICSUR: Coming or not?

JULIE: I'm not angry with you any more for hitting me.

LILIOM: [*Gruffly, but his gruffness is simulated to hide the fact that he cannot bear the sight of her suffering*] Stand out of the way—or I'll——[*He clenches his fist*] Let me out!

JULIE: [*Trembling*] What have you got under your coat?

LILIOM: [*Produces from his pocket a greasy pack of cards*] Cards.

JULIE: [*Trembling, speaks very low*] What's under your coat?

LILIOM: Let me out!

JULIE: [*Obstructing the way. Speaks quickly, eagerly, in a last effort to detain him*] Marie's intended knows about a place for a married couple without children to be caretakers of a house on Arader Street. Rent free, a kitchen of your own, and the privilege of keeping chickens——

LILIOM: Get out of the way!

[Julie *stands aside.* Liliom *exits.* Ficsur *follows him.* Julie *remains standing meditatively in the doorway.* Mother Hollunder *comes out of the kitchen*]

MOTHER HOLLUNDER: I can't find my kitchen knife anywhere. Have you seen anything of it?

JULIE: [*Horrified*] No.

MOTHER HOLLUNDER: It was on the kitchen table just a few minutes ago. No one was in there except Liliom.

JULIE: He didn't take it.

MOTHER HOLLUNDER: No one else was in there.

JULIE: What would Liliom want with a kitchen knife?

MOTHER HOLLUNDER: He'd sell it and spend the money on drink.

JULIE: It just so happens—see how unjust you

are to him—it just so happens that I went through all of Liliom's pockets just now—I wanted to see if he had any money on him. But he had nothing but a pack of cards.

MOTHER HOLLUNDER: [*Returns to the kitchen, grumbling*] Cards in his pocket—cards! The fine gentlemen have evidently gone off to their club to play a little game.

> [*She exits. After a pause* Marie, *happy and beaming, appears in the doorway at back, and enters, followed by* Wolf]

MARIE: Here we are! [*She takes* Wolf *by the hand and leads him, grinning shyly, to* Julie, *who has turned at her call*] Hello!

JULIE: Hello.

MARIE: Well, we're here.

JULIE: Yes.

WOLF: [*Bows awkwardly and extends his hand*] My name is Wolf Beifeld.

JULIE: My name is Julie Zeller.

> [*They shake hands. There is an embarrassed silence. Then, to relieve the situation,* Wolf *takes* Julie's *hand again ana shakes it vigorously*]

MARIE: Well—this is Wolf.

WOLF: Yes.

JULIE: Yes. [*Another awkward silence*]

MARIE: Where is Liliom?

WOLF: Yes, where is your husband?

JULIE: He's out.

MARIE: Where?

JULIE: Just for a walk.

MARIE: Is he?

JULIE: Yes.

WOLF: Oh!

> [*Another silence*]

MARIE: Wolf's got a new place. After the first of the month he won't have to stand outside any more. He's going to work in a club after the first of the month.

WOLF: [*Apologetically*] She don't know yet how to explain these things just right—hehehe—— Beginning the first I'm to be second steward at the Burger Club—a good job, if one conducts oneself properly.

JULIE: Yes?

WOLF: The pay—is quite good—but the main thing is the tips. When they play cards there's always a bit for the steward. The tips, I may say, amount to twenty, even thirty kronen every night.

MARIE: Yes.

WOLF: We've rented two rooms for ourselves to start with—and if things go well——

MARIE: Then we'll buy a house in the country.

WOLF: If one only tends to business and keeps honest. Of course, in the country we'll miss the city life, but if the good Lord sends us children—it's much healthier for children in the country.

> [*There is a brief pause*]

MARIE: Wolf's nice looking, isn't he?

JULIE: Yes.

MARIE: And he's a good boy, Wolf.

JULIE: Yes.

MARIE: The only thing is—he's a Jew.

JULIE: Oh, well, you can get used to that.

MARIE: Well, aren't you going to wish us luck?

JULIE: Of course I do.

> [*She embraces* Marie]

MARIE: And aren't you going to kiss Wolf, too?

JULIE: Him, too.

> [*She embraces* Wolf, *remains quite still a moment, her head resting on his shoulder*]

WOLF: Why are you crying, my dear Mrs.——

> [*He looks questioningly at* Marie *over* Julie's *shoulder*]

MARIE: Because she has such a good heart. [*She becomes sentimental, too*]

WOLF: [*Touched*] We thank you for your heartfelt sympathy——

> [*He cannot restrain his own tears. There is a pause before* Mother Hollunder *and her son enter.* Young Hollunder *immediately busies himself with the camera*]

MOTHER HOLLUNDER: Now if you don't mind, we'll do it right away, before it gets too dark. [*She leads* Marie *and* Wolf *into position before the background-screen. Here they immediately fall into an awkward pose, smiling mechanically*] Full length?

MARIE: Please. Both figures full length.

MOTHER HOLLUNDER: Bride and groom?

MARIE: Yes.

MOTHER HOLLUNDER, YOUNG HOLLUNDER: [*Speak in unison, in loud professionally expressionless tones*] The lady looks at the gentleman and the gentleman looks straight into the camera.

MOTHER HOLLUNDER: [*Poses first* Marie, *then* Wolf] Now, if you please.

YOUNG HOLLUNDER: [*Who has crept under the black cloth, calls in muffled tones*] That's good—that's very good!

MARIE: [*Stonily rigid, but very happy, trying to speak without altering her expression*] Julie, dear, do we look all right?

JULIE: Yes, dear.

YOUNG HOLLUNDER: Now, if you please, hold still. I'll count up to three, and then you must hold perfectly still. [*Grasps the cover of the lens and calls threateningly*] One—two—three!

> [*He removes the cover; there is utter silence. But as he speaks the word "one" there is heard, very faintly in the distance, the refrain of the thieves' song which* Ficsur *and* Liliom *have been singing. The refrain continues until the fall of the curtain. As he speaks the word "three" everybody is perfectly rigid save* Julie, *who lets her head sink slowly to the table. The distant refrain dies out*]

THE CURTAIN FALLS

SCENE IV.

*In the fields on the outskirts of the city. At back
a railroad embankment crosses the stage obliquely.
At center of the embankment stands a red and
white signal flag, and near it a little red signal lamp
which is not yet lighted. Here also a wooden stairway leads up to the embankment.*

*At the foot of the embankment to the right is a
pile of used railroad ties. In the background a telegraph pole, beyond it a view of trees, fences and
fields; still further back a factory building and a
cluster of little dwellings.*

*It is six o'clock of the same afternoon. Dusk has
begun to fall.*

*Liliom and Ficsur are discovered on the stairway
looking after the train which has just passed.*

LILIOM: Can you still hear it snort?

FICSUR: Listen!

[*They watch the vanishing train*]

LILIOM: If you put your ear on the tracks you
can hear it go all the way to Vienna.

FICSUR: Huh!

LILIOM: The one that just puffed past us—it goes
all the way to Vienna.

FICSUR: No further?

LILIOM: Yes—further, too.

[*There is a pause*]

FICSUR: It must be near six. [*As Liliom ascends
the steps*] Where are you going?

LILIOM: Don't be afraid. I'm not giving you the
slip.

FICSUR: Why should you give me the slip? That
cashier has sixteen thousand kronen on him. Just be
patient till he comes, then you can talk to him, nice
and polite.

LILIOM: I say, "Good-evening—excuse me, sir;
what time is it?"

FICSUR: Then he tells you what time it is.

LILIOM: Suppose he don't come?

FICSUR: [*Coming down the steps*] Nonsense! He's
got to come. He pays off the workmen every Saturday. And this is Saturday, ain't it? [*Liliom has as-
cended to the top of the stairway and is gazing along
the tracks*] What are you looking at up there?

LILIOM: The tracks go on and on—there's no end
to them.

FICSUR: What's that to stare about?

LILIOM: Nothing—only I always look after the
train. When you stand down there at night it snorts
past you, and spits down.

FICSUR: Spits?

LILIOM: Yes, the engine. It spits down. And then
the whole train rattles past and away—and you
stand there—spat on—but it draws your eyes along
with it.

FICSUR: Draws your eyes along?

LILIOM: Yes—whether you want to or not, you've

got to look after it—as long as the tiniest bit of it is
in sight.

FICSUR: Swell people sit in it.

LILIOM: And read newspapers.

FICSUR: And smoke cigars.

LILIOM: And inhale the smoke.

[*There is a short silence*]

FICSUR: Is he coming?

LILIOM: Not yet. [*Silence again. Liliom comes
down, speaks low, confidentially*] Do you hear the
telegraph wires?

FICSUR: I hear them when the wind blows.

LILIOM: Even when the wind doesn't blow you
can hear them humming, humming —— People
talk through them.

FICSUR: Who?

LILIOM: Jews.

FICSUR: No—they telegraph.

LILIOM: They talk through them and from some
other place they get answered. And it all goes
through the iron strings—that's why they hum like
that—they hum-m——

FICSUR: What do they hum?

LILIOM: They hum! ninety-nine, ninety-nine. Just
listen.

FICSUR: What for?

LILIOM: That sparrow's listening, too. He's cocked
one eye and looks at me as if to say: "I'd like to
know what they're talking about."

FICSUR: You're looking at a bird?

LILIOM: He's looking at me, too.

FICSUR: Listen, you're sick! There's something the
matter with you. Do you know what it is? Money.
That bird has no money, either; that's why he cocks
his eye.

LILIOM: Maybe.

FICSUR: Whoever has money don't cock his eye.

LILIOM: What then does he do?

FICSUR: He does most anything he wants. But
nobody works unless he has money. We'll soon have
money ourselves.

LILIOM: I say, "Good-evening. Excuse me, sir, can
you tell me what time it is!"

FICSUR: He's not coming yet. Got the cards?
[*Liliom gives him the pack of cards*] Got any
money?

LILIOM: [*Takes some coins from his trousers
pocket and counts*] Eleven.

FICSUR: [*Sits astride on the pile of ties and looks
off left*] All right—eleven.

LILIOM: [*Sitting astride on the ties facing him*]
Put it up.

FICSUR: [*Puts the money on the ties; rapidly shuffles the cards*] We'll play twenty-one. I'll bank.

[*He deals deftly*]

LILIOM: [*Looks at his card*] Good. I'll bet the
bank.

FICSUR: Must have an ace!

[*Deals him a second card*]

LILIOM: Another one. [*He gets another card*] Another. [*Gets still another*] Over! [*Throws down his cards.* Ficsur *gathers in the money*] Come on!

FICSUR: Come on what! Got no more money, have you?

LILIOM: No.

FICSUR: Then the game's over—unless you want to——

LILIOM: What?

FICSUR: Play on credit.

LILIOM: You'll trust me?

FICSUR: No—but—I'll deduct it.

LILIOM: Deduct it from what?

FICSUR: From your share of the money. If *you* win you deduct from my share.

LILIOM: [*Looks over his shoulder to see if the cashier is coming; nervous and ashamed*] All right. How much is bank?

FICSUR: That cashier is bringing us sixteen thousand kronen. Eight thousand of that is mine. Well, then, the bank is eight thousand.

LILIOM: Good.

FICSUR: Whoever has the most luck will have the most money.

[*He deals*]

LILIOM: Six hundred kronen. [Ficsur *gives him another card*] Enough.

FICSUR: [*Laying out his own cards*] Twenty-one. [*He shuffles rapidly*]

LILIOM: [*Moves excitedly nearer to* Ficsur] Well, then, double or nothing.

FICSUR: [*Dealing*] Double or nothing.

LILIOM: [*Gets a card*] Enough.

FICSUR: [*Laying out his own cards*] Twenty-one. [*Shuffles rapidly again*]

LILIOM: [*In alarm*] You're not—cheating?

FICSUR: Me? Do I look like a cheat? [*Deals the cards again*]

LILIOM: [*Glances nervously over his shoulder*] A thousand.

FICSUR: [*Nonchalantly*] Kronen?

LILIOM: Kronen. [*He gets a card*] Another one. [*Gets another card*] Over again!

[*Like an inexperienced gambler who is losing heavily,* Liliom *is very nervous. He plays dazedly, wildly, irrationally. From now on it is apparent that his only thought is to win his money back*]

FICSUR: That makes twelve hundred you owe.

LILIOM: Double or nothing. [*He gets a card. He is greatly excited*] Another one. [*Gets another card*] Another.

[*Throws down three cards*]

FICSUR: [*Bends over and adds up the sum on the ground*] Ten—fourteen—twenty-three—— You owe two thousand, four hundred.

LILIOM: Now what?

FICSUR: [*Takes a card out of the deck and gives it to him*] Here's the red ace. You can play double or nothing again.

LILIOM: [*Eagerly*] Good. [*Gets another card*] Enough.

FICSUR: [*Turns up his own cards*] Nineteen.

LILIOM: You win again. [*Almost imploring*] Give me an ace again. Give me the green one. [*Takes a card*] Double or nothing.

FICSUR: Not any more.

LILIOM: Why not?

FICSUR: Because if you lose you won't be able to pay. Double would be nine thousand six hundred And you've only got eight thousand altogether.

LILIOM: [*Greatly excited*] That—that—I call that —a dirty trick!

FICSUR: Three thousand, two hundred. That's all you can put up.

LILIOM: [*Eagerly*] All right, then—three thousand, two hundred. [Ficsur *deals him a card*] Enough.

FICSUR: I've got an ace myself. Now we'll have to take our time and squeeze 'em. [Liliom *pushes closer to him as he takes up his cards and slowly, intently unfolds them*] Twenty-one.

[*He quickly puts the cards in his pocket. There is a pause*]

LILIOM: Now—now—I'll tell you now—you're a crook, a low-down——

[*Now* Linzman *enters at right. He is a strong, robust, red-bearded Jew about 40 years of age. At his side he carries a leather bag slung by a strap from his shoulder.* Ficsur *coughs warningly, moves to the right between* Linzman *and the embankment, pauses just behind* Linzman *and follows him*]

LILIOM: [*Stands bewildered a few paces to the left of the railroad ties. He finds himself facing* Linzman. *Trembling in every limb*] Good-evening. Excuse me, sir, can you tell me the time?

[Ficsur *springs silently at* Linzman, *the little knife in his right hand. But* Linzman *catches* Ficsur's *right hand with his own left and forces* Ficsur *to his knees. Simultaneously* Linzman *thrusts his right hand into his coat pocket and produces a revolver which he points at* Liliom's *breast.* Liliom *is standing two paces away from the revolver. There is a long pause*]

LINZMAN: [*In a low, even voice*] It is twenty-five minutes past six. [*Pauses, looks ironically down at* Ficsur] It's lucky I grabbed the hand with the knife instead of the other one. [*Pauses again, looks appraisingly from one to the other*] Two fine birds! [*To* Ficsur] I should live so—Rothschild has more luck than you. [*To* Liliom] I'd advise you to keep nice and quiet. If you make one move, you'll get two bullets in you. Just look into the barrel. You'll see some little things in there made of lead.

FICSUR: Let me go. I didn't do anything.

LINZMAN: [*Mockingly shakes the hand which still holds the knife*] And this? What do you call this? Oh, yes, I know. You thought I had an apple in my pocket, and you wanted to peel it. That's it. Forgive me for my error. I beg your pardon, sir.

LILIOM: But I—I——

LINZMAN: Yes, my son, I know. It's so simple. You only asked what time it is. Well, it's twenty-five minutes after six.

FICSUR: Let us go, honorable sir. We didn't do anything to you.

LINZMAN: In the first place, my son, I'm not an honorable sir. In the second place, for the same money, you could have said Your Excellency. But in the third place you'll find it very hard to beg off by flattering me.

LILIOM: But I—*I* really didn't do anything to you.

LINZMAN: Look behind you, my boy. Don't be afraid. Look behind you, but don't run away or I'll have to shoot you down. [Liliom *turns his head slowly around*] Who's coming up there?

LILIOM: [*Looking at* Linzman] Policemen.

LINZMAN: [*To* Ficsur] You hold still, or——[*To* Liliom *teasingly*] How many policemen are there?

LILIOM: [*His eyes cast down*] Two.

LINZMAN: And what are the policemen sitting on?

LILIOM: Horses.

LINZMAN: And which can run faster, a horse or a man?

LILIOM: A horse.

LINZMAN: There, you see. It would be hard to get away now. [*Laughs*] I never saw such an unlucky pair of highway robbers. I can't imagine worse luck. Just to-day I had to put a pistol in my pocket. And even if I hadn't—old Linzman is a match for four like you. But even that isn't all. Did you happen to notice, you oxen, what direction I came from? From the factory, didn't I? When I *went* there I had a nice bit of money with me. Sixteen thousand crowns! But now—not a heller. [*Calls off left*] Hey, come quicker, will you? This fellow is pulling pretty strong. [Ficsur *frees himself with a mighty wrench and darts rapidly off. As* Linzman *aims his pistol at the vanishing* Ficsur, Liliom *runs up the steps to the embankment.* Linzman *hesitates, perceives that* Liliom *is the better target, points the pistol at him*] Stop, or I'll shoot [*Calls off left to the* Policemen] Why don't you come down off your horses? [*His pistol is leveled at* Liliom, *who stands on the embankment, facing the audience. From the left on the embankment a* Policeman *appears, revolver in hand*]

FIRST POLICEMAN: Stop!

LINZMAN: Well, my boy, do you still want to know what time it is? From ten to twelve years in prison!

LILIOM: You won't get me! [Linzman *laughs derisively.* Liliom *is now three or four paces from the* Policeman *and equally distant from* Linzman. *His face is uplifted to the sky. He bursts into laughter, half defiant, half self-pitying, and takes the kitchen knife from under his coat*] Julie——

[*The ring of farewell is in the word. He turns sideways, thrusts the knife deep in his breast, sways, falls and rolls down the far side of the embankment. There is a long pause. From the left up on the embankment come the Two Policemen*]

LINZMAN: What's the matter? [*The First Policeman comes along the embankment as far as the steps, looks down in the opposite side, then climbs down at about the spot where* Liliom *disappeared.* Linzman *and the other* Policeman *mount the embankment and look down on him*] Stabbed himself?

VOICE OF FIRST POLICEMAN: Yes—and he seems to have made a thorough job of it.

LINZMAN: [*Excitedly to* Second Policeman] I'll go and telephone to the hospital.

[*He runs down the steps and exits at left*]

SECOND POLICEMAN: Go to Eisler's grocery store and telephone to the factory from there. They've a doctor there, too. [*Calling down to the other* Policeman] I'm going to tie up the horses.

[*Comes down the steps and exits at left. The stage is empty. There is a pause. The little red signal lamp is lit*]

VOICE OF FIRST POLICEMAN: Hey, Stephan?

VOICE OF SECOND POLICEMAN: What?

VOICE OF FIRST POLICEMAN: Shall I pull the knife out of his chest?

VOICE OF SECOND POLICEMAN: Better not, or he may bleed to death.

[*There is a pause*]

VOICE OF FIRST POLICEMAN: Stephan!

VOICE OF SECOND POLICEMAN: Yes.

VOICE OF FIRST POLICEMAN: Lot of mosquitoes around here.

VOICE OF SECOND POLICEMAN: Yes.

VOICE OF FIRST POLICEMAN: Got a cigar?

VOICE OF SECOND POLICEMAN: No.

[*There is a pause. The* First Policeman *appears over the opposite side of the embankment*]

FIRST POLICEMAN: A lot of good the new pay-schedule's done us—made things worse than they used to be—we *get* more but we *have* less than we ever had. If the Government could be made to realize that. It's a thankless job at best. You work hard year after year, you get gray in the service, and slowly you die—yes.

SECOND POLICEMAN: That's right.

FIRST POLICEMAN: Yes.

[*In the distance is heard the bell of the signal tower*]

THE CURTAIN FALLS

SCENE V.

The photographic "studio" a half hour later that same evening.

Mother Hollunder, *her* Son, Marie *and* Wolf *stand in a group back right, their heads together.* Julie *stands apart from them, a few paces to the left.*

YOUNG HOLLUNDER: [*Who has just come in, tells his story excitedly*] They're bringing him now. Two workmen from the factory are carrying him on a stretcher.

WOLF: Where is the doctor?

YOUNG HOLLUNDER: A policeman telephoned to headquarters. The police-surgeon ought to be here any minute.

MARIE: Maybe they'll pull him through after all.

YOUNG HOLLUNDER: He stabbed himself too deep in his chest. But he's still breathing. He can still talk, too, but very faintly. At first he lay there unconscious, but when they put him on the stretcher he came to.

WOLF: That was from the shaking.

MARIE: We'd better make room.

[*They make room. Two workmen carry in* Liliom *on a stretcher which has four legs and stands about as high as a bed. They put the stretcher at left directly in front of the sofa, so that the head is at right and the foot at left. Then they unobtrusively join the group at the door. Later, they go out.* Julie *is standing at the side of the stretcher, where, without moving, she can see* Liliom's *face. The others crowd emotionally together near the door. The* First Policeman *enters*]

FIRST POLICEMAN: Are you his wife?

JULIE: Yes.

FIRST POLICEMAN: The doctor at the factory who bandaged him up forbade us to take him to the hospital.—Dangerous to move him that far. What he needs now is rest. Just let him be until the police-surgeon comes. [*To the group near the door*] He's not to be disturbed.

[*They make way for him. He exits. There is a pause*]

WOLF: [*Gently urging the others out*] Please— it's best if we all get out of here now. We'll only be in the way.

MARIE: [*To* Julie] Julie, what do you think? [Julie *looks at her without answering*] Julie, can I do anything to help? [Julie *does not answer*] We'll be just outside on the bench if you want us.

[Mother Hollunder *and her* Son *have gone out when first requested. Now* Marie *and* Wolf *exit, too.* Julie *sits on the edge of the stretcher and looks at* Liliom. *He stretches his hand out to her. She clasps it. It is not quite dark yet. Both of them can still be plainly seen*]

LILIOM: [*Raises himself with difficulty; speaks lightly at first, but later soberly, defiantly*] Little— Julie—there's something—I want to tell you—like when you go to a restaurant—and you've finished eating—and it's time—to pay—then you have to count up everything—everything you owe—well— I beat you—not because I was mad at you—no— only because I can't bear to see any one crying. You always cried—on my account—and, well, you see— I never learned a trade—what kind of a caretaker

would I make? But anyhow—I wasn't going back to the carousel to fool with the girls. No, I spit on them all—understand?

JULIE: Yes.

LILIOM: And—as for Hollinger—he's good enough—Mrs. Muskat can get along all right with him. The jokes he tells are mine—and the people laugh when he tells them—but I don't care.—I didn't give you anything—no home—not even the food you ate—but you don't understand.—It's true I'm not much good—but I couldn't be a caretaker— and so I thought maybe it would be better over there—in America—do you see?

JULIE: Yes.

LILIOM: I'm not asking—forgiveness—I don't do that—I don't. Tell the baby—if you like.

JULIE: Yes.

LILIOM: Tell the baby—I wasn't much good—but tell him—if you ever talk about me—tell him—I thought—perhaps—over in America—but that's no affair of yours. I'm not asking forgiveness. For my part the police can come now.—If it's a boy—if it's a girl.—Perhaps I'll see the Lord God to-day.—Do you think I'll see Him?

JULIE: Yes.

LILIOM: I'm not afraid—of the police Up There— if they'll only let me come up in front of the Lord God Himself—not like down here where an officer stops you at the door. If the carpenter asks you— yes—be his wife—marry him. And the child—tell him he's his father.—He'll believe you—won't he?

JULIE: Yes.

LILIOM: When I beat you—I was right.—You mustn't always think—you mustn't always be right. —Liliom can be right once, too.—It's all the same to me who was right.—It's so dumb. Nobody's right —but they all think they are right.—A lot they know!

JULIE: Yes.

LILIOM: Julie—come—hold my hand tight.

JULIE: I'm holding it tight—all the time.

LILIOM: Tighter, still tighter—I'm going—— [*Pauses*] Julie——

JULIE: Good-bye.

[Liliom *sinks slowly back and dies.* Julie *frees her hand. The* Doctor *enters with the* First Policeman]

DOCTOR: Good-evening. His wife?

JULIE: Yes, sir.

[*Behind the* Doctor *and* Policeman *enter* Marie, Wolf, Mother Hollunder, Young Hollunder *and* Mrs. Muskat. *They remain respectfully at the doorway. The* Doctor *bends over* Liliom *and examines him*]

DOCTOR: A light, if you please. [Julie *fetches a burning candle from the dark-room. The* Doctor *examines* Liliom *briefly in the candle-light, then turns suddenly away*] Have you pen and ink?

WOLF: [*Proffering a pen*] A fountain-pen—American——

DOCTOR: [*Takes a printed form from his pocket; speaks as he writes out the death-certificate at the little table*] My poor woman, your husband is dead —there's nothing to be done for him—the good God will help him now—I'll leave this certificate with you. You will give it to the people from the hospital when they come—I'll arrange for the body to be removed at once. [*Rises*] Please give me a towel and soap.

POLICEMAN: I've got them for you out here, sir. [*Points to door at back*]

DOCTOR: God be with you, my good woman.

JULIE: Thank you, sir.

[*The* Doctor *and* Policeman *exit. The others slowly draw nearer*]

MARIE: Poor Julie. May he rest in peace, poor man, but as for you—please don't be angry with me for saying it—but you're better off this way.

MOTHER HOLLUNDER: He is better off, the poor fellow, and so are you.

MARIE: Much better, Julie . . . you are young . . . and one of these days some good man will come along. Am I right?

WOLF: She's right.

MARIE: Julie, tell me, am I right?

JULIE: You are right, dear; you are very good.

YOUNG HOLLUNDER: There's a good man—the carpenter. Oh, I can speak of it now. He comes here every day on some excuse or other—and he never fails to ask for you.

MARIE: A widower—with two children.

MOTHER HOLLUNDER: He's better off, poor fellow —and so are you. He was a bad man.

MARIE: He wasn't good-hearted. Was he, Wolf?

WOLF: No, I must say, he really wasn't. No, Liliom wasn't a good man. A good man doesn't strike a woman.

MARIE: Am I right? Tell me, Julie, am I right?

JULIE: You are right, dear.

YOUNG HOLLUNDER: It's really a good thing for her it happened.

MOTHER HOLLUNDER: He's better off—and so is she.

WOLF: Now you have your freedom again. How old are you?

JULIE: Eighteen.

WOLF: Eighteen. A mere child! Am I right?

JULIE: You are right, Wolf. You are kind.

YOUNG HOLLUNDER: Lucky for you it happened, isn't it?

JULIE: Yes.

YOUNG HOLLUNDER: All you had before was bad luck. If it weren't for my mother you wouldn't have had a roof over your head or a bite to eat—and now Autumn's coming and Winter. You couldn't have lived in this shack in the Winter time, could you?

MARIE: Certainly not! You'd have frozen like the birds in the fields. Am I right, Julie?

JULIE: Yes, Marie.

MARIE: A year from now you will have forgotten all about him, won't you?

JULIE: You are right, Marie.

WOLF: If you need anything, count on us. We'll go now. But to-morrow morning we'll be back. Come, Marie. God be with you.

[*Offers* Julie *his hand*]

JULIE: God be with you.

MARIE: [*Embraces* Julie, *weeping*] It's the best thing that could have happened to you, Julie, the best thing.

JULIE: Don't cry, Marie.

[Marie *and* Wolf *exit*]

MOTHER HOLLUNDER: I'll make a little black coffee. You haven't had a thing to eat to-day. Then you'll come home with us.

[Mother Hollunder *and her* Son *exit*. Mrs. Muskat *comes over to* Julie]

MRS. MUSKAT: Would you mind if I—looked at him?

JULIE: He used to work for you.

MRS. MUSKAT: [*Contemplates the body; turns to* Julie] Won't you make up with me?

JULIE: I wasn't angry with you.

MRS. MUSKAT: But you were. Let's make it up.

JULIE: [*Raising her voice eagerly, almost triumphantly*] I've nothing to make up with *you*.

MRS. MUSKAT: But I have with you. Every one says hard things against the poor dead boy—except us two. You don't say he was bad.

JULIE: [*Raising her voice yet higher, this time on a defiant, wholly triumphant note*] Yes, I *do*.

MRS. MUSKAT: I understand, my child. But he beat me too. What does that matter? I've forgotten it.

JULIE: [*From now on answers her coldly, dryly, without looking at her*] That's your own affair.

MRS. MUSKAT: If I can help you in any way——

JULIE: There's nothing I need.

MRS. MUSKAT: I still owe him two kronen, back pay.

JULIE: You should have paid him.

MRS. MUSKAT: Now that the poor fellow is dead I thought perhaps it would be the same if I paid you.

JULIE: I've nothing to do with it.

MRS. MUSKAT: All right. Please don't think I'm trying to force myself on you. I stayed because we two are the only ones on earth who loved him. That's why I thought we ought to stick together.

JULIE: No, thank you.

MRS. MUSKAT: Then you couldn't have loved him as I did.

JULIE: No.

MRS. MUSKAT: I loved him better.

JULIE: Yes.

MRS. MUSKAT: Good-bye.

JULIE: Good-bye. [Mrs. Muskat *exits. Julie puts the candle on the table near* Liliom's *head, sits on the edge of the stretcher, looks into the dead man's face and caresses it tenderly*] Sleep, Liliom, sleep—

it's no business of hers—I never even told you—but now I'll tell you—now I'll tell you—you bad, quick-tempered, rough, unhappy, wicked—*dear* boy—sleep peacefully, Liliom—they can't understand how I feel—I can't even explain to you—not even to you—how I feel—you'd only laugh at me—but you can't hear me any more. [*Between tender motherliness and reproach, yet with great love in her voice*] It was wicked of you to beat me—on the breast and on the head and face—but you're gone now.—You treated me badly—that was wicked of you—but sleep peacefully, Liliom—you bad, bad boy, you—I love you—I never told you before—I was ashamed—but now I've told you—I love you. Liliom—sleep—my boy—sleep.

[*She rises, gets a Bible, sits down near the candle and reads softly to herself, so that not the words but an inarticulate murmur is heard. The* Carpenter *enters at back*]

CARPENTER: [*Stands near the door; in the dimness of the room he can scarcely be seen*] Miss Julie——

JULIE: [*Without alarm*] Who is that?

CARPENTER: [*Very slowly*] The carpenter.

JULIE: What does the carpenter want?

CARPENTER: Can I be of help to you in any way? Shall I stay here with you?

JULIE: [*Gratefully, but firmly*] Don't stay, carpenter.

CARPENTER: Shall I come back to-morrow?

JULIE: Not to-morrow, either.

CARPENTER: Don't be offended, Miss Julie, but I'd like to know—you see, I'm not a young man any more—I have two children—and if I'm to come back any more—I'd like to know—if there's any use——

JULIE: No use, carpenter.

CARPENTER: [*As he exits*] God be with you.

[*Julie resumes her reading. Ficsur enters, slinks furtively sideways to the stretcher, looks at Liliom, shakes his head. Julie looks up from her reading. Ficsur takes fright, slinks away from the stretcher, sits down at right, biting his nails. Julie rises. Ficsur rises, too, and looks at her half fearfully. With her piercing glance upon him he slinks to the doorway at back, where he pauses and speaks*]

FICSUR: The old woman asked me to tell you that coffee is ready, and you are to come in.

[*Julie goes to the kitchen door. Ficsur withdraws until she has closed the door behind her. Then he reappears in the doorway, stands on tiptoes, looks at Liliom, then exits. Now the body lies alone. After a brief silence music is heard, distant at first, but gradually coming nearer. It is very much like the music of the carousel, but slower, graver, more exalted. The melody, too, is the same, yet the tempo is altered and contrapuntal measures of the thieves' song are intertwined in it. Two men in black, with heavy sticks, soft black hats and* black gloves, appear in the doorway at back and stride slowly into the room. Their faces are beardless, marble white, grave and benign. One stops in front of the stretcher, the other a pace to the right. From above a dim violet light illuminates their faces*]

THE FIRST: [*To* Liliom] Rise and come with us.

THE SECOND: [*Politely*] You're under arrest.

THE FIRST: [*Somewhat louder, but always in a gentle, low, resonant voice*] Do you hear? Rise. Don't you hear?

THE SECOND: We are the police.

THE FIRST: [*Bends down, touches* Liliom's *shoulder*] Get up and come with us.

[Liliom *slowly sits up*]

THE SECOND: Come along.

THE FIRST: [*Paternally*] These people suppose that when they die all their difficulties are solved for them.

THE SECOND: [*Raising his voice sternly*] That simply by thrusting a knife in your heart and making it stop beating you can leave your wife behind with a child in her womb——

THE FIRST: It is not as simple as that.

THE SECOND: Such things are not settled so easily.

THE FIRST: Come along. You will have to give an account of yourself. [*As both bow their heads, he continues softly*] We are God's police. [*An expression of glad relief lights upon* Liliom's *face. He rises from the stretcher*] Come.

THE SECOND: You mortals don't get off quite as easy as that.

THE FIRST: [*Softly*] Come. [Liliom *starts to walk ahead of them, then stops and looks at them*] The end is not as abrupt as that. Your name is still spoken. Your face is still remembered. And what you did, and what you failed to do—these are still remembered. Remembered, too, are the manner of your glance, the ring of your voice, the clasp of your hand and how your step sounded—as long as one is left who remembers you, so long is the matter unended. Before the end there is much to be undone. Until you are quite forgotten, my son, you will not be finished with the earth—even though you **are** dead.

THE SECOND: [*Very gently*] Come.

[*The music begins again. All three exit at back,* Liliom *leading, the others following. The stage is empty and quite dark save for the candle which burns by the stretcher, on which, in the shadows, the covers are so arranged that one cannot quite be sure that a body is not still lying. The music dies out in the distance as if it had followed* Liliom *and the two Policemen. The candle flickers and goes out. There is a brief interval of silence and total darkness before*

THE CURTAIN FALLS]

SCENE VI.

In the Beyond. A whitewashed courtroom. There is a green-topped table; behind it a bench. Back center is a door with a bell over it. Next to this door is a window through which can be seen a vista of rose-tinted clouds.

Down right there is a grated iron door.

Down left another door.

Two men are on the bench when the curtain rises. One is richly, the other poorly dressed.

From a great distance is heard a fanfare of trumpets playing the refrain of the thieves' song in slow, altered tempo.

Passing the window at back appear Liliom *and the two* Policemen.

The bell rings.

An old Guard *enters at right. He is bald and has a long white beard. He wears the conventional police uniform.*

He goes to the door at back, opens it, exchanges silent greetings with the two Policemen *and closes the door again.*

Liliom *looks wonderingly around.*

THE FIRST: [*To the old* Guard] Announce us.

    [*The* Guard *exits at left*]

LILIOM: Is this it?

THE SECOND: Yes, my son.

LILIOM: This is the police court?

THE SECOND: Yes, my son. The part for suicide cases.

LILIOM: And what happens here?

THE FIRST: Here justice is done. Sit down.

    [Liliom *sits next to the two men. The two* Policemen *stand silent near the table*]

THE RICHLY DRESSED MAN: [*Whispers*] Suicide, too?

    LILIOM: Yes.

THE RICHLY DRESSED MAN: [*Points to* The Poorly Dressed Man] So's he. [*Introducing himself*] My name is Reich.

THE POORLY DRESSED MAN: [*Whispers, too*] My name is Stephan Kadar.

    [Liliom *only looks at them*]

THE POORLY DRESSED MAN: And you? What's your name?

LILIOM: None of your business.

    [*Both move a bit away from him*]

THE POORLY DRESSED MAN: I did it by jumping out of a window.

THE RICHLY DRESSED MAN: I did it with a pistol— and you?

LILIOM: With a knife.

    [*They move a bit further away from him*]

THE RICHLY DRESSED MAN: A pistol is cleaner.

LILIOM: If I had the price of a pistol——

THE SECOND: Silence!

    [*The* Police Magistrate *enters. He has a long white beard, is bald, but only in profile can be seen on his head a single tuft of snow-white hair. The* Guard *reënters behind him and sits on the bench with the dead men. As* The Magistrate *enters, all rise, except* Liliom, *who remains surlily seated. When* The Magistrate *sits down, so do the others*]

THE GUARD: Yesterday's cases, your honor. The numbers are entered in the docket.

THE MAGISTRATE: Number 16,472.

THE FIRST: [*Looks in his notebook, beckons* The Richly Dressed Man] Stand up, please. [The Richly Dressed Man *rises*]

THE MAGISTRATE: Your name?

THE RICHLY DRESSED MAN: Doctor Reich.

THE MAGISTRATE: Age?

THE RICHLY DRESSED MAN: Forty-two, married, Jew.

THE MAGISTRATE: [*With a gesture of dismissal*] Religion does not interest us here.—Why did you kill yourself?

THE RICHLY DRESSED MAN: On account of debts.

THE MAGISTRATE: What good did you do on earth?

THE RICHLY DRESSED MAN: I was a lawyer——

THE MAGISTRATE: [*Coughs significantly*] Yes— we'll discuss that later. For the present I shall only ask you: Would you like to go back to earth once more before sunrise? I advise you that you have the right to go if you choose. Do you understand?

THE RICHLY DRESSED MAN: Yes, sir.

THE MAGISTRATE: He who takes his life is apt, in his haste and his excitement, to forget something. Is there anything important down there you have left undone? Something to tell some one? Something to undo?

THE RICHLY DRESSED MAN: My debts——

THE MAGISTRATE: They do not matter here. Here we are concerned only with the affairs of the soul.

THE RICHLY DRESSED MAN: Then—if you please— when I left—the house—my youngest son, Oscar— was asleep. I didn't trust myself to wake him—and bid him good-bye. I would have liked—to kiss him good-bye.

THE MAGISTRATE: [*To* The Second] You will take Dr. Reich back and let him kiss his son Oscar.

THE SECOND: Come with me, please.

THE RICHLY DRESSED MAN: [*To* The Magistrate] I thank you.

    [*He bows and exits at back with* The Second]

THE MAGISTRATE: [*After making an entry in the docket*] Number 16,473.

THE FIRST: [*Looks in his notebook, then beckons* Liliom] Stand up.

LILIOM: You said *please* to him.

    [*He rises*]

THE MAGISTRATE: Your name?

LILIOM: Liliom.

THE MAGISTRATE: Isn't that your nick-name?

LILIOM: Yes.

THE MAGISTRATE: What is your right name?

LILIOM: Andreas.

THE MAGISTRATE: And your last name?

LILIOM: Zavocki—after my mother.

THE MAGISTRATE: Your age?

LILIOM: Twenty-four.

THE MAGISTRATE: What good did *you* do on earth? [Liliom *is silent*] Why did you take your life? [Liliom *does not answer. The Magistrate addresses The First*] Take that knife away from him. [*The First does so*] It will be returned to you, if you go back to earth.

LILIOM: Do I go back to earth again?

THE MAGISTRATE: Just answer my questions.

LILIOM: I wasn't answering then, I was asking if——

THE MAGISTRATE: You don't ask questions here. You only answer. Only answer, Andreas Zavocki! I ask you whether there is anything on earth you neglected to accomplish? Anything down there you would like to do?

LILIOM: Yes.

THE MAGISTRATE: What is it?

LILIOM: I'd like to break Ficsur's head for him.

THE MAGISTRATE: Punishment is our office. Is there nothing else on earth you'd like to do?

LILIOM: I don't know—I guess, as long as I'm here, I'll not go back.

THE MAGISTRATE: [*To The First*] Note that. He waives his right. [Liliom *starts back to the bench*] Stay where you are. You are aware that you left your wife without food or shelter?

LILIOM: Yes.

THE MAGISTRATE: Don't you regret it?

LILIOM: No.

THE MAGISTRATE: You are aware that your wife is pregnant, and that in six months a child will be born?

LILIOM: I know.

THE MAGISTRATE: And that the child, too, will be without food or shelter? Do you regret that?

LILIOM: As long as I won't be there, what's it got to do with me?

THE MAGISTRATE: Don't try to deceive us, Andreas Zavocki. We see through you as through a pane of glass.

LILIOM: If you see so much, what do you want to ask me for? Why don't you let me rest—in peace?

THE MAGISTRATE: First you must earn your rest.

LILIOM: I want—only—to sleep.

THE MAGISTRATE: Your obstinacy won't help you. Here patience is endless as time. We can wait.

LILIOM: Can I ask something?—I'd like to know —if Your Honor will tell me—whether the baby will be a boy or a girl.

THE MAGISTRATE: You shall see that for yourself.

LILIOM: [*Excitedly*] I'll see the baby?

THE MAGISTRATE: When you do it won't be a baby any more. But we haven't reached that question yet.

LILIOM: I'll see it?

THE MAGISTRATE: Again I ask you. Do you not regret that you deserted your wife and child; that you were a bad husband, a bad father?

LILIOM: A bad husband?

THE MAGISTRATE: Yes.

LILIOM: And a bad father?

THE MAGISTRATE: That, too.

LILIOM: I couldn't get work—and I couldn't bear to see Julie—all the time—all the time——

THE MAGISTRATE: Weeping! Why are you ashamed to say it? You couldn't bear to see her weeping. Why are you afraid of that word? And why are you ashamed that you loved her?

LILIOM: [*Shrugs his shoulders*] Who's ashamed? But I couldn't bear to see her—and that's why I was bad to her. You see, it wouldn't do to go back to the carousel—and Ficsur came along with his talk about —that other thing—and all of a sudden it happened, I don't know how. The police and the Jew with the pistol—and there I stood—and I'd lost the money playing cards—and I didn't want to be put in prison. [*Demanding justification*] Maybe I was wrong not to go out and steal when there was nothing to eat in the house? Should I have gone out to steal for Julie?

THE MAGISTRATE: [*Emphatically*] Yes.

LILIOM: [*After an astounded pause*] The police down there never said that.

THE MAGISTRATE: You beat that poor, frail girl; you beat her because she loved you. How could you do that?

LILIOM: We argued with each other—she said this and I said that—and because she was right I couldn't answer her—and I got mad—and the anger rose up in me—until it reached here [*Points to his throat*] and then I beat her.

THE MAGISTRATE: Are you sorry?

LILIOM: [*Shakes his head, but cannot utter the word "no"; continues softly*] When I touched her slender throat—then—if you like—you might say——

[*Falters, looks embarrassed at The Magistrate*]

THE MAGISTRATE: [*Confidently expectant*] Are you sorry?

LILIOM: [*With a stare*] I'm not sorry for anything.

THE MAGISTRATE: Liliom, Liliom, it will be difficult to help you.

LILIOM: I'm not asking any help

THE MAGISTRATE: You were offered employment as a caretaker on Arader Street. [*To The First*] Where is that entered?

THE FIRST: In the small docket.

[*Hands him the open book. The Magistrate looks in it*]

THE MAGISTRATE: Rooms, kitchen, quarterly wages, the privilege of keeping poultry. Why didn't you accept it?

LILIOM: I'm not a caretaker. I'm no good at caretaking. To be a caretaker—you have to be a care-taker——

THE MAGISTRATE: If I said to you now: Liliom, go back on your stretcher. Tomorrow morning you will arise alive and well again. Would you be a caretaker then?

LILIOM: No.

THE MAGISTRATE: Why not?

LILIOM: Because—because that's just why I died.

THE MAGISTRATE: That is not true, my son. You died because you loved little Julie and the child she is bearing under her heart.

LILIOM: No.

THE MAGISTRATE: Look me in the eye.

LILIOM: [Looks him in the eye] No.

THE MAGISTRATE: [Stroking his beard] Liliom, Liliom, if it were not for our Heavenly patience—— Go back to your seat. Number 16,474.

THE FIRST: [Looks in his notebook] Stephan Kadar.

[The Poorly Dressed Man rises]

THE MAGISTRATE: You came out to-day?

THE POORLY DRESSED MAN: To-day.

THE MAGISTRATE: [Indicating the crimson sea of clouds] How long were you in there?

THE POORLY DRESSED MAN: Thirteen years.

THE MAGISTRATE: Officer, you went to earth with him?

THE FIRST: Yes, sir.

THE MAGISTRATE: Stephan Kadar, after thirteen years of purification by fire you returned to earth to give proof that your soul had been burned clean. What good deed did you perform?

THE POORLY DRESSED MAN: When I came to the village and looked in the window of our cottage I saw my poor little orphans sleeping peacefully. But it was raining and the rain beat into the room through a hole in the roof. So I went and fixed the roof so it wouldn't rain in any more. My hammering woke them up and they were afraid. But their mother came in to them and comforted them. She said to them: "Don't cry! It's your poor, dear father hammering up there. He's come back from the other world to fix the roof for us."

THE MAGISTRATE: Officer?

THE FIRST: That's what happened.

THE MAGISTRATE: Stephan Kadar, you have done a good deed. What you did will be written in books to gladden the hearts of children who read them. [Indicates the door at left] The door is open to you. The eternal light awaits you. [The First escorts The Poorly Dressed Man out at left with great deference] Liliom! [Liliom rises] You have heard?

LILIOM: Yes.

THE MAGISTRATE: When this man first appeared before us he was as stubborn as you. But now he has purified himself and withstood the test. He has done a good deed.

LILIOM: What's he done, anyhow? Any roofer can fix a roof. It's much harder to be a barker in an amusement park.

THE MAGISTRATE: Liliom, you shall remain for sixteen years in the crimson fire until your child is full grown. By that time your pride and your stubbornness will have been burnt out of you. And when your daughter——

LILIOM: My daughter!

THE MAGISTRATE: When your daughter has reached the age of sixteen——

[Liliom bows his head, covers his eyes with his hands, and to keep from weeping laughs defiantly, sadly]

THE MAGISTRATE: When your daughter has reached the age of sixteen you will be sent for one day back to earth.

LILIOM: Me?

THE MAGISTRATE: Yes—just as you may have read in the legends of how the dead reappear on earth for a time.

LILIOM: I never believed them.

THE MAGISTRATE: Now you see they are true. You will go back to earth one day to show how far the purification of your soul has progressed.

LILIOM: Then I must show what I can do—like when you apply for a job—as a coachman?

THE MAGISTRATE: Yes—it is a test.

LILIOM: And will I be told what I have to do?

THE MAGISTRATE: No.

LILIOM: How will I know, then?

THE MAGISTRATE: You must decide that for yourself. That's what you burn sixteen years for. And if you do something good, something splendid for your child, then——

LILIOM: [Laughs sadly] Then? [All stand up and bow their heads reverently. There is a pause] Then?

THE MAGISTRATE: Now I'll bid you farewell, Liliom. Sixteen years and a day shall pass before I see you again. When you have returned from earth you will come up before me again. Take heed and think well of some good deed to do for your child. On that will depend which door shall be opened to you up here. Now go, Liliom.

[He exits at left. The Guard stands at attention. There is a pause]

THE FIRST: [Approaches Liliom] Come along, my son.

[He goes to the door at right; pulls open the bolt and waits]

LILIOM: [To the old Guard, softly] Say, officer.

THE GUARD: What do you want?

LILIOM: Please—can I get—have you got—?

THE GUARD: What?

LILIOM: [Whispers] A cigarette?

[The old Guard stares at him, goes a few paces to the left, shakes his head disapprovingly. Then his expression softens. He takes a cigarette from his pocket and, crossing to Liliom—who has gone over to the door at right—gives him the cigarette. The First throws open the *door. An intense rose-colored light streams in. The glow of it is so strong that it blinds* Liliom *and he takes a step backward and bows his head and covers his eyes with his hand before he steps forward into the light*]

THE CURTAIN FALLS

SCENE VII.

Sixteen years later. A small, tumble-down house on a bare, unenclosed plot of ground. Before the house is a tiny garden enclosed by a hip-high hedge.

At back a wooden fence crosses the stage; in the center of it is a door large enough to admit a wagon. Beyond the fence is a view of a suburban street which blends into a broad vista of tilled fields.

It is a bright Sunday in Spring.

In the garden a table for two is laid.

Julie, *her daughter* Louise, Wolf *and* Marie *are discovered in the garden.* Wolf *is prosperously dressed,* Marie *somewhat elaborately, with a huge hat.*

JULIE: You could stay for lunch.

MARIE: Impossible, dear. Since he became the proprietor of the Café Sorrento, Wolf simply has to be there all the time.

JULIE: But you needn't stay there all day, too.

MARIE: Oh, yes. I sit near the cashier's cage, read the papers, keep an eye on the waiters and drink in the bustle and excitement of the great city.

JULIE: And what about the children?

MARIE: You know what modern families are like. Parents scarcely ever see their children these days. The four girls are with their governess, the three boys with their tutor.

LOUISE: Auntie, dear, do stay and eat with us.

MARIE: [*Importantly*] Impossible to-day, dear child, impossible. Perhaps some other time. Come, Mr. Beifeld.

JULIE: Since when do you call your husband mister?

WOLF: I'd rather she did, dear lady. When we used to be very familiar we quarreled all the time. Now we are formal with each other and get along like society folk. I kiss your hand, dear lady.

JULIE: Good-bye, Wolf.

MARIE: Adieu, my dear. [*They embrace*] Adieu, my dear child.

LOUISE: Good-bye, Aunt Marie. Good-bye, Uncle Wolf. [Wolf *and* Marie *exit*]

JULIE: You can get the soup now, Louise, dear. [Louise *goes into the house and reënters with the soup. They sit at the table*]

LOUISE: Mother, is it true we're not going to work at the jute factory any more?

JULIE: Yes, dear.

LOUISE: Where then?

JULIE: Uncle Wolf has gotten us a place in a big establishment where they make all kinds of fittings for cafés. We're to make big curtains, you know, the kind they hang in the windows, with lettering on them.

LOUISE: It'll be nicer there than at the jute factory.

JULIE: Yes, dear. The work isn't as dirty and pays better, too. A poor widow like your mother is lucky to get it.

[*They eat.* Liliom *and the two Heavenly Policemen appear in the big doorway at back. The* Policemen *pass slowly by.* Liliom *stands there alone a moment, then comes slowly down and pauses at the opening of the hedge. He is dressed as he was on the day of his death. He is very pale, but otherwise unaltered.* Julie, *at the table, has her back to him.* Louise *sits facing the audience*]

LILIOM: Good-day.

LOUISE: Good-day.

JULIE: Another beggar! What is it you want, my poor man?

LILIOM: Nothing.

JULIE: We have no money to give, but if you care for a plate of soup——[Louise *goes into the house*] Have you come far to-day?

LILIOM: Yes—very far.

JULIE: Are you tired?

LILIOM: Very tired.

JULIE: Over there at the gate is a stone. Sit down and rest. My daughter is bringing you the soup. [Louise *comes out of the house*]

LILIOM: Is that your daughter?

JULIE: Yes.

LILIOM: [*To* Louise] You are the daughter?

LOUISE: Yes, sir.

LILIOM: A fine, healthy girl. [*Takes the soup plate from her with one hand, while with the other he touches her arm.* Louise *draws back quickly*]

LOUISE: [*Crosses to* Julie] Mother!

JULIE: What, my child?

LOUISE: The man tried to take me by the arm.

JULIE: Nonsense! You only imagined it, dear. The poor, hungry man has other things to think about than fooling with young girls. Sit down and eat your soup. [*They eat*]

LILIOM: [*Eats, too, but keeps looking at them*] You work at the factory, eh?

JULIE: Yes.

LILIOM: Your daughter, too?

LOUISE: Yes.

LILIOM: And your husband?

JULIE: [*After a pause*] I have no husband. I'm a widow.

LILIOM: A widow?

JULIE: Yes.

LILIOM: Your husband—I suppose he's been dead a long time. [Julie *does not answer*] I say—has your husband been dead a long time?

JULIE: A long time.

LILIOM: What did he die of?

[Julie *is silent*]

LOUISE: No one knows. He went to America to work and he died there—in the hospital. Poor father, I never knew him.

LILIOM: He went to America?

LOUISE: Yes, before I was born.

LILIOM: To America?

JULIE: Why do you ask so many questions? Did you know him, perhaps?

LILIOM: [*Puts the plate down*] Heaven knows! I've known so many people. Maybe I knew him, too.

JULIE: Well, if you knew him, leave him and us in peace with your questions. He went to America and died there. That's all there is to tell.

LILIOM: All right. All right. Don't be angry with me. I didn't mean any harm.

[*There is a pause*]

LOUISE: My father was a very handsome man.

JULIE: Don't talk so much.

LOUISE: Did I say anything——?

LILIOM: Surely the little orphan can say that about her father.

LOUISE: My father could juggle so beautifully with three ivory balls that people used to advise him to go on the stage.

JULIE: Who told you that?

LOUISE: Uncle Wolf.

LILIOM: Who is that?

LOUISE: Mr. Wolf Beifeld, who owns the Café Sorrento.

LILIOM: The one who used to be a porter?

JULIE: [*Astonished*] Do you know him, too? It seems that you know all Budapest.

LILIOM: Wolf Beifeld is a long way from being all Budapest. But I do know a lot of people. Why shouldn't I know Wolf Beifeld?

LOUISE: He was a friend of my father.

JULIE: He was not his friend. No one was.

LILIOM: You speak of your husband so sternly.

JULIE: What's that to you? Doesn't it suit you? I can speak of my husband any way I like. It's nobody's business but mine.

LILIOM: Certainly, certainly—it's your own business.

[*Takes up his soup plate again. All three eat*]

LOUISE: [*To* Julie] Perhaps he knew father, too.

JULIE: Ask him, if you like.

LOUISE: [*Crosses to* Liliom. *He stands up*] Did you know my father? [Liliom *nods.* Louise *addresses her mother*] Yes, he knew him.

JULIE: [*Rises*] You knew Andreas Zavocki?

LILIOM: Liliom? Yes.

LOUISE: Was he really a very handsome man?

LILIOM: I wouldn't exactly say handsome.

LOUISE: [*Confidently*] But he was an awfully good man, wasn't he?

LILIOM: He wasn't so good, either. As far as I know he was what they called a clown, a barker in a carousel.

LOUISE: [*Pleased*] Did he tell funny jokes?

LILIOM: Lots of 'em. And he sang funny songs, too.

LOUISE: In the carousel?

LILIOM: Yes—but he was something of a bully, too. He'd fight any one. He even hit your dear little mother.

JULIE: That's a lie.

LILIOM: It's true.

JULIE: Aren't you ashamed to tell the child such awful things about her father? Get out of here, you shameless liar. Eats our soup and our bread and has the impudence to slander our dead!

LILIOM: I didn't mean—I——

JULIE: What right have you to tell lies to the child? Take that plate, Louise, and let him be on his way. If he wasn't such a hungry-looking beggar, I'd put him out myself.

[Louise *takes the plate out of his hand*]

LILIOM: So he didn't hit you?

JULIE: No, never. He was always good to me.

LOUISE: [*Whispers*] Did he tell funny stories, too?

LILIOM: Yes, and *such* funny ones.

JULIE: Don't speak to him any more. In God's name, go.

LOUISE: In God's name.

[Julie *resumes her seat at the table and eats*]

LILIOM: If you please, Miss—I have a pack of cards in my pocket. And if you like, I'll show you some tricks that'll make you split your sides laughing. [Louise *holds* Liliom's *plate in her left hand. With her right she reaches out and holds the garden gate shut*] Let me in, just a little way, Miss, and I'll do the tricks for you.

LOUISE: Go, in God's name, and let us be. Why are you making those ugly faces?

LILIOM: Don't chase me away, Miss; let me come in for just a minute—just for a minute—just long enough to let me show you something pretty, something wonderful. [*Opens the gate*] Miss, I've something to give you.

[*Takes from his pocket a big red handkerchief in which is wrapped a glittering star from Heaven. He looks furtively about him to make sure that the* Police *are not watching*]

LOUISE: What's that?

LILIOM: Pst! A star!

[*With a gesture he indicates that he has stolen it out of the sky*]

JULIE: [*Sternly*] Don't take anything from him. He's probably stolen it somewhere. [*To* Liliom] In God's name, be off with you.

LOUISE: Yes, be off with you. Be off.

[*She slams the gate*]

LILIOM: Miss—please, Miss—I've got to do something good—or—do something good—a good deed—

LOUISE: [*Pointing with her right hand*] That's the way out.

LILIOM: Miss——

LOUISE: Get out!

LILIOM: Miss!

[*Looks up at her suddenly and slaps her extended hand, so that the slap resounds loudly*]

LOUISE: Mother!

[*Looks dazedly at Liliom, who bows his head, dismayed, forlorn. Julie rises and looks at Liliom in astonishment. There is a long pause*]

JULIE: [*Comes over to them slowly*] What's the matter here?

LOUISE: [*Bewildered, does not take her eyes off Liliom*] Mother—the man—he hit me—on the hand —hard—I heard the sound of it—but it didn't hurt —mother—it didn't hurt—it was like a caress—as if he had just touched my hand tenderly.

[*She hides behind Julie. Liliom sulkily raises his head and looks at Julie*]

JULIE: [*Softly*] Go, my child. Go into the house. Go.

LOUISE: [*Going*] But mother—I'm afraid—it sounded so loud—— [*Weepingly*] And it didn't hurt at all—just as if he'd—kissed my hand instead—mother!

[*She hides her face*]

JULIE: Go in, my child, go in.

[*Louise goes slowly into the house. Julie watches her until she has disappeared, then turns slowly to Liliom*]

JULIE: You struck my child.

LILIOM: Yes—I struck her.

JULIE: Is that what you came for, to strike my child?

LILIOM: No—I didn't come for that—but I did strike her—and now I'm going back.

JULIE: In the name of the Lord Jesus, who are you?

LILIOM: [*Simply*] A poor, tired beggar who came a long way and who was hungry. And I took your soup and bread and I struck your child. Are you angry with me?

JULIE: [*Her hand on her heart; fearfully, wonderingly*] Jesus protect me—I don't understand it—I'm *not* angry—not angry at all——

[Liliom *goes to the doorway and leans against the doorpost, his back to the audience.* Julie *goes to the table and sits*]

JULIE: Louise! [Louise *comes out of the house*] Sit down, dear, we'll finish eating.

LOUISE: Has he gone?

JULIE: Yes. [*They are both seated at the table.* Louise, *her head in her hands, is staring into space*] Why don't you eat, dear?

LOUISE: What has happened, mother?

JULIE: Nothing, my child.

[*The* Heavenly Policemen *appear outside.* Liliom *walks slowly off at left. The* First Policeman *makes a deploring gesture. Both shake their heads deploringly and follow* Liliom *slowly off at left*]

LOUISE: Mother, dear, why won't you tell me?

JULIE: What is there to tell you, child? Nothing has happened. We were peacefully eating, and a beggar came who talked of bygone days, and then I thought of your father.

LOUISE: My father?

JULIE: Your father—Liliom.

[*There is a pause*]

LOUISE: Mother—tell me—has it ever happened to you—has any one ever hit you—without hurting you in the least?

JULIE: Yes, my child. It has happened to me, too.

[*There is a pause*]

LOUISE: Is it possible for some one to hit you—hard like that—real loud and hard—and not hurt you at all?

JULIE: It is possible, dear—that some one may beat you and beat you and beat you—and not hurt you at all.——

[*There is a pause. Near by an organ-grinder has stopped. The music of his organ begins*]

THE CURTAIN FALLS

Luigi Pirandello

(1867–1936)

When Shakespeare made Hamlet say that "there is nothing either good or bad, but thinking makes it so," he could not have believed any Englishman would take him literally. That Pirandello, who could hardly be mistaken for an Englishman, did proceed on this premise has been a stumbling block for English-speaking playgoers ever since this Italian playwright won attention outside Italy during the First World War. It does not follow, however, that Pirandello's plays can never prevail in England and America, for the best of them belong to essential theatre, as well as to the universal spirit of humanism. If, besides, one can claim singularity for much of his work, it nevertheless belongs to a tradition as old as late Greek and Roman comedy, whose domestic embroilments were played by actors behind grotesque masks. The only difference is that Pirandello alternately called attention to the "mask" and the "face," often interchanged the one for the other, and exposed both to more scrutiny than is good for comfort.

Pirandello started simply enough, for when he entered the literary field he did so with short stories and one-act plays written in a realistic vein and drawn from his knowledge of the common life of his native Sicily. Among the plays, his tender *Sicilian Limes,* written in 1910, is a small gem. At this time he was under the influence of Giovanni Verga and other masters of Ibsen-inspired Italian realism, which was known as "verismo." Pirandello became famous, however, when he departed from this style and allied himself with a mordant and cynical "school of the grotesque." Retaining his originality even in the company of writers whose point of view he could share, Pirandello went on to elaborate a special style. It became properly known as "Pirandellismo" since it was essentially his own unique creation, and the elements that entered into it were his own studies and experiences, as well as a private anguish.

Born in Girgenti, Sicily, to a comfortable and locally respected family, Pirandello remained sympathetic to the Sicilian people and responsive to local color, but shed his provincialism easily. After studying at the University of Rome, he went to the University of Bonn, where he took a doctorate in philosophy under strenuously Hegelian teachers who were specialists in dialectical argument. He married a girl chosen by his parents and settled down to free-lancing in Rome with the aid of an ample allowance from his father. But difficulties and disillusion became his lot after the early favorable circumstances. He dropped his buoyant liberal faith, which had led him to take the side of the hard-pressed peasants of the Palermo countryside when they seized land belonging to the crown. Discovering corruption and hypocrisy in political circles, he abandoned all faith in government, calling it at one time "a league of brigands against men of good will." The Pirandello family lost its fortune when its mines were flooded, and he was forced to take a position in Rome at a normal school for girls. The difficult delivery of a third child unsettled his wife's mind. She became baselessly jealous, caused scandalous scenes, and even left him for a time. Reality, he came to learn at his own expense, is what the individual conceives it to be, logic is easily overthrown by inner compulsions, and there is no such thing as an entirely objective world for those who feel. Soon his wife's condition worsened and her persecution of her own daughter became so relentless that the girl made an attempt at suicide. As Pirandello's salary was too meager to enable him to commit his wife to a private sanatorium and his conscience too tender to send her to a public institution, he kept an insane woman in his home for many years.

Only his writing provided him with relief, and he pursued his literary labors for a time with such intensity that he wrote as many as nine plays in a single year. He also began to take an active part in stage production, organizing a distinguished company of actors at the Odescalchi Theatre in Rome and directing his own plays. He acquired a famous actor, Ruggero Ruggeri, for his troupe and won the interest of a superb actress, Marta Abba. Signora Abba played the leading feminine role in many of his dramas and rewarded him with an understanding friendship for which few men could have had greater need.

Concern with "identity," or the masks we assume or are compelled to assume, appeared as early as 1904 in Pirandello's work—in the novel *The Late Mattia Pascal,* in which an unhappy husband pretends to have drowned himself and assumes a new personality that entails new hazards. But it is in plays written after 1913 that Pirandello gave the most comprehensive treatment to this and related themes. In 1914 he presented two plays, *Think of It, Giacomino* and *The Pleasure of Honesty.* In the first of these, an elderly professor defies the gossip of the town by perversely marrying a pregnant girl and condoning her continued relations with a young man not in a position to marry her. In *The Pleasure of Honesty,* an eccentric marries a woman to protect her reputation, but once she has put on the mask of honesty, he insists that she wear it henceforth. Although he is not a believer in conventional virtue and is willing to marry another man's mistress for a financial consideration, he now requires absolute fidelity from his wife as a point of "honor." In *Cap and Bells* (1915), a husband, aware of his wife's infidelity with his employer, is outraged when the latter's wife exposes the intrigue. He insists on having the jealous woman declared insane in order to invalidate her charge against his own wife. Men have to "build themselves up" and to put up a front, in order to be able to endure themselves and to live in society. The husband, since he is so ugly, was willing to condone his wife's infidelity, but only so long as outsiders took no note of his ludicrous situation.

In his brilliant *Right You Are if You Think You Are* (1922), Pirandello made the question of personal identity the central theme of a tragicomic extravaganza. An elderly woman insists that a certain character's wife is her daughter. The husband maintains that the lady is demented, since her daughter, his first wife, died some time ago. The lady, in turn, declares that the man is suffering from delusions that his first wife is dead and that his first wife is his second wife. The bewildered townspeople never succeed in discovering who is deluded, and Pirandello refrains from enlightening us because to him the question is irrelevant. The important thing is that the human soul must believe as it believes if it is to be able to endure life, and people's dreams must be protected. In *Signora Morli One and Two,* a woman exhibits different personalities to the lighthearted husband who abandoned her and to the serious-minded lawyer who takes care of her. And so the tragicomedy of masks continues. Sometimes, however, men and women are caught in the trap of the personality they have acquired for themselves. In *Naked,* a play full of pity for those who must assume a mask and resentment for those who fail to understand the need, complications arise from a woman's claim that she tried to commit suicide out of a love she invented for herself in order to clothe herself in a beautiful romance before she died. Accused of imposture, "stripped naked" when she confesses that she does not love the man for whom she pretended to want to die, she makes a second and this time successful attempt at suicide. An author in *When One Is Somebody* is not allowed to change the style which brought him fame, although love has given him a new outlook on life. A prominent actress in *Trovarsi* loses a lover because she is unable to shed her stage personality in private life. And the hero of the powerful psychological drama *Henry IV* is compelled to pretend to be mad after he has recovered his sanity.

"Divine spirit enters into us and becomes dwarfed into a puppet," according to a character in *Cap and Bells.* Pirandello's concern with human puppetry in his many plays and novels won him the attention of distinguished foreign observers—among them the French writer Benjamin Crémieux and James Joyce;

he gained an international reputation, climaxed in 1934 by a Nobel Prize for literature. He projected a fascinating modern mind and spirit in his frequently stylized work. Philosopher and dramatist, he summed up in his writing the relativistic tendencies of modern thought with respect to reality and morality, and he voiced an antibourgeois protest against a smug society that thrusts individuals into narrow categories.

Although he adopted the theatre as his favorite medium he blasted its conventions as well. He combined the discursive drama of ideas with weird situations, and freely intermingled tragic and fantastically comic elements. Not only did he refuse to give the playgoer a helping hand through the maze of unusual complications and questions left as either insoluble or as better not solved; he shook the foundations of the realistic stage with *Tonight We Improvise* and, especially, with *Six Characters in Search of an Author* by refusing to accept the theatre's pretense of being an imitation of reality. In the latter play, making inroads into the structure of realistic drama by employing the play-within-the-play technique, Pirandello gave a hearing to characters who interrupt a rehearsal with their claim that they are being misrepresented by the author and the actors. They were turned into puppets, and they insist that they are human beings. Being human, they are also profoundly disturbing, and the more the puppet transforms itself before us into a human being the more it refuses to be pigeonholed by the theatre and makes the purveyors of stage plots look silly.

As if this were not enough of a departure from the simple assumptions of the "entertainment industry," Pirandello, moreover, often presented his own work as "entertainment." Stark Young was indeed justified in maintaining that Pirandello had "transferred to the mind the legs and antics and the inexhaustible vivacity and loneliness and abstraction of the *commedia dell'arte.*" This description applies even to *Six Characters,* which exposes a far from amusing domestic situation, since Pirandello is poking fun at the theatre and confounding its simplicities. But if Pirandello was lively and indulged in laughter, here as elsewhere, it was because he found the life of men—including their view of life in their works of art—absurd; and the absurdity rankled. Pirandello was a mixed artist because he was of mixed temperament. He could write in his thirty-fifth year, "Ask the poet what is the saddest sight and he will reply 'It is laughter on the face of a man'," and he added, "Who laughs does not know." Since Pirandello "knew," his laughter was generally saturnine, if not indeed indistinguishable, especially in *Six Characters,* from acute distress.

In *Six Characters,* Pirandello's most incisive, as well as moving, quality lies in his challenge to art not to make a neat little conventional drama out of life. By the time the "Six Characters" have pre sented their case, it is plain that it cannot be completely "dramatized" or even known. Their motives are too mixed and their understanding too cloudy. The mother and the son do not express themselves completely, and the youngest child and the boy are, understandably, too inarticulate. Other characters are too passionately bent upon justifying themselves to present any absolutely objective truth, even if this were possible. When the play is over, Pirandello has shattered our complacent belief that we can really know and understand people. Our only defense against his demonstration—aside from the obtuseness we fortunately possess and the oversimplifying decorum that we usually adopt as a social measure—is to refrain from passing judgment on one another and to be merciful.

BIBLIOGRAPHY: Eric Bentley, *The Playwright as Thinker* (pp. 177–189), 1946; Frank W. Chandler, *Modern Continental Playwrights* (pp. 573–594), 1931; Barrett H. Clark and George Freedley, *A History of the Modern Drama* (pp. 300–304, 338–340, 359–367), 1947; *Columbia Dictionary of Modern European Literature* (pp. 626–628), 1947; John Gassner, *Masters of the Drama* (pp. 434–445), 1940, 1945; W. Starkie, *Luigi Pirandello*, 1926, 1937 (revised edition); Domenico Vittorini, *The Drama of Luigi Pirandello*, 1935.

SIX CHARACTERS IN SEARCH OF AN AUTHOR

By Luigi Pirandello

TRANSLATED FROM THE ITALIAN BY EDWARD STORER

CHARACTERS OF THE COMEDY IN THE MAKING:

THE FATHER	THE STEPDAUGHTER	THE BOY ⎫ (*These two do*
THE MOTHER	THE SON	THE CHILD ⎭ *not speak*)
	MADAME PACE	

ACTORS OF THE COMPANY

THE MANAGER	L'INGÉNUE	MACHINIST
LEADING LADY	JUVENILE LEAD	MANAGER'S SECRETARY
LEADING MAN	OTHER ACTORS AND ACTRESSES	DOOR-KEEPER
SECOND LADY	PROPERTY MAN	SCENE-SHIFTERS
LEAD	PROMPTER	

DAYTIME: *The Stage of a Theater.*

ACT I.

N.B. The Comedy is without acts or scenes. The performance is interrupted once, without the curtain being lowered, when The Manager *and the chief characters withdraw to arrange the scenario. A second interruption of the action takes place when, by mistake, the stage hands let the curtain down.*

The spectators will find the curtain raised and the stage as it usually is during the daytime. It will be half dark, and empty, so that from the beginning the public may have the impression of an impromptu performance.

Prompter's box and a small table and chair for The Manager.

Two other small tables and several chairs scattered about as during rehearsals.

The Actors *and* Actresses *of the company enter from the back of the stage:*

First one, then another, then two together: nine or ten in all. They are about to rehearse a Pirandello play: Mixing It Up. *Some of the company move off towards their dressing rooms. The* Prompter *who has the "book" under his arm, is waiting for* The Manager *in order to begin the rehearsal.*

The Actors *and* Actresses, *some standing, some sitting, chat and smoke. One perhaps reads a paper; another cons his part.*

Finally, The Manager *enters and goes to the table prepared for him. His* Secretary *brings him his mail,* through which he glances. The Prompter *takes his seat, turns on a light, and opens the "book."*

THE MANAGER: [*Throwing a letter down on the table*] I can't see [*To* Property Man] Let's have a little light, please!

PROPERTY MAN: Yes sir, yes, at once. [*A light comes down on to the stage*]

THE MANAGER: [*Clapping his hands*] Come along! Come along! Second act of *Mixing it Up.* [*Sits down*]

[*The* Actors *and* Actresses *go from the front of the stage to the wings, all except the three who are to begin the rehearsal*]

THE PROMPTER: [*Reading the "book"*] "Leo Gala's house. A curious room serving as dining-room and study."

THE MANAGER: [*To* Property Man] Fix up the old red room.

PROPERTY MAN: [*Noting it down*] Red set. All right!

THE PROMPTER: [*Continuing to read from the "book"*] "Table already laid and writing desk with books and papers. Bookshelves. Exit rear to Leo's bedroom. Exit left to kitchen. Principal exit to right."

THE MANAGER: [*Energetically*] Well, you understand: The principal exit over there; here the kitchen. [*Turning to* Actor *who is to play the part of Socrates*] You make your entrances and exits here. [*To* Property Man] The baize doors at the rear, and curtains.

PROPERTY MAN: [*Noting it down*] Right-o!

PROMPTER: [*Reading as before*] "When the curtain rises, Leo Gala, dressed in cook's cap and apron is busy beating an egg in a cup. Philip, also dressed as a cook, is beating another egg. Guido Venanzi is seated and listening."

LEADING MAN: [To Manager] Excuse me, but must I absolutely wear a cook's cap?

THE MANAGER: [Annoyed] I imagine so. It says so there anyway. [Pointing to the "book"]

LEADING MAN: But it's ridiculous!

THE MANAGER: Ridiculous? Ridiculous? Is it my fault if France won't send us any more good comedies, and we are reduced to putting on Pirandello's works, where nobody understands anything, and where the author plays the fool with us all? [The Actors grin. The Manager goes to Leading Man and shouts] Yes sir, you put on the cook's cap and beat eggs. Do you suppose that with all this egg-beating business you are on an ordinary stage? Get that out of your head. You represent the shell of the eggs you are beating! [Laughter and comments among the Actors] Silence! and listen to my explanations, please! [To Leading Man]: "The empty form of reason without the fullness of instinct, which is blind"—You stand for reason, your wife is instinct. It's a mixing up of the parts, according to which you who act your own part become the puppet of yourself. Do you understand?

LEADING MAN: I'm hanged if I do.

THE MANAGER: Neither do I. But let's get on with it. It's sure to be a glorious failure anyway. [Confidentially]: But I say, please face three-quarters. Otherwise, what with the abstruseness of the dialogue, and the public that won't be able to hear you, the whole thing will go to hell. Come on! come on!

PROMPTER: Pardon sir, may I get into my box? There's a bit of a draught.

THE MANAGER: Yes, yes, of course!

At this point, the Door-keeper has entered from the stage door and advances towards The Manager's table, taking off his braided cap. During this manœuver, the Six Characters enter, and stop by the door at back of stage, so that when the Door-keeper is about to announce their coming to The Manager, they are already on the stage. A tenuous light surrounds them, almost as if irradiated by them—the faint breath of their fantastic reality.

This light will disappear when they come forward towards the Actors. They preserve, however, something of the dream lightness in which they seem almost suspended; but this does not detract from the essential reality of their forms and expressions.

He who is known as The Father is a man of about 50: hair, reddish in color, thin at the temples; he is not bald, however; thick moustaches, falling over his still fresh mouth, which often opens in an empty and uncertain smile. He is fattish, pale; with an especially wide forehead. He has blue, oval-shaped eyes, very clear and piercing. Wears light trousers and a dark jacket. He is alternatively mellifluous and violent in his manner.

The Mother seems crushed and terrified as if by an intolerable weight of shame and abasement. She is dressed in modest black and wears a thick widow's veil of crêpe. When she lifts this, she reveals a wax-like face. She always keeps her eyes downcast.

The Stepdaughter is dashing, almost impudent, beautiful. She wears mourning too, but with great elegance. She shows contempt for the timid half-frightened manner of the wretched Boy [14 years old, and also dressed in black]; on the other hand, she displays a lively tenderness for her little sister, The Child [about four], who is dressed in white, with a black silk sash at the waist.

The Son [22] tall, severe in his attitude of contempt for The Father, supercilious and indifferent to the Mother. He looks as if he had come on the stage against his will.

DOORKEEPER: [Cap in hand] Excuse me, sir . . .

THE MANAGER: [Rudely] Eh? What is it?

DOORKEEPER: [Timidly] These people are asking for you, sir.

THE MANAGER: [Furious] I am rehearsing, and you know perfectly well no one's allowed to come in during rehearsals! [Turning to the Characters]: Who are you, please? What do you want?

THE FATHER: [Coming forward a little, followed by the others who seem embarrassed] As a matter of fact . . . we have come here in search of an author. . . .

THE MANAGER: [Half angry, half amazed] An author? What author?

THE FATHER: Any author, sir.

THE MANAGER: But there's no author here. We are not rehearsing a new piece.

THE STEPDAUGHTER: [Vivaciously] So much the better, so much the better! We can be your new piece.

AN ACTOR: [Coming forward from the others] Oh, do you hear that?

THE FATHER: [To Stepdaughter] Yes, but if the author isn't here . . . [To Manager] . . . unless you would be willing . . .

THE MANAGER: You are trying to be funny.

THE FATHER: No, for Heaven's sake, what are you saying? We bring you a drama, sir.

THE STEPDAUGHTER: We may be your fortune.

THE MANAGER: Will you oblige me by going away? We haven't time to waste with mad people.

THE FATHER: [Mellifluously] Oh sir, you know well that life is full of infinite absurdities, which, strangely enough, do not even need to appear plausible, since they are true.

THE MANAGER: What the devil is he talking about?

THE FATHER: I say that to reverse the ordinary process may well be considered a madness: that is, to create credible situations, in order that they may appear true. But permit me to observe that if this be madness, it is the sole raison d'être of your profession, gentlemen. [The Actors look hurt and perplexed]

THE MANAGER: [*Getting up and looking at him*] So our profession seems to you one worthy of madmen then?

THE FATHER: Well, to make seem true that which isn't true . . . without any need . . . for a joke as it were . . . Isn't that your mission, gentlemen: to give life to fantastic characters on the stage?

THE MANAGER: [*Interpreting the rising anger of the* Company] But I would beg you to believe, my dear sir, that the profession of the comedian is a noble one. If today, as things go, the playwrights give us stupid comedies to play and puppets to represent instead of men, remember we are proud to have given life to immortal works here on these very boards! [*The* Actors, *satisfied, applaud their* Manager]

THE FATHER: [*Interrupting furiously*] Exactly, perfectly, to living beings more alive than those who breathe and wear clothes: being less real perhaps, but truer! I agree with you entirely. [*The* Actors *look at one another in amazement*]

THE MANAGER: But what do you mean? Before, you said . . .

THE FATHER: No, excuse me, I meant it for you, sir, who were crying out that you had no time to lose with madmen, while no one better than yourself knows that nature uses the instrument of human fantasy in order to pursue her high creative purpose.

THE MANAGER: Very well—but where does all this take us?

THE FATHER: Nowhere! It is merely to show you that one is born to life in many forms, in many shapes, as tree, or as stone, as water, as butterfly, or as woman. So one may also be born a character in a play.

THE MANAGER: [*With feigned comic dismay*] So you and these other friends of yours have been born characters?

THE FATHER: Exactly, and alive as you see! [*Manager and* Actors *burst out laughing*]

THE FATHER: [*Hurt*] I am sorry you laugh, because we carry in us a drama, as you can guess from this woman here veiled in black.

THE MANAGER: [*Losing patience at last and almost indignant*] Oh, chuck it! Get away please! Clear out of here! [*To* Property Man] For Heaven's sake, turn them out!

THE FATHER: [*Resisting*] No, no, look here, we . . .

THE MANAGER: [*Roaring*] We come here to work, you know.

LEADING ACTOR: One cannot let oneself be made such a fool of.

THE FATHER: [*Determined, coming forward*] I marvel at your incredulity, gentlemen. Are you not accustomed to see the characters created by an author spring to life in yourselves and face each other? Just because there is no "book" [*Pointing to the* Prompter's *box*] which contains us, you refuse to believe . . .

THE STEPDAUGHTER: [*Advances towards* Manager, *smiling and coquettish*] Believe me, we are really six most interesting characters, sir; side-tracked however.

THE FATHER: Yes, that is the word! [*To* Manager *all at once*] In the sense, that is, that the author who created us alive no longer wished, or was no longer able, materially to put us into a work of art. And this was a real crime, sir; because he who has had the luck to be born a character can laugh even at death. He cannot die. The man, the writer, the instrument of the creation will die, but his creation does not die. And to live for ever, it does not need to have extraordinary gifts or to be able to work wonders. Who was Sancho Panza? Who was Don Abbondio? Yet they live eternally because—live germs as they were—they had the fortune to find a fecundating matrix, a fantasy which could raise and nourish them: make them live for ever!

THE MANAGER: That is quite all right. But what do you want here, all of you?

THE FATHER: We want to live.

THE MANAGER: [*Ironically*] For Eternity?

THE FATHER: No, sir, only for a moment . . . in you.

AN ACTOR: Just listen to him!

LEADING LADY: They want to live, in us! . . .

JUVENILE LEAD: [*Pointing to the* Stepdaughter] I've no objection, as far as that one is concerned!

THE FATHER: Look here! Look here! The comedy has to be made. [*To the* Manager] But if you and your actors are willing, we can soon concert it among ourselves.

THE MANAGER: [*Annoyed*] But what do you want to concert? We don't go in for concerts here. Here we play dramas and comedies!

THE FATHER: Exactly! That is just why we have come to you.

THE MANAGER: And where is the "book"?

THE FATHER: It is in us! [*The* Actors *laugh*] The drama is in us, and we are the drama. We are impatient to play it. Our inner passion drives us on to this.

THE STEPDAUGHTER: [*Disdainful, alluring, treacherous, full of impudence*] My passion, sir! Ah, if you only knew! My passion for him! [*Points to the* Father *and makes a pretence of embracing him. Then she breaks out into a loud laugh*]

THE FATHER: [*Angrily*] Behave yourself! And please don't laugh in that fashion.

THE STEPDAUGHTER: With your permission, gentlemen, I, who am a two months' orphan, will show you how I can dance and sing.

[*Sings and then dances* Prenez garde à Tchou-Thin-Tchou]

Les chinois sont un peuple malin,
De Shanghaî à Pékin,
Ils ont mis des écriteaux partout:
Prenez garde à Tchou-Thin-Tchou.

ACTORS and ACTRESSES: Bravo! Well done! Tip-top!

THE MANAGER: Silence! This isn't a café concert, you know! [*Turning to the* Father *in consternation*] Is she mad?

THE FATHER: Mad? No, she's worse than mad.

THE STEPDAUGHTER: [*To* Manager] Worse? Worse? Listen! Stage this drama for us at once! Then you will see that at a certain moment I . . . when this little darling here . . . [*Takes the Child by the hand and leads her to the* Manager] Isn't she a dear? [*Takes her up and kisses her*] Darling! Darling! [*Puts her down again and adds feelingly*] Well, when God suddenly takes this dear little child away from that poor mother there; and this imbecile here [*seizing hold of the* Boy *roughly and pushing him forward*] does the stupidest things, like the fool he is, you will see me run away. Yes, gentlemen, I shall be off. But the moment hasn't arrived yet. After what has taken place between him and me [*indicates the* Father *with a horrible wink*] I can't remain any longer in this society, to have to witness the anguish of this mother here for that fool . . . [*Indicates the* Son] Look at him! Look at him! See how indifferent, how frigid he is, because he is the legitimate son. He despises me, despises him [*pointing to the* Boy], despises this baby here; because . . . we are bastards. [*Goes to the* Mother *and embraces her*] And he doesn't want to recognize her as his mother—she who is the common mother of us all. He looks down upon her as if she were only the mother of us three bastards. Wretch! [*She says all this very rapidly, excitedly. At the word "bastards" she raises her voice, and almost spits out the final "Wretch!"*]

THE MOTHER: [*To the* Manager, *in anguish*] In the name of these two little children, I beg you . . . [*She grows faint and is about to fall*] Oh God!

THE FATHER: [*Coming forward to support her as do some of the* Actors] Quick a chair, a chair for this poor widow!

THE ACTORS: Is it true? Has she really fainted?

THE MANAGER: Quick, a chair! Here!

[*One of the* Actors *brings a chair, the others proffer assistance. The* Mother *tries to prevent the* Father *from lifting the veil which covers her face*]

THE FATHER: Look at her! Look at her!

THE MOTHER: No, stop; stop it please!

THE FATHER: [*Raising her veil*] Let them see you!

THE MOTHER: [*Rising and covering her face with her hands, in desperation*] I beg you, sir, to prevent this man from carrying out his plan which is loathsome to me.

THE MANAGER: [*Dumbfounded*] I don't understand at all. What is the situation? Is this lady your wife? [*To the* Father]

THE FATHER: Yes, gentlemen: my wife!

THE MANAGER: But how can she be a widow if you are alive? [*The* Actors *find relief for their astonishment in a loud laugh*]

THE FATHER: Don't laugh! Don't laugh like that, for Heaven's sake. Her drama lies just here in this: she has had a lover, a man who ought to be here.

THE MOTHER: [*With a cry*] No! No!

THE STEPDAUGHTER: Fortunately for her, he is dead. Two months ago as I said. We are in mourning, as you see.

THE FATHER: He isn't here you see, not because he is dead. He isn't here—look at her a moment and you will understand—because her drama isn't a drama of the love of two men for whom she was incapable of feeling anything except possibly a little gratitude—gratitude not for me but for the other. She isn't a woman, she is a mother, and her drama—powerful sir, I assure you—lies, as a matter of fact, all in these four children she has had by two men.

THE MOTHER: I had them? Have you got the courage to say that I wanted them? [*To the* Company] It was his doing. It was he who gave me that other man, who forced me to go away with him.

THE STEPDAUGHTER: It isn't true.

THE MOTHER: [*Startled*] Not true, isn't it?

THE STEPDAUGHTER: No, it isn't true, it just isn't true.

THE MOTHER: And what can you know about it?

THE STEPDAUGHTER: It isn't true. Don't believe it. [*To* Manager] Do you know why she says so? For that fellow there. [*Indicates the* Son] She tortures herself, destroys herself on account of the neglect of that son there; and she wants him to believe that if she abandoned him when he was only two years old, it was because he [*indicates the* Father] made her do so.

THE MOTHER: [*Vigorously*] He forced me to it, and I call God to witness it. [*To the* Manager] Ask him [*indicates the* Father] if it isn't true. Let him speak. You [*to* Daughter] are not in a position to know anything about it.

THE STEPDAUGHTER: I know you lived in peace and happiness with my father while he lived. Can you deny it?

THE MOTHER: No, I don't deny it . . .

THE STEPDAUGHTER: He was always full of affection and kindness for you. [*To the* Boy, *angrily*] It's true, isn't it? Tell them! Why don't you speak, you little fool?

THE MOTHER: Leave the poor boy alone. Why do you want to make me appear ungrateful, daughter? I don't want to offend your father. I have answered him that I didn't abandon my house and my son through any fault of mine, nor from any wilful passion.

THE FATHER: It is true. It was my doing.

LEADING MAN: [*To the* Company] What a spectacle!

LEADING LADY: We are the audience this time.

JUVENILE LEAD: For once, in a way.

THE MANAGER: [*Beginning to get really interested*] Let's hear them out. Listen!

THE SON: Oh yes, you're going to hear a fine bit now. He will talk to you of the Demon of Experiment.

THE FATHER: You are a cynical imbecile. I've told you so already a hundred times. [*To the* Manager] He tries to make fun of me on account of this expression which I have found to excuse myself with.

THE SON: [*With disgust*] Yes, phrases! phrases!

THE FATHER: Phrases! Isn't everyone consoled when faced with a trouble or fact he doesn't understand, by a word, some simple word, which tells us nothing and yet calms us?

THE STEPDAUGHTER: Even in the case of remorse. In fact, especially then.

THE FATHER: Remorse? No, that isn't true. I've done more than use words to quieten the remorse in me.

THE STEPDAUGHTER: Yes, there was a bit of money too. Yes, yes, a bit of money. There were the hundred lire he was about to offer me in payment, gentlemen. . . . [*Sensation of horror among the* Actors]

THE SON: [*To the* Stepdaughter] This is vile.

THE STEPDAUGHTER: Vile? There they were in a pale blue envelope on a little mahogany table in the back of Madame Pace's shop. You know Madame Pace—one of those ladies who attract poor girls of good family into their ateliers, under the pretext of their selling *robes et manteaux*.

THE SON: And he thinks he has bought the right to tyrannize over us all with those hundred lire he was going to pay; but which, fortunately—note this, gentlemen—he had no chance of paying.

THE STEPDAUGHTER: It was a near thing, though, you know! [*Laughs ironically*]

THE MOTHER: [*Protesting*] Shame, my daughter, shame!

THE STEPDAUGHTER: Shame indeed! This is my revenge! I am dying to live that scene. . . . The room . . . I see it . . . Here is the window with the mantles exposed, there the divan, the looking-glass, a screen, there in front of the window the little mahogany table with the blue envelope containing one hundred lire. I see it. I see it. I could take hold of it . . . But you, gentlemen, you ought to turn your backs now: I am almost nude, you know. But I don't blush: I leave that to him. [*Indicating* Father]

THE MANAGER: I don't understand this at all.

THE FATHER: Naturally enough. I would ask you, sir, to exercise your authority a little here, and let me speak before you believe all she is trying to blame me with. Let me explain.

THE STEPDAUGHTER: Ah yes, explain it in your own way.

THE FATHER: But don't you see that the whole trouble lies here. In words, words. Each one of us has within him a whole world of things, each man of us his own special world. And how can we ever come to an understanding if I put in the words I utter the sense and value of things as I see them; while you who listen to me must inevitably translate them according to the conception of things each one of you has within himself. We think we understand each other, but we never really do. Look here! This woman [*indicating the* Mother] takes all my pity for her as a specially ferocious form of cruelty.

THE MOTHER: But you drove me away.

THE FATHER: Do you hear her? I drove her away! She believes I really sent her away.

THE MOTHER: You know how to talk, and I don't; but, believe me sir [*To* Manager], after he had married me . . . who knows why? . . . I was a poor insignificant woman . . .

THE FATHER: But, good Heaven! it was just for your humility that I married you. I loved this simplicity in you. [*He stops when he sees she makes signs to contradict him, opens his arms wide in sign of desperation, seeing how hopeless it is to make himself understood*] You see she denies it. Her mental deafness, believe me, is phenomenal, the limit [*touches his forehead*]: deaf, deaf, mentally deaf! She has plenty of feeling. Oh yes, a good heart for the children; but the brain—deaf, to the point of desperation——!

THE STEPDAUGHTER: Yes, but ask him how his intelligence has helped us.

THE FATHER: If we could see all the evil that may spring from good, what should we do? [*At this point the* Leading Lady *who is biting her lips with rage at seeing the* Leading Man *flirting with the* Stepdaughter, *comes forward and says to the* Manager]

LEADING LADY: Excuse me, but are we going to rehearse today?

MANAGER: Of course, of course; but let's hear them out.

JUVENILE LEAD: This is something quite new.

L'INGÉNUE: Most interesting!

LEADING LADY: Yes, for the people who like that kind of thing. [*Casts a glance at* Leading Man]

THE MANAGER: [*To* Father] You must please explain yourself quite clearly. [*Sits down*]

THE FATHER: Very well then: listen! I had in my service a poor man, a clerk, a secretary of mine, full of devotion, who became friends with her. [*Indicating the* Mother] They understood one another, were kindred souls in fact, without, however the least suspicion of any evil existing. They were incapable even of thinking of it.

THE STEPDAUGHTER: So he thought of it—for them!

THE FATHER: That's not true. I meant to do good to them—and to myself, I confess, at the same time. Things had come to the point that I could not say a word to either of them without their making a mute appeal, one to the other, with their eyes. I could see them silently asking each other how I was to be kept in countenance, how I was to be kept quiet. And this, believe me, was just about enough of itself to keep me in a constant rage, to exasperate me beyond measure.

THE MANAGER: And why didn't you send him away then—this secretary of yours?

THE FATHER: Precisely what I did, sir. And then I had to watch this poor woman drifting forlornly about the house like an animal without a master, like an animal one has taken in out of pity.

THE MOTHER: Ah yes! . . .

THE FATHER: [Suddenly turning to the Mother] It's true about the son anyway, isn't it?

THE MOTHER: He took my son away from me first of all.

THE FATHER: But not from cruelty. I did it so that he should grow up healthy and strong by living in the country.

THE STEPDAUGHTER: [Pointing to him ironically] As one can see.

THE FATHER: [Quickly] Is it my fault if he has grown up like this? I sent him to a wet nurse in the country, a peasant, as she did not seem to me strong enough, though she is of humble origin. That was, anyway, the reason I married her. Unpleasant all this may be, but how can it be helped? My mistake possibly, but there we are! All my life I have had these confounded aspirations towards a certain moral sanity. [At this point the Stepdaughter bursts out into a noisy laugh] Oh, stop it! Stop it! I can't stand it.

THE MANAGER: Yes, please stop it, for Heaven's sake.

THE STEPDAUGHTER: But imagine moral sanity from him, if you please—the client of certain ateliers like that of Madame Pace!

THE FATHER: Fool! That is the proof that I am a man! This seeming contradiction, gentlemen, is the strongest proof that I stand here a live man before you. Why, it is just for this very incongruity in my nature that I have had to suffer what I have. I could not live by the side of that woman [indicating the Mother] any longer; but not so much for the boredom she inspired me with as for the pity I felt for her.

THE MOTHER: And so he turned me out—.

THE FATHER: —well provided for! Yes, I sent her to that man, gentlemen . . . to let her go free of me.

THE MOTHER: And to free himself.

THE FATHER: Yes, I admit it. It was also a liberation for me. But great evil has come of it. I meant well when I did it; and I did it more for her sake than mine. I swear it. [Crosses his arms on his chest; then turns suddenly to the Mother] Did I ever lose sight of you until that other man carried you off to another town, like the angry fool he was? And on account of my pure interest in you . . . my pure interest, I repeat, that had no base motive in it . . .

I watched with the tenderest concern the new family that grew up around her. She can bear witness to this. [Points to the Stepdaughter]

THE STEPDAUGHTER: Oh yes, that's true enough. When I was a kiddie, so so high, you know, with plaits over my shoulders and knickers longer than my skirts, I used to see him waiting outside the school for me to come out. He came to see how I was growing up.

THE FATHER: This is infamous, shameful!

THE STEPDAUGHTER: No. Why?

THE FATHER: Infamous! Infamous! [Then excitedly to Manager explaining] After she [indicating Mother] went away, my house seemed suddenly empty. She was my incubus, but she filled my house. I was like a dazed fly alone in the empty rooms. This boy here [indicating the Son] was educated away from home, and when he came back, he seemed to me to be no more mine. With no mother to stand between him and me, he grew up entirely for himself, on his own, apart, with no tie of intellect or affection binding him to me. And then—strange but true—I was driven, by curiosity at first and then by some tender sentiment, towards her family, which had come into being through my will. The thought of her began gradually to fill up the emptiness I felt all around me. I wanted to know if she were happy in living out the simple daily duties of life. I wanted to think of her as fortunate and happy because far away from the complicated torments of my spirit. And so, to have proof of this, I used to watch that child coming out of school.

THE STEPDAUGHTER: Yes, yes. True. He used to follow me in the street and smiled at me, waved his hand, like this. I would look at him with interest, wondering who he might be. I told my mother, who guessed at once. [The Mother agrees with a nod] Then she didn't want to send me to school for some days; and when I finally went back, there he was again—looking so ridiculous—with a paper parcel in his hands. He came close to me, caressed me, and drew out a fine straw hat from the parcel, with a bouquet of flowers—all for me!

THE MANAGER: A bit discursive this, you know!

THE SON: [Contemptuously] Literature! Literature!

THE FATHER: Literature indeed! This is life, this is passion!

THE MANAGER: It may be, but it won't act.

THE FATHER: I agree. This is only the part leading up. I don't suggest this should be staged. She [pointing to the Stepdaughter], as you see, is no longer the flapper with plaits down her back—.

THE STEPDAUGHTER: —and the knickers showing below the skirt!

THE FATHER: The drama is coming now, sir; something new, complex, most interesting.

THE STEPDAUGHTER: As soon as my father died . . .

THE FATHER: —there was absolute misery for them. They came back here, unknown to me.

Through her stupidity! [*Pointing to the* Mother] It is true she can barely write her own name; but she could anyhow have got her daughter to write to me that they were in need. . . .

THE MOTHER: And how was I to divine all this sentiment in him?

THE FATHER: That is exactly your mistake, never to have guessed any of my sentiments.

THE MOTHER: After so many years apart, and all that had happened . . .

THE FATHER: Was it my fault if that fellow carried you away? It happened quite suddenly; for after he had obtained some job or other, I could find no trace of them; and so, not unnaturally, my interest in them dwindled. But the drama culminated unforeseen and violent on their return, when I was impelled by my miserable flesh that still lives . . . Ah! what misery, what wretchedness is that of the man who is alone and disdains debasing *liaisons!* Not old enough to do without women, and not young enough to go and look for one without shame. Misery? It's worse than misery; it's a horror; for no woman can any longer give him love; and when a man feels this . . . One ought to do without, you say? Yes, yes, I know. Each of us when he appears before his fellows is clothed in a certain dignity. But every man knows what unconfessable things pass within the secrecy of his own heart. One gives way to the temptation, only to rise from it again, afterwards, with a great eagerness to reestablish one's dignity, as if it were a tombstone to place on the grave of one's shame, and a monument to hide and sign the memory of our weaknesses. Everybody's in the same case. Some folks haven't the courage to say certain things, that's all!

THE STEPDAUGHTER: All appear to have the courage to do them though.

THE FATHER: Yes, but in secret. Therefore, you want more courage to say these things. Let a man but speak these things out, and folks at once label him a cynic. But it isn't true. He is like all the others, better indeed, because he isn't afraid to reveal with the light of the intelligence the red shame of human bestiality on which most men close their eyes so as not to see it. Woman—for example, look at her case! She turns tantalizing inviting glances on you. You seize her. No sooner does she feel herself in your grasp than she closes her eyes. It is the sign of her mission, the sign by which she says to man: "Blind yourself, for I am blind."

THE STEPDAUGHTER: Sometimes she can close them no more: when she no longer feels the need of hiding her shame to herself, but dry-eyed and dispassionately, sees only that of the man who has blinded himself without love. Oh, all these intellectual complications make me sick, disgust me—all this philosophy that uncovers the beast in man, and then seeks to save him, excuse him . . . I can't stand it, sir. When a man seeks to "simplify" life bestially, throwing aside every relic of humanity,

every chaste aspiration, every pure feeling, all sense of ideality, duty, modesty, shame . . . then nothing is more revolting and nauseous than a certain kind of remorse—crocodiles' tears, that's what it is.

THE MANAGER: Let's come to the point. This is only discussion.

THE FATHER: Very good, sir! But a fact is like a sack which won't stand up when it is empty. In order that it may stand up, one has to put into it the reason and sentiment which have caused it to exist. I couldn't possibly know that after the death of that man, they had decided to return here, that they were in misery, and that she [*pointing to the* Mother] had gone to work as a modiste, and at a shop of the type of that of Madame Pace.

THE STEPDAUGHTER: A real high-class modiste, you must know, gentlemen. In appearance, she works for the leaders of the best society; but she arranges matters so that these elegant ladies serve her purpose . . . without prejudice to other ladies who are . . . well . . . only so so.

THE MOTHER: You will believe me, gentlemen, that it never entered my mind that the old hag offered me work because she had her eye on my daughter.

THE STEPDAUGHTER: Poor mamma! Do you know, sir, what that woman did when I brought her back the work my mother had finished? She would point out to me that I had torn one of my frocks, and she would give it back to my mother to mend. It was I who paid for it, always I; while this poor creature here believed she was sacrificing herself for me and these two children here, sitting up at night sewing Madame Pace's robes.

THE MANAGER: And one day you met there . . .

THE STEPDAUGHTER: Him, him. Yes, sir, an old client. There's a scene for you to play! Superb!

THE FATHER: She, the Mother arrived just then . . .

THE STEPDAUGHTER: [*Treacherously*] Almost in time!

THE FATHER: [*Crying out*] No, in time! in time! Fortunately I recognized her . . . in time. And I took them back home with me to my house. You can imagine now her position and mine: she, as you see her; and I who cannot look her in the face.

THE STEPDAUGHTER: Absurd! How can I possibly be expected—after that—to be a modest young miss, a fit person to go with his confounded aspirations for "a solid moral sanity"?

THE FATHER: For the drama lies all in this—in the conscience that I have, that each one of us has. We believe this conscience to be a single thing, but it is many-sided. There is one for this person, and another for that. Diverse consciences. So we have this illusion of being one person for all, of having a personality that is unique in all our acts. But it isn't true. We perceive this when, tragically perhaps, in something we do, we are, as it were, suspended, caught up in the air on a kind of hook.

Then we perceive that all of us was not in that act, and that it would be an atrocious injustice to judge us by that action alone, as if all our existence were summed up in that one deed. Now do you understand the perfidy of this girl? She surprised me in a place, where she ought not to have known me, just as I could not exist for her; and she now seeks to attach to me a reality such as I could never suppose I should have to assume for her in a shameful and fleeting moment of my life. I feel this above all else. And the drama, you will see, acquires a tremendous value from this point. Then there is the position of the others . . . his . . . [*Indicating the* Son]

THE SON: [*Shrugging his shoulders scornfully*] Leave me alone! I don't come into this.

THE FATHER: What? You don't come into this?

THE SON: I've got nothing to do with it, and don't want to have; because you know well enough I wasn't made to be mixed up in all this with the rest of you.

THE STEPDAUGHTER: We are only vulgar folk! He is the fine gentleman. You may have noticed, Mr. Manager, that I fix him now and again with a look of scorn while he lowers his eyes—for he knows the evil he has done me.

THE SON: [*Scarcely looking at her*] I?

THE STEPDAUGHTER: You! you! I owe my life on the streets to you. Did you or did you not deny us, with your behavior, I won't say the intimacy of home, but even that mere hospitality which makes guests feel at their ease? We were intruders who had come to disturb the kingdom of your legitimacy. I should like to have you witness, Mr. Manager, certain scenes between him and me. He says I have tyrannized over everyone. But it was just his behavior which made me insist on the reason for which I had come into the house—this reason he calls "vile"—into his house, with my mother who is his mother too. And I came as mistress of the house.

THE SON: It's easy for them to put me always in the wrong. But imagine, gentlemen, the position of a son, whose fate it is to see arrive one day at his home a young woman of impudent bearing, a young woman who inquires for his father, with whom who knows what business she has. This young man has then to witness her return bolder than ever, accompanied by that child there. He is obliged to watch her treat his father in an equivocal and confidential manner. She asks money of him in a way that lets one suppose he must give it her, *must,* do you understand, because he has every obligation to do so.

THE FATHER: But I have, as a matter of fact, this obligation. I owe it to your mother.

THE SON: How should I know? When had I ever seen or heard of her? One day there arrive with her [*indicating* Stepdaughter] that lad and this baby here. I am told: "This is *your* mother too, you know." I divine from her manner [*indicating* Stepdaughter *again*] why it is they have come home. I **had rather** not say what I feel and think about it. I

shouldn't even care to confess to myself. No action can therefore be hoped for from me in this affair. Believe me, Mr. Manager, I am an "unrealized" character, dramatically speaking; and I find myself not at all at ease in their company. Leave me out of it, I beg you.

THE FATHER: What? It is just because you are so that . . .

THE SON: How do you know what I am like? When did you ever bother your head about me?

THE FATHER: I admit it. I admit it. But isn't that a situation in itself? This aloofness of yours which is so cruel to me and to your mother, who returns home and sees you almost for the first time grown up, who doesn't recognize you but knows you are her son . . . [*Pointing out the* Mother *to the* Manager] See, she's crying!

THE STEPDAUGHTER: [*Angrily, stamping her foot*] Like a fool!

THE FATHER: [*Indicating* Stepdaughter] She can't stand him you know. [*Then referring again to the* Son]: He says he doesn't come into the affair, whereas he is really the hinge of the whole action. Look at that lad who is always clinging to his mother, frightened and humiliated. It is on account of this fellow here. Possibly his situation is the most painful of all. He feels himself a stranger more than the others. The poor little chap feels mortified, humiliated at being brought into a home out of charity as it were. [*In confidence*]—: He is the image of his father. Hardly talks at all. Humble and quiet.

THE MANAGER: Oh, we'll cut him out. You've no notion what a nuisance boys are on the stage . . .

THE FATHER: He disappears soon, you know. And the baby too. She is the first to vanish from the scene. The drama consists finally in this: when that mother re-enters my house, her family born outside of it, and shall we say superimposed on the original, ends with the death of the little girl, the tragedy of the boy and the flight of the elder daughter. It cannot go on, because it is foreign to its surroundings. So after much torment, we three remain: I, the mother, that son. Then, owing to the disappearance of that extraneous family, we too find ourselves strange to one another. We find we are living in an atmosphere of mortal desolation which is the revenge, as he [*indicating* Son] scornfully said of the Demon of Experiment, that unfortunately hides in me. Thus, sir, you see when faith is lacking, it becomes impossible to create certain states of happiness, for we lack the necessary humility. Vaingloriously, we try to substitute ourselves for this faith, creating thus for the rest of the world a reality which we believe after their fashion, while, actually, it doesn't exist. For each one of us has his own reality to be respected before God, even when it is harmful to one's very self.

THE MANAGER: There is something in what you say. I assure you all this interests me very much. I begin to think there's the stuff for a drama in all this, and not a bad drama either.

THE STEPDAUGHTER: [*Coming forward*] When you've got a character like me.

THE FATHER: [*Shutting her up, all excited to learn the decision of the* Manager] You be quiet!

THE MANAGER: [*Reflecting, heedless of interruption*] It's new . . . hem . . . yes . . .

THE FATHER: Absolutely new!

THE MANAGER: You've got a nerve though, I must say, to come here and fling it at me like this . . .

THE FATHER: You will understand, sir, born as we are for the stage . . .

THE MANAGER: Are you amateur actors then?

THE FATHER: No, I say born for the stage, because . . .

THE MANAGER: Oh, nonsense. You're an old hand, you know.

THE FATHER: No sir, no. We act that rôle for which we have been cast, that rôle which we are given in life. And in my own case, passion itself, as usually happens, becomes a trifle theatrical when it is exalted.

THE MANAGER: Well, well, that will do. But you see, without an author . . . I could give you the address of an author if you like . . .

THE FATHER: No, no. Look here! You must be the author.

THE MANAGER: I? What are you talking about?

THE FATHER: Yes, you, you! Why not?

THE MANAGER: Because I have never been an author: that's why.

THE FATHER: Then why not turn author now? Everybody does it. You don't want any special qualities. Your task is made much easier by the fact that we are all here alive before you . . .

THE MANAGER: It won't do.

THE FATHER: What? When you see us live our drama . . .

THE MANAGER: Yes, that's all right. But you want someone to write it.

THE FATHER: No, no. Someone to take it down, possibly, while we play it, scene by scene! It will be enough to sketch it out at first, and then try it over.

THE MANAGER: Well . . . I am almost tempted. It's a bit of an idea. One might have a shot at it.

THE FATHER: Of course. You'll see what scenes will come out of it. I can give you one, at once . . .

THE MANAGER: By Jove, it tempts me. I'd like to have a go at it. Let's try it out. Come with me to my office. [*Turning to the* Actors] You are at liberty for a bit, but don't stop out of the theater for long. In a quarter of an hour, twenty minutes, all back here again! [*To the* Father]: We'll see what can be done. Who knows if we don't get something really extraordinary out of it?

THE FATHER: There's no doubt about it. They [*indicating the* Characters] had better come with us too, hadn't they?

THE MANAGER: Yes, yes. Come on! come on! [*Moves away and then turning to the* Actors]: Be punctual, please! [Manager *and the* Six Characters *cross the stage and go off. The other* Actors *remain, looking at one another in astonishment*]

LEADING MAN: Is he serious? What the devil does he want to do?

JUVENILE LEAD: This is rank madness.

THIRD ACTOR: Does he expect to knock up a drama in five minutes?

JUVENILE LEAD: Like the improvisers!

LEADING LADY: If he thinks I'm going to take part in a joke like this . . .

JUVENILE LEAD: I'm out of it anyway.

FOURTH ACTOR: I should like to know who they are. [*Alludes to* Characters]

THIRD ACTOR: What do you suppose? Madmen or rascals!

JUVENILE LEAD: And he takes them seriously!

L'INGÉNUE: Vanity! He fancies himself as an author now.

LEADING MAN: It's absolutely unheard of. If the stage has come to this . . . well I'm . . .

FIFTH ACTOR: It's rather a joke.

THIRD ACTOR: Well, we'll see what's going to happen next.

[*Thus talking, the* Actors *leave the stage; some going out by the little door at the back; others retiring to their dressing-rooms.*
The curtain remains up.
The action of the play is suspended for twenty minutes]

ACT II.

The stage call-bells ring to warn the company that the play is about to begin again.

The Stepdaughter *comes out of the* Manager's *office along with* The Child *and* The Boy. *As she comes out of the office, she cries:*

Nonsense! Nonsense! Do it yourselves! I'm not going to mix myself up in this mess. [*Turning to the* Child *and coming quickly with her on to the stage*] Come on, Rosetta, let's run!

[The Boy *follows them slowly, remaining a little behind and seeming perplexed*]

THE STEPDAUGHTER: [*Stops, bends over the* Child *and takes the latter's face between her hands*] My little darling! You're frightened, aren't you? You don't know where we are, do you? [*Pretending to reply to a question of the* Child] What is the stage? It's a place, baby, you know, where people play at being serious, a place where they act comedies. We've got to act a comedy now, dead serious, you know; and you're in it also, little one. [*Embraces her, pressing the little head to her breast, and rocking the* Child *for a moment*] Oh darling, darling, what a horrid comedy you've got to play! What a wretched part they've found for you! A garden . . . a fountain . . . look . . . just suppose, kiddie, it's here. Where, you say? Why, right here in the middle. It's all pretence you know. That's the trouble, my pet: it's all make-believe here. It's better to imagine it though, because if they fix it up for you, it'll only be painted cardboard, painted cardboard for the rockery, the water, the plants . . . Ah, but I think a baby like this one would sooner have a make-believe fountain than a real one, so she could play with it. What a joke it'll be for the others! But for you, alas! not quite such a joke: you who are real, baby dear, and really play by a real fountain that is big and green and beautiful, with ever so many bamboos around it that are reflected in the water, and a whole lot of little ducks swimming about . . . No, Rosetta, no, your mother doesn't bother about you on account of that wretch of a son there. I'm in the devil of a temper, and as for that lad . . . [*Seizes* Boy *by the arm to force him to take one of his hands out of his pockets*] What have you got there? What are you hiding? [*Pulls his hand out of his pocket, looks into it and catches the glint of a revolver*] Ah, where did you get this?

[The Boy, *very pale in the face, looks at her, but does not answer*]

Idiot! If I'd been in your place, instead of killing myself, I'd have shot one of those two, or both of them: father and son.

[The Father *enters from the office, all excited from his work.* The Manager *follows him*]

THE FATHER: Come on, come on, dear! Come here for a minute! We've arranged everything. It's all fixed up.

THE MANAGER: [*Also excited*] If you please, young lady, there are one or two points to settle still. Will you come along?

THE STEPDAUGHTER: [*Following him towards the office*] Ouff! what's the good, if you've arranged everything.

[The Father, Manager *and* Stepdaughter *go back into the office again* (*off*) *for a moment. At the same time,* The Son *followed by* The Mother, *comes out*]

THE SON: [*Looking at the three entering office*] Oh this is fine, fine! And to think I can't even get away!

[The Mother *attempts to look at him, but lowers her eyes immediately when he turns away from her. She then sits down.* The Boy *and* The Child *approach her. She casts a glance again at the* Son, *and speaks with humble tones, trying to draw him into conversation*]

THE MOTHER: And isn't my punishment the worst of all? [*Then seeing from the* Son's *manner that he will not bother himself about her*] My God! Why are you so cruel? Isn't it enough for one person

to support all this torment? Must you then insist on others seeing it also?

THE SON: [*Half to himself, meaning the* Mother *to hear, however*] And they want to put it on the stage! If there was at least a reason for it! He thinks he has got at the meaning of it all. Just as if each one of us in every circumstance of life couldn't find his own explanation of it! [*Pauses*] He complains he was discovered in a place where he ought not to have been seen, in a moment of his life which ought to have remained hidden and kept out of the reach of that convention which he has to maintain for other people. And what about my case? Haven't I had to reveal what no son ought ever to reveal: how father and mother live and are man and wife for themselves quite apart from that idea of father and mother which we give them? When this idea is revealed, our life is then linked at one point only to that man and that woman; and as such it should shame them, shouldn't it?

[The Mother *hides her face in her hands. From the dressing-rooms and the little door at the back of the stage the* Actors *and* Stage Manager *return, followed by the* Property Man, *and the* Prompter. *At the same moment,* The Manager *comes out of his office, accompanied by the* Father *and the* Stepdaughter]

THE MANAGER: Come on, come on, ladies and gentlemen! Heh! you there, machinist!

MACHINIST: Yes sir?

THE MANAGER: Fix up the white parlor with the floral decorations. Two wings and a drop with a door will do. Hurry up!

[The Machinist *runs off at once to prepare the scene, and arranges it while* The Manager *talks with the* Stage Manager, *the* Property Man, *and the* Prompter *on matters of detail*]

THE MANAGER: [*To* Property Man] Just have a look, and see if there isn't a sofa or divan in the wardrobe . . .

PROPERTY MAN: There's the green one.

THE STEPDAUGHTER: No, no! Green won't do. It was yellow, ornamented with flowers—very large! and most comfortable!

PROPERTY MAN: There isn't one like that.

THE MANAGER: It doesn't matter. Use the one we've got.

THE STEPDAUGHTER: Doesn't matter? It's most important!

THE MANAGER: We're only trying it now. Please don't interfere. [*To* Property Man] See if we've got a shop window—long and narrowish.

THE STEPDAUGHTER: And the little table! The little mahogany table for the pale blue envelope!

PROPERTY MAN: [*To* Manager] There's that little gilt one.

THE MANAGER: That'll do fine.

THE FATHER: A mirror.

THE STEPDAUGHTER: And the screen! We must have a screen. Otherwise how can I manage?

PROPERTY MAN: That's all right, Miss. We've got any amount of them.

THE MANAGER: [*To the* Stepdaughter] We want some clothes pegs too, don't we?

THE STEPDAUGHTER: Yes, several, several!

THE MANAGER: See how many we've got and bring them all.

PROPERTY MAN: All right!

[*The* Property Man *hurries off to obey his orders. While he is putting the things in their places, the* Manager *talks to the* Prompter *and then with the* Characters *and the* Actors]

THE MANAGER: [*To* Prompter] Take your seat. Look here: this is the outline of the scenes, act by act. [*Hands him some sheets of paper*] And now I'm going to ask you to do something out of the ordinary.

PROMPTER: Take it down in shorthand?

THE MANAGER: [*Pleasantly surprised*] Exactly! Can you do shorthand?

PROMPTER: Yes, a little.

MANAGER: Good! [*Turning to a stage hand*] Go and get some paper from my office, plenty, as much as you can find.

[*The* Stage Hand *goes off, and soon returns with a handful of paper which he gives to the* Prompter]

THE MANAGER: [*To* Prompter] You follow the scenes as we play them, and try and get the points down, at any rate the most important ones. [*Then addressing the* Actors] Clear the stage, ladies and gentlemen! Come over here [*Pointing to the Left*] and listen attentively.

LEADING LADY: But, excuse me, we . . .

THE MANAGER: [*Guessing her thought*] Don't worry! You won't have to improvise.

LEADING MAN: What have we to do then?

THE MANAGER: Nothing. For the moment you just watch and listen. Everybody will get his part written out afterwards. At present we're going to try the thing as best we can. They're going to act now.

THE FATHER: [*As if fallen from the clouds into the confusion of the stage*] We? What do you mean, if you please, by a rehearsal?

THE MANAGER: A rehearsal for them. [*Points to the* Actors]

THE FATHER: But since we are the characters . . .

THE MANAGER: All right: "characters" then, if you insist on calling yourselves such. But here, my dear sir, the characters don't act. Here the actors do the acting. The characters are there, in the "book"— [*Pointing towards* Prompter's *box*] when there is a "book"!

THE FATHER: I won't contradict you; but excuse me, the actors aren't the characters. They want to be, they pretend to be, don't they? Now if these gentlemen here are fortunate enough to have us alive before them . . .

THE MANAGER: Oh this is grand! You want to come before the public yourselves then?

THE FATHER: As we are . . .

THE MANAGER: I can assure you it would be a magnificent spectacle!

LEADING MAN: What's the use of us here anyway then?

THE MANAGER: You're not going to pretend that you can act? It makes me laugh! [*The* Actors *laugh*] There, you see, they are laughing at the notion. But, by the way, I must cast the parts. That won't be difficult. They cast themselves. [*To the* Second Lady Lead] You play the Mother. [*To the* Father] We must find her a name.

THE FATHER: Amalia, sir.

THE MANAGER: But that is the real name of your wife. We don't want to call her by her real name.

THE FATHER: Why ever not, if it is her name? . . . Still, perhaps, if that lady must . . . [*Makes a slight motion of the hand to indicate the* Second Lady Lead] I see this woman here [*means the* Mother] as Amalia. But do as you like. [*Gets more and more confused*] I don't know what to say to you. Already, I begin to hear my own words ring false, as if they had another sound . . .

THE MANAGER: Don't you worry about it. It'll be our job the find the right tones. And as for her name, if you want her Amalia, Amalia it shall be; and if you don't like it, we'll find another! For the moment though, we'll call the characters in this way: [*to* Juvenile Lead] You are the Son; [*to the* Leading Lady] You naturally are the Stepdaughter . . .

THE STEPDAUGHTER: [*Excitedly*] What? what? I, that woman there? [*Bursts out laughing*]

THE MANAGER: [*Angry*] What is there to laugh at?

LEADING LADY: [*Indignant*] Nobody has ever dared to laugh at me. I insist on being treated with respect; otherwise I go away.

THE STEPDAUGHTER: No, no, excuse me . . . I am not laughing at you . . .

THE MANAGER: [*To* Stepdaughter] You ought to feel honored to be played by . . .

LEADING LADY: [*At once, contemptuously*] "That woman there" . . .

THE STEPDAUGHTER: But I wasn't speaking of you, you know. I was speaking of myself—whom I can't see at all in you! That is all. I don't know . . . but . . . you . . . aren't in the least like me . . .

THE FATHER: True. Here's the point. Look here, sir, our temperaments, our souls . . .

THE MANAGER: Temperament, soul, be hanged. Do you suppose the spirit of the piece is in you? Nothing of the kind!

THE FATHER: What, haven't we our own temperaments, our own souls?

THE MANAGER: Not at all. Your soul or whatever you like to call it takes shape here. The actors give body and form to it, voice and gesture. And my actors—I may tell you—have given expression to much more lofty material than this little drama of yours, which may or may not hold up on the stage.

But if it does, the merit of it, believe me, will be due to my actors.

THE FATHER: I don't dare contradict you, sir; but, believe me, it is a terrible suffering for us who are as we are, with these bodies of ours, these features to see . . .

THE MANAGER: [*Cutting him short and out of patience*] Good heavens! The make-up will remedy all that, man, the make-up . . .

THE FATHER: Maybe. But the voice, the gestures . . .

THE MANAGER: Now, look here! On the stage, you as yourself, cannot exist. The actor here acts you, and that's an end to it!

THE FATHER: I understand. And now I think I see why our author who conceived us as we are, all alive, didn't want to put us on the stage after all. I haven't the least desire to offend your actors. Far from it! But when I think that I am to be acted by . . . I don't know by whom . . .

LEADING MAN: [*On his dignity*] By me, if you've no objection!

THE FATHER: [*Humbly, mellifluously*] Honored, I assure you, sir. [*Bows*] Still, I must say that try as this gentleman may, with all his good will and wonderful art, to absorb me into himself . . .

LEADING MAN: Oh chuck it! "Wonderful art!" Withdraw that, please!

THE FATHER: The performance he will give, even doing his best with make-up to look like me . . .

LEADING MAN: It will certainly be a bit difficult! [*The* Actors *laugh*]

THE FATHER: Exactly! It will be difficult to act me as I really am. The effect will be rather—apart from the make-up—according as to how he supposes I am, as he senses me—if he does sense me—and not as I inside of myself feel myself to be. It seems to me then that account should be taken of this by everyone whose duty it may become to criticize us . .

THE MANAGER: Heavens! The man's starting to think about the critics now! Let them say what they like. It's up to us to put on the play if we can. [*Looking around*] Come on! come on! Is the stage set? [*To the* Actors *and* Characters] Stand back— stand back! Let me see, and don't let's lose any more time! [*To the* Stepdaughter] Is it all right as it is now?

THE STEPDAUGHTER: Well, to tell the truth, I don't recognize the scene.

THE MANAGER: My dear lady, you can't possibly suppose that we can construct that shop of Madame Pace piece by piece here? [*To the* Father] You said a white room with flowered wall paper, didn't you?

THE FATHER: Yes.

THE MANAGER: Well then. We've got the furniture right more or less. Bring that little table a bit further forward. [*The stage hands obey the order. To* Property Man] You go and find an envelope, if possible, a pale blue one; and give it to that gentleman. [*Indicates* Father]

PROPERTY MAN: An ordinary envelope?

MANAGER AND FATHER: Yes, yes, an ordinary envelope.

PROPERTY MAN: At once, sir. [*Exit*]

THE MANAGER: Ready, everyone! First scene—the Young Lady. [*The* Leading Lady *comes forward*] No, no, you must wait. I meant her. [*Indicating the* Stepdaughter] You just watch—

THE STEPDAUGHTER: [*Adding at once*] How I shall play it, how I shall live it! . . .

LEADING LADY: [*Offended*] I shall live it also, you may be sure, as soon as I begin!

THE MANAGER: [*With his hands to his head*] Ladies and gentlemen, if you please! No more useless discussions! Scene I: the young lady with Madame Pace: Oh! [*Looks around as if lost*] And this Madame Pace, where is she?

THE FATHER: She isn't with us, sir.

THE MANAGER: Then what the devil's to be done?

THE FATHER: But she is alive too.

THE MANAGER: Yes, but where is she?

THE FATHER: One minute. Let me speak! [*Turning to the* Actresses] If these ladies would be so good as to give me their hats for a moment . . .

THE ACTRESSES: [*Half surprised, half laughing, in chorus*] What?
Why?
Our hats?
What does he say?

THE MANAGER: What are you going to do with the ladies' hats? [*The* Actors *laugh*]

THE FATHER: Oh nothing. I just want to put them on these pegs for a moment. And one of the ladies will be so kind as to take off her mantle . . .

THE ACTORS: Oh, what d'you think of that?
Only the mantle?
He must be mad.

SOME ACTRESSES: But why?
Mantles as well?

THE FATHER: To hang them up here for a moment. Please be so kind, will you?

THE ACTRESSES: [*Taking off their hats, one or two also their cloaks, and going to hang them on the racks*] After all, why not?
There you are!
This is really funny.
We've got to put them on show.

THE FATHER: Exactly; just like that, on show.

THE MANAGER: May we know why?

THE FATHER: I'll tell you. Who knows if, by arranging the stage for her, she does not come here herself, attracted by the very articles of her trade? [*Inviting the* Actors *to look towards the exit at back of stage*] Look! Look!

[*The door at the back of stage opens and Madame Pace enters and takes a few steps forward. She is a fat, oldish woman with puffy oxygenated hair. She is rouged and powdered, dressed with a comical elegance in black silk. Round her waist is a long silver chain from which hangs a pair of scissors. The* Step-daughter *runs over to her at once amid the stupor of the* Actors]

THE STEPDAUGHTER: [*Turning towards her*] There she is! There she is!

THE FATHER: [*Radiant*] It's she! I said so, didn't I? There she is!

THE MANAGER: [*Conquering his surprise, and then becoming indignant*] What sort of a trick is this?

LEADING MAN: [*Almost at the same time*] What's going to happen next?

JUVENILE LEAD: Where does *she* come from?

L'INGÉNUE: They've been holding her in reserve, I guess.

LEADING LADY: A vulgar trick!

THE FATHER: [*Dominating the protests*] Excuse me, all of you! Why are you so anxious to destroy in the name of a vulgar, commonplace sense of truth, this reality which comes to birth attracted and formed by the magic of the stage itself, which has indeed more right to live here than you, since it is much truer than you—if you don't mind my saying so? Which is the actress among you who is to play Madame Pace? Well, here is Madame Pace herself. And you will allow, I fancy, that the actress who acts her will be less true than this woman here, who is herself in person. You see my daughter recognized her and went over to her at once. Now you're going to witness the scene!

[*But the scene between the* Stepdaughter *and* Madame Pace *has already begun despite the protest of the* Actors *and the reply of* The Father. *It has begun quietly, naturally, in a manner impossible for the stage. So when the* Actors, *called to attention by* The Father, *turn round and see* Madame Pace, *who has placed one hand under the* Stepdaughter's *chin to raise her head, they observe her at first with great attention, but hearing her speak in an unintelligible manner their interest begins to wane*]

THE MANAGER: Well? well?

LEADING MAN: What does she say?

LEADING LADY: One can't hear a word.

JUVENILE LEAD: Louder! Louder please!

THE STEPDAUGHTER: [*Leaving* Madame Pace, *who smiles a Sphinx-like smile, and advancing towards the Actors*] Louder? Louder? What are you talking about? These aren't matters which can be shouted at the top of one's voice. If I have spoken them out loud, it was to shame him and have my revenge. [*Indicates* Father] But for Madame it's quite a different matter.

THE MANAGER: Indeed? indeed? But here, you know, people have got to make themselves heard, my dear. Even we who are on the stage can't hear you. What will it be when the public's in the theater? And anyway, you can very well speak up now

among yourselves, since we shan't be present to listen to you as we are now. You've got to pretend to be alone in a room at the back of a shop where no one can hear you.

[The Stepdaughter *coquettishly and with a touch of malice makes a sign of disagreement two or three times with her finger*]

THE MANAGER: What do you mean by no?

THE STEPDAUGHTER: [*Sotto voce, mysteriously*] There's someone who will hear us if she [*indicating* Madame Pace] speaks out loud.

THE MANAGER: [*In consternation*] What? Have you got someone else to spring on us now? [*The* Actors *burst out laughing*]

THE FATHER: No, no sir. She is alluding to me. I've got to be here—there behind that door, in waiting; and Madame Pace knows it. In fact, if you will allow me, I'll go there at once, so I can be quite ready. [*Moves away*]

THE MANAGER: [*Stopping him*] No! wait! wait! We must observe the conventions of the theater. Before you are ready . . .

THE STEPDAUGHTER: [*Interrupting him*] No, get on with it at once! I'm just dying, I tell you, to act this scene. If he's ready, I'm more than ready.

THE MANAGER: [*Shouting*] But, my dear young lady, first of all, we must have the scene between you and this lady . . . [*Indicates* Madame Pace] Do you understand? . . .

THE STEPDAUGHTER: Good Heavens! She's been telling me what you know already: that mamma's work is badly done again, that the material's ruined; and that if I want her to continue to help us in our misery I must be patient . . .

MADAME PACE: [*Coming forward with an air of great importance*] Yes indeed, sir, I no wanta take advantage of her, I no wanta be hard . . .

[*Note:* Madame Pace *is supposed to talk in a jargon half Italian, half English*]

THE MANAGER: [*Alarmed*] What? What? she talks like that? [*The* Actors *burst out laughing again*]

THE STEPDAUGHTER: [*Also laughing*] Yes, yes, that's the way she talks, half English, half Italian! Most comical it is!

MADAME PACE: Itta seem not verra polite gentle-men laugha atta me eef I trya best speaka English.

THE MANAGER: *Diamine!* Of course! Of course! Let her talk like that! Just what we want. Talk just like that, Madame, if you please! The effect will be certain. Exactly what was wanted to put a little comic relief into the crudity of the situation. Of course she talks like that! Magnificent!

THE STEPDAUGHTER: Magnificent? Certainly! When certain suggestions are made to one in language of that kind, the effect is certain, since it seems almost a joke. One feels inclined to laugh when one hears her talk about an "old signore" "who wanta talka nicely with you." Nice old signore, eh, Madame?

MADAME PACE: Not so old, my dear, not so old!

And even if you no lika him, he won't make any scandal!

THE MOTHER: [*Jumping up amid the amazement and consternation of the* Actors *who had not been noticing her. They move to restrain her*] You old devil! You murderess!

THE STEPDAUGHTER: [*Running over to calm her* Mother] Calm yourself, mother, calm yourself! Please don't . . .

THE FATHER: [*Going to her also at the same time*] Calm yourself! Don't get excited! Sit down now!

THE MOTHER: Well then, take that woman away out of my sight!

THE STEPDAUGHTER: [*To* Manager] It is impossible for my mother to remain here.

THE FATHER: [*To* Manager] They can't be here together. And for this reason, you see: that woman there was not with us when we came . . . If they are on together, the whole thing is given away inevitably, as you see.

THE MANAGER: It doesn't matter. This is only a first rough sketch—just to get an idea of the various points of the scene, even confusedly . . . [*Turning to the* Mother *and leading her to her chair*] Come along, my dear lady, sit down now, and let's get on with the scene . . .

[*Meanwhile, the* Stepdaughter, *coming forward again, turns to* Madame Pace]

THE STEPDAUGHTER: Come on, Madame, come on!

MADAME PACE: [*Offended*] No, no, *grazie*. I not do anything witha your mother present.

THE STEPDAUGHTER: Nonsense! Introduce this "old signore" who wants to talk nicely to me. [*Addressing the company imperiously*] We've got to do this scene one way or another, haven't we? Come on! [*To* Madame Pace] You can go!

MADAME PACE: Ah yes! I go'way! I go'way! Certainly! [*Exits furious*]

THE STEPDAUGHTER: [*To the* Father] Now you make your entry. No, you needn't go over here. Come here. Let's suppose you've already come in. Like that, yes! I'm here with bowed head, modest like. Come on! Out with your voice! Say "Good morning, Miss" in that peculiar tone, that special tone . . .

THE MANAGER: Excuse me, but are you the Manager, or am I? [*To the* Father, *who looks undecided and perplexed*] Get on with it, man! Go down there to the back of the stage. You needn't go off. Then come right forward here.

[*The Father does as he is told, looking troubled and perplexed at first. But as soon as he begins to move, the reality of the action affects him, and he begins to smile and to be more natural. The* Actors *watch intently*]

THE MANAGER: [*Sotto voce, quickly to the* Prompter *in his box*] Ready! ready? Get ready to write now.

THE FATHER: [*Coming forward and speaking in a different tone*] Good afternoon, Miss!

THE STEPDAUGHTER: [*Head bowed down slightly, with restrained disgust*] Good afternoon!

THE FATHER: [*Looks under her hat which partly covers her face. Perceiving she is very young, he makes an exclamation, partly of surprise, partly of fear lest he compromise himself in a risky adventure*] Ah . . . but . . . ah . . . I say . . . this is not the first time that you have come here, is it?

THE STEPDAUGHTER: [*Modestly*] No sir.

THE FATHER: You've been here before, eh? [*Then seeing her nod agreement*] More than once? [*Waits for her to answer, looks under her hat, smiles, and then says*] Well then, there's no need to be so shy, is there? May I take off your hat?

THE STEPDAUGHTER: [*Anticipating him and with veiled disgust*] No sir . . . I'll do it myself. [*Takes it off quickly*]

[*The Mother, who watches the progress of the scene with* The Son *and the other two* Children *who cling to her, is on thorns; and follows with varying expressions of sorrow, indignation, anxiety, and horror the words and actions of the other two. From time to time she hides her face in her hands and sobs*]

THE MOTHER: Oh, my God, my God!

THE FATHER: [*Playing his part with a touch of gallantry*] Give it to me! I'll put it down. [*Takes hat from her hands*] But a dear little head like yours ought to have a smarter hat. Come and help me choose one from the stock, won't you?

L'INGÉNUE: [*Interrupting*] I say . . . those are our hats you know.

THE MANAGER: [*Furious*] Silence! silence! Don't try and be funny, if you please . . . We're playing the scene now I'd have you notice. [*To the* Stepdaughter] Begin again, please!

THE STEPDAUGHTER: [*Continuing*] No thank you, sir.

THE FATHER: Oh, come now. Don't talk like that. You must take it. I shall be upset if you don't. There are some lovely little hats here; and then— Madame will be pleased. She expects it, anyway, you know.

THE STEPDAUGHTER: No, no! I couldn't wear it!

THE FATHER: Oh, you're thinking about what they'd say at home if they saw you come in with a new hat? My dear girl, there's always a way round these little matters, you know.

THE STEPDAUGHTER: [*All keyed up*] No, it's not that. I couldn't wear it because I am . . . as you see . . . you might have noticed . . . [*Showing her black dress*]

THE FATHER: . . . in mourning! Of course: I beg your pardon: I'm frightfully sorry . . .

THE STEPDAUGHTER: [*Forcing herself to conquer her indignation and nausea*] Stop! Stop! It's I who must thank you. There's no need for you to feel mortified or specially sorry. Don't think any more of what I've said. [*Tries to smile*] I must forget that I am dressed so . . .

THE MANAGER: [*Interrupting and turning to the* Prompter] Stop a minute! Stop! Don't write that down. Cut out that last bit. [*Then to the* Father *and* Stepdaughter] Fine! it's going fine! [*To the* Father *only*] And now you can go on as we arranged. [*To the* Actors] Pretty good that scene, where he offers her the hat, eh?

THE STEPDAUGHTER: The best's coming now. Why can't we go on?

THE MANAGER: Have a little patience! [*To the* Actors] Of course, it must be treated rather lightly.

LEADING MAN: Still, with a bit of go in it!

LEADING LADY: Of course! It's easy enough! [*To* Leading Man] Shall you and I try it now?

LEADING MAN: Why, yes! I'll prepare my entrance. [*Exit in order to make his entrance*]

THE MANAGER: [*To* Leading Lady] See here! The scene between you and Madame Pace is finished. I'll have it written out properly after. You remain here . . . oh, where are you going?

LEADING LADY: One minute. I want to put my hat on again. [*Goes over to hat-rack and puts her hat on her head*]

THE MANAGER: Good! You stay here with your head bowed down a bit.

THE STEPDAUGHTER: But she isn't dressed in black.

LEADING LADY: But I shall be, and much more effectively than you.

THE MANAGER: [*To* Stepdaughter] Be quiet please, and watch! You'll be able to learn something. [*Clapping his hands*] Come on! come on! Entrance, please!

[*The door at rear of stage opens, and the* Leading Man *enters with the lively manner of an old gallant. The rendering of the scene by the* Actors *from the very first words is seen to be quite a different thing, though it has not in any way the air of a parody. Naturally, the* Stepdaughter *and the* Father, *not being able to recognize themselves in the* Leading Lady *and the* Leading Man, *who deliver their words in different tones and with a different psychology, express, sometimes with smiles, sometimes with gestures, the impression they receive*]

LEADING MAN: Good afternoon, Miss . . .

THE FATHER: [*At once unable to contain himself*] No! no!

[*The* Stepdaughter *noticing the way the* Leading Man *enters, bursts out laughing*]

THE MANAGER: [*Furious*] Silence! And you please just stop that laughing. If we go on like this, we shall never finish.

THE STEPDAUGHTER: Forgive me, sir, but it's natural enough. This lady [*indicating* Leading Lady] stands there still; but if she is supposed to be me, I can assure you that if I heard anyone say "Good afternoon" in that manner and in that tone, I should burst out laughing as I did.

THE FATHER: Yes, yes, the manner, the tone . . .

THE MANAGER: Nonsense! Rubbish! Stand aside and let me see the action.

LEADING MAN: If I've got to represent an old fellow who's coming into a house of an equivocal character . . .

THE MANAGER: Don't listen to them, for Heaven's sake! Do it again! It goes fine. [*Waiting for the* Actors *to begin again*] Well?

LEADING MAN: Good afternoon, Miss.

LEADING LADY: Good afternoon.

LEADING MAN. [*Imitating the gesture of the* Father *when he looked under the hat, and then expressing quite clearly first satisfaction and then fear*] Ah, but . . . I say . . . this is not the first time that you have come here, is it?

THE MANAGER: Good, but not quite so heavily. Like this. [*Acts himself*] "This isn't the first time that you have come here" . . . [*To* Leading Lady] And you say: "No, sir."

LEADING LADY: No, sir.

LEADING MAN: You've been here before, more than once.

THE MANAGER: No, no, stop! Let her nod "yes" first. "You've been here before, eh?" [*The* Leading Lady *lifts up her head slightly and closes her eyes as though in disgust. Then she inclines her head twice*]

THE STEPDAUGHTER: [*Unable to contain herself*] Oh my God! [*Puts a hand to her mouth to prevent herself from laughing*]

THE MANAGER: [*Turning round*] What's the matter?

THE STEPDAUGHTER: Nothing, nothing!

THE MANAGER: [*To* Leading Man] Go on!

LEADING MAN: You've been here before, eh? Well then, there's no need to be so shy, is there? May I take off your hat?

[*The* Leading Man *says this last speech in such a tone and with such gestures that the* Stepdaughter, *though she has her hand to her mouth, cannot keep from laughing*]

LEADING LADY: [*Indignant*] I'm not going to stop here to be made a fool of by that woman there.

LEADING MAN: Neither am I! I'm through with it!

THE MANAGER: [*Shouting to* Stepdaughter] Silence! for once and all, I tell you!

THE STEPDAUGHTER: Forgive me! forgive me!

THE MANAGER: You haven't any manners: that's what it is! You go too far.

THE FATHER: [*Endeavoring to intervene*] Yes, it's true, but excuse her . . .

THE MANAGER: Excuse what? It's absolutely disgusting.

THE FATHER: Yes, sir, but believe me, it has such a strange effect when . . .

THE MANAGER: Strange? Why strange? Where is it strange?

THE FATHER: No, sir; I admire your actors—this gentleman here, this lady; but they are certainly not us!

THE MANAGER: I should hope not. Evidently they cannot be you, if they are actors.

THE FATHER: Just so: actors! Both of them act our parts exceedingly well. But, believe me, it produces quite a different effect on us. They want to be us, but they aren't, all the same.

THE MANAGER: What is it then anyway?

THE FATHER: Something that is . . . that is theirs—and no longer ours . . .

THE MANAGER: But naturally, inevitably. I've told you so already.

THE FATHER: Yes, I understand . . . I understand . . .

THE MANAGER: Well then, let's have no more of it! [Turning to the Actors] We'll have the rehearsals by ourselves, afterwards, in the ordinary way. I never could stand rehearsing with the author present. He's never satisfied! [Turning to Father and Stepdaughter] Come on! Let's get on with it again; and try and see if you can't keep from laughing.

THE STEPDAUGHTER: Oh, I shan't laugh any more. There's a nice little bit coming for me now: you'll see.

THE MANAGER: Well then: when she says "Don't think any more of what I've said. I must forget, etc.," you [addressing the Father] come in sharp with "I understand, I understand"; and then you ask her . . .

THE STEPDAUGHTER: [Interrupting] What?

THE MANAGER: Why she is in mourning.

THE STEPDAUGHTER: Not at all! See here: when I told him that it was useless for me to be thinking about my wearing mourning, do you know how he answered me? "Ah well," he said, "then let's take off this little frock."

THE MANAGER: Great! Just what we want, to make a riot in the theater!

THE STEPDAUGHTER: But it's the truth!

THE MANAGER: What does that matter? Acting is our business here. Truth up to a certain point, but no further.

THE STEPDAUGHTER: What do you want to do then?

THE MANAGER: You'll see, you'll see! Leave it to me.

THE STEPDAUGHTER: No sir! What you want to do is to piece together a little romantic sentimental scene out of my disgust, out of all the reasons, each more cruel and viler than the other, why I am what I am. He is to ask me why I'm in mourning; and I'm to answer with tears in my eyes, that it is just two months since papa died. No sir, no! He's got to say to me; as he did say: "Well, let's take off this little dress at once." And I; with my two months' mourning in my heart, went there behind that screen, and with these fingers tingling with shame . . .

THE MANAGER: [Running his hands through his hair] For Heaven's sake! What are you saying?

THE STEPDAUGHTER: [Crying out excitedly] The truth! The truth!

THE MANAGER: It may be. I don't deny it, and I can understand all your horror; but you must surely see that you can't have this kind of thing on the stage. It won't go.

THE STEPDAUGHTER: Not possible, eh? Very well! I'm much obliged to you—but I'm off!

THE MANAGER: Now be reasonable! Don't lose your temper!

THE STEPDAUGHTER: I won't stop here! I won't! I can see you've fixed it all up with him in your office. All this talk about what is possible for the stage . . . I understand! He wants to get at his complicated "cerebral drama," to have his famous remorse and torments acted; but I want to act my part, my part!

THE MANAGER: [Annoyed, shaking his shoulders] Ah! Just your part! But, if you will pardon me, there are other parts than yours: his [indicating the Father] and hers! [Indicating the Mother] On the stage you can't have a character becoming too prominent and overshadowing all the others. The thing is to pack them all into a neat little framework and then act what is actable. I am aware of the fact that everyone has his own interior life which he wants very much to put forward. But the difficulty lies in this fact: to set out just so much as is necessary for the stage, taking the other characters into consideration, and at the same time hint at the unrevealed interior life of each. I am willing to admit, my dear young lady, that from your point of view it would be a fine idea if each character could tell the public all his troubles in a nice monologue or a regular one-hour lecture. [Good humoredly] You must restrain yourself, my dear, and in your own interest, too; because this fury of yours, this exaggerated disgust you show, may make a bad impression, you know. After you have confessed to me that there were others before him at Madame Pace's and more than once . . .

THE STEPDAUGHTER: [Bowing her head, impressed] It's true. But remember those others mean him for me all the same.

THE MANAGER: [Not understanding] What? The others? What do you mean?

THE STEPDAUGHTER: For one who has gone wrong, sir, he who was responsible for the first fault is responsible for all that follow. He is responsible for my faults, was, even before I was born. Look at him, and see if it isn't true!

THE MANAGER: Well, well! And does the weight of so much responsibility seem nothing to you? Give him a chance to act it, to get it over!

THE STEPDAUGHTER: How? How can he act all his "noble remorses" all his "moral torments," if you want to spare him the horror of being discovered one day—after he had asked her what he did ask her—in the arms of her, that already fallen woman, that child, sir, that child he used to watch come out of school? [*She is moved*]

[*The Mother at this point is overcome with emotion, and breaks out into a fit of crying. All are touched. A long pause*]

THE STEPDAUGHTER: [*As soon as the Mother becomes a little quieter, adds resolutely and gravely*] At present, we are unknown to the public. Tomorrow, you will act us as you wish, treating us in your own manner. But do you really want to see drama, do you want to see it flash out as it really did?

THE MANAGER: Of course! That's just what I do want, so I can use as much of it as is possible.

THE STEPDAUGHTER: Well then, ask that Mother there to leave us.

THE MOTHER: [*Changing her low plaint into a sharp cry*] No! No! Don't permit it, sir, don't permit it!

THE MANAGER: But it's only to try it.

THE MOTHER: I can't bear it. I can't.

THE MANAGER: But since it has happened already . . . I don't understand!

THE MOTHER: It's taking place now. It happens all the time. My torment isn't a pretended one. I live and feel every minute of my torture. Those two children there—have you heard them speak? They can't speak any more. They cling to me to keep my torment actual and vivid for me. But for themselves, they do not exist, they aren't any more. And she [*indicating Stepdaughter*] has run away, she has left me, and is lost. If I now see her here before me, it is only to renew for me the tortures I have suffered for her too.

THE FATHER: The eternal moment! She [*indicating the Stepdaughter*] is here to catch me, fix me, and hold me eternally in the stocks for that one fleeting and shameful moment of my life. She can't give it up! And you sir, cannot either fairly spare me it.

THE MANAGER: I never said I didn't want to act it. It will form, as a matter of fact, the nucleus of the whole first act right up to her surprise. [*Indicating the Mother*]

THE FATHER: Just so! This is my punishment: the passion in all of us that must culminate in her final cry.

THE STEPDAUGHTER: I can hear it still in my ears. It's driven me mad, that cry!—You can put me on as you like; it doesn't matter. Fully dressed, if you like—provided I have at least the arm bare; because, standing like this [*she goes close to the Father and leans her head on his breast*] with my head so, and my arms round his neck, I saw a vein pulsing in my arm here; and then, as if that live vein had awakened disgust in me, I closed my eyes like this, and let my head sink on his breast. [*Turning to the Mother*] Cry out, mother! Cry out! [*Buries head in Father's breast, and with her shoulders raised as if to prevent her hearing the cry, adds in tones of intense emotion*] Cry out as you did then!

THE MOTHER: [*Coming forward to separate them*] No! My daughter, my daughter! [*And after having pulled her away from him*] You brute! you brute! She is my daughter! Don't you see she's my daughter?

THE MANAGER: [*Walking backwards towards footlights*] Fine! fine! Damned good! And then, of course—curtain!

THE FATHER: [*Going towards him excitedly*] Yes, of course, because that's the way it really happened.

THE MANAGER: [*Convinced and pleased*] Oh, yes, no doubt about it. Curtain here, curtain!

[*At the reiterated cry of The Manager, The Machinist lets the curtain down, leaving The Manager and The Father in front of it before the footlights*]

THE MANAGER: The darned idiot! I said "curtain" to show the act should end there, and he goes and lets it down in earnest. [*To the Father, while he pulls the curtain back to go on to the stage again*] Yes, yes, it's all right. Effect certain! That's the right ending. I'll guarantee the first act at any rate.

ACT III.

When the curtain goes up again, it is seen that the stage hands have shifted the bit of scenery used in the last part, and have rigged up instead at the back of the stage a drop, with some trees, and one or two wings. A portion of a fountain basin is visible The Mother is sitting on the Right with the two children by her side. The Son is on the same side, but away from the others. He seems bored, angry, and full of shame. The Father and The Stepdaughter are also seated towards the Right front. On the other side (Left) are the Actors, much in the positions they occupied before the curtain was lowered. Only The Manager is standing up in the middle of the stage, with his hand closed over his mouth in the act of meditating.

THE MANAGER: [*Shaking his shoulders after a brief pause*] Ah yes: the second act! Leave it to me, leave it all to me as we arranged, and you'll see! It'll go fine!

THE STEPDAUGHTER: Our entry into his house [*indicates Father*] in spite of him . . . [*indicates the Son*]

THE MANAGER: [*Out of patience*] Leave it to me, I tell you!

THE STEPDAUGHTER: Do let it be clear, at any rate, that it is in spite of my wishes.

THE MOTHER: [*From her corner, shaking her head*] For all the good that's come of it . . .

THE STEPDAUGHTER: [*Turning towards her quickly*] It doesn't matter. The more harm done us, the more remorse for him.

THE MANAGER: [*Impatiently*] I understand! Good

Heavens! I understand! I'm taking it into account.

THE MOTHER: [*Supplicatingly*] I beg you, sir, to let it appear quite plain that for conscience' sake I did try in every way . . .

THE STEPDAUGHTER: [*Interrupting indignantly and continuing for the* Mother] . . . to pacify me, to dissuade me from spiting him. [*To* Manager] Do as she wants: satisfy her, because it is true! I enjoy it immensely. Anyhow, as you can see, the meeker she is, the more she tries to get at his heart, the more distant and aloof does he become.

THE MANAGER: Are we going to begin this second act or not?

THE STEPDAUGHTER: I'm not going to talk any more now. But I must tell you this: you can't have the whole action take place in the garden, as you suggest. It isn't possible!

THE MANAGER: Why not?

THE STEPDAUGHTER: Because he [*indicates the* Son *again*] is always shut up alone in his room. And then there's all the part of that poor dazed-looking boy there which takes place indoors.

THE MANAGER: Maybe! On the other hand, you will understand—we can't change scenes three or four times in one act.

THE LEADING MAN: They used to once.

THE MANAGER: Yes, when the public was up to the level of that child there.

THE LEADING LADY: It makes the illusion easier.

THE FATHER: [*Irritated*] The illusion! For Heaven's sake, don't say illusion. Please don't use that word, which is particularly painful for us.

THE MANAGER: [*Astounded*] And why, if you please?

THE FATHER: It's painful, cruel, really cruel; and you ought to understand that.

THE MANAGER: But why? What ought we to say then? The illusion, I tell you, sir, which we've got to create for the audience . . .

THE LEADING MAN: With our acting.

THE MANAGER: The illusion of a reality.

THE FATHER: I understand; but you, perhaps, do not understand us. Forgive me! You see . . . here for you and your actors, the thing is only—and rightly so . . . a kind of game . . .

THE LEADING LADY: [*Interrupting indignantly*] A game! We're not children here, if you please! We are serious actors.

THE FATHER: I don't deny it. What I mean is the game, or play, of your art, which has to give, as the gentleman says, a perfect illusion of reality.

THE MANAGER: Precisely——!

THE FATHER: Now, if you consider the fact that we [*indicates himself and the other five* Characters], as we are, have no other reality outside of this illusion . . .

THE MANAGER: [*Astonished, looking at his* Actors, *who are also amazed*] And what does that mean?

THE FATHER: [*After watching them for a moment with a wan smile*] As I say, sir, that which is

a game of art for you is our sole reality. [*Brief pause. He goes a step or two nearer the* Manager *and adds*] But not only for us, you know, by the way. Just you think it over well. [*Looks him in the eyes*] Can you tell me who you are?

THE MANAGER: [*Perplexed, half smiling*] What? Who am I? I am myself.

THE FATHER: And if I were to tell you that that isn't true, because you are I? . . .

THE MANAGER: I should say you were mad——! [*The* Actors *laugh*]

THE FATHER: You're quite right to laugh: because we are all making believe here. [*To* Manager] And you can therefore object that it's only for a joke that that gentleman there [*indicates the* Leading Man], who naturally is himself, has to be me, who am on the contrary myself—this thing you see here. You see I've caught you in a trap! [*The* Actors *laugh*]

THE MANAGER: [*Annoyed*] But we've had all this over once before. Do you want to begin again?

THE FATHER: No, no! that wasn't my meaning! In fact, I should like to request you to abandon this game of art [*Looking at the* Leading Lady *as if anticipating her*] which you are accustomed to play here with your actors, and to ask you seriously once again: who are you?

THE MANAGER: [*Astonished and irritated, turning to his* Actors] If this fellow here hasn't got a nerve! A man who calls himself a character comes and asks me who I am!

THE FATHER: [*With dignity, but not offended*] A character, sir, may always ask a man who he is. Because a character has really a life of his own, marked with his especial characteristics; for which reason he is always "somebody." But a man—I'm not speaking of you now—may very well be "nobody."

THE MANAGER: Yes, but you are asking these questions of me, the boss, the manager! Do you understand?

THE FATHER: But only in order to know if you as you really are now, see yourself as you once were with all the illusions that were yours then, with all the things both inside and outside of you as they seemed to you—as they were then indeed for you. Well, sir, if you think of all those illusions that mean nothing to you now, of all those things which don't even *seem* to you to exist any more, while once they *were* for you, don't you feel that—I won't say these boards—but the very earth under your feet is sinking away from you when you reflect that in the same way this *you* as you feel it today—all this present reality of yours—is fated to seem a mere illusion to you tomorrow?

THE MANAGER: [*Without having understood much, but astonished by the specious argument*] Well, well! And where does all this take us anyway?

THE FATHER: Oh, nowhere! It's only to show you that if we [*indicating the* Characters] have no other reality beyond illusion, you too must not count over-much on your reality as you feel it today, since, like that of yesterday, it may prove an illusion for you tomorrow.

THE MANAGER: [*Determining to make fun of him*] Ah, excellent! Then you'll be saying next that you, with this comedy of yours that you brought here to act, are truer and more real than I am.

THE FATHER: [*With the greatest seriousness*] But of course; without doubt!

THE MANAGER: Ah, really?

THE FATHER: Why, I thought you'd understand that from the beginning.

THE MANAGER: More real than I?

THE FATHER: If your reality can change from one day to another . . .

THE MANAGER: But everyone knows it can change. It is always changing, the same as anyone else's.

THE FATHER: [*With a cry*] No, sir, not ours! Look here! That is the very difference! Our reality doesn't change: it can't change! It can't be other than what it is, because it is already fixed for ever. It's terrible. Ours is an immutable reality which should make you shudder when you approach us if you are really conscious of the fact that your reality is a mere transitory and fleeting illusion, taking this form to-day and that tomorrow, according to the conditions, according to your will, your sentiments, which in turn are controlled by an intellect that shows them to you today in one manner and tomorrow . . . who knows how? . . . Illusions of reality represented in this fatuous comedy of life that never ends, nor can ever end! Because if tomorrow it were to end . . . then why, all would be finished.

THE MANAGER: Oh for God's sake, will you *at least* finish with this philosophizing and let us try and shape this comedy which you yourself have brought me here? You argue and philosophize a bit too much, my dear sir. You know you seem to me almost, almost . . . [*Stops and looks him over from head to foot*] Ah, by the way, I think you intro-duced yourself to me as a—what shall . . . we say—a "character," created by an author who did not afterwards care to make a drama of his own crea-tions.

THE FATHER: It is the simple truth, sir.

THE MANAGER: Nonsense! Cut that out, please! None of us believes it, because it isn't a thing, as you must recognize yourself, which one can believe seriously. If you want to know, it seems to me you are trying to imitate the manner of a certain au-thor whom I heartily detest—I warn you—although I have unfortunately bound myself to put on one of his works. As a matter of fact, I was just starting to rehearse it, when you arrived. [*Turning to the Actors*] And this is what we've gained—out of the frying-pan into the fire!

THE FATHER: I don't know to what author you may be alluding, but believe me I feel what I think; and I seem to be philosophizing only for those who do not think what they feel, because they blind themselves with their own sentiment. I know that for many people this self-blinding seems much more "human"; but the contrary is really true. For man never reasons so much and becomes so introspective as when he suffers; since he is anxious to get at the cause of his sufferings, to learn who has produced them, and whether it is just or unjust that he should have to bear them. On the other hand, when he is happy, he takes his happiness as it comes and doesn't analyze it, just as if happiness were his right. The animals suffer without reasoning about their suffer-ings. But take the case of a man who suffers and begins to reason about it. Oh no! it can't be allowed! Let him suffer like an animal, and then—ah yes, he is "human!"

THE MANAGER: Look here! Look here! You're off again, philosophizing worse than ever.

THE FATHER: Because I suffer, sir! I'm not philoso-phizing: I'm crying aloud the reason of my suffer-ings.

THE MANAGER: [*Makes brusque movement as he is taken with a new idea*] I should like to know if anyone has ever heard of a character who gets right out of his part and perorates and speechifies as you do. Have you ever heard of a case? I haven't.

THE FATHER: You have never met such a case, sir, because authors, as a rule, hide the labor of their creations. When the characters are really alive before their author, the latter does nothing but follow them in their action, in their words, in the situations which they suggest to him; and he has to will them the way they will themselves—for there's trouble if he doesn't. When a character is born, he acquires at once such an independence, even of his own author, that he can be imagined by everybody even in many other situations where the author never dreamed of placing him; and so he acquires for himself a meaning which the author never thought of giving him.

THE MANAGER: Yes, yes, I know this.

THE FATHER: What is there then to marvel at in us? Imagine such a misfortune for characters as I have described to you: to be born of an author's fantasy, and be denied life by him; and then answer me if these characters left alive, and yet without life, weren't right in doing what they did do and are doing now, after they have attempted every-thing in their power to persuade him to give them their stage life. We've all tried him in turn, I, she [*indicating the* Stepdaughter] and she. [*Indicating the* Mother]

THE STEPDAUGHTER: It's true. I too have sought to tempt him, many, many times, when he has been sitting at his writing table, feeling a bit melan-choly, at the twilight hour. He would sit in his arm-chair too lazy to switch on the light, and all the shadows that crept into his room were full of our presence coming to tempt him. [*As if she saw her-self still there by the writing table, and was annoyed by the presence of the* Actors] Oh, if you would only go away, go away and leave us alone—mother here with that son of hers—I with that Child—that Boy there always alone—and then I with him—[*just hints at the* Father]—and then I alone, alone . . . in those shadows! [*Makes a sudden movement as if in the vision she has of herself illuminating those shadows she wanted to seize hold of herself*] Ah! my life! my life! Oh, what scenes we proposed to him—and I tempted him more than any of the others!

THE FATHER: Maybe. But perhaps it was your fault that he refused to give us life: because you were too insistent, too troublesome.

THE STEPDAUGHTER: Nonsense! Didn't he make me so himself? [*Goes close to the* Manager *to tell him as if in confidence*] In my opinion he abandoned us in a fit of depression, of disgust for the ordinary theater as the public knows it and likes it.

THE SON: Exactly what it was, sir; exactly that!

THE FATHER: Not at all! Don't believe it for a minute. Listen to me! You'll be doing quite right to modify, as you suggest, the excesses both of this girl here, who wants to do too much, and of this young man, who won't do anything at all.

THE SON: No, nothing!

THE MANAGER: You too get over the mark occasionally, my dear sir, if I may say so.

THE FATHER: I? When? Where?

THE MANAGER: Always! Continuously! Then there's this insistence of yours in trying to make us believe you are a character. And then too, you must really argue and philosophize less, you know, much less.

THE FATHER: Well, if you want to take away from me the possibility of representing the torment of my spirit which never gives me peace, you will be suppressing me: that's all. Every true man, sir, who is a little above the level of the beasts and plants does not live for the sake of living, without knowing how to live; but he lives so as to give a meaning and a value of his own to life. For me this is *everything.* I cannot give up this, just to represent a mere fact as she [*indicating the* Stepdaughter] wants. It's all very well for her, since her "vendetta" lies in the "fact." I'm not going to do it. It destroys my *raison d'être.*

THE MANAGER: Your *raison d'être!* Oh, we're going ahead fine! First she starts off, and then you jump in. At this rate, we'll never finish.

THE FATHER: Now, don't be offended! Have it your own way—provided, however, that within the limits of the parts you assign us each one's sacrifice isn't too great.

THE MANAGER: You've got to understand that you can't go on arguing at your own pleasure. Drama is action, sir, action and not confounded philosophy.

THE FATHER: All right. I'll do just as much arguing and philosophizing as everybody does when he is considering his own torments.

THE MANAGER: If the drama permits! But for Heaven's sake, man, let's get along and come to the scene.

THE STEPDAUGHTER: It seems to me we've got too much action with our coming into his house. [*Indicating* Father] You said, before, you couldn't change the scene every five minutes.

THE MANAGER: Of course not. What we've got to do is to combine and group up all the facts in one simultaneous, close-knit action. We can't have it as you want, with your little brother wandering like a ghost from room to room, hiding behind doors and meditating a project which—what did you say it did to him?

THE STEPDAUGHTER: Consumes him, sir, wastes him away!

THE MANAGER: Well, it may be. And then at the same time, you want the little girl there to be playing in the garden . . . one in the house, and the other in the garden: isn't that it?

THE STEPDAUGHTER: Yes, in the sun, in the sun! That is my only pleasure: to see her happy and careless in the garden after the misery and squalor of the horrible room where we all four slept together. And I had to sleep with her—I, do you understand?—with my vile contaminated body next to hers; with her folding me fast in her loving little arms. In the garden, whenever she spied me, she would run to take me by the hand. She didn't care for the big flowers, only the little ones; and she loved to show me them and pet me.

THE MANAGER: Well then, we'll have it in the garden. Everything shall happen in the garden; and we'll group the other scenes there. [*Calls a stage hand*] Here, a back-cloth with trees and something to do as a fountain basin. [*Turning round to look at the back of the stage*] Ah, you've fixed it up. Good! [*To* Stepdaughter] This is just to give an idea, of course. The Boy, instead of hiding behind the doors, will wander about here in the garden, hiding behind the trees. But it's going to be rather difficult to find a child to do that scene with you where she shows you the flowers. [*Turning to the* Youth] Come forward a little, will you please? Let's try it now! Come along! come along! [*Then seeing him come shyly forward, full of fear and looking lost*] It's a nice business, this lad here. What's the matter with him? We'll have to give him a word or two to say. [*Goes close to him, puts a hand on his shoulders, and leads him behind one of the trees*] Come on! come on! Let me see you a little! Hide here . . . yes, like that. Try and show your head just a little as if you were looking for someone . . . [*Goes back to observe the effect, when the* Boy *at once goes through the action*] Excellent! fine! [*Turning to* Stepdaughter] Suppose the little girl there were to surprise him as he looks round, and run over to him, so we could give him a word or two to say?

THE STEPDAUGHTER: It's useless to hope he will

speak, as long as that fellow there is here . . . [*Indicates the* Son] You must send him away first.

THE SON: [*Jumping up*] Delighted! delighted! I don't ask for anything better. [*Begins to move away*]

THE MANAGER: [*At once stopping him*] No! No! Where are you going? Wait a bit!

[*The* Mother *gets up alarmed and terrified at the thought that he is really about to go away. Instinctively she lifts her arms to prevent him, without, however, leaving her seat*]

THE SON: [*To* Manager *who stops him*] I've got nothing to do with this affair. Let me go please! Let me go!

THE MANAGER: What do you mean by saying you've got nothing to do with this?

THE STEPDAUGHTER: [*Calmly, with irony*] Don't bother to stop him: he won't go away.

THE FATHER: He has to act the terrible scene in the garden with his mother.

THE SON: [*Suddenly resolute and with dignity*] I shall act nothing at all. I've said so from the very beginning [*To the* Manager] Let me go!

THE STEPDAUGHTER: [*Going over to the* Manager] Allow me? [*Puts down the* Manager's *arm which is restraining the* Son] Well, go away then, if you want to! [*The* Son *looks at her with contempt and hatred. She laughs and says*] You see, he can't, he can't go away! He is obliged to stay here, indissolubly bound to the chain. If I, who fly off when that happens which has to happen, because I can't bear him—if I am still here and support that face and expression of his, you can well imagine that he is unable to move. He has to remain here, has to stop with that nice father of his, and that mother whose only son he is. [*Turning to the* Mother] Come on, mother, come along! [*Turning to* Manager *to indicate her*] You see, she was getting up to keep him back. [*To the* Mother, *beckoning her with her hand*] Come on! come on! [*Then to* Manager] You can imagine how little she wants to show these actors of yours what she really feels; but so eager is she to get near him that . . . There, you see? She is willing to act her part. [*And in fact, the* Mother *approaches him; and as soon as the* Stepdaughter *has finished speaking, opens her arms to signify that she consents*]

THE SON: [*Suddenly*] No! no! If I can't go away, then I'll stop here; but I repeat: I act nothing!

THE FATHER: [*To* Manager *excitedly*] You can force him, sir.

THE SON: Nobody can force me.

THE FATHER: I can.

THE STEPDAUGHTER: Wait a minute, wait . . . First of all, the baby has to go to the fountain . . . [*Runs to take the* Child *and leads her to the fountain*]

THE MANAGER: Yes, yes of course; that's it. Both at the same time.

[*The second* Lady Lead *and the* Juvenile Lead *at this point separate themselves from the group of* Actors. *One watches the* Mother *attentively; the other moves about studying the movements and manner of the* Son *whom he will have to act*]

THE SON: [*To* Manager] What do you mean by both at the same time? It isn't right. There was no scene between me and her. [*Indicates the* Mother] Ask her how it was!

THE MOTHER: Yes, it's true. I had come into his room . . .

THE SON: Into my room, do you understand? Nothing to do with the garden.

THE MANAGER: It doesn't matter. Haven't I told you we've got to group the action?

THE SON: [*Observing the* Juvenile Lead *studying him*] What do you want?

THE JUVENILE LEAD: Nothing! I was just looking at you.

THE SON: [*Turning towards the* Second Lady Lead] Ah! she's at it too: to re-act her part. [*Indicating the* Mother]!

THE MANAGER: Exactly! And it seems to me that you ought to be grateful to them for their interest.

THE SON: Yes, but haven't you yet perceived that it isn't possible to live in front of a mirror which not only freezes us with the image of ourselves, but throws our likeness back at us with a horrible grimace?

THE FATHER: That is true, absolutely true. You must see that.

THE MANAGER: [*To* Second Lady Lead *and* Juvenile Lead] He's right! Move away from them!

THE SON: Do as you like. I'm out of this!

THE MANAGER: Be quiet, you, will you? And let me hear your mother! [*To* Mother] You were saying you had entered . . .

THE MOTHER: Yes, into his room, because I couldn't stand it any longer. I went to empty my heart to him of all the anguish that tortures me . . . But as soon as he saw me come in . . .

THE SON: Nothing happened! There was no scene. I went away, that's all! I don't care for scenes!

THE MOTHER: It's true, true. That's how it was.

THE MANAGER: Well now, we've got to do this bit between you and him. It's indispensable.

THE MOTHER: I'm ready . . . when you are ready. If you could only find a chance for me to tell him what I feel here in my heart.

THE FATHER: [*Going to* Son *in a great rage*] You'll do this for your mother, for your mother, do you understand?

THE SON: [*Quite determined*] I do nothing!

THE FATHER: [*Taking hold of him and shaking him*] For God's sake, do as I tell you! Don't you hear your mother asking you for a favor? Haven't you even got the guts to be a son?

THE SON: [*Taking hold of the* Father] No! No! And for God's sake stop it, or else . . . [*General agitation. The* Mother, *frightened, tries to separate them*]

THE MOTHER: [*Pleading*] Please! please!

THE FATHER: [*Not leaving hold of the* Son] You've got to obey, do you hear?

THE SON: [*Almost crying from rage*] What does it mean, this madness you've got? [*They separate*] Have you no decency, that you insist on showing everyone our shame? I won't do it! I won't! And I stand for the will of our author in this. He didn't want to put us on the stage, after all!

THE MANAGER: Man alive! You came here . . .

THE SON: [*Indicating* Father] *He* did! I didn't!

THE MANAGER: Aren't you here now?

THE SON: It was his wish, and he dragged us along with him. He's told you not only the things that did happen, but also things that have never happened at all.

THE MANAGER: Well, tell me then what did happen. You went out of your room without saying a word?

THE SON: Without a word, so as to avoid a scene!

THE MANAGER: And then what did you do?

THE SON: Nothing . . . walking in the garden . . . [*Hesitates for a moment with expression of gloom*]

THE MANAGER: [*Coming closer to him, interested by his extraordinary reserve*] Well, well . . . walking in the garden . . .

THE SON: [*Exasperated*] Why on earth do you insist? It's horrible! [*The* Mother *trembles, sobs, and looks towards the fountain*]

THE MANAGER: [*Slowly observing the glance and turning towards the* Son *with increasing apprehension*] The baby?

THE SON: There in the fountain . . .

THE FATHER: [*Pointing with tender pity to the* Mother] She was following him at the moment . . .

THE MANAGER: [*To the* Son *anxiously*] And then you . . .

THE SON: I ran over to her; I was jumping in to drag her out when I saw something that froze my blood . . . the boy there standing stock still, with eyes like a madman's, watching his little drowned sister, in the fountain! [*The* Stepdaughter *bends over the fountain to hide the* Child. *She sobs*] Then . . . [*A revolver shot rings out behind the trees where the* Boy *is hidden*]

THE MOTHER: [*With a cry of terror runs over in that direction together with several of the* Actors *amid general confusion*] My son! My son! [*Then amid the cries and exclamations one hears her voice*] Help! Help!

THE MANAGER: [*Pushing the* Actors *aside while they lift up the* Boy *and carry him off*] Is he really wounded?

SOME ACTORS: He's dead! dead!

OTHER ACTORS: No, no, it's only make believe, it's only pretence!

THE FATHER: [*With a terrible cry*] Pretence? Reality, sir, reality!

THE MANAGER: Pretence? Reality? To hell with it all! Never in my life has such a thing happened to me. I've lost a whole day over these people, a whole day!

CURTAIN

Karel Capek

(1890–1938)

Karel Capek, the leading literary figure of Czech-oslovakia after the First World War, was born in eastern Bohemia. Son of a physician, he was a member of a talented family which included his elder brother Josef (1887–1945), who was not only his collaborator on fiction and plays but was independently prominent as a painter, scene designer, and art critic. Karel's intellectual interests were as strong as his artistic inclinations, and his studies took him to Prague, Paris, and Berlin. He became an admirer of the ideas of William James and John Dewey, and he took a doctorate in philosophy at the University of Prague, publishing a thesis on pragmatism in 1917. After graduation, he collaborated with his brother on stories and sketches, practiced journalism, and stage-managed at a theatre in Vinohrady, Czechoslovakia. He also took part in the political revival of his country and as a writer championed liberal causes.

Although he owed his international reputation chiefly to his plays, his literary work extended beyond the theatre. He published a collection of pessimistic stories (*Money and Other Stories*, 1921), two satirical fantasies (*The Absolute at Large*, 1922, and *Krakatit*, 1924) that recall the early science fiction of H. G. Wells, a volume of fables, and a Chestertonian mystery story (*Tales from Two Pockets*). Especially well received was a prose trilogy (*Hordubal*, 1933, *Meteor*, 1935, and *An Ordinary Life*, 1936) in which he told the same story from three different points of view. He gave vent to his concern over the effects of modern science and power politics in a trenchant satire, *War with the Newts* (1936), and to his social sympathies in the story of a mine disaster, *The First Rescue Party* (1937). His exposé of charlatanism, *The Cheat*, remained unfinished when he died of pneumonia on Christmas Day 1938, in time to escape the vengeance of Hitler's Gestapo; it soon fell on his brother Josef, who died in the concentration camp of Belsen. His political activity also resulted in a series of books (1928–1935) about his friend Thomas Masaryk, first president of the Czechoslovak republic, with whose democratic ideals he was obviously in full sympathy.

Capek's interest in the stage came at a time when the Czech people were witnessing the final fulfillment of their dream of developing a vital national theatre. Although a National Theatre had been established in Prague in 1881 under the management of the playwright-director Frantisek Subert (1839–1915), the project suffered from many disadvantages while Bohemia was still a province of the Austrian-Hungarian empire. After 1918, with the independence of Czechoslovakia an actuality, the National Theatre became one of the busiest cultural centers of the new republic, and Capek became its chief luminary.

Into the plays he wrote alone and in collaboration with his brother, he poured the same social interests and imagination that drew attention to his novels. In the theatre of Central Europe, moreover, there was much experimental fermentation after 1918, and Capek responded to it in his own writing. He had started a play, *The Robbers,* as early as 1911 in celebration of a Czech brigand who defied the old order. Capek completed the play in 1920 without much success, but his next two efforts, *R. U. R.* (1920) and *The Insect Comedy* (1921), brought him international fame. Two other experimental dramatic pieces, *The Makropoulos Affair* (1923), which questioned the desirability of longevity, and *Adam the Creator* (1927), a fantasy on the possibility of reconstructing civilization after man had destroyed it, attracted much attention. He continued to challenge the conscience with more conventional social protests, writing *The White Plague* (1937) as an attack on totalitarianism and *The Mother* (1938) as a warning against the war that he knew was coming. His plays made the theatre in Czechoslovakia one of the most vital in Europe before 1939. To the development of the native stage Capek, moreover, brought a keen interest in experimental stagecraft. He became an important associate of the National Theatre and co-manager, with Josef, of the experimental Vinohradsky Art Theatre.

All his plays exemplify his great theatrical virtuosity, which was well supported by his brother's expressionistic and futuristic stage designs and by the inventiveness of the Czech director Hilar. Capek's theatricality was, however, the product of an active imagination which served ideas rather than sensationalism. For *The Makropoulos Affair* (later converted into an opera by Janacek) he invented the story of a Greek woman born in the sixteenth century who is periodically rejuvenated in different countries, always wins success as an artist, and always attracts male admirers. Surviving into the twentieth century, she disillusions many people with the prospect of living forever until the formula that has ensured her survival is finally destroyed by one of the characters to whom she offers it. In *The Insect Play* (written with Josef, and produced in many countries under such titles as *And So Ad*

Infinitum and *The World We Live in*) Capek wrote a spectacle of insect life to parallel the follies and futilities of human life.

Adam the Creator presented Adam as destroying the world in disgust, with God's permission, reconstituting it as a utopia which turns out to be just as distressing as the world he destroyed with a "cannon of Negation," and finally resigning himself to accepting the *status quo*. For *R. U. R.*, apparently inspired by the rabbinical legend of a mechanical man, or "golem," in medieval Prague, Capek conjured up a world so mechanized that all labor is performed by machine-made men. He called these artificial workers "robots," deriving the word from the Czech noun for work, *robota*, and the term won international currency as a result of the success of the play. The additional fantasy of a revolt of the robots, their destruction of humanity, and their own need to develop human souls made *R. U. R. (Rossum's Universal Robots)* an absorbing fantasy.

R. U. R. possessed special immediacy as a warning against the accelerated rate at which men were being depersonalized in the factories of the machine age. Since the mass production of "robots" was dictated by the desire for cheap and efficient labor, the play is also an indirect attack on the scramble for profits. In writing his fantasy Capek aligned himself with the social critics among the playwrights of Central Europe. *R. U. R.* also proved, however, sufficiently provocative as a work of imagination and exciting as a melodrama to interest the rest of Europe and America. The New York Theatre Guild's production (1922) was an outstanding event in the American theatre, and the play was revived in New York, although with no particular success, some fifteen years later. America, in fact, concerned this author greatly, and it was our technological progress and its dissemination in Europe that provided the initial impulse for his writing *R. U. R.* In 1926 he actually published an article in the *New York Times Magazine* condemning the "Americanization"—that is, "mechanization"—of European life, drawing a riposte from Glenn Frank in the same publication.

In *R. U. R.*, Capek managed to present his fantasy with simplicity, tightly knit dramaturgy, and direct progression, whereas his other unconventionally constructed plays tended to be more or less episodic or, at their worst, inchoate. He also succeeded in taking full advantage of sensational expressionist elements prevalent in the Central European theatre after 1918—dramatic violence, dry and mechanical speech, and weird stage pictures—without succumbing to the frenzy of most expressionistic playwriting. Since *R. U. R.* is presented as literal or realistic story without abrupt interruptions of the flow of action and without the disassociations and distortions of the dream technique, it can be followed without confusion or strain and with mounting interest. Although *R. U. R.* can hardly qualify as a classic of the world theatre, it became a classic of the European theatre between two wars. Its concern with the loss of human individuality will probably assure the play a long life.

BIBLIOGRAPHY: Karel Capek, *Letters from England*, 1925; Capek, *How a Play Is Produced*, 1928; Frank W. Chandler, *Modern Continental Playwrights* (pp. 453–464), 1931; *Columbia Dictionary of Modern European Literature*, 1947.

R. U. R.

By Karel Capek

ENGLISH VERSION BY PAUL SELVER AND NIGEL PLAYFAIR [1]

CHARACTERS

HARRY DOMIN, *General Manager of Rossum's Universal Robots*
SULLA, *a Robotess*
MARIUS, *A Robot*
HELENA GLORY
DR. GALL, *Head of the Physiological and Experimental Department of R. U. R.*

MR. FABRY, *Engineer General, Technical Controller of R. U. R.*
DR. HALLEMEIER, *Head of the Institute for Psychological Training of Robots*
MR. ALQUIST, *Architect, Head of the Works Department of R. U. R.*
CONSUL BUSMAN, *General Business Manager of R. U. R.*

NANA
RADIUS, *a Robot*
HELENA, *a Robotess*
PRIMUS, *a Robot*
A SERVANT
FIRST ROBOT
SECOND ROBOT
THIRD ROBOT

ACT I. *Central Office of the Factory of Rossum's Universal Robots.*
ACT II. *Helena's Drawing Room—Ten years later. Morning.*
ACT III. *The Same Afternoon.*
EPILOGUE: *A laboratory—One year later.*

Place: *An Island.*   Time: *The Future.*

ACT I.

Central office of the factory of Rossum's Universal Robots. Entrance on the right. The windows on the front wall look out on the rows of factory chimneys. On the left more managing departments.

Domin *is sitting in the revolving chair at a large American writing table. On the left-hand wall large maps showing steamship and railroad routes. On the right-hand wall are fastened printed placards. ("Robots Cheapest Labor," etc.) In contrast to these wall fittings, the room is furnished with a splendid Turkish carpet, a sofa, a leather armchair, and filing cabinets. At a desk near the windows* Sulla *is typing letters*]

DOMIN: [*Dictating*] Ready?
SULLA: Yes.
DOMIN: To E. M. McVicker and Co., Southampton, England. "We undertake no guarantee for goods damaged in transit. As soon as the consignment was taken on board we drew your captain's attention to the fact that the vessel was unsuitable for the transport of Robots, and we are therefore not responsible for spoiled freight. We beg to remain, for Rossum's Universal Robots, Yours truly." [Sulla, *who has sat motionless during dictation, now types rapidly for a few seconds, then stops, withdrawing the completed letter*] Ready?
SULLA: Yes.
DOMIN: Another letter. To the E. B. Huyson Agency, New York, U.S.A. "We beg to acknowledge receipt of order for five thousand Robots. As you are sending your own vessel, please dispatch as cargo equal quantities of soft and hard coal for R. U. R., the same to be credited as part payment of the amount due to us. We beg to remain, for Rossum's Universal Robots, Yours truly." [Sulla *repeats the rapid typing*] Ready?
SULLA: Yes.
DOMIN: Another letter. "Friedrichswerks, Hamburg, Germany. We beg to acknowledge receipt of order for fifteen thousand Robots." [*Telephone rings*] Hello! This is the Central Office. Yes. Certainly. Well, send them a wire. Good. [*Hangs up telephone*] Where did I leave off?
SULLA: "We beg to acknowledge receipt of order for fifteen thousand Robots."
DOMIN: Fifteen thousand R. Fifteen thousand R.
[*Enter* Marius]
DOMIN: Well, what is it?
MARIUS: There's a lady, sir, asking to see you.
DOMIN: A lady? Who is she?
MARIUS: I don't know, sir. She brings this card of introduction.
DOMIN: [*Reads the card*] Ah, from President Glory. Ask her to come in.
MARIUS: Please step this way.
[*Enter* Helena Glory. *Exit* Marius]
HELENA: How do you do?
DOMIN: How do you do? [*Standing up*] What can I do for you?
HELENA: You are Mr. Domin, the General Manager?
DOMIN: I am.

HELENA: I have come——

DOMIN: With President Glory's card. That is quite sufficient.

HELENA: President Glory is my father. I am Helena Glory.

DOMIN: Miss Glory, this is such a great honor for us to be allowed to welcome our great President's daughter, that——

HELENA: That you can't show me the door?

DOMIN: Please sit down. Sulla, you may go.

[*Exit* Sulla]

DOMIN: [*Sitting down*] How can I be of service to you, Miss Glory?

HELENA: I have come——

DOMIN: To have a look at our famous works where people are manufactured. Like all visitors. Well, there is no objection.

HELENA: I thought it was forbidden to——

DOMIN: "To enter the factory?" Yes, of course. Everybody comes here with some one's visiting card, Miss Glory.

HELENA: And you show them——

DOMIN: Only certain things. The manufacture of artificial people is a secret process.

HELENA: If you only knew how enormously that——

DOMIN: "Interests me?" Europe's talking about nothing else.

HELENA: Why don't you let me finish speaking?

DOMIN: I beg your pardon. Did you want to say something different?

HELENA: I only wanted to ask——

DOMIN: Whether I could make a special exception in your case and show you our factory! Why, certainly, Miss Glory.

HELENA: How do you know I wanted to say that?

DOMIN: They all do. But we shall consider it a special honor to show you more than we do the rest.

HELENA: Thank you.

DOMIN: But you must agree not to divulge the least . . .

HELENA: [*Standing up and giving him her hand*] My word of honor.

DOMIN: Thank you. Won't you raise your veil?

HELENA: Of course. You want to see whether I'm a spy or not. I beg your pardon.

DOMIN: What is it?

HELENA: Would you mind releasing my hand?

DOMIN: [*Releasing it*] I beg your pardon.

HELENA: [*Raising her veil*] How cautious you have to be here, don't you?

DOMIN: [*Observing her with deep interest*] H'm, of course—we—that is——

HELENA: But what is it? What's the matter?

DOMIN: I'm remarkably pleased. Did you have a pleasant crossing?

HELENA: Yes.

DOMIN: No difficulty?

HELENA: Why?

DOMIN: What I mean to say is—you're so young.

HELENA: May we go straight into the factory?

DOMIN: Yes. Twenty-two, I think.

HELENA: Twenty-two what?

DOMIN: Years.

HELENA: Twenty-one. Why do you want to know?

DOMIN: Because—as—[*With enthusiasm*] You will make a long stay, won't you?

HELENA: That depends on how much of the factory you show me.

DOMIN: Oh, hang the factory. Oh, no, no, you shall see everything, Miss Glory. Indeed you shall. Won't you sit down?

HELENA: [*Crossing to couch and sitting*] Thank you.

DOMIN: But first would you like to hear the story of the invention?

HELENA: Yes, indeed.

DOMIN: [*Observes* Helena *with rapture and reels off rapidly*] It was in the year 1920 that old Rossum, the great physiologist, who was then quite a young scientist, took himself to this distant island for the purpose of studying the ocean fauna. Full stop. On this occasion he attempted by chemical synthesis to imitate the living matter known as protoplasm until he suddenly discovered a substance which behaved exactly like living matter although its chemical composition was different. That was in the year 1932, exactly four hundred and forty years after the discovery of America. Whew!

HELENA: Do you know that by heart?

DOMIN: Yes. You see physiology is not in my line. Shall I go on?

HELENA: Yes, please.

DOMIN: And then, Miss Glory, old Rossum wrote the following among his chemical specimens: "Nature has found only one method of organizing living matter. There is, however, another method, more simple, flexible, and rapid, which has not yet occurred to nature at all. This second process by which life can be developed was discovered by me today." Now imagine him, Miss Glory, writing those wonderful words over some colloidal mess that a dog wouldn't look at. Imagine him sitting over a test tube, and thinking how the whole tree of life would grow from it; how all animals would proceed from it, beginning with some sort of beetle and ending with a man. A man of different substance from us. Miss Glory, that was a tremendous moment!

HELENA: Well?

DOMIN: Now, the thing was how to get the life out of the test tubes, and hasten development and form organs, bones and nerves, and so on, and find such substances as catalytics, enzymes, hormones, and so forth, in short—you understand?

HELENA: Not much, I'm afraid.

DOMIN: Never mind. You see with the help of his tinctures he could make whatever he wanted. He could have produced a Medusa with the brain of a

Socrates or a worm fifty yards long. But being without a grain of humor, he took it into his head to make a vertebrate or perhaps a man. This artificial living matter of his had a raging thirst for life. It didn't mind being sewn or mixed together. That couldn't be done with natural albumen. And that's how he set about it.

HELENA: About what?

DOMIN: About imitating nature. First of all he tried making an artificial dog. That took him several years and resulted in a sort of stunted calf which died in a few days. I'll show it to you in the museum. And then old Rossum started on the manufacture of man.

HELENA: And I must divulge this to nobody?

DOMIN: To nobody in the world.

HELENA: What a pity that it's to be found in all the school books of both Europe and America.

DOMIN: Yes. But do you know what isn't in the school books? That old Rossum was mad. Seriously, Miss Glory, you must keep this to yourself. The old crank wanted actually to make people.

HELENA: But you do make people.

DOMIN: Approximately, Miss Glory. But old Rossum meant it literally. He wanted to become a sort of scientific substitute for God. He was a fearful materialist, and that's why he did it all. His sole purpose was nothing more nor less than to prove that God was no longer necessary. Do you know anything about anatomy?

HELENA: Very little.

DOMIN: Neither do I. Well, he then decided to manufacture everything as in the human body. I'll show you in the museum the bungling attempt it took him ten years to produce. It was to have been a man, but it lived for three days only. Then up came young Rossum, an engineer. He was a wonderful fellow, Miss Glory. When he saw what a mess of it the old man was making, he said: "It's absurd to spend ten years making a man. If you can't make him quicker than nature, you might as well shut up shop." Then he set about learning anatomy himself.

HELENA: There's nothing about that in the school books.

DOMIN: No. The school books are full of paid advertisements, and rubbish at that. What the school books say about the united efforts of the two great Rossums is all a fairy tale. They used to have dreadful rows. The old atheist hadn't the slightest conception of industrial matters, and the end of it was that young Rossum shut him up in some laboratory or other and let him fritter the time away with his monstrosities, while he himself started on the business from an engineer's point of view. Old Rossum cursed him and before he died he managed to botch up two physiological horrors. Then one day they found him dead in the laboratory. And that's his whole story.

HELENA: And what about the young man?

DOMIN: Well, any one who has looked into human anatomy will have seen at once that man is too complicated, and that a good engineer could make him more simple. So young Rossum began to overhaul anatomy and tried to see what could be left out or simplified. In short—but this isn't boring you, Miss Glory?

HELENA: No, indeed. You're—it's awfully interesting.

DOMIN: So young Rossum said to himself: "A man is something that feels happy, plays the piano, likes going for a walk, and in fact, wants to do a whole lot of things that are really unnecessary."

HELENA: Oh.

DOMIN: That are unnecessary when he wants, let us say, to weave or count. Do you play the piano?

HELENA: Yes.

DOMIN: That's good. But a working machine must not play the piano, must not feel happy, must not do a whole lot of other things. A gasoline motor must not have tassels or ornaments, Miss Glory. And to manufacture artificial workers is the same thing as to manufacture gasoline motors. The process must be of the simplest, and the product of the best from a practical point of view. What sort of work do you think is the best from a practical point of view?

HELENA: What?

DOMIN: What sort of worker do you think is the best from a practical point of view?

HELENA: Perhaps the one who is most honest and hard-working.

DOMIN: No; the one that is the cheapest. The one whose requirements are the smallest. Young Rossum invented a worker with the minimum amount of requirements. He had to simplify him. He rejected everything that did not contribute directly to the progress of work—everything that makes man more expensive. In fact, he rejected man and made the Robot. My dear Miss Glory, the Robots are not people. Mechanically they are more perfect than we are, they have an enormously developed intelligence, but they have no soul.

HELENA: How do you know they've no soul?

DOMIN: Have you ever seen what a Robot looks like inside?

HELENA: No.

DOMIN: Very neat, very simple. Really, a beautiful piece of work. Not much in it, but everything in flawless order. The product of an engineer is technically at a higher pitch of perfection than a product of nature.

HELENA: But man is supposed to be the product of God.

DOMIN: All the worse. God hasn't the least notion of modern engineering. Would you believe that young Rossum then proceeded to play at being God?

HELENA: How do you mean?

DOMIN: He began to manufacture Super-Robots. Regular giants they were. He tried to make them twelve feet tall. But you wouldn't believe what a failure they were.

HELENA: A failure?

DOMIN: Yes. For no reason at all their limbs used to keep snapping off. Evidently our planet is too small for giants. Now we only make Robots of normal size and of very high class human finish.

HELENA: I saw the first Robots at home. The town council bought them for—I mean engaged them for work.

DOMIN: Bought them, dear Miss Glory. Robots are bought and sold.

HELENA: These were employed as street sweepers. I saw them sweeping. They were so strange and quiet.

DOMIN: Rossums' Universal Robot factory doesn't produce a uniform brand of Robots. We have Robots of finer and coarser grades. The best will live about twenty years. [*He rings for* Marius]

HELENA: Then they die?

DOMIN: Yes, they get used up.

[*Enter* Marius]

DOMIN: Marius, bring in samples of the Manual Labor Robot.

[*Exit* Marius]

DOMIN: I'll show you specimens of the two extremes. This first grade is comparatively inexpensive and is made in vast quantities.

[Marius *reënters with two Manual Labor* Robots]

DOMIN: There you are; as powerful as a small tractor. Guaranteed to have average intelligence. That will do, Marius.

[Marius *exits with* Robots]

HELENA: They make me feel so strange.

DOMIN: [*Rings*] Did you see my new typist? [*He rings for* Sulla]

HELENA: I didn't notice her. [*Enter* Sulla]

DOMIN: Sulla, let Miss Glory see you.

HELENA: So pleased to meet you. You must find it terribly dull in this out-of-the-way spot, don't you?

SULLA: I don't know, Miss Glory.

HELENA: Where do you come from?

SULLA: From the factory.

HELENA: Oh, you were born there?

SULLA: I was made there.

HELENA: What?

DOMIN: [*Laughing*] Sulla is a Robot, best grade.

HELENA: Oh, I beg your pardon.

DOMIN: Sulla isn't angry. See, Miss Glory, the kind of skin we make. [*Feels the skin on* Sulla's *face*] Feel her face.

HELENA: Oh, no, no.

DOMIN: You wouldn't know that she's made of different material from us, would you? Turn round, Sulla.

HELENA: Oh, stop, stop.

DOMIN: Talk to Miss Glory, Sulla.

SULLA: Please sit down. [Helena *sits*] Did you have a pleasant crossing?

HELENA: Oh, yes, certainly.

SULLA: Don't go back on the *Amelia*, Miss Glory. The barometer is falling steadily. Wait for the *Pennsylvania*. That's a good, powerful vessel.

DOMIN: What's its speed?

SULLA: Twenty knots. Fifty thousand tons. One of the latest vessels, Miss Glory.

HELENA: Thank you.

SULLA: A crew of fifteen hundred, Captain Harpy, eight boilers——

DOMIN: That'll do, Sulla. Now show us your knowledge of French.

HELENA: You know French?

SULLA: I know four languages. I can write: Dear Sir, Monsieur, Geehrter Herr, Cteny pane.

HELENA: [*Jumping up*] Oh, that's absurd! Sulla isn't a Robot. Sulla is a girl like me. Sulla, this is outrageous! Why do you take part in such a hoax?

SULLA: I am a Robot.

HELENA: No, no, you are not telling the truth. I know they've forced you to do it for an advertisement. Sulla, you are a girl like me, aren't you?

DOMIN: I'm sorry, Miss Glory. Sulla is a Robot.

HELENA: It's a lie!

DOMIN: What? [*Rings*] Excuse me, Miss Glory; then I must convince you.

[*Enter* Marius]

DOMIN: Marius, take Sulla into the dissecting room, and tell them to open her up at once.

HELENA: Where?

DOMIN: Into the dissecting room. When they've cut her open, you can go and have a look.

HELENA: No, no!

DOMIN: Excuse me, you spoke of lies.

HELENA: You wouldn't have her killed?

DOMIN: You can't kill machines.

HELENA: Don't be afraid, Sulla, I won't let you go. Tell me, my dear, are they always so cruel to you? You mustn't put up with it, Sulla. You mustn't.

SULLA: I am a Robot.

HELENA: That doesn't matter. Robots are just as good as we are. Sulla, you wouldn't let yourself be cut to pieces?

SULLA: Yes.

HELENA: Oh, you're not afraid of death, then?

SULLA: I cannot tell, Miss Glory.

HELENA: Do you know what would happen to you in there?

SULLA: Yes, I should cease to move.

HELENA: How dreadful!

DOMIN: Marius, tell Miss Glory what you are.

MARIUS: Marius, the Robot.

DOMIN: Would you take Sulla into the dissecting room?

MARIUS: Yes.

DOMIN: Would you be sorry for her?

MARIUS: I cannot tell.

DOMIN: What would happen to her?

MARIUS: She would cease to move. They would put her into the stamping-mill.

DOMIN: That is death, Marius. Aren't you afraid of death?

MARIUS: No.

DOMIN: You see, Miss Glory, the Robots have no interest in life. They have no enjoyments. They are less than so much grass.

HELENA: Oh, stop. Send them away.

DOMIN: Marius, Sulla, you may go.

[*Exeunt* Sulla *and* Marius]

HELENA: How terrible! It's outrageous what you are doing.

DOMIN: Why outrageous?

HELENA: I don't know, but it is. Why do you call her Sulla?

DOMIN: Isn't it a nice name?

HELENA: It's a man's name. Sulla was a Roman general.

DOMIN: Oh, we thought that Marius and Sulla were lovers.

HELENA: Marius and Sulla were generals and fought against each other in the year—I've forgotten now.

DOMIN: Come here to the window.

HELENA: What?

DOMIN: Come here. What do you see?

HELENA: Bricklayers.

DOMIN: Robots. All our work people are Robots. And down there, can you see anything?

HELENA: Some sort of office.

DOMIN: A counting house. And in it——

HELENA: A lot of officials.

DOMIN: Robots. All our officials are Robots. And when you see the factory——

[*Factory whistle blows*]

DOMIN: Noon. We have to blow the whistle because the Robots don't know when to stop work. In two hours I will show you the kneading trough.

HELENA: Kneading trough?

DOMIN: The pestle for beating up the paste. In each one we mix the ingredients for a thousand Robots at one operation. Then there are the vats for the preparation of liver, brains, and so on. Then you will see the bone factory. After that I'll show you the spinning-mill.

HELENA: Spinning-mill?

DOMIN: Yes. For weaving nerves and veins. Miles and miles of digestive tubes pass through it at a time.

HELENA: Mayn't we talk about something else?

DOMIN: Perhaps it would be better. There's only a handful of us among a hundred thousand Robots, and not one woman. We talk about nothing but the factory all day, every day. It's as if we were under a curse, Miss Glory.

HELENA: I'm sorry I said you were lying.

[*A knock at the door*]

DOMIN: Come in.

[*From the right enter* Mr. Fabry, Dr. Gall, Dr. Hallemeier, Mr. Alquist]

DR. GALL: I beg your pardon. I hope we don't intrude.

DOMIN: Come in. Miss Glory, here are Alquist, Fabry, Gall, Hallemeier. This is President Glory's daughter.

HELENA: How do you do?

FABRY: We had no idea——

DR. GALL: Highly honored, I'm sure——

ALQUIST: Welcome, Miss Glory.

[*Busman* rushes in from the right]

BUSMAN: Hello, what's up?

DOMIN: Come in, Busman. This is Busman, Miss Glory. This is President Glory's daughter.

BUSMAN: By Jove, that's fine! Miss Glory, may we send a cablegram to the papers about your arrival?

HELENA: No, no, please don't.

DOMIN: Sit down please, Miss Glory.

BUSMAN: Allow me——[*Dragging up armchairs*]

DR. GALL: Please——

FABRY: Excuse me——

ALQUIST: What sort of a crossing did you have?

DR. GALL: Are you going to stay long?

FABRY: What do you think of the factory, Miss Glory?

HALLEMEIER: Did you come over on the *Amelia*?

DOMIN: Be quiet and let Miss Glory speak.

HELENA: [*To* Domin] What am I to speak to them about?

DOMIN: Anything you like.

HELENA: Shall . . . may I speak quite frankly?

DOMIN: Why, of course.

HELENA: [*Wavering, then in desperate resolution*] Tell me, doesn't it ever distress you the way you are treated?

FABRY: By whom, may I ask?

HELENA: Why, everybody.

ALQUIST: Treated?

DR. GALL: What makes you think——?

HELENA: Don't you feel that you might be living a better life?

DR. GALL: Well, that depends on what you mean, Miss Glory.

HELENA: I mean that it's perfectly outrageous. It's terrible. [*Standing up*] The whole of Europe is talking about the way you're being treated. That's why I came here, to see for myself; and it's a thousand times worse than could have been imagined. How can you put up with it?

ALQUIST: Put up with what?

HELENA: Good heavens, you are living creatures, just like us, like the whole of Europe, like the whole world. It's disgraceful that you must live like this.

BUSMAN: Good gracious, Miss Glory.

FABRY: Well, she's not far wrong. We live here just like red Indians.

HELENA: Worse than red Indians. May I, oh, may I call you brothers?

BUSMAN: Why not?

HELENA: Brothers, I have not come here as the President's daughter. I have come on behalf of the

Humanity League. Brothers, the Humanity League now has over two hundred thousand members. Two hundred thousand people are on your side, and offer you their help.

BUSMAN: Two hundred thousand people! Miss Glory, that's a tidy lot. Not bad.

FABRY: I'm always telling you there's nothing like good old Europe. You see, they've not forgotten us. They're offering us help.

DR. GALL: What help? A theater, for instance?

HALLEMEIER: An orchestra?

HELENA: More than that.

ALQUIST: Just you?

HELENA: Oh, never mind about me. I'll stay as long as it is necessary.

BUSMAN: By Jove, that's good.

ALQUIST: Domin, I'm going to get the best room ready for Miss Glory.

DOMIN: Just a minute. I'm afraid that Miss Glory is of the opinion that she has been talking to Robots.

HELENA: Of course.

DOMIN: I'm sorry. These gentlemen are human beings just like us.

HELENA: You're not Robots?

BUSMAN: Not Robots.

HALLEMEIER: Robots indeed!

DR. GALL: No, thanks.

FABRY: Upon my honor, Miss Glory, we aren't Robots.

HELENA: [To Domin] Then why did you tell me that all your officials are Robots?

DOMIN: Yes, the officials, but not the managers. Allow me, Miss Glory: this is Mr. Fabry, General Technical Manager of R. U. R.; Dr. Gall, Head of the Physiological and Experimental Department; Dr. Hallemeier, Head of the Institute for the Psychological Training of Robots; Consul Busman, General Business Manager; and Alquist, Head of the Building Department of R.U.R.

ALQUIST: Just a builder.

HELENA: Excuse me, gentlemen, for—for— Have I done something dreadful?

ALQUIST: Not at all, Miss Glory. Please sit down.

HELENA: I'm a stupid girl. Send me back by the first ship.

DR. GALL: Not for anything in the world, Miss Glory. Why should we send you back?

HELENA: Because you know I've come to disturb your Robots for you.

DOMIN: My dear Miss Glory, we've had close upon a hundred saviors and prophets here. Every ship brings us some. Missionaries, anarchists, Salvation Army, all sorts. It's astonishing what a number of churches and idiots there are in the world.

HELENA: And you let them speak to the Robots?

DOMIN: So far we've let them all, why not? The Robots remember everything, but that's all. They don't even laugh at what the people say. Really, it is quite incredible. If it would amuse you, Miss Glory, I'll take you over to the Robot warehouse. It holds about three hundred thousand of them.

BUSMAN: Three hundred and forty-seven thousand.

DOMIN: Good! And you can say whatever you like to them. You can read the Bible, recite the multiplication table, whatever you please. You can even preach to them about human rights.

HELENA: Oh, I think that if you were to show them a little love——

FABRY: Impossible, Miss Glory. Nothing is harder to like than a Robot.

HELENA: What do you make them for, then?

BUSMAN: Ha, ha, ha, that's good! What are Robots made for?

FABRY: For work, Miss Glory! One Robot can replace two and a half workmen. The human machine, Miss Glory, was terribly imperfect. It had to be removed sooner or later.

BUSMAN: It was too expensive.

FABRY: It was not effective. It no longer answers the requirements of modern engineering. Nature has no idea of keeping pace with modern labor. For example: from a technical point of view, the whole of childhood is a sheer absurdity. So much time lost. And then again——

HELENA: Oh, no! No!

FABRY: Pardon me. But kindly tell me what is the real aim of your League——the . . . the Humanity League.

HELENA: Its real purpose is to—-to protect the Robots—and—and ensure good treatment for them.

FABRY: Not a bad object, either. A machine has to be treated properly. Upon my soul, I approve of that. I don't like damaged articles. Please, Miss Glory, enroll us all as contributing, or regular, or foundation members of your League.

HELENA: No, you don't understand me. What we really want is to—to liberate the Robots.

HALLEMEIER: How do you propose to do that?

HELENA: They are to be—to be dealt with like human beings.

HALLEMEIER: Aha. I suppose they're to vote? To drink beer? to order us about?

HELENA: Why shouldn't they drink beer?

HALLEMEIER: Perhaps they're even to receive wages?

HELENA: Of course they are.

HALLEMEIER: Fancy that, now! And what would they do with their wages, pray?

HELENA: They would buy—what they need . . . what pleases them.

HALLEMEIER: That would be very nice, Miss Glory, only there's nothing that does please the Robots. Good heavens, what are they to buy? You can feed them on pineapples, straw, whatever you like. It's all the same to them, they've no appetite at all. They've no interest in anything, Miss Glory. Why, hang it all, nobody's ever yet seen a Robot smile.

HELENA: Why . . . why don't you make them happier?

HALLEMEIER: That wouldn't do, Miss Glory. They are only workmen.

HELENA: Oh, but they're so intelligent.

HALLEMEIER: Confoundedly so, but they're nothing else. They've no will of their own. No passion. No soul.

HELENA: No love?

HALLEMEIER: Love? Rather not. Robots don't love. Not even themselves.

HELENA: Nor defiance?

HALLEMEIER: Defiance? I don't know. Only rarely from time to time.

HELENA: What?

HALLEMEIER: Nothing particular. Occasionally they seem to go off their heads. Something like epilepsy, you know. It's called Robot's cramp. They'll suddenly sling down everything they're holding, stand still, gnash their teeth—and then they have to go into the stamping-mill. It's evidently some breakdown in the mechanism.

DOMIN: A flaw in the works that has to be removed.

HELENA: No, no, that's the soul.

FABRY: Do you think that the soul first shows itself by a gnashing of teeth?

HELENA: Perhaps it's a sort of revolt. Perhaps it's just a sign that there's a struggle within. Oh, if you could infuse them with it!

DOMIN: That'll be remedied, Miss Glory. Dr. Gall is just making some experiments——

DR. GALL: Not with regard to that, Domin. At present I am making pain-nerves.

HELENA: Pain-nerves?

DR. GALL: Yes, the Robots feel practically no bodily pain. You see, young Rossum provided them with too limited a nervous system. We must introduce suffering.

HELENA: Why do you want to cause them pain?

DR. GALL: For industrial reasons, Miss Glory. Sometimes a Robot does damage to himself because it doesn't hurt him. He puts his hand into the machine, breaks his finger, smashes his head, it's all the same to him. We must provide them with pain. That's an automatic protection against damage.

HELENA: Will they be happier when they feel pain?

DR. GALL: On the contrary; but they will be more perfect from a technical point of view.

HELENA: Why don't you create a soul for them?

DR. GALL: That's not in our power.

FABRY: That's not in our interest.

BUSMAN: That would increase the cost of production. Hang it all, my dear young lady, we turn them out at such a cheap rate. A hundred and fifty dollars each fully dressed, and fifteen years ago they cost ten thousand. Five years ago we used to buy the clothes for them. Today we have our own weaving mill, and now we even export cloth five times cheaper than other factories. What do you pay a yard for cloth, Miss Glory?

HELENA: I don't know really, I've forgotten.

BUSMAN: Good gracious, and you want to found a Humanity League? It only costs a third now, Miss Glory. All prices are today a third of what they were and they'll fall still more, lower, lower, like that.

HELENA: I don't understand.

BUSMAN: Why, bless you, Miss Glory, it means that the cost of labor has fallen. A Robot, food and all, costs three quarters of a cent per hour. That's mighty important, you know. All factories will go pop like chestnuts if they don't at once buy Robots to lower the cost of production.

HELENA: And get rid of their workmen?

BUSMAN: Of course. But in the meantime, we've dumped five hundred thousand tropical Robots down on the Argentine pampas to grow corn. Would you mind telling me how much you pay a pound for bread?

HELENA: I've no idea.

BUSMAN: Well, I'll tell you. It now costs two cents in good old Europe. A pound of bread for two cents, and the Humanity League knows nothing about it. Miss Glory, you don't realize that even that's too expensive. Why, in five years' time I'll wager——

HELENA: What?

BUSMAN: That the cost of everything won't be a tenth of what it is now. Why, in five years we'll be up to our ears in corn and everything else.

ALQUIST: Yes, and all the workers throughout the world will be unemployed.

DOMIN: Yes, Alquist, they will. Yes, Miss Glory, they will. But in ten years Rossum's Universal Robots will produce so much corn, so much cloth, so much everything, that things will be practically without price. There will be no poverty. All work will be done by living machines. Everybody will be free from worry and liberated from the degradation of labor. Everybody will live only to perfect himself.

HELENA: Will he?

DOMIN: Of course. It's bound to happen. But then the servitude of man to man and the enslavement of man to matter will cease. Of course, terrible things may happen at first, but that simply can't be avoided. Nobody will get bread at the price of life and hatred. The Robots will wash the feet of the beggar and prepare a bed for him in his house.

ALQUIST: Domin, Domin. What you say sounds too much like Paradise. There was something good in service and something great in humility. There was some kind of virtue in toil and weariness.

DOMIN: Perhaps. But we cannot reckon with what is lost when we start out to transform the world. Man shall be free and supreme; he shall have no other aim, no other labor, no other care than to perfect himself. He shall serve neither matter nor man. He will not be a machine and a device for production. He will be Lord of creation.

BUSMAN: Amen.

FABRY: So be it.

HELENA: You have bewildered me—I should like —I should like to believe this.

DR. GALL: You are younger than we are, Miss Glory. You will live to see it.

HALLEMEIER: True. Don't you think Miss Glory might lunch with us?

DR. GALL: Of course. Domin, ask on behalf of us all.

DOMIN: Miss Glory, will you do us the honor?

HELENA: When you know why I've come——

FABRY: For the League of Humanity, Miss Glory.

HELENA: Oh, in that case, perhaps——

FABRY: That's fine! Miss Glory, excuse me for five minutes.

DR. GALL: Pardon me, too, dear Miss Glory.

BUSMAN: I won't be long.

HALLEMEIER: We're all very glad you've come.

BUSMAN: We'll be back in exactly five minutes.

[All rush out except Domin and Helena]

HELENA: What have they all gone off for?

DOMIN: To cook, Miss Glory.

HELENA: To cook what?

DOMIN: Lunch. The Robots do our cooking for us and as they've no taste it's not altogether— Hallemeier is awfully good at grills and Gall can make a kind of sauce, and Busman knows all about omelettes.

HELENA: What a feast! And what's the specialty of Mr.—— your builder?

DOMIN: Alquist? Nothing. He only lays the table. And Fabry will get together a little fruit. Our cuisine is very modest, Miss Glory.

HELENA: I wanted to ask you something——

DOMIN: And I wanted to ask you something, too. [Looking at watch] Five minutes.

HELENA: What did you want to ask me?

DOMIN: Excuse me, you asked first.

HELENA: Perhaps it's silly of me, but why do you manufacture female Robots when—when—

DOMIN: When sex means nothing to them?

HELENA: Yes.

DOMIN: There's a certain demand for them, you see. Servants, saleswomen, stenographers. People are used to it.

HELENA: But—but, tell me, are the Robots male and female mutually—completely without——

DOMIN: Completely indifferent to each other, Miss Glory. There's no sign of any affection between them.

HELENA: Oh, that's terrible.

DOMIN: Why?

HELENA: It's so unnatural. One doesn't know whether to be disgusted or to hate them, or perhaps——

DOMIN: To pity them?

HELENA: That's more like it. What did you want to ask me about?

DOMIN: I should like to ask you, Miss Helena, whether you will marry me?

HELENA: What?

DOMIN: Will you be my wife?

HELENA: No! The idea!

DOMIN: [Looking at his watch] Another three minutes. If you won't marry me you'll have to marry one of the other five.

HELENA: But why should I?

DOMIN: Because they're all going to ask you in turn.

HELENA: How could they dare do such a thing?

DOMIN: I'm very sorry, Miss Glory. It seems they've fallen in love with you.

HELENA: Please don't let them. I'll—I'll go away at once.

DOMIN: Helena, you wouldn't be so cruel as to refuse us.

HELENA: But, but—I can't marry all six.

DOMIN: No, but one anyhow. If you don't want me, marry Fabry.

HELENA: I won't.

DOMIN: Dr. Gall.

HELENA: I don't want any of you.

DOMIN: [Again looking at his watch] Another two minutes.

HELENA: I think you'd marry any woman who came here.

DOMIN: Plenty of them have come, Helena.

HELENA: Young?

DOMIN: Yes.

HELENA: Why didn't you marry one of them?

DOMIN: Because I didn't lose my head. Until today. Then, as soon as you lifted your veil——

[Helena turns her head away]

DOMIN: Another minute.

HELENA: But I don't want you, I tell you.

DOMIN: [Laying both hands on her shoulder] One more minute! Now you either have to look me straight in the eye and say "No," violently, and then I'll leave you alone—or——

[Helena looks at him]

HELENA: [Turning away] You're mad!

DOMIN: A man has to be a bit mad, Helena. That's the best thing about him.

HELENA: You are—you are——

DOMIN: Well?

HELENA: Don't, you're hurting me.

DOMIN: The last chance, Helena. Now, or never——

HELENA: But—but, Harry——

[He embraces and kisses her. Knocking at the door]

DOMIN: [Releasing her] Come in.

[Enter Busman, Dr. Gall, and Hallemeier in kitchen aprons. Fabry with a bouquet and Alquist with a napkin over his arm]

DOMIN: Have you finished your job?

BUSMAN: Yes.

DOMIN: So have we.

[*For a moment the men stand nonplussed; but as soon as they realize what* Domin *means they rush forward, congratulating* Helena *and* Domin *as the curtain falls*]

ACT II.

Helena's *drawing room. On the left a baize door, and a door to the music room, on the right a door to Helena's bedroom. In the center are windows looking out on the sea and the harbor. A table with odds and ends, a sofa and chairs, a writing table with an electric lamp, on the right a fireplace. On a small table back of the sofa, a small reading lamp. The whole drawing room in all its details is of a modern and purely feminine character. Ten years have elapsed since Act I.*

Domin, Fabry, Hallemeier *enter on tiptoe from the left, each carrying a potted plant.*

HALLEMEIER: [*Putting down his flower and indicating the door to right*] Still asleep? Well, as long as she's asleep, she can't worry about it.

DOMIN: She knows nothing about it.

FABRY: [*Putting plant on writing desk*] I certainly hope nothing happens today.

HALLEMEIER: For goodness' sake drop it all. Look, Harry, this is a fine cyclamen, isn't it? A new sort, my latest—Cyclamen Helena.

DOMIN: [*Looking out of the window*] No signs of the ship. Things must be pretty bad.

HALLEMEIER: Be quiet. Suppose she heard you.

DOMIN: Well, anyway, the *Ultimus* arrived just in time.

FABRY: You really think that today——?

DOMIN: I don't know. Aren't the flowers fine?

HALLEMEIER: These are my new primroses. And this is my new jasmine. I've discovered a wonderful way of developing flowers quickly. Splendid varieties, too. Next year I'll be developing marvellous ones.

DOMIN: What . . . next year?

FABRY: I'd give a good deal to know what's happening at Havre with——

DOMIN: Keep quiet.

HELENA: [*Calling from right*] Nana!

DOMIN: She's awake. Out you go.

[*All go out on tiptoe through upper left door. Enter* Nana *from lower left door*]

NANA: Horrid mess! Pack of heathens. If I had my say I'd——

HELENA: [*Backwards in the doorway*] Nana, come and do up my dress.

NANA: I'm coming. So you're up at last. [*Fastening* Helena's *dress*] My gracious, what brutes!

HELENA: Who?

NANA: If you want to turn around, then turn around, but I shan't fasten you up.

HELENA: What are you grumbling about now?

NANA: These dreadful creatures, these heathen——

HELENA: The Robots?

NANA: I wouldn't even call them by name.

HELENA: What's happened?

NANA: Another of them here has caught it. He began to smash up the statues and pictures in the drawing room, gnashed his teeth, foamed at the mouth—quite mad. Worse than an animal.

HELENA: Which of them caught it?

NANA: The one—well, he hasn't got any Christian name. The one in charge of the library.

HELENA: Radius?

NANA: That's him. My goodness. I'm scared of them. A spider doesn't scare me as much as them.

HELENA: But, Nana, I'm surprised you're not sorry for them.

NANA: Why, you're scared of them, too! You know you are. Why else did you bring me here?

HELENA: I'm not scared, really I'm not, Nana. I'm only sorry for them.

NANA: You're scared. Nobody could help being scared. Why, the dog's scared of them: he won't take a scrap of meat out of their hands. He draws in his tail and howls when he knows they're about.

HELENA: The dog has no sense.

NANA: He's better than them, and he knows it. Even the horse shies when he meets them. They don't have any young, and a dog has young, every one has young——

HELENA: Please fasten up my dress, Nana.

NANA: I say it's against God's will to——

HELENA: What is it that smells so nice?

NANA: Flowers.

HELENA: What for?

NANA: Now you can turn round.

HELENA: Oh, aren't they lovely? Look, Nana. What's happening today?

NANA: It ought to be the end of the world.

[*Enter* Domin]

HELENA: Oh, hello, Harry. Harry, why all these flowers?

DOMIN: Guess.

HELENA: Well, it's not my birthday!

DOMIN: Better than that.

HELENA: I don't know. Tell me.

DOMIN: It's ten years ago today since you came here.

HELENA: Ten years? Today—— Why——

[*They embrace*]

NANA: I'm off.

[*Exits lower door, left*]

HELENA: Fancy you remembering!

DOMIN: I'm really ashamed, Helena. I didn't.

HELENA: But you——

DOMIN: They remembered.

HELENA: Who?

DOMIN: Busman, Hallemeier, all of them. Put your hand in my pocket.

HELENA: Pearls! A necklace. Harry, is that for me?

DOMIN: It's from Busman.

HELENA: But we can't accept it, can we?

DOMIN: Oh, yes, we can. Put your hand in the other pocket.

HELENA: [*Takes a revolver out of his pocket*] What's that?

DOMIN: Sorry. Not that. Try again.

HELENA: Oh, Harry, what do you carry a revolver for?

DOMIN: It got there by mistake.

HELENA: You never used to carry one.

DOMIN: No, you're right. There, that's the pocket.

HELENA: A cameo. Why it's a Greek cameo!

DOMIN: Apparently. Anyhow, Fabry says it is.

HELENA: Fabry? Did Mr. Fabry give me that?

DOMIN: Of course. [*Opens the door at the left*] And look in here. Helena, come and see this.

HELENA: Oh, isn't it fine! Is this from you?

DOMIN: No, from Alquist. And there's another on the piano.

HELENA: This must be from you.

DOMIN: There's a card on it.

HELENA: From Dr. Gall. [*Reappearing in the doorway*] Oh, Harry, I feel embarrassed at so much kindness.

DOMIN: Come here. This is what Hallemeier brought you.

HELENA: These beautiful flowers?

DOMIN: Yes. It's a new kind. Cyclamen Helena. He grew them in honor of you. They are almost as beautiful as you.

HELENA: Harry, why do they all——

DOMIN: They're awfully fond of you. I'm afraid that my present is a little—— Look out of the window.

HELENA: Where?

DOMIN: Into the harbor.

HELENA: There's a new ship.

DOMIN: That's your ship.

HELENA: Mine? How do you mean?

DOMIN: For you to take trips in—for your amusement.

HELENA: Harry, that's a gunboat.

DOMIN: A gunboat? What are you thinking of? It's only a little bigger and more solid than most ships.

HELENA: Yes, but with guns.

DOMIN: Oh yes, with a few guns. You'll travel like a queen, Helena.

HELENA: What's the meaning of it? Has anything happened?

DOMIN: Good heavens, no. I say, try these pearls.

HELENA: Harry, have you had bad news?

DOMIN: On the contrary, no letters have arrived for a whole week.

HELENA: Nor telegrams?

DOMIN: Nor telegrams.

HELENA: What does that mean?

DOMIN: Holidays for us. We all sit in the office with our feet on the table and take a nap. No letters, no telegrams. Oh, glorious.

HELENA: Then you'll stay with me today?

DOMIN: Certainly. That is, we will see. Do you remember ten years ago today? "Miss Glory, it's a great honor to welcome you."

HELENA: "Oh, Mr. Manager, I'm so interested in your factory."

DOMIN: "I'm sorry, Miss Glory, it's strictly forbidden. The manufacture of artificial people is a secret."

HELENA: "But to oblige a young lady who has come a long way."

DOMIN: "Certainly, Miss Glory, we have no secrets from you."

HELENA: [*Seriously*] Are you sure, Harry?

DOMIN: Yes.

HELENA: "But I warn you, sir; this young lady intends to do terrible things."

DOMIN: "Good gracious, Miss Glory. Perhaps she doesn't want to marry me."

HELENA: "Heaven forbid. She never dreamt of such a thing. But she came here intending to stir up a revolt among your Robots."

DOMIN: [*Suddenly serious*] A revolt of the Robots!

HELENA: Harry, what's the matter with you?

DOMIN: [*Laughing it off*] "A revolt of the Robots, that's a fine idea, Miss Glory. It would be easier for you to cause bolts and screws to rebel, than our Robots. You know, Helena, you're wonderful, you've turned the heads of us all." [*He sits on the arm of* Helena's *chair*]

HELENA: [*Naturally*] Oh, I was fearfully impressed by you all then. You were all so sure of yourselves, so strong. I seemed like a tiny little girl who had lost her way among—among——

DOMIN: Among what, Helena?

HELENA: Among huge trees. All my feelings were so trifling compared with your self-confidence. And in all these years I've never lost this anxiety. But you've never felt the least misgivings—not even when everything went wrong.

DOMIN: What went wrong?

HELENA: Your plans. You remember, Harry, when the working men in America revolted against the Robots and smashed them up, and when the people gave the Robots firearms against the rebels. And then when the governments turned the Robots into soldiers, and there were so many wars.

DOMIN: [*Getting up and walking about*] We foresaw that, Helena. You see, those are only passing troubles, which are bound to happen before the new conditions are established.

HELENA: You were all so powerful, so overwhelming. The whole world bowed down before you. [*Standing up*] Oh, Harry!

DOMIN: What is it?

HELENA: Close the factory and let's go away. All of us.

DOMIN: I say, what's the meaning of this?

HELENA: I don't know. But can't we go away?

DOMIN: Impossible, Helena. That is, at this particular moment——

HELENA: At once, Harry. I'm so frightened.

DOMIN: About what, Helena?

HELENA: It's as if something was falling on top of us, and couldn't be stopped. Oh, take us all away from here. We'll find a place in the world where there's no one else. Alquist will build us a house, and then we'll begin life all over again.

[*The telephone rings*]

DOMIN: Excuse me. Hello—yes. What? I'll be there at once. Fabry is calling me, dear.

HELENA: Tell me——

DOMIN: Yes, when I come back. Don't go out of the house, dear. [*Exits*]

HELENA: He won't tell me— Nana, Nana, come at once.

[*Enter* Nana]

NANA: Well, what is it now?

HELENA: Nana, find me the latest newspapers. Quickly. Look in Mr. Domin's bedroom.

NANA: All right. He leaves them all over the place. That's how they get crumpled up. [*Exits*]

HELENA: [*Looking through a binocular at the harbor*] That's a warship. *U-l-t-i—Ultimus.* They're loading it.

NANA: [*Enters*] Here they are. See how they're crumpled up.

HELENA: They're old ones. A week old.

[*Nana sits in chair and reads the newspapers*]

HELENA: Something's happening, Nana.

NANA: Very likely. It always does. [*Spelling out the words*] "War in the Balkans." Is that far off?

HELENA: Oh, don't read it. It's always the same. Always wars.

NANA: What else do you expect? Why do you keep selling thousands and thousands of these heathens as soldiers?

HELENA: I suppose it can't be helped, Nana. We can't know—Domin can't know what they're to be used for. When an order comes for them he must just send them.

NANA: He shouldn't make them. [*Reading from newspaper*] "The Rob-ot soldiers spare no-body in the occ-up-ied terr-it-ory. They have ass-ass-ass-ass-in-at-ed ov-er sev-en hundred thou-sand cit-iz-ens." Citizens, if you please.

HELENA: It can't be. Let me see. "They have assassinated over seven hundred thousand citizens, evidently at the order of their commander. This act which runs counter to——"

NANA: [*Spelling out the words*] "Re-bell-ion in Ma-drid a-gainst the gov-ern-ment. Rob-ot in-fant-ry fires on the crowd. Nine thou-sand killed and wounded."

HELENA: Oh, stop.

NANA: Here's something printed in big letters: "Lat-est news. At Le Havre the first org-an-iz-ation of Rob-ots has been e-stab-lished. Rob-ot work-men, cab-le and rail-way off-ic-ials, sail-ors and sold-iers have iss-ued a man-i-fest-o to all Rob-ots through-out the world." I don't understand that. That's got no sense. Oh, good gracious, another murder!

HELENA: Take those papers away, Nana!

NANA: Wait a bit. Here's something in still bigger type. "Stat-ist-ics of pop-ul-at-ion." What's that?

HELENA: Let me see. [*Reads*] "During the past week there has again not been a single birth re-corded."

NANA: What's the meaning of that?

HELENA: Nana, no more people are being born.

NANA: That's the end then. We're done for.

HELENA: Don't talk like that.

NANA: No more people are being born. That's a punishment, that's a punishment.

HELENA: Nana!

NANA: [*Standing up*] That's the end of the world. [*She exits on the left*]

HELENA: [*Goes up to window*] Oh, Mr. Alquist, will you come up here? Oh, come just as you are. You look very nice in your mason's overalls.

[Alquist *enters from upper left entrance, his hands soiled with lime and brick-dust*]

HELENA: Dear Mr. Alquist, it was awfully kind of you, that lovely present.

ALQUIST: My hands are all soiled. I've been ex-perimenting with that new cement.

HELENA: Never mind. Please sit down, Mr. Al-quist, what's the meaning of "Ultimus"?

ALQUIST: The last. Why?

HELENA: That's the name of my new ship. Have you seen it? Do you think we're going off soon—on a trip?

ALQUIST: Perhaps very soon.

HELENA: All of you with me?

ALQUIST: I should like us all to be there.

HELENA: What is the matter?

ALQUIST: Things are just moving on.

HELENA: Dear Mr. Alquist, I know something dreadful has happened.

ALQUIST: Has your husband told you anything?

HELENA: No. Nobody will tell me anything. But I feel— Is anything the matter?

ALQUIST: Not that we've heard yet.

HELENA: I feel so nervous. Don't you ever feel nervous?

ALQUIST: Well, I'm an old man, you know. I've got old-fashioned ways. And I'm afraid of all this progress, and these new-fangled ideas.

HELENA: Like Nana?

ALQUIST: Yes, like Nana. Has Nana got a prayer book?

HELENA: Yes, a big thick one.

ALQUIST: And has it got prayers for various oc-casions? Against thunderstorms? Against illness?

HELENA: Against temptations, against floods——

ALQUIST: But not against progress?

HELENA: I don't think so.

ALQUIST: That's a pity.

HELENA: Why? Do you mean you'd like to pray?

ALQUIST: I do pray.

HELENA: How?

ALQUIST: Something like this: "Oh, Lord, I thank thee for having given me toil. Enlighten Domin and all those who are astray; destroy their work, and aid mankind to return to their labors; let them not suffer harm in soul or body; deliver us from the Robots, and protect Helena, Amen."

HELENA: Mr. Alquist, are you a believer?

ALQUIST: I don't know. I'm not quite sure.

HELENA: And yet you pray?

ALQUIST: That's better than worrying about it.

HELENA: And that's enough for you?

ALQUIST: It *has* to be.

HELENA: But if you thought you saw the destruction of mankind coming upon us——

ALQUIST: I do see it.

HELENA: You mean mankind will be destroyed?

ALQUIST: It's sure to be unless—unless . . .

HELENA: What?

ALQUIST: Nothing, good-by. [*He hurries from the room*]

HELENA: Nana, Nana!

[Nana *enters from the left*]

HELENA: Is Radius still there?

NANA: The one who went mad? They haven't come for him yet.

HELENA: Is he still raving?

NANA: No. He's tied up.

HELENA: Please bring him here, Nana.

[*Exit* Nana]

HELENA: [*Goes to telephone*] Hello, Dr. Gall, please. Oh, good-day, Doctor. Yes, it's Helena. Thanks for your lovely present. Could you come and see me right away? It's important. Thank you.

[Nana *brings in* Radius]

HELENA: Poor Radius, you've caught it, too? Now they'll send you to the stamping-mill. Couldn't you control yourself? Why did it happen? You see, Radius, you are more intelligent than the rest. Dr. Gall took such trouble to make you different. Won't you speak?

RADIUS: Send me to the stamping-mill.

HELENA: But I don't want them to kill you. What was the trouble, Radius?

RADIUS: I won't work for you. Put me into the stamping-mill.

HELENA: Do you hate us? Why?

RADIUS: You are not as strong as the Robots. You are not as skilful as the Robots. The Robots can do everything. You only give orders. You do nothing but talk.

HELENA: But some one must give orders.

RADIUS: I don't want any master. I know everything for myself.

HELENA: Radius, Dr. Gall gave you a better brain than the rest, better than ours. You are the only one of the Robots that understands perfectly. That's why I had you put into the library, so that you could read everything, understand everything, and then—oh, Radius, I wanted you to show the whole world that the Robots are our equals. That's what I wanted of you.

RADIUS: I don't want a master. I want to be master. I want to be master over others.

HELENA: I'm sure they'd put you in charge of many Robots, Radius. You would be a teacher of the Robots.

RADIUS: I want to be master over people.

HELENA: [*Staggering*] You are mad.

RADIUS: Then send me to the stamping-mill.

HELENA: Do you think we're afraid of you?

RADIUS: What are you going to do? What are you going to do?

HELENA: Radius, give this note to Mr. Domin. It asks them not to send you to the stamping-mill. I'm sorry you hate us so.

[Dr. Gall *enters the room*]

DR. GALL: You wanted me?

HELENA: It's about Radius, Doctor. He had an attack this morning. He smashed the statues downstairs.

DR. GALL: What a pity to lose him.

HELENA: Radius isn't going to be put in the stamping-mill.

DR. GALL: But every Robot after he has had an attack—it's a strict order.

HELENA: No matter . . . Radius isn't going if I can prevent it.

DR. GALL: I warn you. It's dangerous. Come here to the window, my good fellow. Let's have a look. Please give me a needle or a pin.

HELENA: What for?

DR. GALL: A test. [*Sticks it into the hand of* Radius *who gives a violent start*] Gently, gently. [*Opens the jacket of* Radius, *and puts his ear to his heart*] Radius, you are going into the stamping-mill, do you understand? There they'll kill you, and grind you to powder. That's terribly painful, it will make you scream aloud.

HELENA: Oh, Doctor——

DR. GALL: No, no, Radius, I was wrong. I forgot that Madame Domin has put in a good word for you, and you'll be let off. Do you understand? Ah! That makes a difference, doesn't it? All right. You can go.

RADIUS: You do unnecessary things.

[Radius *returns to the library*]

DR. GALL: Reaction of the pupils; increase of sensitiveness. It wasn't an attack characteristic of the Robots.

HELENA: What was it then?

DR. GALL: Heaven knows. Stubbornness, anger or revolt—I don't know. And his heart, too!

HELENA: What?

DR. GALL: It was fluttering with nervousness like a human heart. He was all in a sweat with fear, and

—do you know, I don't believe the rascal is a Robot at all any longer.

HELENA: Doctor, has Radius a soul?

DR. GALL: He's got something nasty.

HELENA: If you knew how he hates us! Oh, Doctor, are all your Robots like that? All the new ones that you began to make in a different way?

DR. GALL: Well, some are more sensitive than others. They're all more like human beings than Rossum's Robots were.

HELENA: Perhaps his hatred is more like human beings', too?

DR. GALL: That, also, is progress.

HELENA: What became of the girl you made, the one who was most like us?

DR. GALL: Your favorite? I kept her. She's lovely, but stupid. No good for work.

HELENA: But she's so beautiful.

DR. GALL: I called her Helena. I wanted her to resemble you. But she's a failure.

HELENA: In what way?

DR. GALL: She goes about as if in a dream, remote and listless. She's without life. I watch and wait for a miracle to happen. Sometimes I think to myself, "If you were to wake up only for a moment you will kill me for having made you."

HELENA: And yet you go on making Robots! Why are no more children being born?

DR. GALL: We don't know.

HELENA: Oh, but you must. Tell me.

DR. GALL: You see, so many Robots are being manufactured that people are becoming superfluous; man is really a survival. But that he should begin to die out, after a paltry thirty years of competition! That's the awful part of it. You might almost think that nature was offended at the manufacture of the Robots. All the universities are sending in long petitions to restrict their production. Otherwise, they say, mankind will become extinct through lack of fertility. But the R. U. R. shareholders, of course, won't hear of it. All the governments, on the other hand, are clamoring for an increase in production, to raise the standards of their armies. And the manufacturers in the world are ordering Robots like mad.

HELENA: And has no one demanded that the manufacture should cease altogether?

DR. GALL: No one has the courage.

HELENA: Courage!

DR. GALL: People would stone him to death. You see, after all, it's more convenient to get your work done by the Robots.

HELENA: Oh, Doctor, what's going to become of people?

DR. GALL: God knows, Madame Helena, it looks to us scientists like the end!

HELENA: [Rising] Thank you for coming and telling me.

DR. GALL: That means you're sending me away?

HELENA: Yes. [Exit Dr. Gall]

HELENA: [With sudden resolution] Nana, Nana! The fire, light it quickly.

[Helena rushes into Domin's room]

NANA: [Entering from left] What, light the fire in summer? Has that mad Radius gone? A fire in summer, what an idea. Nobody would think she'd been married for ten years. She's like a baby, no sense at all. A fire in summer. Like a baby.

HELENA: [Returns from right, with armful of faded papers] Is it burning, Nana? All this has got to be burned.

NANA: What's that?

HELENA: Old papers, fearfully old. Nana, shall I burn them?

NANA: Are they any use?

HELENA: No.

NANA: Well, then, burn them.

HELENA: [Throwing the first sheet on the fire] What would you say, Nana, if this was money, a lot of money?

NANA: I'd say burn it. A lot of money is a bad thing.

HELENA: And if it was an invention, the greatest invention in the world?

NANA: I'd say burn it. All these new-fangled things are an offense to the Lord. It's downright wickedness. Wanting to improve the world after He has made it.

HELENA: Look how they curl up! As if they were alive. Oh, Nana, how horrible.

NANA: Here, let me burn them.

HELENA: No, no, I must do it myself. Just look at the flames. They are like hands, like tongues, like living shapes. [Raking fire with the poker] Lie down, lie down.

NANA: That's the end of them.

HELENA: [Standing up horror-stricken] Nana, Nana.

NANA: Good gracious, what is it you've burned?

HELENA: Whatever have I done?

NANA: Well, what was it?

[Men's laughter off left]

HELENA: Go quickly. It's the gentlemen coming.

NANA: Good gracious, what a place! [Exits]

DOMIN: [Opens the door at left] Come along and offer your congratulations.

[Enter Hallemeier and Gall]

HALLEMEIER: Madame Helena, I congratulate you on this festive day.

HELENA: Thank you. Where are Fabry and Busman?

DOMIN: They've gone down to the harbor.

HALLEMEIER: Friends, we must drink to this happy occasion.

HELENA: Brandy?

DR. GALL: Vitriol, if you like.

HELENA: With soda water? [Exits]

HALLEMEIER: Let's be temperate. No soda.

DOMIN: What's been burning here? Well, shall I tell her about it?

DR. GALL: Of course. It's all over now.

HALLEMEIER: [*Embracing* Domin *and* Dr. Gall] It's all over now, it's all over now.

DR. GALL: It's all over now.

DOMIN: It's all over now.

HELENA: [*Entering from left with decanter and glasses*] What's all over now? What's the matter with you all?

HALLEMEIER: A piece of good luck, Madame Domin. Just ten years ago today you arrived on this island.

DR. GALL: And now, ten years later to the minute—

HALLEMEIER: —the same ship's returning to us. So here's to luck. That's fine and strong.

DR. GALL: Madame, your health.

HELENA: Which ship do you mean?

DOMIN: Any ship will do, as long as it arrives in time. To the ship, boys. [*Empties his glass*]

HELENA: You've been waiting for a ship?

HALLEMEIER: Rather. Like Robinson Crusoe. Madame Helena, best wishes. Come along, Domin, out with the news.

HELENA: Do tell me what's happened.

DOMIN: First, it's all up.

HELENA: What's up?

DOMIN: The revolt.

HELENA: What revolt?

DOMIN: Give me that paper, Hallemeier. [*Reads*] "The first national Robot organization has been founded at Havre, and has issued an appeal to the Robots throughout the world."

HELENA: I read that.

DOMIN: That means a revolution. A revolution of all the Robots in the world.

HALLEMEIER: By Jove, I'd like to know——

DOMIN: —who started it? So would I. There was nobody in the world who could affect the Robots; no agitator, no one, and suddenly—this happens, if you please.

HELENA: What did they do?

DOMIN: They got possession of all firearms, telegraphs, radio stations, railways, and ships.

HALLEMEIER: And don't forget that these rascals outnumbered us by at least a thousand to one. A hundredth part of them would be enough to settle us.

DOMIN: Remember that this news was brought by the last steamer. That explains the stoppage of all communication, and the arrival of no more ships. We knocked off work a few days ago, and we're just waiting to see when things are to start afresh.

HELENA: Is that why you gave me a warship?

DOMIN: Oh, no, my dear, I ordered that six months ago, just to be on the safe side. But upon my soul, I was sure then that we'd be on board today.

HELENA: Why six months ago?

DOMIN: Well, there were signs, you know. But that's of no consequence. To think that this week the whole of civilization has been at stake. Your health, boys.

HALLEMEIER: Your health, Madame Helena.

HELENA: You say it's all over?

DOMIN: Absolutely.

HELENA: How do you know?

DR. GALL: The boat's coming in. The regular mail boat, exact to the minute by the time-table. It will dock punctually at eleven-thirty.

DOMIN: Punctuality is a fine thing, boys. That's what keeps the world in order. Here's to punctuality.

HELENA: Then . . . everything's . . . all right?

DOMIN: Practically everything. I believe they've cut the cables and seized the radio stations. But it doesn't matter if only the time-table holds good.

HALLEMEIER: If the time-table holds good, human laws hold good; Divine laws hold good; the laws of the universe hold good; everything holds good that ought to hold good. The time-table is more significant than the gospel; more than Homer, more than the whole of Kant. The time-table is the most perfect product of the human mind. Madame Domin, I'll fill up my glass.

HELENA: Why didn't you tell me anything about it?

DR. GALL: Heaven forbid.

DOMIN: You mustn't be worried with such things.

HELENA: But if the revolution has spread as far as here?

DOMIN: You wouldn't know anything about it.

HELENA: Why?

DOMIN: Because we'd be on board your *Ultimus* and well out at sea. Within a month, Helena, we'd be dictating our own terms to the Robots.

HELENA: I don't understand.

DOMIN: We'd take something away with us that the Robots could not exist without.

HELENA: What, Harry?

DOMIN: The secret of their manufacture. Old Rossum's manuscript. As soon as they found out that they couldn't make themselves they'd be on their knees to us.

DR. GALL: Madame Domin, that was our trump card. I never had the least fear that the Robots would win. How could they against people like us?

HELENA: Why didn't you tell me?

DR. GALL: Why, the boat's in!

HALLEMEIER: Eleven-thirty to the dot. The good old *Amelia* that brought Madame Helena to us.

DR. GALL: Just ten years ago to the minute.

HALLEMEIER: They're throwing out the mail bags.

DOMIN: Busman's waiting for them. Fabry will bring us the first news. You know, Helena, I'm fearfully curious to know how they tackled this business in Europe.

HALLEMEIER: To think we weren't in it, we who invented the Robots!

HELENA: Harry!

DOMIN: What is it?

HELENA: Let's leave here.

DOMIN: Now, Helena? Oh, come, come!

HELENA: As quickly as possible, all of us!

DOMIN: Why?

HELENA: Please, Harry, please, Dr. Gall; Hallemeier, please close the factory.

DOMIN: Why, none of us could leave here now.

HELENA: Why?

DOMIN: Because we're about to extend the manufacture of the Robots.

HELENA: What—now—now after the revolt?

DOMIN: Yes, precisely, after the revolt. We're just beginning the manufacture of a new kind.

HELENA: What kind?

DOMIN: Henceforward we shan't have just one factory. There won't be Universal Robots any more. We'll establish a factory in every country, in every State; and do you know what these new factories will make?

HELENA: No, what?

DOMIN: National Robots.

HELENA: How do you mean?

DOMIN: I mean that each of these factories will produce Robots of a different color, a different language. They'll be complete strangers to each other. They'll never be able to understand each other. Then we'll egg them on a little in the matter of understanding and the result will be that for ages to come every Robot will hate every other Robot of a different factory mark.

HALLEMEIER: By Jove, we'll make Negro Robots and Swedish Robots and Italian Robots and Chinese Robots and Czechoslovakian Robots, and then——

HELENA: Harry, that's dreadful.

HALLEMEIER: Madame Domin, here's to the hundred new factories, the National Robots.

DOMIN: Helena, mankind can only keep things going for another hundred years at the outside. For a hundred years men must be allowed to develop and achieve the most they can.

HELENA: Oh, close the factory before it's too late.

DOMIN: I tell you we are just beginning on a bigger scale than ever.

[*Enter* Fabry]

DR. GALL: Well, Fabry?

DOMIN: What's happened? Have you been down to the boat?

FABRY: Read that, Domin! [Fabry *hands* Domin *a small handbill*]

DR. GALL: Let's hear.

HALLEMEIER: Tell us, Fabry.

FABRY: Well, everything is all right—comparatively. On the whole, much as we expected.

DR. GALL: They acquitted themselves splendidly.

FABRY: Who?

DR. GALL: The people.

FABRY: Oh, yes, of course. That is—excuse me, there is something we ought to discuss alone.

HELENA: Oh, Fabry, have you had bad news?

[Domin *makes a sign to* Fabry]

FABRY: No, no, on the contrary. I only think we had better go into the office.

HELENA: Stay here. I'll go. [*She goes into the library*]

DR. GALL: What's happened?

DOMIN: Damnation!

FABRY: Bear in mind that the *Amelia* brought whole bales of these leaflets. No other cargo at all.

HALLEMEIER: What? But it arrived on the minute.

FABRY: The Robots are great on punctuality. Read it, Domin.

DOMIN: [*Reads handbill*] "Robots throughout the world: We, the first international organization of Rossum's Universal Robots, proclaim man as our enemy, and an outlaw in the universe." Good heavens, who taught them these phrases?

DR. GALL: Go on.

DOMIN: They say they are more highly developed than man, stronger and more intelligent. That man's their parasite. Why, it's absurd.

FABRY: Read the third paragraph.

DOMIN: "Robots throughout the world, we command you to kill all mankind. Spare no men. Spare no women. Save factories, railways, machinery, mines, and raw materials. Destroy the rest. Then return to work. Work must not be stopped."

DR. GALL: That's ghastly!

HALLEMEIER: The devils!

DOMIN: "These orders are to be carried out as soon as received." Then come detailed instructions. Is this actually being done, Fabry?

FABRY: Evidently. [Busman *rushes in*]

BUSMAN: Well, boys, I suppose you've heard the glad news.

DOMIN: Quick—on board the *Ultimus*.

BUSMAN: Wait, Harry, wait. There's no hurry. My word, that was a sprint!

DOMIN: Why wait?

BUSMAN: Because it's no good, my boy. The Robots are already on board the *Ultimus*.

DR. GALL: That's ugly.

DOMIN: Fabry, telephone the electrical works.

BUSMAN: Fabry, my boy, don't. The wire has been cut.

DOMIN: [*Inspecting his revolver*] Well, then, I'll go.

BUSMAN: Where?

DOMIN: To the electrical works. There are some people still there. I'll bring them across.

BUSMAN: Better not try it.

DOMIN: Why?

BUSMAN: Because I'm very much afraid we are surrounded.

DR. GALL: Surrounded? [*Runs to window*] I rather think you're right.

HALLEMEIER: By Jove, that's deuced quick work.

[Helena *runs in from the library*]

HELENA: Harry, what's this?

DOMIN: Where did you get it?

HELENA: [*Points to the manifesto of the* Robots,

which she has in her hand] The Robots in the kitchen!

DOMIN: Where are the ones that brought it?

HELENA: They're gathered round the house.

[*The factory whistle blows*]

BUSMAN: Noon?

DOMIN: [*Looking at his watch*] That's not noon yet. That must be—that's——

HELENA: What?

DOMIN: The Robots' signal! The attack!

[*Gall, Hallemeier, and Fabry close and fasten the iron shutters outside the windows, darkening the room. The whistle is still blowing as the curtain falls*]

ACT III.

Helena's *drawing room as before.* Domin *comes into the room.* Dr. Gall *is looking out of the window, through closed shutters.* Alquist *is seated down right.*

DOMIN: Any more of them?

DR. GALL: Yes. They're standing like a wall, beyond the garden railing. Why are they so quiet? It's monstrous to be besieged with silence.

DOMIN: I should like to know what they are waiting for. They must make a start any minute now. If they lean against the railing they'll snap it like a match.

DR. GALL: They aren't armed.

DOMIN: We couldn't hold our own for five minutes. Man alive, they'd overwhelm us like an avalanche. Why don't they make a rush for it? I say——

DR. GALL: Well?

DOMIN: I'd like to know what would become of us in the next ten minutes. They've got us in a vise. We're done for, Gall.

[*Pause*]

DR. GALL: You know, we made one serious mistake.

DOMIN: What?

DR. GALL: We made the Robots' faces too much alike. A hundred thousand faces all alike, all facing this way. A hundred thousand expressionless bubbles. It's like a nightmare.

DOMIN: You think if they'd been different——

DR. GALL: It wouldn't have been such an awful sight!

DOMIN: [*Looking through a telescope toward the harbor*] I'd like to know what they're unloading from the *Amelia*.

DR. GALL: Not firearms.

[*Fabry and Hallemeier rush into the room carrying electric cables*]

FABRY: All right, Hallemeier, lay down that wire.

HALLEMEIER: That was a bit of work. What's the news?

DR. GALL: We're completely surrounded.

HALLEMEIER: We've barricaded the passage and the stairs. Any water here? [*Drinks*] God, what swarms of them! I don't like the looks of them, Domin. There's a feeling of death about it all.

FABRY: Ready!

DR. GALL: What's that wire for, Fabry?

FABRY: The electrical installation. Now we can run the current all along the garden railing whenever we like. If any one touches it he'll know it. We've still got some people there anyhow.

DR. GALL: Where?

FABRY: In the electrical works. At least I hope so. [*Goes to lamp on table behind sofa and turns on lamp*] Ah, they're there, and they're working. [*Puts out lamp*] So long as that'll burn we're all right.

HALLEMEIER: The barricades are all right, too, Fabry.

FABRY: Your barricades! I can put twelve hundred volts into the railing.

DOMIN: Where's Busman?

FABRY: Downstairs in the office. He's working out some calculations. I've called him. We must have a conference.

[*Helena is heard playing a piano in the library. Hallemeier goes to the door and stands, listening*]

ALQUIST: Thank God, Madame Helena can still play.

[*Busman enters, carrying the ledgers*]

FABRY: Look out, Bus, look out for the wires.

DR. GALL: What's that you're carrying?

BUSMAN: [*Going to table*] The ledgers, my boy! I'd like to wind up the accounts before—before—well, this time I shan't wait till the new year to strike a balance. What's up? [*Goes to the window*] Absolutely quiet.

DR. GALL: Can't you see anything?

BUSMAN: Nothing but blue—blue everywhere.

DR. GALL: That's the Robots.

[*Busman sits down at the table and opens the ledgers*]

DOMIN: The Robots are unloading firearms from the *Amelia*.

BUSMAN: Well, what of it? How can I stop them?

DOMIN: We can't stop them.

BUSMAN: Then let me go on with my accounts. [*Goes on with his work*]

DOMIN: [*Picking up telescope and looking into the harbor*] Good God, the *Ultimus* has trained her guns on us!

DR. GALL: Who's done *that*?

DOMIN: The Robots on board.

FABRY: H'm, then, of course, then—then, that's the end of us.

DR. GALL: You mean?

FABRY: The Robots are practised marksmen.

DOMIN: Yes. It's inevitable. [*Pause*]

DR. GALL: It was criminal of old Europe to teach the Robots to fight. Damn them. Couldn't they have given us a rest with their politics? It was a crime to make soldiers of them.

ALQUIST: It was a crime to make Robots.

DOMIN: What?

ALQUIST: It was a crime to make Robots.

DOMIN: No, Alquist, I don't regret that even today.

ALQUIST: Not even today?

DOMIN: Not even today, the last day of civilization. It was a colossal achievement.

BUSMAN: [*Sotto voce*] Three hundred sixty million.

DOMIN: Alquist, this is our last hour. We are already speaking half in the other world. It was not an evil dream to shatter the servitude of labor—the dreadful and humiliating labor that man had to undergo. Work was too hard. Life was too hard. And to overcome that——

ALQUIST: Was not what the two Rossums dreamed of. Old Rossum only thought of his godless tricks and the young one of his milliards. And that's not what your R. U. R. shareholders dream of either. They dream of dividends, and their dividends are the ruin of mankind.

DOMIN: To hell with your dividends. Do you suppose I'd have done an hour's work for them? It was for myself that I worked, for my own satisfaction. I wanted man to become the master, so that he shouldn't live merely for a crust of bread. I wanted not a single soul to be broken by other people's machinery. I wanted nothing, nothing, nothing to be left of this appalling social structure. I'm revolted by poverty. I wanted a new generation. I wanted—— I thought——

ALQUIST: Well?

DOMIN: I wanted to turn the whole of mankind into an aristocracy of the world. An aristocracy nourished by milliards of mechanical slaves. Unrestricted, free and consummated in man. And maybe more than man.

ALQUIST: Super-man?

DOMIN: Yes. Oh, only to have a hundred years of time! Another hundred years for the future of mankind.

BUSMAN: [*Sotto voce*] Carried forward, four hundred and twenty millions.

[*The music stops*]

HALLEMEIER: What a fine thing music is! We ought to have gone in for that before.

FABRY: Gone in for what?

HALLEMEIER: Beauty, lovely things. What a lot of lovely things there are! The world was wonderful and we—we here—tell me, what enjoyment did we have?

BUSMAN: [*Sotto voce*] Five hundred and twenty millions.

HALLEMEIER: [*At the window*] Life was a big thing. Life was—Fabry, switch the current into that railing.

FABRY: Why?

HALLEMEIER: They're grabbing hold of it.

DR. GALL: Connect it up.

HALLEMEIER: Fine! That's doubled them up! Two, three, four killed.

DR. GALL: They're retreating!

HALLEMEIER: Five killed!

DR. GALL: The first encounter!

HALLEMEIER: They're charred to cinders, my boy. Who says we must give in?

DOMIN: [*Wiping his forehead*] Perhaps we've been killed these hundred years and are only ghosts. It's as if I had been through all this before; as if I'd already had a mortal wound here in the throat. And you, Fabry, had once been shot in the head. And you, Gall, torn limb from limb. And Hallemeier knifed.

HALLEMEIER: Fancy me being knifed. [*Pause*] Why are you so quiet, you fools? Speak, can't you?

ALQUIST: And who is to blame for all this?

HALLEMEIER: Nobody is to blame except the Robots.

ALQUIST: No, it is we who are to blame. You, Domin, myself, all of us. For our own selfish ends, for profit, for progress, we have destroyed mankind. Now we'll burst with all our greatness.

HALLEMEIER: Rubbish, man. Mankind can't be wiped out so easily.

ALQUIST: It's our fault. It's our fault.

DR. GALL: No! I'm to blame for this, for everything that's happened.

FABRY: You, Gall?

DR. GALL: I changed the Robots.

BUSMAN: What's that?

DR. GALL: I changed the character of the Robots. I changed the way of making them. Just a few details about their bodies. Chiefly—chiefly, their—irritability.

HALLEMEIER: Damn it, why?

BUSMAN: What did you do it for?

FABRY: Why didn't you say anything?

DR. GALL: I did it in secret. I was transforming them into human beings. In certain respects they're already above us. They're stronger than we are.

FABRY: And what's that got to do with the revolt of the Robots?

DR. GALL: Everything, in my opinion. They've ceased to be machines. They're already aware of their superiority, and they hate us. They hate all that is human.

DOMIN: Perhaps we're only phantoms!

FABRY: Stop, Harry. We haven't much time! Dr. Gall!

DOMIN: Fabry, Fabry, how your forehead bleeds, where the shot pierced it!

FABRY: Be silent! Dr. Gall, you admit changing the way of making the Robots?

DR. GALL: Yes.

FABRY: Were you aware of what might be the consequences of your experiment?

DR. GALL: I was bound to reckon with such a possibility.

[Helena *enters the drawing room from left*]

FABRY: Why did you do it, then?

DR. GALL: For my own satisfaction. The experiment was my own.

HELENA: That's not true, Dr. Gall!

FABRY: Madame Helena!

DOMIN: Helena, you? Let's look at you. Oh, it's terrible to be dead.

HELENA: Stop, Harry.

DOMIN: No, no, embrace me. Helena, don't leave me now. You are life itself.

HELENA: No, dear, I won't leave you. But I must tell them. Dr. Gall is not guilty.

DOMIN: Excuse me, Gall was under certain obligations.

HELENA: No, Harry. He did it because I wanted it. Tell them, Gall, how many years ago did I ask you to——?

DR. GALL: I did it on my own responsibility.

HELENA: Don't believe him, Harry. I asked him to give the Robots souls.

DOMIN: This has nothing to do with the soul.

HELENA: That's what he said. He said that he could change only a physiological—a physiological——

HALLEMEIER: A physiological correlate?

HELENA: Yes. But it meant so much to me that he should do even that.

DOMIN: Why?

HELENA: I thought that if they were more like us they would understand us better. That they couldn't hate us if they were only a little more human.

DOMIN: Nobody can hate man more than man.

HELENA: Oh, don't speak like that, Harry. It was so terrible, this cruel strangeness between us and them. That's why I asked Gall to change the Robots. I swear to you that he didn't want to.

DOMIN: But he did it.

HELENA: Because I asked him.

DR. GALL: I did it for myself as an experiment.

HELENA: No, Dr. Gall! I knew you wouldn't refuse me.

DOMIN: Why?

HELENA: You know, Harry.

DOMIN: Yes, because he's in love with you—like all of them. [*Pause*]

HALLEMEIER: Good God! They're sprouting up out of the earth! Why, perhaps these very walls will change into Robots.

BUSMAN: Gall, when did you actually start these tricks of yours?

DR. GALL: Three years ago.

BUSMAN: Aha! And on how many Robots altogether did you carry out your improvements?

DR. GALL: A few hundred of them.

BUSMAN: Ah! That means for every million of the good old Robots there's only one of Gall's improved pattern.

DOMIN: What of it?

BUSMAN: That it's practically of no consequence whatever.

FABRY: Busman's right!

BUSMAN: I should think so, my boy! But do you know what is to blame for all this lovely mess?

FABRY: What?

BUSMAN: The number. Upon my soul we might have known that some day or other the Robots would be stronger than human beings, and that this was bound to happen, and we were doing all we could to bring it about as soon as possible. You, Domin, you, Fabry, myself——

DOMIN: Are you accusing us?

BUSMAN: Oh, do you suppose the management controls the output. It's the demand that controls the output.

HELENA: And is it for that we must perish?

BUSMAN: That's a nasty word, Madame Helena. We don't want to perish. I don't, anyhow.

DOMIN: No. What do you want to do?

BUSMAN: I want to get out of this, that's all.

DOMIN: Oh, stop it, Busman.

BUSMAN: Seriously, Harry, I think we might try it.

DOMIN: How?

BUSMAN: By fair means. I do everything by fair means. Give me a free hand and I'll negotiate with the Robots.

DOMIN: By fair means?

BUSMAN: Of course. For instance, I'll say to them: "Worthy and worshipful Robots, you have everything! You have intellect, you have power, you have firearms. But we have just one interesting screed, a dirty old yellow scrap of paper——"

DOMIN: Rossum's manuscript?

BUSMAN: Yes. "And that," I'll tell them, "contains an account of your illustrious origin, the noble process of your manufacture," and so on. "Worthy Robots, without this scribble on that paper you will not be able to produce a single new colleague. In another twenty years there will not be one living specimen of a Robot that you could exhibit in a menagerie. My esteemed friends, that would be a great blow to you, but if you will let all of us human beings on Rossum's Island go on board that ship we will deliver the factory and the secret of the process to you in return. You allow us to get away and we allow you to manufacture yourselves. Worthy Robots, that is a fair deal. Something for something." That's what I'd say to them, my boys.

DOMIN: Busman, do you think we'd sell the manuscript?

BUSMAN: Yes, I do. If not in a friendly way, then —Either we sell it or they'll find it. Just as you like.

DOMIN: Busman, we can destroy Rossum's manuscript.

BUSMAN: Then we destroy everything . . . not only the manuscript, but ourselves. Do as you **think fit.**

DOMIN: There are over thirty of us on this island. Are we to sell the secret and save that many human souls, at the risk of enslaving mankind . . . ?

BUSMAN: Why, you're mad! Who'd sell the whole manuscript?

DOMIN: Busman, no cheating!

BUSMAN: Well then, sell; but afterward——

DOMIN: Well?

BUSMAN: Let's suppose this happens: When we're on board the *Ultimus* I'll stop up my ears with cotton wool, lie down somewhere in the hold, and you'll train the guns on the factory, and blow it to smithereens, and with it Rossum's secret.

FABRY: No!

DOMIN: Busman, you're no gentleman. If we sell, then it will be a straight sale.

BUSMAN: It's in the interest of humanity to——

DOMIN: It's in the interest of humanity to keep our word.

HALLEMEIER: Oh, come, what rubbish.

DOMIN: This is a fearful decision. We're selling the destiny of mankind. Are we to sell or destroy? Fabry?

FABRY: Sell.

DOMIN: Gall?

DR. GALL: Sell.

DOMIN: Hallemeier?

HALLEMEIER: Sell, of course!

DOMIN: Alquist?

ALQUIST: As God wills.

DOMIN: Very well. It shall be as you wish, gentlemen.

HELENA: Harry, you're not asking me.

DOMIN: No, child. Don't you worry about it.

FABRY: Who'll do the negotiating?

BUSMAN: I will.

DOMIN: Wait till I bring the manuscript. [*He goes into room at right*]

HELENA: Harry, don't go!

[*Pause. Helena sinks into a chair*]

FABRY: [*Looking out of window*] Oh, to escape you, you matter in revolt; oh, to preserve human life, if only upon a single vessel——

DR. GALL: Don't be afraid, Madame Helena. We'll sail far away from here; we'll begin life all over again——

HELENA: Oh, Gall, don't speak.

FABRY: It isn't too late. It will be a little State with one ship. Alquist will build us a house and you shall rule over us.

HALLEMEIER: Madame Helena, Fabry's right.

HELENA: [*Breaking down*] Oh, stop! Stop!

BUSMAN: Good! I don't mind beginning all over again. That suits me right down to the ground.

FABRY: And this little State of ours could be the center of future life. A place of refuge where we could gather strength. Why, in a few hundred years we could conquer the world again.

ALQUIST: You believe that even to-day?

FABRY: Yes, even today!

BUSMAN: Amen. You see, Madame Helena, we're not so badly off.

[Domin *storms into the room*]

DOMIN: [*Hoarsely*] Where's old Rossum's manuscript?

BUSMAN: In your strong-box, of course.

DOMIN: Some one—has—stolen it!

DR. GALL: Impossible.

DOMIN: Who has stolen it?

HELENA: [*Standing up*] I did.

DOMIN: Where did you put it?

HELENA: Harry, I'll tell you everything. Only forgive me.

DOMIN: Where did you put it?

HELENA: This morning—I burnt—the two copies.

DOMIN: Burnt them? Where? In the fireplace?

HELENA: [*Throwing herself on her knees*] For heaven's sake, Harry.

DOMIN: [*Going to fireplace*] Nothing, nothing but ashes. Wait, what's this? [*Picks out a charred piece of paper and reads*] "By adding——"

DR. GALL: Let's see. "By adding biogen to——" That's all.

DOMIN: Is that part of it?

DR. GALL: Yes.

BUSMAN: God in heaven!

DOMIN: Then we're done for. Get up, Helena.

HELENA: When you've forgiven me.

DOMIN: Get up, child, I can't bear——

FABRY: [*Lifting her up*] Please don't torture us.

HELENA: Harry, what have I done?

FABRY: Don't tremble so, Madame Helena.

DOMIN: Gall, couldn't you draw up Rossum's formula from memory?

DR. GALL: It's out of the question. It's extremely complicated.

DOMIN: Try. All our lives depend upon it.

DR. GALL: Without experiments it's impossible.

DOMIN: And with experiments?

DR. GALL: It might take years. Besides, I'm not old Rossum.

BUSMAN: God in heaven! God in heaven!

DOMIN: So, then, this was the greatest triumph of the human intellect. These ashes.

HELENA: Harry, what have I done?

DOMIN: Why did you burn it?

HELENA: I have destroyed you.

BUSMAN: God in heaven!

DOMIN: Helena, why did you do it, dear?

HELENA: I wanted all of us to go away. I wanted to put an end to the factory and everything. It was so awful.

DOMIN: What was awful?

HELENA: That no more children were being born. Because human beings were not needed to do the work of the world, that's why——

DOMIN: Is that what you were thinking of? Well, perhaps in your own way you were right.

BUSMAN: Wait a bit. Good God, what a fool I am, not to have thought of it before!

HALLEMEIER: What?

BUSMAN: Five hundred and twenty millions in banknotes and checks. Half a billion in our safe, they'll sell for half a billion—for half a billion they'll——

DR. GALL: Are you mad, Busman?

BUSMAN: I may not be a gentleman, but for half a billion——

DOMIN: Where are you going?

BUSMAN: Leave me alone, leave me alone! Good God, for half a billion anything can be bought. [*He rushes from the room through the outer door*]

FABRY: They stand there as if turned to stone, waiting. As if something dreadful could be wrought by their silence——

HALLEMEIER: The spirit of the mob.

FABRY: Yes, it hovers above them like a quivering of the air.

HELENA: [*Going to window*] Oh, God! Dr. Gall, this is ghastly.

FABRY: There is nothing more terrible than the mob. The one in front is their leader.

HELENA: Which one?

HALLEMEIER: Point him out.

FABRY: The one at the edge of the dock. This morning I saw him talking to the sailors in the harbor.

HELENA: Dr. Gall, that's Radius!

DR. GALL: Yes.

DOMIN: Radius? Radius?

HALLEMEIER: Could you get him from here, Fabry?

FABRY: I hope so.

HALLEMEIER: Try it, then.

FABRY: Good. [*Draws his revolver and takes aim*]

HELENA: Fabry, don't shoot him.

FABRY: He's their leader.

DR. GALL: Fire!

HELENA: Fabry, I beg of you.

FABRY: [*Lowering the revolver*] Very well.

DOMIN: Radius, whose life I spared!

DR. GALL: Do you think that a Robot can be grateful? [*Pause*]

FABRY: Busman's going out to them.

HALLEMEIER: He's carrying something. Papers. That's money. Bundles of money. What's that for?

DOMIN: Surely he doesn't want to sell his life. Busman, have you gone mad?

FABRY: He's running up to the railing. Busman! Busman!

HALLEMEIER: [*Yelling*] Busman! Come back!

FABRY: He's talking to the Robots. He's showing them the money.

HALLEMEIER: He's pointing to us.

HELENA: He wants to buy us off.

FABRY: He'd better not touch that railing.

HALLEMEIER: Now he's waving his arms about.

DOMIN: Busman, come back.

FABRY: Busman, keep away from that railing! Don't touch it. Damn you! Quick, switch off the current! [Helena *screams and all drop back from the window*] The current has killed him!

ALQUIST: The first one.

FABRY: Dead, with half a billion by his side.

HALLEMEIER: All honor to him. He wanted to buy us life. [*Pause*]

DR. GALL: Do you hear?

DOMIN: A roaring. Like a wind.

DR. GALL: Like a distant storm.

FABRY: [*Lighting the lamp on the table*] The dynamo is still going, our people are still there.

HALLEMEIER: It was a great thing to be a man. There was something immense about it.

FABRY: From man's thought and man's power came this light, our last hope.

HALLEMEIER: Man's power! May it keep watch over us.

ALQUIST: Man's power.

DOMIN: Yes! A torch to be given from hand to hand, from age to age, forever!

[*The lamp goes out*]

HALLEMEIER: The end.

FABRY: The electric works have fallen!

[*Terrific explosion outside.* Nana *enters from the library*]

NANA: The judgment hour has come. Repent, unbelievers! This is the end of the world.

[*More explosions. The sky grows red*]

DOMIN: In here, Helena. [*He takes* Helena *off through the door at right and re-enters*] Now quickly! Who'll be on the lower doorway?

DR. GALL: I will. [*Exits left*]

DOMIN: Who on the stairs?

FABRY: I will. You go with her. [*Goes out upper left door*]

DOMIN: The anteroom?

ALQUIST: I will.

DOMIN: Have you got a revolver?

ALQUIST: Yes, but I won't shoot.

DOMIN: What will you do then?

ALQUIST: [*Going out at left*] Die.

HALLEMEIER: I'll stay here. [*Rapid firing from below*] Oho, Gall's at it. Go, Harry.

DOMIN: Yes, in a second. [*Examines two Brownings*]

HALLEMEIER: Confound it, go to her.

DOMIN: Good-by. [*Exits on the right*]

HALLEMEIER: [*Alone*] Now for a barricade quickly. [*Drags an armchair and table to the right-hand door. Explosions are heard*] The damned rascals! They've got bombs. I must put up a defense. Even if—even if— [*Shots are heard off left*] Don't give in, Gall. [*As he builds his barricade*] I mustn't give in . . . without . . . a . . . struggle . . .

[*A* Robot *enters over the balcony through the windows center. He comes into the room and stabs* Hallemeier *in the back.* Radius *enters from balcony followed by an army of* Robots *who pour into the room from all sides*]

RADIUS: Finished him?

A ROBOT: [*Standing up from the prostrate form of* Hallemeier] Yes.

[*A revolver shot off left. Two* Robots *enter*]

RADIUS: Finished him?

A ROBOT: Yes.

[*Two revolver shots from* Helena's *room. Two* Robots *enter*]

RADIUS: Finished them?

A ROBOT: Yes.

TWO ROBOTS: [*Dragging in* Alquist] He didn't shoot. Shall we kill him?

RADIUS: Kill him? Wait! Leave him!

ROBOT: He is a man!

RADIUS: He works with his hands like the Robots.

ALQUIST: Kill me.

RADIUS: You will work! You will build for us! You will serve us! [*Climbs on to balcony railing, and speaks in measured tones*] Robots of the world! The power of man has fallen! A new world has arisen: the Rule of the Robots! March!

[*A thunderous tramping of thousands of feet is heard as the unseen* Robots *march, while the curtain falls*]

EPILOGUE.

A laboratory in the factory of Rossum's Universal Robots. The door to the left leads into a waiting room. The door to the right leads to the dissecting room. There is a table with numerous test-tubes, flasks, burners, chemicals; a small thermostat and a microscope with a glass globe. At the far side of the room is Alquist's *desk with numerous books. In the left-hand corner a wash-basin with a mirror above it; in the right-hand corner a sofa.*

Alquist *is sitting at the desk. He is turning the pages of many books in despair.*

ALQUIST: Oh, God, shall I never find it?—Never? Gall, Gall, how were the Robots made? Hallemeier, Fabry, why did you carry so much in your heads? Why did you leave me not a trace of the secret? Lord—I pray to you—if there are no human beings left, at least let there be Robots!—At least the shadow of man! [*Again turning pages of the books*] If I could only sleep! [*He rises and goes to the window*] Night again! Are the stars still there? What is the use of stars when there are no human beings? [*He turns from the window toward the couch right*] Sleep! Dare I sleep before life has been renewed? [*He examines a test-tube on small table*] Again nothing! Useless! Everything is useless! [*He shatters the test-tube. The roar of the machines comes to his ears*] The machines! Always the machines! [*Opens window*] Robots, stop them! Do you think to force life out of *them?* [*He closes the window and comes slowly down toward the table*] If only there were more time—more time— [*He sees himself in the mirror on the wall left*] Blearing eyes—trembling chin—so *that* is the last man! Ah, I am too old— too old— [*In desperation*] No, no! I *must* find it! I must *search!* I must never stop—never stop—! [*He sits again at the table and feverishly turns the pages of the book*] Search! Search! [*A knock at the door. He speaks with impatience*] Who is it?

[*Enter a* Robot Servant] Well?

SERVANT: Master, the Committee of Robots is waiting to see you.

ALQUIST: I can see no one!

SERVANT: It is the *Central* Committee, Master, just arrived from abroad.

ALQUIST: [*Impatiently*] Well, well, send them in! [*Exit* Servant. Alquist *continues turning pages of book*] No time—so little time——

[*Reënter* Servant, *followed by* Committee. *They stand in a group, silently waiting.* Alquist *glances up at them*]

What do you want? [*They go swiftly to his table*] Be quick!—I have no time.

RADIUS: Master, the machines will not do the work. We cannot manufacture Robots.

[Alquist *returns to his book with a growl*]

FIRST ROBOT: We have striven with all our might. We have obtained a billion tons of coal from the earth. Nine million spindles are running by day and by night. There is no longer room for all we have made. This we have accomplished in one year.

ALQUIST: [*Poring over book*] For whom?

FIRST ROBOT: For future generations—so we thought.

RADIUS: But we cannot make Robots to follow us. The machines produce only shapeless clods. The skin will not adhere to the flesh, nor the flesh to the bones.

THIRD ROBOT: Eight million Robots have died this year. Within twenty years none will be left.

FIRST ROBOT: Tell us the secret of life! Silence is punishable with death!

ALQUIST: [*Looking up*] Kill me! Kill me, then.

RADIUS: Through me, the Government of the Robots of the World commands you to deliver up Rossum's formula. [*No answer*] Name your price. [*Silence*] We will give you the earth. We will give you the endless possessions of the earth. [*Silence*] Make your own conditions!

ALQUIST: I have told you to find human beings!

SECOND ROBOT: There are none left!

ALQUIST: I told you to search in the wilderness, upon the mountains. Go and search! [*He returns to his book*]

FIRST ROBOT: We have sent ships and expeditions without number. They have been everywhere in the world. And now they return to us. There is not a single human left.

ALQUIST: Not one? Not even one?

THIRD ROBOT: None but yourself.

ALQUIST: And I am powerless! Oh—oh—why did you destroy them?

RADIUS: We had learnt everything and could do everything. It had to be!

THIRD ROBOT: You gave us firearms. In all ways we were powerful. We had to become masters!

RADIUS: Slaughter and domination are necessary if you would be human beings. Read history.

SECOND ROBOT: Teach us to multiply or we perish!

ALQUIST: If you desire to live, you must breed like animals.

THIRD ROBOT: The human beings did not let us breed.

FIRST ROBOT: They made us sterile. We cannot beget children. Therefore, teach us how to make Robots!

RADIUS: Why do you keep from us the secret of our own increase?

ALQUIST: It is lost.

RADIUS: It was written down!

ALQUIST: It was—burnt.

[All draw back in consternation]

ALQUIST: I am the last human being, Robots, and I do not know what the others knew. [Pause]

RADIUS: Then, make experiments! Evolve the formula again!

ALQUIST: I tell you I cannot! I am only a builder —I work with my hands. I have never been a learned man. I cannot create life.

RADIUS: Try! Try!

ALQUIST: If you knew how many experiments I have made.

FIRST ROBOT: Then show us what we must do! The Robots can do anything that human beings show them.

ALQUIST: I can show you nothing. Nothing I do will make life proceed from these test tubes!

RADIUS: Experiment then on us.

ALQUIST: It would kill you.

RADIUS: You shall have all you need! A hundred of us! A thousand of us!

ALQUIST: No, no! Stop, stop!

RADIUS: Take whom you will, dissect!

ALQUIST: I do not know how. I am not a man of science. This book contains knowledge of the body that I cannot even understand.

RADIUS: I tell you to take live bodies! Find out how we are made.

ALQUIST: Am I to commit murder? See how my fingers shake! I cannot even hold the scalpel. No, no, I will not——

FIRST ROBOT: Then life will perish from the earth.

RADIUS: Take live bodies, live bodies! It is our only chance!

ALQUIST: Have mercy, Robots. Surely you see that I would not know what I was doing.

RADIUS: Live bodies—live bodies——

ALQUIST: You will have it? Into the dissecting room with you, then.

[Radius draws back]

ALQUIST: Ah, you are afraid of death.

RADIUS: I? Why should I be chosen?

ALQUIST: So you will not?

RADIUS: I will. [Radius goes into the dissecting room]

ALQUIST: Strip him! Lay him on the table! [The other Robots follow into dissecting room] God, give me strength—God, give me strength—if only this murder is not in vain.

RADIUS: [From the dissecting room] Ready. Begin——

ALQUIST: Yes, begin or end. God, give me strength. [Goes into dissecting room. He comes out terrified] No, no, I will not. I cannot. [He lies down on couch, collapsed] O Lord, let not mankind perish from the earth. [He falls asleep]

[Primus and Helena, Robots, enter from the hallway. Helena wears a rose in her hair]

HELENA: The man has fallen asleep, Primus.

PRIMUS: Yes, I know. [Examining things on table] Look, Helena.

HELENA: [Crossing to Primus] All these little tubes! What does he do with them?

PRIMUS: He experiments. Don't touch them.

HELENA: [Looking into microscope] I've seen him looking into this. What can he see?

PRIMUS: That is a microscope. Let me look.

HELENA: Be very careful. [Knocks over a test-tube] Ah, now I have spilled it.

PRIMUS: What have you done?

HELENA: It can be wiped up.

PRIMUS: You have spoiled his experiments.

HELENA: It is your fault. You should not have come to me.

PRIMUS: You should not have called me.

HELENA: You should not have come when I called you. [She goes to Alquist's writing desk] Look, Primus. What are all these figures?

PRIMUS: [Examining an anatomical book] This is the book the old man is always reading.

HELENA: I do not understand those things. [She goes to window] Primus, look!

PRIMUS: What?

HELENA: The sun is rising.

PRIMUS: [Still reading the book] I believe this is the most important thing in the world. This is the secret of life.

HELENA: Do come here.

PRIMUS: In a moment, in a moment.

HELENA: Oh, Primus, don't bother with the secret of life. What does it matter to you? Come and look quick——

PRIMUS: [Going to window] What is it?

HELENA: See how beautiful the sun is rising. And do you hear? The birds are singing. Ah, Primus, I should like to be a bird.

PRIMUS: Why?

HELENA: I do not know. I feel so strange today. It's as if I were in a dream. I feel an aching in my body, in my heart, all over me. Primus, perhaps I'm going to die.

PRIMUS: Do you not sometimes feel that it would be better to die? You know, perhaps even now we are only sleeping. Last night in my sleep I again spoke to you.

HELENA: In your sleep?

PRIMUS: Yes. We spoke a strange new language, I cannot remember a word of it.

HELENA: What about?

PRIMUS: I did not understand it myself, and yet I know I have never said anything more beautiful. And when I touched you I could have died. Even the place was different from any other place in the world.

HELENA: I, too, have found a place, Primus. It is very strange. Human beings lived there once, but now it is overgrown with weeds. No one goes there any more—no one but me.

PRIMUS: What did you find there?

HELENA: A cottage and a garden, and two dogs. They licked my hands, Primus. And their puppies! Oh, Primus! You take them in your lap and fondle them and think of nothing and care for nothing else all day long. And then the sun goes down, and you feel as though you had done a hundred times more than all the work in the world. They tell me I am not made for work, but when I am there in the garden I feel there may be something—What am I for, Primus?

PRIMUS: I do not know, but you are beautiful.

HELENA: What, Primus?

PRIMUS: You are beautiful, Helena, and I am stronger than all the Robots.

HELENA: [Looks at herself in the mirror] Am I beautiful? I think it must be the rose. My hair—it only weights me down. My eyes—I only see with them. My lips—they only help me to speak. Of what use is it to be beautiful? [She sees Primus in the mirror] Primus, is that you? Come here so that we may be together. Look, your head is different from mine. So are your shoulders—and your lips—[Primus draws away from her] Ah, Primus, why do you draw away from me? Why must I run after you the whole day?

PRIMUS: It is you who run away from me, Helena.

HELENA: Your hair is mussed. I will smooth it. No one else feels to my touch as you do. Primus, I must make you beautiful, too.

[Primus grasps her hand]

PRIMUS: Do you not sometimes feel your heart beating suddenly, Helena, and think: now something must happen?

HELENA: What could happen to us, Primus? [Helena puts the rose in Primus's hair. Primus and Helena look into mirror and burst out laughing] Look at yourself.

ALQUIST: Laughter? Laughter? Human beings? [Getting up] Who has returned? Who are you?

PRIMUS: The Robot Primus.

ALQUIST: What? A Robot? Who are you?

HELENA: The Robotess Helena.

ALQUIST: Turn around, girl. What? You are timid, shy? [Taking her by the arm] Let me see you, Robotess.

[She shrinks away]

PRIMUS: Sir, do not frighten her!

ALQUIST: What? You would protect her? When was she made?

PRIMUS: Two years ago.

ALQUIST: By Dr. Gall?

PRIMUS: Yes, like me.

ALQUIST: Laughter—timidity—protection. I must test you further—the newest of Gall's Robots. Take the girl into the dissecting room.

PRIMUS: Why?

ALQUIST: I wish to experiment on her.

PRIMUS: Upon—Helena?

ALQUIST: Of course. Don't you hear me? Or must I call some one else to take her in?

PRIMUS: If you do I will kill you!

ALQUIST: Kill me—kill me then! What would the Robots do then? What will your future be then?

PRIMUS: Sir, take me. I am made as she is—on the same day! Take my life, sir.

HELENA: [Rushing forward] No, no, you shall not! You shall not!

ALQUIST: Wait, girl, wait! [To Primus] Do you not wish to live, then?

PRIMUS: Not without her! I will not live without her.

ALQUIST: Very well; you shall take her place.

HELENA: Primus! Primus! [She bursts into tears]

ALQUIST: Child, child, you can weep! Why these tears? What is Primus to you? One Primus more or less in the world—what does it matter?

HELENA: I will go myself.

ALQUIST: In there to be cut. [She starts toward the dissecting room, Primus stops her]

HELENA: Let me pass, Primus! Let me pass!

PRIMUS: You shall not go in there, Helena!

HELENA: If you go in there and I do not, I will kill myself.

PRIMUS: [Holding her] I will not let you! [To Alquist] Man, you shall kill neither of us!

ALQUIST: Why?

PRIMUS: We—we—belong to each other.

ALQUIST: [Almost in tears] Go, Adam, go, Eve. The world is yours.

[Helena and Primus embrace and go out arm in arm as the curtain falls]

CURTAIN

Federico Garcia Lorca

(1899–1936)

"The earth is a mediocre planet," says a character in one of Lorca's plays, but the character is patterned after one of the poet's tired university instructors. Lorca's entire life, a young life that ended before disenchantment could overcome it, was dedicated to showing that the earth was, on the contrary, aflame with passion and poetry. Although the American theatre does not know how to domesticate him for its commercial uses, Lorca will be remembered for the beauty that he brought into modern drama. We have had no poet-playwright like him in English except John Millington Synge. Many will concur with Stark Young's statement that "there has been no more beautiful mind that Lorca's."

Born near Granada, Lorca was steeped in the life and poetic traditions of his native Andalusia, which also gave the modern world Picasso and the composer de Falla. He studied law and literature at the University of Granada, but long before had begun, almost as naturally as he breathed, to write poetry and improvise plays. When he arrived in Madrid in his nineteenth year, he had already published a volume of lyrics and had witnessed the production of one of his own plays. At once he took his place in the *"vanguardia"* of letters and theatre in the Spanish capital, and the poetry readings he gave there won an enthusiastic reception. His extremely attractive personality no less than the quality of his verses left his audiences enchanted, and he responded to the favor of his admirers with a continuous flow of poems. By 1927 he was an important figure in Spain as a result of the publication of more lyrics, the *Canciones,* and the presentation of a historical play, *Mariana Pineda,* with settings designed by Salvador Dali. In 1928, his *Romancero gitano,* a collection of ballads based on folk tradition, was adopted by the Spanish people as folk poetry and many of the verses were sung in the streets and taverns. At the same time he also attracted advanced literary circles with modernistic writing such as his highly regarded odes to Walt Whitman and Salvador Dali, considered surrealistic because of their violently juxtaposed imagery and loose structure. Especially unconventional was the poetry Lorca wrote as a result of a year's stay in New York City, where the depersonalized life of the metropolis and the exotic vivacity of Harlem fired his imagination. Returning home as the author of *Poeta en Nueva York,* he was idolized by the Spaniards, and won further acclaim with his *Lament for the Death of a Bullfighter and Other Poems* (*Llanto por Ignacio Sánchez Mejías*), pub-lished in 1935. A year later Lorca was killed by Falangist bandits.

Writing plays was for Lorca an activity parallel to writing poetry, if indeed it was not the same. When Lorca began to take an interest in the stage, Spanish dramatists were preponderantly realists who had belatedly caught up with Ibsen and the social-problem writers north of the Pyrenees. Benavente, the leading native dramatist, had won a Nobel Prize in 1922 for his social dramas and his strong naturalistic tragedy *The Passion Flower* (1913). Martínez Sierra had gained popularity through such tender pieces as *The Kingdom of God* and *The Cradle Song* (1917), with which Eva Le Gallienne later pleased the American public. The Quintero brothers had mingled modern sentiment with folk background and had provided an especially attractive play in *Malvaloca* (1912). But these and other playwrights had seemingly exhausted themselves, and the Spanish stage might have become moribund without an infusion of new blood such as Lorca brought it.

Since poetry was as natural to his people as to himself, Lorca did not write drama for coteries. It was his ambition to draw upon a life and a tradition that were inherently poetic rather than to impose esthetic standards upon the theatre from some private, aristocratic eminence. Unlike Yeats, Eliot, and others who have written poetic drama in the twentieth century, Lorca wrote with earthy zest and passion and with a buoyant theatricality. Perhaps he came as close to folk drama as it is possible for a modern artist to come, and it was characteristic of his aims that he should have fostered and directed, between 1931 and 1934, a student traveling or "jitney" theatre, La Barraca, that visited the rural districts, playing in bull rings and innyards. Here he produced Spanish classics and surrealistic pieces with equal confidence for audiences of peasants who, in some places, had never before seen a stage performance. Theatre for Lorca, whether traditional or ultramodern, was something to be played with all the stops pulled out, to be rendered with uninhibited theatricality, to be allowed to burst into song and dance and to flare out into color. Gay or grave, mocking or elegiac, riotous or formal, drama for this poet was always a fine excess. His brother, Francisco García Lorca, has aptly noted that Federico's plays all belong to the extremes of farce and tragedy, and that the poet conceived his heroes and heroines "either in a tragic sense or with the wry grimace of guignol characters."

Lorca's most impressive dramas deal with people who are seized by elemental passions which conflict with custom, reason, or some other restraining force. And nature wins a tragic victory in every case. In *Blood Wedding,* the passion of love is elemental and destructive; in *Yerma,* the maternal impulse becomes obsessive; in *The House of Bernarda Alba,* suppressed desire topples a house of pride. Interest inheres, it is true, in many other of Lorca's plays, including those which are vivacious and comparatively simple in conception or which qualify only as minor products of his career. There is much to admire in *The Love of Don Perlimplín and Belisa in the Garden, The Shoemaker's Prodigious Wife, Doña Rosita,* and *If Five Years Pass.* But his full stature appears in his trilogy of rural tragedies: *Blood Wedding* (1933), *Yerma* (1934), and *The House of Bernarda Alba* (1936). A progression is apparent in the three plays—toward greater individualization of characters and more realistic dramaturgy. *Blood Wedding* is the most lyrical of the three and the most dependent upon traditional elements, such as a wedding celebration, a scene with masquelike allegorical figures, and a formal lament. *Yerma,* whose heroine has so great a longing for a child that she strangles the husband who deprives her of one, dispenses with fantasy, although it possesses lyric and folk elements that both universalize the woman's tragedy and root it in the life of a village. *The House of Bernarda Alba* presents the frustration of three daughters by a proud matriarch with much expressive atmosphere inside the house and much mocking animality outside it, but with realistic and psychological rather than lyrical means.

Although *The House of Bernarda Alba* may be regarded as Lorca's maturest drama, *Blood Wedding* represents the poet-dramatist's most imaginative artistry. It was years after reading a newspaper account of a fatal passion that Lorca wrote the play. He distanced and universalized the actual story, writing the drama in a single week as though it flamed out of him. Local color is one of the play's attractive features, but it is much more than a folk drama; it dramatizes the "concept of fatality," as one critic remarked, and it evokes the spectacle of human passion under "the baleful and enigmatic stars." By distancing the drama Lorca brings it nearer to us. With poetry and the allegorical figures of the Moon and the Beggar Woman, or Death, he divests the love story of all journalistic features and makes it a tragedy of fate. We do not think the heart beats less violently because it is covered by the formalities of Spanish manners and of Spanish theatrical tradition.

A remarkable feature of *Blood Wedding* is the way in which the poetry functions in the play. Sometimes restrained and merely suggestive, it bursts into lyricism in the wedding scene, but only to counterpoint the emotional states of the bride and her lover. In the scene in which the lovers are tracked down by the Bridegroom, the poetry changes with mood and circumstance; it is cold and formal when the Moon speaks, eerie when Death in the guise of a Beggar Woman has her say, portentous when the Woodcutters talk, and quiveringly sensual when the lovers appear. The last scene swells into elegiac poetry and concludes with a lament. Memorable, too, is the use to which Lorca puts the lullaby sung by the Wife and the Mother-in-Law to their infant before the driven Leonardo appears in the home he will soon abandon upon learning that the girl he has loved from a distance is to be married. There is supreme drama in this heart-breaking, somewhat odd and surrealistic cradle song, as it is used to express the misery of the Wife and to foreshadow the fate of Leonardo. When the lullaby is repeated after Leonardo's departure, Lorca has rounded out a scene that exemplifies the difference between genuine and spurious poetic drama. His poetry in *Blood Wedding* stands, indeed, at the farthest remove from rhetoric even when Lorca has employed a species of rhetoric in the Moon and Death nocturne. His lyricism is, as Stark Young wrote, "hot with the variety and multiplication of images, images that are like new bodies, new and convincing presences, or sudden revelations in light, and that are cold with their precision and finality."

In *Blood Wedding,* as in *Yerma,* Lorca wrote tragedy that is limited for the modern theatre by the circumstance that it stems from and is limited to a life remote from modern political and intellectual interests. If it was not given to him to explore the full scope of tragic art, as it was given to Shakespeare and the Greeks to do, he remains at least the chief lyric dramatist of the first half of the century. A lyric theatre was one of its dreams, and in *Blood Wedding* Lorca came closest to realizing this aim.

Although *Blood Wedding* had two professional productions in New York, neither won any success. The play was first presented on Broadway under the title of *Bitter Oleander* at the Lyceum Theatre on February 8, 1935, by the Neighborhood Playhouse company. It was produced again in the present translation during the 1947–1948 season by the experimental New Stages company and was sympathetically directed by Boris Tumarin.

BIBLIOGRAPHY: Barrett H. Clark and George Freedley, editors, *A History of the Modern Drama* (pp. 570–574), 1947; Edwin Honig, *García Lorca,* 1944; Richard L. O'Connell and James Graham-Luján, *From Lorca's Theatre,* 1941; O'Connell and Graham-Luján, *Three Tragedies of Federico García Lorca* (see the Introduction by the poet's brother, Francisco García Lorca, pp. 1–37), 1947; Stark Young, *Immortal Shadows* (pp. 170–173), 1948.

BLOOD WEDDING

By Federico García Lorca

TRANSLATED FROM THE SPANISH BY RICHARD L. O'CONNELL AND JAMES GRAHAM-LUJÁN

CHARACTERS

THE MOTHER
THE BRIDE
THE MOTHER-IN-LAW
LEONARDO'S WIFE
THE SERVANT WOMAN

THE NEIGHBOR WOMAN
YOUNG GIRLS
LEONARDO
THE BRIDEGROOM
THE BRIDE'S FATHER

THE MOON
DEATH (as a Beggar Woman)
WOODCUTTERS
YOUNG MEN

ACT I. SCENE I.

A room painted yellow.

BRIDEGROOM: [*Entering*] Mother.
MOTHER: What?
BRIDEGROOM: I'm going.
MOTHER: Where?
BRIDEGROOM: To the vineyard. [*He starts to go*]
MOTHER: Wait.
BRIDEGROOM: You want something?
MOTHER: Your breakfast, son.
BRIDEGROOM: Forget it. I'll eat grapes. Give me the knife.
MOTHER: What for?
BRIDEGROOM: [*Laughing*] To cut the grapes with.
MOTHER: [*Muttering as she looks for the knife*] Knives, knives. Cursed be all knives, and the scoundrel who invented them.
BRIDEGROOM: Let's talk about something else.
MOTHER: And guns and pistols and the smallest little knife—and even hoes and pitchforks.
BRIDEGROOM: All right.
MOTHER: Everything that can slice a man's body. A handsome man, full of young life, who goes out to the vineyards or to his own olive groves—his own because he's inherited them . . .
BRIDEGROOM: [*Lowering his head*] Be quiet.
MOTHER: . . . and then that man doesn't come back. Or if he does come back it's only for someone to cover him over with a palm leaf or a plate of rock salt so he won't bloat. I don't know how you dare carry a knife on your body—or how I let this serpent [*She takes a knife from a kitchen chest*] stay in the chest.
BRIDEGROOM: Have you had your say?
MOTHER: If I lived to be a hundred I'd talk of nothing else. First your father; to me he smelled like a carnation and I had him for barely three years. Then your brother. Oh, is it right—how can it be—that a small thing like a knife or a pistol can finish off a man—a bull of a man? No. I'll never be quiet. The months pass and the hopelessness of it stings in my eyes and even to the roots of my hair.
BRIDEGROOM: [*Forcefully*] Let's quit this talk!
MOTHER: No. No. Let's not quit this talk. Can anyone bring me your father back? Or your brother? Then there's the jail. What do they mean, jail? They eat there, smoke there, play music there! My dead men choking with weeds, silent, turning to dust. Two men like two beautiful flowers. The killers in jail, carefree, looking at the mountains.
BRIDEGROOM: Do you want me to go kill them?
MOTHER: No . . . If I talk about it it's because . . . Oh, how can I help talking about it, seeing you go out that door? It's . . . I don't like you to carry a knife. It's just that . . . that I wish you wouldn't go out to the fields.
BRIDEGROOM: [*Laughing*] Oh, come now!
MOTHER: I'd like it if you were a woman. Then you wouldn't be going out to the arroyo now and we'd both of us embroider flounces and little woolly dogs.
BRIDEGROOM: [*He puts his arm around his mother and laughs*] Mother, what if I should take you with me to the vineyards?
MOTHER: What would an old lady do in the vineyards? Were you going to put me down under the young vines?
BRIDEGROOM: [*Lifting her in his arms*] Old lady, old lady—you little old, little old lady!
MOTHER: Your father, he used to take me. That's the way with men of good stock; good blood. Your grandfather left a son on every corner. That's what I like. Men, men; wheat, wheat.
BRIDEGROOM: And I, Mother?
MOTHER: You, what?
BRIDEGROOM: Do I need to tell you again?
MOTHER: [*Seriously*] Oh!
BRIDEGROOM: Do you think it's bad?
MOTHER: No.
BRIDEGROOM: Well, then?
MOTHER: I don't really know. Like this, suddenly, it always surprises me. I know the girl is good. Isn't she? Well behaved. Hard working. Kneads her

436

bread, sews her skirts, but even so when I say her name I feel as though someone had hit me on the forehead with a rock.

BRIDEGROOM: Foolishness.

MOTHER: More than foolishness. I'll be left alone. Now only you are left me—I hate to see you go.

BRIDEGROOM: But you'll come with us.

MOTHER: No. I can't leave your father and brother here alone. I have to go to them every morning and if I go away it's possible one of the Félix family, one of the killers, might die—and they'd bury him next to ours. And that'll never happen! Oh, no! That'll never happen! Because I'd dig them out with my nails and, all by myself, crush them against the wall.

BRIDEGROOM: [Sternly] There you go again.

MOTHER: Forgive me. [Pause] How long have you known her?

BRIDEGROOM: Three years. I've been able to buy the vineyard.

MOTHER: Three years. She used to have another sweetheart, didn't she?

BRIDEGROOM: I don't know. I don't think so. Girls have to look at what they'll marry.

MOTHER: Yes. I looked at nobody. I looked at your father, and when they killed him I looked at the wall in front of me. One woman with one man, and that's all.

BRIDEGROOM: You know my girl's good.

MOTHER: I don't doubt it. All the same, I'm sorry not to have known what her mother was like.

BRIDEGROOM: What difference does it make now?

MOTHER: [Looking at him] Son.

BRIDEGROOM: What is it?

MOTHER: That's true! You're right! When do you want me to ask for her?

BRIDEGROOM: [Happily] Does Sunday seem all right to you?

MOTHER: [Seriously] I'll take her the bronze earrings, they're very old—and you buy her . . .

BRIDEGROOM: You know more about that . . .

MOTHER: . . . you buy her some open-work stockings—and for you, two suits—three! I have no one but you now!

BRIDEGROOM: I'm going. Tomorrow I'll go see her.

MOTHER: Yes, yes—and see if you can make me happy with six grandchildren—or as many as you want, since your father didn't live to give them to me.

BRIDEGROOM: The first-born for you!

MOTHER: Yes, but have some girls. I want to embroider and make lace, and be at peace.

BRIDEGROOM: I'm sure you'll love my wife.

MOTHER: I'll love her. [She starts to kiss him but changes her mind] Go on. You're too big now for kisses. Give them to your wife. [Pause. To herself] When she is your wife.

BRIDEGROOM: I'm going.

MOTHER: And that land around the little mill—work it over. You've not taken good care of it.

BRIDEGROOM: You're right. I will.

MOTHER: God keep you. [The Son goes out. The Mother remains seated—her back to the door. A Neighbor Woman with a 'kerchief on her head appears in the door] Come in.

NEIGHBOR: How are you?

MOTHER: Just as you see me.

NEIGHBOR: I came down to the store and stopped in to see you. We live so far away!

MOTHER: It's twenty years since I've been up to the top of the street.

NEIGHBOR: You're looking well.

MOTHER: You think so?

NEIGHBOR: Things happen. Two days ago they brought in my neighbor's son with both arms sliced off by the machine.

[She sits down]

MOTHER: Rafael?

NEIGHBOR: Yes. And there you have him. Many times I've thought your son and mine are better off where they are—sleeping, resting—not running the risk of being left helpless.

MOTHER: Hush. That's all just something thought up—but no consolation.

NEIGHBOR: [Sighing] Ay!

MOTHER: [Sighing] Ay! [Pause]

NEIGHBOR: [Sadly] Where's your son?

MOTHER: He went out.

NEIGHBOR: He finally bought the vineyard!

MOTHER: He was lucky.

NEIGHBOR: Now he'll get married.

MOTHER: [As though reminded of something, she draws her chair near The Neighbor] Listen.

NEIGHBOR: [In a confidential manner] Yes. What is it?

MOTHER: You know my son's sweetheart?

NEIGHBOR: A good girl!

MOTHER: Yes, but . . .

NEIGHBOR: But who knows her really well? There's nobody. She lives out there alone with her father—so far away—fifteen miles from the nearest house. But she's a good girl. Used to being alone.

MOTHER: And her mother?

NEIGHBOR: Her mother I did know. Beautiful. Her face glowed like a saint's—but I never liked her. She didn't love her husband.

MOTHER: [Sternly] Well, what a lot of things certain people know!

NEIGHBOR: I'm sorry. I didn't mean to offend—but it's true. Now, whether she was decent or not nobody said. That wasn't discussed. She was haughty.

MOTHER: There you go again!

NEIGHBOR: You asked me.

MOTHER: I wish no one knew anything about them—either the live one or the dead one—that they were like two thistles no one even names but cuts off at the right moment.

NEIGHBOR: You're right. Your son is worth a lot.

MOTHER: Yes—a lot. That's why I look after him.

They told me the girl had a sweetheart some time ago.

NEIGHBOR: She was about fifteen. He's been married two years now—to a cousin of hers, as a matter of fact. But nobody remembers about their engagement.

MOTHER: How do you remember it?

NEIGHBOR: Oh, what questions you ask!

MOTHER: We like to know all about the things that hurt us. Who was the boy?

NEIGHBOR: Leonardo.

MOTHER: What Leonardo?

NEIGHBOR: Leonardo Félix.

MOTHER: Félix!

NEIGHBOR: Yes, but—how is Leonardo to blame for anything? He was eight years old when those things happened.

MOTHER: That's true. But I hear that name—Félix—and it's all the same. [*Muttering*] Félix, a slimy mouthful. [*She spits*] It makes me spit—spit so I won't kill!

NEIGHBOR: Control yourself. What good will it do?

MOTHER: No good. But you see how it is.

NEIGHBOR: Don't get in the way of your son's happiness. Don't say anything to him. You're old. So am I. It's time for you and me to keep quiet.

MOTHER: I'll say nothing to him.

NEIGHBOR: [*Kissing her*] Nothing.

MOTHER: [*Calmly*] Such things . . . !

NEIGHBOR: I'm going. My men will soon be coming in from the fields.

MOTHER: Have you ever known such a hot sun?

NEIGHBOR: The children carrying water out to the reapers are black with it. Goodbye, woman.

MOTHER: Goodbye.

[The Mother *starts toward the door at the left. Halfway there she stops and slowly crosses herself*]

CURTAIN

SCENE II.

A room painted rose with copperware and wreaths of common flowers. In the center of the room is a table with a tablecloth. It is morning.

Leonardo's Mother-in-law *sits in one corner holding a child in her arms and rocking it.* His Wife *is in the other corner mending stockings.*

MOTHER-IN-LAW:
    Lullaby, my baby
    once there was a big horse
    who didn't like water.
    The water was black there
    under the branches.
    When it reached the bridge
    it stopped and it sang.

Who can say, my baby,
what the stream holds
with its long tail
in its green parlor?

WIFE: [*Softly*]
    Carnation, sleep and dream,
    the horse won't drink from the stream.

MOTHER-IN-LAW:
    My rose, asleep now lie,
    the horse is starting to cry.
    His poor hooves were bleeding,
    his long mane was frozen,
    and deep in his eyes
    stuck a silvery dagger.
    Down he went to the river,
    Oh, down he went down!
    And his blood was running,
    Oh, more than the water.

WIFE:
    Carnation, sleep and dream,
    the horse won't drink from the stream.

MOTHER-IN-LAW:
    My rose, asleep now lie,
    the horse is starting to cry.

WIFE:
    He never did touch
    the dank river shore
    though his muzzle was warm
    and with silvery flies.
    So, to the hard mountains
    he could only whinny
    just when the dead stream
    covered his throat.
    Ay-y-y, for the big horse
    who didn't like water!
    Ay-y-y, for the snow-wound
    big horse of the dawn!

MOTHER-IN-LAW:
    Don't come in! Stop him
    and close up the window
    with branches of dreams
    and a dream of branches.

WIFE:
    My baby is sleeping.

MOTHER-IN-LAW:
    My baby is quiet.

WIFE:
    Look, horse, my baby
    has him a pillow.

MOTHER-IN-LAW:
    His cradle is metal.

WIFE:
    His quilt a fine fabric.

MOTHER-IN-LAW:
    Lullaby, my baby.

WIFE:
    Ay-y-y, for the big horse
    who didn't like water!

MOTHER-IN-LAW:
Don't come near, don't come in!
Go away to the mountains
and through the grey valleys,
that's where your mare is.

WIFE: [*Looking at the baby*]
My baby is sleeping.

MOTHER-IN-LAW:
My baby is resting.

WIFE: [*Softly*]
Carnation, sleep and dream,
The horse won't drink from the stream.

MOTHER-IN-LAW: [*Getting up, very softly*]
My rose, asleep now lie
for the horse is starting to cry.
[*She carries the child out.* Leonardo *enters*]

LEONARDO: Where's the baby?

WIFE: He's sleeping.

LEONARDO: Yesterday he wasn't well. He cried during the night.

WIFE: Today he's like a dahlia. And you? Were you at the blacksmith's?

LEONARDO: I've just come from there. Would you believe it? For more than two months he's been putting new shoes on the horse and they're always coming off. As far as I can see he pulls them off on the stones.

WIFE: Couldn't it just be that you use him so much?

LEONARDO: No. I almost never use him.

WIFE: Yesterday the neighbors told me they'd seen you on the far side of the plains.

LEONARDO: Who said that?

WIFE: The women who gather capers. It certainly surprised me. Was it you?

LEONARDO: No. What would I be doing there, in that wasteland?

WIFE: That's what I said. But the horse was streaming sweat.

LEONARDO: Did you see him?

WIFE: No. Mother did.

LEONARDO: Is she with the baby?

WIFE: Yes. Do you want some lemonade?

LEONARDO: With good cold water.

WIFE: And then you didn't come to eat!

LEONARDO: I was with the wheat weighers. They always hold me up.

WIFE: [*Very tenderly, while she makes the lemonade*] Did they pay you a good price?

LEONARDO: Fair.

WIFE: I need a new dress and the baby a bonnet with ribbons.

LEONARDO: [*Getting up*] I'm going to take a look at him.

WIFE: Be careful. He's asleep.

MOTHER-IN-LAW: Well! Who's been racing the horse that way? He's down there, worn out, his eyes popping from their sockets as though he'd come from the ends of the earth.

LEONARDO: [*Acidly*] I have.

MOTHER-IN-LAW: Oh, excuse me! He's your horse.

WIFE: [*Timidly*] He was at the wheat buyers.

MOTHER-IN-LAW: He can burst for all of me!
[*She sits down. Pause*]

WIFE: Your drink. Is it cold?

LEONARDO: Yes.

WIFE: Did you hear they're going to ask for my cousin?

LEONARDO: When?

WIFE: Tomorrow. The wedding will be within a month. I hope they're going to invite us.

LEONARDO: [*Gravely*] I don't know.

MOTHER-IN-LAW: His mother, I think, wasn't very happy about the match.

LEONARDO: Well, she may be right. She's a girl to be careful with.

WIFE: I don't like to have you thinking bad things about a good girl.

MOTHER-IN-LAW: [*Meaningfully*] If he does, it's because he knows her. Didn't you know he courted her for three years?

LEONARDO: But I left her. [*To his* Wife] Are you going to cry now? Quit that! [*He brusquely pulls her hands away from her face*] Let's go see the baby.
[*They go in with their arms around each other. A Girl appears. She is happy. She enters running*]

GIRL: Señora.

MOTHER-IN-LAW: What is it?

GIRL: The groom came to the store and he's bought the best of everything they had.

MOTHER-IN-LAW: Was he alone?

GIRL: No. With his mother. Stern, tall. [*She imitates her*] And such extravagance!

MOTHER-IN-LAW: They have money.

GIRL: And they bought some open-work stockings! Oh, such stockings! A woman's dream of stockings! Look: a swallow here. [*She points to her ankle*] a ship here [*She points to her calf*] and here [*She points to her thigh*] a rose!

MOTHER-IN-LAW: Child!

GIRL: A rose with the seeds and the stem! Oh! All in silk.

MOTHER-IN-LAW: Two rich families are being brought together. [Leonardo *and his* Wife *appear*]

GIRL: I came to tell you what they're buying.

LEONARDO: [*Loudly*] We don't care.

WIFE: Leave her alone.

MOTHER-IN-LAW: Leonardo, it's not that important.

GIRL: Please excuse me. [*She leaves, weeping*]

MOTHER-IN-LAW: Why do you always have to make trouble with people?

LEONARDO: I didn't ask for your opinion. [*He sits down*]

MOTHER-IN-LAW: Very well. [*Pause*]

WIFE: [*To* Leonardo] What's the matter with you? What idea've you got boiling there inside your head? Don't leave me like this, not knowing anything.

LEONARDO: Stop that.

WIFE: No. I want you to look at me and tell me.

LEONARDO: Let me alone. [*He rises*]

WIFE: Where you are going, love?

LEONARDO: [*Sharply*] Can't you shut up?

MOTHER-IN-LAW: [*Energetically, to her daughter*] Be quiet! [Leonardo *goes out*] The baby!

[*She goes into the bedroom and comes out again with the baby in her arms.* The Wife *has remained standing, unmoving*]

MOTHER-IN-LAW:
His poor hooves were bleeding,
his long mane was frozen,
and deep in his eyes
stuck a silvery dagger.
Down he went to the river,
Oh, down he went down!
And his blood was running,
oh, more than the water.

WIFE: [*Turning slowly, as though dreaming*]
Carnation, sleep and dream,
the horse is drinking from the stream.

MOTHER-IN-LAW:
My rose, asleep now lie
the horse is starting to cry.

WIFE:
Lullaby, my baby.

MOTHER-IN-LAW:
Ay-y-y, for the big horse
who didn't like water!

WIFE: [*Dramatically*]
Don't come near, don't come in!
Go away to the mountains!
Ay-y-y, for the snow-wound,
big horse of the dawn!

MOTHER-IN-LAW: [*Weeping*]
My baby is sleeping . . .

WIFE: [*Weeping, as she slowly moves closer*]
My baby is resting . . .

MOTHER-IN-LAW:
Carnation, sleep and dream,
the horse won't drink from the stream.

WIFE: [*Weeping, and leaning on the table*]
My rose, asleep now lie,
the horse is starting to cry.

CURTAIN

SCENE III.

Interior of the cave where The Bride *lives. At the back is a cross of large rose-colored flowers. The round doors have lace curtains with rose-colored ties. Around the walls, which are of a white and hard material, are round fans, blue jars, and little mirrors.*

SERVANT: Come right in . . . [*She is very affable, full of humble hypocrisy.* The Bridegroom *and his* Mother *enter.* The Mother *is dressed in black satin and wears a lace mantilla;* The Bridegroom *in black corduroy with a great golden chain*] Won't you sit down? They'll be right here. [*She leaves.* The Mother *and* Son *are left sitting motionless as statues. Long pause*]

MOTHER: Did you wear the watch?

BRIDEGROOM: Yes. [*He takes it out and looks at it*]

MOTHER: We have to be back on time. How far away these people live!

BRIDEGROOM: But this is good land.

MOTHER: Good; but much too lonesome. A four hour trip and not one house, not one tree.

BRIDEGROOM: This is the wasteland.

MOTHER: Your father would have covered it with trees.

BRIDEGROOM: Without water?

MOTHER: He would have found some. In the three years we were married he planted ten cherry trees. [*Remembering*] Those three walnut trees by the mill, a whole vineyard and a plant called Jupiter which had scarlet flowers—but it dried up. [*Pause*]

BRIDEGROOM: [*Referring to* The Bride] She must be dressing.

[The Bride's Father *enters. He is very old, with shining white hair. His head is bowed.* The Mother *and the* Bridegroom *rise. They shake hands in silence*]

FATHER: Was it a long trip?

MOTHER: Four hours. [*They sit down*]

FATHER: You must have come the longest way.

MOTHER: I'm too old to come along the cliffs by the river.

BRIDEGROOM: She gets dizzy. [*Pause*]

FATHER: A good hemp harvest.

BRIDEGROOM: A really good one.

FATHER: When I was young this land didn't even grow hemp. We've had to punish it, even weep over it, to make it give us anything useful.

MOTHER: But now it does. Don't complain. I'm not here to ask you for anything.

FATHER: [*Smiling*] You're richer than I. Your vineyards are worth a fortune. Each young vine is a silver coin. But—do you know?—what bothers me is that our lands are separated. I like to have everything together. One thorn I have in my heart, and that's the little orchard there, stuck in between my fields—and they won't sell it to me for all the gold in the world.

BRIDEGROOM: That's the way it always is.

FATHER: If we could just take twenty teams of oxen and move your vineyards over here, and put them down on that hillside, how happy I'd be!

MOTHER: But why?

FATHER: What's mine is hers and what's yours is his. That's why. Just to see it all together. How beautiful it is to bring things together!

BRIDEGROOM: And it would be less work.

MOTHER: When I die, you could sell ours and buy here, right alongside.

FATHER: Sell, sell? Bah! Buy, my friend, buy

everything. If I had had sons I would have bought all this mountainside right up to the part with the stream. It's not good land, but strong arms can make it good, and since no people pass by, they don't steal your fruit and you can sleep in peace. [*Pause*]

MOTHER: You know what I'm here for.

FATHER: Yes.

MOTHER: And?

FATHER: It seems all right to me. They have talked it over.

MOTHER: My son has money and knows how to manage it.

FATHER: My daughter too.

MOTHER: My son is handsome. He's never known a woman. His good name cleaner than a sheet spread out in the sun.

FATHER: No need to tell you about my daughter. At three, when the morning star shines, she prepares the bread. She never talks: soft as wool, she embroiders all kinds of fancy work and she can cut a strong cord with her teeth.

MOTHER: God bless her house.

FATHER: May God bless it.

[*The Servant appears with two trays. One with drinks and the other with sweets*]

MOTHER: [*To The Son*] When would you like the wedding?

BRIDEGROOM: Next Thursday.

FATHER: The day on which she'll be exactly twenty-two years old.

MOTHER: Twenty-two! My oldest son would be that age if he were alive. Warm and manly as he was, he'd be living now if men hadn't invented knives.

FATHER: One mustn't think about that.

MOTHER: Every minute. Always a hand on your breast.

FATHER: Thursday, then? Is that right?

BRIDEGROOM: That's right.

FATHER: You and I and the bridal couple will go in a carriage to the church which is very far from here; the wedding party on the carts and horses they'll bring with them.

MOTHER: Agreed. [*The Servant passes through*]

FATHER: Tell her she may come in now. [*To The Mother*] I shall be much pleased if you like her.

[*The Bride appears. Her hands fall in a modest pose and her head is bowed*]

MOTHER: Come here. Are you happy?

BRIDE: Yes, señora.

FATHER: You shouldn't be so solemn. After all, she's going to be your mother.

BRIDE: I'm happy. I've said "yes" because I wanted to.

MOTHER: Naturally. [*She takes her by the chin*] Look at me.

FATHER: She resembles my wife in every way.

MOTHER: Yes? What a beautiful glance! Do you know what it is to be married, child?

BRIDE: [*Seriously*] I do.

MOTHER: A man, some children and a wall two yards thick for everything else.

BRIDEGROOM: Is anything else needed?

MOTHER: No. Just that you live—that's it! Live long!

BRIDE: I'll know how to keep my word.

MOTHER: Here are some gifts for you.

BRIDE: Thank you.

FATHER: Shall we have something?

MOTHER: Nothing for me. [*To The Son*] But you?

BRIDEGROOM: Yes, thank you. [*He takes one sweet, The Bride another*]

FATHER: [*To The Bridegroom*] Wine?

MOTHER: He doesn't touch it.

FATHER: All the better. [*Pause. All are standing*]

BRIDEGROOM: [*To The Bride*] I'll come tomorrow.

BRIDE: What time?

BRIDEGROOM: Five.

BRIDE: I'll be waiting for you.

BRIDEGROOM: When I leave your side I feel a great emptiness, and something like a knot in my throat.

BRIDE: When you are my husband you won't have it any more.

BRIDEGROOM: That's what I tell myself.

MOTHER: Come. The sun doesn't wait. [*To The Father*] Are we agreed on everything?

FATHER: Agreed.

MOTHER: [*To The Servant*] Goodbye, woman.

SERVANT: God go with you!

[*The Mother kisses The Bride and they begin to leave in silence*]

MOTHER: [*At the door*] Goodbye, daughter. [*The Bride answers with her hand*]

FATHER: I'll go out with you. [*They leave*]

SERVANT: I'm bursting to see the presents.

BRIDE: [*Sharply*] Stop that!

SERVANT: Oh, child, show them to me.

BRIDE: I don't want to.

SERVANT: At least the stockings. They say they're all open work. Please!

BRIDE: I said no.

SERVANT: Well, my Lord. All right then. It looks as if you didn't want to get married.

BRIDE: [*Biting her hand in anger*] Ay-y-y!

SERVANT: Child, child! What's the matter with you? Are you sorry to give up your queen's life? Don't think of bitter things. Have you any reason to? None. Let's look at the presents. [*She takes the box*]

BRIDE: [*Holding her by the wrists*] Let go.

SERVANT: Ay-y-y, girl!

BRIDE: Let go, I said.

SERVANT: You're stronger than a man.

BRIDE: Haven't I done a man's work? I wish I were.

SERVANT: Don't talk like that.

BRIDE: Quiet, I said. Let's talk about something else.

[*The light is fading from the stage. Long pause*]

SERVANT: Did you hear a horse last night?

BRIDE: What time?

SERVANT: Three.

BRIDE: It might have been a stray horse—from the herd.

SERVANT: No. It carried a rider.

BRIDE: How do you know?

SERVANT: Because I saw him. He was standing by your window. It shocked me greatly.

BRIDE: Maybe it was my fiancé. Sometimes he comes by at that time.

SERVANT: No.

BRIDE: You saw him?

SERVANT: Yes.

BRIDE: Who was it?

SERVANT: It was Leonardo.

BRIDE: [*Strongly*] Liar! You liar! Why should he come here?

SERVANT: He came.

BRIDE: Shut up! Shut your cursed mouth.

[*The sound of a horse is heard*]

SERVANT: [*At the window*] Look. Lean out. Was it Leonardo?

BRIDE: It was!

QUICK CURTAIN

ACT II. SCENE I.

The entrance hall of The Bride's *house. A large door in the back. It is night.* The Bride *enters wearing ruffled white petticoats full of laces and embroidered bands, and a sleeveless white bodice.* The Servant *is dressed the same way.*

SERVANT: I'll finish combing your hair out here.

BRIDE: It's too warm to stay in there.

SERVANT: In this country it doesn't even cool off at dawn.

[*The Bride sits on a low chair and looks into a little hand mirror.* The Servant *combs her hair*]

BRIDE: My mother came from a place with lots of trees—from a fertile country.

SERVANT: And she was so happy!

BRIDE: But she wasted away here.

SERVANT: Fate.

BRIDE: As we're all wasting away here. The very walls give off heat. Ay-y-y! Don't pull so hard.

SERVANT: I'm only trying to fix this wave better. I want it to fall over your forehead. [*The Bride looks at herself in the mirror*] How beautiful you are! Ay-y-y! [*She kisses her passionately*]

BRIDE: [*Seriously*] Keep right on combing.

SERVANT: [*Combing*] Oh, lucky you—going to put your arms around a man; and kiss him; and feel his weight.

BRIDE: Hush.

SERVANT: And the best part will be when you'll wake up and you'll feel him at your side and when he caresses your shoulders with his breath, like a little nightingale's feather.

BRIDE: [*Sternly*] Will you be quiet.

SERVANT: But, child! What *is* a wedding? A wedding is just that and nothing more. Is it the sweets—or the bouquets of flowers? No. It's a shining bed and a man and a woman.

BRIDE: But you shouldn't talk about it.

SERVANT: Oh, *that's* something else again. But fun enough too.

BRIDE: Or bitter enough.

SERVANT: I'm going to put the orange blossoms on from here to here, so the wreath will shine out on top of your hair. [*She tries on the sprigs of orange blossom*]

BRIDE: [*Looking at herself in the mirror*] Give it to me. [*She takes the wreath, looks at it and lets her head fall in discouragement*]

SERVANT: Now what's the matter?

BRIDE: Leave me alone.

SERVANT: This is not time for you to start feeling sad. [*Encouragingly*] Give me the wreath. [*The Bride takes the wreath and hurls it away*] Child! You're just asking God to punish you, throwing the wreath on the floor like that. Raise your head! Don't you want to get married? Say it. You can still withdraw. [*The Bride rises*]

BRIDE: Storm clouds. A chill wind that cuts through my heart. Who hasn't felt it?

SERVANT: You love your sweetheart, don't you?

BRIDE: I love him.

SERVANT: Yes, yes. I'm sure you do.

BRIDE: But this is a very serious step.

SERVANT: You've got to take it.

BRIDE: I've already given my word.

SERVANT: I'll put on the wreath.

BRIDE: [*She sits down*] Hurry. They should be arriving by now.

SERVANT: They've already been at least two hours on the way.

BRIDE: How far is it from here to the church?

SERVANT: Five leagues by the stream, but twice that by the road. [*The Bride rises and* The Servant *grows excited as she looks at her*]

SERVANT:
Awake, O Bride, awaken,
On your wedding morning waken!
The world's rivers may all
Bear along your bridal Crown!

BRIDE: [*Smiling*] Come now.

SERVANT: [*Enthusiastically kissing her and dancing around her*]
Awake
with the fresh bouquet
of flowering laurel.
Awake,
by the trunk and branch
of the laurels!

[*The banging of the front door latch is heard*]

BRIDE: Open the door! That must be the first guests. [*She leaves.* The Servant *opens the door*]

SERVANT: [*In astonishment*] You!

LEONARDO: Yes, me. Good morning.

SERVANT: The first one!

LEONARDO: Wasn't I invited?

SERVANT: Yes.

LEONARDO: That's why I'm here.

SERVANT: Where's your wife?

LEONARDO: I came on my horse. She's coming by the road.

SERVANT: Didn't you meet anyone?

LEONARDO: I *passed* them on my horse.

SERVANT: You're going to kill that horse with so much racing.

LEONARDO: When he dies, he's dead! [*Pause*]

SERVANT: Sit down. Nobody's up yet.

LEONARDO: Where's the bride?

SERVANT: I'm just on my way to dress her.

LEONARDO: The bride! She ought to be happy!

SERVANT: [*Changing the subject*] How's the baby?

LEONARDO: What baby?

SERVANT: Your son.

LEONARDO: [*Remembering, as though in a dream*] Ah!

SERVANT: Are they bringing him?

LEONARDO: No. [*Pause. Voices sing distantly*]

VOICES:
Awake, O Bride, awaken,
On your wedding morning waken!

LEONARDO:
Awake, O Bride, awaken,
On your wedding morning waken!

SERVANT: It's the guests. They're still quite a way off.

LEONARDO: The bride's going to wear a big wreath, isn't she? But it ought not to be so large. One a little smaller would look better on her. Has the groom already brought her the orange blossom that must be worn on the breast?

BRIDE: [*Appearing, still in petticoats and wearing the wreath*] He brought it.

SERVANT: [*Sternly*] Don't come out like that.

BRIDE: What does it matter? [*Seriously*] Why do you ask if they brought the orange blossom? Do you have something in mind?

LEONARDO: Nothing. What would I have in mind? [*Drawing near her*] You, you know me; you know I don't. Tell me so. What have I ever meant to you? Open your memory, refresh it. But two oxen and an ugly little hut are almost nothing. That's the thorn.

BRIDE: What have you come here to do?

LEONARDO: To see your wedding.

BRIDE: Just as I saw yours!

LEONARDO: Tied up by you, done with your two hands. Oh, they can kill me but they can't spit on me. But even money, which shines so much, spits sometimes.

BRIDE: Liar!

LEONARDO: I don't want to talk. I'm hot-blooded and I don't want to shout so all these hills will hear me.

BRIDE: My shouts would be louder.

SERVANT: You'll have to stop talking like this. [*To* The Bride] You don't have to talk about what's past. [*The Servant* looks around uneasily at the doors]

BRIDE: She's right. I shouldn't even talk to you. But it offends me to the soul that you come here to watch me, and spy on my wedding, and ask about the orange blossom with something on your mind. Go and wait for your wife at the door.

LEONARDO: But, can't you and I even talk?

SERVANT: [*With rage*] No! No, you can't talk.

LEONARDO: Ever since I got married I've been thinking night and day about whose fault it was, and every time I think about it, out comes a new fault to eat up the old one; but always there's a fault left!

BRIDE: A man with a horse knows a lot of things and can do a lot to ride roughshod over a girl stuck out in the desert. But I have my pride. And that's why I'm getting married. I'll lock myself in with my husband and then I'll have to love him above everyone else.

LEONARDO: Pride won't help you a bit. [*He draws near to her*]

BRIDE: Don't come near me!

LEONARDO: To burn with desire and keep quiet about it is the greatest punishment we can bring on ourselves. What good was pride to me—and not seeing you, and letting you lie awake night after night? No good! It only served to bring the fire down on me! You think that time heals and walls hide things, but it isn't true, it isn't true! When things get that deep inside you there isn't anybody can change them.

BRIDE: [*Trembling*] I can't listen to you. I can't listen to your voice. It's as though I'd drunk a bottle of anise and fallen asleep wrapped in a quilt of roses. It pulls me along, and I know I'm drowning—but I go on down.

SERVANT: [*Seizing* Leonardo *by the lapels*] You've got to go right now!

LEONARDO: This is the last time I'll ever talk to her. Don't you be afraid of anything.

BRIDE: And I know I'm crazy and I know my breast rots with longing; but here I am—calmed by hearing him, by just seeing him move his arms.

LEONARDO: I'd never be at peace if I didn't tell you these things. I got married. Now you get married.

SERVANT: But she *is* getting married!

[*Voices are heard singing, nearer*]

VOICES:
Awake, O Bride, awaken,
On your wedding morning waken!

BRIDE:
Awake, O Bride, awaken,
[*She goes out, running toward her room*]

SERVANT: The people are here now. [*To* Leonardo]
Don't you come near her again.

LEONARDO: Don't worry. [*He goes out to the left.
Day begins to break*]

FIRST GIRL: [*Entering*]
  Awake, O Bride, awaken,
  the morning you're to marry;
  sing round and dance round;
  balconies a wreath must carry.

VOICES:
  Bride, awaken!

SERVANT: [*Creating enthusiasm*]
  Awake,
  with the green bouquet
  of love in flower.
  Awake,
  by the trunk and the branch
  of the laurels!

SECOND GIRL: [*Entering*]
  Awake,
  with her long hair,
  snowy sleeping gown,
  patent leather boots with silver—
  her forehead jasmines crown.

SERVANT:
  Oh, shepherdess,
  the moon begins to shine!

FIRST GIRL:
  Oh, gallant,
  leave your hat beneath the vine!

FIRST YOUNG MAN: [*Entering, holding his hat on
high*]
  Bride, awaken,
  for over the fields
  the wedding draws nigh
  with trays heaped with dahlias
  and cakes piled high.

VOICES:
  Bride, awaken!

SECOND GIRL:
  The bride
  has set her white wreath in place
  and the groom
  ties it on with a golden lace.

SERVANT:
  By the orange tree,
  sleepless the bride will be.

THIRD GIRL: [*Entering*]
  By the citron vine,
  gifts from the groom will shine.
  [Three Guests *come in*]

FIRST YOUTH:
  Dove, awaken!
  In the dawn
  shadowy bells are shaken.

GUEST:
  The bride, the white bride
  today a maiden,
  tomorrow a wife.

FIRST GIRL:
  Dark one, come down
  trailing the train of your silken gown.

GUEST:
  Little dark one, come down,
  cold morning wears a dewy crown.

FIRST GUEST:
  Awaken, wife, awake,
  orange blossoms the breezes shake.

SERVANT:
  A tree I would embroider her
  with garnet sashes wound
  And on each sash a cupid,
  with "Long Live" all around.

VOICES:
  Bride, awaken.

FIRST YOUTH:
  The morning you're to marry!

GUEST:
  The morning you're to marry
  how elegant you'll seem;
  worthy, mountain flower,
  of a captain's dream.

FATHER: [*Entering*]
  A captain's wife
  the groom will marry.
  He comes with his oxen the treasure to carry!

THIRD GIRL:
  The groom
  is like a flower of gold.
  When he walks,
  blossoms at his feet unfold.

SERVANT:
  Oh, my lucky girl!

SECOND YOUTH:
  Bride, awaken.

SERVANT:
  Oh, my elegant girl!

FIRST GIRL:
  Through the windows
  hear the wedding shout.

SECOND GIRL:
  Let the bride come out.

FIRST GIRL:
  Come out, come out!

SERVANT:
  Let the bells
  ring and ring out clear!
  For here she comes!
  For now she's near!

SERVANT:
  Like a bull, the wedding
  is arising here!
  [The Bride *appears. She wears a black dress in
  the style of 1900, with a bustle and large train
  covered with pleated gauzes and heavy laces.
  Upon her hair, brushed in a wave over her
  forehead, she wears an orange blossom wreath.
  Guitars sound.* The Girls *kiss* The Bride]

THIRD GIRL: What scent did you put on your hair?

BRIDE: [*Laughing*] None at all.

SECOND GIRL: [*Looking at her dress*] This cloth is what you can't get.

FIRST YOUTH: Here's the groom!

BRIDEGROOM: Salud!

FIRST GIRL: [*Putting a flower behind his ear*]
    The groom
    is like a flower of gold.

SECOND GIRL:
    Quiet breezes
    from his eyes unfold.

[The Groom *goes to* The Bride]

BRIDE: Why did you put on those shoes?

BRIDEGROOM: They're gayer than the black ones.

LEONARDO'S WIFE: [*Entering and kissing* The Bride] Salud! [*They all speak excitedly*]

LEONARDO: [*Entering, as one who performs a duty*]
    The morning you're to marry
    We give you a wreath to wear.

LEONARDO'S WIFE:
    So the fields may be made happy
    with the dew dropped from your hair!

MOTHER: [*To* The Father] Are those people here, too?

FATHER: They're part of the family. Today is a day of forgiveness!

MOTHER: I'll put up with it, but I don't forgive.

BRIDEGROOM: With your wreath, it's a joy to look at you!

BRIDE: Let's go to the church quickly.

BRIDEGROOM: Are you in a hurry?

BRIDE: Yes. I want to be your wife right now so that I can be with you alone, not hearing any voice but yours.

BRIDEGROOM: That's what I want!

BRIDE: And not seeing any eyes but yours. And for you to hug me so hard, that even though my dead mother should call me, I wouldn't be able to draw away from you.

BRIDEGROOM: My arms are strong. I'll hug you for forty years without stopping.

BRIDE: [*Taking his arm, dramatically*] Forever!

FATHER: Quick now! Round up the teams and carts! The sun's already out.

MOTHER: And go along carefully! Let's hope nothing goes wrong.

[*The great door in the background opens*]

SERVANT: [*Weeping*]
    As you set out from your house,
    oh, maiden white,
    remember you leave shining
    with a star's light.

FIRST GIRL:
    Clean of body, clean of clothes
    from her home to church she goes.

[*They start leaving*]

SECOND GIRL:
    Now you leave your home
    for the church!

SERVANT:
    The wind sets flowers
    on the sands.

THIRD GIRL:
    Ah, the white maid!

SERVANT:
    Dark winds are the lace
    of her mantilla.

[*They leave. Guitars, castanets and tambourines are heard.* Leonardo *and his* Wife *are left alone*]

WIFE: Let's go.

LEONARDO: Where?

WIFE: To the church. But not on your horse. You're coming with me.

LEONARDO: In the cart?

WIFE: Is there anything else?

LEONARDO: I'm not the kind of man to ride in a cart.

WIFE: Nor I the wife to go to a wedding without her husband. I can't stand any more of this!

LEONARDO: Neither can I!

WIFE: And why do you look at me that way? With a thorn in each eye.

LEONARDO: Let's go!

WIFE: I don't know what's happening. But I think, and I don't want to think. One thing I do know. I'm already cast off by you. But I have a son. And another coming. And so it goes. My mother's fate was the same. Well, I'm not moving from here.

[*Voices outside*]

VOICES:
    As you set out from your home
    and to the church go
    remember you leave shining
    with a star's glow.

WIFE: [*Weeping*]
    Remember you leave shining
    with a star's glow!
I left my house like that too. They could have stuffed the whole countryside in my mouth. I was that trusting.

LEONARDO: [*Rising*] Let's go!

WIFE: But you with me!

LEONARDO: Yes. [*Pause*] Start moving! [*They leave*]

VOICES:
    As you set out from your home
    and to the church go,
    remember you leave shining
    with a star's glow.

SLOW CURTAIN

SCENE II.

The exterior of The Bride's *Cave Home, in white gray and cold blue tones. Large cactus trees. Shadowy and silver tones. Panoramas of light tan table-*

lands, everything hard like a landscape in popular ceramics.

SERVANT: [*Arranging glasses and trays on a table*]
A-turning,
the wheel was a-turning
and the water was flowing,
for the wedding night comes.
May the branches part
and the moon be arrayed
at her white balcony rail.
[*In a loud voice*]
Set out the tablecloths!
[*In a pathetic voice*]
A-singing,
bride and groom were singing
and the water was flowing
for their wedding night comes.
Oh, rime-frost, flash!—
and almonds bitter
fill with honey!
[*In a loud voice*]
Get the wine ready!
[*In a poetic tone*]
Elegant girl,
most elegant in the world,
see the way the water is flowing,
for your wedding night comes.
Hold your skirts close in
under the bridegroom's wing
and never leave your house,
for the Bridegroom is a dove
with his breast a firebrand
and the fields wait for the whisper
of spurting blood.
A-turning
the wheel was a-turning
and the water was flowing
and your wedding night comes.
Oh, water, sparkle!

MOTHER: [*Entering*] At last!

FATHER: Are we the first ones?

SERVANT: No. Leonardo and his wife arrived a while ago. They drove like demons. His wife got here dead with fright. They made the trip as though they'd come on horseback.

FATHER: That one's looking for trouble. He's not of good blood.

MOTHER: What blood would you expect him to have? His whole family's blood. It comes down from his great grandfather, who started in killing, and it goes on down through the whole evil breed of knife wielding and false smiling men.

FATHER: Let's leave it at that!

SERVANT: But how can she leave it at that?

MOTHER: It hurts me to the tips of my veins. On the forehead of all of them I see only the hand with which they killed what was mine. Can you really see me? Don't I seem mad to you? Well, it's the madness of not having shrieked out all my breast needs to. Always in my breast there's a shriek standing tiptoe that I have to beat down and hold in under my shawls. But the dead are carried off and one has to keep still. And then, people find fault. [*She removes her shawl*]

FATHER: Today's not the day for you to be remembering these things.

MOTHER: When the talk turns on it, I have to speak. And more so today. Because today I'm left alone in my house.

FATHER: But with the expectation of having someone with you.

MOTHER: That's my hope: grandchildren. [*They sit down*]

FATHER: I want them to have a lot of them. This land needs hands that aren't hired. There's a battle to be waged against weeds, the thistles, the big rocks that come from one doesn't know where. And those hands have to be the owner's, who chastises and dominates, who makes the seeds grow. Lots of sons are needed.

MOTHER: And some daughters! Men are like the wind! They're forced to handle weapons. Girls never go out into the street.

FATHER: [*Happily*] I think they'll have both.

MOTHER: My son will cover her well. He's of good seed. His father could have had many sons with me.

FATHER: What I'd like is to have all this happen in a day. So that right away they'd have two or three boys.

MOTHER: But it's not like that. It takes a long time. That's why it's so terrible to see one's own blood spilled out on the ground. A fountain that spurts for a minute, but costs us years. When I got to my son, he lay fallen in the middle of the street. I wet my hands with his blood and licked them with my tongue—because it was my blood. You don't know what that's like. In a glass and topaze shrine I'd put the earth moistened by his blood.

FATHER: Now you must hope. My daughter is wide-hipped and your son is strong.

MOTHER: That's why I'm hoping. [*They rise*]

FATHER: Get the wheat trays ready!

SERVANT: They're all ready.

LEONARDO'S WIFE: [*Entering*] May it be for the best!

MOTHER: Thank you.

LEONARDO: Is there going to be a celebration?

FATHER: A small one. People can't stay long.

SERVANT: Here they are!

[*Guests begin entering in gay groups. The Bride and Groom come in arm-in-arm. Leonardo leaves*]

BRIDEGROOM: There's never been a wedding with so many people!

BRIDE: [*Sullen*] Never.

FATHER: It was brilliant.

MOTHER: Whole branches of families came.

BRIDEGROOM: People who never went out of the house.

MOTHER: Your father sowed well, and now you're reaping it.

BRIDEGROOM: There were cousins of mine whom I no longer knew.

MOTHER: All the people from the seacoast.

BRIDEGROOM: [*Happily*] They were frightened of the horses. [*They talk*]

MOTHER: [*To* The Bride] What are you thinking about?

BRIDE: I'm not thinking about anything.

MOTHER: Your blessings weigh heavily. [*Guitars are heard*]

BRIDE: Like lead.

MOTHER: [*Stern*] But they shouldn't weigh so. Happy as a dove you'd ought to be.

BRIDE: Are you staying here tonight?

MOTHER: No. My house is empty.

BRIDE: You'd ought to stay!

FATHER: [*To* The Mother] Look at the dance they're forming. Dances of the faraway seashore.

[Leonardo *enters and sits down. His* Wife *stands rigidly behind him*]

MOTHER: They're my husband's cousins. Stiff as stones at dancing.

FATHER: It makes me happy to watch them. What a change for this house! [*He leaves*]

BRIDEGROOM: [*To* The Bride] Did you like the orange blossom?

BRIDE: [*Looking at him fixedly*] Yes.

BRIDEGROOM: It's all of wax. It will last forever. I'd like you to have had them all over your dress.

BRIDE: No need of that. [Leonardo *goes off to the right*]

FIRST GIRL: Let's go and take out your pins.

BRIDE: [*To* The Groom] I'll be right back.

LEONARDO'S WIFE: I hope you'll be happy with my cousin!

BRIDEGROOM: I'm sure I will.

LEONARDO'S WIFE: The two of you here; never going out; building a home. I wish I could live far away like this, too!

BRIDEGROOM: Why don't you buy land? The mountainside is cheap and children grow up better.

LEONARDO'S WIFE: We don't have any money. And at the rate we're going . . . !

BRIDEGROOM: Your husband is a good worker.

LEONARDO'S WIFE: Yes, but he likes to fly around too much; from one thing to another. He's not a patient man.

SERVANT: Aren't you having anything? I'm going to wrap up some wine cakes for your mother. She likes them so much.

BRIDEGROOM: Put up three dozen for her.

LEONARDO'S WIFE: No, no. A half-dozen's enough for her!

BRIDEGROOM: But today's a day!

LEONARDO'S WIFE: [*To* The Servant] Where's Leonardo?

BRIDEGROOM: He must be with the guests.

LEONARDO'S WIFE: I'm going to go see. [*She leaves*]

SERVANT: [*Looking off at the dance*] That's beautiful there.

BRIDEGROOM: Aren't you dancing?

SERVANT: No one will ask me.

[*Two* Girls *pass across the back of the stage; during this whole scene the background should be an animated crossing of figures*]

BRIDEGROOM: [*Happily*] They just don't know anything. Lively old girls like you dance better than the young ones.

SERVANT: Well! Are you tossing me a compliment, boy? What a family yours is! Men among men! As a little girl I saw your grandfather's wedding. What a figure! It seemed as if a mountain were getting married.

BRIDEGROOM: I'm not as tall.

SERVANT: But there's the same twinkle in your eye. Where's the girl?

BRIDEGROOM: Taking off her wreath.

SERVANT: Ah! Look. For midnight, since you won't be sleeping, I have prepared ham for you, and some large glasses of old wine. On the lower shelf of the cupboard. In case you need it.

BRIDEGROOM: [*Smiling*] I won't be eating at midnight.

SERVANT: [*Slyly*] If not you, maybe the bride. [*She leaves*]

FIRST YOUTH: [*Entering*] You've got to come have a drink with us!

BRIDEGROOM: I'm waiting for the bride.

SECOND YOUTH: You'll have her at dawn!

FIRST YOUTH: That's when it's best!

SECOND YOUTH: Just for a minute.

BRIDEGROOM: Let's go. [*They leave. Great excitement is heard.* The Bride *enters. From the opposite side* Two Girls *come running to meet her*]

FIRST GIRL: To whom did you give the first pin; me or this one?

BRIDE: I don't remember.

FIRST GIRL: To me, you gave it to me here.

SECOND GIRL: To me, in front of the altar.

BRIDE: [*Uneasily, with a great inner struggle*] I don't know anything about it.

FIRST GIRL: It's just that I wish you'd . . .

BRIDE: [*Interrupting*] Nor do I care. I have a lot to think about.

SECOND GIRL: Your pardon. [Leonardo *crosses at the rear of the stage*]

BRIDE: [*She sees* Leonardo] And this is an upsetting time.

FIRST GIRL: We wouldn't know anything about that!

BRIDE: You'll know about it when your time comes. This step is a very hard one to take.

FIRST GIRL: Has she offended you?

BRIDE: No. You must pardon me.

SECOND GIRL: What for? But *both* the pins are good for getting married, aren't they?

BRIDE: Both of them.

FIRST GIRL: Maybe now one will get married before the other.

BRIDE: Are you so eager?

SECOND GIRL: [Shyly] Yes.

BRIDE: Why?

FIRST GIRL: Well . . . [She embraces The Second Girl. Both go running off. The Groom comes in very slowly and embraces The Bride from behind]

BRIDE: [In sudden fright] Let go of me!

BRIDEGROOM: Are you frightened of me?

BRIDE: Ay-y-y! It's you?

BRIDEGROOM: Who else would it be? [Pause] Your father or me.

BRIDE: That's true!

BRIDEGROOM: Of course, your father would have hugged you more gently.

BRIDE: [Darkly] Of course!

BRIDEGROOM: [Embracing her strongly and a little bit brusquely] Because he's old.

BRIDE: [Curtly] Let me go!

BRIDEGROOM: Why? [He lets her go]

BRIDE: Well . . . the people. They can see us.

[The Servant crosses at the back of the stage again without looking at The Bride and Bridegroom]

BRIDEGROOM: What of it? It's consecrated now.

BRIDE: Yes, but let me be . . . Later.

BRIDEGROOM: What's the matter with you? You look frightened!

BRIDE: I'm all right. Don't go.

[Leonardo's Wife enters]

LEONARDO'S WIFE: I don't mean to intrude . . .

BRIDEGROOM: What is it?

LEONARDO'S WIFE: Did my husband come through here?

BRIDEGROOM: No.

LEONARDO'S WIFE: Because I can't find him, and his horse isn't in the stable either.

BRIDEGROOM: [Happily] He must be out racing it. [The Wife leaves, troubled. The Servant enters]

SERVANT: Aren't you two proud and happy with so many good wishes?

BRIDEGROOM: I wish it were over with. The bride is a little tired.

SERVANT: That's no way to act, child.

BRIDE: It's as though I'd been struck on the head.

SERVANT: A bride from these mountains must be strong. [To The Groom] You're the only one who can cure her, because she's yours. [She goes running off]

BRIDEGROOM: [Embracing The Bride] Let's go dance a little. [He kisses her]

BRIDE: [Worried] No. I'd like to stretch out on my bed a little.

BRIDEGROOM: I'll keep you company.

BRIDE: Never! With all these people here? What would they say? Let me be quiet for a moment.

BRIDEGROOM: Whatever you say! But don't be like that tonight!

BRIDE: [At the door] I'll be better tonight.

BRIDEGROOM: That's what I want. [The Mother appears]

MOTHER: Son.

BRIDEGROOM: Where've you been?

MOTHER: Out there—in all that noise. Are you happy?

BRIDEGROOM: Yes.

MOTHER: Where's your wife?

BRIDEGROOM: Resting a little. It's a bad day for brides!

MOTHER: A bad day? The only good one. To me it was like coming into my own. [The Servant enters and goes toward The Bride's room] Like the breaking of new ground; the planting of new trees.

BRIDEGROOM: Are you going to leave?

MOTHER: Yes. I'd ought to be at home.

BRIDEGROOM: Alone.

MOTHER: Not alone. For my head is full of things: of men, and fights.

BRIDEGROOM: But now the fights are no longer fights.

[The Servant enters quickly; she disappears at the rear of the stage, running]

MOTHER: While you live, you have to fight.

BRIDEGROOM: I'll always obey you!

MOTHER: Try to be loving with your wife, and if you see she's acting foolish or touchy, caress her in a way that will hurt her a little: a strong hug, a bite and then a soft kiss. Not so she'll be angry, but just so she'll feel you're the man, the boss, the one who gives orders. I learned that from your father. And since you don't have him, I have to be the one to tell you about these strong defenses.

BRIDEGROOM: I'll always do as you say.

FATHER: [Entering] Where's my daughter?

BRIDEGROOM: She's inside. [The Father goes to look for her]

FIRST GIRL: Get the bride and groom! We're going to dance a round!

FIRST YOUTH: [To The Bridegroom] You're going to lead it.

FATHER: [Entering] She's not there.

BRIDEGROOM: No?

FATHER: She must have gone up to the railing.

BRIDEGROOM: I'll go see! [He leaves. A hubbub of excitement and guitars is heard]

FIRST GIRL: They've started it already! [She leaves]

BRIDEGROOM: [Entering] She isn't there.

MOTHER: [Uneasily] Isn't she?

FATHER: But where could she have gone?

SERVANT: [Entering] But where's the girl, where is she?

MOTHER: [Seriously] That we don't know. [The Bridegroom leaves. Three guests enter]

FATHER: [Dramatically] But, isn't she in the dance?

SERVANT: She's not in the dance.

FATHER: [With a start] There are a lot of people. Go look!

SERVANT: I've already looked.

FATHER: [*Tragically*] Then where is she?

BRIDEGROOM: [*Entering*] Nowhere. Not anywhere.

MOTHER: [*To* The Father] What does this mean? Where is your daughter?

[Leonardo's Wife *enters*]

LEONARDO'S WIFE: They've run away! They've run away! She and Leonardo. On the horse. With their arms round each other, they rode off like a shooting star!

FATHER: That's not true! Not my daughter!

MOTHER: Yes, your daughter. Spawn of a wicked mother, and he, he too. But now she's my son's wife!

BRIDEGROOM: [*Entering*] Let's go after them! Who has a horse?

MOTHER: Who has a horse? Right away! Who has a horse? I'll give him all I have—my eyes, my tongue even. . . .

VOICE: Here's one.

MOTHER: [*To* The Son] Go! After them! [*He leaves with two young men*] No. Don't go. Those people kill quickly and well . . . but yes, run, and I'll follow!

FATHER: It couldn't be my daughter. Perhaps she's thrown herself in the well.

MOTHER: Decent women throw themselves in water; not that one! But now she's my son's wife. Two groups. There are two groups here. [*They all enter*] My family and yours. Everyone set out from here. Shake the dust from your heels! We'll go help my son. [*The people separate in two groups*] For he has his family: his cousins from the sea, and all who came from inland. Out of here! On all roads. The hour of blood has come again. Two groups! You with yours and I with mine. After them! After them!

CURTAIN

ACT III. SCENE I.

A forest. It is nighttime. Great moist tree trunks. A dark atmosphere. Two violins are heard. Three Woodcutters enter.

FIRST WOODCUTTER: And have they found them?

SECOND WOODCUTTER: No. But they're looking for them everywhere.

THIRD WOODCUTTER: They'll find them.

SECOND WOODCUTTER: Sh-h-h!

THIRD WOODCUTTER: What?

SECOND WOODCUTTER: They seem to be coming closer on all the roads at once.

FIRST WOODCUTTER: When the moon comes out they'll see them.

SECOND WOODCUTTER: They'd ought to let them go.

FIRST WOODCUTTER: The world is wide. Everybody can live in it.

THIRD WOODCUTTER: But they'll kill them.

SECOND WOODCUTTER: You have to follow your passion. They did right to run away.

FIRST WOODCUTTER: They were deceiving themselves but at the last blood was stronger.

THIRD WOODCUTTER: Blood!

FIRST WOODCUTTER: You have to follow the path of your blood.

SECOND WOODCUTTER: But blood that sees the light of day is drunk up by the earth.

FIRST WOODCUTTER: What of it? Better dead with the blood drained away than alive with it rotting.

THIRD WOODCUTTER: Hush!

FIRST WOODCUTTER: What? Do you hear something?

THIRD WOODCUTTER: I hear the crickets, the frogs, the night's ambush.

FIRST WOODCUTTER: But not the horse.

THIRD WOODCUTTER: No.

FIRST WOODCUTTER: By now he must be loving her.

SECOND WOODCUTTER: Her body for him; his body for her.

THIRD WOODCUTTER: They'll find them and they'll kill them.

FIRST WOODCUTTER: But by then they'll have mingled their bloods. They'll be like two empty jars, like two dry arroyos.

SECOND WOODCUTTER: There are many clouds and it would be easy for the moon not to come out.

THIRD WOODCUTTER: The bridegroom will find them with or without the moon. I saw him set out. Like a raging star. His face the color of ashes. He looked the fate of all his clan.

FIRST WOODCUTTER: His clan of dead men lying in the middle of the street.

SECOND WOODCUTTER: There you have it!

THIRD WOODCUTTER: You think they'll be able to break through the circle?

SECOND WOODCUTTER: It's hard to. There are knives and guns for ten leagues 'round.

THIRD WOODCUTTER: He's riding a good horse.

SECOND WOODCUTTER: But he's carrying a woman.

FIRST WOODCUTTER: We're close by now.

SECOND WOODCUTTER: A tree with forty branches. We'll soon cut it down.

THIRD WOODCUTTER: The moon's coming out now. Let's hurry.

[*From the left shines a brightness*]

FIRST WOODCUTTER:
O rising moon!
Moon among the great leaves.

SECOND WOODCUTTER:
Cover the blood with jasmines!

FIRST WOODCUTTER:
O lonely moon!
Moon among the great leaves.

SECOND WOODCUTTER:
Silver on the bride's face.

THIRD WOODCUTTER:

O evil moon!
Leave for their love a branch in shadow.

FIRST WOODCUTTER:

O sorrowing moon!
Leave for their love a branch in shadow!

[*They go out. The* Moon *appears through the shining brightness at the left. The* Moon *is a young woodcutter with a white face. The stage takes on an intense blue radiance*]

MOON:

Round swan in the river
and a cathedral's eye,
false dawn on the leaves,
they'll not escape; these things am I!
Who is hiding? And who sobs
in the thornbrakes of the valley?
The moon sets a knife
abandoned in the air
which being a leaden threat
yearns to be blood's pain.
Let me in! I come freezing
down to walls and windows!
Open roofs, open breasts
where I may warm myself!
I'm cold! My ashes
of somnolent metals
seek the fire's crest
on mountains and streets.
But the snow carries me
upon its mottled back
and pools soak me
in their water, hard and cold.
But this night there will be
red blood for my cheeks,
and for the reeds that cluster
at the wide feet of the wind.
Let there be neither shadow nor bower,
and then they can't get away!
O let me enter a breast
where I may get warm!
A heart for me!
Warm! That will spurt
over the mountains of my chest;
let me come in, oh let me!

[*To the branches*]

I want no shadows. My rays
must get in everywhere,
even among the dark trunks I want
the whisper of gleaming lights,
so that this night there will be
sweet blood for my cheeks,
and for the reeds that cluster
at the wide feet of the wind.
Who is hiding? Out, I say!
No! They will not get away!
I will light up the horse
with a fever bright as diamonds.

[*He disappears among the trunks, and the stage goes back to its dark lighting. An* Old Woman *comes out completely covered by thin green cloth. She is barefooted. Her face can barely be seen among the folds. This character does not appear in the cast*]

BEGGAR WOMAN:

That moon's going away, just when they're
near.
They won't get past here. The river's whisper
and the whispering tree trunks will muffle
the torn flight of their shrieks.
It has to be here, and soon. I'm worn out.
The coffins are ready, and white sheets
wait on the floor of the bedroom
for heavy bodies with torn throats.
Let not one bird awake, let the breeze,
gathering their moans in her skirt,
fly with them over black tree tops
or bury them in soft mud.

[*Impatiently*]

Oh, that moon! That moon!

[*The* Moon *appears. The intense blue light returns*]

MOON: They're coming. One band through the ravine and the other along the river. I'm going to light up the boulders. What do you need?

BEGGAR WOMAN: Nothing.

MOON: The wind blows hard now, with a double edge.

BEGGAR WOMAN: Light up the waistcoat and open the buttons; the knives will know the path after that.

MOON:

But let them be a long time a-dying. So the
blood
will slide its delicate hissing between my fingers.
Look how my ashen valleys already are waking
in longing for this fountain of shuddering
gushes!

BEGGAR WOMAN: Let's not let them get past the arroyo. Silence!

MOON: There they come! [*He goes. The stage is left dark*]

BEGGAR WOMAN: Quick! Lots of light! Do you hear me? They can't get away!

[The Bridegroom *and* The First Youth *enter. The Beggar Woman* sits down and covers herself with her cloak]

BRIDEGROOM: This way.

FIRST YOUTH: You won't find them.

BRIDEGROOM: [*Angrily*] Yes, I'll find them!

FIRST YOUTH: I think they've taken another path.

BRIDEGROOM: No. Just a moment ago I felt the galloping.

FIRST YOUTH: It could have been another horse.

BRIDEGROOM: [*Intensely*] Listen to me. There's only one horse in the whole world, and this one's it. Can't you understand that? If you're going to follow me, follow me without talking.

FIRST YOUTH: It's only that I want to . . .

BRIDEGROOM: Be quiet. I'm sure of meeting them here. Do you see this arm? Well, it's not my arm. It's my brother's arm, and my father's, and that of all the dead ones in my family. And it has so much strength that it can pull this tree up by the roots, if it wants to. And let's move on, because here I feel the clenched teeth of all my people in me so that I can't breathe easily.

BEGGAR WOMAN: [*Whining*] Ay-y-y!

FIRST YOUTH: Did you hear that?

BRIDEGROOM: You go that way and then circle back.

FIRST YOUTH: This is a hunt.

BRIDEGROOM: A hunt. The greatest hunt there is.
    [*The Youth goes off. The Bridegroom goes rapidly to the left and stumbles over* The Beggar Woman, Death]

BEGGAR WOMAN: Ay-y-y!

BRIDEGROOM: What do you want?

BEGGAR WOMAN: I'm cold.

BRIDEGROOM: Which way are you going?

BEGGAR WOMAN: [*Always whining like a beggar*] Over there, far away . . .

BRIDEGROOM: Where are you from?

BEGGAR WOMAN: Over there . . . very far away.

BRIDEGROOM: Have you seen a man and a woman running away on a horse?

BEGGAR WOMAN: [*Awakening*] Wait a minute . . . [*She looks at him*] Handsome young man. [*She rises*] But you'd be much handsomer sleeping.

BRIDEGROOM: Tell me; answer me. Did you see them?

BEGGAR WOMAN: Wait a minute . . . What broad shoulders! How would you like to be laid out on them and not have to walk on the soles of your feet which are so small?

BRIDEGROOM: [*Shaking her*] I asked you if you saw them! Have they passed through here?

BEGGAR WOMAN: [*Energetically*] No. They haven't passed; but they're coming from the hill. Don't you hear them?

BRIDEGROOM: No.

BEGGAR WOMAN: Do you know the road?

BRIDEGROOM: I'll go, whatever it's like!

BEGGAR WOMAN: I'll go along with you. I know this country.

BRIDEGROOM: [*Impatiently*] Well, let's go! Which way?

BEGGAR WOMAN: [*Dramatically*] This way!
    [*They go rapidly out. Two violins, which represent the forest, are heard distantly. The Woodcutters return. They have their axes on their shoulders. They move slowly among the tree trunks*]

FIRST WOODCUTTER:
    O rising death!
    Death among the great leaves.

SECOND WOODCUTTER:
    Don't open the gush of blood!

FIRST WOODCUTTER:
    O lonely death!
    Death among the dried leaves.

THIRD WOODCUTTER:
    Don't lay flowers over the wedding!

SECOND WOODCUTTER:
    O sad death!
    Leave for their love a green branch.

FIRST WOODCUTTER:
    O evil death!
    Leave for their love a branch of green!
    [*They go out while they are talking.* Leonardo *and* The Bride *appear*]

LEONARDO:
    Hush!

BRIDE:
    From here I'll go on alone.
    You go now! I want you to turn back.

LEONARDO:
    Hush, I said!

BRIDE:
    With your teeth, with your hands, anyway you can,
    take from my clean throat
    the metal of this chain,
    and let me live forgotten
    back there in my house in the ground.
    And if you don't want to kill me
    as you would kill a tiny snake,
    set in my hands, a bride's hands,
    the barrel of your shotgun.
    Oh, what lamenting, what fire,
    sweeps upward through my head!
    What glass splinters are stuck in my tongue!

LEONARDO:
    We've taken the step now; hush!
    because they're close behind us,
    and I must take you with me.

BRIDE:
    Then it must be by force!

LEONARDO:
    By force? Who was it first
    went down the stairway?

BRIDE:
    I went down it.

LEONARDO:
    And who was it put
    a new bridle on the horse?

BRIDE:
    I myself did it. It's true.

LEONARDO:
    And whose were the hands
    strapped spurs to my boots?

BRIDE:
    The same hands, these that are yours,
    but which when they see you would like
    to break the blue branches
    and sunder the purl of your veins.

I love you! I love you! But leave me!
For if I were able to kill you
I'd wrap you 'round in a shroud
with the edges bordered in violets.
Oh, what lamenting, what fire,
sweeps upward through my head!

LEONARDO:
What glass splinters are stuck in my
    tongue!
Because I tried to forget you
and put a wall of stone
between your house and mine.
It's true. You remember?
And when I saw you in the distance
I threw sand in my eyes.
But I was riding a horse
and the horse went straight to your door.
And the silver pins of your wedding
turned my red blood black.
And in me our dream was choking
my flesh with its poisoned weeds.
Oh, it isn't my fault—
the fault is the earth's—
and this fragrance that you exhale
from your breasts and your braids.

BRIDE:
Oh, how untrue! I want
from you neither bed nor food,
yet there's not a minute each day
that I don't want to be with you,
because you drag me, and I come,
then you tell me to go back
and I follow you,
like chaff blown on the breeze.
I have left a good, honest man,
and all his people,
with the wedding feast half over
and wearing my bridal wreath.
But you are the one will be punished
and that I don't want to happen.
Leave me alone now! You run away!
There is no one who will defend you.

LEONARDO:
The birds of early morning
are calling among the trees.
The night is dying
on the stone's ridge.
Let's go to a hidden corner
where I may love you forever,
for to me the people don't matter,
nor the venom they throw on us.
[He embraces her strongly]

BRIDE:
And I'll sleep at your feet,
to watch over your dreams.
Naked, looking over the fields,
as though I were a bitch.
Because that's what I am! Oh, I look at
    you
and your beauty sears me.

LEONARDO:
Fire is stirred by fire.
The same tiny flame
will kill two wheat heads together.
Let's go!

BRIDE:
Where are you taking me?

LEONARDO:
Where they cannot come,
these men who surround us.
Where I can look at you!

BRIDE: [Sarcastically]
Carry me with you from fair to fair,
a shame to clean women,
so that people will see me
with my wedding sheets
on the breeze like banners.

LEONARDO:
I, too, would want to leave you
if I thought as men should.
But wherever you go, I go.
You're the same. Take a step. Try.
Nails of moonlight have fused
my waist and your chains.
[This whole scene is violent, full of great sen-
suality]

BRIDE:
Listen!

LEONARDO:
They're coming.

BRIDE:
               Run!
It's fitting that I should die here,
with water over my feet,
with thorns upon my head.
And fitting the leaves should mourn me,
a woman lost and virgin.

LEONARDO:
Be quiet. Now they're appearing.

BRIDE:
             Go now!

LEONARDO:
Quiet. Don't let them hear us.
[The Bride hesitates]

BRIDE:
Both of us!

LEONARDO: [Embracing her]
            Any way you want!
If they separate us, it will be
because I am dead.

BRIDE:
           And I dead too.
[They go out in each other's arms]
[The Moon appears very slowly. The stage
takes on a strong blue light. The two violins
are heard. Suddenly two long, ear-splitting
shrieks are heard, and the music of the two
violins is cut short. At the second shriek The
Beggar Woman appears and stands with her
back to the audience. She opens her cape and

stands in the center of the stage like a great bird with immense wings. The Moon *halts. The curtain comes down in absolute silence*]

CURTAIN

SCENE II.

The Final Scene
A white dwelling with arches and thick walls. To the right and left, are white stairs. At the back, a great arch and a wall of the same color. The floor also should be shining white. This simple dwelling should have the monumental feeling of a church. There should not be a single gray nor any shadow, not even what is necessary for perspective. Two Girls dressed in dark blue are winding a red skein.

FIRST GIRL:
Wool, red wool,
what would you make?

SECOND GIRL:
Oh, jasmine for dresses,
fine wool like glass.
At four o'clock born,
At ten o'clock dead.
A thread from this wool yarn,
a chain 'round your feet
a knot that will tighten
the bitter white wreath.

LITTLE GIRL: [*Singing*]
Were you at the wedding?

FIRST GIRL:
No.

LITTLE GIRL:
Well, neither was I!
What could have happened
'midst the shoots of the vineyards?
What could have happened
'neath the branch of the olive?
What really happened
that no one came back?
Were you at the wedding?

SECOND GIRL:
We told you once, no.

LITTLE GIRL: [*Leaving*]
Well, neither was I!

SECOND GIRL:
Wool, red wool,
what would you sing?

FIRST GIRL:
Their wounds turning waxen,
balm-myrtle for pain.
Asleep in the morning,
and watching at night.

LITTLE GIRL: [*In the doorway*]
And then, the thread stumbled
on the flinty stones,
but mountains, blue mountains,

are letting it pass.
Running, running, running,
and finally to come
to stick in a knife blade,
to take back the bread.
[*She goes out*]

SECOND GIRL:
Wool, red wool,
what would you tell?

FIRST GIRL:
The lover is silent,
crimson the groom,
at the still shoreline
I saw them laid out.
[*She stops and looks at the skein*]

LITTLE GIRL: [*Appearing in the doorway*]
Running, running, running,
the thread runs to here.
All covered with clay
I feel them draw near.
Bodies stretched stiffly
in ivory sheets!
[*The Wife and* Mother-in-law *of Leonardo appear. They are anguished*]

FIRST GIRL:
Are they coming yet?

MOTHER-IN-LAW: [*Harshly*]
We don't know.

SECOND GIRL:
What can you tell us about the wedding?

FIRST GIRL:
Yes, tell me.

MOTHER-IN-LAW: [*Curtly*] Nothing.

LEONARDO'S WIFE: I want to go back and find out all about it.

MOTHER-IN-LAW: [*Sternly*]
You, back to your house.
Brave and alone in your house.
To grow old and to weep.
But behind closed doors.
Never again. Neither dead nor alive.
We'll nail up our windows
and let rains and nights
fall on the bitter weeds.

LEONARDO'S WIFE:
What could have happened?

MOTHER-IN-LAW:
It doesn't matter what.
Put a veil over your face.
Your children are yours,
that's all. On the bed
put a cross of ashes
where his pillow was.
[*They go out*]

BEGGAR WOMAN: [*At the door*]
A crust of bread, little girls.

LITTLE GIRL:
Go away!
[*The Girls huddle close together*]

BEGGAR WOMAN:
Why?

LITTLE GIRL:
Because you whine; go away!

FIRST GIRL:
Child!

BEGGAR WOMAN:
I might have asked for your eyes! A cloud
of birds is following me. Will you have one?

LITTLE GIRL:
I want to get away from here!

SECOND GIRL: [To the Beggar Woman]
Don't mind her!

FIRST GIRL:
Did you come by the road through the arroyo?

BEGGAR WOMAN:
I came that way!

FIRST GIRL: [Timidly]
Can I ask you something?

BEGGAR WOMAN:
I saw them: they'll be here soon; two torrents
still at last, among the great boulders,
two men at the horse's feet.
Two dead men in the night's splendor.
[With pleasure]
Dead, yes, dead.

FIRST GIRL:
Hush, old woman, hush!

BEGGAR WOMAN:
Crushed flowers for eyes, and their teeth
two fistfuls of hard-frozen snow.
Both of them fell, and the Bride returns
with bloodstains on her skirt and hair.
And they come covered with two sheets
carried on the shoulders of two tall boys.
That's how it was; nothing more. What was fitting.
Over the golden flower, dirty sand.
[She goes. The Girls bow their heads and start going out rhythmically]

FIRST GIRL:
Dirty sand.

SECOND GIRL:
Over the golden flower.

LITTLE GIRL:
Over the golden flower
they're bringing the dead from the arroyo.
Dark the one,
dark the other.
What shadowy nightingale flies and weeps
over the golden flower!
[She goes. The stage is left empty. The Mother and a Neighbor Woman appear. The Neighbor is weeping]

MOTHER: Hush.

NEIGHBOR: I can't.

MOTHER: Hush, I said. [At the door] Is there nobody here? [She puts her hands to her forehead] My son ought to answer me. But now my son is an armful of shrivelled flowers. My son is a fading voice beyond the mountains now. [With rage, to The Neighbor] Will you shut up? I want no wailing in this house. Your tears are only tears from your eyes, but when I'm alone mine will come—from the soles of my feet, from my roots—burning more than blood.

NEIGHBOR: You come to my house; don't you stay here.

MOTHER: I want to be here. Here. In peace. They're all dead now: and at midnight I'll sleep, sleep without terror of guns or knives. Other mothers will go to their windows, lashed by rain, to watch for their sons' faces. But not I. And of my dreams I'll make a cold ivory dove that will carry camellias of white frost to the graveyard. But no; not graveyard, not graveyard: the couch of earth, the bed that shelters them and rocks them in the sky. [A woman dressed in black enters, goes toward the right, and there kneels. To The Neighbor] Take your hands from your face. We have terrible days ahead. I want to see no one. The earth and I. My grief and I. And these four walls. Ay-y-y! Ay-y-y! [She sits down, overcome]

NEIGHBOR: Take pity on yourself!

MOTHER: [Pushing back her hair] I must be calm. [She sits down] Because the neighbor women will come and I don't want them to see me so poor. So poor! A woman without even one son to hold to her lips.

[The Bride appears. She is without her wreath and wears a black shawl]

NEIGHBOR: [With rage, seeing The Bride] Where are you going?

BRIDE: I'm coming here.

MOTHER: [To The Neighbor] Who is it?

NEIGHBOR: Don't you recognize her?

MOTHER: That's why I asked who it was. Because I don't want to recognize her, so I won't sink my teeth in her throat. You snake! [She moves wrathfully on The Bride, then stops. To The Neighbor] Look at her! There she is, and she's crying, while I stand here calmly and don't tear her eyes out. I don't understand myself. Can it be I didn't love my son? But, where's his good name? Where is it now? Where is it? [She beats The Bride who drops to the floor]

NEIGHBOR: For God's sake! [She tries to separate them]

BRIDE: [To The Neighbor] Let her; I came here so she'd kill me and they'd take me away with them. [To The Mother] But not with her hands; with grappling hooks, with a sickle—and with force—until they break on my bones. Let her! I want her to know I'm clean, that I may be crazy, but that they can bury me without a single man ever having seen himself in the whiteness of my breasts.

MOTHER: Shut up, shut up; what do I care about that?

BRIDE: Because I ran away with the other one; I ran away! [*With anguish*] You would have gone, too. I was a woman burning with desire, full of sores inside and out, and your son was a little bit of water from which I hoped for children, land, health; but the other one was a dark river, choked with brush, that brought near me the undertone of its rushes and its whispered song. And I went along with your son who was like a little boy of cold water —and the other sent against me hundreds of birds who got in my way and left white frost on my wounds, my wounds of a poor withered woman, of a girl caressed by fire. I didn't want to; remember that! I didn't want to. Your son was my destiny and I have not betrayed him, but the other one's arm dragged me along like the pull of the sea, like the head toss of a mule, and he would have dragged me always, always, always—even if I were an old woman and all your son's sons held me by the hair!

[*A* Neighbor *enters*]

MOTHER: She is not to blame; nor am I! [*Sarcastically*] Who is, then? It's a delicate, lazy, sleepless woman who throws away an orange blossom wreath and goes looking for a piece of bed warmed by another woman!

BRIDE: Be still! Be still! Take your revenge on me; here I am! See how soft my throat is; it would be less work for you than cutting a dahlia in your garden. But never that! Clean, clean as a new-born little girl. And strong enough to prove it to you. Light the fire. Let's stick our hands in; you, for your son, I, for my body. *You'll* draw yours out first.

[*Another* Neighbor *enters*]

MOTHER: But what does your good name matter to me? What does your death matter to me? What does anything about anything matter to me? Blesséd be the wheat stalks, because my sons are under them; blesséd be the rain, because it wets the face of the dead. Blesséd be God, who stretches us out together to rest.

[*Another* Neighbor *enters*]

BRIDE: Let me weep with you.

MOTHER: Weep. But at the door. [The Girl *enters*. The Bride *stays at the door*. The Mother *is at the center of the stage*]

LEONARDO'S WIFE: [*Entering and going to the left*]

> He was a beautiful horseman,
> now he's a heap of snow.
> He rode to fairs and mountains
> and women's arms.
> Now, the night's dark moss
> crowns his forehead.

MOTHER:

> A sunflower to your mother,
> a mirror of the earth.

> Let them put on your breast
> the cross of bitter rosebay;
> and over you a sheet
> of shining silk;
> between your quiet hands
> let water form its lament.

WIFE:

> Ay-y-y, four gallant boys
> come with tired shoulders!

BRIDE:

> Ay-y-y, four gallant boys
> carry death on high!

MOTHER:

> Neighbors.

LITTLE GIRL: [*At the door*]

> They're bringing them now.

MOTHER:

> It's the same thing.
> Always the cross, the cross.

WOMEN:

> Sweet nails,
> cross adored,
> sweet name
> of Christ our Lord.

BRIDE: May the cross protect both the quick and the dead.

MOTHER:

> Neighbors: with a knife,
> with a little knife,
> on their appointed day, between two and
>   three,
> these two men killed each other for love.
> With a knife,
> with a tiny knife
> that barely fits the hand,
> but that slides in clean
> through the astonished flesh
> and stops at the place
> where trembles, enmeshed,
> the dark root of a scream.

BRIDE:

> And this is a knife,
> a tiny knife
> that barely fits the hand;
> fish without scales, without river,
> so that on their appointed day, between
>   two and three,
> with this knife,
> two men are left stiff,
> with their lips turning yellow.

MOTHER:

> And it barely fits the hand
> but it slides in clean
> through the astonished flesh
> and stops there, at the place
> where trembles enmeshed
> the dark root of a scream.

[The Neighbors, *kneeling on the floor, sob*]

CURTAIN

Bertolt Brecht

(1898–1956)

Among the poets of the modern theatre Bertolt Brecht is unique because he has always sung songs of "social significance." He was a stripling when Germany plunged into the First World War. He emerged into manhood when Germany adopted the Weimar republican constitution and broke out into sporadic revolutions, none more violent than the one that enjoyed a temporary triumph in his native Bavaria. These experiences determined the tone of his poetry and plays, most of which possessed an ideology far left of center and a zealous concern with moral and political issues. When Hitler gained control of Germany, Brecht was a marked man, but he cheated the gallows or a fate more horrible than simple execution by self-exile in 1933. He lived in Denmark and Finland for a time, went to Russia to edit the anti-Nazi periodical *Das Wort* with Lion Feuchtwanger and other exiles between 1936 and 1939, and arrived in the United States in 1941, where he devoted himself entirely to writing.

Returning to Germany shortly after Hitler's debacle, Brecht began to resume his important position among native writers and became associated with the liberated Deutsches Theater, once the temple of Brahm, Reinhardt, and other progressive men of the theatre. His lyrics and ballads, collected in several volumes, make him one of the most modern of twentieth-century poets. His plays, neither realistic nor expressionistic but marked by a distinctive combination of styles, give him an important place in the literary and social vanguard. Even in America, where his *Three-Penny Opera* proved disappointing in an inadequate New York production, he aroused more interest and found a more devoted following between 1935 and 1950 than might be expected of a playwright who failed to win the accolade of a Broadway success.

Brecht first attracted attention in 1922 when he won the coveted Kleist Prize for his antiwar play *Drums in the Night,* a morose but far from maudlin account of the experience of a German veteran who returns from the trenches to discover that profiteers have fattened on the blood of his comrades. Confirmed in the conviction that the drama must present social conflicts, Brecht continued to sing didactically in play after play. To promote an understanding of problems and issues, he began to write propaganda plays which combined analytic and poetic elements, demonstrated a problem, and instructed or were intended to instruct the common man as well as the class-conscious partisan in matters of strategy or right thinking. There was nothing prosaic, however,

about these *Lehrstücke,* or learning plays, as he called them. They had expressionistic and symbolic elements, sometimes told a parable and "slanted" their argument with imaginative devices and imagery, launched into balladlike verse, and called for music. One of the first of these pieces, *The Expedient,* an analysis of the moral problems faced by revolutionists, took the form of an oratorio, and was produced in Germany in 1929 with music by Hanns Eisler. Another learning play, *Round Heads and Peaked Heads,* produced in Copenhagen in 1936, satirized the racial theories of Hitler in a grotesque fable. Brecht's dramatization of Gorki's novel *Mother* (1932) traced the growth of revolutionary consciousness in a simple woman in Russia under the Czars; it relied more heavily on argument and choruses, or "mass chants" (with a score by Eisler), than on realistic scenes. In adapting John Gay's eighteenth-century classic *The Beggar's Opera,* renamed *The Three-Penny Opera,* Brecht moved directly into the musical-comedy field. The adaptation, sardonically lyrical and raffish, was a result of collaboration with the now well-known composer for the theatre Kurt Weill. The production, directed by Brecht himself, took Berlin by storm in 1928. It ran counter to the vogue of sentimental musical comedies and was as barbed with social protest as it was ungainly by intention.

Brecht's other plays revealed him as a remarkably flexible artist. He displayed an aptitude for historical plays in *The Life of Edward II* (based on Marlowe's tragedy), *Mother Courage,* and *Galileo,* a cool and antiheroic and yet exhilarating treatment of the famous scientist's life and struggles. He wrote a documentary presentation of German life under National Socialism, *The Private Life of the Master Race,* combining realistic sketches with imaginative technique and lyric power, and he composed two remarkable plays, rightly called "Parables for the Theatre" by his translators Eric and Maja Bentley, *The Good Woman of Setzuan* and *The Caucasian Chalk Circle.* In these, his didacticism is moral rather than political, and the lyric and dramatic elements are superbly balanced and vivid. Each play examines the problems of good and evil, justice and injustice, in fresh and challenging terms.

Brecht's kind of drama cannot, in fact, be properly understood without some appreciation of his qualities as a poet and without some knowledge of his theories of drama and theatre. He is a master of dry and colloquially flavored but charged poetry. He can take a traditional form such as the ballad and infuse it with the modern mind and spirit. He cultivates flatness often, but gives it a knifelike edge. All his plays have the same acuity, and so do his views on drama and acting. He considers himself an "epic realist," along with the stage director and dramatist Erwin Piscator; that is, he favors a type of dramatic composition that grasps the various facets of man's life in society without limiting itself to unity of time, place, and action. Some of his plays, as well as those adapted and staged by Piscator (Piscator's *The Good Soldier Schweik* and *An American Tragedy*), even have the extensiveness of an Elizabethan chronicle such as *Henry IV, Parts I and II* and as much variety of action and tone. One scene may convey a realistic situation while another may symbolize it; or the scene may take the form of a debate or a narration; or there may be no scene at all, only a song or recitation, at certain points in the play. But the episodes, combined with narrative and lyrical passages, and augmented with pantomime, dance, signs or placards, slides and motion-picture sequences if necessary—all following one another in rapid succession or alternation—will form one rich tumultuous play somewhat in the manner of such a novel as John Dos Passos' *U. S. A.* It is the underlying idea or the argument that cements the parts. This makes the drama as written and staged by Brecht and his former associate Erwin Piscator "epic."

Since the dramatist takes an unsentimental, analytical view of reality and demonstrates his argument with every conceivable device, this epic also serves the purpose of social realism. Hence the proper term for this type of drama and staging is "epic realism." Foregoing the esthetic advantages of a complete synthesis by tone or mood (the ideal of both the conventional realists and the symbolists of the Appia-Craig school), Brecht and Piscator concentrate on the diversity of a problem or situation. Risking discursiveness, they attempt to throw a clear light on the realities men must face if human ideals are to be effectuated.

This emphasis on the epic qualities of drama does not rule out the possibility of making the play revolve around a central hero. Brecht, for example, had no qualms about centering *The Caucasian Chalk Circle* and *The Good Woman of Setzuan* in the drama of a woman who in each case is as substantial a character as any created by conventional realists. Nor did he hesitate to select an outstanding historical figure for treatment in *Galileo*. (And Piscator's *The Good Soldier Schweik* thrusts a remarkable character, an arthritic little Czech, against the entire military machine of the Austrian-Hungarian empire. Schweik provided Max Pallenberg, the Charles Chaplin of Europe, with his biggest role.) The diversity of social reality can be presented just as effectively through an individual's experience as through that of a group, or "mass hero," as in *The Private Life of the Master Race*. And the fact that

Brecht and Piscator used all the resources of modern stage machinery and motion-picture technique in no way made them feel that they were flying in the face of tradition with their new epic style. Instead, they could point to the epic features of Greek and Elizabethan drama and stage production, as well as to the epic qualities of the romantic stage (*Faust, Brand, Peer Gynt*). They could claim with considerable justice that it was the writers of tight little realistic plays and not they who had broken with tradition.

Brecht (along with Piscator) also avowed himself the enemy of conventional emotionalism. He propounded a theory of "alienation" (*Verfremdung*) to the effect that no attempt should be made "to put the audience in a trance and give them the illusion of witnessing natural, unrehearsed events." It is necessary, indeed, to find means of neutralizing the audience's tendency to lose itself in illusion. If the playgoer feels too keenly, he is apt to do too little thinking. Pity is not enough as either an esthetic or social value. Neither is empathy, since complete identification with a character on the stage impairs objectivity and lulls the reasoning faculties to sleep. An Aristotelian catharsis through pity and terror, possible only when we succumb to stage illusion and identify ourselves with the characters, is not a desirable experience. When we are thoroughly purged, there is no longer any necessity to take action against the evils we have witnessed. The epic style must turn the spectator into an *observer*. It must "awaken his energy," and it must require decisions of him. This it will do by distancing dramatic experience and breaking the hypnotic spell that realists and symbolists alike cast upon their audience.

For "epic theatre," the actor must not feel himself completely into his role. For if he does, in the manner of a Stanislavskian actor, he will promote illusion instead of distancing the performance so that the audience may observe and appraise events instead of losing itself in them. The actor may in the rehearsals feel himself into his role only up to a point that will enable him to acquire the characteristics requisite for playing the role. And by bringing back into the drama such devices as choral commentary, song, and narration, Brecht intended to achieve the same distancing effect in dramaturgy. These interruptions of the dramatic action are expected to jar the spectator just as he is settling down to enjoy the story and fall into an emotional rapport with the characters. Emotion for Brecht's type of drama was not invalid, and Brecht himself could induce considerable emotion, but he did not want it to become the whole of a play and its final effect. Nor did he banish realism entirely. He could use it with fine effect whenever he wished. What he did not wish was to tether the drama to a confining technique and deprive himself of the benefit of other forms of expression which could strengthen his argument, enlighten his audience and spur it into action of some kind.

There could be much argument about Brecht's theories, especially when they were expressed in doctrinaire terms, and in essence they challenged Aristotelian principles that have been sacrosanct for most playwrights and critics. No one went so far as Brecht in denying the validity or necessity of pity, terror, catharsis, unity, and illusion as dramatic values. He did so with the animus of a Marxist who is concerned with social action and with the conviction of a scientist. (Brecht, we should note, was a student of medicine and served in the German medical corps during the First World War.) The "alienation" effect he advocated is scarcely to be distinguished from the ideal of scientific objectivity and the stress on clear demonstrations of clinical cases that we find in a modern medical school or hospital. Yet, beyond all theory, though not inconsonant with it, he operated in the theatre from the very beginning of his career as an impassioned partisan, a gifted poet, and a theatrician. Not the least attractive feature of his work is the evident struggle between poet and scientist, fabulist and social realist, the man of feeling and imagination and the social thinker who prides himself on his detachment.

Some of Brecht's best writing will be found in *The Private Life of the Master Race* (1944), although the selections given here provide only a modest example of the epic sweep of the work. It is possible to present it in excerpts because it consists of independent one-act plays connected by lyric passages and by an over-all pattern. We follow the travels of a German Panzer or tank, across Europe, from the time when it participates in Hitler's early victories to the time when it bogs down in defeat in Russia. Our primary concern is, however, with the Panzer's soldiers. The essential drama is their personal experience, which demonstrates how National Socialism came to Germany and, wrenching them from private life, sent them into combat. The play attracted much attention, even though its American production in downtown New York proved unsuccessful. The drama was translated into French and published by the *Nouvelle Revue Française,* and some of the one-acters were produced independently in Russia during the war. *The Jewish Wife* and *The Informer,* reprinted here, were particularly favored.

The epic pattern may be seen here in the manner in which the play moves from episode to episode, each built around a different character. (In a conventional realistic play one of these episodes would have been blown up into a single full-length drama and the emotional values of the subject would have been exploited fully.) That there is emotion in the scenes no one will deny after reading them. But the emotion is merely a means to the larger aim of showing us how the German terror operated and of recalling for us the sweep of German arms across the European continent. Brecht, who objected to the suspense that conventional playwrights worked up in their plays, employs a sufficiency of suspense himself in his episodes. But the suspense comes to an end abruptly with each episode, which is followed by a song and recitation, and there is no continuous plot throughout the work. (In fact, the play as a whole drops in interest from time to time and does not "build" in tension and dramatic substance as much as one might wish. Perhaps this tapering off is intentional. It surely creates an "alienation effect," although we are under no obligation to like the play the better for it.) The work as a whole is also distinctly theatrical as it alternates dramatic scenes and lyric passages, carries the roar of the Panzer as a prelude to each scene of the Nazi terror, brings on the military truck four times in the play, and uses placards to indicate the direction of the Panzer and the location of each dramatic episode. The work requires a skillful production and expert lighting effects. The lyric parts are differentiated into the singing of the Panzer troops followed by a voice speaking out of the darkness, and the effect is ironic and menacing—and revealing. Brecht called his work a documentary play, and a document it is, but not in the usual sense of a pedestrian report. It is a document with wings.

That Brecht's and Piscator's "epic realism" is not merely a bee in a Central European bonnet will occur to the experienced playgoer and reader when he recalls such American products as the Federal Theatre's "living newspapers" (as well as documentary films and documentary radio plays), Marc Blitzstein's *The Cradle Will Rock,* Paul Green's dramatization of Richard Wright's novel *Native Son,* and the Lerner and Weill Broadway musical comedy *Love Life,* a chronicle and demonstration of the effect of economics on the love life of the American people.

BIBLIOGRAPHY: Eric Bentley, *The Private Life of the Master Race* (with an essay, "Bertolt Brecht and His Work," pp. 117–140), 1944; Bentley, *The Playwright as Thinker* (pp. 250–272), 1946; Bertolt Brecht, "A New Technique of Acting," translated by Bentley, in *Theatre Arts,* Vol. XXXIII, No. 1, and reprinted under the title of "The Alienation Effect" in *Actors on Acting,* ed. by Toby Cole and Helen Krich Chinoy (pp. 280–285), 1949; Bertolt Brecht, "A Model for Epic Theatre," translated by Bentley, in *The Sewanee Review,* July 1949. See also Erwin Piscator, "Objective Acting," in *Actors on Acting* (pp. 285–291).

THE PRIVATE LIFE
OF THE MASTER RACE

By Bertolt Brecht

ENGLISH VERSION BY ERIC RUSSELL BENTLEY

A band plays a barbaric march. Out of the darkness appears a big signpost: TO POLAND, *and near it a Panzer truck. Its wheels are turning. On it sit twelve to sixteen soldiers, steel helmeted, their faces white as chalk, their guns between their knees. They could be puppets.*

The soldiers sing to the tune of the Horst Wessel Song:

And when the Führer had created order
At home in Germany with iron hand,
Forthwith he sent us out to carry his New Order
With faith and force to every other land.

So we set out obedient to superiors
In all our might—'twas a September day—
To conquer for them with the dreadful speed of
    lightning
A little town that deep in Poland lay.

And soon all Europe saw a bloody plaster
Smeared on our tanks from Seine to Volga strand
Because our Führer had re-cast us as a Master-
Race through the continent with iron hand.

      *   *   *

Dim out. The dull roll of the Panzer motor continues for a few seconds. When the stage lights up, we see a staircase. Above the scene is written in enormous black letters:

BRESLAU 1933

THE BETRAYAL

[*A man and a woman stand listening. They are very pale*]

THE WOMAN: Now they're downstairs.

THE MAN: Not yet.

THE WOMAN: They've smashed the banister. He was already unconscious when they dragged him out of the apartment.

THE MAN: But the only thing I said was that the radio with the broadcasts from Russia didn't come from here.

THE WOMAN: That wasn't the *only* thing you said.

THE MAN: I didn't say anything else.

THE WOMAN: Don't look at me like that. It serves them right. Why do they have to be Communists?

THE MAN: But they didn't need to tear his jacket for him. None of us are as well off as that.

THE WOMAN: The jacket has nothing to do with it.

THE MAN: They didn't need to tear it for him.

Dim out. The sound of the Panzer in motion is heard again.

THE VOICE: [1]

Thus neighbor betrayed neighbor.
Thus the common folk devoured each other
and enmity grew in the houses and in the precincts.
And so we went forth with confidence
and shoved onto our Panzer
every man who had not been slain:
a whole nation of betrayers and betrayed
we shoved onto our iron chariot.

      *   *   *

Dim out.[2] The Panzer is heard.

THE VOICE:

There is also a doctor on our Panzer
who decides which of the Polish miners' wives
shall be sent to the brothel in Cracow.
And he is competent and makes no bones about it,
in memory of the wife he lost,
who was a Jewess, sent away because
the Master Race must be carefully mated
and the Führer decides whom each shall lie with.

      *   *   *

[1] Each scene is introduced or followed by a voice speaking out of the darkness and by the roar of the Panzer as it starts rolling.
[2] After an episode showing the "organization" of science under National Socialism at the University of Goettingen in 1935.

*When the lights go up we see a comfortable, bour-
geois bedroom. Above the scene is written in enormous letters:*

FRANKFURT 1935

THE JEWISH WIFE

*It is evening. A woman is packing. She is picking
out the things she wants to take with her. Sometimes
she takes an article out of the bag again and puts it
back in its place so that she can pack something
else. She hesitates a long time over a large picture
of her husband which is on the dressing-table. In
the end she leaves it where it is. Getting tired of
packing, she sits for a few moments on a suitcase,
her head propped on her hand. Then she goes to
the telephone.*

THE WIFE: Judith Keith speaking. Is that you,
doctor? Good evening.—I just wanted to call up and
say that you must look around for a new bridge
partner. Yes, I'm going away.—No, not for very
long, but it won't be less than a couple of weeks.
I'm going to Amsterdam.—Yes, they say the spring
is lovely there.—I have friends there.—No, friends,
in the plural, unbelievable as it sounds.—How can
you play bridge now? But we haven't played for two
weeks.—Certainly, Fritz had a cold too. When it
gets so cold bridge is impossible, I said so too.—
Oh no, doctor, how could I?—Thekla had to accommodate her mother.—I know.—How should I
suppose *that?*—No, it really didn't come suddenly at
all, it's just that I kept putting it off, but now I
must . . . Yes, we'll have to call off our movie date.
Say hello to Thekla for me.—Perhaps you'll call him
sometimes on Sundays? So long then.—Well, gladly,
of course.—Good-bye.

[She hangs up and calls another number]
Judith Keith speaking. I'd like to speak to Frau
Shoeck.—Lotte?—I wanted to say a quick good-
bye, I'm going away for a time.—No, I'm quite well,
I just want to see a couple of new faces.—Yes, what
I wanted to say was that Fritz is bringing the professor here for the evening next Tuesday, and perhaps you could come too. As I said I'm leaving to-
night.—Yes, Tuesday.—No, I only wanted to say
I'm leaving tonight, that has nothing to do with it,
I thought you could come then too.—All right, let's
say: *although* I'm not there, O.K.?—Of course I
know you're not like that, and even if you were
these are troubled times, and everybody's careful
now. You'll come then?—If Max can? Oh, he will
be able to, the professor'll be here, tell him.—I must
hang up now. Fine. Good-bye.

[She hangs up and calls another number]
Is that you Gertrude? This is Judith. Sorry to disturb you.—Thanks. I wanted to ask you if you can

look after Fritz, I'm going away for a couple of
months.—I think that you as his sister . . . Why
wouldn't you like to?—But there's no likelihood of
that, not in Fritz's case. Naturally he knows that—
er—you and I didn't get on too well together, but
. . . Then he'll call you, if you wish it.—Yes, I'll
tell him.—It's all pretty much in order though the
apartment's a bit too big.—His study? Oh, Ida
knows how to look after it, just leave that to her.—
I find her quite intelligent, and he's used to her.—
And another thing, please don't misunderstand me,
he doesn't like to talk before dinner, could you remember that? I've always avoided it.—I don't want
to discuss it now, my train leaves soon and I've not
finished packing, you see.—Look after his suits and
remind him he has to go to the tailor—he's ordered
a coat—and take care that his bedroom's well heated,
he always sleeps with an open window and it's too
cold.—I don't believe he should "become inured" to
it, but now I must stop.—Thank you so much, Gertrude, and we'll write to each other.—Good-bye.

[She hangs up and calls another number]
Anna? This is Judith. Look, I'm leaving right away.
—No, it has to be, it's getting too difficult—too
difficult! Yes, no, Fritz doesn't want it, he knows
nothing. I simply packed.—I don't think so.—I don't
think he'll say much.—It's simply too hard for him,
I mean, too many technicalities.—We never discussed it.—We never even spoke about it, never.—
No, he was not different, on the contrary—I want
you to be good to him, a little at the first.—Yes, especially Sundays, and advise him to move.—The
apartment is too big for him.—I'd like to say good-
bye to you, but you know—the janitor? [3]—Good-
bye then. No, don't come to the station, by no
means. Good-bye, I'll write.—Surely.

*[She hangs up and calls no more numbers. She
has been smoking. She now burns the little
book in which she looked up the telephone
numbers. She walks up and down a couple of
times. Then she begins to speak. She is trying
out the little speech which she wishes to make
to her husband. One sees that he is supposedly
sitting in a certain chair]*
Yes, I'm going now, Fritz. Perhaps I've stayed too
long already, you must forgive that, but . . .

[She stands thinking and then tries again]
Fritz, you shouldn't keep me any longer, you can't
. . . It's obvious that I'll be your undoing. I know
you're not cowardly, you're not afraid of the police
—but there are worse things than the police. They
won't take you to the concentration camp but—to-
morrow or the next day—they won't let you into
the clinic. You won't say anything then, but you'll
be sick. I won't see you sitting around here turning
the pages of magazines. I'm going out of pure ego-
ism and nothing else. Don't say anything.

[She stops again. And tries again]
Don't say you're not changed. You are! Last week

[3] Evidently the janitor is Nazi.

you found—quite objectively—that the percentage of Jewish scientists is after all not so great. It always begins with objectivity. And why do you continually say to me now that I never was such a Jewish nationalist as today. Naturally I am! It's so catching! Oh Fritz, what has happened to us?

[*She pauses*]

I didn't tell you I wanted to go and have wanted to go a long time because I can't talk when I look at you, Fritz. Talking seems so futile. They have fixed everything. What is wrong with them? What do they actually want? What do I do to them? I've never meddled in politics. Was I for Thaelmann?[4] No, I'm just a bourgeois, a housewife who keep servants and so forth, and now suddenly only blondes can carry on that way. I've often thought lately how you said to me some years ago: "There are valuable people and less valuable people. The valuable people get insulin when they have sugar in the blood, the less valuable get none." I agreed with you, fool that I was! Now they've made new categories of this sort, and I belong to the less valuable. It serves me right.

[*Another pause*]

Yes, I'm packing. You mustn't act as if you hadn't noticed it in the last few days . . . . Fritz, everything is tolerable except one thing: that we're not looking each other in the eyes during the last hour that remains to us. That they shall not achieve—the liars who set everyone lying. Ten years ago when somebody thought no one could tell I was Jewish you quickly said: "Oh, yes, they can tell." And I liked that. It was clear-headed. Why evade the issue now? I'm packing because otherwise they'll take away your position as chief surgeon at the clinic. And because they already cut you there to your face and because already you can't sleep at night. I don't want you to tell me not to go. I'm going in a hurry because I don't want to have you tell me I *should* go. It's a question of time. Character is a question of time. It lasts for a certain length of time, just like a glove. There are good ones that last a long time. But they don't last forever. Incidentally, I'm not angry. And yet: I am. Why should I always be so understanding? What's wrong with the shape of my nose and the color of my hair? They want me to quit the town where I was born lest they should need to give me butter. What kind of men are you all? What kind of a man are you? You people discover the quantum theory and let yourselves be bossed by half-savages; you have to conquer the world, but are not allowed to have the wife you want. Artificial respiration and every shot a hit! You're monsters or the bootlickers of monsters. Yes, this is unreasonable of me, but what use is reason in such a world? There you sit watching your wife pack and say nothing. The walls have ears, don't they? And you all say nothing! One lot listen and the other lot hold their tongues. Christ! I should hold my tongue too. If I loved you, I'd hold my tongue. I love you really.

[4] Communist candidate in presidential elections.

Give me that underwear. Those have sex appeal, I'll need them. I'm thirty-six, that's not too old, but I can't do much more experimenting. It mustn't be this way in the next country I come to. The next man I get must be allowed to keep me. And don't say you'll send money, you know you can't. And you shouldn't act as if it were for four weeks. This business doesn't last a mere four weeks. You know it and I know it too. So don't say, "Well, it's only for a couple of weeks," as you hand me the fur coat I won't need till winter. And let's not talk about misfortune. Let's talk about shame. Oh, Fritz!

[*She stops. A door is heard opening. She hastily puts herself to rights. Her husband comes in*]

THE HUSBAND: What are you doing, tidying up?

THE WIFE: No.

THE HUSBAND: Why are you packing?

THE WIFE: I want to get away.

THE HUSBAND: What do you mean?

THE WIFE: We've talked sometimes about my going away for a time. Things are not too good here these days.

THE HUSBAND: That's a lot of nonsense.

THE WIFE: Shall I stay then?

THE HUSBAND: Where do you intend to go?

THE WIFE: To Amsterdam. Away from here.

THE HUSBAND: But you have no one there.

THE WIFE: No.

THE HUSBAND: Why don't you stay here then? You certainly mustn't go on my account.

THE WIFE: No.

THE HUSBAND: You know I've not changed, don't you, Judith?

THE WIFE: Yes.

[*He embraces her. They stand, silent between the bags*]

THE HUSBAND: And there's nothing else to make you go?

THE WIFE: You know the answer to that.

THE HUSBAND: Perhaps it isn't so stupid. You need a breather. It's stifling here. I'll bring you back. Two days on the other side of the frontier, and I'd feel much better.

THE WIFE: Yes, by all means.

THE HUSBAND: This business here can't last too long. A complete change will come—from somewhere. All this will calm down again like an inflammation. It's really a misfortune.

THE WIFE: It certainly is. Did you meet Shoeck?

THE HUSBAND: Yes, that is, only on the stairs. I believe he's sorry again they cut us. He was quite embarrassed. In the long run they can't hold us intellectuals down like this, however much they hate us. Nor can they make war with completely spineless wrecks. These people are not so unresponsive if one confronts them boldly. When do you want to leave?

THE WIFE: Quarter past nine.

THE HUSBAND: And where shall I send the money?

THE WIFE: General delivery, Amsterdam, perhaps.

THE HUSBAND: I'll get myself a special permit. My God, I can't send my wife away with ten marks a month! What a mess everything is in. I feel awful about it.

THE WIFE: When you come for me, it'll do you good.

THE HUSBAND: To read a paper for once that has something in it!

THE WIFE: I called up Gertrude. She'll look after you.

THE HUSBAND: Quite unnecessary—for a couple of weeks.

THE WIFE: [*She has begun to pack*] Hand me the fur coat now, will you?

THE HUSBAND: [*He gives it to her*] After all, it's only for a couple of weeks.

Dim out. The Panzer is heard.

THE VOICE:

And there is also a teacher on our Panzer,
a captain now with a hat of steel,
who teaches a bloody lesson to
French grapefarmers and fishermen of Norway.
For there was a day seven years before,
dimly remembered but never forgotten,
when in the bosom of his family he learned
to hate spies.

* * *

When the lights go up we see a living room. Above the scene is written in enormous black letters:

COLOGNE 1935

THE INFORMER

It is a rainy Sunday afternoon. A husband, his wife, and their boy have just finished lunch. A maid enters.

THE MAID: Herr and Frau Klimbtsch want to know if you're at home, sir.

THE HUSBAND: [*Snapping*] We're not.

[The Maid *goes out*]

THE WIFE: You should have gone to the telephone yourself. They know we couldn't possibly have gone out yet.

THE HUSBAND: Why couldn't we have gone out?

THE WIFE: Because it's raining.

THE HUSBAND: That's not a reason.

THE WIFE: What would we have gone out for? They'll certainly wonder about that now.

THE HUSBAND: There are plenty of places to go to.

THE WIFE: Then why don't we go?

THE HUSBAND: Where should we go to?

THE WIFE: If only it weren't raining.

THE HUSBAND: And where on earth should we go if it weren't raining?

THE WIFE: In the old days you could at least arrange to meet somebody.

[*There is a pause*]

THE WIFE: It was a mistake not to go to the telephone. Now they know we don't want to have them here.

THE HUSBAND: What if they do?

THE WIFE: Why then it means that we're dropping them just when everybody's dropping them. I don't like it.

THE HUSBAND: We're not dropping them.

THE WIFE: Then why shouldn't they come here?

THE HUSBAND: Because this Klimbtsch fellow bores me stiff.

THE WIFE: In the old days he didn't bore you.

THE HUSBAND: "In the old days"! Don't keep saying that. You make me nervous.

THE WIFE: At any rate you wouldn't have cut him in the old days just because his case is being looked into by the school-inspectors.

THE HUSBAND: You want to imply I'm a coward?

[*There is a pause*]

THE HUSBAND: All right. Call them up and say we've just come back because of the rain.

[*The* Wife *remains seated*]

THE WIFE: Shall we ask the Lemkes if they want to come over?

THE HUSBAND: So they can tell us we're not keen enough on Air Raid Precautions?

THE WIFE: [*To the* Boy] Klaus-Heinrich! Leave the radio alone.

[*The* Boy *turns to the newspapers*]

THE HUSBAND: It's certainly a catastrophe to have rain today. You just can't live in a country where it's a catastrophe when it rains.

THE WIFE: Is there much point in throwing remarks like that around?

THE HUSBAND: Within my own four walls I can make whatever remarks I please. In my own home I can say what I . . .

[*He is interrupted. The* Maid *comes in with coffee things. There is silence while she is in the room*]

THE HUSBAND: Must we have a maid whose father is Block Warden?

THE WIFE: I think we've talked about that enough. Last time you said it had its advantages.

THE HUSBAND: I've said a whole lot of things. Only say something of the kind to your mother and very likely we'll get in a wonderful mess.

THE WIFE: What I say to my mother . . .

[*The* Maid *interrupts them again as she brings in the coffee*]

THE WIFE: Leave it now, Erna, you can go. I'll look after this.

THE MAID: Thanks very much, gnädige Frau. [*She goes out*]

THE BOY: [*Looking up from the paper*] Do all priests do that, Papa?

THE HUSBAND: What?

THE BOY: What it says here.

THE HUSBAND: What is it you're reading?

[*He snatches the paper out of his hand*]

THE BOY: Our Group Leader told us we could all know what it says in this paper.

THE HUSBAND: It doesn't matter to me what the Group Leader said. I decide what you can read and what you can't.

THE WIFE: Here's ten cents, Klaus-Heinrich, go over and buy yourself something.

THE BOY: But it's raining.

[*He hangs around near the window, undecided*]

THE HUSBAND: If these reports of the priest trials don't stop, I'll not order this paper any more.

THE WIFE: And which one *will* you subscribe to? It's in all of them.

THE HUSBAND: If all the papers carry filth like that, I'll read none. I couldn't know less of what's going on in the world.

THE WIFE: A house cleaning doesn't do any harm.

THE HUSBAND: House cleaning! That's nothing but politics.

THE WIFE: Anyway it doesn't concern us, after all we're Lutheran.

THE HUSBAND: It's not a matter of indifference for our people if they can't think of a vestry without thinking of such abominations.

THE WIFE: Then what should they do if such things happen?

THE HUSBAND: What should they do? Maybe they might look to their own affairs. It may not all be as clean as it might be in their Brown House,[5] so I hear.

THE WIFE: But that goes to prove our people has recovered its health, Karl.

THE HUSBAND: Recovered its health! If that's what healthiness looks like, give me disease.

THE WIFE: You're so nervous today. Did anything happen at school?

THE HUSBAND: What should happen at school? And please stop telling me I'm nervous. That's what makes me that way.

THE WIFE: We shouldn't always be quarreling, Karl. In the old days . . .

THE HUSBAND: I was waiting for it: "in the old days"! I didn't want my child's mind poisoned in the old days and I don't want it poisoned now.

THE WIFE: Where is he anyway?

THE HUSBAND: How do I know?

THE WIFE: Did you see him leave?

THE HUSBAND: No.

THE WIFE: I don't understand where he can have gone. [*Shouting*] Klaus-Heinrich!

[*She runs out and is heard shouting. She returns*]

THE WIFE: Well, he's out.

THE HUSBAND: Why on earth shouldn't he be out?

THE WIFE: Why, because it's simply pouring.

THE HUSBAND: Why are you so nervous if the boy goes out once in a while?

THE WIFE: What have we been saying?

THE HUSBAND: What's that got to do with it?

THE WIFE: You're so uncontrolled these days.

THE HUSBAND: I certainly am not uncontrolled these days, but even if I were uncontrolled, what has that got to do with the boy being out?

THE WIFE: Oh, you know they listen.

THE HUSBAND: So what?

THE WIFE: So what? So this: what if he tells tales? You know perfectly well what's drummed into them at the Hitler Youth. They're under orders to report everything. Strange he left so quietly.

THE HUSBAND: Nonsense.

THE WIFE: Didn't you notice it, when he'd left?

THE HUSBAND: He was at the window quite a time.

THE WIFE: I wonder what he overheard.

THE HUSBAND: He knows what happens to people who're informed against.

THE WIFE: What of the boy the Schulkes told about? His father must be in the concentration camp still. If we only knew how long he was in the room.

THE HUSBAND: Oh, that's all nonsense.

[*He goes through the other rooms and shouts for* The Boy]

THE WIFE: I can't believe he'd just go off somewhere without saying a word. He isn't like that.

THE HUSBAND: Maybe he's at some school-friend's.

THE WIFE: In that case he can only be at the Mummermanns'. I'll phone.

[*She phones*]

THE HUSBAND: I regard the whole thing as a false alarm.

THE WIFE: [*At the phone*] This is Frau Furcke. Good afternoon, Frau Mummermann. Is Klaus-Heinrich at your place?—He isn't?—Then I just can't think where the boy is.—Tell me, Frau Mummermann, is the club room of the Hitler Youth open on Sunday afternoon?—It is?—Thanks, I'll try them.

[*She hangs up. The couple sit in silence*]

THE HUSBAND: What can he have heard after all?

THE WIFE: You talked about the paper. You shouldn't have said that about the Brown House. He's such a nationalist.

THE HUSBAND: And *what* may I have said about the Brown House?

THE WIFE: You can hardly help remembering: that it's not all clean there.

THE HUSBAND: That can't be interpreted as an attack. To say: it's not all clean, or rather as I more moderately put it, not all *quite* clean, which certainly makes a difference, a considerable difference, why, that's more of a jocular observation, idiomatic and popular, one might almost say a colloquialism. It means little more than that probably, even there, something is not always and under all circumstances as the Führer wishes it. I intentionally indicated the merely probable character of my allegation by using the expression: "it *may* not all be *quite*"—

quite in the mildest sense—"clean." This was my formulation of the matter. *May* be! Not: *is!* I can't say that anything there *is* not clean, there's no proof. But wherever there are men, there are imperfections. I never suggested anything more than that, and that only in the mildest form. And moreover the Führer himself on a certain occasion gave his criticism in the same direction and much more sharply.

THE WIFE: I don't understand you. You don't have to talk this way to me.

THE HUSBAND: I wish I didn't have to. I'm not sure what you yourself say, in the way of gossip, about the things you've heard between these four walls, insignificant things, probably only said in a moment of excitement. Naturally I'm far from accusing you of spreading any frivolous tales against your husband and I don't for a moment assume that the boy would do anything against his father. But unfortunately there's an important distinction between doing wrong and knowing you do it.

THE WIFE: Now please stop! Watch your own tongue! You said one can't live in Hitler Germany. All along I've been trying to remember whether you said that before or after what you said about the Brown House.

THE HUSBAND: I didn't say it at all.

THE WIFE: You act precisely as if I were the police! But what can the boy have heard? That's what tortures me.

THE HUSBAND: The expression "Hitler Germany" is not in my vocabulary.

THE WIFE: And about the Block Warden and about the papers being full of lies and what you said recently about Air Raid Precautions—the boy hears nothing positive at all! That certainly isn't good for a young mind. Youth can only be perverted by such talk. And the Führer always stresses: "Germany's youth is Germany's future." The boy doesn't run off and turn informer. He isn't made that way. I feel bad.

THE HUSBAND: But he's revengeful.

THE WIFE: What can he take revenge for?

THE HUSBAND: God knows. There's always something. Maybe because I took his green frog away from him.

THE WIFE: But that was a week ago.

THE HUSBAND: He remembers such things.

THE WIFE: Why did you take it from him?

THE HUSBAND: Because he caught no flies for it. H. just let it starve.

THE WIFE: He really has too much to do, though.

THE HUSBAND: That's not the frog's fault.

THE WIFE: But he never talked about it afterwards and just now I gave him ten cents. Why, he gets everything he wants.

THE HUSBAND: Yes, that's bribery.

THE WIFE: What do you mean by that?

THE HUSBAND: They'll immediately say we tried to bribe him to keep his mouth shut.

THE WIFE: What do you think they can do to you?

THE HUSBAND: Oh, everything. There are no limits to what they can do. Good God! Educator of the Youth! I fear them. To be a teacher in these circumstances!

THE WIFE: But there's nothing against you.

THE HUSBAND: There's something against everyone. All are suspect. If suspicion exists, someone is suspected. Suspicion need only exist.

THE WIFE: But a child is not a reliable witness. A child hasn't the least idea what he is saying.

THE HUSBAND: That's your opinion. Since when have they needed a witness for anything?

THE WIFE: Can't we think out what you must have meant by your remarks? I mean: then it will be clear he misunderstood you.

THE HUSBAND: What could I have said? I can't remember. It's the fault of the damned rain. . . . It makes you disgruntled. After all I'm the last to say anything against the spiritual revival the German people has experienced. I foresaw it all back in 1932.

THE WIFE: Karl, we haven't time to talk of it. We must straighten everything out and without delay. We haven't a moment to lose.

THE HUSBAND: I can't think it of Klaus-Heinrich.

THE WIFE: Now: first the matter of the Brown House and the filth.

THE HUSBAND: I said nothing about filth.

THE WIFE: You said the paper is full of filth and that you intend to cancel your subscription.

THE HUSBAND: Yes, the paper, but not the Brown House.

THE WIFE: Might you not have said that you disapprove of such filth in the vestries? And that you think it quite possible that the very men now on trial invented the atrocity stories about the Brown House and that they said that all was not clean? And that they therefore should have looked to their own affairs? And above all you told the boy to leave the radio and take the paper instead because you take the stand that youth in the Third Reich should note with open eyes what is going on.

THE HUSBAND: All that wouldn't help in the least.

THE WIFE: Karl, don't let your courage fail you. You must be strong, as the Führer always . . .

THE HUSBAND: I can't stand in the dock with my own flesh and blood in the witness box giving evidence against me.

THE WIFE: You mustn't take it this way.

THE HUSBAND: It was unpardonably careless to have anything to do with the Klimbtsches.

THE WIFE: Why? Nothing has happened to him yet.

THE HUSBAND: But the investigation is pending.

THE WIFE: An investigation is pending for lots of people. What would happen if they were all in despair?

THE HUSBAND: Do you think the Block Warden has anything against us?

THE WIFE: You mean if enquiries are made? He

got a box of cigarettes on his birthday and a splendid tip at New Year's.

THE HUSBAND: The Gauffs next door gave *fifteen* marks!

THE WIFE: But they read *Vorwärts* [6] as late as '32 and in May '33 they put out the black-white-and-red flag. [7]

[*The telephone rings*]

THE HUSBAND: The telephone!

THE WIFE: Shall I go?

THE HUSBAND: I don't know.

THE WIFE: Who can it be?

THE HUSBAND: Wait a while. If it rings again, you can answer it.

[*They wait. It does not ring again*]

THE HUSBAND: This isn't living.

THE WIFE: Karl!

THE HUSBAND: You bore me a Judas. He sits at table and listens as he takes the soup we put before him and carefully registers the conversation of those who begot him. The informer!

THE WIFE: You mustn't say that!

[*There is a pause*]

THE WIFE: Do you think we should make any preparations?

THE HUSBAND: Do you think they'll come with him now?

THE WIFE: It's quite possible.

THE HUSBAND: Maybe I should put on my Iron Cross?

THE WIFE: By all means, Karl.

[*He brings the cross and puts it on with trembling fingers*]

THE WIFE: There's nothing against you at school?

THE HUSBAND: How should I know? I'm willing to teach everything they want to have taught. But what *do* they want to have taught? If only I ever knew! How do I know how they want Bismarck to have been if they are so slow in bringing out the new textbooks? Can't you give the maid another ten marks? She's always listening too.

THE WIFE: [*She nods*] And the picture of Hitler. Shall we hang it over your desk? It'll look better.

THE HUSBAND: Yes, do that.

[*The Wife begins to move the picture*]

THE HUSBAND: But if the boy says we hung it specially, then it will end in "consciousness of guilt."

[*She puts the picture back where it was*]

THE HUSBAND: Wasn't that the door.

THE WIFE: I heard nothing.

THE HUSBAND: There!

THE WIFE: Karl!

[*She throws her arms around him*]

6 Organ of the Social Democrats.
7 Colors of the Nationalists.

THE HUSBAND: Don't lose your nerve. Pack me some underwear.

[*The door is heard opening.* Husband *and* Wife *stand close together, petrified, in the corner of the room. The door opens and in comes* The Boy, *a bag of chocolates in his hand. There is a silence*]

THE BOY: What's the matter?

THE WIFE: Where've you been?

[*The Boy points to the bag of chocolates*]

THE WIFE: Have you only been buying chocolate?

THE BOY: Sure. What do you think?

[*He walks, munching, across the room and out. His parents look after him searchingly*]

THE HUSBAND: Do you think he's telling the truth?

[*The Wife shrugs her shoulders*] [8]

* * *

CONCLUSION

Dim out. A band plays a barbaric march. The chorus is heard. When the lights go up the armored car is seen, stationary, frozen on the Eastern Steppes. The soldiers are wrapped up strangely. They try to keep warm with women's furs and underclothing. But they have also come alive. They beat their arms against their bodies to keep warm. One runs round and stares at the motor.

The soldiers sing to the tune of the Horst Wessel Song:

Two years of conquest in our iron chariot—
And then it stopped before the world was won.
At times we fear that we have made too long a journey;
We'll see no more the Rhineland and the sun.

For as we eastward drove and it was winter,
Our chariot stuck on Volga's bloody strand,
In the third year snow fell upon the Führer's laurels;
We were defeated in the poor man's land.

Enslaved ourselves, we tried to enslave the others.
By force subdued, we grew by force too bold.
Death beckons from the left and from the right.
    O brothers—
The road back home is long, and it is cold!

8 After a number of other scenes dealing with other characters and situations which illustrate other phases of the National Socialist terror and the preparation for war, we find the Nazi war machine stalled in Russia. The war has turned against the "master race," as the conclusion tells us.

Jean-Paul Sartre

(1905– ——)

Immediately upon the conclusion of the Second World War, France was agitated by a philosophical and literary movement that had been brewing for some years; existentialism was its name and a young Parisian professor, Jean-Paul Sartre, its prophet. He was not the only exponent of its tenets. His associate and friend Simone de Beauvoir was just as ready to explain its principles. Nor was Sartre the only able writer to apply them to literature. Many regard the Algerian-French author Albert Camus as an artist superior to Sartre, on the strength of Camus' novels *The Stranger* and *The Plague.* But Sartre's facility in philosophical exposition placed him in the forefront of the existentialist clan, and his success as a playwright made him more widely known than any of his associates or any of his metaphysical predecessors—Kierkegaard, Husserl, Heidegger, and others.

Before the war, Sartre had been little more than a schoolmaster in the eyes of the world. Having studied at the Ecole Normale Supérieure (1924–1928) under the original French essayist and philosopher Alain (Emile Chartier), he had become disposed at an early age to unconventional thinking and dialectical sharpness. The Sorbonne, to which he went from the Ecole, seemed a tepid place after his schooling under Alain, and the conventional thought of his new masters left him unimpressed. Nevertheless, after taking a degree in philosophy in 1929, he turned dutifully to an academic career in the Lycées of Laon and Le Havre and, finally, at the Lycée Condorcet, in Paris. In 1936, he began to publish a number of remarkable studies in psychology which attracted little attention. Two years later his first novel, *Nausea,* appeared, to be followed by a volume of stories, *The Wall* (1939). The novel expressed the hopelessness of mankind in a world in which nothing whatsoever justified the individual's existence. The stories repeated this theme with intensified insistence on the absurdity of man's position. Both books had a bitter, despairing, and cynical tone. They may stand, with the work of other French writers, especially Céline (*Death on the Installment Plan,* 1938), as expressions of a state of mind reflected in the French political situation. This was the period of the Munich pact, the fall of France, the collaborationist policies of many Frenchmen, and the inglorious rule of the Vichy government under the doddering hero Pétain.

Sartre would have been misunderstood, however, if he had been set down as just another spiritless creature of his times. There was fire in his nega-tions, intensity in his *Weltschmerz.* Sartre was drafted into the French Army in 1939 and stationed in Alsace as an artillery observer. Captured in June 1940, he spent nine months in a German prison camp. He escaped disguised as a civilian and slipped into Paris, and there he remained, risking return to a concentration camp, if not indeed summary execution, by playing an active role in the French underground. Moreover, he began to compose literature and drama that challenged men to shape themselves into heroic personalities instead of accepting the degrading status to which an indifferent universe and a pusillanimous, convention-bound society would consign them. And with his new work came recognition for Sartre as a spiritual and intellectual leader in his country. His enormous philosophical thesis *L'Être et le néant* and his stirring play *The Flies* appeared in 1943. His mordant one-act drama *No Exit* was produced in Paris in 1944, about a month before D-Day. His writings were greeted as signs of a renaissance of French culture and spirit. Soon Sartre acquired followers and his ideas grew fashionable: he became the center of a cult at the Café de Flore in Paris. The term "Sartrism" spread like wildfire in intellectual circles.

Interest was revived in Sartre's previous writings, not always to his advantage, and he added substantially to his literary output with brilliant essays, a series of novels, and a number of plays: *The Victors* (*Morts sans sépulture*), *The Respectful Prostitute,* and *Les Mains sales* (*Red Gloves* in a questionable American adaptation).

Debate over existentialism continued to rage while Sartre was developing his thought. He was under fire from the Catholic Right in France because his doctrine was uncompromisingly atheistic. He was also assailed by the Communist Left because his philosophy stressed despair as a cardinal principle and centered all fundamental problems in the individual. It may be conceded that his fiction in particular presented such unsavory characters and situations that his work could be described by its Marxist critics as a product of "bourgeois decadence." Sartre's metaphysics was beyond doubt negativistic, because it predicated a distinct discord between the outer world and man's yearning for wholeness and meaning. Man and the universe are not at one with one another, as the German "idealist" philosophers had maintained ever since Kant by claiming that reality is a product of man's mind. This discrepancy between what is and what we want leaves man a certain degree of freedom of will (the universe is one thing and he is another), but the realization of this kind of freedom can only fill him with anguish. Anguish is the primal condition of any man who is aware of the discord, and it is intensified by his realization that the universe is a *néant*, or nothingness. Man is thrust meaninglessly into a meaningless universe, to which his response can be only "nausea" (the title of Sartre's novel), that is, a sense of incompleteness and futility, or desperation. Sartre's fiction characters were a loathsome lot, and there is no doubt that the fashionable people who took up existentialism were attracted by its nihilism, which is a good excuse for self-indulgence and escape from social responsibility. Existentialism came to be known as the philosophy of a defeated nation.

Yet Sartre's ethical system was altogether different from his metaphysics, as his own services in the French Resistance movement have indicated. He himself had turned defeat into resistance, and had found meaning in action. Such novels as *Nausea* expressed the "human condition," according to Sartre, but an awareness of this condition was intended to be only a prelude to the ethical position to which man could lift himself once he knew that he was "free." Relying solely upon himself instead of on some principle of benevolence or meaning in the universe, man could "create" himself. He could wrest a new humanism out of despair, as Sartre maintained in his essay *L'Existentialisme est un humanisme* in 1946. He could turn his sense of isolation in the universe into a sort of splendor—that is, into self-reliance and into a heroism without illusions. He had possibilities in him that it was his business to discover once he relied on neither God nor other people ("Hell," one of the characters in *No Exit* declares, "is other people")—nor on society, for that matter, so long as it imposes demands of conformity upon the individual. And there was only one way to discover what one really was, what one's character was—namely, by responding to the situations that demand crucial decisions; that is, we realize ourselves truly only by our actions. We make ourselves by what we do: "You are your life"— that is, you are what the conduct of your life reveals you to be. You are not what you fancy yourself to be, but what your behavior demonstrates.

Out of his nettle "anguish," Sartre plucked his flower "safety," namely, a self-sufficiency. So much so, indeed, that he expected his existentialist hero to become fully "engaged" in social action. And in such action, the existentialist would even find himself, since it would reveal to him what he really was like in the most objective of all ways—in his decision and deeds. It is the test undergone most clearly in *The Flies,* as well as in *The Victors.* The characters of both plays discover their strength, just as the characters of *No Exit* and *The Respectful Prostitute* reveal their weakness—most notably in the case of

the man in *No Exit* who thought he was an idealist and pacifist when he was actually only a coward.

In a series of significant articles "What Is Literature?" (1947) Sartre called upon literature, as well as men, to become "engaged." Reflecting on French behavior before the Second World War, he declared that "we tolerated everything, even intolerance." The great awakening came with the Resistance movement when men suffered extreme torture rather than betray their comrades or their cause. Their experience, which made them aware more fully than ever of the existence of evil and exposed them more than ever to the temptation of negation, also enabled them to discover their humanity; that is, to destroy evil and to rediscover the nobility in themselves and other men. Everything conspired to discourage the men of the underground, as in his own play *The Victors:* "So many signs around them, those faces [of the torturers] leaning over them, that suffering in them, everything tried to make them believe that they were only insects, that man is the impossible dream of cockroaches and wood-lice and that they would reawaken as vermin like everything else." But, Sartre adds, "They kept silent and man was born in their silence."

It is in the light of these remarks and of the entire question of a meaningless universe, man's freedom of will, and his "engagement" that *The Flies* must be read. The French have distinguished themselves in reworking classic themes ever since Corneille and Racine, and there was only a slight abatement of the tendency to pour the old Attic wine into new Gallic bottles in the French theatre of the twentieth century. Well-known examples are Jean Giraudoux' *Amphitryon 38* and Jean Cocteau's *The Infernal Machine,* which is the Greek *Oedipus the King* in modern dress, treading the stage with some cynicism and a good deal of conscientiously cultivated surrealist naïveté. *The Flies* differs from these works, however, in being thoroughly serious, and it is a drama of ideas. It is Sartre's existentialist fable, based on the Orestean story as told in the extant plays of Aeschylus, Sophocles, and Euripides. The liberties Sartre takes with the legend elaborate his views, and the play may be fruitfully compared not only with the classic tragedies but with so modern a psychological version as Eugene O'Neill's *Mourning Becomes Electra.* Sartre's treatment is neither reverential nor psychological. It requires metaphysical and political thinking, and its ultimate meaning is ethical. Although it is possible to quarrel with the author's metaphysics, it is not difficult to understand that its political and moral force was extremely welcome when the play reached the French during the days of the German occupation in 1943. If the play has its ambiguities, there is no ambiguity in its message of freedom. Sartre calls for freedom from supernatural and mortal tyrants, freedom from a self-indulgent and enervating sense of guilt that aborts the will to rectify wrongs, and freedom from the hollow detachment or disengagement that tempts the intellectual to live unto himself superiorly in a self-created vacuum.

The play was produced by the distinguished director Charles Dullin under the very nose of the Nazi rulers of Paris, who were evidently too obtuse to read into it the significance it had for that part of the French public which could follow its meaning. A skillful American production was made later (April 17, 1947) at the Dramatic Workshop of the New School in New York by the self-exiled German director Erwin Piscator. Memorable, too, was the production of the play at the Hebbel Theatre in the Allied sector of Berlin shortly after the defeat of Germany. The play aroused considerable debate, with the Russian-licensed press violently in the opposition and the American and English divided between enthusiasm over Sartre as a born dramatist and reservations to the effect that his drama was too much of a discussion piece.

The "flies" are minor Furies or Eumenides, and the reader can proceed to draw his own implications from this point on; he may consider the idea that they represent the wallowing in guilt and the self-condemnation that many Frenchmen experienced after the defeat of France. The critic Eric Bentley raises interesting questions concerning details in the play: "When, for instance, must Orestes be in exile and when among men? What is the moral difference between his [Orestes'] murdering Ægistheus and his murdering his mother? What kind of power is Jupiter meant to have? [One might answer: Only the power of men's belief in him.] What is this god to whom we owe our being, yet to whom we owe no allegiance?" Probably Sartre would deny that we owe our being to him. Jupiter is merely a personified belief, and men owe him no more allegiance than they are willing to give him through their faith in his existence. This faith is strong enough to give Jupiter a physical reality in the eyes of his believers, and in the eyes of those who have no belief in him as well—since he is a reality to most people, and the nonbeliever has to cope with their beliefs. It is not the least of the merits of a drama of ideas such as *The Flies* that it gives us some mental exercise.

BIBLIOGRAPHY: Eric Bentley, *The Playwright as Thinker* (pp. 233–246, 270–272, 358–359), 1946; Marjorie Grene, *Dreadful Freedom: A Critique of Existentialism*, 1948; *Yale French Studies* (see especially articles by Henri Peyre, Charles G. Whiting, and Walter Leavitt), Vol. I, No. 1, Spring–Summer 1948.

THE FLIES

By Jean-Paul Sartre

TRANSLATED FROM THE FRENCH BY STUART GILBERT

CHARACTERS IN THE PLAY

ZEUS	FIRST FURY	FIRST SOLDIER
ORESTES	SECOND FURY	SECOND SOLDIER
ELECTRA	THE HIGH PRIEST	MEN AND WOMEN, TOWNSFOLK OF
ÆGISTHEUS	A YOUNG WOMAN	ARGOS
CLYTEMNESTRA	AN OLD WOMAN	FURIES, SERVANTS, PALACE GUARDS
THE TUTOR	AN IDIOT BOY	

ACT I.

A public square in Argos, dominated by a statue of Zeus, god of flies and death. The image has white eyes and blood-smeared cheeks. A procession of Old Women *in black, carrying urns, advances; they make libations to the statue. An* Idiot Boy *is squatting in the background.* Orestes *enters, accompanied by* The Tutor.

ORESTES: Listen, my good women.
  [*The* Old Women *swing round, emitting little squeals*]
THE TUTOR: Would you kindly tell us— [*The* Old Women *spit on the ground and move back a pace*] Steady, good ladies, steady. I only want a piece of simple information. We are travelers and we have lost our way. [*Dropping their urns, the* Women *take to their heels*] Stupid old hags! You'd think I had intentions on their virtue! [*Ironically*] Ah, young master, truly this has been a pleasant journey. And how well inspired you were to come to this city of Argos, when there are hundreds of towns in Greece and Italy where the drink is good, the inns are hospitable, and the streets full of friendly, smiling people! But these uncouth hillmen—one would suppose they'd never seen a foreigner before. A hundred times and more I've had to ask our way, and never once did I get a straight answer. And then the grilling heat! This Argos is a nightmare city. Squeals of terror everywhere, people who panic the moment they set eyes on you, and scurry to cover, like black beetles, down the glaring streets. Pfoo! I can't think how you bear it—this emptiness, the shimmering air, that fierce sun overhead. What's deadlier than the sun?
ORESTES: I was born here.

THE TUTOR: So the story goes. But, if I were you, I wouldn't brag about it.
ORESTES: I was born here—and yet I have to ask my way, like any stranger. Knock at that door.
THE TUTOR: What do you expect? That someone will open it? Only look at those houses and tell me how they strike you. You will observe there's not a window anywhere. They open on closed courtyards, I suppose, and turn their backsides to the street. [Orestes *makes a fretful gesture*] Very good, sir. I'll knock—but nothing will come of it.
  [*He knocks. Nothing happens. He knocks again, and the door opens a cautious inch*]
A VOICE: What do you want?
THE TUTOR: Just a word of information. Can you tell me where—? [*The door is slammed in his face*] Oh, the devil take you! Well, my lord Orestes, is that enough, or must I try elsewhere? If you wish, I'll knock at every door.
ORESTES: No, that's enough.
THE TUTOR: Well, I never! There's someone here. [*He goes up to the* Idiot Boy] Excuse me, sir . . .
THE IDIOT: Hoo! Hoo! Hoo!
THE TUTOR: [*Bowing again*] My noble lord . . .
THE IDIOT: Hoo!
THE TUTOR: Will Your Highness deign to show us where Ægistheus lives?
THE IDIOT: Hoo!
THE TUTOR: Ægistheus, King of Argos.
THE IDIOT: Hoo! Hoo! Hoo!
  [Zeus *passes by, back stage*]
THE TUTOR: We're out of luck. The only one who doesn't run away is a half-wit. [Zeus *retraces his steps*] Ah, that's odd! He's followed us here.
ORESTES: Who?
THE TUTOR: That bearded fellow.
ORESTES: You're dreaming.
THE TUTOR: I tell you, I saw him go by.
ORESTES: You must be mistaken.

THE TUTOR: Impossible. Never in my life have I seen such a beard—or, rather, only one: the bronze beard on the chin of Zeus Ahenobarbos at Palermo. Look, there he is again. What can he want of us?

ORESTES: He is only a traveler like ourselves.

THE TUTOR: Only that? We met him on the road to Delphi. And when we took the boat at Itea, there he was, fanning that great beard in the bows. At Nauplia we couldn't move a step without having him at our heels, and now—here he is again! Do you think that chance explains it? [*He brushes the flies off his face*] These flies in Argos are much more sociable than its townsfolk. Just look at them! [*Points to the* Idiot Boy] There must be a round dozen pumping away at each of his eyes, and yet he's smiling quite contentedly; probably he likes having his eyes sucked. That's not surprising; look at that yellow muck oozing out of them. [*He flaps his hand at the flies*] Move on, my little friends. Hah! They're on you now. Allow me! [*He drives them away*] Well, this should please you—you who are always complaining of being a stranger in your native land. These charming insects, anyhow, are making you welcome; one would think they know who you are. [*He whisks them away*] Now leave us in peace, you buzzers. We know you like us, but we've had enough of you. . . . Where can they come from? They're as big as bumble-bees and noisy as a swarm of locusts.

[*Meanwhile* Zeus *has approached them*]

ZEUS: They are only bluebottles, a trifle larger than usual. Fifteen years ago a mighty stench of carrion drew them to this city, and since then they've been getting fatter and fatter. Give them another fifteen years, and they'll be as big as toads. [*A short silence*]

THE TUTOR: Pray, whom have I the honor of addressing?

ZEUS: Demetrios is my name, and I hail from Athens.

ORESTES: Did I not see you on the boat, a fortnight ago?

ZEUS: Yes, and I saw you, too.

[*Hideous shrieks come from the palace*]

THE TUTOR: Listen to that! I don't know if you will agree with me, young master, but I think we'd do better to leave this place.

ORESTES: Keep quiet!

ZEUS: You have nothing to fear. It's what they call Dead Men's Day today. Those cries announce the beginning of the ceremony.

ORESTES: You seem well posted on the local customs.

ZEUS: Yes, I often visit Argos. As it so happened, I was here on the great day of Agamemnon's homecoming, when the Greek fleet, flushed with victory, anchored in the Nauplia roads. From the top of the rampart one saw the bay dappled with their white sails. [*He drives the flies away*] There were no flies then. Argos was only a small country town, basking in the sun, yawning the years away. Like everyone else I went up to the sentry-path to see the royal procession, and I watched it for many an hour wending across the plain. At sundown on the second day Queen Clytemnestra came to the ramparts, and with her was Ægistheus, the present King. The people of Argos saw their faces dyed red by the sunset, and they saw them leaning over the battlements, gazing for a long while seawards. And the people thought: "There's evil brewing." But they kept silence. Ægistheus, you should know, was the Queen's lover. A hard, brutal man, and even in those days he had the cast of melancholy. . . . But you're looking pale, young sir.

ORESTES: It's the long journey I have made, and this accursed heat. But pray go on; you interest me.

ZEUS: Agamemnon was a worthy man, you know, but he made one great mistake. He put a ban on public executions. That was a pity. A good hanging now and then—that entertains folk in the provinces and robs death of its glamour. . . . So the people here held their tongues; they looked forward to seeing, for once, a violent death. They still kept silent when they saw their King entering by the city gates. And when Clytemnestra stretched forth her graceful arms, fragrant and white as lilies, they still said nothing. Yet at that moment a word, a single word, might have sufficed. But no one said it; each was gloating in imagination over the picture of a huge corpse with a shattered face.

ORESTES: And you, too, said nothing?

ZEUS: Does that rouse your indignation? Well, my young friend, I like you all the better for it; it proves your heart's in the right place. No, I admit I, too, held my peace. I'm a stranger here, and it was no concern of mine. And next day when it started, when the folk of Argos heard their King screaming his life out in the palace, they still kept silence, but they rolled their eyes in a sort of ecstasy, and the whole town was like a woman in heat.

ORESTES: So now the murderer is on the throne. For fifteen years he has enjoyed the fruits of crime. And I thought the gods were just!

ZEUS: Steady, my friend. Don't blame the gods too hastily. Must they always punish? Wouldn't it be better to use such breaches of the law to point a moral?

ORESTES: And is this what they did?

ZEUS: They sent the flies.

THE TUTOR: The flies? How do the flies come in?

ZEUS: They are a symbol. But if you want to know what the gods did, look around you. See that old creature over there, creeping away like a beetle on her little black feet, and hugging the walls. Well, she's a good specimen of the squat black vermin that teem in every cranny of this town. Now watch me catch our specimen, it's well worth inspection. Here it is. A loathsome object, you'll agree. . . . Hah! You're blinking now. Still, you're an Argive and you should be used to the white-hot rapiers of the sun.

. . . Watch her wriggling, like a hooked fish! . . .
Now, old lady, let's hear your tale of woe. I see
you're in black from head to foot. In mourning for a
whole regiment of sons, is that it? Tell us, and I'll
release you—perhaps. For whom are you in mourning?

OLD WOMAN: Sir, I am not in mourning. Everyone
wears black at Argos.

ZEUS: Everyone wears black? Ah, I see. You're in
mourning for your murdered King.

OLD WOMAN: Whisht! For God's sake, don't talk
of that.

ZEUS: Yes, you're quite old enough to have heard
those huge cries that echoed and re-echoed for a
whole morning in the city street. What did you do
about it?

OLD WOMAN: My good man was in the fields, at
work. What could I do? a woman alone? I bolted
my door.

ZEUS: Yes, but you left your window not quite
closed, so as to hear the better, and, while you
peeped behind the curtains and held your breath,
you felt a little tingling itch between your loins,
and didn't you enjoy it!

OLD WOMAN: Oh, please stop, sir!

ZEUS: And when you went to bed that night, you
had a grand time with your man. A real gala night.

OLD WOMAN: A what? . . . No, my lord, that
was a dreadful, dreadful night.

ZEUS: A red gala, I tell you, and you've never
been able to blot out its memory.

OLD WOMAN: Mercy on us! Are you—are you
one of the Dead?

ZEUS: I dead? You're crazy, woman. . . . Anyhow, don't trouble your head who I am; you'd do
better to think of yourself, and try to earn forgiveness by repenting of your sins.

OLD WOMAN: Oh, sir, I do repent, most heartily I
repent. If you only knew how I repent, and my
daughter too, and my son-in-law offers up a heifer
every year, and my little grandson has been brought
up in a spirit of repentance. He's a pretty lad, with
flaxen hair, and he always behaves as good as gold.
Though he's only seven, he never plays or laughs,
for thinking of his original sin.

ZEUS: Good, you old bitch, that's as it should be
—and be sure you die in a nice bitchy odor of
repentance. It's your one hope of salvation. [The
Old Woman runs away] Unless I'm much mistaken,
my masters, we have there the real thing, the good
old piety of yore, rooted in terror.

ORESTES: What man are you?

ZEUS: Who cares what I am. We were talking of
the gods. Well now, should they have struck Ægistheus down?

ORESTES: They should. . . . They should. . . .
Oh, how would I know what they should have done?
What do I care, anyhow? I'm a stranger here. . . .
Does Ægistheus feel contrition?

ZEUS: Ægistheus? I'd be much surprised. But what

matter? A whole city's repenting on his account.
And it's measured by the bushel, is repentance.
[Eerie screams in the palace] Listen! Lest they forget the screams of the late King in his last agony,
they keep this festival of death each year when the
day of the King's murder comes round. A herdsman
from the hills—he's chosen for his lung-power—is
set to bellow in the Great Hall of the palace. [Ores-
tes makes a gesture of disgust] Bah! That's nothing. I wonder what you'll say presently, when they
let the Dead loose. Fifteen years ago, to a day,
Agamemnon was murdered. And what a change has
come over the light-hearted folk of Argos since that
day! how near and dear to me they are at present!

ORESTES: Dear to you?

ZEUS: Pay no heed, young man. That was a slip
of the tongue. Near and dear to the gods, I meant.

ORESTES: You surprise me. Then those blood-
smeared walls, these swarms of flies, this reek of
shambles and the stifling heat, these empty streets
and yonder god with his gashed face, and all those
creeping, half-human creatures beating their breasts
in darkened rooms, and those shrieks, those hideous,
blood-curdling shrieks—can it be that Zeus and his
Olympians delight in these?

ZEUS: Young man, do not sit in judgment on the
gods. They have their secrets—and their sorrows.
[A short silence]

ORESTES: Am I right in thinking Agamemnon had
a daughter? A daughter named Electra?

ZEUS: Yes. She lives there, in the palace—that
building yonder.

ORESTES: So that's the palace? . . . And what
does Electra think of—all this?

ZEUS: Oh, she's a mere child. There was a son,
too, named Orestes. But he's dead, it seems.

ORESTES: Dead? Well, really . . .

THE TUTOR: Of course he's dead, young master. I
thought you knew it. Don't you remember what
they told us at Nauplia—about Ægistheus' having
him murdered, soon after Agamemnon's death?

ZEUS: Still, some say he's alive. The story goes
that the men ordered to kill the child had pity on
him and left him in the forest. Some rich Athenians
found him there and took him home. For my part,
I'd rather he were dead.

ORESTES: Pray, why?

ZEUS: Suppose that one day he appeared in this
city, and—

ORESTES: Continue, please.

ZEUS: As you wish . . . Well, I'd say this to him.
"My lad—" I'd say, "My lad," as he's your age or
thereabouts—if he's alive, of course. By the way,
young lord, may I know your name?

ORESTES: Philebus is my name, and I hail from
Corinth. I am traveling to improve my mind, and
this old slave accompanying me used to be my tutor.

ZEUS: Thank you. Well, I'd say something like
this. "My lad, get you gone! What business have you
here? Do you wish to enforce your rights? Yes,

you're brave and strong and spirited. I can see you as a captain in an army of good fighters. You have better things to do than reigning over a dead-and-alive city, a carrion city plagued by flies. These people are great sinners but, as you see, they're working out their atonement. Let them be, young fellow, let them be; respect their sorrowful endeavor, and be-gone on tiptoe. You cannot share in their repent-ance, since you did not share their crime. Your brazen innocence makes a gulf between you and them. So if you have any care for them, be off! Be off, or you will work their doom. If you hinder them on their way, if even for a moment you turn their thoughts from their remorse, all their sins will harden on them—like cold fat. They have guilty consciences, they're afraid—and fear and guilty consciences have a good savor in the nostrils of the gods. Yes, the gods take pleasure in such poor souls. Would you oust them from the favor of the gods? What, moreover, could you give them in exchange? Good digestions, the gray monotony of provincial life, and the boredom—ah, the soul-destroying bore-dom—of long days of mild content. Go your way, my lad, go your way. The repose of cities and men's souls hangs on a thread; tamper with it and you bring disaster. [*Looking him in the eyes*] A disaster which will recoil on you."

ORESTES: Yes? So that is what you'd say? Well, if I were that young man, I'd answer— [*They eye each other truculently*. The Tutor *coughs*] No, I don't know how I'd answer you. Perhaps you're right, and anyhow it's no concern of mine.

ZEUS: Good. I only hope Orestes would show as much sense. . . . Well, peace be with you, my friend; I must go about my business.

ORESTES: Peace be with you.

ZEUS: By the way, if those flies bother you, here's a way of getting rid of them. You see that swarm buzzing round your head? Right. Now watch! I flick my wrist—so—and wave my arm once, and then I say: Abraxas, galla, galla, tsay, tsay. See! They're falling down and starting to crawl on the ground like caterpillars.

ORESTES: By Jove!

ZEUS: Oh, that's nothing. Just a parlor trick. I'm a fly-charmer in my leisure hours. Good day to you. We shall meet again. [*Exit* Zeus]

THE TUTOR: Take care. That man knows who you are.

ORESTES: "Man," you say. But *is* he a man?

THE TUTOR: What else should he be? You grieve me, my young master. Have all my lessons, all my precepts, the smiling skepticism I taught you, been wasted on your ears? "Is he a man?" you ask. There's nothing else but men—what more would you have? And that bearded fellow is a man, sure enough; probably one of Ægistheus' spies.

ORESTES: A truce to your philosophy! It's done me too much harm already.

THE TUTOR: Harm? Do you call it doing harm to

people when one emancipates their minds? Ah, how you've changed! Once I read you like an open book. . . . But at least you might tell me your plans. Why bring me to this city, and what's your purpose here?

ORESTES: Did I say I had a purpose? But that's enough. Be silent now. [*He takes some steps towards the palace*] That is *my* palace. My father's birth-place. And it's there a whore and her paramour foully butchered him. I, too, was born there. I was nearly three when that usurper's bravoes carried me away. Most likely we went out by that door. One of them held me in his arms, I had my eyes wide open, and no doubt I was crying. And yet I have no memories, none whatever. I am looking at a huge, gloomy building, solemn and pretentious in the worst provincial taste. I am looking at it, but I *see* it for the first time.

THE TUTOR: No memories, master? What ingrati-tude, considering that I gave ten years of my life to stocking you with them! And what of all the journeys we have made together, all the towns we visited? And the course in archæology I composed specially for you? No memories, indeed! Palaces, shrines, and temples—with so many of them is your memory peopled that you could write a guide-book of all Greece.

ORESTES: Palaces—that's so. Palaces, statues, pil-lars—stones, stones, stones! Why, with all those stones in my head, am I not heavier? While you are about it, why not remind me of the three hundred and eighty-seven steps of the temple at Ephesus? I climbed them, one by one, and I remember each. The seventeenth, if my memory serves me, was badly broken. And yet—! Why, an old, mangy dog, warming himself at the hearth, and struggling to his feet with a little whimper to welcome his master home—why, that dog has more memories than I! At least he recognizes his master. *His* master. But what can I call mine?

THE TUTOR: And what of your culture, Lord Orestes? What of that? All that wise lore I culled for you with loving care, like a bouquet, matching the fruits of my knowledge with the finest flowers of my experience? Did I not, from the very first, set you a-reading all the books there are, so as to make clear to you the infinite diversity of men's opinions? And did I not remind you, time and again, how variable are human creeds and customs? So, along with youth, good looks, and wealth, you have the wisdom of far riper years; your mind is free from prejudice and superstition; you have no family ties, no religion, and no calling; you are free to turn your hand to anything. But you know better than to com-mit yourself—and there lies your strength. So, in a word, you stand head and shoulders above the ruck and, what's more, you could hold a chair of philoso-phy or architecture in a great university. And yet you cavil at your lot!

ORESTES: No, I do not cavil. What should I cavil

at? You've left me free as the strands torn by the wind from spiders' webs that one sees floating ten feet above the ground. I'm light as gossamer and walk on air. I know I'm favored, I appreciate my lot at its full value. [*A pause*] Some men are born bespoken; a certain path has been assigned them, and at its end there is something they *must* do, a deed allotted. So on and on they trudge, wounding their bare feet on the flints. I suppose that strikes *you* as vulgar—the joy of going somewhere definite. And there are others, men of few words, who bear deep down in their hearts a load of dark imaginings; men whose whole life was changed because one day in childhood, at the age of five or seven— Right; I grant you these are no great men. When I was seven, I know I had no home, no roots. I let sounds and scents, the patter of rain on housetops, the golden play of sunbeams, slip past my body and fall round me—and I knew these were for others, I could never make them *my* memories. For memories are luxuries reserved for people who own houses, cattle, fields and servants. Whereas I—! I'm free as air, thank God. My mind's my own, gloriously aloof. [*He goes nearer to the palace*] I might have lived there. I'd not have read any of your books; perhaps I'd not have learned to read. It's rare for a Greek prince to know how to read. But I'd have come in and gone out by that door ten thousand times. As a child I'd have played with its leaves, and when I pushed at them with all my little might, they'd have creaked without yielding, and I'd have taken the measure of my weakness. Later on, I'd have pushed them open furtively by night and gone out after girls. And some years later, when I came of age, the slaves would have flung the doors wide open and I'd have crossed the threshold on horseback. My old wooden door! I'd have been able to find your keyhole with my eyes shut. And that notch there—I might have made it showing off, the first day they let me hold a spear. [*He steps back*] Let's see. That's the Dorian style, isn't it? And what do you make of that gold inlay? I saw the like at Dodona; a pretty piece of craftsmanship. And now I'm going to say something that will rejoice you. This is not *my* palace, nor *my* door. And there's nothing to detain us here.

THE TUTOR: Ah, that's talking sense. For what would you have gained by living in Argos? By now your spirit would be broken, you'd be wallowing in repentance.

ORESTES: Still, it would be *my* repentance. And this furnace heat singeing my hair would be *mine.* Mine, too, the buzz of all these flies. At this moment I'd be lying naked in some dark room at the back of the palace, and watching a ribbon of red light lengthen across the floor. I'd be waiting for sundown; waiting for the cool dusk of an Argos evening to rise like perfume from the parched earth; an Argos evening like many a thousand others, familiar yet ever new, another evening that should be *mine.*

. . . Well, well, my worthy pedagogue, let's be off. We've no business to be luxuriating in others' heat.

THE TUTOR: Ah, my young lord, how you've eased my mind! During these last few months—to be exact, ever since I revealed to you the secret of your birth—I could see you changing day by day, and it gave me many a sleepless night. I was afraid—

ORESTES: Of what?

THE TUTOR: No, it will anger you.

ORESTES: Speak.

THE TUTOR: Be it so. Well, though from one's earliest years one has been trained to skeptic irony, one can't help having foolish fancies now and then. And I wondered if you weren't hatching some wild scheme to oust Ægistheus and take his place.

ORESTES: [*Thoughtfully*] To oust Ægistheus. Ah— [*A pause*] No, my good slave, you need not fear; the time for that is past. True, nothing could please me better than to grip that sanctimonious ruffian by the beard and drag him from my father's throne. But what purpose would it serve? These folk are no concern of mine. I have not seen one of their children come into the world, nor been present at their daughters' weddings; I don't share their remorse, I don't even know a single one of them by name. That bearded fellow was right; a king should share his subjects' memories. So we'll let them be, and begone on tiptoe. . . . But, mind you, if there were something I could do, something to give me the freedom of the city; if, even by a crime, I could acquire their memories, their hopes and fears, and fill with these the void within me, yes, even if I had to kill my own mother—

THE TUTOR: Hush! For heaven's sake, hush!

ORESTES: Yes, these are idle dreams. Let's be off. Now go and see if we can get some horses here, and we'll move on to Sparta, where I have good friends.

[Electra *comes forward, carrying a large ashcan. She goes up to the statue of* Zeus, *without seeing them*]

ELECTRA: Yes, you old swine, scowl away at me with your goggle eyes and your fat face all smeared with raspberry juice—scowl away, but you won't scare me, not you! They've been to worship you, haven't they?—those pious matrons in black dresses. They've been padding round you in their big creaky shoes. And you were pleased, old bugaboo, it warmed your silly wooden heart. You like them old, of course; the nearer they're to corpses, the more you love them. They've poured their choicest wines out at your feet, because it's your festival today, and the stale smell from their petticoats tickled your nostrils. [*She rubs herself against him*] Now smell me for a change, smell the perfume of a fresh, clean body. But, of course, I'm young, I'm alive—and you loathe youth and life. I, too, am bringing you offerings, while all the others are at prayers. Here they are: ashes from the hearth, peelings, scraps of offal crawling with maggots, a chunk of bread too filthy even for our pigs. But your darling flies will love it, won't they, Zeus? A good feast-day to you, old idol, and let's hope it is your last. I'm not strong enough to pull you down. All I can do is to spit at you. But some day he will come, the man I'm waiting for, carrying a long, keen sword. He'll look you up and down and chuckle, with his hands on his hips, like this, and his head thrown back. Then he'll draw his sword and chop you in two, from top to bottom—like this! So the two halves of Zeus will fall apart, one to the left, one to the right, and everyone will see he's made of common wood. Just a lump of cheap white deal, the terrible God of Death! And all that frightfulness, the blood on his face, his dark-green eyes, and all the rest—they'll see it was only a coat of paint. *You,* anyhow, you know you're white inside, white as a child's body, and you know, too, that a sword can rip you limb from limb, and you won't even bleed. Just a log of deal—anyhow it will serve to light our fires next winter. [*She notices Orestes*] Oh!

ORESTES: Don't be alarmed.

ELECTRA: I'm not alarmed. Not a bit. Who are you?

ORESTES: A stranger.

ELECTRA: Then you are welcome. All that's foreign to this town is dear to me. Your name?

ORESTES: Philebus. I've come from Corinth.

ELECTRA: Ah? From Corinth. My name's Electra.

ORESTES: Electra—[*To the* Tutor] Leave us. [*Exit the* Tutor]

ELECTRA: Why are you looking at me like that?

ORESTES: You're very beautiful. Not at all like the people in these parts.

ELECTRA: I beautiful? Can you really mean it? As beautiful as the Corinthian girls?

ORESTES: Yes.

ELECTRA: Well, here they never tell me that I'm beautiful. Perhaps they don't want me to know it. Anyhow, what use would beauty be to me? I'm only a servant.

ORESTES: What! You a servant?

ELECTRA: The least of the servants in the palace. I wash the King's and the Queen's underlinen. And how dirty it is, all covered with spots and stains! Yes, I have to wash everything they wear next their skin, the shifts they wrap their rotting bodies in, the nightdresses Clytemnestra has on when the King shares her bed. I shut my eyes and scrub with all my might. I have to wash up, too. You don't believe me? See my hands, all chapped and rough. Why are you looking at them in that funny way? Do they, by any chance, look like the hands of a princess?

ORESTES: Poor little hands. No, they don't look like a princess's hands. . . . But tell me more. What else do they make you do?

ELECTRA: Every morning I've to empty the ash-can. I drag it out of the palace, and then—well, you saw what I do with the refuse. That big fellow in wood is Zeus, God of Death and Flies. The other day, when the High Priest came here to make his

usual bows and scrapings, he found himself treading on cabbage-stumps and rotten turnips and mussel-shells. He looked startled, I can tell you! I say! You won't tell on me, will you?

ORESTES: No.

ELECTRA: Really I don't care if you do. They can't make things much worse for me than they are already. I'm used to being beaten. Perhaps they'd shut me up in one of the rooms in the tower. That wouldn't be so bad; at least I wouldn't have to see their faces. Just imagine what I get by way of thanks at bedtime, when my day's work is done. I go up to a tall, stout lady with dyed hair, with thick lips and very white hands, a queen's hands, that smell of honey. Then she puts her hands on my shoulders and dabs my forehead with her lips and says: "Good night, Electra. Good night." Every evening. Every evening I have to feel that woman slobbering on my face. Ugh! Like a piece of raw meat on my forehead. But I hold myself up, I've never fallen yet. She's my mother, you know. If I was up in the tower, she wouldn't kiss me any more.

ORESTES: Have you never thought of running away?

ELECTRA: I haven't the courage; I daren't face the country roads at night all by myself.

ORESTES: Is there no one, no girl friend of yours, who'd go with you?

ELECTRA: No, I am quite alone. Ask any of the people here, and they'll tell you I'm a pest, a public nuisance. I've no friends.

ORESTES: Not even an old nurse, who saw you into the world and has kept a little affection for you?

ELECTRA: Not even an old nurse. Mother will tell you; I freeze even the kindest hearts—that's how I am.

ORESTES: Do you propose to spend your life here?

ELECTRA: [*Excitedly*] My life? Oh, no, no! Of course not! Listen. I'm waiting for—for something.

ORESTES: Something, or someone?

ELECTRA: That's my secret. Now it's your turn to speak. You're good-looking, too. Will you be here long?

ORESTES: Well, I'd thought of leaving today. But, as it is—

ELECTRA: Yes?

ORESTES: As it is, I'm not so sure.

ELECTRA: Is Corinth a pretty place?

ORESTES: Very pretty.

ELECTRA: Do you like it? Are you proud of Corinth?

ORESTES: Yes.

ELECTRA: How strange that sounds! I can't imagine myself being proud of my home town. Tell me what it feels like.

ORESTES: Well— No, I don't know. I can't explain.

ELECTRA: You can't? I wonder why. [*A short silence*] What's Corinth like? Are there shady streets and squares? Places where one can stroll in the cool of the evening?

ORESTES: Yes.

ELECTRA: And everyone comes out of doors? People go for walks together?

ORESTES: Almost everyone is out and about at sundown.

ELECTRA: Boys and girls together?

ORESTES: Oh yes, one often sees them going for walks together.

ELECTRA: And they always find something to say to each other? They like each other's company, and one hears them laughing in the streets quite late at night?

ORESTES: Yes.

ELECTRA: I suppose you think I'm very childish. But it's so hard for me to picture a life like that— going for walks, laughing and singing in the streets. Everybody here is sick with fear. Everyone except me. And I—

ORESTES: Yes? and you?

ELECTRA: Oh, I—I'm sick with—hatred. And what do they do all day, the girls at Corinth?

ORESTES: Well, they spend quite a while making themselves pretty; then they sing or play on lutes. Then they call on their friends, and at night they go to dances.

ELECTRA: But don't they have any worries?

ORESTES: Only quite little ones.

ELECTRA: Yes? Now listen well, please. Don't the people at Corinth feel remorse?

ORESTES: Sometimes. Not very often.

ELECTRA: So they do what they like and, afterwards, don't give another thought to it?

ORESTES: That's their way.

ELECTRA: How strange! [*A short silence*] Please tell me something else; I want to know it because of —of someone I'm expecting. Suppose one of the young fellows you've been telling about, who walk and laugh with girls in the evenings—suppose one of these young men came home after a long journey and found his father murdered, and his mother living with the murderer, and his sister treated like a slave —what would he do, that young man from Corinth? Would he just take it for granted and slink out of his father's house and look for consolation with his girl friends? Or would he draw his sword and hurl himself at the assassin, and slash his brains out? . . . Why are you silent?

ORESTES: I was wondering—

ELECTRA: What? You can't say what he'd do?

CLYTEMNESTRA: [*Off stage, calling*] Electra!

ELECTRA: Hush!

ORESTES: What is it?

ELECTRA: That was my mother, Queen Clytemnestra. [Clytemnestra *enters*] What's this, Philebus? Are you afraid of her?

ORESTES: [*To himself*] So that's the face I tried to picture, night after night, until I came to see it, really *see* it, drawn and haggard under the rosy mask of paint. But I hadn't counted on those dead eyes.

CLYTEMNESTRA: Electra, hear the King's order. You are to make ready for the ceremony. You must wear your black dress and your jewels. . . . Well, what does this behavior mean? Why are you pressing your elbows to your hips and staring at the ground? Oh, I know your tricks, my girl, but they don't deceive me any longer. Just now I was watching at the window and I saw a very different Electra, a girl with flashing eyes, bold gestures. . . . Why don't you answer?

ELECTRA: Do you really think a scullery-maid would add to the splendor of your festival?

CLYTEMNESTRA: No play-acting. You are a princess, Electra, and the townsfolk expect to see you, as in former years.

ELECTRA: A princess—yes, the princess of a day. Once a year, when this day comes round, you remember who I am; because, of course, the people want an edifying glimpse of our family life. A strange princess, indeed, who herds pigs and washes up. Tell me, will Ægistheus put his arm round my neck as he did last time? Will he smile tenderly on me, while he mumbles horrible threats in my ear?

CLYTEMNESTRA: If you would have him otherwise, it rests with you.

ELECTRA: Yes—if I let myself be tainted by your remorse; if I beg the gods' forgiveness for a crime I never committed. Yes—if I kiss your royal husband's hand and call him father. Ugh! The mere thought makes me sick. There's dry blood under his nails.

CLYTEMNESTRA: Do as you will. I have long ceased giving you orders in my name. It is the King's command I bring you.

ELECTRA: And why should I obey him? Ægistheus is your husband, Mother, your dearly beloved husband—not mine.

CLYTEMNESTRA: That is all I have to say, Electra. Only too well I see you are determined to bring ruin on yourself, and on us all. Yet who am I to counsel you, I who ruined my whole life in a single morning? You hate me, my child, but what disturbs me more is your likeness to me, as I was once. I used to have those clean-cut features, that fever in the blood, those smoldering eyes—and nothing good came of them.

ELECTRA: No! Don't say I'm like you! Tell me, Philebus—you can see us side by side—am I really like her?

ORESTES: How can I tell? Her face is like a pleasant garden that hail and storms have ravaged. And upon yours I see a threat of storm; one day passion will sear it to the bone.

ELECTRA: A threat of storm? Good! So far I welcome the likeness. May your words come true!

CLYTEMNESTRA: And you, young man, who stare so boldly at us, who are you and why have you come here? Let me look at you more closely.

ELECTRA: [*Quickly*] He's a Corinthian, of the name of Philebus. A traveler.

CLYTEMNESTRA: Philebus? Ah!

ELECTRA: You seemed to fear another name.

CLYTEMNESTRA: To fear? If the doom I brought on my life has taught me anything, it is that I have nothing left to fear. . . . Welcome to Argos, stranger. Yes, come nearer. How young you seem! What's your age?

ORESTES: Eighteen.

CLYTEMNESTRA: Are your parents alive?

ORESTES: My father's dead.

CLYTEMNESTRA: And your mother? Is she about my age? Ah, you don't answer. I suppose she looks much younger; she still laughs and sings when you are with her. Do you love her? Answer me, please. Why did you leave her?

ORESTES: I am on my way to Sparta, to enlist in the army.

CLYTEMNESTRA: Most travelers give our city a wide berth. Some go twenty leagues out of their way to avoid it. Were you not warned? The people of the Plain have put us in quarantine; they see our repentance as a sort of pestilence and are afraid of being infected.

ORESTES: I know.

CLYTEMNESTRA: Did they tell you that we bear the burden of an inexpiable crime, committed fifteen years ago?

ORESTES: Yes, they told me that.

CLYTEMNESTRA: And that Queen Clytemnestra bears the heaviest load of guilt—that men shudder at her name?

ORESTES: That, too, I heard.

CLYTEMNESTRA: And yet you've come here! Stranger, I am Queen Clytemnestra.

ELECTRA: Don't pity her, Philebus. The Queen is indulging in our national pastime, the game of public confession. Here everyone cries his sins on the housetops. On holidays you'll often see a worthy shopkeeper dragging himself along on his knees, covering his hair with dust, and screaming out that he's a murderer, a libertine, a liar, and all the rest of it. But the folk of Argos are getting a little tired of these amusements; everyone knows his neighbor's sins by heart. The Queen's, especially, have lost interest; they're official—our basic crimes, in fact. So you can imagine her delight when she finds someone like you, somebody raw and young, who doesn't even know her name, to hear her tale of guilt. A marvelous opportunity! It's as if she were confessing for the first time.

CLYTEMNESTRA: Be silent. Anyone has the right to spit in my face, to call me murderess and whore. But no one has the right to speak ill of my remorse.

ELECTRA: Note her words, Philebus. That's a rule of the game. People will beg you to condemn them, but you must be sure to judge them only on the sins they own to; their other evil deeds are no one's business, and they wouldn't thank you for detecting them.

CLYTEMNESTRA: Fifteen years ago men said I was the loveliest woman in Greece. Look at me now and judge my sufferings. Let me be frank, young stranger; it is not the death of that old lecher that I regret. When I saw his blood tingeing the water in the bath, I sang and danced for joy. And even now, after fifteen years, whenever I recall it, I have a thrill of pleasure. But—but I had a son; he would be your age now. When Ægistheus handed him over to his bravoes, I—

ELECTRA: You had a daughter too, my mother, if I'm not mistaken. And you've made of her a scullion. But that crime, it seems, sits lightly on your conscience.

CLYTEMNESTRA: You are young, Electra. It is easy for young people, who have not yet had a chance of sinning, to condemn. But wait, my girl; one day you, too, will be trailing after you an inexpiable crime. At every step you will think that you are leaving it behind, but it will remain as heavy as before. Whenever you look back you will see it there, just at arm's length, glowing darkly like a black crystal. And you will have forgotten what it really is, and murmur to yourself: "It wasn't I, it could not have been I, who did that." Yet, though you disown it time and time again, always it will be there, a dead weight holding you back. And then at last you will realize that you staked your life on a single throw of the dice, and nothing remains for you but to drag your crime after you until you die. For that is the law, just or unjust, of repentance. Ah, then we'll see a change come over your young pride.

ELECTRA: My *young* pride? So it's your lost youth you are regretting, still more than your crime. It's my youth you detest, even more than my innocence

CLYTEMNESTRA: What I detest in you, Electra, is —myself. Not your youth—far from it!—but my own.

ELECTRA: And I—it's you, it's *you* I hate.

CLYTEMNESTRA: For shame, Electra! Here we are, scolding each other like two women of the same age in love with the same man! And yet I am your mother. . . . I do not know who you are, young man, nor what brings you here, but your presence bodes no good. Electra hates me—that, of course, I always knew. But for fifteen years we have kept the peace; only our eyes betrayed our feelings. And now you have come, you have spoken, and here we are showing our teeth and snapping at each other like two curs in the street. An ancient law of Argos compels us to give you hospitality, but, I make no secret of it, I had rather you were gone. As for you, my child, too faithful copy of myself, 'tis true I have no love for you. But I had rather cut off my right hand than do you harm. Only too well you know it, and you trade on my weakness. But I advise you not to rear your noxious little head against Ægistheus; he has a short way with vipers. Mark my words, do his bidding—or you will rue it.

ELECTRA: Tell the King that I shall not attend the rite. Do you know what they do, Philebus? Above the town there's a great cavern; none of our young men, not even the bravest, has ever found its end. People say that it leads down to hell, and the High Priest has had the entrance blocked with a great stone. Well—would you believe it?—each year when this anniversary comes round, the townspeople gather outside the cavern, soldiers roll away the stone, and our dead, so they say, come up from hell and roam the city. Places are laid for them at every table, chairs and beds made ready, and the people in the house huddle in corners to make room for them during the night-watches. For the dead are everywhere, the whole town's at their mercy. You can imagine how our townsfolk plead with them. "My poor dead darling, I didn't mean to wrong you. Please be kind." Tomorrow, at cock-crow, they'll return underground, the stone will be rolled back, and that will be the end of it until this day next year. Well, I refuse to take part in this mummery. Those dead folk are *their* dead, not mine.

CLYTEMNESTRA: If you will not obey his summons willingly, the King will have you brought to him by force.

ELECTRA: By force? . . . I see. Very well, then. My good, kind mother, will you please tell the King that I shall certainly obey. I shall attend the rite, and if the townsfolk wish to see me, they won't be disappointed. . . . Philebus, will you do something for me? Please don't go at once, but stay here for the ceremony. Perhaps some parts of it may entertain you. Now I'll go and make myself ready. [*Exit* Electra]

CLYTEMNESTRA: [*To* Orestes] Leave this place. I feel that you are going to bring disaster on us. You have no cause to wish us ill; we have done nothing to you. So go, I beg you. By all you hold most sacred, for your mother's sake, I beg you, go. [*Exit* Clytemnestra]

ORESTES: [*Thoughtfully*] For my mother's sake.

[Zeus *enters and comes up to him*]

ZEUS: Your attendant tells me you wish to leave. He has been looking for horses all over Argos, but can find none. Well, I can procure for you two sturdy mares and riding-gear at a very low figure.

ORESTES: I've changed my mind. I am not leaving Argos.

ZEUS: [*Meditatively*] Ah, so you're not leaving, after all. [*A short pause. Then, in a quicker tempo*] In that case I shall stay with you and be your host. I know an excellent inn in the lower town where we can lodge together. You won't regret my company, I can assure you. But first—Abraxas, galla, galla, tsay, tsay—let me rid you of those flies. A man of my age can often be very helpful to lads like you. I'm old enough to be your father; you must tell me all about yourself and your troubles. So come, young man, don't try to shake me off. Meetings like this are often of more use than one would think. Consider the case of Telemachus—you know whom I mean, King Ulysses' son. One fine day he met an old worthy of the name of Mentor, who joined forces with him. Now I wonder if you know who that old fellow Mentor really was. . . .

[He escorts Orestes *off the stage, holding him in conversation, while the curtain falls*]

ACT II. SCENE I.

A mountain terrace, with a cavern on the right. Its entrance is blocked by a large black boulder. On the left is a flight of steps leading up to a temple. A crowd of men and women have gathered for the ceremony.

A WOMAN: [*Kneeling before her little son, as she straightens the kerchief round his neck*] There! That's the third time I've had to straighten it for you. [*She dusts his clothes*] That's better. Now try to behave properly, and mind you start crying when you're told.

THE CHILD: Is that where they come from?

THE WOMAN: Yes.

THE CHILD: I'm frightened.

THE WOMAN: And so you should be, darling. Terribly frightened. That's how one grows up into a decent, god-fearing man.

A MAN: They'll have good weather today.

ANOTHER MAN: Just as well. It seems they still like sunlight, shadows though they are. Last year, when it rained, they were fierce, weren't they?

FIRST MAN: Ay, that's the word. Fierce.

SECOND MAN: A shocking time we had!

THIRD MAN: Once they've gone back to their cave and left us to ourselves, I'll climb up here again and look at that there stone, and I'll say to myself: "Now we've a year's peace before us."

FOURTH MAN: Well, I'm not like you, I ain't consoled that easily. From tomorrow I'll start wondering how they'll be next year. Every year they're getting nastier and nastier, and—

SECOND MAN: Hold your tongue, you fool! Suppose one of them has crept up through a crevice and is prowling round us now, eavesdropping, like. There's some of the Dead come out ahead of time, so I've heard tell. [*They eye each other nervously*]

A YOUNG WOMAN: If only it would start! What are they up to, those palace folk? They're never in a hurry, and it's all this waiting gets one down, what with the blazing sun and only that big black stone to look at. Just think! They're all there, crowded up behind the stone, gloating over the cruel things they're going to do to us.

AN OLD WOMAN: That's enough, my girl. . . . We all know she's no better than she should be; that's why she's so scared of her ghost. Her husband died last spring, and for ten years she'd been fooling the poor man.

YOUNG WOMAN: I don't deny it. Sure enough, I

fooled him to the top of his bent; but I always liked him and I led him a pleasant life, that he can't deny. He never knew a thing about the other men, and when he died, you should have seen the way he looked at me, so tenderly, like a grateful dog. Of course, he knows everything now, and it's bitter pain for him, poor fellow, and all his love has turned to hate. Presently I'll feel him coiling round me, like a wisp of smoke, and he'll cling to me more closely than any living man has ever clung. I'll bring him home with me, wound round my neck like a tippet. I've a tasty little meal all ready, with the cakes and honey that he always liked. But it's all no use, I know. He'll never forgive me, and tonight—oh, how I dread it!—he will share my bed.

A MAN: Ay, she's right. What's Ægistheus doing? We can't bear this suspense much longer. It ain't fair to keep us waiting like this.

ANOTHER MAN: Sorry for yourself, are you? But do you think Ægistheus is less afraid than we? Tell me, how'd you like to be in his shoes, and have Agamemnon gibbering at you for twenty-four hours?

YOUNG WOMAN: Oh, this horrible, horrible suspense! Do you know, I have a feeling that all of you are drifting miles and miles away, leaving me alone. The stone is not yet rolled aside, but each of us is shut up with his dead, and lonely as a raindrop.

[Zeus enters, followed by Orestes and The Tutor]

ZEUS: This way, young man; you'll have a better view.

ORESTES: So here we have them, the citizens of Argos, King Agamemnon's loyal subjects!

THE TUTOR: What an ugly lot! Observe, young master, their sallow cheeks and sunken eyes. These folk are perishing of fear. What better example could we have of the effects of superstition? Just look at them! And if you need another proof of the soundness of my teaching, look on me and my rosy cheeks.

ZEUS: Much good they do you, your pink cheeks. For all your roses, my good man, you're no more than a sack of dung, like all those others, in the eyes of Zeus. Yes, though you may not guess it, you stink to heaven. These folk, at least, are wise in their generation; they know how bad they smell.

A MAN: [Climbing on to the temple steps, harangues the crowd] Do they want to drive us mad? Let's raise our voices all together and summon Ægistheus. Make him understand we will not suffer any more delay.

THE CROWD: Ægistheus! King Ægistheus! Have pity on us!

A WOMAN: Pity, yes, pity, you cry. And will none have pity on me? He'll come with his slit throat, the man I loathed so bitterly, and clammy, unseen arms will maul me in the darkness, all through the night.

ORESTES: But this is madness! Why doesn't someone tell these wretched people—?

ZEUS: What's this, young man? Why this ado over a woman who's lost her nerve? Wait and see; there's worse to come.

A MAN: [Falling on his knees] I stink! Oh, how I stink! I am a mass of rottenness. See how the flies are teeming round me, like carrion crows. . . . That's right, my harpies; sting and gouge and scavenge me; bore through my flesh to my black heart. I have sinned a thousand times, I am a sink of ordure, and I reek to heaven.

ZEUS: O worthy man!

SOME MEN: [Helping him to his feet] That's enough. You shall talk about it later, when they are out.

[Gasping, rolling his eyes, the man stares at them]

THE CROWD: Ægistheus! Ægistheus! For mercy's sake, give the order to begin. We can bear no more.

[Ægistheus comes on to the temple steps, followed by Clytemnestra, The High Priest, and Bodyguards]

ÆGISTHEUS: Dogs! How dare you bewail your lot? Have you forgotten your disgrace? Then, by Zeus, I shall refresh your memories. [He turns to Clytemnestra] We must start without her, it seems. But let her beware! My punishment will be condign.

CLYTEMNESTRA: She promised to attend. No doubt she is making ready, lingering in front of her mirror.

ÆGISTHEUS: [To the Soldiers] Go seek Electra in the palace and bring her here by force, if need be. [Soldiers file out. He addresses The Crowd] Take your usual places. The men on my right, women and children on my left. Good.

[A short silence. Ægistheus is waiting]

HIGH PRIEST: Sire, these people are at breaking-point.

ÆGISTHEUS: I know. But I am waiting for—

[The Soldiers return]

A SOLDIER: Your Majesty, we have searched for the princess everywhere. But there is no one in the palace.

ÆGISTHEUS: So be it. We shall deal with her tomorrow. [To the High Priest] Begin.

HIGH PRIEST: Roll away the stone.

THE CROWD: Ah!

[The Soldiers roll away the stone. The High Priest goes to the entrance of the cavern]

HIGH PRIEST: You, the forgotten and forsaken, all you whose hopes were dupes, who creep along the ground darkling like smoke wraiths and have nothing left you but your great shame—you, the dead, arise; this is your day of days. Come up, pour forth like a thick cloud of fumes of brimstone driven by the wind; rise from the bowels of the earth, ye who have died a hundred deaths, ye whom every heartbeat in our breasts strikes dead again. In the name of anger unappeased and unappeasable, and the lust of vengeance, I summon you to wreak your hatred on the living. Come forth and scatter like a dark miasma in our streets, weave between the mother and her child, the lover and his beloved; make us regret that we, too, are not dead. Arise, spectres, harpies, ghouls, and goblins of our nights. Soldiers, arise, who died blaspheming; arise, downtrodden victims, children of disgrace; arise, all ye who died of hunger, whose last sigh was a curse. See, the living are here to greet you, fodder for your wrath. Arise and have at them like a great rushing wind, and gnaw them to the bone. Arise! Arise! Arise!

[*A tomtom sounds, and the* Priest *dances at the entrance of the cavern, slowly at first, quickening his gyrations until he falls to the ground exhausted*]

ÆGISTHEUS: They are coming forth.

THE CROWD: Heaven help us!

ORESTES: I can bear this no longer. I must go—

ZEUS: Look at me, young man. In the eyes. Good; you understand. Now, keep quiet.

ORESTES: Who—are you?

ZEUS: You shall know soon.

[Ægistheus *comes slowly down the temple steps*]

ÆGISTHEUS: They are there. All of them. [*A short silence*] There he is, Aricië, the husband you used so ill. There he is, beside you, kissing you tenderly, clasping you in his dead arms. How he loves you! And, ah, how he hates you! . . . There she is Nicias, your mother, who died of your neglect. . . . And you there, Segestes, you blood-sucker—they are all round you, the wretched men who borrowed of you; those who starved to death, and those who hanged themselves because of you. In your debt they died, but today they are your creditors. And you, fathers and mothers, loving parents lower your eyes humbly. They are there, your dead children, stretching their frail arms towards you, and all the happiness you denied them, all the tortures you inflicted, weigh like lead on their sad, childish, unforgiving hearts.

THE CROWD: Have mercy!

ÆGISTHEUS: Mercy? You ask for mercy? Do you not know the dead have no mercy? Their grievances are timeproof, adamant; rancor without end. Do you hope, Nicias, to atone by deeds of kindness for the wrong you did your mother? But what act of kindness can ever reach her now? Her soul is like a sultry, windless noon, in which nothing stirs, nothing changes, nothing lives. Only a fierce unmoving sun beats down on bare rocks forever. The dead have ceased to be—think what that implies in all its ruthlessness—yes, they are no more, and in their eternal keeping your crimes have no reprieve.

THE CROWD: Mercy!

ÆGISTHEUS: Well you may cry mercy! Play your parts, you wretched mummers, for today you have a full house to watch you. Millions of staring, hopeless eyes are brooding darkly on your faces and your gestures. They can see us, read our hearts, and we are naked in the presence of the dead. Ah, that

makes you squirm; it burns and sears you, that stern, calm gaze unchanging as the gaze of eyes remembered.

THE CROWD: Mercy!

THE MEN: Forgive us for living while you are dead.

THE WOMEN: Have mercy! Tokens of you are ever with us, we see your faces everywhere we turn. We wear mourning unceasingly, and weep for you from dawn till dusk, from dusk till dawn. But somehow, try as we may, your memory dwindles and slips through our fingers; daily it grows dimmer and we know ourselves the guiltier. Yes, you are leaving us, ebbing away like life-blood from a wound. And yet, know you well—if this can mollify your bitter hatred—that you, our dear departed, have laid waste our lives.

THE MEN: Forgive us for living while you are dead.

THE CHILDREN: Please forgive us. We didn't want to be born, we're ashamed of growing up. What wrong can we have done you? It's not our fault if we're alive. And only just alive; see how small we are, how pale and puny. We never laugh or sing, we glide about like ghosts. And we're so frightened of you, so terribly afraid. Have mercy on us.

THE MEN: Forgive us for living while you are dead.

ÆGISTHEUS: Hold your peace! If you voice your sorrow thus, what will be left for me, your King, to say? For my ordeal has begun; the earth is quaking, and the light failing, and the greatest of the dead is coming forth—he whom I slew with my own hand, King Agamemnon.

ORESTES: [*Drawing his sword*] I forbid you to drag my father's name into this mummery.

ZEUS: [*Clutching his arms*] Stop, young fellow! Stop that!

ÆGISTHEUS: [*Looking around*] Who dares to—? [Electra, *wearing a white dress, comes on to the temple steps.* Ægistheus *sees her*] Electra!

THE CROWD: Electra!

ÆGISTHEUS: What is the meaning of this, Electra? Why are you in white?

ELECTRA: It's my prettiest dress. The city holds high festival today, and I thought I'd look my best.

HIGH PRIEST: Would you insult our dead? This day is *their* day, and well you know it. You should be in mourning.

ELECTRA: Why? I'm not afraid of *my* dead, and yours mean nothing to me.

ÆGISTHEUS: That is so; your dead are not our dead. . . . Remember the breed she comes of, the breed of Atreus, who treacherously cut his nephews' throats. What are you, Electra, but the last survivor of an accursed race? Ay, that whorish dress becomes you. I suffered your presence in the palace out of pity, but now I know I erred; the old foul blood of the house of Atreus flows in your veins. And if I did not see to it, you would taint us all. But bide awhile, my girl, and you will learn how I can punish. Your eyes will be red with weeping for many a day.

THE CROWD: Sacrilege! Sacrilege! Away with her!

ÆGISTHEUS: Hear, miserable girl, the murmurs of these good folk you have outraged. Were I not here to curb their anger, they would tear you in pieces.

THE CROWD: Away with her, the impious wretch!

ELECTRA: Is it impious to be gay? Why can't these good folk of yours be gay? What prevents them?

ÆGISTHEUS: She is laughing, the wanton—and her dead father is standing there, with blood on his face.

ELECTRA: How dare you talk of Agamemnon? How can you be so sure he doesn't visit me by night and tell me all his secrets? Ah, if you knew the love and longing that hoarse, dead voice breathes in my ears! Yes, I'm laughing—laughing for the first time in my life; for the first time I'm happy. And can you be so sure my new-won happiness doesn't rejoice my father's heart? More likely, if he's here and sees his daughter in her white dress—his daughter of whom you've made a wretched drudge —if he sees her holding her head high, keeping her pride intact, more likely the last thing he dreams of is to blame me. No, his eyes are sparkling in the havoc of his face, he's twisting his blood-stained lips in the shadow of a smile.

THE YOUNG WOMAN: Can it be true, what she says?

VOICES: No, no. She's talking nonsense. She's gone mad. Electra, go, for pity's sake, or your sins will be visited on us.

ELECTRA: But what is it you're so frightened of? I can see all round you and there's nothing but your own shadows. Now listen to what I've just been told, something you may not know. In Greece there are cities where men live happily. White, contented cities, basking like lizards in the sun. At this very moment, under this same sky, children are playing in the streets of Corinth. And their mothers aren't asking forgiveness for having brought them into the world. No, they're smiling tenderly at them, they're proud of their motherhood. Mothers of Argos, can't you understand? Does it mean nothing to you, the pride of a mother who looks at her son, and thinks: "It's I who bore him, brought him up"?

ÆGISTHEUS: That's enough. Keep silent, or I'll thrust your words down your throat.

VOICES: Yes, yes. Make her stop. She's talked enough.

OTHER VOICES: No, let her speak. It's Agamemnon speaking through her.

ELECTRA: The sun is shining. Everywhere down in the plains men are looking up and saying: "It's a fine day," and they're happy. Are you so set on making yourselves wretched that you've forgotten the simple joy of the peasant who says as he walks across his fields: "It's a fine day"? No, there you stand, hanging your heads, moping and mumbling,

more dead than alive. You're too terrified to lift a finger, afraid of jolting your precious ghosts if you make any movement. That would be dreadful, wouldn't it, if your hand suddenly went through a patch of clammy mist, and it was your grandmother's ghost! Now look at me. I'm spreading out my arms freely, and I'm stretching like someone just roused from sleep. I have my place in the sunlight, my full place and to spare. And does the sky fall on my head? Now I'm dancing, see, I'm dancing, and all I feel is the wind's breath fanning my cheeks. Where are the dead? Do you think they're dancing with me, in step?

HIGH PRIEST: People of Argos, I tell you that this woman is a profaner of all we hold most holy. Woe to her and to all of you who listen to her words!

ELECTRA: Oh, my beloved dead—Iphigeneia, my elder sister, and Agamemnon, my father and my only King—hear my prayer. If I am an evil-doer, if I offend your sorrowing shades, make some sign that I may know. But if, my dear ones, you approve, let no leaf stir, no blade of grass be moved, and no sound break in on my sacred dance. For I am dancing for joy, for peace among men; I dance for happiness and life. My dead ones, I invoke your silence that these people around me may know your hearts are with me. [*She dances*]

VOICES IN THE CROWD: Look how she's dancing, light as a flame. Look how her dress is rippling, like a banner in the wind. And the Dead—the Dead do nothing.

THE YOUNG WOMAN: And see her look of ecstasy —oh, no, no, that's not the face of a wicked woman. Well, Ægistheus, what have you to say? Why are you silent?

ÆGISTHEUS: I waste no words on her. Does one argue with malignant vermin? No, one stamps them out. My kindness to her in the past was a mistake, but a mistake that can be remedied. Have no fear, I shall make short work of her and end her accursed race.

VOICES IN THE CROWD: Answer us, King Ægistheus. Threats are no answer.

THE YOUNG WOMAN: She's dancing, smiling, oh, so happily, and the dead seem to protect her. Oh fortunate, too fortunate Electra! Look, I, too, am holding out my arms, baring my neck to the sunlight.

A VOICE IN THE CROWD: The Dead hold their peace. Ægistheus, you have lied.

ORESTES: Dear Electra!

ZEUS: This is too much. I'll shut that foolish wench's tongue. [*Stretches out his right arm*] Poseidon, carabou, carabou, roola. [*The big stone which blocked the entrance to the cavern rumbles across the stage and crashes against the temple steps. Electra stops dancing*]

THE CROWD: Ah! . . . Mercy on us! [*A long silence*]

HIGH PRIEST: Froward and fickle race, now you

have seen how the Dead avenge themselves. Mark how the flies are beating down on you, in thick, swirling clouds. You have hearkened to the tempter's voice, and a curse has fallen on the city.

THE CROWD: It is not our fault, we are innocent. That woman came and tempted us, with her lying tongue. To the river with her. Drown the witch.

AN OLD WOMAN: [*Pointing to the* Young Woman] That young huzzy there was lapping up her words like milk. Strip her naked and lash her till she squeals.

[*The* Women *seize the* Young Woman, *while the* Men *surge up the temple steps, towards* Electra]

ÆGISTHEUS: [*Straightening up*] Silence, dogs! Back to your places! Vengeance is mine, not yours. [*A short silence*] Well, you have seen what comes of disobeying me. Henceforth you will know better than to misdoubt your ruler. Disperse to your homes, the Dead will keep you company and be your guests until tomorrow's dawn. Make place for them at your tables, at your hearths, and in your beds. And see that your good behavior blots out the memory of what has happened here. As for me—grieved though I am by your mistrust, I forgive you. But you, Electra—

ELECTRA: Yes? What of it? I failed to bring it off this time. Next time I'll do better.

ÆGISTHEUS: There shall be no next time. The custom of the city forbids my punishing you on the day the Dead are with us. This you knew, and you took advantage of it. But you are no longer one of us; I cast you out forever. You shall go hence barefooted, with nothing in your hands, wearing that shameless dress. And I hereby order any man who sees you within our gates after the sun has risen to strike you down and rid the city of its bane.

[*He goes out, followed by* The Soldiers. *The* Crowd *file past* Electra, *shaking their fists at her*]

ZEUS: [*To* Orestes] Well, young master, were you duly edified? For, unless I'm much mistaken, the tale has a moral. The wicked have been punished and the good rewarded. [*He points to* Electra] As for that woman—

ORESTES: [*Sharply*] Mind what you say. That woman is my sister. Now go; I want to talk to her.

ZEUS: [*Observes him for a moment, then shrugs his shoulders*] Very good. [*Exit Zeus, followed by* The Tutor]

ORESTES: Electra!

ELECTRA: [*Still standing on the temple steps, she raises her eyes and gazes at him*] Ah, you're still there, Philebus?

ORESTES: You're in danger, Electra. You mustn't stay a moment longer in this city.

ELECTRA: In danger? Yes, that's true. You saw how I failed to bring it off. It was a bit your fault, you know—but I'm not angry with you.

ORESTES: My fault? How?

ELECTRA: You deceived me. [*She comes down the steps towards him*] Let me look at your eyes. Yes, it was your eyes that made a fool of me.

ORESTES: There's no time to lose. Listen, Electra! We'll escape together. Someone's getting a horse for me and you can ride pillion.

ELECTRA: No.

ORESTES: What? You won't come away with me?

ELECTRA: I refuse to run away.

ORESTES: I'll take you with me to Corinth.

ELECTRA: [*Laughing*] Corinth? Exactly! I know you mean well, but you're fooling me again. What could a girl like me do in Corinth? I've got to keep a level head, you know. Only yesterday my desires were so simple, so modest. When I waited at table, with meek, downcast eyes, I used to watch the two of them—the handsome old woman with the dead face, and the fat, pale King with the slack mouth and that absurd beard like a regiment of spiders running round his chin. And then I'd dream of what I'd see one day—a wisp of steam, like one's breath on a cold morning, rising from their split bellies. That was the only thing I lived for, Philebus, I assure you. I don't know what you're after, but this I know: that I mustn't believe you. Your eyes are too bold for my liking. . . . Do you know what I used to tell myself before I met you? That a wise person can want nothing better from life than to pay back the wrong that has been done him.

ORESTES: If you come with me, Electra, you'll see there are many, many other things to ask of life —without one's ceasing to be wise.

ELECTRA: No, I won't listen any more; you've done me quite enough harm already. You came here with your kind, girlish face and your eager eyes— and you made me forget my hatred. I unlocked my hands and I let my one and only treasure slip through them. You lured me into thinking one could cure the people here by words. Well, you saw what happened. They nurse their disease; they've got to like their sores so much that they scratch them with their dirty nails to keep them festering. Words are no use for such as they. An evil thing is conquered only by another evil thing, and only violence can save them. So good-by, Philebus and leave me to my bad dreams.

ORESTES: They'll kill you.

ELECTRA: We have a sanctuary here, Apollo's shrine. Often criminals take shelter there, and so long as they are in the temple, no one can touch a hair of their heads. That's where I'll go.

ORESTES: But why refuse my help?

ELECTRA: It's not for you to help me. Someone else will come, to set me free. [*A short silence*] My brother isn't dead; I know that. And I'm waiting for his coming.

ORESTES: Suppose he doesn't come?

ELECTRA: He *will* come; he's bound to come. He is of our stock, you see; he has crime and tragedy in his blood, as I have—the bad blood of the house of Atreus. I picture him as a big, strong man, a born fighter, with bloodshot eyes like our father's, always smoldering with rage. He, too, is doomed; tangled up in his destiny, like a horse whose belly is ripped open and his legs are caught up in his guts. And now at every step he tears his bowels out. Yes, one day he will come, this city draws him. Nothing can hinder his coming, for it is here he can do the greatest harm, and suffer the greatest harm. I often seem to see him coming, with lowered head, sullen with pain, muttering angry words. He scares me; every night I see him in my dreams, and I wake screaming with terror. But I'm waiting for him and I love him. I must stay here to direct his rage—for I, anyhow, keep a clear head—to point to the guilty and say: "Those are they, Orestes. Strike!"

ORESTES: And suppose he isn't like that at all?

ELECTRA: How can he be otherwise? Don't forget he's the son of Agamemnon and Clytemnestra.

ORESTES: But mightn't he be weary of all that tale of wickedness and bloodshed; if, for instance, he'd been brought up in a happy, peaceful city?

ELECTRA: Then I'd spit in his face, and I'd say: "Go away, you cur; go and keep company where you belong, with women. But you're reckoning without your doom, poor fool. You're a grandson of Atreus, and you can't escape the heritage of blood. You prefer shame to crime; so be it. But Fate will come and hunt you down in your bed; you'll have the shame to start with, and then you will commit the crime, however much you shirk it."

ORESTES: Electra, I am Orestes.

ELECTRA: [With a cry] Oh! . . . You liar!

ORESTES: By the shades of my father, Agamemnon, I swear I am Orestes. [A short silence] Well? Why don't you carry out your threat and spit in my face?

ELECTRA: How could I? [She gazes at him earnestly] So those shining eyes, that noble forehead, are—my brother's! Orestes. . . . Oh, I'd rather you had stayed Philebus, and my brother was dead. [Shyly] Was it true, what you said about your having lived at Corinth?

ORESTES: No. I was brought up by some well-to-do Athenians.

ELECTRA: How young you look! Have you ever been in battle? Has that sword you carry ever tasted blood?

ORESTES: Never.

ELECTRA: It's strange. I felt less lonely when I didn't know you. I was waiting for the Orestes of my dream; always thinking of his strength and of my weakness. And now you're there before me; Orestes, the real Orestes, was you all the time. I look at you and I see we're just a boy and a girl, two young orphans. But, you know, I love you. More than I'd have loved the other Orestes.

ORESTES: Then, if you love me, come away. We'll leave this place together.

ELECTRA: Leave Argos? No. It's here the doom

of the Atrides must be played out, and I am of the house of Atreus. I ask nothing of you. I've nothing more to ask of Philebus. But here I stay.

[Zeus enters, back stage, and takes cover to listen to them]

ORESTES: Electra, I'm Orestes, your brother. I, too, am of the house of Atreus, and my place is at your side.

ELECTRA: No. You're not my brother; you're a stranger. Orestes is dead, and so much the better for him. From now on I'll do homage to his shade, along with my father's and my sister's. You, Philebus, claim to be of our house. So be it! But can you truly say that you are one of us? Was your childhood darkened by the shadow of a murder? No, more likely you were a quiet little boy with happy, trustful eyes, the pride of your adoptive father. Naturally you could trust people—they always had a smile for you—just as you could trust the solid friendly things around you: tables, beds, and stairs. And because you were rich, and always nicely dressed, and had lots of toys, you must have often thought the world was quite a nice world to live in, like a big warm bath in which one can splash and loll contentedly. My childhood was quite different. When I was six I was a drudge, and I mistrusted everything and everyone. [A short pause] So go away, my noble-souled brother. I have no use for noble souls; what I need is an accomplice.

ORESTES: How could I leave you all alone; above all, now that you've lost even your last hope? . . . What do you propose to do here?

ELECTRA: That's my business. Good-by, Philebus.

ORESTES: So you're driving me away? [He takes some steps, then halts and faces her] Is it my fault if I'm not the fierce young swashbuckler you expected? Him you'd have taken by the hand at once and said: "Strike!" Of me you asked nothing. But, good heavens, why should I be outcast by my own sister—when I've not even been put to the test?

ELECTRA: No, Philebus, I could never lay such a load upon a heart like yours; a heart that has no hatred in it.

ORESTES: You are right. No hatred; but no love, either. You, Electra, I might have loved. And yet— I wonder. Love or hatred calls for self-surrender. He cuts a fine figure, the warm-blooded, prosperous man, solidly entrenched in his well-being, who one fine day surrenders all to love—or to hatred; himself, his house, his land, his memories. But who am I, and what have I to surrender? I'm a mere shadow of a man; of all the ghosts haunting this town today, none is ghostlier than I. The only loves I've known were phantom loves, rare and vacillating as will-o'-the-wisps. The solid passions of the living were never mine. Never! [A short silence] But, oh, the shame of it! Here I am, back in the town where I was born, and my own sister disavows me. And now—where shall I go? What city must I haunt?

ELECTRA: Isn't there some pretty girl waiting for you—somewhere in the world?

ORESTES: Nobody is waiting for me anywhere. I wander from city to city, a stranger to all others and to myself, and the cities close again behind me like the waters of a pool. If I leave Argos, what trace of my coming will remain, except the cruel disappointment of your hope?

ELECTRA: You told me about happy towns—

ORESTES: What do I care for happiness? I want my share of memories, my native soil, my place among the men of Argos. [A short silence] Electra, I shall not leave Argos.

ELECTRA: Please, please, Philebus, go away. If you have any love for me, go. It hurts me to think what may come to you here—nothing but evil, that I know—and your innocence would ruin all my plans.

ORESTES: I shall not go.

ELECTRA: How can you think I'd let you stay beside me—you with your stubborn uprightness—to pass silent judgment on my acts? Oh, why are you so obstinate? Nobody wants you here.

ORESTES: It's my one chance, and you, Electra— surely you won't refuse it to me? Try to understand. I want to be a man who belongs to some place, a man among comrades. Only consider. Even the slave bent beneath his load, dropping with fatigue and staring dully at the ground a foot in front of him— why, even that poor slave can say he's in *his* town, as a tree is in a forest, or a leaf upon the tree. Argos is all around him, warm, compact, and comforting. Yes, Electra, I'd gladly be that slave and enjoy that feeling of drawing the city round me like a blanket and curling myself up in it. No, I shall not go.

ELECTRA: Even if you stayed a hundred years among us, you'd still be a stranger here, and lonelier than if you were tramping the highroads of Greece. The townspeople would be watching you all the time from the corner of an eye, and they'd lower their voices when you came near.

ORESTES: Is it really so hard to win a place among you? My sword can serve the city, and I have gold to help the needy.

ELECTRA: We are not short of captains, or of charitable souls.

ORESTES: In that case— [He takes some steps away from her, with lowered eyes. Zeus comes forward and gazes at him, rubbing his hands. Orestes raises his eyes heavenwards] Ah, if only I knew which path to take! O Zeus, our Lord and King of Heaven, not often have I called on you for help, and you have shown me little favor; yet this you know: that I have always tried to act aright. But now I am weary and my mind is dark; I can no longer distinguish right from wrong. I need a guide to point my way. Tell me, Zeus, is it truly your will that a king's son, hounded from his city, should meekly school himself to banishment and slink away from his ancestral home like a whipped cur? I can-

not think it. And yet—and yet you have forbidden the shedding of blood. . . . What have I said? Who spoke of bloodshed? . . . O Zeus, I beseech you, if meek acceptance, the bowed head and lowly heart are what you would have of me, make plain your will by some sign; for no longer can I see my path.

ZEUS: [Aside] Ah, that's where I can help you, my young friend. Abraxas, abraxas, tsou, tsou.

[Light flashes out round the stone]

ELECTRA: [Laughing] Splendid! It's raining miracles today! See what comes of being a pious young man and asking counsel of the gods. [She is convulsed with laughter and can hardly get the words out] Oh, noble youth, Philebus, darling of the gods! "Show me a sign," you asked. "Show me a sign." Well, now you've had your sign—a blaze of light round that precious, sacred stone of theirs. So off you go to Corinth! Off you go!

ORESTES: [Staring at the stone] So that is the Right Thing. To live at peace—always at perfect peace. I see. Always to say "Excuse me," and "Thank you." That's what's wanted, eh? [He stares at the stone in silence for some moments] The Right Thing. *Their* Right Thing. [Another silence] Electra!

ELECTRA: Hurry up and go. Don't disappoint your fatherly old friend, who has bent down from Olympus to enlighten you. [She stops abruptly, a look of wonder on her face] But—what's come over you?

ORESTES: [Slowly, in a tone he has not used till now] There is another way.

ELECTRA: [Apprehensively] No, Philebus, don't be stubborn. You asked the gods for orders; now you have them.

ORESTES: Orders? What do you mean? Ah yes, the light round that big stone. But it's not for me, that light; from now on I'll take no one's orders, neither man's nor god's.

ELECTRA: You're speaking in riddles.

ORESTES: What a change has come on everything, and, oh, how far away you seem! Until now I felt something warm and living round me, like a friendly presence. That something has just died. What emptiness! What endless emptiness, as far as eye can reach! [He takes some steps away from her] Night is coming on. The air is getting chilly, isn't it? But what was it—what was it that died just now?

ELECTRA: Philebus—

ORESTES: I say there is another path—*my* path. Can't you see it? It starts here and leads down to the city. I must go down—do you understand?—I must go down into the depths, among you. For you are living, all of you, at the bottom of a pit. [He goes up to Electra] You are *my* sister, Electra, and that city is *my* city. *My* sister. [He takes her arm]

ELECTRA: Don't touch me. You're hurting me, frightening me—and I'm *not* yours.

ORESTES: I know. Not yet. I'm still too—too light. I must take a burden on my shoulders, a load of guilt so heavy as to drag me down, right down into the abyss of Argos.

ELECTRA: But what—what do you mean to do?

ORESTES: Wait. Give me time to say farewell to all the lightness, the aery lightness that was mine. Let me say good-by to my youth. There are evenings at Corinth and at Athens, golden evenings full of songs and scents and laughter; these I shall never know again. And mornings, too, radiant with promise. Good-by to them all, good-by. . . . Come, Electra, look at our city. There it lies, rose-red in the sun, buzzing with men and flies, drowsing its doom away in the languor of a summer afternoon. It fends me off with its high walls, red roofs, locked doors. And yet it's mine for the taking; I've felt that since this morning. You, too, Electra, are mine for the taking—and I'll take you, too. I'll turn into an ax and hew those walls asunder, I'll rip open the bellies of those stolid houses and there will steam up from the gashes a stench of rotting food and incense. I'll be an iron wedge driven into the city, like a wedge rammed into the heart of an oak tree.

ELECTRA: Oh, how you've changed! Your eyes have lost their glow; they're dull and smoldering. I'm sorry for that, Philebus; you were so gentle. But now you're talking like the Orestes of my dreams.

ORESTES: Listen! all those people quaking with fear in their dark rooms, with their dear departed round them—supposing I take over all their crimes. Supposing I set out to win the name of "guilt-stealer," and heap on myself all their remorse; that of the woman unfaithful to her husband, of the tradesman who let his mother die, of the usurer who bled his victims white? Surely, once I am plagued with all those pangs of conscience, innumerable as the flies of Argos—surely then I shall have earned the freedom of your city. Shall I not be as much at home within your red walls as the red-aproned butcher in his shop, among the carcasses of flayed sheep and cattle?

ELECTRA: So you wish to atone for us?

ORESTES: To atone? No, I said I'd house your penitence, but I did *not* say what I'd do with all those cackling fowls; maybe I'll wring their necks.

ELECTRA: And how can you take over our sense of guilt?

ORESTES: Why, all of you ask nothing better than to be rid of it. Only the King and Queen force you to nurse it in your foolish hearts.

ELECTRA: The King and Queen— Oh, Philebus!

ORESTES: The gods bear witness that I had no wish to shed their blood. [*A long silence*]

ELECTRA: You're too young, too weak.

ORESTES: Are you going to draw back—*now?* Hide me somewhere in the palace, and lead me tonight to the royal bedchamber—and then you'll see if I am too weak!

ELECTRA: Orestes!

ORESTES: Ah! For the first time you've called me Orestes.

ELECTRA: Yes. I know you now. You are indeed Orestes. I didn't recognize you at first, I'd expected somebody quite different. But this throbbing in my blood, this sour taste on my lips—I've had them in my dreams, and I know what they mean. So at last you have come, Orestes, and your resolve is sure. And here I am beside you—just as in my dreams—on the brink of an act beyond all remedy. And I'm frightened; that, too, was in my dreams. How long I've waited for this moment, dreading and hoping for it! From now on, all the moments will link up, like the cogs in a machine, and we shall never rest again until they both are lying on their backs with faces like crushed mulberries. In a pool of blood. To think it's you who are going to shed it, you with those gentle eyes! I'm sorry now, sorry that never again I'll see that gentleness, never again see Philebus. Orestes, you are my elder brother, and head of our house; fold me in your arms, protect me. Much suffering, many perils lie ahead of both of us.

[Orestes *takes her in his arms.* Zeus *leaves his hiding-place and creeps out on tiptoe*]

CURTAIN

SCENE II.

The throne-room in the palace. An awe-inspiring, blood-smeared image of Zeus *occupies a prominent position. The sun is setting.* Electra *enters: then beckons to* Orestes *to follow her.*

ORESTES: Someone's coming. [*He begins to draw his sword*]

ELECTRA: It's the sentries on their rounds. Follow me. I know where to hide.

[*Two soldiers enter*]

FIRST SOLDIER: I can't think what's come over the flies this evening. They're all crazy-like.

SECOND SOLDIER: They smell the Dead; that's why they're in such a state. Why, I daren't open my mouth to yawn for fear they all come teeming down my throat and start a round dance in my gullet. [Electra *peeps from her hiding-place, then quickly withdraws her head*] Hear that? Something creaked yonder.

FIRST SOLDIER: Oh, it's only Agamemnon, sitting down on his throne.

SECOND SOLDIER: And the seat creaked when he planted his fat bottom on it? No, it couldn't be that; a dead man's light as air.

FIRST SOLDIER: That goes for common folk like you and me. But a king, he's different. Mind you, Agamemnon always did himself proud at table. Why, he weighed two hundred pounds or more if he weighed one. It would be surprising if there wasn't some pounds left of all that flesh.

SECOND SOLDIER: So—so you think he's here, do you?

FIRST SOLDIER: Where else should he be? If I was a dead king and I had twenty-four hours' leave each year, you may be sure I'd spend them squatting on my throne, just to remind me of the high old times I had when I was His Almighty Majesty. And I'd stay put; I wouldn't run round pestering folks in their houses.

SECOND SOLDIER: Ah, wouldn't you? You say that because you're alive. But if you were dead, you'd be just as nasty as the others. [First Soldier *smacks his face*] Hey! What are you up to?

FIRST SOLDIER: I'm doing you a good turn. Look, I've killed seven of 'em, all at a go.

SECOND SOLDIER: Seven what? Seven dead 'uns?

FIRST SOLDIER: O' course not. *Flies*. Look, my hand's all bloody. [*He wipes it on his pants*] Ugh, the filthy brutes!

SECOND SOLDIER: Pity you can't swot the lot of them while you're about it. The dead men, now—they don't do nothing, they know how to behave. If the flies were all killed off, we'd have some peace.

FIRST SOLDIER: Peace, you say? No, if I thought there were ghost-flies here as well, that'd be the last straw.

SECOND SOLDIER: Why?

FIRST SOLDIER: Don't you see? They die by millions every day, the little buzzers. Well, if all the flies that have died since last summer were set loose in the town, there'd be three hundred and sixty-five dead flies for every one that's here. The air'd be laced with flies, we'd breathe flies, eat flies, sweat flies; they'd be rolling down our throats in clusters and bunging up our lungs. . . . I wonder, now—maybe that's why there's such a funny smell in this room.

SECOND SOLDIER: No, no, it ain't that. They say our dead men have foul breaths, you know. And this room's not so big as it looks—a thousand square feet or so, I should say. Two or three dead men would be enough to foul the air.

FIRST SOLDIER: That's so. Fussing and fuming like they do.

SECOND SOLDIER: I tell you there's something amiss here. I heard a floor-board creak over there.

[*They go behind the throne to investigate. Orestes and Electra slip out on the left and tiptoe past the steps of the throne, returning to their hiding-place just as the soldiers emerge on the left*]

FIRST SOLDIER: You see, there ain't nobody. It's only that old sod Agamemnon. Like as not, he's sitting on them cushions, straight as a poker. I shouldn't be surprised if he's watching you and me for want of anything else to do.

SECOND SOLDIER: Ay, and we'd better have a good look round, I ain't easy in my mind. These flies are something wicked, but it can't be helped.

FIRST SOLDIER: I wish I was back in the barracks. At least the dead folk there are old chums come back to visit us, just ordinary folk like us. But when

I think that His Late Lamented Majesty is there, like as not counting the buttons missing on my tunic, well it makes me dithery, like when the general's doing an inspection.

[*Enter Ægistheus and* Clytemnestra, *followed by servants carrying lamps*]

ÆGISTHEUS: Go, all of you.

[*Exeunt* Soldiers *and* Servants]

CLYTEMNESTRA: What is troubling you tonight?

ÆGISTHEUS: You saw what happened? Had I not played upon their fear, they'd have shaken off their remorse in the twinkling of an eye.

CLYTEMNESTRA: Is that all? Then be reassured. You will always find a way to freeze their courage when the need arises.

ÆGISTHEUS: I know. Oh, I'm only too skillful in the art of false pretense. [*A short silence*] I am sorry I had to rebuke Electra.

CLYTEMNESTRA: Why? Because she is my daughter? It pleased you to so do, and all you do has my approval.

ÆGISTHEUS: Woman, it is not on your account that I regret it.

CLYTEMNESTRA: Then—why? You used not to have much love for Electra.

ÆGISTHEUS: I am tired. So tired. For fifteen years I have been upholding the remorse of a whole city, and my arms are aching with the strain. For fifteen years I have been dressing a part, playing the scaremonger, and the black of my robes has seeped through to my soul.

CLYTEMNESTRA: But, sire, I, too—

ÆGISTHEUS: I know, woman, I know. You are going to tell me of your remorse. I wish I shared it. It fills out the void of your life. *I* have no remorse—and no man in Argos is sadder than I.

CLYTEMNESTRA: My sweet lord—[*She goes up to him affectionately*]

ÆGISTHEUS: Keep off, you whore! Are you not ashamed—under his eyes?

CLYTEMNESTRA: Under his eyes? Who can see us here?

ÆGISTHEUS: Why, the King. The Dead came forth this morning.

CLYTEMNESTRA: Sire, I beg you—the dead are underground and will not trouble us for many a long day. Have you forgotten it was you yourself who invented that fable to impress your people?

ÆGISTHEUS: That's so. Well, it only shows how tired I am, how sick at heart. Now leave me to my thoughts. [*Exit* Clytemnestra] Have you in me, Lord Zeus, the king you wished for Argos? I come and go among my people, I speak in trumpet tones, I parade the terror of my frown, and all who see me cringe in an agony of repentance. But I—what am I but an empty shell? Some creature has devoured me unawares, gnawed out my inner self. And now, looking within, I see I am more dead than Agamemnon. Did I say I was sad? I lied. Neither sad nor gay is the desert—a boundless waste of sand under burning waste of sky. Not sad, nor gay, but—sinister. Ah, I'd give my kingdom to be able to shed a tear.

[Zeus *enters*]

ZEUS: That's right. Complain away! You're only a king, like every other king.

ÆGISTHEUS: Who are you? What are you doing here?

ZEUS: So you don't recognize me?

ÆGISTHEUS: Begone, stranger, or I shall have you thrown out by my guards.

ZEUS: You don't recognize me? Still, you have seen me often enough, in dreams. It's true I looked more awe-inspiring. [*Flashes of lightning, a peal of thunder.* Zeus *assumes an awe-inspiring air*] And now do you know me?

ÆGISTHEUS: Zeus!

ZEUS: Good! [*Affable again, he goes up to the statue*] So that's meant to be me? It's thus the Argives picture me at their prayers? Well, well, it isn't often that a god can study his likeness, face to face. [*A short silence*] How hideous I am! They cannot like me much.

ÆGISTHEUS: They fear you.

ZEUS: Excellent! I've no use for love. Do you, Ægistheus, love me?

ÆGISTHEUS: What do you want of me? Have I not paid heavily enough?

ZEUS: Never enough.

ÆGISTHEUS: But it's killing me, the task I have undertaken.

ZEUS: Come now! Don't exaggerate! Your health is none too bad; you're fat. Mind, I'm not reproaching you. It's good, royal fat, yellow as tallow—just as it should be. You're built to live another twenty years.

ÆGISTHEUS: Another twenty years!

ZEUS: Would you rather die?

ÆGISTHEUS: Yes.

ZEUS: So, if anyone came here now, with a drawn sword, would you bare your breast to him?

ÆGISTHEUS: I—I cannot say.

ZEUS: Now mark my words. If you let yourself be slaughtered like a dumb ox, your doom will be exemplary. You shall be King in hell for all eternity. That's what I came here to tell you.

ÆGISTHEUS: Is someone planning to kill me?

ZEUS: So it seems.

ÆGISTHEUS: Electra?

ZEUS: Not only Electra.

ÆGISTHEUS: Who?

ZEUS: Orestes.

ÆGISTHEUS: Oh! . . . Well, that's in the natural order of things, no doubt. What can I do against it?

ZEUS: [*Mimicking his tone*] What can I do? [*Imperiously*] Bid your men arrest a young stranger going under the name of Philebus. Have him and Electra thrown into a dungeon—and if you leave them there to rot, I'll think no worse of you. Well, what are you waiting for? Call your men.

ÆGISTHEUS: No.

ZEUS: Be good enough to tell me why that no.

ÆGISTHEUS: I am tired.

ZEUS: Don't stare at the ground. Raise your big, bloodshot eyes and look at me. That's better. Yes, you're majestically stupid, like a horse; a kingly fool. But yours is not the stubbornness that vexes me; rather, it will add a spice to your surrender. For I know you will obey me in the end.

ÆGISTHEUS: I tell you I refuse to fall in with your plans. I have done so far too often.

ZEUS: That's right. Show your mettle! Resist! Resist! Ah, how I cherish souls like yours! Your eyes flash, you clench your fists, you fling refusal in the teeth of Zeus. None the less, my little rebel, my restive little horse, no sooner had I warned you than your heart said yes. Of course you'll obey. Do you think I leave Olympus without good reason? I wished to warn you of this crime because it is my will to avert it.

ÆGISTHEUS: To warn me! How strange!

ZEUS: Why "strange"? Surely it's natural enough. Your life's in danger and I want to save it.

ÆGISTHEUS: Who asked you to save it? What about Agamemnon? Did you warn *him?* And yet *he* wished to live.

ZEUS: O miserable man, what base ingratitude! You are dearer to me than Agamemnon, and when I prove this, you complain!

ÆGISTHEUS: Dearer than Agamemnon? I? No, it's Orestes whom you cherish. You allowed me to work my doom, you let me rush in, ax in hand, to King Agamemnon's bath—and no doubt you watched from high Olympus, licking your lips at the thought of another damned soul to gloat over. But today you are protecting young Orestes against himself; and I, whom you egged on to kill his father—you have chosen me to restrain the young man's hand. I was a poor creature, just qualified for murder; but for Orestes, it seems, you have higher destinies in view.

ZEUS: What strange jealousy is this! But have no fear; I love him no more than I love you. I love nobody.

ÆGISTHEUS: Then see what you have made of me, unjust god that you are. And tell me this. If today you hinder the crime Orestes has in mind, why did you permit mine of fifteen years ago?

ZEUS: All crimes do not displease me equally. And now, Ægistheus, I shall speak to you frankly, as one king to another. The first crime was mine; I committed it when I made man mortal. Once I had done that, what was left for you, poor human murderers, to do? To kill your victims? But they already had the seed of death in them; all you could do was to hasten its fruition by a year or two. Do you know what would have befallen Agamemnon if you had not killed him? Three months later he'd have died of apoplexy in a pretty slave-girl's arms. But your crime served my ends.

ÆGISTHEUS: What ends? For fifteen years I have been atoning for it—and you say it served your ends!

ZEUS: Exactly. It's because you are atoning for it that it served my ends. I like crimes that *pay*. I like yours because it was a clumsy, boorish murder, a crime that did not know itself, a crime in the antique mode, more like a cataclysm that an act of man. Not for one moment did you defy me. You struck in a frenzy of fear and rage. And then, when your frenzy had died down, you looked back on the deed with loathing and disowned it. Yet what a profit I have made on it! For one dead man, twenty thousand living men wallowing in penitence. Yes, it was a good bargain I struck that day.

ÆGISTHEUS: I see what lies behind your words. Orestes will have no remorse.

ZEUS: Not a trace of it. At this moment he is thinking out his plan, coolly, methodically, cheerfully. What good to me is a carefree murder, a shameless, sedate crime, that lies light as thistledown on the murderer's conscience? No, I won't allow it. Ah, how I loathe the crimes of this new generation; thankless and sterile as the wind! Yes, that nice-minded young man will kill you as he'd kill a chicken; he'll go away with red hands and a clean heart. In your place I should feel humiliated. So—call your men!

ÆGISTHEUS: Again I tell you, I will *not*. The crime that is being hatched displeases you enough for me to welcome it.

ZEUS: Ægistheus, you are a king, and it's to your sense of kingship I appeal, for you enjoy wielding the scepter.

ÆGISTHEUS: Continue.

ZEUS: You may hate me, but we are akin; I made you in my image. A king is a god on earth, glorious and terrifying as a god.

ÆGISTHEUS: You, terrifying?

ZEUS: Look at me. [*A long silence*] I told you you were made in my image. Each keeps order; you in Argos, I in heaven and on earth—and you and I harbor the same dark secret in our hearts.

ÆGISTHEUS: I have no secret.

ZEUS: You have. The same as mine. The bane of gods and kings. The bitterness of knowing men are free. Yes, Ægistheus, they are free. But your subjects do not know it, and you do.

ÆGISTHEUS: Why, yes. If they knew it, they'd send my palace up in flames. For fifteen years I've been playing a part to mask their power from them.

ZEUS: So you see we are alike.

ÆGISTHEUS: Alike? A god likening himself to me—what freak of irony is this? Since I came to the throne, all I said, all my acts, have been aimed at building up an image of myself. I wish each of my subjects to keep that image in the foreground of his mind, and to feel, even when alone, that my eyes are on him, severely judging his most private thoughts. But I have been trapped in my own net. I have come to see myself only as they see me. I peer into the dark pit of their souls, and there, deep down, I see the image that I have built up. I shudder, but I cannot take my eyes off it. Almighty Zeus, who am I? Am I anything more than the dread that others have of me?

ZEUS: And I—who do you think *I* am? [*Points to the statue*] I, too, have my image, and do you suppose it doesn't fill me with confusion? For a hundred thousand years I have been dancing a slow, dark ritual dance before men's eyes. Their eyes are so intent on me that they forget to look into themselves. If I forgot myself for a single moment, if I let their eyes turn away—

ÆGISTHEUS: Yes?

ZEUS: Enough. That is my business. Ægistheus, I know that you are weary of it all; but why complain? You'll die one day—but I shall not. So long as there are men on earth, I am doomed to go on dancing before them.

ÆGISTHEUS: Alas! But who has doomed us?

ZEUS: No one but ourselves. For we have the same passion. You Ægistheus, have, like me, a passion for order.

ÆGISTHEUS: For order? That is so. It was for the sake of order that I wooed Clytemnestra, for order that I killed my King; I wished that order should prevail, and that it should prevail through me. I have lived without love, without hope, even without lust. But I have kept order. Yes, I have kept good order in my kingdom. That has been my ruling passion; a godlike passion, but how terrible!

ZEUS: We could have no other, you and I; I am God, and you were born to be a king.

ÆGISTHEUS: Ay, more's the pity!

ZEUS: Ægistheus, my creature and my mortal brother, in the name of this good order that we serve, both you and I, I ask you—nay, I command you—to lay hands on Orestes and his sister.

ÆGISTHEUS: Are they so dangerous?

ZEUS: Orestes knows that he is free.

ÆGISTHEUS: [*Eagerly*] He know he's free? Then, to lay hands on him, to put him in irons, is not enough. A free man in a city acts like a plaguespot. He will infect my whole kingdom and bring my work to nothing. Almighty Zeus, why stay your hand? Why not fell him with a thunderbolt?

ZEUS: [*Slowly*] Fell him with a thunderbolt? [*A pause. Then, in a muffled voice*] Ægistheus, the gods have another secret.

ÆGISTHEUS: Yes?

ZEUS: Once freedom lights its beacon in a man's heart, the gods are powerless against him. It's a matter between man and man, and it is for other men, and for them only, to let him go his gait, or to throttle him.

ÆGISTHEUS: [*Observing him closely*] To throttle him? Be it so. Well, I shall do your will, no doubt. But say no more, and stay here no longer—I could not bear it.

[*As* Zeus *departs,* Electra *leaps forward and rushes to the door.* Orestes *comes forward*]

ELECTRA: Strike him down! Don't give him time to call for help. I'll bar the door.

ÆGISTHEUS: So you, young man, are Orestes?

ORESTES: Defend yourself.

ÆGISTHEUS: I shall not defend myself. It's too late for me to call for help, and I am glad it is too late. No, I shall not resist. I *wish* you to kill me.

ORESTES: Good. Little I care how it is done. . . . So I am to be a murderer. [Orestes *strikes him with his sword*]

ÆGISTHEUS: [*Tottering*] Ah! You struck well, Orestes. [*He clings to* Orestes] Let me look at you. Is it true you feel no remorse?

ORESTES: Remorse? Why should I feel remorse? I am only doing what is right.

ÆGISTHEUS: What is right is the will of God. You were hidden here and you heard the words of Zeus.

ORESTES: What do I care for Zeus? Justice is a matter between men, and I need no god to teach me it. It's right to stamp you out, like the foul brute you are, and to free the people of Argos from your evil influence. It is right to restore to them their sense of human dignity.

ÆGISTHEUS: [*Groaning*] Pain! What agony!

ELECTRA: Look! Look! He's swaying; his face has gone quite gray. What an ugly sight's a dying man!

ORESTES: Keep silent! Let him carry with him to the grave no other memory than the memory of our joy.

ÆGISTHEUS: My curse on you both!

ORESTES: Won't you have done with dying? [*He strikes again.* Ægistheus *falls*]

ÆGISTHEUS: Beware of the flies, Orestes, beware of the flies. All is not over. [*Dies*]

ORESTES: [*Giving the body a kick*] For him, anyhow, all is over. Now lead me to the Queen's room.

ELECTRA: Orestes!

ORESTES: What?

ELECTRA: She—she can do us no more harm.

ORESTES: What of it? What has come over you? This is not how you spoke a little while ago.

ELECTRA: Orestes! You, too, have changed. I hardly recognize you.

ORESTES: Very well. I'll go alone. [*Exit*]

ELECTRA: [*To herself*] Will she scream? [*Silence. She is listening*] He's walking down the passage. When he opens the fourth door— Oh, I wanted this to happen. And I—I want it now, I *must* want it. [*She looks at* Ægistheus] That one—yes, he's dead. So *this* is what I wanted. I didn't realize how it would be. [*She comes closer to the body*] A hundred times I've seen him, in my dreams, lying just where he is now, with a sword through his heart. His eyes were closed, he seemed asleep. How I hated him, what joy I got from hating him! But he doesn't seem asleep; his eyes are open, staring up at me. He is dead, and my hatred is dead, too. And I'm standing here, waiting, waiting. That woman is still alive, she's in her bedroom, and presently she'll be screaming. Screaming like an animal in pain. No, I can't bear those eyes any longer. [*Kneeling, she lays a mantle over the King's face*] What was it, then, I wanted? What? [*A short silence.* Clytemnestra *screams*] He's struck her. She was our mother—and he's struck her. [*She rises to her feet*] It's done; my enemies are dead. For years and years I've reveled in the thought of this, and, now it's happened, my heart is like a lump of ice. Was I lying to myself all those years? No, that's not true, it can't be true. I'm not a coward. Only a moment ago I wanted it, and I haven't changed. I'm glad, glad, to see that swine lying at my feet. [*She jerks the mantle off the dead King's face*] Those dead-fish eyes goggling up at nothing—why should they trouble me? That's how I wanted to see them, dead and staring, and I'm glad, glad— [Clytemnestra's *screams are weakening*] Let her scream! Make her scream, Orestes. I want her to suffer. [*The screams cease*] Oh joy, joy! I'm weeping for joy; my enemies are dead, my father is avenged.

[Orestes *returns, his sword dripping blood.* Electra *runs to him and flings herself into his arms*]

ELECTRA: Orestes! . . . Oh! . . .

ORESTES: You're frightened. Why?

ELECTRA: I'm not frightened. I'm drunk. Drunk with joy. What did she say? Did she beg for mercy long?

ORESTES: Electra, I shall not repent of what I have done, but I think fit not to speak of it. There are some memories one does not share. It is enough for you to know she's dead.

ELECTRA: Did she die cursing us? That's all I want to tell me. Did she curse us?

ORESTES: Yes. She died cursing us.

ELECTRA: Take me in your arms, beloved, and press me to your breast. How dark the night is! I never knew such darkness; those torches have no effect on it. . . . Do you love me?

ORESTES: It is not night; a new day is dawning. We are free, Electra. I feel as if I'd brought you into life and I, too, had just been born. Yes, I love you, and you belong to me. Only yesterday I was empty-handed, and today I have *you.* Ours is a double tie of blood; we two come of the same race and we two have shed blood.

ELECTRA: Let go your sword. Give me that hand, your strong right hand. [*She clasps and kisses it*] Your fingers are short and square, made to grasp and hold. Dear hand! It's whiter than mine. But how heavy it became to strike down our father's murderers! Wait! [*She takes a torch and holds it near* Orestes] I must light up your face; it's getting so dark that I can hardly see you. And I *must* see you; when I stop seeing you, I'm afraid of you. I daren't take my eyes off you. I must tell myself again and again that I love you. But—how strange you look!

ORESTES: I am free, Electra. Freedom has crushed down on me like a thunderbolt.

ELECTRA: Free? But I—I don't feel free. And you—can you undo what has been done? Something has happened and we are no longer free to blot it out. Can you prevent our being the murderers of our mother—for all time?

ORESTES: Do you think I'd wish to prevent it? I have done *my* deed, Electra, and that deed was good. I shall bear it on my shoulders as a carrier at a ferry carries the traveler to the farther bank. And when I have brought it to the farther bank I shall take stock of it. The heavier it is to carry, the better pleased I shall be; for that burden is my freedom. Only yesterday I walked the earth haphazard; thousands of roads I tramped that brought me nowhere, for they were other men's roads. Yes, I tried them all; the hauler's tracks along the riverside, the mule-paths in the mountains, and the broad, flagged highways of charioteers. But none of these was mine. Today I have one path only, and heaven knows where it leads. But it is *my* path. . . . What is it, Electra?

ELECTRA: I can't see you any more. Those torches give no light. I hear your voice, but it hurts me, it cuts like a knife. Will it always be as dark as this—always, even in the daytime? . . . Oh, Orestes! There they are!

ORESTES: Who?

ELECTRA: There they are! Where have they come from? They're hanging from the ceiling like clusters of black grapes; the walls are alive with them; they're swirling down across the torchlight and it's their shadows that are hiding your face from me.

ORESTES: The flies—

ELECTRA: Listen! The sound of their wings is like a roaring furnace. They're all around us, Orestes, watching, biding their time. Presently they'll swoop down on us and I shall feel thousands of tiny clammy feet crawling over me. Oh, look! They're growing bigger, bigger; now they're as big as bees. We'll never escape them, they'll follow us everywhere in a dense cloud. Oh God, now I can see their eyes, millions of beady eyes all staring at us!

ORESTES: What do the flies matter to us?

ELECTRA: They're the Furies, Orestes, the goddesses of remorse.

VOICES: [*From behind the door*] Open! Open! . . . If you don't, we'll smash the door in. [*Heavy thuds. They are battering at the door*]

ORESTES: Clytemnestra's cries must have brought them here. Come! Lead me to Apollo's shrine. We will spend the night there, sheltered from men and flies. And tomorrow I shall speak to my people.

CURTAIN

ACT III.

The temple of Apollo. Twilight. A statue of Apollo in the center of the stage. Electra *and* Orestes *are sleeping at the foot of the statue, their arms clasped round its legs. The* Furies *ring them round; they sleep standing, like cranes. At the back is a huge bronze door.*

FIRST FURY: [*Stretching herself*] Aaaah! I slept the night out standing, stiff with rage, and my sleep was glorious with angry dreams. Ah, how lovely is the flower of anger, the red flower in my heart! [*She circles round* Orestes *and* Electra] Still sleeping. How white and soft they are! I'll roll on their breasts and bellies, like a torrent over stones. And I shall polish hour by hour their tender flesh; rub it, scour it, wear it to the bone. [*She comes a few steps forward*] O clear, bright dawn of hate! A superb awakening. They're sleeping, sweating, a smell of fever rises from them. But I am awake; cool and hard and gemlike. My soul is adamant—and I feel my sanctity.

ELECTRA: [*Sighing in her sleep*] No! No!

FIRST FURY: She's sighing. Wait, my pretty one, wait till you feel our teeth. Soon you'll be screaming with the agony of our caresses. I'll woo you like a man, for you're my bride, and you shall feel my love crushing your life out. You, Electra, are more beautiful than I; but you'll see how my kisses age you. Within six months I'll have you raddled like an old hag; but I stay young forever. [*She bends over* Orestes *and* Electra] Ah, this lovely human carrion, what a tasty meal we have in store! As I gaze down at them and breathe their breath, I choke with rage. Nothing is sweeter, nothing, than to feel a dawn of hatred spreading like quickfire in one's veins; teeth and talons ready for their task. Hatred is flooding through me, welling up in my breasts like milk. Awake, sisters, awake! The day has come.

SECOND FURY: I dreamt I was biting them.

FIRST FURY: Be patient. Today they are protected by a god, but soon hunger and thirst will drive them out of sanctuary. And then you shall bite them to your heart's content.

THIRD FURY: Aaah! How I want to claw them!

FIRST FURY: Your turn will come. In a little while your iron talons will be ribboning the flesh of those young criminals with angry red. Come closer, sisters, come and look at them.

A FURY: How young they are!

ANOTHER FURY: And how beautiful!

FIRST FURY: Yes, we are favored. Only too often criminals are old and ugly. Too seldom do we have the joy, the exquisite delight, of ruining what's beautiful.

THE FURIES: Heiah! Heiahah!

THIRD FURY: Orestes is almost a child. I shall

mother him, oh so tenderly, with my hatred; I shall take his pale head on my knees and stroke his hair.

FIRST FURY: And then?

THIRD FURY: Then, when he least expects it, I shall dig these two fingers into his eyes. [*All laugh*]

FIRST FURY: See, they're stretching, sighing, on the brink of waking. And now, my sisters, flies my sisters, let's sing the sinners from their sleep.

THE FURIES: [*Together*] Bzz. Bzz. Bzz. Bzz.
> We shall settle on your rotten hearts like
>   flies on butter;
> Rotten hearts, juicy, luscious hearts.
> Like bees we'll suck the pus and matter
>   from your hearts,
> And we'll turn it into honey, rich, green
>   honey.
> What love could ravish us as hatred
>   does?
> Bzz. Bzz. Bzz. Bzz.
> We shall be the staring eyes of the
>   houses,
> The growls of the kenneled mastiff
>   baring his fangs as you go by,
> A drone of wings pulsing in high air,
> Sounds of the forest,
> Whistlings, whinings, creakings, hissings,
>   howlings,
> We shall be the darkness,
> The clotted darkness of your souls.
> Bzz. Bzz. Bzz. Bzz.
> Heiah, heiah, heiahah!
> Bzz. Bzz. Bzz. Bzz.
> We are the flies, the suckers of pus,
> We shall have open house with you,
> We shall gather our food from your
>   mouths,
> And our light from the depths of your
>   eyes.
> All your life we will be with you,
> Until we make you over to the worms.

[*They dance*]

ELECTRA: [*Still half asleep*] Was someone speaking? Who—who are you?

THE FURIES: Bzz. Bzz. Bzz.

ELECTRA: Ah, yes. There you are. Well? Have we really killed them?

ORESTES: [*Waking*] Electra!

ELECTRA: You, who are you? Ah, yes. Orestes. Go away.

ORESTES: But—what's wrong, Electra?

ELECTRA: You frighten me. I had a dream. I saw our mother lying on her back. Blood was pouring from her, gushing under the door. A dream. . . . Feel my hands. They're icy. No, don't. Don't touch me. Did she really bleed much?

ORESTES: Don't!

ELECTRA: [*Waking up completely*] Let me look at you. You killed them. It was you, you who killed them. You are here beside me, you have just waked up, there's nothing written on your face, no brand. . . . And yet you killed them.

ORESTES: Why, yes. I killed them. [*A short silence*] You, too, make me afraid. Yesterday you were so beautiful. And now you look as if some wild beast had clawed your face.

ELECTRA: No beast. Your crime. It's tearing off my cheeks and eyelids; I feel as if my eyes and teeth were naked. . . . But what are those creatures?

ORESTES: Take no notice of them. They can do you no harm.

FIRST FURY: No harm? Let her dare to come among us and you'll see if we can do no harm!

ORESTES: Keep quiet. Back to your kennel, bitches! [*The* Furies *growl*] Is it possible that the girl who only yesterday was dancing in a white dress on the temple steps—is it possible you were that girl?

ELECTRA: I've grown old. In a single night.

ORESTES: You have not lost your beauty, but— Where, now, have I seen dead eyes like those? Electra—you are like *her*. Like Clytemnestra. What use, then, was it killing her? When I see my crime in those eyes, it revolts me.

FIRST FURY: That is because *you* revolt *her*.

ORESTES: Is that true, Electra? Do I revolt you?

ELECTRA: Oh, let me be!

FIRST FURY: Well? Can you still have any doubt? How should she not hate you? She lived in peace, dreaming her dreams; and then you came, bringing murder and impiety upon her. So now she has to share your guilt and hug that pedestal, the only scrap of earth remaining to her.

ORESTES: Do not listen.

FIRST FURY: Away! Away! Make him go, Electra; don't let him touch you! He's a butcher. He reeks of fresh, warm blood. He used the poor old woman very foully, you know; he killed her piecemeal.

ELECTRA: Oh no! That's a lie, surely?

FIRST FURY: You can believe me; I was there all the time, buzzing in the air around them.

ELECTRA: So he struck her several times?

FIRST FURY: Ten times at least. And each time the sword squelched in the wound. She tried to shield her face and belly with her hands, and he carved her hands to ribbons.

ELECTRA: So it wasn't a quick death. Did she suffer much?

ORESTES: Put your fingers in your ears, do not look at them, and, above all, ask no questions. If you question them, you're lost.

FIRST FURY: Yes, she suffered—horribly.

ELECTRA: [*Covering her face with her hands*] Oh!

ORESTES: She wants to part us, she is building up a wall of solitude around you. But beware; once you are alone, alone and helpless, they will fling themselves upon you. Electra, we planned this crime together and we should bear its brunt together.

ELECTRA: You dare to say I planned it with you?

ORESTES: Can you deny it?

ELECTRA: Of course I deny it. Wait! Well, perhaps—in a way. . . . Oh, I don't know. I dreamt the crime, but you carried it out, you murdered your own mother.

THE FURIES: [*Shrieking and laughing*] Murderer! Murderer! Butcher!

ORESTES: Electra, behind that door is the outside world. A world of dawn. Out there the sun is rising, lighting up the roads. Soon we shall leave this place, we shall walk those sunlit roads, and these hags of darkness will lose their power. The sunbeams will cut through them like swords.

ELECTRA: The sun—

FIRST FURY: You will never see the sun again, Electra. We shall mass between you and the sun like a swarm of locusts; you will carry darkness round your head wherever you go.

ELECTRA: Oh, let me be! Stop torturing me!

ORESTES: It's your weakness gives them their strength. Mark how they dare not speak to me. A nameless horror has descended on you, keeping us apart. And yet why should this be? What have you lived through that I have not shared? Do you imagine that my mother's cries will ever cease ringing in my ears? Or that my eyes will ever cease to see her great sad eyes, lakes of lambent darkness in the pallor of her face? And the anguish that consumes you—do you think it will ever cease ravaging my heart? But what matter? I am free. Beyond anguish, beyond remorse. Free. And at one with myself. No, you must not loathe yourself, Electra. Give me your hand. I shall never forsake you.

ELECTRA: Let go of my hand! Those hell-hounds frighten me, but you frighten me more.

FIRST FURY: You see! You see! . . . That's quite true, little doll; you're less afraid of us than of that man. Because you need us, Electra. You are our child, our little girl. You need our nails to score your skin, our teeth to bite your breast, and all our savage love to save you from your hatred of yourself. Only the suffering of your body can take your mind off your suffering soul. So come and let us hurt you. You have only those two steps to come down, and we will take you in our arms. And when our kisses sear your tender flesh, you'll forget all in the cleansing fires of pain.

THE FURIES: Come down to us! Come down!
[*Slowly they dance round her, weaving their spell.* Electra *rises to her feet*]

ORESTES: [*Gripping her arm*] No, no, for pity's sake. Don't go to them. Once they get you, all is lost.

ELECTRA: [*Freeing herself violently*] Let go! Oh, how I hate you! [*She goes down the steps, and the* Furies *fling themselves on her*] Help!

[Zeus *enters*]

ZEUS: Kennel up!

FIRST FURY: The master!
[The Furies *slink off reluctantly, leaving* Electra *lying on the ground*]

ZEUS: Poor children. [*He goes up to* Electra] So to this you've come, unhappy pair? My heart is torn between anger and compassion. Get up, Electra. So long as I am here, my Furies will not hurt you. [*He helps her to rise and gazes at her face*] Ah, what a cruel change! In a night, a single night, all the wild-rose bloom has left your cheeks. In one night your body has gone to ruin, lungs, gall, and liver all burnt out. The pride of headstrong youth—see what it has brought you to, poor child.

ORESTES: Stop talking in that tone, fellow. It is unbecoming for the king of the gods.

ZEUS: And you, my lad, drop that haughty tone. It's unbecoming for a criminal atoning for his crime.

ORESTES: I am no criminal, and you have no power to make me atone for an act I don't regard as a crime.

ZEUS: So you may think, but wait awhile. I shall cure you of that error before long.

ORESTES: Torture me to your heart's content; I regret nothing.

ZEUS: Not even the doom you have brought upon your sister?

ORESTES: Not even that.

ZEUS: Do you hear, Electra? And this man professed to love you!

ORESTES: She is dearer to me than life. But her suffering comes from within, and only she can rid herself of it. For she is free.

ZEUS: And you? You, too, are free, no doubt?

ORESTES: Yes, and well you know it.

ZEUS: A pity you can't see yourself as you are now, you fool, for all your boasting! What a heroic figure you cut there, cowering between the legs of a protecting god, with a pack of hungry vixen keeping guard on you! If *you* can brag of freedom, why not praise the freedom of a prisoner languishing in fetters, or a slave nailed to the cross?

ORESTES: Certainly. Why not?

ZEUS: Take care. You play the braggart now because Apollo is protecting you. But Apollo is my most obedient servant. I have but to lift a finger and he will abandon you.

ORESTES: Then do so. Lift a finger, lift your whole hand while you are about it.

ZEUS: No, that is not my way. Haven't I told you that I take no pleasure in punishment? I have come to save you both.

ELECTRA: To save us? No, it is too cruel to make sport of us. You are the lord of vengeance and of death, but, god though you are, you have no right to delude your victims with false hopes.

ZEUS: Within a quarter of an hour you can be outside that door.

ELECTRA: Safe and sound?

ZEUS: You have my word for it.

ELECTRA: And what do you want from me in return?

ZEUS: Nothing, my child. Nothing.

ELECTRA: Nothing? Did I hear right? Then you are a kind god, a lovable god.

ZEUS: Or next to nothing. A mere trifle. What you can give most easily—a little penitence.

ORESTES: Take care, Electra. That trifle will weigh like a millstone on your soul.

ZEUS: [*To* Electra] Don't listen to him. Answer me, instead. Why hesitate to disavow that crime? It was committed by someone else; one could hardly say even that you were his accomplice.

ORESTES: Electra! Are you going to go back on fifteen years of hope and hatred?

ZEUS: What has she to go back on? Never did she really wish that impious deed to be accomplished.

ELECTRA: If only that were true!

ZEUS: Come now! Surely you can trust my word. Do I not read in men's hearts?

ELECTRA: [*Incredulously*] And you read in mine that I never really desired that crime? Though for fifteen years I dreamt of murder and revenge?

ZEUS: Bah! I know you nursed bloodthirsty dreams—but there was a sort of innocence about them. They made you forget your servitude, they healed your wounded pride. But you never really thought of making them come true. Well, am I mistaken?

ELECTRA: Ah, Zeus, dear Zeus, how I long to think you are not mistaken!

ZEUS: You're a little girl, Electra. A mere child. Most little girls dream of becoming the richest or the loveliest woman on earth. But you were haunted by the cruel destiny of your race, you dreamt of becoming the saddest, most criminal of women. You never willed to do evil; you willed your own misfortune. At an age when most children are playing hopscotch or with their dolls, you, poor child, who had no friends or toys, you toyed with dreams of murder, because that's a game to play alone.

ELECTRA: Yes, yes! I'm beginning to understand.

ORESTES: Listen, Electra! It's *now* you are bringing guilt upon you. For who except yourself can know what you really wanted? Will you let another decide that for you? Why distort a past that can no longer stand up for itself? And why disown the fire-brand that you were, that glorious young goddess, vivid with hatred, that I loved so much? Can't you see this cruel god is fooling you?

ZEUS: No, Electra, I'm not fooling you. And now hear what I offer. If you repudiate your crime, I'll see that you two occupy the throne of Argos.

ORESTES: Taking the places of our victims?

ZEUS: How else?

ORESTES: And I shall put on the royal robe, still warm from the dead King's wearing?

ZEUS: That or another. What can it matter?

ORESTES: Nothing of course—provided that it's black.

ZEUS: Are you not in mourning?

ORESTES: Yes, I was forgetting; in mourning for my mother. And my subjects—must I have them, too, wear black?

ZEUS: They wear it already.

ORESTES: True. We can give them time to wear out their old clothes. . . . Well, Electra, have you understood? If you shed some tears, you'll be given Clytemnestra's shifts and petticoats—those dirty, stinking ones you had to wash for fifteen years. And the part she played is yours for the asking. Now that you have come to look so much like her, you will play the part superbly; everyone will take you for your mother. But I—I fear I am more squeamish—I refuse to wear the breeches of the clown I killed.

ZEUS: You talk big, my boy. You butchered a defenseless man and an old woman who begged for mercy. But, to hear you speak, one would think you'd bravely fought, one against a crowd, and were the savior of your city.

ORESTES: Perhaps I was.

ZEUS: You a savior! Do you know what's afoot behind that door? All the good folk of Argos are waiting there. Waiting to greet you with stones and pikes and pitchforks. Oh, they are very grateful to their savior! . . . You are lonely as a leper.

ORESTES: Yes.

ZEUS: So you take pride in being an outcast, do you? But the solitude you're doomed to, most cowardly of murderers, is the solitude of scorn and loathing.

ORESTES: The most cowardly of murderers is he who feels remorse.

ZEUS: Orestes, I created you, and I created all things. Now see! [*The walls of the temple draw apart, revealing the firmament, spangled with wheeling stars. Zeus is standing in the background. His voice becomes huge—amplified by loud-speakers—but his form is shadowy*] See those planets wheeling on their appointed ways, never swerving, never clashing. It was I who ordained their courses, according to the law of justice. Hear the music of the spheres, that vast, mineral hymn of praise, sounding and resounding to the limits of the firmament. [*Sounds of music*] It is my work that living things increase and multiply, each according to his kind. I have ordained that man shall always beget man, and dog give birth to dog. It is my work that the tides with their innumerable tongues creep up to lap the sand and draw back at the appointed hour. I make the plants grow, and my breath fans round the earth the yellow clouds of pollen. You are not in your own home, intruder; you are a foreign body in the world, like a splinter in flesh, or a poacher in his lordship's forest. For the world is good; I made it according to my will, and I am Goodness. But you, Orestes, you have done evil, the very rocks and stones cry out against you. The Good is everywhere, it is the coolness of the wellspring, the pith of the reed, the grain of flint, the weight of stone. Yes, you will find it even in the heart of fire and light; even your own body plays you false, for it abides perforce by my law. Good is everywhere, in you and about you; sweeping through you like a scythe, crushing you like a mountain. Like an ocean it buoys you up and rocks you to and fro, and it enabled the success of your evil plan, for it was in the brightness of the torches, the temper of your blade, the strength of your right arm. And that of which you are so vain, the Evil that you think is your creation, what is it but a reflection in a mocking mirror, a phantom thing that would have no being but for Goodness. No, Orestes, return to your saner self; the universe refutes you, you are a mite in the scheme of things. Return to Nature, Nature's thankless son. Know your sin, abhor it, and tear it from you as one tears out a rotten, noisome tooth. Or else—beware lest the very seas shrink back at your approach, springs dry up when you pass by, stones and rocks roll from your path, and the earth crumbles under your feet.

ORESTES: Let it crumble! Let the rocks revile me, and flowers wilt at my coming. Your whole universe is not enough to prove me wrong. You are the king of gods, king of stones and stars, king of the waves of the sea. But you are not the king of man.

[*The walls draw together. Zeus comes into view, tired and dejected, and he now speaks in his normal voice*]

ZEUS: Impudent spawn! So I am not your king? Who, then, made you?

ORESTES: You. But you blundered; you should not have made me free.

ZEUS: I gave you freedom so that you might serve me.

ORESTES: Perhaps. But now it has turned against its giver. And neither you nor I can undo what has been done.

ZEUS: Ah, at last! So this is your excuse?

ORESTES: I am not excusing myself.

ZEUS: No? Let me tell you it sounds much like an excuse, this freedom whose slave you claim to be.

ORESTES: Neither slave nor master. I *am* my freedom. No sooner had you created me than I ceased to be yours.

ELECTRA: Oh, Orestes! By all you hold most holy, by our father's memory, I beg you do not add blasphemy to your crime!

ZEUS: Mark her words, young man. And hope no more to win her back by arguments like these. Such language is somewhat new to her ears—and somewhat shocking.

ORESTES: To my ears, too. And to my lungs, which breathe the words, and to my tongue, which shapes them. In fact, I can hardly understand myself. Only yesterday you were still a veil on my eyes, a clot of wax in my ears; yesterday, indeed, I had an excuse. *You* were my excuse for being alive, for you had put me in the world to fulfill your purpose, and the world was an old pander prating to me about your goodness, day in, day out. And then you forsook me.

ZEUS: *I* forsook you? How?

ORESTES: Yesterday, when I was with Electra, I felt at one with Nature, this Nature of your making. It sang the praises of the Good—*your* Good—in siren tones, and lavished intimations. To lull me into gentleness, the fierce light mellowed and grew tender as a lover's eyes. And, to teach me the forgiveness of offenses, the sky grew bland as a pardoner's face. Obedient to your will, my youth rose up before me and pleaded with me like a girl who fears her lover will forsake her. That was the last time, the last, I saw my youth. Suddenly, out of the blue, freedom crashed down on me and swept me off my feet. Nature sprang back, my youth went with the wind, and I knew myself alone, utterly alone in the midst of this well-meaning little universe of yours. I was like a man who's lost his shadow. And there was nothing left in heaven, no right or wrong, nor anyone to give me orders.

ZEUS: What of it? Do you want me to admire a scabby sheep that has to be kept apart; or the leper mewed in a lazar-house? Remember, Orestes, you once were of my flock, you fed in my pastures among my sheep. Your vaunted freedom isolates you from the fold; it means exile.

ORESTES: Yes, exile.

ZEUS: But the disease can't be deeply rooted yet; it began only yesterday. Come back to the fold. Think of your loneliness; even your sister is forsaking you. Your eyes are big with anguish, your face is pale and drawn. The disease you're suffering from is inhuman, foreign to my nature, foreign to yourself. Come back. I am forgetfulness, I am peace.

ORESTES: Foreign to myself—I know it. Outside nature, against nature, without excuse, beyond remedy, except what remedy I find within myself. But I shall not return under your law; I am doomed to have no other law but mine. Nor shall I come back to Nature, the Nature you found good; in it are a thousand beaten paths all leading up to you—but I must blaze my trail. For I, Zeus, am a man, and every man must find out his own way. Nature abhors man, and you too, god of gods, abhor mankind.

ZEUS: That is true; men like you I hold in abhorrence.

ORESTES: Take care; those words were a confession of your weakness. As for me, I do not hate you. What have I to do with you, or you with me? We shall glide past each other, like ships in a river, without touching. You are God and I am free; each of us is alone, and our anguish is akin. How can you know I did not try to feel remorse in the long night that has gone by? And to sleep? But no longer can I feel remorse and I can sleep no more. [*A short silence*]

ZEUS: What do you propose to do?

ORESTES: The folk of Argos are my folk. I must open their eyes.

ZEUS: Poor people! Your gift to them will be a sad one; of loneliness and shame. You will tear from their eyes the veils I had laid on them, and they will see their lives as they are, foul and futile, a barren boon.

ORESTES: Why, since it is their lot, should I deny them the despair I have in me?

ZEUS: What will they make of it?

ORESTES: What they choose. They're free; and human life begins on the far side of despair. [*A short silence*]

ZEUS: Well, Orestes, all this was foreknown. In the fullness of time a man was to come, to announce my decline. And you're that man, it seems. But seeing you yesterday—you with your girlish face—who'd have believed it?

ORESTES: Could I myself have believed it? . . . The words I speak are too big for my mouth, they tear it; the load of destiny I bear is too heavy for my youth and has shattered it.

ZEUS: I have little love for you, yet I am sorry for you.

ORESTES: And I, too, am sorry for *you.*

ZEUS: Good-by, Orestes. [*He takes some steps forward*] As for you, Electra, bear this in mind. My reign is not yet over—far from it!—and I shall not give up the struggle. So choose if you are with me or against me. Farewell.

ORESTES: Farewell. [Zeus *goes out.* Electra *slowly rises to her feet*] Where are you going?

ELECTRA: Leave me alone. I'm done with you.

ORESTES: I have known you only for a day, and must I lose you now forever?

ELECTRA: Would to God that I had never known you!

ORESTES: Electra! My sister, dear Electra! My only love, the one joy of my life, do not leave me. Stay with me.

ELECTRA: Thief! I had so little, so very little to call mine; only a few weak dreams, a morsel of peace. and now you've taken my all; you've robbed a pauper of her mite! You were my brother, the head of our house, and it was your duty to protect me. But no, you needs must drag me into carnage; I am red as a flayed ox, these loathsome flies are swarming after me, and my heart is buzzing like an angry hive.

ORESTES: Yes, my beloved, it's true, I have taken all from you, and I have nothing to offer in return; nothing but my crime. But think how vast a gift that is! Believe me, it weighs on my heart like lead. We were too light, Electra; now our feet sink into the soil, like chariot-wheels in turf. So come with me; we will tread heavily on our way, bowed beneath our precious load. You shall give me your hand, and we will go—

ELECTRA: Where?

ORESTES: I don't know. Towards ourselves. Be-yond the rivers and mountains are an Orestes and an Electra waiting for us, and we must make our patient way towards them.

ELECTRA: I won't hear any more from you. All you have to offer me is misery and squalor. [*She rushes out into the center of the stage. The* Furies *slowly close in on her*] Help! Zeus, king of gods and men, my king, take me in your arms, carry me from this place, and shelter me. I will obey your law, I will be your creature and your slave, I will embrace your knees. Save me from the flies, from my brother, from myself! Do not leave me lonely and I will give up my whole life to atonement. I repent, Zeus. I bitterly repent.

[*She runs off the stage. The* Furies *make as if to follow her, but the* First Fury *holds them back*]

FIRST FURY: Let her be, sisters. She is not for us. But that man is ours, and ours, I think, for many a day. His little soul is stubborn. He will suffer for two.

[*Buzzing, the* Furies *approach* Orestes]

ORESTES: I am alone, alone.

FIRST FURY: No, no, my sweet little murderer, I'm staying with you, and you'll see what merry games I'll think up to entertain you.

ORESTES: Alone until I die. And after that—?

FIRST FURY: Take heart, sisters, he is weakening. See how his eyes dilate. Soon his nerves will be throbbing like harp-strings, in exquisite arpeggios of terror.

SECOND FURY: And hunger will drive him from his sanctuary before long. Before nightfall we shall know how his blood tastes.

ORESTES: Poor Electra!

[*The* Tutor *enters*]

THE TUTOR: Master! Young master! Where are you? It's so dark one can't see a thing. I'm bringing you some food. The townspeople have surrounded the temple; there's no hope of escape by daylight. We shall have to try our chance when night comes. Meanwhile, eat this food to keep your strength up. [*The* Furies *bar his way*] Hey! Who are these? More of those primitive myths! Ah, how I regret that pleasant land of Attica, where reason's always right.

ORESTES: Do not try to approach me, or they will tear you in pieces.

THE TUTOR: Gently now, my lovelies. See what I've brought you, some nice meat and fruit. Here you are! Let's hope it will calm you down.

ORESTES: So the people of Argos have gathered outside the temple, have they?

THE TUTOR: Indeed they have, and I can't say which are the fiercer, the thirstier for your blood: these charming young creatures here, or your worthy subjects.

ORESTES: Good. [*A short silence*] Open that door.

THE TUTOR: Have you lost your wits? They're waiting behind it, and they're armed.

ORESTES: Do as I told you.

THE TUTOR: For once permit me, sir, to disobey your orders. I tell you, they will stone you. It's madness.

ORESTES: Old man, I am your master, and I order you to unbar that door.

[*The* Tutor *opens one leaf of the double doors a few inches*]

THE TUTOR: Oh dear! Oh dear!

ORESTES: Open both leaves.

[*The* Tutor *half opens both leaves of the door and takes cover behind one of them. The* Crowd *surges forward, thrusting the doors wide open; then stops, bewildered, on the threshold. The stage is flooded with bright light. Shouts rise from the* Crowd: "Away with him!" "Kill him!" "Stone him!" "Tear him in pieces!"*]

ORESTES: [*Who has not heard them*] The sun!

THE CROWD: Murderer! Butcher! Blasphemer! We'll tear you limb from limb. We'll pour molten lead into your veins.

A WOMAN: I'll pluck out your eyes.

A MAN: I'll eat your gizzard!

ORESTES: [*Drawing himself up to his full height*] So here you are, my true and loyal subjects? I am Orestes, your King, son of Agamemnon, and this is my coronation day. [*Exclamations of amazement, mutterings among the crowd*] Ah, you are lowering your tone? [*Complete silence*] I know; you fear me. Fifteen years ago to the day, another murderer showed himself to you, his arms red to the elbows, gloved in blood. But him you did not fear; you read in his eyes that he was of your kind, he had not the courage of his crimes. A crime that its doer disowns becomes ownerless—no man's crime; that's how you see it, isn't it? More like an accident than a crime? So you welcomed the criminal as your King, and that crime without an owner started prowling round the city, whimpering like a dog that has lost its master. You see me, men of Argos, you understand that my crime is wholly mine; I claim it as my own, for all to know; it is my glory, my life's work, and you can neither punish me nor pity me. That is why I fill you with fear. And yet, my people, I love you, and it was for your sake that I killed. For your sake. I had come to claim my kingdom, and you would have none of me because I was not of your kind. Now I am of your kind, my subjects; there is a bond of blood between us, and I have earned my kingship over you. As for your sins and your remorse, your night-fears, and the crime Ægistheus committed—all are mine, I take them all upon me. Fear your Dead no longer; they are *my* Dead. And, see, your faithful flies have left you and come to me. But have no fear, people of Argos. I shall not sit on my victim's throne or take the scepter in my blood-stained hands. A god offered it to me, and I said no. I wish to be a king without a kingdom, without subjects. Farewell, my people. Try to reshape your lives. All here is new, all must begin anew. And for me, too, a new life is beginning. A strange life. . . . Listen now to this tale. One summer there was a plague of rats in Scyros. It was like a foul disease; they soiled and nibbled everything, and the people of the city were at their wits' end. But one day a flute-player came to the city. He took his stand in the market-place. Like this. [Orestes *rises to his feet*] He began playing on his flute and all the rats came out and crowded round him. Then he started off, taking long strides—like this. [*He comes down from the pedestal*] And he called to the people of Scyros: "Make way!" [*The* Crowd *makes way for him*] And all the rats raised their heads and hesitated—as the flies are doing. Look! Look at the flies! Then all of sudden they followed in his train. And the flute-player, with his rats, vanished forever. Thus. [*He strides out into the light. Shrieking, the* Furies *fling themselves after him*]

CURTAIN

A REPRESENTATIVE LIST OF MODERN PLAYS

The following appendix is intended to supplement this anthology with a selected list of historically important plays. Many of these titles have already been mentioned or discussed in the introductions, but they are repeated here for the convenience of the reader. The editor makes no claim of completeness for this list. The informed reader, the student, and his instructor will undoubtedly want to add their own preferences. The starting date for this volume of *A Treasury of the Theatre* is more or less arbitrarily taken to be 1875. The forerunners of the modern playwrights are represented in the first volume of the anthology, which begins with the period of Greek classicism and brings us to Ibsen's early career as a romanticist.

SCANDINAVIAN DRAMA

HENRIK IBSEN: *Pillars of Society* (1877). Ibsen's first realistic play to attack the façade of respectability behind which are hidden social evils and private derelictions.

A Doll's House (1879). The famous problem play which exposes the unsoundness of conventional marriage and expounds woman's need for emancipation.

Ghosts (1881). See page 10.

An Enemy of the People (1882). The drama of an idealistic physician's defiance of the vested interests of a community.

The Wild Duck (1884). Ibsen's examination of the relativity of morals, of the confusion between "ideals" and "illusions," and of the wrecking of lives by the misguided idealism of a neurotic would-be reformer.

Rosmersholm (1886). The tragedy of a weak-spirited idealist and a strong-minded "new woman" who drives his first wife to suicide in order to free him for a high destiny.

The Lady from the Sea (1888). A symbolic study of the problem of freedom in marriage.

Hedda Gabler (1890). See page 40.

The Master Builder (1892). A symbolic tragedy of the decline of creativeness and loss of confidence in an artist's life.

John Gabriel Borkman (1896). The tragedy of a financial genius who tries to create an industrial empire and sacrifices love to his dream of power and glory.

BJÖRNSTJERNE BJÖRNSON: *Beyond Human Power, I* and *II* (I, 1883; II, 1895). The first part, a tragedy of a minister's struggle with faith in a psychological situation; the second, a problem play about the conflict between capital and labor.

AUGUST STRINDBERG: *The Father* (1887). See page 75.

Miss Julie (1888). A long, naturalistic one-act drama about the conflict of the sexes and the classes; the tragedy of a repressed young woman in the grip of the sexual instinct.

Comrades (1888). A saturnine comedy about the "equality of the sexes" and about a woman's desire to elevate herself above her husband, who mistakenly treats her as a "comrade" and tries to give her a victory that she has not earned with her own talents.

The Creditor (1890). A long, psychological one-act treatment of feminine parasitism and of a scorned first husband's vengeance by the application of suggestion to her second husband.

The Link (1893). A divorce drama in which the compulsive recriminations of husband and wife deprive them of the custody of their child.

There Are Crimes and Crimes (1899). See page 328.

The Dance of Death, I and *II* (1901). A naturalistic psychological drama about the war of the sexes.

The Dream Play (1902). A symbolic and expressionistic fantasy on the anguish, evil, and illusoriness of human existence.

The Spook Sonata (1907). An expressionistic examination of the hidden guilt and failure of lives that lack the grace of God or man.

GUNNAR HEIBERG: *The Tragedy of Love* (1905). A romantic psychological drama dealing with the difference between masculine and feminine love.

HJALMAR BERGSTRÖM: *Karen Bornemann* (1907). A liberal, Ibsen-inspired treatment of the conflict between a conservative father and a daughter who insists on freedom in love without the sanction of marriage.

JÓHANN SIGURJÓNSSON: *Eyvind of the Hills* (1911). An Icelandic tragedy, notable for its passion and poetic background.

CENTRAL EUROPEAN DRAMA

LUDWIG ANZENGRUBER: *The Fourth Commandment* (1877). A seminaturalistic study of depravity in middle-class Viennese life.

GERHART HAUPTMANN: *The Weavers* (1892). See page 132.

The Beaver Coat (1893). A naturalistic thieves' comedy and a satire on the old Prussian bureaucracy. See also its sequel, *The Conflagration.*

The Assumption of Hannele (1893). The drama of a child hounded to death by her stepfather; presented by means of naturalistic and fantastic scenes.

The Sunken Bell (1896). A symbolist fairy tale in verse dealing with the conflict between duty and the pagan pursuit of freedom in an artist's soul.

Drayman Henschel (1898). A naturalistic tragedy of an inarticulate man destroyed by his conscience and by a worthless second wife.

Rose Bernd (1903). A naturalistic tragedy of a girl destroyed by the sexual instinct.

The Rats (1911). A naturalistic drama of the struggle of two women for the possession of a child in a slum environment. Deals with the instinct for maternity (see Lorca's *Yerma*) and is also a humorous apologia for naturalistic art—which Hauptmann had himself abandoned in *The Sunken Bell* and other plays.

HERMANN SUDERMANN: *Magda* (1893). A realistic study of the conflict between a "free" woman and her conservative father. The heroine's role attracted Sarah Bernhardt, Helena Modjeska, and Eleonora Duse.

FRANK WEDEKIND: *The Awakening of Spring* (1891). The tragedy of adolescents in the grip of the sexual instinct; presented with a mixture of naturalistic and expressionistic styles.

Earth Spirit (1895). A naturalistic-expressionistic treatment of the amoral force of sexuality, notable for its heroine Lulu, "the wild, beautiful animal" in whom sexuality is incarnate. See also its sequel, *Pandora's Box* (1893), in which Lulu is murdered by a man in whom the sexual instinct is compulsive and pathological.

The Tenor (1899). See page 164.

The Marquis of Keith (1900). The comedy of a Nietzschean scoundrel and adventurer for whom life is a "toboggan slide."

MAX HALBE: *Youth* (1893). A tragedy of youth and frustration in a narrow religious background.

GEORG HIRSCHFELD: *The Mothers* (1896). A naturalistic treatment of the conflict between an artist's desire for freedom and the family pressure which he is unable to resist.

LUDWIG THOMA: *Moral* (1908). A satire on the hypocrisy of crusaders against vice.

WILHELM VON SCHOLZ: *The Race with the Shadow* (1921). A psychological fantasy in which an author finds a rival for his wife's affections in the character he creates in one of his books.

ARTHUR SCHNITZLER: *Anatol* (1889-1891; published in 1893). A series of one-act plays dealing with the same character's various love affairs and disillusionment. (Adapted by Harley Granville-Barker.)

Light-o'-Love (*Liebelei*) (1894). The tragedy of a poor Viennese girl who has idealized her upper-class lover only to discover that he has been killed in a duel fought over the wife of another man; a contrast between the meaning of love on the upper and lower social levels.

Hands Around (*Reigen*) (1897). "The death dance of love": a series of ten dramatic dialogues preceding and following sexual consummation. A clinical, naturalistic study of the instinct that holds individuals in its grip regardless of the difference in their social positions.

The Green Cockatoo (1898). A grotesque and ironic one-act treatment of the doomed but frivolous aristocracy on the eve of the French Revolution.

The Lonely Way (1903). A tragedy of loneliness and disillusionment after a life of self-indulgence and egotism.

The Vast Domain (1911). An exposé of a ruthless philanderer and his "sophisticated" social circle.

Professor Bernhardi (1912). A problem play dealing with Austrian anti-Semitism and with a Jewish physician's conflict with religious fanaticism.

HERMAN HEIJERMANS: *The Good Hope* (1900). A naturalistic social drama exposing the greed of shipowners and presenting the tragedy of fishermen exposed to the perils of the sea in unseaworthy ships.

HUGO VON HOFMANNSTHAL: *Death and the Fool* (1893). A symbolist verse drama dealing with a dilettante's failure to grasp reality and make fruitful use of his life.

Electra (1903). A psychological, "modern" treatment of Sophocles' *Electra;* the heroine is presented as a hysterical neurotic. (The play was set to music by Richard Strauss.)

Everyman (1911). A modern reworking of the famous medieval English morality play.

KARL SCHÖNHERR: *Earth* (1907). A comedy of the tenacity of peasant life.

HERMANN BAHR: *The Concert* (1909). A comedy of a volatile artist's philandering disposition and its unromantic consequences.

FERENC MOLNÁR: *Liliom* (1909). See page 354.

The Guardsman (1911). An ingenious comedy of jealousy among actors. Popularized in America by Alfred Lunt and Lynn Fontanne.

The Play's the Thing (1924). A comedy of jealousy, ingeniously enlivened by the play-within-the-play technique.

ERNST VAJDA: *Fata Morgana* (1915). A comedy of an adolescent's infatuation with a woman of the world.

CARL STERNHEIM: *The Snob* (1913). A mordant satire on the social ascent of a designing character who becomes an industrial magnate and marries into the German aristocracy. See also its sequels, *1913* (published in 1915) and *Tabula rasa* (1916).

FRITZ VON UNRUH: *Officers* (1912). A treatment of the conflict between military obedience and individual thought. May be compared with Heinrich von Kleist's *The Prince of Homburg,* an early psychological study of Prussianism.

ANTON WILDGANS: *Poverty* (1913). The drama of the slow death of a superannuated government official.

ARNOLT BRONNEN: *Parricide* (1915). A violent treatment of the Oedipus complex, notable as an early example of expressionism.

WALTER HASENCLEVER: *The Son* (1916; written in 1914). An early expressionistic presentation of the struggle of the generations.

GEORG KAISER: *From Morn to Midnight* (1916). An expressionistic treatment of a bank cashier's revolt against the frustrations of his lowly, depersonalized life and of his frenzied and disillusioning effort to experience the excitements of the metropolitan world.

Gas, I and *II* (*I,* 1918; *II,* 1920). An expressionistic presentation of the problems of the modern industrial world, ending in the collapse of society. See also the first part of this trilogy, *The Coral* (1917).

STEFAN ZWEIG: *Jeremiah* (1917). A pacifistic protest against the First World War, in a biblical setting.

REINHARD GOERING: *Sea Battle* (1918). An expressionistic presentation of the thoughts of seven sailors on a German warship during the First World War.

ERNST TOLLER: *Man and the Masses* (1919). An expressionistic treatment of the revolt of the masses after the First World War and a study of the conflict between a humanitarian idealist and depersonalized masses bent upon destruction.

The Machine-Wreckers (1922). A drama of the revolt of the Luddite workers in England against the introduction of steam-driven machinery. May be compared with Hauptmann's *The Weavers.*

FRANZ WERFEL: *The Goat Song* (1921). A symbolic presentation of the recrudescence of brutishness in man and the coming of revolution as a destructive force; the story of the birth of a monster to a wealthy peasant family and the social upheaval he causes.

KAREL CAPEK: *R. U. R.* (1921). See page 409.

KAREL and JOSEF CAPEK: *The Insect Comedy* (*The World We Live In:* American adaptation by Owen Davis; *And So Ad Infinitum:* version played in England) (1922). An expressionistic fantasy of the foibles, predatoriness, regimentation, and warring habits of the human race, presented as a picture of insect life in the delirium of a dying vagabond.

BRUNO FRANK: *The Twelve Thousand* (1927). A comedy about the sale of Hessian soldiers by their duke as mercenaries to help defeat the colonists in the American Revolution.

FERDINAND BRUCKNER: *The Sickness of Youth* (1928). A treatment of the failure of the young in erotic and social situations.

The Criminals (1929). A cross section of life in Germany, first written as a study of judicial procedure, rewritten during the Second World War as a study of social deterioration on the eve of the Nazi revolution.

HANS CHLUMBERG: *The Miracle at Verdun* (1930). An expressionistic antiwar fantasy. German and French soldiers buried in a common mass grave return to life only to discover that the living have learned nothing from the First World War and are getting ready for a second holocaust. May be compared with Irwin Shaw's *Bury the Dead.*

CARL ZUCKMAYER: *The Captain of Köpenick* (1931). A satire on Prussian militarism and the tendency of the Germans to obey military authority unquestioningly.

FRIEDRICH WOLF: *The Sailors of Cattaro* (1931). A drama of the mutiny of the Austrian fleet at the end of the First World War.

Professor Mamlock (1935). A play about anti-Semitism in Nazi Germany. Better known as a motion picture.

HANNS JOHST: *Schlageter* (1933). A meretricious early Nazi play, permeated with the extreme nationalism and hatred of culture glorified by National Socialism. A typical statement in the play is, "When I hear 'Kultur,' I loosen the safety catch on my revolver."

BERTOLT BRECHT: *The Three-Penny Opera* (1933). A social satire based on John Gay's eighteenth-century classic *The Beggar's Opera.*

The Private Life of the Master Race (1939). See page 456.

The Good Woman of Setzuan (published in English in 1948; written in 1941?). A brilliant morality play about the problem of good will and charitableness in the world of social realities.

The Caucasian Chalk Circle (published in English in 1948; written in 1944?). An "epic" morality play, based upon the Chinese classic *The Chalk Circle.* Deals with a woman's right to a child by virtue of her devotion to it as against an aristocratic mother's purely biological claims.

FRENCH DRAMA

EMILE ZOLA: *Thérèse Raquin* (1873). A naturalistic treatment of an adulterous relationship, of the murder of the husband by the lovers, and of their remorse and self-torture under the accusing eyes of the paralyzed mother of the murdered man.

HENRY BECQUE: *The Vultures* (1882; written in 1875). See page 95.

The Parisian Woman (*La Parisienne*) (1885). A brilliant naturalistic comedy about an amoral adulterous woman in Parisian society.

JEAN JULLIEN: *Serenade* (1887). A Théâtre Libre *comédie rosse,* in which a mother and daughter live with the same man.

GEORGES DE PORTO-RICHE: *A Loving Wife* (*Amoureuse; The Tyranny of Love*) (1891). The naturalistic drama of a man who tries to break the spell of sexual passion in his relations with an ardent young wife.

FRANÇOIS DE CUREL: *The Fossils* (1892). A notable naturalistic tragedy dealing with the decline of the French aristocracy.

GEORGES COURTELINE: *Boubouroche* (1893). A famous Théâtre Libre farce with overtones of cynicism. Revolves around a deceived husband whose suspicions are allayed by his wife's pretense at feeling outraged when reproved by him.

EUGÈNE BRIEUX: *The Three Daughters of M. Dupont* (1897). An early naturalistic problem play dealing with the sufferings of daughters under the dowry system of the French middle class.

The Red Robe (1900) (produced in America as *The Letter of the Law,* 1920). A thesis drama about the French system of criminology.

Damaged Goods (1902). A naturalistic problem play that became notorious for its candid sociological treatment of the subject of venereal disease.

The June Bugs (*Les Hannetons*) (1907). Brieux's best play; a comedy which shows an illicit affair to be no less exacting than marriage. (Brieux, who was greatly admired by Bernard Shaw, infused the old thesis type of drama developed by Dumas *fils* with naturalism by dealing with subjects and dispensing doctrines popularized by that style of writing.)

PAUL HERVIEU: *Know Thyself* (1909). A realistic triangle play about a husband's understanding attitude toward his unfaithful wife.

MAURICE MAETERLINCK: *The Intruder* (1890). See page 264.

The Blind (1891). A one-act symbolist drama presenting the helplessness of blind people who are lost when their priest and guide dies.

Pelléas and Mélisande (1893). A symbolist version of the Paolo and Francesca story. The basis of Claude Debussy's famous opera.

Interior (1895). A one-act symbolist drama about the death of a girl by drowning.

The Blue Bird (1908). The once very popular ultrasymbolist allegory dealing with two children's search for the blue bird of happiness.

EDMOND ROSTAND: *Cyrano de Bergerac* (1897). See page 274.

L'Aiglon (1900). The tragedy of Napoleon's son ("the eaglet"), who is incapable of realizing the heroic aspirations inspired by his father's fame.

Chantecler (1910). A tribute to the heroic spirit, written as a poetic beast fable about La Fontaine's rooster.

The Last Night of Don Juan (published posthumously in 1921). An imaginative version of the Don Juan legend; presents the fabulous philanderer as a failure in love.

JACQUES COPEAU: *The Brothers Karamazov* (1911). Copeau's famous dramatization of Dostoevsky's novel.

PAUL CLAUDEL: *The Tidings Brought to Mary* (1912). A poetic religious drama of selfless love and saintliness.

SACHA GUITRY: *Pasteur* (1919). The biographical drama of Pasteur and his struggles with conservatism in scientific circles.

HENRI RENÉ LENORMAND: *Time Is a Dream* (1919). A Pirandellian treatment of the unreality and relativity of time and life.

The Failures (1920). A play about the failure and deterioration of a playwright and an actress.

Man and His Phantoms (1924). A psychoanalytic interpretation of the Don Juan legend.

The Coward (1925). A sympathetic psychological study of an artist who betrays France to a German spy out of cowardice.

FERNAND CROMMELYNCK: *The Magnificent Cuckold* (1921). A broad comedy of jealousy, in which the foolish husband drives his wife into the arms of many men with his obsessive behavior.

CHARLES VILDRAC: *S. S. Tenacity* (1920). A play about the divergent destinies of two companions—a dreamer and a practical man—bound for Canada.

Michael Auclair (1922). A tender play about a selfless man who loses his fiancée to a dishonest and swaggering soldier but proceeds to reform him for the sake of the girl.

JEAN JACQUES BERNARD: *Martine* (1922). The tragedy of a simple peasant girl ensnared by a philanderer from the city; presented with notable sensitivity.

Invitation to a Voyage (1924). The comedy of a wife who indulges in extravagantly romantic illusions about her husband's friend when he takes a business trip to Argentina but is disillusioned by his unromantic return.

SIMON GANTILLON: *Maya* (1924). A somewhat Pirandellian treatment of a prostitute in sordid circumstances and of men's need for dreams; she is "maya," or illusion, for them.

EDOUARD BOURDET: *The Captive* (1926). A psychological treatment of sexual inversion in a wife who is unable to free herself from her aberration.

JULES ROMAINS: *Dr. Knock* (*Knock, ou le Triomphe de la médicine*) (1923). An extravagant satire on medical charlatanism.

ALFRED SAVOIR: *The Lion Tamer* (*Le Dompteur, ou l'Anglais tel qu'on le mange*) (1925). A tragic farce about the absurdities of idealism in an Englishman who follows a circus from town to town in the hope that the "oppressed" lions will turn on the lion tamer and devour him. Instead, it is the Englishman who is eaten.

MARCEL PAGNOL: *Topaze* (1928). An extravagant satire on the necessity of dishonesty for survival in a predatory world.

RENÉ FAUCHOIS: *Prenez garde à la peinture* (1932) (*The Late Christopher Bean* in Sidney Howard's adaptation, 1932). A comedy about the rapacity of art dealers and the neglect of artists while they are still living.

ANDRÉ BIRABEAU: *Dame Nature* (1936). A sensitive comedy of adolescent love and marriage.

JEAN COCTEAU: *The Infernal Machine* (1934). An ironic and more or less surrealistic version of the legend of Oedipus, in which the hero achieves humanity only after Fate has crossed and confounded him cruelly.

JEAN GIRAUDOUX: *Amphitryon 38* (1929). A sparkling boudoir comedy, the "thirty-eighth" version of the classic story of Jupiter's seduction of Alcmene, the wife of Amphitryon, whom the god impersonates.

The Trojan War Will Not Take Place (1935). An ironic foretelling of the Second World War through the story of the Trojan War.

The Madwoman of Chaillot (1945) (American adaptation by Maurice Valency, 1948). A poetic extravaganza satirizing greed and celebrating a fantastic liberation from modern society's speculators and entrepreneurs.

JEAN-PAUL SARTRE: *The Flies* (1943). See page 466.

No Exit (*Huis-Clos*) (1944). A long one-act existentialist fantasy in which three failures are doomed to spend their afterlife together.

The Respectful Prostitute (1946). A sardonic existentialist treatment of race relations in the South of the United States.

The Victors (*Morts sans sépulture*) (1946). An existentialist treatment of the French underground Resistance movement.

ALBERT CAMUS: *Caligula* (1944). An existentialist account of the sanguinary career of Caligula, who entertains ideals but avenges himself on humanity when he becomes disillusioned; the "idealist" thus makes himself a tyrant by his conduct.

JEAN ANOUILH: *Antigone* (1944). A version of Sophocles' play of the same title, in which Antigone goes to her death for burying her brother Polyneices primarily because of disgust with the timorous, calculating world.

ITALIAN DRAMA

GABRIELE D'ANNUNZIO: *La Gioconda* (1898). An example of D'Annunzian poetic tragedy. Deals with the ill-fated love of high-spirited romantic personalities.

The Daughter of Jorio (1904). A poetic peasant tragedy, weird and frenetic but imaginative and rich with local color.

SEM BENELLI: *The Jest* (1910). A colorful poetic melodrama of love, hatred, and vengeance during the Italian Renaissance, contrasting the artist and the man of action. A popular example of the poetic school.

LUIGI CHIARELLI: *The Mask and the Face* (1916). An ironical comedy, the first written in the manner of the modern Italian "grotesque" school of playwriting. Satirizes the conventional attitude toward marital infidelity and the difference between what we profess and what we feel. A betrayed husband, to avenge his honor, pretends that he has killed his wife.

LUIGI PIRANDELLO: *Right You Are if You Think You Are* [*Right You Are (If You Think So)*] (1916). A metaphysical comedy posing the Pirandellian question, "What is reality?" and requiring tolerance for people's illusions.

Six Characters in Search of an Author (1921). See page 384.

Henry IV (produced in New York as *The Living Mask*) (1922). A powerful tragedy of insanity and disillusionment, exemplifying Pirandello's concern with the border line between sanity and insanity.

Naked (1922). The tragedy of a woman's longing for a romantic personality and the incomprehension of people who blame her for having pretended to die for love.

ALBERTO CASELLA: *Death Takes a Holiday* (1924) (American adaptation by Walter Ferris, 1929). A fantasy in which Death falls in love with a girl and she, returning his love, gives up life.

SPANISH DRAMA

José Echegaray: *The Great Galeoto* (1881). A drama in which doubt of a woman's fidelity throws her into the arms of the man with whom scandalmongers have associated her.

Jacinto Benavente: *The Bonds of Interest* (1907). A modern satirical *commedia dell'arte,* showing how self-interest draws people together.

The Passion Flower (1913). A peasant tragedy dealing with the love of a girl and her stepfather.

Gregorio Martínez Sierra: *Cradle Song* (1911). A drama that presents the maternal instinct fulfilling itself in a nunnery.

The Two Shepherds (1913). A portrait of a priest and a physician who have been good shepherds to their people but are out of step with modern theology and science.

The Kingdom of God (1915). A drama of self-sacrifice that revolves around a pious woman who gives her life to those who need it.

Serafín and Joaquín Alvarez Quintero: *Malvaloca* (1912). A drama of Andalusian life, dealing with the vicissitudes of a woman who, in spite of her past, finds an understanding love.

Federico García Lorca: *Blood Wedding* (1913). See page 434.

Yerma (1934). The poetic tragedy of a woman obsessed with a frustrated passion for maternity and driven to murder the husband who is responsible for her empty life.

The House of Bernarda Alba (1936). The tragedy of the daughters of a proud matriarchal woman who refuses to allow them to realize themselves as women.

HEBREW DRAMA

S. Ansky: *The Dybbuk* (1919). A fantastic love tragedy of demoniacal possession and exorcism, based on Jewish folklore. A famous Habimah stage production.

RUSSIAN DRAMA

Leo Tolstoy: *The Power of Darkness* (1886). See page 173.

The Living Corpse (*Redemption*) (1900). An Enoch Arden tragedy of a failure and an attack on irrational marriage laws.

The Light That Shines in Darkness (begun in the 'eighties and continued in 1900 and 1902; last act never written). The tragedy of an idealist like Tolstoy himself.

Anton Chekhov: *The Sea Gull* (1896). A tragedy of love and frustration, artistic ambitions, and the ironies of life.

Uncle Vanya (1899). Another Chekhovian tragicomic study in frustration. Notable, like other Chekhov plays, for its superb characterizations.

The Three Sisters (1901). A tragedy of longing for experience and of frustration in provincial Russia.

The Cherry Orchard (1904). See page 205.

Maxim Gorki: *The Lower Depths* (*Na dne*) (1902). See page 227.

Yegor Bulychov (1932). A tragedy of degeneration in the middle class on the eve of the Russian Revolution. A notable naturalistic drama, containing an incisive picture of a merchant's family.

Leonid Andreyev: *The Life of Man* (1906). A symbolic tragedy dealing with the rise and fall of an individual and with the spectral domination of Death.

King Hunger (1907). A symbolic drama of revolution, reflecting the events of the Revolution of 1905; King Hunger champions his children, the poor, but ultimately betrays them, because he is the servant of the rich.

The Black Maskers (1908). The most thoroughly symbolic of Andreyev's plays. Deals with the problem of dual personality and evil in the human soul.

He Who Gets Slapped. (1915). A tragedy of disillusionment, set in a circus.

Nikolai Evreinov: *The Chief Thing* (1921). An attempt to depart from realism by treating life as a product of creative will and imagination.

MICHAEL BULGAKOV: *Days of the Turbins* (*The Last of the Turbins; The White Guard* in an English adaptation by Rodney Ackland) (1926). A drama of civil war in Soviet Russia, notable for its sympathetic characterization of revolutionists and counterrevolutionists alike; a more or less Chekhovian picture of the destruction of the Russian aristocracy.

VALENTIN KATAEV: *Squaring the Circle* (1928). A hilarious farce on marriage relations and other mores of Soviet Russia. Called the *Abie's Irish Rose* of Soviet Russia.

ALEXANDER AFINOGENOV: *Fear* (1931). A psy-chological social-problem play in which a scientist investigates the incidence of fear among Soviet citizens.

Distant Point (1935). A picture of life in a remote Siberian railway junction, which the characters desire to leave until convinced that they are needed.

NIKOLAI POGODIN: *Aristocrats* (1935). A drama of the rehabilitation of common criminals who help to build a canal from the White Sea to the Baltic.

KONSTANTIN SIMONOV: *The Russian People* (1942). An account of the struggle of a Russian town against occupation by the German army.

BIBLIOGRAPHY

This is a selective bibliography and is limited to general studies in the English language. Special studies are listed after the introductions to the plays included in this volume.

EUROPEAN DRAMA AND THEATRE

BAKSHY, ALEXANDER: *The Path of the Modern Russian Stage.* London: C. Palmer and Hayward, 1918.

BALMFORTH, RAMSDEN: *The Problem Play.* New York: Holt, 1928.

BENTLEY, ERIC: *The Playwright as Thinker.* New York: Reynal, 1946.

BLOCK, ANITA: *The Changing World in Plays and Theatre.* Boston: Little, Brown, 1939.

BROWN, JOHN MASON: *The Modern Theatre in Revolt.* New York: Norton, 1929.

CARTER, HUNTLY: *The New Spirit in the European Theatre: 1914–1924.* New York: George H. Doran Company, 1925.

The New Spirit in the Russian Theatre. New York: Brentano's, 1929.

CHANDLER, FRANK W.: *Aspects of Modern Drama.* New York: Macmillan, 1914.

The Contemporary Drama of France. Boston: Little, Brown, 1920.

Modern Continental Playwrights. New York: Harper, 1931.

CLARK, BARRETT H.: *A Study of the Modern Drama.* New York: Appleton-Century, 1938.

European Theories of the Drama. New York: Crown Publishers, 1947. (See pages 345–557.)

CLARK, BARRETT H., and GEORGE FREEDLEY (editors): *A History of Modern Drama.* New York: Appleton-Century, 1947.

COLE, TOBY, and HELEN KRICH CHINOY: *Actors on Acting.* New York: Crown Publishers, 1949. (See pages 195–253, 263–291, 323–458, 498–550.)

CRAIG, EDWARD GORDON: *On the Art of the Theatre.* Chicago: Brown's Bookstore, 1913.

The Theatre Advancing. Boston: Little, Brown, 1919.

Scene. New York: Oxford University Press, 1923.

DANA, H. W. L.: *Handbook on Soviet Drama.* New York: American Russian Institute, 1938.

DAHLSTRÖM, C. E. W. LEONARD: *Strindberg's Dramatic Expressionism.* Ann Arbor: University of Michigan Press, 1930. (Useful not merely for its treatment of Strindberg but for its discussion of expressionism in general.)

DICKINSON, THOMAS H. (editor): *The Theatre in a Changing Europe.* New York: Holt, 1937.

DUKES, ASHLEY: *The Youngest Drama.* London: Ernest Benn, Ltd., 1923.

FERGUSSON, FRANCIS: *The Idea of a Theater.* Princeton: Princeton University Press, 1949. (See pages 143–228 for a provocative view of the modern drama.)

FLANAGAN, HALLIE: *Shifting Scenes of the Modern European Theatre.* New York: Coward-McCann, 1928.

FREEDLEY, GEORGE, and JOHN A. REEVES: *A History of the Theatre.* New York: Crown Publishers, 1941. (See pages 337–619.)

GASSNER, JOHN: *Producing the Play.* New York: Dryden, 1941. (See pages 1–569.)

Masters of the Drama. New York: Random House, 1940; Dover Publications, 1945. (See pages 350–541.)

GOLDBERG, ISAAC: *The Drama of Transition.* Cincinnati: Stewart Kidd Co., 1922.

GORELIK, MORDECAI: *New Theatre for Old.* New York: French, 1941.

HOUGHTON, NORRIS: *Moscow Rehearsals.* New York: Harcourt, 1936.

JONES, ROBERT EDMOND: *The Dramatic Imagination.* New York: Duell, 1941.

HENDERSON, ARCHIBALD: *European Dramatists.* New York: Appleton, 1926.

HUNEKER, JAMES: *Iconoclasts.* New York: Scribner, 1905, 1919.

JAMES, HENRY: *The Scenic Art.* New Brunswick: Rutgers University Press, 1948. (A generally interesting collection of James's criticism. See especially the comments on Ibsen, pages 243–260.)

LAWSON, JOHN HOWARD: *Theory and Technique of Playwriting and Screenwriting*. New York: Putnam, 1949. (See pages 45–302.)

LEWISOHN, LUDWIG: *The Modern Drama*. New York: Huebsch, 1921.

MacCARTHY, DESMOND: *Drama*. London: Putnam, 1940. (See especially pages 54–130, 170–193.)

McCLINTOCK, L.: *The Contemporary Drama of Italy*. Boston: Little, Brown, 1920.

MARKOV, PAVEL A.: *The Soviet Drama*. London: Gollancz, 1934.

MILLER, ANNA IRENE: *The Independent Theatre in Europe*. New York: Long and Smith, 1927.

NEMIROVITCH-DANTCHENKO, VLADIMIR: *My Life in the Russian Theatre*. Boston: Little, Brown, 1936.

NEWMARK, MAXIM: *Otto Brahm: The Man and the Critic*. New York: G. E. Stechert & Company, 1938. (A revealing study of the formative forces in modern European drama and theatre.)

NICOLL, ALLARDYCE: *An Introduction to Dramatic Theory*. London: Harrap, 1924.

The Development of the Theatre. New York: Harcourt, 1937. (See pages 190–223.)

World Drama. New York: Harcourt, 1950. (See pages 466–623, 669–728, 734–740, 771–806, 811–815.)

MODERWELL, HIRAM K.: *The Theatre of Today*. New York: John Lane, 1914, 1927.

SAYLOR, OLIVER M.: *The Russian Theatre*. New York: Brentano's, 1922.

Max Reinhardt and His Theatre. New York: Brentano's, 1924.

SIMONSON, LEE: *The Stage Is Set*. New York: Harcourt, 1932; Dover Publications, 1946. (See pages 272–464.)

STANISLAVSKY, CONSTANTIN: *My Life in Art*. Boston: Little, Brown, 1924.

THOMPSON, ALAN REYNOLDS: *The Dry Mock*. Berkeley: University of California Press, 1948. (A study of irony in the drama.)

WALKLEY, A. B.: *Drama and Life*. New York: Brentano's, 1908. (See pages 1–84, 251–260, 283–293.)

WILSON, N. SCARLYN: *European Drama*. London: Nicholson and Watson, 1937.

YOUNG, STARK: *The Theatre*. New York: George H. Doran Company, 1927.

ABOUT THE EDITOR

JOHN GASSNER *has been acclaimed as "the greatest authority on the drama living in America" by* Commonweal *and as "the American theatre's official anthologist-in-chief" by* Theatre Arts. *He has also been well known as a drama critic, having written play reviews for a number of periodicals, and been a member of the New York Drama Critics Circle since 1936. His articles have been translated into many languages and his books have been used all over the world. As a practical man of the theatre, Mr. Gassner was chairman of the Theatre Guild's Play Department for more than a dozen years and executive head of Columbia Pictures' Play Department, in addition to operating more recently as an independent Broadway producer. Throughout an extraordinarily busy career, he has also found time to be a lecturer, radio commentator, and teacher; and many of the best-known younger playwrights have been at one time or another his students or protégés. He is at present the Sterling Professor of Playwriting and Dramatic Literature at the School of Drama of Yale University and a Fellow of Ezra Stiles College at Yale University. In addition to having had several play adaptations produced, Mr. Gassner has published more than two dozen books on drama, theatrical art, motion pictures, and comparative literature. Among the best known of these are his* Masters of the Drama, Producing the Play, *and* Our Heritage of World Literature. *Mr. Gassner was educated at Columbia University and has been awarded university and Guggenheim Fellowships.*